START-UP
HISTORY
TOYS

Stewart Ross

Evans Brothers Limited

Published by Evans Brothers Limited
2A Portman Mansions
Chiltern Street
London W1U 6NR

© Evans Brothers Limited 2002
Reprinted 2003 (twice), 2005

Produced for Evans Brothers Limited by
White-Thomson Publishing Ltd,
Bridgewater Business Centre,
210 High Street, Lewes, East Sussex BN7 2NH

Printed in China by WKT Company Limited.

Editor: Anna Lee
Consultant: Norah Granger
Designer: Tessa Barwick

Cover (centre): Noah's Ark.
Cover (top left): Victorian alphabet blocks and modern
    teddy bear.
Cover (top right): clockwork car and Barbie doll.

The right of Stewart Ross to be identified as the author of
this work has been asserted by him in accordance with the
Copyright, Designs and Patents Act 1988.

British Library Cataloguing in Publication Data

Ross, Stewart
  Toys. - (Start-up history)
  1.Toys - History - Juvenile literature
  I.Title
  790.1'33'09

ISBN: 0 237 52408 2

Acknowledgements: The publishers would like to
thank Big Kids Toy Shop, Lewes, for their assistance
with this book.

Picture Acknowledgements: Beamish Open Air Museum
(cover, top centre right), 5 *(top)*, 10-11, 13 *(bottom)*; Hodder
Wayland Picture Library 7; Mary Evans Picture Library 11;
Zul Mukhida *(cover, top centre left)*, 4 *(top)*, 6, 12, 14,
20 *(top)*, 21 *(right)*; Robert Opie *(cover, top far left)*, 13 *(top)*,
15 *(right)*; Topham Picturepoint *(cover, top far right)*,
15 *(left)*, 19 *(left)*; Victoria and Albert Museum Picture
Library 4 *(bottom)*, 9 *(top)*, 16, 18, 19 *(right)*, 20 *(bottom)*,
21 *(left)*; Richard Stansfield/York Castle Museum *(cover,
centre)*, 5 *(bottom)*, 8, 9 *(right)*, 17 *(left and right)*.

VISIT OUR WEBSITE
www.evansbooks.co.uk
Evans

Contents

Toys now and then 4

What is it made of? 6

Looking at the past 8

A Victorian steam engine 10

Making toys move 12

Toys to help us learn 14

Toys from long ago 16

How do we know? 18

The same and different 20

Further information for Parents and Teachers 22

Index 24

Toys now and then

▼ **This is a** new computer game.

It plays **a** football **game.**

► **Your parents may have played with a** doll **like this.**

It was made 40 years ago.

◄ This toy car is 70 years old.
How is it different from
modern toy cars?

▼ This doll's house is
more than 100 years old.

doll   years   ago   car   old   modern

What is it made of?

Here is a modern toy dog.
Like most modern toys,
it was made in
a factory.

The dog is
very shiny.
It is made
of plastic.

dog   factory   shiny

These children are playing with a plastic tea set.

Many toys are made of plastic nowadays.

What others can you think of?

plastic   tea set   nowadays   **7**

Looking at the past

This Noah's Ark was made long ago.

In the past, many toys were made of wood.

They were painted by hand.

Noah's Ark long ago past wood

▼ These old Minibrix are made of rubber.

► This toy soldier is made from lead. How is it different from a modern toy?

painted   minibrix   rubber   soldier   lead   9

A Victorian steam engine

▶ These children are playing with a Victorian steam engine.

Victorian   steam engine

Steam engines have a **burner** to heat the **water**.

The water turns into steam. The steam drives the engine.

burner   water

11

Making toys move

This modern boat works
with batteries.
It is radio-controlled.

boat batteries radio-controlled

► Your grandparents may have played with a train like this.

It has a clockwork motor inside. How can you tell it is clockwork?

◄ This very old toy camel has no motor.

It is pulled by a string.

train   clockwork   motor   camel   string

Toys to help us learn

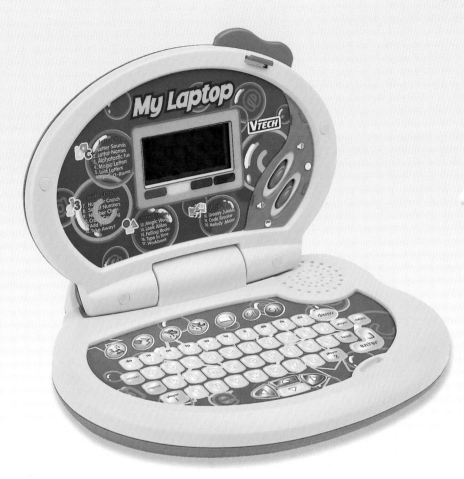

▲ Here is a modern computer for children.

It helps them learn to read and do sums.

Meccano build

▼ **Meccano** teaches children how to **build** things. Your grandparents may have played with Meccano.

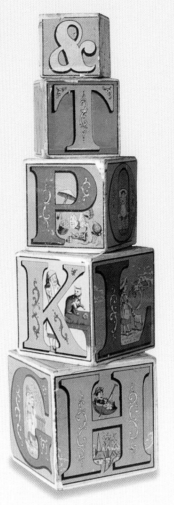

▲ These alphabet bricks are more than 100 years old.

What did children learn with these bricks?

alphabet bricks   **15**

Toys from long ago

These toys are from long ago.
Can you see how they work?

◄ This is an old puppet.

◄ Here is a spinning top.

work   puppet

◀ **This toy is called a zoetrope.**

▼ **This card slots into the zoetrope.**

When the zoetrope spins around, the figures move.

spinning top   zoetrope   17

How do we know?

▶ A rag doll.

These dolls were made at different times.

Can you tell which is the oldest and which is the newest?

How can you tell?

18

oldest   newest

◀ **A plastic doll.**

◀ **A china doll.**

rag   china

The same and different

One toy car is modern and one is 70 years old.
How can you tell which is which?

teddy bears   different

These teddy bears were made at different times.
One is new and one is about 90 years old.

Some modern toys are like toys made long ago.
Other toys have changed over time.

times   changed

Further information for

New history and toys words listed in the text:

ago	computer game	motor	puppet	teddy bears
alphabet bricks	different	new	radio-controlled	times
batteries	dog	newest	rag	train
boat	doll	Noah's Ark	rubber	Victorian
build	factory	nowadays	shiny	water
burner	football	old	soldier	wood
camel	lead	oldest	spinning top	work
car	long ago	painted	soldier	years
changed	Meccano	past	steam engine	zoetrope
china	Minibrix	plastic	string	
clockwork	modern	plays	tea set	

Background Information

A SELECT CHRONOLOGY OF TWENTIETH CENTURY TOYS

1901 First electric train.
Meccano (then called Mechanics) invented.

1902 Teddy bears available.

1903 First crayons.

1909 Bakelite, the first modern plastic, invented.

1927 Polystyrene invented.

1928 Mickey Mouse is born.

1929 Yo-yo popular.

1934 Nylon manufactured.
First Dinky Toys appear.

1936 Monopoly board game produced.

1940s Cheap plastic model airplane kits for sale.

1949 Lego first made.

1950s Matchbox models appear.

1956 Play-doh first appears.

1959 Barbie dolls make their first appearance.
Hula hoops appear.

1972 First video game machine.

1978 Personal computers available.

1983 Nintendo games system appears.

1989 Game Boy appears.

1993 Beanie Babies are born.

Parents and Teachers

Possible Activities:

Make a frieze timeline.

Invite adults in to talk about the toys they played with when they were young.

Make a collection of toys (class toy museum) and arrange them by age.

Make simple toys from paper and wood.

Some Topics for Discussion:

Adventures of individual toys.

Changing materials that toys are made from.

How can we work out how old a toy might be?

How might toys be arranged – by age, by type, by material.

What toys might your parents/grandparents have had?

What toys from the past are no longer available?

PLACES TO VISIT

Victoria and Albert Museum, London.

Bethnal Green Museum of Childhood, Bethnal Green, London.

Toy Museum, Isle of Skye, Scotland.

The Vina Cooke Museum of Dolls and Bygone Childhood, Cromwell, Newark, Nottinghamshire.

The National Trust Museum of Childhood, Sudbury Hall, Ashbourne, Derbyshire.

Many local museums have sections on toys, for example the Royal Cornwall Museum, Truro.

Further Information

BOOKS

FOR CHILDREN

Don L. Wulffson, *Toys!: Amazing Stories behind Some Great Inventions* (Henry Holt, 2000)

Karen Bryant-Mole, *History from Objects: Toys* (Hodder Wayland, 1996)

Philip Steele, *Toys and Games (Everyday History)* (Franklin Watts, 2000)

Chris Oxlade, *Toys Through Time* (Raintree Steck-Vaughn, 1996)

Jane Shuter, *Toys* (Heinemann, 1997)

Simon Adams, *20th Century: A Visual History* (Dorling Kindersley, 1996)

FOR ADULTS

Andrew McClary, *Toys with Nine Lives, A Social History of American Toys* (Linnet, 1997)

Kenneth D. Brown, *The British Toy Business: A History Since 1700* (Hambledon and London, 1996)

Gary Cross, *Kid's Stuff* (Harvard University Press, 1997)

WEBSITES

http://www.historychannel.com/exhibits/toys

http://www.discovery.com/stories/history/toys/toys.html

http://www.woodentoymuseum.com

Index

a
alphabet bricks 15

b
batteries 12
boat 12
build 15
burner 11

c
camel 13
car 5, 20
children 7, 10, 15
clockwork 13
computer game 4, 14

d
dog 6
doll 4, 5
  china 19
  plastic 19
  rag 18
doll's house 5

e
engine 10, 11

f
football game 4

l
lead 9

m
Meccano 14, 15
Minibrix 9
motor 13

n
Noah's Ark 8

p
painted 8
plastic 6, 7, 19
puppet 16

r
radio-controlled 12
rubber 9

s
soldier 9
spinning top 16, 17
steam engine 10, 11
string 13

t
tea set 7
teddy bears 20, 21
train 13

v
Victorian 10

w
water 11
wood 8

z
zoetrope 17

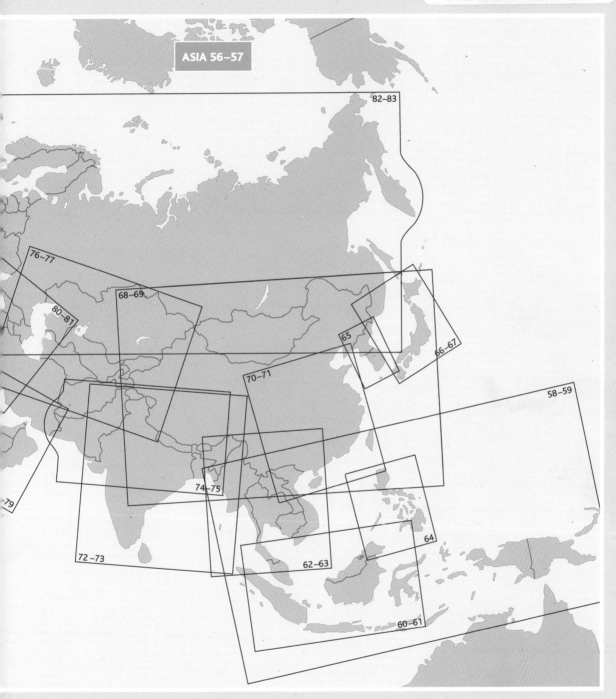

ASIA 56–57

82–83

76–77

68–69

80–81

65

66–67

70–71

58–59

74–75

79

64

72–73

62–63

60–61

THE TIMES

ATLAS

OF THE

WORLD

DESKTOP EDITION

Times Books, 77-85 Fulham Palace Road, London W6 8JB

The Times is a registered trademark of Times Newspapers Ltd

First published 2006

The contents of this edition of The Times World Atlas are believed correct at the time of printing.
Nevertheless the publisher can accept no responsibility for errors or omissions,
changes in the detail given or for any expense or loss thereby caused.

Printed in Singapore

British Library Cataloguing in Publication Data.
A catalogue record for this book is available from the British Library.

ISBN 0 00 722296 3

SH12099 Imp 001

All mapping in this atlas is generated from Collins Bartholomew digital databases.
Collins Bartholomew, the UK's leading independent geographical information supplier,
can provide a digital, custom, and premium mapping service to a variety of markets.
For further information:
Tel: +44 (0) 141 306 3752
e-mail: collinsbartholomew@harpercollins.co.uk

or visit our website at: www.collinsbartholomew.com

www.harpercollins.co.uk
visit the book lover's website

THE TIMES
ATLAS
OF THE
WORLD

DESKTOP EDITION

TIMES BOOKS
London

CONTENTS

THE WORLD TODAY

Pages	Title	Scale
6–29	STATES AND TERRITORIES OF THE WORLD	
30–33	CONTINENTS AND OCEANS	
34–35	CLIMATE	
36–37	ENVIRONMENT	
38–39	POPULATION AND CITIES	
40–41	TELECOMMUNICATIONS	

ATLAS OF THE WORLD

Pages	Title	Scale
42–43	INTRODUCTION TO ATLAS OF THE WORLD	
44–45	**WORLD** PHYSICAL FEATURES	
46–47	**WORLD** COUNTRIES	
48–49	**OCEANIA**	**1:40 000 000**
50–51	AUSTRALIA	1:16 000 000
52–53	AUSTRALIA Southeast	1:6 000 000
54	NEW ZEALAND	1:6 000 000
55	ANTARCTICA	1:36 000 000
56–57	**ASIA**	**1:44 000 000**
58–59	SOUTHEAST ASIA	1:20 000 000
60–61	MALAYSIA AND INDONESIA West	1:9 600 000
62–63	CONTINENTAL SOUTHEAST ASIA	1:9 600 000
64	PHILIPPINES	1:9 600 000
65	NORTH KOREA AND SOUTH KOREA	1:5 200 000
66–67	JAPAN	1:6 000 000
68–69	CHINA AND MONGOLIA	1:20 000 000
70–71	CHINA Central	1:9 600 000
72–73	SOUTH ASIA	1:12 000 000
74–75	PAKISTAN, INDIA North AND BANGLADESH	1:9 600 000
76–77	CENTRAL ASIA	1:12 000 000
78–79	ARABIAN PENINSULA	1:9 600 000
80–81	EAST MEDITERRANEAN	1:9 600 000
82–83	RUSSIAN FEDERATION	1:24 000 000
84–85	**EUROPE**	**1:20 000 000**
86–87	EUROPEAN RUSSIAN FEDERATION	1:12 000 000
88–89	NORTHEAST EUROPE	1:4 800 000
90–91	UKRAINE AND MOLDOVA	1:4 800 000
92–93	SCANDINAVIA AND ICELAND	1:6 000 000
94–95	BRITISH ISLES	1:4 800 000
96	SCOTLAND	1:2 400 000
97	IRELAND	1:2 400 000
98–99	ENGLAND AND WALES	1:2 400 000

Pages	Title	Scale
100–101	NORTHWEST EUROPE	1:2 400 000
102–103	CENTRAL EUROPE	1:4 800 000
104–105	FRANCE AND SWITZERLAND	1:4 800 000
106–107	SPAIN AND PORTUGAL	1:4 800 000
108–109	ITALY AND THE BALKANS	1:4 800 000
110–111	SOUTHEAST EUROPE	1:4 800 000

Pages	Title	Scale
112–113	**AFRICA**	**1:36 000 000**
114–115	NORTHWEST AFRICA	1:16 000 000
116–117	NORTHEAST AFRICA	1:16 000 000
118–119	CENTRAL AFRICA	1:12 000 000
120–121	SOUTHERN AFRICA	1:12 000 000
122–123	REPUBLIC OF SOUTH AFRICA	1:6 000 000

Pages	Title	Scale
124–125	**NORTH AMERICA**	**1:32 000 000**
126–127	CANADA	1:20 000 000
128–129	CANADA West	1:9 600 000
130–131	CANADA East	1:9 600 000
132–133	UNITED STATES OF AMERICA	1:16 000 000
134–135	USA West	1:6 400 000
136–137	USA North Central	1:6 400 000
138–139	USA Northeast	1:6 400 000
140–141	USA Southeast	1:6 400 000
142–143	USA South Central	1:6 400 000

Pages	Title	Scale
144–145	MEXICO	1:9 600 000
146–147	CENTRAL AMERICA AND THE CARIBBEAN	1:12 000 000

Pages	Title	Scale
148–149	**SOUTH AMERICA**	**1:28 000 000**
150–151	SOUTH AMERICA North	1:16 000 000
152–153	SOUTH AMERICA South	1:16 000 000
154–155	BRAZIL Southeast	1:6 000 000

Pages	Title	Scale
156–160	**OCEANS**	
156–157	PACIFIC OCEAN	1:72 000 000
158	ATLANTIC OCEAN	1:72 000 000
159	INDIAN OCEAN	1:72 000 000
160	ARCTIC OCEAN	1:36 000 000

WORLD FACTS AND FIGURES

161	CONTENTS
162–167	WORLD STATISTICS
168–169	WORLD TIME ZONES
170–171	GEOGRAPHICAL TABLES
172–173	CLIMATE AROUND THE WORLD
174–175	USEFUL FACTS AND WEB LINKS
176	DISTANCE AND CONVERSION CHARTS

177–240 INDEX

STATES AND TERRITORIES OF THE WORLD

6 All independent countries and populated dependent and disputed territories are included in this list of the states and territories of the world; the list is arranged in alphabetical order by the conventional name form. For independent states, the full name is given below the conventional name, if this is different; for territories, the status is given. The capital city name is the same form as shown on the reference maps.

The statistics used for the area and population are the latest available and include estimates. The information on languages and religions is based on the latest information on 'de facto' speakers of the language or 'de facto' adherents to the religion. The information available on languages and religions varies greatly from country to country. Some countries include questions in censuses, others do not, in which case best estimates are used. The order of the languages and religions reflect their relative importance within the country; generally, languages or religions are included when more than one per cent of the population are estimated to be speakers or adherents.

Membership of selected international organizations is shown for each independent country. Territories are not shown as having separate memberships of these organizations.

ABBREVIATIONS

Currencies

CFA Communauté Financière Africaine
CFP Comptoirs Français du Pacifique

Organizations

APEC Asia-Pacific Economic Cooperation
ASEAN Association of Southeast Asian Nations
CARICOM Caribbean Community
CIS Commonwealth of Independent States
Comm. The Commonwealth
EU European Union
OECD Organization of Economic Cooperation and Development
OPEC Organization of Petroleum Exporting Countries
SADC Southern African Development Community
UN United Nations

AFGHANISTAN
Islamic State of Afghanistan

Area Sq Km	652 225	Religions	Sunni Muslim, Shi'a Muslim
Area Sq Miles	251 825		
Population	23 897 000	Currency	Afghani
Capital	Kābul	Organizations	UN
Languages	Dari, Pushtu, Uzbek,Turkmen	Map page	76–77

ALBANIA
Republic of Albania

Area Sq Km	28 748	Religions	Sunni Muslim, Albanian Orthodox, Roman Catholic
Area Sq Miles	11 100		
Population	3 166 000		
Capital	Tirana (Tiranë)	Currency	Lek
Languages	Albanian, Greek	Organizations	UN
		Map page	109

ALGERIA
People's Democratic Republic of Algeria

Area Sq Km	2 381 741	Religions	Sunni Muslim
Area Sq Miles	919 595	Currency	Algerian dinar
Population	31 800 000	Organizations	OPEC, UN
Capital	Algiers (Alger)	Map page	114–115
Languages	Arabic, French, Berber		

American Samoa
United States Unincorporated Territory

Area Sq Km	197	Religions	Protestant, Roman Catholic
Area Sq Miles	76		
Population	67 000	Currency	United States dollar
Capital	Fagatogo	Map page	49
Languages	Samoan, English		

ANDORRA
Principality of Andorra

Area Sq Km	465	Religions	Roman Catholic
Area Sq Miles	180	Currency	Euro
Population	71 000	Organizations	UN
Capital	Andorra la Vella	Map page	104
Languages	Spanish, Catalan, French		

ANGOLA
Republic of Angola

Area Sq Km	1 246 700	Religions	Roman Catholic, Protestant, traditional beliefs
Area Sq Miles	481 354		
Population	13 625 000		
Capital	Luanda	Currency	Kwanza
Languages	Portuguese, Bantu, local languages	Organizations	SADC, UN
		Map page	120

Anguilla

United Kingdom Overseas Territory

Area Sq Km	155	Religions	Protestant, Roman Catholic
Area Sq Miles	60		
Population	12 000	Currency	East Caribbean dollar
Capital	The Valley	Map page	147
Languages	English		

ANTIGUA AND BARBUDA

Area Sq Km	442	Religions	Protestant, Roman Catholic
Area Sq Miles	171		
Population	73 000	Currency	East Caribbean dollar
Capital	St John's	Organizations	CARICOM, Comm., UN
Languages	English, creole	Map page	147

ARGENTINA
Argentine Republic

Area Sq Km	2 766 889	Religions	Roman Catholic, Protestant
Area Sq Miles	1 068 302		
Population	38 428 000	Currency	Argentinian peso
Capital	Buenos Aires	Organizations	UN
Languages	Spanish, Italian, Amerindian languages	Map page	152–153

ARMENIA
Republic of Armenia

Area Sq Km	29 800	Religions	Armenian Orthodox
Area Sq Miles	11 506	Currency	Dram
Population	3 061 000	Organizations	CIS, UN
Capital	Yerevan (Erevan)	Map page	81
Languages	Armenian, Azeri		

Aruba
Self-governing Netherlands Territory

Area Sq Km	193	Religions	Roman Catholic, Protestant
Area Sq Miles	75		
Population	100 000	Currency	Aruban florin
Capital	Oranjestad	Map page	147
Languages	Papiamento, Dutch, English		

Ascension
Dependency of St Helena

Area Sq Km	88	Religions	Protestant, Roman Catholic
Area Sq Miles	34		
Population	1 122	Currency	Pound sterling
Capital	Georgetown	Map page	113
Languages	English		

AUSTRALIA
Commonwealth of Australia

Area Sq Km	7 692 024	Religions	Protestant, Roman Catholic, Orthodox
Area Sq Miles	2 969 907		
Population	19 731 000	Currency	Australian dollar
Capital	Canberra	Organizations	APEC, Comm., OECD, UN
Languages	English, Italian, Greek	Map page	50–51

Australian Capital Territory (Federal Territory)

Area Sq Km	2 358	Population	321 680
Area Sq Miles	910	Capital	Canberra

Jervis Bay Territory (Territory)

Area Sq Km	73	Population	611
Area Sq Miles	28		

New South Wales (State)

Area Sq Km	800 642	Population	6 609 304
Area Sq Miles	309 130	Capital	Sydney

Northern Territory (Territory)

Area Sq Km	1 349 129	Population	200 019
Area Sq Miles	520 902	Capital	Darwin

Queensland (State)

Area Sq Km	1 730 648	Population	3 635 121
Area Sq Miles	668 207	Capital	Brisbane

South Australia (State)

Area Sq Km	983 482	Population	1 514 854
Area Sq Miles	379 725	Capital	Adelaide

Tasmania (State)

Area Sq Km	68 401	Population	472 931
Area Sq Miles	26 410	Capital	Hobart

Victoria (State)

Area Sq Km	227 416	Population	4 822 663
Area Sq Miles	87 806	Capital	Melbourne

Western Australia (State)

Area Sq Km	2 529 875	Population	1 906 114
Area Sq Miles	976 790	Capital	Perth

AUSTRIA
Republic of Austria

Area Sq Km	83 855	Religions	Roman Catholic, Protestant
Area Sq Miles	32 377		
Population	8 116 000	Currency	Euro
Capital	Vienna (Wien)	Organizations	EU, OECD, UN
Languages	German, Croatian, Turkish	Map page	102–103

AZERBAIJAN

Azerbaijani Republic

Area Sq Km	86 600	Religions	Shi'a Muslim, Sunni Muslim, Russian and Armenian Orthodox
Area Sq Miles	33 436		
Population	8 370 000		
Capital	Baku (Bakı)	Currency	Azerbaijani manat
Languages	Azeri, Armenian, Russian, Lezgian	Organizations	CIS, UN
		Map page	81

Azores (Arquipélago dos Açores)
Autonomous Region of Portugal

Area Sq Km	2 300	Religions	Roman Catholic, Protestant
Area Sq Miles	888		
Population	242 073	Currency	Euro
Capital	Ponta Delgada	Map page	112
Languages	Portuguese		

 ## THE BAHAMAS
Commonwealth of The Bahamas

Area Sq Km	13 939	Religions	Protestant, Roman Catholic
Area Sq Miles	5 382		
Population	314 000	Currency	Bahamian dollar
Capital	Nassau	Organizations	CARICOM, Comm., UN
Languages	English, creole		
		Map page	146–147

 ## BAHRAIN
Kingdom of Bahrain

Area Sq Km	691	Religions	Shi'a Muslim, Sunni Muslim, Christian
Area Sq Miles	267		
Population	724 000	Currency	Bahraini dinar
Capital	Manama	Organizations	UN
	(Al Manāmah)	Map page	79
Languages	Arabic, English		

 ## BANGLADESH
People's Republic of Bangladesh

Area Sq Km	143 998	Religions	Sunni Muslim, Hindu
Area Sq Miles	55 598	Currency	Taka
Population	146 736 000	Organizations	Comm., UN
Capital	Dhaka (Dacca)	Map page	75
Languages	Bengali, English		

 ## BARBADOS

Area Sq Km	430	Religions	Protestant, Roman Catholic
Area Sq Miles	166		
Population	270 000	Currency	Barbados dollar
Capital	Bridgetown	Organizations	CARICOM, Comm., UN
Languages	English, creole		
		Map page	147

 ## BELARUS
Republic of Belarus

Area Sq Km	207 600	Religions	Belorussian Orthodox, Roman Catholic
Area Sq Miles	80 155		
Population	9 895 000	Currency	Belarus rouble
Capital	Minsk	Organizations	CIS, UN
Languages	Belorussian, Russian	Map page	88–89

 ## BELGIUM
Kingdom of Belgium

Area Sq Km	30 520	Religions	Roman Catholic, Protestant
Area Sq Miles	11 784		
Population	10 318 000	Currency	Euro
Capital	Brussels (Bruxelles)	Organizations	EU, OECD, UN
Languages	Dutch (Flemish), French (Walloon), German	Map page	100

 ## BELIZE

Area Sq Km	22 965	Religions	Roman Catholic, Protestant
Area Sq Miles	8 867		
Population	256 000	Currency	Belize dollar
Capital	Belmopan	Organizations	CARICOM, Comm., UN
Languages	English, Spanish, Mayan, creole		
		Map page	147

 ## BENIN
Republic of Benin

Area Sq Km	112 620	Religions	Traditional beliefs, Roman Catholic, Sunni Muslim
Area Sq Miles	43 483		
Population	6 736 000		
Capital	Porto-Novo	Currency	CFA franc
Languages	French, Fon, Yoruba, Adja, local languages	Organization	UN
		Map page	114

 ## Bermuda
United Kingdom Overseas Territory

Area Sq Km	54	Religions	Protestant, Roman Catholic
Area Sq Miles	21		
Population	82 000	Currency	Bermuda dollar
Capital	Hamilton	Map page	125
Languages	English		

 ## BHUTAN
Kingdom of Bhutan

Area Sq Km	46 620	Religions	Buddhist, Hindu
Area Sq Miles	18 000	Currency	Ngultrum, Indian rupee
Population	2 257 000		
Capital	Thimphu	Organizations	UN
Languages	Dzongkha, Nepali, Assamese	Map page	75

 ## BOLIVIA
Republic of Bolivia

Area Sq Km	1 098 581	Religions	Roman Catholic, Protestant, Baha'i
Area Sq Miles	424 164		
Population	8 808 000	Currency	Boliviano
Capital	La Paz/Sucre	Organizations	UN
Languages	Spanish, Quechua, Aymara	Map page	152

 ## Bonaire
part of Netherlands Antilles

Area Sq Km	288	Religions	Roman Catholic, Protestant
Area Sq Miles	111		
Population	10 114	Currency	Netherlands Antilles guilder
Capital	Kralendijk		
Languages	Dutch, Papiamento	Map page	147

Bonin Islands (Ogasawara-shotō)
part of Japan

Area Sq Km	104	Religions	Shintoist, Buddhist, Christian
Area Sq Miles	40		
Population	2 300	Currency	Yen
Capital	Omura	Map page	69
Languages	Japanese		

BOSNIA-HERZEGOVINA

Republic of Bosnia and Herzegovina

Area Sq Km	51 130	Religions	Sunni Muslim, Serbian
Area Sq Miles	19 741		Orthodox, Roman
Population	4 161 000		Catholic, Protestant
Capital	Sarajevo	Currency	Marka
Languages	Bosnian, Serbian,	Organizations	UN
	Croatian	Map page	109

BOTSWANA

Republic of Botswana

Area Sq Km	581 370	Religions	Traditional beliefs,
Area Sq Miles	224 468		Protestant, Roman
Population	1 785 000		Catholic
Capital	Gaborone	Currency	Pula
Languages	English, Setswana,	Organizations	Comm., SADC, UN
	Shona, local	Map page	120
	languages		

BRAZIL

Federative Republic of Brazil

Area Sq Km	8 514 879	Religions	Roman Catholic,
Area Sq Miles	3 287 613		Protestant
Population	178 470 000	Currency	Real
Capital	Brasília	Organizations	UN
Languages	Portuguese	Map page	150–151

BRUNEI

State of Brunei Darussalam

Area Sq Km	5 765	Religions	Sunni Muslim, Buddhist,
Area Sq Miles	2 226		Christian
Population	358 000	Currency	Brunei dollar
Capital	Bandar Seri Begawan	Organizations	APEC, ASEAN,
Languages	Malay, English,		Comm., UN
	Chinese	Map page	61

BULGARIA

Republic of Bulgaria

Area Sq Km	110 994	Religions	Bulgarian Orthodox,
Area Sq Miles	42 855		Sunni Muslim
Population	7 897 000	Currency	Lev
Capital	Sofia (Sofiya)	Organizations	UN
Languages	Bulgarian, Turkish,	Map page	110
	Romany,		
	Macedonian		

BURKINA

Democratic Republic of Burkina Faso

Area Sq Km	274 200	Religions	Sunni Muslim,
Area Sq Miles	105 869		traditional beliefs,
Population	13 002 000		Roman Catholic
Capital	Ouagadougou	Currency	CFA franc
Languages	French, Moore	Organizations	UN
	(Mossi), Fulani, local	Map page	114
	languages		

BURUNDI

Republic of Burundi

Area Sq Km	27 835	Religions	Roman Catholic,
Area Sq Miles	10 747		traditional beliefs,
Population	6 825 000		Protestant
Capital	Bujumbura	Currency	Burundian franc
Languages	Kirundi (Hutu,	Organizations	UN
	Tutsi), French	Map page	119

CAMBODIA

Kingdom of Cambodia

Area Sq Km	181 000	Religions	Buddhist, Roman
Area Sq Miles	69 884		Catholic, Sunni
Population	14 144 000		Muslim
Capital	Phnum Pénh	Currency	Riel
	(Phnom Penh)	Organizations	ASEAN, UN
Languages	Khmer, Vietnamese	Map page	63

CAMEROON

Republic of Cameroon

Area Sq Km	475 442	Religions	Roman Catholic,
Area Sq Miles	183 569		traditional beliefs,
Population	16 018 000		Sunni Muslim,
Capital	Yaoundé		Protestant
Languages	French, English,	Currency	CFA franc
	Fang, Bamileke,	Organizations	Comm., UN
	local languages	Map page	118

CANADA

Area Sq Km	9 984 670	Religions	Roman Catholic,
Area Sq Miles	3 855 103		Protestant, Eastern
Population	31 510 000		Orthodox, Jewish
Capital	Ottawa	Currency	Canadian dollar
Languages	English, French,	Organizations	APEC, Comm.,
	local languages		OECD, UN
		Map page	126–127

Alberta (Province)

Area Sq Km	661 848	Population	3 113 600
Area Sq Miles	255 541	Capital	Edmonton

British Columbia (Province)

Area Sq Km	944 735	Population	4 141 300
Area Sq Miles	364 764	Capital	Victoria

Manitoba (Province)

Area Sq Km	647 797	Population	1 150 800
Area Sq Miles	250 116	Capital	Winnipeg

New Brunswick (Province)

Area Sq Km	72 908	Population	756 700
Area Sq Miles	28 150	Capital	Fredericton

Newfoundland and Labrador (Province)

Area Sq Km	405 212	Population	531 600
Area Sq Miles	156 453	Capital	St John's

Northwest Territories (Territory)

Area Sq Km	1 346 106	Population	41 400
Area Sq Miles	519 734	Capital	Yellowknife

CANADA

Nova Scotia (Province)

Area Sq Km	55 284	Population	944 800
Area Sq Miles	21 345	Capital	Halifax

Nunavut (Territory)

Area Sq Km	2 093 190	Population	28 700
Area Sq Miles	808 185	Capital	Iqaluit (Frobisher Bay)

Ontario (Province)

Area Sq Km	1 076 395	Population	12 068 300
Area Sq Miles	415 598	Capital	Toronto

Prince Edward Island (Province)

Area Sq Km	5 660	Population	139 900
Area Sq Miles	2 185	Capital	Charlottetown

Québec (Province)

Area Sq Km	1 542 056	Population	7 455 200
Area Sq Miles	595 391	Capital	Québec

Saskatchewan (Province)

Area Sq Km	651 036	Population	1 011 800
Area Sq Miles	251 366	Capital	Regina

Yukon Territory (Territory)

Area Sq Km	482 443	Population	29 900
Area Sq Miles	186 272	Capital	Whitehorse

Canary Islands (Islas Canarias)
Autonomous Community of Spain

Area Sq Km	7 447	Languages	Spanish
Area Sq Miles	2 875	Religions	Roman Catholic
Population	1 694 477	Currency	Euro
Capital	Santa Cruz de Tenerife/Las Palmas	Map page	114

CAPE VERDE
Republic of Cape Verde

Area Sq Km	4 033	Religions	Roman Catholic, Protestant
Area Sq Miles	1 557		
Population	463 000	Currency	Cape Verde escudo
Capital	Praia	Organizations	UN
Languages	Portuguese, creole	Map page	46

Cayman Islands
United Kingdom Overseas Territory

Area Sq Km	259	Religions	Protestant, Roman Catholic
Area Sq Miles	100		
Population	40 000	Currency	Cayman Islands dollar
Capital	George Town	Map page	146
Languages	English		

CENTRAL AFRICAN REPUBLIC

Area Sq Km	622 436	Religions	Protestant, Roman Catholic, traditional beliefs, Sunni Muslim
Area Sq Miles	240 324		
Population	3 865 000		
Capital	Bangui	Currency	CFA franc
Languages	French, Sango, Banda, Baya, local languages	Organizations	UN
		Map page	118

Ceuta
Autonomous Community of Spain

Area Sq Km	19	Religions	Roman Catholic, Muslim
Area Sq Miles	7		
Population	71 505	Currency	Euro
Capital	Ceuta	Map page	106
Languages	Spanish, Arabic		

CHAD
Republic of Chad

Area Sq Km	1 284 000	Religions	Sunni Muslim, Roman Catholic, Protestant, traditional beliefs
Area Sq Miles	495 755		
Population	8 598 000		
Capital	Ndjamena	Currency	CFA franc
Languages	Arabic, French,Sara, local languages	Organizations	UN
		Map page	115

Chatham Islands
part of New Zealand

Area Sq Km	963	Religions	Protestant
Area Sq Miles	372	Currency	New Zealand dollar
Population	717	Map page	49
Capital	Waitangi		
Languages	English		

CHILE
Republic of Chile

Area Sq Km	756 945	Religions	Roman Catholic, Protestant
Area Sq Miles	292 258		
Population	15 805 000	Currency	Chilean peso
Capital	Santiago	Organizations	APEC, UN
Languages	Spanish, Amerindian languages	Map page	152–153

CHINA
People's Republic of China

Area Sq Km	9 584 492	Religions	Confucian, Taoist, Buddhist, Christian, Sunni Muslim
Area Sq Miles	3 700 593		
Population	1 289 161 000		
Capital	Beijing (Peking)	Currency	Yuan, Hong Kong dollar, Macao pataca
Languages	Mandarin, Wu, Cantonese, Hsiang, regional languages	Organizations	APEC, UN
		Map page	68–69

Anhui (Province)

Area Sq Km	139 000	Population	59 860 000
Area Sq Miles	53 668	Capital	Hefei

Bejing (Municipality)

Area Sq Km	16 800	Population	13 820 000
Area Sq Miles	6 487	Capital	Beijing (Peking)

Chongqing (Municipality)

Area Sq Km	23 000	Population	30 900 000
Area Sq Miles	8 880	Capital	Chongqing

Fujian (Province)

Area Sq Km	121 400	Population	34 710 000
Area Sq Miles	46 873	Capital	Fuzhou

Gansu (Province)

Area Sq Km	453 700	Population	25 620 000
Area Sq Miles	175 175	Capital	Lanzhou

Guangdong (Province)

Area Sq Km	178 000	Population	86 420 000
Area Sq Miles	68 726	Capital	Guangzhou (Canton)

Guangxi Zhuangzu Zizhiqu (Autonomous Region)

Area Sq Km	236 000	Population	44 890 000
Area Sq Miles	91 120	Capital	Nanning

Guizhou (Province)

Area Sq Km	176 000	Population	35 250 000
Area Sq Miles	67 954	Capital	Guiyang

Hainan (Province)

Area Sq Km	34 000	Population	7 870 000
Area Sq Miles	13 127	Capital	Haikou

Hebei (Province)

Area Sq Km	187 700	Population	67 440 000
Area Sq Miles	72 471	Capital	Shijiazhuang

Heilongjiang (Province)

Area Sq Km	454 600	Population	36 890 000
Area Sq Miles	175 522	Capital	Harbin

Henan (Province)

Area Sq Km	167 000	Population	92 560 000
Area Sq Miles	64 479	Capital	Zhengzhou

Hong Kong (Special Administrative Region)

Area Sq Km	1 075	Population	6 780 000
Area Sq Miles	415	Capital	Hong Kong

Hubei (Province)

Area Sq Km	185 900	Population	60 280 000
Area Sq Miles	71 776	Capital	Wuhan

Hunan (Province)

Area Sq Km	210 000	Population	64 400 000
Area Sq Miles	81 081	Capital	Changsha

Jiangsu (Province)

Area Sq Km	102 600	Population	74 380 000
Area Sq Miles	39 614	Capital	Nanjing

Jiangxi (Province)

Area Sq Km	166 900	Population	41 400 000
Area Sq Miles	64 440	Capital	Nanchang

Jilin (Province)

Area Sq Km	187 000	Population	27 280 000
Area Sq Miles	72 201	Capital	Changchun

Liaoning (Province)

Area Sq Km	147 400	Population	42 380 000
Area Sq Miles	56 911	Capital	Shenyang

Macao (Special Administrative Region)

Area Sq Km	17	Population	440 000
Area Sq Mile	7		

Nei Mongol Zizhiqu (Inner Mongolia) (Autonomous Region)

Area Sq Km	1 183 000	Population	23 760 000
Area Sq Miles	456 759	Capital	Hohhot

Ningxia Huizu Zizhiqu (Autonomous Region)

Area Sq Km	66 400	Population	5 620 000
Area Sq Miles	25 637	Capital	Yinchuan

Qinghai (Province)

Area Sq Km	721 000	Population	5 180 000
Area Sq Miles	278 380	Capital	Xining

Shaanxi (Province)

Area Sq Km	205 600	Population	36 050 000
Area Sq Miles	79 383	Capital	Xi'an

Shandong (Province)

Area Sq Km	153 300	Population	90 790 000
Area Sq Miles	59 189	Capital	Jinan

Shanghai (Municipality)

Area Sq Km	6 300	Population	16 740 000
Area Sq Miles	2 432	Capital	Shanghai

Shanxi (Province)

Area Sq Km	156 300	Population	32 970 000
Area Sq Miles	60 348	Capital	Taiyuan

Sichuan (Province)

Area Sq Km	569 000	Population	83 290 000
Area Sq Miles	219 692	Capital	Chengdu

Tianjin (Municipality)

Area Sq Km	11 300	Population	10 010 000
Area Sq Miles	4 363	Capital	Tianjin

Xinjiang Uygur Zizhiqu (Sinkiang) (Autonomous Region)

Area Sq Km	1 600 000	Population	19 250 000
Area Sq Miles	617 763	Capital	Ürümqi

Xizang Zizhiqu (Tibet) (Autonomous Region)

Area Sq Km	1 228 400	Population	2 620 000
Area Sq Miles	474 288	Capital	Lhasa

Yunnan (Province)

Area Sq Km	394 000	Population	42 880 000
Area Sq Miles	152 124	Capital	Kunming

Zhejiang (Province)

Area Sq Km	101 800	Population	46 770 000
Area Sq Miles	39 305	Capital	Hangzhou

Christmas Island
Australian External Territory

Area Sq Km	135	Religions	Buddhist, Sunni
Area Sq Miles	52		Muslim, Protestant,
Population	1 560		Roman Catholic
Capital	The Settlement	Currency	Australian dollar
Languages	English	Map page	58

Cook Islands
Self-governing New Zealand Territory

Area Sq Km	293	Religions	Protestant, Roman
Area Sq Miles	113		Catholic
Population	18 000	Currency	New Zealand dollar
Capital	Avarua	Map page	49
Languages	English, Maori		

Cocos Islands (Keeling Islands)
Australian External Territory

Area Sq Km	14	Religions	Sunni Muslim,
Area Sq Miles	5		Christian
Population	632	Currency	Australian dollar
Capital	West Island	Map page	58
Languages	English		

COSTA RICA
Republic of Costa Rica

Area Sq Km	51 100	Religions	Roman Catholic,
Area Sq Miles	19 730		Protestant
Population	4 173 000	Currency	Costa Rican colón
Capital	San José	Organizations	UN
Languages	Spanish	Map page	146

COLOMBIA
Republic of Colombia

Area Sq Km	1 141 748	Religions	Roman Catholic,
Area Sq Miles	440 831		Protestant
Population	44 222 000	Currency	Colombian peso
Capital	Bogotá	Organizations	APEC, UN
Languages	Spanish, Amerindian	Map page	150
	languages		

CÔTE D'IVOIRE
Republic of Côte d'Ivoire

Area Sq Km	322 463	Religions	Sunni Muslim, Roman
Area Sq Miles	124 504		Catholic, traditonal
Population	16 631 000		beliefs, Protestant
Capital	Yamoussoukro	Currency	CFA franc
Languages	French, creole, Akan,	Organizations	UN
	local languages	Map page	114

COMOROS
Union of the Comoros

Area Sq Km	1 862	Religions	Sunni Muslim, Roman
Area Sq Miles	719		Catholic
Population	768 000	Currency	Comoros franc
Capital	Moroni	Organizations	UN
Languages	Comorian, French,	Map page	121
	Arabic		

CROATIA
Republic of Croatia

Area Sq Km	56 538	Religions	Roman Catholic,
Area Sq Miles	21 829		Serbian Orthodox,
Population	4 428 000		Sunni Muslim
Capital	Zagreb	Currency	Kuna
Languages	Croatian, Serbian	Organizations	UN
		Map page	109

CONGO
Republic of the Congo

Area Sq Km	342 000	Religions	Roman Catholic,
Area Sq Miles	132 047		Protestant, traditional
Population	3 724 000		beliefs, Sunni Muslim
Capital	Brazzaville	Currency	CFA franc
Languages	French, Kongo,	Organizations	UN
	Monokutuba, local	Map page	118
	languages		

CUBA
Republic of Cuba

Area Sq Km	110 860	Religions	Roman Catholic,
Area Sq Miles	42 803		Protestant
Population	11 300 000	Currency	Cuban peso
Capital	Havana (La Habana)	Organizations	UN
Languages	Spanish	Map page	146

Curaçao
part of Netherlands Antilles

Area Sq Km	444	Religions	Roman Catholic,
Area Sq Miles	171		Protestant
Population	126 816	Currency	Netherlands Antilles
Capital	Willemstad		guilder
Languages	Dutch, Papiamento	Map page	147

CONGO, DEMOCRATIC REPUBLIC OF THE

Area Sq Km	2 345 410	Religions	Christian, Sunni
Area Sq Miles	905 568		Muslim
Population	52 771 000	Currency	Congolese franc
Capital	Kinshasa	Organizations	SADC, UN
Languages	French, Lingala,	Map page	118–119
	Swahili, Kongo,		
	local languages		

CYPRUS
Republic of Cyprus

Area Sq Km	9 251	Religions	Greek Orthodox,
Area Sq Miles	3 572		Sunni Muslim
Population	802 000	Currency	Cyprus pound
Capital	Nicosia (Lefkosia)	Organizations	Comm., UN
Languages	Greek, Turkish,	Map page	80
	English		

CZECH REPUBLIC

Area Sq Km	78 864	Religions	Roman Catholic, Protestant
Area Sq Miles	30 450		
Population	10 236 000	Currency	Czech koruna
Capital	Prague (Praha)	Organizations	UN
Languages	Czech, Moravian, Slovakian	Map page	102–103

DENMARK
Kingdom of Denmark

Area Sq Km	43 075	Religions	Protestant
Area Sq Miles	16 631	Currency	Danish krone
Population	5 364 000	Organizations	EU, OECD, UN
Capital	Copenhagen (København)	Map page	93
Languages	Danish		

DJIBOUTI
Republic of Djibouti

Area Sq Km	23 200	Religions	Sunni Muslim, Christian
Area Sq Miles	8 958		
Population	703 000	Currency	Djibouti franc
Capital	Djibouti	Organizations	UN
Languages	Somali, Afar, French, Arabic	Map page	117

DOMINICA
Commonwealth of Dominica

Area Sq Km	750	Religions	Roman Catholic, Protestant
Area Sq Miles	290		
Population	79 000	Currency	East Caribbean dollar
Capital	Roseau	Organizations	CARICOM, Comm., UN
Languages	English, creole		
		Map page	147

DOMINICAN REPUBLIC

Area Sq Km	48 442	Religions	Roman Catholic, Protestant
Area Sq Miles	18 704		
Population	8 745 000	Currency	Dominican peso
Capital	Santo Domingo	Organizations	UN
Languages	Spanish, creole	Map page	147

Easter Island (Isla de Pascua)
part of Chile

Area Sq Km	171	Religions	Roman Catholic
Area Sq Miles	66	Currency	Chilean peso
Population	3 791	Map page	157
Capital	Hanga Roa		
Languages	Spanish		

EAST TIMOR
Democratic Republic of East Timor

Area Sq Km	14 874	Religions	Roman Catholic
Area Sq Miles	5 743	Currency	United States dollar
Population	778 000	Organisations	UN
Capital	Dili	Map page	59
Languages	Portuguese, Tetun, English		

ECUADOR
Republic of Ecuador

Area Sq Km	272 045	Religions	Roman Catholic
Area Sq Miles	105 037	Currency	United States dollar
Population	13 003 000	Organizations	APEC, UN
Capital	Quito	Map page	150
Languages	Spanish, Quechua, Amerindian languages		

EGYPT
Arab Republic of Egypt

Area Sq Km	1 000 250	Religions	Sunni Muslim, Coptic Christian
Area Sq Miles	386 199		
Population	71 931 000	Currency	Egyptian pound
Capital	Cairo (Al Qāhira)	Organizations	UN
Languages	Arabic	Map page	116

EL SALVADOR
Republic of El Salvador

Area Sq Km	21 041	Religions	Roman Catholic, Protestant
Area Sq Miles	8 124		
Population	6 515 000	Currency	El Salvador colón, United States dollar
Capital	San Salvador		
Languages	Spanish	Organizations	UN
		Map page	146

EQUATORIAL GUINEA
Republic of Equatorial Guinea

Area Sq Km	28 051	Religions	Roman Catholic, traditional beliefs
Area Sq Miles	10 831		
Population	494 000	Currency	CFA franc
Capital	Malabo	Organizations	UN
Languages	Spanish, French, Fang	Map page	118

ERITREA
State of Eritrea

Area Sq Km	117 400	Religions	Sunni Muslim, Coptic Christian
Area Sq Miles	45 328		
Population	4 141 000	Currency	Nakfa
Capital	Asmara	Organizations	UN
Languages	Tigrinya, Tigre	Map page	116

ESTONIA
Republic of Estonia

Area Sq Km	45 200	Religions	Protestant, Estonian and Russian Orthodox
Area Sq Miles	17 452		
Population	1 323 000	Currency	Kroon
Capital	Tallinn	Organizations	UN
Languages	Estonian, Russian	Map page	88

ETHIOPIA
Federal Democratic Republic of Ethiopia

Area Sq Km	1 133 880	Religions	Ethiopian Orthodox, Sunni Muslim, traditional beliefs
Area Sq Miles	437 794		
Population	70 678 000		
Capital	Addis Ababa (Ādīs Ābeba)	Currency	Birr
		Organizations	UN
Languages	Oromo, Amharic, Tigrinya, local languages	Map page	117

STATES AND TERRITORIES

Falkland Islands
United Kingdom Overseas Territory

Area Sq Km	12 170	Religions	Protestant, Roman Catholic
Area Sq Miles	4 699		
Population	3 000	Currency	Falkland Islands pound
Capital	Stanley		
Languages	English	Map page	153

Faroe Islands
Self-governing Danish Territory

Area Sq Km	1 399	Religions	Protestant
Area Sq Miles	540	Currency	Danish krone
Population	47 000	Map page	94
Capital	Tórshavn (Thorshavn)		
Languages	Faroese, Danish		

FIJI
Sovereign Democratic Republic of Fiji

Area Sq Km	18 330	Religions	Christian, Hindu, Sunni Muslim
Area Sq Miles	7 077		
Population	839 000	Currency	Fiji dollar
Capital	Suva	Organizations	UN, Comm.
Languages	English, Fijian, Hindi	Map page	49

FINLAND
Republic of Finland

Area Sq Km	338 145	Religions	Protestant, Greek Orthodox
Area Sq Miles	130 559		
Population	5 207 000	Currency	Euro
Capital	Helsinki (Helsingfors)	Organizations	EU, OECD, UN
Languages	Finnish, Swedish	Map page	92–93

FRANCE
French Republic

Area Sq Km	543 965	Religions	Roman Catholic, Protestant, Sunni Muslim
Area Sq Miles	210 026		
Population	60 144 000		
Capital	Paris	Currency	Euro
Languages	French, Arabic	Organizations	EU, OECD, UN
		Map page	104–105

French Guiana
French Overseas Department

Area Sq Km	90 000	Religions	Roman Catholic
Area Sq Miles	34 749	Currency	Euro
Population	178 000	Map page	151
Capital	Cayenne		
Languages	French, creole		

French Polynesia
French Overseas Territory

Area Sq Km	3 265	Religions	Protestant, Roman Catholic
Area Sq Miles	1 261		
Population	244 000	Currency	CFP franc
Capital	Papeete	Map page	49
Languages	French, Tahitian, Polynesian languages		

GABON
Gabonese Republic

Area Sq Km	267 667	Religions	Roman Catholic, Protestant, traditonal beliefs
Area Sq Miles	103 347		
Population	1 329 000		
Capital	Libreville	Currency	CFA franc
Languages	French, Fang, local languages	Organizations	UN
		Map page	118

Galapagos Islands (Islas Galápagos)
part of Ecuador

Area Sq Km	8 010	Religions	Roman Catholic
Area Sq Miles	3 093	Currency	United States dollar
Population	18 640	Map page	125
Capital	Puerto Baquerizo Moreno		
Languages	Spanish		

THE GAMBIA
Republic of The Gambia

Area Sq Km	11 295	Religions	Sunni Muslim, Protestant
Area Sq Miles	4 361		
Population	1 426 000	Currency	Dalasi
Capital	Banjul	Organizations	Comm., UN
Languages	English, Malinke, Fulani, Wolof	Map page	114

Gaza
semi-autonomous region

Area Sq Km	363	Religions	Sunni Muslim, Shi'a Muslim
Area Sq Miles	140		
Population	1 203 591	Currency	Israeli shekel
Capital	Gaza	Map page	80
Languages	Arabic		

GEORGIA
Republic of Georgia

Area Sq Km	69 700	Religions	Georgian Orthodox, Russian Orthodox, Sunni Muslim
Area Sq Miles	26 911		
Population	5 126 000		
Capital	T'bilisi	Currency	Lari
Languages	Georgian, Russian, Armenian, Azeri, Ossetian, Abkhaz	Organizations	CIS, UN
		Map page	81

GERMANY
Federal Republic of Germany

Area Sq Km	357 022	Religions	Protestant, Roman Catholic
Area Sq Miles	137 847		
Population	82 476 000	Currency	Euro
Capital	Berlin	Organizations	EU, OECD, UN
Languages	German, Turkish	Map page	102

GHANA
Republic of Ghana

Area Sq Km	238 537	Religions	Christian, Sunni Muslim, traditional beliefs
Area Sq Miles	92 100		
Population	20 922 000		
Capital	Accra	Currency	Cedi
Languages	English, Hausa, Akan, local languages	Organizations	Comm., UN
		Map page	114

Gibraltar
United Kingdom Overseas Territory

Area Sq Km	7	Religions	Roman Catholic,
Area Sq Miles	3		Protestant, Sunni
Population	27 000		Muslim
Capital	Gibraltar	Currency	Gibraltar pound
Languages	English, Spanish	Map page	106

Guernsey
United Kingdom Crown Dependency

Area Sq Km	78	Religions	Protestant, Roman
Area Sq Miles	30		Catholic
Population	62 701	Currency	Pound sterling
Capital	St Peter Port	Map page	95
Languages	English, French		

GREECE
Hellenic Republic

Area Sq Km	131 957	Religions	Greek Orthodox,
Area Sq Miles	50 949		Sunni Muslim
Population	10 976 000	Currency	Euro
Capital	Athens (Athina)	Organizations	EU, OECD, UN
Languages	Greek	Map page	111

GUINEA
Republic of Guinea

Area Sq Km	245 857	Religions	Sunni Muslim,
Area Sq Miles	94 926		traditional beliefs,
Population	8 480 000		Christian
Capital	Conakry	Currency	Guinea franc
Languages	French, Fulani,	Organizations	UN
	Malinke, local	Map page	114
	languages		

Greenland
Self-governing Danish Territory

Area Sq Km	2 175 600	Religions	Protestant
Area Sq Miles	840 004	Currency	Danish krone
Population	57 000	Map page	127
Capital	Nuuk (Godthâb)		
Languages	Greenlandic, Danish		

GUINEA-BISSAU
Republic of Guinea-Bissau

Area Sq Km	36 125	Religions	Traditional beliefs,
Area Sq Miles	13 948		Sunni Muslim,
Population	1 493 000		Christian
Capital	Bissau	Currency	CFA franc
Languages	Portuguese, crioulo,	Organizations	UN
	local languages	Map page	114

GRENADA

Area Sq Km	378	Religions	Roman Catholic,
Area Sq Miles	146		Protestant
Population	80 000	Currency	East Caribbean dollar
Capital	St George's	Organizations	CARICOM, Comm.,
Languages	English, creole		UN
		Map page	147

GUYANA
Co-operative Republic of Guyana

Area Sq Km	214 969	Religions	Protestant, Hindu,
Area Sq Miles	83 000		Roman Catholic,
Population	765 000		Sunni Muslim
Capital	Georgetown	Currency	Guyana dollar
Languages	English, creole,	Organizations	CARICOM, Comm.,
	Amerindian		UN
	languages	Map page	150

Guadeloupe
French Overseas Department

Area Sq Km	1 780	Religions	Roman Catholic
Area Sq Miles	687	Currency	Euro
Population	440 000	Map page	147
Capital	Basse-Terre		
Languages	French, creole		

HAITI
Republic of Haiti

Area Sq Km	27 750	Religions	Roman Catholic,
Area Sq Miles	10 714		Protestant, Voodoo
Population	8 326 000	Currency	Gourde
Capital	Port au-Prince	Organizations	CARICOM, UN
Languages	French, creole	Map page	147

Guam
United States Unincorporated Territory

Area Sq Km	541	Religions	Roman Catholic
Area Sq Miles	209	Currency	United States dollar
Population	163 000	Map page	59
Capital	Hagåtña		
Languages	Chamorro, English,		
	Tagalog		

HONDURAS
Republic of Honduras

Area Sq Km	112 088	Religions	Roman Catholic,
Area Sq Miles	43 277		Protestant
Population	6 941 000	Currency	Lempira
Capital	Tegucigalpa	Organizations	UN
Languages	Spanish, Amerindian	Map page	147
	languages		

GUATEMALA
Republic of Guatemala

Area Sq Km	108 890	Religion	Roman Catholic,
Area Sq Miles	42 043		Protestant
Population	12 347 000	Currency	Quetzal, United
Capital	Guatemala City		States dollar
Languages	Spanish, Mayan	Organizations	UN
	languages	Map page	146

HUNGARY
Republic of Hungary

Area Sq Km	93 030	Religions	Roman Catholic,
Area Sq Miles	35 919		Protestant
Population	9 877 000	Currency	Forint
Capital	Budapest	Organizations	OECD, UN
Languages	Hungarian	Map page	103

 ICELAND
Republic of Iceland

Area Sq Km	102 820	Religions	Protestant
Area Sq Miles	39 699	Currency	Icelandic króna
Population	290 000	Organizations	OECD, UN
Capital	Reykjavík	Map page	92
Languages	Icelandic		

 INDIA
Republic of India

Area Sq Km	3 064 898	Religions	Hindu, Sunni Muslim,
Area Sq Miles	1 183 364		Shi'a Muslim, Sikh,
Population	1 065 462 000		Christian
Capital	New Delhi	Currency	Indian rupee
Languages	Hindi, English, many	Organizations	Comm., UN
	regional languages	Map page	72–73

 INDONESIA
Republic of Indonesia

Area Sq Km	1 919 445	Religions	Sunni Muslim,
Area Sq Miles	741 102		Protestant, Roman
Population	219 883 000		Catholic, Hindu,
Capital	Jakarta		Buddhist
Languages	Indonesian, local	Currency	Rupiah
	languages	Organizations	APEC, ASEAN,
			OPEC, UN
		Map page	58–59

 IRAN
Islamic Republic of Iran

Area Sq Km	1 648 000	Religions	Shi'a Muslim, Sunni
Area Sq Miles	636 296		Muslim
Population	68 920 000	Currency	Iranian rial
Capital	Tehrān	Organizations	OPEC, UN
Languages	Farsi, Azeri, Kurdish,	Map page	81
	regional languages		

 IRAQ
Republic of Iraq

Area Sq Km	438 317	Religions	Shi'a Muslim, Sunni
Area Sq Miles	169 235		Muslim, Christian
Population	25 175 000	Currency	Iraqi dinar
Capital	Baghdād	Organizations	OPEC, UN
Languages	Arabic, Kurdish,	Map page	81
	Turkmen		

 IRELAND

Area Sq Km	70 282	Religions	Roman Catholic,
Area Sq Miles	27 136		Protestant,
Population	3 956 000	Currency	Euro
Capital	Dublin	Organizations	EU, OECD, UN
	(Baile Átha Cliath)	Map page	97
Languages	English, Irish		

 Isle of Man
United Kingdom Crown Dependency

Area Sq Km	572	Religions	Protestant, Roman
Area Sq Miles	221		Catholic
Population	75 000	Currency	Pound sterling
Capital	Douglas	Map page	98
Languages	English		

 ISRAEL
State of Israel

Area Sq Km	20 770	Religions	Jewish, Sunni Muslim,
Area Sq Miles	8 019		Christian, Druze
Population	6 433 000	Currency	Shekel
Capital	Jerusalem*	Organizations	UN
	(Yerushalayim)	Map page	80
	(El Quds)		
Languages	Hebrew, Arabic		

*De facto capital. Disputed.

 ITALY
Italian Republic

Area Sq Km	301 245	Religions	Roman Catholic
Area Sq Miles	116 311	Currency	Euro
Population	57 423 000	Organizations	EU, OECD, UN
Capital	Rome (Roma)	Map page	108–109
Languages	Italian		

 JAMAICA

Area Sq Km	10 991	Religions	Protestant, Roman
Area Sq Miles	4 244		Catholic
Population	2 651 000	Currency	Jamaican dollar
Capital	Kingston	Organizations	CARICOM, Comm.,
Languages	English, creole		UN
		Map page	146

Jammu and Kashmir
Disputed territory (India/Pakistan)

Area Sq Km	222 236	Map page	74–75
Area Sq Miles	85 806		
Population	13 000 000		
Capital	Srinagar		

 JAPAN

Area Sq Km	377 727	Religions	Shintoist, Buddhist,
Area Sq Miles	145 841		Christian
Population	127 654 000	Currency	Yen
Capital	Tōkyō	Organizations	APEC, OECD, UN
Languages	Japanese	Map page	66–67

 Jersey
United Kingdom Crown Dependency

Area Sq Km	116	Religions	Protestant, Roman
Area Sq Miles	45		Catholic
Population	87 186	Currency	Pound sterling
Capital	St Helier	Map page	95
Languages	English, French		

 JORDAN
Hashemite Kingdom of Jordan

Area Sq Km	89 206	Religions	Sunni Muslim,
Area Sq Miles	34 443		Christian
Population	5 473 000	Currency	Jordanian dinar
Capital	'Ammān	Organizations	UN
Languages	Arabic	Map page	80

Juan Fernández Islands
part of Chile

Area Sq Km	179	Religions	Roman Catholic, Protestant
Area Sq Miles	69		
Population	633	Currency	Chilean peso
Capital	San Juan Bautista	Map page	157
Languages	Spanish, Amerindian languages		

KAZAKHSTAN
Republic of Kazakhstan

Area Sq Km	2 717 300	Religions	Sunni Muslim, Russian Orthodox, Protestant
Area Sq Miles	1 049 155		
Population	15 433 000	Currency	Tenge
Capital	Astana (Akmola)	Organizations	CIS, UN
Languages	Kazakh, Russian, Ukrainian, German, Uzbek, Tatar	Map page	76–77

KENYA
Republic of Kenya

Area Sq Km	582 646	Religions	Christian, traditional beliefs
Area Sq Miles	224 961		
Population	31 987 000	Currency	Kenyan shilling
Capital	Nairobi	Organizations	Comm., UN
Languages	Swahili, English, local languages	Map page	119

KIRIBATI
Republic of Kiribati

Area Sq Km	717	Religions	Roman Catholic, Protestant
Area Sq Miles	277		
Population	88 000	Currency	Australian dollar
Capital	Bairiki	Organizations	Comm., UN
Languages	Gilbertese, English	Map page	49

KUWAIT
State of Kuwait

Area Sq Km	17 818	Religions	Sunni Muslim, Shi'a Muslim, Christian, Hindu
Area Sq Miles	6 880		
Population	2 521 000		
Capital	Kuwait (Al Kuwayt)	Currency	Kuwaiti dinar
Languages	Arabic	Organizations	OPEC, UN
		Map page	78

KYRGYZSTAN
Kyrgyz Republic

Area Sq Km	198 500	Religions	Sunni Muslim, Russian Orthodox
Area Sq Miles	76 641		
Population	5 138 000	Currency	Kyrgyz som
Capital	Bishkek (Frunze)	Organizations	CIS, UN
Languages	Kyrgyz, Russian, Uzbek	Map page	77

LAOS
Lao People's Democratic Republic

Area Sq Km	236 800	Religions	Buddhist, traditional beliefs
Area Sq Miles	91 429		
Population	5 657 000	Currency	Kip
Capital	Vientiane (Viangchan)	Organizations	ASEAN, UN
		Map page	62–63
Languages	Lao, local languages		

LATVIA
Republic of Latvia

Area Sq Km	63 700	Religions	Protestant, Roman Catholic, Russian Orthodox
Area Sq Miles	24 595		
Population	2 307 000		
Capital	Rīga	Currency	Lats
Languages	Latvian, Russian	Organizations	UN
		Map page	88

LEBANON
Republic of Lebanon

Area Sq Km	10 452	Religions	Shi'a Muslim, Sunni Muslim, Christian
Area Sq Miles	4 036		
Population	3 653 000	Currency	Lebanese pound
Capital	Beirut (Beyrouth)	Organizations	UN
Languages	Arabic, Armenian, French	Map page	80

LESOTHO
Kingdom of Lesotho

Area Sq Km	30 355	Religions	Christian, traditional beliefs
Area Sq Miles	11 720		
Population	1 802 000	Currency	Loti, South African rand
Capital	Maseru		
Languages	Sesotho, English, Zulu	Organizations	Comm., SADC, UN
		Map page	123

LIBERIA
Republic of Liberia

Area Sq Km	111 369	Religions	Traditional beliefs, Christian, Sunni Muslim
Area Sq Miles	43 000		
Population	3 367 000		
Capital	Monrovia	Currency	Liberian dollar
Languages	English, creole, local languages	Organizations	UN
		Map page	114

LIBYA
Socialist People's Libyan Arab Jamahiriya

Area Sq Km	1 759 540	Religions	Sunni Muslim
Area Sq Miles	679 362	Currency	Libyan dinar
Population	5 551 000	Organizations	OPEC, UN
Capital	Tripoli (Ṭarābulus)	Map page	115
Languages	Arabic, Berber		

LIECHTENSTEIN
Principality of Liechtenstein

Area Sq Km	160	Religions	Roman Catholic, Protestant
Area Sq Miles	62		
Population	34 000	Currency	Swiss franc
Capital	Vaduz	Organizations	UN
Languages	German	Map page	105

LITHUANIA
Republic of Lithuania

Area Sq Km	65 200	Religions	Roman Catholic, Protestant, Russian Orthodox
Area Sq Miles	25 174		
Population	3 444 000		
Capital	Vilnius	Currency	Litas
Languages	Lithuanian, Russian, Polish	Organizations	UN
		Map page	88

Lord Howe Island
part of Australia

Area Sq Km	17	Religions	Protestant,
Area Sq Miles	6		Roman Catholic
Population	397	Currency	Australian dollar
Languages	English	Map page	51

LUXEMBOURG
Grand Duchy of Luxembourg

Area Sq Km	2 586	Religions	Roman Catholic
Area Sq Miles	998	Currency	Euro
Population	453 000	Organizations	EU, OECD, UN
Capital	Luxembourg	Map page	100
Languages	Letzeburgish, German, French		

MACEDONIA (F.Y.R.O.M.)
Republic of Macedonia

Area Sq Km	25 713	Religions	Macedonian Orthodox,
Area Sq Miles	9 928		Sunni Muslim
Population	2 056 000	Currency	Macedonian denar
Capital	Skopje	Organizations	UN
Languages	Macedonian, Albanian, Turkish	Map page	111

MADAGASCAR
Republic of Madagascar

Area Sq Km	587 041	Religions	Traditional beliefs,
Area Sq Miles	226 658		Christian, Sunni
Population	17 404 000		Muslim
Capital	Antananarivo	Currency	Malagasy ariary,
Languages	Malagasy, French		Malagasy franc
		Organizations	UN
		Map page	121

Madeira
Autonomous Region of Portugal

Area Sq Km	779	Religions	Roman Catholic,
Area Sq Miles	301		Protestant
Population	242 603	Currency	Euro
Capital	Funchal	Map page	114
Languages	Portuguese		

MALAWI
Republic of Malawi

Area Sq Km	118 484	Religions	Christian, traditional
Area Sq Miles	45 747		beliefs, Sunni Muslim
Population	12 105 000	Currency	Malawian kwacha
Capital	Lilongwe	Organizations	Comm.,SADC, UN
Languages	Chichewa, English, local languages	Map page	121

MALAYSIA
Federation of Malaysia

Area Sq Km	332 965	Religions	Sunni Muslim,
Area Sq Miles	128 559		Buddhist,
Population	24 425 000		Hindu, Christian,
Capital	Kuala Lumpur/		traditional beliefs
	Putrajaya	Currency	Ringgit
Languages	Malay, English,	Organizations	APEC, ASEAN,
	Chinese, Tamil,		Comm., UN
	local languages	Map page	60–61

MALDIVES
Republic of the Maldives

Area Sq Km	298	Religions	Sunni Muslim
Area Sq Miles	115	Currency	Rufiyaa
Population	318 000	Organizations	Comm., UN
Capital	Male	Map page	56
Languages	Divehi (Maldivian)		

MALI
Republic of Mali

Area Sq Km	1 240 140	Religions	Sunni Muslim,
Area Sq Miles	478 821		traditional beliefs,
Population	13 007 000		Christian
Capital	Bamako	Currency	CFA franc
Languages	French, Bambara,	Organizations	UN
	local languages	Map page	114

MALTA
Republic of Malta

Area Sq Km	316	Religions	Roman Catholic
Area Sq Miles	122	Currency	Maltese lira
Population	394 000	Organizations	Comm., UN
Capital	Valletta	Map page	84
Languages	Maltese, English		

MARSHALL ISLANDS
Republic of the Marshall Islands

Area Sq Km	181	Religions	Protestant, Roman
Area Sq Miles	70		Catholic
Population	53 000	Currency	United States dollar
Capital	Delap-Uliga-Djarrit	Organizations	UN
Languages	English, Marshallese	Map page	48

Martinique
French Overseas Department

Area Sq Km	1 079	Religions	Roman Catholic,
Area Sq Miles	417		traditional beliefs
Population	393 000	Currency	Euro
Capital	Fort-de-France	Map page	147
Languages	French, creole		

MAURITANIA
Islamic Arab and African Republic of Mauritania

Area Sq Km	1 030 700	Religions	Sunni Muslim
Area Sq Miles	397 955	Currency	Ouguiya
Population	2 893 000	Organizations	UN
Capital	Nouakchott	Map page	114
Languages	Arabic, French, local languages		

MAURITIUS
Republic of Mauritius

Area Sq Km	2 040	Religions	Hindu, Roman
Area Sq Miles	788		Catholic, Sunni
Population	1 221 000		Muslim
Capital	Port Louis	Currency	Mauritius rupee
Languages	English, creole,	Organizations	Comm., SADC, UN
	Hindi, Bhojpuri,	Map page	113
	French		

Mayotte
French Territorial Collectivity

Area Sq Km	373	Religions	Sunni Muslim,
Area Sq Miles	144		Christian
Population	170 879	Currency	Euro
Capital	Dzaoudzi	Map page	121
Languages	French, Mahorian		

Melilla
Autonomous Community of Spain

Area Sq Km	13	Languages	Spanish, Arabic
Area Sq Miles	5	Religions	Roman Catholic,
Population	66 411		Muslim
Capital	Melilla	Currency	Euro
		Map page	114

MEXICO
United Mexican States

Area Sq Km	1 972 545	Religions	Roman Catholic,
Area Sq Miles	761 604		Protestant
Population	103 457 000	Currency	Mexican peso
Capital	Mexico City	Organizations	APEC, OECD, UN
Languages	Spanish, Amerindian languages	Map page	144–145

MICRONESIA, FEDERATED STATES OF

Area Sq Km	701	Religions	Roman Catholic,
Area Sq Miles	271		Protestant
Population	109 000	Currency	United States dollar
Capital	Palikir	Organizations	UN
Languages	English, Chuukese, Pohnpeian, local languages	Map page	48

MOLDOVA
Republic of Moldova

Area Sq Km	33 700	Religions	Romanian Orthodox,
Area Sq Miles	13 012		Russian Orthodox
Population	4 267 000	Currency	Moldovan leu
Capital	Chişinău (Kishinev)	Organizations	CIS, UN
Languages	Romanian, Ukrainian, Gagauz, Russian	Map page	90

MONACO
Principality of Monaco

Area Sq Km	2	Religions	Roman Catholic
Area Sq Miles	1	Currency	Euro
Population	34 000	Organizations	UN
Capital	Monaco-Ville	Map page	105
Languages	French, Monégasque, Italian		

MONGOLIA

Area Sq Km	1 565 000	Religions	Buddhist,
Area Sq Miles	604 250		Sunni Muslim
Population	2 594 000	Currency	Tugrik (tögrög)
Capital	Ulan Bator (Ulaanbaatar)	Organizations	UN
Languages	Khalka (Mongolian), Kazakh, local languages	Map page	68–69

Montserrat
United Kingdom Overseas Territory

Area Sq Km	100	Religions	Protestant, Roman
Area Sq Miles	39		Catholic
Population	4 000	Currency	East Caribbean dollar
Capital	Plymouth	Organizations	CARICOM
Languages	English	Map page	147

MOROCCO
Kingdom of Morocco

Area Sq Km	446 550	Religions	Sunni Muslim
Area Sq Miles	172 414	Currency	Moroccan dirham
Population	30 566 000	Organizations	UN
Capital	Rabat	Map page	114
Languages	Arabic, Berber, French		

MOZAMBIQUE
Republic of Mozambique

Area Sq Km	799 380	Religions	Traditional beliefs,
Area Sq Miles	308 642		Roman Catholic,
Population	18 863 000		Sunni Muslim
Capital	Maputo	Currency	Metical
Languages	Portuguese, Makua, Tsonga, local languages	Organizations	Comm., SADC, UN
		Map page	121

MYANMAR
Union of Myanmar

Area Sq Km	676 577	Religions	Buddhist, Christian,
Area Sq Miles	261 228		Sunni Muslim
Population	49 485 000	Currency	Kyat
Capital	Rangoon (Yangôn)	Organizations	ASEAN, UN
Languages	Burmese, Shan, Karen, local languages	Map page	62–63

NAMIBIA
Republic of Namibia

Area Sq Km	824 292	Religions	Protestant, Roman
Area Sq Miles	318 261		Catholic
Population	1 987 000	Currency	Namibian dollar
Capital	Windhoek	Organizations	Comm., SADC, UN
Languages	English, Afrikaans, German, Ovambo, local languages	Map page	121

20

STATES AND TERRITORIES

NAURU
Republic of Nauru

Area Sq Km	21	Religions	Protestant, Roman Catholic
Area Sq Miles	8		
Population	13 000	Currency	Australian dollar
Capital	Yaren	Organizations	Comm., UN
Languages	Nauruan, English	Map page	48

NEPAL
Kingdom of Nepal

Area Sq Km	147 181	Religions	Hindu, Buddhist, Sunni Muslim
Area Sq Miles	56 827		
Population	25 164 000	Currency	Nepalese rupee
Capital	Kathmandu	Organizations	UN
Languages	Nepali, Maithili, Bhojpuri, English, local languages	Map page	75

NETHERLANDS
Kingdom of the Netherlands

Area Sq Km	41 526	Religions	Roman Catholic, Protestant, Sunni Muslim
Area Sq Miles	16 033		
Population	16 149 000		
Capital	Amsterdam/ The Hague ('s-Gravenhage)	Currency	Euro
		Organizations	EU, OECD, UN
		Map page	100
Languages	Dutch, Frisian		

Netherlands Antilles
Self-governing Netherlands Territory

Area Sq Km	800	Religions	Roman Catholic, Protestant
Area Sq Miles	309		
Population	221 000	Currency	Netherlands Antilles guilder
Capital	Willemstad		
Languages	Dutch, Papiamento, English	Map page	147

New Caledonia
French Overseas Territory

Area Sq Km	19 058	Religions	Roman Catholic, Protestant, Sunni Muslim
Area Sq Miles	7 358		
Population	228 000		
Capital	Nouméa	Currency	CFP franc
Languages	French, local languages	Map page	48

NEW ZEALAND

Area Sq Km	270 534	Religions	Protestant, Roman Catholic
Area Sq Miles	104 454		
Population	3 875 000	Currency	New Zealand dollar
Capital	Wellington	Organizations	APEC, Comm., OECD, UN
Languages	English, Maori		
		Map page	54

NICARAGUA
Republic of Nicaragua

Area Sq Km	130 000	Religions	Roman Catholic, Protestant
Area Sq Miles	50 193		
Population	5 466 000	Currency	Córdoba
Capital	Managua	Organizations	UN
Languages	Spanish, Amerindian languages	Map page	146

NIGER
Republic of Niger

Area Sq Km	1 267 000	Religions	Sunni Muslim, traditional beliefs
Area Sq Miles	489 191		
Population	11 972 000	Currency	CFA franc
Capital	Niamey	Organizations	UN
Languages	French, Hausa, Fulani, local languages	Map page	115

NIGERIA
Federal Republic of Nigeria

Area Sq Km	923 768	Religions	Sunni Muslim, Christian, traditional beliefs
Area Sq Miles	356 669		
Population	124 009 000		
Capital	Abuja	Currency	Naira
Languages	English, Hausa, Yoruba, Ibo, Fulani, local languages	Organizations	Comm., OPEC, UN
		Map page	115

Niue
Self-governing New Zealand Overseas Territory

Area Sq Km	258	Religions	Christian
Area Sq Miles	100	Currency	New Zealand dollar
Population	2 000	Map page	48
Capital	Alofi		
Languages	English, Polynesian		

Norfolk Island
Australian External Territory

Area Sq Km	35	Religions	Protestant, Roman Catholic
Area Sq Miles	14		
Population	2 037	Currency	Australian dollar
Capital	Kingston	Map page	48
Languages	English		

Northern Mariana Islands
United States Commonwealth

Area Sq Km	477	Religions	Roman Catholic
Area Sq Miles	184	Currency	United States dollar
Population	79 000	Map page	59
Capital	Capitol Hill		
Languages	English, Chamorro, local languages		

NORTH KOREA
People's Democratic Republic of North Korea

Area Sq Km	120 538	Religions	Traditional beliefs, Chondoist, Buddhist
Area Sq Miles	46 540		
Population	22 664 000	Currency	North Korean won
Capital	P'yŏngyang	Organizations	UN
Languages	Korean	Map page	65

NORWAY
Kingdom of Norway

Area Sq Km	323 878	Religions	Protestant, Roman
Area Sq Miles	125 050		Catholic
Population	4 533 000	Currency	Norwegian krone
Capital	Oslo	Organizations	OECD, UN
Languages	Norwegian	Map page	92–93

 ## OMAN
Sultanate of Oman

Area Sq Km	309 500	Religions	Ibadhi Muslim, Sunni
Area Sq Miles	119 499		Muslim
Population	2 851 000	Currency	Omani riyal
Capital	Muscat (Masqaṭ)	Organizations	UN
Languages	Arabic, Baluchi, Indian languages	Map page	79

 ## PAKISTAN
Islamic Republic of Pakistan

Area Sq Km	803 940	Religions	Sunni Muslim, Shi'a
Area Sq Miles	310 403		Muslim, Christian,
Population	153 578 000		Hindu
Capital	Islamabad	Currency	Pakistani rupee
Languages	Urdu, Punjabi, Sindhi, Pushtu, English	Organizations	Comm., UN
		Map page	74

 ## PALAU
Republic of Palau

Area Sq Km	497	Religions	Roman Catholic,
Area Sq Miles	192		Protestant, traditional
Population	20 000		beliefs
Capital	Koror	Currency	United States dollar
Languages	Palauan, English	Organizations	UN
		Map page	59

 ## PANAMA
Republic of Panama

Area Sq Km	77 082	Religions	Roman Catholic,
Area Sq Miles	29 762		Protestant, Sunni
Population	3 120 000		Muslim
Capital	Panama City	Currency	Balboa
Languages	Spanish, English, Amerindian languages	Organizations	UN
		Map page	146

 ## PAPUA NEW GUINEA
Independent State of Papua New Guinea

Area Sq Km	462 840	Religions	Protestant, Roman
Area Sq Miles	178 704		Catholic, traditional
Population	5 711 000		beliefs
Capital	Port Moresby	Currency	Kina
Languages	English, Tok Pisin (creole), local languages	Organizations	Comm., UN
		Map page	59

 ## PARAGUAY
Republic of Paraguay

Area Sq Km	406 752	Religions	Roman Catholic,
Area Sq Miles	157 048		Protestant
Population	5 878 000	Currency	Guaraní
Capital	Asunción	Organizations	UN
Languages	Spanish, Guaraní	Map page	152

 ## PERU
Republic of Peru

Area Sq Km	1 285 216	Religions	Roman Catholic,
Area Sq Miles	496 225		Protestant
Population	27 167 000	Currency	Sol
Capital	Lima	Organizations	APEC, UN
Languages	Spanish, Quechua, Aymara	Map page	150

 ## PHILIPPINES
Republic of the Philippines

Area Sq Km	300 000	Religions	Roman Catholic,
Area Sq Miles	115 831		Protestant, Sunni
Population	79 999 000		Muslim, Aglipayan
Capital	Manila	Currency	Philippine peso
Languages	English, Filipino, Tagalog, Cebuano, local languages	Organizations	APEC, ASEAN, UN
		Map page	64

 ## Pitcairn Islands
United Kingdom Overseas Territory

Area Sq Km	45	Religions	Protestant
Area Sq Miles	17	Currency	New Zealand dollar
Population	51	Map page	49
Capital	Adamstown		
Languages	English		

 ## POLAND
Polish Republic

Area Sq Km	312 683	Religions	Roman Catholic,
Area Sq Miles	120 728		Polish Orthodox
Population	38 587 000	Currency	Złoty
Capital	Warsaw (Warszawa)	Organizations	OECD, UN
Languages	Polish, German	Map page	103

 ## PORTUGAL
Portuguese Republic

Area Sq Km	88 940	Religions	Roman Catholic,
Area Sq Miles	34 340		Protestant
Population	10 062 000	Currency	Euro
Capital	Lisbon (Lisboa)	Organizations	EU, OECD, UN
Languages	Portuguese	Map page	106

 ## Puerto Rico
United States Commonwealth

Area Sq Km	9 104	Religions	Roman Catholic,
Area Sq Miles	3 515		Protestant
Population	3 879 000	Currency	United States dollar
Capital	San Juan	Map page	147
Languages	Spanish, English		

QATAR
State of Qatar

Area Sq Km	11 437	Religions	Sunni Muslim
Area Sq Miles	4 416	Currency	Qatari riyal
Population	610 000	Organizations	OPEC, UN
Capital	Doha (Ad Dawḩah)	Map page	79
Languages	Arabic		

Réunion
French Overseas Department

Area Sq Km	2 551	Religions	Roman Catholic
Area Sq Miles	985	Currency	Euro
Population	756 000	Map page	113
Capital	St-Denis		
Languages	French, creole		

St Helena
United Kingdom Overseas Territory

Area Sq Km	121	Religions	Protestant, Roman
Area Sq Miles	47		Catholic,
Population	5 644	Currency	St Helena pound
Capital	Jamestown	Map page	113
Languages	English		

Rodrigues Island
part of Mauritius

Area Sq Km	104	Religions	Christian
Area Sq Miles	40	Currency	Rupee
Population	36 306	Map page	159
Capital	Port Mathurin		
Languages	English, creole		

ST KITTS AND NEVIS
Federation of St Kitts and Nevis

Area Sq Km	261	Religions	Protestant, Roman
Area Sq Miles	101		Catholic
Population	42 000	Currency	East Caribbean dollar
Capital	Basseterre	Organizations	CARICOM, Comm.,
Languages	English, creole		UN
		Map page	147

ROMANIA

Area Sq Km	237 500	Religions	Romanian Orthodox,
Area Sq Miles	91 699		Protestant, Roman
Population	22 334 000		Catholic
Capital	Bucharest (Bucureşti)	Currency	Romanian leu
Languages	Romanian,	Organizations	UN
	Hungarian	Map page	110

ST LUCIA

Area Sq Km	616	Religions	Roman Catholic,
Area Sq Miles	238		Protestant
Population	149 000	Currency	East Caribbean dollar
Capital	Castries	Organizations	CARICOM, Comm.,
Languages	English, creole		UN
		Map page	147

RUSSIAN FEDERATION

Area Sq Km	17 075 400	Religions	Russian Orthodox,
Area Sq Miles	6 592 849		Sunni Muslim,
Population	143 246 000		Protestant
Capital	Moscow (Moskva)	Currency	Russian rouble
Languages	Russian, Tatar,	Organizations	APEC, CIS, UN
	Ukrainian, local	Map page	82–83
	languages		

St Martin
Dependency of Guadeloupe

Area Sq Km	54	Religions	Roman Catholic
Area Sq Miles	21	Currency	Euro
Population	29 078	Map page	147
Capital	Marigot		
Languages	French, creole		

RWANDA
Republic of Rwanda

Area Sq Km	26 338	Religions	Roman Catholic,
Area Sq Miles	10 169		traditional beliefs,
Population	8 387 000		Protestant
Capital	Kigali	Currency	Rwandan franc
Languages	Kinyarwanda,	Organizations	UN
	French, English	Map page	119

St Pierre and Miquelon
French Territorial Collectivity

Area Sq Km	242	Religions	Roman Catholic
Area Sq Miles	93	Currency	Euro
Population	6 000	Map page	131
Capital	St-Pierre		
Languages	French		

Saba
part of Netherlands Antilles

Area Sq Km	13	Religions	Roman Catholic,
Area Sq Miles	5		Protestant
Population	1 387	Currency	Netherlands Antilles
Capital	Bottom		guilder
Languages	Dutch, English	Map page	147

ST VINCENT AND THE GRENADINES

Area Sq Km	389	Religions	Protestant, Roman
Area Sq Miles	150		Catholic
Population	120 000	Currency	East Caribbean dollar
Capital	Kingstown	Organizations	CARICOM, Comm.,
Languages	English, creole		UN
		Map page	147

St Barthélémy
Dependency of Guadeloupe

Area Sq Km	21	Religions	Roman Catholic
Area Sq Miles	8	Currency	Euro
Population	6 852	Map page	147
Capital	Gustavia		
Languages	French, creole		

SAMOA
Independent State of Samoa

Area Sq Km	2 831	Religions	Protestant, Roman
Area Sq Miles	1 093		Catholic
Population	178 000	Currency	Tala
Capital	Apia	Organizations	Comm., UN
Languages	Samoan, English	Map page	49

SAN MARINO
Republic of San Marino

Area Sq Km	61	Religions	Roman Catholic
Area Sq Miles	24	Currency	Euro
Population	28 000	Organizations	UN
Capital	San Marino	Map page	108
Languages	Italian		

SÃO TOMÉ AND PRÍNCIPE
Democratic Republic of São Tomé and Príncipe

Area Sq Km	964	Religions	Roman Catholic,
Area Sq Miles	372		Protestant
Population	161 000	Currency	Dobra
Capital	São Tomé	Organizations	UN
Languages	Portuguese, creole	Map page	113

SAUDI ARABIA
Kingdom of Saudi Arabia

Area Sq Km	2 200 000	Religions	Sunni Muslim, Shi'a
Area Sq Miles	849 425		Muslim
Population	24 217 000	Currency	Saudi Arabian riyal
Capital	Riyadh (Ar Riyāḍ)	Organizations	OPEC, UN
Languages	Arabic	Map page	78–79

SENEGAL
Republic of Senegal

Area Sq Km	196 720	Religions	Sunni Muslim,
Area Sq Miles	75 954		Roman Catholic,
Population	10 095 000		traditional beliefs
Capital	Dakar	Currency	CFA franc
Languages	French, Wolof, Fulani,	Organizations	UN
	local languages	Map page	114

SERBIA AND MONTENEGRO

Area Sq Km	102 173	Religions	Serbian Orthodox,
Area Sq Miles	39 449		Montenegrin Orthodox,
Population	10 527 000		Sunni Muslim
Capital	Belgrade (Beograd)	Currency	Serbian dinar, Euro
Languages	Serbian, Albanian,	Organizations	UN
	Hungarian	Map page	109

SEYCHELLES
Republic of the Seychelles

Area Sq Km	455	Religions	Roman Catholic,
Area Sq Miles	176		Protestant
Population	81 000	Currency	Seychelles rupee
Capital	Victoria	Organizations	Comm., SADC, UN
Languages	English, French,	Map page	113
	creole		

SIERRA LEONE
Republic of Sierra Leone

Area Sq Km	71 740	Religions	Sunni Muslim,
Area Sq Miles	27 699		traditional beliefs
Population	4 971 000	Currency	Leone
Capital	Freetown	Organizations	Comm., UN
Languages	English, creole,	Map page	114
	Mende, Temne,		
	local languages		

 (see SINGAPORE below)

SINGAPORE
Republic of Singapore

Area Sq Km	639	Religions	Buddhist, Taoist, Sunni
Area Sq Miles	247		Muslim, Christian,
Population	4 253 000		Hindu
Capital	Singapore	Currency	Singapore dollar
Languages	Chinese, English,	Organizations	APEC, ASEAN,
	Malay, Tamil		Comm., UN
		Map page	60

Sint Eustatius
part of Netherlands Antilles

Area Sq Km	21	Religions	Protestant, Roman
Area Sq Miles	8		Catholic
Population	2 829	Currency	Netherlands Antilles
Capital	Oranjestad		guilder
Languages	Dutch, English	Map page	147

Sint Maarten
part of Netherlands Antilles

Area Sq Km	34	Religions	Protestant, Roman
Area Sq Miles	13		Catholic
Population	31 882	Currency	Netherlands Antilles
Capital	Philipsburg		guilder
Languages	Dutch, English	Map page	147

SLOVAKIA
Slovak Republic

Area Sq Km	49 035	Religions	Roman Catholic,
Area Sq Miles	18 933		Protestant, Orthodox
Population	5 402 000	Currency	Slovakian koruna
Capital	Bratislava	Organizations	UN
Languages	Slovakian,	Map page	103
	Hungarian, Czech		

SLOVENIA
Republic of Slovenia

Area Sq Km	20 251	Religions	Roman Catholic,
Area Sq Miles	7 819		Protestant
Population	1 984 000	Currency	Tólar
Capital	Ljubljana	Organizations	UN
Languages	Slovene, Croatian,	Map page	108–109
	Serbian		

SOLOMON ISLANDS

Area Sq Km	28 370	Religions	Protestant, Roman
Area Sq Miles	10 954		Catholic
Population	477 000	Currency	Solomon Islands dollar
Capital	Honiara	Organizations	Comm., UN
Languages	English, creole,	Map page	48
	local languages		

STATES AND TERRITORIES

SOMALIA
Somali Democratic Republic

Area Sq Km	637 657	Religions	Sunni Muslim
Area Sq Miles	246 201	Currency	Somali shilling
Population	9 890 000	Organizations	UN
Capital	Mogadishu (Muqdisho)	Map page	117
Languages	Somali, Arabic		

SOUTH AFRICA, REPUBLIC OF

Area Sq Km	1 219 080	Religions	Protestant, Roman Catholic, Sunni Muslim, Hindu
Area Sq Miles	470 689		
Population	45 026 000		
Capital	Pretoria (Tshwane) /Cape Town	Currency	Rand
		Organizations	Comm., SADC, UN
Languages	Afrikaans, English, nine official local languages	Map page	122–123

SOUTH KOREA
Republic of Korea

Area Sq Km	99 274	Religions	Buddhist, Protestant, Roman Catholic
Area Sq Miles	38 330		
Population	47 700 000	Currency	South Korean won
Capital	Seoul (Sŏul)	Organizations	APEC, UN
Languages	Korean	Map page	65

SPAIN
Kingdom of Spain

Area Sq Km	504 782	Religions	Roman Catholic
Area Sq Miles	194 897	Currency	Euro
Population	41 060 000	Organizations	EU, OECD, UN
Capital	Madrid	Map page	106–107
Languages	Castilian, Catalan, Galician, Basque		

SRI LANKA
Democratic Socialist Republic of Sri Lanka

Area Sq Km	65 610	Religions	Buddhist, Hindu, Sunni Muslim, Roman Catholic
Area Sq Miles	25 332		
Population	19 065 000		
Capital	Sri Jayewardenepura Kotte	Currency	Sri Lankan rupee
		Organizations	Comm., UN
Languages	Sinhalese, Tamil, English	Map page	73

SUDAN
Republic of the Sudan

Area Sq Km	2 505 813	Religions	Sunni Muslim, traditional beliefs, Christian
Area Sq Miles	967 500		
Population	33 610 000		
Capital	Khartoum	Currency	Sudanese dinar
Languages	Arabic, Dinka, Nubian, Beja, Nuer, local languages	Organizations	UN
		Map page	116–117

SURINAME
Republic of Suriname

Area Sq Km	163 820	Religions	Hindu, Roman Catholic, Protestant, Sunni Muslim
Area Sq Miles	63 251		
Population	436 000		
Capital	Paramaribo	Currency	Suriname guilder
Languages	Dutch, Surinamese, English, Hindi	Organizations	CARICOM, UN
		Map page	151

Svalbard
part of Norway

Area Sq Km	61 229	Religions	Protestant
Area Sq Miles	23 641	Currency	Norwegian krone
Population	2 515	Map page	82
Capital	Longyearbyen		
Languages	Norwegian		

SWAZILAND
Kingdom of Swaziland

Area Sq Km	17 364	Currency	Emalangeni, South African rand
Area Sq Miles	6 704		
Population	1 077 000	Organizations	Comm., SADC, UN
Capital	Mbabane	Map page	123
Languages	Swazi, English		
Religions	Christian, traditional beliefs		

SWEDEN
Kingdom of Sweden

Area Sq Km	449 964	Religions	Protestant, Roman Catholic
Area Sq Miles	173 732		
Population	8 876 000	Currency	Swedish krona
Capital	Stockholm	Organizations	EU, OECD, UN
Languages	Swedish	Map page	92–93

SWITZERLAND
Swiss Confederation

Area Sq Km	41 293	Religions	Roman Catholic, Protestant
Area Sq Miles	15 943		
Population	7 169 000	Currency	Swiss franc
Capital	Bern (Berne)	Organizations	OECD, UN
Languages	German, French, Italian, Romansch	Map page	105

SYRIA
Syrian Arab Republic

Area Sq Km	185 180	Religions	Sunni Muslim, Shi'a Muslim, Christian
Area Sq Miles	71 498		
Population	17 800 000	Currency	Syrian pound
Capital	Damascus (Dimashq)	Organizations	UN
Languages	Arabic, Kurdish, Armenian	Map page	80

TAIWAN
Republic of China

Area Sq Km	36 179	Religions	Buddhist, Taoist, Confucian, Christian
Area Sq Miles	13 969		
Population	22 548 009	Currency	Taiwan dollar
Capital	T'aipei	Organizations	APEC
Languages	Mandarin, Min, Hakka, local languages	Map page	71

TAJIKISTAN
Republic of Tajikistan

Area Sq Km	143 100	Religions	Sunni Muslim
Area Sq Miles	55 251	Currency	Somoni
Population	6 245 000	Organizations	CIS, UN
Capital	Dushanbe	Map page	77
Languages	Tajik, Uzbek, Russian		

TANZANIA
United Republic of Tanzania

Area Sq Km	945 087	Religions	Shi'a Muslim, Sunni
Area Sq Miles	364 900		Muslim, traditional
Population	36 977 000		beliefs, Christian
Capital	Dodoma	Currency	Tanzanian shilling
Languages	Swahili, English,	Organizations	Comm., SADC, UN
	Nyamwezi, local	Map page	119
	languages		

THAILAND
Kingdom of Thailand

Area Sq Km	513 115	Religions	Buddhist, Sunni
Area Sq Miles	198 115		Muslim
Population	62 833 000	Currency	Baht
Capital	Bangkok	Organizations	APEC, ASEAN, UN
	(Krung Thep)	Map page	62–63
Languages	Thai, Lao, Chinese,		
	Malay, Mon-Khmer		
	languages		

TOGO
Republic of Togo

Area Sq Km	56 785	Religions	Traditional beliefs,
Area Sq Miles	21 925		Christian, Sunni
Population	4 909 000		Muslim
Capital	Lomé	Currency	CFA franc
Languages	French, Ewe, Kabre,	Organizations	UN
	local languages	Map page	114

Tokelau
New Zealand Overseas Territory

Area Sq Km	10	Religions	Christian
Area Sq Miles	4	Currency	New Zealand dollar
Population	2 000	Map page	49
Capital	none		
Languages	English, Tokelauan		

TONGA
Kingdom of Tonga

Area Sq Km	748	Religions	Protestant, Roman
Area Sq Miles	289		Catholic
Population	104 000	Currency	Pa'anga
Capital	Nuku'alofa	Organizations	Comm., UN
Languages	Tongan, English	Map page	49

TRINIDAD AND TOBAGO
Republic of Trinidad and Tobago

Area Sq Km	5 130	Religions	Roman Catholic,
Area Sq Miles	1 981		Hindu, Protestant,
Population	1 303 000		Sunni Muslim
Capital	Port of Spain	Currency	Trinidad and Tobago
Languages	English, creole,		dollar
	Hindi	Organizations	CARICOM, Comm.,
			UN
		Map page	147

Tristan da Cunha
Dependency of St Helena

Area Sq Km	98	Religions	Protestant, Roman
Area Sq Miles	38		Catholic
Population	284	Currency	Pound sterling
Capital	Settlement of	Map page	113
	Edinburgh		
Languages	English		

TUNISIA
Republic of Tunisia

Area Sq Km	164 150	Religions	Sunni Muslim
Area Sq Miles	63 379	Currency	Tunisian dinar
Population	9 832 000	Organizations	UN
Capital	Tunis	Map page	115
Languages	Arabic, French		

TURKEY
Republic of Turkey

Area Sq Km	779 452	Religions	Sunni Muslim, Shi'a
Area Sq Miles	300 948		Muslim
Population	71 325 000	Currency	Turkish lira
Capital	Ankara	Organizations	OECD, UN
Languages	Turkish, Kurdish	Map page	80

TURKMENISTAN
Republic of Turkmenistan

Area Sq Km	488 100	Religions	Sunni Muslim, Russian
Area Sq Miles	188 456		Orthodox
Population	4 867 000	Currency	Turkmen manat
Capital	Ashgabat (Ashkhabad)	Organizations	CIS, UN
Languages	Turkmen, Uzbek,	Map page	76
	Russian		

Turks and Caicos Islands
United Kingdom Overseas Territory

Area Sq Km	430	Religions	Protestant
Area Sq Miles	166	Currency	United States dollar
Population	21 000	Map page	147
Capital	Grand Turk		
Languages	English		

TUVALU

Area Sq Km	25	Religions	Protestant
Area Sq Miles	10	Currency	Australian dollar
Population	11 000	Organizations	Comm.
Capital	Vaiaku	Map page	49
Languages	Tuvaluan, English		

STATES AND TERRITORIES

UGANDA
Republic of Uganda

Area Sq Km	241 038	Religions	Roman Catholic, Protestant, Sunni Muslim, traditional beliefs
Area Sq Miles	93 065		
Population	25 827 000		
Capital	Kampala		
Languages	English, Swahili, Luganda, local languages	Currency	Ugandan shilling
		Organizations	Comm., UN
		Map page	119

UKRAINE
Republic of Ukraine

Area Sq Km	603 700	Religions	Ukrainian Orthodox, Ukrainian Catholic, Roman Catholic
Area Sq Miles	233 090		
Population	48 523 000		
Capital	Kiev (Kyiv)		
Languages	Ukrainian, Russian	Currency	Hryvnia
		Organizations	CIS, UN
		Map page	90–91

UNITED ARAB EMIRATES
Federation of Emirates

Area Sq Km	77 700	Religions	Sunni Muslim, Shi'a Muslim
Area Sq Miles	30 000		
Population	2 995 000		
Capital	Abu Dhabi (Abū Ẓabī)	Currency	United Arab Emirates dirham
Languages	Arabic, English	Organizations	OPEC, UN
		Map page	79

Abu Dhabi (Abū Ẓabī) (Emirate)

Area Sq Km	67 340	Population	1 248 000
Area Sq Miles	26 000	Capital	Abu Dhabi (Abū Ẓabī)

Ajman (Emirate)

Area Sq Km	259	Population	189 000
Area Sq Miles	100	Capital	Ajman

Dubai (Emirate)

Area Sq Km	3 885	Population	971 000
Area Sq Miles	1 500	Capital	Dubai

Fujairah (Emirate)

Area Sq Km	1 165	Population	103 000
Area Sq Miles	450	Capital	Fujairah

Ras al Khaimah (Emirate)

Area Sq Km	1 684	Population	179 000
Area Sq Miles	650	Capital	Ras al Khaimah

Sharjah (Emirate)

Area Sq Km	2 590	Population	551 000
Area Sq Miles	1 000	Capital	Sharjah

Umm al Qaiwain (Emirate)

Area Sq Km	777	Population	49 000
Area Sq Miles	300	Capital	Umm al Qaiwain

UNITED KINGDOM
of Great Britain and Northern Ireland

Area Sq Km	243 609	Religions	Protestant, Roman Catholic, Muslim
Area Sq Miles	94 058		
Population	58 789 194	Currency	Pound sterling
Capital	London	Organizations	Comm., EU, OECD, UN
Languages	English, Welsh, Gaelic		
		Map page	94–95

England (Constituent country)

Area Sq Km	130 433	Population	49 138 831
Area Sq Miles	50 360	Capital	London

Northern Ireland (Province)

Area Sq Km	13 576	Population	1 685 267
Area Sq Miles	5 242	Capital	Belfast

Scotland (Constituent country)

Area Sq Km	78 822	Population	5 062 011
Area Sq Miles	30 433	Capital	Edinburgh

Wales (Principality)

Area Sq Km	20 778	Population	2 903 085
Area Sq Miles	8 022	Capital	Cardiff

UNITED STATES OF AMERICA
Federal Republic

Area Sq Km	9 826 635	Religions	Protestant, Roman Catholic, Sunni Muslim, Jewish
Area Sq Miles	3 794 085		
Population	294 043 000		
Capital	Washington D.C.	Currency	United States dollar
Languages	English, Spanish	Organizations	APEC, OECD, UN
		Map page	132–133

Alabama (State)

Area Sq Km	135 765	Population	4 486 508
Area Sq Miles	52 419	Capital	Montgomery

Alaska (State)

Area Sq Km	1 717 854	Population	643 786
Area Sq Miles	663 267	Capital	Juneau

Arizona (State)

Area Sq Km	295 253	Population	5 456 453
Area Sq Miles	113 998	Capital	Phoenix

Arkansas (State)

Area Sq Km	137 733	Population	2 710 079
Area Sq Miles	53 179	Capital	Little Rock

California (State)

Area Sq Km	423 971	Population	35 116 033
Area Sq Miles	163 696	Capital	Sacramento

Colorado (State)

Area Sq Km	269 602	Population	4 506 542
Area Sq Miles	104 094	Capital	Denver

Connecticut (State)

Area Sq Km	14 356	Population	3 460 503
Area Sq Miles	5 543	Capital	Hartford

Delaware (State)

Area Sq Km	6 446	Population	807 385
Area Sq Miles	2 489	Capital	Dover

District of Columbia (District)

Area Sq Km	176	Population	570 898
Area Sq Miles	68	Capital	Washington

Florida (State)

Area Sq Km	170 305	Population	16 713 149
Area Sq Miles	65 755	Capital	Tallahassee

Georgia (State)

Area Sq Km	69 700	Population	5 126 000
Area Sq Miles	26 911	Capital	Atlanta

Hawaii (State)

Area Sq Km	28 311	Population	1 244 898
Area Sq Miles	10 931	Capital	Honolulu

Idaho (State)

Area Sq Km	216 445	Population	1 341 131
Area Sq Miles	83 570	Capital	Boise

Illinois (State)

Area Sq Km	149 997	Population	12 600 620
Area Sq Miles	57 914	Capital	Springfield

Indiana (State)

Area Sq Km	94 322	Population	6 159 068
Area Sq Miles	36 418	Capital	Indianapolis

Iowa (State)

Area Sq Km	145 744	Population	2 936 760
Area Sq Miles	56 272	Capital	Des Moines

Kansas (State)

Area Sq Km	213 096	Population	2 715 884
Area Sq Miles	82 277	Capital	Topeka

Kentucky (State)

Area Sq Km	104 659	Population	4 092 891
Area Sq Miles	40 409	Capital	Frankfort

Louisiana (State)

Area Sq Km	134 265	Population	4 482 646
Area Sq Miles	51 840	Capital	Baton Rouge

Maine (State)

Area Sq Km	91 647	Population	1 294 464
Area Sq Miles	35 385	Capital	Augusta

Maryland (State)

Area Sq Km	32 134	Population	5 458 137
Area Sq Miles	12 407	Capital	Annapolis

Massachusetts (State)

Area Sq Km	27 337	Population	6 427 801
Area Sq Miles	10 555	Capital	Boston

Michigan (State)

Area Sq Km	250 493	Population	10 050 446
Area Sq Miles	96 716	Capital	Lansing

Minnesota (State)

Area Sq Km	225 171	Population	5 019 720
Area Sq Miles	86 939	Capital	St Paul

Mississippi (State)

Area Sq Km	125 433	Population	2 871 782
Area Sq Miles	48 430	Capital	Jackson

Missouri (State)

Area Sq Km	180 533	Population	5 672 579
Area Sq Miles	69 704	Capital	Jefferson City

Montana (State)

Area Sq Km	380 837	Population	909 453
Area Sq Miles	147 042	Capital	Helena

Nebraska (State)

Area Sq Km	200 346	Population	1 729 180
Area Sq Miles	77 354	Capital	Lincoln

Nevada (State)

Area Sq Km	286 352	Population	2 173 491
Area Sq Miles	110 561	Capital	Carson City

New Hampshire (State)

Area Sq Km	24 216	Population	1 275 056
Area Sq Miles	9 350	Capital	Concord

New Jersey (State)

Area Sq Km	22 587	Population	8 590 300
Area Sq Miles	8 721	Capital	Trenton

STATES AND TERRITORIES

UNITED STATES OF AMERICA
Federal Republic

New Mexico (State)

Area Sq Km	314 914	Population	1 855 059
Area Sq Miles	121 589	Capital	Santa Fe

New York (State)

Area Sq Km	141 299	Population	19 157 532
Area Sq Miles	54 556	Capital	Albany

North Carolina (State)

Area Sq Km	139 391	Population	8 320 146
Area Sq Miles	53 819	Capital	Raleigh

North Dakota (State)

Area Sq Km	183 112	Population	634 110
Area Sq Miles	70 700	Capital	Bismarck

Ohio (State)

Area Sq Km	116 096	Population	11 421 267
Area Sq Miles	44 825	Capital	Columbus

Oklahoma (State)

Area Sq Km	181 035	Population	3 493 714
Area Sq Miles	69 898	Capital	Oklahoma City

Oregon (State)

Area Sq Km	254 806	Population	3 521 515
Area Sq Miles	98 381	Capital	Salem

Pennsylvania (State)

Area Sq Km	119 282	Population	12 335 091
Area Sq Miles	46 055	Capital	Harrisburg

Rhode Island (State)

Area Sq Km	4 002	Population	1 069 725
Area Sq Miles	1 545	Capital	Providence

South Carolina (State)

Area Sq Km	82 931	Population	4 107 183
Area Sq Miles	32 020	Capital	Columbia

South Dakota (State)

Area Sq Km	199 730	Population	761 063
Area Sq Miles	77 116	Capital	Pierre

Tennessee (State)

Area Sq Km	109 150	Population	5 797 289
Area Sq Miles	42 143	Capital	Nashville

Texas (State)

Area Sq Km	695 622	Population	21 779 893
Area Sq Miles	268 581	Capital	Austin

Utah (State)

Area Sq Km	219 887	Population	2 316 256
Area Sq Miles	84 899	Capital	Salt Lake City

Vermont (State)

Area Sq Km	24 900	Population	616 592
Area Sq Miles	9 614	Capital	Montpelier

Virginia (State)

Area Sq Km	110 784	Population	7 293 542
Area Sq Miles	42 774	Capital	Richmond

Washington (State)

Area Sq Km	184 666	Population	6 068 996
Area Sq Miles	71 300	Capital	Olympia

West Virginia (State)

Area Sq Km	62 755	Population	1 801 873
Area Sq Miles	24 230	Capital	Charleston

Wisconsin (State)

Area Sq Km	169 639	Population	5 441 196
Area Sq Miles	65 498	Capital	Madison

Wyoming (State)

Area Sq Km	253 337	Population	498 703
Area Sq Miles	97 814	Capital	Cheyenne

URUGUAY
Oriental Republic of Uruguay

Area Sq Km	176 215	Religions	Roman Catholic,
Area Sq Miles	68 037		Protestant, Jewish
Population	3 415 000	Currency	Uruguayan peso
Capital	Montevideo	Organizations	UN
Languages	Spanish	Map page	153

UZBEKISTAN
Republic of Uzbekistan

Area Sq Km	447 400	Religions	Sunni Muslim, Russian
Area Sq Miles	172 742		Orthodox
Population	26 093 000	Currency	Uzbek som
Capital	Tashkent	Organizations	CIS, UN
Languages	Uzbek, Russian,	Map page	76–77
	Tajik, Kazakh		

VANUATU
Republic of Vanuatu

Area Sq Km	12 190	Religions	Protestant, Roman
Area Sq Miles	4 707		Catholic, traditional
Population	212 000		beliefs
Capital	Port Vila	Currency	Vatu
Languages	English, Bislama	Organizations	Comm., UN
	(creole), French	Map page	48

VATICAN CITY
Vatican City State

Area Sq Km	0.5	Religions	Roman Catholic
Area Sq Miles	0.2	Currency	Euro
Population	472	Map page	108
Capital	Vatican City		
Languages	Italian		

VENEZUELA
Republic of Venezuela

Area Sq Km	912 050	Religions	Roman Catholic,
Area Sq Miles	352 144		Protestant
Population	25 699 000	Currency	Bolívar
Capital	Caracas	Organizations	OPEC, UN
Languages	Spanish, Amerindian	Map page	150
	languages		

VIETNAM
Socialist Republic of Vietnam

Area Sq Km	329 565	Religions	Buddhist, Taoist,
Area Sq Miles	127 246		Roman Catholic,
Population	81 377 000		Cao Dai, Hoa Hoa
Capital	Ha Nôi (Hanoi)	Currency	Dong
Languages	Vietnamese, Thai,	Organizations	APEC, ASEAN, UN
	Khmer, Chinese,	Map page	62–63
	local languages		

Virgin Islands (U.K.)
United Kingdom Overseas Territory

Area Sq Km	153	Religions	Protestant, Roman
Area Sq Miles	59		Catholic
Population	21 000	Currency	United States dollar
Capital	Road Town	Map page	147
Languages	English		

Virgin Islands (U.S.)
United States Unincorporated Territory

Area Sq Km	352	Religions	Protestant,
Area Sq Miles	136		Roman Catholic
Population	111 000	Currency	United States dollar
Capital	Charlotte Amalie	Map page	147
Languages	English, Spanish		

Wallis and Futuna Islands
French Overseas Territory

Area Sq Km	274	Religions	Roman Catholic
Area Sq Miles	106	Currency	CFP franc
Population	15 000	Map page	49
Capital	Matā'utu		
Languages	French, Wallisian,		
	Futunian		

West Bank
Disputed Territory

Area Sq Km	5 860	Religions	Sunni Muslim, Jewish,
Area Sq Miles	2 263		Shi'a Muslim, Christian
Population	2 303 660	Currency	Jordanian dinar,
Capital	none		Isreali shekel
Languages	Arabic, Hebrew	Map page	80

Western Sahara
Disputed territory (Morocco)

Area Sq Km	266 000	Religions	Sunni Muslim
Area Sq Miles	102 703	Currency	Moroccan dirham
Population	308 000	Map page	114
Capital	Laâyoune		
Languages	Arabic		

YEMEN
Republic of Yemen

Area Sq Km	527 968	Religions	Sunni Muslim, Shi'a
Area Sq Miles	203 850		Muslim
Population	20 010 000	Currency	Yemeni riyal
Capital	San'a'	Organizations	UN
Languages	Arabic	Map page	78–79

ZAMBIA
Republic of Zambia

Area Sq Km	752 614	Religions	Christian, traditional
Area Sq Miles	290 586		beliefs
Population	10 812 000	Currency	Zambian kwacha
Capital	Lusaka	Organizations	Comm., SADC, UN
Languages	English, Bemba,	Map page	120–121
	Nyanja, Tonga,		
	local languages		

ZIMBABWE
Republic of Zimbabwe

Area Sq Km	390 759	Religions	Christian, traditional
Area Sq Miles	150 873		beliefs
Population	12 891 000	Currency	Zimbabwean dollar
Capital	Harare	Organizations	SADC, UN
Languages	English, Shona,	Map page	121
	Ndebele		

ANTARCTICA

Total Land Area
12 093 000 sq km
4 669 292 sq miles
(excluding ice shelves)

HIGHEST MOUNTAIN
Vinson Massif
4 897 m / 16 066 ft

OCEANIA

Total land area
8 844 516 sq km
3 414 887 sq miles
(includes New Guinea and
Pacific Island nations)

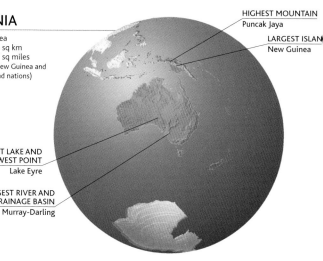

HIGHEST MOUNTAIN
Puncak Jaya

LARGEST ISLAND
New Guinea

LARGEST LAKE AND
LOWEST POINT
Lake Eyre

LONGEST RIVER AND
LARGEST DRAINAGE BASIN
Murray-Darling

HIGHEST MOUNTAINS	HEIGHT metres	feet	LARGEST ISLANDS	AREA sq km	sq miles	LARGEST LAKES	AREA sq km	sq miles	LONGEST RIVERS	LENGTH km	miles
Puncak Jaya	5 030	16 502	New Guinea	808 510	312 167	Lake Eyre	0–8 900	0–3 436	Murray-Darling	3 750	2 330
Puncak Trikora	4 730	15 518	South Island	151 215	58 384	Lake Torrens	0–5 780	0–2 232	Darling	2 739	1 702
Puncak Mandala	4 700	15 420	North Island	115 777	44 702				Murray	2 589	1 608
Puncak Yamin	4 595	15 075	Tasmania	67 800	26 178				Murrumbidgee	1 690	1 050
Mt Wilheim	4 509	14 793							Lachlan	1 480	919

ASIA

Total Land Area
45 036 492 sq km
17 388 686 sq miles

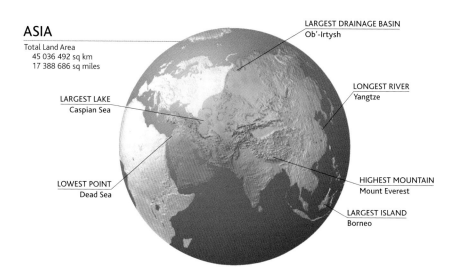

LARGEST DRAINAGE BASIN
Ob'-Irtysh

LONGEST RIVER
Yangtze

LARGEST LAKE
Caspian Sea

LOWEST POINT
Dead Sea

HIGHEST MOUNTAIN
Mount Everest

LARGEST ISLAND
Borneo

HIGHEST MOUNTAINS	HEIGHT metres	feet	LARGEST ISLANDS	AREA sq km	sq miles	LARGEST LAKES	AREA sq km	sq miles	LONGEST RIVERS	LENGTH km	miles
Mt Everest	8 848	29 028	Borneo	745 561	287 863	Caspian Sea	371 000	143 244	Yangtze	6 380	3 964
K2	8 611	28 251	Sumatra	473 606	182 860	Lake Baikal	30 500	11 776	Ob'-Irtysh	5 568	3 460
Kangchenjunga	8 586	28 169	Honshū	227 414	87 805	Lake Balkhash	17 400	6 718	Yenisey-Angara-Selenga	5 550	3 448
Lhotse	8 516	27 939	Celebes	189 216	73 057	Aral Sea	17 158	6 625	Yellow	5 464	3 395
Makalu	8 463	27 765	Java	132 188	51 038	Ysyk-Köl	6 200	2 393	Irtysh	4 440	2 759

EUROPE

Total Land Area
9 908 599 sq km
3 825 731 sq miles

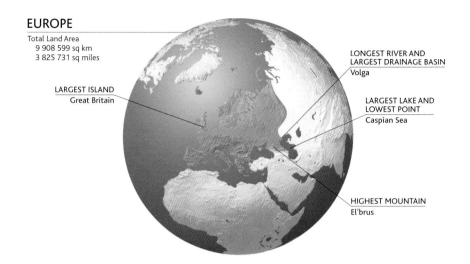

LARGEST ISLAND
Great Britain

LONGEST RIVER AND
LARGEST DRAINAGE BASIN
Volga

LARGEST LAKE AND
LOWEST POINT
Caspian Sea

HIGHEST MOUNTAIN
El'brus

HIGHEST MOUNTAINS	HEIGHT metres	feet	LARGEST ISLANDS	AREA sq km	sq miles	LARGEST LAKES	AREA sq km	sq miles	LONGEST RIVERS	LENGTH km	miles
El'brus	5 642	5 642	Great Britain	218 476	84 354	Caspian Sea	371 000	143 244	Volga	3 688	2 291
Gora Dykh-Tau	5 204	17 073	Iceland	102 820	39 699	Lake Ladoga	18 390	7 100	Danube	2 850	1 770
Shkhara	5 201	17 063	Novaya Zemlya	90 650	35 000	Lake Onega	9 600	3 706	Dnieper	2 285	1 419
Kazbek	5 047	16 558	Ireland	83 045	32 064	Vänern	5 585	2 156	Kama	2 028	1 260
Mont Blanc	4 808	15 774	Spitsbergen	37 814	14 600	Rybinskoye Vdkhr.	5 180	2 000	Don	1 931	1 199

AFRICA

Total Land Area
30 343 578 sq km
11 715 721 sq miles

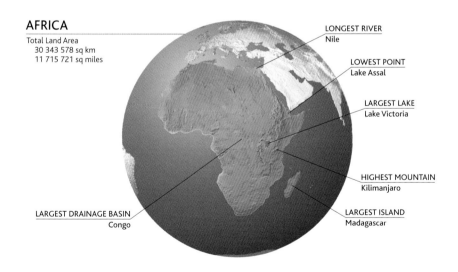

LONGEST RIVER
Nile

LOWEST POINT
Lake Assal

LARGEST LAKE
Lake Victoria

HIGHEST MOUNTAIN
Kilimanjaro

LARGEST ISLAND
Madagascar

LARGEST DRAINAGE BASIN
Congo

HIGHEST MOUNTAINS	HEIGHT metres	feet	LARGEST ISLANDS	AREA sq km	sq miles	LARGEST LAKES	AREA sq km	sq miles	LONGEST RIVERS	LENGTH km	miles
Kilimanjaro	5 892	19 331	Madagascar	587 040	226 657	Lake Victoria	68 800	26 564	Nile	6 695	4 160
Mt Kenya	5 199	17 057				Lake Tanganyika	32 900	12 702	Congo	4 667	2 900
Margherita Peak	5 110	16 765				Lake Nyasa	30 044	11 600	Niger	4 184	2 599
Meru	4 565	14 977				Lake Volta	8 485	3 276	Zambezi	2 736	1 700
Ras Dejen	4 533	14 872				Lake Turkana	6 475	2 500	Webi Shabeelle	2 490	1 547

NORTH AMERICA

Total Land Area
24 680 331 sq km
9 529 129 sq miles
(includes Hawai'ian Islands)

HIGHEST MOUNTAIN
Mt McKinley

LOWEST POINT
Death Valley

LARGEST ISLAND
Greenland

LARGEST LAKE
Lake Superior

LONGEST RIVER AND
LARGEST DRAINAGE BASIN
Mississippi-Missouri

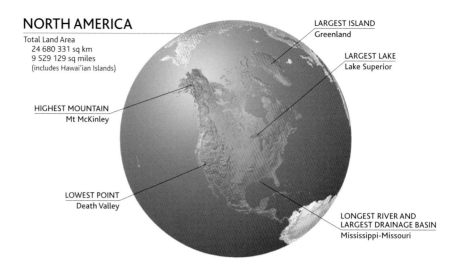

HIGHEST MOUNTAINS	HEIGHT metres	feet	LARGEST ISLANDS	AREA sq km	sq miles	LARGEST LAKES	AREA sq km	sq miles	LONGEST RIVERS	LENGTH km	miles
Mt McKinley	6 194	20 321	Greenland	2 175 600	840 004	Lake Superior	82 100	31 699	Mississippi-Missouri	5 969	3 709
Mt Logan	5 959	19 550	Baffin Island	507 451	195 928	Lake Huron	59 600	23 012	Mackenzie-Peace-Finlay	4 241	2 635
Pico de Orizaba	5 747	18 855	Victoria Island	217 291	83 897	Lake Michigan	57 800	22 317	Missouri	4 086	2 539
Mt St Elias	5 489	18 008	Ellesmere Island	196 236	75 767	Great Bear Lake	31 328	12 095	Mississippi	3 765	2 339
Volcán Popocatépetl	5 452	17 887	Cuba	110 860	42 803	Great Slave Lake	28 568	11 030	Yukon	3 185	1 979

SOUTH AMERICA

Total Land Area
17 815 420 sq km
6 878 572 sq miles

LONGEST RIVER AND
LARGEST DRAINAGE BASIN
Amazon

LARGEST LAKE
Lake Titicaca

HIGHEST MOUNTAIN
Cerro Aconcagua

LARGEST ISLAND
Isla Grande de Tierra del Fuego

LOWEST POINT
Península Valdés

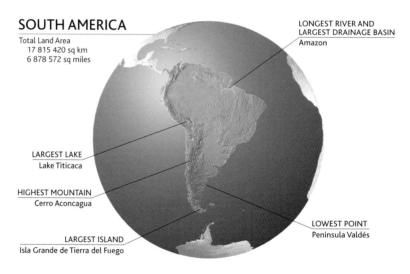

HIGHEST MOUNTAINS	HEIGHT metres	feet	LARGEST ISLANDS	AREA sq km	sq miles	LARGEST LAKES	AREA sq km	sq miles	LONGEST RIVERS	LENGTH km	miles
Cerro Aconcagua	6 959	22 831	Isla Grande de Tierra del Fuego	47 000	18 147	Lake Titicaca	8 340	3 220	Amazon	6 516	4 049
Nevado Ojos del Salado	6 908	22 664	Isla de Chiloé	8 394	3 240				Río de la Plata-Paraná	4 500	2 796
Cerro Bonete	6 872	22 546	East Falkland	6 760	2 610				Purus	3 218	1 999
Cerro Pissis	6 858	22 500	West Falkland	5 413	2 090				Madeira	3 200	1 988
Cerro Tupungato	6 800	22 211							Sao Francisco	2 900	1 802

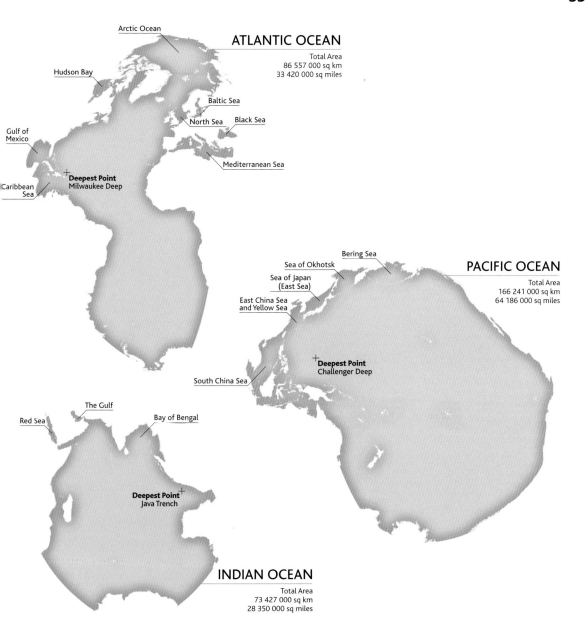

ATLANTIC OCEAN
Total Area
86 557 000 sq km
33 420 000 sq miles

PACIFIC OCEAN
Total Area
166 241 000 sq km
64 186 000 sq miles

INDIAN OCEAN
Total Area
73 427 000 sq km
28 350 000 sq miles

Arctic Ocean · Hudson Bay · Baltic Sea · North Sea · Black Sea · Gulf of Mexico · Mediterranean Sea · Caribbean Sea · Deepest Point Milwaukee Deep · Bering Sea · Sea of Okhotsk · Sea of Japan (East Sea) · East China Sea and Yellow Sea · Deepest Point Challenger Deep · South China Sea · The Gulf · Bay of Bengal · Red Sea · Deepest Point Java Trench

ATLANTIC OCEAN	AREA sq km	sq miles	DEEPEST POINT metres	feet
Extent	86 557 000	33 420 000	8 605	28 231
Arctic Ocean	9 485 000	3 662 000	5 450	17 880
Caribbean Sea	2 512 000	970 000	7 680	25 196
Mediterranean Sea	2 510 000	969 000	5 121	16 800
Gulf of Mexico	1 544 000	596 000	3 504	11 495
Hudson Bay	1 233 000	476 000	259	849
North Sea	575 000	222 000	661	2 168
Black Sea	508 000	196 000	2 245	7 365
Baltic Sea	382 000	147 000	460	1 509

INDIAN OCEAN	AREA sq km	sq miles	DEEPEST POINT metres	feet
Extent	73 427 000	28 350 000	7 125	23 376
Bay of Bengal	2 172 000	839 000	4 500	14 763
Red Sea	453 000	175 000	3 040	9 973
The Gulf	238 000	92 000	73	239

PACIFIC OCEAN	AREA sq km	sq miles	DEEPEST POINT metres	feet
Extent	166 241 000	64 186 000	10 920	35 826
South China Sea	2 590 000	1 000 000	5 514	18 090
Bering Sea	2 261 000	873 000	4 150	13 615
Sea of Okhotsk	1 392 000	537 000	3 363	11 033
Sea of Japan (East Sea)	1 013 000	391 000	3 743	12 280
East China Sea and Yellow Sea	1 202 000	464 000	2 717	8 913

CLIMATE

MAJOR CLIMATIC REGIONS AND SUB-TYPES

Winkel Tripel Projection
1:120 000 000

Köppen classification system

A Rainy climate with no winter:
coolest month above 18°C (64.4°F).

B Dry climates; limits are defined by formulae
based on rainfall effectiveness:
   BS Steppe or semi-arid climate.
   BW Desert or arid climate.

*C Rainy climates with mild winters:
coolest month above 0°C (32°F), but
below 18°C (64.4°F); warmest month
above 10°C (50°F).

*D Rainy climates with severe winters:
coldest month below 0°C (32°F);
warmest month above 10°C (50°F).

E Polar climates with no warm season:
warmest month below 10°C (50°F).
   ET Tundra climate: warmest month
   below 10°C (50°F) but above
   0°C (32°F).
   EF Perpetual frost: all months below
   0°C (32°F).

a Warmest month above 22°C (71.6°F).

b Warmest month below 22°C (71.6°F).

c Less than four months over 10°C (50°F).

d As 'c', but with severe cold: coldest
month below -38°C (-36.4°F).

f Constantly moist rainfall throughout the year.

*h Warmer dry: all months above 0°C (32°F).

*k Cooler dry: at least one month below
0°C (32°F).

m Monsoon rain: short dry season, but is
compensated by heavy rains during rest
of the year.

n Frequent fog.

s Dry season in summer.

* Modification of Köppen definition

	World weather extremes– see table

Polar

EF	Ice cap
ET	Tundra

Cooler humid

Dc Dd	Subarctic
Db	Continental cool summer
Da	Continental warm summer

Warmer humid

Cb Cc	Temperate
Ca	Humid subtropical
Cs	Mediterranean

Dry

BS	Steppe
BW	Desert

Tropical humid

Aw As	Savanna
Af Am	Rain forest

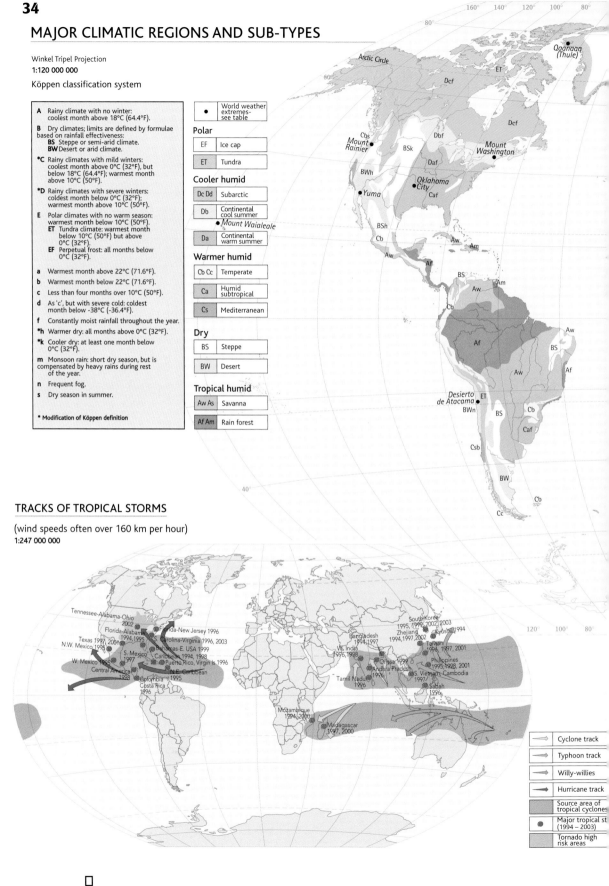

TRACKS OF TROPICAL STORMS

(wind speeds often over 160 km per hour)
1:247 000 000

→	Cyclone track
→	Typhoon track
→	Willy-willies
→	Hurricane track
	Source area of tropical cyclones
●	Major tropical storm (1994 – 2003)
	Tornado high risk areas

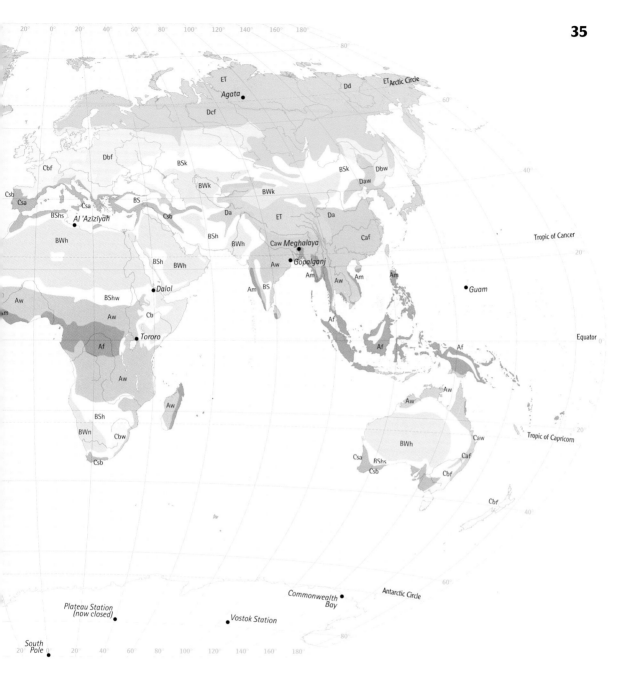

WORLD WEATHER EXTREMES

		Highest surface wind speed	
Highest shade temperature	57.8°C/136°F **Al 'Azīzīyah**, Libya (13th September 1922)		
Hottest place – Annual mean	34.4°C/93.9°F **Dalol**, Ethiopia	High altitude	372 km per hour/231 miles per hour **Mount Washington**, New Hampshire, USA (12th April 1934)
Driest place – Annual mean	0.1 mm/0.004 inches **Atacama Desert**, Chile	Low altitude	333 km per hour/207 miles per hour **Qaanaaq (Thule)**, Greenland (8th March 1972)
Most sunshine – Annual mean	90% **Yuma**, Arizona, USA (over 4 000 hours)	Tornado	512 km per hour/318 miles per hour **Oklahoma City**, Oklahoma, USA (3rd May 1999)
Least sunshine	Nil for 182 days each year, **South Pole**		
Lowest screen temperature	-89.2°C/-128.6°F **Vostok Station**, Antarctica (21st July 1983)	Greatest snowfall	31 102 mm/1 224.5 inches **Mount Rainier**, Washington, USA (19th February 1971–18th February 1972)
Coldest place – Annual mean	-56.6°C/-69.9°F **Plateau Station**, Antarctica	Heaviest hailstones	1 kg/2.21 lb **Gopalganj**, Bangladesh (14th April 1986)
Wettest place – Annual mean	11 873 mm/467.4 inches **Meghalaya**, India	Thunder-days Average	251 days per year **Tororo**, Uganda
Most rainy days	Up to 350 per year **Mount Waialeale**, Hawaii, USA	Highest barometric pressure	1 083.8 mb **Agata**, Siberia, Rus. Fed. (31st December 1968)
Windiest place	322 km per hour/200 miles per hour in gales, **Commonwealth Bay**, Antarctica	Lowest barometric pressure	870 mb 483 km/300 miles west of **Guam**, Pacific Ocean (12th October 1979)

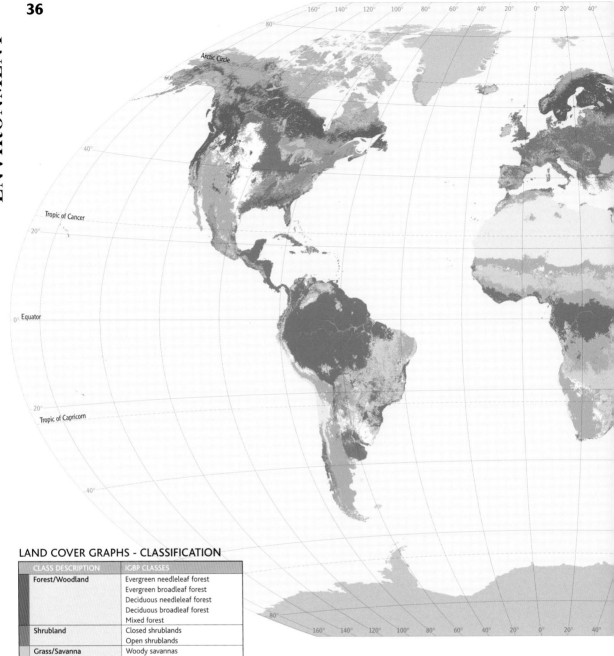

LAND COVER GRAPHS - CLASSIFICATION

CLASS DESCRIPTION	IGBP CLASSES
Forest/Woodland	Evergreen needleleaf forest
	Evergreen broadleaf forest
	Deciduous needleleaf forest
	Deciduous broadleaf forest
	Mixed forest
Shrubland	Closed shrublands
	Open shrublands
Grass/Savanna	Woody savannas
	Savannas
	Grasslands
Wetland	Permanent wetlands
Crops/Mosaic	Croplands
	Cropland/Natural vegetation mosaic
Urban	Urban and built-up
Snow/Ice	Snow and Ice
Barren	Barren or sparsely vegetated

GLOBAL LAND COVER COMPOSITION

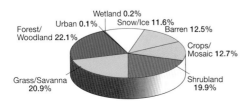

Wetland 0.2%
Urban 0.1%
Snow/Ice 11.6%
Barren 12.5%
Forest/Woodland 22.1%
Crops/Mosaic 12.7%
Grass/Savanna 20.9%
Shrubland 19.9%

CONTINENTAL LAND COVER COMPOSITION

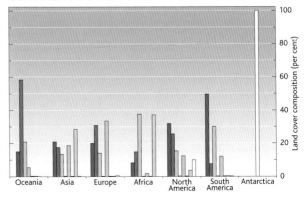

Oceania, Asia, Europe, Africa, North America, South America, Antarctica

Land cover composition (per cent)

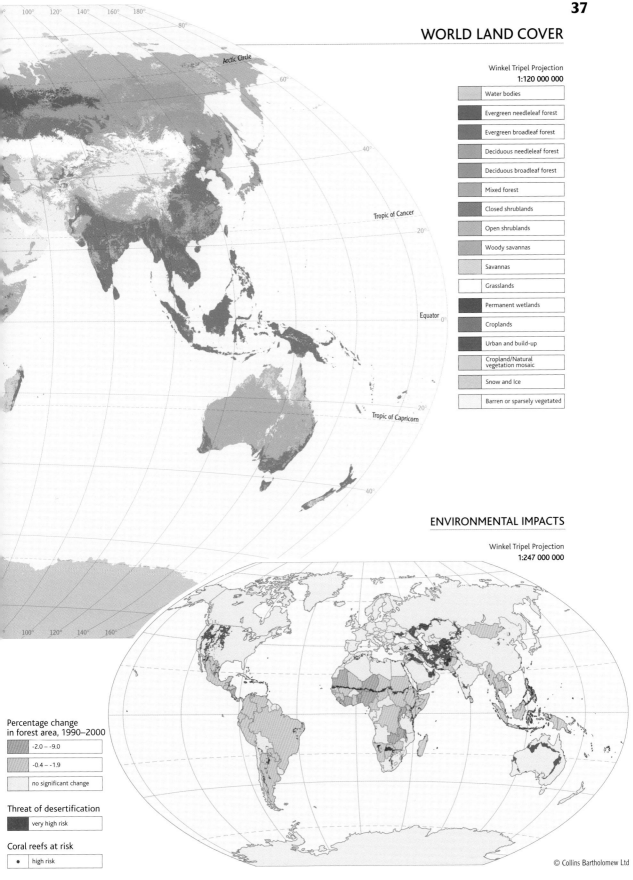

WORLD LAND COVER

Winkel Tripel Projection
1:120 000 000

	Water bodies
	Evergreen needleleaf forest
	Evergreen broadleaf forest
	Deciduous needleleaf forest
	Deciduous broadleaf forest
	Mixed forest
	Closed shrublands
	Open shrublands
	Woody savannas
	Savannas
	Grasslands
	Permanent wetlands
	Croplands
	Urban and build-up
	Cropland/Natural vegetation mosaic
	Snow and Ice
	Barren or sparsely vegetated

ENVIRONMENTAL IMPACTS

Winkel Tripel Projection
1:247 000 000

Percentage change in forest area, 1990–2000

	-2.0 – -9.0
	-0.4 – -1.9
	no significant change

Threat of desertification

	very high risk

Coral reefs at risk

•	high risk

© Collins Bartholomew Ltd

WORLD POPULATION DISTRIBUTION AND THE WORLD'S MAJOR CITIES

Winkel Tripel Projection
1:120 000 000

Population Density

per sq mile
1 250   250   62.5   2.5   0
Inhabitants   Uninhabited
500   100   25   1   0
per sq km

Major Urban Agglomerations

●	5 million–10 million
●	10 million–20 million
○	over 20 million

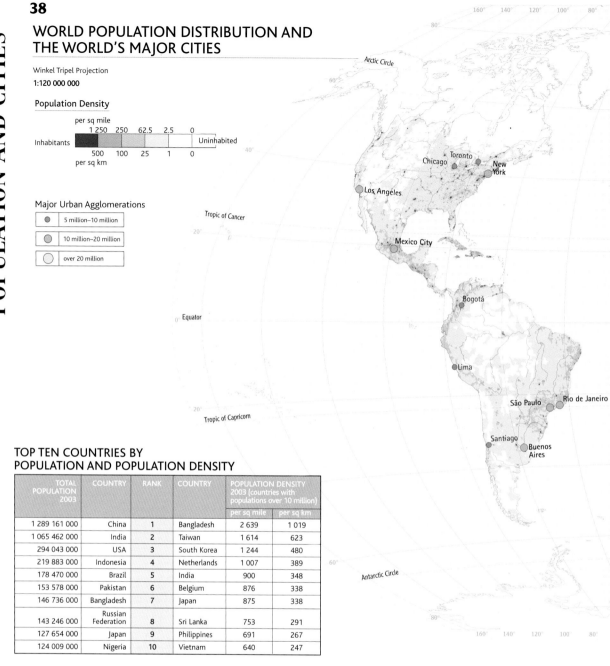

TOP TEN COUNTRIES BY POPULATION AND POPULATION DENSITY

TOTAL POPULATION 2003	COUNTRY	RANK	COUNTRY	POPULATION DENSITY 2003 (countries with populations over 10 million)	
				per sq mile	per sq km
1 289 161 000	China	1	Bangladesh	2 639	1 019
1 065 462 000	India	2	Taiwan	1 614	623
294 043 000	USA	3	South Korea	1 244	480
219 883 000	Indonesia	4	Netherlands	1 007	389
178 470 000	Brazil	5	India	900	348
153 578 000	Pakistan	6	Belgium	876	338
146 736 000	Bangladesh	7	Japan	875	338
143 246 000	Russian Federation	8	Sri Lanka	753	291
127 654 000	Japan	9	Philippines	691	267
124 009 000	Nigeria	10	Vietnam	640	247

KEY POPULATION STATISTICS FOR MAJOR REGIONS

	POPULATION 2003 (millions)	GROWTH (per cent)	INFANT MORTALITY RATE	TOTAL FERTILITY RATE	LIFE EXPECTANCY (years)	% AGED 60 OR OVER	
						2000	2050
World	6 301	1.2	56	2.7	65	10	21
More developed regions	1 203	0.3	8	1.6	76	19	32
Less developed regions	5 098	1.5	61	2.9	63	8	20
Africa	851	2.2	89	4.9	49	5	10
Asia	3 823	1.3	53	2.6	67	9	23
Europe	726	-0.1	9	1.4	74	20	35
Latin America and the Caribbean	543	1.4	32	2.5	70	8	24
North America	326	1.0	7	2.1	77	16	26
Oceania	32	1.2	26	2.3	74	13	25

Except for population (2003) and % aged 60 and over figures, the data are annual averages projected for the period 2000–2005.

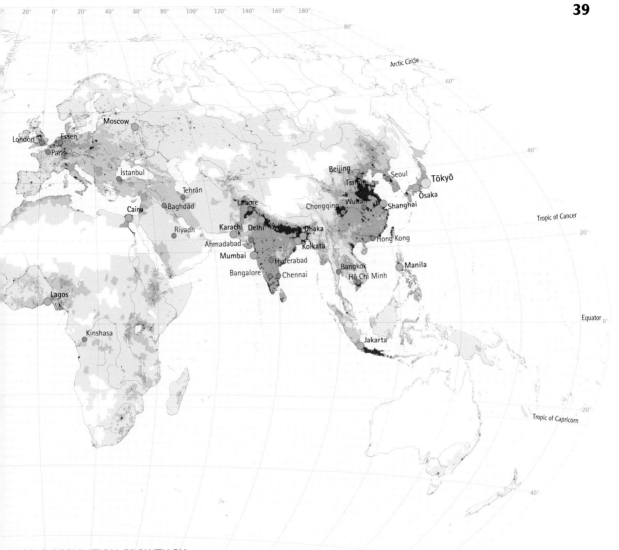

WORLD POPULATION GROWTH BY CONTINENT 1750–2050

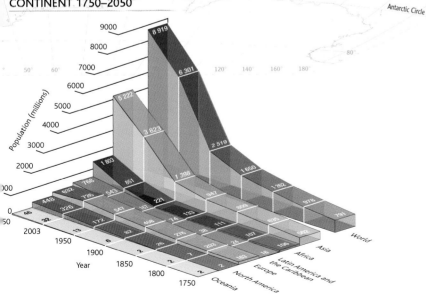

THE WORLD'S LARGEST CITIES

CITY	COUNTRY	POPULATION
Tōkyō	Japan	35 327 000
Mexico City	Mexico	19 013 000
New York	USA	18 498 000
Mumbai	India	18 336 000
São Paulo	Brazil	18 333 000
Delhi	India	15 334 000
Kolkata	India	14 299 000
Buenos Aires	Argentina	13 349 000
Jakarta	Indonesia	13 194 000
Shanghai	China	12 665 000
Dhaka	Bangladesh	12 560 000
Los Angeles	USA	12 146 000
Karachi	Pakistan	11 819 000
Rio de Janeiro	Brazil	11 469 000
Ōsaka	Japan	11 286 000
Cairo	Egypt	11 146 000
Lagos	Nigeria	11 135 000
Beijing	China	10 849 000
Manila	Philippines	10 677 000
Moscow	Russian Fed.	10 672 000

TELECOMMUNICATIONS

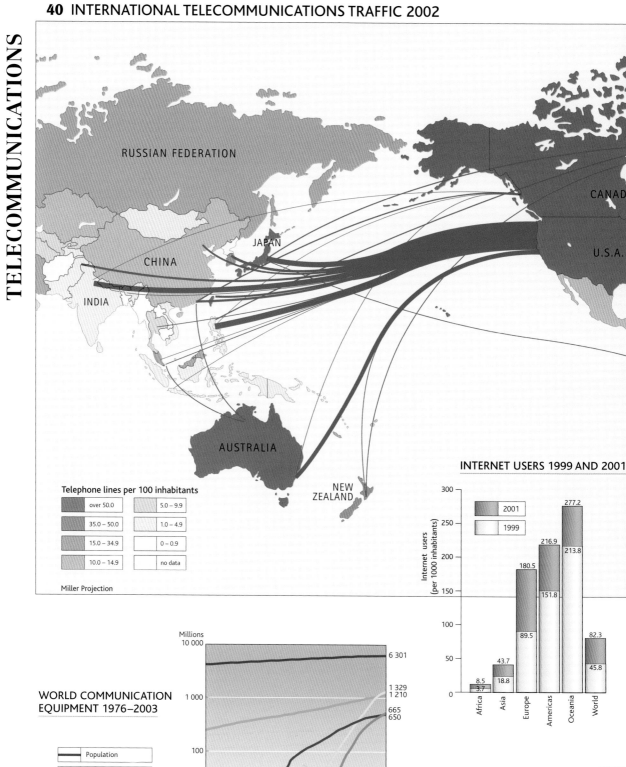

RUSSIAN FEDERATION

CANADA

JAPAN

U.S.A.

CHINA

INDIA

AUSTRALIA

NEW ZEALAND

Telephone lines per 100 inhabitants

over 50.0		5.0 – 9.9	
35.0 – 50.0		1.0 – 4.9	
15.0 – 34.9		0 – 0.9	
10.0 – 14.9		no data	

Miller Projection

INTERNET USERS 1999 AND 2001

Internet users (per 1000 inhabitants)

2001
1999

	1999	2001
Africa	3.7	8.5
Asia	18.8	43.7
Europe	89.5	180.5
Americas	151.8	216.9
Oceania	213.8	277.2
World	45.8	82.3

WORLD COMMUNICATION EQUIPMENT 1976–2003

Millions

Population	
Main telephone lines	
Mobile cellular subscribers	
Personal computers	
Internet users	

6 301

1 329
1 210

665
650

1976 1979 1982 1985 1988 1991 1994 1997 2000 2003

INTERN

1.7% 1.4

29.3%

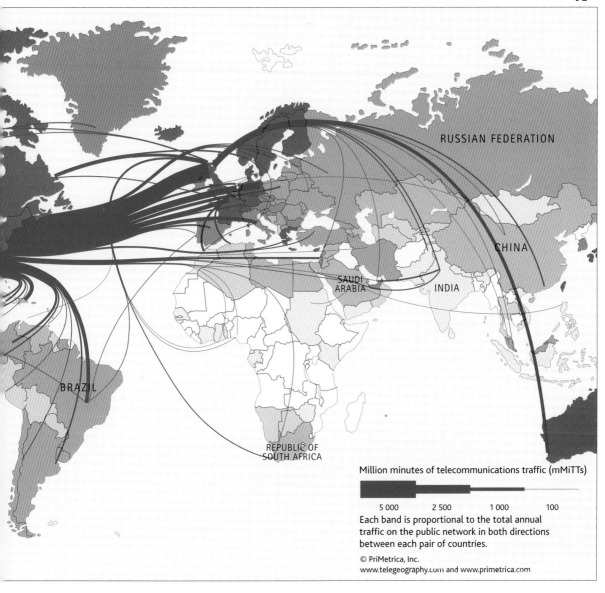

RUSSIAN FEDERATION

CHINA

SAUDI
ARABIA

INDIA

BRAZIL

REPUBLIC OF
SOUTH AFRICA

Million minutes of telecommunications traffic (mMiTTs)

5 000   2 500   1 000   100

Each band is proportional to the total annual
traffic on the public network in both directions
between each pair of countries.

© PriMetrica, Inc.
www.telegeography.com and www.primetrica.com

TELEPHONE MAIN LINES

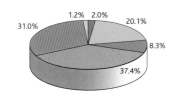

1.2% 2.0%
31.0%   20.1%
                8.3%
         37.4%

TOP 10 INTERNET SERVICE PROVIDERS (ISPs)

INTERNET SERVICE PROVIDER	WEB ADDRESS	SUBSCRIBERS
AOL (USA)	www.aol.com	20 500 000
T-Online (Germany)	www.t-online.de	4 151 000
Nifty-Serve (Japan)	www.nifty.com	3 500 000
EarthLink (USA)	www.earthlink.com	3 122 000
Biglobe (Japan)	www.biglobe.ne.jp	2 720 000
MSN (USA)	www.msn.com	2 700 000
Chollian (South Korea)	www.chollian.net	2 000 000
Tin.it (Italy)	www.tin.it	1 990 000
Freeserve (UK)	www.freeserve.com	1 575 000
AT&T WorldNet (USA)	www.att.net	1 500 000

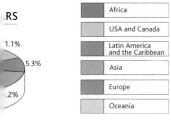

RS
1.1%
5.3%
.2%

	Africa
	USA and Canada
	Latin America and the Caribbean
	Asia
	Europe
	Oceania

CELLULAR SUBSCRIBERS

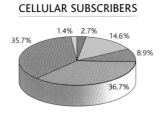

1.4% 2.7% 14.6%
35.7%   8.9%
        36.7%

MAP POLICIES AND ABBREVIATIONS

Place Names

The spelling of place names on maps has always been a matter of great complexity, because of the variety of the world's languages and the systems used to write them down. There is no standard way of spelling names or of converting them from one alphabet, or symbol set, to another. Instead, conventional ways of spelling have evolved in each of the world's major languages, and the results often differ significantly from the name as it is spelled in the original language. Familiar examples of English conventional names include Munich (München), Florence (Firenze) and Moscow (from the transliterated form, Moskva).

In this atlas, local name forms are used where these are in the Roman alphabet, though for major cities, and main physical features, conventional English names are given first. The local forms are those which are officially recognized by the government of the country concerned, usually as represented by its official mapping agency. This is a basic principle laid down by the United Kingdom government's Permanent Committee on Geographical Names (PCGN) and the equivalent United States Board on Geographic Names, (BGN). Prominent English-language and historic names are not neglected, however. These, and significant superseded names and alternate spellings, are included in brackets on the maps where space permits, and are cross-referenced in the index.

Country names are shown in conventional English form and include any recent changes promulgated by national governments and adopted by the United Nations. The names of continents, oceans, seas and under-water features in international waters also appear in English throughout the atlas, as do those of other international features where such an English form exists and is in common use. International features are defined as features crossing one or more international boundary.

Boundaries

The status of nations, their names and their boundaries, are shown in this atlas as they are at the time of going to press, as far as can be ascertained. Where an international boundary symbol appears in the sea or ocean it does not necessarily infer a legal maritime boundary, but shows which offshore islands belong to which country. The extent of island nations is shown by a short boundary symbol at the extreme limits of the area of sea or ocean within which all land is part of that nation.

Where international boundaries are the subject of dispute it may be that no portrayal of them will meet with the approval of any of the countries involved, but it is not seen as the function of this atlas to try to adjudicate between the rights and wrongs of political issues. Although reference mapping at atlas scales is not the ideal medium for indicating the claims of many separatist and irredentist movements, every reasonable attempt is made to show where an active territorial dispute exists, and where there is an important difference between 'de facto' (existing in fact, on the ground) and 'de jure' (according to law) boundaries. This is done by the use of a different symbol where international boundaries are disputed, or where the alignment is unconfirmed, to that used for settled international boundaries. Ceasefire lines are also shown by a separate symbol. For clarity, disputed boundaries and areas are annotated where this is considered necessary. The atlas aims to take a strictly neutral viewpoint of all such cases, based on advice from expert consultants.

Map Projections

Map projections have been selected specifically for the area and scale of each map, or suite of maps. As the only way to show the Earth with absolute accuracy is on a globe, all map projections are compromises. Some projections seek to maintain correct area relationships (equal area projections), true distances and bearings from a point (equidistant projections) or correct angles and shapes (conformal projections); others attempt to achieve a balance between these properties. The choice of projections used in this atlas has been made on an individual continental and regional basis. Projections used, and their individual parameters, have been defined to minimize distortion and to reduce scale errors as much as possible. The projection used is indicated at the bottom left of each map page.

Scale

In order to directly compare like with like throughout the world it would be necessary to maintain a single scale throughout the atlas. However, the desirability of mapping the more densely populated areas of the world at larger scales, and other geographical considerations, such as the need to fit a homogeneous physical region within a uniform rectangular page format, mean that a range of scales have been used. Scales for continental maps range between 1:25 000 000 and 1:55 000 000, depending on the size of the continental land mass being covered. Scales for regional maps are typically in the range 1:15 000 000 to 1:25 000 000. Mapping for most countries is at scales between 1:6 000 000 and 1:12 000 000, although for the more densely populated areas of Europe the scale increases to 1:3 000 000.

ABBREVIATIONS

Arch.	Archipelago			L.	Lake			Ra.	Range		mountain range
B.	Bay				Loch	(Scotland)	lake	S.	South, Southern		
	Bahía, Baía	Portuguese	bay		Lough	(Ireland)	lake		Salar, Salina,		
	Bahía	Spanish	bay		Lac	French	lake		Salinas	Spanish	salt pan, salt pans
	Baie	French	bay		Lago	Portuguese, Spanish	lake	Sa	Serra	Portuguese	mountain range
C.	Cape			M.	Mys	Russian	cape, point		Sierra	Spanish	mountain range
	Cabo	Portuguese, Spanish	cape, headland	Mt	Mount			Sd	Sound		
					Mont	French	hill, mountain	S.E.	Southeast,		
	Cap	French	cape, headland	Mt.	Mountain				Southeastern		
Co	Cerro	Spanish	hill, peak, summit	Mte	Monte	Portuguese, Spanish	hill, mountain	St	Saint		
E.	East, Eastern			Mts	Mountains				Sankt	German	
Est.	Estrecho	Spanish	strait		Monts	French	hills, mountains		Sint	Dutch	saint
G.	Gebel	Arabic	hill, mountain	N.	North, Northern			Sta	Santa	Italian, Portuguese,	
Gt	Great			O.	Ostrov	Russian	island			Spanish	saint
I.	Island, Isle			Pk	Puncak	Indonesian, Malay	hill, mountain	Ste	Sainte	French	saint
	Ilha	Portuguese	island	Pt	Point			Str.	Strait		
	Islas	Spanish	island	Pta	Punta	Italian, Spanish	cape, point	Tk	Teluk	Indonesian, Malay	bay, gulf
Is	Islands, Isles			R.	River			Tg	Tanjong, Tanjung	Indonesian, Malay	cape, point
	Islas	Spanish	islands		Rio	Portuguese	river	Vdkhr.	Vodokhranilishche	Russian	reservoir
Kep.	Kepulauan	Indonesian	islands		Río	Spanish	river	W.	West, Western		
Khr.	Khrebet	Russian	mountain range		Rivière	French	river		Wadi, Wâdi, Wādī	Arabic	watercourse

MAP SYMBOLS

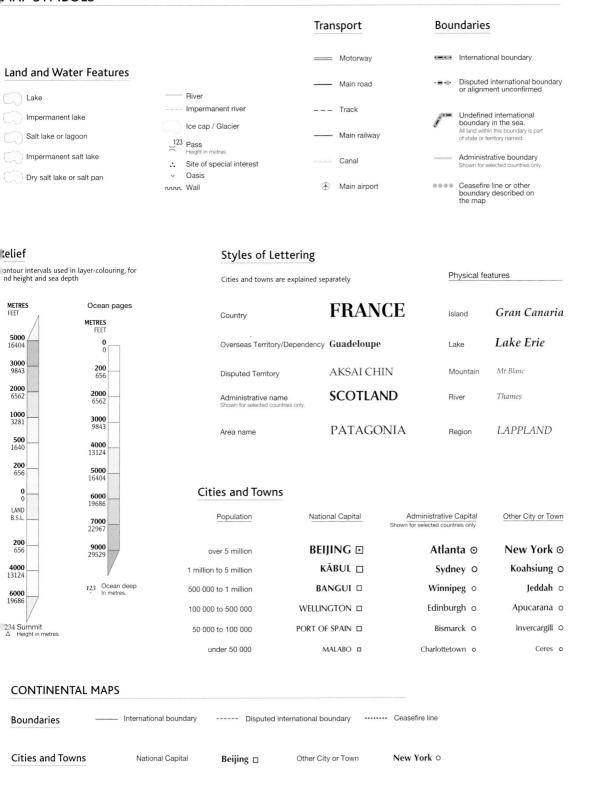

Land and Water Features

- Lake
- Impermanent lake
- Salt lake or lagoon
- Impermanent salt lake
- Dry salt lake or salt pan

--- River
---- Impermanent river

Ice cap / Glacier

123 Pass
Height in metres

∴ Site of special interest

⌄ Oasis

nnnn Wall

Transport

═══ Motorway

── Main road

--- Track

── Main railway

⊢⊢⊢ Canal

✈ Main airport

Boundaries

International boundary

Disputed international boundary or alignment unconfirmed

Undefined international boundary in the sea.
All land within this boundary is part of state or territory named.

Administrative boundary
Shown for selected countries only.

Ceasefire line or other boundary described on the map

Relief

Contour intervals used in layer-colouring, for land height and sea depth

METRES	FEET
5000	16404
3000	9843
2000	6562
1000	3281
500	1640
200	656
0	0
LAND B.S.L.	
200	656
4000	13124
6000	19686

234 Summit
△ Height in metres

Ocean pages

METRES	FEET
0	0
200	656
2000	6562
3000	9843
4000	13124
5000	16404
6000	19686
7000	22967
9000	29529

123 Ocean deep
In metres.

Styles of Lettering

Cities and towns are explained separately

Country	**FRANCE**
Overseas Territory/Dependency	**Guadeloupe**
Disputed Territory	AKSAI CHIN
Administrative name	**SCOTLAND**
Shown for selected countries only.	
Area name	PATAGONIA

Physical features

Island	*Gran Canaria*
Lake	*Lake Erie*
Mountain	*Mt Blanc*
River	*Thames*
Region	*LAPPLAND*

Cities and Towns

Population	National Capital	Administrative Capital *Shown for selected countries only*	Other City or Town
over 5 million	**BEIJING** ⊡	**Atlanta** ⊙	**New York** ⊙
1 million to 5 million	**KĀBUL** ☐	**Sydney** ⊙	**Koahsiung** ⊙
500 000 to 1 million	**BANGUI** ☐	**Winnipeg** ○	**Jeddah** ○
100 000 to 500 000	WELLINGTON ☐	Edinburgh ○	Apucarana ○
50 000 to 100 000	PORT OF SPAIN ☐	Bismarck ○	Invercargill ○
under 50 000	MALABO ☐	Charlottetown ○	Ceres ○

CONTINENTAL MAPS

Boundaries

── International boundary   ------ Disputed international boundary   ········ Ceasefire line

Cities and Towns

National Capital   **Beijing** ☐   Other City or Town   **New York** ○

WORLD PHYSICAL FEATURES

EARTH'S DIMENSIONS

Mass	5.974 X 10^{21} tonnes
Total area	509 450 000 sq km / 196 699 746 sq miles
Land area	148 721 936 sq km / 57 421 861 sq miles
Water area	360 728 064 sq km / 139 277 885 sq miles
Volume	1 083 207 X 10^6 cu km / 259 911 X 10^6 cu miles

Winkel Tripel Projection

HIGHEST MOUNTAINS

	LOCATION	HEIGHT	
		metres	feet
Mt Everest	China/Nepal	8 848	29 028
K2	China/Jammu and Kashmir	8 611	28 251
Kangchenjunga	India/Nepal	8 586	28 169
Lhotse	China/Nepal	8 516	27 939
Makalu	China/Nepal	8 463	27 765

LARGEST ISLANDS

	LOCATION	AREA	
		sq km	sq miles
Greenland	North America	2 175 600	840 004
New Guinea	Oceania	808 510	312 167
Borneo	Asia	745 561	287 863
Madagascar	Africa	587 040	266 657
Baffin Island	North America	507 451	195 928

METRES
FEET

METRES	FEET
6000	19686
4000	13124
2000	6562
1000	3281
500	1640
200	656
0	0
	LAND
	B.S.L.
200	656
3000	9843
5000	16404
7000	22967

Equatorial diameter	12 756 km / 7 927 miles
Polar diameter	12 714 km / 7 901 miles
Equatorial circumference	40 075 km / 24 903 miles
Meridional circumference	40 008 km / 24 861 miles

1: 100 800 000

© Collins Bartholomew Ltd

LARGEST LAKES

	LOCATION	AREA	
		sq km	sq miles
Caspian Sea	Asia/Europe	371 000	143 244
Lake Superior	North America	82 100	31 699
Lake Victoria	Africa	68 800	26 564
Lake Huron	North America	59 600	23 012
Lake Michigan	North America	57 800	22 317

LONGEST RIVERS

	LOCATION	LENGTH	
		km	miles
Nile	Africa	6 695	4 160
Amazon	South America	6 516	4 049
Yangtze	Asia	6 380	3 965
Mississippi-Missouri	North America	5 969	3 709
Ob'-Irtysh	Asia	5 568	3 460

WORLD COUNTRIES

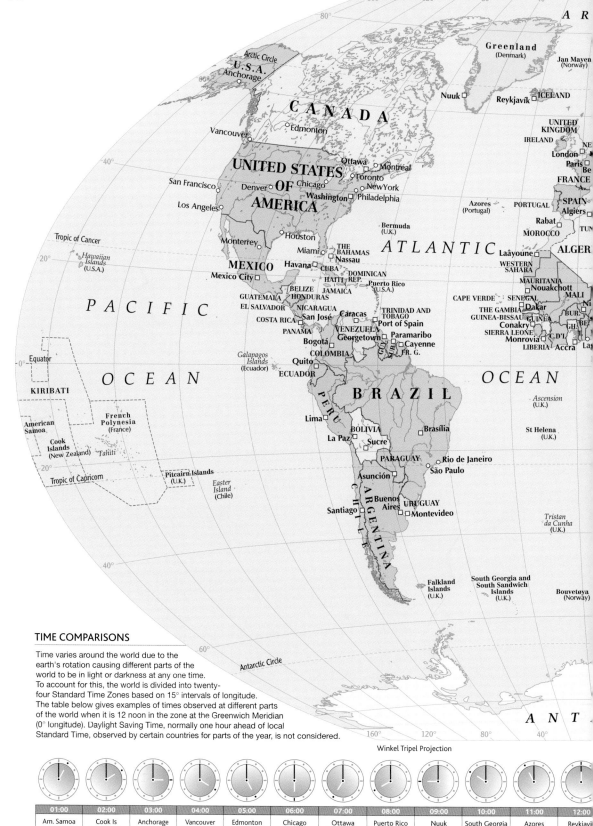

A R

Greenland
(Denmark)

Jan Mayen
(Norway)

Nuuk □   Reykjavík □ ICELAND

Arctic Circle
U.S.A.
Anchorage ○

C A N A D A

UNITED
KINGDOM

IRELAND

London □   NE

Paris □   Be

FRANCE

Edmonton ○

Vancouver ○

Ottawa ○   Montreal
Toronto

UNITED STATES
OF
AMERICA

San Francisco ○

Los Angeles ○

Denver ○ Chicago ○
Washington ○   NewYork
□ Philadelphia

Azores
(Portugal)   PORTUGAL

Rabat ○
MOROCCO

SPAIN

Algiers □

ALGER

TUN

Tropic of Cancer

Hawaiian
Islands
(U.S.A.)

Monterrey ○

Houston ○

Miami ○

Bermuda
(U.K.)

A T L A N T I C

Laâyoune □

WESTERN
SAHARA

MEXICO

Mexico City ○

THE
BAHAMAS
Nassau

Havana □

CUBA

HAITI

DOMINICAN
REP.

JAMAICA

Puerto Rico
(U.S.A.)

MAURITANIA
Nouakchott □

CAPE VERDE ○   SENEGAL

THE GAMBIA   Dakar □

GUINEA-BISSAU   GUINEA

Conakry □

SIERRA LEONE □   C.D'I

Monrovia □

LIBERIA   Accra

MALI

BUR.

BE

GH.

La

P A C I F I C

O C E A N

KIRIBATI

GUATEMALA
EL SALVADOR

BELIZE
HONDURAS

NICARAGUA

COSTA RICA   San José ○

PANAMA

Bogotá ○

Caracas ○

Port of Spain

Georgetown □   Paramaribo □

TRINIDAD AND
TOBAGO

VENEZUELA

□ Cayenne
FR. G.

COLOMBIA

Galapagos
Islands
(Ecuador)

Quito ○

ECUADOR

Equator

American
Samoa

French
Polynesia
(France)

Cook
Islands
(New Zealand)   Tahiti

Pitcairn Islands
(U.K.)

Easter
Island
(Chile)

Tropic of Capricorn

B R A Z I L

Lima ○

PERU

BOLIVIA

La Paz ○

Brasília ○

Sucre □

Ascension
(U.K.)

St Helena
(U.K.)

O C E A N

PARAGUAY

Asunción ○

Rio de Janeiro ○
São Paulo ○

Buenos
Aires □

URUGUAY

Santiago ○

ARGENTINA

CHILE

□ Montevideo

Tristan
da Cunha
(U.K.)

Falkland
Islands
(U.K.)

South Georgia and
South Sandwich
Islands
(U.K.)

Bouvetøya
(Norway)

TIME COMPARISONS

Time varies around the world due to the
earth's rotation causing different parts of the
world to be in light or darkness at any one time.
To account for this, the world is divided into twenty-
four Standard Time Zones based on 15° intervals of longitude.
The table below gives examples of times observed at different parts
of the world when it is 12 noon in the zone at the Greenwich Meridian
(0° longitude). Daylight Saving Time, normally one hour ahead of local
Standard Time, observed by certain countries for parts of the year, is not considered.

Antarctic Circle

A N T

Winkel Tripel Projection

01:00	02:00	03:00	04:00	05:00	06:00	07:00	08:00	09:00	10:00	11:00	12:00
Am. Samoa
Samoa	Cook Is
Hawaiian Is
Tahiti	Anchorage	Vancouver
San Francisco
Los Angeles
Pitcairn Is	Edmonton
Denver	Chicago
Houston
Monterrey
Mexico City
Easter Island	Ottawa
Washington
Havana
Bogotá
Lima	Puerto Rico
Caracas
La Paz
Asunción	Nuuk
Brasília
Rio de Janeiro
Buenos Aires	South Georgia
S. Sandwich Is	Azores
Cape Verde	Reykjavi
London
Rabat
Nouakch
Accra

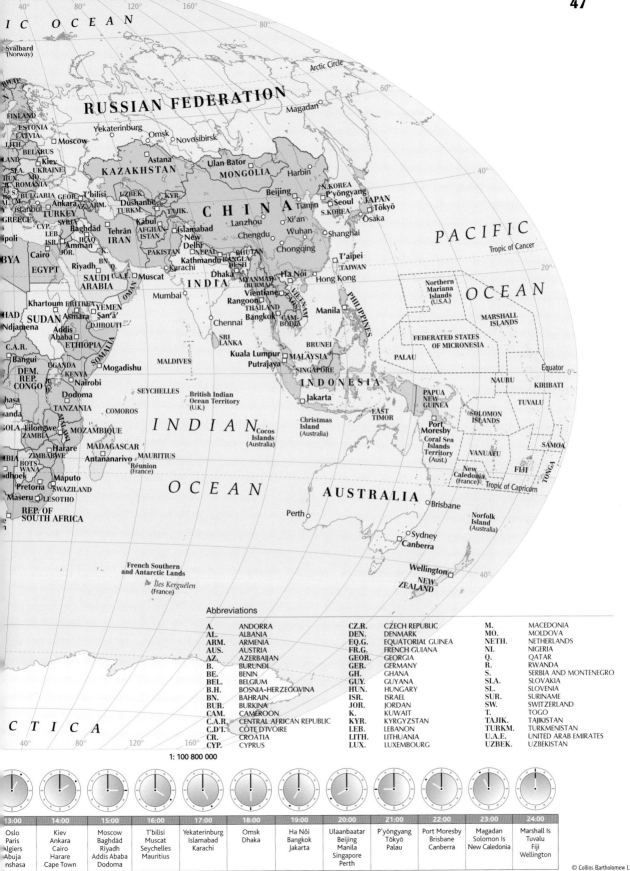

Abbreviations

A.	ANDORRA	CZ.R.	CZECH REPUBLIC	M.	MACEDONIA
AL.	ALBANIA	DEN.	DENMARK	MO.	MOLDOVA
ARM.	ARMENIA	EQ.G.	EQUATORIAL GUINEA	NETH.	NETHERLANDS
AUS.	AUSTRIA	FR.G.	FRENCH GUIANA	NI.	NIGERIA
AZ.	AZERBAIJAN	GEOR.	GEORGIA	Q.	QATAR
B.	BURUNDI	GER.	GERMANY	R.	RWANDA
BE.	BENIN	GH.	GHANA	S.	SERBIA AND MONTENEGRO
BEL.	BELGIUM	GUY.	GUYANA	SLA.	SLOVAKIA
B.H.	BOSNIA-HERZEGOVINA	HUN.	HUNGARY	SL.	SLOVENIA
BN.	BAHRAIN	ISR.	ISRAEL	SUR.	SURINAME
BUR.	BURKINA	JOR.	JORDAN	SW.	SWITZERLAND
CAM.	CAMEROON	K.	KUWAIT	T.	TOGO
C.A.R.	CENTRAL AFRICAN REPUBLIC	KYR.	KYRGYZSTAN	TAJIK.	TAJIKISTAN
C.D'I.	CÔTE D'IVOIRE	LEB.	LEBANON	TURKM.	TURKMENISTAN
CR.	CROATIA	LITH.	LITHUANIA	U.A.E.	UNITED ARAB EMIRATES
CYP.	CYPRUS	LUX.	LUXEMBOURG	UZBEK.	UZBEKISTAN

1: 100 800 000

13:00	14:00	15:00	16:00	17:00	18:00	19:00	20:00	21:00	22:00	23:00	24:00
Oslo	Kiev	Moscow	T'bilisi	Yekaterinburg	Omsk	Ha Nôi	Ulaanbaatar	P'yŏngyang	Port Moresby	Magadan	Marshall Is
Paris	Ankara	Baghdād	Muscat	Islamabad	Dhaka	Bangkok	Beijing	Tōkyō	Brisbane	Solomon Is	Tuvalu
Algiers	Cairo	Riyadh	Seychelles	Karachi		Jakarta	Manila	Palau	Canberra	New Caledonia	Fiji
Abuja	Harare	Addis Ababa	Mauritius				Singapore				Wellington
nshasa	Cape Town	Dodoma					Perth				

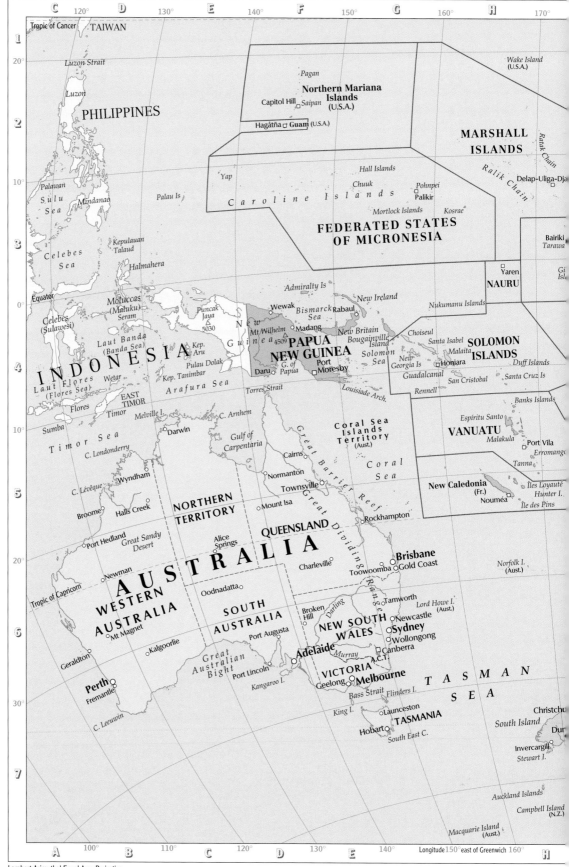

Lambert Azimuthal Equal Area Projection

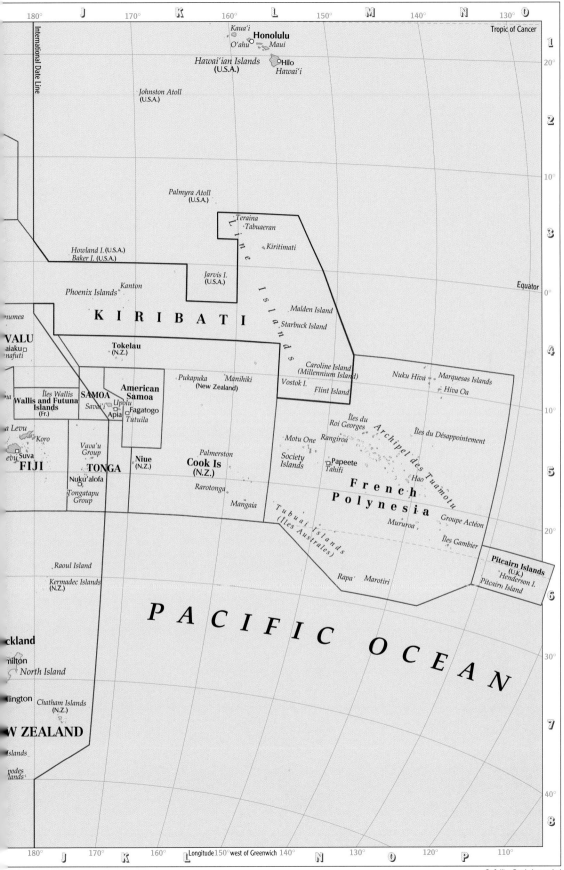

J 180° 170° K 160° L 150° M 140° N 130° O

Tropic of Cancer

1

Kaua'i
Honolulu
O'ahu Maui
Hawai'ian Islands
(U.S.A.) ○ Hilo
Hawai'i 20°

Johnston Atoll
(U.S.A.)

2

10°

Palmyra Atoll
(U.S.A.)

Teraina
Tabuaeran

3

Kiritimati

Howland I. (U.S.A.)
Baker I. (U.S.A.)

Jarvis I.
(U.S.A.)

Equator 0°

Phoenix Islands
Kanton

Malden Island

K I R I B A T I

Starbuck Island

4

Tokelau
(N.Z.)

numea

Caroline Island
(Millennium Island)

Nuku Hiva • Marquesas Islands

VALU
aiaku
nafuti

Pukapuka Manihiki
(New Zealand)

Vostok I.

Flint Island

• Hiva Oa

10°

Îles Wallis
Wallis and Futuna
Islands
(Fr.)

SAMOA
Savai'i
Upolu
Apia
Tuutila

**American
Samoa**
Fagatogo

Motu One

Îles du
Roi Georges

Rangiroa

Îles du Désappointement

5

a Levu
Koro
ebu Suva
FIJI

Vava'u
Group

Niue
(N.Z.)

TONGA
Nuku'alofa
Tongatapu
Group

Palmerston

Cook Is
(N.Z.)

Rarotonga

Mangaia

Society
Islands

Papeete
Tahiti

Hao

**F r e n c h
P o l y n e s i a**

Groupe Actéon

20°

Tubuai Islands
(Îles Australes)

Mururoa

Îles Gambier

Pitcairn Islands
(U.K.)
Henderson I.
Pitcairn Island

Raoul Island

Kermadec Islands
(N.Z.)

Rapa Marotiri

6

P A C I F I C   O C E A N

30°

ckland
milton
North Island

lington Chatham Islands
(N.Z.)

7

W ZEALAND

slands

podes
lands

40°

8

J 180° 170° K 160° L 150° Longitude west of Greenwich 140° N 130° O 120° P 110°

© Collins Bartholomew Ltd

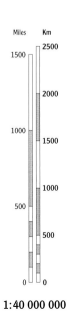

Miles   Km
2500
1500
2000
1000
1500
1000
500
500
0   0

1:40 000 000

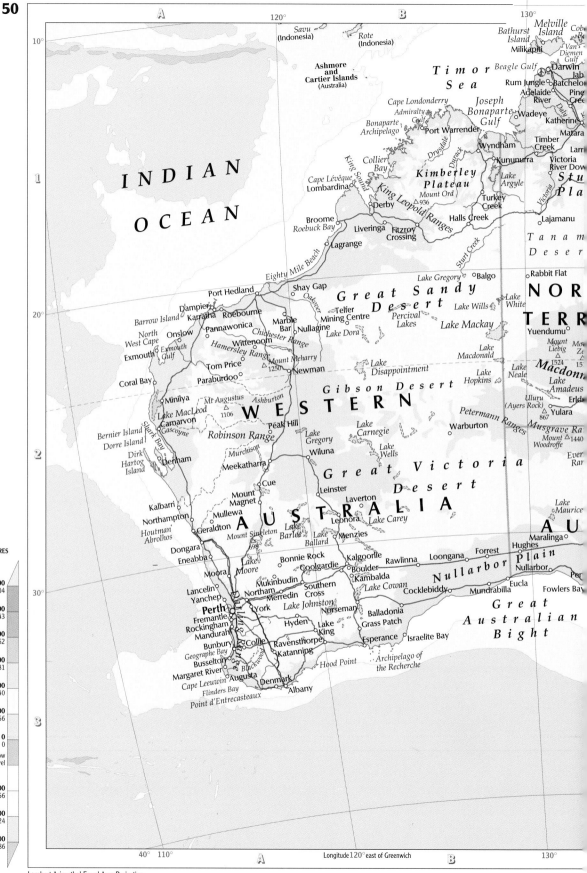

A 120° B 130°

METRES
FEET

5000
16404

3000
9843

2000
6562

1000
3281

500
1640

200
656

0
0

Land below
sea level

200
656

4000
13124

6000
19686

Lambert Azimuthal Equal Area Projection

INDIAN OCEAN

Savu (Indonesia)
Rote (Indonesia)

Melville Island
Bathurst Island
Milikapiti
Van Diemen Gulf
Darwin
Batchelor
Rum Jungle
Adelaide River
Wadeye
Katherine
Mataranka

Ashmore and Cartier Islands (Australia)

Timor Sea

Beagle Gulf

Cape Londonderry
Admiralty Gulf
Bonaparte Archipelago
Port Warrender
Joseph Bonaparte Gulf
Wyndham
Timber Creek
Victoria River Downs

Cape Lévêque
Lombardina
King Sound
Collier Bay
Kimberley Plateau
Mount Ord 936
Derby
Kununurra
Lake Argyle
Turkey Creek
Halls Creek
Lajamanu

Broome
Roebuck Bay
Liveringa
Fitzroy Crossing
Sturt Creek

Lagrange
Eighty Mile Beach

Lake Gregory
Balgo
Rabbit Flat

Port Hedland
Shay Gap
Great Sandy Desert
Telfer
Mining Centre
Percival Lakes
Lake Wills
Lake White
Lake Mackay

Dampier
Karratha
Roebourne
Oakover
Marble Bar
Nullagine
Yuendumu

Barrow Island
Pannawonica
Chichester Range
Lake Dora
Mount Liebig 1524

North West Cape
Onslow
Hamersley Range
Wittenoom
Lake Disappointment
Lake Macdonald
Macdonnell

Exmouth
Exmouth Gulf
Tom Price
Mount Meharry 1250
Newman

Coral Bay
Paraburdoo
Gibson Desert
Lake Hopkins
Lake Neale
Lake Amadeus
Uluru (Ayers Rock) 867
Yulara

Minilya
Mt Augustus 1106
Ashburton
WESTERN
Lake Carnegie
Petermann Ranges
Musgrave Range
Mount Woodroffe 1440

Lake MacLeod
Carnarvon
Gascoyne
Robinson Range
Murchison
Peak Hill
Lake Gregory
Warburton

Bernier Island
Dorre Island
Shark Bay
Meekatharra
Wiluna
Lake Wells

Dirk Hartog Island
Denham
AUSTRALIA
Great Victoria Desert

Cue
Mount Magnet
Leinster
Lake Maurice

Kalbarri
Mullewa
Laverton
Lake Carey

Northampton
Geraldton
Mount Singleton 698
Leonora
Maralinga

Houtman Abrolhos
Lake Barlee
Lake Ballard
Menzies

Dongara
Eneabba
Lake Moore
Bonnie Rock
Coolgardie
Kalgoorlie
Boulder
Rawlinna
Loongana
Forrest
Hughes
Nullarbor Plain
Nullarbor
Eucla

Moora
Mukinbudin
Southern Cross
Kambalda
Lake Cowan
Cocklebiddy
Mundrabilla
Fowlers Bay

Lancelin
Yanchep
Northam
Merredin
Lake Johnston
Norseman
Great Australian Bight

Perth
Fremantle
Rockingham
Mandurah
York
Hyden
Lake King
Balladonia
Grass Patch
Esperance
Israelite Bay

Bunbury
Collie
Ravensthorpe
Katanning
Archipelago of the Recherche

Geographe Bay
Busselton
Blackwood
Hood Point

Margaret River
Cape Leeuwin
Augusta
Denmark
Albany

Flinders Bay
Point d'Entrecasteaux

NOR TERR

Tanam Deser

Stu Pla

Longitude 120° east of Greenwich

40° 110° A B 130°

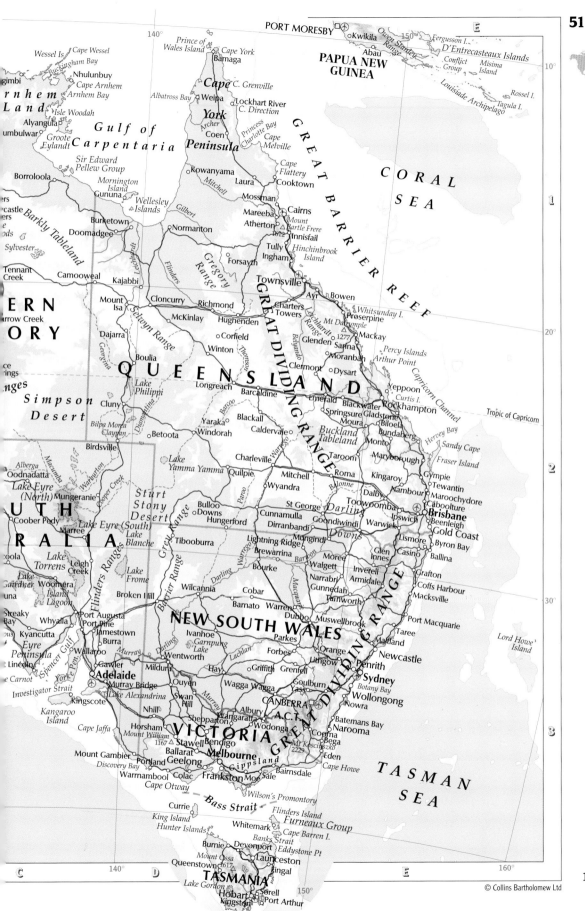

PORT MORESBY
Kwikila
Abau
PAPUA NEW GUINEA
Fergusson I.
D'Entrecasteaux Islands
Conflict Group
Misima Island
Rossel I.
Louisiade Archipelago
Tagula I.

Wessel Is
Cape Wessel
gimbi
Buckingham Bay
Nhulunbuy
Cape Arnhem
Arnhem Bay
Arnhem Land
Isle Woodah
Alyangula
mbulwar
Groote Eylandt
Sir Edward Pellew Group
Mornington Island
Wellesley Islands
Borroloola
Gunuma

Gulf of Carpentaria

Prince of Wales Island
Cape York
Bamaga
Cape York Peninsula
C. Grenville
Weipa
Lockhart River
C. Direction
Albatross Bay
Archer
Coen
Princess Charlotte Bay
Cape Melville
Kowanyama
Laura
Cape Flattery
Cooktown
Mitchell
Mossman
Mareeba
Cairns
Atherton
Mount Bartle Frere 1612
Innisfail
Tully
Hinchinbrook Island
Ingham

CORAL SEA

GREAT BARRIER REEF

castle
ers
ers
Sylvester
Barkly Tableland
Burketown
Doomadgee
Normanton
Forsayth
Gregory Range
Gilbert

Tennant Creek
Camooweal
Kajabbi
Cloncurry
Richmond
Townsville
Ayr
Bowen
Proserpine
Whitsunday I.

NORTHERN TERRITORY
rrow Creek
Mount Isa
McKinlay
Hughenden
Charters Towers
Mt Dalrymple 1277
Mackay
Dajarra
Corfield
Glenden
Sarina
Moranbah
Belyando
Percy Islands
Arthur Point

ce
rings
ges
Simpson Desert
Boulia
Winton
Clermont
Dysart
Lake Philippi
QUEENSLAND
Thomson
Longreach
Barcaldine
Emerald
Blackwater
Gladstone
Yeppoon
Curtis I.
Rockhampton
Capricorn Channel
Cluny
Diamantina
Yaraka
Blackall
Caldervale
Springsure
Moura
Biloela
Bilpa Morea Claypan
Betoota
Windorah
Charleville
Taroom
Monto
Bundaberg
Hervey Bay
Sandy Cape
Birdsville
Lake Yamma Yamma
Quilpie
Mitchell
Maryborough
Fraser Island
Warrego
Roma
Kingaroy
Gympie

Tropic of Capricorn

Alberga
Macumba
Warburton
Oodnadatta
Mungeranie
Lake Eyre (North)
Sturt Stony Desert
Bulloo Downs
Hungerford
St George
Darling
Wyandra
Balonne
Dalby
Toowoomba
Nambour
Maroochydore
Caboolture
Brisbane
Beenleigh
Ipswich
Gold Coast
Coober Pedy
Marree
Lake Eyre (South)
Lake Blanche
Tibooburra
Cunnamulla
Dirranbandi
Goondiwindi
Warwick
Lismore
Byron Bay
Casino
Ballina
Lightning Ridge
Mungindi
Downs
Glen Innes
Leigh Creek
Lake Torrens
Flinders Ranges
Lake Frome
Brewarrina
Bourke
Moree
Narrabri
Inverell
Armidale
Grafton
Coffs Harbour
Macksville
Lake
Gairdner
una
Woomera
Island Lagoon
Broken Hill
Wilcannia
Cobar
Walgett
Gunnedah
Tamworth
Streaky Bay
Whyalla
Kyancutta
Port Augusta
Port Pirie
Jamestown
Ivanhoe
NEW SOUTH WALES
Barnato
Warren
Dubbo
Muswellbrook
Taree
Port Macquarie
Eyre Peninsula
Lincoln
Carnot
Cleve
Wallaroo
Burra
Garnpung Lake
Parkes
Forbes
Orange
Maitland
Newcastle
Lord Howe Island

York
Gawler
Adelaide
Murray Bridge
Mildura
Wentworth
Hay
Lachlan
Griffith
Grenfell
Lithgow
Penrith
Sydney
Botany Bay
Wollongong

Investigator Strait
Kingscote
Lake Alexandrina
Ouyen
Swan Hill
Wagga Wagga
Yass
CANBERRA
A.C.T.
Nowra
Kangaroo Island
Cape Jaffa
Nhill
Albury
Wangaratta
Shepparton
Wodonga
Cooma
Batemans Bay
Narooma
Bega
Eden
Mount Gambier
Mount William 1167
Horsham
Stawell
Bendigo
VICTORIA
Mt Kosciuszko 2229
Cape Howe
Ballarat
Melbourne
Gippsland
GREAT DIVIDING RANGE
Portland
Geelong
Sale
Bairnsdale
TASMAN SEA
Warrnambool
Colac
Frankston
Moe
Cape Otway
Wilson's Promontory
Currie
Bass Strait
Flinders Island
Furneaux Group
King Island
Whitemark
Cape Barren I.
Hunter Islands
Banks Strait
Burnie
Devonport
Eddystone Pt
Mount Ossa 1617
Launceston
Queenstown
Fingal
TASMANIA
Lake Gordon
Hobart
Sorell
Kingston
Port Arthur

Miles | Km
700 | 1000
600 | 800
500 |
400 | 600
300 | 400
200 |
100 | 200
0 | 0

1:16 000 000

AUSTRALIA Southeast

A 140° B

Lake Eyre (North)

Macumba

Warburton

Cooper Creek
Innamincka

Noccundra

Thargomindah

Grey Range

Mungeranie

Tirari Desert

Moomba

Bulloo

QUE

Cooper Creek

Sturt Stony Desert

Bulloo Downs

William Creek

Etadunna

1

Hungerford

Lake Blanche

Caryapundy Swamp

Parroo

Tilcha

Mount Sturt 427 △

Tibooburra

Marree

Moolawatana

Lake Callabonna

Milparinka

Wanaaring

SOUTH

Hawkers Gate

Millers Creek

30°

Lyndhurst

Leigh Creek

Balcanoona

Packsaddle

Tongo

Parakylia

Roxby Downs

Lake Frome

White Cliffs

Darli

AUSTRALIA

Beltana

Parachilna

Lake Torrens

Flinders Ranges

Momba

Tilpa

Wirraminna

Woomera

Frome Downs

Barrier Range

Mootwingee

Island Lagoon

Pernatty Lagoon

Hawker

Curnamona

Mount Robe 486 △

Euriowie

Wilcannia

Woocalla

Lake Macfarlane

Cradock

Broken Hill

Stephens Creek

Lake Gairdner

Quorn

Mannahill

Cockburn
Mingary

NEW

Nonning

Port Augusta

Stirling North
Wilmington

Yunta

Olary

Menindee Lake

Menindee

Gawler Ranges

Mount Ramarkable △969

Orroroo

Paratoo

Tandou Lake

Mount Man

2

Buckleboo

Iron Knob

Wirrabara

Oakbank

Coombah

Darnick

Ivanh

Whyalla

Peterborough
Terowie

Popiltah

Pooncarie

Mossgiel

Kimba

Jamestown

Canopus

Darling

Garnpung Lake

Kyancutta

Port Pirie

Crystal Brook

Gladstone

Burtundy

Hatfield

Bool

Lock

Cleve

Snowtown

Burra

Lake Victoria

Wentworth

Oxley

Sheringa

Cowell

Clare

Morgan

Murray

Renmark

Merbein

Mildura

Murrumbidgee

Eyre Peninsula

Arno Bay

Wallaroo

Blyth

Port Wakefield

Waikerie

Barmera

Berri

Werrimull

Red Cliffs

Robinvale

Balranald

Ungarra

Kadina

Moonta

Balaklava

Loxton

RI

Cockaleechie

Maitland

Kapunda
Nuriootpa

Alawoona

Hattah

Tooleybuc

Booroorb

Tumby Bay

Ardrossan

Gawler

Mannum

Mindarie

Ouyen

Swan Hill

Moulan

Minlaton

Gulf St Vincent

Adelaide

York Peninsula

Lake Tyrrell

Denil

Coffin Bay

Port Lincoln

Mount Barker

Murray Bridge

Pinnaroo

Murrayville

Underbool

Sea Lake

Ultima

Barham

Cape Carnot

35°

Gambier Is

Yorketown

Tailem Bend

Lameroo

Hopetoun

Birchip

Kerang

Cohur

Marion Bay

Willunga

Goolwa

Lake Alexandrina

Coonalpyn

Lake Hindmarsh

Wycheproof

Charlton

Echuc

Investigator Strait

Victor Harbor

Meningie

Tintinara

Warracknabeal
Nhill

Donald

Rocheste

Cape Borda

Kingscote

Penneshaw

Backstairs Passage

Younghusband Peninsula

Keith

Dimboola

Cape de Couedic

Kangaroo Island

Bordertown

Kaniva

Padthaway

Horsham

St Arnaud

Bendigo

Lacepede Bay

Kingston South East

Cape Jaffa

Naracoorte

Goroke

Edenhope

Stawell
Mount William △1167

Avoca

VICT

Castlemaine

Kyneton

3

Robe

Lake George

Penola

Balmoral

Glenelg

The Grampians

Ararat

Daylesford

Beachport

Millicent

Casterton

Coleraine

Beaufort

Skipton

Ballarat

Bacchus Marsh

Melton

Sunbu

Mount Gambier

Hamilton

Mortlake

Lake Corangamite

Wyndham-
Werribee

Port MacDonnell

Heywood

Portland

Camperdown
Terang

Colac

Geelong

Queenscliff

Torq

Discovery Bay

Cape Nelson

Port Fairy

Warrnambool

Anglese

Lorne

Port Campbell

Apollo Bay

Cape Otway

135°

A

Longitude 140° east of Greenwich

B

Conic Equidistant Projection

METRES
FEET

5000
16404

3000
9843

2000
6562

1000
3281

500
1640

200
656

0
0

Land below sea level

200
656

4000
13124

6000
19686

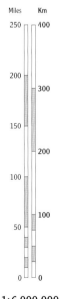

Miles Km

1:6 000 000

© Collins Bartholomew Ltd

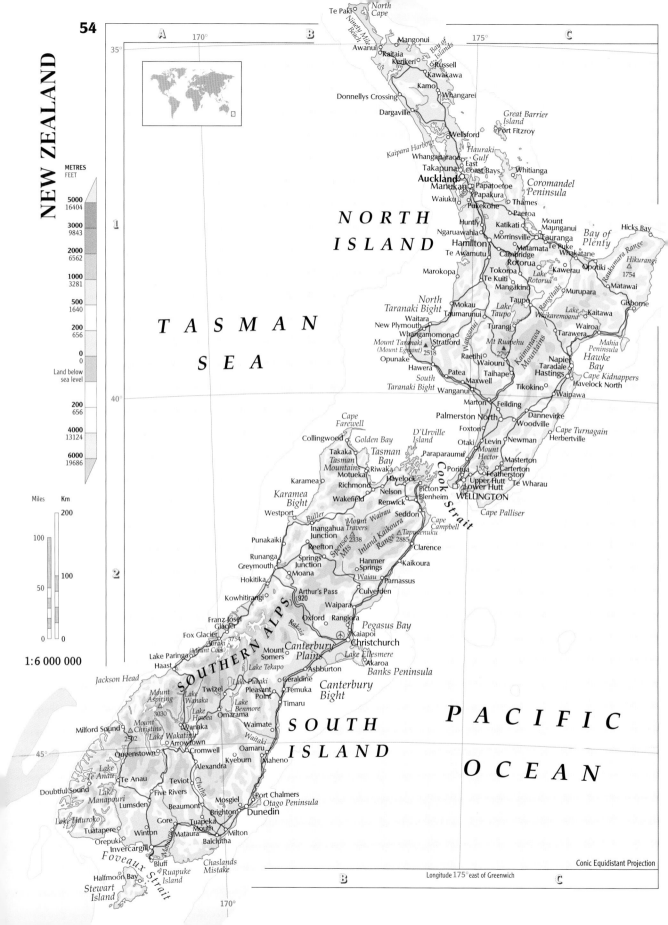

NEW ZEALAND

METRES
FEET

5000	16404
3000	9843
2000	6562
1000	3281
500	1640
200	656
0	0

Land below
sea level

200	656
4000	13124
6000	19686

Miles   Km

1:6 000 000

Te Paki
North Cape
Ninety Mile Beach
Mangonui
Awanui
Kaitaia
Kerikeri
Bay of Islands
Russell
Kawakawa
Kamo
Donnellys Crossing
Whangarei
Dargaville
Great Barrier Island
Wellsford
Port Fitzroy
Kaipara Harbour
Whangaparaoa
Hauraki Gulf
East Coast Bays
Whitianga
Takapuna
Auckland
Coromandel Peninsula
Manukau
Papatoetoe
Papakura
Thames
Waiuku
Pukekohe
Paeroa
Huntly
Katikati
Mount Maunganui
Ngaruawahia
Morrinsville
Tauranga
Hicks Bay
NORTH
Hamilton
Matamata
Te Puke
Bay of Plenty
Raukumara Range
Te Awamutu
Cambridge
Rotorua
Whakatane
Opotiki
Hikurangi
1754
ISLAND
Marokopa
Te Kuiti
Lake Rotorua
Kawerau
Murupara
Matawai
Mangakino
Gisborne
North Taranaki Bight
Mokau
Taumarunui
Lake Taupo
Taupo
Kaitawa
Waitara
Turangi
Lake Waikaremoana
Wairoa
New Plymouth
Whangamomona
Tarawera
Stratford
Mt Ruapehu
Mahia Peninsula
Mount Taranaki (Mount Egmont)
2518
2797
Napier
Hawke Bay
Opunake
Raetihi
Waiouru
Taradale
Hawera
Patea
Taihape
Hastings
Cape Kidnappers
Maxwell
Tikokino
Havelock North
South Taranaki Bight
Wanganui
Waipawa
Marton
Feilding
Palmerston North
Danevirke
Woodville
Cape Turnagain
Foxton
Herbertville
Cape Farewell
Otaki
Levin
Newman
Collingwood
Golden Bay
D'Urville Island
Mount Hector
Masterton
Takaka
Tasman Bay
Paraparaumu
1529
Tasman Mountains
Riwaka
Porirua
Carterton
Karamea
Motueka
Upper Hutt
Featherston
Richmond
Hayelock
Lower Hutt
Te Wharau
Karamea Bight
Nelson
Picton
WELLINGTON
Wakefield
Renwick
Blenheim
Westport
Buller
Seddon
Cape Palliser
Punakaiki
Inangahua Junction
Mount Travers
Wairau
2338
Inland Kaikoura Range
Tapuaenuku
Reefton
Spenser Mts
2885
Cape Campbell
Runanga
Springs Junction
Clarence
Greymouth
Moana
Hanmer Springs
Kaikoura
Hokitika
Waiau
Parnassus
Kowhitirangi
Arthur's Pass
(920)
Waipara
Culverden
Oxford
Rangiora
Pegasus Bay
Franz Josef Glacier
Rakaia
Kaiapoi
Fox Glacier
Christchurch
Aoraki
3754
Mount Somers
Canterbury Plains
(Mount Cook)
Lake Ellesmere
Akaroa
Lake Paringa
Mount Aspiring
Ashburton
Banks Peninsula
Haast
Lake Tekapo
Jackson Head
Geraldine
Lake Pukaki
Pleasant Point
Canterbury Bight
Twizel
Temuka
3030
Lake Hawea
Lake Benmore
Timaru
Milford Sound
Mount Christina
Wanaka
Omarama
Waimate
2502
Lake Wakatipu
Waitaki
Arrowtown
Oamaru
Doubtful Sound
Queenstown
Cromwell
Maheno
Lake Te Anau
Alexandra
Kyeburn
Te Anau
Teviot
Lake Manapouri
Five Rivers
Mosgiel
Otago Peninsula
Lumsden
Beaumont
Port Chalmers
Lake Hauroko
Gore
Brighton
Dunedin
Tuatapere
Winton
Tuapeka Mouth
Orepuki
Mataura
Milton
Invercargill
Balclutha
Foveaux Strait
Bluff
Chaslands Mistake
Ruapuke Island
Halfmoon Bay
Stewart Island

TASMAN

SEA

SOUTH

SOUTHERN ALPS

ISLAND

PACIFIC

OCEAN

35°
170°
175°
40°
45°
170°

Conic Equidistant Projection

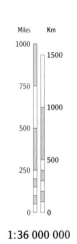

© Collins Bartholomew Ltd

ASIA

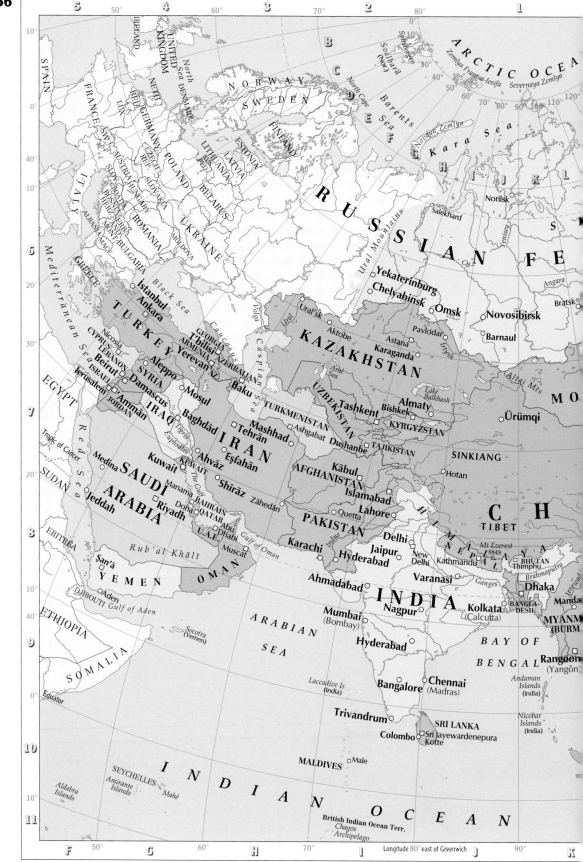

Two Point Equidistant Projection

80° **2** 180° 170° 160° **4** 50° **5** 40° **6** 30°

East Siberian Sea

Kolyma Siberia Islands

Arctic Circle

Wrangel Island

U.S.A.

I S

R U

BERING

SEA

Aleutian Islands (U.S.A.)

170°

Midway Islands (U.S.A.)

SIBERIA

FEDERATION

Lena

Kamchatka Peninsula

Magadan

Yakutsk

Sea of Okhotsk

Petropavlovsk-Kamchatskiy

7

180°

Tropic of Cancer

20°

170°

Kure Atoll

Lake Baikal

utsk

Amur

Heilong Jiang

Khabarovsk

Sakhalin

Kuril Islands

Sapporo

Hokkaidō

Wake Atoll (U.S.A.)

P A C I F I C

O C E A N

Qiqihar **Harbin**

Vladivostok

Ulan Bator

MONGOLIA

o b i

Changchun

INNER MONGOLIA **Shenyang**

Baotou **Beijing**

Tianjin

Taiyuan

NORTH KOREA

P'yŏngyang

Dalian

SOUTH KOREA

Seoul

Sea of Japan (East Sea)

Honshū

Tōkyō

Ōsaka

J A P A N

10°

160°

Lanzhou

Xi'an

Fukuoka

Kyūshū

Bonin Islands (Japan)

Yellow

Sea

Huang He

Shanghai

East

China

Sea

Ryukyu Islands

Volcano Islands (Japan)

9

ongqing

hengdu

Nanjing

Wuhan

Yangtze

Changsha

Fuzhou

T'aipei

TAIWAN

Northern Mariana Is (U.S.A.)

Kunming

Guangzhou

Hong Kong

Guam (U.S.A.)

Nanning

Luzon

Caroline Islands

0°

Equator

Ha Nôi

Hainan

South

China

Sea

Manila **Quezon City**

PHILIPPINES

ntiane

VIETNAM

Koror

Mindanao

PALAU

Admiralty Is

New Britain

AILAND

Bangkok

CAMBODIA

Phnom Pénh

Hô Chi Minh City

Gulf of Thailand

Palawan

Sulu Sea

Davao

Jayapura

N e w

G u i n e a

PAPUA

NEW GUINEA

10

10°

Bandar Seri Begawan **BRUNEI**

Celebes Sea

Manado

Halmahera

Puncak Jaya △ 5030

MALAYSIA

edan

Kuala Lumpur

Putrajaya

SINGAPORE

Kuching

B o r n e o

Moluccas (Maluku)

Seram

Kepulauan Aru

11

Balikpapan

Celebes (Sulawesi)

Kepulauan Tanimbar

Pulau Dolak

Banjarmasin

Makassar

Palembang

umatra)

Laut Java

I N D O N E S I A

Laut Banda

Arafura Sea

C. Arnhem

AUSTRALIA

Jakarta

Java

Bandung **Surabaya**

Sumbawa

Sumba

Laut Sawu

Dili

Timor

EAST TIMOR

0 140° P 150°

1:44 000 000

Miles Km

2000 3000

1500 2500

2000

1000 1500

1000

500 500

0 0

© Collins Bartholomew Ltd

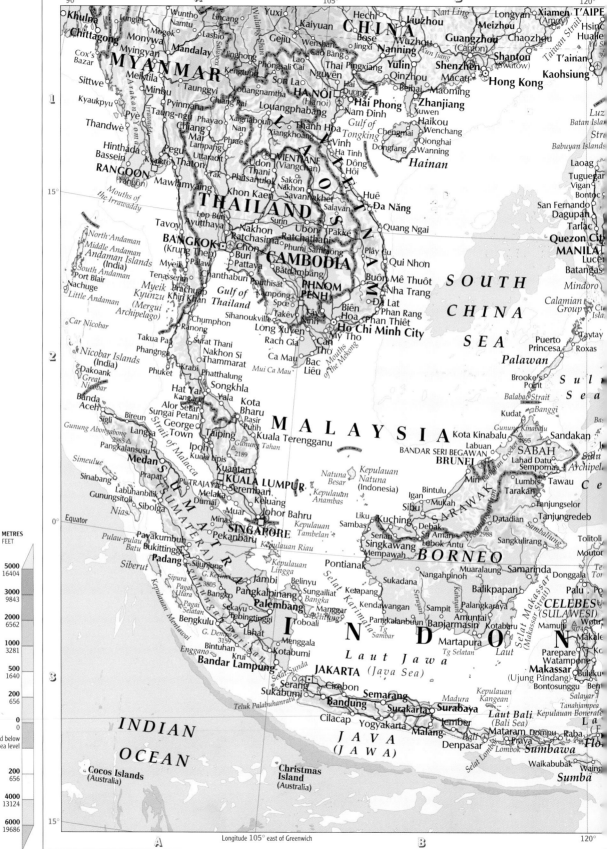

METRES
FEET

5000
16404

3000
9843

2000
6562

1000
3281

500
1640

200
656

0
0

Land below
sea level

200
656

4000
13124

6000
19686

Longitude 105° east of Greenwich

Albers Equal Area Conic Projection

C 135° D 150° E

Tropic of Cancer

Ryukyu Islands
(Nansei-shotō)
(Japan)

AIWAN

P A C I F I C

Northern
Mariana
Islands
(U.S.A.)

Pagan

Philippine
Sea

O C E A N

1

rri

an

15°

CAPITOL HILL • □ *Saipan*
□ *Tinian*

uzon

Rota

llo

HAGÅTÑA •⊕
Guam
(U.S.A.)

PHILIPPINES

et

Catanduanes

• Legaspi
• Sorsogon
nblon
Irosin • Catarman
Masbate **Samar**
• Roxas • Catbalogan
nay • Tacloban

Ulithi
Fais

FEDERATED STATES
OF MICRONESIA

Yap
Colonia ⊕

Faraulep

2

• Bacolod
Cebu
gros *Bohol*
biliran *Bohol Sea*
• Butuan

Ngulu

Sorol

Eauripik *C a r o l i n e*
I s l a n d s

quieta • Cagayan de Oro
adian • Iligan
amboanga • Cotabato *Mindanao*
bela **Davao**
Moro • Mati
Gulf
• General Santos

PALAU
KOROR •
Babeldaob

East Caroline
Basin

1:20 000 000

bes

Kepulauan
Talaud
Sangir

Morotai

a

Kepulauan
Sangir

• Daruba
• Tobelo

St Matthias
Group *Mussau Island*
Pelleluhu *Admiralty* • Lorengau *New Hanover*
Islands *Islands* *Ysabel Channel* • Kavieng
Hermit Is *Umbukul* *New*
• Manado *Wuvulu* *Manus Island* **Bismarck Archipelago** *Ireland*
Island

enanjung • Manado
Minahasa
• Kwandang • Tondano
• Gorontalo *Laut Maluku*
(*Molucca Sea*) • Sao-Siu
• Ternate *Halmahera*

Waigeo
Selat Dampir *Kwoka* *Biak* Manokwari *Biak*
3000 Jazirah *Numfoor* *Selat Yapen*
Sorong Doberai *Yapen*
Luwuk Misoöl Fafanlap Ransiki *Serui* *Sarmi* *Taritatu* Jayapura

Bismarck Sea
• Rabaul
2438
• Ulamona
• Kimbe *New Britain*
Manam Island • Madang *Long* • Lae *Gasmata*
Island

Kepulauan
Logian

• Tabuna
• Bacan
Obi

• Vanimo
Maprik • Wewak • Bogia
Aitape *Schouten Islands*
Sepik

Peleng • Todeli *Mangole* *Obi*
Moluccas *Teluk Berau* Babo
Banggai *Tallabu* Dofa (*Maluku*) Fakfak Nabire
Sula *Kepulauan* G. Binaja
Banggai Piru *3019* Bula Kaimana
• Namlea *Seram* Saparua *Ceram Sea*

Inanwatan
Teluk
Cenderawasih *Pegunungan* *Van Rees* **PAPUA**
Pk Trikora (IRIAN JAYA) *Pk Mandala*
Enarotali *Pegunungan Maoke*
Pk *4700*
Jaya *5030* *4730*

Mt **NEW**
Wilhelm **GUINEA** **PAPUA**
4509 • Goroka • Madang
Mount *Huon* • Lae
Hagen *Peninsula* • Morobe
Mount

Manui
Kendari
Raha
Buton

S
Buru **I** Adi
Ambon *Ambon*
Wowoni

Kepulauan
Watubela

• Fakfak
Kaimana
• Mendi
• Kiunga
Lake
Murray

• Goroka
Mount
Hagen
NEW GUINEA
• Kikori
• Balimo
• Morehead

Central Ra.
4509
Mount
Victoria
4073

Trobriand
Islands
• Wau
D'Entrecasteaux Is.
• Kwikila
Goschen Strait
• Alotau
Samarai

Kepulauan
Banda
(*Banda Sea*)

Kepulauan
Namlea *Kai*
A Tual • Dobo Wokam
Kai Kecil *Kai* Benjina
Besar

• Kerema
Gulf
of Papua
PORT
MORESBY Abau

Lores
Sea)

Lubau
Tukangbesi

Manuatuto
Leti

Kobroör
Kepulauan *Tanjung Deyong*
Aru • Sia *Trangan*
Kaiwatu *Kepulauan Tanimbar*

Digul
Pulau
Dolak
• Merauke

• Daru
Bamaga

C. Grenville
• Weipa
• Lockhart River

L a u t B a n d a

Kalabahi • Atapupu
Alor *Kepulauan Barat Daya* *Damar* *Wuliaru* *Larat*
Wetar Roma Babar *Selaru* *Kepulauan*
Kepulauan *Sermata* Saumlakki
DILI Maliana *Leti*

Tanjung Vals

A r a f u r a   S e a

Thursday
Island *C. York*
Prince of Wales Bamaga
Island

C. York

C. Melville
C. Flattery

aranutaka
OCUSSI
wu *2960*
Sea) *2215* *Timor*
Kupang

Maliana
• Kefamenanu
EAST
TIMOR

AUSTRALIA

Melville *Croker I.* *Wessel Is*
Island
Van Diemen Nhulunbuy
• Milikapiti *Gulf* • Milingimbi *C. Arnhem*
Bathurst Island • Jabiru *Gulf*
Beagle Gulf • Darwin *Arnhem* *of*
• Batchelor *Land* *Carpentaria*
Adelaide River • Pine Creek • Alyangula

Coen
Cape York
Peninsula *C. Melville*

Rote

T i m o r   S e a

• Laura
• Cooktown

© Collins Bartholomew Ltd

Miles Km
750 1250

1000

500 750

500

250
250

0 0

THAILAND

VIETNAM

Andaman Sea

MALAYSIA

PENINSULAR

MALAYSIA

KUALA LUMPUR

PUTRAJAYA

SINGAPORE

Strait of Malacca

Medan

Pematangsiantar

S U M A T E R A

Padang

Siberut

Kepulauan Mentawai

Palembang

Bangka

Belitung

Bandar Lampung

JAKARTA

Bandung

JAVA
(JAWA)

INDIAN

OCEAN

S O U T H   C H I

Natuna Besar

Kepulauan
Anambas

Kepulauan
Natuna
(Indonesia)

Kepulauan
Tambelan
(Indonesia)

Pontianak

Singkawang

Kuchi

Selat Karimata

I N D

L A U T
(J A V

Phangnga
Ban Khok Kloi
Thalang
Phuket
Krabi
Trang
Thung Song
Nakhon Si Thammarat
Khao Chum Thong
Phatthalung
Thale Luang
Songkhla
Hat Yai
Satun
Sadao
Pattani
Yala
Narathiwat
Kota Bharu
Rangae
Kangar
Alor Setar
Sungai Petani
George Town
Butterworth
Kuala Kerai
Pasir Putih
Kuala Terengganu
Taiping
Kuala Kangsar
Ipoh
Kampar
Gunung Tahan △2189
Tasik Kenyir
Kuala Lipis
Dungun
Cukai
Teluk Intan
Bagan Datuk
Kuantan
Klang
Temerluh
Pekan
Bahau
Seremban
Padang Endau
Melaka
Segamat
Mersing
Muar
Keluang
Batu Pahat
Bengkalis
Johor Bahru
Labuhanbilik
Bagansiapiapi
Dumai
Duri
Daludalu
Minas
Pekanbaru
Bangkinang
Tembilahan
Rengat
Bintan
Tanjungpinang
Kepulauan Riau
Daik
Lingga
Kepulauan Lingga
Singkep
Belinyu
Mentok
Sungailiat
Pangkalpinang
Koba
Rajik
Tanjungpandan
Toboali
Dendang
Manggar
Kualatungal
Jambi
Muaratembesi
Simpang
Bangko
Sarolangun
Surulangun
Sekayu
Plaju
Kayuagung
Prabumulih
Lahat
Lubuklinggau
Tebingtinggi
Curup
Martapura
Menggala
Muaradua
Kotabumi
Metro
Kotaagung
Krui
Bintuhan
Bengkulu
Mega
Sijunjung
Solok
Muarabungo
Gunung Kerinci △3805
Sungaipenuh
Bangko
Mukomuko
Buriai
Pagai Utara
Pagai Selatan
Enggano
Sipura
Kaliet
Muarasiberut
Painan
Bukittinggi
Padangpanjang
Kagologolo
Payakumbuh
Telo
Tanahmasa
Tanahbala
Pulau-pulau Batu
Equator
Natal
Airbangis
Talu
Hutanopan
Padangsidimpuan
Sirombu
Telukdalam
Nias
Gunungsitoli
Pulau-pulau Banyak
Sibolga
Gunungtua
Rantauprapat
Balige
Danau Toba
Prapat
Singkil
Tanjungbalai
Risaran
Sidikalang
Tebingtinggi
Binjai
Belawan
Gunung Leuser △3145
Blangkejeren
Pangkalansusu
Langsa
Gunung Abongabong △2985
Takengon
Peureula
Lhokseumawe
Bireun
Sigli
Calang
Banda Aceh
Sabang
Pulau We
Tapaktuan
Sinabang
Simeulue
Muaradua
Gunung Dempo △3159
Gunung Resag △2232
Bandar Lampung
Bintuhan
Kotaagung
Teluk Semangka
Krakatau
Selat Sunda
Tanjung Cina
Panaitan
Deli
Teluk Palabuhanratu
Sindangbarang
Rangkasbitung
Serang
Karawang
Bogor
Gunung △3019
Sukabumi
Garut
Ciamis
Cilacap
Kebume
Temanggu
Gunung Slamet △3428
Tegal
Pekalon
Cirebon
Tanjung Indramayu
Mui Ca Mau
Nam Căn
Côn Son
Laut
Panarik
Subi Besar
Selat Serasan
Liku
Sema
Sambas
Pemangkat
Siluas
Bengkayan
Ngabang
Mempawah
Balaiberk
Kubu
Telukbatang
Sukadana
Ketapang
Suka
Kendawa
Pulau-pulau Karimata
Tanj
Sam

METRES
FEET

5000 / 16404
3000 / 9843
2000 / 6562
1000 / 3281
500 / 1640
200 / 656
0 / 0
Land below sea level
200 / 656
4000 / 13124
6000 / 19686

Longitude 100° east of Greenwich

Albers Equal Area Conic Projection

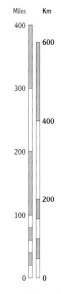

MALAYSIA AND INDONESIA West

1:9 600 000

© Collins Bartholomew Ltd

CONTINENTAL SOUTHEAST ASIA

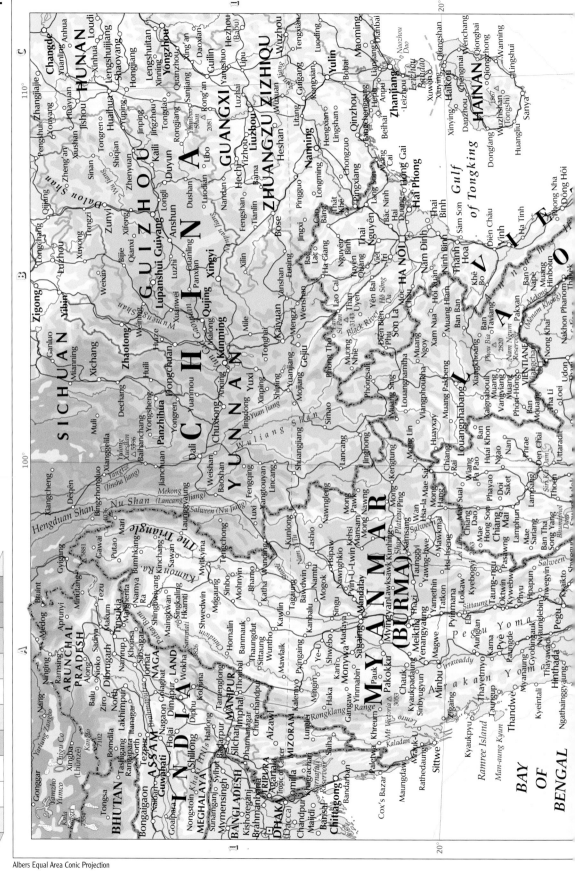

Albers Equal Area Conic Projection

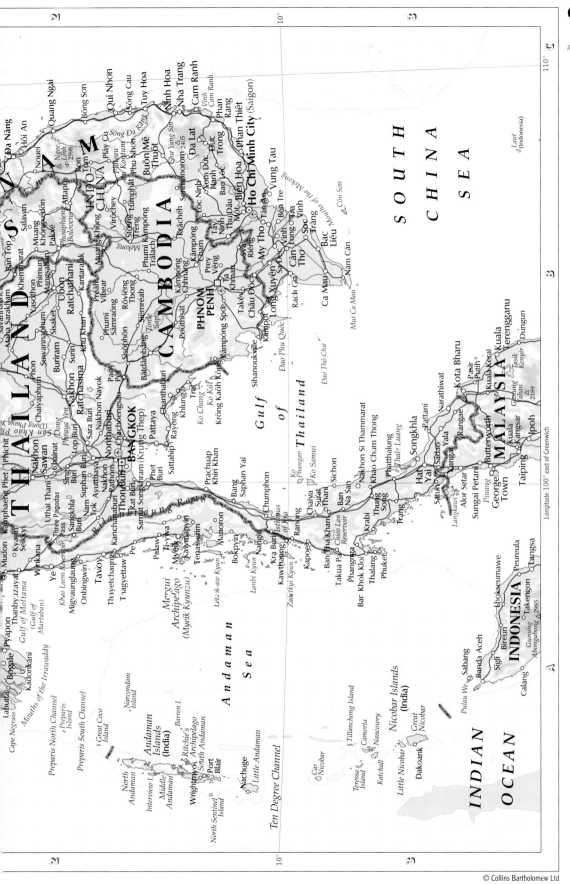

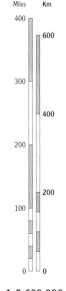

S O U T H   C H I N A   S E A

Laut (Indonesia)

V I E T N A M

Da Nẵng
Hội An
Nquei
Quang Ngai
Bông Sơn
Qui Nhơn
Song Câu
Tuy Hoa
Ninh Hoa
Nha Trang
Cam Ranh
Vịnh Cam Ranh
Phan Rang
Phan Thiêt

Ngọc Linh △2598
Play Cu
Kon Tum
Plei Kon
Tuy Hoa
Buôn Mê Thuột
Shu Yang Sin △2405
Đa Lat
Đức Trong

INDO - CHINA

Xam Nua
Muang Xepon
Attapu
Phouphieng Bolovens
Salavan
Virochey
Stoeng Treng
Phumi Khong
Senmonorom △2405
Bao Lôc
Xom Duc
Phu Nhon
Biên Hoa
Loc Ninh
Ho Chi Minh City (Saigon)
Vung Tau

C A M B O D I A

Muang Khong
Preah Vihéar
Rôviêng
Tbông
Rôcheh
Kâmpông Thum
Kâmpông Cham
Prey Vêng
Svay Riêng
Tây Ninh
Thu Dầu Một
Tân An
Bên Tre
Vĩnh Long
Trà Vinh
Cân Tho
Soc Trang
Bac Liêu
Năm Cân
Ca Mau

Preâh Vihéar
Phumi Sámraông
Siĕmréab
Bătdâmbâng
Tónlé Sap
Pouthisăt
PHNOM PENH
Kâmpóng Spoe
Takêv
Svay Chék
Châu Đôc
Long Xuyên
Rach Gia

Sisôphón
Phumi Prêk
Kâb
Kâmpông Chhnăng
Kâmpót
Mekong
Tralach
Pôipêt
Sên
Mouths of the Mekong
Côn Son

T H A I L A N D

Loei
Udon Thani
Sakon Nakhon
Maha Sarakham
Roi Et
Yasothon
Kalasin
Khon Kaen
Phimun Mangsahan
Ubon Ratchathani
Khemmarat
Sisaket
Surin
Buriram
Nang Rong
Nakhon Ratchasima
Khu Khan
Phon
Chaiyaphum

Phetchabun
Lom Sak
Phichit
Kamphaeng Phet
Nakhon Sawan
Uthai Thani
Sing Buri
Lop Buri
Sara Buri
Nakhon Nayok
Phra Nakhon Si Ayutthaya
Phraya Tem
Chainat
Dong
Suphan Buri
Nam
Nakhon Pathom
Nonthaburi
BANGKOK
(Krung Thep)
Thon Buri
Samut Prakan
Chachoengsao
Chon Buri
Pattaya
Rayong
Chanthaburi
Trat
Ko Chang
Khlung
Krông Kaôh Kong
Ko Kut

△Ban Top

Ban Nao
Muang Phimun
Ban
Kyaing Seikkyi

San Khao Pt.
(Dong Phaya)

Sattahip
Phet Buri
Prachuap Khiri Khan
Bang Saphan Yai
Chumphon
Lang Suan
Ko Phangan
Ko Samui
Sichon
Surat Thani
Ban Na San
Nakhon Si Thammarat
Thung Song
Krabi
Trang
Phatthalung
Phuket
Thalang
Takua Pa
Phangnga
Ban Khok Kloi

Bilauktaung Range

Tenasserim
Myeik
Palaw
Bokpyin
Kawthaung
Nanghin
Ranong
Kapoe
Ban Tha Kham
Chaiya
Khao Chum Thong
Phatthalung
Thale Luang
Songkhla
Hat Yai
Yala
Pattani
Narathiwat
Rangae
Kota Bharu

M A L A Y S I A

Kota Bharu
Pasir Putih
Kuala Terengganu
Dungun
Kuala Kerai
Kuala Krai
Gunung Tahan △2189
Butterworth
George Town
Pinang
Taiping
Ipoh
Sungai Petani
Alor Setar
Kangar
Langkawi
Satun
Kuala Kangsar

Gulf of Thailand

Dao Phu Quôc
Sihanoukville
Dao Tho Chu

Mui Ca Mau

Gulf of Martaban

Mawlamyine
Thanbyuzayat
Ye
Migyaunglaung
Onbingwin
Tavoy
Thayetchaung
Tagyettaw
Pe
Khao Laem Reservoir
Three Pagodas Pass
Kanchanaburi
Ratburi
Thong Pha Phum
Sangkhla Buri

Pyapon
Bogale
Kadonkani
Labutta
Mouths of the Irrawaddy
Kyauktan
Kadonkani

Cape Negrais
Preparis Island
Preparis North Channel
Great Coco Island
Preparis South Channel
Narcondam Island
Barren I.

Merqui Archipelago
(Myeik Kyunzu)
Zadetkyi Kyun
Letsôk-aw Kyun
Lanbi Kyun

Andaman Islands (India)
North Andaman
Interview I.
Middle Andaman
Ritchie's Archipelago
South Andaman
Wrightmyo
Port Blair
Little Andaman
Nachuge
North Sentinel Island

A n d a m a n   S e a

Ten Degree Channel

Tillanchong Island
Car Nicobar
Camorta
Teressa Island
Nancowry
Katchall

Nicobar Islands (India)
Little Nicobar
Great Nicobar
Dakoank

Pulau We
Sabang
Banda Aceh
Sigli
Bireun
Calang
Lhokseumawe
Peureula
Takengon
Tangsa

I N D O N E S I A
Gunung Abongabong △2985

I N D I A N   O C E A N

Longitude 100° east of Greenwich

Miles	Km
400	
	600
300	
	400
200	
100	200
0	0

1:9 600 000

PHILIPPINES

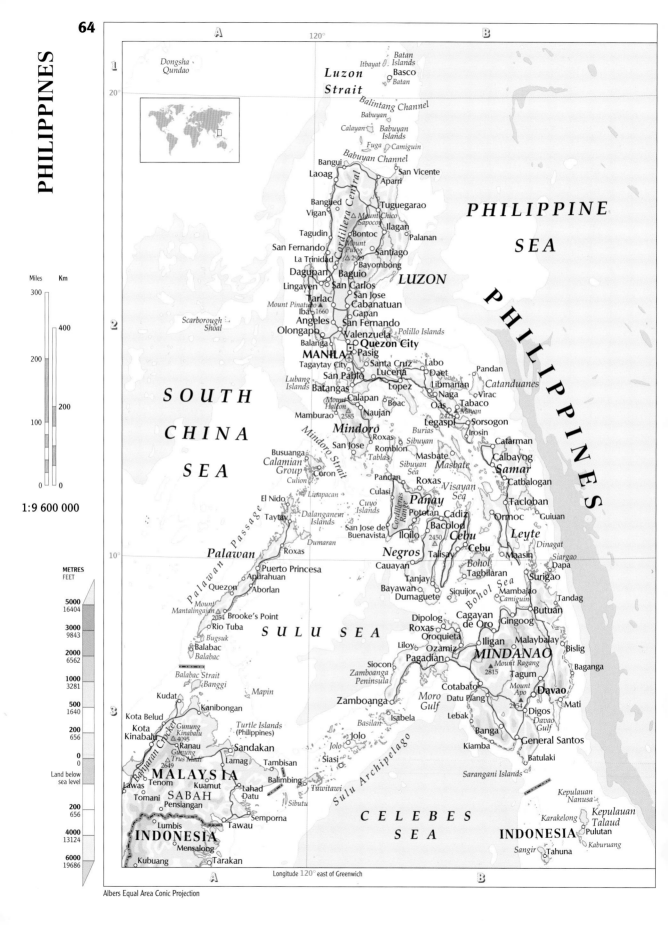

Dongsha
Qundao

Miles Km

300

400

200

200

100
100

0   0

1:9 600 000

SOUTH

CHINA

SEA

METRES
FEET

5000
16404

3000
9843

2000
6562

1000
3281

500
1640

200
656

0
0
Land below
sea level

200
656

4000
13124

6000
19686

Luzon
Strait

Batan
Islands
Itbayat   Basco
            Batan

Balintang Channel
Babuyan
Calayan   Babuyan
           Islands
        Fuga Camiguin
      Babuyan Channel

Bangui   San Vicente
Laoag   Aparri
Banguéd   Tuguegarao
Vigan   Mount Chico
         Sapocoy
Tagudin   Bontoc Ilagan   Palanan
San Fernando Mount
La Trinidad   Pulog   Santiago
Dagupan Baguio △ 2929 Bayombong
Lingayen San Carlos
        San Jose
Tarlac   Cabanatuan   LUZON
Mount Pinatubo Gapan
Iba 1660 Angeles San Fernando
Olongapo Valenzuela   Polillo Islands
Balanga Quezon City
         Pasig
MANILA   Santa Cruz   Labo
Tagaytay City Lucena   Daet   Pandan
San Pablo   Libmanan   Catanduanes
Lubang Batangas   Lopez   Naga   Virac
Islands   Boac   Oas Tabaco
    Mount   Calapan   Mayon
    Halton Naujan   2421 Legaspi
Mamburao 2585   Sorsogon
           Mindoro   Burias   Irosin
        San Jose Roxas Sibuyan   Catarman
Busuanga Romblon Masbate   Calbayog
Calamian   Coron Tablas Masbate   Samar
Group   Sibuyan Masbate   Catbalogan
    Culion   Sea
Liinapacan   Pandan Roxas Visayan Tacloban
El Nido   Culasi Sea   Ormoc Guiuan
Taytay   Cuyo   Panay
         Islands   Pototan Cadiz Leyte
Dalanganem   Cordilleras Bacolod Cebu Dinagat
Islands San Jose de Ranges Iloilo 2450 Cebu Siargao
Dumaran Buenavista   Negros △ Bohol Dapa
Roxas   Talisay   Maasin Surigao
Palawan   Cauayan   Tanjay Tagbilaran Mambajao
Puerto Princesa   Bayawan Siquijor Camiguin Tandag
Aborlan Apurahuan Dumaguete Bohol Butuan
                    Sea
Mount   Dipolog Cagayan Gingoog Bislig
Mantalingajan Roxas de Oro
2054 Brooke's Point Oroquieta Iligan Malaybalay Baganga
Rio Tuba   Ozamiz MINDANAO
Bugsuk   SULU SEA Pagadian Mount Ragang
Balabac Siocon   2815
Balabac   Zamboanga Cotabato Mount Davao
Balabac Strait Peninsula Datu Piang Apo Mati
Banggi   Zamboanga   2954 Digos
Mapin   Lebak Banga Davao
Kudat   Isabela   Gulf
Kota Belud Turtle Islands Moro Kiamba General Santos
Kota Gunung (Philippines) Gulf   Batulaki
Kinabalu Kinabalu Jolo Basilan Sarangani Islands
Ranau △ 4095 Jolo Kepulauan
MALAYSIA Gunung Sandakan Siasi Nanusa
Tenom Trus Madi Lamag Tambisan Karakelong Kepulauan
SABAH 2649   Talaud
Kuamut Balimbing Tuwitawi Pulutan
Lawas Kota Kinabalu   Kaburuang
Tomani Pensiangan Sibutu CELEBES Sangir Tahuna
Lumbis Semporna SEA INDONESIA
INDONESIA Tawau
Mensalong
Kubuang Tarakan

PHILIPPINE

SEA

PHILIPPINES

Scarborough
Shoal

Mindoro
Strait

Mindoro

Palawan Passage

Palawan

Banjaran Crocker

Moro
Gulf

Sulu Archipelago

Albers Equal Area Conic Projection

A   120°   B

20°

10°

1

2

3

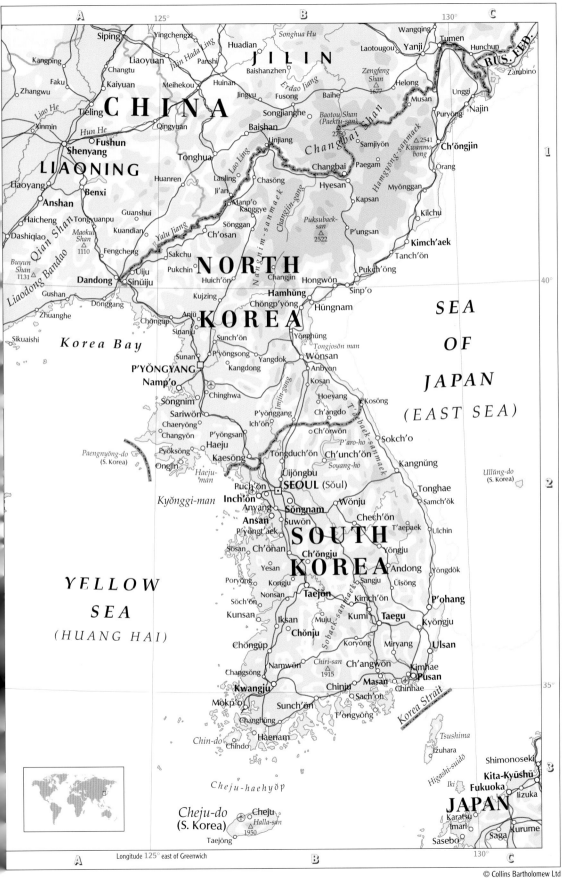

NORTH KOREA AND SOUTH KOREA

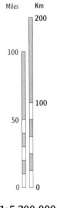

1:5 200 000

© Collins Bartholomew Ltd

JAPAN

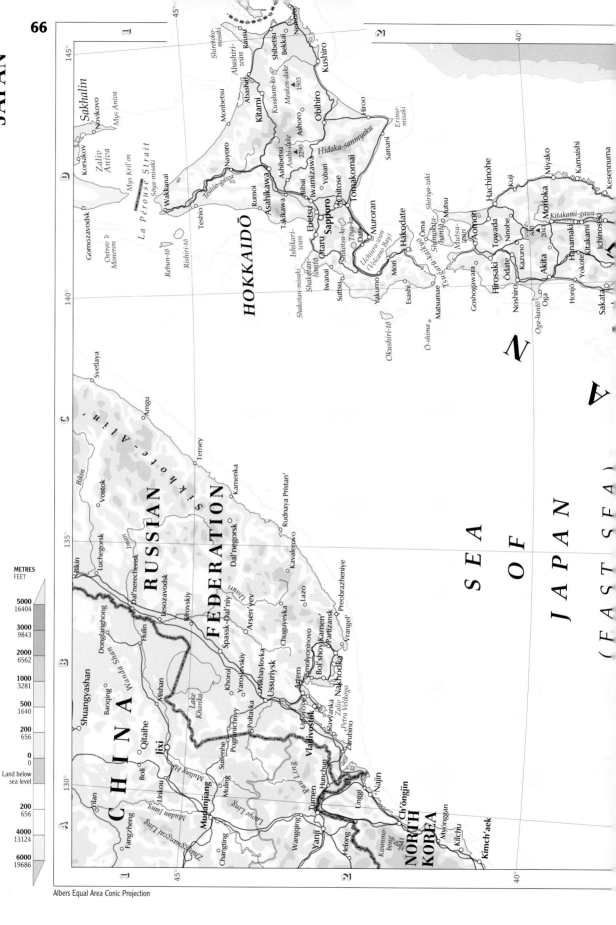

METRES
FEET

5000	16404
3000	9843
2000	6562
1000	3281
500	1640
200	656
0	0
Land below sea level	
200	656
4000	13124
6000	19686

Albers Equal Area Conic Projection

CHINA AND MONGOLIA

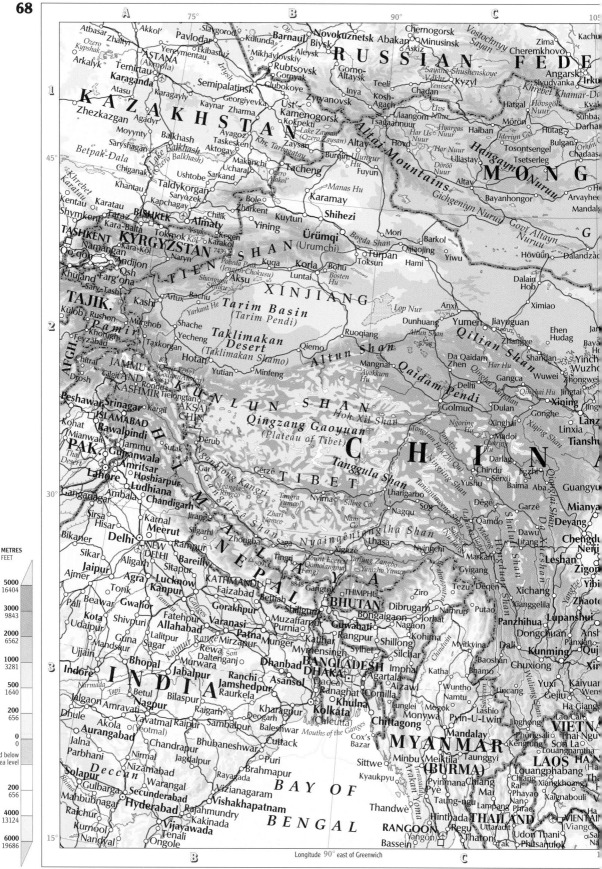

METRES / FEET

5000	16404
3000	9843
2000	6562
1000	3281
500	1640
200	656
0	0
Land below sea level	
200	656
4000	13124
6000	19686

Longitude 90° east of Greenwich

Albers Equal Area Conic Projection

CHINA Central

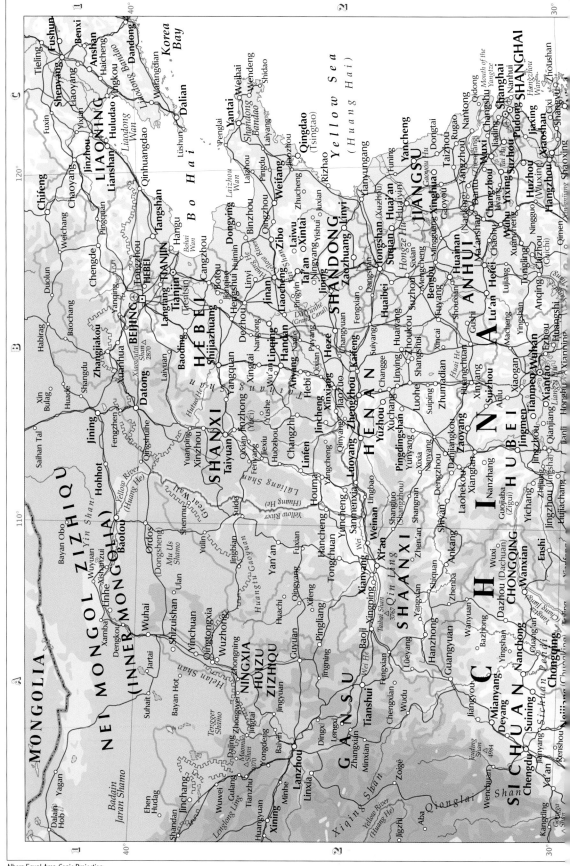

METRES
FEET

5000	16404
3000	9843
2000	6562
1000	3281
500	1640
200	656
0	0
	Land below sea level
200	656
4000	13124
6000	19686

Albers Equal Area Conic Projection

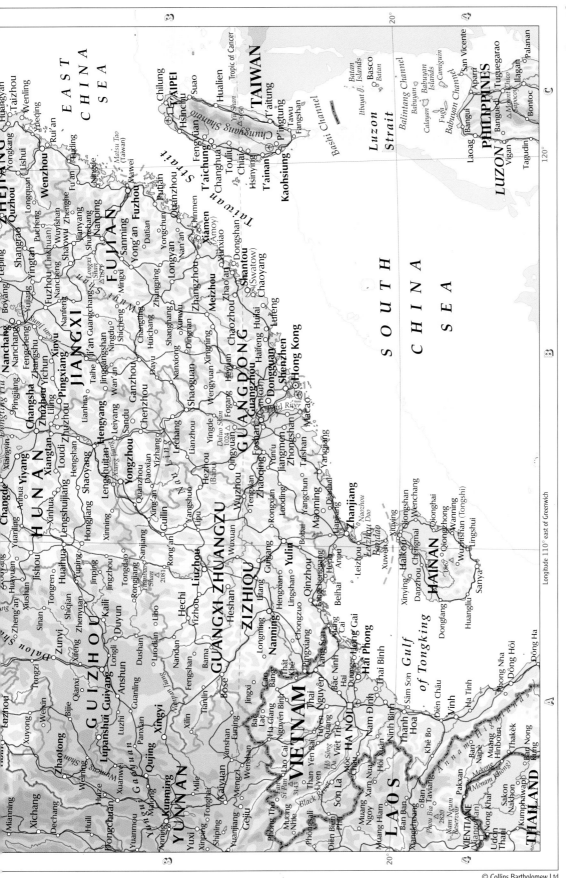

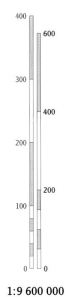

E A S T   C H I N A   S E A

S O U T H   C H I N A   S E A

ZHEJIANG

Huangyan
Taizhou
Wenling
Yongkang
Lishui
Longquan
Yudu
Rui'an
Wenzhou
Qingyuan

FUJIAN

Boyang
Leping
Shangrao
Fengcheng
Guixi
Yingtan
Jianyang
Shunchang
Shaowu
Wuyishan
Nanping

Pucheng
Fu'an
Ningde
Fuzhou (Linhchuan)
Nanchang
Zhangshu

Fuzhou
Putian
Yong'an
Sanming
Datian
Yongchun
Nan'an
Xiamen (Amoy)
Quanzhou
Jinjiang
Chenghai

JIANGXI

Nanchang
Changsha
Zhuzhou
Pingxiang
Xinyu

Ji'an
Taihe
Ningdu
Shicheng
Longyan
Zhangping
Changting

Ganzhou
Dayu
Nanxiong
Wan'an
Lianhua
Jinggangshan

HUNAN

Changde
Yiyang
Xiangyin
Pingjiang
Anhua

Loudi
Xiangtan
Shaoyang
Hengyang
Hongjiang
Hengshan

Lengshuijiang
Quanzhou
Yongzhou
Leiyang
Chenzhou
Yizhang

GUANGDONG

Shaoguan
Lechang
Lianzhou
Yingde
Qingyuan
Heyuan
Huidong
Huilai

Heshan
Zhaoqing
Foshan
Guangzhou
Dongguan
Shenzhen
Hong Kong

Pearl River

Macao

Yunfu
Jiangmen
Zhongshan
Taishan
Yangjiang
Yangchun

Zhanjiang

HAINAN

Haikou
Qionghai
Wanning
Sanya

Gulf of Tongking

GUANGXI ZHUANGZU ZIZHIQU

Hechi
Liuzhou
Guilin
Liuzhou
Laibin
Guigang
Yulin
Qinzhou
Beihai

Nanning

GUIZHOU

Zunyi
Guiyang
Anshun
Duyun
Kaili

YUNNAN

Kunming
Yuxi
Qujing
Xingyi

VIETNAM

HA NOI
Hai Phong
Nam Dinh
Thanh Hoa
Vinh
Ha Tinh

LAOS

WIENTIANE

THAILAND

TAIWAN

T'AIPEI
Chilung
Hsinchu
T'aichung
Changhua
Chiai
T'ainan
Kaohsiung
Hualien
T'aitung
Pingtung
Fangshan

PHILIPPINES

LUZON

Laoag
Vigan
Aparri
Tuguegarao

Luzon Strait

Bashi Channel

Babuyan Islands

Batan Islands

Longitude 110° east of Greenwich

Miles	Km
400	600
300	400
200	200
100	
0	0

1:9 600 000

SOUTH ASIA

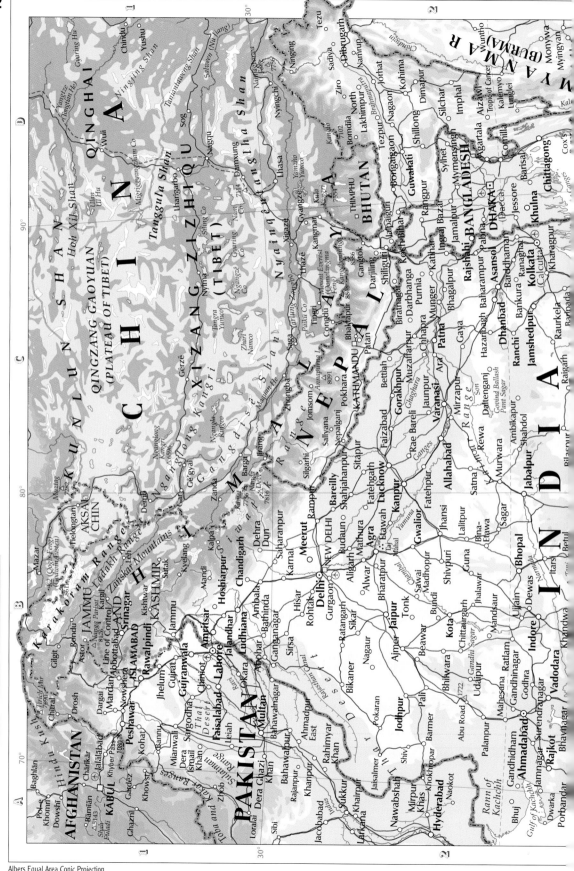

METRES
FEET

5000 / 16404
3000 / 9843
2000 / 6562
1000 / 3281
500 / 1640
200 / 656
0 / 0
Land below
sea level
200 / 656
4000 / 13124
6000 / 19686

Albers Equal Area Conic Projection

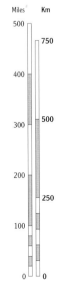

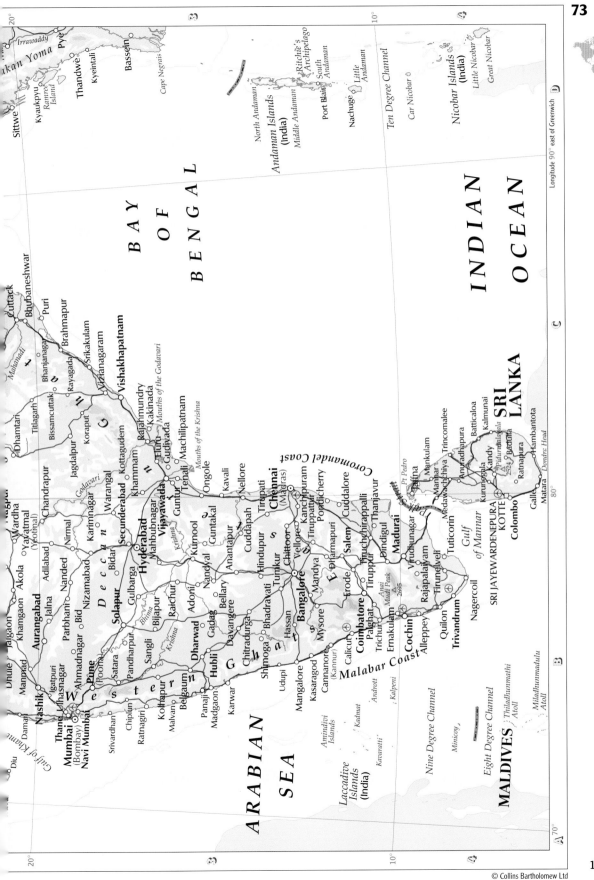

BAY OF BENGAL

INDIAN OCEAN

ARABIAN SEA

Irrawaddy

Arakan Yoma
Pye
Thandwe
Kyaukpyu
Ramree Island
Kyeintali
Bassein
Thandwe
Cape Negrais
Sittwe

Ritchie's
Archipelago
South Andaman
North Andaman
Middle Andaman
Andaman Islands (India)
Port Blair
Nachugo
Little Andaman

Ten Degree Channel
Car Nicobar
Little Nicobar
Nicobar Islands (India)
Great Nicobar

Longitude 90° east of Greenwich

Cuttack
Bhubaneshwar
Puri
Brahmapur
Bhanjanagar
Mahanadi
Dhamtari
Titlagarh
Bissamcuttak
Jagdalpur
Koraput
Rayagada
Srikakulam
Vizianagaram
Vishakhapatnam

Rajahmundry
Kakinada
Eluru
Mouths of the Godavari
Kottagudem
Khammam
Vijayawada
Machilipatnam
Tenali
Mouths of the Krishna

Chandrapur
Wardha
Yavatmal
(Yeotmal)
Adilabad
Nirmal
Karimnagar
Warangal
Nizamabad
Secunderabad
Hyderabad
Mahbubnagar

Coromandel Coast
Ongole
Kavali
Nellore
Tirupati
Chennai
(Madras)

Dhule
Manmad
Nashik
Jalgaon
Khamgaon
Akola
Aurangabad
Jalna
Parbhani
Nanded
Bid
Ahmadnagar
Pune
(Poona)
Igatpuri
Ulhasnagar
Thane
Mumbai
(Bombay)
Navi Mumbai
Srivardhan
Ratnagiri
Chiplun
Solapur
Gulbarga
Bidar
Deccan
Bhima
Bijapur
Raichur
Adoni
Kurnool
Nandyal
Guntakal
Bellary
Anantapur
Cuddapah
Chittoor
Tirupati
Vellore

Damar
Diu
Gulf of Khambat
Gulf of Kutch

Gadag
Dharwad
Hubli
Gadag
Davangere
Chitradurga
Shimoga
Hassan
Bangalore
Mandya
Mysore
Anai
Midi Peak
2695
Palghat
Trichur
Ernakulam
Cochin
Alleppey
Quilon
Trivandrum
Nagercoil

Sangli
Kolhapur
Satara
Panaji
Madgaon
Karwar
Belgaum
Malvan
Western Ghats
Udupi
Mangalore
Kasaragod
Cannanore
(Kannur)
Calicut
Malabar Coast

Laccadive Islands (India)
Amindivi Islands
Kavaratti
Kadmat
Andrott
Kalpeni
Minicoy
Nine Degree Channel
Eight Degree Channel

MALDIVES
Thiladhunmathi Atoll
Miladhunmadulu Atoll

Bhadravati
Tumkur
Erode
Tiruppur
Coimbatore
Dindigul
Madurai
Virudhunagar
Tuticorin
Rajapalaiyam
Tirunelveli

Guntur
Tiruppattur
Kanchipuram
Pondicherry
Cuddalore
Salem
Tiruchchirappalli
Thanjavur
Tiruvannamalai
Bharmapuri

Pt Pedro
Palk Strait
Jaffna
Mankulam
Mannar
Medawachchiya
Anuradhapura
Kalmunai
Batticaloa
Trincomalee
SRI LANKA
Kurunegala
Kandy
254
Pidurutalagala
Badulla
Ratnapura
Hambantota
Dondrc Head
Matara
Galle
SRI JAYEWARDENEPURA
KOTTE
Colombo
Gulf of Mannar

Godavari
Krishna

Miles | Km
500 — 750
400 — 500
300 —
200 — 250
100 —
0 — 0

A   70°   B   K

Kozvyshennost' Karabil'
TURKMENISTAN
Andkhvoy   Feyzābād   Qullai Karl Marks   Buzal Gumbad   6726
Sheberghān   Kholm   Khānābād   Taloqan   Ishkoshim   Battura Glacier   Pasu   Mazar
Mazār-e Sharīf   Baghlān   Tirich Mir 7690   Kush   Mastuj   Gilgit Rakaposhi   K2 (Qogir Feng) Godwin Austen 8611
Bālā Morghāb   Meymaneh   Sar-e Pol   Āybak   Chitral   Drosh   Gilgit   7788   Rondu   Karakoram Range
Gushgy   Murghāb   Dowshī   Pol-e Khomrī   Barikot   Dir   Chilas   Nanga Parbat   Astor   Skardu   Khapalu   Shyok
Qal'eh-ye Now   Hari Rūd   Bāmiān   Chārikār   Jabal as Sirāj   Mehtar Lām   Dargai   Mongora   8126   JAMMU   Kargil   Ladakh Range   H
Paropamisus   Chaghcharān   Kūh-e Bābā   Shah Fuladi 5143   Sikaram 4761   Khyber Pass 1080   Peshawar   Mardan   Abbottābad   Line of Control   AND   Leh   Zanskar Mts
Chalap Dalan   Kūh-e Qeysar 4182   KABUL   Jalālābād   Nowshera   Wah   Haripur   Spopur   KASHMIR   Kishtwar   Kidri
AFGHANISTAN   Ghaznī   Gardēz   Kohat   ISLAMABAD   Srinagar   Anantnag   Chenab   Sutak
HAZARAJAT   Tarīn Kowt   Khowst   Thal   Rawalpindi   Jhelum   Udhampur   Chamba   Kyelang
Delārām   Gereshk   Orgūn   Bannu   Daud Khel   Talagang   Jhelum   Jammu   Kathua   Pathankot   HIMACHAL
Dasht-e Margow   Argandab   Tarnak   Lakki   Tank   Mianwali   Khushab   Bhera   Wazirabad   Sialkot   Sujanpur   Nagri   PRADESH
Lashkar Gah   Kandahār   Kalāt   Kalur Kot   Sargodha   Hafizabad   Gujranwala   Batala   Mandi   Sundarnagar
Helmand   Toba and Kakar Ranges   Zhob   Takht-i-Sulaimān 3374   Dera Ismail Khan   Bhakkar   Jhang   Chiniot   Lahore   Amritsar   Hoshiarpur   Shimla
Chaman   Muslimbagh   Thal Desert   Jhang   Shorkot   Faisalabad   Jalandhar   Ludhiana   Chandigarh
Pishin   Loralai   Taunsa   Leiah   Okara   Sahiwal   Firozpur   PUNJAB   Ambala   De
Dasht-e Arbu Lut   Quetta   Mach   Barkhan   Dera Ghazi Khan   Khanewal   Burewala   Fazilka   Patiala   Saharanpur   Du   UT
30°   Mastung   Beji   Multan   Mandi   Abohar   Bathinda   Tohana   Karnal   Roorkee
Amir Chah   Chagai   Hamun-i-Lora   Rās Koh   Nushki   Sibi   Lahri   Muzaffargarh   Bahawalnagar   Hanumangarh   Ganganagar   Sirsa   HARYANA   Nagina
Dalbandin   3007   Kalat   Jampur   Lodhran   Bahawalpur   Anupgarh   Nohar   Hisar   Rohtak   Sonipat   Kairana
Nok Kundi   Yakmach   Surab   Dera Bugti   Rajanpur   Uch   Fort Abbas   Suratgarh   Mahajan   Rajgarh   Bhiwani   Delhi   Meer
Hamun-i-Mashkel   Qila Ladgasht   Washuk   Siahan Range   Karodi   Khuzdar   Kashmor   Rahimyar Khan   Barsalpur   Pugal   Sardarshahr   Churu   Jhunjhunun   Namaul   Ghaziaba   Morada
Kamarod   Panjgur   Nagha Kalat   Shadadkot   Shikarpur   Ghotki   Ramgarh   Bikaner   Ratangarh   Sikar   Alwar   NEW DEL   Faridaba
Diz   Jacobabad   Sukkur   Khairpur   Sadiqabad   Bap   Nokha   Sujangarh   Mathura
Central Makran Range   Tump   Turbat   Bazdar   Khuzdar   Karodi   Larkana   Ghotaru   Jaisalmer   Pokaran   Phalodi   Nagaur   Sambhar   Jaipur   Bharatpur   Agra
Dasht   Hoshab   Bhairi Hol   Goshanak   Bela   Dadu   Kandiaro   RAJASTHAN   Jodhpur   Merta   Ajmer   Sawai Madhopur   Morena   Gwali
Suntsar   Makran Coast Range   1454   Pab Range   Diwana   Nawabshah   Shiv   Barmer   Balotra   Pali   Beawar   Tonk   Devli   Bundi   Shivpuri
Gwadar   Pasni   Ormara   Sonmiani   Thano Bula Khan   Sakrand   Klupro   Jalore   Deogarh   Bhilwara   Kota   Baran   Jhansi
Tatta   Hyderabad   Mirpur Khas   Mithi   Sirohi   Chittaurgarh   Jhalawar   Lalitpur
Karachi   Sonmiani Bay   Tando Adam   Naokot   Nagar Parkar   Abu Road   1722   Udaipur   Neemuch   Garoth   Guna   I   N
Mouths of the Indus   Badin   Jati   Rann of Kachchh   Palanpur   Siddhpur   Dungarpur   Mandsaur   Bina-Etav   Sag
Tropic of Cancer   Lakhpat   Radhanpur   Mahesana   Himatnagar   Banswara   Jaora   Agar   Gandhi Sagar   Biaora
Bhuj   Gandhidham   Viramgam   Gandhinagar   Ratlam   Ujjain   Dewas   Bhopal   Vidish
Rapur   Kandla   Ahmadabad   Godhra   Dahod   Indore   MADHYA PR
Okha   Surendranagar   Nadiad   Dhar   Mhow   Harda   Itarsi
Dwarka   Jamnagar   Dhandhuka   GUJARAT   Vadodara   Narmada   Chhindw
Gulf of Kachchh   Rajkot   Gondal   Dhasa   Khambhat   Alirajpur   Rajpur   Khargon   Khandwa   Betul
Porbandar   Upleta   Bhavnagar   Bharuch   Nandurbar   Tapi   Burhanpur   Achalpur
Junagadh   Amreli   Satpura Range   Amravati
Keshod   Visavadar   Mahuva   Surat   Vyara   Jalgaon   Bhusawal   Akola   Wardha   63   Hingangh
Veraval   2 Diu   Valsad   Dhule   Chalisgaon   Khamgaon
20°   Gulf of Khambhat   2 Daman   Silvassa   1   Nashik   Manmad   MAHARASHTRA
ARABIAN SEA   Dahanu   igatpuri   Sangamner   Aurangabad   Jalna   Pusad   Adilat
Thane   Kalyan   Godavari   Penganga
Longitude 70° east of Greenwich   Mumbai (Bombay)   Ulhasnagar   Ahmadnagar   Parbhani   Nir
Navi Mumbai   Narayangaon   Nanded

METRES FEET
5000   16404
3000   9843
2000   6562
1000   3281
500   1640
200   656
0   0
Land below sea level
200   656
4000   13124
6000   19686

Administrative areas not named on the map:
INDIA
1. DADRA AND NAGAR HAVELI (B2)
2. DAMAN AND DIU (B2)

Albers Equal Area Conic Projection

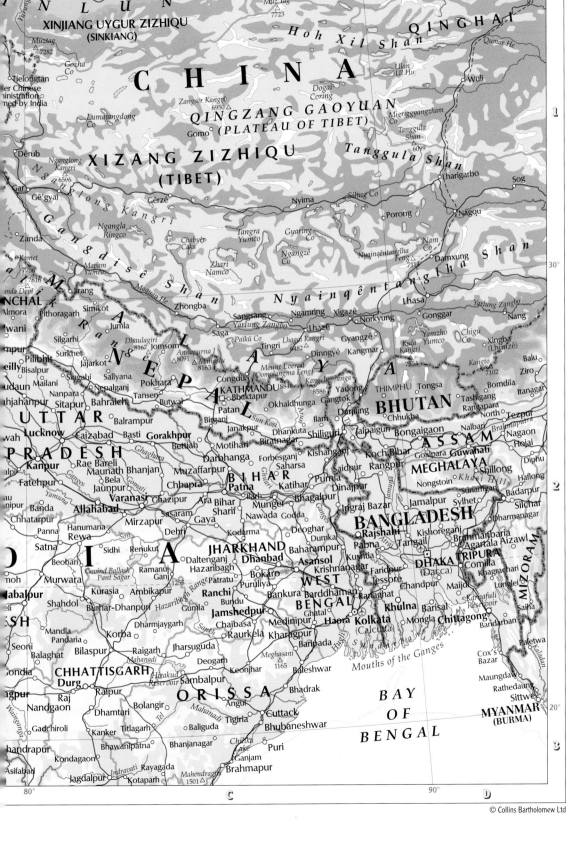

80°

90°

1

Aqqikkol Hu

Golmud

KUNLUN SHAN

Yutian   Minfeng

QINGHAI

XINJIANG UYGUR ZIZHIQU
(SINKIANG)

Muz Tag
7723

Hoh Xil Shan

Qumar He

Müztag △7282

CHINA

Tielongtan

Ulan
Ul Hu

Wuli

Gozha
Co

Dogai
Coring

er Chinese
ministration
ned by India

Lumajangdong
Co

Zangsêr Kangri
6950

QINGZANG GAOYUAN
(PLATEAU OF TIBET)

Tanggula
Shan
6099

Gar

Gomo

Migriggyangzham
Co

Gê'gyai

Zanda

Ng, Ngla Kangri

Ng'anglong
Kangri
6596

XIZANG ZIZHIQU
(TIBET)

Tanggula Shan

Lharigarbo

Sog

Nyaingêntanglha Shan

anda Devi
7816

Kamet
7756

Mapam
Yumco

Gangdisê Shan

Nyima

Gerzê

Siling Co

Porong

Nam
Co

Nagqu

30°

NCHAL

Almora

MA

Jirang

Mapam
Yumco

Ngangla
Ringco

Chabyêr
Caka

Tangra
Yumco

Gyaring
Co

Ngangzê
Co

Nyainqêntanglha
Feng
7114

Damxung

wani

Pithoragarh

Simikot

Ra

Zhongba

Maquan He

Saga

Yarlung Zangbo

Norkyung

Lhasa

Gonggar

Yarlung Zangbo

Nang

mpur

Almora

Silgarhi

Jumla

Sangsang

Ngamring

Xigazê

Yamzho
Yumco

Chigu
Co

Xingba
(Lhünzê)

eilly

Pilibhit

Surkhet

Jajarkot

Dhaulagiri
8167

Jomsom

Annapurna I
8091

Paikü Co

Lhagoi Kangri
6482

Lhazê

Dinngyê

Kangmar

Kula
Kangri
7554

Kangto
7102

Balu

Ziro

udaun

Bisalpur

Singahi

Sallyana

Pokhara

Manaslu
8163

Tingri

Mount Everest
(Qomolangma Feng)
8848

Kangchenjunga
8586

Yadong

THIMPHU

Tongsa

Tashigang

Bomdila

Itanagar

hjahanpur

Mailani

Nanpara

Nepalganj

Tansen

Butwal

CONGDÜ

KATHMANDU

Bhaktapur

Okhaldhunga

Gangtok

Darjiling

Chhukha

North

Rangapara

Tezpur

Sitapur

Bahraich

Patan

Sun Kosi

Ilam

Shiliguri

Nalbari

Brahmaputra

Nagaon

UTTAR

Balrampur

Birganj

Janakpur

Dhankuta

Jalpaiguri

Bongaigaon

ASSAM

Hojai

wah

Lucknow

Faizabad

Basti

Gorakhpur

Ghaghara

Motihari

Biratnagar

Koch Bihar

Goalpara

Guwahati

Diphu

PRADESH

Rae Bareli

Bettiah

Darbhanga

Forbesganj

Kishanganj

Rangpur

MEGHALAYA

Shillong

Haflong

alpi

Kanpur

Maunath Bhanjan

Muzaffarpur

Saharsa

Saidpur

Purnia

Dinajpur

Nongstoin

Khasi Hills

Sunamganj

Badarpur

Fatehpur

Bela

Jaunpur

Chhapra

BIHAR

Katihar

Jamalpur

Sylhet

Silchar

nipur

Banda

Ganges

Gomti

Patna

Barh

Bhagalpur

Ingraj Bazar

BANGLADESH

Dharmanagar

Allahabad

Varanasi

Ghazipur

Ara

Bihar
Sharif

Munger

Godda

Nawada

Purnia

Rajshahi

Kishoreganj

Chhatarpur

Mirzapur

Sasaram

Gaya

Kodarma

Deoghar

Dumka

Pabna

Tangail

Brahmanbaria

Agartala

Aizawl

Panna

Hanumana

Dehri

Baharampur

Kushtia

DHAKA
(Dacca)

Comilla

Khagrachari

TRIPURA

MIZORAM

Satna

Beohari

Sidhi

Renukut

Daltenganj

Dhanbad

Asansol

Krishnanagar

Faridpur

Chandpur

Maijdi

Lunglei

noh

Murwara

Govind Ballash
Pant Sagar

Ramanuj
Ganj

Hazaribagh

Bokaro

Puruliya

WEST

Jessore

Ranaghat

Khulna

Barisal

Chittagong

Bandarban

abalpur

Shahdol

Burhar-Dhanpuri

Hazaribagh Range

Patratu

1255

Kurasia

Ambikapur

Ranchi

Bundu

BENGAL

Ghatal

Haora

Kolkata
(Calcutta)

Mongla

Karnafuli
Reservoir

Saiha

SH

Mandla

Pandaria

Korba

Dharmjaygarh

Jamshedpur

Chaibasa

Medinipur

Kharagpur

Hugli

Sundarbans

Mouths of the Ganges

Cox's
Bazar

Paletwa

Kaladan

Seoni

Balaghat

Bilaspur

Raigarh

Jharsuguda

Raurkela

Baripada

Meghasani
1165

Maungdaw

Rathedaung

ondia

CHHATTISGARH

Durg

Raipur

Mahanadi

Hirakud
Reservoir

Sambalpur

Deogarh

Keonjhar

Baleshwar

BAY

Sittwe

agpur

Raj
Nandgaon

Dhamtari

Bolangir

Tel

Mahanadi

Angul

Tigiria

Bhadrak

OF

MYANMAR
(BURMA)

20°

Gadchiroli

Kanker

Titlagarh

Baliguda

ORISSA

Cuttack

Bhubaneswar

BENGAL

handrapur

Kondagaon

Bhawanipatna

Bhanjanagar

Chilka
Lake

Puri

Asifabad

Jagdalpur

Indravati

Rayagada

Mahendragiri
1501

Brahmapur

Ganjam

Kotaparh

80°

90°

C

D

Miles   Km

400

600

300

400

200

200

100

0   0

CENTRAL ASIA

METRES
FEET

5000
16404

3000
9843

2000
6562

1000
3281

500
1640

200
656

0
0
Land below
sea level

200
656

4000
13124

6000
19686

Albers Equal Area Conic Projection

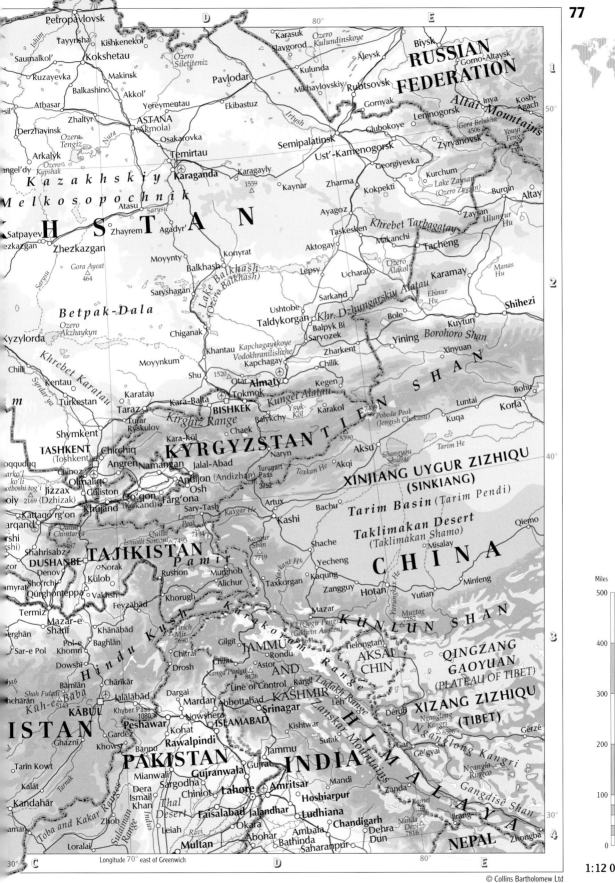

1:12 000 000

Longitude 70° east of Greenwich

Miles   Km

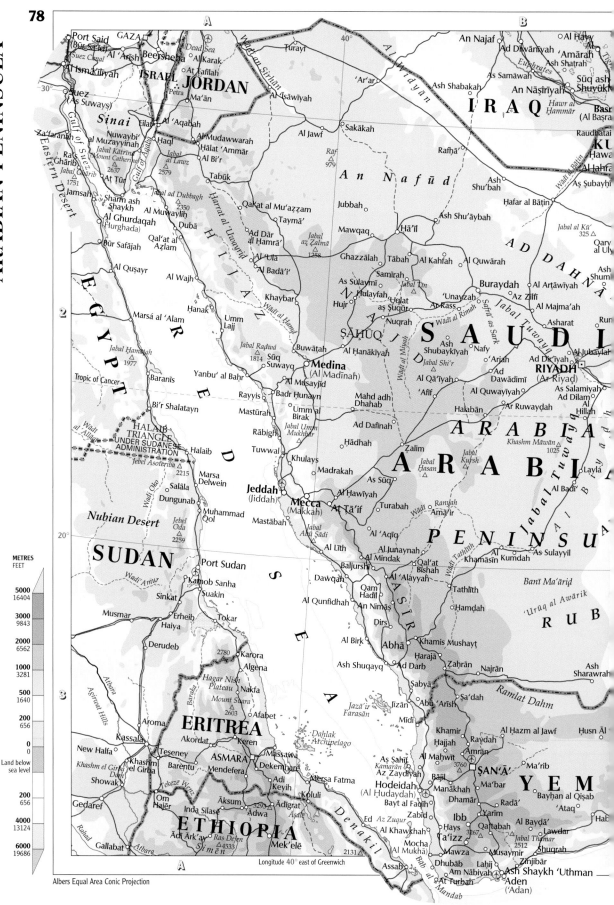

ARABIAN PENINSULA

METRES
FEET

5000
16404

3000
9843

2000
6562

1000
3281

500
1640

200
656

0
0
Land below
sea level

200
656

4000
13124

6000
19686

Albers Equal Area Conic Projection

Longitude 40° east of Greenwich

EGYPT

ISRAEL **JORDAN**

IRAQ

SAUDI

ARABIA

ARABIAN

PENINSULA

SUDAN

ERITREA

ETHIOPIA

YEM

Port Said
(Būr Sa'īd)
GAZA
At 'Arīsh
Al Ismā'īlīyah
Suez
(As Suways)
Dead Sea
Beersheba
At Fafīlah
Al Karak
Petra
Ma'ān
Wādī as Sirhān
Tūrayf
'Ar'ar
An Najaf
Ad Dīwānīyah
Ash Shatrah
'Amārah
As Samāwah
An Nāṣirīyah
Ash Shabakah
Sūq ash
Shuyūkh
Basr
(Al Baṣrah)
Raudhatai
KU
Hawa
Aş Şubayhī
Al Jahrah
Jabal al Kū
325

Sinai
Gulf of Suez
Eastern Desert
Jabal Gharib
1751
Jabal Katrīn
Mount Catherine
2637
Za'farānah
Al Muzayyinah
Sharm ash
Shaykh
Al Ghurdaqah
(Hurghada)
Būr Safājah
Al Quṣayr
Marsā al 'Alam
Baranīs
Bi'r Shalatayn
Nuwaybi'
Haql
Ilat
Al 'Aqabah
Jabal
al Lawz
2579
Al Bi'r
Tabūk
Ḥālat 'Ammār
Al Mudawwarah
Al 'Āsawīyah
Al Jawf
Sakākah
Rafḥā'
Raf
979
An Nafūd
Jubbah
Ḥā'īl
Ash
Shu'bah
Ash Shu'āybah
Ḥafar al Bāṭin
Wādī al Bāṭin

Tropic of Cancer
Rā's
Gharib
Jamsah
At Ṭūr
Jabal ad Dubbagh
2350
Al Muwaylih
Dubā
Qal'at al
Azlam
Al Wajh
Ḥanak
Umm
Lajj
Jabal Raḍwā
1814
Sūq
Suwayq
Yanbu' al Baḥr
Al 'Ula
Al Badā'i'
Khaybar
Ad Dār
al Ḥamrā'
Jabal
az Zalma
1258
Qakat al Mu'azzam
Taymā'
Mawqaq
Ghazzālah
Ṭābah
Al Kahfah
Al Quwārah
Samīrah
Jabal Tin
Hulayfah
As Sulaymī
'Uqlat
aş Şuqūr
Nuqrah
Ḥujr
Buwātah
Ar Rass
'Unayzah
Buraydah
Az Zilfī
Al Arṭāwīyah
Al Majma'ah
Asharat
Run
Jabal Tuwayq
Ash
Shum
Qary
al Uly
Ash
AD DAHNĀ

HIJAZ

NAJD

Marsā ad Dhahab
Medina
(Al Madīnah)
Al Musayjid
Badr Ḥunayn
Rayyis
Masfūrah
Rābigh
Tuwwal
Khulays
Jeddah
(Jiddah)
Mecca
(Makkah)
Mastābah
Al Ḥanākīyah
Umm
Birak
Jabal Umm
Mukhbar
Ṣ AḤŪQ
Ash
Shubaykīyah
Nafy
'Ariah
Ad
Dawādimī
Al Qā'īyah
'Afīf
Jabal Shi'r
Mahd adh
Dhahab
Ad Dafīnah
Ḥāḍhah
Zalim
Al Quwayyah
Halabān
Jabal
Kursh
Ad Dr'īyah
RIYADH
(Ar Riyāḍ)
As Salamiyah
Ad Dilam
Al
Ḥillam
Laylā
Khashm Māwān
1025
Jabal Tuwayq

Al Ḥawīyah
Aṭ Ṭā'if
Turabah
Al 'Aqīq
'Amā'ir
Ranyah
As Sūq
Jabal
Ḥasan
As Sulayyil
Kumdah
Khamāsīn
Qal'at
Bīshah
Tathlīth
Banī Ma'ārīd
'Urūq al Awārik
RUB
Al Badī'

Nubian Desert
Wādī al Allāqī
HALAIB
TRIANGLE
UNDER SUDANESE
ADMINISTRATION
Halaib
Jebel Asoteriba
2215
Marsa
Delwein
Salāla
Dungunab
Muhammad
Qol
Jebel
Oda
2259
Mastūrah
Al Līth
Bāljurshī
Dawqah
Qam
Hadīl
An Nimāş
Dirs
Al Birk
Al Qunfidhah
Ash Shuqayq
Ad Darb
Ḥamdān
Ḥarajā
Khamis Mushayṭ
Zahrān
Najrān
Abḥā
'ASĪR
Ash
Sharawrah
Ṣabyā
Ramlat Dahm

Port Sudan
Wadī Amur
Kamob Sanha
Sinkat
Suakin
Musmar
Erheib
Haiya
Derudeb
Tokar
Karora
Algena
2780
Hagar Nish
Plateau
Mount Shara
2603
Nakfa
Afabet
Jazā'ir
Farasān
Dahlak
Archipelago
Jīzān
Abū 'Arīsh
Ṣa'dah
Khamir
Ḥajjah
Al Ḥazm al Jawf
Husn Āl
Al Mawīt
Amrān
Raydah
3760
ŞAN'Ā'
Ma'rib

New Halfa
Kassala
Teseney
Khashm
el Girba
Khashm el Girba
Dam
Showak
Barēntu
Mendefera
ASMARA
Keren
Akordat
Massawa
Dekemhare
Mersa Fatma
Kamarān
Aẓ Zaydīyah
Bājil
Al Maḥwīt
Manākhah
Bayt al Faqīh
Dhamār
Ma'bar
Bayhān al Qiṣab
'Ataq
YEM
Ma'rib
Hab

Gedaref
Om
Hajer
Gallabat
Āksum
Adwa
Ādigrat
Mek'elē
Adi
Keyih
Koluli
4533
Ras Defen
Simen
Inda Silasē
Ādi Ark'ay
Āshak
2131
Ed
Az Zuqur
Zabīd
Al Khawkhah
Mocha
(Al Mukhā)
Mawza
Ḥays
Ibb
Qaltabah
Ta'izz
Jabal Thamar
2512
3267
Rada'
Yārīm
Dhamār
Al Baydā'
Lawdar
Musaymir
Zinjibār
Ash Shaykh 'Uthman
Aden
('Adan)
Dhubāb
Lahij
Am Nābiyah
At Turbah
Shuqrah
Hodeidah
(Al Ḥudaydah)
Mandab

Red Sea
Denakil
RED SEA

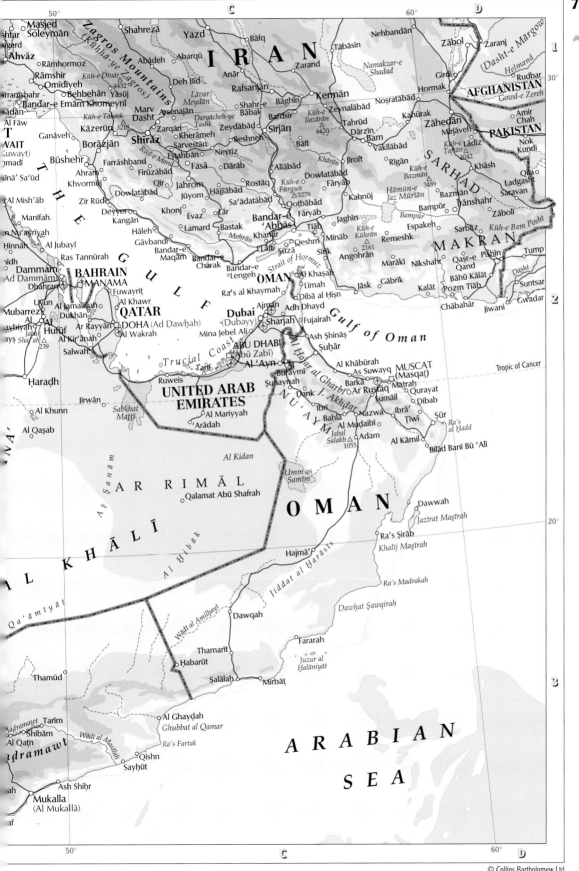

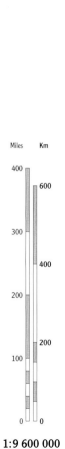

IRAN

Masjed Soleymān
Shahreẕā
Yazd
Bāfq
Tābāsin
Nehbandān
Zābol
Zaranj
Dasht-e Mārgow
Helmand

Ahvāz
Rāmhormoz
Abādeh
Abarqū
Anār
Zarand
Namakzar-e Shadad
Girdī
Hormak
30°

Rāmshīr
Yāsūj
Kūh-e Dīnar
4432
Deh Bīd
Rafsanjān
Kermān
Noṣratābād
Kahūrak
Zāhedān
AFGHANISTAN
Gowd-e Zereh

Behbehān
Bandar-e Emām Khomeynī
Marv Dasht
Shahr-e Bābak
Bardsīr
Kūh-e Ilazārān
Zeynalābād
Tahrūd
Zāhedān
Amīr Chah
PAKISTAN

Al Fāw
Kāzerūn
Zarqān
Zeydābād
Sīrjān
4420
Dārzīn
Bam
Vakīlābād
Kūh-e Lālēzār
Tāftān
1042
Nok Kundi

Ganāveh
Borāzjān
SHIRĀZ
Kherāmeh
Sarvestān
Neyrīz
Bāft
Khārān
Jīroft
Rīgān
Khāsh
Qila Ladgasht
Saravan

Būshehr
Farrāshband
Eṣṭahbān
Fasā
Dārāb
Aliābād
Dowlatābād
Fāryāb
Kahnūj
Kūh-e Bazmān
3489
Bazmān
Īrānshahr
Zābolī

Ahram
Khvormūj
Qīr
Jahrom
Hājjīābād
Rostāq
Kūh-e Fūrgun
3279
Fāryāb
Hāmūn-e Jaz Mūriān
Bampūr
Sarbāz
Kūh-e Bam Posht

Dowlatābād
Jūyom
Saʿādatābād
Bampūr
Espakeh
Remeshk
Tump

Deyyer
Kangān
Khonj
Evaz
Ēvaz
Lamard
Bastak
Bandar-e ʿAbbās
Tīāb
Jaghīn
Kūh-e Kūhrān
2161
Marākī
Nīkshahr
Qaṣr-e Qand
Pīshīn

Gāvbandī
Lār
Mehrān
Khamīr
Qeshm
Mināb
Angohrān
Jāsk
Gābrīk
Kalāt
Bāhū Kalāt
Pozm Tīāb
Chābahār
Suntsar

THE GULF
Strait of Hormuz
OMAN
Līmah
MAKRAN
Dasht
Jiwani
Gwadar

Ras Tannūrah
BAHRAIN
MANAMA
Fuwayriṭ
Raʾs al Khaymah
Dibā al Ḥiṣn
Khaṣab
Gulf of Oman

Dammām
Ad Dammām
Dhahrān
Al Khawr
Ajman
Adh Dhayd
Sharjah
Fujairah

QATAR
Ar Rayyān
DOHA (Ad Dawḥah)
Al Wakrah
Dubai (Dubayy)
Mina Jebel Ali
Ash Shināṣ
Ṣuḥār

Al Kirʿānah
Salwah
Trucial Coast
ABU DHABI (Abū Ẓabī)
Al ʿAyn
Al Ḥajar al Gharbī
Al Khābūrah
As Suwayq
MUSCAT (Masqaṭ)
Tropic of Cancer

Harāḍh
Ruweis
Tarif
Buraymī
Ar Rustāq
Maṭraḥ

Jirwān
Sabkhat Maṭṭī
Al Mariyyah
Suḥaymī
Dank
J. Akhḍar
Nazwa
Ṣumāil
Ibrā
Dibāb
Qurayat

Al Khunn
Arādah
UNITED ARAB EMIRATES
Ibrī
Bahla
Ṭīwī
Sūr
Raʾs al Ḥadd

Al Qaṣab
Al Kidan
Jabal Salakh
1055
Al Mudaibī
Adam
Al Kāmil
Bilād Banī Bū ʿAlī

AS ṢANĀM
AR RIMĀL
Qalamat Abū Shafrah
Umm as Samīm
OMAN
Dawwah
Jazīrat Maṣīrah
20°

AL KHĀLĪ
Al Hibak
Hajmāʾ
Raʾs Ṣīrāb
Khalīj Maṣīrah

Qaʿāmīyāt
Jiddat al Ḥarāsīs
Raʾs Madrakah

Wādī Amīlḥayt
Dawqah
Dawḥat Sawqirah

Thamarīt
Fararah
Juzur al Ḥalāniyāt

Thamūd
Ḥabarūt
Salālah
Mirbāṭ

Ḥadramawt
Tarīm
Shibām
Al Ghaydah
Ghubbat al Qamar
Raʾs Fartak
ARABIAN

Al Qaṭn
Wādī al Masīlah
Qishn
SEA

Sayḥūt
Ash Shiḥr
Mukalla (Al Mukallā)

Miles | Km

400 | 600
300 | 400
200 | 200
100
0 | 0

1:9 600 000

EAST MEDITERRANEAN

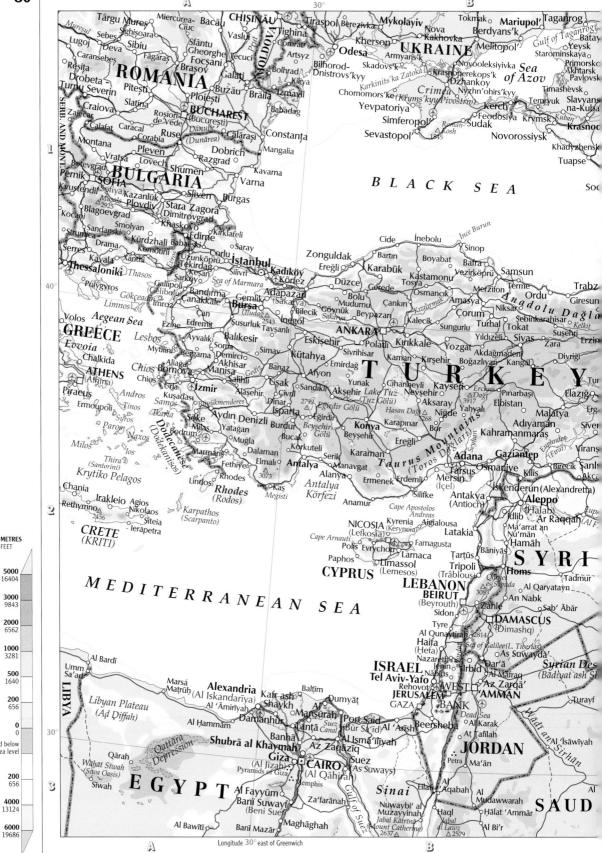

METRES / FEET

METRES	FEET
5000	16404
3000	9843
2000	6562
1000	3281
500	1640
200	656
0	0

Land below sea level

200	656
4000	13124
6000	19686

Longitude 30° east of Greenwich

Albers Equal Area Conic Projection

ocherkassk
ov-na-Donu
norsk

RUSSIAN
FEDERATION

Balykshi

Karakum
Desert
(Peski Karakum)

Barankul

Sor
Donyztau

Sal'sk
Ipatovo
Ozero
Manych-Gudilo Elista
Divnoye
Utta
Ulan-
Khol

KAZAKHSTAN

Beyneu

horetsk
ropotkin
Komsomol'skiy
Lagan'

Burynshyk

Sor
Mertvyy
Kultuk

UZBEKISTAN

avil
Labinsk
kop
Psebay
Kuban Stavropol'
Vozvyshennost'
Budennovsk
Nevinnomyssk

Mys Tyub-
Karagan Fort-Shevchenko
Shetpe
Gora
Besshoky
555

Borsakelmas
sho'rxogi

Ustyurt
Plateau

Uqal Karabaur

Karachayevsk
Pyatigorsk
Kislovodsk
Georgiyevsk
Prokhladnyy
Mozdok

Kizlyar
Mys Sagyndyk

Aktau
432 Mangystau

Zhanaozen

1

Psebay
El'brus
5642 Nal'chik
Groznyy
Khasav'yurt

Kuryk

Kazakhskiy
Zaliv

Sarykamyshskoye
Ozero

Sokhumi
Algir Vladikavkaz
Makhachkala

Tqvarch'eli
Buynaksk
Izberbash

Zugdidi
Derbent
Bekdash

Zaliv
Kara-Bogaz-
Gol

Chagyl

GEORGIA
Khashuri Gori
P'ot'i Samtredia
at'umi Akhalts'ikhe

T'elavi

Gora
Bazardyuzyu
4466

Karabogazkel'

TURKMENISTAN

Karshi

40°

ar Akhalk'alak'
Artvin Ardahan
Lesser Caucasus
(Maly Kavkaz)

T'BILISI
(Tiflis)
Rust'avi
Qazax
Zaqatala
Saki
Quba

Samaxi

Dzhanga

Turkmenbashi
Dzhebel
Balkanabat
Gazandzhyk

Kaçkar
Dağı Yusufeli
3932

Gyumri
Vanadzor
Sevan
Ganca
Mingaçevir
Göyçay Samaxi
Sumqayit

Abşeron
Yarımadası

BAKU
(Bakı)

Cheleken
Gumdag

Gyzylarbat

Oltu
Kars
Sarıkamış

ARMENIA **YEREVAN**
(Erevan)
Iğdır *Arak's*
Ağdam
Qazımämmäd
Alät

Turkmenbashi

Garrygala

Erzurum
Ağrı Mt. Ararat
Van Dağı 5165
Ararat
AZER.
Sisian
Xankändi

Äli Bayramlı
Salyan
Bıläsuvar
Läncäran

Ostrov
Ogurchinskiy

Horasan
Doğubeyazıt
Makū
Naxçıvan

Cälilabad
Āstārā

Hınıs Tutak
Patnos
Ercis
Khvoy
Marand
Ahar
4810

S
E
A

Malazgirt
Süphan Dağı
4058
Van
Salmas
Marägheh
Sarāb
Ardabil

Muş Ahlat
Bitlis
Lake Van
(Van Gölü)
Başkale
Urmia
Lake Urmia
(Daryächeh-ye Orümiyeh)
Miäneh

Bandar-e Anzali
Rasht
Lāhijān

Gomishān
Gorgān
Gonbad-e
Kavus

arbäkir
Tigris Siirt
Hakkäri
Orümiyeh
3711
Fowman
Tonkabon
Now
Shahr Bäbol
Behshahr
Sari

Mayamey

Satman Şırnak
Şemdinli
Haydaräbad

Elburz Mountains
(Reshteh-ye Alborz)

Amol

Emämrüd

Mardin
Al 'Amädiyah
Oshnoviyeh
Miandowäb

Zanjän
Qazvin

Damghan

Al Qāmishli
Zakho
Dahük
Mahäbäd
Saqqez

5601
TEHRĀN

Torüd

asakah
Arbil
Bijār
Abhar
Karaj

Semnän

Dasht-e Kavir

Mosul
As Sulaymāniyah
Sanandaj
Qorveh
Soltänäbäd

faz Ash
vr Sharqät
Halabja
Kirkük
Ravänsar
Kangävar
Hamadän

Daryächeh-ye
Namak

2

Bayji
Tuz Khurmätü
Qom

Jandaq

Kāshān

Al Hadithah
'Änah
Tikrit
Qasr-e
Shirin
Kermänshäh
Maläyer

Sämarrä
Kerend
Naḥävand

Aräk

IRAN

Ardestän

Nä'in

Dokali

Al Muqdädiyah
Eslämäbäd-e
Gharb
Īläm
Borüjerd
Dow
Rüd
Golpäyegän

Khunsar

Äqdä
Meybod

Hit
Ba'qübah

Khorramäbäd
Aligüdarz
Dārān
Küh-e
Garbosh
4294
Najafäbäd

Esfahän
(Isfahan)

Ar Ramādi
Al Käzimiyah
BAGHDĀD

Dehlorän
Dezfül

Shahr-e
Kord
Shahreza

Yazd
Bafq

uthah
Hawr al Habbäniyah
Buhayrat ar
Razäzah

Hillah
Karbalā'

Al Küt
Shushtar

Zagros Mountains (Kühhä-ye Zagros)

Abādeh

Anär

Abarqü

IRAQ
An Najaf
Ad Diwäniyah
Al Hayy
Al 'Amārah
Susangerd
Masjed
Soleymän
Rämhormoz
Küh-e
Dinar
4432

Deh Bid
Shahr-e
Bäbak

As Samäwah
Ash Shatrah
Ahväz
Omidiyeh
Yäsüj

Lavar
Meydän
Arsenaján
Abädeh Tashk

Ash Shabakah
An Näşiriyah
Süq ash
Shuyükh
Khorramshahr
Rämshir
Behbehän

Küh-e Tabask Marv
Dasht
Daryächeh-ye
Tashk

Beshneh

30°

Hawr al
Hammär
Basra
(Al Başrah)
Äbädän

Bandar-e
Emäm Khomeyni

Käzerün
3210
Zarqán

Kherämeh
3

kah
Raudhatain
Al Fäw
Ganäveh
Borâzjän
Farräshband
Shiräz

Salvestän Neyriz
Estahbän
Däräb
Rostäq

KUWAIT
Hawalli
KUWAIT
(Al Kuwayt)
Büshehr
Ahram
Khvormuj

Firüzäbäd
Fasä

Qir Jahrom
Häjjiäbäd

RABIA
Rafha'
Al Jahrah
Al Ahmadi
Aş Şubayhiyah
Mina' Sa'üd
Wädi al Batin

Dowlatäbäd
Jüyom

n Nafüd
Ash
Shu'bah

50°

© Collins Bartholomew Ltd

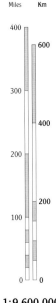

Miles Km
400

600

300

400

200

200

100

0 0

1:9 600 000

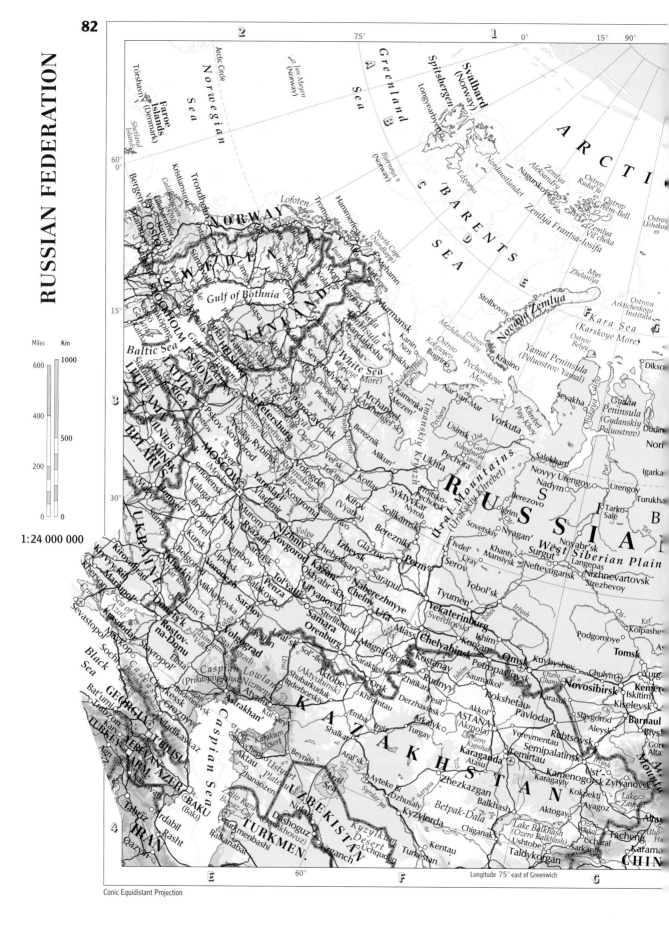

RUSSIAN FEDERATION

Conic Equidistant Projection

EUROPE

2

60°

Greenland
(Denmark)

Bear I.
(Nor.)

Arctic Circle

Denmark Strait

Jan Mayen
(Nor.)

3

ICELAND

Reykjavík

ATLANTIC

OCEAN

NORWEGIAN
SEA

Tromsø

N
O
R
W
A
Y

S
W
E
D
E
N

Faroe
Islands
(Den.)
Tórshavn

Trondheim

Shetland
Islands

Gulf of Both

Bergen

Orkney
Islands

Oslo

Stockho

50°

SCOTLAND

Glasgow
Edinburgh

N
O
R
T
H
S
E
A

Vänern

Gothenburg

Gotland

B
a
l
t
i
c
S
e
a

N. Belfast
IRELAND

IRELAND

Dublin

Manchester

UNITED
KINGDOM

DENMARK
Copenhagen

Malmö

RUS. F

WALES
ENGLAND

Cardiff

Birmingham

London

English Channel

Channel Is.
(U.K.)

NETHERLANDS
Amsterdam

The Hague

Brussels

Essen

BELGIUM

Hamburg

Hannover
Berlin

POLAN

Poznań Warsaw

Łódź

4

LIE. LIECHTENSTEIN
MACE. MACEDONIA

Seine

Paris

Luxembourg
LUXEMBOURG

Loire

Rhine

GERMANY

Frankfurt

Prague

CZECH
REPUBLIC

Katow

B
a
y
of Biscay

Cape Finisterre

Bordeaux

FRANCE

Lyon

SWITZERLAND
Bern
Mont Blanc
4808 ▲

Munich

Danube

LIE.

Vienna

SLOVAKI

Bratislava

AUSTRIA
S

Buda

HUNGARY

40°

Oporto

Bilbao

Pyrenees

Andorra
la Vella ANDORRA

Marseille

Rhône

MONACO

Turin

Milan

A
L
P
S

SLOVENIA

Ljubljana

SAN
MARINO

Zagreb

CROATIA

BOSNIA-
HERZ.

Belgra

SERBI
AND
MONTENE

PORTUGAL

SPAIN

Madrid

Lisbon

Valencia

Barcelona

Corsica

Balearic Islands

Sardinia

I
T
A
L
Y

VATICAN
CITY

Rome

Naples

Sarajevo

Adriatic Sea

Skopje
M

Tirana

ALBANIA

5

Cabo de
São Vicente

Seville

Gibraltar
(U.K.)

MEDITERRANEAN
SEA

Palermo

Sicily

Ionian
Sea

A

MOROCCO

ALGERIA

TUNISIA

MALTA
Valletta

Chamberlin Trimetric Projection

BARENTS SEA

Novaya Zemlya

kapp

Ostrov Kolguyev

Murmansk

Vorkuta

Ostrov Kolguyev

Ural Mountains

RUSSIAN FEDERATION

White Sea

Archangel

Syktyvkar

NLAND

Lake Onega

Perm'

Lake Ladoga

lelsinki

St Petersburg

Volga

Nizhniy Novgorod

Kazan'

allinn

Yaroslavl'

ONIA

Samara

Orenburg

ga
VIA

Moscow

KAZAKHSTAN

GIA
us

Ryazan'

Saratov

Minsk

Voronezh

4

BELARUS

Aral Sea

Homyel'

Volgograd

UZBEKISTAN

Kiev

Kharkiv

Don

UKRAINE

Dnipropetrovs'k

Donets'k

Volga

Astrakhan

Rostov na-Donu

MOLDOVA

Chişinău

Dniepr

Sea of Azov

40°

Odesa

Krasnodar

Grozny

Caspian Sea

MANIA

TURKMENISTAN

Bucharest

Black Sea

Caucasus

GEORGIA

AZERBAIJAN

ofia

ARMENIA

AZER.

LGARIA

Istanbul

5

essaloniki

CE

Athens

TURKEY

IRAN

Aegean Sea

Crete

CYPRUS

Euphrates

30°

LEBANON

SYRIA

IRAQ

Tigris

© Collins Bartholomew Ltd

Miles   Km
              1000
500
              750
250
              500
              250
0   0

1:20 000 000

EUROPEAN RUSSIAN FEDERATION

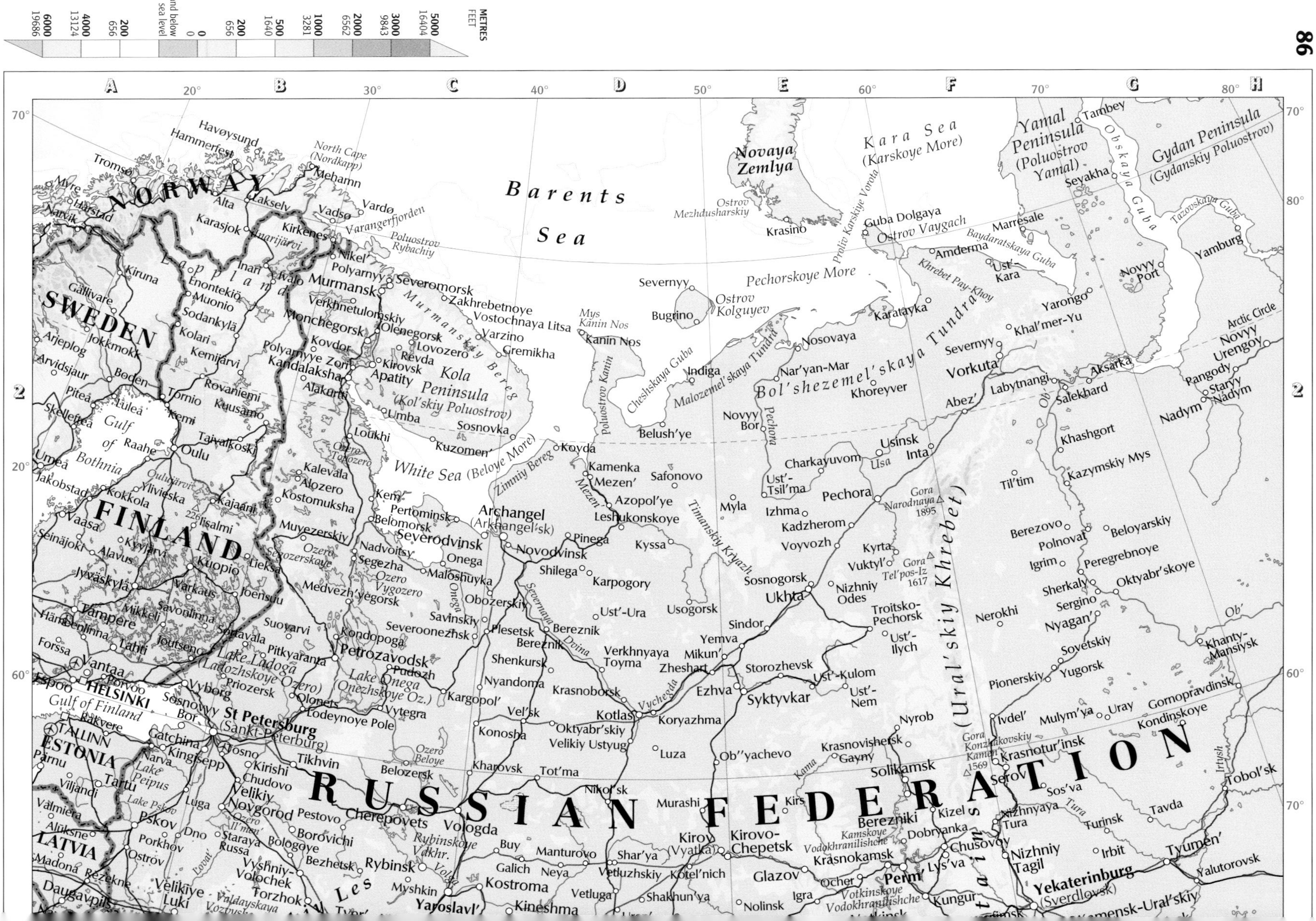

RUSSIAN FEDERATION

NORWAY

SWEDEN

FINLAND

ESTONIA

LATVIA

Barents Sea

Kara Sea (Karskoye More)

White Sea (Beloye More)

Gulf of Finland

Gulf of Bothnia

Novaya Zemlya

Ural'skiy Khrebet (Ural Mountains)

Yamal Peninsula (Poluostrov Yamal)

Gydan Peninsula (Gydanskiy Poluostrov)

Obskaya Guba

Pechorskoye More

Kola Peninsula (Kol'skiy Poluostrov)

Poluostrov Kanin

Timanskiy Kryazh

Arctic Circle

St Petersburg (Sankt-Peterburg)

Archangel (Arkhangel'sk)

Murmansk

Yekaterinburg (Sverdlovsk)

Perm'

Vologda

Kostroma

Yaroslavl'

HELSINKI

TALLINN

RĪGA

Lake Onega

Lake Ladoga

Lake Peipus

METRES / FEET

METRES	FEET
5000	16404
3000	9843
2000	6562
1000	3281
500	1640
200	656
0	0
Land below sea level	
200	656
4000	13124
6000	19686

Conic Equidistant Projection

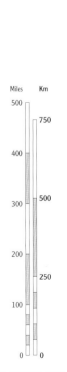

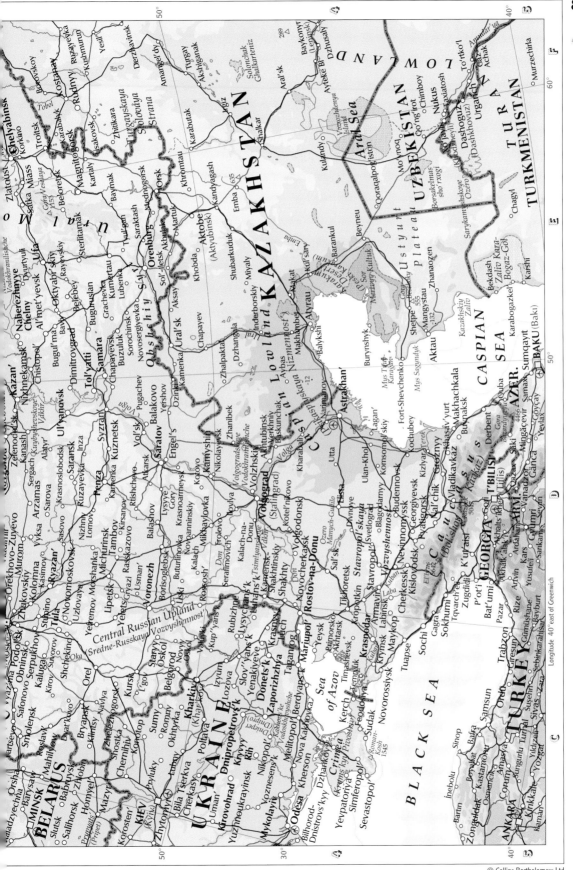

1:12 000 000

NORTHEAST EUROPE

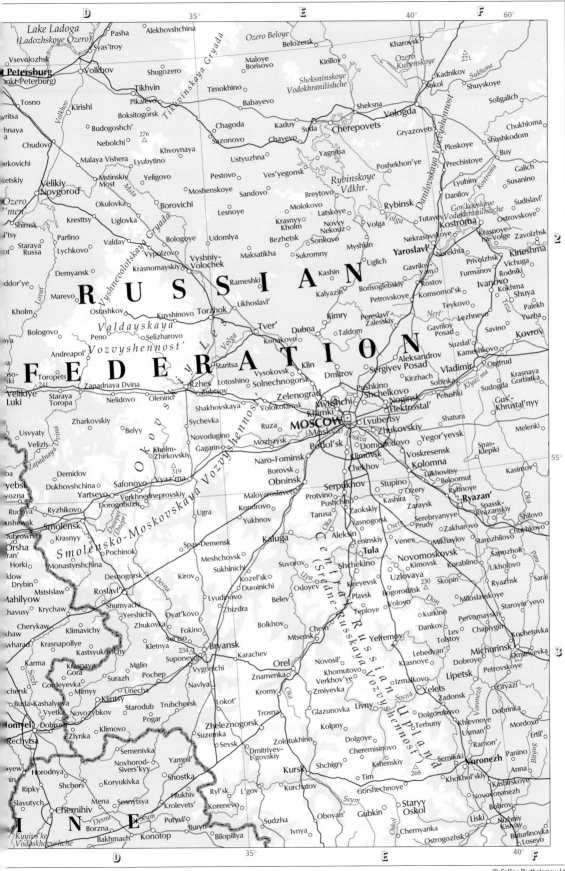

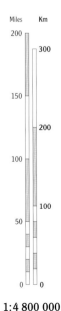

1:4 800 000

UKRAINE AND MOLDOVA

METRES
FEET

5000 / 16404
3000 / 9843
2000 / 6562
1000 / 3281
500 / 1640
200 / 656
0
Land below
sea level
200 / 656
4000 / 13124
6000 / 19686

Conic Equidistant Projection

Longitude 30° east of Greenwi

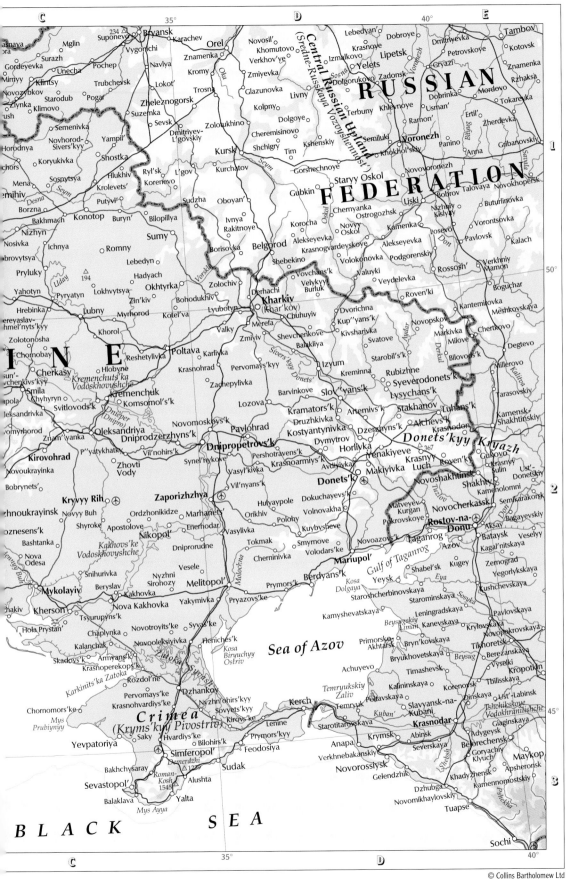

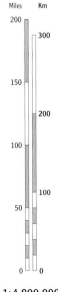

1:4 800 000

SCANDINAVIA AND ICELAND

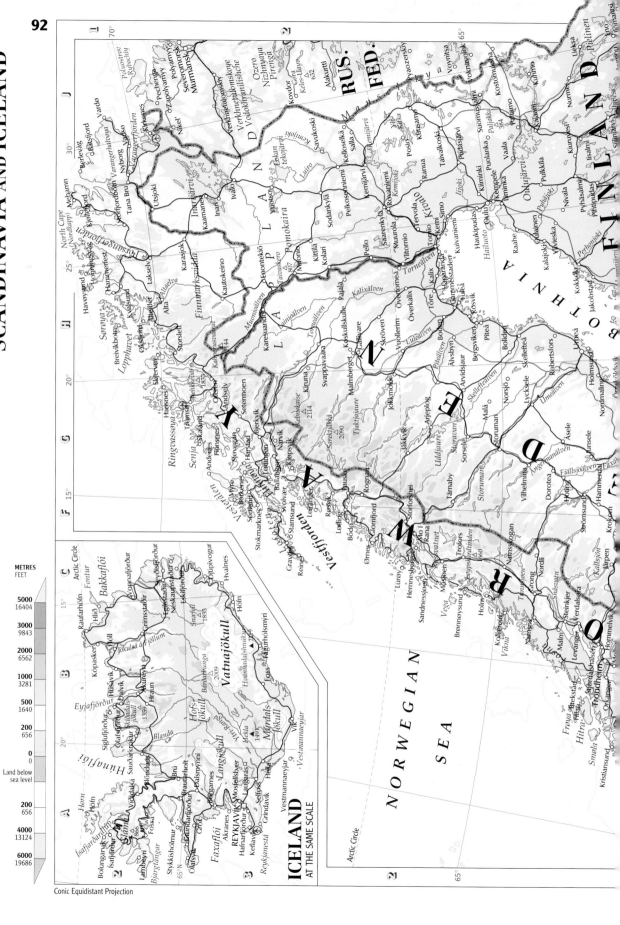

RUS. FED.

FINLAND

SWEDEN

NORWAY

N O R W E G I A N   S E A

GULF OF BOTHNIA

North Cape (Nordkapp)

Arctic Circle

ICELAND
AT THE SAME SCALE

Vatnajökull

Bakkaflói

Faxaflói

Húnaflói

REYKJAVIK

METRES / FEET

METRES	FEET
5000	16404
3000	9843
2000	6562
1000	3281
500	1640
200	656
0	0
Land below sea level	
200	656
4000	13124
6000	19686

Conic Equidistant Projection

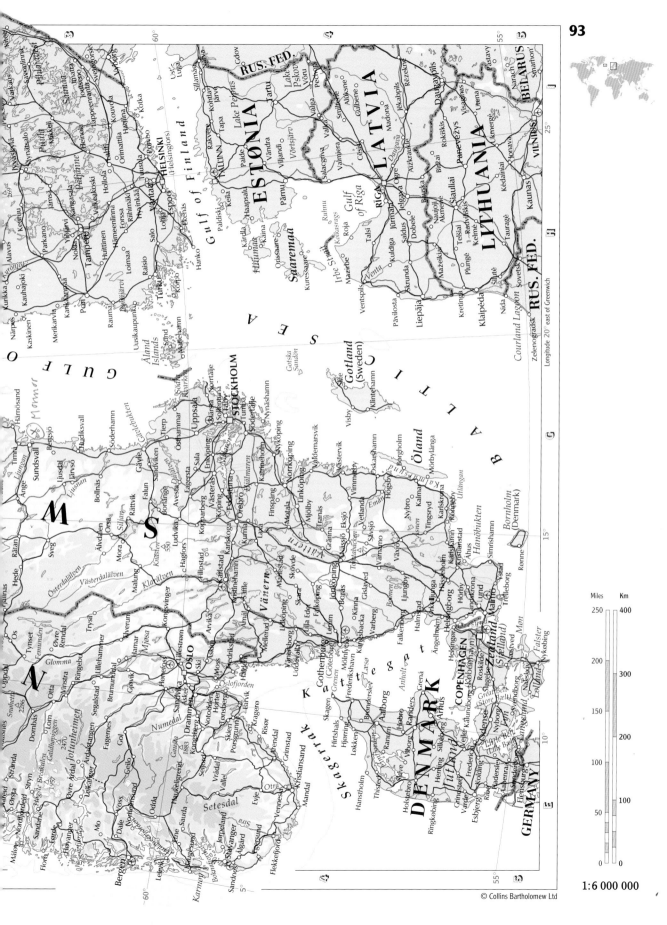

© Collins Bartholomew Ltd

1:6 000 000

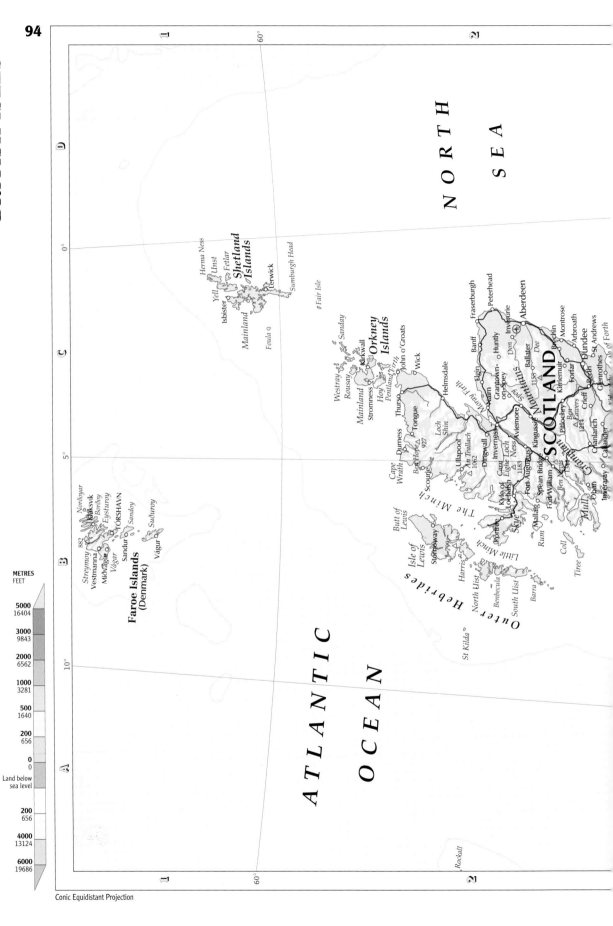

METRES
FEET

5000	16404
3000	9843
2000	6562
1000	3281
500	1640
200	656
0	0
Land below	sea level
200	656
4000	13124
6000	19686

Conic Equidistant Projection

NORTH SEA

ATLANTIC OCEAN

Faroe Islands (Denmark)

Nordoyar
Streymoy
Vestmanna
Miðvágur
Vágar
Eysturoy
Sandoy
Sandur
Vágur
Suðuroy
TÓRSHAVN
Borðoy
Klaksvík
882

Shetland Islands
Herma Ness
Unst
Yell
Fetlar
Isbister
Mainland
Lerwick
Sumburgh Head
Foula
Fair Isle

Orkney Islands
Westray
Sanday
Rousay
Mainland
Stromness
Kirkwall
Hoy
Pentland Firth
John o'Groats
Wick
Helmsdale

SCOTLAND
Cape Wrath
Durness
Ben Hope 927
Tongue
Loch Shin
Ullapool
Scourie
An Teallach 1062
Dingwall
Thurso
Moray Firth
Elgin
Banff
Fraserburgh
Peterhead
Aberdeen
Inverurie
Huntly
Dee
Ballater
Bechin
Montrose
Arbroath
St Andrews
Dundee
Kirriemuir
Forfar
Glenrothes
Firth of Forth
Grantown-on-Spey
Nairn
Inverness
Loch Ness
Fort Augustus
Cairn 1245
Ben Nevis 1344
Fort William
Spean Bridge
Mallaig
Kyle of Lochalsh
Portree
Skye
Rum
Coll
Tiree
Mull
Oban
Inveraray
Callander
Crieff
Dot
Pitlochry
Grampian Mountains 1155
Kingussie
Aviemore
Loch Eil
Ben Lawers 1214
Cromarty

Butt of Lewis
Stornoway
799
Isle of Lewis
Harris
North Uist
Benbecula
South Uist
Barra
St Kilda
Outer Hebrides
The Minch
Little Minch

0°
5°
10°
60°

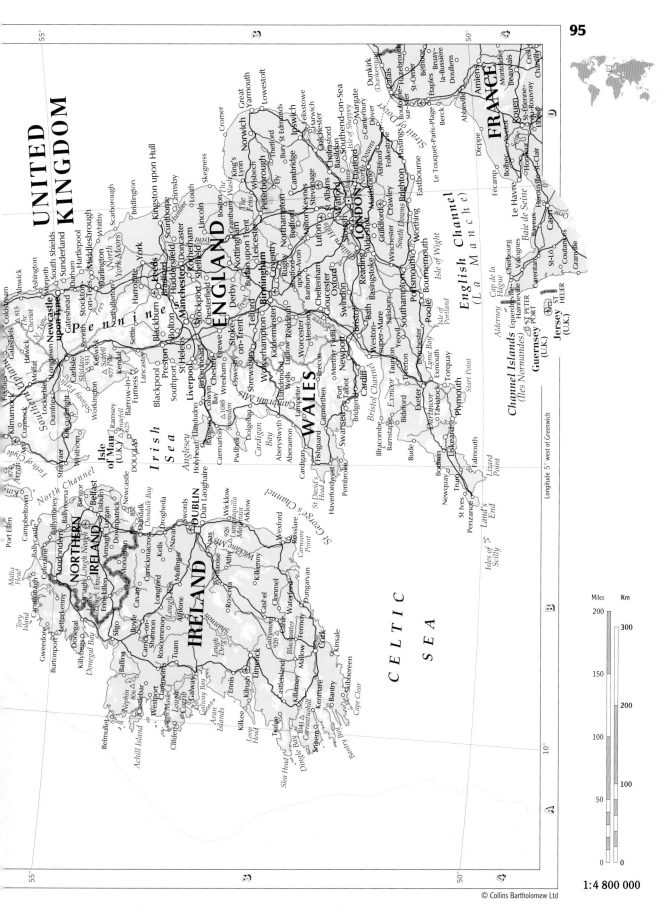

CELTIC SEA

© Collins Bartholomew Ltd

1:4 800 000

SCOTLAND

ATLANTIC OCEAN

Orkney Islands

Westray, North Ronaldsay, Sanday, Rousay, Eday, Loth, Stronsay, Birsay, Shapinsay, Mainland, Kirkwall, Stromness, Gritley, Ward Hill 479, Scapa Flow, Hoy, South Ronaldsay, Longhope, Burwick, Pentland Firth, John o' Groats, Dunnet Head, Duncansby Head

Shetland Islands

Herma Ness, Unst, Haroldswick, Yell, Isbister, Ronas Hill 450, Ulsta, Fetlar, Hillswick, Toft, St Magnus Bay, Papa Stour, Mainland, Walls, Lerwick, Foula, Bressay, Scalloway, Whalsay, Sumburgh, Sumburgh Head, Fair Isle

60°, 2°

Cape Wrath, Durness, Butt of Lewis, Port Ness (Port Nis), Thurso, Dunnet Head, Wick

Ben Hope 927, Tongue, Naver, Thurso, Scourie, Altnaharra, Kinbrace, Dunbeath, Point of Stoer, Ben More Assynt 998, Loch Shin, Helmsdale, Lochinver, Laing, Helmsdale, An Teallach 1062, Ullapool, Dornoch, Golspie, Loch Broom, Dornoch Firth, Tarbat Ness, Gairloch, Invergordon, Cromarty, Lossiemouth, Rosehearty, Fraserburgh, Ben Wyvis 1046, Alness, Moray Firth, Elgin, Banff, Macduff, Aberchirder, Rattray Head, Achnasheen, Dingwall, Black Isle, Nairn, Forres, Rothes, Keith, Turriff, Peterhead, Torridon, Beauly, Fortrose, Findhorn, Dufftown, Huntly, Mintlaw, Boddam, Ben Wyvis, Inverness, Strathspey, Spey, Ellon, Oldmeldrum

Loch Maree, Stromeferry, Carn Eighe 1183, Beauly, Drumnadrochit, Grantown-on-Spey, Inverurie, Dyce, Aberdeen, Glen More, Loch Ness, Aviemore, Don, Alford, Kintore, Westhill, Monadhliath Mountains, Cairngorm Mountains, Cuillin Hills, Sligachan, Kyle of Lochalsh, Fort Augustus, Kingussie, Ben Macdui 1309, Ballater, Banchory, Broadford, Garry, Newtonmore, Lochnagar 1155, Braemar, Stonehaven, Ardvasar, Loch Shiel, Dalwhinnie, Grampian Mountains, North Esk, Inverbervie, Mallaig, Spean Bridge, Ben Nevis 1344, Arisaig, Glenfinnan, Fort William, Edzell, Laurencekirk, Glencoe, Blair Atholl, Pitlochry, Brechin, Montrose, Kinlochleven, Bidean nam Bian 1150, Rannoch Moor, Tay, Aberfeldy, Blairgowrie, Kirriemuir, Forfar, Ballachulish, Ben Lawers 1214, Dunkeld, Sidlaw Hills, Arbroath, Lochaline, Connel, Tyndrum, Killin, Loch Tay, Carnoustie, Ben More 966, Oban, Dalmally, Ben More 1174, Crieff, Perth, Dundee, Tayport, Bell Rock, Fionnphort, Loch Awe, Inveraray, Crianlarich, Callander, Earn, Cupar, St Andrews, Fife Ness

SCOTLAND

Skye, Dunvegan, Portree, Sgurr Alasdair 993, Isle of Lewis, Carloway, Stornoway, Tarbert, Harris, Leverburgh, North Uist, Lochmaddy, Benbecula, Beinn Mhòr 620, South Uist, Lochboisdale, Barra, Castlebay, Mingulay, Clisham 799, Loch Roag, West Loch Roag, Loch a' Tuath, Sound of Harris, Little Minch, The Minch, Outer Hebrides, Inner Sound, Loch Torridon, Raasay

Canna, Rum, Eigg, Point of Ardnamurchan, Coll, Tiree, Mull, Ben More, Iona, Scarinish, Arinagour, Tobermory, Morvern, Firth of Lorn, Colonsay, Scarba, Jura, Beinn an Oir 785, Islay, Port Askaig, Portnahaven, Port Ellen, Mull of Oa, Gigha, Kintyre, Sound of Jura, Crinan, Lochgilphead, Tarbert, Loch Lomond, Ben Lomond 974, Aberfoyle, Stirling, Loch Katrine, Helensburgh, Greenock, Dumbarton, Alloa, Clydebank, Glasgow, Airdrie, Coatbridge, Paisley, Johnstone, Motherwell, Hamilton, Largs, Newton Mearns, East Kilbride, Rothesay, Bute, Lochranza, Ardrossan, Saltcoats, Kilmarnock, Lanark, Goat Fell 874, Brodick, Arran, Irvine, Troon, Prestwick, Cumnock, Ayr, Maybole, Campbeltown, Mull of Kintyre, Firth of Clyde, Dalmellington, Girvan, Merrick 843, New Galloway, Ballantrae, Newton Stewart, Thornhill, Castle Douglas, Sanquhar, Moffat, Teviothead, Hawick

North Berwick, Dunbar, Edinburgh, East Linton, Haddington, Firth of Forth, Musselburgh, Eyemouth, Berwick-upon-Tweed, Livingston, Dalkeith, Duns, Holy Island (Lindisfarne), Falkirk, Cumbernauld, Bathgate, Penicuik, Peebles, Galashiels, Coldstream, Wooler, Bamburgh, Biggar, Melrose, Kelso, Cowdenbeath, Kirkcaldy, Buckhaven, Anstruther, Glenrothes, Dunfermline, Alexandria, Loch Lomond, Selkirk, St Boswells, Jedburgh, The Cheviot 815, Alnwick, Broad Law 840, Clyde, Tweed, Teviot, Cheviot Hills, Rothbury, Amble, Southern Uplands, Langholm, Kielder Water, Otterburn, Morpeth, Ashington, Esk, North Tyne, Bedlington, Nith, Dumfries, Lockerbie, Longtown, Haltwhistle, Hexham, Newcastle upon Tyne, Blaydon, Gateshead, Annan, Carlisle, Brampton, Consett, Dalbeattie, Wigtown, Kirkcudbright, Solway Firth, Silloth, Maryport, Alston, Wear, Durham, Spennymoor, Cross Fell 893, Bishop Auckland, Newton Aycliffe, Cockermouth, Workington, Skiddaw 931, Penrith

NORTH SEA

ENGLAND

NORTHERN IRELAND

Giant's Causeway, Rathlin Island, Mull of Kintyre, Portrush, Portstewart, Ballycastle, Cushendun, Coleraine, Antrim Hills, Trostan 554, Milleur Point, Cairnryan, Limavady, Ballymoney, Dungiven, Ballybackey, Cullybackey, Ballymena, Larne, Stranraer, Portpatrick, Luce Bay, Drummore, Mull of Galloway, Magherafelt, Antrim, Lough Neagh, Newtownabbey, Whitehead, Carrickfergus, Bangor, Donaghadee, North Channel

North Channel, Firth of Clyde, Ailsa Craig

METRES / FEET

METRES	FEET
5000	16404
3000	9843
2000	6562
1000	3281
500	1640
200	656
0	0

Land below sea level

200	656
4000	13124
6000	19686

Conic Equidistant Projection

Longitude 4° west of Greenwich

6°, 4°, 2°

A B C D

1 2 3

58°, 56°

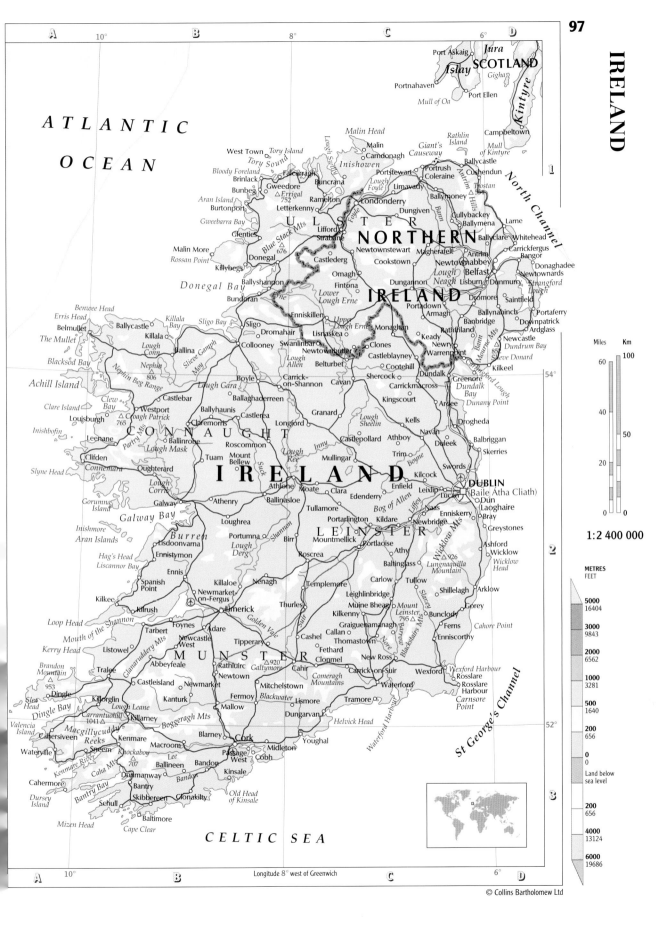

ENGLAND AND WALES

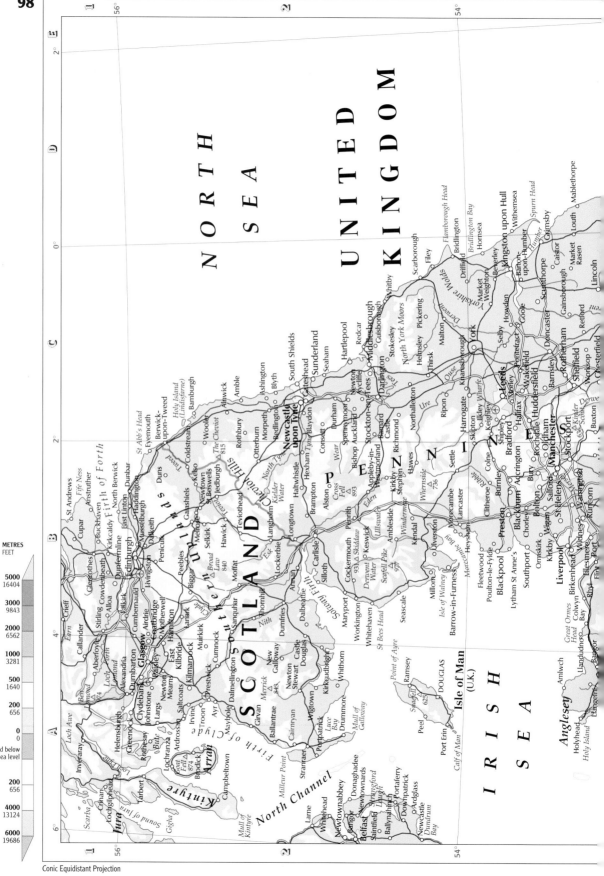

METRES
FEET

5000	16404
3000	9843
2000	6562
1000	3281
500	1640
200	656
0	0
Land below sea level	
200	656
4000	13124
6000	19686

Conic Equidistant Projection

ENGLAND

WALES

FRANCE

Strait of Dover

ENGLISH CHANNEL

(LA MANCHE)

Isle of Wight

Cardigan Bay

Cambrian Mountains

Bristol Channel

Wash

The Fens

Greenwich 0° meridian

52°

50°

1:2 400 000

© Collins Bartholomew Ltd

Miles   Km
                150
80
                100
60
                50
40

20

0   0

North Walsham
Great Yarmouth
Lowestoft
Southwold
Aldeburgh
Orford Ness
Felixstowe
Harwich
Clacton-on-Sea
Foulness Point
Southend-on-Sea
Sheerness
Isle of Sheppey
Whitstable
Margate
North Foreland
Ramsgate
Canterbury
Deal
Dover
Folkestone
Hythe
Ashford
Dungeness
Cap Gris Nez
Wimereux
Boulogne-sur-Mer
Le Touquet-Paris-Plage
Berck
Mers-les-Bains
Le Tréport
Dieppe
Neuville-lès-Dieppe
Eu
Montreuil
Calais

Norwich
Diss
Beccles
Long Stratton
Wymondham
Wroxham
Bungay
Halesworth
Fakenham
Dereham
East Dereham
Hunstanton
King's Lynn
Wisbech
Spalding
Bourne
Stamford
Oakham
Melton Mowbray
Grantham
Leicester
Loughborough
Nuneaton
Hinckley
Coventry
Rugby
Daventry
Northampton
Wellingborough
Kettering
Corby
Market Harborough
Huntingdon
Peterborough
March
Ely
Mildenhall
Newmarket
Thetford
Bury St Edmunds
Stowmarket
Ipswich
Woodbridge
Sudbury
Colchester
Braintree
Maldon
Chelmsford
Brentwood
Basildon
Gravesend
Gillingham
Chatham
Rochester
Maidstone
Royal Tunbridge Wells
Tonbridge
Sevenoaks
Crawley
Brighton
Hove
Worthing
Seaford
Beachy Head
Eastbourne
Bexhill
Hastings
Rye
Uckfield
Lewes
Haywards Heath
Crowborough
Horsham
Chichester
Selsey Bill
Havant
Littlehampton
Bognor Regis

Cambridge
Saffron Walden
Royston
Biggleswade
Letchworth
Stevenage
Hertford
St Albans
Hatfield
Welwyn Garden City
Watford
Hendon
Harlow
Epping
Romford
Ilford
Dartford
Grays
LONDON
Staines
Slough
Windsor
Maidenhead
High Wycombe
Hemel Hempstead
Luton
Dunstable
Leighton Buzzard
Aylesbury
Buckingham
Milton Keynes
Bedford
Banbury
Chipping Norton
Bicester
Witney
Oxford
Abingdon
Wantage
Didcot
Newbury
Reading
Wokingham
Bracknell
Camberley
Aldershot
Farnham
Guildford
Woking
Epsom
Reigate
Redhill
Dorking
Haslemere
Alton
Basingstoke
Andover
Winchester
Eastleigh
Southampton
Portsmouth
Gosport
Fareham
Waterlooville
Cosham
Newport
Ventnor
St Catherine's Point

Bala
Porthmadog
Pwllheli
Aberdaron
Barmouth
Dolgellau
Machynlleth
Penygadair
Plynlimon
Cader Idris
Aberystwyth
Aberaeron
Aberaeron
Newtown
Welshpool
Llanidloes
Llandrindod Wells
Builth Wells
Brecon
Brecon Beacons
Llandovery
Llandeilo
Lampeter
Tregaron
Cardigan
Fishguard
St David's (Tyddewi)
Haverfordwest
Milford Haven
Pembroke
Tenby
St Clears
Carmarthen
Llanelli
Swansea
Gower
Worms Head
Neath
Port Talbot
Porthcawl
Bridgend
Maesteg
Aberdare
Merthyr Tydfil
Aberystwyth
Pontypridd
Barry
Cardiff
Newport
Cwmbran
Pontypool
Abertillery
Ebbw Vale
Abergavenny
Usk
Ross-on-Wye
Monmouth
Chepstow
Hereford
Leominster
Ludlow
Oswestry
Shrewsbury
Telford
Bridgnorth
Kidderminster
Droitwich Spa
Worcester
Great Malvern
Pershore
Evesham
Stratford-upon-Avon
Warwick
Royal Leamington Spa
Redditch
Bromsgrove
Solihull
Birmingham
West Bromwich
Dudley
Walsall
Sutton Coldfield
Cannock
Lichfield
Tamworth
Wolverhampton

Stafford
Stoke-on-Trent
Derby
Burton upon Trent
Uttoxeter
Madeley
Market Drayton
Whitchurch

Tewkesbury
Cheltenham
Gloucester
Stroud
Cirencester
Stow-on-the-Wold
Swindon
Chippenham
Calne
Devizes
Marlborough
Trowbridge
Bath
Keynsham
Bristol
Weston-super-Mare
Bridgwater
Clevedon
Frome
Warminster
Shaftesbury
Salisbury
Stonehenge
Amesbury
Salisbury Plain
Romsey
Ringwood
Fordingbridge
Christchurch
Bournemouth
Poole
Wareham
Swanage
The Needles
Wells
Glastonbury
Street
Wincanton
Yeovil
Sherborne
Blandford Forum
Dorchester
Weymouth
Bill of Portland
Isle of Portland
Bridport
Lyme Regis
Chard
Axminster
Honiton
Sidmouth
Exmouth
Seaton
St Alban's Head

Minehead
Ilfracombe
Barnstaple
Bideford
Great Torrington
Bideford Bay
Lundy
Hartland Point
Bude
Launceston
Okehampton
Tavistock
Tiverton
Crediton
Exeter
Newton Abbot
Teignmouth
Dawlish
Torquay
Paignton
Brixham
Dartmouth
Start Point
Bodmin Moor
Bodmin
Liskeard
Saltash
Callington
Plymouth
Rame Head
Yes Tor
Dartmoor
Camelford
Wadebridge
Padstow
Newquay
Perranporth
St Austell
Truro
Bodmin
St Ives
Camborne
Redruth
Helston
Penzance
Mount's Bay
Land's End
Lizard Point
Trevose Head

Exmoor
Blackdown Hills
Mendip Hills
Chiltern Hills
Cotswold Hills
South Downs
The Weald
The Solent
North Downs

Strumble Head
St David's Head
St Bride's Bay
Stour
Nene
Avon
Severn
Wye
Teme
Teifi
Towy
Usk
Trent
Kennet
Thames
Test
Itchen
Exe
Taw
Tamar
Camel

NORTHWEST EUROPE

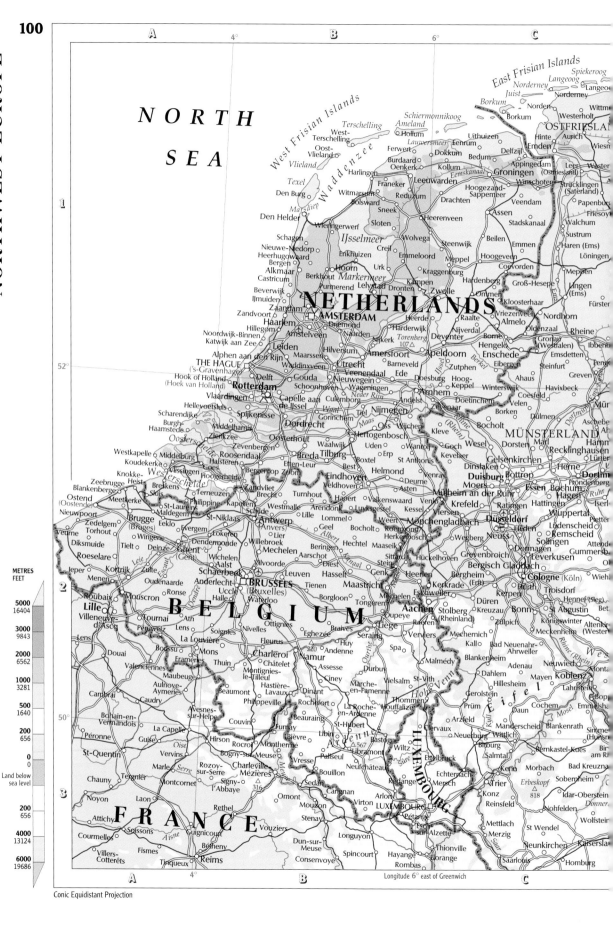

NORTH SEA

NETHERLANDS

OSTFRIESLAND

East Frisian Islands

West Frisian Islands

BELGIUM

LUXEMBOURG

FRANCE

MÜNSTERLAND

EIFEL

METRES
FEET

METRES	FEET
5000	16404
3000	9843
2000	6562
1000	3281
500	1640
200	656
0	0

Land below
sea level

200	656
4000	13124
6000	19686

Longitude 6° east of Greenwich

Conic Equidistant Projection

Miles   Km

150

80   100

60

40   50

20

0   0

1:2 400 000

© Collins Bartholomew Ltd

CENTRAL EUROPE

METRES
FEET

5000
16404

3000
9843

2000
6562

1000
3281

500
1640

200
656

0
0

Land below
sea level

200
656

4000
13124

6000
19686

Conic Equidistant Projection

Longitude 10° east of Greenwich

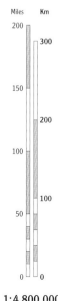

1:4 800 000

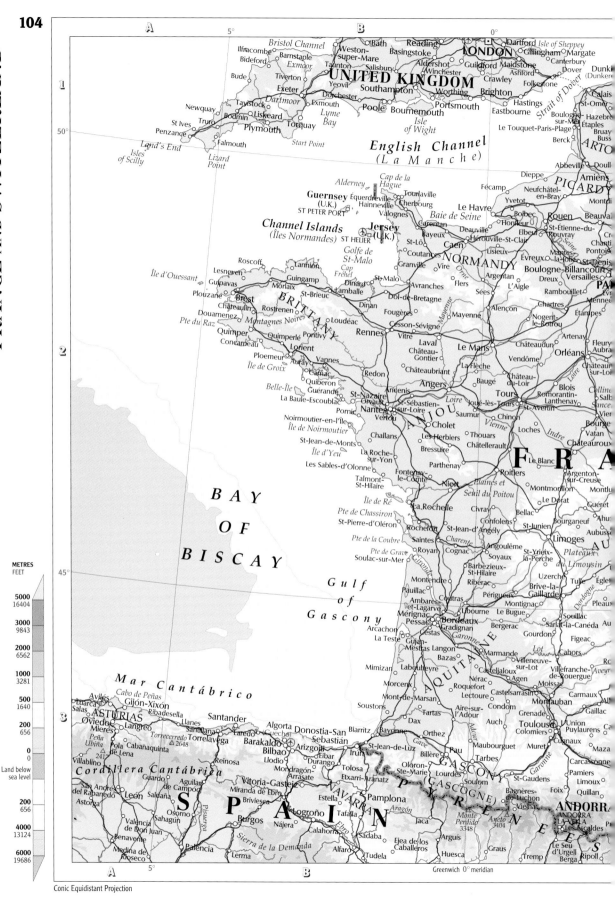

FRANCE AND SWITZERLAND

Conic Equidistant Projection

METRES
FEET

5000
16404

3000
9843

2000
6562

1000
3281

500
1640

200
656

0
0

Land below
sea level

200
656

4000
13124

6000
19686

Greenwich 0° meridian

MEDITERRANEAN SEA

1:4 800 000

© Collins Bartholomew Ltd

SPAIN AND PORTUGAL

ATLANTIC OCEAN

Mar Cantábrico

METRES
FEET

5000	16404
3000	9843
2000	6562
1000	3281
500	1640
200	656
0	0
Land below sea level	
200	656
4000	13124
6000	19686

Conic Equidistant Projection

Cabo Ortegal
Punta da Estaca de Bares
Cervo
Ortigueira
Viveiro
Ribadeo
Luarca
Cabo de Peñas
Gijón-Xixón
Avilés
Ferrol
Gándara
A Coruña
Vilalba
Salas
Oviedo
Ribadesella
Llanes
Santander
Laredo
Algorta
(Getxo)
Betanzos
Santiago de Compostela
Ordes
Melide
Lugo
Cangas del Narcea
Mieres
Pola de Siero
Santillana
Torrelavega
Reinosa
Barakaldo
Bilbao
Muros
Estrada
Becerreá
Villablino
Torrecerredo 2648
Cabañaquinta
Guardo
Aguilar de Campóo
Llodio
Mondrag
Arras
Cape Finisterre
(Cabo Fisterra)
Vilagarcía de Arousa
Lalín
Sarria
Chantada
ASTURIAS
Peña Ubiña
2417
Cordillera Cantábrica
San Andrés del Rabanedo
León
Saldaña
Osorno
Vitoria-Gasteiz
Miranda de Ebro
Briviesca
Logro
Nájera
Santa Uxía de Ribeira
Pontevedra
Marín
Redondela
Monforte
Ourense
Ponferrada
Astorga
Valencia de Don Juan
Sahagún
Palencia
Burgos
Cangas
Vigo
Tui
Xinzo de Limia
Barco
Truchas
El Teleno
2188
Benavente
Medina de Rioseco
Lerma
Aranda de Duero
Ayllón
Miño
Fondevila
Verín
Bragança
Macedo de Cavaleiros
Zamora
Valladolid
Toro
Tordesillas
Cuéllar
Medina del Campo
Segovia
Sigüenza
Sierra de la Dema
Viana do Castelo
Braga
Chaves
Mirandela
Hermosele
Embalse de Almendra
Ledesma
Olmedo
Peñaranda de Bracamonte
Sierra de Guadarrama
Guadalajara
Alcalá de Henares
Emba de Buen
Póvoa de Varzim
Guimarães
Vila Real
Torre de Moncorvo
Salamanca
Arévalo
Ávila
Maia
Matosinhos
Oporto
(Porto)
Lamego
Meda
Sierra de Mogadouro
Lumbrales
Peñalara
2430
Móstoles
Fuenlabrada
Parla
Alcalá de Henares
MADRID
Getafe
Vila Nova de Gaia
Pedroso
São João da Madeira
Douro
Vilari Formoso
Ciudad Rodrigo
Nuñomoral
Béjar
Sierra de Gredos
Aranjuez
Ocaña
Taranc
Ovar
Aveiro
Ílhavo
Águeda
Mangualde
Viseu
Guarda
Torre
1993
Sabugal
Sierra de Estrela
Plasencia
Coria
Navalmoral de la Mata
Valle de Tiétar
Torrijos
Toledo
Mealhada
Coimbra
Figueira da Foz
Covilhã
Fundão
Alcántara
Talavera de la Reina
Tagus Tajo
Castilla-La Mancha
Marinha Grande
Lousã
Serra da Estrela
Castelo Branco
Cáceres
Embalse de Valdecañas
Montes de Toledo
Alcázar de San Juan
Pombal
Leiria
Batalha
Tomar
Abrantes
Trujillo
Herrera del Duque
Madridejos
Caldas da Rainha
Torres Novas
Entroncamento
Ponte de Sor
Portalegre
Sierra de San Pedro
Miajadas
Navalvillar de Pela
Embalse de Cijara
Socuéllamos
Villarroble
Peniche
Santarém
Coruche
Campo Maior
EXTREMADURA
Mérida
Villanueva de la Serena
Ciudad Real
Daimiel
Tomell
Torres Vedras
Vila Franca de Xira
Amadora
Cacém
LISBON
(Lisboa)
Montijo
Estremoz
Elvas
Montijo
Don Benito
Almadén
Jabalón
Valdepeñas
Alca
Cascais
Almada
Redondo
Badajoz
Olivenza
Cabeza del Buey
Villanueva de los Infantes
Cabo Espichel
Setúbal
Alcácer do Sal
Évora
Barragem de Alqueva
Almendralejo
Hinojosa del Duque
Puertollano
Baía de Setúbal
Grândola
Torrão
Amareleja
Zafra
Los Pedroches
Pozoblanco
Morena
Sines
Cabo de Sines
Beja
Moura
Fregenal de la Sierra
Azuaga
Andújar
Linares
Sierra de Se
Aljustrel
Serpa
Rosal de la Frontera
Peñarroya-Pueblonuevo
Sierra
Guadalquivir
Baeza
Úbeda
Odemira
Castro Verde
Cortegana
Constantina
Córdoba
Jaén
Huéso
Almodôvar
Mértola
Valverde del Camino
Palma del Río
Martos
Alcaudete
Baza
Aljezur
ALGARVE
Guadiana
Huelva
Almonte
Coria del Río
Lora del Río
Écija
Montilla
Cabra
Alcalá la Real
Priego de Córdoba
Guadix
Cabo de Lagos
Portimão
Loulé
Ayamonte
Playa de Castilla
Utrera
Marchena
Osuna
Lucena
Loja
Granada
Sierra de
São Vicente
Sagres
Albufeira
Tavira
Olhão
Cabo de Faro Santa Maria
Las Marismas
Lebrija
Morón de la Frontera
Antequera
Sierra Nevada
Mulhacén
3482
Alme
Costa de la Luz
Sanlúcar de Barrameda
El Puerto de Santa María
ANDALUCÍA
Arcos de la Frontera
Ronda
Vélez-Málaga
Motril
Adra
El E
Golfo de Cádiz
Cádiz
Jerez de la Frontera
Torremolinos
Málaga
Almuñécar
Golfo
Alme
San Fernando
Chiclana de la Frontera
Marbella
Costa del Sol
Vejer de la Frontera
Estepona
Barbate de Franco
Algeciras
La Línea de la Concepción
Cabo Trafalgar
Gibraltar (U.K.)
Strait of Gibraltar
Pta Almina
Ceuta
(Spain)
Cap des Trois Fourches
Asilah
Tangier
(Tanger)
Cabo Negro
Tétouan
MOROCCO

GALICIA
PORTUGAL
SPAIN
CASTILLA Y LEÓN

Gulf of Gascony

Arcachon · La Teste · Gujan-Mestras · Gradignan · Langon · Garonne · Marmande · Figeac · Espalion · Marvejols · Mende · Valréas · Nyons · Bollène · Pierrelatte · Sisteron · Digne-les-Bains

Mimizan · Labouheyre · Morcenx · Bazas · Casteljaloux · Lot · Villeneuve-sur-Lot · Cahors · Villefranche-de-Rouergue · Rodez · Sévérac-le-Château · Florac · Les-Vans · Orange · Carpentras · Manosque

Soustons · Mont-de-Marsan · Roquefort · Castelsarrasin · Agen · Moissac · Montauban · Gaillac · Albi · Carmaux · Tarn · Ganges · Alès · Uzès · Avignon · Cavaillon · Salon-de-Provence · Draguignan · Verdon

Biarritz · Bayonne · Dax · Tartas · Adour · Aire-sur-l'Adour · Auch · Colomiers · Toulouse · Castres · Lodève · Nîmes · Istres · Aix-en-Provence · Fréjus

Irún · St-Jean-de-Luz · Orthez · Pau · Billère · Maubourguet · Tarbes · Muret · Puylaurens · Mazamet · Béziers · Sète · Châteauneuf-les- · Martigues · Marignane · Aubagne · Brignoles

Hostia · San Sebastián · Etxarri-Aranatz · Oloron-Ste-Marie · Lourdes · Soulom · St-Gaudens · Carcassonne · Pamiers · Narbonne · Durban-Corbières · Agde · Marseille · La Ciotat · Toulon · St-Tropez

Pamplona · Aragón · Jaca · Monte Perdido 3348 · Aneto 3404 · Le Seu d'Urgell · Les Escaldes · ANDORRA LA VELLA · Prades · Perpignan · Port-Vendres · Six-Fours-les-Plages · Cap Sicié · Hyères

Tafalla · Arguís · Huesca · Tremp · Berga · Ripoll · Olot · Vic · Salt · Girona · Banyoles · Cap de Creus · Figueres · Cap de Begur · Torroella de Montgrí · Palamós

Sádaba · Ejea de los Caballeros · Graus · Barbastro · Monzón · Manresa · Igualada · Sabadell · Santa Coloma de Gramanet · Blanes · Costa Brava

Alfaro · Tudela · Zaragoza · Binéfar · Fraga · Lleida · Tárrega · Martorell · Barcelona · El Prat de Llobregat · Mataró · Vilanova i la Geltrú

Calatayud · Daroca · Cariñena · Quinto · Caspe · Valls · Reus · Tarragona · Costa Dorada

ARAGÓN · Escatrón · Alcañiz · Ebro · Gandesa · Tortosa · Golf de Sant Jordi · Costa del Azahar

Molina de Aragón · Monreal del Campo · Perales del Alfambra · Morella · Amposta · Sant Carles de la Rapita · Vinaròs

Tordesillos · Teruel · Peñarroya 2019 · VALENCIA · Torreblanca · Castelló de la Plana · Burriana

Sarrión · Sierra de Javalambre · Santa Cruz de Moya · Turia · Alcora · Vall de Uxó · Sagunto · Costa del Azahar

Utiel · Requena · Manises · Lliria · Burjassot · Valencia · Catarroja · Golfo de Valencia

Minglanilla · Torrent · Sueca · Cullera

La Roda · Júcar · Algemesí · Carcaixent · Gandía · Oliva · Denia · Cabo de la Nao

Albacete · Almansa · Xàtiva · Ontinyent · Alcoy-Alcoi · Altea · Formentera

Alcaraz · Yecla · Villena · Ibi · Benidorm · Villajoyosa-La Vila Joiosa · Alicante

Hellín · Elda · Novelda · Crevillente · Elche-Elx · Elx

Caravaca de la Cruz · Cieza · Molina de Segura · Murcia · Orihuela · Torrevieja · Costa Blanca

Lorca · Alhama de Murcia · Alcantarilla · Mazarrón · Cabo de Palos

Huércal-Overa · Aguilas · Golfo de Mazarrón

Cartagena

Vera · Cabo de Gata

MEDITERRANEAN SEA

Minorca (Menorca)

Punta Nati · Ciutadella de Menorca · Mercadal · Mahón · Cap de Formentor

Majorca (Mallorca)

Pollença · Alcúdia · Sa Pobla · Sóller · Calvià · Sa Cabaneta · Manacor · Cap des Freu · Sa Dragonera · Palma de Mallorca · Felanitx · Cap de ses Salines · Cabrera

Ibiza (Eivissa)

San Juan Bautista · San Antonio Abad · Santa Eulalia del Río · Ibiza (Eivissa) · San Francisco Javier · Formentera

BALEARIC ISLANDS (ISLAS BALEARES) (Spain)

ALGIERS (Alger) · Aïn Taya · Dellys · Boumerdes · Bejaïa · Jijel

Koléa · Larba · Tizi Ouzou · Bougaa · Sétif

Tipasa · Gouraya · Blida · Bouira · Bordj Bou Arréridj · Aïn Azel

Ténès · Djebel Bissa 1157 · Miliana · Médéa · Berrouaghia · Sour el Ghozlane · Sidi Aïssa · M'Sila

Sidi Ali · Ouled Farès · Aïn Defla · Khemis Miliana · Ksar el Boukhari · Barika

Mostaganem · Aïn Tédélès · Relizane · Bordj Bounaama · Zenzach · Bou Saâda · M'Oukal

Gap Carbon · Arzew · Oued Chélif · Zemmora · Tissemsilt · Mahdia · Tiaret

Oran · Oued Tlélat · Sig · Mohammadia · Mascara

Beni-Saf · Aïn Temouchent

ALGERIA

Greenwich 0° meridian

1:4 800 000

© Collins Bartholomew Ltd

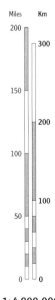

Miles 200 150 100 50 0

Km 300 200 100 0

ITALY AND THE BALKANS

METRES
FEET

5000 / 16404
3000 / 9843
2000 / 6562
1000 / 3281
500 / 1640
200 / 656
0 / 0
Land below sea level
200 / 656
4000 / 13124
6000 / 19686

Conic Equidistant Projection

Longitude 10° east of Greenwich

CROATIA
HUNGARY
ROMANIA
VOJVODINA
BELGRADE (Beograd)
BOSNIA-HERZEGOVINA
SARAJEVO
SRBIJA (SERBIA)
SERBIA AND MONTENEGRO
DALMATIA
CRNA GORA (MONTENEGRO)
KOSOVO
BULGARIA
SOFIA (Sofiya)
Podgorica
ALBANIA
MACEDONIA (F.Y.R.O.M.)
SKOPJE
TIRANA (Tiranë)
A D R I A T I C   S E A
Golfo di Taranto
Strait of Otranto
LA SILA
GREECE
Corfu (Kerkyra)
Cephalonia (Kefallonia)
Ionian Islands (Ionioi Nisoi)
Zakynthos (Zante)
I O N I A N   S E A

Miles   Km
200   300
         200
150
100
         100
50
0   0

1:4 800 000

© Collins Bartholomew Ltd

SOUTHEAST EUROPE

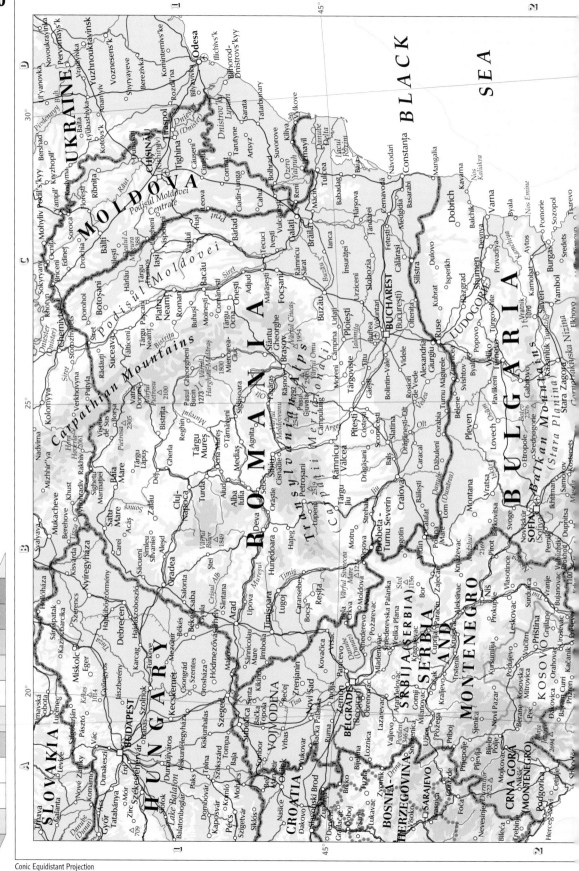

METRES
FEET

5000	16404
3000	9843
2000	6562
1000	3281
500	1640
200	656
0	0

Land below
sea level

200	656
4000	13124
6000	19686

Conic Equidistant Projection

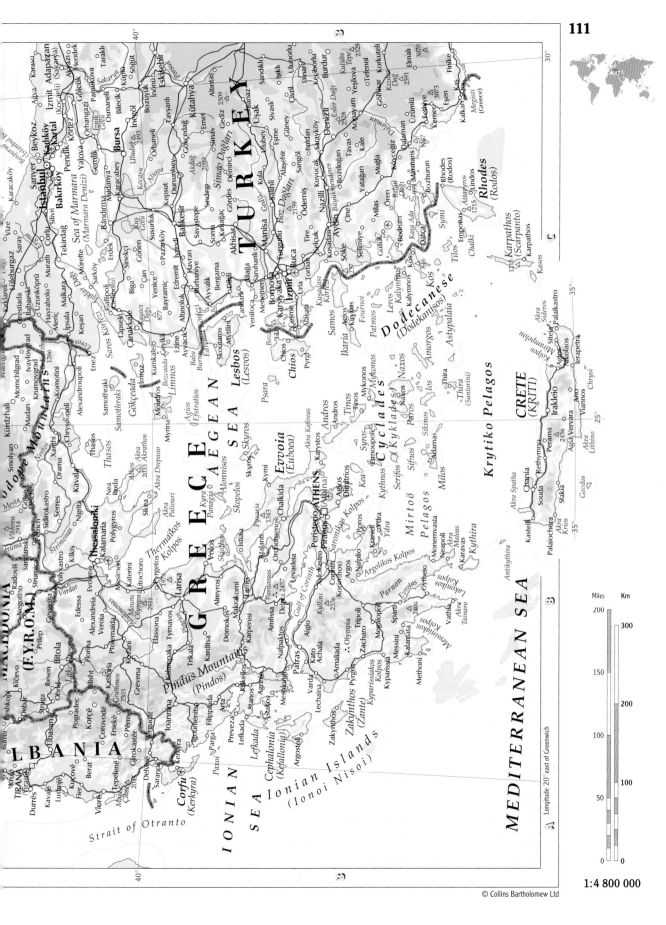

1:4 800 000

AFRICA

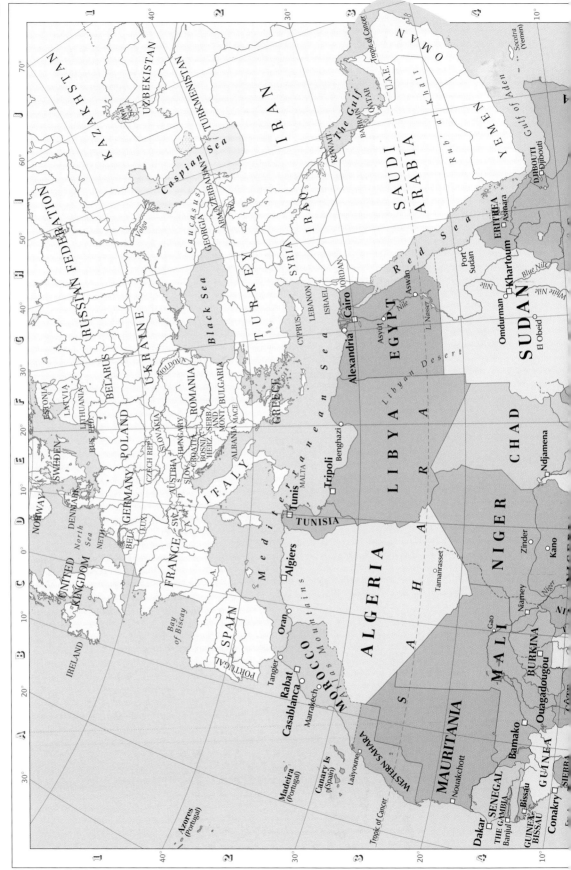

Oblated Stereographic Projection

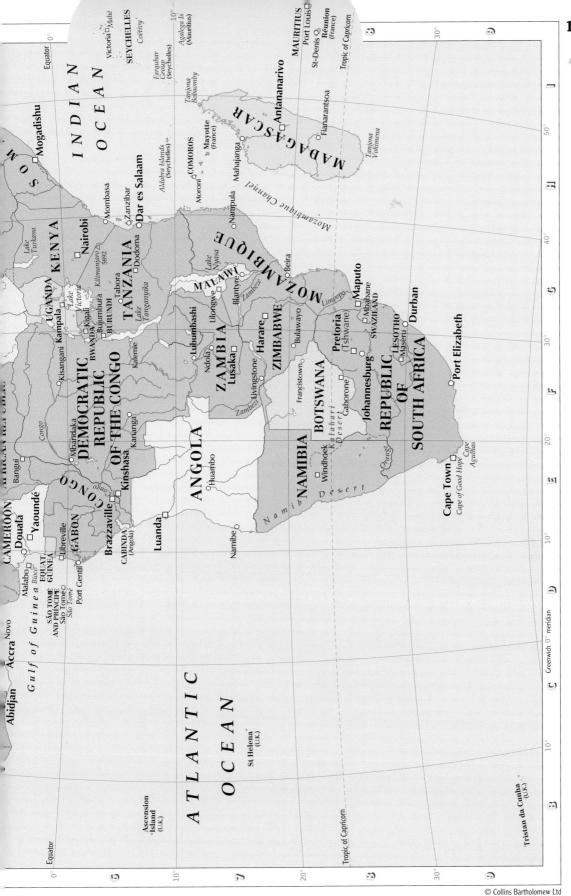

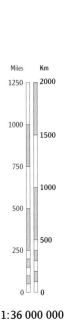

SEYCHELLES
Victoria □ Mahé
Coëtivy

Farquhar Group (Seychelles)

MAURITIUS
Port Louis □
Réunion (France)
St-Denis □
Agalega Is (Mauritius)
Tropic of Capricorn

INDIAN OCEAN

Mogadishu

SOMALIA

Antananarivo
Tanjona Bobaomby

Fianarantsoa

MADAGASCAR

Mayotte (France)
COMOROS
Moroni

Aldabra Islands (Seychelles)

Tanjona Vohimena

Mombasa
Zanzibar
Dar es Salaam

Nampula

Mozambique Channel

Mahajanga

Lake Turkana

KENYA
Nairobi

UGANDA
Kampala

Kilimanjaro 5892
Kigali
RWANDA
Bujumbura
BURUNDI

TANZANIA
Tabora
Dodoma

Lake Victoria

Lake Tanganyika

Lake Nyasa

MALAWI
Lilongwe
Blantyre

MOZAMBIQUE
Beira

Kisangani

DEMOCRATIC REPUBLIC OF THE CONGO

Lubumbashi
Kalemie

ZAMBIA
Ndola
Lusaka
Livingstone

Zambezi

ZIMBABWE
Harare
Bulawayo

Maputo
Mbabane
SWAZILAND

Limpopo

Pretoria (Tshwane)
LESOTHO
Maseru

Durban

CAMEROON
Yaoundé
Douala

Bangui

CONGO
Brazzaville
Kinshasa
Mbandaka
GABON
Libreville
Port Gentil

Kananga

ANGOLA
Huambo

Luanda

CABINDA (Angola)

NAMIBIA
Windhoek

BOTSWANA
Francistown
Gaborone
Kalahari Desert

Johannesburg
REPUBLIC OF SOUTH AFRICA

Port Elizabeth

Namib Desert
Namibe
Orange

Cape Town
Cape of Good Hope
Cape Agulhas

Malabo
Bioco
EQUAT. GUINEA
SÃO TOMÉ AND PRÍNCIPE
São Tomé

Gulf of Guinea

Abidjan
Accra
Novo

ATLANTIC OCEAN

St Helena (U.K.)

Ascension Island (U.K.)

Equator

Greenwich 0° meridian

Tropic of Capricorn

Tristan da Cunha (U.K.)

Miles   Km
1250   2000

1000   1500

750   1000

500

250   500

0   0

1:36 000 000

© Collins Bartholomew Ltd

NORTHWEST AFRICA

20° A 10°

1

Madeira
(Portugal)
FUNCHAL

A T L A N T I C
O C E A N

30°

SPAIN
Gibraltar
Málaga Almería Cartage
Ché
Strait Gibraltar (UK)
Tangier Ceuta (Spain) Mostaganem
Larache (Tanger) Tétouan Oran
Ksar el Kebir Sidi Melilla Sidi Bel
Ben Slimane Taounate Oujda Abbès Saïda
RABAT Kacem Tlemcen
Casablanca Meknès Fès (Fez) Taza Taourirt
El Jadida Oued Hauts Plateaux Atlas
Settat Khouribga Zem Bou Arfa Baya
Safi Beni Mellal Ain Sefra
El Kelaâ Marrakech Haut Atlas (High Atlas) ATLAS MOUNTAINS
des Srarhna Jbel Er
Essaouira Toubkal Rachidia Figuig (Sahar
4167 Béchar Grand Erg
Taroudannt Ouarzazate Abadla Occidenta
Agadir Anti Atlas Zagora Beni-
Tiznit Abbès El Homr
Santa Sidi Ifni Guelmine Tabelbala Timimou
La Palma Cruz de Lanzarote Hammada du Drâa Ksabi Plateau
Pico del Tenerife Tan- Adrar Sbaa
La Gomera Teide Tenerife Fuerteventura Tan Erg Sbaa
El Hierro 3718 807 Jandia Iabès ALGE
Gran Es Semara Bordj Flye
Canary Islands LAS PALMAS Canaria Aïn Ste-Marie Reggane Aoulef In S
(Islas Canarias) DE GRAN Ben Tili El Eglab
(Spain) CANARIA LAÂYOUNE Al Mahbas Chenachane Sebkha Azzel Sebk
Boujdour Tindouf Matti Meker

2
Galtat Chegga
Skaymat Zemmour Bir
Ad Dakhla Mogrein S
Tropic of Cancer El Hammâmi A A Erg Iguidi Erg Chech Taoudenni Tanezrouft Oued Ilarh
WESTERN Tiguesmat El Haus
SAHARA Zouérat OURÂNE Taoudenni Bordj
Awserd Fdérik Aouk Post Mokhtar
Tichla Choûm S Weygand
Nouâdhibou Guelb er Richât Adrar N
485 Adrar des
Atâr Maqteïr Araouane Aguelhok Ifôghas
Akchâr Kidal
Nouâmghâr Akjoujt Azaouâd
MAURITANIA

20°

NOUAKCHOTT Sebkhet Dhar Tichît M A L I
Te-n-Dghâmcha Tidjikja Tichît Anéfis
Boutilimit Moudjéria Dhar
Tiguent Magta Lahjar HÔD Oualâta Araouane
Rosso Aleg Bogué Ayoûn el Irîgui Gourma-
Sénégal Kaédi Atroûs Oualâta Rharous Bourem
St-Louis Dagana Kiffa Néma Vallée du Tilemsi
Louga Linguère Mbout Timbedgha Bassikounou Niger Gao Ménaka
DAKAR Thiès Dara Matam Sélibabi Ballé Nara S Nampala Timbuktu Doro Ansongo
3 Mbour Fatick Kaffrine Yélimané Nioro Diéma Kogoni Mopti (Tombouctou) Hombori
SENEGAL Goudiri Kidira Diéma Douentza
Kaolack Tambacounda Kayes Boron Niono Ténenkou Bandiagara Gorom Filin
Gambia THE GAMBIA Bafoulabé Kolokani Massina Djenné Ouahigouya Gorom Tillabéri NIAM
BANJUL Georgetown Kita Koulikoro Ségou San Tougan Dori Doss
Brikama Sédhiou Kolda Kédougou Satadougou Kati BURKINA Kantcha
Ziguinchor Gabú BAMAKO Bla Koutiala Nouna Bogandé Diapag
GUINEA Bafatâ Koundara Kangaba Dioïla Mahou Koudougou Zorgho Gayeri Porga
BISSAU Gaoual Fouta Siguiri Bougouni Sikasso OUAGADOUGOU Fada-N'Gourma
BISSAU Buba Koubia Lac de Yanfolila Bobo- Manga Léo Pô Bawku BEN
Arquipélago Bolama Pita Labé Djallon Sélingué Kolondiéba Orodara Dioulasso Tenkodogo Natitingo
dos Bijagós Cacine Boké Dinguiraye Dabola Mandiana Kadiolo Lawra Bolgatanga Dapaong Djougo
4 Eria Dubréka Kindia Faranah Kankan Minirian Banfora Gaoua Wa GHANA Bassila
Kissidougou Kérouané Tehini Bimbila Sokodé
CONAKRY Port Loko Fessédougou Boundiali Korhogo Bouna Damongo Salaga Savalou
Lungi Makeni Magburaka Diana Tamale Kete Krachi
FREETOWN Sefadu Touba Mankono Katiola Bondoukou Yendi Krachi
SIERRA Bo Kenema Nzérékoré Séguéla Wenchi Atakpamé Abomey PORTO-N
LEONE Zorzor Lola CÔTE Bouaké Sunyani Techiman Mampong LOMÉ Aného La
Bonthe Zimmi Gbarnga D'IVOIRE Daoukro Kintampo Kumasi Kete Slave Coa
Robertsport Kakata YAMOUSSOUKRO Bongouanou Bekwai ACCRA
MONROVIA Harbel LIBERIA Daloa Divo Obuasi Tarkwa Winneba of Ben
Buchanan Zwedru Tiassalé Adzopé Cape Coast
River Cess Tapeta Gagnoa Abengourou Kofondua
Greenville Lakota Abidjan Sekondi Axim Bigh
Barclayville Sassandra Grand- Cape Gold Coast
Harper San-Pédro Lahou Three Points
Cape Palmas Tabou

G U L F O F G U I N E A

METRES
FEET

5000 16404
3000 9843
2000 6562
1000 3281
500 1640
200 656
0 / 0
Land below sea level
200 656
4000 13124
6000 19686

Lambert Azimuthal Equal Area Projection

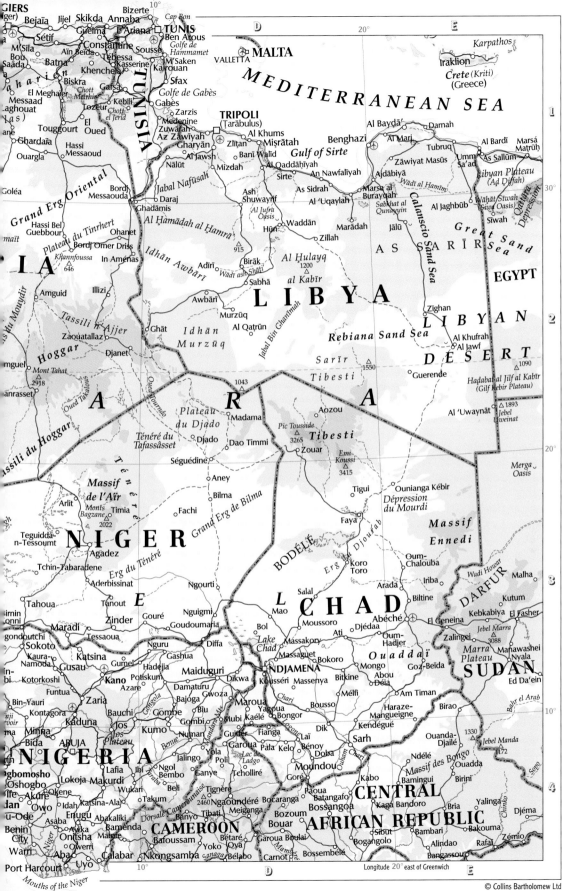

ALGIERS
(Alger)
Bejaïa
Jijel
Skikda
Annaba
Bizerte
Cap Bon
10°
Sétif
Guelma
l'Ariana
TUNIS
M'Sila
Constantine
Sousse
Ben Arous
Aïn Beïda
Tebessa
Batna
Kasserine
M'Saken
Golfe de
Hammamet
VALLETTA
MALTA
Bou
Khenchela
Kairouan
Saâda
Biskra
Gafsa
Sfax
Golfe de Gabès
El Meghaïer
Chott
Melrhir
Medenine
Gabès

MEDITERRANEAN SEA

Karpathos
Iraklion
Crete (Kriti)
(Greece)

Messaad
Laghouat
(as)
El Oued
Touggourt
Ghardaïa
Hassi
Messaoud
Ouargla
Goléa
maït

Tozeur
Chott
el Jerid
Kebili
Zarzis
Zuwārah
TRIPOLI
(Tarābulus)
Al Khums
Zlitan
Mişrātah
Benghazi
Al Bayḍā'
Darnah
Al Marj
Tubruq
Al Bardī
Marsá
Maţrūḥ
Az Zāwiyah
Gharyān
Al Jawsh
Mizdah
Sirte
An Nawfalīyah
Marsá al
Burayqah
Ajdābiyā
Zāwiyat Masūs
Umm
Sa'ad
As Sallūm
Libyan Plateau
(Ad Diffah)

Grand Erg Oriental
Hassi Bel
Guebbour
Bordj
Messaouda
Ghadāmis
Daraj
Nālūt
Al Qaddāḥīyah
As Sidrah
Al 'Uqaylah
Sabkhat
al Qunayyin
Al Jaghbūb
Wahāt Sīwah
(Siwa Oasis)
Qattara
Depression
30°

Plateau du Tinrhert
Bordj Omer Driss
Ohanet
In Amenas
Al Ḥamādah al Ḥamrā'
Al Jufra
Oasis
Waddān
Ghadāmis
Marādah
Jālū
Sīwah
915
TUNISIA
Khannfoussa
646
Idhān Awbārī
Adīrī
Sabhā
Birāk
Wadi ash Shāţi
Al Hulayq
1200
al Kabīr
Zillah
Hūn
As SARĪR
Calanscio Sand Sea
Great Sand Sea
EGYPT

Amguid
Illizi
Awbārī
Murzūq
Jabal Bin Ghanīmah
Zīghan
Al Qaṭrūn
Rebiana Sand Sea
Al Khufrah
Al Jawf
2°
LIBYA
LIBYAN

Tassili n'Ajjer
Zaouatallaz
Ghāt
Idhān
Murzūq
Sarīr
1550
Guerende
Hadabat al Jilf al Kabīr
(Gilf Kebir Plateau)
DESERT

Hoggar
Mont Tahat
2918
Djanet
Oued Takalous
1043
Tibesti
1090
Al 'Uwaynāt
1893
Jebel
Uweinat
3088

anrasset
Oued Tourndo
Plateau
du Djado
Madama
Aozou
A

Tassili du Hoggar
Ténéré du
Tafassâsset
Djado
Dao Timmi
Séguédine
Pic Toussidé
3265
Zouar
Tibesti
Emi
Koussi
3415
Ounianga Kébir
Dépression
du Mourdi
Merga
Oasis
20°

Massif
de l'Aïr
Aney
Bilma
Tigui
Massif
Ennedi

Arlit
Monts
Bagzane
2022
Timia
Fachi
Grand Erg de Bilma
Faya

Teguidda-
n-Tessoumt
NIGER
Agadez
Koro
Toro
BODÉLÉ
Erg du Djourâb
Oum-
Chalouba
Iriba
Wadi Howar
Malha
DARFUR
Kutum
3°

Tchin-Tabaradene
Aderbissinat
Erg du Ténéré
Salal
Biltine
El Geneina
El Fasher
Kebkabiya

Tahoua
Tânout
E
Nguigmi
Mao
Arada
Abéché
Zalingei
Jebel Marra
3088
Manawashei

Zinder
Gouré
Goudoumaria
Bol
Moussoro
Ati
Djédaa
Oum-
Hadjer
Goz-Beïda
Marra
Plateau
Nyala
SUDAN

Maradi
Tessaoua
Nguru
Diffa
Massakory
Mongo
Abou
Déïa
Am Timan
Ed Da'ein

Sokoto
Katsina
Gumel
Hadejia
Massaguet
Bokoro
Bitkine
Massenya
Mélfi
CHAD

Kaura-
Namoda
Gusau
Kotorkoshi
Azare
Maiduguri
Dikwa
NDJAMENA
Kousséri
Chari
Bousso
Haraze-
Mangueigne
Birao

Funtua
Zaria
Bauchi
Gombe
Gwoza
Maroua
Yagoua
Bongor
Dik
Kendégué
Ouanda-
Djalé
1330
Jebel Manda
172
10°

Bin-Yauri
Kontagora
Kaduna
Jos
Jos
Plateau
Kumo
Numan
Mubi
Kaélé
Fianga
Laï
Bénoy
Sarh
Ndélé
Ouadda

Minna
Bida
ABUJA
Lafia
Gombi
Guider
Garoua
Pala
Kelo
Doba
Moundou
Goré
Kabo
Massif des Bongo
Birini

NIGERIA
Makurdi
Wukari
Ngol
Poli
Tcholliré
Bocaranga
Batangafo
Kaga Bandoro
Bria
Yalinga

gbomosho
Oshogbo
Akure
Lokoja
Okene
Idah
Katsina-Ala
Takum
2460
Ngaoundéré
Meiganga
Tignère
Tibati
Bozoum
Bossangoa
Bambari
Bakouma
Djéma

Jan
ife
Owo
Enugu
Abakaliki
Banyo
Bétaré Oya
Bouar
CENTRAL
Sibut
Bangolgolo
Alindao
Rafaï

u-Ode
Benin
City
Asaba
Awka
Onitsha
Owerri
CAMEROON
Bafoussam
Yoko
Garoua Boulaï
Bozoum
AFRICAN REPUBLIC
Bamingui
Bossembélé
Warri
Aba
Calabar
Nkongsamba
Bélabo
Carnot
Bogangolo
Bangassou

Port Harcourt
Uyo
Mouths of the Niger
10°
Longitude 20° east of Greenwich
© Collins Bartholomew Ltd

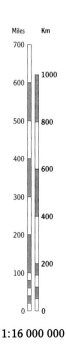

Miles   Km
700
1000
600
500   800
400   600
300
200   400
100   200
0   0

1:16 000 000

NORTHEAST AFRICA

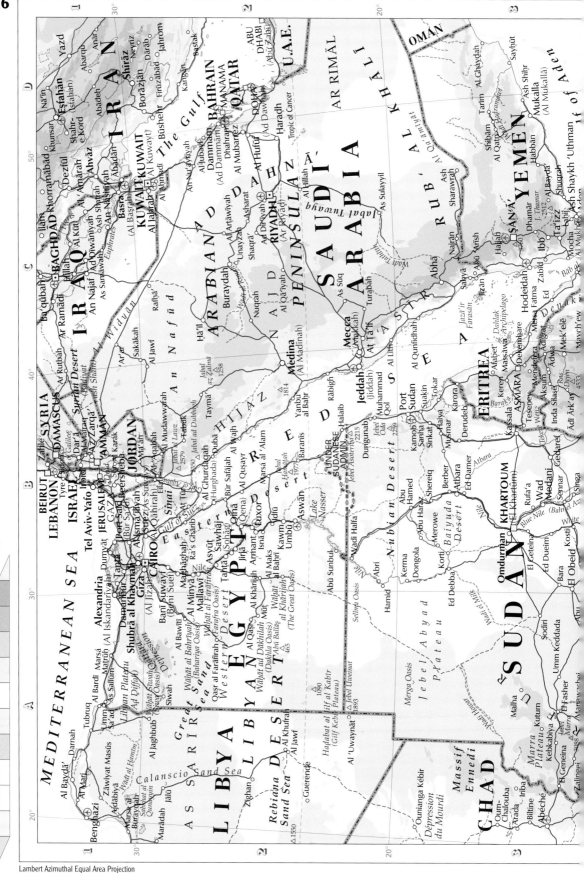

METRES
FEET

5000	16404
3000	9843
2000	6562
1000	3281
500	1640
200	656
0	0
	Land below sea level
200	656
4000	13124
6000	19686

Lambert Azimuthal Equal Area Projection

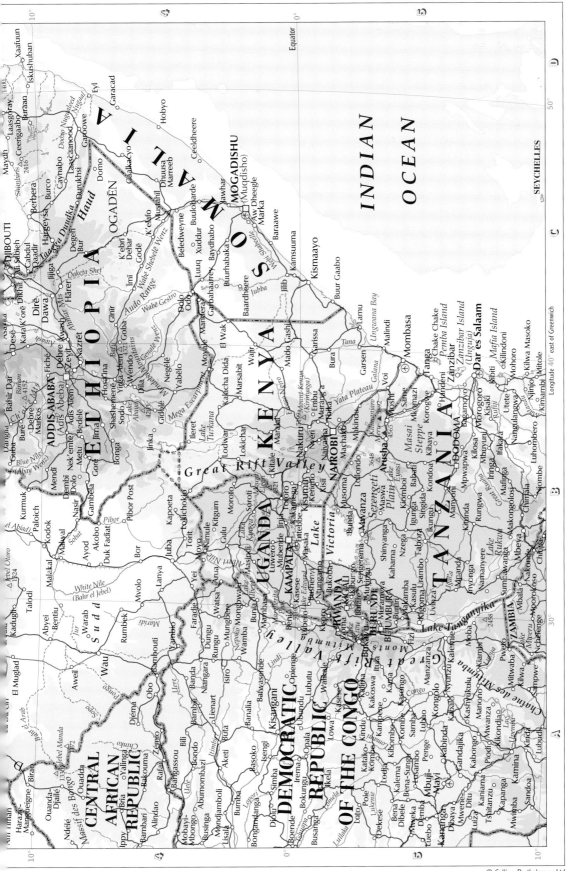

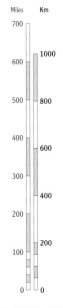

1:16 000 000

© Collins Bartholomew Ltd

CENTRAL AFRICA

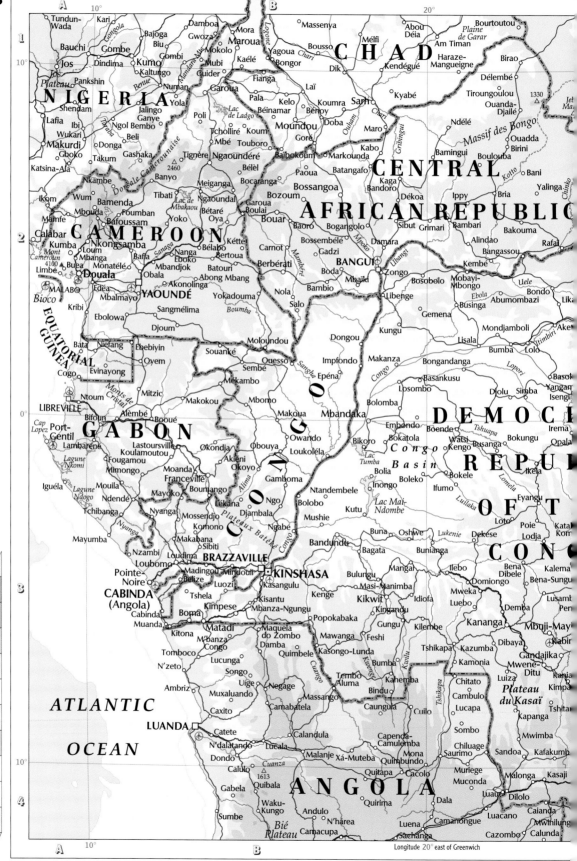

METRES
FEET

5000	16404
3000	9843
2000	6562
1000	3281
500	1640
200	656
0	0

Land below sea level

200	656
4000	13124
6000	19686

Lambert Azimuthal Equal Area Projection

Longitude 20° east of Greenwich

CHAD

CENTRAL AFRICAN REPUBLIC

NIGERIA

CAMEROON

EQUATORIAL GUINEA

GABON

CONGO

DEMOCRATIC REPUBLIC OF THE CONGO

CABINDA (Angola)

ANGOLA

ATLANTIC OCEAN

SUDAN

Da'ein
Babanusa
El Muglad
Kadugli
Talodi
Heiban
Jebel Otoro 1324
Kurmuk
Bure
Chok'ē Mts
Dembech'a
Birhan 4152
Kara K'orē

Sumeih
Abyei
Malakal
Kodok
Paloich
Mendī
Nek'emtē
ADDIS ABABA
(Ādīs Ābeba)
Debre Markos
Debre Sīna
Fichē
Āk'ak'ī Beseka
Awash
Ahmar Mts
Debre Zeyit
Āsbe Teferi

Raga
Aweil
Gogrial
Warab
Jur (Bahr el Jebel)
Daga Post
Dembī Dolo
Bedelē
Giyon
Adis Alem
Nazrēt
Āwash

Sopo
Wau
Tonj
Ayod
Akobo
Nasir
Gambēla
Gorē
Metu
Āgaro
Jima
Hosa'ina
Āsela

ETHIOPIA

Bo River Post
Rumbek
Yirol
Bor
Pibor Post
Veveno
Maji
Jinka
Shashemenē
Sodo
Āwasa
Bonga
Yirga Alem
Wendo
Mendebo Mountains
Goba
Batu 4321
Gīnīr

Mboki
Obo
Tambura
Bambouti
Maridi
Juba
Kapoeta
Lokichokio
Ch'ew Bahir
Īleret
Mēga
Mandera
Yabēlo
Negēlē
Filtu

UGANDA **KENYA** **SOMALIA**

TANZANIA

ZAMBIA

MOZAMBIQUE

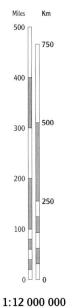

1:12 000 000

© Collins Bartholomew Ltd

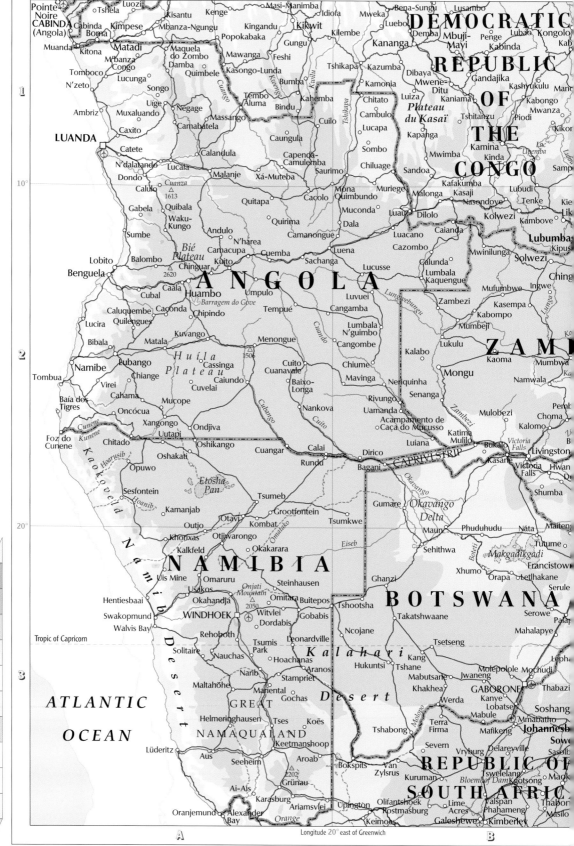

Pointe-Noire
CABINDA (Angola)
Cabinda
Boma
Muanda
Kitona
Matadi
M'banza Congo
Tomboco
Lucunga
N'zeto
Songo
Uíge
Ambriz
Muxaluando
Negage
Caxito

LUANDA

Catete
N'dalatando
Dondo
Calulo
Gabela
Quibala
Waku-Kungo
Sumbe

Lobito
Balombo
Benguela

Lobito
Cubal
Caala
Huambo
Caluquembe
Caconda
Quilengues
Lucira
Matala
Bibala
Namibe
Lubango
Chiange
Tombua
Virei
Cahama
Baía dos Tigres
Oncócua
Foz do Cunene
Chitado
Opuwo
Sesfontein
Kamanjab

Tshela
Luozi
Kisantu
Kenge
Kimpese
Mbanza-Ngungu
Kingandu
Kikwit
Maquela do Zombo
Mawanga
Damba
Quimbele
Kasongo-Lunda
Feshi
Tembo Aluma
Bumba
Bindu
Camabatela
Massango
Caungula

Masi-Manimba
Idiofa
Mweka
Bena-Sungu
Lusambo
Kikwit
Kilembe
Kananga
Demba
Mbuji-Mayi
Penge
Luebo

Calandula
Xá-Muteba
Malanje
Lucala
Quitapa
Quirima
Andulo
N'harea
Camacupa
Cuemba
Koito
Chinguar
Sachanga
Cacolo
Mona Quimbundo
Muconda
Dala

Capenda-Camulemba
Saurimo
Chiluage
Sombo
Luena
Lucusse
Calunda

ANGOLA

Bié Plateau
Umpulo
Tempué
Cangamba
Luvuei
Lumbala N'guimbo
Cangombe
Menongue
Cuito Cuanavale
Baixo-Longa
Mavinga
Neriquinha
Senanga
Rivungo
Uamanda
Acampamento de Caça do Mucusso
Katima Mulilo
Luiana

Huíla Plateau
Cassinga
Caiundo
Cuvelai
Mucope
Xangongo
Ondjiva
Uutapi
Oshikango
Oshakati
Chitado

NAMIBIA

Etosha Pan
Tsumeb
Otavi
Grootfontein
Tsumkwe
Kombat
Outjo
Otjiwarongo
Khorixas
Kalkfeld
Okakarara
Uis Mine
Omaruru
Steinhausen
Onjati Mountain
Okahandja
Omitara
Buitepos
Hentiesbaai
Usakos
WINDHOEK
Witvlei
Dordabis
Gobabis
Swakopmund
Walvis Bay
Rehoboth
Tsumis Park
Leonardville
Solitaire
Nauchas
Hoachanas
Aranos
Maltahöhe
Mariental
Stampriet
Gochas
Helmeringhausen
Tses
Koës
Keetmanshoop
Lüderitz
Aus
Seeheim
Aroab
Grünau
Ai-Ais
Karasburg
Oranjemund
Alexander Bay
Ariamsvlei
Upington

ATLANTIC OCEAN

Tropic of Capricorn

GREAT NAMAQUALAND

BOTSWANA

Gumare
Okavango Delta
Maun
Phuduhudu
Nata
Ghanzi
Xhumo
Orapa
Tetlhakane
Francistown
Tshootsha
Takatshwaane
Serowe
Ncojane
Mahalapye
Tsetseng
Kalahari
Kang
Tshane
Mabutsane
Jwaneng
Molepolole
Mochudi
Hukuntsi
GABORONE
Kanye
Thabazi
Desert
Werda
Lobatse
Soshang
Mabule
Mmabatho
Terra Firma
Tshabong
Mafikeng
Johannesb
Sow
Bokspits
Van Zylsrus
Severn
Vryburg
Delareyville
REPUBLIC OF SOUTH AFRIC
Kuruman
Sweleleng
Kgotsong
Maok
Olifantshoek
Lime Acres
Valspan
Phahameng
Thabon
Postmasburg
Galeshewe
Kimberley
Keimoes

DEMOCRATIC REPUBLIC OF THE CONGO

Kananga
Dibaya
Kamonia
Luiza
Mwene-Ditu
Plateau du Kasaï
Tshitanzu
Gandajika
Kabongo
Mwanza
Piodi
Kikor
Kashyukulu
Kabongo
Kamina
Kinda
Samp
Sandoa
Kafakumba
Kasaji
Muriege
Nasondoye
Lubudi
Tenke
Kolwezi
Kambove
Kie
Caianda
Mwinilunga
Solwezi
Lubumba
Kipusi
Lumbala Kaquengue
Mufumbwe
Ingwe
Ching
Zambezi
Kasempa
Kabompo
Mumbeji
Lukulu
ZAMB
Kalabo
Kaoma
Mumbwa
Mongu
Namwala
Mulobezi
Choma
Kalomo
Peml
Senanga
Zambezi
Katima Mulilo
Bukalo
Victoria Falls
Kasane
Livingston
Victoria Falls
Hwan
Shumba

CAPRIVI STRIP
Rundu
Bagani
Dirico

Cuangar
Calai

Lambert Azimuthal Equal Area Projection

METRES / FEET

METRES	FEET
5000	16404
3000	9843
2000	6562
1000	3281
500	1640
200	656
0	0

Land below sea level

200	656
4000	13124
6000	19686

1:12 000 000

© Collins Bartholomew Ltd

REPUBLIC OF SOUTH AFRICA

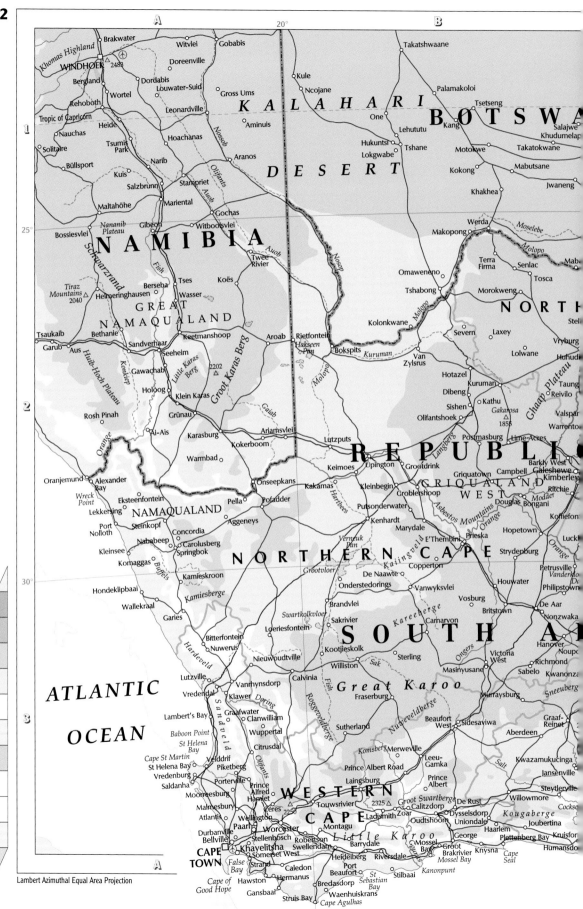

METRES FEET

METRES	FEET
5000	16404
3000	9843
2000	6562
1000	3281
500	1640
200	656
0	0
Land below sea level	
200	656
4000	13124
6000	19686

Lambert Azimuthal Equal Area Projection

NAMIBIA

Brakwater, Witvlei, Gobabis, Takatshwaane, Khomas Highland, WINDHOEK, 2483, Doreenville, Kule, Palamakoloi, Tsetseng, Bergland, Dordabis, Ncojane, One, Lehututu, Kang, Salajwe, Khudumelap, Rehoboth, Louwater-Suid, Gross Ums, Hukuntsi, Tshane, Motokwe, Takatokwane, Wortel, Tropic of Capricorn, Heide, Leonardville, Aminuis, Lokgwabe, Kokong, Mabutsane, Nauchas, Hoachanas, Jwaneng, Solitaire, Tsumis Park, Narib, Aranos, Khakhea, Büllsport, Kuis, Salzbrunn, Stampriet, Maltahöhe, Marleental, Gochas, Werda, Moselebe, Bossiesvlei, Nananib Plateau, Gibeon, Witbooisvlei, Makopong, Terra Firma, Senlac, Mab, Tiraz Mountains 2040, Berseba, Tses, Koës, Auob, Nosop, Omaweneo, Tshabong, Morokweng, Tosca, Helmeringhausen, Wasser, Kolonkwane, Severn, Laxey, Vryburg, Tsaukaib, Bethanie, Seeheim, Keetmanshoop, Aroab, Rietfontein, Hakseen Pan, Bokspits, Kuruman, Van Zylsrus, Lolwane, Huhudi, Garub, Aus, Gawachab, Little Karas Berg, 2202, Hotazel, Kuruman, Taung, Reivilo, Holoog, Klein Karas, Gaiab, Dibeng, Kathu, Gakarosa 1855, Valspar, Rosh Pinah, Grünau, Ariamsvlei, Sishen, Olifantshoek, Warrenton, Oranjemund, Alexander Bay, Karasburg, Kokerboom, Lutzputs, Postmasburg, Lime-Acres, Wreck Point, Eksteenfontein, Warmbad, Keimoes, Upington, Grootdrink, Griquatown, Campbell, Galeshewe, Kimberley, Lekkersing, Onseepkans, Kakamas, Kleinbegin, Groblershoop, Douglas, Bongani, Ritchie, Port Nolloth, Steinkopf, Pella, Pofadder, Putsonderwater, Asbestos Mountains, Hopetown, Koffiefon, Nababeep, Concordia, Aggeneys, Kenhardt, Marydale, Priska, Luck, Kleinsee, Carolusberg, Springbok, Verneuk Pan, E'Thembini, Strydenburg, Petrusville, Vanderklo, Komaggas, Kamieskroon, De Naawte, Copperton, Houwater, Philipstown, Hondeklipbaai, Grootvloer, Onderstedorings, Vanwyksvlei, Vosburg, De Aar, Nonzwaka, Wallekraal, Garies, Brandvlei, Kareeberge, Britstown, Swartkolkvloer, Sakrivier, Carnarvon, Hanover, Noupo, Bitterfontein, Loeriesfontein, Sterling, Victoria West, Richmond, Nuwerus, Kootjieskolk, Williston, Masinyusane, Sabelo, Kwanonza, Nieuwoudtville, Calvinia, Fraserburg, Murraysburg, Sneeuberg, Lutzville, Vanrhynsdorp, Great Karoo, Graaf-Reinet, Vredendal, Klawer, Dering, Nuweveldberge, Beaufort West, Sidesaviwa, Aberdeen, Sandveld, Graafwater, Clanwilliam, Sutherland, Kwazamukucinga, Lambert's Bay, Wuppertal, Komsberg, Merweville, Leeu-Gamka, Jansenville, Baboon Point, St Helena Bay, Citrusdal, Prince Albert Road, Prince Albert, Steytlerville, Cape St Martin, Velddrif, Piketberg, Laingsburg, Willowmore, St Helena Bay, Vredenburg, Porterville, Prince Alfred Hamlet, Touwsrivier, 2325, De Rust, Calitzdorp, Joubertina, Saldanha, Moorreesburg, Ceres, 2250, Ladismith, Zoar, Oudtshoorn, Dysselsdorp, Uniondale, Kruisfon, Malmesbury, Wellington, Montagu, Groot Swartberg, Haarlem, Plettenberg Bay, Cocksc, Atlantis, Durbanville, Paarl, Worcester, Little Karoo, George, Bellville, Stellenbosch, Robertson, Swellendam, Barrydale, Riversdale, Mossel Bay, Knysna, Cape Seal, CAPE TOWN, Khayelitsha, Somerset West, Heidelberg, Groot Brakrivier, Humansdo, False Bay, Strand, Caledon, Port Beaufort, Mossel Bay, St Sebastian Bay, Cape of Good Hope, Hawston, Hermanus, Bredasdorp, Stilbaai, Kanonpunt, Gansbaai, Waenhuiskrans, Struis Bay, Cape Agulhas

KALAHARI DESERT

BOTSWA

NORTH

REPUBLIC

GRIQUALAND WEST

NORTHERN CAPE

SOUTH A

WESTERN CAPE

ATLANTIC OCEAN

NAMAQUALAND

GREAT NAMAQUALAND

Schwarzrand, Fish, Konkiep, Huib-Hoch Plateau, Orange, Buffels, Hardeveld, Kamiesberge, Olifants, Sandveld, Rossveldberge, Fish, Groot Karas Berg, Nossob, Auob, Molopo, Langberg, Chaap Plateau, Modder, Asbestos Mountains, Orange, Kaiingveld, Ongers, Sak, Salt, Kougaberge

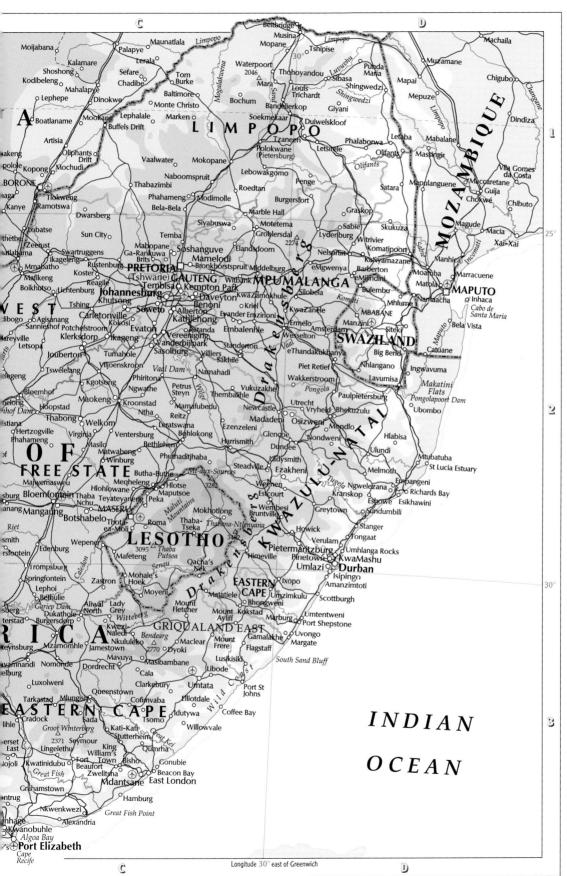

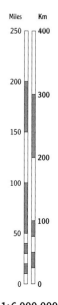

© Collins Bartholomew Ltd

1:6 000 000

NORTH AMERICA

ICELAND

Arctic Circle

70°

Jan Mayen (Nor.)

Denmark Strait

Ammassalik

Kong Frederik VI Kyst

Kong Christian IX Land

Kong Christian X Land

Greenland (Denmark)

Kong Frederik VIII Land

Nuuk

Sisimiut

Davis Strait

Labrador Sea

NEWFOUNDLAND AND LABRADOR

St John's
C. Race
Newfoundland
Gulf of St Lawrence
Cabot Strait
Île d'Anticosti
St Pierre and Miquelon (Fr.)
PRINCE EDWARD ISLAND
Charlottetown
NOVA SCOTIA
NEW BRUNSWICK
Fredericton

QUÉBEC

Québec

Montréal

Baffin Bay

Ellesmere Island

Dundas

Baffin Island

Iqaluit

Hudson Strait

Foxe Basin

Smallwood Res.

Labrador

Chisasibi

ONTARIO

Queen Elizabeth Islands

Parry Islands

Melville Island

Somerset Island

Prince of Wales Island

Devon Island

Victoria Island

Boothia Pen.

NUNAVUT

Repulse Bay

Southampton I.

Coats I.

Mansel I.

Hudson Bay

Churchill

Belcher Is.

Inukjuak

Kuujjuaq

MANITOBA

Thunder Bay

Lake Superior

MICHI

Winnipeg

MINNESOTA

St Paul

WISC

Banks Island

Amundsen Gulf

Sachs Harbour

Bathurst Inlet

NORTHWEST TERRITORIES

Great Bear Lake

Yellowknife

Great Slave Lake

Lake Athabasca

SASKATCHEWAN

Lake Winnipeg

Regina

Saskatoon

NORTH DAKOTA

Bismarck

SOUTH DAKOTA

Rapid City

Pie

ARCTIC OCEAN

Beaufort Sea

Mackenzie

Inuvik

YUKON TERRITORY

Whitehorse

Peace

ALBERTA

Edmonton

Calgary

CANADA

BRITISH COLUMBIA

Prince George

Kamloops

ROCKY MOUNTAIN

MONTANA

Helena

Billings

WYOMING

IDAHO

Boise

MinuteMt McKinley 6194

Barrow

U.S.A.

ALASKA

Yukon

Fairbanks

Anchorage

Nome

Arctic Circle

RUS. FED.

Bering Str.

St Lawrence I.

St Matthew I.

Nunivak I.

Pribilof Is.

Bering Sea

Aleutian Islands

Alaska Pen.

Kodiak I.

Gulf of Alaska

Juneau

Alexander Archipelago

Queen Charlotte Islands

Vancouver Island

Victoria

Vancouver

Seattle

Olympia

WASHINGTON

Portland

Salem

OREGON

Columbia

Seattle

Salt Lake City

Reno

Carson City

Sacramento

San Francisco

CALI

1:32 000 000

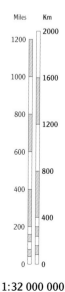

CANADA

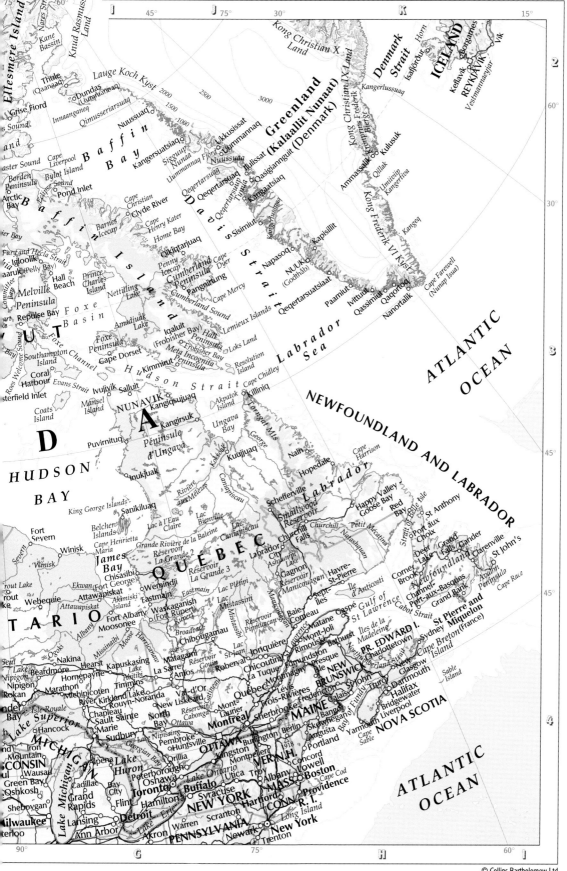

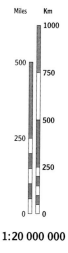

1:20 000 000

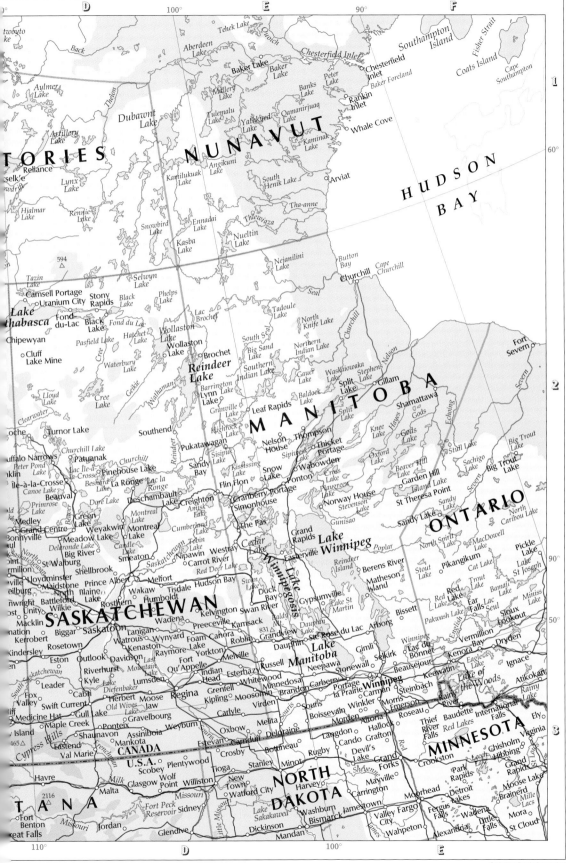

1:9 600 000

© Collins Bartholomew Ltd

CANADA West map labels:

TORIES

NUNAVUT

HUDSON BAY

MANITOBA

ONTARIO

SASKATCHEWAN

MINNESOTA

NORTH DAKOTA

TANA

CANADA / U.S.A.

Miles / Km

400
300
200
100
0

600
400
200
0

100° · 90° · 60° · 1 · 2 · 3 · 50° · 90° · 110° · 100°

CANADA East

HUDSON BAY

NUNAVUT

MANITOBA

ONTARIO

QUÉ...

Belcher Islands

James Bay

Lake Superior

Lake Michigan

Lake Huron

Lake Erie

Lake Ontario

MICHIGAN

WISCONSIN

ILLINOIS

INDIANA

OHIO

NEW YORK

VERM...

CANADA
U.S.A.

Cape Churchill
North Knife Lake
Churchill
Puvirnituq
Gilmour Island
Ottawa Islands
Lac Payne
Lac Tasiat
Tasialuf
Arnaud
Fariba
Stephens Lake
Nelson
Shamattawa
Gods
Fort Severn
Hopewell Islands
Inukjuak
Lac Le Roy
Lac Ned...
Knee Lake
Hayes
Gillam
Echoing
North Belcher Islands
King George Islands
Nastapoka Islands
Lac Chavigny
Lac Bacqueville
Rivière aux Fe...
Gods Lake
Severn
Sanikiluaq
Lac Minto
Nastapoca
Iles des Loups Marins
Stull Lake
Winisk
Sleeper Islands
Lac Guillaume-Delisle
Lac à l'Eau Claire
Sachigo Lake
Sandy Lake
Flaherty Island
Lac Burton
Réservoir La Grande 2
Réservoir La Grande 4
North Spirit Lake
Big Trout Lake
Kasabonika Lake
Cape Henrietta Maria
Long Island
Kuujjuarapik (Poste-de-la-Baleine)
Grande Rivière de la Baleine
Lac Bienville
Stout Lake
Pikangikum
MacDowell Lake
Webequie
Winisk Lake
Wunnummin
Ekwan
Chisasibi (Fort George)
North Twin Island
Réservoir La Grande 3
Réservoir Opinaca
Sandy Lake
North Caribou Lake
Attawapiskat Lake
Attawapiskat
Akimiski Island
Radisson
Eastmain
Red Lake
Cat Lake
St Joseph Lake
Pickle Lake
Missisa Lake
Kapiskau
Fort Albany
South Twin Island
Wemindji
Pakwash Lake
Ear Falls
Bamaji Lake
Whitewater Lake
Ogoki Reservoir
Albany
Charlton Island
Eastmain
Vermilion Bay
Red Lake
Trout Lake
Miniss Lake
Savant Lake
Ogoki
Moosonee
Rupert
Réservoir Opinaca
Lac Mistassini
Kenora
Eagle Lake
Dryden
Sioux Lookout
Sturgeon Lake
Caribou Lake
Pledger Lake
Moose Factory
Rupert
Lac Evans
Broadback
Lake of the Woods
Ignace
Armstrong
Longlac
Nakina
Missinaibi
Moose River
Kesagami Lake
Nottaway
Lac Comencho
Lac Opataca
Mistissini
Fort Frances
Atikokan
Lake Nipigon
Beardmore
Otter Rapids
Hearst
Harricana
Lac au Goéland
Chibougamau
Rainy Lake
Thunder Bay
Nipigon
Terrace Bay
Long Lake
Kapuskasing
Hornepayne
Fraserdale
Lac Matagami
Lac Waswanipi
Grand Marais
Pigeon River
Isle Royale
Thunder Bay
St Ignace Island
Manitouwadge
Kabinakagami Lake
Smooth Rock Falls
Cochrane
Matagami
Lebel-sur-Quévillon
Réservoir Gouin
Dolbe
St-Félicien
Copper Harbor
Michipicoten Island
Marathon
Missinaibi Lake
Groundhog
Iroquois Falls
La Sarre
Lac Parent
Senneterre
St-Félicien
Roberv
Métabetch
Ashland
Gogebic Range
Houghton
Keweenaw Peninsula
Wawa
Michipicoten River
Foleyet
Timmins
Nighthawk Lake
Amos
Dolbe
Bruce Crossing
Hancock
Ishpeming
Batchawana Mountain
Chapleau
Kirkland Lake
Rouyn-Noranda
Malartic
Lac Simard
Réservoir Cabonga
Parent
La Tuque
Park Falls
Crystal Falls
Iron Mountain
Marquette
Newberry
Sault Sainte Marie
Ramsey Lake
New Liskeard
Englehart
Val-d'Or
Gatineau
Lac Kempt
Rhinelander
Merrill
Menominee
Escanaba
St Ignace
St Joseph I.
North Channel
Blind River
Sudbury
Temagami
Lac Kipawa
Réservoir Baskatong
Lac Dozois
St-Michel-des-Saints
Gr...
Wausau
Marinette
Shawano
Sturgeon Falls
North Bay
Mattawa
Maniwaki
Mt Tremblant
Shawinigan
Trois-Rivières
WISCONSIN
Green Bay
Menominee
Cheboygan
Petoskey
Espanola
Manitoulin Island
Manitowaning
Lake Nipissing
Ottawa
Deep River
Petawawa
Pembroke
Ste-Adèle
Joliette
Sor...
Asbe...
Wisconsin Rapids
Appleton
Oshkosh
Sheboygan
Alpena
Gaylord
Baymouth
Tobermory
Wikwemikong
Georgian Bay
South River
Huntsville
Barrys Bay
Bracebridge
Arnprior
Hull
Montreal
Salaberry-de-Valleyfield
Sherbr...
Portage
Fond du Lac
West Bend
Traverse City
Manistee
Cadillac
Grayling
Tawas City
Bruce Peninsula
Parry Sound
Owen Sound
Bancroft
Gravenhurst
Carleton Place
Smiths Falls
Cornwall
St-Jean...
Madison
Milwaukee
Grand Rapids
Muskegon
Ludington
Big Rapids
Mount Pleasant
Midland
Saginaw Bay
Port Elgin
Midland
Kincardine
Kawartha Lakes
Rideau Lake
Ogdensburg
Brockville
Massena
Plattsburgh
Lac Champlain
St John
New...
Waukesha
Racine
Rockford
Kenosha
Battle Creek
Saginaw
Bay City
Owosso
Flint
Port Huron
Goderich
Barrie
Orillia
Lindsay
Peterborough
Belleville
Kingston
Watertown
Burlington
Montpelier
Elgin
Waukegan
Lansing
Pontiac
Hanover
Oshawa
Cobourg
Lowville
Oneida
VERM...
Aurora
Chicago
Kalamazoo
Livonia
Detroit
London
Stratford
Kitchener
Guelph
Toronto
Scarborough
Hamilton
Rochester
Oswego
Rome
Utica
Rutland
Lebanon
Glens Falls
Joliet
Ottawa
South Bend
Jackson
Ann Arbor
Windsor
St Thomas
Brantford
St Catharines
Buffalo
Batavia
Geneva
Syracuse
NEW YORK
Auburn
Schenectady
Troy
Albany
Pittsfield
Watseka
Gary
Michigan City
Elkhart
Adrian
Sylvania
Fort Wayne
Toledo
Lorain
Cleveland
Erie
Ashtabula
Dunkirk
Jamestown
Olean
Hornell
Corning
Ithaca
Cortland
Elmira
Binghamton
Oneonta
Worces...
Springfield
Pontiac
INDIANA
OHIO
Warren
Bradford
Sayre

METRES
FEET

METRES	FEET
5000	16404
3000	9843
2000	6562
1000	3281
500	1640
200	656
0	0

Land below sea level

200	656
4000	13124
6000	19686

Longitude 80° west of Greenwich

Lambert Azimuthal Equal Area Projection

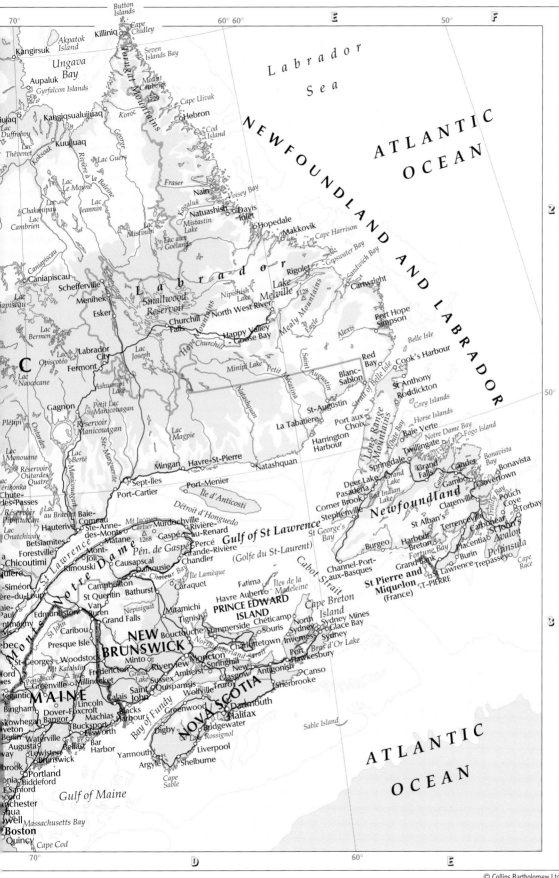

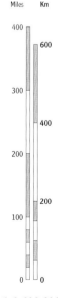

© Collins Bartholomew Ltd

1:9 600 000

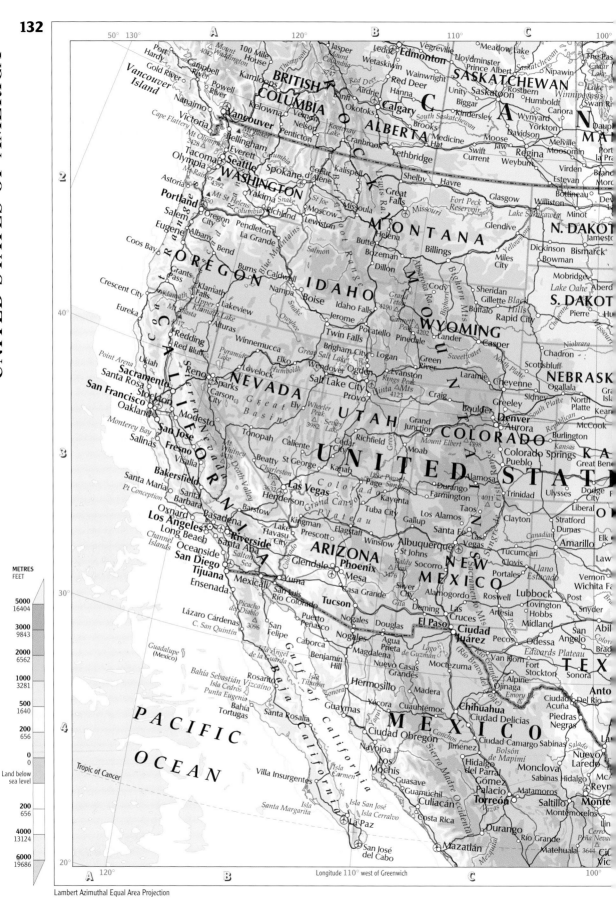

UNITED STATES OF AMERICA

PACIFIC OCEAN

METRES FEET

METRES	FEET
5000	16404
3000	9843
2000	6562
1000	3281
500	1640
200	656
0	0

Land below sea level

200	656
4000	13124
6000	19686

Lambert Azimuthal Equal Area Projection

Longitude 110° west of Greenwich

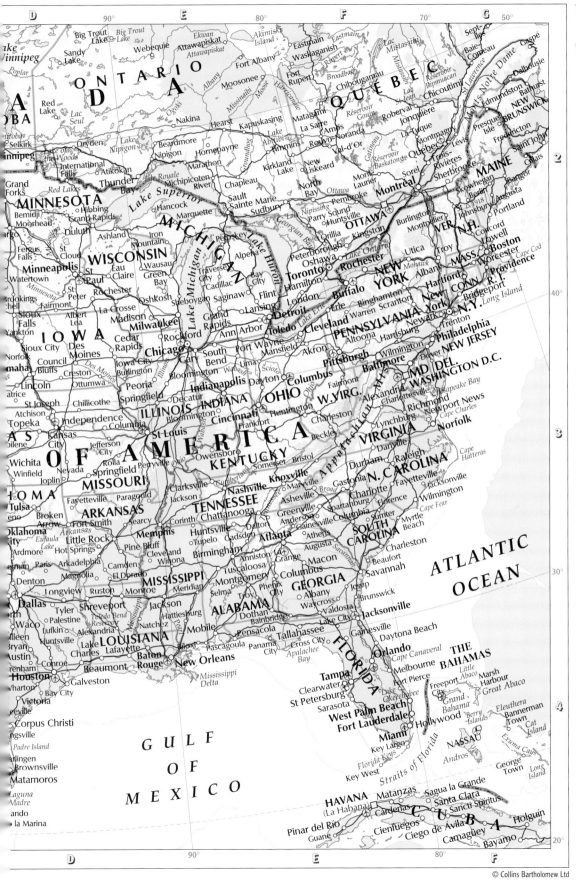

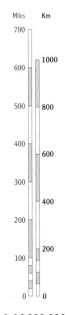

Miles | Km

700

600 | 1000

500 | 800

400 | 600

300 | 400

200 | 200

100

0 | 0

1:16 000 000

USA West

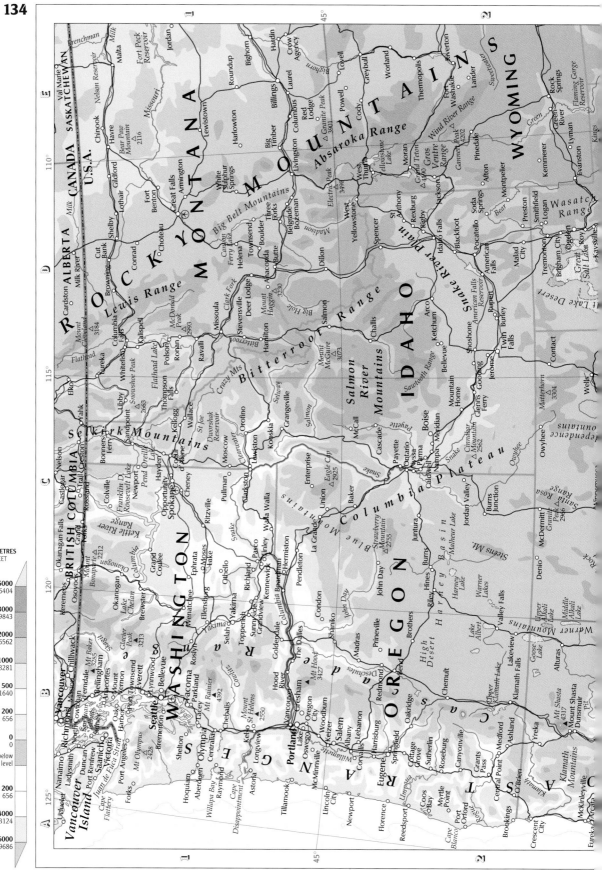

METRES
FEET

5000	16404
3000	9843
2000	6562
1000	3281
500	1640
200	656
0	0

Land below
sea level

200	656
4000	13124
6000	19686

Lambert Azimuthal Equal Area Projection

40°

COLORADO

Roan Plateau

Roosevelt
Duchesne

Gunnison

Grand Junction
Mount Peale
3877
Crescent Junction
Moab

NEW MEXICO

Monticello
Cortez
Shiprock
Gallup
Chinle
Ganado
Chambers
Winslow
Holbrook

St Johns
Springerville
Alpine
Baldy Peak
3476
Show Low
Snowflake
Clifton
Glenwood
Chiricahua Peak
2985
Willcox
Tombstone
Bisbee
Douglas

Blanding
Bluff
Kayenta
Many Farms
Polacca
Tuba City

Green River
San Juan

Colorado

Hanksville

Escalante

Lake Powell

Page
Kanab

Painted Desert

Humphreys Peak
3851
Flagstaff
Sedona
Camp Verde
Verde

Mogollon Plateau

Globe
Superior
Kearny
Safford
Mount Graham
3265
Benson
Sierra Vista
2881
Nogales

UTAH

Provo
Springville
Spanish Fork
American Fork
Utah Lake
Nephi
Mount Nebo
3623

Price
Mount Pleasant
Ephraim
Gunnison
Salina
Richfield
Fillmore
Delta
Beaver

Abajo Peak
3462

Delano Peak
3710

Sevier Lake

Escalante Desert

Richfield

Cedar City

Parowan

Hurricane

Washington
St George

Confusion Range

Milford

Indian Peak
2982

Wheeler Peak
3982

Grand Canyon

Grand Canyon

Williams
Bill Williams Mountain
2824
Prescott
Chino Valley
Bagdad
Yarnell
Wickenburg

ARIZONA

Prescott Valley

Seligman

Phoenix
Glendale
Mesa
Peoria
Tempe
Chandler
Avondale
Buckeye
Gila Bend
Casa Grande
Florence
Eloy
Marana
Mount Wrightson
2881

Tucson
Green Valley
Sells
Ajo
Lukeville

NEVADA

Currie
Eureka
Currant

McGill
Ely

Pioche
Caliente

Alamo

Schell Creek Range

Egan Range

Great

Basin

Troy Peak
3443

Charleston Peak
3632

Las Vegas
Henderson
Boulder City

Overton

Black Mountains

Dolan Springs

Lake Mead

Virgin

Ruby Mts

Shoshone Mountains

Monitor Range

Mount Callaghan
3105
Austin
Mount Jefferson
3642

Eastgate

Tonopah

Goldfield

Coaldale

Death Valley Range
3366

Beatty

Shoshone

Indian Springs

Nipton

Baker

Ludlow

Amboy

Kingman

Mohave Mountains

Lake Havasu City

Needles

Bullhead City

Quartzsite

Parker

Colorado

Blythe

Twentynine Palms

Yucca Valley

Yuma
San Luis
Wellton
Yuma Desert

MEXICO

San Luis Río Colorado
Mexicali
Tecate
Rosarito

Kern

Barstow
Victorville
Hesperia

San Bernardino Mts

San Bernardino

Riverside

Palm Springs
La Quinta
Indio
Coachella

Salton Sea

Niland
Brawley
El Centro

Colorado Desert

Laguna Salada

CALIFORNIA

Reno
Sparks

Carson City
Gardnerville

Walker Lake

Hawthorne

Pyramid Lake

Fallon

Lovelock

Winnemucca

Battle Mountain

Stillwater Range

Carson Sink

Honey Lake
Janesville

Quincy

Paradise
Oroville
Yuba City

Red Bluff
Corning
Chico
Willows

Lake Almanor

Truckee
South Lake Tahoe
Lake Tahoe
Placerville
Auburn
Sonora

SIERRA

Mono Lake
Mammoth Lakes

Bishop

Independence

Lone Pine
Mt Whitney
4418
Owens Lake

Ridgecrest

Mojave Desert

Mojave

Lancaster
Palmdale

Santa Clarita

San Antonio

Chino

Ontario

Fontana

Hemet
Temecula

Escondido
Ramona
Santee
El Cajon

Oceanside
Carlsbad

Encinitas

Del Mar
Chula Vista

San Diego

Tijuana

Placerville
Arden Town
Sacramento
Davis
Vacaville
Fairfield
Napa
Vallejo
Concord
Berkeley
Oakland
Hayward
Fremont

Citrus Heights

Stockton

Lodi

Modesto
Turlock

Merced

Madera

Clovis
Selma
Dinuba
Hanford
Corcoran

Visalia
Tulare
Earlimart
Delano
Wasco

NEVADA

CALIFORNIA

Fresno

Kings

San Joaquin

Bakersfield
Mettler

California Aqueduct

Santa Maria

Lompoc
Point Conception
Goleta
Santa Barbara
Ventura
Oxnard

Los Angeles
Santa Monica
Hollywood
Pasadena
Torrance
Long Beach
Huntington Beach
Santa Ana
Anaheim

Simi Valley

San Francisco
San Mateo
Palo Alto
Santa Clara
San Jose
Sunnyvale
Los Baños
Gilroy

Santa Cruz
Watsonville
Marina
Monterey

Santa Rosa
Healdsburg
Sebastopol
Petaluma

Point Reyes

Monterey Bay

Salinas
Hollister
Soledad
King City
Paso Robles
Atascadero
Arroyo Grande
Grover Beach
San Luis Obispo
San Luis Obispo Bay

Salinas

Garberville
Cummings
Willits
Ukiah
Fort Bragg
Point Arena

Eel
Clear Lake

Sacramento Valley

San Miguel Island
Santa Rosa Island
Santa Cruz Island
Santa Catalina Island
San Clemente Island
San Nicolas Island

Channel Islands

PACIFIC

OCEAN

35°

110°

115°

120°

Longitude 120° west of Greenwich

1:6 400 000

© Collins Bartholomew Ltd

Miles	Km
250	400
200	300
150	200
100	100
50	
0	0

USA North Central

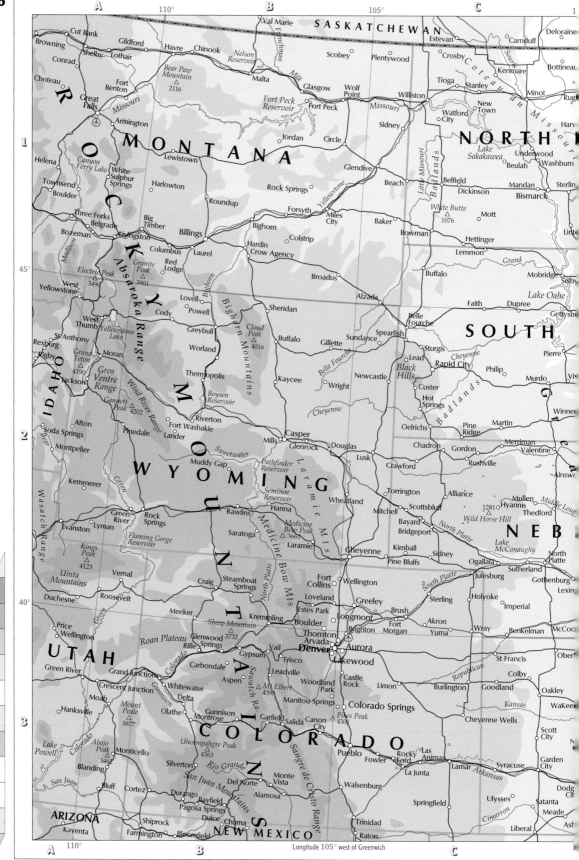

METRES
FEET

5000 16404

3000 9843

2000 6562

1000 3281

500 1640

200 656

0 0
Land below
sea level

200 656

4000 13124

6000 19686

Lambert Azimuthal Equal Area Projection

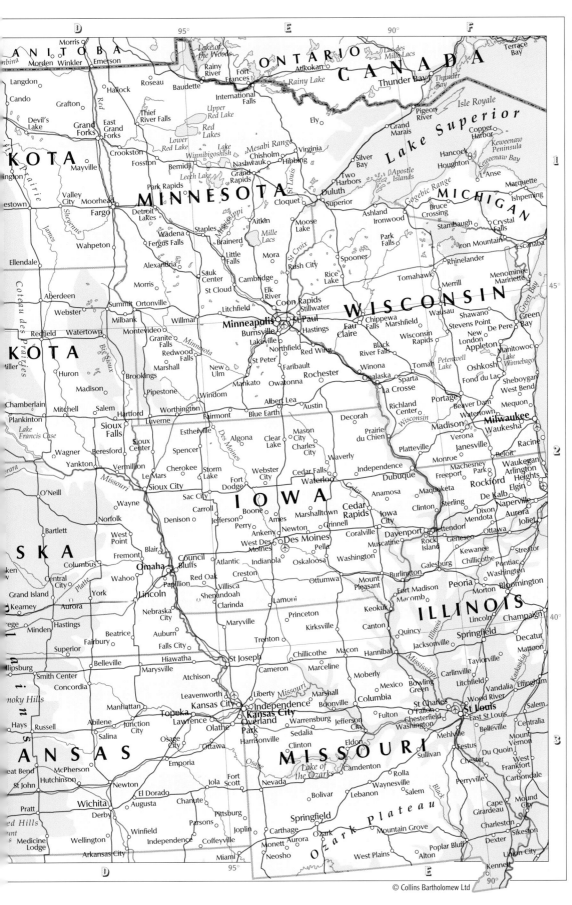

MANITOBA
Morris
Morden Winkler Emerson
bina
Langdon
Cando
Grafton
Devil's Lake
Grand Forks East Grand Forks
KOTA
Mayville
Crookston
Valley City Moorhead
stown
Fargo
Detroit Lakes
Wahpeton
Ellendale

ONTARIO
CANADA

Lake of the Woods
Rainy River
Fort Frances
Baudette
International Falls
Thief River Falls
Upper Red Lake
Red Lakes
Lower Red Lake
Bemidji
Fosston
Park Rapids
Leech Lake

Atikokan
Rainy Lake
Ely
Grand Marais

Des Mille Lacs
Thunder Bay
Thunder Bay

Pigeon River
Isle Royale

Lake Superior

Terrace Bay

Keweenaw Peninsula
Copper Harbor
Keweenaw Bay

KOTA
ington
Summit Ortonville
Aberdeen
Webster
Redfield Watertown
Milbank
Montevideo
KOTA
Huron
Madison
Brookings
Chamberlain
Mitchell
Salem
Hartford
Plankinton
Lake Francis Case
Sioux Falls
Wagner
Beresford
Yankton
Vermillion
O'Neill
Wayne
Norfolk
Bartlett
West Point
SKA
Columbus
Fremont
Central City
Grand Island
Kearney
Aurora
Minden Hastings
ege
Superior
Belleville

MINNESOTA
Mesabi Range
Chisholm Hibbing
Nashwauk
Grand Rapids
Lake Winnibigoshish
Virginia
Silver Bay
Two Harbors
Duluth
Superior

Hallock
Roseau

Hancock
Houghton
L'Anse
Marquette
Ishpeming

MICHIGAN
Ashland
Ironwood
Bruce Crossing
Stambaugh
Iron Mountain
Escanaba
Crystal Falls

1:6 400 000

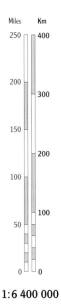

© Collins Bartholomew Ltd

USA Northeast

MINNESOTA

Ely
Virginia
Chisholm
Duluth
Cloquet
Superior

Two Harbors
Silver Bay
Apostle Islands
Grand Marais

Ashland
Ironwood
Park Falls
Spooner

St Croix
Rice Lake

Hastings
Chippewa Falls
Eau Claire
Marshfield
Black River Falls
Wisconsin Rapids
New London
Winona
Sparta
Onalaska
La Crosse

WISCONSIN

Tomahawk
Rhinelander
Merrill
Wausau
Shawano
Stevens Point
Green Bay
De Pere
Appleton
Oshkosh

Decorah
Richland Center
Portage
Fond du Lac

Prairie du Chien
Madison
Watertown
Waukesha
Beaver Dam
West Bend
Mequon
Glendale

Platteville
Verona
Janesville
Monroe

Independence
Dubuque
IOWA
Anamosa
Maquoketa
Cedar Rapids
Iowa City
Clinton
Davenport
Muscatine
Rock Island
Washington
Mount Pleasant
Burlington
Fort Madison
Keokuk

Macomb
Galesburg
Peoria
Canton

ILLINOIS

Springfield
Jacksonville
Carlinville
Decatur
Taylorville
Litchfield

Lake Superior

MICHIGAN

Copper Harbor
Hancock
Houghton
Keweenaw Peninsula
L'Anse
Keweenaw Bay
Gogebic Range
Bruce Crossing
Stambaugh
Crystal Falls
Iron Mountain

Marquette
Ishpeming
Newberry

Menominee
Marinette
Sturgeon Bay
Green Bay
Manitowoc
Sheboygan

Door Peninsula
Manistique
Escanaba
Beaver Island

Lake Michigan

Manistee
Ludington
Shelby
Muskegon
Grand Haven
Holland
South Haven
Benton Harbor
Kalamazoo

Cadillac
Big Rapids
Mount Pleasant
Grand Rapids
Wyoming
Battle Creek
Three Rivers
Sturgis

Traverse City
Frankfort
Au Sable
Grayling
Tawas City
Standish
Midland
Saginaw
Bay City
Owosso
East Lansing
Lansing
Jackson
Adrian
Monroe

ONTARIO

Thunder Bay
Nipigon
Terrace Bay
Marathon
Kabinakagami Lake
Missinaibi Lake
Nighthawk Lake
Timmins
Foleyet

Wawa
Michipicoten Bay
Michipicoten River
Chapleau
Sultan

Sault Sainte Marie
Thessalon
Blind River
Elliot Lake
Sudbury
Espanola

St Joseph I.
Drummond Island
Manitoulin Island
Little Current
Wikwemikong

Cheboygan
Rogers City
Petoskey
Charlevoix
Alpena

South Baymouth
Tobermory
Bruce Peninsula

Georgian Bay

Gaylord
Oscoda

Lake Huron

Port Elgin
Owen Sound
Collingwood
Hanover
Orangeville
Goderich
Kincardine
Stratford
Kitchener
Woodstock
London
Brantford

Saginaw Bay
Harbor Beach
Port Huron
Sarnia
St Thomas
Lake St Clair
Detroit
Windsor
Chatham

Lake Erie
Toledo
Sandusky
Lorain
Cleveland

OHIO

Findlay
Tiffin
Ashland
Mansfield
Wooster
Akron
Canton
Massillon

Columbus
Delaware
Marion
Mount Vernon
Newark
Zanesville

Dayton
Springfield
Middletown
Hamilton
Cincinnati

INDIANA

South Bend
Elkhart
Angola
Auburn
Fort Wayne
Warsaw
Huntington
Peru
Marion
Muncie
Anderson
Kokomo
Logansport
Lafayette
Crawfordsville
Indianapolis
Lawrence
Richmond
Shelbyville
Greensburg
Columbus
Bloomington
Terre Haute
Vincennes
Washington
Bedford
Seymour

Chicago
Gary
Hammond
Michigan City
Joliet
Aurora
Oak Lawn
Merrillville
Plymouth
Rensselaer
Kankakee
Watseka

KENTUCKY

Louisville
Frankfort
Lexington
Richmond
Danville
Campbellsville
Columbia
Bowling Green
Glasgow

MISSOURI
St Louis
TENNESSEE

WEST VIRGINIA

Lambert Azimuthal Equal Area Projection

METRES
FEET

5000	16404
3000	9843
2000	6562
1000	3281
500	1640
200	656
0	0

Land below sea level

200	656
4000	13124
6000	19686

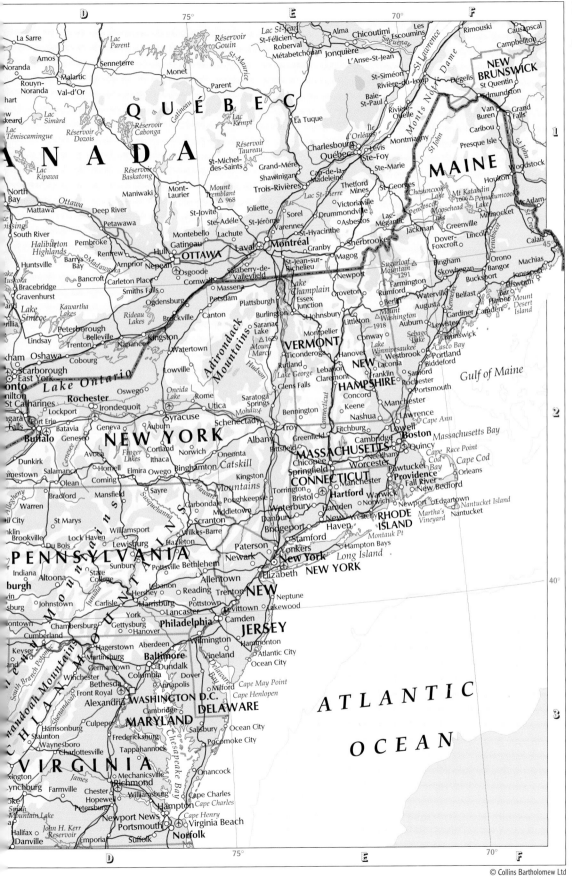

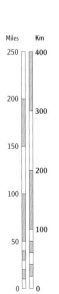

1 : 6 400 000

© Collins Bartholomew Ltd

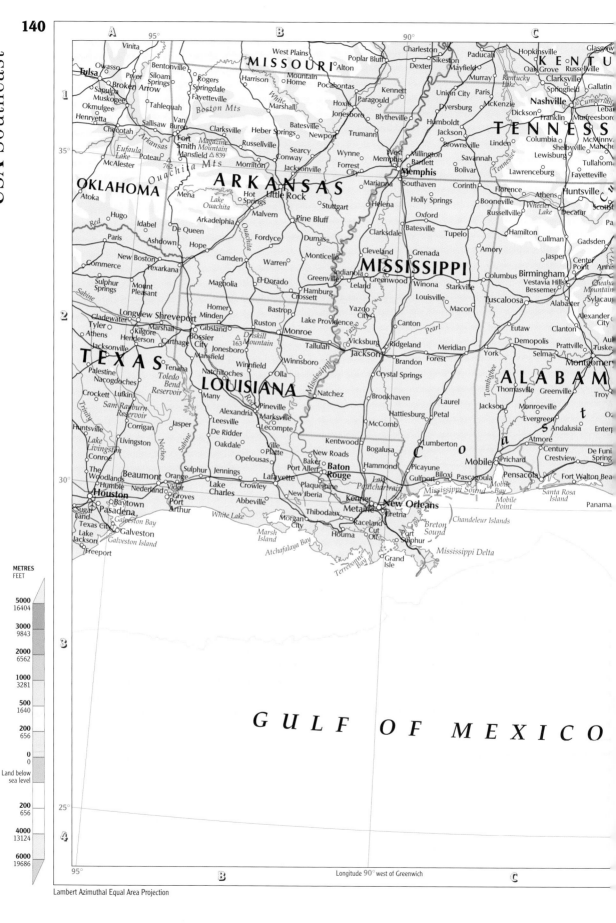

USA Southeast

Vinita
Tulsa Owasso
Broken Arrow Siloam Springs
Pryor
Sapulpa
Muskogee
Okmulgee
Henryetta
Tahlequah
Bentonville
Rogers
Springdale
Fayetteville
Harrison

West Plains
MISSOURI
Mountain Home
Pocahontas
Alton
Poplar Bluff

Charleston
Dexter
Sikeston
Mayfield
Paducah
Hopkinsville
KENTU
Oak Grove Russellville
Glasgow
Clarksville
Gallatin

Union City Paris
Murray
Kentucky Lake
Springfield
Nashville

Checotah
Sallisaw
Van Buren
Fort Smith
Clarksville
Heber Springs
Batesville
Newport
Searcy
Conway
Jacksonville
Russellville
Morrilton

Boston Mts
White
Marshall
Hoxie
Paragould
Jonesboro
Blytheville
Kennett
Trumann
Wynne
West Memphis
Forrest City
Dyersburg
McKenzie
Humboldt
Jackson
Brownsville
Dickson
Franklin
TENNESS
McMinnv.
Shelbyville
Lewisburg
Columbia
Linden
Savannah
Bolivar
Lawrenceburg
Tullaho
Fayetteville

35°
OKLAHOMA
McAlester
Atoka
Hugo
Idabel
ARKANSAS
Eufaula Lake
Magazine Mountain △839
762
Ouachita Mts
Mena
Lake Ouachita
Hot Springs
Little Rock
Stuttgart
Arkadelphia
Malvern
Pine Bluff
Memphis
Southaven
Marianna
Helena
Holly Springs
Oxford
Corinth
Florence
Athens
Huntsville
Scott
Pa
Red
De Queen
Ashdown
Hope
Paris
Fordyce
Dumas
Clarksdale
Batesville
Tupelo
Hamilton
Wheeler Lake
Decatur
Russellville
Booneville
Amory
Cullman
Gadsden

New Boston
Commerce
Texarkana
Camden
Warren
Monticello
Cleveland
Grenada
MISSISSIPPI
Jasper
Center Point
Annis
Sulphur Springs
Mount Pleasant
Magnolia
El Dorado
Greenville
Indianola
Greenwood
Winona
Starkville
Columbus
Birmingham
Vestavia Hills
Bessemer
Cheaha Mountain
Sylacu

Ouachita
Hamburg
Crossett
Leland
Louisville
Macon
Tuscaloosa
Alabaster
Alexander City

Gladewater
Longview Shreveport
Tyler
Athens
Kilgore
Henderson
Jacksonville
Minden
Homer
Gibsland
Bossier City
Monroe
Bastrop
Ruston
Lake Providence
Yazoo City
Canton
Ridgeland
Vicksburg
Jackson
Meridian
York
Eutaw
Clanton
Demopolis
Prattville
Aul
Tuske
ALABAM

TEXAS
Marshall
Carthage
Jonesboro
Mansfield
Driskill Mountain △163
Tallulah
Pearl
Brandon
Forest
Selma
Montgomer
Troy

Palestine
Nacogdoches
Crockett
Lufkin
Tenaha
Toledo Bend Reservoir
Natchitoches
Winnfield
Many
Olla
Winnsboro
LOUISIANA
Natchez
Crystal Springs
Brookhaven
Thomasville
Greenville
Monroeville
Evergreen
Laurel
Jackson
Tombigbee

Huntsville
Corrigan
Livingston
Lake Livingston
Sam Rayburn Reservoir
Jasper
Alexandria
Leesville
De Ridder
Oakdale
Ville Platte
Opelousas
Pineville
Marksville
Lecompte
Hattiesburg
Petal
McComb
Kentwood
Bogalusa
Lumberton
Andalusia
Enterp
Century
Crestview
De Funi
Spring
Atmore

The Woodlands
Humble
Beaumont Orange
Houston
Baytown
Pasadena
Sugar Land
Texas City
Lake Jackson
Freeport
Galveston Bay
Galveston
Galveston Island
Nederland
Vidor
Port Arthur
Groves
Lake Charles
Sulphur
Jennings
Crowley
Abbeville
White Lake
Lafayette
New Iberia
Baker
Port Allen
Baton Rouge
Plaquemine
Morgan City
Marsh Island
Atchafalaya Bay
Thibodaux
Houma
Raceland
Cut Off
Port Sulphur
Grand Isle
Terrebonne Bay
Kenner
Metairie
New Orleans
Gretna
Lake Pontchartrain
Hammond
Picayune
Gulfport
Biloxi
Pascagoula
Mississippi Sound
Mobil Bay
Mobile Point
Santa Rosa Island
Chandeleur Islands
Breton Sound
Mississippi Delta

New Roads
Bogalusa
Mobile
Prichard
Pensacola
Fort Walton Bea
Panama

30°

MISSISSIPPI
Yazoo City
Leland

GULF OF MEXICO

25°

METRES
FEET

5000 / 16404
3000 / 9843
2000 / 6562
1000 / 3281
500 / 1640
200 / 656
0 / 0
Land below sea level
200 / 656
4000 / 13124
6000 / 19686

Lambert Azimuthal Equal Area Projection

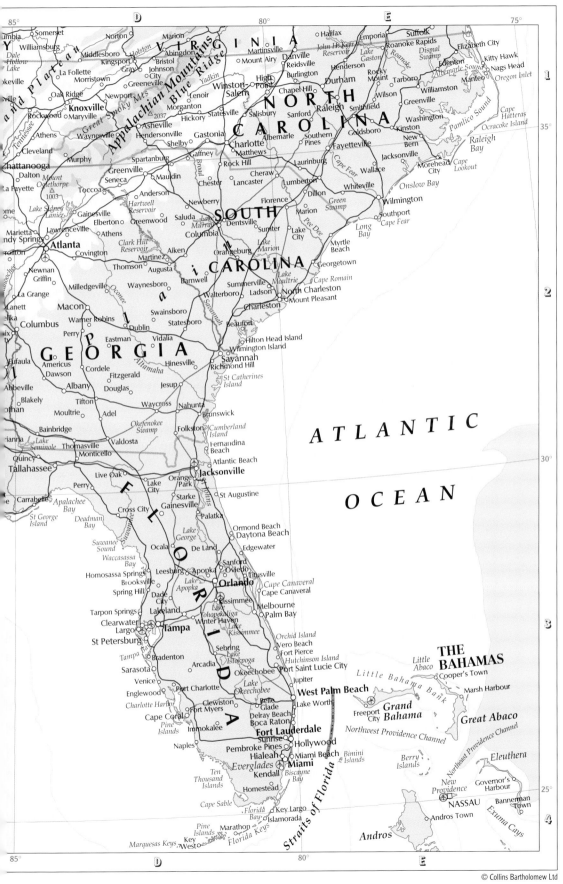

1:6 400 000

© Collins Bartholomew Ltd

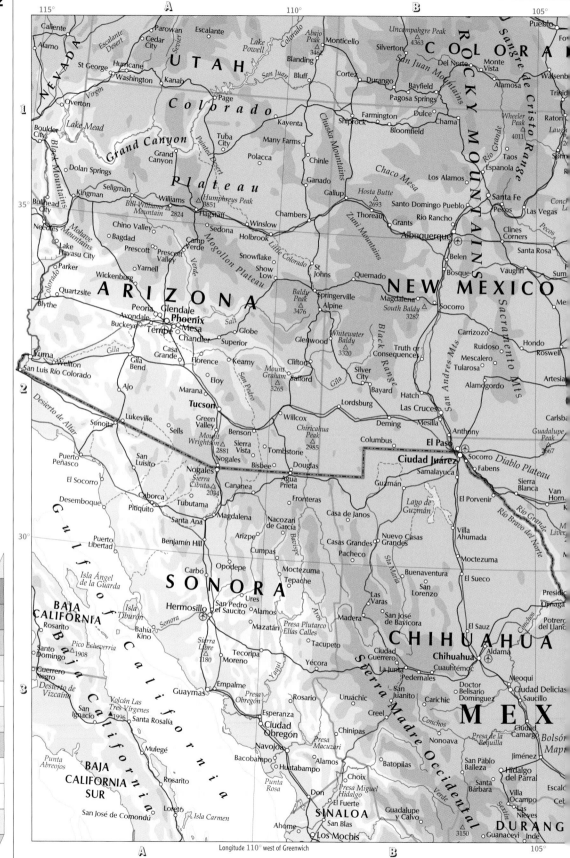

METRES
FEET

5000	16404
3000	9843
2000	6562
1000	3281
500	1640
200	656
0	0
Land below sea level	
200	656
4000	13124
6000	19686

Longitude 110° west of Greenwich

Lambert Azimuthal Equal Area Projection

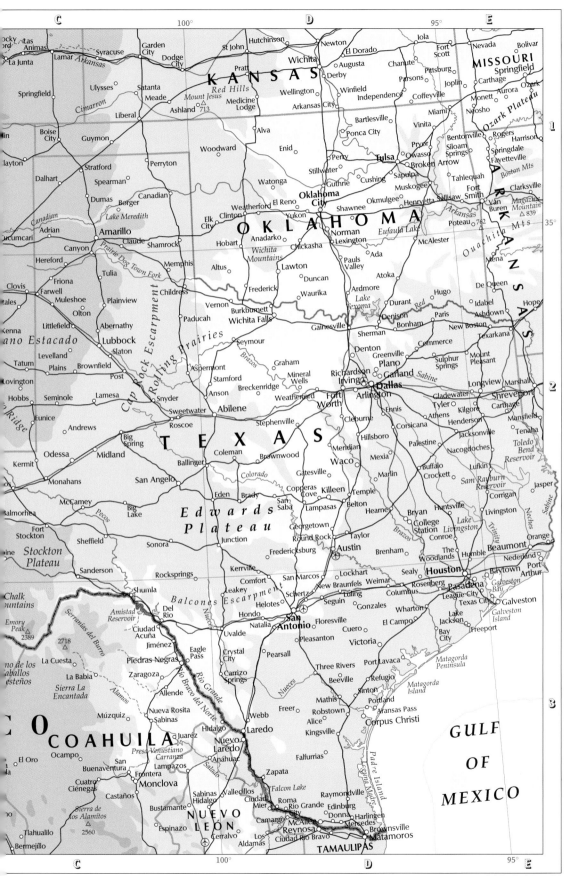

KANSAS

Las Animas
La Junta
Lamar
Arkansas
Syracuse
Garden City
St John
Hutchinson
Newton
Iola
Fort Scott
Nevada
Bolivar
MISSOURI
Springfield

Ulysses
Satanta
Meade
Red Hills
Mount Jesus
713
Medicine Lodge
Pratt
Wellington
Wichita
Augusta
Derby
El Dorado
Chanute
Pittsburg
Carthage
Ozark

Springfield
Liberal
Ashland
Arkansas City
Winfield
Independence
Coffeyville
Joplin
Monett
Aurora
Neosho
Ozark Plateau

Boise City
Guymon
Cimarron
Woodward
Alva
Ponca City
Bartlesville
Miami
Vinita
Bentonville
Rogers
Springdale
Harrison
Fayetteville

layton
Dalhart
Stratford
Spearman
Perryton
Enid
Perry
Stillwater
Pryor
Owasso
Siloam Springs
Boston Mts

Dumas
Borger
Canadian
Lake Meredith
Weatherford
El Reno
Oklahoma City
Shawnee
Okmulgee
Henryetta
Sallisaw
Van Buren
Clarksville
Magazine Mountain 839

Adrian
Amarillo
Canadian
Claude
Shamrock
Elk City
Clinton
Yukon
Norman
Lexington
Ada
McAlester
Poteau
762
35°

cumcari
Canyon
Hereford
Prairie Dog Town Fork
Hobart
Anadarko
Chickasha
Wichita Mountains
Eufaula Lake
Arkansas
Mena
Ouachita Mts

Clovis
Friona
Tulia
Memphis
Altus
Lawton
Duncan
Pauls Valley
Atoka
Hugo
De Queen
Ashdown
Hope

ales
Farwell
Muleshoe
Olton
Plainview
Childress
Vernon
Frederick
Waurika
Ardmore
Durant
Red
Idabel
New Boston

Littlefield
Abernathy
Paducah
Burkburnett
Wichita Falls
Gainesville
Denison
Bonham
Paris
Texarkana

Lubbock
Slaton
Seymour
Graham
Denton
Sherman
Commerce
Mount Pleasant
Marshall

Levelland
Plains
Brownfield
Post
Aspermont
Brazos
Mineral Wells
Richardson
Plano
Garland
Greenville
Sulphur Springs
Sabine
Longview
Shreveport

Hobbs
Seminole
Lamesa
Snyder
Sweetwater
Stamford
Anson
Breckenridge
Weatherford
Dallas
Arlington
Tyler
Kilgore
Gladewater
Carthage

Eunice
Andrews
Big Spring
Roscoe
Abilene
Stephenville
Fort Worth
Cleburne
Athens
Henderson
Jacksonville
Mansfield
Tenaha

Odessa
Midland
Ballinger
Coleman
Brownwood
Hillsboro
Corsicana
Palestine
Nacogdoches
Toledo Bend Reservoir

TEXAS

Kermit
Monahans
San Angelo
Colorado
Gatesville
Meridian
Waco
Mexia
Marlin
Buffalo
Crockett
Lufkin
Jasper

McCamey
Big Lake
Eden
Brady
Copperas Cove
Killeen
Temple
Hearne
Bryan
Huntsville
Sam Rayburn Reservoir
Corrigan

Fort Stockton
Sheffield
Pecos
Sonora
Junction
San Saba
Lampasas
Belton
Georgetown
College Station
Lake Livingston
Livingston

Sanderson
Rocksprings
Edwards Plateau
Round Rock
Taylor
Austin
Brenham
Conroe
The Woodlands
Humble
Neches
Orange

Stockton Plateau
Kerrville
Fredericksburg
Lockhart
Sealy
Houston
Beaumont
Nederland
Port Arthur

Emory Peak 2389
Shumla
Balcones Escarpment
Comfort
Leakey
Helotes
San Marcos
New Braunfels
Weimar
Columbus
Rosenberg
Pasadena
Baytown
Galveston Bay

2718
Amistad Reservoir
Del Rio
Ciudad Acuña
Hondo
Natalia
San Antonio
Seguin
Gonzales
Wharton
Luling
League City
Texas City
Galveston
Galveston Island

La Cuesta
Serranías del Burro
Jiménez
Uvalde
Floresville
Cuero
El Campo
Bay City
Freeport

no de los aballos esteños
Piedras Negras
Eagle Pass
Crystal City
Pearsall
Pleasanton
Victoria
Port Lavaca
Matagorda Peninsula

Zaragoza
Sierra La Encantada
Alamos
Carrizo Springs
Three Rivers
Beeville
Refugio
Matagorda Island

Allende
Rio Grande
Freer
Sinton
Portland

Múzquiz
Nueva Rosita
Sabinas
Webb
Mathis
Robstown
Alice
Aransas Pass
Corpus Christi

COAHUILA
Juárez
Hidalgo
Laredo
Kingsville
Padre Island

El Oro
Ocampo
San Buenaventura
Presa Venustiano Carranza
Nuevo Laredo
Anáhuac
Falfurrias
Zapata
Laguna Madre

Cuatro Ciénegas
Frontera
Lampazos
Monclova
Castaños
Sabinas Hidalgo
Vallecillos
Falcon Lake
Raymondville
Edinburg
Donna
Harlingen

Sierra de los Alamitos
2560
Bustamante
Ciudad Mier
Roma
Rio Grande City
Mercedes
Brownsville

Tlahualilo
Espinazo
NUEVO LEÓN
Cerralvo
Camargo
McAllen
Reynosa
Matamoros

Bermejillo
Los Aldamas
Ciudad Rio Bravo
TAMAULIPAS

GULF
OF
MEXICO

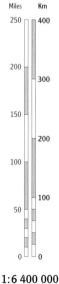

Miles Km
250 400
200 300
150 200
100 100
50 50
0 0

1:6 400 000

MEXICO

METRES
FEET

5000
16404

3000
9843

2000
6562

1000
3281

500
1640

200
656

0
0

Land below
sea level

200
656

4000
13124

6000
19686

Lambert Azimuthal Equal Area Projection

STATES OF AMERICA

TEXAS

LOUISIANA

MISSISSIPPI

ALABAMA

FLORIDA

Dallas
Fort Worth
Abilene
Austin
San Antonio
Houston
Baton Rouge
New Orleans
Mobile
Pensacola

Laredo
Corpus Christi
Brownsville
Matamoros
Monterrey
Reynosa

Laguna Madre

GULF

OF

MEXICO

Tropic of Cancer

Arrecife
Alacrán

Yucatan Channel

Cabo Catoche
Cancún
Cozumel
Isla de Cozumel

Mérida

YUCATÁN

Campeche

MEXICO

Ciudad Madero
Tampico

MEXICO CITY
Toluca
Puebla
Cuernavaca
Veracruz

Bahía de Campeche

Chetumal
Corozal
Orange Walk
Belize
BELMOPAN

BELIZE

Coatzacoalcos
Villahermosa

Gulf of Tehuantepec

GUATEMALA

HONDURAS

GUATEMALA CITY

Miles   Km

300

400

200

200

100

100

0   0

1 : 9 600 000

© Collins Bartholomew Ltd

100°   90°   C   D

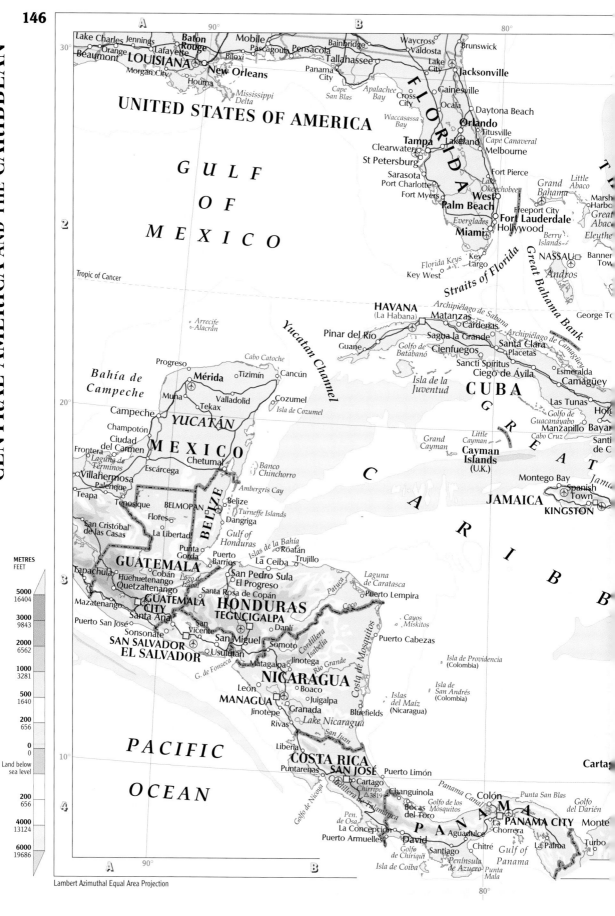

CENTRAL AMERICA AND THE CARIBBEAN

UNITED STATES OF AMERICA

GULF
OF
MEXICO

Tropic of Cancer

PACIFIC

OCEAN

METRES
FEET

5000
16404
3000
9843
2000
6562
1000
3281
500
1640
200
656
0
0
Land below
sea level
200
656
4000
13124
6000
19686

Lambert Azimuthal Equal Area Projection

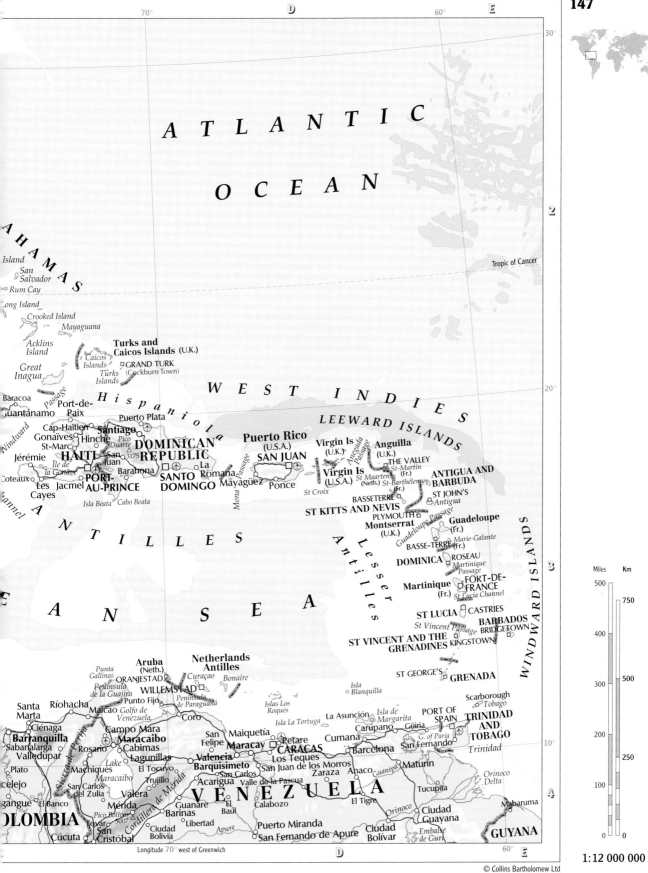

70°   D   60°   E

30°

A T L A N T I C

O C E A N

2

Tropic of Cancer

Island
San
Salvador
Rum Cay
B
A
H
A
M
A
S

Long Island

Crooked Island
Mayaguana
Acklins
Island

Turks and
Caicos Islands (U.K.)
Caicos
Islands
□ **GRAND TURK**
(Cockburn Town)
Turks
Islands

Great
Inagua

Baracoa
Guantánamo

W E S T   I N D I E S

20°

Windward Passage

H i s p a n i o l a

LEEWARD ISLANDS

Port-de-
Paix
Puerto Plata
Cap-Haïtien
Santiago
Gonaïves   Hinche   *Pico*
St-Marc   *Duarte*
Jérémie   **HAITI** San ▲3175
Île de   Juan
la Gonâve   **PORT-**   Barahona
Coteaux   **AU-PRINCE**
Les   Jacmel   **SANTO**
Cayes   **DOMINGO**
Isla Beata Cabo Beata

DOMINICAN
REPUBLIC
La
Romana
Puerto Rico
(U.S.A.)
SAN JUAN
Mayagüez
Ponce

Mona Passage

Virgin Is
(U.K.)
Virgin Is
(U.S.A.)
St Croix

Anegada Passage

Anguilla
(U.K.)
THE VALLEY
St-Martin
(Fr.)
St Maarten
(Neth.) *St-Barthélemy*
(Fr.)

ANTIGUA AND
BARBUDA
ST JOHN'S
Antigua

BASSETERRE
ST KITTS AND NEVIS
PLYMOUTH
Montserrat
(U.K.)
Guadeloupe Passage
Guadeloupe
(Fr.)
BASSE-TERRE *Marie-Galante*
(Fr.)
DOMINICA **ROSEAU**
Martinique
Passage
Martinique **FORT-DE-**
(Fr.) **FRANCE**
St Lucia Channel
ST LUCIA **CASTRIES**
St Vincent Passage
ST VINCENT AND THE
GRENADINES **KINGSTOWN**

BARBADOS
BRIDGETOWN

W I N D W A R D   I S L A N D S

3

G   r   e   a   t   e   r   A   N   T   I   L   L   E   S

Windward Channel

C A R I B B E A N   S E A

L e s s e r   A n t i l l e s

ST GEORGE'S **GRENADA**

Aruba
(Neth.)
ORANJESTAD
Netherlands
Antilles
Curaçao
WILLEMSTAD *Bonaire*
Punta
Gallinas
Península
de la Guajira
Ríohacha Punto Fijo
Maicao *Golfo de*
Venezuela
Barranquilla Rosario Coro
Santa   Ciénaga   Campo Mara
Marta   **Maracaibo**
Sabanalarga   Cabimas
Valledupar   Lagunillas
Plato   Machiques   *Lake*
San Carlos *Maracaibo*
del Zulia   Trujillo
El Banco   Valera
Toyar Mérida
COLOMBIA *Pico Bolívar*
▲5007
Cúcuta Tovar
San
Cristóbal

Península
de Paraguaná

Isla
Blanquilla

Islas Los
Roques
San
Felipe
Maracay
Valencia
Barquisimeto
San Carlos
Acarigua
Guanare
Barinas
Guarico
El
Baúl

Isla La Tortuga

La Asunción
Carúpano
CARACAS Barcelona Cumaná
Los Teques
San Juan de los Morros
Zaraza
Valle de la Pascua
Calabozo
Anaco
Guanipa
El Tigre

Isla de
Margarita
Güiria
PORT OF
SPAIN
G. of Paria
San Fernando
Trinidad

Scarborough
Tobago

TRINIDAD
AND
TOBAGO

10°

Petare
Maiquetía

Orinoco
Delta
Maturín
Tucupita

V E N E Z U E L A

Orinoco
Ciudad
Guayana
Ciudad
Bolívar
Puerto Miranda
San Fernando de Apure
Ciudad
Bolivia
Apure
Libertad

Mabaruma

Embalse
de Guri

GUYANA

4

Longitude 70° west of Greenwich D 60° E

© Collins Bartholomew Ltd

Miles   Km
500
750
400
500
300
250
200
100
0   0

1:12 000 000

SOUTH AMERICA

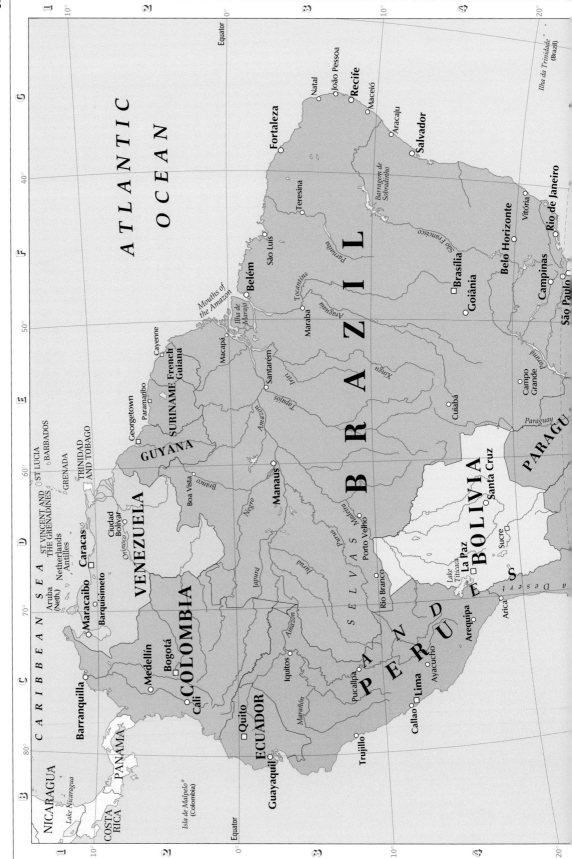

Bi-Polar Oblique Projection

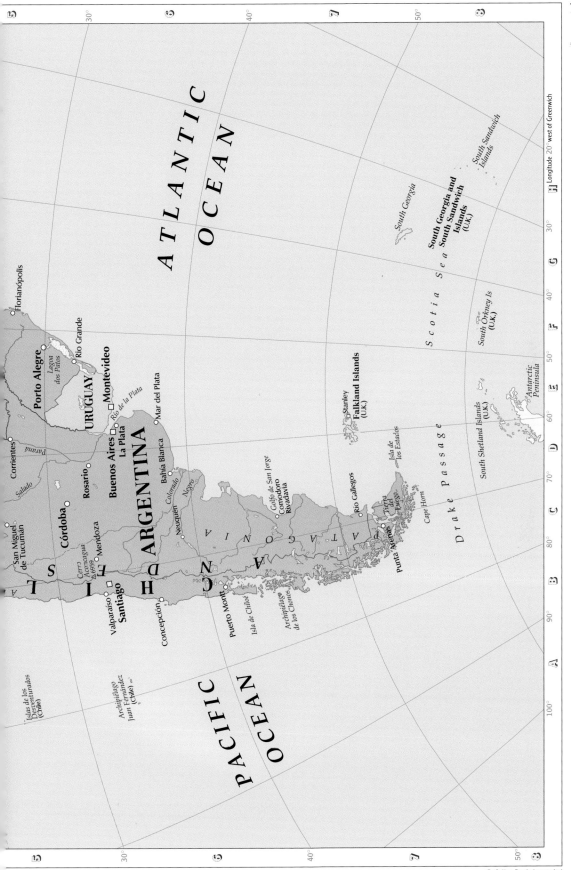

149

30° 40° 50°

Longitude 20 west of Greenwich

30°

40°

50°

60°

70°

80°

90°

100°

H G F E D C B A

A T L A N T I C

O C E A N

P A C I F I C

O C E A N

Florianópolis

Porto Alegre

Rio Grande

Lagoa dos Patos

URUGUAY

Montevideo

La Plata

Río de la Plata

Buenos Aires

Mar del Plata

Corrientes

Paraná

Rosario

Bahía Blanca

Colorado

Negro

Córdoba

Salado

San Miguel de Tucumán

Mendoza

Cerro Aconcagua △ 6959

ARGENTINA

Neuquén

P A T A G O N I A

CHILE

Valparaíso

Santiago

Concepción

Puerto Montt

Isla de Chiloé

Archipiélago de los Chonos

Golfo de San Jorge

Comodoro Rivadavia

Río Gallegos

Tierra del Fuego

Punta Arenas

Cape Horn

Isla de los Estados

D r a k e   P a s s a g e

S c o t i a   S e a

Stanley

Falkland Islands
(U.K.)

South Georgia

South Georgia and
South Sandwich
Islands
(U.K.)

South Sandwich
Islands

South Orkney Is
(U.K.)

South Shetland Islands

Antarctic
Peninsula

Islas de los Desventurados
(Chile)

Archipiélago
Juan Fernández (Chile)

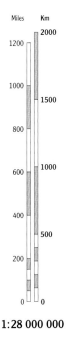

Miles   Km

1200 ─ 2000

1000 ─ 1500

800

600 ─ 1000

400

200 ─ 500

0 ─ 0

1:28 000 000

© Collins Bartholomew Ltd

SOUTH AMERICA North

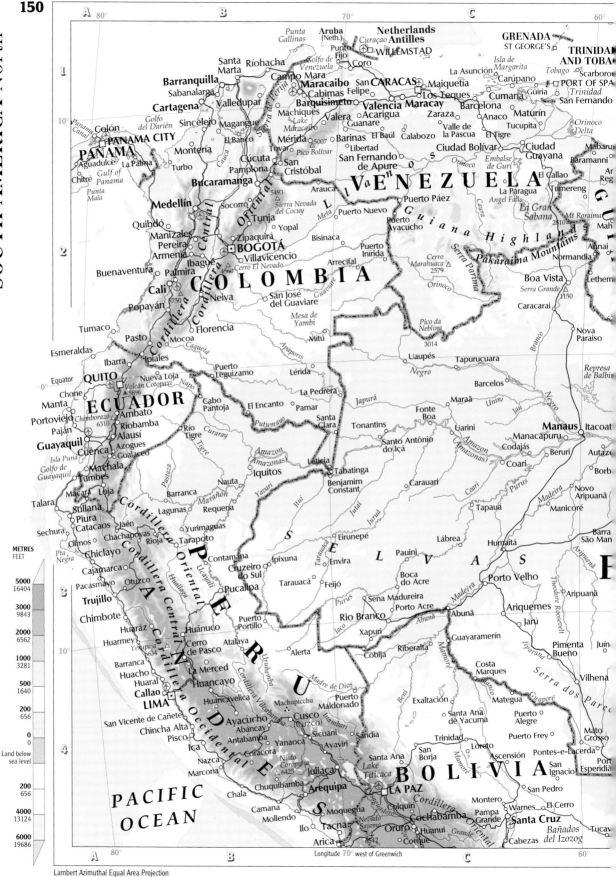

METRES FEET

5000	16404
3000	9843
2000	6562
1000	3281
500	1640
200	656
0	0
Land below sea level	
200	656
4000	13124
6000	19686

PACIFIC OCEAN

Lambert Azimuthal Equal Area Projection

Longitude 70° west of Greenwich

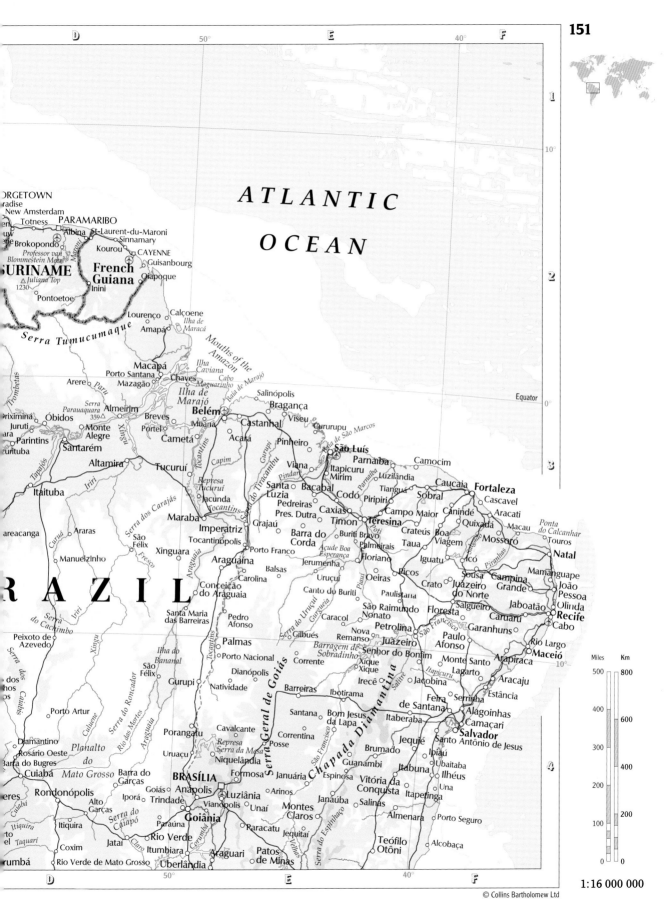

ATLANTIC

OCEAN

Equator

SURINAME
French
Guiana

ORGETOWN
aradise
New Amsterdam
Totness PARAMARIBO
uw Albina St-Laurent-du-Maroni
rie Brokopondo Sinnamary
Professor van Kourou
Blommestein Meer CAYENNE
Guisanbourg
Juliana Top Oiapoque
1230
Pontoetoe Inini

Lourenço Calçoene
Amapá Ilha de
Maracá
Serra Tumucumaque
Macapá
Porto Santana
Arere Paru Mazagão Chaves
Trombetas Ilha de
Marajó Salinópolis
Ilha Bragança
oriximiná Óbidos Almeirim Caviana Cabo
Juruti Serra 359 Breves Viseu
ara Parauaquara Monte Belém Muaná Pinheiro Cururupu
Parintins Alegre Portel Castanhal Acará Ilha de São Marcos
uruba Santarém Cametá Camocim
Tapajós Altamira Tucuruí São Luís Parnaíba
Itaituba Iriri Santa Viana Parnaíba Caucaia Fortaleza
Luzia Itapicuru Luzilândia Sobral Cascavel
Represa Bacabal Mirim Tianguá Aracati
Jacundá Pedreiras Codó Piripiri Campo Maior Canindé Quixadá Macau
Maraba Pres. Dutra Caxias Buriti Bravo Teresina Crateús Boa Mossoró Touros
Imperatriz Grajaú Barra do Palmeirais Viagem Icó Natal
Xinguara Tocantinopolis Corda Açude Boa Iguatu Sousa Mamanguape
Manuelzinho Araguaína Porto Franco Esperança Floriano Picos Crato Juazeiro Campina João
Fresco Balsas Jerumenha Oeiras do Norte Grande Pessoa
RAZIL Carolina Uruçuí Paulistana Salgueiro Jaboatão Recife
Conceição Canto do Buriti São Raimundo Floresta Caruaru Cabo
Santa Maria do Araguaia Caracol Nonato Garanhuns
das Barreiras Pedro Nova Petrolina Rio Largo
Afonso Remanso Juazeiro Paulo Maceió
Peixoto de Gilbués Barragem de Senhor do Bonfim Afonso
Azevedo Palmas Sobradinho Xique Monte Santo Arapiraca
dos Porto Nacional Corrente Xique Lagarto Aracaju
Diamantino Dianópolis Irecê Jacobina Estância
Rosário Oeste Ilha do Natividade Barreiras Feira Serrinha
Barra do Bugres Bananal Gurupi Ibotirama de Santana Alagoinhas
Cuiabá São Santana Bom Jesus Itaberaba Camaçari
Rondonópolis Félix Correntina da Lapa Salvador
Cavalcante Posse Brumado Jequié Santo Antônio de Jesus
Porangatu Represa Januária Guanambi Ipiaú
Uruaçu Serra da Mesa Espinosa Vitória da Itabuna Ubaitaba
Barra do Niquelândia Formosa Janaúba Conquista Ilhéus
Garças Goiás Anápolis BRASÍLIA Arinos Salinas Itapetinga Una
Alto Iporá Trindade Luziânia Montes Almenara Porto Seguro
Garças Serra do Vianópolis Unaí Claros Teófilo Alcobaça
Itiquira Caiapó Goiânia Paracatu Jequitaí Otôni
Rondonópolis Paraúna Salvador

Mouths of the Amazon
Baía de Marajó
Serra dos Carajás
São Félix
Araras
areacanga Curuá
Serra do Cachimbo
Serra do Roncador
Planalto do Mato Grosso
Serra dos Caiás
Xingu
Tocantins
Araguaia
Tocantins
Serra Geral de Goiás
Chapada Diamantina
São Francisco
Serra do Espinhaço

eres
Coxim
Rio Verde
Jataí
Itumbiara
Rio Verde de Mato Grosso
Uberlândia
Araguari
Patos de Minas

1:16 000 000

© Collins Bartholomew Ltd

Miles Km
500 800
400 600
300 400
200 200
100
0 0

SOUTH AMERICA South

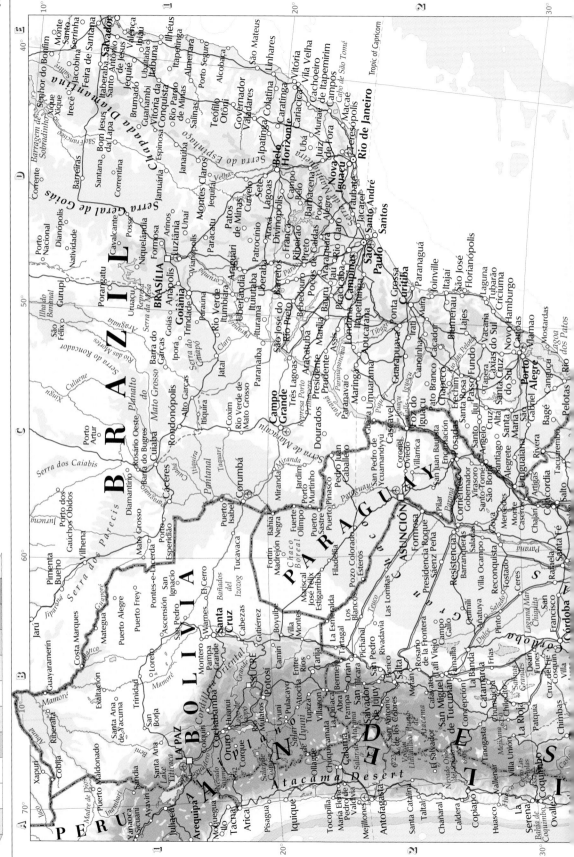

METRES / FEET

METRES	FEET
5000	16404
3000	9843
2000	6562
1000	3281
500	1640
200	656
0	0
Land below sea level	
200	656
4000	13124
6000	19686

Lambert Azimuthal Equal Area Projection

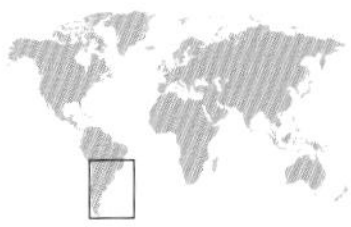

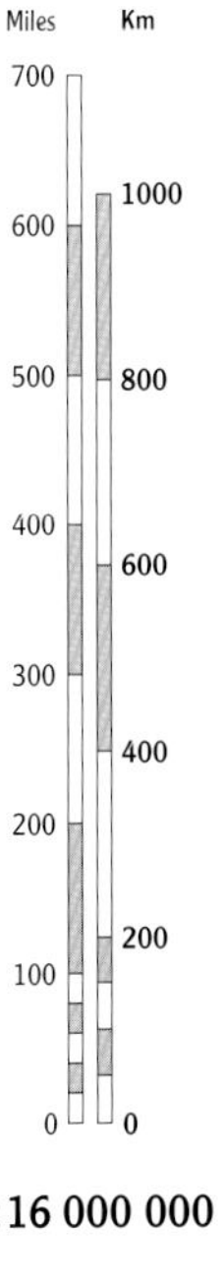

ATLANTIC

OCEAN

South Georgia
(U.K.)

Cape
Alexandra
Mount Paget
2934
Grytviken
Cape
Disappointment

Falkland Islands
(U.K.)

ST STANLEY
Darwin
East
Falkland

West
Falkland
Port
Stephens

Isla de
los Estados

Estrecho de Le Maire

URUGUAY

Florida
Minas
Rocha
Las Piedras
MONTEVIDEO
Pando

Mírim

Punta del Este

BUENOS AIRES
Quilmes
La Plata
Lomas de Zamora
Pilar

Pinamar
Villa Gesell
Mar del Plata
Cabo Corrientes

Bahía
de la Plata
Samborombón
General
Belgrano
Las Flores
Azul

Pergamino
Arroyos
de los
Río
Chascomús

ARGENTINA

Rufino
Junín

Necochea

Bahía
Samborombón

Tandil
Benito Juárez
Olavarría
Coronel
Suárez
Tres
Arroyos

Punta
Alta
Bahía Blanca

Stroeder
Punta
Rasa

Laboulaye

General
Pico
Trenque
Lauquen
Pehuajó
Pigüé

Coronel
Dorrego

Villa
Mercedes

San Rafael

Malargüe

General
Acha

Santa
Isabel

Santa Rosa

Puelén
General
Roca

Cipolletti

Choele
Choel

Río
Colorado

Colorado
Negro

Viedma
San Antonio
Oeste

Golfo San Matías

Península
Valdés

Puerto
Madryn

Rawson

Cabo Dos Bahías

Comodoro Rivadavia
Golfo
de
San Jorge

Cabo Tres Puntas

Deseado
Punta Medanosa

Salado o
Chadileo

Puelches

Maquinchao

Sierra Grande

Trelew

Las
Plumas

Gangán

Chubut

Chico

Sarmiento
Colonia
Las Heras

Pico
Truncado

San
Julián

Bahía
Grande

Nueva
Lubecka

Paso
Río Mayo

Buenos
Aires

Puerto Santa Cruz
Río
Gallegos

Gobernador
Gregores

Río
Grande

Puerto Deseado

Caleta
Olivia

Esperanza

Río Grande

Ushuaia

Tierra del Fuego

Cape
Horn

H

CHILE

SANTIAGO

Quillota
Valparaíso
Viña del Mar

Rancagua

Curicó
Talca

Parral

Chillán

Concepción
Talcahuano
Coihue
Los Angeles

Lebu
Victoria

Carahue
Temuco

Valdivia
La Unión
Osorno

Puerto
Montt

Ancud
Isla
de Chiloé
Castro
Quellón

Archipiélago
de los
Chonos

Golfo
de Penas

Península
de Taitao

Puerto Aisén
Coihaique

Cochrane

Lago
Buenos
Aires
Perito
Moreno

Bajo
Caracoles

Gobernador
Costa

Lago
Viedma
Tres
Lagos

Calafate
Lago
Argentino

Puerto Natales

Isla Contreras
Archipiélago de
la Reina Adelaida

Punta
Arenas

Porvenir

Estrecho de Magallanes

Linares

Colico

Parral

Puente
Alto

Villa
Alemana

Rosario

M

F

D

PAMPAS

PATAGONIA

A R G E N T I N A

San Carlos
de Bariloche

El Bolsón

Esquel

Puerto
Aisén

Puerto
San
Julián

Isla
Wellington

Isla
Campana

Miles   Km
700
600   1000
500   800
400   600
300
200   400
100   200
0   0

1:16 000 000

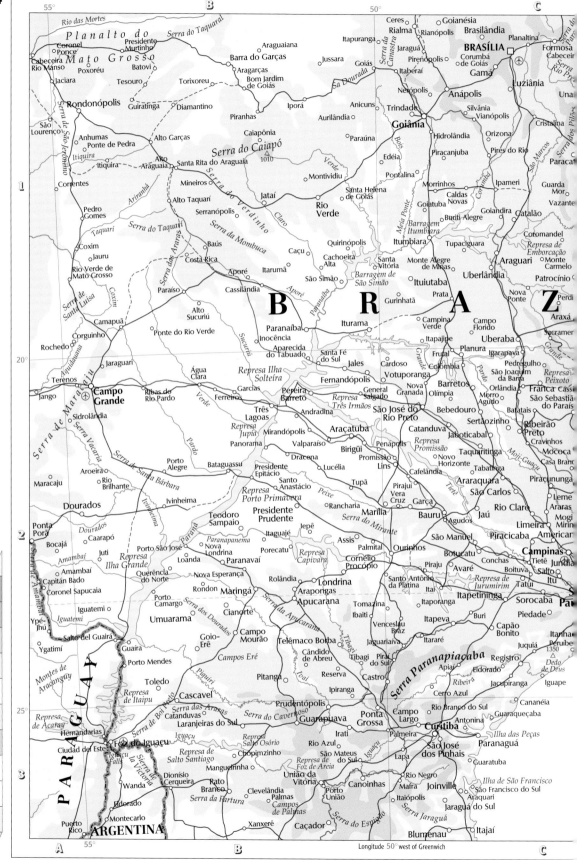

METRES
FEET

5000	16404
3000	9843
2000	6562
1000	3281
500	1640
200	656
0	0

Land below
sea level

200	656
4000	13124
6000	19686

Lambert Azimuthal Equal Area Projection

Longitude 50° west of Greenwich

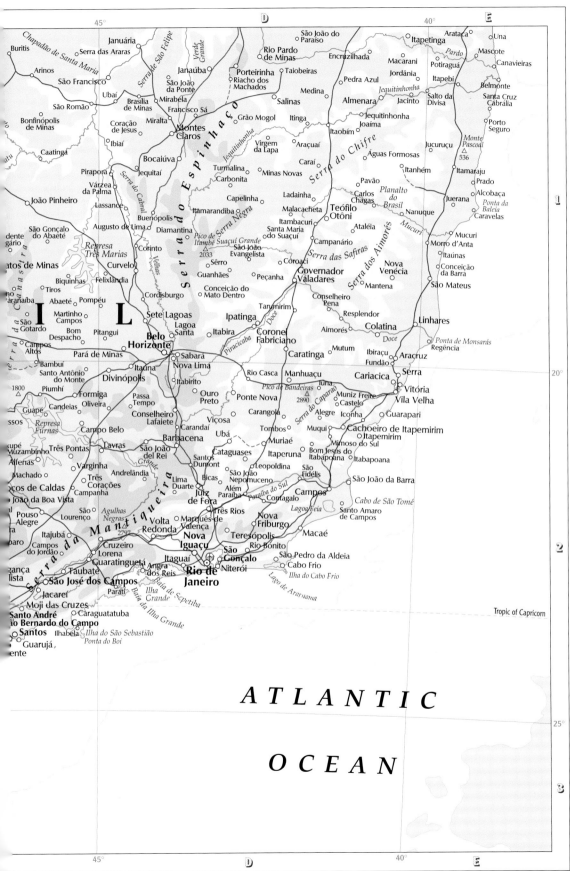

ATLANTIC

OCEAN

Tropic of Capricorn

Miles   Km
250 ┬ ┬ 400

200   ┤ 300

150   ┤

        ┤ 200
100   ┤

 50   ┤ 100

  0 ┴ ┴ 0

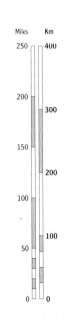

1:6 000 000

PACIFIC OCEAN

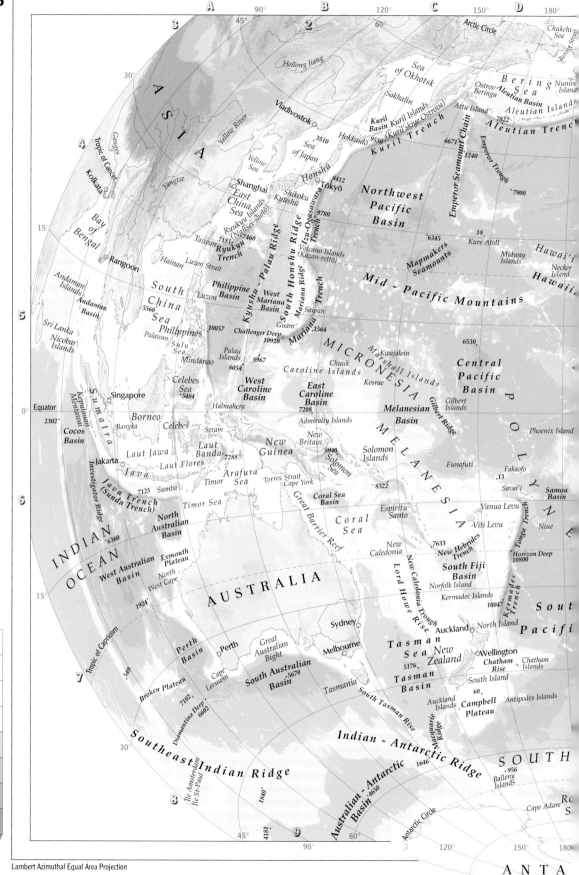

METRES
FEET

0	0
200	656
2000	6562
3000	9843
4000	13124
5000	16404
6000	19686
7000	22967
9000	29529

Lambert Azimuthal Equal Area Projection

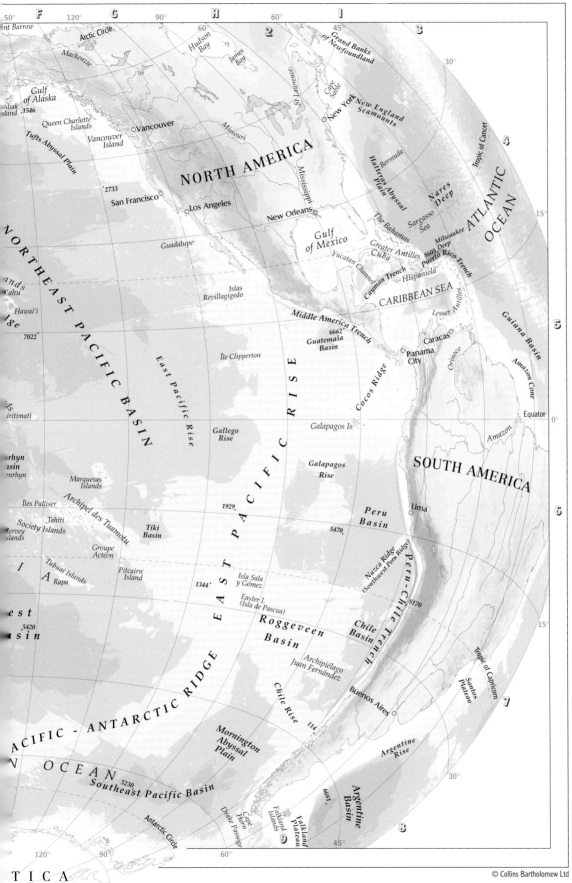

F 150° 120° G 90° H 60° I 2 3

Arctic Circle
nt Barrow
Mackenzie
Gulf
of Alaska
odiak .1546
sland
Queen Charlotte
Islands
Vancouver
Vancouver
Island
Tufts Abyssal Plain
.2733
San Francisco
Los Angeles
Guadalupe
Hudson
Bay
James
Bay
Missouri
St Lawrence
Cape
Sable
Grand Banks
of Newfoundland
New York
New England
Seamounts
Bermuda
Hatteras Abyssal
Plain
Sargasso
Sea
Milwaukee
8605 Deep
Puerto Rico Trench
Nares
Deep
Tropic of Cancer
ATLANTIC
OCEAN

NORTH AMERICA
Mississippi
New Orleans
Gulf
of Mexico
Yucatan Channel
Islas
Revillagigedo
Middle America Trench
6662
Guatemala
Basin
The Bahamas
Cuba
Greater Antilles
Cayman Trench
Hispaniola
CARIBBEAN SEA
Lesser Antilles
Guiana Basin
Amazon Cone

NORTHEAST PACIFIC BASIN
ands
ahu
Hawai'i
7022
Cocos Ridge
Caracas
Panama
City
Orinoco
Amazon
Equator 0°

East Pacific Rise
Île Clipperton
Galapagos Is
Galapagos
Rise
SOUTH AMERICA

EAST PACIFIC RISE
Gallego
Rise
rhyn
sin
enrhyn
Marquesas
Islands
1929.
Peru
Basin
Lima

Îles Palliser
Archipel des Tuamotu
Tahiti
Society Islands
ervey
lands
Tiki
Basin
5470.
Nazca Ridge
(Southwest Peru Ridge)
Peru - Chile Trench

Groupe
Actéon
Tubuai Islands
Rapa
I
A
Pitcairn
Island
1344.
Isla Sala
y Gómez
Easter I.
(Isla de Pascua)
Roggeveen
Basin
8170
Chile
Basin

est
asin
5420
PACIFIC - ANTARCTIC RIDGE
Archipiélago
Juan Fernández
Buenos Aires
Chile Rise
114
Tropic of Capricorn
Santos
Plateau

OCEAN 5230
Southeast Pacific Basin
Mornington
Abyssal
Plain
6689.
Argentine
Rise
Argentine
Basin

120° 90°
Antarctic Circle
60°
Cape
Horn
Drake Passage
Falkland
Islands
Falkland
Plateau
45°

TICA

30°
15°
4
5
6
7
8
9

© Collins Bartholomew Ltd

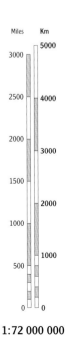

Miles   Km

3000   5000

2500   4000

2000   3000

1500

1000   2000

500   1000

0   0

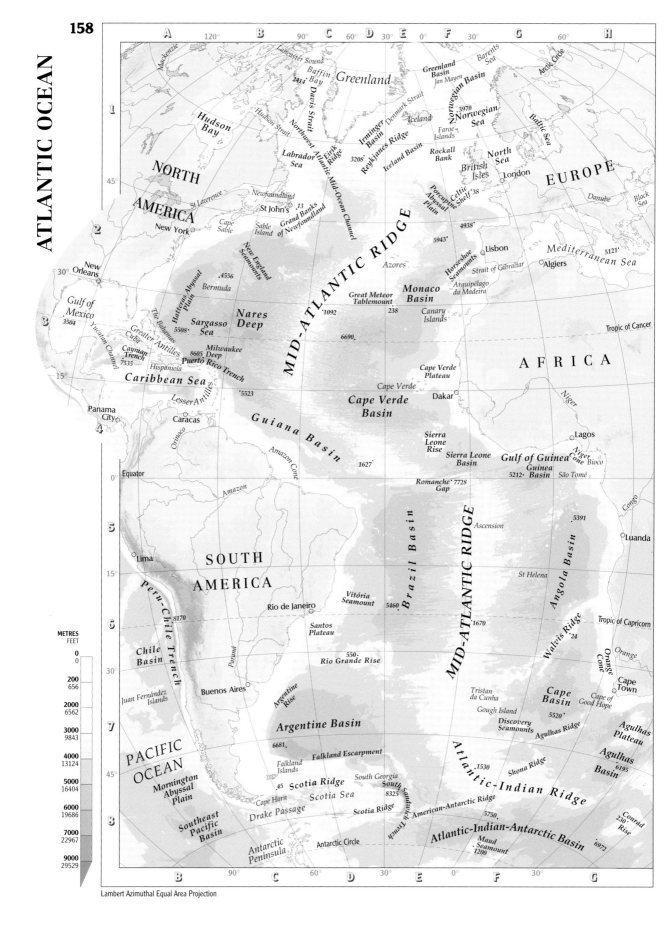

ATLANTIC OCEAN

Lambert Azimuthal Equal Area Projection

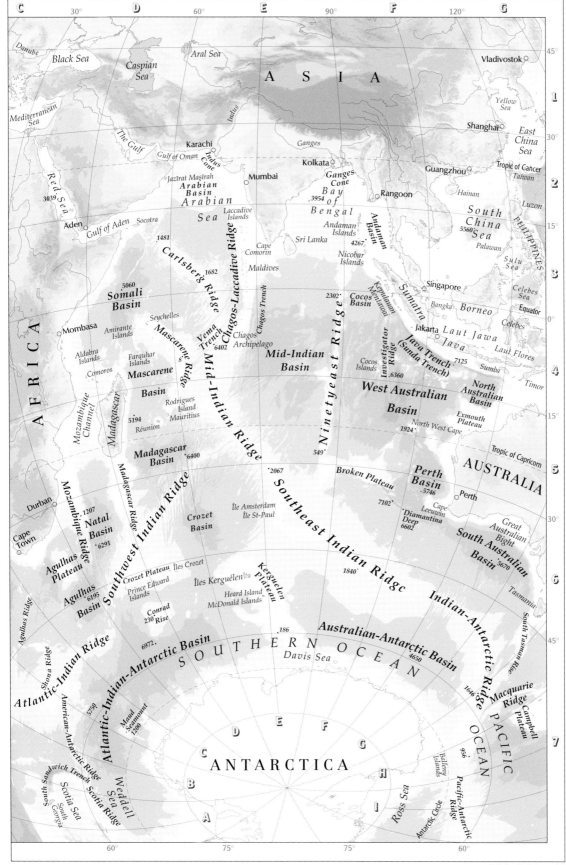

INDIAN OCEAN

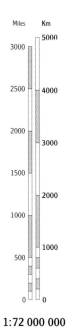

1:72 000 000

ARCTIC OCEAN

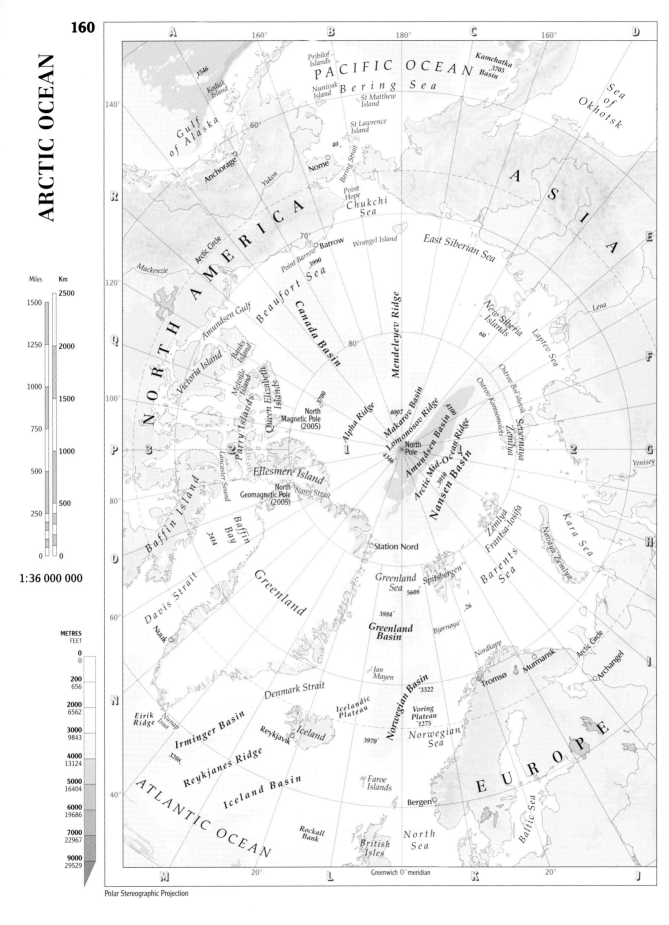

Miles   Km

1500 — 2500

1250 — 2000

1000 — 1500

750 — 1000

500 —

250 — 500

0 — 0

1:36 000 000

METRES
FEET

0 / 0

200 / 656

2000 / 6562

3000 / 9843

4000 / 13124

5000 / 16404

6000 / 19686

7000 / 22967

9000 / 29529

Polar Stereographic Projection

PACIFIC OCEAN

Kamchatka
.3703
Basin

Pribilof
Islands

Nunivak
Island

St Matthew
Island

St Lawrence
Island

Bering Sea

Sea
of
Okhotsk

40.

Nome

Bering Strait

Point
Hope

Chukchi
Sea

ASIA

East Siberian Sea

Wrangel Island

Barrow

Point Barrow

Beaufort Sea
.3990

New Siberia
Islands

60.

Lena

Laptev Sea

Ostrov Bol'shevik

NORTH AMERICA

Mackenzie

Arctic Circle

Amundsen Gulf

Canada Basin

80°

Mendeleyev Ridge

Ostrov Komsomolets

Severnaya
Zemlya

Banks
Island

Victoria Island

Melville
Island

Queen Elizabeth
Islands

Parry Islands

3700

Makarov Basin

4007

Alpha Ridge

1

Lomonosov Ridge

Amundsen Basin

4100

Arctic Mid-Ocean Ridge

3910

Nansen Basin

Zemlya
Frantsa-Iosifa

Kara
Sea

Novaya Zemlya

North
Magnetic Pole
(2005)

North
Pole

4346

Lancaster Sound

Ellesmere Island

North
Geomagnetic Pole
(2005)

Nares Strait

Baffin Island

Baffin
Bay

2444

Station Nord

Spitsbergen

Barents
Sea

Yenisey

Davis Strait

Greenland

Greenland
Sea

5608

Norway Zemlya

Nuuk

3884.

Greenland
Basin

Bjørnøya.

.26

Nordkapp

Tromsø

Murmansk

Archangel

Arctic Circle

Jan
Mayen

Norwegian Basin

.3322

Voring
Plateau
.1275

Norwegian
Sea

EUROPE

Eirik
Ridge

Nunap
Isua

Irminger Basin

Reykjavik

Iceland

Icelandic
Plateau

3970.

Bergen

3208.

Reykjanes Ridge

Iceland Basin

Denmark Strait

Faroe
Islands

ATLANTIC OCEAN

Rockall
Bank

British
Isles

North
Sea

Baltic Sea

Greenwich 0° meridian

WORLD FACTS AND FIGURES

WORLD STATISTICS

	TOTAL POPULATION	2050 PROJECTED POPULATION	GROSS NATIONAL INCOME (GNI) PER CAPITA (US$)	LITERACY RATE (%)	INTERNATIONAL DIALING CODE	TIME ZONE	OFFICIAL WEBSITE TOURISM WEBSITE
WORLD	6 301 000 000	9 075 903 000	5 500	87.3	...	...	
AFGHANISTAN	23 897 000	97 324 000	...	...	93	+4.5	www.afghanistan-mfa.net ...
ALBANIA	3 166 000	3 458 000	1 740	98.2	355	+1	www.keshilliministrave.al www.albaniantourism.com
ALGERIA	31 800 000	49 500 000	1 890	90.4	213	+1	www.el-mouradia.dz www.mta.gov.dz
ANDORRA	71 000	58 000	...	...	376	+1	www.andorra.ad www.andorra.ad
ANGOLA	13 625 000	43 501 000	740	...	244	+1	www.angola.org www.angola.org.uk/prov_tourism.htm
ANTIGUA AND BARBUDA	73 000	112 000	9 160	...	1 268	-4	www.un.int/antigua www.antigua-barbuda.org
ARGENTINA	38 428 000	51 382 000	3 650	98.6	54	-3	www.info.gov.ar www.turismo.gov.ar
ARMENIA	3 061 000	2 506 000	950	99.8	374	+4	www.gov.am www.armeniainfo.am
AUSTRALIA	19 731 000	27 940 000	21 650	...	61	+8 to +11	www.gov.au www.australia.com
AUSTRIA	8 116 000	8 073 000	26 720	...	43	+1	www.oesterreich.at www.austria-tourism.at
AZERBAIJAN	8 370 000	9 631 000	810	...	994	+4	www.president.az ...
THE BAHAMAS	314 000	466 000	15 110	97.4	1 242	-5	www.bahamas.gov.bs www.bahamas.com
BAHRAIN	724 000	1 155 000	11 260	98.6	973	+3	www.bahrain.gov.bh www.bahraintourism.com
BANGLADESH	146 736 000	242 937 000	400	52.1	880	+6	www.bangladesh.gov.bd www.parjatan.org
BARBADOS	270 000	255 000	9 270	...	1 246	-4	www.barbados.gov.bb www.barbados.org/bta.htm
BELARUS	9 895 000	7 017 000	1 590	99.8	375	+2	www.government.by www.mst.by
BELGIUM	10 318 000	10 302 000	25 820	...	32	+1	www.belgium.be www.visitflanders.com Wallonia: www.opt.be
BELIZE	256 000	442 000	3 190	98.2	501	-6	www.belize.gov.bz www.travelbelize.org
BENIN	6 736 000	22 123 000	440	55.5	229	+1	www.gouv.bj www.benintourisme.com
BHUTAN	2 257 000	4 393 000	660	...	975	+6	www.bhutan.gov.bt www.tourism.gov.bt
BOLIVIA	8 808 000	14 908 000	890	96.3	591	-4	www.bolivia.gov.bo ...
BOSNIA-HERZEGOVINA	4 161 000	3 170 000	1 540	...	387	+1	www.fbihvlada.gov.ba www.bhtourism.ba
BOTSWANA	1 785 000	1 658 000	3 430	89.1	267	+2	www.gov.bw www.gov.bw/tourism
BRAZIL	178 470 000	253 105 000	2 710	93.0	55	-2 to -5	www.brazil.gov.br www.embratur.gov.br
BRUNEI	358 000	681 000	...	99.5	673	+8	www.brunei.gov.bn www.tourismbrunei.com
BULGARIA	7 897 000	5 065 000	2 130	99.7	359	+2	www.government.bg www.bulgariatravel.org
BURKINA	13 002 000	39 093 000	300	36.9	226	GMT	www.primature.gov.bf www.culture.gov.bf
BURUNDI	6 825 000	25 812 000	100	66.1	257	+2	www.burundi.gov.bi www.burundi.gov.bi/tour.htm
CAMBODIA	14 144 000	25 972 000	310	80.1	855	+7	www.cambodia.gov.kh www.visit-mekong.com/cambodia/mot/
CAMEROON	16 018 000	26 891 000	640	94.4	237	+1	www.spm.gov.cm www.camnet.cm/mintour/tourisme
CANADA	31 510 000	42 844 000	23 930	...	1	-3.5 to -8	canada.gc.ca www.travelcanada.ca
CAPE VERDE	463 000	1 002 000	1 490	89.2	238	-1	www.governo.cv ...
CENTRAL AFRICAN REPUBLIC	3 865 000	6 747 000	260	69.9	236	+1	... ...

	TOTAL POPULATION	2050 PROJECTED POPULATION	GROSS NATIONAL INCOME (GNI) PER CAPITA (US$)	LITERACY RATE (%)	INTERNATIONAL DIALING CODE	TIME ZONE	OFFICIAL WEBSITE *TOURISM WEBSITE*
CHAD	8 598 000	31 497 000	250	69.9	235	+1	www.tit.td ...
CHILE	15 805 000	20 657 000	4 390	99.0	56	-3	www.gobiernodechile.cl *www.visit-chile.org*
CHINA	1 289 161 000	1 402 062 000	1 100	98.2	86	+8	www.china.org.cn *www.cnta.com/lyen/index.asp*
COLOMBIA	44 222 000	65 679 000	1 810	97.2	57	-5	www.gobiernoenlinea.gov.co *www.idct.gov.co*
COMOROS	768 000	1 781 000	450	59.0	269	+3	www.presidence-uniondescomores.com ...
CONGO	3 724 000	13 721 000	640	97.8	242	+1	www.congo-site.com ...
CONGO, DEMOCRATIC REPUBLIC OF THE	52 771 000	177 271 000	100	83.7	243	+1 to +2	www.un.int/drcongo ...
COSTA RICA	4 173 000	6 426 000	4 280	98.4	506	-6	www.casapres.go.cr *www.visitcostarica.com*
CÔTE D'IVOIRE	16 631 000	33 959 000	660	67.6	225	GMT	www.pr.ci ...
CROATIA	4 428 000	3 686 000	5 350	99.8	385	+1	www.vlada.hr *www.croatia.hr*
CUBA	11 300 000	9 749 000	...	99.8	53	-5	www.cubagob.gov.cu *www.cubatravel.cu*
CYPRUS	802 000	1 174 000	12 320	99.8	357	+2	www.cyprus.gov.cy *www.visitcyprus.org.cy*
CZECH REPUBLIC	10 236 000	8 452 000	6 740	...	420	+1	www.czech.cz *www.visitczech.cz*
DENMARK	5 364 000	5 851 000	33 750	...	45	+1	www.denmark.dk *www.visitdenmark.com*
DJIBOUTI	703 000	1 547 000	910	85.7	253	+3	... *www.office-tourisme.dj*
DOMINICA	79 000	98 000	3 360	...	1 767	-4	www.dominica.co.uk *www.ndcdominica.dm*
DOMINICAN REPUBLIC	8 745 000	12 668 000	2 070	91.7	1 809	-4	www.presidencia.gov.do *www.dominicanrepublic.com/Tourism*
EAST TIMOR	778 000	3 265 000	430	...	670	+9	www.gov.east-timor.org ...
ECUADOR	13 003 000	19 214 000	1 790	97.5	593	-5	www.ec-gov.net *www.vivecuador.com*
EGYPT	71 931 000	125 916 000	1 390	71.3	20	+2	www.sis.gov.eg *www.egypttreasures.gov.eg*
EL SALVADOR	6 515 000	10 823 000	2 200	89.0	503	-6	www.casapres.gob.sv *www.elsalvadorturismo.gob.sv*
EQUATORIAL GUINEA	494 000	1 146 000	930	97.4	240	+1	www.ceiba-equatorial-guinea.org ...
ERITREA	4 141 000	11 229 000	190	72.0	291	+3	shabait.com ...
ESTONIA	1 323 000	1 119 000	4 960	99.8	372	+2	www.riik.ee *visitestonia.com*
ETHIOPIA	70 678 000	170 190 000	90	57.2	251	+3	www.ethiopar.net *www.tourismethiopia.org*
FIJI	839 000	934 000	2 360	99.2	679	+12	www.fiji.gov.fj *www.bulafiji.com*
FINLAND	5 207 000	5 329 000	27 020	...	358	+2	www.valtioneuvosto.fi *www.visitfinland.com*
FRANCE	60 144 000	63 116 000	24 770	...	33	+1	www.premier-ministre.gouv.fr *www.franceguide.com*
GABON	1 329 000	2 279 000	3 580	...	241	+1	www.un.int/gabon *www.tourisme-gabon.com*
THE GAMBIA	1 426 000	3 106 000	310	60.0	220	GMT	www.statehouse.gm *www.visitthegambia.qm*
GEORGIA	5 126 000	2 985 000	830	...	995	+3	www.parliament.ge *www.parliament.ge/TOURISM/*
GERMANY	82 476 000	78 765 000	25 250	...	49	+1	www.bundesregierung.de *www.germany-tourism.de*
GHANA	20 922 000	40 573 000	320	92.1	233	GMT	www.ghana.gov.gh *www.ghanatourism.gov.gh*
GREECE	10 976 000	10 742 000	13 720	99.8	30	+2	www.greece.gov.gr *www.gnto.gr*

	TOTAL POPULATION	2050 PROJECTED POPULATION	GROSS NATIONAL INCOME (GNI) PER CAPITA (US$)	LITERACY RATE (%)	INTERNATIONAL DIALING CODE	TIME ZONE	OFFICIAL WEBSITE / TOURISM WEBSITE
GRENADA	80 000	157 000	3 790	...	1 473	-4	www.grenadaconsulate.org / grenadagrenadines.com
GUATEMALA	12 347 000	25 612 000	1 910	80.3	502	-6	www.congreso.gob.gt / www.mayaspirit.com.gt
GUINEA	8 480 000	22 987 000	430	...	224	GMT	www.guinee.gov.gn / www.mirinet.net.gn/ont/
GUINEA-BISSAU	1 493 000	5 312 000	140	60.9	245	GMT	... / ...
GUYANA	765 000	488 000	900	99.8	592	-4	www.gina.gov.gy / www.guyana-tourism.com
HAITI	8 326 000	12 996 000	380	66.2	509	-5	www.haiti.org / www.haititourisme.org
HONDURAS	6 941 000	12 776 000	970	84.2	504	-6	www.congreso.gob.hn / www.letsgohonduras.com
HUNGARY	9 877 000	8 262 000	6 330	99.8	36	+1	www.magyarorszag.hu / www.hungarytourism.hu
ICELAND	290 000	370 000	30 810	...	354	GMT	eng.stjornarrad.is / www.icetourist.is
INDIA	1 065 462 000	1 592 704 000	530	74.1	91	+5.5	goidirectory.nic.in / www.tourismofindia.com
INDONESIA	219 883 000	284 640 000	810	98.0	62	+7 to +9	www.indonesia.go.id / www.budpar.go.id
IRAN	68 920 000	101 944 000	2 000	94.8	98	+3.5	www.president.ir / www.itto.org
IRAQ	25 175 000	63 693 000	...	45.3	964	+3	www.iraqmofa.net / ...
IRELAND	3 956 000	5 762 000	26 960	...	353	GMT	www.irlgov.ie / www.ireland.travel.ie
ISRAEL	6 433 000	10 403 000	16 020	99.5	972	+2	www.index.gov.il/FirstGov / www.tourism.gov.il
ITALY	57 423 000	50 912 000	21 560	99.8	39	+1	www.governo.it / www.enit.it
JAMAICA	2 651 000	2 586 000	2 760	94.5	1 876	-5	www.jis.gov.jm / www.visitjamaica.com
JAPAN	127 654 000	112 198 000	34 510	...	81	+9	web-japan.org / www.jnto.go.jp
JORDAN	5 473 000	10 225 000	1 850	99.5	962	+2	www.nic.gov.jo / www.see-jordan.com
KAZAKHSTAN	15 433 000	13 086 000	1 780	...	7	+4 to +6	www.president.kz / www.president.kz
KENYA	31 987 000	83 073 000	390	95.8	254	+3	www.kenya.go.ke / www.magicalkenya.com
KIRIBATI	88 000	177 000	880	...	686	+12 to +14	... / ...
KUWAIT	2 521 000	5 279 000	16 340	93.1	965	+3	www.kuwaitmission.com / ...
KYRGYZSTAN	5 138 000	6 664 000	330	...	996	+5	www.gov.kg / ...
LAOS	5 657 000	11 586 000	320	73.3	856	+7	www.un.int/lao / mekongcenter.com
LATVIA	2 307 000	1 678 000	4 070	99.8	371	+2	www.saeima.lv / www.latviatourism.lv
LEBANON	3 653 000	4 702 000	4 040	95.6	961	+2	www.presidency.gov.lb / www.destinationlebanon.com
LESOTHO	1 802 000	1 601 000	590	91.1	266	+2	www.lesotho.gov.ls / www.lesotho.gov.ls/lstourism.htm
LIBERIA	3 367 000	10 653 000	130	71.7	231	GMT	www.embassyofliberia.org
LIBYA	5 551 000	9 553 000	...	97.0	218	+2	www.libya-un.org / ...
LIECHTENSTEIN	34 000	44 000	...	...	423	+1	www.liechtenstein.li / www.tourismus.li
LITHUANIA	3 444 000	2 565 000	4 490	99.8	370	+2	www.lrv.lt / www.tourism.lt
LUXEMBOURG	453 000	721 000	43 940	...	352	+1	www.gouvernement.lu / www.ont.lu
MACEDONIA (F.Y.R.O.M.)	2 056 000	1 884 000	1 980	...	389	+1	www.vlada.mk / ...

	TOTAL POPULATION	2050 PROJECTED POPULATION	GROSS NATIONAL INCOME (GNI) PER CAPITA (US$)	LITERACY RATE (%)	INTERNATIONAL DIALING CODE	TIME ZONE	OFFICIAL WEBSITE / *TOURISM WEBSITE*
MADAGASCAR	17 404 000	43 508 000	290	81.5	261	+3	www.madagascar-diplomatie.ch ...
MALAWI	12 105 000	29 452 000	170	72.5	265	+2	www.malawi.gov.mw *www.tourismmalawi.com*
MALAYSIA	24 425 000	38 924 000	3 780	97.9	60	+8	www.gov.my *tourism.gov.my*
MALDIVES	318 000	682 000	2 300	99.2	960	+5	www.maldivesinfo.gov.mv *www.visitmaldives.com*
MALI	13 007 000	41 976 000	290	69.9	223	GMT	www.maliensdelexterieur.gov.ml *www.malitourisme.com*
MALTA	394 000	428 000	9 260	98.7	356	+1	www.gov.mt *www.visitmalta.com*
MARSHALL ISLANDS	53 000	150 000	2 710	...	692	+12	www.rmiembassyus.org *www.visitmarshallislands.com*
MAURITANIA	2 893 000	7 497 000	430	49.6	222	GMT	www.mauritania.mr ...
MAURITIUS	1 221 000	1 465 000	4 090	94.3	230	+4	www.gov.mu *www.mauritius.net*
MEXICO	103 457 000	139 015 000	6 230	97.2	52	-6 to -8	www.presidencia.gob.mx *www.visitmexico.com*
MICRONESIA, FEDERATED STATES OF	109 000	99 000	2 090	...	691	+10 to +11	www.fsmgov.org *visit-fsm.org*
MOLDOVA	4 267 000	3 312 000	590	99.8	373	+2	www.moldova.md *www.turism.md*
MONACO	34 000	55 000	...	...	377	+1	monaco.gouv.mc *www.monaco-congres.com*
MONGOLIA	2 594 000	3 625 000	480	99.6	976	+8	www.pmis.gov.mn *www.mongoliatourism.gov.mn*
MOROCCO	30 566 000	46 397 000	1 320	69.6	212	GMT	www.mincom.gov.ma *www.tourism-in-morocco.com*
MOZAMBIQUE	18 863 000	37 604 000	210	62.8	258	+2	www.mozambique.mz *www.mozambique.mz/turismo/topics.htm*
MYANMAR	49 485 000	63 657 000	...	91.4	95	+6.5	www.myanmar.com *www.myanmar-tourism.com*
NAMIBIA	1 987 000	3 060 000	1 870	92.3	264	+2	www.grnnet.gov.na *www.namibiatourism.com.na*
NAURU	13 000	18 000	...	...	674	+12	www.un.int/nauru ...
NEPAL	25 164 000	51 172 000	240	62.8	977	+5.75	www.nepalhmg.gov.np *www.welcomenepal.com*
NETHERLANDS	16 149 000	17 139 000	26 310	98.3	31	+1	www.overheid.nl *www.visitholland.com*
NEW ZEALAND	3 875 000	4 790 000	15 870	...	64	+13	www.govt.nz *www.newzealand.com*
NICARAGUA	5 466 000	9 371 000	730	72.3	505	-6	www.asamblea.gob.ni *www.visit-nicaragua.com*
NIGER	11 972 000	50 156 000	200	24.4	227	+1	www.delgi.ne/presidence ...
NIGERIA	124 009 000	258 108 000	320	88.5	234	+1	www.nigeria.gov.ng *www.nigeriatourism.net*
NORTH KOREA	22 664 000	24 192 000	...	...	850	+9	www.korea-dpr.com ...
NORWAY	4 533 000	5 435 000	43 350	...	47	+1	www.norway.no *www.visitnorway.com*
OMAN	2 851 000	4 958 000	7 830	98.5	968	+4	www.moneoman.gov.om *www.omantourism.gov.om*
PAKISTAN	153 578 000	304 700 000	470	58.7	92	+5	www.infopak.gov.pk *www.tourism.gov.pk*
PALAU	20 000	21 000	7 500	...	680	+9	www.palauembassy.com *visit-palau.com*
PANAMA	3 120 000	5 093 000	4 250	97.0	507	-5	www.pa *www.visitpanama.com*
PAPUA NEW GUINEA	5 711 000	10 619 000	510	76.9	675	+10	www.pngonline.gov.pg *www.pngtourism.org.pg/*
PARAGUAY	5 878 000	12 095 000	1 100	97.3	595	-3	www.presidencia.gov.py *www.senatur.gov.py*
PERU	27 167 000	42 552 000	2 150	97.1	51	-5	www.peru.gob.pe *www.peru.org.pe*

	TOTAL POPULATION	2050 PROJECTED POPULATION	GROSS NATIONAL INCOME (GNI) PER CAPITA (US$)	LITERACY RATE (%)	INTERNATIONAL DIALING CODE	TIME ZONE	OFFICIAL WEBSITE / TOURISM WEBSITE
PHILIPPINES	79 999 000	127 068 000	1 080	98.8	63	+8	www.gov.ph / www.tourism.gov.ph
POLAND	38 587 000	31 916 000	5 270	99.8	48	+1	www.poland.gov.pl / www.poland-tourism.pl
PORTUGAL	10 062 000	10 723 000	12 130	99.8	351	GMT	www.portugal.gov.pt / www.portugalinsite.pt
QATAR	610 000	1 330 000	...	95.3	974	+3	english.mofa.gov.qa / www.experienceqatar.com
ROMANIA	22 334 000	16 757 000	2 310	99.7	40	+2	www.guv.ro / www.romaniatravel.com
RUSSIAN FEDERATION	143 246 000	111 752 000	2 610	99.8	7	+2 to +12	www.gov.ru / www.russiatourism.ru
RWANDA	8 387 000	18 153 000	220	84.9	250	+2	www.gov.rw / www.rwandatourism.com
SAMOA	178 000	157 000	1 600	99.8	685	-11	www.govt.ws / www.visitsamoa.ws
ST KITTS AND NEVIS	42 000	59 000	6 880	...	1 869	-4	www.stkittsnevis.net / www.stkitts-tourism.com
ST LUCIA	149 000	188 000	4 050	...	1 758	-4	www.stlucia.gov.lc / www.stlucia.org
ST VINCENT AND THE GRENADINES	120 000	105 000	3 300	...	1 784	-4	... / www.svgtourism.com
SAN MARINO	28 000	30 000	...	...	378	+1	www.consigliograndeegenerale.sm / www.visitsanmarino.com
SÃO TOMÉ AND PRÍNCIPE	161 000	295 000	320	...	239	GMT	www.uns.st / www.saotome.st
SAUDI ARABIA	24 217 000	49 464 000	8 530	93.6	966	+3	www.saudinf.com / www.sauditourism.gov.sa
SENEGAL	10 095 000	23 108 000	550	52.9	221	GMT	www.gouv.sn / www.senegal-tourism.com
SERBIA AND MONTENEGRO	10 527 000	9 426 000	1 910	...	381	+1	www.gov.yu / www.visit-montenegro.com & www.serbia-tourism.org
SEYCHELLES	81 000	99 000	7 480	...	248	+4	www.virtualseychelles.sc / www.virtualseychelles.sc
SIERRA LEONE	4 971 000	13 786 000	150	...	232	GMT	www.statehouse-sl.org / ...
SINGAPORE	4 253 000	5 213 000	21 230	99.8	65	+8	www.gov.sg / www.visitsingapore.com
SLOVAKIA	5 402 000	4 612 000	4 920	...	421	+1	www.government.gov.sk / www.slovakiatourism.sk
SLOVENIA	1 984 000	1 630 000	11 830	99.8	386	+1	www.sigov.si / www.slovenia-tourism.si
SOLOMON ISLANDS	477 000	921 000	600	...	677	+11	www.commerce.gov.sb / www.commerce.gov.sb/Tourism
SOMALIA	9 890 000	21 329 000	...	...	252	+3	... / ...
SOUTH AFRICA, REPUBLIC OF	45 026 000	48 660 000	2 780	91.8	27	+2	www.gov.za / www.southafrica.net
SOUTH KOREA	47 700 000	44 629 000	12 020	99.8	82	+9	www.korea.net / english.tour2korea.com
SPAIN	41 060 000	42 541 000	16 990	99.8	34	+1	www.la-moncloa.es / www.spain.info
SRI LANKA	19 065 000	23 554 000	930	97.1	94	+6	www.priu.gov.lk / www.srilankatourism.org
SUDAN	33 610 000	66 705 000	460	79.1	249	+3	www.sudan.gov.sd / ...
SURINAME	436 000	429 000	1 990	...	597	-3	www.kabinet.sr.org / www.mintct.sr
SWAZILAND	1 077 000	1 026 000	1 350	91.2	268	+2	www.gov.sz / www.mintour.gov.sz
SWEDEN	8 876 000	10 054 000	28 840	...	46	+1	www.sweden.se / www.visit-sweden.com
SWITZERLAND	7 169 000	7 252 000	39 880	...	41	+1	www.admin.ch / myswitzerland.com
SYRIA	17 800 000	35 935 000	1 160	88.3	963	+2	www.moi-syria.com / www.syriatourism.org
TAIWAN	22 548 009	...	...	...	886	+8	www.gov.tw / www.tbroc.gov.tw

	TOTAL POPULATION	2050 PROJECTED POPULATION	GROSS NATIONAL INCOME (GNI) PER CAPITA (US$)	LITERACY RATE (%)	INTERNATIONAL DIALING CODE	TIME ZONE	OFFICIAL WEBSITE *TOURISM WEBSITE*
TAJIKISTAN	6 245 000	10 423 000	190	99.8	992	+5	www.tjus.org *www.tajiktour.tajnet.com*
TANZANIA	36 977 000	66 845 000	290	91.6	255	+3	www.tanzania.go.tz *www.tanzaniatouristboard.com*
THAILAND	62 833 000	74 594 000	2 190	99.0	66	+7	www.thaigov.go.th *www.tourismthailand.org*
TOGO	4 909 000	13 544 000	310	77.4	228	GMT	www.republicoftogo.com *...*
TONGA	104 000	75 000	1 490	...	676	+13	www.pmo.gov.to *www.tongaholiday.com*
TRINIDAD AND TOBAGO	1 303 000	1 230 000	7 260	99.8	1 868	-4	www.gov.tt *www.visittnt.com*
TUNISIA	9 832 000	12 927 000	2 240	94.3	216	+1	www.tunisiaonline.com *www.tourismtunisia.com*
TURKEY	71 325 000	101 208 000	2 790	96.9	90	+2	www.mfa.gov.tr *www.turizm.gov.tr*
TURKMENISTAN	4 867 000	6 780 000	1 120	...	993	+5	www.turkmenistanembassy.org *www.turkmenistanembassy.org*
TUVALU	11 000	12 000	...	...	688	+12	... *www.timelesstuvalu.com*
UGANDA	25 827 000	126 950 000	240	80.3	256	+3	www.government.go.ug *www.visituganda.com*
UKRAINE	48 523 000	26 393 000	970	99.9	380	+2	www.kmu.gov.ua *www.tourism.gov.ua*
UNITED ARAB EMIRATES	2 995 000	9 056 000	...	91.5	971	+4	www.uae.gov.ae *...*
UNITED KINGDOM	58 789 194	67 143 000	28 350	...	44	GMT	www.direct.gov.uk *www.visitbritain.com*
UNITED STATES OF AMERICA	294 043 000	394 976 000	37 610	...	1	-5 to -10	www.firstgov.gov *www.tourstates.com*
URUGUAY	3 415 000	4 043 000	3 790	99.3	598	-3	www.presidencia.gub.uy *www.turismo.gub.uy*
UZBEKISTAN	26 093 000	38 665 000	420	99.7	998	+5	www.gov.uz *www.uzbektourism.uz*
VANUATU	212 000	375 000	1 180	...	678	+11	www.vanuatugovernment.gov.vu *www.vanuatutourism.com*
VATICAN CITY	472	1 000	...	...	39	+1	www.vatican.va *...*
VENEZUELA	25 699 000	41 991 000	3 490	98.2	58	-4	www.gobiernoenlinea.ve *...*
VIETNAM	81 377 000	116 654 000	480	97.3	84	+7	www.na.gov.vn *www.vietnamtourism.com*
YEMEN	20 010 000	59 454 000	520	67.8	967	+3	www.nic.gov.ye *www.yementourism.com*
ZAMBIA	10 812 000	22 781 000	380	89.1	260	+2	www.zambiatourism.com *www.zambiatourism.com*
ZIMBABWE	12 891 000	15 805 000	480	97.6	263	+2	www.zim.gov.zw *www.zimbabwetourism.co.zw*

INDICATOR	DEFINITION
Total population	Interpolated mid-year population, 2003.
2050 projected population	Projected total population for the year 2050.
GNI per capita	Gross National Income per person in U.S. dollars using the World Bank Atlas method, from latest available data.
Literacy rate	Percentage of population aged 15–24 with at least a basic ability to read and write, 2002.
International dialling code	The country code prefix to be used when dialling from another country.
Time zone	Time difference in hours between local standard time and Greenwich Mean Time.
Official Website	The official country website where available.
Tourism website	The country website for tourists where available.

WORLD TIME ZONES

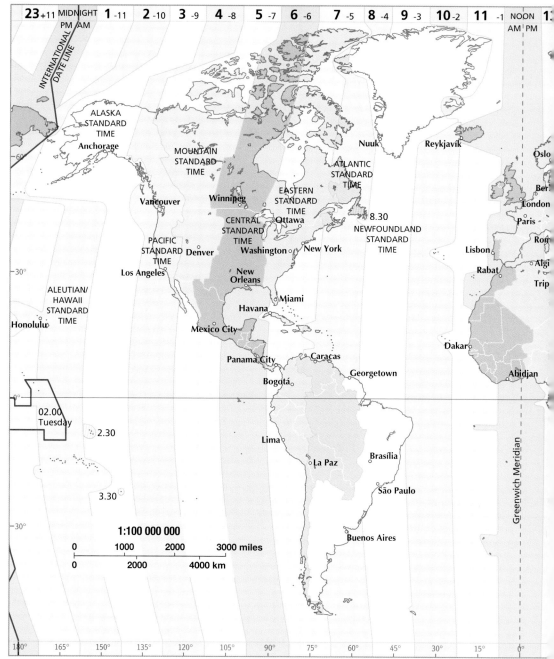

| 23 +11 | MIDNIGHT PM AM | 1 -11 | 2 -10 | 3 -9 | 4 -8 | 5 -7 | 6 -6 | 7 -5 | 8 -4 | 9 -3 | 10 -2 | 11 -1 | NOON AM PM |

The system of timekeeping throughout the world is based on twenty-four time zones, each stretching over fifteen degrees of longitude – the distance equivalent to a time difference of one hour. The Prime, or Greenwich Meridian (0 degrees west), is the basis for Greenwich Mean Time (GMT) or Universal Coordinated Time (UTC), by which other times are measured. This universal reference point was agreed at an international conference in 1884.

Times are the local Standard Times observed compared with 12:00 (noon) Greenwich Mean Time (GMT). Daylight Saving Time, normally one hour ahead of local Standard Time, which is observed by certain countries for part of the year, is not shown on the map.

ORGANIZATION	WEB ADDRESS	THEME
Greenwich Royal Observatory	www.rog.nmm.ac.uk	The home of time
Greenwich Mean Time	wwp.greenwichmeantime.com	World time since 1884
World time zones	www.worldtimezones.com	Detailed time zones information
The Official US time	www.time.gov/	The home of US time
International Date Line	aa.usno.navy.mil/faq/docs/international_date.html	Understanding the interntational date line

Time zone boundaries can be altered to suit international or internal boundaries. China uses only one time zone although it should theoretically have five, while the Russian Federation stretches over eleven zones. The four mainland USA time zones do not always follow state boundaries.

The International Date Line is an imaginary line at approximately 180° west (or east) of Greenwich, across which the date changes by one day. The line has no international legal status and countries near to the line can choose which date they will observe. The line was amended recently so that Caroline Island, in Kiribati in the Pacific Ocean, would be the first land area to greet the year 2000. The island was renamed Millennium Island in recognition of this.

Daylight Saving Time allows nations to adjust their clocks to extend daylight during the working day. It was first introduced to the UK during the First World War to reduce the demand for artificial heating and lighting.

TIME DIFFERENCES FOR MAJOR CITIES FROM GMT (hours)	
Los Angeles	-8
New York	-5
Buenos Aires	-3
Berlin	+1
Cape Town	+2
Mumbai	+5
Singapore	+8
Beijing	+8
Tōkyō	+9
Sydney	+10

GEOGRAPHICAL TABLES

HIGHEST MOUNTAINS	HEIGHT metres	feet	LOCATION
Mt Everest	8 848	29 028	China/Nepal
K2	8 611	28 251	China/Jammu and Kashmir
Kangchenjunga	8 586	28 169	India/Nepal
Lhotse	8 516	27 939	China/Nepal
Makalu	8 463	27 765	China/Nepal
Cho Oyu	8 201	26 906	China/Nepal
Dhaulagiri	8 167	26 794	Nepal
Manaslu	8 163	26 781	Nepal
Nanga Parbat	8 126	26 660	Jammu and Kashmir
Annapurna I	8 091	26 545	Nepal
Gasherbrum I	8 068	26 469	China/Jammu and Kashmir
Broad Peak	8 047	26 401	China/Jammu and Kashmir
Gasherbrum II	8 035	26 361	China/Jammu and Kashmir
Xixabangma Feng	8 012	26 286	China
Annapurna II	7 937	26 040	Nepal
Nuptse	7 885	25 869	Nepal
Himalchul	7 864	25 800	Nepal
Masherbrum	7 821	25 659	Jammu and Kashmir
Nandi Devi	7 816	25 643	India
Rakaposhi	7 788	25 551	Jammu and Kashmir

LONGEST RIVERS	LENGTH km	miles	CONTINENT
Nile	6 695	4 160	Africa
Amazon	6 516	4 049	South America
Yangtze	6 380	3 964	Asia
Mississippi-Missouri	5 969	3 709	North America
Ob'-Irtysh	5 568	3 460	Asia
Yenisey-Angara-Selenga	5 550	3 448	Asia
Yellow River	5 464	3 395	Asia
Congo	4 667	2 900	Africa
Río de la Plata-Paraná	4 500	2 796	South America
Irtysh	4 440	2 759	Asia
Mekong	4 425	2 750	Asia
Heilong Jiang-Argun'	4 416	2 744	Asia
Lena-Kirenga	4 400	2 734	Asia
MacKenzie-Peace-Finlay	4 241	2 635	North America
Niger	4 184	2 599	Africa
Yenisey	4 090	2 542	Asia
Missouri	4 086	2 539	North America
Mississippi	3 765	2 339	North America
Murray-Darling	3 750	2 330	Oceania
Ob'	3 701	2 300	Asia

LARGEST LAKES	AREA sq km	sq miles	CONTINENT
Caspian Sea	371 000	143 244	Asia/Europe
Lake Superior	82 100	31 699	North America
Lake Victoria	68 800	26 564	Africa
Lake Huron	59 600	23 012	North America
Lake Michigan	57 800	22 317	North America
Lake Tanganyika	32 900	12 702	Africa
Great Bear Lake	31 328	12 095	North America
Lake Baikal	30 500	11 776	Asia
Lake Nyasa	30 044	11 600	Africa
Great Slave Lake	28 568	11 030	North America
Lake Erie	25 700	9 922	North America
Lake Winnipeg	24 387	9 415	North America
Lake Ontario	18 960	7 320	North America
Lake Ladoga	18 390	7 100	Europe
Lake Balkhash	17 400	6 718	Asia
Aral Sea	17 158	6 625	Asia
Lake Onega	9 600	3 706	Europe
Lake Volta	8 485	3 276	Africa
Lake Titicaca	8 340	3 220	South America
Lake Nicaragua	8 150	3 147	North America

LARGEST DRAINAGE BASINS	AREA sq km	sq miles	CONTINENT
Amazon	7 050 000	2 722 000	South America
Congo	3 700 000	1 429 000	Africa
Nile	3 349 000	1 293 000	Africa
Mississippi-Missouri	3 250 000	1 255 000	North America
Río de la Plata-Paraná	3 100 000	1 197 000	South America
Ob'-Irtysh	2 990 000	1 154 000	Asia
Yenisey-Angara-Selenga	2 580 000	996 000	Asia
Lena-Kirenga	2 490 000	961 000	Asia
Yangtze	1 959 000	756 000	Asia
Niger	1 890 000	730 000	Africa
Heilong Jiang-Argun'	1 855 000	716 000	Asia
Mackenzie-Peace-Finlay	1 805 000	697 000	North America
Ganges-Brahmaputra	1 621 000	626 000	Asia
St Lawrence-St Louis	1 463 000	565 000	North America
Volga	1 380 000	533 000	Europe
Zambezi	1 330 000	514 000	Africa
Indus	1 166 000	450 000	Asia
Nelson-Saskatchewan	1 150 000	444 000	North America
Shaṭṭ al'Arab	1 114 000	430 000	Asia
Murray-Darling	1 058 000	408 000	Oceania

ATLANTIC OCEAN	AREA sq km	sq miles	DEEPEST POINT metres		feet
Total extent	86 557 000	33 420 000	8 605	Milwaukee Deep	28 231
Arctic Ocean	9 485 000	3 662 000	5 450		17 880
Caribbean Sea	2 512 000	970 000	7 680		25 196
Mediterranean Sea	2 510 000	969 000	5 121		16 800
Gulf of Mexico	1 544 000	596 000	3 504		11 495
Hudson Bay	1 233 000	476 000	259		849
North Sea	575 000	222 000	661		2 168
Black Sea	508 000	196 000	2 245		7 365
Baltic Sea	382 000	147 000	460		1 509

INDIAN OCEAN	AREA sq km	sq miles	DEEPEST POINT metres		feet
Total extent	73 427 000	28 350 000	7 125	Java Trench	23 376
Bay of Bengal	2 172 000	839 000	4 500		14 763
Red Sea	453 000	175 000	3 040		9 973
The Gulf	238 000	92 000	73		239

PACIFIC OCEAN	AREA sq km	sq miles	DEEPEST POINT metres		feet
Total extent	166 241 000	64 186 000	10 920	Challenger Deep	35 826
South China Sea	2 590 000	1 000 000	5 514		18 090
Bering Sea	2 261 000	873 000	4 150		13 615
Sea of Okhotsk	1 392 000	537 000	3 363		11 033
Sea of Japan (East Sea)	1 013 000	391 000	3 743		12 280
East China Sea and Yellow Sea	1 202 000	464 000	2 717		8 913

LARGEST ISLANDS	AREA sq km	sq miles	CONTINENT
Greenland	2 175 600	840 004	North America
New Guinea	808 510	312 167	Oceania
Borneo	745 561	287 863	Asia
Madagascar	587 040	266 657	Africa
Baffin Island	507 451	195 928	North America
Sumatra	473 606	182 860	Asia
Honshū	227 414	87 805	Asia
Great Britain	218 476	84 354	Europe
Victoria Island	217 291	83 897	North America
Ellesmere Island	196 236	75 767	North America
Celebes	189 216	73 057	Asia
South Island, New Zealand	151 215	58 384	Oceania
Java	132 188	51 038	Asia
North Island, New Zealand	115 777	44 702	Oceania
Cuba	110 860	42 803	North America
Newfoundland	108 860	42 031	North America
Luzon	104 690	40 421	Asia
Iceland	102 820	39 699	Europe
Mindanao	94 630	36 537	Asia
Novaya Zemlya	90 650	35 000	Europe

LARGEST COUNTRIES BY POPULATION	POPULATION
China	1 289 161 000
India	1 065 462 000
United States of America	294 043 000
Indonesia	219 883 000
Brazil	178 470 000
Pakistan	153 578 000
Bangladesh	146 736 000
Russian Federation	143 246 000
Japan	127 654 000
Nigeria	124 009 000

LARGEST COUNTRIES BY AREA	AREA sq km	sq miles
Russian Federation	17 075 400	6 592 849
Canada	9 984 670	3 855 103
United States of America	9 826 635	3 794 085
China	9 584 492	3 700 593
Brazil	8 514 879	3 287 613
Australia	7 692 024	2 969 907
India	3 064 898	1 183 364
Argentina	2 766 889	1 068 302
Kazakhstan	2 717 300	1 049 155
Sudan	2 505 813	967 500

DEEPEST LAKES	DEPTH metres	feet	CONTINENT
Lake Baikal	1 741	5 712	Asia
Lake Tanganyika	1 471	4 826	Africa
Caspian Sea	1 025	3 363	Asia/Europe
Lake Nyasa	706	2 316	Africa
Ysyk-Köl	702	2 303	Asia

LARGEST CITIES	POPULATION	LOCATION
Tōkyō	35 327 000	Japan
Mexico City	19 013 000	Mexico
New York	18 498 000	United States of America
Mumbai	18 336 000	India
São Paulo	18 333 000	Brazil
Delhi	15 334 000	India
Kolkata	14 299 000	India
Buenos Aires	13 349 000	Argentina
Jakarta	13 194 000	Indonesia
Shanghai	12 665 000	China
Dhaka	12 560 000	Bangladesh
Los Angeles	12 146 000	United States of America
Karachi	11 819 000	Pakistan
Rio de Janeiro	11 469 000	Brazil
Ōsaka	11 286 000	Japan
Cairo	11 146 000	Egypt
Lagos	11 135 000	Nigeria
Beijing	10 849 000	China
Manila	10 677 000	Philippines
Moscow	10 672 000	Russian Federation

LOWEST POINTS ON LAND	DEPTH BELOW SEA LEVEL metres	feet	LOCATION
Dead Sea	-417	-1 368	Asia
Lake Assal	-156	-512	Djibouti
Turpan Pendi	-154	-505	China
Qattara Depression	-133	-436	Egypt
Poluostrov Mangyshlak	-132	-433	Kazakhstan

HIGHEST WATERFALLS	HEIGHT metres	feet	LOCATION
Angel Falls	979	3 212	Venezuela
Tugela	948	3 110	South Africa
Utigård	800	2 625	Norway
Mongfossen	774	2 539	Norway
Mtarazi	762	2 500	Zimbabwe

BUSIEST AIRPORTS (2004)	LOCATION	PASSENGERS
Atlanta (ATL)	USA	83 606 583
Chicago (ORD)	USA	75 533 822
London (LHR)	UK	67 344 054
Tōkyō (HND)	Japan	62 291 405
Los Angeles (LAX)	USA	60 688 609
Dallas/Fort Worth Airport (DFW)	USA	59 412 217
Paris (CDG)	France	51 260 363
Frankfurt am Main (FRA)	Germany	51 098 271
Amsterdam (AMS)	Netherlands	42 541 180
Denver (DEN)	USA	42 393 766
Las Vegas (LAS)	USA	41 441 531
Phoenix (PHX)	USA	39 504 898
Madrid (MAD)	Spain	38 704 731
Bangkok (BKK)	Thailand	37 960 169
New York (JFK)	USA	37 518 143
Minneapolis/St Paul (MSP)	USA	36 713 173
Hong Kong (HKG)	China	36 711 920
Houston (IAH)	USA	36 506 116
Detroit (DTW)	USA	35 187 517
Beijing (PEK)	China	34 883 190

EARTH'S DIMENSIONS

Mass	5.974×10^{21} tonnes
Total area	509 450 000 sq km /196 672 000 sq miles
Land area	149 450 000 sq km / 57 688 000 sq miles
Water area	360 000 000 sq km /138 984 000 sq miles
Volume	$1\ 083\ 207 \times 10^6$ cubic km / $259\ 875 \times 10^6$ cubic miles
Equatorial diameter	12 756 km / 7 926 miles
Polar diameter	12 714 km / 7 900 miles
Equatorial circumference	40 075 km / 24 903 miles
Meridional circumference	40 008 km / 24 861 miles

Climate is defined by the long-term weather conditions prevalent in any part of the world. The classification of climate types is based on the relationship between temperature and humidity and also on how these are affected by latitude, altitude, ocean currents and wind. Weather is how climatic conditions affect local areas. Weather stations collect data on temperature and rainfall, which can be plotted on graphs as shown here. These are based on average monthly figures over a minimum period of thirty years and can help to monitor climate change.

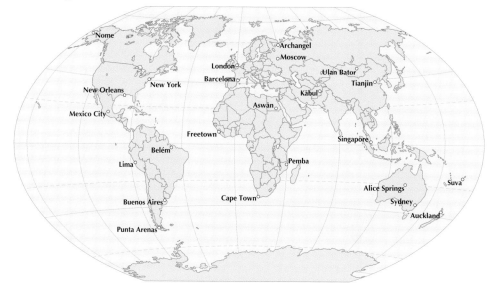

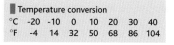

Temperature conversion						
°C	-20	-10	0	10	20	30	40
°F	-4	14	32	50	68	86	104

Rainfall conversion						
mm	25.4	127	254	381	508	635	762
ins	1	5	10	15	20	25	30

AFRICA

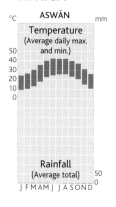

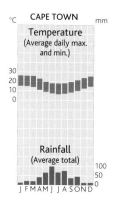

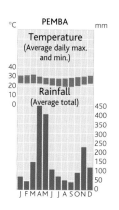

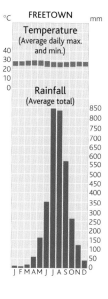

ASIA

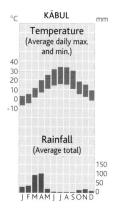

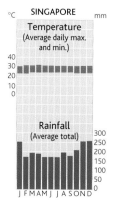

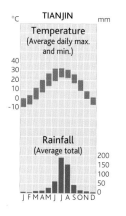

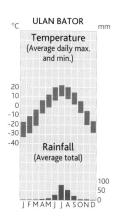

EUROPE

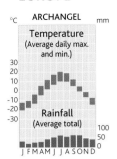

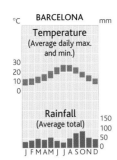

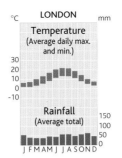

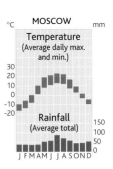

NORTH AMERICA

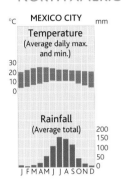

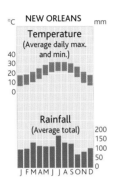

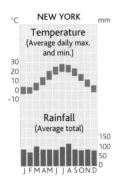

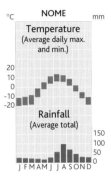

SOUTH AMERICA

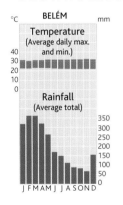

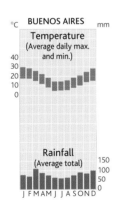

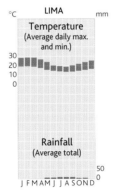

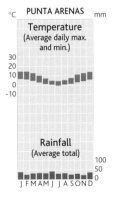

OCEANIA

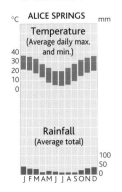

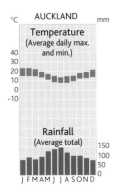

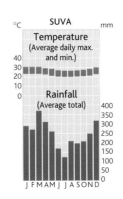

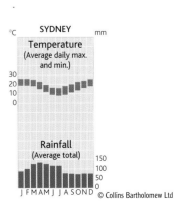

© Collins Bartholomew Ltd

The earth has a rich environment with a wide range of habitats. Forest and woodland form the predominant natural land cover and tropical rain forests are believed to be home to the majority of the world's bird, animal and plant species. These forests are part of a delicate land-atmosphere relationship disturbed by changes in land use. Grassland, shrubland and deserts cover most of the unwooded areas of the earth with low-growing tundra in the far northern latitudes. Grassland and shrubland regions in particular have been altered greatly by man through agriculture, livestock grazing and settlements.

ORGANIZATION	WEB ADDRESS	THEME
Earth Observatory	earthobservatory.nasa.gov	Observing the earth
National Earthquake Information Center	neic.usgs.gov	Monitoring earthquakes
Scripps Institution of Oceanography	sio.ucsd.edu	Exploration of the oceans
Visible Earth	visibleearth.nasa.gov	Satellite images of the earth
United States Geological Survey	Volcanoes.usgs.gov	Volcanic activity
UNESCO World Heritage Centre	whc.unesco.org	World Heritage Sites
British Geological Survey	www.bgs.ac.uk	Geology
The World Conservation Union	www.iucn.org	World and ocean conservation
World Rainforest Information Portal	www.rainforestweb.org	Rainforest information and resources
United Nations Environment Programme	www.unep.org	Environmental protection by the UN
World Conservation Monitoring Centre	www.unep-wcmc.org	Conservation and the environment
World Resources Institute	www.wri.org	Monitoring the environment and resources
IUCN Red List	www.redlist.org	Threatened species

OCEANS

Between them, the world's oceans cover approximately 70 per cent of the earth's surface. They contain 96 per cent of the earth's water and a vast range of flora and fauna. They are a major influence on the world's climate, particularly through ocean currents – the circulation of water within and between the oceans. Our understanding of the oceans has increased enormously over the last twenty years through the development of new technologies, including that of satellite images, which can generate vast amounts of data relating to the sea floor, ocean currents and sea surface temperatures.

ORGANIZATION	WEB ADDRESS	THEME
International Maritime Organisation	www.imo.org	Shipping and the environment
General Bathymetric Chart of the Oceans	www.ngdc.noaa.gov/mgg/gebco	Mapping the oceans
National Oceanography Centre	www.soc.soton.ac.uk	Researching the oceans
Scott Polar Research Institute	www.spri.cam.ac.uk	Polar research

CLIMATE

The Earth's climate system is highly complex. It is recognized and accepted that man's activities are affecting this system, and monitoring climate change, including human influences upon it, is now a major issue. Future climate change depends critically on how quickly and to what extent the concentration of greenhouse gases in the atmosphere increase. Change will not be uniform across the globe and the information from sophisticated mathematical climate models is invaluable in helping governments and industry to assess the impacts climate change will have.

ORGANIZATION	WEB ADDRESS	THEME
BBC Weather	www.bbc.co.uk/weather	Worldwide weather forecasts
Climatic Research Unit	www.cru.uea.ac.uk	Climatic research in the UK
The Meteorological Office	www.met-office.gov.uk	Weather information and climatic research
National Climatic Data Center	www.ncdc.noaa.gov	Global climate data
US National Hurricane Center	www.nhc.noaa.gov	Tracking hurricanes
National Oceanic and Atmospheric Administration	www.noaa.gov	Monitoring climate and the oceans
World Meteorological Organization	www.wmo.ch	The world's climate
El Niño	www.elnino.noaa.gov	El Niño research and observations

POPULATION

The world's population reached 6 billion in 1999. Rates of population growth vary between continents, but overall, the rate of growth has been increasing and it is predicted that by 2050 another 3 billion people will inhabit the planet. The process of urbanization, in particular migration from countryside to city, has led to the rapid growth of many cities. It is estimated that by 2007, for the first time in history, more people will be living in urban areas than in rural areas. There are now 387 cities with over 1 million inhabitants and twenty with over 10 million.

ORGANIZATION	WEB ADDRESS	THEME
UK National Statistics	www.statistics.gov.uk/census2001	The UK 2001 census
City Populations	www.citypopulation.de	Statistics and maps about population
US Census Bureau	www.census.gov	US and world population
World Urbanization Prospects	www.un.org/esa/population/publications/ wup2003/WUP2003Report.pdf	Population estimates and projections
United Nations Population Information Network	www.un.org/popin	World population statistics
UN Population Division	www.un.org/esa/population/unpop	Monitoring world population

COUNTRIES

The present picture of the political world is the result of a long history of exploration, colonialism, conflict and negotiation. In 1950 there were eighty-two independent countries. Since then there has been a significant trend away from colonial influences and although many dependent territories still exist, there are now 193 independent countries. The newest country is East Timor which gained independence from Indonesia in May 2002. The shapes of countries reflect a combination of natural features, such as mountain ranges, and political agreements. There are still areas of the world where boundaries are disputed or only temporarily settled as ceasefire lines.

ORGANIZATION	WEB ADDRESS	THEME
European Union	Europa.eu.int	Gateway to the European Union
Permament Committee on Geographical Names	www.pcgn.org.uk	Place names research in the UK
The World Factbook	www.odci.gov/cia/publications/factbook	Country profiles
Geographic Names Information System	geonames.usgs.gov	Place names research in the USA
United Nations	www.un.org	The United Nations
International Boundaries Research Unit	www-ibru.dur.ac.uk	International boundaries resources and research
Organisation for Economic Cooperation and Development	www.oecd.org	Economic statistics
World Bank	www.worldbank.org/data	World development indicators

TRAVEL

Travelling as a tourist or on business to some countries, or travelling within certain areas can be dangerous because of wars and political unrest. The UK Foreign Office provide the latest travel advice and security warnings. Some areas of the world, particularly tropical regions in the developing world, also carry many risks of disease. Advice should be sought on precautions to take and medications required.

ORGANIZATION	WEB ADDRESS	THEME
UK Foreign Office	www.fco.gov.uk	Travel, trade and country information
US Department of State	www.state.gov	Travel advice
World Health Organization	www.who.int	Health advice and world health issues
Centers for Disease Control and Prevention	www.cdc.gov/travel	Advice for travellers
Airports Council International	www.airports.org	The voice of the world's airports
World Wise Directory	www.brookes.ac.uk/worldwise/directory.html	Basic information for all countries
Travel Daily News	www.traveldailynews.com	Travel and tourism newsletter

ORGANIZATIONS

Throughout the world there are many international, national and local organizations representing the interests of individual countries, groups of countries, regions and specialist groups. These can provide enormous amounts of information on economic, social, cultural, environmental and general geographical issues facing the world. The following is a selection of such sites.

ORGANIZATION	WEB ADDRESS	THEME
United Nations	www.un.org	The United Nations
United Nations Educational, Scientific and Cultural Organization	www.unesco.org	International collaboration
United Nations Children's Fund	www.unicef.org	Health, education, equality and protection for children
United Nations High Commissioner for Refugees	www.unhcr.org	The UN refugee agency
Food and Agriculture Organization	www.fao.org	Agriculture and defeating hunger
United Nations Development Programme	www.undp.org	The UN global development network
North Atlantic Treaty Organization	www.nato.int	North Atlantic freedom and security
European Environment Agency	www.eea.eu.int	Europe's environment
European Centre for Nature conservation	www.ecnc.nl/	Nature conservation in Europe
Europa - The European Union On-line	europe.eu.int	European Union facts and statistics
World Health Organisation	www.who.int	Health issues and advice
Association of Southeast Asian Nations	www.aseansec.org	Economic, social and cultural development
Africawater	www.africawater.org	Water resources in Africa
The Joint United Nations Convention on AIDS	www.unaids.org	The AIDS crisis
African Union	www.africa-union.org	African international relations
World Lakes Network	www.worldlakes.org/searchlakes.asp	Lakes around the world
The Secretariat of the Pacific Commmunity	www.spc.int	The Pacific community
The Maori world	www.maori.org.nz	Maori culture
US National Park Service	www.nps.gov	National Parks of the USA
Parks Canada	www.pc.gc.ca	Natural heritage of Canada
The Panama Canal	www.pancanal.com	Explore the Panama Canal
The Caribbean Community Secretariat	www.caricom.org	Caribbean Community
Organization of American States	www.oas.org	Inter-American cooperation
The Aztec Empire	www.aztecempire.com	Aztec culture
The Latin American Network Information Center	lanic.utexas.edu	Latin America
World Wildlife Fund	www.worldwildlife.org	Global environmental conservation
Amazon Conservation Team	www.amazonteam.org	Conservation in tropical America

DISTANCE AND CONVERSION CHARTS

DISTANCES

This table shows air distances in both kilometres and *miles* for 27 cities around the world. These are the shortest distances between cities and are known as Great Circle routes.

In the table below, each cell gives the distance as **kilometres / *miles***. Reading each origin-city row from left to right, the destination columns run (as printed) Tōkyō, Sydney, Singapore, Seoul, Rome, Rio de Janeiro, Paris, New York, Nairobi, Moscow, Montréal, Mexico City, Melbourne, Madrid, Los Angeles, London, Jerusalem, İstanbul, Delhi, Cape Town, Cairo, Buenos Aires, Berlin, Beijing, Bangkok, Auckland.

From \ To	Tōkyō	Sydney	Singapore	Seoul	Rome	Rio de Janeiro	Paris	New York	Nairobi	Moscow	Montréal	Mexico City	Melbourne	Madrid	Los Angeles	London	Jerusalem	İstanbul	Delhi	Cape Town	Cairo	Buenos Aires	Berlin	Beijing	Bangkok	Auckland
Abu Dhabi	8075 / 5018	9793 / 6085	5905 / 3669	6918 / 4299	4303 / 2674	11764 / 7310	5247 / 3260	11040 / 6860	3422 / 2126	3735 / 2321	10647 / 6616	14374 / 8932	11689 / 7263	5632 / 3500	13481 / 8377	5478 / 3404	2043 / 1270	2987 / 1856	2317 / 1440	7498 / 4659	2367 / 1471	13534 / 8410	4637 / 2881	5972 / 3711	4795 / 3091	14244 / 8851
Auckland	8811 / 5475	2161 / 1343	8411 / 5227	9596 / 5963	18400 / 11433	12288 / 7636	18540 / 11521	14187 / 8816	13966 / 8678	16194 / 10063	14379 / 8935	10947 / 6802	2629 / 1634	19592 / 12174	10479 / 6512	18330 / 11390	16287 / 10121	17042 / 10590	12482 / 7756	11796 / 7330	16573 / 10298	10372 / 6445	17743 / 11025	10388 / 6455	9566 / 5944	
Bangkok	4610 / 2865	7523 / 4675	1427 / 887	3720 / 2312	8842 / 5494	16081 / 9993	9457 / 5877	13949 / 8668	7218 / 4485	7070 / 4393	13417 / 8337	15760 / 9739	7359 / 4573	10196 / 6336	13319 / 8276	9544 / 5931	6895 / 4285	7477 / 4646	2917 / 1813	10144 / 6303	7279 / 4523	16885 / 10492	8613 / 5352	3291 / 2045		
Beijing	2104 / 1307	8923 / 5545	4465 / 2775	958 / 595	8144 / 5061	17325 / 10766	8236 / 5118	11012 / 6843	9216 / 5727	5809 / 3610	10490 / 6518	12478 / 7754	9093 / 5650	9243 / 5744	10082 / 6265	8160 / 5071	7135 / 4434	7072 / 4394	3788 / 2354	12947 / 8045	7557 / 4696	19265 / 11971	7375 / 4583			
Berlin	8942 / 5556	16090 / 9998	9927 / 6169	8150 / 5064	1182 / 735	9989 / 6207	880 / 547	6403 / 3979	6353 / 3948	1612 / 1002	6018 / 3740	9746 / 6056	15970 / 9924	1871 / 1163	9332 / 5799	934 / 580	2903 / 1804	1739 / 1081	5791 / 3599	9588 / 5958	2891 / 1796	11890 / 7388				
Buenos Aires	18365 / 11412	11821 / 7345	15889 / 9873	19429 / 12073	11135 / 6919	1968 / 1223	11029 / 6853	8490 / 5276	10416 / 6472	13461 / 8365	9001 / 5593	7366 / 4577	11629 / 7226	10024 / 6229	9828 / 6107	11105 / 6901	12236 / 7603	12235 / 7603	15800 / 9818	6891 / 4282	11811 / 7339					
Cairo	9587 / 5957	14415 / 8957	8270 / 5139	8504 / 5284	2135 / 1327	9882 / 6141	3215 / 1998	9042 / 5618	3518 / 2186	2899 / 1801	8733 / 5427	12392 / 7700	13966 / 8678	3355 / 2083	12223 / 7595	3513 / 2183	426 / 265	1234 / 767	4436 / 2757	7208 / 4479						
Cape Town	14737 / 9157	11034 / 6856	9671 / 6009	13710 / 8519	8417 / 5230	6075 / 3775	9307 / 5783	12551 / 7799	4090 / 2542	10101 / 6277	12744 / 7919	13703 / 8515	10338 / 6424	8536 / 5304	16054 / 9976	9635 / 5987	7481 / 4649	8367 / 5199	9284 / 5769							
Delhi	5857 / 3640	10415 / 6472	4142 / 2574	4699 / 2920	5929 / 3684	14080 / 8749	6601 / 4102	11779 / 7319	5428 / 3373	4349 / 2702	11286 / 7013	14679 / 9121	10192 / 6333	7288 / 4529	12882 / 8005	6724 / 4178	4032 / 2505	4560 / 2834								
İstanbul	8970 / 5574	14944 / 9286	8652 / 5376	7975 / 4956	1379 / 857	10268 / 6380	2261 / 1405	8089 / 5026	4751 / 2952	1755 / 1091	7730 / 4803	11448 / 7114	14628 / 9090	2744 / 1705	11043 / 6862	2504 / 1556	1170 / 727									
Jerusalem	9171 / 5699	14126 / 8778	7924 / 4924	8083 / 5023	2310 / 1435	10308 / 6405	3339 / 2075	9190 / 5711	3662 / 2276	2671 / 1660	8854 / 5502	12552 / 7800	13713 / 8521	3602 / 2238	12210 / 7587	3615 / 2246										
London	9585 / 5956	16990 / 10557	10860 / 6748	8882 / 5519	1434 / 891	9254 / 5750	341 / 212	5586 / 3471	6805 / 4229	2506 / 1557	5240 / 3256	8947 / 5560	16902 / 10503	1264 / 785	8778 / 5455											
Los Angeles	8828 / 5486	12065 / 7497	14136 / 8784	9605 / 5968	10212 / 6346	10129 / 6294	9106 / 5658	3945 / 2451	15553 / 9664	9793 / 6085	3973 / 2469	2492 / 1549	12762 / 7930	9387 / 5833												
Madrid	10789 / 6704	17687 / 10990	11396 / 7081	10021 / 6227	1365 / 848	8118 / 5044	1054 / 655	5785 / 3595	6177 / 3838	3446 / 2141	5551 / 3449	9083 / 5644	17315 / 10759													
Melbourne	8159 / 5070	711 / 442	6050 / 3759	8552 / 5314	15987 / 9934	13227 / 8219	16793 / 10435	16671 / 10359	11513 / 7154	14418 / 8959	16730 / 10396	13557 / 8424														
Mexico City	11319 / 7034	12972 / 8061	16623 / 10329	12071 / 7501	10260 / 6375	7669 / 4765	9213 / 5725	3362 / 2089	14834 / 9218	10740 / 6674	3728 / 2317															
Montréal	10409 / 6468	16026 / 9958	14816 / 9207	10577 / 6572	6601 / 4102	8175 / 5080	5522 / 3431	533 / 331	11692 / 7265	7077 / 4398																
Moscow	7502 / 4662	14487 / 9002	8426 / 5236	6626 / 4117	2378 / 1478	11529 / 7164	2492 / 1549	7530 / 4679	6323 / 3929																	
Nairobi	11266 / 7001	12162 / 7557	7467 / 4640	10115 / 6285	5374 / 3339	8941 / 5556	6471 / 4021	11849 / 7363																		
New York	10870 / 6755	15990 / 9936	15349 / 9538	11078 / 6884	6907 / 4292	7729 / 4803	5851 / 3636																			
Paris	9738 / 6051	16959 / 10538	10743 / 6676	8990 / 5586	1108 / 689	9146 / 5683																				
Rio de Janeiro	18557 / 10288	13539 / 8413	15740 / 9781	18135 / 11269	9181 / 5705																					
Rome	9881 / 6140	16322 / 10142	10030 / 6232	8991 / 5587																						
Seoul	1160 / 721	8298 / 5156	4666 / 2899																							
Singapore	5317 / 3304	6293 / 3910																								
Sydney	7794 / 4843																									

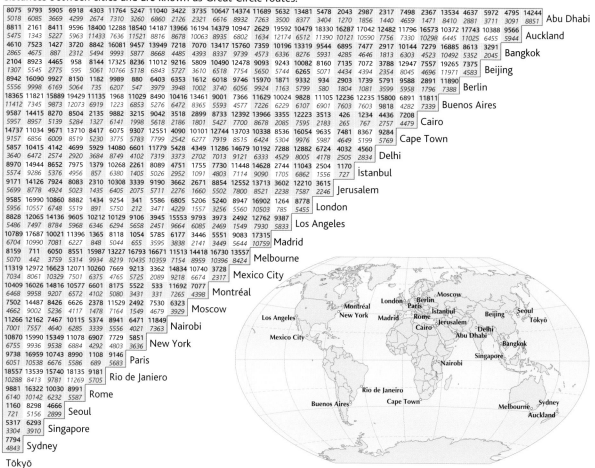

CONVERSION CHARTS

To convert	into	multiply by
LENGTH AND AREA		
millimetres	inches	0.0394
centimetres	inches	0.3937
metres	feet	3.2808
metres	yards	1.0936
kilometres	miles	0.6214
inches	millimetres	25.4
inches	centimetres	2.54
feet	metres	0.3048
yards	metres	0.9144
miles	kilometres	1.6093
acres	hectares	0.4047
hectares	acres	2.4711
square miles	square kilometres	2.5900
square kilometres	square miles	0.3861
TEMPERATURE		
°C	°F	multiply by 1.8 and add 32
°F	°C	subtract 32 and divide by 1.8

To convert	into	multiply by
WEIGHT		
grams	ounces	0.0353
kilograms	pounds	2.2046
metric tonnes (1000 kg)	tons (2 240lbs)	0.9842
ounces	grams	28.3495
pounds	kilograms	0.4536
tons (2 240lbs)	metric tonnes (1000 kg)	1.0161
VOLUME		
pints (20fl oz)	litres	0.5683
imperial gallons	litres	4.5461
litres	pints (20fl oz)	1.7598
litres	imperial gallons	0.2200
SPEED		
km/h	mph	0.6214
mph	km/h	1.6093

INTRODUCTION TO THE INDEX

The index includes all names shown on the maps in the Atlas of the World. Names are referenced by page number and by a grid reference. The grid reference correlates to the alphanumeric values which appear within each map frame. Each entry also includes the country or geographical area in which the feature is located. Entries relating to names appearing on insets are indicated by a small box symbol: ▫, followed by a grid reference if the inset has its own alphanumeric values.

Name forms are as they appear on the maps, with additional alternative names or name forms included as cross-references which refer the user to the entry for the map form of the name. Names beginning with Mc or Mac are alphabetized exactly as they appear. The terms Saint, Sainte, Sankt, etc, are abbreviated to St, Ste, St, etc, but alphabetized as if in the full form.

Names of physical features beginning with generic geographical terms are permuted – the descriptive term is placed after the main part of the name. For example, Lake Superior is indexed as Superior, Lake; Mount Everest as Everest, Mount. This policy is applied to all languages.

Entries, other than those for towns and cities, include a descriptor indicating the type of geographical feature. Descriptors are not included where the type of feature is implicit in the name itself.

Administrative divisions are included to differentiate entries of the same name and feature type within the one country. In such cases, duplicate names are alphabetized in order of administrative division. Additional qualifiers are also included for names within selected geographical areas.

INDEX ABBREVIATIONS

admin. div.	administrative division	**g.**	gulf	**Port.**	Portugal
Afgh.	Afghanistan	**Ger.**	Germany	**prov.**	province
Alg.	Algeria	**Guat.**	Guatemala	**pt**	point
Arg.	Argentina	**hd**	headland	**r.**	river
Austr.	Australia	**Hond.**	Honduras	**r. mouth**	river mouth
aut. comm.	autonomous community	**i.**	island	**reg.**	region
aut. reg.	autonomous region	**imp. l.**	impermanent lake	**resr**	reservoir
aut. rep.	autonomous republic	**Indon.**	Indonesia	**rf**	reef
Azer.	Azerbaijan	**is.**	islands	**Rus. Fed.**	Russian Federation
b.	bay	**isth.**	isthmus	**S.**	South
B.I.O.T.	British Indian Ocean Territory	**Kazakh.**	Kazakhstan	**salt l.**	salt lake
		Kyrg.	Kyrgyzstan	**sea chan.**	sea channel
Bangl.	Bangladesh	**l.**	lake	**Serb. and Mont.**	Serbia and Montenegro
Bol.	Bolivia	**lag.**	lagoon	**special admin. reg.**	special administrative region
Bos.-Herz.	Bosnia Herzegovina	**Lith.**	Lithuania		
Bulg.	Bulgaria	**Lux.**	Luxembourg	**str.**	strait
c.	cape	**Madag.**	Madagascar	**Switz.**	Switzerland
Can.	Canada	**Maur.**	Mauritania	**Tajik.**	Tajikistan
C.A.R.	Central African Republic	**Mex.**	Mexico	**Tanz.**	Tanzania
Col.	Colombia	**Moz.**	Mozambique	**terr.**	territory
Czech Rep.	Czech Republic	**mt.**	mountain	**Thai.**	Thailand
Dem. Rep. Congo	Democratic Republic of Congo	**mts**	mountains	**Trin. and Tob.**	Trinidad and Tobago
		mun.	municipality	**Turkm.**	Turkmenistan
depr.	depression	**N.**	North	**U.A.E.**	United Arab Emirates
des.	desert	**Neth.**	Netherlands	**U.K.**	United Kingdom
Dom. Rep.	Dominican Republic	**Neth. Antilles**	Netherland Antilles	**Ukr.**	Ukraine
Equat. Guinea	Equatorial Guinea	**Nic.**	Nicaragua	**union terr.**	union territory
		N.Z.	New Zealand	**Uru.**	Uruguay
esc.	escarpment	**Pak.**	Pakistan	**U.S.A.**	United States of America
est.	estuary	**Para.**	Paraguay	**Uzbek.**	Uzbekistan
Eth.	Ethiopia	**pen.**	peninsula	**val.**	valley
Fin.	Finland	**Phil.**	Philippines	**Venez.**	Venezuela
for.	forest	**plat.**	plateau	**vol.**	volcano
Fr. Guiana	French Guiana	**P.N.G.**	Papua New Guinea	**vol. crater**	volcanic crater
Fr. Polynesia	French Polynesia	**Pol.**	Poland		

A

93 E4 **Aabenraa** Denmark
100 B3 **Aachen** Ger.
93 E4 **Aalborg** Denmark
102 C2 **Aalen** Ger.
100 B2 **Aalst** Belgium
100 B2 **Aarschot** Belgium
93 I3 **Äänekoski** Fin.
105 D2 **Aarau** Switz.
100 B2 **Aarschot** Belgium
70 A2 **Aba** China
119 D2 **Aba** Dem. Rep. Congo
115 C4 **Aba** Nigeria
81 C2 **Ābādān** Iran
81 D2 **Ābādeh** Iran
81 D3 **Ābādeh Ţashk** Iran
114 B1 **Abadla** Alg.
155 C1 **Abaeté** Brazil
Abagnar Qi China *see Xilinhot*
135 E3 **Abajo Peak** U.S.A.
115 C4 **Abakaliki** Nigeria
83 H3 **Abakan** Rus. Fed.
150 B4 **Abancay** Peru
81 D2 **Abarqū** Iran
66 D2 **Abashiri** Japan
66 D2 **Abashiri-wan** *b.* Japan
59 D3 **Abau** P.N.G.
Abaya, Lake Eth. *see Lake Abaya*
Ābay Wenz *r.* Eth. *see Blue Nile*
83 H3 **Abaza** Rus. Fed.
108 A2 **Abbasanta** *Sardinia* Italy
104 C1 **Abbeville** France
141 C2 **Abbeville** *AL* U.S.A.
140 B3 **Abbeville** *LA* U.S.A.
97 B2 **Abbeyfeale** Ireland
55 R2 **Abbot Ice Shelf** Antarctica
74 B1 **Abbottabad** Pak.
115 E3 **Abéché** Chad
114 B4 **Abengourou** Côte d'Ivoire
114 C4 **Abeokuta** Nigeria
99 A3 **Aberaeron** U.K.
96 C2 **Aberchirder** U.K.
Abercorn Zambia *see Mbala*
99 B4 **Aberdare** U.K.
99 A3 **Aberdaron** U.K.
53 D2 **Aberdeen** Austr.
122 B3 **Aberdeen** S. Africa
96 C2 **Aberdeen** U.K.
139 D3 **Aberdeen** *MD* U.S.A.
137 D1 **Aberdeen** *SD* U.S.A.
134 B1 **Aberdeen** *WA* U.S.A.
129 E1 **Aberdeen Lake** Can.
96 C2 **Aberfeldy** U.K.
96 B2 **Aberfoyle** U.K.
99 B4 **Abergavenny** U.K.
Abergwaun U.K. *see Fishguard*
Aberhonddu U.K. *see Brecon*
143 C2 **Abernathy** U.S.A.
134 B2 **Abert, Lake** U.S.A.
Abertawe U.K. *see Swansea*
Aberteifi U.K. *see Cardigan*
99 B4 **Abertillery** U.K.
99 A3 **Aberystwyth** U.K.
86 F2 **Abez'** Rus. Fed.
78 B3 **Abhā** Saudi Arabia
81 C2 **Abhar** Iran
Abiad, Bahr el *r.* Sudan/Uganda *see White Nile*
114 B4 **Abidjan** Côte d'Ivoire
137 D3 **Abilene** *KS* U.S.A.
143 D2 **Abilene** *TX* U.S.A.
99 C4 **Abingdon** U.K.
138 C3 **Abingdon** U.S.A.
91 D3 **Abinsk** Rus. Fed.
130 B3 **Abitibi, Lake** Can.
Åbo Fin. *see Turku*
74 B1 **Abohar** India
114 B4 **Aboisso** Côte d'Ivoire
114 C4 **Abomey** Benin
60 A1 **Abongabong, Gunung** *mt.* Indon.
118 B2 **Abong Mbang** Cameroon
64 A3 **Aborlan** Phil.
115 D3 **Abou Déia** Chad
106 B2 **Abrantes** Port.
152 B2 **Abra Pampa** Arg.
142 A3 **Abreojos, Punta** *pt* Mex.
116 B2 **'Abri** Sudan
136 A2 **Absaroka Range** *mts* U.S.A.
81 C1 **Abşeron Yarımadası** *pen.* Azer.
78 B3 **Abū 'Arīsh** Saudi Arabia
116 A2 **Abū Ballāş** *hill* Egypt
79 C2 **Abu Dhabi** U.A.E.
116 B3 **Abu Hamed** Sudan
116 B3 **Abu Haraz** Sudan
115 C4 **Abuja** Nigeria
81 C2 **Abū Kamāl** Syria
118 C2 **Abumombazi** Dem. Rep. Congo
152 B1 **Abunā** *r.* Bol.
150 B2 **Abunã** Brazil
74 B2 **Abu Road** India
78 B2 **Abū Şādī, Jabal** *hill* Saudi Arabia
116 B2 **Abū Sunbul** Egypt
116 A3 **Abu Zabad** Sudan
Abū Zabī U.A.E. *see Abu Dhabi*
117 A4 **Abyei** Sudan
145 B2 **Acambaro** Mex.
120 B2 **Acampamento de Caça do Mucusso** Angola
106 B1 **A Cañiza** Spain
144 B2 **Acaponeta** Mex.
145 C3 **Acapulco** Mex.
151 E3 **Acará** Brazil

154 A3 **Acaray, Represa de** *resr* Para.
150 C2 **Acarigua** Venez.
110 B1 **Acâş** Romania
145 C3 **Acatlan** Mex.
145 C3 **Acayucán** Mex.
114 B4 **Accra** Ghana
98 B3 **Accrington** U.K.
74 B2 **Achalpur** India
97 A2 **Achill Island** Ireland
101 D1 **Achim** Ger.
96 B2 **Achnasheen** U.K.
91 D2 **Achuyevo** Rus. Fed.
111 C3 **Acıpayam** Turkey
109 C3 **Acireale** *Sicily* Italy
147 C2 **Acklins Island** Bahamas
153 A3 **Aconcagua, Cerro** *mt.* Arg.
106 B1 **A Coruña** Spain
108 A2 **Acqui Terme** Italy
103 D2 **Ács** Hungary
49 N6 **Actéon, Groupe** *is* Fr. Polynesia
145 C2 **Actopán** Mex.
143 D2 **Ada** U.S.A.
Adabazar Turkey *see Adapazarı*
79 C2 **Adam** Oman
111 B3 **Adamas** Greece
135 B3 **Adams Peak** U.S.A.
'Adan Yemen *see Aden*
80 B2 **Adana** Turkey
111 D2 **Adapazarı** Turkey
97 B2 **Adare** Ireland
55 M2 **Adare, Cape** Antarctica
108 A1 **Adda** *r.* Italy
78 B2 **Ad Dafinah** Saudi Arabia
78 B2 **Ad Dahnā'** *des.* Saudi Arabia
79 B2 **Ad Dahnā'** *des.* Saudi Arabia
114 A2 **Ad Dakhla** Western Sahara
Ad Dammām Saudi Arabia *see Dammam*
78 A2 **Ad Dār al Ḥamrā'** Saudi Arabia
78 B3 **Ad Darb** Saudi Arabia
78 B2 **Ad Dawādimī** Saudi Arabia
Ad Dawḥah Qatar *see Doha*
Aḑ Ḑiffah Egypt *see Libyan Plateau*
78 B2 **Ad Dilam** Saudi Arabia
78 B2 **Ad Dir'īyah** Saudi Arabia
117 B4 **Addis Ababa** Eth.
81 C2 **Ad Dīwānīyah** Iraq
141 D2 **Adel** U.S.A.
52 A2 **Adelaide** Austr.
55 A3 **Adelaide Island** Antarctica
50 C1 **Adelaide River** Austr.
101 D2 **Adelebsen** Ger.
55 K2 **Adélie Land** Antarctica
78 B3 **Aden** Yemen
116 C3 **Aden, Gulf of** Somalia/Yemen
100 C2 **Adenau** Ger.
115 C3 **Aderbissinat** Niger
79 C2 **Adh Dhayd** U.A.E.
59 C3 **Adi** *i.* Indon.
116 B3 **Ādī Ārk'ay** Eth.
108 B1 **Adige** *r.* Italy
116 B3 **Ādīgrat** Eth.
78 A3 **Adi Keyih** Eritrea
74 B3 **Adilabad** India
115 D2 **Adiri** Libya
139 E2 **Adirondack Mountains** U.S.A.
Ādīs Ābeba Eth. *see Addis Ababa*
117 B4 **Ādīs Alem** Eth.
80 B2 **Adıyaman** Turkey
110 C1 **Adjud** Romania
50 B1 **Admiralty Gulf** Austr.
128 A2 **Admiralty Island** U.S.A.
59 D3 **Admiralty Islands** P.N.G.
73 B3 **Adoni** India
104 B3 **Adour** *r.* France
106 C2 **Adra** Spain
114 B2 **Adrar** Alg.
138 C2 **Adrian** *MI* U.S.A.
143 C1 **Adrian** *TX* U.S.A.
108 B2 **Adriatic Sea** Europe
Ādwa Eth. *see Ādwa*
116 B3 **Ādwa** Eth.
83 K2 **Adycha** *r.* Rus. Fed.
91 D3 **Adygeysk** Rus. Fed.
114 B4 **Adzopé** Côte d'Ivoire
111 B3 **Aegean Sea** Greece/Turkey
101 D1 **Aerzen** Ger.
106 B1 **A Estrada** Spain
116 B3 **Afabet** Eritrea
Affreville Alg. *see Khemis Miliana*
76 C3 **Afghanistan** *country* Asia
78 B2 **'Afif** Saudi Arabia
136 A2 **Afton** U.S.A.
80 B2 **Afyon** Turkey
115 C3 **Agadez** Niger
114 B1 **Agadir** Morocco
77 D2 **Agadyr'** Kazakh.
113 I7 **Agalega Islands** Mauritius
Agana Guam *see Hagåtña*
74 B2 **Agar** India
119 D2 **Āgaro** Eth.
75 D2 **Agartala** India
81 C2 **Ağdam** Azer.
105 C3 **Agde** France
104 C3 **Agen** France
122 A2 **Aggeneys** S. Africa
111 C3 **Agia Vervara** Greece
111 B3 **Agios Dimitrios** Greece
111 C3 **Agios Efstratios** *i.* Greece
111 C3 **Agios Kirykos** Greece
111 C3 **Agios Nikolaos** Greece
78 A3 **Agirwat Hills** Sudan
123 C2 **Agisanang** S. Africa
110 B1 **Agnita** Romania

74 B2 **Agra** India
81 C2 **Ağrı** Turkey
Ağrı Dağı *mt.* Turkey *see Ararat, Mount*
108 B3 **Agrigento** *Sicily* Italy
111 B3 **Agrinio** Greece
109 B2 **Agropoli** Italy
87 E3 **Agryz** Rus. Fed.
144 B2 **Agua Brava, Laguna** *lag.* Mex.
154 B2 **Água Clara** Brazil
145 C3 **Aguada** Mex.
146 B4 **Aguadulce** Panama
144 B2 **Aguanaval** *r.* Mex.
144 B1 **Agua Prieta** Mex.
144 B2 **Aguascalientes** Mex.
155 D1 **Águas Formosas** Brazil
154 C2 **Águeda** Brazil
106 B1 **Águeda** Port.
114 C3 **Aguelhok** Mali
106 C1 **Aguilar de Campóo** Spain
107 C2 **Águilas** Spain
144 B3 **Aguililla** Mex.
122 B3 **Agulhas, Cape** S. Africa
158 F7 **Agulhas Basin** *sea feature* Southern Ocean
155 D2 **Agulhas Negras** *mt.* Brazil
158 F7 **Agulhas Plateau** *sea feature* Southern Ocean
158 F7 **Agulhas Ridge** *sea feature* S. Atlantic Ocean
111 C3 **Ağva** Turkey
81 C2 **Ahar** Iran
100 C1 **Ahaus** Ger.
81 C2 **Ahlat** Turkey
100 C2 **Ahlen** Ger.
74 B2 **Ahmadabad** India
74 B3 **Ahmadnagar** India
74 B2 **Ahmadpur East** Pak.
74 B1 **Ahmadpur Sial** Pak.
117 C4 **Ahmar Mountains** Eth.
Ahmedabad India *see Ahmadabad*
Ahmednagar India *see Ahmadnagar*
144 B2 **Ahome** Mex.
81 D3 **Ahram** Iran
101 E1 **Ahrensburg** Ger.
104 C2 **Ahun** France
93 F4 **Åhus** Sweden
81 C2 **Ahvāz** Iran
Ahvenanmaa *is* Fin. *see Åland Islands*
122 A2 **Ai-Ais** Namibia
80 B2 **Aigialousa** Cyprus
111 B3 **Aigio** Greece
Aihui China *see Heihe*
Aijal India *see Aizawl*
141 D2 **Aiken** U.S.A.
155 D1 **Aimorés** Brazil
155 D1 **Aimorés, Serra dos** *hills* Brazil
105 D2 **Ain** *r.* France
107 E2 **Aïn Azel** Alg.
115 C1 **Aïn Beïda** Alg.
114 A2 **'Aïn Ben Tili** Maur.
107 D2 **Aïn Defla** Alg.
114 B1 **Aïn Sefra** Alg.
136 D2 **Ainsworth** U.S.A.
Aintab Turkey *see Gaziantep*
107 D2 **Aïn Taya** Alg.
107 D2 **Aïn Tédélès** Alg.
107 C2 **Aïn Temouchent** Alg.
115 C3 **Aïr, Massif de l'** *mts* Niger
60 A1 **Airbangis** Indon.
128 C2 **Airdrie** Can.
96 C3 **Airdrie** U.K.
104 B3 **Aire-sur-l'Adour** France
101 E3 **Aisch** *r.* Ger.
128 A1 **Aishihik Lake** Can.
100 A3 **Aisne** *r.* France
59 D3 **Aitape** P.N.G.
137 E1 **Aitkin** U.S.A.
110 B1 **Aiud** Romania
105 D3 **Aix-en-Provence** France
Aix-la-Chapelle Ger. *see Aachen*
105 D2 **Aix-les-Bains** France
75 D2 **Aizawl** India
88 C2 **Aizkraukle** Latvia
88 B2 **Aizpute** Latvia
67 C3 **Aizu-wakamatsu** Japan
105 D3 **Ajaccio** *Corsica* France
Ajayameru India *see Ajmer*
115 E1 **Ajdābiyā** Libya
79 C2 **'Ajman** U.A.E.
74 B2 **Ajmer** India
Ajmer-Merwara India *see Ajmer*
142 A2 **Ajo** U.S.A.
119 C2 **Āk'ak'ī Beseka** Eth.
Akamagaseki Japan *see Shimonoseki*
54 B2 **Akaroa** N.Z.
87 E3 **Akbulak** Rus. Fed.
80 B2 **Akçakale** Turkey
114 A3 **Akchâr** *reg.* Maur.
111 C3 **Akdağ** *mt.* Turkey
80 B2 **Akdağmadeni** Turkey
88 A2 **Åkersberga** Sweden
118 C2 **Aketi** Dem. Rep. Congo
81 C1 **Akhalk'alak'i** Georgia
81 C1 **Akhalts'ikhe** Georgia
79 C2 **Akhḑar, Jabal** *mts* Oman
111 C3 **Akhisar** Turkey
87 D4 **Akhtubinsk** Rus. Fed.
118 B3 **Akiéni** Gabon
130 B2 **Akimiski Island** Can.
66 D3 **Akita** Japan

114 A3 **Akjoujt** Maur.
Akkerman Ukr. *see Bilhorod-Dnistrovs'kyy*
77 D1 **Akkol'** Kazakh.
Ak-Mechet Kazakh. *see Kyzylorda*
88 B2 **Akmeņrags** *pt* Latvia
Akmola Kazakh. *see Astana*
Akmolinsk Kazakh. *see Astana*
67 B4 **Akō** Japan
117 B4 **Akobo** Sudan
74 B2 **Akola** India
118 B2 **Akonolinga** Cameroon
78 A3 **Akordat** Eritrea
131 D1 **Akpatok Island** Can.
77 D2 **Akqi** China
92 □A3 **Akranes** Iceland
111 B2 **Akrathos, Akra** *pt* Greece
136 C2 **Akron** *CO* U.S.A.
138 C2 **Akron** *OH* U.S.A.
75 B1 **Aksai Chin** *terr.* Asia
80 B2 **Aksaray** Turkey
86 F2 **Aksarka** Rus. Fed.
76 B1 **Aksay** Kazakh.
91 D2 **Aksay** Rus. Fed.
80 B2 **Akşehir** Turkey
76 C2 **Akshiganak** Kazakh.
77 E2 **Aksu** China
116 B3 **Āksum** Eth.
76 B2 **Aktau** Kazakh.
76 B1 **Aktobe** Kazakh.
77 D1 **Aktogay** Kazakh.
88 C3 **Aktsyabrski** Belarus
Aktyubinsk Kazakh. *see Aktobe*
67 B4 **Akune** Japan
115 C4 **Akure** Nigeria
92 □B2 **Akureyri** Iceland
Akyab Myanmar *see Sittwe*
111 D2 **Akyazı** Turkey
77 C2 **Akzhaykyn, Ozero** *salt l.* Kazakh.
140 C2 **Alabama** *r.* U.S.A.
140 C2 **Alabama** *state* U.S.A.
140 C2 **Alabaster** U.S.A.
111 C3 **Alaçatı** Turkey
145 D2 **Alacrán, Arrecife** *rf* Mex.
81 C1 **Alagir** Rus. Fed.
151 F4 **Alagoinhas** Brazil
107 C1 **Alagón** Spain
78 B2 **Al Aḩmadi** Kuwait
77 E2 **Alakol', Ozero** *salt l.* Kazakh.
92 J2 **Alakurtti** Rus. Fed.
78 B3 **Al 'Alayyah** Saudi Arabia
81 C2 **Al 'Amādīyah** Iraq
81 C2 **Al 'Amārah** Iraq
80 A2 **Al 'Āmirīyah** Egypt
143 C3 **Alamitos, Sierra de los** *mt.* Mex.
135 C3 **Alamo** U.S.A.
142 B2 **Alamogordo** U.S.A.
144 A2 **Alamos** Mex.
144 B2 **Alamos** Mex.
144 B2 **Alamos** *r.* Mex.
136 B3 **Alamosa** U.S.A.
Åland Fin. *see Åland Islands*
93 G3 **Åland Islands** *is* Fin.
80 B2 **Alanya** Turkey
Alappuzha India *see Alleppey*
80 B2 **Al 'Aqabah** Jordan
78 B2 **Al 'Aqiq** Saudi Arabia
107 C2 **Alarcón, Embalse de** *resr* Spain
80 B2 **Al 'Arīsh** Egypt
78 B2 **Al Arţāwīyah** Saudi Arabia
61 C2 **Alas** Indon.
111 C3 **Alaşehir** Turkey
128 A2 **Alaska** *state* U.S.A.
124 D4 **Alaska, Gulf of** U.S.A.
126 B3 **Alaska Peninsula** U.S.A.
126 C2 **Alaska Range** *mts* U.S.A.
81 C2 **Älät** Azer.
87 D3 **Alatyr'** Rus. Fed.
150 B3 **Alausí** Ecuador
93 H3 **Alavus** Fin.
52 B2 **Alawoona** Austr.
79 C2 **Al 'Ayn** U.A.E.
108 A2 **Alba** Italy
107 C2 **Albacete** Spain
78 A2 **Al Badā'i'** Saudi Arabia
78 B2 **Al Badī'** Saudi Arabia
110 B1 **Alba Iulia** Romania
109 C2 **Albania** *country* Europe
50 A3 **Albany** Austr.
130 B2 **Albany** *r.* Can.
141 D2 **Albany** *GA* U.S.A.
139 E2 **Albany** *NY* U.S.A.
134 B2 **Albany** *OR* U.S.A.
115 E1 **Al Bardī** Libya
Al Başrah Iraq *see Basra*
51 D1 **Albatross Bay** Austr.
116 A2 **Al Bawīţī** Egypt
115 E1 **Al Bayḑā'** Libya
78 B3 **Al Bayḑā'** Yemen
141 D1 **Albemarle** U.S.A.
141 E1 **Albemarle Sound** *sea chan.* U.S.A.
108 A2 **Albenga** Italy
51 C2 **Alberga** *watercourse* Austr.
119 D2 **Albert, Lake** Dem. Rep. Congo/Uganda
128 C2 **Alberta** *prov.* Can.
100 B2 **Albert Kanaal** *canal* Belgium
137 E2 **Albert Lea** U.S.A.
117 B4 **Albert Nile** *r.* Sudan/Uganda
123 C2 **Alberton** S. Africa
Albertville Dem. Rep. Congo *see Kalemie*
105 D2 **Albertville** France
104 C3 **Albi** France
151 D2 **Albina** Suriname

78 A2 **Al Bi'r** Saudi Arabia
78 B3 **Al Birk** Saudi Arabia
78 B2 **Al Biyāḍh** *reg.* Saudi Arabia
Alborz, Reshteh-ye Iran *see* Elburz Mountains
107 C2 **Albox** Spain
106 B2 **Albufeira** Port.
142 B1 **Albuquerque** U.S.A.
79 C2 **Al Buraymī** Oman
53 C3 **Albury** Austr.
106 B2 **Alcácer do Sal** Port.
106 C1 **Alcalá de Henares** Spain
106 C2 **Alcalá la Real** Spain
108 B3 **Alcamo** *Sicily* Italy
107 C1 **Alcañiz** Spain
106 B2 **Alcántara** Spain
107 C2 **Alcantarilla** Spain
106 C2 **Alcaraz** Spain
106 C2 **Alcaraz, Sierra de** *mts* Spain
106 C2 **Alcaudete** Spain
106 C2 **Alcázar de San Juan** Spain
Alcazarquivir Morocco *see* Ksar el Kebir
91 D2 **Alchevs'k** Ukr.
155 E1 **Alcobaça** Brazil
107 C1 **Alcora** Spain
107 C2 **Alcoy-Alcoi** Spain
107 D2 **Alcúdia** Spain
113 H6 **Aldabra Islands** Seychelles
142 B3 **Aldama** Mex.
145 C2 **Aldama** Mex.
83 J3 **Aldan** Rus. Fed.
83 J2 **Aldan** *r.* Rus. Fed.
99 D3 **Aldeburgh** U.K.
95 C4 **Alderney** *i.* Channel Is
99 C4 **Aldershot** U.K.
114 A3 **Aleg** Maur.
155 E1 **Alegre** Brazil
152 C2 **Alegrete** Brazil
89 D1 **Alekhovshchina** Rus. Fed.
89 E2 **Aleksandrov** Rus. Fed.
Aleksandrovsk Ukr. *see* Zaporizhzhya
83 K3 **Aleksandrovsk-Sakhalinskiy** Rus. Fed.
82 E1 **Aleksandry, Zemlya** *i.* Rus. Fed.
Alekseyevka Kazakh. *see* Akkol'
91 D1 **Alekseyevka** Rus. Fed.
91 D1 **Alekseyevka** Rus. Fed.
89 E3 **Aleksin** Rus. Fed.
109 D2 **Aleksinac** Serb. and Mont.
118 B3 **Alèmbé** Gabon
155 D2 **Além Paraíba** Brazil
93 F3 **Ålen** Norway
104 C2 **Alençon** France
80 B2 **Aleppo** Syria
150 B4 **Alerta** Peru
128 B2 **Alert Bay** Can.
105 C3 **Alès** France
110 B1 **Aleşd** Romania
Aleshki Ukr. *see* Tsyurupyns'k
108 A2 **Alessandria** Italy
Alessio Albania *see* Lezhë
93 E3 **Ålesund** Norway
156 D2 **Aleutian Basin** *sea feature* Bering Sea
124 A4 **Aleutian Islands** U.S.A.
83 L3 **Alevina, Mys** *c.* Rus. Fed.
128 A2 **Alexander Archipelago** *is* U.S.A.
122 A2 **Alexander Bay** S. Africa
140 C2 **Alexander City** U.S.A.
55 A2 **Alexander Island** Antarctica
53 C3 **Alexandra** Austr.
54 A3 **Alexandra** N.Z.
153 E5 **Alexandra, Cape** S. Georgia
Alexandra Land *i.* Rus. Fed. *see* Aleksandry, Zemlya
111 B2 **Alexandreia** Greece
116 A1 **Alexandria** Egypt
110 C2 **Alexandria** Romania
123 C3 **Alexandria** S. Africa
96 B3 **Alexandria** U.K.
140 B2 **Alexandria** *LA* U.S.A.
137 D1 **Alexandria** *MN* U.S.A.
139 D3 **Alexandria** *VA* U.S.A.
52 A3 **Alexandrina, Lake** Austr.
111 C2 **Alexandroupoli** Greece
131 E2 **Alexis** *r.* Can.
128 B2 **Alexis Creek** Can.
77 E1 **Aleysk** Rus. Fed.
107 C1 **Alfaro** Spain
81 C3 **Al Fāw** Iraq
80 B3 **Al Fayyūm** Egypt
101 D2 **Alfeld (Leine)** Ger.
155 C2 **Alfenas** Brazil
96 C2 **Alford** U.K.
Al Fujayrah U.A.E. *see* Fujairah
Al Furāt *r.* Iraq/Syria *see* Euphrates
93 E4 **Ålgård** Norway
106 B2 **Algarve** *reg.* Port.
106 B2 **Algeciras** Spain
107 C2 **Algemesí** Spain
78 A3 **Algena** Eritrea
Alger Alg. *see* Algiers
114 C2 **Algeria** *country* Africa
79 C3 **Al Ghaydah** Yemen
108 A2 **Alghero** *Sardinia* Italy
80 B2 **Al Ghurdaqah** Egypt
79 B2 **Al Ghwaybiyah** Saudi Arabia
115 C1 **Algiers** Alg.
123 C3 **Algoa Bay** S. Africa
137 E2 **Algona** U.S.A.
106 C1 **Algorta** Spain
Algueirao Moz. *see* Hacufera
81 C2 **Al Ḥadīthah** Iraq

79 C2 **Al Ḥajar al Gharbī** *mts* Oman
115 D2 **Al Ḥamādah al Ḥamrā'** *plat.* Libya
107 C2 **Alhama de Murcia** Spain
80 A2 **Al Ḥammām** Egypt
78 B2 **Al Ḥanākīyah** Saudi Arabia
81 C2 **Al Ḥasakah** Syria
78 B2 **Al Ḥawīyah** Saudi Arabia
81 C2 **Al Ḥayy** Iraq
78 B3 **Al Ḥazm al Jawf** Yemen
79 C3 **Al Ḥibāk** *des.* Saudi Arabia
Al Ḥillah Iraq *see* Hillah
78 B2 **Al Ḥillah** Saudi Arabia
79 B2 **Al Ḥinnāh** Saudi Arabia
Al Ḥudaydah Yemen *see* Hodeidah
79 B2 **Al Ḥufūf** Saudi Arabia
115 D2 **Al Ḥulayq al Kabīr** *hills* Libya
79 C2 **'Alīābād** Iran
111 C3 **Aliağa** Turkey
111 B2 **Aliakmonas** *r.* Greece
81 C2 **Ali Bayramlı** Azer.
107 C2 **Alicante** Spain
143 D3 **Alice** U.S.A.
109 C3 **Alice, Punta** *pt* Italy
51 C2 **Alice Springs** Austr.
77 D3 **Alichur** Tajik.
74 B2 **Aligarh** India
81 C2 **Alīgūdarz** Iran
69 E1 **Alihe** China
118 B3 **Alima** *r.* Congo
118 C2 **Alindao** C.A.R.
111 C3 **Alınca** *r.* Turkey
74 B2 **Alirajpur** India
117 C3 **Ali Sabieh** Djibouti
78 A1 **Al 'Isāwiyah** Saudi Arabia
Al Iskandarīyah Egypt *see* Alexandria
116 B1 **Al Ismā'īlīyah** Egypt
123 C3 **Aliwal North** S. Africa
115 E2 **Al Jaghbūb** Libya
78 B2 **Al Jahrah** Kuwait
79 C2 **Al Jamalīyah** Qatar
115 E2 **Al Jawf** Libya
78 A2 **Al Jawf** Saudi Arabia
115 D1 **Al Jawsh** Libya
106 B2 **Aljezur** Port.
Al Jizah Egypt *see* Giza
79 B2 **Al Jubayl** Saudi Arabia
78 B2 **Al Jubaylah** Saudi Arabia
115 D2 **Al Jufra Oasis** Libya
78 B2 **Al Junaynah** Saudi Arabia
106 B2 **Aljustrel** Port.
78 B2 **Al Kahfah** Saudi Arabia
79 C2 **Al Kāmil** Oman
80 B2 **Al Karak** Jordan
81 C2 **Al Kāẓimīyah** Iraq
79 C2 **Al Khāburah** Oman
78 B2 **Al Khamāsin** Saudi Arabia
116 B2 **Al Khārijah** Egypt
79 C2 **Al Khaṣab** Oman
78 B3 **Al Khawkhah** Yemen
79 C2 **Al Khawr** Qatar
115 E2 **Al Khufrah** Libya
115 D1 **Al Khums** Libya
79 B2 **Al Khunn** Saudi Arabia
79 C2 **Al Kidan** *well* Saudi Arabia
79 C2 **Al Kir'ānah** Qatar
100 B1 **Alkmaar** Neth.
81 C2 **Al Kūt** Iraq
Al Kuwayt Kuwait *see* Kuwait
Al Lādhiqīyah Syria *see* Latakia
75 C2 **Allahabad** India
83 K2 **Allakh-Yun'** Rus. Fed.
78 A2 **'Allāqī, Wādī al** *watercourse* Egypt
139 D2 **Allegheny** *r.* U.S.A.
139 C3 **Allegheny Mountains** U.S.A.
97 B1 **Allen, Lough** *l.* Ireland
145 D2 **Allende** Mex.
145 B2 **Allende** Mex.
139 D2 **Allentown** U.S.A.
73 B4 **Alleppey** India
101 D1 **Aller** *r.* Ger.
136 C2 **Alliance** *NE* U.S.A.
138 C2 **Alliance** *OH* U.S.A.
78 B1 **Al Lith** Saudi Arabia
96 C2 **Alloa** U.K.
131 C3 **Alma** Can.
Alma-Ata Kazakh. *see* Almaty
106 B2 **Almada** Port.
106 C2 **Almadén** Spain
Al Madīnah Saudi Arabia *see* Medina
80 B2 **Al Mafraq** Jordan
114 B2 **Al Mahbas** Western Sahara
78 B3 **Al Maḥwit** Yemen
78 B2 **Al Majma'ah** Saudi Arabia
116 B2 **Al Maks al Baḥrī** Egypt
Al Manāmah Bahrain *see* Manama
135 B2 **Almanor, Lake** U.S.A.
107 C2 **Almansa** Spain
80 B2 **Al Manṣūrah** Egypt
79 C2 **Al Mariyyah** U.A.E.
115 E1 **Al Marj** Libya
77 D2 **Almaty** Kazakh.
Al Mawṣil Iraq *see* Mosul
81 C2 **Al Mayādīn** Syria
106 C1 **Almazán** Spain
151 D3 **Almeirim** Brazil
100 C1 **Almelo** Neth.
155 D1 **Almenara** Brazil
106 B1 **Almendra, Embalse de** *resr* Spain
106 B2 **Almendralejo** Spain
106 C2 **Almería** Spain
106 C2 **Almería, Golfo de** *b.* Spain
87 E3 **Al'met'yevsk** Rus. Fed.

78 B2 **Al Mindak** Saudi Arabia
79 B2 **Al Minyā** Egypt
79 B2 **Al Mish'āb** Saudi Arabia
106 B2 **Almodôvar** Port.
106 B2 **Almonte** Spain
75 B2 **Almora** India
79 B2 **Al Mubarrez** Saudi Arabia
79 C2 **Al Muḍaibī** Oman
80 B3 **Al Mudawwarah** Jordan
Al Mukallā Yemen *see* Mukalla
Al Mukhā Yemen *see* Mocha
106 C2 **Almuñécar** Spain
81 C2 **Al Muqdādīyah** Iraq
78 A2 **Al Musayjid** Saudi Arabia
79 B2 **Al Muwaylih** Saudi Arabia
111 B3 **Almyros** Greece
96 B2 **Alness** U.K.
98 C2 **Alnwick** U.K.
62 A1 **Along** India
111 B3 **Alonnisos** *i.* Greece
59 C3 **Alor** *i.* Indon.
59 C3 **Alor, Kepulauan** *is* Indon.
60 B1 **Alor Setar** Malaysia
Alor Star Malaysia *see* Alor Setar
Alost Belgium *see* Aalst
59 E3 **Alotau** P.N.G.
86 C2 **Alozero** Rus. Fed.
138 C1 **Alpena** U.S.A.
160 Q1 **Alpha Ridge** *sea feature* Arctic Ocean
100 B1 **Alphen aan den Rijn** Neth.
142 B2 **Alpine** *AZ* U.S.A.
143 C2 **Alpine** *TX* U.S.A.
84 E4 **Alps** *mts* Europe
79 B3 **Al Qa'āmiyāt** *reg.* Saudi Arabia
115 D1 **Al Qaddāḥīyah** Libya
Al Qāhirah Egypt *see* Cairo
78 B2 **Al Qā'iyah** Saudi Arabia
81 C2 **Al Qāmishlī** Syria
80 B2 **Al Qaryatayn** Syria
79 B2 **Al Qaṣab** Saudi Arabia
116 A2 **Al Qaṣr** Egypt
79 B3 **Al Qaṭn** Yemen
115 D2 **Al Qaṭrūn** Libya
106 B2 **Alqueva, Barragem de** Portugal
80 B2 **Al Qunayṭirah** Syria
78 B3 **Al Qunfidhah** Saudi Arabia
116 B2 **Al Quṣayr** Egypt
78 B2 **Al Quwārah** Saudi Arabia
78 B2 **Al Quwayʻiyah** Saudi Arabia
101 D2 **Alsfeld** Ger.
98 B2 **Alston** U.K.
92 H2 **Alta** Norway
92 H2 **Altaelva** *r.* Norway
68 B1 **Altai Mountains** Asia
141 D2 **Altamaha** *r.* U.S.A.
151 D3 **Altamira** Brazil
109 C2 **Altamura** Italy
144 A1 **Altar, Desierto de** *des.* Mex.
77 D2 **Altay** China
68 C1 **Altay** Mongolia
105 D2 **Altdorf** Switz.
107 C2 **Altea** Spain
92 H1 **Alteidet** Norway
101 F2 **Altenburg** Ger.
100 C2 **Altenkirchen (Westerwald)** Ger.
101 F1 **Altentreptow** Ger.
111 C3 **Altınoluk** Turkey
111 D3 **Altıntaş** Turkey
152 B1 **Altiplano** *plain* Bol.
96 B1 **Altnaharra** U.K.
154 B1 **Alto Araguaia** Brazil
107 C1 **Alto del Moncayo** *mt.* Spain
154 B1 **Alto Garças** Brazil
121 C2 **Alto Ligonha** Moz.
121 C2 **Alto Molócuè** Moz.
99 C4 **Alton** U.K.
137 E3 **Alton** U.S.A.
129 E3 **Altona** Can.
139 D2 **Altoona** U.S.A.
154 B1 **Alto Sucuriú** Brazil
154 B1 **Alto Taquari** Brazil
102 C2 **Altötting** Ger.
143 D2 **Alturas** U.S.A.
143 D2 **Altus** U.S.A.
88 C2 **Alūksne** Latvia
78 A2 **Al 'Ulā** Saudi Arabia
115 D1 **Al 'Uqaylah** Libya
Al Uqṣur Egypt *see* Luxor
91 C3 **Alushta** Ukr.
115 E2 **Al 'Uwaynāt** Libya
143 D1 **Alva** U.S.A.
145 C3 **Alvarado** Mex.
93 F3 **Älvdalen** Sweden
93 F3 **Älvdalen** *val.* Sweden
92 H2 **Älvsbyn** Sweden
78 A2 **Al Wajh** Saudi Arabia
79 C2 **Al Wakrah** Qatar
74 B2 **Alwar** India
81 C2 **Al Widyān** *plat.* Iraq/Saudi Arabia
Alxa Youqi China *see* Ehen Hudag
Alxa Zuoqi China *see* Bayan Hot
51 C1 **Alyangula** Austr.
88 B3 **Alytus** Lith.
136 C1 **Alzada** U.S.A.
101 D3 **Alzey** Ger.
50 C2 **Amadeus, Lake** *salt flat* Austr.
127 H2 **Amadjuak Lake** Can.
106 B2 **Amadora** Port.
78 B2 **Amā'ir** Saudi Arabia
67 B4 **Amakusa-Shimo-shima** *i.* Japan
93 F4 **Åmål** Sweden
111 B3 **Amaliada** Greece

59 D3 **Amamapare** Indon.
154 A2 **Amambai** Brazil
154 B2 **Amambai** *r.* Brazil
154 A2 **Amambaí, Serra de** *hills* Brazil/Para.
69 E3 **Amami-Ō-shima** *i.* Japan
69 E3 **Amami-shotō** *is* Japan
77 C1 **Amangel'dy** Kazakh.
109 C3 **Amantea** Italy
123 D3 **Amanzimtoti** S. Africa
151 D2 **Amapá** Brazil
106 B2 **Amareleja** Port.
88 B2 **Ämari** Estonia
143 C1 **Amarillo** U.S.A.
108 B2 **Amaro, Monte** *mt.* Italy
80 B1 **Amasya** Turkey
150 D2 **Amazon** *r.* S. America
151 E2 **Amazon, Mouths of the** Brazil
Amazonas *r.* S. America *see* Amazon
157 I5 **Amazon Cone** *sea feature* S. Atlantic Ocean
74 B1 **Ambala** India
121 □D2 **Ambalavao** Madag.
121 □D2 **Ambanja** Madag.
104 B3 **Ambarès-et-Lagrave** France
150 B3 **Ambato** Ecuador
121 □D2 **Ambato Boeny** Madag.
121 □D3 **Ambato Finandrahana** Madag.
121 □D2 **Ambatolampy** Madag.
121 □D2 **Ambatondrazaka** Madag.
101 E3 **Amberg** Ger.
146 B3 **Ambergris Cay** *i.* Belize
75 C2 **Ambikapur** India
121 □D2 **Ambilobe** Madag.
98 C2 **Amble** U.K.
98 B2 **Ambleside** U.K.
121 □D3 **Amboasary** Madag.
121 □D2 **Ambodifotatra** Madag.
121 □D2 **Ambohidratrimo** Madag.
121 □D3 **Ambohimahasoa** Madag.
Amboina Indon. *see* Ambon
59 C3 **Ambon** Indon.
59 C3 **Ambon** *i.* Indon.
121 □D3 **Ambositra** Madag.
121 □D2 **Ambovombe** Madag.
135 C4 **Amboy** U.S.A.
Ambre, Cap d' *c.* Madag. *see* Bobaomby, Tanjona
120 A1 **Ambriz** Angola
Ambrizete Angola *see* N'zeto
86 F2 **Amderma** Rus. Fed.
Amdo China *see* Lharigarbo
145 B2 **Amealco** Mex.
144 B2 **Ameca** Mex.
100 B1 **Ameland** *i.* Neth.
154 C2 **Americana** Brazil
55 D4 **American-Antarctic Ridge** *sea feature* S. Atlantic Ocean
134 D2 **American Falls** U.S.A.
134 D2 **American Falls Reservoir** U.S.A.
135 D2 **American Fork** U.S.A.
49 J5 **American Samoa** *terr.* S. Pacific Ocean
100 D1 **Americus** U.S.A.
100 B1 **Amersfoort** Neth.
55 H2 **Amery Ice Shelf** Antarctica
137 E2 **Ames** U.S.A.
111 B3 **Amfissa** Greece
83 J2 **Amga** Rus. Fed.
66 C1 **Amgu** Rus. Fed.
115 C2 **Amguid** Alg.
83 K3 **Amgun'** *r.* Rus. Fed.
131 D3 **Amherst** Can.
104 C2 **Amiens** France
79 C3 **Amilḥayt, Wādī al** *r.* Oman
73 B3 **Amindivi Islands** India
122 A1 **Aminuis** Namibia
74 A2 **Amir Chah** Pak.
129 D2 **Amisk Lake** Can.
143 C3 **Amistad Reservoir** Mex./U.S.A.
98 A3 **Amlwch** U.K.
80 B2 **'Ammān** Jordan
127 J2 **Ammassalik** Greenland
78 B3 **Am Nābiyah** Yemen
81 D2 **Amol** Iran
111 C3 **Amorgos** *i.* Greece
140 C2 **Amory** U.S.A.
130 C3 **Amos** Can.
Amoy China *see* Xiamen
121 □D3 **Ampanihy** Madag.
155 C2 **Amparo** Brazil
121 □D2 **Ampasimanolotra** Madag.
107 D1 **Amposta** Spain
78 B3 **Amrān** Yemen
Amraoti India *see* Amravati
74 B2 **Amravati** India
74 B2 **Amreli** India
74 B1 **Amritsar** India
100 B1 **Amstelveen** Neth.
100 B1 **Amsterdam** Neth.
123 D2 **Amsterdam** S. Africa
156 A8 **Amsterdam, Île** *i.* Indian Ocean
103 C2 **Amstetten** Austria
115 E3 **Am Timan** Chad
76 B2 **Amudar'ya** *r.* Asia
126 F1 **Amund Ringnes Island** Can.
55 J3 **Amundsen, Mount** Antarctica
160 H1 **Amundsen Basin** *sea feature* Arctic Ocean
126 D2 **Amundsen Gulf** Can.
55 P2 **Amundsen Ridge** *sea feature* Southern Ocean
55 P2 **Amundsen Sea** Antarctica
61 C2 **Amuntai** Indon.

Amur *r.* China/Rus. Fed. *see*
  Heilong Jiang
78 A3 'Amur, Wadi *watercourse* Sudan
61 D2 Anabanua Indon.
83 I2 Anabar *r.* Rus. Fed.
83 I2 Anabarskiy Zaliv *b.* Rus. Fed.
150 C2 Anaco Venez.
134 D1 Anaconda U.S.A.
134 B1 Anacortes U.S.A.
143 D1 Anadarko U.S.A.
80 B1 Anadolu Dağları *mts* Turkey
83 M2 Anadyr' Rus. Fed.
83 M2 Anadyr' *r.* Rus. Fed.
81 C2 'Ānah Iraq
145 B2 Anáhuac Mex.
73 B3 Anai Mudi Peak India
121 □D2 Analalava Madag.
121 □D3 Analavelona *mts* Madag.
60 B1 Anambas, Kepulauan *is* Indon.
137 E2 Anamosa U.S.A.
80 B2 Anamur Turkey
67 B4 Anan Japan
73 B3 Anantapur India
74 B1 Anantnag Jammu and Kashmir
90 B2 Anan'yiv Ukr.
91 D3 Anapa Rus. Fed.
154 C1 Anápolis Brazil
81 D2 Anār Iran
152 B2 Añatuya Arg.
65 B2 Anbyon N. Korea
104 B2 Ancenis France
126 C2 Anchorage U.S.A.
108 B2 Ancona Italy
153 A4 Ancud Chile
  Anda China *see* Daqing
93 E3 Åndalsnes Norway
106 C2 Andalucía *reg.* Spain
  Andalusia *reg.* Spain *see*
    Andalucía
140 C2 Andalusia U.S.A.
159 F3 Andaman Basin *sea feature*
  Indian Ocean
73 D3 Andaman Islands India
63 A2 Andaman Sea Indian Ocean
121 □D2 Andapa Madag.
100 B2 Andelst Neth.
92 G2 Andenes Norway
100 B2 Andenne Belgium
100 B2 Anderlecht Belgium
105 D2 Andermatt Switz.
126 D2 Anderson *r.* Can.
126 C2 Anderson *AK* U.S.A.
138 B2 Anderson *IN* U.S.A.
141 D2 Anderson *SC* U.S.A.
148 C3 Andes *mts* S. America
77 D2 Andijon Uzbek.
121 □D2 Andilamena Madag.
121 □D2 Andilanatoby Madag.
  Andizhan Uzbek. *see* Andijon
74 A1 Andkhvoy Afgh.
121 □D2 Andoany Madag.
  Andong China *see* Dandong
65 B2 Andong S. Korea
104 C3 Andorra *country* Europe
104 C3 Andorra la Vella Andorra
99 C4 Andover U.K.
154 B2 Andradina Brazil
89 D2 Andreapol' Rus. Fed.
155 D2 Andrelândia Brazil
143 C2 Andrews U.S.A.
109 C2 Andria Italy
121 □D3 Androka Madag.
  Andropov Rus. Fed. *see* Rybinsk
146 C2 Andros *i.* Bahamas
111 B3 Andros Greece
111 B3 Andros *i.* Greece
141 E4 Andros Town Bahamas
73 B3 Andrott *i.* India
90 B1 Andrushivka Ukr.
92 G2 Andselv Norway
106 C2 Andújar Spain
120 A2 Andulo Angola
114 C3 Anéfis Mali
147 B3 Anegada Passage Virgin Is (U.K.)
114 C4 Aného Togo
107 D1 Aneto *mt.* Spain
115 D3 Aney Niger
83 H3 Angara *r.* Rus. Fed.
68 C1 Angarsk Rus. Fed.
93 G3 Ånge Sweden
  Angel, Salto del *waterfall* Venez.
  see Angel Falls
144 A2 Ángel de la Guarda, Isla *i.* Mex.
64 A2 Angeles Phil.
150 C2 Angel Falls Venez.
93 F4 Ängelholm Sweden
92 G3 Ångermanälven *r.* Sweden
104 B2 Angers France
129 E1 Angikuni Lake Can.
52 B3 Anglesea Austr.
98 A3 Anglesey *i.* U.K.
121 C2 Angoche Moz.
79 C2 Angohrān Iran
120 A2 Angola *country* Africa
138 C2 Angola U.S.A.
158 F6 Angola Basin *sea feature*
  S. Atlantic Ocean
128 A2 Angoon U.S.A.
104 C2 Angoulême France
155 D2 Angra dos Reis Brazil
77 D2 Angren Uzbek.
147 D3 Anguilla *terr.* West Indies
75 C2 Angul India
93 F4 Anholt *i.* Denmark
71 B3 Anhua China

70 B2 Anhui *prov.* China
154 B1 Anhumas Brazil
  Anhwei *prov.* China *see* Anhui
154 C1 Anicuns Brazil
66 D1 Aniva, Mys *c.* Rus. Fed.
66 D1 Aniva, Zaliv *b.* Rus. Fed.
88 C1 Anjalankoski Fin.
104 B2 Anjou *reg.* France
65 B2 Anjŭ N. Korea
70 A2 Ankang China
80 B2 Ankara Turkey
121 □D3 Ankazoabo Madag.
121 □D2 Ankazobe Madag.
137 E2 Ankeny U.S.A.
102 C1 Anklam Ger.
121 □D2 Ankofa *mt.* Madag.
70 B2 Anlu China
55 G3 Ann, Cape Antarctica
139 E2 Ann, Cape U.S.A.
89 F3 Anna Rus. Fed.
115 C1 Annaba Alg.
101 F2 Annaberg-Buchholtz Ger.
80 B2 An Nabk Syria
78 B2 An Nafūd *des.* Saudi Arabia
150 D2 Annai Guyana
81 C2 An Najaf Iraq
63 B2 Annam Highlands *mts*
  Laos/Vietnam
96 C3 Annan U.K.
139 D3 Annapolis U.S.A.
75 C2 Annapurna I *mt.*
  Jammu and Kashmir/Nepal
138 C2 Ann Arbor U.S.A.
150 D2 Anna Regina Guyana
  An Nás Ireland *see* Naas
81 C2 An Nāşirīyah Iraq
115 D1 An Nawfalīyah Libya
105 C2 Annecy France
78 B3 An Nimāş Saudi Arabia
71 A3 Anning China
140 C2 Anniston U.S.A.
105 C2 Annonay France
79 B2 An Nu'ayrīyah Saudi Arabia
121 □D2 Anorontany, Tanjona *hd* Madag.
111 C3 Ano Viannos Greece
71 B3 Anpu China
70 B2 Anqing China
65 B2 Ansan S. Korea
101 E3 Ansbach Ger.
70 C1 Anshan China
71 A3 Anshun China
78 A1 An Sirhān, Wādī *watercourse*
  Saudi Arabia
143 D2 Anson U.S.A.
114 C3 Ansongo Mali
96 C2 Anstruther U.K.
150 B4 Antabamba Peru
80 B2 Antakya Turkey
121 □E2 Antalaha Madag.
80 B2 Antalya Turkey
80 B2 Antalya Körfezi *g.* Turkey
121 □D2 Antananarivo Madag.
55 A2 Antarctic Peninsula Antarctica
96 B2 An Teallach *mt.* U.K.
106 C2 Antequera Spain
142 B2 Anthony U.S.A.
114 B2 Anti Atlas *mts* Morocco
105 D3 Antibes France
131 D3 Anticosti, Île d' *i.* Can.
131 D3 Antigonish Can.
147 D3 Antigua *i.* Antigua
147 D3 Antigua and Barbuda *country*
  West Indies
145 C2 Antiguo-Morelos Mex.
111 B3 Antikythira *i.* Greece
  Antioch Turkey *see* Antakya
49 I8 Antipodes Islands N.Z.
152 A2 Antofagasta Chile
154 C3 Antonina Brazil
  António Enes Moz. *see* Angoche
97 C1 Antrim U.K.
97 C1 Antrim Hills U.K.
121 □D2 Antsalova Madag.
121 □D2 Antsirañana Madag.
  Antseranana Madag. *see*
    Antsirañana
121 □D2 Antsirabe Madag.
121 □D2 Antsirañana Madag.
121 □D2 Antsohihy Madag.
100 B2 Antwerp Belgium
  Antwerpen Belgium *see* Antwerp
  An Uaimh Ireland *see* Navan
74 B2 Anupgarh India
73 C4 Anuradhapura Sri Lanka
  Anvers Belgium *see* Antwerp
68 C2 Anxi China
51 C3 Anxious Bay Austr.
70 B2 Anyang China
65 B2 Anyang S. Korea
108 B2 Anzio Italy
67 C4 Aoga-shima *i.* Japan
66 D2 Aomori Japan
54 B2 Aoraki N.Z.
108 A1 Aosta Italy
114 B2 Aoukâr *reg.* Mali/Maur.
114 C2 Aoulef Alg.
115 D2 Aozou Chad
141 D3 Apalachee Bay U.S.A.
150 B2 Apaporis *r.* Col.
154 B2 Aparecida do Tabuado Brazil
64 B2 Aparri Phil.
86 C2 Apatity Rus. Fed.
144 B3 Apatzingán Mex.
100 B1 Apeldoorn Neth.
100 C1 Apen Ger.

108 A2 Apennines *mts* Italy
49 J5 Apia Samoa
154 C2 Apiaí Brazil
64 B3 Apo, Mount *vol.* Phil.
101 E2 Apolda Ger.
52 B3 Apollo Bay Austr.
141 D3 Apopka U.S.A.
141 D3 Apopka, Lake U.S.A.
154 B1 Aporé Brazil
154 B1 Aporé *r.* Brazil
138 A1 Apostle Islands U.S.A.
80 B2 Apostolos Andreas, Cape Cyprus
91 C2 Apostolove Ukr.
133 F3 Appalachian Mountains U.S.A.
  Appennino *mts* Italy *see*
  Apennines
53 D2 Appin Austr.
100 C1 Appingedam Neth.
98 B2 Appleby-in-Westmorland U.K.
138 B2 Appleton U.S.A.
108 B2 Aprilia Italy
62 A1 Aprunyi India
91 D3 Apsheronsk Rus. Fed.
  Apsheronskaya Rus. Fed. *see*
  Apsheronsk
154 B2 Apucarana Brazil
154 B2 Apucarana, Serra da *hills* Brazil
64 A3 Apurahuan Phil.
147 D4 Apure *r.* Venez.
78 A2 Aqaba, Gulf of Asia
81 D2 'Aqdá Iran
75 C1 Aqqikkol Hu *salt l.* China
  Arabian Gulf Asia *see* The Gulf
78 B2 Arabian Peninsula Saudi Arabia
56 B4 Arabian Sea Indian Ocean
151 F4 Aracaju Brazil
154 A2 Aracanguy, Montes de *hills* Para.
151 F3 Aracati Brazil
154 B2 Araçatuba Brazil
155 D1 Aracruz Brazil
155 D1 Araçuaí Brazil
110 B1 Arad Romania
115 E3 Arada Chad
79 C2 'Arādah U.A.E.
59 C3 Arafura Sea Austr./Indon.
154 B1 Aragarças Brazil
107 C1 Aragón *r.* Spain
107 C1 Aragón *reg.* Spain
151 E3 Araguaia *r.* Brazil
154 B1 Araguaiana Brazil
151 E3 Araguaína Brazil
154 C1 Araguari Brazil
67 C3 Arai Japan
115 C2 Arak Alg.
81 C2 Arāk Iran
62 A1 Arakan Yoma *mts* Myanmar
81 C1 Arak's *r.* Armenia/Turkey
76 C2 Aral Sea *salt l.* Kazakh./Uzbek.
76 C2 Aral'sk Kazakh.
  Aral'skoye More *salt l.*
  Kazakh./Uzbek. *see* Aral Sea
106 C1 Aranda de Duero Spain
109 D2 Arandelovac Serb. and Mont.
97 B1 Aran Island Ireland
97 B2 Aran Islands Ireland
106 C1 Aranjuez Spain
122 A1 Aranos Namibia
143 D3 Aransas Pass U.S.A.
67 B4 Arao Japan
114 B3 Araouane Mali
151 F3 Arapiraca Brazil
154 B2 Arapongas Brazil
154 C3 Araquari Brazil
78 B1 'Ar'ar Saudi Arabia
154 B2 Araraquara Brazil
151 D3 Araras Brazil
154 C2 Araras Brazil
154 B1 Araras, Serra das *hills* Brazil
154 B3 Araras, Serra das *mts* Brazil
81 C2 Ararat Armenia
52 B3 Ararat Austr.
81 C2 Ararat, Mount Turkey
155 D2 Araruama, Lago de *lag.* Brazil
155 E1 Arataca Brazil
  Aratürük China *see* Yiwu
150 B2 Arauca Col.
154 C1 Araxá Brazil
81 C2 Arbil Iraq
129 E2 Arborg Can.
96 C2 Arbroath U.K.
74 A2 Arbu Lut, Dasht-e *des.* Afgh.
104 B3 Arcachon France
141 D3 Arcadia U.S.A.
134 B2 Arcata U.S.A.
145 B3 Arcelia Mex.
86 C2 Archangel Rus. Fed.
51 D1 Archer *r.* Austr.
49 M5 Archipel des Tuamotu *is*
  Fr. Polynesia
149 B6 Archipiélago Juan Fernández
  S. Pacific Ocean
134 D2 Arco U.S.A.
106 B2 Arcos de la Frontera Spain
127 G2 Arctic Bay Can.
  Arctic Institute Islands Rus. Fed.
  see Arkticheskogo Instituta,
  Ostrova
160 J1 Arctic Mid-Ocean Ridge
  sea feature Arctic Ocean
160 Arctic Ocean
126 D2 Arctic Red *r.* Can.

81 C2 Ardabil Iran
81 C1 Ardahan Turkey
93 E3 Årdalstangen Norway
97 C2 Ardee Ireland
100 B3 Ardennes *plat.* Belgium
135 B2 Arden Town U.S.A.
81 D2 Ardestān Iran
97 D1 Ardglass U.K.
53 C2 Ardlethan Austr.
143 D2 Ardmore U.S.A.
96 A2 Ardnamurchan, Point of U.K.
52 A2 Ardrossan Austr.
96 B3 Ardrossan U.K.
96 B2 Ardvasar U.K.
135 B3 Arena, Point U.S.A.
93 E4 Arendal Norway
100 B2 Arendonk Belgium
101 E1 Arendsee (Altmark) Ger.
150 B4 Arequipa Peru
151 D3 Arere Brazil
106 C1 Arévalo Spain
108 B2 Arezzo Italy
108 B2 Argenta Italy
104 B2 Argentan France
153 B4 Argentina *country* S. America
158 D7 Argentine Basin *sea feature*
  S. Atlantic Ocean
157 I8 Argentine Rise *sea feature*
  S. Atlantic Ocean
153 A5 Argentino, Lago *l.* Arg.
104 C2 Argenton-sur-Creuse France
110 C2 Argeş *r.* Romania
74 A1 Arghandab *r.* Afgh.
111 B3 Argolikos Kolpos *b.* Greece
111 B3 Argos Greece
111 B3 Argostoli Greece
107 C1 Arguis Spain
69 E1 Argun' *r.* China/Rus. Fed.
131 D3 Argyle Can.
50 B1 Argyle, Lake Austr.
  Argyrokastron Albania *see*
  Gjirokastër
  Ar Horqin Qi China *see* Tianshan
93 F4 Århus Denmark
122 A2 Ariamsvlei Namibia
152 A1 Arica Chile
96 A2 Arinagour U.K.
155 C1 Arinos Brazil
150 D4 Aripuanã Brazil
150 C3 Aripuanã *r.* Brazil
150 C3 Ariquemes Brazil
154 B1 Ariranhá *r.* Brazil
96 B2 Arisaig U.K.
96 B2 Arisaig, Sound of *sea chan.* U.K.
104 B3 Arizgoiti Spain
142 A2 Arizona *state* U.S.A.
144 A1 Arizpe Mex.
78 B2 'Arjah Saudi Arabia
61 C2 Arjasa Indon.
92 G2 Arjeplog Sweden
140 B2 Arkadelphia U.S.A.
77 C1 Arkalyk Kazakh.
140 B2 Arkansas *r.* U.S.A.
140 B1 Arkansas *state* U.S.A.
137 D3 Arkansas City U.S.A.
  Arkhangel'sk Rus. Fed. *see*
  Archangel
97 C2 Arklow Ireland
102 C1 Arkona, Kap *c.* Ger.
82 G1 Arkticheskogo Instituta, Ostrova
  is Rus. Fed.
105 C3 Arles France
143 D2 Arlington U.S.A.
138 B2 Arlington Heights U.S.A.
115 C3 Arlit Niger
100 B3 Arlon Belgium
97 C1 Armagh U.K.
116 B2 Armant Egypt
87 D4 Armavir Rus. Fed.
81 C1 Armenia *country* Asia
150 B2 Armenia Col.
  Armenopolis Romania *see*
  Gherla
144 B3 Armeria Mex.
53 C2 Armidale Austr.
134 D1 Armington U.S.A.
130 B2 Armstrong Can.
91 C2 Armyans'k Ukr.
  Armyanskaya S.S.R. *admin. reg.*
  Asia *see* Armenia
147 D3 Arnaoutis, Cape Cyprus *see*
  Arnauti, Cape
130 D2 Arnaud *r.* Can.
80 B2 Arnauti, Cape Cyprus
100 B2 Arnhem Neth.
51 C1 Arnhem, Cape Austr.
51 C1 Arnhem Bay Austr.
51 C1 Arnhem Land *reg.* Austr.
108 B2 Arno *r.* Italy
52 A2 Arno Bay Austr.
130 C3 Arnprior Can.
101 D2 Arnsberg Ger.
101 E2 Arnstadt Ger.
122 A2 Aroab Namibia
154 B2 Aroeira Brazil
101 D2 Arolsen Ger.
78 A3 Aroma Sudan
108 A1 Arona Italy
144 B2 Aros *r.* Mex.
  Arquipélago dos Açores *aut. reg.*
  N. Atlantic Ocean *see* Azores
  Arrah India *see* Ara
81 C2 Ar Ramādī Iraq
96 B3 Arran *i.* U.K.
80 B2 Ar Raqqah Syria

105 C1 Arras France
78 B2 Ar Rass Saudi Arabia
79 C2 Ar Rayyān Qatar
150 C2 Arrecifal Col.
145 C3 Arriagá Mex.
79 C2 Ar Rimāl reg. Saudi Arabia
Ar Riyāḍ Saudi Arabia see Riyadh
54 A2 Arrowtown N.Z.
135 B3 Arroyo Grande U.S.A.
145 C2 Arroyo Seco Mex.
79 C2 Ar Rustāq Oman
81 C2 Ar Ruṭbah Iraq
78 B2 Ar Ruwaydah Saudi Arabia
81 D3 Arsenajān Iran
66 B2 Arsen'yev Rus. Fed.
111 B3 Arta Greece
144 B3 Arteaga Mex.
66 B2 Artem Rus. Fed.
91 C2 Artemivs'k Ukr.
104 C2 Artenay France
142 C2 Artesia U.S.A.
51 E2 Arthur Point Austr.
54 B2 Arthur's Pass N.Z.
152 C3 Artigas Uru.
129 D1 Artillery Lake Can.
123 C1 Artisia Botswana
104 C1 Artois reg. France
90 B2 Artsyz Ukr.
Artur de Paiva Angola see Kuvango
77 D3 Artux China
81 C1 Artvin Turkey
59 C3 Aru, Kepulauan is Indon.
119 D2 Arua Uganda
147 D3 Aruba terr. West Indies
75 C2 Arun r. Nepal
119 D3 Arusha Tanz.
136 B3 Arvada U.S.A.
68 C1 Arvayheer Mongolia
129 E1 Arviat Can.
92 G2 Arvidsjaur Sweden
93 F4 Arvika Sweden
108 A2 Arzachena Sardinia Italy
87 D3 Arzamas Rus. Fed.
107 C2 Arzew Alg.
100 C2 Arzfeld Ger.
Arzila Morocco see Asilah
101 F2 Aš Czech Rep.
115 C4 Asaba Nigeria
66 D2 Asahi-dake vol. Japan
66 D2 Asahikawa Japan
78 B3 Āsalē l. Eth.
75 C2 Asansol India
117 C3 Āsayita Eth.
130 C3 Asbestos Can.
122 B2 Asbestos Mountains S. Africa
119 E2 Āsbe Teferi Eth.
109 C2 Ascea Italy
152 B1 Ascensión Bol.
113 B6 Ascension i. S. Atlantic Ocean
145 D3 Ascensión, Bahía de la b. Mex.
101 D3 Aschaffenburg Ger.
100 C2 Ascheberg Ger.
101 E2 Aschersleben Ger.
108 B2 Ascoli Piceno Italy
119 D2 Āsela Eth.
92 G3 Åsele Sweden
111 B2 Asenovgrad Bulg.
78 B2 Asharat Saudi Arabia
50 A2 Ashburton watercourse Austr.
54 B2 Ashburton N.Z.
140 B2 Ashdown U.S.A.
141 D1 Asheville U.S.A.
53 D1 Ashford Austr.
97 C2 Ashford Ireland
99 D4 Ashford U.K.
76 B3 Ashgabat Turkm.
66 D2 Ashibetsu Japan
98 C2 Ashington U.K.
67 B4 Ashizuri-misaki pt Japan
Ashkhabad Turkm. see Ashgabat
136 D3 Ashland KS U.S.A.
138 C3 Ashland KY U.S.A.
138 C2 Ashland OH U.S.A.
134 B2 Ashland OR U.S.A.
138 A1 Ashland WI U.S.A.
53 C1 Ashley Austr.
88 C3 Ashmyany Belarus
66 D2 Ashoro Japan
81 C2 Ash Shabakah Iraq
78 B3 Ash Sharawrah Saudi Arabia
Ash Shāriqah U.A.E. see Sharjah
81 C2 Ash Sharqāt Iraq
81 C2 Ash Shaṭrah Iraq
78 B3 Ash Shaykh 'Uthman Yemen
79 B3 Ash Shiḥr Yemen
79 C2 Ash Shināş Oman
78 B2 Ash Shu'aybah Saudi Arabia
78 B2 Ash Shu'bah Saudi Arabia
78 B2 Ash Shubaykīyah Saudi Arabia
78 B3 Ash Shumlūl Saudi Arabia
115 D2 Ash Shuwayrif Libya
138 C2 Ashtabula U.S.A.
131 D2 Ashuanipi Lake Can.
75 B3 Asifabad India
106 B2 Asilah Morocco
108 A2 Asinara, Golfo dell' b. Sardinia Italy
108 A2 Asinara, Isola i. Sardinia Italy
82 G3 Asino Rus. Fed.
88 C3 Asipovichy Belarus
78 B2 'Asir reg. Saudi Arabia

93 F4 Asker Norway
93 F4 Askim Norway
68 C1 Askiz Rus. Fed.
116 B3 Asmara Eritrea
93 F4 Åsnen l. Sweden
116 B2 Asoteriba, Jebel mt. Sudan
103 D2 Aspang-Markt Austria
136 B3 Aspen U.S.A.
143 C2 Aspermont U.S.A.
54 A2 Aspiring, Mount N.Z.
116 C3 Assab Eritrea
78 B3 Aş Şaḥif Yemen
Aş Şaḥrā' al Gharbīyah des. Egypt see Western Desert
Aş Şaḥrā' ash Sharqīyah des. Egypt see Eastern Desert
78 B2 As Salamīyah Saudi Arabia
116 A1 As Sallūm Egypt
75 D2 Assam state India
81 C2 As Samāwah Iraq
79 C2 Aş Şanām reg. Saudi Arabia
115 E2 As Sarir reg. Libya
108 A3 Assemini Sardinia Italy
100 C1 Assen Neth.
100 B2 Assesse Belgium
115 D1 As Sidrah Libya
129 D3 Assiniboia Can.
128 C2 Assiniboine, Mount Can.
154 B2 Assis Brazil
78 B2 Aş Şubayḥīyah Kuwait
81 C2 As Sulaymānīyah Iraq
78 B2 As Sulaymī Saudi Arabia
78 B2 As Sulayyil Saudi Arabia
78 B2 As Sūq Saudi Arabia
80 B2 As Suwaydā' Syria
79 C2 As Suwayq Oman
As Suways Egypt see Suez
111 B3 Astakos Greece
77 D1 Astana Kazakh.
81 C2 Āstārā Iran
100 B2 Asten Neth.
Asterabad Iran see Gorgān
108 A2 Asti Italy
74 B1 Astor Jammu and Kashmir
72 B1 Astor Jammu and Kashmir
106 B1 Astorga Spain
134 B1 Astoria U.S.A.
Astrabad Iran see Gorgān
87 D4 Astrakhan' Rus. Fed.
Astrakhan' Bazar Azer. see Cälilabad
88 C3 Astravyets Belarus
Astrida Rwanda see Butare
106 B1 Asturias reg. Spain
111 C3 Astypalaia i. Greece
152 C2 Asunción Para.
116 B2 Aswān Egypt
116 B2 Asyūṭ Egypt
Atacama, Desierto de des. Chile see Atacama Desert
152 B2 Atacama, Puna de plat. Arg.
152 B2 Atacama, Salar de salt flat Chile
152 B2 Atacama Desert des. Chile
114 C4 Atakpamé Togo
111 B3 Atalanti Greece
150 B4 Atalaya Peru
155 D1 Ataléia Brazil
77 C3 Atamyrat Turkm.
78 B3 'Ataq Yemen
114 A2 Atâr Maur.
135 B3 Atascadero U.S.A.
77 D2 Atasu Kazakh.
116 B3 Atbara Sudan
116 B3 Atbara r. Sudan
77 C1 Atbasar Kazakh.
140 B3 Atchafalaya Bay U.S.A.
137 D3 Atchison U.S.A.
Ateransk Kazakh. see Atyrau
108 B2 Aterno r. Italy
108 B2 Atessa Italy
100 A2 Ath Belgium
128 C2 Athabasca Can.
129 C2 Athabasca r. Can.
129 D2 Athabasca, Lake Can.
97 C2 Athboy Ireland
97 B2 Athenry Ireland
111 B3 Athens Greece
140 C2 Athens AL U.S.A.
141 D2 Athens GA U.S.A.
138 C3 Athens OH U.S.A.
141 D1 Athens TN U.S.A.
143 D2 Athens TX U.S.A.
51 D1 Athens Austr.
Athina Greece see Athens
97 C2 Athlone Ireland
111 B3 Athos mt. Greece
97 C2 Athy Ireland
115 D3 Ati Chad
130 A3 Atikokan Can.
87 D4 Atkarsk Rus. Fed.
141 D2 Atlanta U.S.A.
137 D2 Atlantic U.S.A.
141 E2 Atlantic Beach U.S.A.
139 E3 Atlantic City U.S.A.
55 D3 Atlantic-Indian-Antarctic Basin sea feature S. Atlantic Ocean
158 E8 Atlantic-Indian Ridge sea feature Southern Ocean
158 Atlantic Ocean
122 A3 Atlantis S. Africa
114 B1 Atlas Mountains Africa
114 C1 Atlas Saharien mts Alg.
128 C2 Atlin Can.
128 A2 Atlin Lake Can.
140 C2 Atmore U.S.A.

152 B2 Atocha Bol.
143 D2 Atoka U.S.A.
75 C2 Atrai r. India
80 B2 Aṭ Ṭafilah Jordan
78 B2 Aṭ Ṭā'if Saudi Arabia
63 B2 Attapu Laos
111 C3 Attavyros mt. Greece
130 B2 Attawapiskat Can.
130 B2 Attawapiskat r. Can.
130 B2 Attawapiskat Lake Can.
100 C2 Attendorn Ger.
100 A3 Attichy France
116 B2 Aṭ Ṭūr Egypt
78 B3 At Turbah Yemen
135 B3 Atwater U.S.A.
76 B2 Atyrau Kazakh.
105 D3 Aubagne France
105 C3 Aubenas France
126 D2 Aubry Lake Can.
140 C2 Auburn AL U.S.A.
135 B3 Auburn CA U.S.A.
138 B2 Auburn IN U.S.A.
139 E2 Auburn ME U.S.A.
137 D2 Auburn NE U.S.A.
139 D2 Auburn NY U.S.A.
104 C2 Aubusson France
104 C3 Auch France
54 B1 Auckland N.Z.
48 H9 Auckland Islands N.Z.
117 C4 Audo Range mts Eth.
101 F2 Aue Ger.
101 F2 Auerbach Ger.
102 C2 Augsburg Ger.
50 A3 Augusta Austr.
109 C3 Augusta Sicily Italy
141 D2 Augusta GA U.S.A.
137 D3 Augusta KS U.S.A.
139 F2 Augusta ME U.S.A.
155 D1 Augusto de Lima Brazil
103 E1 Augustów Pol.
50 A2 Augustus, Mount Austr.
100 A2 Aulnoye-Aymeries France
Aumale Alg. see Sour el Ghozlane
62 A2 Aunglan Myanmar
122 B2 Auob watercourse Namibia/S. Africa
131 D2 Aupaluk Can.
74 B2 Aurangabad India
104 B2 Auray France
100 C1 Aurich Ger.
154 B1 Aurilândia Brazil
104 C3 Aurillac France
136 C3 Aurora CO U.S.A.
138 B2 Aurora IL U.S.A.
137 E3 Aurora MO U.S.A.
137 D2 Aurora NE U.S.A.
122 A2 Aus Namibia
138 C2 Au Sable r. U.S.A.
137 E2 Austin MN U.S.A.
135 C3 Austin NV U.S.A.
143 D2 Austin TX U.S.A.
Australes, Îles is Fr. Polynesia see Tubuai Islands
50 B2 Australia country Oceania
55 K4 Australian-Antarctic Basin sea feature Southern Ocean
53 C3 Australian Capital Territory admin. div. Austr.
102 C2 Austria country Europe
150 D3 Autazes Brazil
144 B3 Autlán Mex.
105 C2 Autun France
104 C3 Auvergne reg. France
105 C2 Auvergne, Monts d' mts France
105 C2 Auxerre France
105 D2 Auxonne France
105 C2 Avallon France
131 E3 Avalon Peninsula Can.
154 C2 Avaré Brazil
91 C2 Avdiyivka Ukr.
106 B1 Aveiro Port.
109 B2 Avellino Italy
108 B2 Aversa Italy
100 A2 Avesnes-sur-Helpe France
93 G3 Avesta Sweden
104 C3 Aveyron r. France
108 B2 Avezzano Italy
96 C2 Aviemore U.K.
109 C2 Avigliano Italy
105 C3 Avignon France
106 C1 Ávila Spain
106 B1 Avilés Spain
52 B3 Avoca Austr.
139 D2 Avoca U.S.A.
109 C3 Avola Sicily Italy
99 C4 Avon r. England U.K.
99 B4 Avon r. England U.K.
99 C3 Avon r. England U.K.
142 A2 Avondale U.S.A.
104 B2 Avranches France
54 B1 Awanui N.Z.
119 C3 Āwasa Eth.
117 C4 Āwash Eth.
117 C4 Āwash r. Eth.
115 D2 Awbārī Libya
117 C4 Aw Dheegle Somalia
96 B2 Awe, Loch l. U.K.
117 A4 Aweil Sudan
115 C4 Awka Nigeria
114 A2 Awserd Western Sahara
126 F1 Axel Heiberg Island Can.
114 B4 Axim Ghana
150 B4 Ayacucho Peru
77 E2 Ayagoz Kazakh.
Ayaguz Kazakh. see Ayagoz

68 B2 Ayakkum Hu salt l. China
106 B2 Ayamonte Spain
83 K3 Ayan Rus. Fed.
150 B4 Ayaviri Peru
74 A1 Āybak Afgh.
76 A2 Aybas Kazakh.
91 D2 Aydar r. Ukr.
77 C2 Aydarko'l ko'li l. Uzbek.
111 C3 Aydın Turkey
77 C2 Ayeat, Gora hill Kazakh.
Ayers Rock hill Austr. see Uluru
83 I2 Aykhal Rus. Fed.
99 C4 Aylesbury U.K.
106 C2 Ayllón Spain
129 D1 Aylmer Lake Can.
117 B4 Ayod Sudan
83 M2 Ayon, Ostrov i. Rus. Fed.
114 B3 'Ayoûn el 'Atroûs Maur.
51 D1 Ayr Austr.
96 B3 Ayr U.K.
98 A2 Ayre, Point of Isle of Man
76 C2 Ayteke Bi Kazakh.
110 C2 Aytos Bulg.
145 C3 Ayutla Mex.
63 B2 Ayutthaya Thai.
111 C3 Ayvacık Turkey
111 C3 Ayvalık Turkey
91 C3 Ayya, Mys pt Ukr.
114 B3 Azaouâd reg. Mali
114 C3 Azaouagh, Vallée de watercourse Mali/Niger
115 D3 Azare Nigeria
Azbine mts Niger see Aïr, Massif de l'
81 C1 Azerbaijan country Asia
Azerbaydzhanskaya S.S.R. admin. reg. Asia see Azerbaijan
150 B3 Azogues Ecuador
86 D2 Azopol'ye Rus. Fed.
112 A2 Azores aut. reg. N. Atlantic Ocean
91 D2 Azov Rus. Fed.
91 D2 Azov, Sea of Rus. Fed./Ukr.
Azraq, Bahr el r. Sudan see Blue Nile
106 B2 Azuaga Spain
146 B4 Azuero, Península de pen. Panama
153 C3 Azul Arg.
108 A3 Azzaba Alg.
Aẕ Ẕahrān Saudi Arabia see Dhahran
80 B2 Az Zaqāzīq Egypt
80 B2 Az Zarqā' Jordan
115 D1 Az Zāwiyah Libya
78 B3 Az Zaydīyah Yemen
114 C2 Azzel Matti, Sebkha salt pan Alg.
78 B2 Az Zilfī Saudi Arabia
78 B3 Az Zuqur i. Yemen

B

117 C4 Baardheere Somalia
77 C3 Bābā, Kūh-e mts Afgh.
111 C3 Baba Burnu pt Turkey
110 C2 Babadag Romania
111 C2 Babaeski Turkey
116 C3 Bāb al Mandab str. Africa/Asia
61 C2 Babana Indon.
119 C1 Babanusa Sudan
59 D3 Babar i. Indon.
119 D3 Babati Tanz.
89 E2 Babayevo Rus. Fed.
59 C2 Babeldaob i. Palau
128 B2 Babine r. Can.
128 B2 Babine Lake Can.
59 C3 Babo Indon.
81 D2 Bābol Iran
122 A3 Baboon Point S. Africa
88 C3 Babruysk Belarus
Babu China see Hezhou
64 B2 Babuyan i. Phil.
64 B2 Babuyan Channel Phil.
64 B2 Babuyan Islands Phil.
151 E3 Bacabal Brazil
145 D3 Bacalar Mex.
59 C3 Bacan i. Indon.
110 C1 Bacău Romania
52 B3 Bacchus Marsh Austr.
77 D3 Bachu China
129 E1 Back r. Can.
109 C1 Bačka Palanka Serb. and Mont.
109 C1 Bačka Topola Serb. and Mont.
52 A3 Backstairs Passage Austr.
62 B1 Bac Lac Vietnam
63 B3 Bac Liêu Vietnam
62 B1 Băc Ninh Vietnam
142 B3 Bacobampo Mex.
64 B2 Bacolod Phil.
130 C2 Bacqueville, Lac l. Can.
Bada China see Xilin
70 A1 Badain Jaran Shamo des. China
106 B2 Badajoz Spain
Badaojiang China see Baishan
75 D2 Badarpur India
101 D2 Bad Berka Ger.
101 E1 Bad Berleburg Ger.
101 E1 Bad Bevensen Ger.
100 C2 Bad Dürkheim Ger.
100 C2 Bad Ems Ger.
103 D2 Baden Austria
102 C2 Baden-Baden Ger.
101 E2 Bad Harzburg Ger.
101 D2 Bad Hersfeld Ger.

102 C2 **Bad Hofgastein** Austria
101 D2 **Bad Homburg vor der Höhe** Ger.
101 D1 **Bad Iburg** Ger.
74 A2 **Badin** Pak.
　　　Bādiyat ash Shām des. Asia see
　　　Syrian Desert
101 E2 **Bad Kissingen** Ger.
100 C3 **Bad Kreuznach** Ger.
136 C1 **Badlands** reg. ND U.S.A.
136 C2 **Badlands** reg. SD U.S.A.
101 E2 **Bad Lauterberg im Harz** Ger.
101 D2 **Bad Lippspringe** Ger.
101 D3 **Bad Mergentheim** Ger.
101 D2 **Bad Nauheim** Ger.
100 C2 **Bad Neuenahr-Ahrweiler** Ger.
101 E2 **Bad Neustadt an der Saale** Ger.
101 E1 **Bad Oldesloe** Ger.
101 D2 **Bad Pyrmont** Ger.
78 A2 **Badr Ḥunayn** Saudi Arabia
101 D1 **Bad Salzuflen** Ger.
101 E2 **Bad Salzungen** Ger.
102 C1 **Bad Schwartau** Ger.
101 E1 **Bad Segeberg** Ger.
73 C4 **Badulla** Sri Lanka
101 D1 **Bad Zwischenahn** Ger.
106 C2 **Baeza** Spain
114 A3 **Bafatá** Guinea-Bissau
127 H2 **Baffin Bay** sea Can./Greenland
127 H2 **Baffin Island** Can.
118 B2 **Bafia** Cameroon
114 A3 **Bafing** r. Guinea/Mali
114 A3 **Bafoulabé** Mali
118 B2 **Bafoussam** Cameroon
81 D2 **Bāfq** Iran
80 B1 **Bafra** Turkey
79 C2 **Bāft** Iran
119 C2 **Bafwasende** Dem. Rep. Congo
119 D3 **Bagamoyo** Tanz.
　　　Bagan Datoh Malaysia see
　　　Bagan Datuk
60 B1 **Bagan Datuk** Malaysia
64 B3 **Baganga** Phil.
120 A2 **Bagani** Namibia
60 B1 **Bagansiapiapi** Indon.
118 B3 **Bagata** Dem. Rep. Congo
91 E2 **Bagayevskiy** Rus. Fed.
142 A2 **Bagdad** U.S.A.
152 C3 **Bagé** Brazil
81 C2 **Baghdād** Iraq
79 C1 **Bāghīn** Iran
77 C3 **Baghlān** Afgh.
104 C3 **Bagnères-de-Luchon** France
105 C3 **Bagnols-sur-Cèze** France
　　　Bago Myanmar see Pegu
88 B3 **Bagrationovsk** Rus. Fed.
　　　Bagrax China see Bohu
64 B2 **Baguio** Phil.
115 C3 **Bagzane, Monts** mts Niger
146 C2 **Bahamas, The** country West Indies
75 C2 **Baharampur** India
　　　Bahariya Oasis Egypt see
　　　Bahrīyah, Wāḥāt al
60 B1 **Bahau** Malaysia
74 B2 **Bahawalnagar** Pak.
74 B2 **Bahawalpur** Pak.
　　　Bahia Brazil see Salvador
146 B3 **Bahía, Islas de la** is Hond.
153 B3 **Bahía Blanca** Arg.
144 A2 **Bahía Kino** Mex.
152 C2 **Bahía Negra** Para.
144 A2 **Bahía Tortugas** Mex.
117 B3 **Bahir Dar** Eth.
79 C2 **Bahlā** Oman
75 C2 **Bahraich** India
79 C2 **Bahrain** country Asia
116 A2 **Bahrīyah, Wāḥāt al** Egypt
79 D2 **Bāhū Kālāt** Iran
89 D3 **Bahushewsk** Belarus
110 C2 **Baia** Romania
120 A2 **Baía dos Tigres** Angola
110 B1 **Baia Mare** Romania
118 B2 **Baïbokoum** Chad
69 E1 **Baicheng** China
　　　Baidoa Somalia see Baydhabo
　　　Baie-aux-Feuilles Can. see
　　　Tasiujaq
131 D3 **Baie-Comeau** Can.
　　　Baie-du-Poste Can. see
　　　Mistissini
131 C3 **Baie-St-Paul** Can.
131 E3 **Baie Verte** Can.
62 A1 **Baihanchang** China
65 B1 **Baihe** China
69 D1 **Baikal, Lake** Rus. Fed.
　　　Baile Átha Cliath Ireland see
　　　Dublin
110 B2 **Băileşti** Romania
68 C2 **Baima** China
141 D2 **Bainbridge** U.S.A.
　　　Baingoin China see Porong
48 I3 **Bairiki** Kiribati
　　　Bairin Youqi China see Daban
53 C3 **Bairnsdale** Austr.
65 B1 **Baishan** Jilin China
65 B1 **Baishanzhen** Jilin China
120 A2 **Baixo-Longa** Angola
70 A2 **Baiyin** China
116 B3 **Baiyuda Desert** Sudan
103 D2 **Baja** Hungary
144 A1 **Baja California** pen. Mex.
61 D2 **Bajawa** Indon.
78 B3 **Bājil** Yemen
115 D3 **Bajoga** Nigeria
109 D2 **Bajram Curri** Albania
114 A3 **Bakel** Senegal

135 C3 **Baker** CA U.S.A.
140 B2 **Baker** LA U.S.A.
136 C1 **Baker** MT U.S.A.
134 C2 **Baker** OR U.S.A.
134 B1 **Baker, Mount** vol. U.S.A.
129 I1 **Baker Foreland** hd Can.
49 J3 **Baker Island** terr. N. Pacific Ocean
129 E1 **Baker Lake** Can.
129 E1 **Baker Lake** l. Can.
135 C3 **Bakersfield** U.S.A.
　　　Bakharden Turkm. see
　　　Bakherden
91 C3 **Bakhchysaray** Ukr.
76 B3 **Bakherden** Turkm.
91 C1 **Bakhmach** Ukr.
　　　Bakhmut Ukr. see Artemivs'k
　　　Bākhtarān Iran see Kermānshāh
　　　Bakı Azer. see Baku
111 C2 **Bakırköy** Turkey
92 □C2 **Bakkaflói** b. Iceland
118 C2 **Bakouma** C.A.R.
81 C1 **Baku** Azer.
99 B3 **Bala** U.K.
64 A3 **Balabac** Phil.
64 A3 **Balabac** i. Phil.
61 C1 **Balabac Strait** Malaysia/Phil.
75 C2 **Balaghat** India
60 C2 **Balaiberkuak** Indon.
52 A2 **Balaklava** Austr.
91 C3 **Balaklava** Ukr.
91 D2 **Balakliya** Ukr.
87 D3 **Balakovo** Rus. Fed.
76 C3 **Bālā Morghāb** Afgh.
145 C3 **Balancán** Mex.
111 C3 **Balan Daği** hill Turkey
64 B2 **Balanga** Phil.
87 D3 **Balashov** Rus. Fed.
　　　Balaton, Lake Hungary see
　　　Lake Balaton
103 D2 **Balatonboglár** Hungary
150 D3 **Balbina, Represa de** resr Brazil
97 C2 **Balbriggan** Ireland
52 A2 **Balcanoona** Austr.
110 C2 **Balchik** Bulg.
54 A3 **Balclutha** N.Z.
143 C3 **Balcones Escarpment** U.S.A.
129 E2 **Baldock Lake** Can.
138 D2 **Baldwin** U.S.A.
129 D2 **Baldy Mountain** hill Can.
142 B2 **Baldy Peak** U.S.A.
　　　Baleares, Islas is Spain see
　　　Balearic Islands
107 D2 **Balearic Islands** is Spain
155 E1 **Baleia, Ponta da** pt Brazil
130 C2 **Baleine, Grande Rivière de la** r.
　　　Can.
131 D2 **Baleine, Rivière à la** r. Can.
75 C2 **Baleshwar** India
50 B2 **Balgo** Austr.
79 B3 **Bālḥaf** Yemen
61 C2 **Bali** i. Indon.
60 A1 **Balige** Indon.
75 C2 **Baliguda** India
111 C3 **Balıkesir** Turkey
61 C2 **Balikpapan** Indon.
64 A3 **Balimbing** Phil.
59 D3 **Balimo** P.N.G.
102 B2 **Balingen** Ger.
64 B2 **Balintang Channel** Phil.
　　　Bali Sea Indon. see Laut Bali
78 B3 **Baljurshi** Saudi Arabia
76 B3 **Balkanabat** Turkm.
110 B2 **Balkan Mountains**
　　　Bulg./Serb. and Mont.
77 C1 **Balkashino** Kazakh.
77 D2 **Balkhash** Kazakh.
77 D2 **Balkhash, Lake** Kazakh.
　　　Balkhash, Ozero l. Kazakh. see
　　　Balkhash, Lake
　　　Balla Balla Zimbabwe see
　　　Mbalabala
96 B2 **Ballachulish** U.K.
50 B3 **Balladonia** Austr.
97 B2 **Ballaghaderreen** Ireland
92 G2 **Ballangen** Norway
96 B3 **Ballantrae** U.K.
52 B3 **Ballarat** Austr.
50 B2 **Ballard, Lake** salt flat Austr.
96 C2 **Ballater** U.K.
114 B3 **Ballé** Mali
55 M3 **Balleny Islands** Antarctica
53 D1 **Ballina** Austr.
97 B1 **Ballina** Ireland
97 B2 **Ballinasloe** Ireland
97 B3 **Ballineen** Ireland
143 D2 **Ballinger** U.S.A.
97 B2 **Ballinrobe** Ireland
97 B1 **Ballycastle** Ireland
97 C1 **Ballycastle** U.K.
97 D1 **Ballyclare** U.K.
97 B2 **Ballyhaunis** Ireland
97 C1 **Ballymena** U.K.
97 C1 **Ballymoney** U.K.
97 D1 **Ballynahinch** U.K.
97 B1 **Ballyshannon** Ireland
95 B2 **Ballyvoy** U.K.
52 B3 **Balmoral** Austr.
143 C2 **Balmorhea** U.S.A.
120 A2 **Balombo** Angola
51 D2 **Balonne** r. Austr.
74 B2 **Balotra** India
77 D2 **Balpyk Bi** Kazakh.
75 C2 **Balrampur** India
52 B2 **Balranald** Austr.
110 B2 **Balş** Romania

151 E3 **Balsas** Brazil
145 C3 **Balsas** Mex.
145 B3 **Balsas** r. Mex.
90 B2 **Balta** Ukr.
90 B2 **Bălţi** Moldova
93 G4 **Baltic Sea** g. Europe
80 B2 **Balţīm** Egypt
97 B3 **Baltimore** Ireland
123 C1 **Baltimore** S. Africa
139 D3 **Baltimore** U.S.A.
97 C2 **Baltinglass** Ireland
88 A3 **Baltiysk** Rus. Fed.
75 D2 **Balu** India
52 A2 **Balumbah** Austr.
88 C2 **Balvi** Latvia
77 D2 **Balykchy** Kyrg.
87 E4 **Balykshi** Kazakh.
79 C2 **Bam** Iran
71 A3 **Bama** China
51 D1 **Bamaga** Austr.
130 A2 **Bamaji Lake** Can.
114 B3 **Bamako** Mali
118 C2 **Bambari** C.A.R.
101 E3 **Bamberg** Ger.
119 C2 **Bambili** Dem. Rep. Congo
118 B2 **Bambio** C.A.R.
119 C2 **Bambouti** C.A.R.
155 C2 **Bambuí** Brazil
98 C2 **Bamburgh** U.K.
118 B2 **Bamenda** Cameroon
77 C3 **Bāmiān** Afgh.
118 C2 **Bamingui** C.A.R.
79 D2 **Bampūr** Iran
79 C2 **Bampūr** watercourse Iran
152 B1 **Bañados del Izozog** swamp Bol.
119 C2 **Banalia** Dem. Rep. Congo
71 A3 **Banan** China
151 D4 **Bananal, Ilha do** i. Brazil
74 B2 **Banas** r. India
111 C3 **Banaz** Turkey
62 B2 **Ban Ban** Laos
97 C1 **Banbridge** U.K.
99 C3 **Banbury** U.K.
96 C2 **Banchory** U.K.
130 C3 **Bancroft** Can.
　　　Bancroft Zambia see
　　　Chililabombwe
119 C2 **Banda** Dem. Rep. Congo
75 C2 **Banda** India
59 C3 **Banda, Kepulauan** is Indon.
59 C3 **Banda, Laut** Indon.
60 A1 **Banda Aceh** Indon.
　　　Bandar India see Machilipatnam
　　　Bandar Abbas Iran see
　　　Bandar-e 'Abbās
75 D2 **Bandarban** Bangl.
79 C2 **Bandar-e 'Abbās** Iran
81 C2 **Bandar-e Anzalī** Iran
79 C2 **Bandar-e Chārak** Iran
81 C2 **Bandar-e Emām Khomeynī** Iran
79 C2 **Bandar-e Lengeh** Iran
79 C2 **Bandar-e Maqām** Iran
　　　Bandar-e Pahlavi Iran see
　　　Bandar-e Anzalī
　　　Bandar-e Shāhpūr Iran see
　　　Bandar-e Emām Khomeynī
60 B2 **Bandar Lampung** Indon.
61 C1 **Bandar Seri Begawan** Brunei
　　　Banda Sea Indon. see Banda, Laut
155 C2 **Bandeiras, Pico de** mt. Brazil
123 C1 **Bandelierkop** S. Africa
144 B2 **Banderas, Bahía de** b. Mex.
114 B3 **Bandiagara** Mali
111 C2 **Bandırma** Turkey
　　　Bandjarmasin Indon. see
　　　Banjarmasin
97 B3 **Bandon** Ireland
97 B3 **Bandon** r. Ireland
118 B3 **Bandundu** Dem. Rep. Congo
60 B2 **Bandung** Indon.
128 C2 **Banff** Can.
96 C2 **Banff** U.K.
114 B3 **Banfora** Burkina
64 B3 **Banga** Phil.
73 B3 **Bangalore** India
118 C2 **Bangassou** C.A.R.
61 D2 **Banggai** Indon.
59 C3 **Banggai, Kepulauan** is Indon.
61 D2 **Banggai, Kepulauan** is Indon.
61 C1 **Banggi** i. Sabah Malaysia
　　　Banghāzī Libya see Benghazi
60 B2 **Bangka** i. Indon.
60 B2 **Bangka, Selat** sea chan. Indon.
61 C2 **Bangkalan** Indon.
60 B1 **Bangkinang** Indon.
60 B2 **Bangko** Indon.
63 B2 **Bangkok** Thai.
75 C2 **Bangladesh** country Asia
97 D1 **Bangor** Northern Ireland U.K.
98 A3 **Bangor** Wales U.K.
139 F2 **Bangor** U.S.A.
63 A2 **Bang Saphan Yai** Thai.
64 B2 **Bangued** Phil.
118 B2 **Bangui** C.A.R.
64 B2 **Bangui** Phil.
121 B2 **Bangweulu, Lake** Zambia
80 B2 **Banhā** Egypt
62 B2 **Ban Huai Khon** Thai.
118 C2 **Bani** C.A.R.
80 B3 **Banī Mazār** Egypt
116 B2 **Banī Suwayf** Egypt
115 D1 **Banī Walīd** Libya
80 B2 **Bāniyās** Syria
109 C2 **Banja Luka** Bos.-Herz.
61 C2 **Banjarmasin** Indon.

114 A3 **Banjul** Gambia
63 A3 **Ban Khok Kloi** Thai.
128 A2 **Banks Island** B.C. Can.
126 D2 **Banks Island** N.W.T. Can.
48 H5 **Banks Islands** Vanuatu
129 E1 **Banks Lake** Can.
54 B2 **Banks Peninsula** N.Z.
51 D4 **Banks Strait** Austr.
75 C2 **Bankura** India
62 A1 **Banmauk** Myanmar
62 B2 **Ban Mouang** Laos
97 C1 **Bann** r. U.K.
62 B2 **Ban Napè** Laos
63 A3 **Ban Na San** Thai.
146 C2 **Bannerman Town** Bahamas
　　　Banningville Dem. Rep. Congo see
　　　Bandundu
71 A4 **Ban Nong Kung** Thai.
74 B1 **Bannu** Pak.
103 D2 **Banská Bystrica** Slovakia
111 B2 **Bansko** Bulg.
74 B2 **Banswara** India
62 B2 **Ban Taviang** Laos
63 A3 **Ban Tha Kham** Thai.
62 A1 **Ban Tha Song Yang** Thai.
63 B2 **Ban Tôp** Laos
97 B3 **Bantry** Ireland
97 B3 **Bantry Bay** Ireland
60 A1 **Banyak, Pulau-pulau** is Indon.
118 B2 **Banyo** Cameroon
107 D1 **Banyoles** Spain
61 C2 **Banyuwangi** Indon.
　　　Banzyville Dem. Rep. Congo see
　　　Mobayi-Mbongo
　　　Bao'an China see Shenzhen
70 B1 **Baochang** China
70 B2 **Baoding** China
70 A2 **Baoji** China
63 B2 **Bao Lôc** Vietnam
66 B1 **Baoqing** China
118 B2 **Baoro** C.A.R.
62 A1 **Baoshan** China
70 B1 **Baotou** China
65 B1 **Baotou Shan** mt. China/N. Korea
74 B2 **Bap** India
81 C2 **Ba'qūbah** Iraq
109 C2 **Bar** Serb. and Mont.
90 B2 **Bar** Ukr.
116 B3 **Bara** Sudan
117 C4 **Baraawe** Somalia
147 C3 **Baracoa** Cuba
53 C2 **Baradine** Austr.
147 C3 **Barahona** Dom. Rep.
116 B3 **Baraka** watercourse Eritrea/Sudan
106 C1 **Barakaldo** Spain
61 C1 **Baram** r. Sarawak Malaysia
150 B2 **Baramanni** Guyana
89 D3 **Baran'** Belarus
74 B2 **Baran** India
88 C3 **Baranavichy** Belarus
116 B2 **Baranis** Egypt
90 B1 **Baranivka** Ukr.
76 B2 **Barankul** Kazakh.
128 A2 **Baranof Island** U.S.A.
　　　Baranowicze Belarus see
　　　Baranavichy
59 C3 **Barat Daya, Kepulauan** is Indon.
155 C2 **Barbacena** Brazil
147 E3 **Barbados** country West Indies
107 D1 **Barbastro** Spain
106 B2 **Barbate de Franco** Spain
123 C3 **Barberton** S. Africa
104 B2 **Barbezieux-St-Hilaire** France
51 D2 **Barcaldine** Austr.
107 D1 **Barcelona** Spain
150 C1 **Barcelona** Venez.
105 D3 **Barcelonnette** France
150 C3 **Barcelos** Brazil
114 B4 **Barclayville** Liberia
51 D2 **Barcoo** watercourse Austr.
　　　Barcoo Creek watercourse Austr.
　　　see Cooper Creek
103 D2 **Barcs** Hungary
92 □B3 **Bárðarbunga** mt. Iceland
75 C2 **Barddhaman** India
103 E2 **Bardejov** Slovakia
　　　Bardera Somalia see
　　　Baardheere
79 C2 **Bardsir** Iran
75 B2 **Bareilly** India
82 C1 **Barents Sea** Arctic Ocean
78 A3 **Barentu** Eritrea
72 C1 **Barga** China
108 D2 **Barga** Italy
75 C2 **Barh** India
52 B3 **Barham** Austr.
139 F2 **Bar Harbor** U.S.A.
109 C2 **Bari** Italy
107 E2 **Barika** Alg.
74 B1 **Barikot** Afgh.
150 B2 **Barinas** Venez.
75 C2 **Baripada** India
75 C2 **Barisal** Bangl.
60 B2 **Barisan, Pegunungan** mts Indon.
61 C2 **Barito** r. Indon.
79 C2 **Barkā** Oman
88 C2 **Barkava** Latvia
74 A2 **Barkhan** Pak.
51 C1 **Barkly Tableland** reg. Austr.
122 B2 **Barkly West** S. Africa
68 C2 **Barkol** China
110 C1 **Bârlad** Romania
105 D2 **Bar-le-Duc** France
50 A2 **Barlee, Lake** salt flat Austr.
109 C2 **Barletta** Italy

53 C2 **Barmedman** Austr.
Barmen-Elberfeld Ger. *see* Wuppertal
74 B1 **Barmer** India
52 B2 **Barmera** Austr.
99 A3 **Barmouth** U.K.
101 D1 **Barmstedt** Ger.
98 C2 **Barnard Castle** U.K.
53 B2 **Barnato** Austr.
82 G3 **Barnaul** Rus. Fed.
127 H2 **Barnes Icecap** Can.
100 B1 **Barneveld** Neth.
98 C3 **Barnsley** U.K.
99 A4 **Barnstaple** U.K.
Barnstaple Bay U.K. *see* Bideford Bay
141 D2 **Barnwell** U.S.A.
Baroda India *see* Vadodara
150 C1 **Barquisimeto** Venez.
96 A2 **Barra** i. U.K.
53 D2 **Barraba** Austr.
151 D4 **Barra do Bugres** Brazil
151 E3 **Barra do Corda** Brazil
154 B1 **Barra do Garças** Brazil
150 D3 **Barra do São Manuel** Brazil
Barraigh i. U.K. *see* Barra
150 B4 **Barranca** Peru
150 B3 **Barranca** Peru
152 C2 **Barranqueras** Arg.
150 B1 **Barranquilla** Col.
105 D3 **Barre des Ecrins** mt. France
151 E4 **Barreiras** Brazil
63 A2 **Barren Island** India
154 C2 **Barretos** Brazil
128 C2 **Barrhead** Can.
130 C3 **Barrie** Can.
128 B2 **Barrière** Can.
52 B2 **Barrier Range** hills Austr.
53 D2 **Barrington** Austr.
129 D2 **Barrington Lake** Can.
53 C1 **Barringun** Austr.
97 C2 **Barrow** r. Ireland
126 B2 **Barrow** U.S.A.
126 B2 **Barrow, Point** U.S.A.
51 C2 **Barrow Creek** Austr.
98 B2 **Barrow-in-Furness** U.K.
50 A2 **Barrow Island** Austr.
126 F2 **Barrow Strait** Can.
99 B4 **Barry** U.K.
122 B3 **Barrydale** S. Africa
130 C3 **Barrys Bay** Can.
74 B2 **Barsalpur** India
101 D1 **Barsinghausen** Ger.
135 C4 **Barstow** U.S.A.
105 C2 **Bar-sur-Aube** France
102 C1 **Barth** Ger.
80 B1 **Bartın** Turkey
51 D1 **Bartle Frere, Mount** Austr.
143 D1 **Bartlesville** U.S.A.
137 D2 **Bartlett** NE U.S.A.
140 C1 **Bartlett** TN U.S.A.
98 C3 **Barton-upon-Humber** U.K.
103 E1 **Bartoszyce** Pol.
61 C2 **Barung** i. Indon.
69 D1 **Baruun-Urt** Mongolia
91 D2 **Barvinkove** Ukr.
53 C2 **Barwon** r. Austr.
88 C3 **Barysaw** Belarus
118 C2 **Basankusu** Dem. Rep. Congo
110 C2 **Basarabi** Romania
64 B1 **Basco** Phil.
105 D2 **Basel** Switz.
71 C3 **Bashi Channel** Taiwan
91 C2 **Bashtanka** Ukr.
64 B3 **Basilan** i. Phil.
99 D4 **Basildon** U.K.
99 C4 **Basingstoke** U.K.
81 C2 **Başkale** Turkey
130 C3 **Baskatong, Réservoir** resr Can.
Basle Switz. *see* Basel
118 C2 **Basoko** Dem. Rep. Congo
81 C2 **Basra** Iraq
128 C2 **Bassano** Can.
114 C4 **Bassar** Togo
63 A2 **Bassein** Myanmar
147 D3 **Basse-Terre** Guadeloupe
147 D3 **Basseterre** St Kitts and Nevis
114 B3 **Bassikounou** Maur.
114 C4 **Bassila** Benin
51 D3 **Bass Strait** Austr.
79 C2 **Bastak** Iran
101 E2 **Bastheim** Ger.
75 C2 **Basti** India
105 D3 **Bastia** Corsica France
100 B2 **Bastogne** Belgium
140 B2 **Bastrop** U.S.A.
Basuo China *see* Dongfang
Basutoland country Africa *see* Lesotho
118 A2 **Bata** Equat. Guinea
146 B2 **Batabanó, Golfo de** b. Cuba
83 J2 **Batagay** Rus. Fed.
154 B2 **Bataguassu** Brazil
74 B1 **Batala** India
106 B2 **Batalha** Port.
64 B1 **Batan** i. Phil.
118 B2 **Batangafo** C.A.R.
64 B1 **Batangas** Phil.
60 B2 **Batanghari** r. Indon.
64 B1 **Batan Islands** Phil.
154 C2 **Batatais** Brazil
130 B3 **Batavia** U.S.A.
91 D2 **Bataysk** Rus. Fed.
130 B3 **Batchawana Mountain** hill Can.
50 C1 **Batchelor** Austr.

63 B2 **Bătdâmbâng** Cambodia
118 B3 **Batéké, Plateaux** Congo
53 D3 **Batemans Bay** Austr.
140 B1 **Batesville** AR U.S.A.
140 C2 **Batesville** MS U.S.A.
89 D2 **Batetskiy** Rus. Fed.
99 B4 **Bath** U.K.
96 C3 **Bathgate** U.K.
74 B1 **Bathinda** India
53 C2 **Bathurst** Austr.
131 D3 **Bathurst** Can.
Bathurst Gambia *see* Banjul
126 E2 **Bathurst Inlet** Can.
126 E2 **Bathurst Inlet** inlet Can.
50 C1 **Bathurst Island** Austr.
126 F1 **Bathurst Island** Can.
78 B1 **Bāṭin, Wādī al** watercourse Asia
53 C1 **Batlow** Austr.
81 C2 **Batman** Turkey
115 C1 **Batna** Alg.
140 B2 **Baton Rouge** U.S.A.
144 B2 **Batopilas** Mex.
118 B2 **Batouri** Cameroon
154 B1 **Batovi** Brazil
92 I1 **Båtsfjord** Norway
73 C4 **Batticaloa** Sri Lanka
109 B2 **Battipaglia** Italy
128 D2 **Battle** r. Can.
138 B2 **Battle Creek** U.S.A.
135 C2 **Battle Mountain** U.S.A.
74 B1 **Battura Glacier** Jammu and Kashmir
117 B4 **Batu** mt. Eth.
60 A2 **Batu, Pulau-pulau** is Indon.
61 D2 **Batuata** i. Indon.
61 D2 **Batudaka** i. Indon.
64 B3 **Batulaki** Phil.
Batum Georgia *see* Bat'umi
81 C1 **Bat'umi** Georgia
60 B1 **Batu Pahat** Malaysia
61 D2 **Baubau** Indon.
115 C3 **Bauchi** Nigeria
137 E1 **Baudette** U.S.A.
Baudouinville Dem. Rep. Congo *see* Moba
104 B2 **Baugé** France
105 D2 **Baume-les-Dames** France
154 C2 **Bauru** Brazil
154 B1 **Baús** Brazil
88 B2 **Bauska** Latvia
102 C1 **Bautzen** Ger.
102 C2 **Bavaria** reg. Ger.
144 B2 **Bavispe** r. Mex.
87 E3 **Bavly** Rus. Fed.
62 A1 **Bawdwin** Myanmar
61 C2 **Bawean** i. Indon.
114 B3 **Bawku** Ghana
Baxian China *see* Banan
146 C2 **Bayamo** Cuba
Bayan Gol China *see* Dengkou
68 C1 **Bayanhongor** Mongolia
70 A2 **Bayan Hot** China
70 A1 **Bayan Obo** China
136 C2 **Bayard** NE U.S.A.
142 B2 **Bayard** NM U.S.A.
64 B3 **Bayawan** Phil.
81 C1 **Bayburt** Turkey
138 C2 **Bay City** MI U.S.A.
143 D3 **Bay City** TX U.S.A.
86 F2 **Baydaratskaya Guba** Rus. Fed.
117 C4 **Baydhabo** Somalia
104 B2 **Bayeux** France
136 B3 **Bayfield** U.S.A.
78 B3 **Bayḥan al Qişab** Yemen
Bay Islands is Hond. *see* Bahía, Islas de la
81 C2 **Bayjī** Iraq
Baykal, Ozero l. Rus. Fed. *see* Baikal, Lake
Baykal Range mts Rus. Fed. *see* Baykal'skiy Khrebet
83 I3 **Baykal'skiy Khrebet** mts Rus. Fed.
76 C2 **Baykonyr** Kazakh.
87 E3 **Baymak** Rus. Fed.
64 B2 **Bayombong** Phil.
104 B3 **Bayonne** France
76 C3 **Bayramaly** Turkm.
111 C3 **Bayramiç** Turkey
101 E3 **Bayreuth** Ger.
78 B3 **Bayt al Faqīh** Yemen
143 D3 **Baytown** U.S.A.
106 C2 **Baza** Spain
106 C2 **Baza, Sierra de** mts Spain
76 A2 **Bazardyuzyu, Gora** mt. Azer./Rus. Fed.
104 B3 **Bazas** France
74 A2 **Bazdar** Pak.
70 B2 **Bazhong** China
79 C2 **Bazmān** Iran
79 D2 **Bazmān, Küh-e** mt. Iran
Bé, Nossi i. Madag. *see* Nosy Bé
136 C1 **Beach** U.S.A.
52 B3 **Beachport** Austr.
99 D4 **Beachy Head** hd U.K.
123 C3 **Beacon Bay** S. Africa
50 C1 **Beagle Gulf** Austr.
121 □D2 **Bealanana** Madag.
121 □D3 **Beampingaratra** mts Madag.
134 D2 **Bear** r. U.S.A.
130 B3 **Beardmore** Can.
53 C1 **Beardmore Reservoir** Austr.
Bear Island i. Arctic Ocean *see* Bjørnøya
134 E1 **Bear Paw Mountain** U.S.A.

147 C3 **Beata, Cabo** c. Dom. Rep.
147 C3 **Beata, Isla** i. Dom. Rep.
137 D2 **Beatrice** U.S.A.
135 C3 **Beatty** U.S.A.
53 D1 **Beaudesert** Austr.
52 B3 **Beaufort** Austr.
61 C1 **Beaufort** Sabah Malaysia
141 D2 **Beaufort** U.S.A.
126 D2 **Beaufort Sea** Can./U.S.A.
122 B3 **Beaufort West** S. Africa
96 B2 **Beauly** U.K.
96 B2 **Beauly** r. U.K.
100 B2 **Beaumont** Belgium
54 A3 **Beaumont** N.Z.
143 E2 **Beaumont** U.S.A.
105 C2 **Beaune** France
100 B2 **Beauraing** Belgium
129 E2 **Beauséjour** Can.
104 C2 **Beauvais** France
129 D2 **Beauval** Can.
129 D2 **Beaver** r. Can.
135 D3 **Beaver** U.S.A.
128 A1 **Beaver Creek** Can.
138 B2 **Beaver Dam** U.S.A.
129 E2 **Beaver Hill Lake** Can.
138 B1 **Beaver Island** U.S.A.
128 C2 **Beaverlodge** Can.
74 B2 **Beawar** India
154 C2 **Bebedouro** Brazil
101 D2 **Bebra** Ger.
99 D3 **Beccles** U.K.
109 D1 **Bečej** Serb. and Mont.
106 B1 **Becerreá** Spain
114 B1 **Béchar** Alg.
Bechuanaland country Africa *see* Botswana
138 C3 **Beckley** U.S.A.
117 B4 **Bedelē** Eth.
99 C3 **Bedford** U.K.
138 B3 **Bedford** U.S.A.
98 C2 **Bedlington** U.K.
100 C1 **Bedum** Neth.
53 C3 **Beechworth** Austr.
53 D2 **Beecroft Peninsula** Austr.
101 F1 **Beelitz** Ger.
53 D1 **Beenleigh** Austr.
80 B2 **Beersheba** Israel
Be'ér Sheva' Israel *see* Beersheba
143 D3 **Beeville** U.S.A.
121 □D2 **Befandriana Avaratra** Madag.
53 C3 **Bega** Austr.
107 D1 **Begur, Cap de** c. Spain
81 D2 **Behbehān** Iran
81 D2 **Behshahr** Iran
69 E1 **Bei'an** China
71 A3 **Beihai** China
70 B2 **Beijing** China
100 C1 **Beilen** Neth.
118 B2 **Béinamar** Chad
96 B3 **Beinn an Oir** hill U.K.
96 A2 **Beinn Mhòr** hill U.K.
Beinn na Faoghla i. U.K. *see* Benbecula
121 C2 **Beira** Moz.
80 B2 **Beirut** Lebanon
123 C1 **Beitbridge** Zimbabwe
106 B2 **Beja** Port.
115 C1 **Bejaïa** Alg.
106 B1 **Béjar** Spain
74 A2 **Beji** r. Pak.
76 B2 **Bekdash** Turkm.
103 E2 **Békés** Hungary
103 E2 **Békéscsaba** Hungary
121 □D3 **Bekily** Madag.
66 D2 **Bekkai** Japan
114 B4 **Bekwai** Ghana
75 C2 **Bela** India
74 A2 **Bela** Pak.
123 C1 **Bela-Bela** S. Africa
118 B2 **Bélabo** Cameroon
109 D2 **Bela Crkva** Serb. and Mont.
61 C1 **Belaga** Sarawak Malaysia
88 C3 **Belarus** country Europe
123 C3 **Bela Vista** Moz.
60 A1 **Belawan** Indon.
83 M2 **Belaya** r. Rus. Fed.
103 E1 **Bełchatów** Pol.
Belchatow Pol. *see* Bełchatów
130 C2 **Belcher Islands** Can.
87 E3 **Belebey** Rus. Fed.
117 C4 **Beledweyne** Somalia
118 B2 **Bélèl** Cameroon
151 E3 **Belém** Brazil
142 B2 **Belen** U.S.A.
110 C2 **Belene** Bulg.
89 E3 **Belev** Rus. Fed.
97 D1 **Belfast** U.K.
139 F2 **Belfast** U.S.A.
136 C1 **Belfield** U.S.A.
105 D2 **Belfort** France
73 B3 **Belgaum** India
Belgian Congo country Africa *see* Congo, Democratic Republic of the
100 B2 **Belgium** country Europe
91 D1 **Belgorod** Rus. Fed.
109 D2 **Belgrade** Serb. and Mont.
134 D1 **Belgrade** U.S.A.
115 D4 **Beli** Nigeria
109 C2 **Beli Manastir** Croatia
60 B2 **Belinyu** Indon.
60 B2 **Belitung** i. Indon.
118 B3 **Belize** Angola
146 B3 **Belize** Belize
146 B3 **Belize** country Central America
83 K1 **Bel'kovskiy, Ostrov** i. Rus. Fed.

128 B2 **Bella Bella** Can.
104 C2 **Bellac** France
128 B2 **Bella Coola** Can.
73 B3 **Bellary** India
53 C1 **Bellata** Austr.
138 C2 **Bellefontaine** U.S.A.
136 C2 **Belle Fourche** U.S.A.
136 C2 **Belle Fourche** r. U.S.A.
141 D3 **Belle Glade** U.S.A.
104 B2 **Belle-Île** i. France
131 E2 **Belle Isle** i. Can.
131 E2 **Belle Isle, Strait of** Can.
130 C3 **Belleville** Can.
138 B3 **Belleville** IL U.S.A.
137 D3 **Belleville** KS U.S.A.
134 D2 **Bellevue** ID U.S.A.
134 B1 **Bellevue** WA U.S.A.
Bellin Can. *see* Kangirsuk
53 D2 **Bellingen** Austr.
134 B1 **Bellingham** U.S.A.
55 R2 **Bellingshausen Sea** Antarctica
105 D2 **Bellinzona** Switz.
96 C2 **Bell Rock** i. U.K.
108 B1 **Belluno** Italy
122 A3 **Bellville** S. Africa
53 D2 **Belmont** Austr.
155 E1 **Belmonte** Brazil
146 B3 **Belmopan** Belize
97 B1 **Belmullet** Ireland
69 E1 **Belogorsk** Rus. Fed.
121 □D3 **Beloha** Madag.
155 D1 **Belo Horizonte** Brazil
138 B2 **Beloit** U.S.A.
86 C2 **Belomorsk** Rus. Fed.
89 E3 **Beloomut** Rus. Fed.
91 D3 **Belorechensk** Rus. Fed.
Belorechenskaya Rus. Fed. *see* Belorechensk
87 E3 **Beloretsk** Rus. Fed.
Belorussia country Europe *see* Belarus
Belorusskaya S.S.R. admin. reg. Europe *see* Belarus
121 □D2 **Belo Tsiribihina** Madag.
86 F2 **Beloyarskiy** Rus. Fed.
89 E1 **Beloye, Ozero** l. Rus. Fed.
Beloye More sea Rus. Fed. *see* White Sea
89 E1 **Belozersk** Rus. Fed.
52 A2 **Beltana** Austr.
143 D2 **Belton** U.S.A.
Bel'ts' Moldova *see* Bălţi
Bel'tsy Moldova *see* Bălţi
97 C1 **Belturbet** Ireland
77 E2 **Belukha, Gora** mt. Kazakh./Rus. Fed.
86 D2 **Belush'ye** Rus. Fed.
138 B2 **Belvidere** U.S.A.
51 D2 **Belyando** r. Austr.
89 D2 **Belyy** Rus. Fed.
82 F2 **Belyy, Ostrov** i. Rus. Fed.
101 F1 **Belzig** Ger.
137 E1 **Bemidji** U.S.A.
118 C3 **Bena Dibele** Dem. Rep. Congo
53 C3 **Benalla** Austr.
Benares India *see* Varanasi
115 D1 **Ben Arous** Tunisia
118 C3 **Bena-Sungu** Dem. Rep. Congo
106 B1 **Benavente** Spain
96 A2 **Benbecula** i. U.K.
134 B2 **Bend** U.S.A.
123 C3 **Bendearg** mt. S. Africa
Bender Moldova *see* Tighina
Bendery Moldova *see* Tighina
52 B3 **Bendigo** Austr.
121 C2 **Bene** Moz.
102 C2 **Benešov** Czech Rep.
109 B2 **Benevento** Italy
73 C3 **Bengal, Bay of** sea Indian Ocean
70 B2 **Bengbu** China
115 E1 **Benghazi** Libya
60 B1 **Bengkalis** Indon.
60 B1 **Bengkayang** Indon.
60 B2 **Bengkulu** Indon.
120 A2 **Benguela** Angola
Benha Egypt *see* Banhā
96 B1 **Ben Hope** hill U.K.
152 B1 **Beni** r. Bol.
119 C2 **Beni** Dem. Rep. Congo
114 B1 **Beni-Abbès** Alg.
107 C2 **Benidorm** Spain
114 B1 **Beni Mellal** Morocco
114 C4 **Benin** country Africa
114 C4 **Benin, Bight of** g. Africa
115 C4 **Benin City** Nigeria
107 C2 **Beni-Saf** Alg.
Beni Suef Egypt *see* Banī Suwayf
153 C3 **Benito Juárez** Arg.
150 C3 **Benjamin Constant** Brazil
144 A1 **Benjamin Hill** Mex.
59 C3 **Benjina** Indon.
136 C2 **Benkelman** U.S.A.
96 B2 **Ben Lawers** mt. U.K.
96 B2 **Ben Lomond** hill U.K.
96 C2 **Ben Macdui** mt. U.K.
96 A2 **Ben More** hill U.K.
96 B2 **Ben More** hill U.K.
54 B2 **Benmore, Lake** N.Z.
96 B1 **Ben More Assynt** hill U.K.
128 A2 **Bennett** Can.
83 K1 **Bennetta, Ostrov** i. Rus. Fed.
Bennett Island Rus. Fed. *see* Bennetta, Ostrov

Ben Nevis

184

96 B2 Ben Nevis *mt.* U.K.
139 E2 Bennington U.S.A.
123 C2 Benoni S. Africa
115 D4 Bénoy Chad
101 D3 Bensheim Ger.
114 B1 Ben Slimane Morocco
142 A2 Benson U.S.A.
61 D2 Benteng Indon.
117 A4 Bentiu Sudan
138 B2 Benton Harbor U.S.A.
140 B1 Bentonville U.S.A.
63 B2 Bên Tre Vietnam
115 C4 Benue *r.* Nigeria
97 B1 Benwee Head *hd* Ireland
96 B2 Ben Wyvis *mt.* U.K.
70 C1 Benxi China
Beograd Serb. and Mont. *see*
Belgrade
75 C2 Beohari India
114 B4 Béoumi Côte d'Ivoire
67 B4 Beppu Japan
109 C2 Berane Serb. and Mont.
109 C2 Berat Albania
59 C3 Berau, Teluk *b.* Indon.
116 B3 Berber Sudan
117 C3 Berbera Somalia
118 B2 Berbérati C.A.R.
104 C1 Berck France
91 D2 Berdyans'k Ukr.
90 B2 Berdychiv Ukr.
90 A2 Berehove Ukr.
59 D3 Bereina P.N.G.
129 E2 Berens River Can.
137 D2 Beresford U.S.A.
91 D2 Berezanskaya Rus. Fed.
90 A2 Berezhany Ukr.
90 C2 Berezivka Ukr.
90 B1 Berezne Ukr.
86 D2 Bereznik Rus. Fed.
86 E3 Berezniki Rus. Fed.
Berezov Rus. Fed. *see* Berezovo
86 F2 Berezovo Rus. Fed.
107 D1 Berga Spain
111 C3 Bergama Turkey
108 A1 Bergamo Italy
102 C1 Bergen Ger.
101 D1 Bergen Ger.
100 B1 Bergen Neth.
93 E3 Bergen Norway
100 B2 Bergen op Zoom Neth.
104 C3 Bergerac France
100 C2 Bergheim (Erft) Ger.
100 C2 Bergisch Gladbach Ger.
122 A1 Bergland Namibia
93 G3 Bergsjö Sweden
92 H2 Bergsviken Sweden
Berhampur India *see*
Baharampur
83 M3 Beringa, Ostrov *i.* Rus. Fed.
100 B2 Beringen Belgium
124 A4 Bering Sea N. Pacific Ocean
124 B3 Bering Strait Rus. Fed./U.S.A.
100 C1 Berkel *r.* Neth.
135 B3 Berkeley U.S.A.
100 B1 Berkhout Neth.
55 B2 Berkner Island Antarctica
110 B2 Berkovitsa Bulg.
92 I1 Berlevåg Norway
101 F1 Berlin Ger.
139 E2 Berlin U.S.A.
101 E2 Berlingerode Ger.
53 D3 Bermagui Austr.
144 B2 Bermejillo Mex.
152 B2 Bermejo Bol.
131 D2 Bermen, Lac *l.* Can.
125 L6 Bermuda *terr.* N. Atlantic Ocean
105 D2 Bern Switz.
101 E2 Bernburg (Saale) Ger.
127 G2 Bernier Bay Can.
50 A2 Bernier Island Austr.
100 C3 Bernkastel-Kues Ger.
121 □D3 Beroroha Madag.
52 B2 Berri Austr.
115 C1 Berriane Alg.
53 C3 Berrigan Austr.
107 D2 Berrouaghia Alg.
53 D2 Berry Austr.
146 C2 Berry Islands Bahamas
122 A2 Berseba Namibia
101 C1 Bersenbrück Ger.
90 B2 Bershad' Ukr.
131 D2 Berté, Lac *l.* Can.
118 B2 Bertoua Cameroon
150 C3 Beruri Brazil
98 B2 Berwick-upon-Tweed U.K.
91 C2 Beryslav Ukr.
121 □D2 Besalampy Madag.
105 D2 Besançon France
81 D3 Beshneh Iran
129 D2 Besnard Lake Can.
140 C2 Bessemer U.S.A.
76 B2 Besshoky, Gora *hill* Kazakh.
100 B2 Best Neth.
121 □D2 Betafo Madag.
106 B1 Betanzos Spain
118 B2 Bétaré Oya Cameroon
122 A2 Bethanie Namibia
100 B3 Bétheny France
139 D3 Bethesda U.S.A.
123 C2 Bethlehem S. Africa
139 D2 Bethlehem U.S.A.
123 C3 Bethulie S. Africa
105 C1 Béthune France
121 □D3 Betioky Madag.
51 D2 Betoota Austr.

77 D2 Betpak-Dala *plain* Kazakh.
121 □D3 Betroka Madag.
131 D3 Betsiamites Can.
121 □D2 Betsiboka *r.* Madag.
137 E2 Bettendorf U.S.A.
75 C2 Bettiah India
74 B2 Betul India
74 B2 Betwa *r.* India
99 B3 Betws-y-coed U.K.
100 C2 Betzdorf Ger.
136 C1 Beulah U.S.A.
98 C3 Beverley U.K.
101 D2 Beverungen Ger.
100 B1 Beverwijk Neth.
99 D4 Bexhill U.K.
111 C2 Beykoz Turkey
114 B4 Beyla Guinea
76 B2 Beyneu Kazakh.
80 B1 Beypazarı Turkey
Beyrouth Lebanon *see* Beirut
80 B2 Beyşehir Turkey
80 B2 Beyşehir Gölü *l.* Turkey
91 D2 Beysug *r.* Rus. Fed.
91 D2 Beysugskiy Liman *lag.* Rus. Fed.
88 C2 Bezhanitsy Rus. Fed.
89 E2 Bezhetsk Rus. Fed.
105 C3 Béziers France
Bhadgaon Nepal *see* Bhaktapur
75 C2 Bhadrak India
73 B3 Bhadravati India
75 C2 Bhagalpur India
74 A2 Bhairi Hol *mt.* Pak.
74 B1 Bhakkar Pak.
75 C2 Bhaktapur Nepal
62 A1 Bhamo Myanmar
75 C3 Bhanjanagar India
74 B2 Bharatpur India
74 B2 Bharuch India
74 B2 Bhavnagar India
75 C3 Bhawanipatna India
123 D2 Bhekuzulu S. Africa
74 B1 Bhera Pak.
74 B2 Bhilwara India
73 B3 Bhima *r.* India
74 B2 Bhind India
74 B2 Bhiwani India
123 C3 Bhongweni S. Africa
74 B2 Bhopal India
75 C2 Bhubaneshwar India
Bhubaneswar India *see*
Bhubaneshwar
74 A2 Bhuj India
62 A2 Bhumiphol Dam Thai.
74 B2 Bhusawal India
75 D2 Bhutan *country* Asia
62 B2 Bia, Phou *mt.* Laos
Biafra, Bight of *g.* Africa *see*
Benin, Bight of
59 D3 Biak Indon.
59 D3 Biak *i.* Indon.
103 E1 Biała Podlaska Pol.
103 D1 Białogard Pol.
103 E1 Białystok Pol.
109 C3 Bianco Italy
74 B2 Biaora India
104 B3 Biarritz France
105 D2 Biasca Switz.
66 D2 Bibai Japan
120 A2 Bibala Angola
53 C3 Bibbenluke Austr.
102 B2 Biberach an der Riß Ger.
155 D2 Bicas Brazil
73 B3 Bid India
115 C4 Bida Nigeria
73 B3 Bidar India
139 E2 Biddeford U.S.A.
96 B2 Bidean nam Bian *mt.* U.K.
99 A4 Bideford U.K.
99 A4 Bideford Bay U.K.
Bié Angola *see* Kuito
101 D2 Biedenkopf Ger.
105 D2 Biel Switz.
101 D1 Bielefeld Ger.
108 A1 Biella Italy
103 D1 Bielsko-Biała Pol.
63 B2 Biên Hoa Vietnam
130 C2 Bienville, Lac *l.* Can.
120 A2 Bié Plateau Angola
100 B3 Bièvre Belgium
118 B3 Bifoun Gabon
111 C2 Biga Turkey
134 D1 Big Belt Mountains U.S.A.
123 D2 Big Bend Swaziland
129 D2 Biggar Can.
96 C3 Biggar U.K.
99 C3 Biggleswade U.K.
134 D1 Big Hole *r.* U.S.A.
134 E1 Bighorn U.S.A.
136 B1 Bighorn *r.* U.S.A.
136 B2 Bighorn Mountains U.S.A.
143 C2 Big Lake U.S.A.
138 B2 Big Rapids U.S.A.
129 D2 Big River Can.
129 E2 Big Sand Lake Can.
137 D2 Big Sioux *r.* U.S.A.
143 C2 Big Spring U.S.A.
134 E1 Big Timber U.S.A.
130 B2 Big Trout Lake Can.
130 A2 Big Trout Lake *l.* Can.
109 C2 Bihać Croatia
75 C2 Bihar *state* India
75 C2 Bihar Sharif India
110 B1 Bihor, Vârful *mt.* Romania
114 A3 Bijagós, Arquipélago dos *is*
Guinea-Bissau

73 B3 Bijapur India
81 C2 Bijār Iran
109 C2 Bijeljina Bos.-Herz.
109 C2 Bijelo Polje Serb. and Mont.
71 A3 Bijie China
74 B2 Bikaner India
66 B1 Bikin Rus. Fed.
66 B1 Bikin *r.* Rus. Fed.
118 B3 Bikoro Dem. Rep. Congo
79 C2 Bilād Banī Bū 'Alī Oman
75 C2 Bilaspur India
81 C2 Biläsuvar Azer.
90 C2 Bila Tserkva Ukr.
63 A2 Bilauktaung Range *mts*
Myanmar/Thai.
106 C1 Bilbao Spain
109 C2 Bileća Bos.-Herz.
111 C2 Bilecik Turkey
103 E1 Biłgoraj Pol.
119 D3 Bilharamulo Tanz.
90 C2 Bilhorod-Dnistrovs'kyy Ukr.
119 C2 Bili Dem. Rep. Congo
83 M2 Bilibino Rus. Fed.
109 D2 Bilisht Albania
104 B3 Billère France
134 E1 Billings U.S.A.
99 B4 Bill of Portland *hd* U.K.
142 A1 Bill Williams Mountain U.S.A.
115 D3 Bilma Niger
51 E2 Biloela Austr.
91 C2 Bilohirs'k Ukr.
90 B1 Bilohir"ya Ukr.
91 C1 Bilopillya Ukr.
91 D2 Bilovods'k Ukr.
140 C2 Biloxi U.S.A.
51 C2 Bilpa Morea Claypan *salt flat*
Austr.
101 E2 Bilshausen Ger.
115 E3 Biltine Chad
90 C2 Bilyayivka Ukr.
114 C4 Bimbila Ghana
141 E3 Bimini Islands Bahamas
74 B2 Bina-Etawa India
59 C3 Binaija, Gunung *mt.* Indon.
53 C1 Bindle Austr.
118 B3 Bindu Dem. Rep. Congo
121 C2 Bindura Zimbabwe
107 D1 Binefar Spain
120 B2 Binga Zimbabwe
53 D1 Bingara Austr.
100 C3 Bingen am Rhein Ger.
114 B4 Bingerville Côte d'Ivoire
139 F1 Bingham U.S.A.
139 D2 Binghamton U.S.A.
115 D2 Bin Ghanimah, Jabal *hills* Libya
81 C2 Bingöl Turkey
62 A1 Bingzhongluo China
60 A1 Binjai Indon.
53 C2 Binnaway Austr.
60 B1 Bintan *i.* Indon.
60 B2 Bintuhan Indon.
61 C1 Bintulu *Sarawak* Malaysia
115 C3 Bin-Yauri Nigeria
70 B2 Binzhou China
118 A2 Bioco *i.* Equat. Guinea
109 C2 Biograd na Moru Croatia
155 C1 Biquinhas Brazil
115 D2 Birāk Libya
118 C1 Birao C.A.R.
75 C2 Biratnagar Nepal
52 B3 Birchip Austr.
128 C2 Birch Mountains Can.
51 C2 Birdsville Austr.
80 B2 Birecik Turkey
Birendranagar Nepal *see* Surkhet
60 A1 Bireun Indon.
75 C2 Birganj Nepal
117 B3 Birhan *mt.* Eth.
154 B2 Birigüi Brazil
118 C2 Birini C.A.R.
76 B3 Birjand Iran
98 B3 Birkenhead U.K.
99 C3 Birmingham U.K.
140 C2 Birmingham U.S.A.
114 A2 Bîr Mogreïn Maur.
115 C3 Birnin-Kebbi Nigeria
115 C3 Birnin Konni Niger
69 E1 Birobidzhan Rus. Fed.
97 C2 Birr Ireland
96 C1 Birsay U.K.
78 A2 Bi'r Shalatayn Egypt
88 B2 Biržai Lith.
75 B2 Bisalpur India
142 B2 Bisbee U.S.A.
104 A2 Biscay, Bay of *sea* France/Spain
141 D3 Biscayne Bay U.S.A.
102 C2 Bischofshofen Austria
77 D2 Bishkek Kyrg.
123 C3 Bisho S. Africa
135 C3 Bishop U.S.A.
98 C2 Bishop Auckland U.K.
69 E1 Bishui China
150 C2 Bisinaca Col.
115 C1 Biskra Alg.
64 B3 Bislig Phil.
136 C1 Bismarck U.S.A.
59 D3 Bismarck Archipelago *is* P.N.G.
59 D3 Bismarck Sea P.N.G.
107 D2 Bissa, Djebel *mt.* Alg.
114 A3 Bissau Guinea-Bissau
129 E2 Bissett Can.
128 C2 Bistcho Lake Can.
110 B1 Bistriţa Romania
110 C1 Bistriţa *r.* Romania
100 C3 Bitburg Ger.

105 D2 Bitche France
115 D3 Bitkine Chad
81 C2 Bitlis Turkey
111 B2 Bitola Macedonia
Bitolj Macedonia *see* Bitola
109 C2 Bitonto Italy
101 F2 Bitterfeld Ger.
122 A3 Bitterfontein S. Africa
134 D1 Bitterroot *r.* U.S.A.
134 C1 Bitterroot Range *mts* U.S.A.
89 E3 Bityug *r.* Rus. Fed.
115 D3 Biu Nigeria
67 C3 Biwa-ko *l.* Japan
77 E1 Biysk Rus. Fed.
Bizerta Tunisia *see* Bizerte
115 C1 Bizerte Tunisia
92 □A2 Bjargtangar *hd* Iceland
92 G3 Bjästa Sweden
109 C1 Bjelovar Croatia
92 G2 Bjerkvik Norway
Björneborg Fin. *see* Pori
82 C2 Bjørnøya Arctic Ocean
114 B3 Bla Mali
137 E3 Black *r.* U.S.A.
51 D2 Blackall Austr.
98 B3 Blackburn U.K.
134 D2 Blackfoot U.S.A.
102 B2 Black Forest *mts* Ger.
136 C2 Black Hills U.S.A.
96 B2 Black Isle *pen.* U.K.
129 D2 Black Lake Can.
129 D2 Black Lake *l.* Can.
99 B4 Black Mountains *hills* U.K.
142 A1 Black Mountains U.S.A.
98 B3 Blackpool U.K.
142 B2 Black Range *mts* U.S.A.
62 B1 Black River *r.* Vietnam
138 A2 Black River Falls U.S.A.
134 C2 Black Rock Desert U.S.A.
138 C3 Blacksburg U.S.A.
80 B1 Black Sea Asia/Europe
131 D3 Blacks Harbour Can.
97 A1 Blacksod Bay Ireland
97 C2 Blackstairs Mountains *hills*
Ireland
114 B4 Black Volta *r.* Africa
51 D2 Blackwater Austr.
97 C2 Blackwater *r.* Ireland
128 B1 Blackwater Lake Can.
50 A3 Blackwood *r.* Austr.
87 D4 Blagodarnyy Rus. Fed.
111 B2 Blagoevgrad Bulg.
69 E1 Blagoveshchensk Rus. Fed.
129 D2 Blaine Lake Can.
137 D2 Blair U.S.A.
96 C2 Blair Atholl U.K.
96 C2 Blairgowrie U.K.
141 D2 Blakely U.S.A.
105 D2 Blanc, Mont *mt.* France/Italy
153 B3 Blanca, Bahía *b.* Arg.
52 A1 Blanche, Lake *salt flat* Austr.
152 B1 Blanco *r.* Bol.
134 B2 Blanco, Cape U.S.A.
131 E2 Blanc-Sablon Can.
92 □A2 Blanda *r.* Iceland
99 B4 Blandford Forum U.K.
135 E3 Blanding U.S.A.
107 D1 Blanes Spain
60 A1 Blangkejeren Indon.
100 A2 Blankenberge Belgium
100 C2 Blankenheim Ger.
100 C2 Blankenrath Ger.
147 D3 Blanquilla, Isla *i.* Venez.
103 D2 Blansko Czech Rep.
121 C2 Blantyre Malawi
97 B3 Blarney Ireland
98 C2 Blaydon U.K.
53 C2 Blayney Austr.
54 B2 Blenheim N.Z.
115 C1 Blida Alg.
130 B3 Blind River Can.
123 C2 Bloemfontein S. Africa
123 C2 Bloemhof S. Africa
123 C2 Bloemhof Dam S. Africa
104 C2 Blois France
92 □A2 Blönduós Iceland
97 B1 Bloody Foreland *pt*
Ireland
142 B1 Bloomfield U.S.A.
138 B2 Bloomington IL U.S.A.
138 B3 Bloomington IN U.S.A.
102 B2 Bludenz Austria
137 E2 Blue Earth U.S.A.
138 C3 Bluefield U.S.A.
146 B3 Bluefields Nic.
53 C2 Blue Mountains Austr.
134 C1 Blue Mountains U.S.A.
116 B3 Blue Nile *r.* Eth./Sudan
126 E2 Bluenose Lake Can.
138 C3 Blue Ridge *mts* U.S.A.
128 C2 Blue River Can.
97 B1 Blue Stack Mountains *hills* Ireland
54 A3 Bluff N.Z.
135 E3 Bluff U.S.A.
154 C3 Blumenau Brazil
52 A2 Blyth Austr.
98 C2 Blyth U.K.
135 D4 Blythe U.S.A.
140 C2 Blytheville U.S.A.
114 A4 Bo Sierra Leone
64 B2 Boac Phil.
146 B3 Boaco Nic.
151 E3 Boa Esperança, Açude *resr* Brazil
134 C1 Boardman U.S.A.

123 C1 **Boatlaname** Botswana
151 F3 **Boa Viagem** Brazil
150 C2 **Boa Vista** Brazil
53 C2 **Bobadah** Austr.
71 B3 **Bobai** China
121 □D2 **Bobaomby, Tanjona** c. Madag.
114 B3 **Bobo-Dioulasso** Burkina
121 B3 **Bobonong** Botswana
Bobriki Rus. Fed. *see* Novomoskovsk
89 F3 **Bobrov** Rus. Fed.
91 C2 **Bobrovytsya** Ukr.
91 C2 **Bobrynets'** Ukr.
121 □D3 **Boby** mt. Madag.
150 C3 **Boca do Acre** Brazil
155 D1 **Bocaiúva** Brazil
154 A2 **Bocajá** Brazil
118 B2 **Bocaranga** C.A.R.
141 D3 **Boca Raton** U.S.A.
146 B4 **Bocas del Toro** Panama
103 E2 **Bochnia** Pol.
100 B2 **Bocholt** Belgium
100 C2 **Bocholt** Ger.
100 C2 **Bochum** Ger.
123 C1 **Bochum** S. Africa
101 E1 **Bockenem** Ger.
110 B1 **Bocşa** Romania
118 B2 **Boda** C.A.R.
83 I3 **Bodaybo** Rus. Fed.
96 D2 **Boddam** U.K.
115 D3 **Bodélé** reg. Chad
92 H2 **Boden** Sweden
Bodensee l. Ger./Switz. *see* Constance, Lake
99 A4 **Bodmin** U.K.
99 A4 **Bodmin Moor** moorland U.K.
92 F2 **Bodø** Norway
111 C3 **Bodrum** Turkey
118 C3 **Boende** Dem. Rep. Congo
63 A2 **Bogale** Myanmar
140 C2 **Bogalusa** U.S.A.
114 B3 **Bogandé** Burkina
118 B2 **Bogangolo** C.A.R.
80 B2 **Boğazlıyan** Turkey
68 B2 **Bogda Shan** mts China
53 D1 **Boggabilla** Austr.
53 D2 **Boggabri** Austr.
97 B2 **Boggeragh Mountains** hills Ireland
Boghari Alg. *see* Ksar el Boukhari
59 D3 **Bogia** P.N.G.
100 B3 **Bogny-sur-Meuse** France
97 C2 **Bog of Allen** reg. Ireland
53 C2 **Bogong, Mount** Austr.
60 B2 **Bogor** Indon.
89 E3 **Bogoroditsk** Rus. Fed.
150 B2 **Bogotá** Col.
83 G3 **Bogotol** Rus. Fed.
Bogoyavlenskoye Rus. Fed. *see* Pervomayskiy
83 H3 **Boguchany** Rus. Fed.
91 E2 **Boguchar** Rus. Fed.
114 A3 **Bogué** Maur.
70 B2 **Bo Hai** g. China
100 A3 **Bohain-en-Vermandois** France
70 B2 **Bohai Wan** b. China
Bohemian Forest mts Ger. *see* Böhmer Wald
123 C2 **Bohlokong** S. Africa
101 F3 **Böhmer Wald** mts Ger.
91 D1 **Bohodukhiv** Ukr.
64 B3 **Bohol** i. Phil.
64 B3 **Bohol Sea** Phil.
77 E2 **Bohu** China
155 C1 **Boi, Ponta do** pt Brazil
123 C2 **Boikhutso** S. Africa
154 B3 **Boi Preto, Serra de** hills Brazil
154 B1 **Bols** r. Brazil
126 D2 **Bois, Lac des** l. Can.
134 C2 **Boise** U.S.A.
143 C1 **Boise City** U.S.A.
129 D3 **Boissevain** Can.
123 C2 **Boitumelong** S. Africa
154 C2 **Boituva** Brazil
101 E1 **Boizenburg** Ger.
76 B2 **Bojnurd** Iran
75 C2 **Bokaro** India
118 B3 **Bokatola** Dem. Rep. Congo
114 A3 **Boké** Guinea
118 C3 **Bokele** Dem. Rep. Congo
93 E4 **Boknafjorden** sea chan. Norway
115 D3 **Bokoro** Chad
63 A2 **Bokpyin** Myanmar
89 D2 **Boksitogorsk** Rus. Fed.
122 B2 **Bokspits** S. Africa
118 C3 **Bokungu** Dem. Rep. Congo
115 D3 **Bol** Chad
114 A3 **Bolama** Guinea-Bissau
75 C2 **Bolangir** India
104 C2 **Bolbec** France
77 E2 **Bole** China
118 B3 **Boleko** Dem. Rep. Congo
114 B3 **Bolgatanga** Ghana
90 B2 **Bolhrad** Ukr.
66 B1 **Boli** China
118 B3 **Bolia** Dem. Rep. Congo
92 H3 **Boliden** Sweden
110 C2 **Bolintin-Vale** Romania
137 E3 **Bolivar** MO U.S.A.
140 C1 **Bolivar** TN U.S.A.
150 A2 **Bolívar, Pico** mt. Venez.
152 B1 **Bolivia** country S. America
83 E3 **Bolkhov** Rus. Fed.
105 C3 **Bollène** France
93 G3 **Bollnäs** Sweden
53 C1 **Bollon** Austr.

101 E2 **Bollstedt** Ger.
93 F4 **Bolmen** l. Sweden
118 B3 **Bolobo** Dem. Rep. Congo
108 B2 **Bologna** Italy
89 D2 **Bologovo** Rus. Fed.
89 D2 **Bologoye** Rus. Fed.
123 C2 **Bolokanang** S. Africa
118 B2 **Bolomba** Dem. Rep. Congo
63 B2 **Bolovens, Phouphieng** plat. Laos
108 B2 **Bolsena, Lago di** l. Italy
83 H1 **Bol'shevik, Ostrov** i. Rus. Fed.
86 E2 **Bol'shezemel'skaya Tundra** lowland Rus. Fed.
83 L2 **Bol'shoy Aluy** r. Rus. Fed.
66 B2 **Bol'shoy Kamen'** Rus. Fed.
Bol'shoy Kavkaz mts Asia/Europe *see* Caucasus
83 K2 **Bol'shoy Lyakhovskiy, Ostrov** i. Rus. Fed.
Bol'shoy Tokmak Kyrg. *see* Tokmok
Bol'shoy Tokmak Ukr. *see* Tokmak
100 B1 **Bolsward** Neth.
98 B3 **Bolton** U.K.
80 B1 **Bolu** Turkey
59 E3 **Bolubolu** P.N.G.
92 □A2 **Bolungarvík** Iceland
108 B1 **Bolzano** Italy
118 B3 **Boma** Dem. Rep. Congo
53 D2 **Bomaderry** Austr.
53 C3 **Bombala** Austr.
Bombay India *see* Mumbai
155 C1 **Bom Despacho** Brazil
75 D2 **Bomdila** India
154 B1 **Bom Jardim de Goiás** Brazil
151 E4 **Bom Jesus da Lapa** Brazil
155 D2 **Bom Jesus do Itabapoana** Brazil
115 D1 **Bon, Cap** c. Tunisia
147 D3 **Bonaire** i. Neth. Antilles
134 C1 **Bonaparte, Mount** U.S.A.
50 B1 **Bonaparte Archipelago** is Austr.
131 E3 **Bonavista** Can.
131 E3 **Bonavista Bay** Can.
118 C2 **Bondo** Dem. Rep. Congo
114 B4 **Bondoukou** Côte d'Ivoire
Bône Alg. *see* Annaba
61 D2 **Bonerate, Kepulauan** is Indon.
155 C1 **Bonfinópolis de Minas** Brazil
117 B4 **Bonga** Eth.
75 D2 **Bongaigaon** India
118 C2 **Bongandanga** Dem. Rep. Congo
122 B2 **Bongani** S. Africa
118 C2 **Bongo, Massif des** mts C.A.R.
121 □D2 **Bongolava** mts Botswana
115 D3 **Bongor** Chad
114 B4 **Bonguanou** Côte d'Ivoire
63 B2 **Bông Son** Vietnam
143 D2 **Bonham** U.S.A.
105 D3 **Bonifacio** Corsica France
108 A2 **Bonifacio, Strait of** France/Italy
69 F3 **Bonin Islands** is Japan
100 C2 **Bonn** Ger.
134 C1 **Bonners Ferry** U.S.A.
105 C2 **Bonneville** France
50 A3 **Bonnie Rock** Austr.
129 C2 **Bonnyville** Can.
108 A2 **Bonorva** Sardinia Italy
53 D1 **Bonshaw** Austr.
61 C1 **Bontang** Indon.
114 A4 **Bonthe** Sierra Leone
64 B2 **Bontoc** Phil.
61 C2 **Bontosunggu** Indon.
123 C3 **Bontrug** S. Africa
53 C1 **Boolba** Austr.
52 B2 **Booligal** Austr.
53 C1 **Boomi** Austr.
53 D1 **Boonah** Austr.
137 E2 **Boone** U.S.A.
140 C2 **Booneville** U.S.A.
137 E3 **Boonville** U.S.A.
52 B2 **Booroorban** Austr.
53 C2 **Boorowa** Austr.
117 C3 **Boosaaso** Somalia
126 G2 **Boothia, Gulf of** Can.
126 F2 **Boothia Peninsula** Can.
118 B3 **Booué** Gabon
100 C2 **Boppard** Ger.
144 B2 **Boquilla, Presa de la** resr Mex.
109 D2 **Bor** Serb. and Mont.
117 B4 **Bor** Sudan
80 B2 **Bor** Turkey
93 F4 **Borås** Sweden
81 D3 **Borāzjān** Iran
150 D3 **Borba** Brazil
104 B3 **Bordeaux** France
126 E1 **Borden Island** Can.
127 G2 **Borden Peninsula** Can.
52 B3 **Bordertown** Austr.
107 D2 **Bordj Bou Arréridj** Alg.
107 D2 **Bordj Bounaama** Alg.
114 B2 **Bordj Flye Ste-Marie** Alg.
115 C1 **Bordj Messaouda** Alg.
114 C2 **Bordj Mokhtar** Alg.
Bordj Omer Driss Alg. *see* Bordj Omer Driss
115 C2 **Bordj Omer Driss** Alg.
94 B1 **Borðoy** i. Faroe Is
Borgá Fin. *see* Porvoo
92 □A3 **Borgarnes** Iceland
143 C1 **Borger** U.S.A.
93 G4 **Borgholm** Sweden
100 B2 **Borgloon** Belgium
108 A1 **Borgosesia** Italy
87 D3 **Borisoglebsk** Rus. Fed.
89 E2 **Borisoglebskiy** Rus. Fed.

91 D1 **Borisovka** Rus. Fed.
119 C2 **Bo River Post** Sudan
100 C2 **Borken** Ger.
92 G2 **Borkenes** Norway
100 C1 **Borkum** Ger.
100 C1 **Borkum** i. Ger.
93 G3 **Borlänge** Sweden
101 F2 **Borna** Ger.
100 C1 **Borne** Neth.
61 C1 **Borneo** i. Asia
93 F4 **Bornholm** i. Denmark
111 C3 **Bornova** Turkey
90 B1 **Borodyanka** Ukr.
77 E2 **Borohoro Shan** mts China
114 B3 **Boron** Mali
89 D2 **Borovichi** Rus. Fed.
89 E2 **Borovsk** Rus. Fed.
76 C1 **Borovskoy** Kazakh.
51 C1 **Borroloola** Austr.
110 B1 **Borşa** Romania
76 B2 **Borsakelmas sho'rxogi** salt marsh Uzbek.
90 B2 **Borshchiv** Ukr.
69 D1 **Borshchovochnyy Khrebet** mts Rus. Fed.
101 E1 **Börßum** Ger.
Bortala China *see* Bole
81 C2 **Borūjerd** Iran
90 A2 **Boryslav** Ukr.
90 C1 **Boryspil'** Ukr.
91 C1 **Borzna** Ukr.
69 D1 **Borzya** Rus. Fed.
109 C1 **Bosanska Dubica** Bos.-Herz.
109 C1 **Bosanska Gradiška** Bos.-Herz.
109 C1 **Bosanska Krupa** Bos.-Herz.
109 C1 **Bosanski Novi** Bos.-Herz.
109 C2 **Bosansko Grahovo** Bos.-Herz.
71 A3 **Bose** China
123 C2 **Boshof** S. Africa
109 C2 **Bosnia-Herzegovina** country Europe
118 B2 **Bosobolo** Dem. Rep. Congo
111 C2 **Bosporus** str. Turkey
142 B2 **Bosque** U.S.A.
118 B2 **Bossangoa** C.A.R.
118 B2 **Bossembélé** C.A.R.
140 B2 **Bossier City** U.S.A.
122 A2 **Bossievlei** Namibia
68 B2 **Bosten Hu** l. China
99 C3 **Boston** U.K.
139 E2 **Boston** U.S.A.
140 B1 **Boston Mountains** U.S.A.
53 D2 **Botany Bay** Austr.
120 B3 **Boteti** r. Botswana
110 B2 **Botev** mt. Bulg.
80 A1 **Botevgrad** Bulg.
92 G3 **Bothnia, Gulf of** Fin./Sweden
110 C1 **Botoşani** Romania
70 B2 **Botou** China
123 C2 **Botshabelo** S. Africa
120 B3 **Botswana** country Africa
109 C3 **Botte Donato, Monte** mt. Italy
136 C1 **Bottineau** U.S.A.
100 C2 **Bottrop** Ger.
154 C2 **Botucatu** Brazil
114 B4 **Bouaké** Côte d'Ivoire
118 B2 **Bouar** C.A.R.
114 B1 **Bouârfa** Morocco
131 D3 **Bouctouche** Can.
107 C2 **Bougaa** Alg.
48 G4 **Bougainville Island** P.N.G.
Bougie Alg. *see* Bejaïa
114 B3 **Bougouni** Mali
100 B3 **Bouillon** Belgium
107 D2 **Bouira** Alg.
114 A2 **Boujdour** Western Sahara
50 D3 **Boulder** Austr.
136 B2 **Boulder** CO U.S.A.
134 D1 **Boulder** MT U.S.A.
135 D3 **Boulder City** U.S.A.
Boulhaut Morocco *see* Ben Slimane
51 C2 **Boulia** Austr.
104 C1 **Boulogne-Billancourt** France
104 C1 **Boulogne-sur-Mer** France
118 C2 **Boulouba** C.A.R.
118 B3 **Boumango** Gabon
118 B2 **Boumba** r. Cameroon
107 D2 **Boumerdes** Alg.
114 B4 **Bouna** Côte d'Ivoire
114 B4 **Boundiali** Côte d'Ivoire
134 D2 **Bountiful** U.S.A.
49 I8 **Bounty Islands** N.Z.
114 B3 **Bourem** Mali
104 C2 **Bourganeuf** France
105 D2 **Bourg-en-Bresse** France
104 C2 **Bourges** France
Bourgogne reg. France *see* Burgundy
105 D2 **Bourgoin-Jallieu** France
53 C2 **Bourke** Austr.
99 C3 **Bourne** U.K.
99 C4 **Bournemouth** U.K.
118 C1 **Bourtoutou** Chad
115 C1 **Bou Saâda** Alg.
115 D3 **Bousso** Chad
100 A2 **Boussu** Belgium
114 A3 **Boutilimit** Maur.
128 C2 **Bow** r. Can.
Bowa China *see* Muli
51 D2 **Bowen** Austr.
53 C3 **Bowen, Mount** Austr.
129 C2 **Bow Island** Can.
138 B3 **Bowling Green** KY U.S.A.
137 E3 **Bowling Green** MO U.S.A.

138 C2 **Bowling Green** OH U.S.A.
136 C1 **Bowman** U.S.A.
53 C2 **Bowral** Austr.
101 D3 **Boxberg** Ger.
100 B2 **Boxtel** Neth.
80 B1 **Boyabat** Turkey
71 B3 **Boyang** China
97 B2 **Boyle** Ireland
97 C2 **Boyne** r. Ireland
136 B2 **Boysen Reservoir** U.S.A.
152 B2 **Boyuibe** Bol.
111 C3 **Bozburun** Turkey
111 C3 **Bozcaada** i. Turkey
111 C3 **Bozdağ** mt. Turkey
111 C3 **Boz Dağları** mts Turkey
111 C3 **Bozdoğan** Turkey
134 D1 **Bozeman** U.S.A.
118 B2 **Bozoum** C.A.R.
80 B2 **Bozüyük** Turkey
109 C2 **Brač** i. Croatia
130 C3 **Bracebridge** Can.
131 D3 **Brachet, Lac au** l. Can.
93 G3 **Bräcke** Sweden
99 C4 **Bracknell** U.K.
108 B2 **Bradano** r. Italy
141 D3 **Bradenton** U.S.A.
98 C3 **Bradford** U.K.
139 D2 **Bradford** U.S.A.
143 D2 **Brady** U.S.A.
96 C2 **Braemar** U.K.
106 B1 **Braga** Port.
151 E3 **Bragança** Brazil
106 B1 **Bragança** Port.
155 C2 **Bragança Paulista** Brazil
89 D3 **Brahin** Belarus
75 D2 **Brahmanbaria** Bangl.
75 C3 **Brahmapur** India
62 A1 **Brahmaputra** r. China/India
53 C3 **Braidwood** Austr.
110 C1 **Brăila** Romania
137 E1 **Brainerd** U.S.A.
99 D4 **Braintree** U.K.
100 B2 **Braives** Belgium
101 D1 **Brake (Unterweser)** Ger.
122 A1 **Brakwater** Namibia
98 B2 **Brampton** U.K.
101 D1 **Bramsche** Ger.
150 C3 **Branco** r. Brazil
101 F1 **Brandenburg** Ger.
129 E3 **Brandon** Can.
140 C2 **Brandon** U.S.A.
97 A2 **Brandon Mountain** hill Ireland
122 B3 **Brandvlei** S. Africa
103 D1 **Braniewo** Pol.
130 B3 **Brantford** Can.
53 D2 **Branxton** Austr.
131 E3 **Bras d'Or Lake** Can.
155 C1 **Brasil, Planalto do** plat. Brazil
154 C1 **Brasilândia** Brazil
155 C1 **Brasília** Brazil
155 C1 **Brasília de Minas** Brazil
88 C2 **Braslaw** Belarus
110 C1 **Braşov** Romania
103 D2 **Bratislava** Slovakia
83 H3 **Bratsk** Rus. Fed.
102 C2 **Braunau am Inn** Austria
101 E1 **Braunschweig** Ger.
92 □A2 **Brautarholt** Iceland
Bravo del Norte, Rio r. Mex./U.S.A. *see* Rio Grande
135 C4 **Brawley** U.S.A.
97 C2 **Bray** Ireland
150 D2 **Brazil** country S. America
158 E6 **Brazil Basin** sea feature S. Atlantic Ocean
143 D3 **Brazos** r. U.S.A.
118 B3 **Brazzaville** Congo
109 C2 **Brčko** Bos.-Herz.
96 C2 **Brechin** U.K.
100 B2 **Brecht** Belgium
143 D2 **Breckenridge** U.S.A.
103 D2 **Břeclav** Czech Rep.
99 B4 **Brecon** U.K.
99 B4 **Brecon Beacons** reg. U.K.
100 B2 **Breda** Neth.
122 B3 **Bredasdorp** S. Africa
102 B2 **Bregenz** Austria
92 H1 **Breivikbotn** Norway
92 E3 **Brekstad** Norway
101 D1 **Bremen** Ger.
101 D1 **Bremerhaven** Ger.
134 B1 **Bremerton** U.S.A.
101 D1 **Bremervörde** Ger.
143 D2 **Brenham** U.S.A.
108 B1 **Brennero** Italy
102 C2 **Brenner Pass** Austria/Italy
99 D4 **Brentwood** U.K.
108 B1 **Brescia** Italy
100 A2 **Breskens** Neth.
108 B1 **Bressanone** Italy
96 □ **Bressay** i. U.K.
104 B2 **Bressuire** France
88 B3 **Brest** Belarus
104 B2 **Brest** France
Brest-Litovsk Belarus *see* Brest
Bretagne reg. France *see* Brittany
140 C2 **Breton Sound** b. U.S.A.
151 D3 **Breves** Brazil
53 C1 **Brewarrina** Austr.
134 C1 **Brewster** U.S.A.
89 E2 **Breytovo** Rus. Fed.
Brezhnev Rus. Fed. *see* Naberezhnyye Chelny

109 C1 Brezovo Polje hill Croatia
118 C2 Bria C.A.R.
105 D3 Briançon France
90 B2 Briceni Moldova
Brichany Moldova see Briceni
99 B4 Bridgend U.K.
139 E2 Bridgeport CT U.S.A.
136 C2 Bridgeport NE U.S.A.
147 E3 Bridgetown Barbados
131 D3 Bridgewater Can.
99 B3 Bridgnorth U.K.
99 B4 Bridgwater U.K.
99 B4 Bridgwater Bay U.K.
98 C2 Bridlington U.K.
98 C2 Bridlington Bay U.K.
99 B4 Bridport U.K.
105 D2 Brig Switz.
134 D2 Brigham City U.S.A.
53 C3 Bright Austr.
54 B3 Brighton N.Z.
99 C4 Brighton U.K.
136 C3 Brighton CO U.S.A.
138 C2 Brighton MI U.S.A.
105 D3 Brignoles France
114 A3 Brikama Gambia
101 D2 Brilon Ger.
109 C2 Brindisi Italy
97 B1 Brinlack Ireland
53 D1 Brisbane Austr.
99 B4 Bristol U.K.
139 E2 Bristol CT U.S.A.
141 D1 Bristol TN U.S.A.
99 A4 Bristol Channel est. U.K.
128 B2 British Columbia prov. Can.
British Guiana country S. America see Guyana
British Honduras country Central America see Belize
56 C6 British Indian Ocean Territory terr. Indian Ocean
British Solomon Islands country S. Pacific Ocean see Solomon Islands
123 C2 Brits S. Africa
122 B3 Britstown S. Africa
104 B2 Brittany reg. France
104 C2 Brive-la-Gaillarde France
106 C1 Briviesca Spain
99 B4 Brixham U.K.
103 D2 Brno Czech Rep.
Broach India see Bharuch
141 D1 Broad r. Can.
130 C2 Broadback r. Can.
53 C3 Bradford Austr.
96 B2 Broadford U.K.
96 C3 Broad Law hill U.K.
136 B3 Broadus U.S.A.
129 D2 Brochet Can.
129 D2 Brochet, Lac l. Can.
101 E1 Bröckel Ger.
101 E2 Brocken mt. Ger.
126 E1 Brock Island Can.
130 C2 Brockville Can.
127 G2 Brodeur Peninsula Can.
96 B3 Brodick U.K.
103 D1 Brodnica Pol.
90 B1 Brody Ukr.
143 D1 Broken Arrow U.S.A.
137 D2 Broken Bow U.S.A.
52 B2 Broken Hill Austr.
Broken Hill Zambia see Kabwe
159 F6 Broken Plateau sea feature Indian Ocean
151 D2 Brokopondo Suriname
99 B3 Bromsgrove U.K.
93 E4 Brønderslev Denmark
123 C3 Bronkhorstspruit S. Africa
92 F2 Brønnøysund Norway
64 A3 Brooke's Point Phil.
140 B2 Brookhaven U.S.A.
134 B2 Brookings OR U.S.A.
137 D2 Brookings SD U.S.A.
128 C2 Brooks Can.
126 C2 Brooks Range mts U.S.A.
141 D3 Brooksville U.S.A.
139 D2 Brookville U.S.A.
96 B2 Broom, Loch inlet U.K.
50 B1 Broome Austr.
134 B2 Brothers U.S.A.
Broughton Island Can. see Qikiqtarjuaq
90 C1 Brovary Ukr.
143 C2 Brownfield U.S.A.
128 C3 Browning U.S.A.
140 C1 Brownsville TN U.S.A.
143 D3 Brownsville TX U.S.A.
143 D2 Brownwood U.S.A.
92 □A2 Brú Iceland
104 C1 Bruay-la-Bussière France
138 B1 Bruce Crossing U.S.A.
130 B3 Bruce Peninsula Can.
103 D2 Bruck an der Mur Austria
Bruges Belgium see Brugge
100 A2 Brugge Belgium
62 A1 Bruint India
128 C2 Brûlé Can.
151 E4 Brumado Brazil
93 F3 Brumunddal Norway
61 C1 Brunei country Asia
Brunei Brunei see Bandar Seri Begawan
102 C2 Brunico Italy
Brünn Czech Rep. see Brno
101 D1 Brunsbüttel Ger.
141 D2 Brunswick GA U.S.A.

139 F2 Brunswick ME U.S.A.
53 D1 Brunswick Head Austr.
123 D2 Bruntville S. Africa
136 C2 Brush U.S.A.
100 B2 Brussels Belgium
Bruxelles Belgium see Brussels
143 D2 Bryan U.S.A.
89 D3 Bryansk Rus. Fed.
91 D2 Bryn'kovskaya Rus. Fed.
91 D2 Bryukhovetskaya Rus. Fed.
103 D1 Brzeg Pol.
Brześć nad Bugiem Belarus see Brest
114 A3 Buba Guinea-Bissau
111 C3 Buca Turkey
80 B2 Bucak Turkey
150 B2 Bucaramanga Col.
90 B2 Buchach Ukr.
53 C3 Buchan Austr.
114 A4 Buchanan Liberia
110 C2 Bucharest Romania
101 D1 Bucholz in der Nordheide Ger.
110 C1 Bucin, Pasul pass Romania
101 D1 Bückeburg Ger.
142 A2 Buckeye U.S.A.
96 C2 Buckhaven U.K.
96 C2 Buckie U.K.
99 C3 Buckingham U.K.
51 C1 Buckingham Bay Austr.
51 D2 Buckland Tableland reg. Austr.
52 A2 Buckleboo Austr.
139 F2 Bucksport U.S.A.
103 D2 Bučovice Czech Rep.
Bucureşti Romania see Bucharest
89 D3 Buda-Kashalyova Belarus
103 D2 Budapest Hungary
75 B2 Budaun India
108 A2 Buddusò Sardinia Italy
99 A4 Bude U.K.
87 D4 Budennovsk Rus. Fed.
Budennoye Rus. Fed. see Krasnogvardeyskoye
89 D2 Budogoshch' Rus. Fed.
108 A2 Budoni Sardinia Italy
Budweis Czech Rep. see České Budějovice
118 A2 Buea Cameroon
135 B4 Buellton U.S.A.
150 B2 Buenaventura Col.
144 B2 Buenaventura Mex.
Buena Vista i. N. Mariana Is see Tinian
106 C1 Buendia, Embalse de resr Spain
155 D1 Buenópolis Brazil
153 C3 Buenos Aires Arg.
153 A4 Buenos Aires, Lago l. Arg./Chile
139 D2 Buffalo NY U.S.A.
136 C1 Buffalo SD U.S.A.
143 D2 Buffalo TX U.S.A.
136 B2 Buffalo WY U.S.A.
129 D2 Buffalo Narrows Can.
121 C3 Buffalo Range Zimbabwe
122 A2 Buffels watercourse S. Africa
123 C1 Buffels Drift S. Africa
110 C2 Buftea Romania
103 E1 Bug r. Pol.
61 C2 Bugel, Tanjung pt Indon.
109 C2 Bugojno Bos.-Herz.
86 D2 Bugrino Rus. Fed.
64 A3 Bugsuk i. Phil.
87 E3 Bugul'ma Rus. Fed.
87 E3 Buguruslan Rus. Fed.
121 C2 Buhera Zimbabwe
110 C1 Buhuşi Romania
99 B3 Builth Wells U.K.
69 D1 Buir Nur l. Mongolia
120 A3 Buitepos Namibia
109 D2 Bujanovac Serb. and Mont.
119 C3 Bujumbura Burundi
69 D1 Bukachacha Rus. Fed.
120 B2 Bukalo Namibia
119 C3 Bukavu Dem. Rep. Congo
Bukhara Uzbek. see Buxoro
60 B2 Bukittinggi Indon.
119 D3 Bukoba Tanz.
103 D1 Bukowiec hill Pol.
59 C3 Bula Indon.
53 D2 Bulahdelal Austr.
121 B3 Bulawayo Zimbabwe
111 C3 Buldan Turkey
123 D2 Bulembu Swaziland
68 C1 Bulgan Mongolia
110 C2 Bulgaria country Europe
54 B2 Buller r. N.Z.
142 A1 Bullhead City U.S.A.
52 B1 Bulloo watercourse Austr.
52 B1 Bulloo Downs Austr.
122 A1 Büllsport Namibia
61 C2 Bulukumba Indon.
118 B3 Bulungu Dem. Rep. Congo
118 B3 Bumba Dem. Rep. Congo
118 C2 Bumba Dem. Rep. Congo
62 A1 Bumhkang Myanmar
118 B3 Buna Dem. Rep. Congo
97 B1 Bunbeg Ireland
50 A3 Bunbury Austr.
97 C2 Bunclody Ireland
97 C1 Buncrana Ireland
119 D3 Bunda Tanz.
51 E2 Bundaberg Austr.
53 C1 Bundaleer Austr.
53 D2 Bundarra Austr.
74 B2 Bundi India
97 B1 Bundoran Ireland

75 C2 Bundu India
53 C3 Bungendore Austr.
119 D2 Bungoma Kenya
67 B4 Bungo-suidō sea chan. Japan
119 D2 Bunia Dem. Rep. Congo
118 C3 Bunianga Dem. Rep. Congo
63 B2 Buôn Mê Thuôt Vietnam
119 D3 Bura Kenya
117 C3 Buraan Somalia
Burang China see Jirang
78 B2 Buraydah Saudi Arabia
101 D2 Burbach Ger.
117 C4 Burco Somalia
100 B1 Burdaard Neth.
111 D3 Burdur Turkey
117 B3 Burē Eth.
99 D3 Bure r. U.K.
69 E1 Bureinskiy Khrebet mts Rus. Fed.
101 D2 Büren Ger.
Bureya Range mts Rus. Fed. see Bureinskiy Khrebet
110 C2 Burgas Bulg.
101 E1 Burg bei Magdeburg Ger.
101 E1 Burgdorf Ger.
101 E1 Burgdorf Ger.
131 E3 Burgeo Can.
123 C3 Burgersdorp S. Africa
123 D1 Burgersfort S. Africa
100 A2 Burgh-Haamstede Neth.
101 F3 Burglengenfeld Ger.
145 C2 Burgos Mex.
106 C1 Burgos Spain
105 C2 Burgundy reg. France
111 C3 Burhaniye Turkey
74 B2 Burhanpur India
75 C2 Burhar-Dhanpuri India
101 D1 Burhave (Butjadingen) Ger.
154 C1 Buri Brazil
60 B2 Buriai Indon.
64 B2 Burias i. Phil.
131 E3 Burin Can.
63 B2 Buriram Thai.
154 C1 Buriti Alegre Brazil
151 E3 Buriti Bravo Brazil
155 C1 Buritis Brazil
107 C2 Burjassot Spain
143 D2 Burkburnett U.S.A.
51 C1 Burketown Austr.
114 B3 Burkina country Africa
134 D2 Burley U.S.A.
136 C3 Burlington CO U.S.A.
137 E2 Burlington IA U.S.A.
141 E1 Burlington NC U.S.A.
139 E2 Burlington VT U.S.A.
Burma country see Myanmar
134 B2 Burney U.S.A.
51 D4 Burnie Austr.
98 B3 Burnley U.K.
134 C2 Burns U.S.A.
134 C2 Burns Junction U.S.A.
128 B2 Burns Lake Can.
137 E2 Burnsville U.S.A.
101 F1 Burow Ger.
77 E2 Burqin China
52 A2 Burra Austr.
109 D2 Burrel Albania
97 B2 Burren reg. Ireland
53 C2 Burrendong Reservoir Austr.
53 C2 Burren Junction Austr.
107 C2 Burriana Spain
53 C2 Burrinjuck Reservoir Austr.
144 B2 Burro, Serranías del mts Mex.
111 C2 Bursa Turkey
116 B2 Bûr Safâjah Egypt
Bûr Sa'îd Egypt see Port Said
Bûr Sa'îd Egypt see Port Said
Bûr Sudan Sudan see Port Sudan
130 C2 Burton, Lac l. Can.
97 B1 Burtonport Ireland
99 C3 Burton upon Trent U.K.
52 B2 Burundy Austr.
59 C3 Buru i. Indon.
119 C3 Burundi country Africa
119 C3 Bururi Burundi
96 C1 Burwick U.K.
98 B3 Bury U.K.
91 C1 Buryn' Ukr.
76 B2 Burynshyk Kazakh.
99 D3 Bury St Edmunds U.K.
118 C3 Busanga Dem. Rep. Congo
81 D3 Büshehr Iran
119 D3 Bushenyi Uganda
Bushire Iran see Büshehr
118 C2 Businga Dem. Rep. Congo
50 A3 Busselton Austr.
143 C3 Bustamante Mex.
108 A1 Busto Arsizio Italy
64 A2 Busuanga Phil.
118 C2 Buta Dem. Rep. Congo
119 C3 Butare Rwanda
96 B3 Bute i. U.K.
119 C2 Butembo Dem. Rep. Congo
123 C2 Butha-Buthe Lesotho
139 D2 Butler U.S.A.
61 C2 Buton i. Indon.
134 D1 Butte U.S.A.
60 B1 Butterworth Malaysia
96 A1 Butt of Lewis hd U.K.
129 C2 Button Bay Can.
131 D1 Button Islands Can.
64 B3 Butuan Phil.
89 F3 Buturlinovka Rus. Fed.
75 C2 Butwal Nepal
101 D2 Butzbach Ger.

117 C4 Buulobarde Somalia
117 C5 Buur Gaabo Somalia
117 C4 Buurhabaka Somalia
78 A2 Buwâṭah Saudi Arabia
76 C3 Buxoro Uzbek.
101 D1 Buxtehude Ger.
98 C3 Buxton U.K.
89 F2 Buy Rus. Fed.
87 D4 Buynaksk Rus. Fed.
111 C3 Büyükmenderes r. Turkey
65 A1 Buyun Shan mt. China
74 B1 Buzai Gumbad Afgh.
110 C1 Buzău Romania
110 C1 Buzău r. Romania
121 C2 Búzi Moz.
87 E3 Buzuluk Rus. Fed.
88 C3 Byahoml' Belarus
110 C2 Byala Bulg.
110 C2 Byala Bulg.
88 C3 Byalynichy Belarus
88 D3 Byarezina r. Belarus
88 B3 Byaroza Belarus
88 C3 Byarozawka Belarus
103 D1 Bydgoszcz Pol.
Byelorussia country Europe see Belarus
88 C3 Byerazino Belarus
88 C2 Byeshankovichy Belarus
89 D3 Bykhaw Belarus
127 G2 Bylot Island Can.
53 C2 Byrock Austr.
53 D1 Byron Bay Austr.
83 J2 Bytantay r. Rus. Fed.
103 D1 Bytom Pol.
103 D1 Bytów Pol.

C

120 A2 Caála Angola
154 B2 Caarapó Brazil
155 C1 Caatinga Brazil
144 B2 Caballos Mesteños, Llano de los plain Mex.
106 B1 Cabañaquinta Spain
64 B2 Cabanatuan Phil.
117 C3 Cabdul Qaadir Somalia
154 A1 Cabeceira Rio Manso Brazil
154 C1 Cabeceiras Brazil
106 B2 Cabeza del Buey Spain
152 B1 Cabezas Bol.
150 B1 Cabimas Venez.
120 A1 Cabinda Angola
118 B3 Cabinda prov. Angola
151 F3 Cabo Brazil
155 D2 Cabo Frio Brazil
155 D2 Cabo Frio, Ilha do i. Brazil
130 C3 Cabonga, Réservoir resr Can.
53 D1 Caboolture Austr.
150 B3 Cabo Pantoja Peru
121 C2 Cabora Bassa, Lake resr Moz.
144 A1 Caborca Mex.
131 D3 Cabot Strait Can.
106 C2 Cabra Spain
155 D1 Cabral, Serra do mts Brazil
107 D2 Cabrera i. Spain
106 B1 Cabrera, Sierra de la mts Spain
129 D2 Cabri Can.
107 C2 Cabriel r. Spain
154 B3 Caçador Brazil
109 D2 Čačak Serb. and Mont.
108 A2 Caccia, Capo c. Sardinia Italy
106 B2 Cacém Port.
151 D4 Cáceres Brazil
106 B2 Cáceres Spain
128 B2 Cache Creek Can.
114 A3 Cacheu Guinea-Bissau
151 D3 Cachimbo, Serra do hills Brazil
154 B1 Cachoeira Alta Brazil
155 D2 Cachoeiro de Itapemirim Brazil
114 A3 Cacine Guinea-Bissau
120 A2 Cacolo Angola
120 A2 Caconda Angola
154 B1 Caçu Brazil
103 D2 Čadca Slovakia
101 D1 Cadenberge Ger.
145 B2 Cadereyta Mex.
138 B2 Cadillac U.S.A.
64 B2 Cadiz Phil.
106 B2 Cádiz Spain
106 B2 Cádiz, Golfo de g. Spain
128 B2 Cadotte Lake Can.
104 B2 Caen France
Caerdydd U.K. see Cardiff
Caerfyrddin U.K. see Carmarthen
Caergybi U.K. see Holyhead
98 A3 Caernarfon U.K.
99 A3 Caernarfon Bay U.K.
Caernarvon U.K. see Caernarfon
152 B2 Cafayate Arg.
154 C2 Cafelândia Brazil
64 B3 Cagayan de Oro Phil.
108 B2 Cagli Italy
108 A3 Cagliari Sardinia Italy
108 A3 Cagliari, Golfo di b. Sardinia Italy
120 A2 Cahama Angola
97 B3 Caha Mountains hills Ireland
97 A3 Cahermore Ireland
97 B3 Cahersiveen Ireland
97 C2 Cahir Ireland
Cahora Bassa, Lago de resr Moz. see Cabora Bassa, Lake
97 C2 Cahore Point Ireland
104 C3 Cahors France

90 B2 **Cahul** Moldova
121 C2 **Caia** Moz.
151 D4 **Caiabis, Serra dos** hills Brazil
120 B2 **Caianda** Angola
154 B1 **Caiapó, Serra de** mts Brazil
154 B1 **Caiapônia** Brazil
147 C2 **Caicos Islands** Turks and Caicos Is
96 C2 **Cairngorm Mountains** U.K.
96 B3 **Cairnryan** U.K.
51 D1 **Cairns** Austr.
116 B1 **Cairo** Egypt
Caisleán an Bharraigh Ireland *see* Castlebar
98 C3 **Caistor** U.K.
120 A2 **Caiundo** Angola
150 B3 **Cajamarca** Peru
109 C1 **Čakovec** Croatia
123 C3 **Cala** S. Africa
115 C4 **Calabar** Nigeria
150 B2 **Calabozo** Venez.
110 B2 **Calafat** Romania
153 A5 **Calafate** Arg.
107 C1 **Calahorra** Spain
120 A2 **Calai** Angola
104 C1 **Calais** France
139 F1 **Calais** U.S.A.
152 B2 **Calama** Chile
64 A2 **Calamian Group** *is* Phil.
107 C1 **Calamocha** Spain
120 A1 **Calandula** Angola
60 A1 **Calang** Indon.
115 E1 **Calanscio Sand Sea** *des.* Libya
64 B2 **Calapan** Phil.
110 C2 **Călăraşi** Romania
107 C1 **Calatayud** Spain
64 B2 **Calayan** *i.* Phil.
64 B2 **Calbayog** Phil.
151 F3 **Calcanhar, Ponta do** *pt* Brazil
151 D2 **Calçoene** Brazil
Calcutta India *see* Kolkata
106 B2 **Caldas da Rainha** Port.
154 C1 **Caldas Novas** Brazil
152 A2 **Caldera** Chile
51 D2 **Caldervale** Austr.
134 C2 **Caldwell** U.S.A.
123 C3 **Caledon** *r.* Lesotho/S. Africa
122 A3 **Caledon** S. Africa
153 B4 **Caleta Olivia** Arg.
98 A2 **Calf of Man** *i.* Isle of Man
128 C2 **Calgary** Can.
150 B2 **Cali** Col.
73 B3 **Calicut** India
135 D3 **Caliente** U.S.A.
135 B2 **California** *state* U.S.A.
144 A1 **California, Gulf of** *g.* Mex.
135 B3 **California Aqueduct** *canal* U.S.A.
81 C2 **Cälilabad** Azer.
122 B3 **Calitzdorp** S. Africa
145 C2 **Calkini** Mex.
52 B1 **Callabonna, Lake** *salt flat* Austr.
135 C3 **Callaghan, Mount** U.S.A.
97 C2 **Callan** Ireland
96 B2 **Callander** U.K.
150 B4 **Callao** Peru
99 A4 **Callington** U.K.
108 B3 **Caltagirone** *Sicily* Italy
108 B3 **Caltanissetta** *Sicily* Italy
120 A1 **Calulo** Angola
120 B2 **Calunda** Angola
120 A2 **Caluquembe** Angola
117 D3 **Caluula** Somalia
105 D3 **Calvi** *Corsica* France
107 C2 **Calvià** Spain
144 B2 **Calvillo** Mex.
122 A3 **Calvinia** S. Africa
109 C2 **Calvo, Monte** *mt.* Italy
120 A1 **Camabatela** Angola
151 F4 **Camaçari** Brazil
144 B2 **Camacho** Mex.
120 A2 **Camacupa** Angola
146 C2 **Camagüey** Cuba
146 C2 **Camagüey, Archipiélago de** *is* Cuba
150 B4 **Camana** Peru
120 B2 **Camanongue** Angola
154 B1 **Camapuã** Brazil
145 C2 **Camargo** Mex.
63 B3 **Ca Mau** Vietnam
Cambay India *see* Khambhat
63 B2 **Cambodia** *country* Asia
99 A4 **Camborne** U.K.
105 C1 **Cambrai** France
99 B3 **Cambrian Mountains** *hills* U.K.
138 C2 **Cambridge** Can.
54 C1 **Cambridge** N.Z.
99 D3 **Cambridge** U.K.
139 E2 **Cambridge** *MA* U.S.A.
139 D3 **Cambridge** *MD* U.S.A.
137 E1 **Cambridge** *MN* U.S.A.
138 C2 **Cambridge** *OH* U.S.A.
126 E2 **Cambridge Bay** Can.
131 D2 **Cambrien, Lac** *l.* Can.
120 B1 **Cambulo** Angola
53 D2 **Camden** Austr.
140 B2 **Camden** *AR* U.S.A.
139 F2 **Camden** *ME* U.S.A.
139 D3 **Camden** *NJ* U.S.A.
134 C2 **Camdenton** U.S.A.
137 E3 **Cameron** U.S.A.
118 A2 **Cameroon** *country* Africa
118 A2 **Cameroun, Mont** *vol.* Cameroon
151 E3 **Cametá** Brazil
64 B2 **Camiguin** *i.* Phil.
64 B3 **Camiguin** *i.* Phil.
152 B2 **Camiri** Bol.

151 E3 **Camocim** Brazil
51 C1 **Camooweal** Austr.
63 A3 **Camorta** *i.* India
153 A4 **Campana, Isla** *i.* Chile
155 D1 **Campanário** Brazil
122 B2 **Campanha** Brazil
122 B2 **Campbell** S. Africa
54 B2 **Campbell, Cape** N.Z.
48 H9 **Campbell Island** N.Z.
156 D9 **Campbell Plateau** *sea feature* S. Pacific Ocean
128 B2 **Campbell River** Can.
138 B3 **Campbellsville** U.S.A.
131 D3 **Campbellton** Can.
53 D2 **Campbelltown** Austr.
96 B3 **Campbeltown** U.K.
145 C3 **Campeche** Mex.
145 C3 **Campeche, Bahía de** *g.* Mex.
52 B3 **Camperdown** Austr.
110 C1 **Câmpina** Romania
151 F3 **Campina Grande** Brazil
154 C2 **Campinas** Brazil
154 C1 **Campina Verde** Brazil
108 B2 **Campobasso** Italy
155 C2 **Campo Belo** Brazil
154 C1 **Campo Florido** Brazil
152 B2 **Campo Gallo** Arg.
154 B2 **Campo Grande** Brazil
154 C3 **Campo Largo** Brazil
151 E3 **Campo Maior** Brazil
106 B2 **Campo Maior** Port.
150 B1 **Campo Mara** Venez.
109 C2 **Campomarino** Italy
154 B2 **Campo Mourão** Brazil
155 D2 **Campos** Brazil
155 C1 **Campos Altos** Brazil
155 C2 **Campos do Jordão** Brazil
110 C1 **Câmpulung** Romania
142 A2 **Camp Verde** U.S.A.
63 B2 **Cam Ranh** Vietnam
63 B2 **Cam Ranh, Vinh** *b.* Vietnam
Cam Ranh Bay Vietnam *see* Cam Ranh, Vinh
128 C2 **Camrose** Can.
129 D2 **Camsell Portage** Can.
111 C2 **Çan** Turkey
126 F2 **Canada** *country* N. America
160 A2 **Canada Basin** *sea feature* Arctic Ocean
143 C1 **Canadian** U.S.A.
143 D1 **Canadian** *r.* U.S.A.
111 C2 **Çanakkale** Turkey
144 A1 **Cananea** Mex.
154 C2 **Cananéia** Brazil
114 A2 **Canary Islands** *terr.* N. Atlantic Ocean
154 C1 **Canastra, Serra da** *mts Goiás* Brazil
155 C1 **Canastra, Serra da** *mts Minas Gerais* Brazil
144 B2 **Cantalán** Mex.
141 D3 **Canaveral, Cape** U.S.A.
155 E1 **Canavieiras** Brazil
53 C2 **Canbelego** Austr.
53 C3 **Canberra** Austr.
145 D2 **Cancún** Mex.
111 C3 **Çandarlı** Turkey
155 C2 **Candeias** Brazil
145 C3 **Candelaria** Mex.
154 B2 **Cândido de Abreu** Brazil
129 D2 **Candle Lake** Can.
137 D1 **Cando** U.S.A.
120 A2 **Cangamba** Angola
106 B1 **Cangas** Spain
106 B1 **Cangas del Narcea** Spain
120 B2 **Cangombe** Angola
152 C3 **Canguçu** Brazil
70 B2 **Cangzhou** China
131 D2 **Caniapiscau** Can.
131 D2 **Caniapiscau** *r.* Can.
131 C2 **Caniapiscau, Lac** *l.* Can.
Caniçado Moz. *see* Guija
108 B3 **Canicattì** *Sicily* Italy
151 F3 **Canindé** Brazil
144 B2 **Cañitas de Felipe Pescador** Mex.
80 B1 **Çankırı** Turkey
128 C2 **Canmore** Can.
96 A2 **Canna** *i.* U.K.
73 B3 **Cannanore** India
105 D3 **Cannes** France
99 B3 **Cannock** U.K.
53 C3 **Cann River** Austr.
152 C2 **Canoas** Brazil
129 D2 **Canoe Lake** Can.
154 B3 **Canoinhas** Brazil
136 B3 **Canon City** U.S.A.
52 B2 **Canopus** Austr.
129 D2 **Canora** Can.
53 C2 **Canowindra** Austr.
131 D3 **Canso** Can.
Cantabrian Mountains Spain *see* Cantábrica, Cordillera
Cantabrian Sea Spain *see* Cantábrico, Mar
106 C1 **Cantábrica, Cordillera** *mts* Spain
106 B1 **Cantábrico, Mar** *sea* Spain
99 D4 **Canterbury** U.K.
54 B2 **Canterbury Bight** *b.* N.Z.
54 B2 **Canterbury Plains** N.Z.
63 B2 **Cân Thơ** Vietnam
151 E3 **Canto do Buriti** Brazil
Canton China *see* Guangzhou
137 E2 **Canton** *MO* U.S.A.
140 C2 **Canton** *MS* U.S.A.
139 D2 **Canton** *NY* U.S.A.

138 C2 **Canton** *OH* U.S.A.
143 C1 **Canyon** U.S.A.
134 D1 **Canyon Ferry Lake** U.S.A.
134 B2 **Canyonville** U.S.A.
62 B1 **Cao Bằng** Vietnam
109 C2 **Capaccio** Italy
154 C2 **Capão Bonito** Brazil
155 D2 **Caparaó, Serra de** *mts* Brazil
139 E1 **Cap-de-la-Madeleine** Can.
51 D4 **Cape Barren Island** Austr.
158 F7 **Cape Basin** *sea feature* S. Atlantic Ocean
52 A3 **Cape Borda** Austr.
131 D3 **Cape Breton Island** Can.
141 D3 **Cape Canaveral** U.S.A.
139 D3 **Cape Charles** U.S.A.
114 B4 **Cape Coast** Ghana
139 E2 **Cape Cod Bay** U.S.A.
141 D3 **Cape Coral** U.S.A.
127 G2 **Cape Dorset** Can.
141 E2 **Cape Fear** *r.* U.S.A.
137 F3 **Cape Girardeau** U.S.A.
155 D1 **Capelinha** Brazil
100 B2 **Capelle aan de IJssel** Neth.
Capelongo Angola *see* Kuvango
139 E3 **Cape May Point** U.S.A.
120 A1 **Capenda-Camulemba** Angola
122 A3 **Cape Town** S. Africa
158 E3 **Cape Verde** *country* N. Atlantic Ocean
158 D4 **Cape Verde Basin** *sea feature* N. Atlantic Ocean
51 D1 **Cape York Peninsula** Austr.
147 C3 **Cap-Haïtien** Haiti
151 E3 **Capim** *r.* Brazil
154 A2 **Capitán Bado** Para.
58 D1 **Capitol Hill** N. Mariana Is
154 B2 **Capivara, Represa** *resr* Brazil
109 C2 **Čapljina** Bos.-Herz.
109 B3 **Capo d'Orlando** *Sicily* Italy
108 A2 **Capraia, Isola d'** *i.* Italy
108 A2 **Caprara, Punta** *pt Sardinia* Italy
108 B2 **Capri, Isola di** *i.* Italy
51 E2 **Capricorn Channel** Austr.
120 B2 **Caprivi Strip** *reg.* Namibia
143 C2 **Cap Rock Escarpment** U.S.A.
143 C1 **Capulin** U.S.A.
150 C3 **Caquetá** *r.* Col.
110 B2 **Caracal** Romania
150 C2 **Caracarai** Brazil
150 C1 **Caracas** Venez.
151 E3 **Caracol** Brazil
155 C2 **Caraguatatuba** Brazil
153 A3 **Carahue** Chile
155 D1 **Caraí** Brazil
151 D3 **Carajás, Serra dos** *hills* Brazil
155 D2 **Carandaí** Brazil
155 D2 **Carangola** Brazil
110 B1 **Caransebeş** Romania
131 D3 **Caraquet** Can.
146 B3 **Caratasca, Laguna de** *lag.* Hond.
155 D1 **Caratinga** Brazil
150 C3 **Carauari** Brazil
107 C2 **Caravaca de la Cruz** Spain
155 E1 **Caravelas** Brazil
129 E3 **Carberry** Can.
144 A2 **Carbó** Mex.
108 A3 **Carbonara, Capo** *c. Sardinia* Italy
136 B3 **Carbondale** *CO* U.S.A.
138 B3 **Carbondale** *IL* U.S.A.
139 D2 **Carbondale** *PA* U.S.A.
131 E3 **Carbonear** Can.
155 D1 **Carbonita** Brazil
107 C2 **Carcaixent** Spain
104 C3 **Carcassonne** France
128 A1 **Carcross** Can.
146 B2 **Cárdenas** Cuba
145 C3 **Cárdenas** Mex.
99 B4 **Cardiff** U.K.
99 A3 **Cardigan** U.K.
99 A3 **Cardigan Bay** U.K.
154 C2 **Cardoso** Brazil
128 C3 **Cardston** Can.
110 B1 **Carei** Romania
104 B2 **Carentan** France
50 B2 **Carey, Lake** *salt flat* Austr.
154 C2 **Cariacica** Brazil
146 B3 **Caribbean Sea** N. Atlantic Ocean
128 B2 **Cariboo Mountains** Can.
139 F1 **Caribou** U.S.A.
130 B2 **Caribou Lake** Can.
128 C2 **Caribou Mountains** Can.
144 B2 **Carichic** Mex.
100 B3 **Carignan** France
53 C2 **Carinda** Austr.
107 C1 **Cariñena** Spain
130 C3 **Carleton Place** Can.
123 C3 **Carletonville** S. Africa
135 C2 **Carlin** U.S.A.
97 C1 **Carlingford Lough** *inlet* Ireland/U.K.
138 B3 **Carlinville** U.S.A.
98 B2 **Carlisle** U.K.
139 D2 **Carlisle** U.S.A.
155 D1 **Carlos Chagas** Brazil
97 C2 **Carlow** Ireland
96 A1 **Carloway** U.K.
135 C4 **Carlsbad** *CA* U.S.A.
142 C2 **Carlsbad** *NM* U.S.A.
129 D3 **Carlyle** Can.
128 A1 **Carlyle** Can.
99 A4 **Carman** Can.
99 A4 **Carmarthen** U.K.
99 A4 **Carmarthen Bay** U.K.
104 C3 **Carmaux** France

145 C3 **Carmelita** Guat.
144 A2 **Carmen, Isla** *i.* Mex.
155 C1 **Carmo do Paranaíba** Brazil
Carmona Angola *see* Uige
106 B2 **Carmona** Spain
104 B2 **Carnac** France
50 A2 **Carnarvon** Austr.
122 B3 **Carnarvon** S. Africa
97 C1 **Carndonagh** Ireland
129 D3 **Carnduff** Can.
50 B2 **Carnegie, Lake** *salt flat* Austr.
96 B2 **Carn Eighe** *mt.* U.K.
55 P2 **Carney Island** Antarctica
73 D4 **Car Nicobar** *i.* India
118 B2 **Carnot** C.A.R.
52 A2 **Carnot, Cape** Austr.
96 C2 **Carnoustie** U.K.
97 C2 **Carnsore Point** Ireland
151 E3 **Carolina** Brazil
49 L4 **Caroline Island** Kiribati
59 D2 **Caroline Islands** N. Pacific Ocean
122 A2 **Carolusberg** S. Africa
103 D2 **Carpathian Mountains** Europe
Carpaţii Meridionali *mts* Romania *see* Transylvanian Alps
51 C1 **Carpentaria, Gulf of** Austr.
105 D3 **Carpentras** France
108 B2 **Carpi** Italy
141 D3 **Carrabelle** U.S.A.
97 B3 **Carrantuohill** *mt.* Ireland
108 B2 **Carrara** Italy
97 C1 **Carrickfergus** U.K.
97 C2 **Carrickmacross** Ireland
97 B2 **Carrick-on-Shannon** Ireland
97 C2 **Carrick-on-Suir** Ireland
137 D1 **Carrington** U.S.A.
143 D3 **Carrizo Springs** U.S.A.
142 B2 **Carrizozo** U.S.A.
137 E2 **Carroll** U.S.A.
141 C2 **Carrollton** U.S.A.
129 D2 **Carrot River** Can.
135 C3 **Carson City** U.S.A.
135 C3 **Carson Sink** *l.* U.S.A.
Carstensz-top *mt.* Indon. *see* Jaya, Puncak
150 B1 **Cartagena** Col.
107 C2 **Cartagena** Spain
146 B4 **Cartago** Costa Rica
54 C2 **Carterton** N.Z.
137 E3 **Carthage** *MO* U.S.A.
143 E2 **Carthage** *TX* U.S.A.
131 E2 **Cartwright** Can.
151 F3 **Caruaru** Brazil
150 C1 **Carúpano** Venez.
52 B1 **Caryapundy Swamp** Austr.
114 B1 **Casablanca** Morocco
154 C2 **Casa Branca** Brazil
144 B1 **Casa de Janos** Mex.
142 A2 **Casa Grande** U.S.A.
108 A1 **Casale Monferrato** Italy
109 C2 **Casarano** Italy
144 B1 **Casas Grandes** Mex.
134 C2 **Cascade** U.S.A.
134 B2 **Cascade Range** *mts* Can./U.S.A.
106 B2 **Cascais** Port.
151 F3 **Cascavel** Brazil
154 B2 **Cascavel** Brazil
139 F2 **Casco Bay** U.S.A.
108 B2 **Caserta** Italy
97 C2 **Cashel** Ireland
153 B3 **Casilda** Arg.
53 D1 **Casino** Austr.
Casnewydd U.K. *see* Newport
107 C1 **Caspe** Spain
136 B2 **Casper** U.S.A.
76 A2 **Caspian Lowland** Kazakh./Rus. Fed.
81 C1 **Caspian Sea** Asia/Europe
Cassaigne Alg. *see* Sidi Ali
154 C2 **Cássia** Brazil
128 B2 **Cassiar** Can.
128 A2 **Cassiar Mountains** Can.
154 B1 **Cassilândia** Brazil
120 A2 **Cassinga** Angola
108 B2 **Cassino** Italy
96 B2 **Cassley** *r.* U.K.
151 E3 **Castanhal** Brazil
152 B3 **Castaño** *r.* Arg.
144 B2 **Castaños** Mex.
104 C3 **Casteljaloux** France
105 C3 **Castellane** France
107 C2 **Castelló de la Plana** Spain
155 C2 **Castelo** Brazil
106 B2 **Castelo Branco** Port.
104 C3 **Castelsarrasin** France
108 B3 **Castelvetrano** *Sicily* Italy
52 B3 **Casterton** Austr.
108 B2 **Castiglione della Pescaia** Italy
106 C2 **Castilla - La Mancha** *reg.* Spain
106 C1 **Castilla y León** *reg.* Spain
97 C2 **Castlebar** Ireland
96 A2 **Castlebay** U.K.
97 C1 **Castleblayney** Ireland
97 C1 **Castlederg** U.K.
96 C3 **Castle Douglas** U.K.
128 C3 **Castlegar** Can.
97 B2 **Castleisland** Ireland
52 B3 **Castlemaine** Austr.
97 C2 **Castlepollard** Ireland
97 B2 **Castlerea** Ireland
53 C2 **Castlereagh** *r.* Austr.
136 B3 **Castle Rock** U.S.A.
128 C2 **Castor** Can.
104 C3 **Castres** France
100 B1 **Castricum** Neth.

147 D3 **Castries** St Lucia
154 C2 **Castro** Brazil
153 A4 **Castro** Chile
106 B2 **Castro Verde** Port.
109 C3 **Castrovillari** Italy
150 A3 **Catacaos** Peru
155 D2 **Cataguases** Brazil
154 C1 **Catalão** Brazil
Catalonia reg. Spain see **Cataluña**
107 D1 **Cataluña** reg. Spain
152 B2 **Catamarca** Arg.
64 B2 **Catanduanes** i. Phil.
154 C2 **Catanduva** Brazil
154 B3 **Catanduvas** Brazil
109 C3 **Catania** Sicily Italy
109 C3 **Catanzaro** Italy
64 B2 **Catarman** Phil.
107 C2 **Catarroja** Spain
64 B2 **Catbalogan** Phil.
145 C3 **Catemaco** Mex.
120 A1 **Catete** Angola
Catherine, Mount mt. Egypt see
Kātrīnā, Jabal
147 D3 **Cat Island** Bahamas
130 A2 **Cat Lake** Can.
145 D2 **Catoche, Cabo** c. Mex.
139 E2 **Catskill Mountains** U.S.A.
123 D2 **Catuane** Moz.
64 B3 **Cauayan** Phil.
131 D2 **Caubvick, Mount** Can.
150 B2 **Cauca** r. Col.
151 F3 **Caucaia** Brazil
81 C1 **Caucasus** mts Asia/Europe
100 A2 **Caudry** France
109 C3 **Caulonia** Italy
120 A1 **Caungula** Angola
150 D2 **Caura** r. Venez.
131 D3 **Causapscal** Can.
90 B2 **Căuşeni** Moldova
105 D3 **Cavaillon** France
151 E4 **Cavalcante** Brazil
114 B4 **Cavally** r. Côte d'Ivoire
97 C2 **Cavan** Ireland
154 B3 **Cavernoso, Serra do** mts Brazil
151 D2 **Caviana, Ilha** i. Brazil
Cawnpore India see Kanpur
151 E3 **Caxias** Brazil
152 C4 **Caxias do Sul** Brazil
120 A1 **Caxito** Angola
151 E2 **Cayenne** Fr. Guiana
146 B3 **Cayman Islands** terr. West Indies
158 C3 **Cayman Trench** sea feature
Caribbean Sea
117 C4 **Caynabo** Somalia
120 B2 **Cazombo** Angola
Ceará Brazil see Fortaleza
Ceatharlach Ireland see Carlow
144 B2 **Ceballos** Mex.
64 B2 **Cebu** Phil.
64 B2 **Cebu** i. Phil.
108 B2 **Cecina** Italy
137 F2 **Cedar** r. U.S.A.
135 D3 **Cedar City** U.S.A.
137 E2 **Cedar Falls** U.S.A.
129 D2 **Cedar Lake** Can.
137 E2 **Cedar Rapids** U.S.A.
144 A2 **Cedros, Isla** i. Mex.
51 C3 **Ceduna** Austr.
117 C4 **Ceeldheere** Somalia
117 C3 **Ceerigaabo** Somalia
108 B3 **Cefalù** Sicily Italy
145 B2 **Celaya** Mex.
61 D2 **Celebes** i. Indon.
156 C5 **Celebes Sea** Indon./Phil.
145 C2 **Celestún** Mex.
101 E1 **Celle** Ger.
95 B3 **Celtic Sea** Ireland/U.K.
59 D3 **Cenderawasih, Teluk** b. Indon.
140 C2 **Center Point** U.S.A.
150 B2 **Central, Cordillera** mts Col.
150 B4 **Central, Cordillera** mts Peru
64 B2 **Central, Cordillera** mts Phil.
Central African Empire country
Africa see **Central African Republic**
118 C2 **Central African Republic** country
Africa
74 A2 **Central Brahui Range** mts Pak.
137 D2 **Central City** U.S.A.
138 B3 **Centralia** IL U.S.A.
134 B1 **Centralia** WA U.S.A.
74 A2 **Central Makran Range** mts Pak.
156 D5 **Central Pacific Basin** sea feature
Pacific Ocean
134 B2 **Central Point** U.S.A.
Central Provinces state India see
Madhya Pradesh
59 D3 **Central Range** mts P.N.G.
89 D3 **Central Russian Upland** hills
Rus. Fed.
83 I2 **Central Siberian Plateau** plat.
Rus. Fed.
140 C2 **Century** U.S.A.
Ceos i. Greece see Kea
111 B3 **Cephalonia** i. Greece
Ceram i. Indon. see Seram
Ceram Sea Indon. see Laut Seram
101 F3 **Čerchov** mt. Czech Rep.
152 B2 **Ceres** Arg.
154 C1 **Ceres** Brazil
122 A3 **Ceres** S. Africa
105 C3 **Céret** France
106 C1 **Cerezo de Abajo** Spain
109 C2 **Cerignola** Italy
Cerigo i. Greece see Kythira
110 C2 **Cernavodă** Romania

145 C2 **Cerralvo** Mex.
144 B2 **Cerralvo, Isla** i. Mex.
145 B2 **Cerritos** Mex.
154 C2 **Cerro Azul** Brazil
145 C2 **Cerro Azul** Mex.
150 B4 **Cerro de Pasco** Peru
105 C3 **Cervione** Corsica France
106 B1 **Cervo** Spain
108 B2 **Cesena** Italy
108 B2 **Cesenatico** Italy
88 C2 **Cēsis** Latvia
102 C2 **České Budějovice** Czech Rep.
101 F3 **Český Les** mts Czech Rep./Ger.
111 C3 **Çeşme** Turkey
53 D2 **Cessnock** Austr.
104 B2 **Cesson-Sévigné** France
104 B3 **Cestas** France
109 C2 **Cetinje** Serb. and Mont.
109 C3 **Cetraro** Italy
106 B2 **Ceuta** N. Africa
105 C3 **Cévennes** mts France
Ceylon country Asia see Sri Lanka
79 D2 **Chābahār** Iran
75 C1 **Chabyêr Caka** salt l. China
150 B3 **Chachapoyas** Peru
89 D3 **Chachersk** Belarus
63 B2 **Chachoengsao** Thai.
152 C2 **Chaco Boreal** reg. Para.
142 B1 **Chaco Mesa** plat. U.S.A.
115 D3 **Chad** country Africa
115 D3 **Chad, Lake** Africa
68 C1 **Chadaasan** Mongolia
68 C1 **Chadan** Rus. Fed.
123 C1 **Chadibe** Botswana
136 C2 **Chadron** U.S.A.
Chadyr-Lunga Moldova see
Ciadîr-Lunga
77 D2 **Chaek** Kyrg.
65 B2 **Chaerŏng** N. Korea
74 A2 **Chagai** Pak.
77 C3 **Chaghcharān** Afgh.
89 E2 **Chagoda** Rus. Fed.
56 I10 **Chagos Archipelago** is B.I.O.T.
159 E4 **Chagos-Laccadive Ridge**
sea feature Indian Ocean
159 E4 **Chagos Trench** sea feature
Indian Ocean
76 B2 **Chagyl** Turkm.
75 C2 **Chaibasa** India
63 B2 **Chainat** Thai.
63 A3 **Chaiya** Thai.
63 B2 **Chaiyaphum** Thai.
152 C3 **Chajarí** Arg.
119 D3 **Chake Chake** Tanz.
131 D2 **Chakonipau, Lake** Can.
150 B4 **Chala** Peru
74 A1 **Chalap Dalan** mts Afgh.
121 C2 **Chalāua** Moz.
131 D3 **Chaleur Bay** inlet Can.
74 B2 **Chalisgaon** India
111 C3 **Chalki** i. Greece
111 B3 **Chalkida** Greece
143 C3 **Chalk Mountains** U.S.A.
104 B2 **Challans** France
134 D2 **Challis** U.S.A.
105 C2 **Châlons-en-Champagne** France
Châlons-sur-Marne France see
Châlons-en-Champagne
105 C2 **Chalon-sur-Saône** France
101 F3 **Cham** Ger.
142 B1 **Chama** U.S.A.
121 C2 **Chama** Zambia
74 A1 **Chaman** Pak.
74 B1 **Chamba** India
74 B2 **Chambal** r. India
137 D2 **Chamberlain** U.S.A.
142 B1 **Chambers** U.S.A.
139 D3 **Chambersburg** U.S.A.
105 D2 **Chambéry** France
121 C2 **Chambeshi** Zambia
121 B2 **Chambeshi** r. Zambia
Chamdo China see Qamdo
105 D2 **Chamonix-Mont-Blanc** France
105 C2 **Champagne** reg. France
138 B2 **Champaign** U.S.A.
139 E2 **Champlain, Lake** Can./U.S.A.
145 C3 **Champotón** Mex.
Chanak Turkey see Çanakkale
152 A2 **Chañaral** Chile
Chanda India see Chandrapur
126 C2 **Chandalar** r. U.S.A.
140 C3 **Chandeleur Islands** U.S.A.
74 B1 **Chandigarh** India
131 D3 **Chandler** Can.
142 A2 **Chandler** U.S.A.
75 D2 **Chandpur** Bangl.
75 B3 **Chandrapur** India
63 B2 **Chang, Ko** i. Thai.
Chang'an China see Rong'an
121 C3 **Changane** r. Moz.
121 C2 **Changara** Moz.
65 B1 **Changbai** China
65 B1 **Changbai Shan** mts
China/N. Korea
69 E2 **Changchun** China
71 B3 **Changde** China
65 B2 **Ch'angdo** N. Korea
70 B2 **Changge** China
71 C3 **Changhua** Taiwan
65 B3 **Changhŭng** S. Korea
Chang Jiang r. China see Yangtze
Changjiang Kou r. mouth China
see Yangtze, Mouth of the

65 B1 **Changjin** N. Korea
65 B1 **Changjin-gang** r. N. Korea
Changkiang China see Zhanjiang
Changning China see Xunwu
Ch'ang-pai Shan mts
China/N. Korea see Changbai Shan
71 B3 **Changsha** China
70 C2 **Changshu** China
65 B2 **Changsŏng** S. Korea
Changteh China see Changde
71 B3 **Changting** Fujian China
66 A2 **Changting** Heilong. China
65 A1 **Changtu** China
146 B4 **Changuinola** Panama
65 B2 **Ch'angwŏn** S. Korea
65 B2 **Changyŏn** N. Korea
70 B2 **Changyuan** China
70 B2 **Changzhi** China
70 B2 **Changzhou** China
111 B3 **Chania** Greece
95 C4 **Channel Islands** English Chan.
135 C4 **Channel Islands** U.S.A.
131 E3 **Channel-Port-aux-Basques** Can.
106 B1 **Chantada** Spain
63 B2 **Chanthaburi** Thai.
104 C2 **Chantilly** France
137 D3 **Chanute** U.S.A.
82 G3 **Chany, Ozero** salt l. Rus. Fed.
70 B2 **Chaohu** China
71 B3 **Chaoyang** Guangdong China
Chaoyang China see Huinan
70 C1 **Chaoyang** Liaoning China
71 B3 **Chaozhou** China
144 B2 **Chapala, Laguna de** l. Mex.
76 B1 **Chapayev** Kazakh.
87 D3 **Chapayevsk** Rus. Fed.
152 C2 **Chapecó** Brazil
141 E1 **Chapel Hill** U.S.A.
130 B3 **Chapleau** Can.
89 E3 **Chaplygin** Rus. Fed.
91 C2 **Chaplynka** Ukr.
Chapra India see Chhapra
145 B2 **Charcas** Mex.
99 B4 **Chard** U.K.
Chardzhev Turkm. see
Turkmenabat
Chardzhou Turkm. see
Turkmenabat
104 B2 **Charente** r. France
118 B1 **Chari** r. Cameroon/Chad
77 C3 **Chārīkār** Afgh.
86 E2 **Charkayuvom** Rus. Fed.
Charkhlik China see Ruoqiang
100 B2 **Charleroi** Belgium
139 D3 **Charles, Cape** U.S.A.
139 E1 **Charlesbourg** Can.
137 E2 **Charles City** U.S.A.
138 B3 **Charleston** IL U.S.A.
137 F3 **Charleston** MO U.S.A.
141 E2 **Charleston** SC U.S.A.
138 C3 **Charleston** WV U.S.A.
135 C3 **Charleston Peak** U.S.A.
51 D2 **Charleville** Austr.
105 C2 **Charleville-Mézières** France
138 B1 **Charlevoix** U.S.A.
141 D1 **Charlotte** U.S.A.
141 D3 **Charlotte Harbor** b. U.S.A.
139 D3 **Charlottesville** U.S.A.
131 D3 **Charlottetown** Can.
52 B3 **Charlton** Austr.
130 C2 **Charlton Island** Can.
51 D2 **Charters Towers** Austr.
104 C2 **Chartres** France
128 C2 **Chase** Can.
88 C3 **Chashniki** Belarus
54 A3 **Chaslands Mistake** c. N.Z.
65 B1 **Chasŏng** N. Korea
104 B2 **Chassiron, Pointe de** pt France
104 C2 **Châteaubriant** France
104 C2 **Château-du-Loir** France
104 C2 **Châteaudun** France
104 B2 **Château-Gontier** France
104 B2 **Châteaulin** France
105 D3 **Châteauneuf-les-Martigues**
France
104 C2 **Châteauneuf-sur-Loire** France
104 C2 **Châteauroux** France
105 C2 **Château-Thierry** France
128 C2 **Chateh** Can.
100 B2 **Châtelet** Belgium
104 C2 **Châtellerault** France
138 C2 **Chatham** Can.
99 D4 **Chatham** U.K.
49 J8 **Chatham Islands** N.Z.
105 C2 **Châtillon-sur-Seine** France
141 D2 **Chattahoochee** r. U.S.A.
141 C1 **Chattanooga** U.S.A.
63 B2 **Châu Đốc** Vietnam
62 A1 **Chauk** Myanmar
105 D2 **Chaumont** France
Chau Phu Vietnam see Châu Đốc
151 E3 **Chaves** Brazil
106 B1 **Chaves** Port.
130 C2 **Chavigny, Lac** l. Can.
89 D3 **Chavusy** Belarus
89 E2 **Chayevo** Rus. Fed.
86 E3 **Chaykovskiy** Rus. Fed.
140 C2 **Cheaha Mountain** hill U.S.A.
102 C1 **Cheb** Czech Rep.
87 D3 **Cheboksary** Rus. Fed.
138 C1 **Cheboygan** U.S.A.
65 B2 **Chech'ŏn** S. Korea
140 A1 **Checotah** U.S.A.
Chefoo China see Yantai

126 B2 **Chefornak** U.S.A.
114 B2 **Chegga** Maur.
121 C2 **Chegutu** Zimbabwe
134 B1 **Chehalis** U.S.A.
65 B3 **Cheju** S. Korea
65 B3 **Cheju-do** i. S. Korea
65 B3 **Cheju-haehyŏp** sea chan. S. Korea
89 E2 **Chekhov** Rus. Fed.
Chekiang prov. China see Zhejiang
134 B1 **Chelan, Lake** U.S.A.
81 D2 **Cheleken** Turkm.
107 D2 **Chélif, Oued** r. Alg.
103 E1 **Chełm** Pol.
99 D4 **Chelmer** r. U.K.
103 D1 **Chełmno** Pol.
99 D4 **Chelmsford** U.K.
99 B4 **Cheltenham** U.K.
87 F3 **Chelyabinsk** Rus. Fed.
83 H1 **Chelyuskin** Rus. Fed.
101 F2 **Chemnitz** Ger.
Chemulpo S. Korea see Inch'ŏn
134 B2 **Chemult** U.S.A.
74 B2 **Chenab** r. India/Pak.
114 B2 **Chenachane** Alg.
134 C1 **Cheney** U.S.A.
Chengchow China see Zhengzhou
70 B1 **Chengde** China
70 A2 **Chengdu** China
Chengjiang China see Taihe
71 B4 **Chengmai** China
Chengshou China see Yingshan
Chengtu China see Chengdu
70 A2 **Chengxian** China
Chengxiang China see Wuxi
Chengxiang China see Mianning
Chengyang China see Juxian
73 C3 **Chennai** India
Chenstokhov Pol. see
Częstochowa
71 B3 **Chenzhou** China
99 B4 **Chepstow** U.K.
141 E2 **Cheraw** U.S.A.
104 B2 **Cherbourg** France
Cherchen China see Qiemo
89 E3 **Cheremisinovo** Rus. Fed.
68 C1 **Cheremkhovo** Rus. Fed.
89 E2 **Cherepovets** Rus. Fed.
91 C2 **Cherkasy** Ukr.
87 D4 **Cherkessk** Rus. Fed.
89 E3 **Chern'** Rus. Fed.
91 C1 **Chernihiv** Ukr.
90 B2 **Cherninivka** Ukr.
90 B2 **Chernivtsi** Ukr.
68 C1 **Chernogorsk** Rus. Fed.
90 B1 **Chernyakhiv** Ukr.
88 B3 **Chernyakhovsk** Rus. Fed.
89 E3 **Chernyanka** Rus. Fed.
69 D1 **Chernyshevsk** Rus. Fed.
83 I2 **Chernyshevskiy** Rus. Fed.
Chernyy Rynok Rus. Fed. see
Kochubey
137 D2 **Cherokee** U.S.A.
83 L2 **Cherskiy** Rus. Fed.
83 K2 **Cherskogo, Khrebet** mts
Rus. Fed.
91 E2 **Chertkovo** Rus. Fed.
Chervonoarmeyskoye Ukr. see
Vil'nyans'k
Chervonoarmiys'k Ukr. see
Krasnoarmiys'k
Chervonoarmiys'k Ukr. see
Radyvyliv
90 A1 **Chervonohrad** Ukr.
88 C3 **Chervyen'** Belarus
89 D3 **Cherykaw** Belarus
139 D3 **Chesapeake Bay** U.S.A.
86 D2 **Cheshskaya Guba** b. Rus. Fed.
98 B3 **Chester** U.K.
138 B3 **Chester** IL U.S.A.
141 D2 **Chester** SC U.S.A.
139 D3 **Chester** VA U.S.A.
98 C3 **Chesterfield** U.K.
137 E3 **Chesterfield** U.S.A.
129 E1 **Chesterfield Inlet** Can.
129 E1 **Chesterfield Inlet** inlet Can.
139 F1 **Chesuncook Lake** U.S.A.
108 A3 **Chetaïbi** Alg.
131 D3 **Chéticamp** Can.
145 D3 **Chetumal** Mex.
128 B2 **Chetwynd** Can.
98 B2 **Cheviot Hills** U.K.
119 D2 **Che'w Bahir** salt l. Eth.
136 C2 **Cheyenne** U.S.A.
136 C2 **Cheyenne** r. U.S.A.
136 C3 **Cheyenne Wells** U.S.A.
75 C2 **Chhapra** India
75 B2 **Chhatarpur** India
75 C2 **Chhattisgarh** state India
74 B2 **Chhindwara** India
75 C2 **Chhukha** Bhutan
62 A2 **Chiai** Taiwan
120 A2 **Chiange** Angola
62 A2 **Chiang Mai** Thai.
62 A2 **Chiang Rai** Thai.
145 C3 **Chiapa** Mex.
108 A1 **Chiavenno** Italy
69 F2 **Chiba** Japan
70 B3 **Chibi** China
Chibizovka Rus. Fed. see
Zherdevka
121 C2 **Chiboma** Moz.
130 C3 **Chibougamau** Can.
123 D1 **Chibuto** Moz.
138 B2 **Chicago** U.S.A.

128 A2 Chichagof Island U.S.A.
99 C4 Chichester U.K.
50 A2 Chichester Range mts Austr.
143 D1 Chickasha U.S.A.
106 B2 Chiclana de la Frontera Spain
150 B3 Chiclayo Peru
153 B4 Chico r. Arg.
153 B4 Chico r. Arg.
135 B3 Chico U.S.A.
139 E2 Chicopee U.S.A.
64 B2 Chico Sapocoy, Mount Phil.
131 C3 Chicoutimi Can.
131 D1 Chidley, Cape Can.
63 A3 Chieo Lan Reservoir Thai.
108 B2 Chieti Italy
145 C3 Chietla Mex.
70 B1 Chifeng China
155 D1 Chifre, Serra do mts Brazil
121 C2 Chifunde Moz.
77 D2 Chiganak Kazakh.
145 C3 Chignahuapán Mex.
121 C3 Chigubo Moz.
62 A1 Chigu Co l. China
144 B2 Chihuahua Mex.
77 C3 Chiili Kazakh.
88 C2 Chikhachevo Rus. Fed.
67 C3 Chikuma-gawa r. Japan
128 B2 Chilanko r. Can.
74 B1 Chilas Jammu and Kashmir
143 C2 Childress U.S.A.
153 A3 Chile country S. America
158 C6 Chile Basin sea feature
         S. Pacific Ocean
152 B2 Chilecito Arg.
157 G8 Chile Rise sea feature
         S. Pacific Ocean
77 D2 Chilik Kazakh.
75 C3 Chilika Lake India
121 B2 Chililabombwe Zambia
128 B2 Chilko r. Can.
128 B2 Chilko Lake Can.
153 A3 Chillán Chile
138 B2 Chillicothe IL U.S.A.
137 E3 Chillicothe MO U.S.A.
138 C3 Chillicothe OH U.S.A.
128 B3 Chilliwack Can.
153 A4 Chiloé, Isla de i. Chile
145 C3 Chilpancingo Mex.
53 C3 Chiltern Austr.
99 C4 Chiltern Hills U.K.
120 B1 Chiluage Angola
71 C3 Chilung Taiwan
119 D3 Chimala Tanz.
121 C2 Chimanimani Zimbabwe
152 B2 Chimbas Arg.
150 B3 Chimborazo mt. Ecuador
150 B3 Chimbote Peru
76 B2 Chimboy Uzbek.
       Chimishliya Moldova see Cimişlia
       Chimkent Kazakh. see Shymkent
121 C2 Chimoio Moz.
77 C3 Chimtargha, Qullai mt. Tajik.
68 C2 China country Asia
145 C2 China Mex.
150 B4 Chincha Alta Peru
128 C2 Chinchaga r. Can.
145 D3 Chinchorro, Banco sea feature Mex.
121 C2 Chinde Moz.
65 B3 Chindo S. Korea
65 B3 Chin-do i. S. Korea
68 C2 Chindu China
62 A1 Chindwin r. Myanmar
65 B3 Chinghwa N. Korea
121 B2 Chingola Zambia
120 A2 Chinguar Angola
65 B2 Chinhae S. Korea
121 C2 Chinhoyi Zimbabwe
       Chini India see Kalpa
       Chining China see Jining
74 B1 Chiniot Pak.
144 B2 Chinipas Mex.
65 B2 Chinju S. Korea
118 C2 Chinko r. C.A.R.
142 B1 Chinle U.S.A.
71 B3 Chinmen Taiwan
       Chinnamp'o N. Korea see Namp'o
67 C3 Chino Japan
135 C4 Chino U.S.A.
104 C2 Chinon France
134 E1 Chinook U.S.A.
142 A2 Chino Valley U.S.A.
77 C2 Chinoz Uzbek.
121 C2 Chinsali Zambia
108 B1 Chioggia Italy
111 C3 Chios Greece
111 C3 Chios i. Greece
121 C2 Chipata Zambia
120 A2 Chipindo Angola
       Chipinga Zimbabwe see Chipinge
121 C3 Chipinge Zimbabwe
73 B3 Chiplun India
99 B4 Chippenham U.K.
138 A2 Chippewa Falls U.S.A.
99 C4 Chipping Norton U.K.
       Chipuriro Zimbabwe see Guruve
145 D3 Chiquimula Guat.
77 C2 Chirchiq Uzbek.
121 C3 Chiredzi Zimbabwe
142 B2 Chiricahua Peak U.S.A.
146 B4 Chiriqui, Golfo de b. Panama
65 B3 Chiri-san mt. S. Korea
146 B4 Chirripo mt. Costa Rica
121 C2 Chirundu Zimbabwe
130 C2 Chisasibi Can.
137 E1 Chisholm U.S.A.

       Chisimaio Somalia see Kismaayo
90 B2 Chişinău Moldova
87 E3 Chistopol' Rus. Fed.
69 D1 Chita Rus. Fed.
120 A2 Chitado Angola
121 C2 Chitambo Zambia
120 B1 Chitato Angola
121 C1 Chitipa Malawi
121 C3 Chitobe Moz.
       Chitor India see Chittaurgarh
66 D2 Chitose Japan
73 B3 Chitradurga India
74 B1 Chitral Pak.
146 B4 Chitré Panama
75 D2 Chittagong Bangl.
74 B2 Chittaurgarh India
73 B3 Chittoor India
       Chittorgarh India see Chittaurgarh
121 C2 Chitungwiza Zimbabwe
120 B2 Chiume Angola
121 C2 Chivhu Zimbabwe
70 B2 Chizhou China
       Chkalov Rus. Fed. see Orenburg
101 F2 Chodov Czech Rep.
153 B3 Choele Choel Arg.
       Chogori Feng mt.
       China/Jammu and Kashmir see K2
48 G4 Choiseul i. Solomon Is
144 B2 Choix Mex.
102 C1 Chojna Pol.
103 D1 Chojnice Pol.
117 B3 Ch'ok'ē Mountains Eth.
       Chokue Moz. see Chókwé
83 K2 Chokurdakh Rus. Fed.
121 C3 Chókwé Moz.
104 B2 Cholet France
145 C3 Cholula Mex.
120 B2 Choma Zambia
       Chomo China see Yadong
102 C1 Chomutov Czech Rep.
83 I2 Chona r. Rus. Fed.
65 B2 Ch'ŏnan S. Korea
58 A2 Chon Buri Thai.
150 A3 Chone Ecuador
       Chong'an China see Wuyishan
65 B1 Ch'ŏngjin N. Korea
65 B2 Ch'ŏngju N. Korea
65 B2 Ch'ŏngju S. Korea see Chŏngŭp
65 B2 Chŏngp'yŏng N. Korea
70 A3 Chongqing China
70 A2 Chongqing mun. China
65 B2 Chŏngŭp S. Korea
121 B2 Chongwe Zambia
71 A3 Chongzuo China
65 B2 Chŏnju S. Korea
153 A4 Chonos, Archipiélago de los is Chile
154 B3 Chopimzinho Brazil
98 B3 Chorley U.K.
91 C2 Chornobay Ukr.
90 C1 Chornobyl' Ukr.
91 C2 Chornomors'ke Ukr.
90 B2 Chortkiv Ukr.
65 B2 Ch'ŏrwŏn S. Korea
65 B1 Ch'osan N. Korea
66 D3 Chōshi Japan
153 A3 Chos Malal Arg.
103 D1 Choszczno Pol.
134 D1 Choteau U.S.A.
114 A2 Choûm Maur.
69 D1 Choybalsan Mongolia
69 D1 Choyr Mongolia
54 B2 Christchurch N.Z.
99 C4 Christchurch U.K.
127 H2 Christian, Cape Can.
123 C2 Christiana S. Africa
       Christianshåb Greenland see
       Qasigiannguit
54 A2 Christina, Mount U.S.A.
58 B3 Christmas Island terr.
       Indian Ocean
111 C3 Chrysi i. Greece
111 B2 Chrysoupoli Greece
       Chu Kazakh. see Shu
       Chubarovka Ukr. see Polohy
153 B4 Chubut r. Arg.
89 F3 Chuchkovo Rus. Fed.
90 B1 Chudniv Ukr.
89 D2 Chudovo Rus. Fed.
126 C2 Chugach Mountains U.S.A.
67 B4 Chūgoku-sanchi mts Japan
       Chuguchak China see Tacheng
66 B2 Chuguyevka Rus. Fed.
91 D2 Chuhuyiv Ukr.
       Chukchi Peninsula Rus. Fed. see
       Chukotskiy Poluostrov
160 J3 Chukchi Sea sea Rus. Fed./U.S.A.
89 F2 Chukhloma Rus. Fed.
83 N2 Chukotskiy Poluostrov pen.
       Rus. Fed.
       Chulaktau Kazakh. see Karatau
135 C4 Chula Vista U.S.A.
82 G3 Chulym Rus. Fed.
152 B2 Chumbicha Arg.
83 K3 Chumikan Rus. Fed.
63 A2 Chumphon Thai.
65 B2 Ch'unch'ŏn S. Korea
       Chungking China see Chongqing
       Ch'ungmu S. Korea see T'ongyŏng
71 C3 Chungyang Shanmo mts Taiwan
83 H2 Chunya r. Rus. Fed.
119 D3 Chunya Tanz.
150 B4 Chuquibamba Peru
152 B2 Chuquicamata Chile

105 D2 Chur Switz.
82 A1 Churachandpur India
83 J2 Churapcha Rus. Fed.
129 E2 Churchill Can.
131 D2 Churchill r. Man. Can.
131 D2 Churchill r. Nfld and Lab. Can.
129 E2 Churchill, Cape Can.
131 D2 Churchill Falls Can.
129 D2 Churchill Lake Can.
74 B2 Churu India
142 B1 Chuska Mountains U.S.A.
86 E3 Chusovoy Rus. Fed.
131 C3 Chute-des-Passes Can.
48 G3 Chuuk is Micronesia
62 B1 Chuxiong China
63 B2 Chu Yang Sin mt. Vietnam
91 C2 Chyhyryn Ukr.
       Chymyshliya Moldova see Cimişlia
       Ciadâr-Lunga Moldova see
       Ciadîr-Lunga
90 B2 Ciadîr-Lunga Moldova
60 B2 Ciamis Indon.
60 B2 Cianjur Indon.
154 B2 Cianorte Brazil
142 A2 Cibuta, Sierra mt. Mex.
103 E1 Ciechanów Pol.
146 C2 Ciego de Ávila Cuba
147 C3 Ciénaga Col.
146 B2 Cienfuegos Cuba
107 C2 Cieza Spain
106 C2 Cigüela r. Spain
80 B2 Cihanbeyli Turkey
144 B3 Cihuatlán Mex.
106 C2 Cijara, Embalse de resr Spain
109 C2 Çikes, Maja e mt. Albania
60 B2 Cilacap Indon.
       Cill Airne Ireland see Killarney
       Cill Chainnigh Ireland see Kilkenny
143 C1 Cimarron r. U.S.A.
90 B2 Cimişlia Moldova
108 B2 Cimone, Monte mt. Italy
       Cîmpina Romania see Câmpina
       Cîmpulung Romania see
       Câmpulung
60 B2 Cina, Tanjung c. Indon.
138 C3 Cincinnati U.S.A.
       Cinco de Outubro Angola see
       Xá-Muteba
111 C3 Çine Turkey
100 B2 Ciney Belgium
134 C2 Cinnabar Mountain U.S.A.
145 C3 Cintalapa Mex.
       Ciping China see Jinggangshan
153 B3 Cipolletti Arg.
126 C2 Circle AK U.S.A.
136 D1 Circle MT U.S.A.
60 B2 Cirebon Indon.
99 C4 Cirencester U.K.
108 A1 Ciriè Italy
109 C3 Cirò Marina Italy
110 B1 Cisnădie Romania
109 C2 Čitluk Bos.-Herz.
122 A3 Citrusdal S. Africa
135 B3 Citrus Heights U.S.A.
110 C1 Ciucaş, Vârful mt. Romania
145 B2 Ciudad Acuña Mex.
145 B3 Ciudad Altamirano Mex.
150 C2 Ciudad Bolívar Venez.
147 C4 Ciudad Bolivia Venez.
144 B2 Ciudad Camargo Mex.
144 A2 Ciudad Constitución Mex.
145 C3 Ciudad Cuauhtémoc Mex.
154 C3 Ciudad del Carmen Mex.
154 C3 Ciudad del Este Para.
144 B2 Ciudad Delicias Mex.
145 C2 Ciudad de Valles Mex.
150 C2 Ciudad Guayana Venez.
142 B3 Ciudad Guerrero Mex.
144 B3 Ciudad Guzmán Mex.
145 C3 Ciudad Hidalgo Mex.
145 C3 Ciudad Ixtepec Mex.
144 B1 Ciudad Juárez Mex.
145 C2 Ciudad Madero Mex.
145 C2 Ciudad Mante Mex.
145 C2 Ciudad Mier Mex.
144 B2 Ciudad Obregón Mex.
106 C2 Ciudad Real Spain
145 C2 Ciudad Río Bravo Mex.
106 B1 Ciudad Rodrigo Spain
       Ciudad Trujillo Dom. Rep. see
       Santo Domingo
145 C2 Ciudad Victoria Mex.
107 D1 Ciutadella de Menorca Spain
108 B1 Cividale del Friuli Italy
108 B2 Civitanova Marche Italy
108 B2 Civitavecchia Italy
104 C2 Civray France
111 C3 Çivril Turkey
70 C2 Cixi China
99 D4 Clacton-on-Sea U.K.
128 C2 Claire, Lake Can.
105 C2 Clamecy France
140 C2 Clanton U.S.A.
122 A3 Clanwilliam S. Africa
97 C2 Clara Ireland
52 A2 Clare Austr.
138 C2 Clare U.S.A.
97 A2 Clare Island Ireland
139 E2 Claremont U.S.A.
97 B2 Claremorris Ireland
54 B2 Clarence N.Z.
55 B3 Clarence Island Antarctica
131 E3 Clarenville Can.
128 C2 Claresholm Can.

137 D2 Clarinda U.S.A.
144 A3 Clarión, Isla i. Mex.
123 C3 Clarkebury S. Africa
134 C1 Clark Fork r. U.S.A.
141 D2 Clark Hill Reservoir U.S.A.
138 C3 Clarksburg U.S.A.
140 B2 Clarksdale U.S.A.
134 C1 Clarkston U.S.A.
140 B1 Clarksville AR U.S.A.
140 C1 Clarksville TN U.S.A.
154 B1 Claro r. Brazil
143 C1 Claude U.S.A.
143 C1 Clayton U.S.A.
97 B3 Clear, Cape Ireland
126 C3 Cleare, Cape U.S.A.
137 E2 Clear Lake U.S.A.
135 B3 Clear Lake l. U.S.A.
128 C2 Clearwater r. Can.
129 C2 Clearwater r. Can.
141 D3 Clearwater U.S.A.
134 C1 Clearwater r. U.S.A.
143 D2 Cleburne U.S.A.
101 E1 Clenze Ger.
51 D2 Clermont Austr.
105 C2 Clermont-Ferrand France
100 C2 Clervaux Lux.
52 A2 Cleve Austr.
140 B2 Cleveland MS U.S.A.
138 C2 Cleveland OH U.S.A.
141 D1 Cleveland TN U.S.A.
134 D1 Cleveland, Mount U.S.A.
154 B3 Clevelândia Brazil
97 B2 Clew Bay Ireland
141 D3 Clewiston U.S.A.
97 A2 Clifden Ireland
53 D1 Clifton Austr.
142 B2 Clifton U.S.A.
142 B1 Clines Corners U.S.A.
128 B2 Clinton Can.
137 E2 Clinton IA U.S.A.
137 E3 Clinton MO U.S.A.
143 D1 Clinton OK U.S.A.
125 H8 Clipperton, Île terr.
       N. Pacific Ocean
96 A2 Clisham hill U.K.
98 B3 Clitheroe U.K.
97 B3 Clonakilty Ireland
51 D2 Cloncurry Austr.
97 C1 Clones Ireland
97 C2 Clonmel Ireland
101 D1 Cloppenburg Ger.
137 E1 Cloquet U.S.A.
136 B2 Cloud Peak U.S.A.
135 C3 Clovis CA U.S.A.
143 C2 Clovis NM U.S.A.
       Cluain Meala Ireland see Clonmel
129 D2 Cluff Lake Mine Can.
110 B1 Cluj-Napoca Romania
51 C2 Cluny Austr.
105 D2 Cluses France
54 A3 Clutha r. N.Z.
96 B3 Clyde r. U.K.
96 B3 Clyde, Firth of est. U.K.
96 B3 Clydebank U.K.
127 H2 Clyde River Can.
144 B3 Coalcomán Mex.
128 C3 Coaldale Can.
135 C3 Coaldale Can.
128 B2 Coal River Can.
150 B3 Coari Brazil
150 C3 Coari r. Brazil
141 C2 Coastal Plain U.S.A.
128 B2 Coast Mountains Can.
134 B2 Coast Ranges mts U.S.A.
96 B3 Coatbridge U.K.
129 F1 Coats Island Can.
55 C2 Coats Land reg. Antarctica
145 C3 Coatzacoalcos Mex.
146 A3 Cobán Guat.
53 C2 Cobar Austr.
97 B3 Cóbh Ireland
152 B1 Cobija Bol.
       Coblenz Ger. see Koblenz
130 C3 Cobourg Can.
50 C1 Cobourg Peninsula Austr.
53 C3 Cobram Austr.
101 E2 Coburg Ger.
152 B1 Cochabamba Bol.
100 C2 Cochem Ger.
73 B4 Cochin India
128 C2 Cochrane Alta Can.
130 B3 Cochrane Ont. Can.
153 A4 Cochrane Chile
52 A2 Cockaleechie Austr.
52 B2 Cockburn Austr.
       Cockburn Town
       Turks and Caicos Is see Grand Turk
98 B2 Cockermouth U.K.
50 B3 Cocklebiddy Austr.
122 B3 Cockscomb mt. S. Africa
146 B3 Coco r. Hond./Nic.
125 J9 Coco, Isla de i. N. Pacific Ocean
159 F4 Cocos Basin sea feature
       Indian Ocean
58 A3 Cocos Islands terr. Indian Ocean
144 B2 Cocula Mex.
150 B2 Cocuy, Sierra Nevada del mt. Col.
139 E2 Cod, Cape U.S.A.
150 C3 Codajás Brazil
108 B2 Codigoro Italy
131 D2 Cod Island Can.
151 E2 Codó Brazil
136 B2 Cody U.S.A.
51 D1 Coen Austr.
100 C2 Coesfeld Ger.

113 I6 **Coëtivy** *i.* Seychelles
134 C1 **Coeur d'Alene** U.S.A.
100 C1 **Coevorden** Neth.
123 C3 **Coffee Bay** S. Africa
137 D3 **Coffeyville** U.S.A.
52 A2 **Coffin Bay** Austr.
53 D2 **Coffs Harbour** Austr.
123 C3 **Cofimvaba** S. Africa
104 B2 **Cognac** France
118 A2 **Cogo** Equat. Guinea
52 B3 **Cohuna** Austr.
146 B4 **Coiba, Isla de** *i.* Panama
153 A4 **Coihaique** Chile
73 B3 **Coimbatore** India
106 B1 **Coimbra** Port.
152 B1 **Coipasa, Salar de** *salt flat* Bol.
52 B3 **Colac** Austr.
155 D1 **Colatina** Brazil
136 C3 **Colby** U.S.A.
99 D4 **Colchester** U.K.
129 C2 **Cold Lake** Can.
96 C3 **Coldstream** U.K.
53 C2 **Coleambally** Austr.
143 D2 **Coleman** U.S.A.
52 B3 **Coleraine** Austr.
97 C1 **Coleraine** U.K.
123 C3 **Colesberg** S. Africa
153 A3 **Colico** Chile
144 B3 **Colima** Mex.
144 B3 **Colima, Nevado de** *vol.* Mex.
96 A2 **Coll** *i.* U.K.
53 C1 **Collarenebri** Austr.
143 D2 **College Station** U.S.A.
53 C1 **Collerina** Austr.
50 A3 **Collie** Austr.
50 B1 **Collier Bay** Austr.
138 C2 **Collingwood** Can.
54 B2 **Collingwood** N.Z.
126 F2 **Collinson Peninsula** Can.
101 F2 **Collmberg** *hill* Ger.
108 A3 **Collo** Alg.
97 B1 **Collooney** Ireland
105 D2 **Colmar** France
98 B3 **Colne** U.K.
100 C2 **Cologne** Ger.
Colomb-Béchar Alg. *see* Béchar
154 C2 **Colômbia** Brazil
150 B2 **Colombia** *country* S. America
73 B4 **Colombo** Sri Lanka
104 C3 **Colomiers** France
152 C3 **Colón** Arg.
146 C4 **Colón** Panama
59 D2 **Colonia** Micronesia
153 B4 **Colonia Las Heras** Arg.
109 C3 **Colonna, Capo** *c.* Italy
96 A2 **Colonsay** *i.* U.K.
153 B3 **Colorado** *r.* Arg.
142 A2 **Colorado** *r.* Mex./U.S.A.
143 D3 **Colorado** *r.* U.S.A.
136 B3 **Colorado** *state* U.S.A.
135 C4 **Colorado Desert** U.S.A.
135 E3 **Colorado Plateau** U.S.A.
136 C3 **Colorado Springs** U.S.A.
144 B2 **Colotlán** Mex.
152 B1 **Colquiri** Bol.
136 B1 **Colstrip** U.S.A.
138 B3 **Columbia** *KY* U.S.A.
139 D3 **Columbia** *MD* U.S.A.
137 E3 **Columbia** *MO* U.S.A.
141 D2 **Columbia** *SC* U.S.A.
140 C1 **Columbia** *TN* U.S.A.
134 B1 **Columbia** *r.* U.S.A.
128 C2 **Columbia, Mount** Can.
134 D1 **Columbia Falls** U.S.A.
128 B2 **Columbia Mountains** Can.
134 C1 **Columbia Plateau** U.S.A.
141 D2 **Columbus** *GA* U.S.A.
138 B3 **Columbus** *IN* U.S.A.
140 C2 **Columbus** *MS* U.S.A.
134 E1 **Columbus** *MT* U.S.A.
137 D2 **Columbus** *NE* U.S.A.
142 B2 **Columbus** *NM* U.S.A.
138 C3 **Columbus** *OH* U.S.A.
143 D3 **Columbus** *TX* U.S.A.
134 C1 **Colville** U.S.A.
126 B2 **Colville** *r.* U.S.A.
126 D2 **Colville Lake** Can.
98 B3 **Colwyn Bay** U.K.
108 B2 **Comacchio** Italy
145 C3 **Comalcalco** Mex.
110 C1 **Comăneşti** Romania
130 C2 **Comencho, Lac** *l.* Can.
97 C2 **Comeragh Mountains** *hills* Ireland
143 D2 **Comfort** U.S.A.
75 D2 **Comilla** Bangl.
108 A2 **Comino, Capo** *c.* Sardinia Italy
145 C3 **Comitán de Domínguez** Mex.
105 C2 **Commentry** France
143 D2 **Commerce** U.S.A.
127 G2 **Committee Bay** Can.
108 A1 **Como** Italy
Como, Lago di Italy *see*
Como, Lake
108 A1 **Como, Lake** *l.* Italy
153 B4 **Comodoro Rivadavia** Arg.
145 B2 **Comonfort** Mex.
121 D2 **Comoros** *country* Africa
128 B3 **Comox** Can.
105 C2 **Compiègne** France
144 B2 **Compostela** Mex.
90 B2 **Comrat** Moldova
114 A4 **Conakry** Guinea
104 B2 **Concarneau** France
155 E1 **Conceição da Barra** Brazil
151 E3 **Conceição do Araguaia** Brazil

155 D1 **Conceição do Mato Dentro** Brazil
152 B2 **Concepción** Arg.
153 A3 **Concepción** Chile
144 B2 **Concepción** Mex.
135 B4 **Conception, Point** U.S.A.
154 C2 **Conchas** Brazil
142 C1 **Conchas Lake** U.S.A.
144 B2 **Conchos** *r.* Mex.
145 C2 **Conchos** *r.* Mex.
135 B3 **Concord** *CA* U.S.A.
139 E2 **Concord** *NH* U.S.A.
152 C3 **Concordia** Arg.
122 A2 **Concordia** S. Africa
137 D3 **Concordia** U.S.A.
53 C2 **Condobolin** Austr.
104 C3 **Condom** France
134 B1 **Condon** U.S.A.
108 B1 **Conegliano** Italy
51 E1 **Conflict Group** *is* P.N.G.
104 C2 **Confolens** France
135 D3 **Confusion Range** *mts* U.S.A.
75 C2 **Congdü** China
98 B3 **Congleton** U.K.
118 B3 **Congo** *country* Africa
118 B3 **Congo** *r.* Congo/Dem. Rep. Congo
118 C3 **Congo, Democratic Republic of the** *country* Africa
118 C3 **Congo Basin** Dem. Rep. Congo
Congo (Brazzaville) *country* Africa *see* Congo
Congo Free State *country* Africa *see* Congo, Democratic Republic of Congo (Kinshasa) *country* Africa *see* Congo, Democratic Republic of
129 C2 **Conklin** Can.
97 C1 **Conn, Lough** *l.* Ireland
97 B2 **Connaught** *reg.* Ireland
139 E2 **Connecticut** *r.* U.S.A.
139 E2 **Connecticut** *state* U.S.A.
96 B2 **Connel** U.K.
97 B2 **Connemara** *reg.* Ireland
134 D1 **Conrad** U.S.A.
159 D7 **Conrad Rise** *sea feature* Southern Ocean
143 D2 **Conroe** U.S.A.
155 D2 **Conselheiro Lafaiete** Brazil
155 D1 **Conselheiro Pena** Brazil
100 B3 **Consenvoye** France
98 C2 **Consett** U.K.
63 B3 **Côn Son** *i.* Vietnam
Constance Ger. *see* Konstanz
105 D2 **Constance, Lake** Ger./Switz.
110 C2 **Constanţa** Romania
106 B2 **Constantina** Spain
115 C1 **Constantine** Alg.
134 D2 **Contact** U.S.A.
155 D2 **Contagalo** Brazil
150 B3 **Contamana** Peru
153 A5 **Contreras, Isla** *i.* Chile
126 F2 **Contwoyto Lake** Can.
140 B1 **Conway** *AR* U.S.A.
139 E2 **Conway** *NH* U.S.A.
51 C2 **Coober Pedy** Austr.
Cooch Behar India *see* Koch Bihar
Cook, Mount *mt.* N.Z. *see* Aoraki
141 C1 **Cookeville** U.S.A.
126 B2 **Cook Inlet** *sea chan.* U.S.A.
49 K5 **Cook Islands** *terr.* S. Pacific Ocean
131 E2 **Cook's Harbour** Can.
97 C1 **Cookstown** U.K.
54 B2 **Cook Strait** N.Z.
51 D1 **Cooktown** Austr.
53 C2 **Coolabah** Austr.
53 C2 **Coolamon** Austr.
53 D1 **Coolangatta** Austr.
50 B3 **Coolgardie** Austr.
53 C3 **Cooma** Austr.
52 B2 **Coombah** Austr.
53 C2 **Coonabarabran** Austr.
52 A3 **Coonalpyn** Austr.
53 C2 **Coonamble** Austr.
53 C1 **Coongoola** Austr.
137 E1 **Coon Rapids** U.S.A.
52 A1 **Cooper Creek** *watercourse* Austr.
141 E3 **Cooper's Town** Bahamas
134 B2 **Coos Bay** U.S.A.
53 C2 **Cootamundra** Austr.
97 C1 **Cootehill** Ireland
145 C3 **Copainalá** Mex.
145 C3 **Copala** Mex.
93 F4 **Copenhagen** Denmark
109 C2 **Copertino** Italy
53 D1 **Copeton Reservoir** Austr.
152 A2 **Copiapó** Chile
143 D2 **Copperas Cove** U.S.A.
138 B1 **Copper Harbor** U.S.A.
Coppermine Can. *see* Kugluktuk
126 E2 **Coppermine** *r.* Can.
122 B2 **Copperton** S. Africa
Coquilhatville Dem. Rep. Congo *see* Mbandaka
152 A2 **Coquimbo** Chile
152 A2 **Coquimbo, Bahía de** *b.* Chile
110 B2 **Corabia** Romania
155 D1 **Coração de Jesus** Brazil
150 B4 **Coracora** Peru
53 D1 **Coraki** Austr.
50 A2 **Coral Bay** Austr.
127 G2 **Coral Harbour** Can.
51 E1 **Coral Sea** S. Pacific Ocean
48 G5 **Coral Sea Islands Territory** *terr.* Austr.
137 E2 **Coralville** U.S.A.
52 B3 **Corangamite, Lake** Austr.

99 C3 **Corby** U.K.
Corcaigh Ireland *see* Cork
135 C2 **Corcoran** U.S.A.
153 A4 **Corcovado, Golfo de** *sea chan.* Chile
141 D2 **Cordele** U.S.A.
64 B2 **Cordilleras Range** *mts* Phil.
155 D1 **Cordisburgo** Brazil
152 B3 **Córdoba** Arg.
145 C3 **Córdoba** Mex.
106 C2 **Córdoba** Spain
153 B3 **Córdoba, Sierras de** *mts* Arg.
126 C2 **Cordova** U.S.A.
51 D2 **Corfield** Austr.
111 A3 **Corfu** *i.* Greece
154 B1 **Corguinho** Brazil
106 B2 **Coria** Spain
106 B2 **Coria del Río** Spain
53 D2 **Coricudgy** *mt.* Austr.
111 B3 **Corinth** Greece
140 C2 **Corinth** U.S.A.
Corinth, Gulf of *sea chan.* Greece *see* Gulf of Corinth
155 D1 **Corinto** Brazil
97 B3 **Cork** Ireland
111 C2 **Çorlu** Turkey
154 B2 **Cornélio Procópio** Brazil
131 E3 **Corner Brook** Can.
53 C3 **Corner Inlet** *b.* Austr.
135 B3 **Corning** *CA* U.S.A.
139 D2 **Corning** *NY* U.S.A.
Corn Islands *is* Nic. *see* Maíz, Islas del
108 B2 **Corno, Monte** *mt.* Italy
130 C3 **Cornwall** Can.
126 F1 **Cornwallis Island** Can.
150 C1 **Coro** Venez.
155 D1 **Coroaci** Brazil
154 C1 **Coromandel** Brazil
73 C4 **Coromandel Coast** India
54 C1 **Coromandel Peninsula** N.Z.
64 B2 **Coron** Phil.
129 C2 **Coronation** Can.
126 E2 **Coronation Gulf** Can.
55 B3 **Coronation Island** S. Atlantic Ocean
155 D1 **Coronel Fabriciano** Brazil
152 C2 **Coronel Oviedo** Para.
154 B1 **Coronel Ponce** Brazil
153 B3 **Coronel Pringles** Arg.
154 A2 **Coronel Sapucaia** Brazil
153 B3 **Coronel Suárez** Arg.
109 D2 **Çorovodë** Albania
145 D3 **Corozal** Belize
143 D3 **Corpus Christi** U.S.A.
152 B1 **Corque** Bol.
151 E4 **Corrente** Brazil
154 B1 **Correntes** Brazil
151 E4 **Correntina** Brazil
97 B2 **Corrib, Lough** *l.* Ireland
152 C2 **Corrientes** Arg.
153 C3 **Corrientes, Cabo** *c.* Arg.
144 B2 **Corrientes, Cabo** *c.* Mex.
143 E2 **Corrigan** U.S.A.
53 C3 **Corryong** Austr.
Corse *i.* France *see* Corsica
105 D3 **Corse, Cap** *c.* Corsica France
105 D3 **Corsica** *i.* France
143 D2 **Corsicana** U.S.A.
105 D3 **Corte** Corsica France
106 B2 **Cortegana** Spain
136 B3 **Cortez** U.S.A.
108 B1 **Cortina d'Ampezzo** Italy
139 D2 **Cortland** U.S.A.
108 B2 **Cortona** Italy
106 B2 **Coruche** Port.
Çoruh Turkey *see* Artvin
80 B1 **Çorum** Turkey
151 D4 **Corumbá** Brazil
154 C1 **Corumbá** *r.* Brazil
154 C1 **Corumbá de Goiás** Brazil
Corunna Spain *see* A Coruña
134 B2 **Corvallis** U.S.A.
99 B3 **Corwen** U.K.
Cos *i.* Greece *see* Kos
144 B2 **Cosalá** Mex.
145 C3 **Cosamaloapan** Mex.
109 C3 **Cosenza** Italy
105 C2 **Cosne-Cours-sur-Loire** France
152 B3 **Cosquín** Arg.
107 C2 **Costa Blanca** *coastal area* Spain
107 D1 **Costa Brava** *coastal area* Spain
106 B2 **Costa de la Luz** *coastal area* Spain
107 C2 **Costa del Azahar** *coastal area* Spain
106 C2 **Costa del Sol** *coastal area* Spain
146 B3 **Costa de Mosquitos** *coastal area* Nic.
107 D1 **Costa Dorada** *coastal area* Spain
150 C4 **Costa Marques** Brazil
154 B1 **Costa Rica** Brazil
146 B3 **Costa Rica** *country* Central America
144 B2 **Costa Rica** Mex.
Costermansville Dem. Rep. Congo *see* Bukavu
110 B2 **Costeşti** Romania
64 B3 **Cotabato** Phil.
137 D1 **Coteau des Prairies** *slope* U.S.A.
136 C1 **Coteau du Missouri** *slope* U.S.A.
147 C3 **Coteaux** Haiti
105 D3 **Côte d'Azur** *coastal area* France
114 B4 **Côte d'Ivoire** *country* Africa
Côte Française de Somalis *country* Africa *see* Djibouti

105 C2 **Côtes de Meuse** *ridge* France
150 B3 **Cotopaxi, Volcán** *vol.* Ecuador
99 B4 **Cotswold Hills** U.K.
134 B2 **Cottage Grove** U.S.A.
102 C1 **Cottbus** Ger.
105 D3 **Cottian Alps** *mts* France/Italy
104 B2 **Coubre, Pointe de la** *pt* France
52 A3 **Couëdic, Cape de** Austr.
105 C2 **Coulommiers** France
137 D2 **Council Bluffs** U.S.A.
88 B2 **Courland Lagoon** *b.* Lith./Rus. Fed.
100 A3 **Courmelles** France
128 B3 **Courtenay** Can.
104 B2 **Coutances** France
104 B2 **Coutras** France
100 B2 **Couvin** Belgium
99 C3 **Coventry** U.K.
106 B1 **Covilhã** Port.
141 D2 **Covington** *GA* U.S.A.
138 C3 **Covington** *KY* U.S.A.
138 C3 **Covington** *VA* U.S.A.
96 C2 **Cowan, Lake** *salt flat* Austr.
96 C2 **Cowdenbeath** U.K.
52 A2 **Cowell** Austr.
53 C3 **Cowes** Austr.
134 B1 **Cowlitz** *r.* U.S.A.
53 C2 **Cowra** Austr.
154 B1 **Coxim** Brazil
154 B1 **Coxim** *r.* Brazil
75 D2 **Cox's Bazar** Bangl.
145 B3 **Coyuca de Benitez** Mex.
145 D2 **Cozumel** Mex.
145 D2 **Cozumel, Isla de** *i.* Mex.
52 A2 **Cradock** Austr.
123 C3 **Cradock** S. Africa
136 B2 **Craig** U.S.A.
102 C2 **Crailsheim** Ger.
110 B2 **Craiova** Romania
129 D2 **Cranberry Portage** Can.
53 C3 **Cranbourne** Austr.
128 C3 **Cranbrook** Can.
151 E3 **Crateús** Brazil
151 F3 **Crato** Brazil
154 B1 **Cravinhos** Brazil
136 C2 **Crawford** U.S.A.
138 B2 **Crawfordsville** U.S.A.
99 C4 **Crawley** U.K.
134 D1 **Crazy Mountains** U.S.A.
129 C2 **Cree** *r.* Can.
144 B2 **Creel** Mex.
129 D2 **Cree Lake** Can.
129 D2 **Creighton** Can.
104 C2 **Creil** France
100 B1 **Creil** Neth.
108 A1 **Crema** Italy
108 B1 **Cremona** Italy
108 B2 **Cres** *i.* Croatia
134 B2 **Crescent City** U.S.A.
53 D2 **Crescent Head** Austr.
135 E3 **Crescent Junction** U.S.A.
128 C3 **Creston** Can.
137 E2 **Creston** U.S.A.
140 C2 **Crestview** U.S.A.
111 B3 **Crete** *i.* Greece
107 D1 **Creus, Cap de** *c.* Spain
107 C2 **Crevillente** Spain
98 B3 **Crewe** U.K.
96 B2 **Crianlarich** U.K.
152 D2 **Criciúma** Brazil
96 C2 **Crieff** U.K.
108 B1 **Crikvenica** Croatia
91 C2 **Crimea** *pen.* Ukr.
101 F2 **Crimmitschau** Ger.
96 B2 **Crinan** U.K.
118 B2 **Cristal, Monts de** *mts* Equat. Guinea/Gabon
154 C1 **Cristalina** Brazil
110 B1 **Crişul Alb** *r.* Romania
101 E1 **Crivitz** Ger.
109 C2 **Crna Gora** *aut. rep.* Serb. and Mont.
109 C1 **Črnomelj** Slovenia
97 B2 **Croagh Patrick** *hill* Ireland
109 C1 **Croatia** *country* Europe
61 C1 **Crocker, Banjaran** *mts* Malaysia
143 D2 **Crockett** U.S.A.
59 C3 **Croker Island** Austr.
96 B2 **Cromarty** U.K.
99 D3 **Cromer** U.K.
54 A3 **Cromwell** N.Z.
147 C2 **Crooked Island** Bahamas
137 D1 **Crookston** U.S.A.
53 C2 **Crookwell** Austr.
53 D1 **Croppa Creek** Austr.
136 C1 **Crosby** U.S.A.
141 D3 **Cross City** U.S.A.
140 B2 **Crossett** U.S.A.
98 B2 **Cross Fell** *hill* U.K.
129 E2 **Cross Lake** Can.
141 C1 **Crossville** U.S.A.
109 C3 **Crotone** Italy
134 E1 **Crow Agency** U.S.A.
99 D4 **Crowborough** U.K.
140 B2 **Crowley** U.S.A.
53 C1 **Crows Nest** Austr.
128 C3 **Crowsnest Pass** Can.
159 D7 **Crozet, Îles** *is* Indian Ocean
146 C3 **Cruz, Cabo** *c.* Cuba
152 C2 **Cruz Alta** Brazil
152 B3 **Cruz del Eje** Arg.
155 D2 **Cruzeiro** Brazil
150 B3 **Cruzeiro do Sul** Brazil
52 A2 **Crystal Brook** Austr.
143 D3 **Crystal City** U.S.A.
138 B1 **Crystal Falls** U.S.A.
140 B2 **Crystal Springs** U.S.A.

103 E2 Csongrád Hungary
103 D2 Csorna Hungary
121 C2 Cuamba Moz.
120 B2 Cuando r. Angola/Zambia
120 A2 Cuangar Angola
118 B3 Cuango r. Angola/Dem. Rep. Congo
120 A1 Cuanza r. Angola
144 A2 Cuatro Ciénegas Mex.
144 B2 Cuauhtémoc Mex.
145 C3 Cuautla Mex.
146 B2 Cuba country West Indies
120 A2 Cubal Angola
120 B2 Cubango r. Angola/Namibia
150 B2 Cúcuta Col.
73 B3 Cuddalore India
73 B3 Cuddapah India
50 A2 Cue Austr.
106 C1 Cuéllar Spain
120 A2 Cuemba Angola
150 B3 Cuenca Ecuador
107 C1 Cuenca Spain
107 C1 Cuenca, Serranía de mts Spain
145 C3 Cuernavaca Mex.
143 D3 Cuero U.S.A.
104 C3 Cugnaux France
151 D4 Cuiabá Brazil
151 D4 Cuiabá r. Brazil
96 A2 Cuillin Sound sea chan. U.K.
120 A1 Cuilo Angola
120 B2 Cuito r. Angola
120 A2 Cuito Cuanavale Angola
60 B1 Cukai Malaysia
64 B2 Culasi Phil.
53 C3 Culcairn Austr.
100 B2 Culemborg Neth.
53 C1 Culgoa Austr.
144 B2 Culiacán Mex.
64 A2 Culion i. Phil.
107 C2 Cullera Spain
140 C2 Cullman U.S.A.
97 C1 Cullybackey U.K.
139 D3 Culpeper U.S.A.
151 D4 Culuene r. Brazil
54 B2 Culverden N.Z.
150 C1 Cumaná Venez.
139 D3 Cumberland U.S.A.
138 B3 Cumberland r. U.S.A.
141 D2 Cumberland Island U.S.A.
129 D2 Cumberland Lake Can.
127 H2 Cumberland Peninsula Can.
140 C3 Cumberland Plateau U.S.A.
127 H2 Cumberland Sound sea chan. Can.
96 C3 Cumbernauld U.K.
135 B3 Cummings U.S.A.
96 B3 Cumnock U.K.
144 B1 Cumpas Mex.
145 C3 Cunduacán Mex.
120 A2 Cunene r. Angola/Namibia
108 A2 Cuneo Italy
53 C1 Cunnamulla Austr.
108 A1 Cuorgnè Italy
96 C2 Cupar U.K.
110 B2 Ćuprija Serb. and Mont.
147 D3 Curaçao i. Neth. Antilles
150 B3 Curaray r. Ecuador
153 A3 Curicó Chile
154 C3 Curitiba Brazil
52 A2 Curnamona Austr.
135 C3 Currant U.S.A.
51 D3 Currie Austr.
135 D2 Currie U.S.A.
51 E2 Curtis Island Austr.
151 D3 Curuá r. Brazil
60 B2 Curup Indon.
151 E3 Curvelo Brazil
155 D1 Curwood U.S.A.
150 B4 Cusco Peru
97 C1 Cushendun U.K.
143 D1 Cushing U.S.A.
136 C2 Custer U.S.A.
134 D1 Cut Bank U.S.A.
140 B3 Cut Off U.S.A.
75 C2 Cuttack India
120 A2 Cuvelai Angola
101 D1 Cuxhaven Ger.
64 B2 Cuyo Islands Phil.
　　 Cuzco Peru see Cusco
99 B4 Cwmbrân U.K.
119 C3 Cyangugu Rwanda
111 B3 Cyclades is Greece
129 C3 Cypress Hills Can.
80 B2 Cyprus country Asia
80 B2 Cyprus i. Asia
102 C2 Czech Republic country Europe
103 D1 Czersk Pol.
103 D1 Częstochowa Pol.

D

　　 Đa, Sông r. Vietnam see Black River
69 D2 Daban China
103 D2 Dabas Hungary
114 A3 Dabola Guinea
103 D1 Dąbrowa Górnicza Pol.
110 B2 Dăbuleni Romania
　　 Dacca Bangl. see Dhaka
102 C2 Dachau Ger.
　　 Dachuan China see Dazhou
141 D3 Dade City U.S.A.
　　 Dadong China see Donggang
　　 Dadra India see Achalpur
74 B2 Dadra and Nagar Haveli
　　 union terr. India

74 A2 Dadu Pak.
　　 Daegu S. Korea see Taegu
64 B2 Daet Phil.
114 A3 Dagana Senegal
119 D2 Daga Post Sudan
88 C2 Dagda Latvia
64 B2 Dagupan Phil.
　　 Dahalach, Isole is Eritrea see
　　 Dahlak Archipelago
74 B3 Dahanu India
69 D2 Da Hinggan Ling mts China
116 C3 Dahlak Archipelago is Eritrea
100 C2 Dahlem Ger.
78 B3 Dahm, Ramlat des.
　　 Saudi Arabia/Yemen
74 B2 Dahod India
　　 Dahomey country Africa see Benin
　　 Dahra Senegal see Dara
81 C2 Dahūk Iraq
60 B2 Daik Indon.
106 C2 Daimiel Spain
　　 Dairen China see Dalian
51 C2 Dajarra Austr.
70 A2 Dajing China
114 A3 Dakar Senegal
117 C4 Daketa Shet' watercourse Eth.
116 C2 Dākhilah, Wāḥāt ad Egypt
　　 Dakhla Oasis Egypt see Dākhilah,
　　 Wāḥāt ad
63 A3 Dakoank India
88 C3 Dakol'ka r. Belarus
109 D2 Đakovica Serb. and Mont.
109 C1 Đakovo Croatia
120 B2 Dala Angola
70 A1 Dalain Hob China
93 G3 Dalälven r. Sweden
111 C3 Dalaman Turkey
111 C3 Dalaman r. Turkey
68 C2 Dalandzadgad Mongolia
64 B2 Dalanganem Islands Phil.
63 B2 Đa Lat Vietnam
　　 Dalatando Angola see
　　 N'dalatando
74 A2 Dalbandin Pak.
96 C3 Dalbeattie U.K.
53 D1 Dalby Austr.
93 E3 Dale Norway
141 C1 Dale Hollow Lake U.S.A.
53 C2 Dalgety Austr.
143 C1 Dalhart U.S.A.
131 D3 Dalhousie Can.
70 B2 Dali China
70 C2 Dalian China
96 C3 Dalkeith U.K.
143 D2 Dallas U.S.A.
128 B2 Dall Island U.S.A.
　　 Dalmacija reg. Croatia see
　　 Dalmatia
96 B2 Dalmally U.K.
109 C2 Dalmatia reg. Croatia
96 B3 Dalmellington U.K.
66 C2 Dal'negorsk Rus. Fed.
66 B1 Dal'nerechensk Rus. Fed.
　　 Dalny China see Dalian
114 B4 Daloa Côte d'Ivoire
71 A3 Dalou Shan mts China
51 D2 Dalrymple, Mount Austr.
92 □A3 Dalsmynni Iceland
75 C2 Daltenganj India
141 D2 Dalton U.S.A.
　　 Daltonganj India see Daltenganj
60 B1 Daludalu Indon.
71 B3 Daluo Shan mt. China
92 □B2 Dalvík Iceland
96 B2 Dalwhinnie U.K.
50 C1 Daly r. Austr.
51 C1 Daly Waters Austr.
74 B2 Daman India
74 B2 Daman and Diu union terr. India
116 B1 Damanhūr Egypt
59 C3 Damar i. Indon.
118 B2 Damara C.A.R.
80 B2 Damascus Syria
115 D3 Damaturu Nigeria
76 B3 Damāvand, Qolleh-ye mt. Iran
120 A1 Damba Angola
118 B1 Damboa Nigeria
81 D2 Damghan Iran
　　 Damietta Egypt see Dumyāţ
79 C2 Dammam Saudi Arabia
101 D1 Damme Ger.
75 B2 Damoh India
114 B4 Damongo Ghana
50 A2 Dampier Austr.
59 C3 Dampir, Selat sea chan. Indon.
75 D1 Damxung China
114 B4 Danané Côte d'Ivoire
63 B2 Đa Năng Vietnam
139 E2 Danbury U.S.A.
70 B2 Dandong China
117 B3 Dangila Eth.
146 B3 Dangriga Belize
70 B2 Dangshan China
89 F2 Danilov Rus. Fed.
89 E2 Danilovskaya Vozvyshennost' hills Rus. Fed.
70 B2 Danjiangkou China
79 C2 Dank Oman
89 E3 Dankov Rus. Fed.
146 B3 Danlí Hond.
101 E1 Dannenberg (Elbe) Ger.
54 C2 Dannevirke N.Z.
62 B2 Dan Sai Thai.
70 B2 Dantu China
110 A1 Danube r. Europe

110 C1 Danube Delta Romania
138 B2 Danville IL U.S.A.
138 C3 Danville KY U.S.A.
139 D3 Danville VA U.S.A.
　　 Danxian China see Danzhou
71 A4 Danzhou China
　　 Danzig, Gulf of Pol./Rus. Fed. see
　　 Gdańsk, Gulf of
　　 Daojiang China see Daoxian
115 D2 Dao Timmi Niger
　　 Daoud Alg. see Aïn Beïda
114 B4 Daoukro Côte d'Ivoire
71 B3 Daoxian China
64 B3 Dapa Phil.
68 C2 Dapaong Togo
69 E1 Daqing China
114 A3 Dara Senegal
80 B2 Dar'ā Syria
81 D3 Dārāb Iran
115 D1 Daraj Libya
81 D2 Dārān Iran
63 B2 Đa Răng, Sông r. Vietnam
109 D2 Đaravica mt. Serb. and Mont.
75 C2 Darbhanga India
　　 Dardo China see Kangding
117 A3 Darfur reg. Sudan
119 D3 Dar es Salaam Tanz.
74 B1 Dargai Pak.
54 B1 Dargaville N.Z.
53 C3 Dargo Austr.
68 D1 Darhan Mongolia
150 B2 Darién, Golfo del g. Col.
　　 Darjeeling India see Darjiling
75 C2 Darjiling India
68 C2 Darlag China
52 B2 Darling r. Austr.
53 C1 Darling Downs hills Austr.
50 A3 Darling Range hills Austr.
98 C2 Darlington U.K.
53 C2 Darlington Point Austr.
103 D1 Darłowo Pol.
101 D3 Darmstadt Ger.
115 E1 Darnah Libya
52 B2 Darnick Austr.
55 H3 Darnley, Cape Antarctica
107 C1 Daroca Spain
99 D4 Dartford U.K.
99 A4 Dartmoor hills U.K.
131 D3 Dartmouth Can.
99 B4 Dartmouth U.K.
59 D3 Daru P.N.G.
59 C2 Daruba Indon.
50 C1 Darwin Austr.
153 C5 Darwin Falkland Is
79 C2 Dārzīn Iran
65 A1 Dashiqiao China
　　 Dashkhovuz Turkm. see Dashoguz
76 B2 Dashoguz Turkm.
74 A2 Dasht r. Pak.
61 C1 Datadian Indon.
111 C3 Datça Turkey
66 D2 Date Japan
71 B3 Datian China
70 B1 Datong China
64 B3 Datu Piang Phil.
74 B1 Daud Khel Pak.
88 B2 Daugava r. Latvia
88 C2 Daugavpils Latvia
100 C2 Daun Ger.
129 D2 Dauphin Can.
129 E2 Dauphin Lake Can.
73 B3 Davangere India
64 B3 Davao Phil.
64 B3 Davao Gulf Phil.
137 E2 Davenport U.S.A.
99 C3 Daventry U.K.
123 C2 Daveyton S. Africa
146 B4 David Panama
129 D2 Davidson Can.
126 F3 Davidson Lake Can.
135 B3 Davis U.S.A.
131 D2 Davis Inlet Can.
55 I3 Davis Sea sea Antarctica
127 I2 Davis Strait str. Can./Greenland
105 D2 Davos Switz.
88 C3 Davyd-Haradok Belarus
79 C3 Dawqah Oman
78 B3 Dawqah Saudi Arabia
126 C2 Dawson Can.
141 D2 Dawson U.S.A.
128 B2 Dawson Creek Can.
128 B2 Dawsons Landing Can.
68 C2 Dawu China
　　 Dawukou China see Shizuishan
79 C2 Dawwah Oman
104 C3 Dax France
　　 Daxian China see Dazhou
68 C2 Da Xueshan mts China
52 B3 Daylesford Austr.
　　 Dayong China see Zhangjiajie
81 C2 Dayr az Zawr Syria
138 C3 Dayton U.S.A.
141 D3 Daytona Beach U.S.A.
71 B3 Dayu China
70 B2 Da Yunhe canal China
70 A2 Dazhou China
122 B3 De Aar S. Africa
141 D3 Deadman Bay U.S.A.
80 B2 Dead Sea salt l. Asia
99 D4 Deal U.K.
71 B3 De'an China
152 B3 Deán Funes Arg.
128 B2 Dease Lake Can.
126 E2 Dease Strait Can.

135 C3 Death Valley depr. U.S.A.
104 C2 Deauville France
61 C1 Debak Sarawak Malaysia
111 B2 Debar Macedonia
103 E1 Dębica Pol.
103 E1 Dęblin Pol.
114 B3 Débo, Lac l. Mali
103 E2 Debrecen Hungary
117 B3 Debre Markos Eth.
119 C3 Debre Sina Eth.
117 B3 Debre Tabor Eth.
117 B4 Debre Zeyit Eth.
140 C2 Decatur AL U.S.A.
138 B3 Decatur IL U.S.A.
73 B3 Deccan plat. India
53 D1 Deception Bay Austr.
71 A3 Dechang China
102 C1 Děčín Czech Rep.
137 E2 Decorah U.S.A.
154 C2 Dedo de Deus mt. Brazil
88 C2 Dedovichi Rus. Fed.
121 C2 Dedza Malawi
99 B3 Dee r. England/Wales U.K.
96 C2 Dee r. Scotland U.K.
130 C3 Deep River Can.
53 D1 Deepwater Austr.
131 E3 Deer Lake Can.
134 D1 Deer Lodge U.S.A.
138 C2 Defiance U.S.A.
140 C2 De Funiak Springs U.S.A.
68 C2 Dêgê China
117 C4 Degeh Bur Eth.
139 F1 Dégelis Can.
102 C2 Deggendorf Ger.
91 E2 Degtevo Rus. Fed.
81 D2 Deh Bid Iran
81 C2 Dehlorān Iran
74 B1 Dehra Dun India
75 C2 Dehri India
69 E2 Dehui China
100 A2 Deinze Belgium
110 B1 Dej Romania
138 B2 De Kalb U.S.A.
116 B3 Dekemhare Eritrea
118 C3 Dekese Dem. Rep. Congo
118 B2 Dékoa C.A.R.
141 D3 De Land U.S.A.
135 C3 Delano U.S.A.
135 D3 Delano Peak U.S.A.
48 I3 Delap-Uliga-Djarrit Marshall Is
74 A1 Delārām Afgh.
123 C2 Delareyville S. Africa
129 D2 Delaronde Lake Can.
138 C2 Delaware U.S.A.
139 D3 Delaware r. U.S.A.
139 D3 Delaware state U.S.A.
139 D3 Delaware Bay U.S.A.
53 C3 Delegate Austr.
118 C2 Délembé C.A.R.
105 D2 Delémont Switz.
100 B1 Delft Neth.
100 C1 Delfzijl Neth.
121 D2 Delgado, Cabo c. Moz.
68 C2 Delhi China
74 B2 Delhi India
60 B2 Deli i. Indon.
128 B1 Déline Can.
　　 Delingha China see Delhi
101 F2 Delitzsch Ger.
107 D2 Dellys Alg.
135 C4 Del Mar U.S.A.
101 D1 Delmenhorst Ger.
109 B1 Delnice Croatia
136 B3 Del Norte U.S.A.
83 L1 De-Longa, Ostrova is Rus. Fed.
　　 De Long Islands Rus. Fed. see
　　 De-Longa, Ostrova
　　 De Long Strait Rus. Fed. see
　　 Longa, Proliv
129 D3 Deloraine Can.
111 B3 Delphi tourist site Greece
141 D3 Delray Beach U.S.A.
143 C3 Del Rio U.S.A.
136 B3 Delta CO U.S.A.
135 D3 Delta UT U.S.A.
126 C2 Delta Junction U.S.A.
109 D3 Delvinë Albania
106 C1 Demanda, Sierra de la mts Spain
　　 Demavend Iran see
　　 Damāvand, Qolleh-ye
118 C3 Demba Dem. Rep. Congo
119 D1 Dembech'a Eth.
117 B4 Dembī Dolo Eth.
　　 Demerara Guyana see
　　 Georgetown
91 C3 Demerdzhi mt. Ukr.
89 D2 Demidov Rus. Fed.
142 B3 Deming U.S.A.
111 C3 Demirci Turkey
111 C2 Demirköy Turkey
102 C1 Demmin Ger.
140 C2 Demopolis U.S.A.
60 B2 Dempo, Gunung vol. Indon.
89 D2 Demyansk Rus. Fed.
122 B3 De Naawte S. Africa
117 C3 Denakil reg. Eritrea/Eth.
98 B3 Denbigh U.K.
100 B1 Den Burg Neth.
62 B1 Den Chai Thai.
60 B2 Dendang Indon.
100 B2 Dendermonde Belgium
100 B2 Dendre r. Belgium
　　 Dengjiabu China see Yujiang
70 A1 Dengkou China
　　 Dengxian China see Dengzhou

Dengzhou
192

70 B2 **Dengzhou** China
Dengzhou China *see* **Penglai**
Den Haag Neth. *see* **The Hague**
50 A2 **Denham** Austr.
100 B1 **Den Helder** Neth.
107 D2 **Denia** Spain
52 B3 **Deniliquin** Austr.
134 C2 **Denio** U.S.A.
137 D2 **Denison** *IA* U.S.A.
143 D2 **Denison** *TX* U.S.A.
111 C3 **Denizli** Turkey
53 D2 **Denman** Austr.
50 A3 **Denmark** Austr.
93 E4 **Denmark** *country* Europe
84 B2 **Denmark Strait** Greenland/Iceland
77 C3 **Denov** Uzbek.
61 C2 **Denpasar** Indon.
143 D2 **Denton** U.S.A.
50 A3 **D'Entrecasteaux, Point** Austr.
59 E3 **D'Entrecasteaux Islands** P.N.G.
141 D2 **Dentsville** U.S.A.
136 B3 **Denver** U.S.A.
75 C2 **Deogarh** *Orissa* India
74 B2 **Deogarh** *Rajasthan* India
75 C2 **Deoghar** India
138 B2 **De Pere** U.S.A.
83 K2 **Deputatskiy** Rus. Fed.
62 A1 **Dêqên** China
140 B2 **De Queen** U.S.A.
74 A2 **Dera Bugti** Pak.
74 B1 **Dera Ghazi Khan** Pak.
74 B1 **Dera Ismail Khan** Pak.
87 D4 **Derbent** Rus. Fed.
50 B1 **Derby** Austr.
99 C3 **Derby** U.K.
137 D3 **Derby** U.S.A.
99 D3 **Dereham** U.K.
97 B2 **Derg, Lough** *l.* Ireland
91 D1 **Derhachi** Ukr.
140 B2 **De Ridder** U.S.A.
91 D2 **Derkul** *r.* Rus. Fed./Ukr.
75 B1 **Dêrub** China
116 B3 **Derudeb** Sudan
122 B3 **De Rust** S. Africa
109 C2 **Derventa** Bos.-Herz.
98 C3 **Derwent** *r. England* U.K.
98 C3 **Derwent** *r. England* U.K.
98 B2 **Derwent Water** *l.* U.K.
77 C1 **Derzhavinsk** Kazakh.
Derzhavinskiy Kazakh. *see* Derzhavinsk
152 B1 **Desaguadero** *r.* Bol.
49 M5 **Désappointement, Îles du** *is* Fr. Polynesia
129 D2 **Deschambault Lake** Can.
134 B1 **Deschutes** *r.* U.S.A.
117 B3 **Desē** Eth.
153 B4 **Deseado** Arg.
153 B4 **Deseado** *r.* Arg.
142 A2 **Desemboque** Mex.
137 E2 **Des Moines** U.S.A.
137 E2 **Des Moines** *r.* U.S.A.
91 C1 **Desna** *r.* Rus. Fed./Ukr.
89 D3 **Desnogorsk** Rus. Fed.
101 F2 **Dessau** Ger.
Dessye Eth. *see* **Desē**
128 A1 **Destruction Bay** Can.
149 C5 **Desventurados, Islas de los** *is* S. Pacific Ocean
128 C1 **Detah** Can.
120 B2 **Dete** Zimbabwe
101 D2 **Detmold** Ger.
138 C2 **Detroit** U.S.A.
137 D1 **Detroit Lakes** U.S.A.
Dett Zimbabwe *see* **Dete**
100 B2 **Deurne** Neth.
110 B1 **Deva** Romania
100 C1 **Deventer** Neth.
96 C2 **Deveron** *r.* U.K.
103 D2 **Devét Skal** *hill* Czech Rep.
137 D1 **Devil's Lake** U.S.A.
128 A2 **Devil's Paw** *mt.* U.S.A.
99 C4 **Devizes** U.K.
74 B2 **Devli** India
110 C2 **Devnya** Bulg.
128 C2 **Devon** Can.
126 F1 **Devon Island** Can.
51 D4 **Devonport** Austr.
74 B2 **Dewas** India
137 F3 **Dexter** U.S.A.
70 A2 **Deyang** China
59 D3 **Deyong, Tanjung** *pt* Indon.
79 C2 **Deyyer** Iran
81 C2 **Dezfūl** Iran
70 B2 **Dezhou** China
79 C2 **Dhahran** Saudi Arabia
75 D2 **Dhaka** Bangl.
78 B3 **Dhamār** Yemen
75 C2 **Dhamtari** India
75 C2 **Dhanbad** India
74 B2 **Dhandhuka** India
75 C2 **Dhankuta** Nepal
74 B2 **Dhar** India
75 D2 **Dharmanagar** India
73 B3 **Dharmapuri** India
75 C2 **Dharmjaygarh** India
114 B3 **Ḍhar Oualâta** *hills* Maur.
114 B3 **Ḍhar Tîchît** *hills* Maur.
73 B3 **Dharwad** India
Dharwar India *see* **Dharwad**
74 B2 **Dhasa** India
75 C2 **Dhaulagiri** *mt.* Nepal
78 B3 **Dhubāb** Yemen
74 B2 **Dhule** India
Dhulia India *see* **Dhule**
117 C4 **Dhuusa Marreeb** Somalia
144 A1 **Diablo, Picacho del** *mt.* Mex.
142 B2 **Diablo Plateau** U.S.A.
121 C2 **Diaca** Moz.
51 C2 **Diamantina** *watercourse* Austr.
155 D1 **Diamantina** Brazil
151 E4 **Diamantina, Chapada** *plat.* Brazil
159 F6 **Diamantina Deep** *sea feature* Indian Ocean
154 B1 **Diamantino** Brazil
151 D4 **Diamantino** Brazil
71 B3 **Dianbai** China
151 E4 **Dianópolis** Brazil
114 B4 **Dianra** Côte d'Ivoire
114 C3 **Diapaga** Burkina
79 C2 **Dibā al Ḥiṣn** U.A.E.
79 C2 **Ḍibab** Oman
118 C3 **Dibaya** Dem. Rep. Congo
122 B2 **Dibeng** S. Africa
72 D2 **Dibrugarh** India
136 C1 **Dickinson** U.S.A.
140 C1 **Dickson** U.S.A.
Dicle *r.* Turkey *see* **Tigris**
105 D3 **Die** France
Diedenhofen France *see* Thionville
129 D2 **Diefenbaker, Lake** Can.
Diégo Suarez Madag. *see* Antsirañana
114 B3 **Diéma** Mali
101 D2 **Diemel** *r.* Ger.
62 B1 **Điên Biên Phu** Vietnam
62 B2 **Diên Châu** Vietnam
101 D1 **Diepholz** Ger.
104 C2 **Dieppe** France
100 B2 **Diest** Belgium
115 D3 **Diffa** Niger
131 D3 **Digby** Can.
105 D3 **Digne-les-Bains** France
105 C2 **Digoin** France
64 B3 **Digos** Phil.
59 D3 **Digul** *r.* Indon.
105 D2 **Dijon** France
115 D4 **Dik** Chad
117 C3 **Dikhil** Djibouti
111 C3 **Dikili** Turkey
100 A2 **Diksmuide** Belgium
82 G2 **Dikson** Rus. Fed.
115 D3 **Dikwa** Nigeria
117 B4 **Dīla** Eth.
59 C3 **Dili** East Timor
101 D2 **Dillenburg** Ger.
117 A3 **Dilling** Sudan
126 B3 **Dillingham** U.S.A.
134 D1 **Dillon** *MT* U.S.A.
141 E2 **Dillon** *SC* U.S.A.
118 C4 **Dilolo** Dem. Rep. Congo
72 D2 **Dimapur** India
Dimashq Syria *see* **Damascus**
52 B3 **Dimboola** Austr.
110 C2 **Dimitrovgrad** Bulg.
87 D3 **Dimitrovgrad** Rus. Fed.
Dimitrovo Bulg. *see* **Pernik**
64 B2 **Dinagat** *i.* Phil.
75 C2 **Dinajpur** Bangl.
104 B2 **Dinan** France
100 B2 **Dinant** Belgium
111 D3 **Dinar** Turkey
81 D2 **Dīnār, Kūh-e** *mt.* Iran
104 B2 **Dinard** France
Dinbych U.K. *see* **Denbigh**
73 B3 **Dindigul** India
118 B1 **Dindima** Nigeria
123 D1 **Dindiza** Moz.
101 E2 **Dingelstädt** Ger.
97 A2 **Dingle** Ireland
97 A2 **Dingle Bay** Ireland
71 B3 **Dingnan** China
102 C2 **Dingolfing** Ger.
114 A3 **Dinguiraye** Guinea
96 B2 **Dingwall** U.K.
70 A2 **Dingxi** China
75 C2 **Dinngyê** China
123 C1 **Dinokwe** Botswana
91 D2 **Dinskaya** Rus. Fed.
100 C2 **Dinslaken** Ger.
135 C3 **Dinuba** U.S.A.
114 B3 **Dioïla** Mali
154 B3 **Dionísio Cerqueira** Brazil
114 A3 **Diourbel** Senegal
75 D2 **Diphu** India
64 B3 **Dipolog** Phil.
74 B1 **Dir** Pak.
51 D1 **Direction, Cape** Austr.
117 C4 **Dirē Dawa** Eth.
120 B2 **Dirico** Angola
50 A2 **Dirk Hartog Island** Austr.
53 C1 **Dirranbandi** Austr.
78 B3 **Ḍirs** Saudi Arabia
153 E5 **Disappointment, Cape** S. Georgia
134 B1 **Disappointment, Cape** U.S.A.
50 B2 **Disappointment, Lake** *salt flat* Austr.
52 B3 **Discovery Bay** Austr.
Disko *i.* Greenland *see* Qeqertarsuaq
141 E1 **Dismal Swamp** U.S.A.
99 D3 **Diss** U.K.
108 B3 **Dittaino** *r. Sicily* Italy
74 B2 **Diu** India
155 D2 **Divinópolis** Brazil
87 D4 **Divnoye** Rus. Fed.
114 B4 **Divo** Côte d'Ivoire
80 B2 **Divriği** Turkey
74 A2 **Diwana** Pak.
138 B2 **Dixon** U.S.A.
128 A2 **Dixon Entrance** *sea chan.* Can./U.S.A.
81 C2 **Diyarbakır** Turkey
74 A2 **Diz** Pak.
115 D2 **Djado** Niger
115 D2 **Djado, Plateau du** Niger
Djakarta Indon. *see* **Jakarta**
118 B3 **Djambala** Congo
115 C2 **Djanet** Alg.
115 D3 **Djédaa** Chad
115 C1 **Djelfa** Alg.
119 C2 **Djéma** C.A.R.
114 B3 **Djenné** Mali
114 B3 **Djibo** Burkina
117 C3 **Djibouti** *country* Africa
117 C3 **Djibouti** Djibouti
Djidjelli Alg. *see* **Jijel**
118 C2 **Djolu** Dem. Rep. Congo
114 C4 **Djougou** Benin
118 B2 **Djoum** Cameroon
115 D3 **Djourab, Erg du** *des.* Chad
92 □C3 **Djúpivogur** Iceland
89 F3 **Dmitriyevka** Rus. Fed.
89 E3 **Dmitriyev-L'govskiy** Rus. Fed.
Dmitriyevsk Ukr. *see* **Makiyivka**
89 E2 **Dmitrov** Rus. Fed.
Dmytriyevs'k Ukr. *see* **Makiyivka**
Dnepr *r.* Rus. Fed. *see* **Dnieper**
89 D3 **Dnieper** *r.* Rus. Fed.
91 C2 **Dnieper** *r.* Ukr.
90 B2 **Dniester** *r.* Ukr.
Dnipro *r.* Ukr. *see* **Dnieper**
91 C2 **Dniprodzerzhyns'k** Ukr.
91 D2 **Dnipropetrovs'k** Ukr.
91 C2 **Dniprorudne** Ukr.
Dnister *r.* Ukr. *see* **Dniester**
90 C2 **Dnistrov'ky Lyman** *l.* Ukr.
88 C2 **Dno** Rus. Fed.
121 C2 **Doa** Moz.
115 D4 **Doba** Chad
88 B2 **Dobele** Latvia
101 F2 **Döbeln** Ger.
59 C3 **Doberai, Jazirah** *pen.* Indon.
Doberai Peninsula Indon. *see* Doberai, Jazirah
59 C3 **Dobo** Indon.
109 C2 **Doboj** Bos.-Herz.
103 E1 **Dobre Miasto** Pol.
110 C2 **Dobrich** Bulg.
89 F3 **Dobrinka** Rus. Fed.
89 E3 **Dobroye** Rus. Fed.
89 D3 **Dobrush** Belarus
86 E3 **Dobryanka** Rus. Fed.
155 E1 **Doce** *r.* Brazil
145 B2 **Doctor Arroyo** Mex.
144 B2 **Doctor Belisario Domínguez** Mex.
Doctor Petru Groza Romania *see* Ștei
111 C3 **Dodecanese** *is* Greece
Dodekanisos *is* Greece *see* Dodecanese
136 C3 **Dodge City** U.S.A.
119 D3 **Dodoma** Tanz.
100 C1 **Doesburg** Neth.
100 C2 **Doetinchem** Neth.
59 C3 **Dofa** Indon.
75 C1 **Dogai Coring** *salt l.* China
128 B2 **Dog Creek** Can.
67 B3 **Dōgo** *i.* Japan
115 C3 **Dogondoutchi** Niger
81 C2 **Doğubeyazıt** Turkey
79 C2 **Doha** Qatar
62 A2 **Doi Saket** Thai.
81 D2 **Dokali** Iran
100 B1 **Dokkum** Neth.
88 C3 **Dokshytsy** Belarus
91 D2 **Dokuchayevs'k** Ukr.
59 D3 **Dolak, Pulau** *i.* Indon.
142 A1 **Dolan Springs** U.S.A.
130 C3 **Dolbeau** Can.
104 B2 **Dol-de-Bretagne** France
105 D2 **Dole** France
91 D2 **Dolgaya, Kosa** *spit* Rus. Fed.
99 B3 **Dolgellau** U.K.
89 E3 **Dolgorukovo** Rus. Fed.
89 E3 **Dolgoye** Rus. Fed.
69 F1 **Dolinsk** Rus. Fed.
103 D2 **Dolný Kubín** Slovakia
108 B1 **Dolomites** *mts* Italy
Dolomiti *mts* Italy *see* **Dolomites**
Dolonnur China *see* **Duolun**
117 C4 **Dolo Odo** Eth.
144 A2 **Dolores** Mex.
126 E2 **Dolphin and Union Strait** Can.
90 A2 **Dolyna** Ukr.
102 C2 **Domažlice** Czech Rep.
93 E3 **Dombås** Norway
103 D2 **Dombóvár** Hungary
Dombrovitsa Ukr. *see* **Dubrovytsya**
Dombrowa Pol. *see* Dąbrowa Górnicza
128 B2 **Dome Creek** Can.
147 D3 **Dominica** *country* West Indies
147 C3 **Dominican Republic** *country* West Indies
118 C3 **Domiongo** Dem. Rep. Congo
117 C4 **Domo** Eth.
89 E2 **Domodedovo** Rus. Fed.
111 B3 **Domokos** Greece
61 C2 **Dompu** Indon.
153 A3 **Domuyo, Volcán** *vol.* Arg.
142 B3 **Don** Mex.
89 E3 **Don** *r.* Rus. Fed.
96 C2 **Don** *r.* U.K.
97 D1 **Donaghadee** U.K.
52 B3 **Donald** Austr.
Donau *r.* Austria/Ger. *see* **Danube**
102 C2 **Donauwörth** Ger.
106 B2 **Don Benito** Spain
98 C3 **Doncaster** U.K.
120 A1 **Dondo** Angola
121 C2 **Dondo** Moz.
73 C4 **Dondra Head** *hd* Sri Lanka
97 B1 **Donegal** Ireland
97 B1 **Donegal Bay** Ireland
91 D2 **Donets'k** Ukr.
91 D2 **Donets'kyy Kryazh** *hills* Rus. Fed./Ukr.
118 B2 **Donga** Nigeria
50 A2 **Dongara** Austr.
71 A3 **Dongchuan** China
71 A4 **Dongfang** China
66 B1 **Dongfanghong** China
61 C2 **Donggala** Indon.
65 A2 **Donggang** China
Donggou China *see* **Donggang**
71 B3 **Dongguan** China
62 B2 **Đông Ha** Vietnam
Dong Hai *sea* N. Pacific Ocean *see* East China Sea
62 B2 **Đông Hôi** Vietnam
116 B3 **Dongola** Sudan
118 B2 **Dongou** Congo
Dong Phaya Yen Range *mts* Thai. *see* **San Khao Phang Hoei**
63 B2 **Dong Phraya Yen** *esc.* Thai.
Dongping China *see* **Anhua**
71 B3 **Dongshan** China
Dongsheng China *see* **Ordos**
70 C2 **Dongtai** China
71 B3 **Dongting Hu** *l.* China
Dong Ujimqin Qi China *see* **Uliastai**
71 C3 **Dongyang** China
70 B2 **Dongying** China
143 D3 **Donna** U.S.A.
54 B1 **Donnellys Crossing** N.Z.
100 C3 **Donnersberg** *hill* Ger.
107 C1 **Donostia - San Sebastián** Spain
81 D1 **Donyztau, Sor** *dry lake* Kazakh.
51 C1 **Doomadgee** Austr.
138 B2 **Door Peninsula** U.S.A.
117 C4 **Dooxo Nugaaleed** *val.* Somalia
50 B2 **Dora, Lake** *salt flat* Austr.
99 B4 **Dorchester** U.K.
122 A1 **Dordabis** Namibia
104 B2 **Dordogne** *r.* France
100 B2 **Dordrecht** Neth.
123 C3 **Dordrecht** S. Africa
122 A1 **Doreenville** Namibia
129 D2 **Doré Lake** Can.
101 D1 **Dorfmark** Ger.
114 B3 **Dori** Burkina
122 A3 **Doring** *r.* S. Africa
100 C2 **Dormagen** Ger.
96 B2 **Dornoch** U.K.
96 B2 **Dornoch Firth** *est.* U.K.
114 B3 **Doro** Mali
89 D3 **Dorogobuzh** Rus. Fed.
110 C1 **Dorohoi** Romania
68 C1 **Döröö Nuur** *salt l.* Mongolia
92 G3 **Dorotea** Sweden
50 A2 **Dorre Island** Austr.
53 D2 **Dorrigo** Austr.
118 B2 **Dorsale Camerounaise** *slope* Cameroon/Nigeria
100 C2 **Dorsten** Ger.
100 C2 **Dortmund** Ger.
100 C2 **Dortmund-Ems-Kanal** *canal* Ger.
153 B4 **Dos Bahías, Cabo** *c.* Arg.
101 F1 **Dosse** *r.* Ger.
114 C3 **Dosso** Niger
141 C2 **Dothan** U.S.A.
101 D1 **Dötlingen** Ger.
105 C1 **Douai** France
118 A2 **Douala** Cameroon
104 B2 **Douarnenez** France
105 D2 **Doubs** *r.* France/Switz.
54 A3 **Doubtful Sound** N.Z.
114 B3 **Douentza** Mali
98 A2 **Douglas** Isle of Man
122 B2 **Douglas** S. Africa
128 A2 **Douglas** *AK* U.S.A.
142 B2 **Douglas** *AZ* U.S.A.
141 D2 **Douglas** *GA* U.S.A.
136 B2 **Douglas** *WY* U.S.A.
104 C1 **Doullens** France
154 B1 **Dourada, Serra** *hills* Brazil
154 B2 **Dourados** Brazil
154 B2 **Dourados** *r.* Brazil
154 B2 **Dourados, Serra dos** *hills* Brazil
106 B1 **Douro** *r.* Port.
99 D4 **Dover** U.K.
139 D3 **Dover** U.S.A.
95 D3 **Dover, Strait of** France/U.K.
139 F1 **Dover-Foxcroft** U.S.A.
121 C2 **Dowa** Malawi
81 D3 **Dowlatābād** Iran
79 C2 **Dowlatābād** Iran
97 D1 **Downpatrick** U.K.
81 C2 **Dow Rūd** Iran
77 C3 **Dowshī** Afgh.
67 B3 **Dōzen** *is* Japan
130 C3 **Dozois, Réservoir** *resr* Can.
154 B2 **Dracena** Brazil
100 C1 **Drachten** Neth.
110 B2 **Drăgănești-Olt** Romania
110 B2 **Drăgășani** Romania
105 D3 **Draguignan** France
88 C3 **Drahichyn** Belarus

53 D1 **Drake** Austr.
123 C2 **Drakensberg** *mts* Lesotho/S. Africa
123 C2 **Drakensberg** *mts* S. Africa
149 C8 **Drake Passage** S. Atlantic Ocean
111 B2 **Drama** Greece
93 F4 **Drammen** Norway
109 C1 **Drava** *r.* Europe
128 C2 **Drayton Valley** Can.
101 D2 **Dreieich** Ger.
111 B3 **Drepano, Akra** *pt* Greece
102 C1 **Dresden** Ger.
104 C2 **Dreux** France
100 B1 **Driemond** Neth.
98 C2 **Driffield** U.K.
137 D1 **Drift Prairie** *reg.* U.S.A.
109 C2 **Drina** *r.* Bos.-Herz./Serb. and Mont.
140 B2 **Driskill Mountain** *hill* U.S.A.
Drissa Belarus *see*
Vyerkhnyadzvinsk
109 C1 **Drniš** Croatia
110 B2 **Drobeta-Turnu Severin** Romania
90 B2 **Drochia** Moldova
101 D1 **Drochtersen** Ger.
97 C2 **Drogheda** Ireland
90 A2 **Drohobych** Ukr.
99 B3 **Droitwich Spa** U.K.
Drokiya Moldova *see* **Drochia**
97 B1 **Dromahair** Ireland
97 C1 **Dromore** U.K.
100 B1 **Dronten** Neth.
74 B1 **Drosh** Pak.
53 C3 **Drouin** Austr.
128 C2 **Drumheller** Can.
138 C1 **Drummond Island** U.S.A.
131 C3 **Drummondville** Can.
96 B3 **Drummore** U.K.
96 B2 **Drumnadrochit** U.K.
Druskieniki Lith. *see* **Druskininkai**
88 B3 **Druskininkai** Lith.
88 C2 **Druya** Belarus
91 D2 **Druzhkivka** Ukr.
88 D2 **Druzhnaya Gorka** Rus. Fed.
89 D3 **Drybin** Belarus
130 A3 **Dryden** Can.
50 B1 **Drysdale** *r.* Austr.
147 C3 **Duarte, Pico** *mt.* Dom. Rep.
78 A2 **Ḍubā** Saudi Arabia
79 C2 **Dubai** U.A.E.
90 B2 **Dubăsari** Moldova
129 D1 **Dubawnt Lake** Can.
Dubayy U.A.E. *see* **Dubai**
78 A2 **Dubbagh, Jabal ad** *mt.*
Saudi Arabia
53 C2 **Dubbo** Austr.
Dubesar' Moldova *see* **Dubăsari**
97 C2 **Dublin** Ireland
141 D2 **Dublin** U.S.A.
89 E2 **Dubna** Rus. Fed.
90 B1 **Dubno** Ukr.
139 D2 **Du Bois** U.S.A.
Dubossary Moldova *see* **Dubăsari**
114 A4 **Dubréka** Guinea
109 C2 **Dubrovnik** Croatia
90 B1 **Dubrovytsya** Ukr.
89 D3 **Dubrowna** Belarus
137 E2 **Dubuque** U.S.A.
135 D2 **Duchesne** U.S.A.
129 D2 **Duck Bay** Can.
63 B2 **Đức Trọng** Vietnam
101 E2 **Duderstadt** Ger.
82 G2 **Dudinka** Rus. Fed.
99 B3 **Dudley** U.K.
106 B1 **Duero** *r.* Spain
48 H4 **Duff Islands** Solomon Is
131 C2 **Duffreboy, Lac** *l.* Can.
96 C2 **Dufftown** U.K.
109 C2 **Dugi Otok** *i.* Croatia
109 C2 **Dugi Rat** Croatia
100 C2 **Duisburg** Ger.
123 C1 **Duiwelskloof** S. Africa
123 C3 **Dukathole** S. Africa
117 B4 **Duk Fadiat** Sudan
79 C2 **Dukhān** Qatar
89 D2 **Dukhovshchina** Rus. Fed.
Dukou China *see* **Panzhihua**
88 C2 **Dūkštas** Lith.
68 C2 **Dulan** China
152 B3 **Dulce** *r.* Arg.
142 B1 **Dulce** U.S.A.
97 C2 **Duleek** Ireland
100 C2 **Dülmen** Ger.
110 C2 **Dulovo** Bulg.
137 E1 **Duluth** U.S.A.
64 B3 **Dumaguete** Phil.
60 B1 **Dumai** Indon.
64 B2 **Dumaran** *i.* Phil.
140 B2 **Dumas** AR U.S.A.
143 C1 **Dumas** TX U.S.A.
96 B3 **Dumbarton** U.K.
103 D2 **Ďumbier** *mt.* Slovakia
96 C3 **Dumfries** U.K.
89 E3 **Duminichi** Rus. Fed.
75 C2 **Dumka** India
55 L3 **Dumont d'Urville Sea** Antarctica
116 B1 **Dumyâṭ** Egypt
Duna *r.* Hungary *see* **Danube**
Dünaburg Latvia *see* **Daugavpils**
103 D2 **Dunakeszi** Hungary
97 C2 **Dunany Point** Ireland
Dunărea *r.* Romania *see* **Danube**
Dunării, Delta Romania *see*
Danube Delta
103 D2 **Dunaújváros** Hungary
Dunav *r.* Bulg./Croatia/
Serb. and Mont. *see* **Danube**

90 B2 **Dunayivtsi** Ukr.
96 C2 **Dunbar** U.K.
96 C1 **Dunbeath** U.K.
128 B3 **Duncan** Can.
143 D2 **Duncan** U.S.A.
96 C1 **Duncansby Head** *hd* U.K.
88 B2 **Dundaga** Latvia
97 C1 **Dundalk** Ireland
139 D3 **Dundalk** U.S.A.
97 C2 **Dundalk Bay** Ireland
127 H1 **Dundas** Greenland
Dún Dealgan Ireland *see* **Dundalk**
123 D2 **Dundee** S. Africa
96 C2 **Dundee** U.K.
97 D1 **Dundrum Bay** U.K.
54 B3 **Dunedin** N.Z.
53 C2 **Dunedoo** Austr.
96 C2 **Dunfermline** U.K.
97 C1 **Dungannon** U.K.
74 B2 **Dungarpur** India
97 C2 **Dungarvan** Ireland
99 D4 **Dungeness** *hd* U.K.
97 C1 **Dungiven** U.K.
53 D2 **Dungog** Austr.
119 C2 **Dungu** Dem. Rep. Congo
60 B1 **Dungun** Malaysia
116 B2 **Dungunab** Sudan
69 E2 **Dunhua** China
68 C2 **Dunhuang** China
96 C2 **Dunkeld** U.K.
Dunkerque France *see* **Dunkirk**
104 C1 **Dunkirk** France
139 D2 **Dunkirk** U.S.A.
97 C2 **Dún Laoghaire** Ireland
97 B3 **Dunmanway** Ireland
97 D1 **Dunmurry** U.K.
96 C1 **Dunnet Head** *hd* U.K.
96 C3 **Duns** U.K.
134 B2 **Dunsmuir** U.S.A.
99 C4 **Dunstable** U.K.
100 B3 **Dun-sur-Meuse** France
96 A2 **Dunvegan** U.K.
70 B1 **Duolun** China
Duperré Alg. *see* **Aïn Defla**
110 B2 **Dupnitsa** Bulg.
136 C1 **Dupree** U.S.A.
Duque de Bragança Angola *see*
Calandula
138 B3 **Du Quoin** U.S.A.
50 B1 **Durack** *r.* Austr.
105 C3 **Durance** *r.* France
144 B2 **Durango** Mex.
106 C1 **Durango** Spain
136 B3 **Durango** U.S.A.
143 D2 **Durant** U.S.A.
153 C3 **Durazno** Uru.
Durazzo Albania *see* **Durrës**
123 D2 **Durban** S. Africa
105 C3 **Durban-Corbières** France
122 A3 **Durbanville** S. Africa
100 B2 **Durbuy** Belgium
100 C2 **Düren** Ger.
75 C2 **Durg** India
98 C2 **Durham** U.K.
141 E1 **Durham** U.S.A.
60 B1 **Duri** Indon.
109 C2 **Durmitor** *mt.* Serb. and Mont.
96 B1 **Durness** U.K.
109 C2 **Durrës** Albania
97 A3 **Dursey Island** Ireland
111 C3 **Dursunbey** Turkey
117 C4 **Durukhsi** Somalia
59 D3 **D'Urville, Tanjung** *pt* Indon.
54 B2 **D'Urville Island** N.Z.
71 A3 **Dushan** China
77 C3 **Dushanbe** Tajik.
100 C2 **Düsseldorf** Ger.
Dutch East Indies *country* Asia
see **Indonesia**
Dutch Guiana *country* S. America
see **Suriname**
Dutch West Indies *terr.* West Indies
see **Netherlands Antilles**
Duvno Bos.-Herz. *see*
Tomislavgrad
71 A3 **Duyun** China
80 B1 **Düzce** Turkey
91 D2 **Dvorichna** Ukr.
74 A2 **Dwarka** India
123 C1 **Dwarsberg** S. Africa
134 C1 **Dworshak Reservoir** U.S.A.
89 D3 **Dyat'kovo** Rus. Fed.
96 C2 **Dyce** U.K.
127 H2 **Dyer, Cape** Can.
140 C1 **Dyersburg** U.S.A.
99 B3 **Dyfi** *r.* U.K.
103 D2 **Dyje** *r.* Austria/Czech Rep.
103 D1 **Dylewska Góra** *hill* Pol.
91 D2 **Dymytrov** Ukr.
123 C3 **Dyoki** S. Africa
51 D2 **Dysart** Austr.
122 B3 **Dysselsdorp** S. Africa
87 E3 **Dyurtyuli** Rus. Fed.
69 D1 **Dzamïn Üüd** Mongolia
121 D2 **Dzaoudzi** Mayotte
91 D2 **Dzerzhyns'k** Ukr.
Dzhaltyr Kazakh. *see* **Zhaltyr**
Dzhambul Kazakh. *see* **Taraz**
81 D1 **Dzhanga** Turkm.
76 B2 **Dzhangala** Kazakh.
91 C2 **Dzhankoy** Ukr.
Dzharkent Kazakh. *see* **Zharkent**
81 D2 **Dzhebel** Turkm.
Dzhetygara Kazakh. *see* **Zhitikara**

Dzhezkazgan Kazakh. *see*
Zhezkazgan
Dzhizak Uzbek. *see* **Jizzax**
91 D3 **Dzhubga** Rus. Fed.
83 K3 **Dzhugdzhur, Khrebet** *mts*
Rus. Fed.
77 D2 **Dzhungarskiy Alatau, Khrebet**
mts China/Kazakh.
76 C2 **Dzhusaly** Kazakh.
103 E1 **Działdowo** Pol.
145 D2 **Dzilam de Bravo** Mex.
69 D1 **Dzuunmod** Mongolia
88 C3 **Dzyarzhynsk** Belarus
88 C3 **Dzyatlavichy** Belarus

E

131 E2 **Eagle** *r.* Can.
134 C1 **Eagle Cap** *mt.* U.S.A.
130 A3 **Eagle Lake** Can.
134 B2 **Eagle Lake** U.S.A.
143 C3 **Eagle Pass** U.S.A.
126 C2 **Eagle Plain** Can.
Eap *i.* Micronesia *see* **Yap**
130 A2 **Ear Falls** Can.
135 C3 **Earlimart** U.S.A.
96 C2 **Earn** *r.* U.K.
55 J2 **East Antarctica** *reg.* Antarctica
East Bengal *country* Asia *see*
Bangladesh
99 D4 **Eastbourne** U.K.
59 C2 **East Caroline Basin** *sea feature*
N. Pacific Ocean
69 E2 **East China Sea** N. Pacific Ocean
54 B1 **East Coast Bays** N.Z.
East Dereham U.K. *see* **Dereham**
129 D3 **Eastend** Can.
157 G7 **Easter Island** S. Pacific Ocean
123 C3 **Eastern Cape** *prov.* S. Africa
116 B2 **Eastern Desert** Egypt
73 B3 **Eastern Ghats** *mts* India
Eastern Samoa *terr.*
S. Pacific Ocean *see*
American Samoa
Eastern Sayan Mountains
Rus. Fed. *see* **Vostochnyy Sayan**
Eastern Transvaal *prov.* S. Africa
see **Mpumalanga**
129 E2 **Easterville** Can.
153 C5 **East Falkland** *i.* Falkland Is
100 C1 **East Frisian Islands** Ger.
135 C3 **Eastgate** U.S.A.
137 D1 **East Grand Forks** U.S.A.
96 B3 **East Kilbride** U.K.
138 C2 **East Lansing** U.S.A.
99 C4 **Eastleigh** U.K.
96 C3 **East Linton** U.K.
138 C2 **East Liverpool** U.S.A.
123 C3 **East London** S. Africa
130 C2 **Eastmain** Can.
130 C2 **Eastmain** *r.* Can.
141 D2 **Eastman** U.S.A.
157 G8 **East Pacific Rise** *sea feature*
N. Pacific Ocean
East Pakistan *country* Asia *see*
Bangladesh
East Sea N. Pacific Ocean *see*
Japan, Sea of
83 K2 **East Siberian Sea** Rus. Fed.
138 A3 **East St Louis** U.S.A.
59 C3 **East Timor** *country* Asia
53 C2 **East Toorale** Austr.
139 D2 **East York** Can.
138 A2 **Eau Claire** U.S.A.
130 C2 **Eau Claire, Lac à l'** *l.* Can.
59 D2 **Eauripik** *atoll* Micronesia
145 D2 **Ebano** Mex.
99 B4 **Ebbw Vale** U.K.
118 B2 **Ebebiyin** Equat. Guinea
102 C1 **Eberswalde-Finow** Ger.
66 D2 **Ebetsu** Japan
77 E2 **Ebinur Hu** *salt l.* China
118 C2 **Ebola** *r.* Dem. Rep. Congo
109 C2 **Eboli** Italy
118 B2 **Ebolowa** Cameroon
107 D1 **Ebro** *r.* Spain
114 C1 **Ech Chélif** Alg.
Echeng China *see* **Ezhou**
144 A2 **Echeverria, Pico** *mt.* Mex.
129 E2 **Echoing** *r.* Can.
100 C3 **Echternach** Lux.
52 B3 **Echuca** Austr.
106 B2 **Écija** Spain
102 B1 **Eckernförde** Ger.
127 G2 **Eclipse Sound** *sea chan.* Can.
150 B3 **Ecuador** *country* S. America
116 C3 **Ed** Eritrea
96 C1 **Eday** *i.* U.K.
117 A3 **Ed Da'ein** Sudan
117 B3 **Ed Damazin** Sudan
116 B3 **Ed Damer** Sudan
116 B3 **Ed Debba** Sudan
116 B3 **Ed Dueim** Sudan
51 D4 **Eddystone Point** Austr.
100 B1 **Ede** Neth.
118 B2 **Edéa** Cameroon
154 C1 **Edéia** Brazil
53 C3 **Eden** Austr.
98 B2 **Eden** *r.* U.K.
143 D2 **Eden** U.S.A.
123 C2 **Edenburg** S. Africa
97 C2 **Edenderry** Ireland
52 B3 **Edenhope** Austr.

141 E1 **Edenton** U.S.A.
111 B2 **Edessa** Greece
139 E2 **Edgartown** U.S.A.
Edge Island Svalbard *see* **Edgeøya**
82 C1 **Edgeøya** *i.* Svalbard
141 D3 **Edgewater** U.S.A.
138 C2 **Edinboro** U.S.A.
143 D3 **Edinburg** U.S.A.
96 C3 **Edinburgh** U.K.
90 B2 **Edineţ** Moldova
111 C2 **Edirne** Turkey
Edith Ronne Land *ice feature*
Antarctica *see* **Ronne Ice Shelf**
128 C2 **Edmonton** Can.
131 D3 **Edmundston** Can.
111 C3 **Edremit** Turkey
111 C3 **Edremit Körfezi** *b.* Turkey
128 C2 **Edson** Can.
119 C3 **Edward, Lake**
Dem. Rep. Congo/Uganda
Edwardesabad Pak. *see* **Bannu**
143 D2 **Edwards Plateau** U.S.A.
55 O2 **Edward VII Peninsula** Antarctica
96 C2 **Edzell** U.K.
100 A2 **Eeklo** Belgium
135 B2 **Eel** *r.* U.S.A.
100 C1 **Eemskanaal** *canal* Neth.
100 C1 **Eenrum** Neth.
138 B3 **Effingham** U.S.A.
135 C3 **Egan Range** *mts* U.S.A.
103 E2 **Eger** Hungary
93 E4 **Egersund** Norway
100 B2 **Eghezée** Belgium
92 □C2 **Egilsstaðir** Iceland
80 B2 **Eğirdir** Turkey
80 B2 **Eğirdir Gölü** *l.* Turkey
104 C2 **Égletons** France
Egmont, Mount *vol.* N.Z. *see*
Taranaki, Mount
83 M2 **Egvekinot** Rus. Fed.
116 A2 **Egypt** *country* Africa
70 A2 **Ehen Hudag** China
106 C1 **Eibar** Spain
100 C1 **Eibergen** Neth.
100 C2 **Eifel** *hills* Ger.
96 A2 **Eigg** *i.* U.K.
73 B4 **Eight Degree Channel**
India/Maldives
50 B1 **Eighty Mile Beach** Austr.
80 B3 **Eilat** Israel
101 F2 **Eilenburg** Ger.
101 D2 **Einbeck** Ger.
100 B2 **Eindhoven** Neth.
160 N4 **Eirik Ridge** *sea feature*
N. Atlantic Ocean
150 C3 **Eirunepé** Brazil
120 B2 **Eiseb** *watercourse* Namibia
101 E2 **Eisenach** Ger.
101 E2 **Eisenberg** Ger.
102 C1 **Eisenhüttenstadt** Ger.
103 D2 **Eisenstadt** Austria
101 E2 **Eisleben Lutherstadt** Ger.
Eivissa Spain *see* **Ibiza**
Eivissa *i.* Spain *see* **Ibiza**
107 C1 **Ejea de los Caballeros** Spain
121 □D3 **Ejeda** Madag.
Ejin Qi China *see* **Dalain Hob**
93 H4 **Ekenäs** Fin.
77 D1 **Ekibastuz** Kazakh.
93 F4 **Eksjö** Sweden
122 A2 **Eksteenfontein** S. Africa
130 B2 **Ekwan** *r.* Can.
62 A2 **Ela** Myanmar
El Aaiún Western Sahara *see*
Laâyoune
123 C2 **Elandsdoorn** S. Africa
El Araïche Morocco *see* **Larache**
El Asnam Alg. *see* **Ech Chélif**
111 B3 **Elassona** Greece
Elat Israel *see* **Eilat**
80 B2 **Elazığ** Turkey
108 B2 **Elba, Isola d'** *i.* Italy
150 B2 **El Banco** Col.
109 D2 **Elbasan** Albania
150 C2 **El Baúl** Venez.
114 C1 **El Bayadh** Alg.
101 D1 **Elbe** *r.* Ger.
136 B3 **Elbert, Mount** U.S.A.
141 D2 **Elberton** U.S.A.
104 C2 **Elbeuf** France
80 B2 **Elbistan** Turkey
103 D1 **Elbląg** Pol.
153 A4 **El Bolsón** Arg.
87 D4 **El'brus** *mt.* Rus. Fed.
81 C2 **Elburz Mountains** *mts* Iran
150 C2 **El Callao** Venez.
143 D3 **El Campo** U.S.A.
135 C4 **El Centro** U.S.A.
152 B1 **El Cerro** Bol.
107 C2 **Elche-Elx** Spain
145 C3 **El Chichónal** *vol.* Mex.
107 C2 **Elda** Spain
119 D2 **Eldama Ravine** Kenya
137 E3 **Eldon** U.S.A.
154 B3 **Eldorado** Arg.
154 B2 **Eldorado** Brazil
144 B2 **El Dorado** Mex.
140 B2 **El Dorado** AR U.S.A.
137 D3 **El Dorado** KS U.S.A.
134 D1 **Electric Peak** U.S.A.
114 B2 **El Eglab** Alg.
106 C2 **El Ejido** Spain
89 E2 **Elektrostal'** Rus. Fed.
150 B3 **El Encanto** Col.
146 C2 **Eleuthera** *i.* Bahamas

116 A3 El Fasher Sudan
144 B2 El Fuerte Mex.
117 A3 El Fula Sudan
116 A3 El Geneina Sudan
116 B3 El Geteina Sudan
 96 C2 Elgin U.K.
138 B2 Elgin U.S.A.
 83 K2 El'ginskiy Rus. Fed.
        El Giza Egypt see Giza
115 C1 El Goléa Alg.
144 A1 El Golfo de Santa Clara Mex.
119 D2 Elgon, Mount Uganda
108 A3 El Hadjar Alg.
114 A2 El Hammâmi reg. Maur.
114 B2 El Hank esc. Mali/Maur.
114 A2 El Hierro i. Canary Is
145 C2 El Higo Mex.
114 C2 El Homr Alg.
        Elichpur India see Achalpur
126 B2 Elim U.S.A.
        Élisabethville Dem. Rep. Congo
        see Lubumbashi
        El Iskandarîya Egypt see
        Alexandria
 87 D4 Elista Rus. Fed.
139 E2 Elizabeth Ger.
141 E1 Elizabeth City U.S.A.
138 B3 Elizabethtown U.S.A.
114 B1 El Jadida Morocco
103 E1 Elk Pol.
108 A3 El Kala Alg.
 88 C2 Elkas kalns hill Latvia
143 D1 Elk City U.S.A.
114 B1 El Kelaâ des Srarhna Morocco
128 C2 Elkford Can.
138 B2 Elkhart U.S.A.
        El Khartûm Sudan see Khartoum
110 C2 Elkhovo Bulg.
139 D3 Elkins U.S.A.
128 C3 Elko Can.
134 C2 Elko U.S.A.
129 C2 Elk Point Can.
137 E1 Elk River U.S.A.
126 F1 Ellef Ringnes Island Can.
137 D1 Ellendale U.S.A.
134 B1 Ellensburg U.S.A.
 54 B2 Ellesmere, Lake N.Z.
127 G1 Ellesmere Island Can.
 98 B3 Ellesmere Port U.K.
126 F2 Ellice r. Can.
        Ellice Islands country
        S. Pacific Ocean see Tuvalu
123 C3 Elliotdale S. Africa
138 C1 Elliot Lake Can.
 96 C2 Ellon U.K.
139 F2 Ellsworth U.S.A.
 55 R2 Ellsworth Mountains Antarctica
111 C3 Elmalı Turkey
115 C1 El Meghaïer Alg.
139 D2 Elmira U.S.A.
107 C2 El Moral Spain
101 D1 Elmshorn Ger.
117 A3 El Muglad Sudan
150 B2 El Nevado, Cerro mt. Col.
 64 A2 El Nido Phil.
116 B3 El Obeid Sudan
144 B2 El Oro Mex.
115 C1 El Oued Alg.
142 A2 Eloy U.S.A.
        El Paso U.S.A. see Derby
142 B2 El Paso U.S.A.
145 D3 El Pinalón, Cerro mt. Guat.
144 B1 El Porvenir Mex.
107 D1 El Prat de Llobregat Spain
146 B3 El Progreso Hond.
106 B2 El Puerto de Santa María Spain
        El Qâhira Egypt see Cairo
        El Quds Israel/West Bank see
        Jerusalem
143 D1 El Reno U.S.A.
128 A1 Elsa Can.
145 B2 El Salado Mex.
144 B2 El Salto Mex.
146 B3 El Salvador country
        Central America
152 B2 El Salvador Chile
145 B2 El Salvador Mex.
142 B3 El Sauz Mex.
144 A1 El Socorro Mex.
142 B3 El Sueco Mex.
        El Suweis Egypt see Suez
108 A3 El Tarf Alg.
106 B1 El Teleno mt. Spain
145 C2 El Temascal Mex.
150 C2 El Tigre Venez.
147 D4 El Tocuyo Venez.
        El Uqsur Egypt see Luxor
 73 C3 Eluru India
 88 C2 Elva Estonia
106 B2 Elvas Port.
 93 F3 Elverum Norway
119 E2 El Wak Kenya
 99 D3 Ely U.K.
137 E1 Ely MN U.S.A.
135 D3 Ely NV U.S.A.
 81 D2 Emämrüd Iran
 93 G4 Emån r. Sweden
 76 B2 Emba Kazakh.
 76 B2 Emba r. Kazakh.
123 C2 Embalenhle S. Africa
118 B2 Embondo Dem. Rep. Congo
154 C1 Emborcação, Represa de resr
        Brazil
119 D3 Embu Kenya
100 C1 Emden Ger.

 51 D2 Emerald Austr.
129 E3 Emerson Can.
111 C3 Emet Turkey
123 D2 eMgwenya S. Africa
123 D2 eMijindini S. Africa
115 D3 Emi Koussi mt. Chad
145 C3 Emiliano Zapata Mex.
110 C2 Emine, Nos pt Bulg.
 80 B2 Emirdağ Turkey
 88 B2 Emmaste Estonia
100 B1 Emmeloord Neth.
100 C2 Emmelshausen Ger.
100 C1 Emmen Neth.
143 C3 Emory Peak U.S.A.
144 A2 Empalme Mex.
123 D2 Empangeni S. Africa
156 D2 Emperor Trough sea feature
        N. Pacific Ocean
108 B2 Empoli Italy
111 C3 Emponas Greece
137 D3 Emporia KS U.S.A.
139 D3 Emporia VA U.S.A.
        Empty Quarter des. Saudi Arabia
        see Rub' al Khālī
100 C1 Ems r. Ger.
100 C1 Emsdetten Ger.
 88 C2 Emumägi hill Estonia
123 C2 Emzinoni S. Africa
 59 D3 Enarotali Indon.
144 B2 Encarnación Mex.
152 C2 Encarnación Para.
155 D1 Encruzilhada Brazil
 61 D2 Ende Indon.
 55 G2 Enderby Land reg. Antarctica
126 B2 Endicott Mountains U.S.A.
 50 A2 Eneabba Austr.
 91 C2 Enerhodar Ukr.
111 C2 Eşen Turkey
 97 C2 Enfield Ireland
 87 D3 Engel's Rus. Fed.
 60 B2 Enggano i. Indon.
 99 C3 England admin. div. U.K.
130 C3 Englehart Can.
141 D3 Englewood U.S.A.
130 A2 English r. Can.
        English Bazar India see
        Ingraj Bazar
 95 C4 English Channel France/U.K.
143 D1 Enid U.S.A.
100 B1 Enkhuizen Neth.
 93 G4 Enköping Sweden
108 B3 Enna Sicily Italy
129 D1 Ennadai Lake Can.
116 A3 En Nahud Sudan
115 E3 Ennedi, Massif mts Chad
 53 C1 Enngonia Austr.
 97 B2 Ennis Ireland
143 D2 Ennis U.S.A.
 97 C2 Enniscorthy Ireland
 97 C2 Enniskerry Ireland
 97 C1 Enniskillen U.K.
 97 B2 Ennistymon Ireland
102 C2 Enns Austria
102 C2 Enns r. Austria
 92 J3 Eno Fin.
 92 H2 Enontekiö Fin.
 53 C3 Ensay Austr.
100 C1 Enschede Neth.
144 A1 Ensenada Mex.
 70 A2 Enshi China
119 D2 Entebbe Uganda
128 C1 Enterprise Can.
140 C2 Enterprise AL U.S.A.
134 C1 Enterprise OR U.S.A.
152 B3 Entre Ríos Arg.
106 B2 Entroncamento Port.
115 C4 Enugu Nigeria
150 B3 Envira Brazil
118 B2 Épéna Congo
105 C2 Épernay France
135 D3 Ephraim U.S.A.
134 C1 Ephrata U.S.A.
105 D2 Épinal France
 99 D4 Epping U.K.
 99 C4 Epsom U.K.
118 A2 Equatorial Guinea country Africa
104 B2 Équerdreville-Hainneville France
101 D3 Erbach Ger.
101 F3 Erbendorf Ger.
100 C3 Erbeskopf hill Ger.
 81 C2 Erciş Turkey
 80 B2 Erciyes Dağı mt. Turkey
103 D2 Érd Hungary
        Erdaobaihe China see Baihe
 65 B1 Erdao Jiang r. China
111 C2 Erdek Turkey
 80 B2 Erdemli Turkey
154 B2 Eré, Campos hills Brazil
 55 M2 Erebus, Mount vol. Antarctica
152 C2 Erechim Brazil
 69 D1 Ereentsav Mongolia
 80 B2 Ereğli Turkey
 80 B1 Ereğli Turkey
 69 D2 Erenhot China
        Erevan Armenia see Yerevan
101 E2 Erfurt Ger.
 80 B2 Ergani Turkey
114 B2 'Erg Chech des. Alg./Mali
111 C2 Ergene r. Turkey
 78 A3 Erheib Sudan
 96 B2 Ericht, Loch l. U.K.
138 C2 Erie U.S.A.
138 C2 Erie, Lake Can./U.S.A.
 66 D2 Erimo-misaki c. Japan

116 B3 Eritrea country Africa
101 E3 Erlangen Ger.
 50 C2 Erldunda Austr.
123 C2 Ermelo S. Africa
 80 B2 Ermenek Turkey
111 B3 Ermoupoli Greece
 73 B4 Ernakulam India
 97 B1 Erne r. Ireland/U.K.
 73 B3 Erode India
100 B2 Erp Neth.
114 B1 Er Rachidia Morocco
116 B3 Er Rahad Sudan
 97 B1 Errigal hill Ireland
 97 A1 Erris Head hd Ireland
 48 H5 Erromango i. Vanuatu
109 D2 Ersekë Albania
 89 F3 Ertil' Rus. Fed.
101 D2 Erwitte Ger.
101 F2 Erzgebirge mts Czech Rep./Ger.
 80 B2 Erzincan Turkey
 81 C2 Erzurum Turkey
 66 D2 Esashi Japan
 93 E4 Esbjerg Denmark
135 D3 Escalante U.S.A.
135 D3 Escalante Desert U.S.A.
144 B2 Escalón Mex.
138 B1 Escanaba U.S.A.
145 C3 Escárcega Mex.
107 C1 Escatrón Spain
100 A2 Escaut r. Belgium
101 E1 Eschede Ger.
100 B3 Esch-sur-Alzette Lux.
101 E2 Eschwege Ger.
100 C2 Eschweiler Ger.
135 C4 Escondido U.S.A.
144 B2 Escuinapa Mex.
111 C3 Eşen Turkey
 81 D2 Eşfahān Iran
123 D2 Eshowe S. Africa
123 D2 Esikhawini S. Africa
 98 B2 Esk r. U.K.
131 D2 Esker Can.
 92 □C2 Eskifjörður Iceland
 93 G4 Eskilstuna Sweden
        Eskimo Point Can. see Arviat
111 D3 Eskişehir Turkey
 81 C2 Eslāmābād-e Gharb Iran
111 C3 Esler Dağı mt. Turkey
111 C3 Eşme Turkey
146 C2 Esmeralda Cuba
150 B2 Esmeraldas Ecuador
 79 D2 Espakeh Iran
105 C3 Espalion France
130 B3 Espanola Can.
142 B1 Espanola U.S.A.
 50 B3 Esperance Austr.
153 A5 Esperanza Arg.
144 B2 Esperanza Mex.
106 B2 Espichel, Cabo c. Port.
154 B3 Espigão, Serra do mts Brazil
143 C3 Espinazo Mex.
155 D1 Espinhaço, Serra do mts Brazil
151 E4 Espinosa Brazil
        Espírito Santo Brazil see Vila Velha
 48 H5 Espíritu Santo i. Vanuatu
144 A2 Espíritu Santo, Isla i. Mex.
 93 H3 Espoo Fin.
153 A4 Esquel Arg.
114 B1 Essaouira Morocco
114 A2 Es Semara Western Sahara
100 C2 Essen Ger.
150 D2 Essequibo r. Guyana
139 E2 Essex Junction U.S.A.
 83 L1 Esso Rus. Fed.
106 B1 Estaca de Bares, Punta da pt
        Spain
153 B5 Estados, Isla de los i. Arg.
 81 D3 Eṣṭahbān Iran
151 F4 Estância Brazil
123 C2 Estcourt S. Africa
107 C1 Estella Spain
106 B2 Estepona Spain
106 C1 Esteras de Medinaceli Spain
129 D2 Esterhazy Can.
152 B2 Esteros Para.
136 B2 Estes Park U.S.A.
129 D3 Estevan Can.
137 E2 Estherville U.S.A.
129 D2 Eston Can.
 88 C2 Estonia country Europe
        Estonskaya S.S.R. admin. reg.
        Europe see Estonia
106 B1 Estrela, Serra da mts Port.
106 B2 Estremoz Port.
 52 A1 Etadunna Austr.
104 C2 Étampes France
104 C1 Étaples France
 75 B2 Etawah India
123 D2 eThandakukhanya S. Africa
122 B2 E'Thembini S. Africa
117 B4 Ethiopia country Africa
        Etna, Monte vol. Italy see
        Etna, Mount
109 C3 Etna, Mount vol. Sicily Italy
 93 E4 Etne Norway
128 A2 Etolin Island U.S.A.
120 A2 Etosha Pan salt pan Namibia
110 B2 Etropole Bulg.
100 C3 Ettelbruck Lux.
100 B2 Etten-Leur Neth.
107 C1 Etxarri-Aranatz Spain
 99 D4 Eu France
 53 C2 Euabalong Austr.
        Euboea i. Greece see Evvoia
 50 B3 Eucla Austr.

138 C2 Euclid U.S.A.
141 C2 Eufaula U.S.A.
143 D1 Eufaula Lake resr U.S.A.
134 B2 Eugene U.S.A.
144 A2 Eugenia, Punta pt Mex.
 53 C1 Eulo Austr.
 53 C2 Eumungerie Austr.
143 C2 Eunice U.S.A.
 81 C2 Euphrates r. Asia
134 B2 Eureka CA U.S.A.
134 C1 Eureka MT U.S.A.
135 C3 Eureka NV U.S.A.
 52 B2 Euriowie Austr.
 53 C2 Euroa Austr.
106 B2 Europa Point Gibraltar
140 C2 Eutaw U.S.A.
128 B2 Eutsuk Lake Can.
123 C2 Evander S. Africa
130 C2 Evans, Lac l. Can.
 53 C1 Evans Head Austr.
127 G2 Evans Strait Can.
138 B2 Evanston IL U.S.A.
136 A2 Evanston WY U.S.A.
138 B3 Evansville U.S.A.
        Eva Perón Arg. see La Plata
123 C2 Evaton S. Africa
 79 C2 Evaz Iran
 83 L2 Evensk Rus. Fed.
 50 C2 Everard Range hills Austr.
 75 C2 Everest, Mount China/Nepal
134 B1 Everett U.S.A.
100 A2 Evergem Belgium
141 D3 Everglades swamp U.S.A.
140 C2 Evergreen U.S.A.
 99 C3 Evesham U.K.
118 B2 Evinayong Equat. Guinea
 93 E4 Evje Norway
106 B2 Évora Port.
 69 F1 Evoron, Ozero l. Rus. Fed.
111 B3 Evosmo Greece
104 C2 Évreux France
111 C2 Evros r. Greece/Turkey
111 B3 Evrotas r. Greece
104 C2 Évry France
 80 B2 Evrychou Cyprus
111 B3 Evvoia i. Greece
119 E2 Ewaso Ngiro r. Kenya
152 B1 Exaltación Bol.
 99 B4 Exe r. U.K.
 99 B4 Exeter U.K.
 99 B4 Exmoor hills U.K.
 50 A2 Exmouth Austr.
 99 B4 Exmouth U.K.
 50 A2 Exmouth Gulf Austr.
106 B2 Extremadura reg. Spain
146 C2 Exuma Cays is Bahamas
 91 D2 Eya r. Rus. Fed.
118 C3 Eyangu Dem. Rep. Congo
119 D3 Eyasi, Lake salt l. Tanz.
 96 C3 Eyemouth U.K.
 92 □B2 Eyjafjörður inlet Iceland
117 C4 Eyl Somalia
 52 A1 Eyre, Lake salt flat Austr.
 52 A1 Eyre Peninsula Austr.
 94 B1 Eysturoy i. Faroe Is
123 C2 Ezakheni S. Africa
123 C2 Ezenzeleni S. Africa
 70 B2 Ezhou China
 86 E2 Ezhva Rus. Fed.
111 C3 Ezine Turkey

F

102 C1 Faaborg Denmark
142 B2 Fabens U.S.A.
108 B2 Fabriano Italy
115 D3 Fachi Niger
114 B3 Fada-N'Gourma Burkina
108 B2 Faenza Italy
        Faeroes terr. N. Atlantic Ocean see
        Faroe Islands
 59 C3 Fafanlap Indon.
110 B1 Făgăraş Romania
 49 J5 Fagatogo American Samoa
 93 E3 Fagernes Norway
 93 G4 Fagersta Sweden
153 B5 Fagnano, Lago l. Arg./Chile
114 B3 Faguibine, Lac l. Mali
 92 □B3 Fagurhólsmýri Iceland
126 C2 Fairbanks U.S.A.
137 D2 Fairbury U.S.A.
135 B3 Fairfield CA U.S.A.
138 C3 Fairfield OH U.S.A.
 96 □ Fair Isle i. U.K.
137 E2 Fairmont MN U.S.A.
138 C3 Fairmont WV U.S.A.
128 C2 Fairview Can.
128 A2 Fairweather, Mount Can./U.S.A.
 59 D2 Fais i. Micronesia
 74 B1 Faisalabad Pak.
136 C1 Faith U.S.A.
 75 C2 Faizabad India
156 E6 Fakaofo atoll Tokelau
 99 D3 Fakenham U.K.
 59 C3 Fakfak Indon.
 65 A1 Faku China
114 A4 Falaba Sierra Leone
 97 B1 Falcarragh Ireland
143 D3 Falcon Lake Mex./U.S.A.
        Faleshty Moldova see Fălești
 90 B2 Fălești Moldova
143 D3 Falfurrias U.S.A.
128 C2 Falher Can.

Franca 195

101 F2 Falkenberg Ger.
93 F4 Falkenberg Sweden
101 F1 Falkensee Ger.
96 C3 Falkirk U.K.
158 D8 Falkland Escarpment *sea feature* S. Atlantic Ocean
153 C5 Falkland Islands *terr.* S. Atlantic Ocean
157 I9 Falkland Plateau *sea feature* S. Atlantic Ocean
93 F4 Falköping Sweden
101 D1 Fallingbostel Ger.
135 C3 Fallon U.S.A.
139 E2 Fall River U.S.A.
137 D2 Falls City U.S.A.
99 A4 Falmouth U.K.
122 A3 False Bay S. Africa
144 B2 Falso, Cabo *c.* Mex.
93 F5 Falster *i.* Denmark
110 C1 Fălticeni Romania
93 G3 Falun Sweden
152 B2 Famailla Arg.
121 □D3 Fandriana Madag.
Fangcheng China *see* Fangchenggang
71 A3 Fangchenggang China
71 C3 Fangshan Taiwan
66 A1 Fangzheng China
108 B2 Fano Italy
62 B1 Fan Si Pan *mt.* Vietnam
119 C2 Faradje Dem. Rep. Congo
121 □D3 Farafangana Madag.
116 A2 Farāfirah, Wāḥāt al Egypt
Farafra Oasis Egypt *see* Farāfirah, Wāḥāt al
76 C3 Farāh Afgh.
114 A3 Faranah Guinea
79 C3 Fararah Oman
78 B3 Farasān, Jazā'ir *is* Saudi Arabia
59 D2 Faraulep *atoll* Micronesia
127 J2 Farewell, Cape *c.* Greenland
54 B2 Farewell, Cape N.Z.
137 D1 Fargo U.S.A.
77 D2 Farg'ona Uzbek.
137 E2 Faribault U.S.A.
130 C2 Faribault, Lac *l.* Can.
74 B2 Faridabad India
75 C2 Faridpur Bangl.
139 E2 Farmington *ME* U.S.A.
142 B1 Farmington *NM* U.S.A.
139 D3 Farmville U.S.A.
99 C4 Farnborough U.K.
128 C2 Farnham, Mount Can.
128 A1 Faro Can.
106 B2 Faro Port.
88 A2 Fårö *i.* Sweden
147 C3 Faro, Punta *pt* Col.
106 B1 Faro, Serra do *mts* Spain
94 B1 Faroe Islands *terr.* N. Atlantic Ocean
113 I6 Farquhar Group *atoll* Seychelles
81 D3 Farrāshband Iran
Farrukhabad India *see* Fatehgarh
79 C3 Fartak, Ra's *c.* Yemen
154 B3 Fartura, Serra da *mts* Brazil
143 C2 Farwell U.S.A.
79 C2 Fāryāb Iran
79 C2 Fāryāb Iran
81 D3 Fasā Iran
109 C2 Fasano Italy
90 B1 Fastiv Ukr.
119 D2 Fataki Dem. Rep. Congo
75 B2 Fatehgarh India
75 C2 Fatehpur India
114 A3 Fatick Senegal
131 D3 Fatima Can.
123 C2 Fauresmith S. Africa
92 G2 Fauske Norway
92 □A3 Faxaflói *b.* Iceland
92 G3 Faxälven *r.* Sweden
115 D3 Faya Chad
140 B1 Fayetteville *AR* U.S.A.
141 E1 Fayetteville *NC* U.S.A.
140 C1 Fayetteville *TN* U.S.A.
74 B1 Fazilka India
114 A2 Fdérik Maur.
141 E2 Fear, Cape U.S.A.
54 C2 Featherston N.Z.
104 C2 Fécamp France
Federated Malay States *country* Asia *see* Malaysia
48 G3 Federated States of Micronesia *country* N. Pacific Ocean
102 C1 Fehmarn *i.* Ger.
101 F1 Fehrbellin Ger.
155 D2 Feia, Lagoa *lag.* Brazil
150 B3 Feijó Brazil
54 C2 Feilding N.Z.
151 F4 Feira de Santana Brazil
107 D2 Felanitx Spain
101 F1 Feldberg Ger.
145 D3 Felipe C. Puerto Mex.
155 D1 Felixlândia Brazil
99 D4 Felixstowe U.K.
101 D2 Felsberg Ger.
108 B1 Feltre Italy
93 F3 Femunden *l.* Norway
Fénérive Madag. *see* Fenoarivo Atsinanana
Fengcheng China *see* Fengshan
71 B3 Fengcheng *Jiangxi* China
65 A1 Fengcheng *Liaoning* China
62 A1 Fengqing China
71 A3 Fengshan China
Fengshan China *see* Fengqing
70 B2 Fengxian *Jiangsu* China
70 A2 Fengxian *Shaanxi* China
Fengxiang China *see* Lincang
Fengyi China *see* Zheng'an
71 C3 Fengyüan Taiwan
70 B1 Fengzhen China
105 D3 Feno, Capo di *c. Corsica* France
121 □D2 Fenoarivo Atsinanana Madag.
70 B2 Fenyang China
91 D2 Feodosiya Ukr.
108 A3 Fer, Cap de *c.* Alg.
137 D1 Fergus Falls U.S.A.
51 E1 Fergusson Island P.N.G.
114 B4 Ferkessédougou Côte d'Ivoire
108 B2 Fermo Italy
131 D2 Fermont Can.
106 B1 Fermoselle Spain
97 B2 Fermoy Ireland
141 D2 Fernandina Beach U.S.A.
154 B2 Fernandópolis Brazil
Fernando Poó *i.* Equat. Guinea *see* Bioco
134 B1 Ferndale U.S.A.
99 C4 Ferndown U.K.
128 C3 Fernie Can.
135 C3 Fernley U.S.A.
97 C2 Ferns Ireland
Ferozepore India *see* Firozpur
108 B2 Ferrara Italy
154 B2 Ferreiros Brazil
108 A2 Ferro, Capo *c. Sardinia* Italy
106 B1 Ferrol Spain
Ferryville Tunisia *see* Menzel Bourguiba
100 B1 Ferwert Neth.
114 B1 Fès Morocco
118 B3 Feshi Dem. Rep. Congo
137 E3 Festus U.S.A.
110 C2 Fetești Romania
97 C2 Fethard Ireland
111 C3 Fethiye Turkey
96 □ Fetlar *i.* U.K.
130 C2 Feuilles, Rivière aux *r.* Can.
77 D3 Feyzābād Afgh.
Fez Morocco *see* Fès
121 □D3 Fianarantsoa Madag.
115 D4 Fianga Chad
117 B4 Fichē Eth.
109 C2 Fier Albania
96 C2 Fife Ness *pt* U.K.
104 C3 Figeac France
106 B1 Figueira da Foz Port.
107 D1 Figueres Spain
114 B1 Figuig Morocco
49 I5 Fiji *country* S. Pacific Ocean
152 B2 Filadelfia Para.
55 B2 Filchner Ice Shelf Antarctica
98 C2 Filey U.K.
108 B3 Filicudi, Isola *i.* Italy
114 C3 Filingué Niger
111 B3 Filippiada Greece
93 F4 Filipstad Sweden
92 E3 Fillan Norway
135 D3 Fillmore U.S.A.
119 E2 Filtu Eth.
55 D2 Fimbull Ice Shelf Antarctica
96 C2 Findhorn *r.* U.K.
138 C2 Findlay U.S.A.
51 D4 Fingal Austr.
139 D2 Finger Lakes U.S.A.
111 D3 Finike Turkey
106 B1 Finisterre, Cape *c.* Spain
93 I3 Finland *country* Europe
93 H4 Finland, Gulf of Europe
128 B2 Finlay *r.* Can.
53 C3 Finley Austr.
134 C1 Finley U.S.A.
101 E2 Finne *ridge* Ger.
92 H2 Finnmarksvidda *reg.* Norway
92 G2 Finnsnes Norway
93 G4 Finspång Sweden
97 C1 Fintona U.K.
96 A2 Fionnphort U.K.
Fırat *r.* Turkey *see* Euphrates
Firenze Italy *see* Florence
105 C2 Firminy France
74 B2 Firozabad India
74 B1 Firozpur India
81 D3 Fīrūzābād Iran
122 A2 Fish *watercourse* Namibia
122 B3 Fish *r.* S. Africa
129 F1 Fisher Strait Can.
99 A4 Fishguard U.K.
105 C2 Fismes France
Fisterra, Cabo Spain *see* Finisterre, Cape
139 E2 Fitchburg U.S.A.
128 C2 Fitzgerald Can.
141 D2 Fitzgerald U.S.A.
50 B1 Fitzroy Crossing Austr.
Fiume Croatia *see* Rijeka
54 A3 Five Rivers N.Z.
108 B2 Fivizzano Italy
119 C3 Fizi Dem. Rep. Congo
93 F3 Fjällnäs Sweden
92 G3 Fjällsjöälven *r.* Sweden
123 C3 Flagstaff S. Africa
142 A1 Flagstaff U.S.A.
130 C2 Flaherty Island Can.
98 C2 Flamborough Head *hd* U.K.
101 F1 Fläming *hills* Ger.
136 B2 Flaming Gorge Reservoir U.S.A.
134 D1 Flathead *r.* U.S.A.
134 D1 Flathead Lake U.S.A.
51 D1 Flattery, Cape Austr.
134 B1 Flattery, Cape U.S.A.
98 B3 Fleetwood U.K.
93 E4 Flekkefjord Norway
102 B1 Flensburg Ger.
104 B2 Flers France
100 B2 Fleurus Belgium
104 C2 Fleury-les-Aubrais France
51 D1 Flinders *r.* Austr.
50 A3 Flinders Bay Austr.
51 D3 Flinders Island Austr.
52 A2 Flinders Ranges *mts* Austr.
129 D2 Flin Flon Can.
98 B3 Flint U.K.
138 C2 Flint U.S.A.
49 L5 Flint Island Kiribati
101 F2 Flöha Ger.
107 D1 Florac France
100 C3 Florange France
108 B2 Florence Italy
140 C2 Florence *AL* U.S.A.
142 A2 Florence *AZ* U.S.A.
134 B2 Florence *OR* U.S.A.
141 E2 Florence *SC* U.S.A.
150 B2 Florencia Col.
146 B3 Flores Guat.
61 D2 Flores *i.* Indon.
61 C2 Flores, Laut Indon.
Floreshty Moldova *see* Florești
Flores Sea Indon. *see* Flores, Laut
151 F3 Floresta Brazil
90 B2 Florești Moldova
143 D3 Floresville U.S.A.
151 E3 Floriano Brazil
152 D2 Florianópolis Brazil
153 C3 Florida Uru.
141 D2 Florida *state* U.S.A.
141 D4 Florida, Straits of Bahamas/U.S.A.
141 D4 Florida Bay U.S.A.
141 D4 Florida Keys *is* U.S.A.
111 B2 Florina Greece
93 E3 Florø Norway
129 D2 Foam Lake Can.
109 C2 Foča Bos.-Herz.
110 C1 Focșani Romania
71 B3 Fogang China
109 C2 Foggia Italy
131 E3 Fogo Island Can.
104 C3 Foix France
89 D3 Fokino Rus. Fed.
130 B3 Foleyet Can.
108 B2 Foligno Italy
99 D4 Folkestone U.K.
141 D2 Folkston U.S.A.
108 B2 Follonica Italy
129 D2 Fond-du-Lac Can.
129 D2 Fond du Lac *r.* Can.
138 B2 Fond du Lac U.S.A.
106 B1 Fondevila Spain
108 B2 Fondi Italy
146 B3 Fonseca, Golfo do *b.* Central America
150 C3 Fonte Boa Brazil
104 B2 Fontenay-le-Comte France
92 □C2 Fontur *pt* Iceland
Foochow China *see* Fuzhou
53 C2 Forbes Austr.
75 C2 Forbesganj India
101 E3 Forchheim Ger.
93 E3 Førde Norway
53 C1 Fords Bridge Austr.
140 B2 Fordyce U.S.A.
140 C2 Forest U.S.A.
53 C3 Forest Hill Austr.
131 D3 Forestville Can.
96 C2 Forfar U.K.
134 B1 Forks U.S.A.
108 B2 Forlì Italy
107 D2 Formentera *i.* Spain
107 D2 Formentor, Cap de *c.* Spain
155 C2 Formiga Brazil
152 C2 Formosa Arg.
Formosa Asia *see* Taiwan
154 C1 Formosa Brazil
Formosa Strait China/Taiwan *see* Taiwan Strait
Føroyar *terr.* N. Atlantic Ocean *see* Faroe Islands
96 C2 Forres U.K.
50 B3 Forrest Austr.
140 B1 Forrest City U.S.A.
51 D1 Forsayth Austr.
93 H3 Forssa Fin.
53 D2 Forster Austr.
136 B1 Forsyth U.S.A.
74 B2 Fort Abbas Pak.
130 B2 Fort Albany Can.
151 F3 Fortaleza Brazil
Fort Archambault Chad *see* Sarh
128 C2 Fort Assiniboine Can.
96 B2 Fort Augustus U.K.
123 C3 Fort Beaufort S. Africa
134 D1 Fort Benton U.S.A.
Fort Brabant Can. *see* Tuktoyaktuk
135 B3 Fort Bragg U.S.A.
Fort Carnot Madag. *see* Ikongo
Fort Charlet Alg. *see* Djanet
Fort Chimo Can. *see* Kuujjuaq
129 C2 Fort Chipewyan Can.
136 B2 Fort Collins U.S.A.
Fort Crampel C.A.R. *see* Kaga Bandoro
Fort-Dauphin Madag. *see* Tôlañaro
147 D3 Fort-de-France Martinique
Fort de Polignac Alg. *see* Illizi
137 E2 Fort Dodge U.S.A.
139 D2 Fort Erie Can.
Fort Flatters Alg. *see* Bordj Omer Driss
Fort Foureau Cameroon *see* Kousséri
130 A3 Fort Frances Can.
Fort Franklin Can. *see* Déljne
Fort Gardel Alg. *see* Zaouatallaz
Fort George Can. *see* Chisasibi
126 D2 Fort Good Hope Can.
Fort Gouraud Maur. *see* Fdérik
96 C2 Forth *r.* U.K.
96 C2 Forth, Firth of *est.* U.K.
Fort Hall Kenya *see* Murang'a
Fort Hertz Myanmar *see* Putao
152 C2 Fortín Madrejón Para.
Fort Jameson Zambia *see* Chipata
Fort Johnston Malawi *see* Mangochi
Fort Lamy Chad *see* Ndjamena
Fort Laperrine Alg. *see* Tamanrasset
141 D3 Fort Lauderdale U.S.A.
128 B1 Fort Liard Can.
128 C2 Fort Mackay Can.
137 E2 Fort Madison U.S.A.
Fort Manning Malawi *see* Mchinji
128 C2 Fort McMurray Can.
126 D2 Fort McPherson Can.
136 C2 Fort Morgan U.S.A.
141 D3 Fort Myers U.S.A.
128 B2 Fort Nelson Can.
128 B2 Fort Nelson *r.* Can.
Fort Norman Can. *see* Tulita
140 C2 Fort Payne U.S.A.
136 B1 Fort Peck U.S.A.
136 B1 Fort Peck Reservoir U.S.A.
141 D3 Fort Pierce U.S.A.
119 D2 Fort Portal Uganda
128 C1 Fort Providence Can.
129 D2 Fort Qu'Appelle Can.
128 C1 Fort Resolution Can.
96 B2 Fortrose U.K.
Fort Rosebery Zambia *see* Mansa
Fort Rousset Congo *see* Owando
Fort Rupert Can. *see* Waskaganish
Fort Sandeman Pak. *see* Zhob
128 C2 Fort Saskatchewan Can.
137 E3 Fort Scott U.S.A.
130 B2 Fort Severn Can.
76 B2 Fort-Shevchenko Kazakh.
128 B1 Fort Simpson Can.
128 C1 Fort Smith Can.
140 B1 Fort Smith U.S.A.
128 B2 Fort St James Can.
128 B2 Fort St John Can.
143 C2 Fort Stockton U.S.A.
142 C2 Fort Sumner U.S.A.
Fort Trinquet Maur. *see* Bîr Mogreïn
134 B2 Fortuna U.S.A.
131 E3 Fortune Bay Can.
128 C2 Fort Vermilion Can.
Fort Victoria Zimbabwe *see* Masvingo
Fort Walton U.S.A. *see* Fort Walton Beach
140 C2 Fort Walton Beach U.S.A.
136 B2 Fort Washakie U.S.A.
138 B2 Fort Wayne U.S.A.
96 B2 Fort William U.K.
143 D2 Fort Worth U.S.A.
126 C2 Fort Yukon U.S.A.
71 B3 Foshan China
92 F3 Fosna *pen.* Norway
93 E3 Fosnavåg Norway
92 □B3 Foss Iceland
92 □A2 Fossá Iceland
108 A2 Fossano Italy
137 D1 Fosston U.S.A.
53 C3 Foster Austr.
118 B3 Fougamou Gabon
104 B2 Fougères France
96 □ Foula *i.* U.K.
99 D4 Foulness Point U.K.
118 B2 Foumban Cameroon
111 C3 Fournoi *i.* Greece
114 A3 Fouta Djallon *reg.* Guinea
54 A3 Foveaux Strait N.Z.
136 C3 Fowler U.S.A.
50 C3 Fowlers Bay Austr.
81 C2 Fowman Iran
128 C2 Fox Creek Can.
127 G2 Foxe Basin *g.* Can.
127 G2 Foxe Channel Can.
127 G2 Foxe Peninsula Can.
54 B2 Fox Glacier N.Z.
128 C2 Fox Lake Can.
128 A1 Fox Mountain Can.
54 C2 Foxton N.Z.
129 D2 Fox Valley Can.
97 C1 Foyle *r.* Ireland/U.K.
97 C1 Foyle, Lough *b.* Ireland/U.K.
97 B2 Foynes Ireland
154 B3 Foz de Areia, Represa de *resr* Brazil
120 A2 Foz do Cunene Angola
154 B3 Foz do Iguaçu Brazil
107 D1 Fraga Spain
100 A2 Frameries Belgium
154 C2 Franca Brazil

109 C2 **Francavilla Fontana** Italy
104 C2 **France** country Europe
118 B3 **Franceville** Gabon
137 D2 **Francis Case, Lake** U.S.A.
155 C1 **Francisco Sá** Brazil
120 B3 **Francistown** Botswana
128 B2 **François Lake** Can.
100 B1 **Franeker** Neth.
101 D2 **Frankenberg (Eder)** Ger.
101 D3 **Frankenthal (Pfalz)** Ger.
101 E2 **Frankenwald** mts Ger.
138 C3 **Frankfort** KY U.S.A.
138 B2 **Frankfort** MI U.S.A.
        Frankfurt Ger. see
        Frankfurt am Main
101 D2 **Frankfurt am Main** Ger.
102 C1 **Frankfurt an der Oder** Ger.
102 C2 **Fränkische Alb** hills Ger.
101 E3 **Fränkische Schweiz** reg. Ger.
139 E2 **Franklin** NH U.S.A.
139 D2 **Franklin** PA U.S.A.
140 C1 **Franklin** TN U.S.A.
126 C2 **Franklin Bay** Can.
134 C1 **Franklin D. Roosevelt Lake** U.S.A.
128 B1 **Franklin Mountains** Can.
126 F2 **Franklin Strait** Can.
53 C3 **Frankston** Austr.
82 E1 **Frantsa-Iosifa, Zemlya** is
        Rus. Fed.
54 B2 **Franz Josef Glacier** N.Z.
        Franz Josef Land is Rus. Fed. see
        Frantsa-Iosifa, Zemlya
108 A3 **Frasca, Capo della** c. Sardinia Italy
128 B3 **Fraser** r. B.C. Can.
131 D2 **Fraser** r. Nfld and Lab. Can.
122 B3 **Fraserburg** S. Africa
96 C2 **Fraserburgh** U.K.
130 B3 **Fraserdale** Can.
51 E2 **Fraser Island** Austr.
128 B2 **Fraser Lake** Can.
128 B2 **Fraser Plateau** Can.
153 C3 **Fray Bentos** Uru.
93 E4 **Fredericia** Denmark
143 D2 **Frederick** U.S.A.
143 D2 **Fredericksburg** TX U.S.A.
139 D3 **Fredericksburg** VA U.S.A.
128 A2 **Frederick Sound** sea chan. U.S.A.
131 D3 **Fredericton** Can.
        Frederikshåb Greenland see
        Paamiut
93 F4 **Frederikshavn** Denmark
        Frederikshamn Fin. see **Hamina**
93 F4 **Fredrikstad** Norway
138 B2 **Freeport** IL U.S.A.
143 D3 **Freeport** TX U.S.A.
146 C2 **Freeport City** Bahamas
143 D3 **Freer** U.S.A.
123 C2 **Free State** prov. S. Africa
114 A4 **Freetown** Sierra Leone
106 B2 **Fregenal de la Sierra** Spain
104 B2 **Fréhel, Cap** c. France
102 B2 **Freiburg im Breisgau** Ger.
102 C2 **Freising** Ger.
102 C2 **Freistadt** Austria
105 D3 **Fréjus** France
50 A3 **Fremantle** Austr.
135 B3 **Fremont** CA U.S.A.
137 D2 **Fremont** NE U.S.A.
138 C2 **Fremont** OH U.S.A.
        French Congo country Africa see
        Congo
151 D2 **French Guiana** terr. S. America
        French Guinea country Africa see
        Guinea
134 E1 **Frenchman** r. U.S.A.
49 M5 **French Polynesia** terr.
        S. Pacific Ocean
        French Somaliland country Africa
        see **Djibouti**
        French Sudan country Africa see
        Mali
        **French Territory of the Afars and
        Issas** country Africa see **Djibouti**
151 D3 **Fresco** r. Brazil
144 B2 **Fresnillo** Mex.
135 C3 **Fresno** U.S.A.
107 D2 **Freu, Cap des** c. Spain
105 D2 **Freyming-Merlebach** France
114 A3 **Fria** Guinea
152 B2 **Frias** Arg.
101 D2 **Friedberg (Hessen)** Ger.
102 B2 **Friedrichshafen** Ger.
101 F1 **Friesack** Ger.
100 C1 **Friesoythe** Ger.
143 C2 **Friona** U.S.A.
136 B3 **Frisco** U.S.A.
        Frobisher Bay Can. see **Iqaluit**
127 H2 **Frobisher Bay** b. Can.
101 F2 **Frohburg** Ger.
87 D4 **Frolovo** Rus. Fed.
103 D1 **Frombork** Pol.
99 B4 **Frome** U.K.
52 A2 **Frome, Lake** salt flat Austr.
52 A2 **Frome Downs** Austr.
100 C2 **Fröndenberg** Ger.
143 C3 **Frontera** Mex.
145 C3 **Frontera** Mex.
144 B1 **Fronteras** Mex.
139 D3 **Front Royal** U.S.A.
108 B2 **Frosinone** Italy
92 E3 **Frøya** i. Norway
        Frunze Kyrg. see **Bishkek**
154 C2 **Frutal** Brazil
105 D2 **Frutigen** Switz.
103 D2 **Frýdek-Místek** Czech Rep.

71 B3 **Fu'an** China
71 C3 **Fuding** China
106 C1 **Fuenlabrada** Spain
152 C2 **Fuerte Olimpo** Para.
114 A2 **Fuerteventura** i. Canary Is
64 B2 **Fuga** i. Phil.
79 C2 **Fujairah** U.A.E.
67 C3 **Fuji** Japan
71 B3 **Fujian** prov. China
67 C3 **Fujinomiya** Japan
67 C3 **Fuji-san** vol. Japan
        Fukien prov. China see **Fujian**
67 A4 **Fukue** Japan
67 A4 **Fukue-jima** i. Japan
67 C3 **Fukui** Japan
67 B4 **Fukuoka** Japan
67 D3 **Fukushima** Japan
101 D2 **Fulda** Ger.
101 D2 **Fulda** r. Ger.
70 A3 **Fuling** China
137 E3 **Fulton** U.S.A.
105 C2 **Fumay** France
49 I4 **Funafuti** atoll Tuvalu
114 A1 **Funchal** Madeira
155 D1 **Fundão** Brazil
106 B1 **Fundão** Port.
131 D3 **Fundy, Bay of** g. Can.
121 C3 **Funhalouro** Moz.
70 B2 **Funing** Jiangsu China
71 A3 **Funing** Yunnan China
115 C3 **Funtua** Nigeria
79 C2 **Fürgun, Küh-e** mt. Iran
89 F2 **Furmanov** Rus. Fed.
        Furmanovka Kazakh. see
        Moyynkum
        Furmanovo Kazakh. see
        Zhalpaktal
155 D1 **Furnas, Represa** resr Brazil
51 D4 **Furneaux Group** is Austr.
        Furong China see **Wan'an**
100 C1 **Fürstenau** Ger.
101 E3 **Fürth** Ger.
66 D3 **Furukawa** Japan
127 G2 **Fury and Hecla Strait** Can.
70 C1 **Fushun** China
65 B1 **Fusong** China
79 C2 **Fuwayriṭ** Qatar
        Fuxian China see **Wafangdian**
70 A3 **Fuxian** China
70 C1 **Fuxin** China
70 B2 **Fuyang** China
69 E1 **Fuyu** China
        Fuyu China see **Songyuan**
68 B1 **Fuyun** China
71 B3 **Fuzhou** China
71 B3 **Fuzhou** China
93 F4 **Fyn** i. Denmark
96 B3 **Fyne, Loch** inlet U.K.
        F.Y.R.O.M. country Europe see
        Macedonia

G

117 C4 **Gaalkacyo** Somalia
120 A2 **Gabela** Angola
        Gaberones Botswana see
        Gaborone
115 D1 **Gabès** Tunisia
115 D1 **Gabès, Golfe de** g. Tunisia
118 B3 **Gabon** country Africa
123 C1 **Gaborone** Botswana
79 C2 **Gâbrik** Iran
110 C2 **Gabrovo** Bulg.
114 A3 **Gabú** Guinea-Bissau
73 B3 **Gadag** India
75 C2 **Gadchiroli** India
101 E1 **Gadebusch** Ger.
140 C2 **Gadsden** U.S.A.
118 B2 **Gadzi** C.A.R.
110 C2 **Găeşti** Romania
108 B2 **Gaeta** Italy
108 B2 **Gaeta, Golfo di** g. Italy
141 D1 **Gaffney** U.S.A.
115 C1 **Gafsa** Tunisia
89 E2 **Gagarin** Rus. Fed.
109 C3 **Gagliano del Capo** Italy
114 B4 **Gagnoa** Côte d'Ivoire
131 D2 **Gagnon** Can.
        Gago Coutinho Angola see
        Lumbala N'guimbo
81 C1 **Gagra** Georgia
122 A2 **Gaiab** watercourse Namibia
104 C3 **Gaillac** France
        Gaillimh Ireland see **Galway**
141 D3 **Gainesville** FL U.S.A.
141 D2 **Gainesville** GA U.S.A.
143 D2 **Gainesville** TX U.S.A.
98 C3 **Gainsborough** U.K.
52 A2 **Gairdner, Lake** salt flat Austr.
96 B2 **Gairloch** U.K.
122 B2 **Gakarosa** mt. S. Africa
119 E3 **Galana** r. Kenya
103 D2 **Galanta** Slovakia
        Galápagos, Islas is Pacific Ocean
        see **Galapagos Islands**
125 I10 **Galapagos Islands** is
        Pacific Ocean
157 G6 **Galapagos Rise** sea feature
        Pacific Ocean
96 C2 **Galashiels** U.K.
110 C1 **Galaţi** Romania
93 E3 **Galdhøpiggen** mt. Norway
145 B2 **Galeana** Mex.

128 C2 **Galena Bay** Can.
138 A2 **Galesburg** U.S.A.
122 B2 **Galeshewe** S. Africa
89 F2 **Galich** Rus. Fed.
106 B1 **Galicia** reg. Spain
80 B2 **Galilee, Sea of** l. Israel
78 A3 **Gallabat** Sudan
140 C1 **Gallatin** U.S.A.
73 C4 **Galle** Sri Lanka
157 G6 **Gallego Rise** sea feature
        Pacific Ocean
150 B1 **Gallinas, Punta** pt Col.
109 C2 **Gallipoli** Italy
111 C2 **Gallipoli** Turkey
92 H2 **Gällivare** Sweden
142 B1 **Gallup** U.S.A.
114 A2 **Galtat Zemmour**
        Western Sahara
97 B2 **Galtymore** hill Ireland
143 E3 **Galveston** U.S.A.
143 E3 **Galveston Bay** U.S.A.
143 E3 **Galveston Island** U.S.A.
97 B2 **Galway** Ireland
97 B2 **Galway Bay** Ireland
154 C1 **Gamá** Brazil
123 D3 **Gamalakhe** S. Africa
117 B4 **Gambêla** Eth.
114 A3 **Gambia** r. Gambia
114 A3 **Gambia, The** country Africa
49 N6 **Gambier, Îles** is Fr. Polynesia
52 A3 **Gambier Islands** Austr.
131 E3 **Gambo** Can.
118 B3 **Gamboma** Congo
92 H2 **Gammelstaden** Sweden
142 B1 **Ganado** U.S.A.
81 D3 **Ganāveh** Iran
81 C1 **Gäncä** Azer.
61 C2 **Gandadiwata, Bukit** mt. Indon.
118 C3 **Gandajika** Dem. Rep. Congo
106 B1 **Gándara** Spain
131 E3 **Gander** Can.
131 E3 **Gander** r. Can.
101 D1 **Ganderkesee** Ger.
107 D1 **Gandesa** Spain
74 B2 **Gandhidham** India
74 B2 **Gandhinagar** India
74 B2 **Gandhi Sagar** resr India
107 C2 **Gandia** Spain
        Ganga r. Bangl./India see **Ganges**
153 B4 **Gangán** Arg.
74 B2 **Ganganagar** India
62 A1 **Gangaw** Myanmar
68 C2 **Gangca** China
75 C1 **Gangdisê Shan** mts China
75 D2 **Ganges** r. Bangl./India
105 C3 **Ganges** France
75 C2 **Ganges, Mouths of the**
        Bangl./India
159 E2 **Ganges Cone** sea feature
        Indian Ocean
75 C2 **Gangtok** India
75 C3 **Ganjam** India
71 B3 **Gan Jiang** r. China
71 A3 **Ganluo** China
105 C2 **Gannat** France
136 B2 **Gannett Peak** U.S.A.
122 A3 **Gansbaai** S. Africa
70 A1 **Gansu** prov. China
115 D4 **Ganye** Nigeria
71 B3 **Ganzhou** China
114 B3 **Gao** Mali
        Gaoleshan China see **Xianfeng**
114 B3 **Gaoua** Burkina
114 A3 **Gaoual** Guinea
70 B2 **Gaoyou** China
70 B2 **Gaoyou Hu** l. China
105 D3 **Gap** France
64 B2 **Gapan** Phil.
107 C2 **Gap Carbon** hd Alg.
75 C1 **Gar** China
72 C1 **Gar** China
97 B2 **Gara, Lough** l. Ireland
117 C4 **Garacad** Somalia
53 C1 **Garah** Austr.
151 F3 **Garanhuns** Brazil
123 C2 **Ga-Rankuwa** S. Africa
118 C1 **Garar, Plaine de** plain Chad
117 C4 **Garbahaarrey** Somalia
135 B2 **Garberville** U.S.A.
81 D2 **Garbosh, Küh-e** mt. Iran
101 D1 **Garbsen** Ger.
154 C2 **Garça** Brazil
154 B2 **Garcias** Brazil
108 B1 **Garda, Lake** l. Italy
108 A3 **Garde, Cap de** c. Alg.
101 E1 **Gardelegen** Ger.
136 C3 **Garden City** U.S.A.
129 E2 **Garden Hill** Can.
77 C3 **Gardēz** Afgh.
139 F2 **Gardiner** U.S.A.
        Gardner atoll Micronesia see
        Faraulep
135 C3 **Gardnerville** U.S.A.
136 B3 **Garfield** U.S.A.
88 B2 **Gargždai** Lith.
123 C2 **Gariep Dam** resr S. Africa
122 A3 **Garies** S. Africa
119 D3 **Garissa** Kenya
88 B2 **Garkalne** Latvia
143 D2 **Garland** U.S.A.
102 C2 **Garmisch-Partenkirchen** Ger.
52 B2 **Garnpung Lake** imp. l. Austr.
104 B3 **Garonne** r. France
117 C4 **Garoowe** Somalia
74 B2 **Garoth** India

118 B2 **Garoua** Cameroon
118 B2 **Garoua Boulai** Cameroon
        Gargêntang China see **Sog**
96 B2 **Garry** r. U.K.
81 D2 **Garrygala** Turkm.
126 F2 **Garry Lake** Can.
119 E3 **Garsen** Kenya
122 A2 **Garub** Namibia
60 B2 **Garut** Indon.
138 B2 **Gary** U.S.A.
145 B2 **Garza García** Mex.
68 C2 **Garzê** China
        Gascogne reg. France see
        Gascony
        Gascogne, Golfe de g.
        France/Spain see **Gascony, Gulf of**
104 B3 **Gascony** reg. France
104 B3 **Gascony, Gulf of** France/Spain
50 A2 **Gascoyne** r. Austr.
118 B2 **Gashaka** Nigeria
115 D3 **Gashua** Nigeria
59 E3 **Gasmata** P.N.G.
131 D3 **Gaspé** Can.
131 D3 **Gaspé, Péninsule de** pen. Can.
141 E1 **Gaston, Lake** U.S.A.
141 D1 **Gastonia** U.S.A.
107 C2 **Gata, Cabo de** c. Spain
88 D2 **Gatchina** Rus. Fed.
98 C2 **Gateshead** U.K.
143 D2 **Gatesville** U.S.A.
139 D1 **Gatineau** Can.
130 C3 **Gatineau** r. Can.
        Gatooma Zimbabwe see **Kadoma**
53 D1 **Gatton** Austr.
129 E2 **Gauer Lake** Can.
93 E4 **Gausta** mt. Norway
123 C2 **Gauteng** prov. S. Africa
79 C2 **Gävbandi** Iran
111 B3 **Gavdos** i. Greece
104 B3 **Gave** r. France
93 G3 **Gävle** Sweden
93 G3 **Gävlebukten** b. Sweden
89 F2 **Gavrilov Posad** Rus. Fed.
89 E2 **Gavrilov-Yam** Rus. Fed.
122 A2 **Gawachab** Namibia
62 A1 **Gawai** Myanmar
52 A2 **Gawler** Austr.
52 A2 **Gawler Ranges** hills Austr.
75 C2 **Gaya** India
114 C3 **Gaya** Niger
114 C3 **Gayéri** Burkina
138 C1 **Gaylord** U.S.A.
86 E2 **Gayny** Rus. Fed.
116 B1 **Gaza** terr. Asia
80 B2 **Gaza** Gaza
76 B2 **Gaz-Achak** Turkm.
76 B3 **Gazandzhyk** Turkm.
80 B2 **Gaziantep** Turkey
114 B4 **Gbarnga** Liberia
118 A2 **Gboko** Nigeria
103 D1 **Gdańsk** Pol.
88 A3 **Gdańsk, Gulf of** Pol./Rus. Fed.
88 C2 **Gdov** Rus. Fed.
103 D1 **Gdynia** Pol.
116 B3 **Gedaref** Sudan
101 D2 **Gedern** Ger.
111 C3 **Gediz** Turkey
111 C3 **Gediz** r. Turkey
102 C1 **Gedser** Denmark
100 B2 **Geel** Belgium
52 B3 **Geelong** Austr.
101 E1 **Geesthacht** Ger.
75 C1 **Gê'gyai** China
129 D2 **Geikie** r. Can.
93 E3 **Geilo** Norway
119 D3 **Geita** Tanz.
71 A3 **Gejiu** China
108 B3 **Gela** Sicily Italy
108 B3 **Gela, Golfo di** g. Sicily Italy
91 D3 **Gelendzhik** Rus. Fed.
        Gelibolu Turkey see **Gallipoli**
100 C2 **Gelsenkirchen** Ger.
118 B2 **Gemena** Dem. Rep. Congo
111 C2 **Gemlik** Turkey
108 B1 **Gemona del Friuli** Italy
117 C4 **Genalë Wenz** r. Eth.
153 B3 **General Acha** Arg.
153 B3 **General Alvear** Arg.
153 C3 **General Belgrano** Arg.
144 B2 **General Cepeda** Mex.
        General Freire Angola see
        Muxaluando
        General Machado Angola see
        Camacupa
153 R3 **General Pico** Arg.
153 B3 **General Roca** Arg.
154 B2 **General Salgado** Brazil
64 B2 **General Santos** Phil.
139 D2 **Genesee** r. U.S.A.
138 A2 **Geneseo** IL U.S.A.
139 D2 **Geneseo** NY U.S.A.
105 D2 **Geneva** Switz.
139 D2 **Geneva** U.S.A.
105 D2 **Geneva, Lake** l. France/Switz.
        Genève Switz. see **Geneva**
106 B2 **Genil** r. Spain
100 B2 **Genk** Belgium
53 C3 **Genoa** Austr.
108 A2 **Genoa** Italy
108 A2 **Genoa, Gulf of** g. Italy
        Genova Italy see **Genoa**
        Gent Belgium see **Ghent**
61 C2 **Genteng** i. Indon.
101 F1 **Genthin** Ger.
50 A3 **Geographe Bay** Austr.

131 D2 **George** r. Can.
122 B3 **George** S. Africa
52 A3 **George, Lake** Austr.
141 D3 **George, Lake** FL U.S.A.
139 E2 **George, Lake** NY U.S.A.
146 C2 **George Town** Bahamas
114 A3 **Georgetown** Gambia
151 D2 **Georgetown** Guyana
60 B1 **Georgetown** Malaysia
138 C3 **Georgetown** KY U.S.A.
141 E2 **Georgetown** SC U.S.A.
143 D2 **Georgetown** TX U.S.A.
55 L2 **George V Land** reg. Antarctica
81 C1 **Georgia** country Asia
141 D2 **Georgia** state U.S.A.
130 B3 **Georgian Bay** Can.
51 C2 **Georgina** watercourse Austr.
Georgiu-Dezh Rus. Fed. see Liski
77 E2 **Georgiyevka** Kazakh.
87 D4 **Georgiyevsk** Rus. Fed.
101 F2 **Gera** Ger.
151 E4 **Geral de Goiás, Serra** hills Brazil
54 B2 **Geraldine** N.Z.
50 A2 **Geraldton** Austr.
80 B1 **Gerede** Turkey
76 C3 **Gereshk** Afgh.
102 C2 **Geretsried** Ger.
135 C2 **Gerlach** U.S.A.
103 E2 **Gerlachovský štit** mt. Slovakia
139 D3 **Germantown** U.S.A.
102 C1 **Germany** country Europe
100 C2 **Gerolstein** Ger.
101 E3 **Gerolzhofen** Ger.
53 D2 **Gerringong** Austr.
101 D2 **Gersfeld (Rhön)** Ger.
Géryville Alg. see El Bayadh
75 C1 **Gêrzê** China
106 C1 **Getafe** Spain
139 D3 **Gettysburg** PA U.S.A.
136 D1 **Gettysburg** SD U.S.A.
55 P2 **Getz Ice Shelf** Antarctica
111 B2 **Gevgelija** Macedonia
111 C3 **Geyikli** Turkey
122 B3 **Ghaap Plateau** S. Africa
Ghadámes Libya see Ghadāmis
115 C1 **Ghadāmis** Libya
75 C2 **Ghaghara** r. India
76 C2 **Ghalkarteniz, Solonchak** salt marsh Kazakh.
114 B4 **Ghana** country Africa
120 B3 **Ghanzi** Botswana
115 C1 **Ghardaïa** Alg.
78 A2 **Ghārib, Jabal** mt. Egypt
115 D1 **Gharyān** Libya
115 D2 **Ghāt** Libya
75 C2 **Ghatal** India
75 B2 **Ghaziabad** Uttar Prad. India
75 C2 **Ghazipur** India
77 C3 **Ghazni** Afgh.
78 B2 **Ghazzālah** Saudi Arabia
100 A2 **Ghent** Belgium
Gheorghe Gheorghiu-Dej Romania see Oneşti
110 C1 **Gheorgheni** Romania
110 B1 **Gherla** Romania
105 D3 **Ghisonaccia** Corsica France
74 B2 **Ghotaru** India
74 A2 **Ghotki** Pak.
75 C2 **Ghuari** r. India
76 C3 **Ghurian** Afgh.
91 E3 **Giaginskaya** Rus. Fed.
97 C1 **Giant's Causeway** lava field U.K.
61 C2 **Gianyar** Indon.
109 C3 **Giarre** Sicily Italy
108 A1 **Giaveno** Italy
120 A2 **Gibeon** Namibia
106 B2 **Gibraltar** terr. Europe
106 B2 **Gibraltar, Strait of** Morocco/Spain
140 B2 **Gibsland** U.S.A.
50 B2 **Gibson Desert** Austr.
68 C1 **Gichgeniyn Nuruu** mts Mongolia
117 B4 **Gidolē** Eth.
105 C2 **Gien** France
101 D2 **Gießen** Ger.
101 E1 **Gifhorn** Ger.
128 C2 **Gift Lake** Can.
67 C3 **Gifu** Japan
96 B3 **Gigha** i. U.K.
76 C2 **G'ijduvon** Uzbek.
106 B1 **Gijón-Xixón** Spain
142 A2 **Gila** r. U.S.A.
142 A2 **Gila Bend** U.S.A.
51 D1 **Gilbert** r. Austr.
48 I4 **Gilbert Islands** country Pacific Ocean
156 D5 **Gilbert Ridge** sea feature Pacific Ocean
151 E3 **Gilbués** Brazil
134 D1 **Gildford** U.S.A.
Gilf Kebir Plateau Egypt see Ḥaḍabat al Jilf al Kabir
53 C2 **Gilgandra** Austr.
74 B1 **Gilgit** Jammu and Kashmir
74 B1 **Gilgit** r. Jammu and Kashmir
53 C2 **Gilgunnia** Austr.
129 E2 **Gillam** Can.
136 B2 **Gillette** U.S.A.
99 D4 **Gillingham** U.K.
135 B3 **Gilmour Island** Can.
135 B3 **Gilroy** U.S.A.
129 E2 **Gimli** Can.
129 E2 **Gingoog** Phil.
117 C4 **Ginir** Eth.
109 C2 **Ginosa** Italy

109 C2 **Gioia del Colle** Italy
53 C3 **Gippsland** reg. Austr.
74 A2 **Girdar Dhor** r. Pak.
79 D1 **Girdi** Iran
80 B1 **Giresun** Turkey
Girgenti Italy see Agrigento
53 C2 **Girilambone** Austr.
Giron Sweden see Kiruna
107 D1 **Girona** Spain
104 B2 **Gironde** est. France
53 C2 **Girral** Austr.
96 B3 **Girvan** U.K.
54 C1 **Gisborne** N.Z.
93 F4 **Gislaved** Sweden
119 C3 **Gitarama** Rwanda
119 C3 **Gitega** Burundi
Giuba r. Somalia see Jubba
108 B2 **Giulianova** Italy
110 C2 **Giurgiu** Romania
110 C1 **Giuvala, Pasul** pass Romania
105 C2 **Givors** France
123 D1 **Giyani** S. Africa
119 D2 **Giyon** Eth.
116 B2 **Giza** Egypt
103 E1 **Giżycko** Pol.
109 D2 **Gjirokastër** Albania
126 F2 **Gjoa Haven** Can.
93 F3 **Gjøvik** Norway
131 E3 **Glace Bay** Can.
134 B1 **Glacier Peak** vol. U.S.A.
143 E2 **Gladewater** U.S.A.
51 E2 **Gladstone** Qld Austr.
52 A2 **Gladstone** S.A. Austr.
92 □A2 **Gláma** mts Iceland
109 C2 **Glamoč** Bos.-Herz.
100 C3 **Glan** r. Ger.
97 B2 **Glanaruddery Mountains** hills Ireland
96 B3 **Glasgow** U.K.
138 B3 **Glasgow** KY U.S.A.
136 B1 **Glasgow** MT U.S.A.
99 B4 **Glastonbury** U.K.
101 F2 **Glauchau** Ger.
86 E3 **Glazov** Rus. Fed.
89 E3 **Glazunovka** Rus. Fed.
123 D2 **Glencoe** S. Africa
96 B2 **Glen Coe** val. U.K.
142 A2 **Glendale** AZ U.S.A.
138 B2 **Glendale** WI U.S.A.
53 D2 **Glen Davis** Austr.
51 D1 **Glenden** Austr.
136 C1 **Glendive** U.S.A.
52 B3 **Glenelg** r. Austr.
96 B2 **Glenfinnan** U.K.
53 D1 **Glen Innes** Austr.
96 B2 **Glen More** val. U.K.
53 C1 **Glenmorgan** Austr.
126 C2 **Glennallen** U.S.A.
134 C2 **Glenns Ferry** U.S.A.
136 B2 **Glenrock** U.S.A.
96 C2 **Glenrothes** U.K.
139 E2 **Glens Falls** U.S.A.
96 C2 **Glen Shee** val. U.K.
97 B1 **Glenties** Ireland
142 B2 **Glenwood** U.S.A.
136 B3 **Glenwood Springs** U.S.A.
101 E1 **Glinde** Ger.
103 D1 **Gliwice** Pol.
142 A2 **Globe** U.S.A.
103 D1 **Głogów** Pol.
92 F2 **Glomfjord** Norway
93 F4 **Glomma** r. Norway
53 D2 **Gloucester** Austr.
99 B4 **Gloucester** U.K.
131 E3 **Glovertown** Can.
101 E1 **Glöwen** Ger.
77 E1 **Glubokoye** Kazakh.
101 D2 **Glückstadt** Ger.
103 C2 **Gmünd** Austria
102 C2 **Gmunden** Austria
101 D1 **Gnarrenburg** Ger.
103 D1 **Gniezno** Pol.
109 D2 **Gnjilane** Serb. and Mont.
75 D2 **Goalpara** India
96 B3 **Goat Fell** hill U.K.
117 C4 **Goba** Eth.
122 A1 **Gobabis** Namibia
153 A4 **Gobernador Gregores** Arg.
152 C2 **Gobernador Virasoro** Arg.
68 D2 **Gobi** des. China/Mongolia
67 C4 **Gobō** Japan
100 C2 **Goch** Ger.
122 A1 **Gochas** Namibia
74 B3 **Godavari** r. India
73 C3 **Godavari, Mouths of the** India
75 C3 **Godda** India
117 C4 **Godē** Eth.
130 B3 **Goderich** Can.
Godhavn Greenland see Qeqertarsuaq
74 B2 **Godhra** India
129 E2 **Gods** r. Can.
129 E2 **Gods Lake** Can.
Godthåb Greenland see Nuuk
Godwin-Austen, Mount China/Jammu and Kashmir see K2
Goedgegun Swaziland see Nhlangano
130 C3 **Goéland, Lac au** l. Can.
131 D2 **Goélands, Lac aux** l. Can.
100 A2 **Goes** Neth.
138 B1 **Gogebic Range** hills U.S.A.
88 C1 **Gogland, Ostrov** i. Rus. Fed.
Gogra r. India see Ghaghara
119 C2 **Gogrial** Sudan

154 C1 **Goiandira** Brazil
154 C1 **Goianésia** Brazil
154 C1 **Goiânia** Brazil
154 B1 **Goiás** Brazil
154 C1 **Goiatuba** Brazil
154 B2 **Goio-Erê** Brazil
111 C2 **Gökçeada** i. Turkey
111 C3 **Gökçedağ** Turkey
121 B2 **Gokwe** Zimbabwe
93 E3 **Gol** Norway
75 C2 **Golaghat** India
62 A1 **Golaghat** India
111 C2 **Gölcük** Turkey
103 E1 **Goldap** Pol.
101 F1 **Goldberg** Ger.
Gold Coast country Africa see Ghana
53 D1 **Gold Coast** Austr.
114 B4 **Gold Coast** coastal area Ghana
128 C2 **Golden** Can.
54 B2 **Golden Bay** N.Z.
134 B1 **Goldendale** U.S.A.
128 B3 **Golden Hinde** mt. Can.
97 B2 **Golden Vale** lowland Ireland
135 C3 **Goldfield** U.S.A.
128 B3 **Gold River** Can.
141 E1 **Goldsboro** U.S.A.
103 C1 **Goleniów** Pol.
135 C4 **Goleta** U.S.A.
Golfe du St-Laurent g. Can. see St Lawrence, Gulf of
111 C3 **Gölhisar** Turkey
Gollel Swaziland see Lavumisa
75 D1 **Golmud** China
81 D2 **Golpāyegān** Iran
96 C2 **Golspie** U.K.
Golyshi Rus. Fed. see Vetluzhskiy
119 C3 **Goma** Dem. Rep. Congo
75 C2 **Gomati** r. India
115 D3 **Gombe** Nigeria
115 D3 **Gombi** Nigeria
Gomel' Belarus see Homyel'
144 B2 **Gómez Palacio** Mex.
81 D2 **Gomīshān** Iran
75 C1 **Gomo** China
147 C3 **Gonaïves** Haiti
147 C3 **Gonâve, Île de la** i. Haiti
81 D2 **Gonbad-e Kavus** Iran
74 B2 **Gondal** India
116 B3 **Gonder** Eth. see Gonder
75 C2 **Gondia** India
111 C2 **Gönen** Turkey
62 A1 **Gonggar** China
70 A3 **Gongga Shan** mt. China
68 C2 **Gonghe** China
115 D4 **Gongola** r. Nigeria
53 C2 **Gongolgon** Austr.
Gongtang China see Damxung
123 C3 **Gonubie** S. Africa
145 C2 **Gonzáles** Mex.
143 D3 **Gonzales** U.S.A.
122 A3 **Good Hope, Cape of** S. Africa
134 D2 **Gooding** U.S.A.
136 C3 **Goodland** U.S.A.
53 C1 **Goodooga** Austr.
98 C3 **Goole** U.K.
53 C2 **Goolgowi** Austr.
52 A3 **Goolwa** Austr.
53 D1 **Goondiwindi** Austr.
134 B2 **Goose Lake** U.S.A.
102 B2 **Göppingen** Ger.
75 C2 **Gorakhpur** India
109 C2 **Goražde** Bos.-Herz.
111 C3 **Gördes** Turkey
89 D3 **Gordeyevka** Rus. Fed.
Gordon, U.S.A.
51 D4 **Gordon, Lake** Austr.
115 D4 **Goré** Chad
117 B4 **Gorē** Eth.
54 A3 **Gore** N.Z.
97 C2 **Gorey** Ireland
81 D2 **Gorgān** Iran
81 C1 **Gori** Georgia
100 B2 **Gorinchem** Neth.
108 B1 **Gorizia** Italy
Gor'kiy Rus. Fed. see Nizhniy Novgorod
89 F2 **Gor'kovskoye Vodokhranilishche** resr Rus. Fed.
103 E2 **Gorlice** Pol.
103 C1 **Görlitz** Ger.
Gorna Dzhumaya Bulg. see Blagoevgrad
109 D2 **Gornji Milanovac** Serb. and Mont.
109 C2 **Gornji Vakuf** Bos.-Herz.
77 E1 **Gorno-Altaysk** Rus. Fed.
86 F2 **Gornopravdinsk** Rus. Fed.
110 C2 **Gornotrakiyska Nizina** lowland Bulg.
66 D1 **Gornozavodsk** Rus. Fed.
77 E1 **Gornyak** Rus. Fed.
59 D3 **Goroka** P.N.G.
52 B3 **Goroke** Austr.
121 C2 **Gorom Gorom** Burkina
61 D1 **Gorontalo** Indon.
89 E3 **Gorshechnoye** Rus. Fed.
97 B2 **Gorumna Island** Ireland
91 D3 **Goryachiy Klyuch** Rus. Fed.
103 D1 **Gorzów Wielkopolski** Pol.
59 D3 **Goschen Strait** P.N.G.
53 D2 **Gosford** Austr.
74 A2 **Goshanak** Pak.
66 D3 **Goshogawara** Japan
101 E2 **Goslar** Ger.

109 C2 **Gospić** Croatia
99 C4 **Gosport** U.K.
111 B2 **Gostivar** Macedonia
Göteborg Sweden see Gothenburg
101 E2 **Gotha** Ger.
93 F4 **Gothenburg** Sweden
136 C2 **Gothenburg** U.S.A.
93 G4 **Gotland** i. Sweden
111 B2 **Gotse Delchev** Bulg.
93 G4 **Gotska Sandön** i. Sweden
67 B4 **Gōtsu** Japan
101 D2 **Göttingen** Ger.
128 B2 **Gott Peak** Can.
100 B1 **Gouda** Neth.
114 A3 **Goudiri** Senegal
115 D3 **Goudoumaria** Niger
158 E7 **Gough Island** S. Atlantic Ocean
130 C3 **Gouin, Réservoir** resr Can.
53 C2 **Goulburn** Austr.
53 C2 **Goulburn** r. N.S.W. Austr.
53 C3 **Goulburn** r. Vic. Austr.
114 B3 **Goundam** Mali
107 B3 **Gouraya** Alg.
114 B3 **Gourcy** Burkina
104 C3 **Gourdon** France
115 D3 **Gouré** Niger
122 B3 **Gourits** r. S. Africa
114 B3 **Gourma-Rharous** Mali
53 C3 **Gourock Range** mts Austr.
155 D1 **Governador Valadares** Brazil
147 E3 **Governor's Harbour** Bahamas
68 C2 **Govi Altayn Nuruu** mts Mongolia
75 C2 **Govind Ballash Pant Sagar** resr India
76 C4 **Gowd-e Zereh** plain Afgh.
99 A3 **Gower** pen. U.K.
152 C2 **Goya** Arg.
81 C1 **Göyçay** Azer.
80 B1 **Göynük** Turkey
115 E3 **Goz-Beïda** Chad
75 C1 **Gozha Co** salt l. China
122 B3 **Graaf-Reinet** S. Africa
122 A3 **Graafwater** S. Africa
101 E1 **Grabow** Ger.
109 C2 **Gračac** Croatia
87 E3 **Grachevka** Rus. Fed.
109 C2 **Gradačac** Bos.-Herz.
104 B3 **Gradignan** France
101 F2 **Gräfenhainichen** Ger.
53 D1 **Grafton** Austr.
137 D1 **Grafton** U.S.A.
143 D2 **Graham** U.S.A.
142 B2 **Graham, Mount** U.S.A.
Graham Bell Island Rus. Fed. see Greem-Bell, Ostrov
128 A2 **Graham Island** Can.
55 A3 **Graham Land** reg. Antarctica
123 C3 **Grahamstown** S. Africa
97 C2 **Graiguenamanagh** Ireland
151 E3 **Grajaú** Brazil
103 E1 **Grajewo** Pol.
111 B2 **Grammos** mt. Greece
96 B2 **Grampian Mountains** U.K.
146 B3 **Granada** Nic.
106 C2 **Granada** Spain
97 C2 **Granard** Ireland
139 E1 **Granby** Can.
114 A2 **Gran Canaria** i. Canary Is
152 B3 **Gran Chaco** reg. Arg./Para.
136 F2 **Grand** r. MO U.S.A.
136 C1 **Grand** r. SD U.S.A.
147 C3 **Grand Bahama** i. Bahamas
131 E3 **Grand Bank** Can.
158 D2 **Grand Banks of Newfoundland** sea feature N. Atlantic Ocean
Grand Canal China see Da Yunhe
Grand Canary i. Canary Is see Gran Canaria
142 A1 **Grand Canyon** U.S.A.
142 A1 **Grand Canyon** gorge U.S.A.
146 B3 **Grand Cayman** i. Cayman Is
129 C2 **Grand Centre** Can.
134 C1 **Grand Coulee** U.S.A.
152 B1 **Grande** r. Bol.
154 B2 **Grande** r. Brazil
153 B5 **Grande, Bahía** b. Arg.
155 D1 **Grande, Ilha** i. Brazil
150 C2 **Grande, Serra** mt. Brazil
128 C2 **Grande Cache** Can.
Grande Comore i. Comoros see Njazidja
128 C2 **Grande Prairie** Can.
115 D3 **Grand Erg de Bilma** des. Niger
114 B1 **Grand Erg Occidental** des. Alg.
115 C2 **Grand Erg Oriental** des. Alg.
131 D3 **Grande-Rivière** Can.
152 B3 **Grandes, Salinas** salt marsh Arg.
131 D3 **Grand Falls** N.B. Can.
131 E3 **Grand Falls** Nfld and Lab. Can.
128 C2 **Grand Forks** Can.
137 D1 **Grand Forks** U.S.A.
138 B2 **Grand Haven** U.S.A.
128 C1 **Grandin, Lac** l. Can.
137 D2 **Grand Island** U.S.A.
140 B3 **Grand Isle** U.S.A.
136 B3 **Grand Junction** U.S.A.
114 B4 **Grand-Lahou** Côte d'Ivoire
131 D3 **Grand Lake** N.B. Can.
131 E3 **Grand Lake** Nfld and Lab. Can.
137 E1 **Grand Marais** U.S.A.
130 C3 **Grand-Mère** Can.
106 B2 **Grândola** Port.

129 E2 **Grand Rapids** Can.
138 B2 **Grand Rapids** *MI* U.S.A.
137 E1 **Grand Rapids** *MN* U.S.A.
136 A2 **Grand Teton** *mt.* U.S.A.
147 C2 **Grand Turk** Turks and Caicos Is
129 D2 **Grandview** Can.
134 C1 **Grandview** U.S.A.
134 C1 **Grangeville** U.S.A.
128 B2 **Granisle** Can.
137 D3 **Granite Falls** U.S.A.
134 E1 **Granite Peak** *MT* U.S.A.
134 C2 **Granite Peak** *NV* U.S.A.
108 B3 **Granitola, Capo** *c. Sicily* Italy
93 F4 **Gränna** Sweden
101 F1 **Gransee** Ger.
99 C3 **Grantham** U.K.
96 C2 **Grantown-on-Spey** U.K.
142 B1 **Grants** U.S.A.
134 B2 **Grants Pass** U.S.A.
104 B2 **Granville** France
129 D2 **Granville Lake** Can.
155 D1 **Grão Mogol** Brazil
123 D1 **Graskop** S. Africa
105 D3 **Grasse** France
50 B3 **Grass Patch** Austr.
107 D1 **Graus** Spain
92 F2 **Gravdal** Norway
104 B2 **Grave, Pointe de** *pt* France
129 D3 **Gravelbourg** Can.
130 C3 **Gravenhurst** Can.
53 D1 **Gravesend** Austr.
99 D4 **Gravesend** U.K.
105 D2 **Gray** France
141 D1 **Gray** U.S.A.
138 C2 **Grayling** U.S.A.
99 D4 **Grays** U.K.
103 D2 **Graz** Austria
146 C2 **Great Abaco** *i.* Bahamas
50 B3 **Great Australian Bight** *g.* Austr.
146 C2 **Great Bahama Bank** *sea feature*
Bahamas
54 C1 **Great Barrier Island** N.Z.
51 D1 **Great Barrier Reef** Austr.
135 C3 **Great Basin** U.S.A.
128 C1 **Great Bear Lake** Can.
93 F4 **Great Belt** *sea chan.* Denmark
137 D3 **Great Bend** U.S.A.
63 A2 **Great Coco Island** Cocos Is
53 B3 **Great Dividing Range** *mts* Austr.
Great Eastern Erg *des.* Alg. *see*
Grand Erg Oriental
146 B2 **Greater Antilles** *is*
Caribbean Sea
Greater Khingan Mountains
China *see* Da Hinggan Ling
134 D1 **Great Falls** U.S.A.
123 C3 **Great Fish** *r.* S. Africa
123 C3 **Great Fish Point** S. Africa
147 C2 **Great Inagua** *i.* Bahamas
122 B3 **Great Karoo** *plat.* S. Africa
123 C3 **Great Kei** *r.* S. Africa
99 B3 **Great Malvern** U.K.
122 A2 **Great Namaqualand** *reg.* Namibia
73 D4 **Great Nicobar** *i.* India
98 B3 **Great Ormes Head** *hd* U.K.
99 D3 **Great Ouse** *r.* U.K.
136 C2 **Great Plains** U.S.A.
119 D3 **Great Rift Valley** Africa
119 D3 **Great Ruaha** *r.* Tanz.
134 D2 **Great Salt Lake** U.S.A.
134 D2 **Great Salt Lake Desert** U.S.A.
116 A2 **Great Sand Sea** *des.* Egypt/Libya
50 B2 **Great Sandy Desert** Austr.
128 C1 **Great Slave Lake** Can.
141 D1 **Great Smoky Mountains** U.S.A.
99 A4 **Great Torrington** U.K.
50 B2 **Great Victoria Desert** Austr.
70 B1 **Great Wall** *tourist site* China
Great Western Erg *des.* Alg. *see*
Grand Erg Occidental
99 D3 **Great Yarmouth** U.K.
Grebenkovskiy Ukr. *see* Hrebinka
106 B1 **Gredos, Sierra de** *mts* Spain
111 B3 **Greece** *country* Europe
136 C2 **Greeley** U.S.A.
82 F1 **Greem-Bell, Ostrov** *i.* Rus. Fed.
138 F1 **Green** *r.* Can.
138 B3 **Green** *r. KY* U.S.A.
136 B3 **Green** *r. WY* U.S.A.
138 B2 **Green Bay** U.S.A.
138 B1 **Green Bay** *b.* U.S.A.
138 C3 **Greenbrier** *r.* U.S.A.
138 B3 **Greencastle** U.S.A.
141 D1 **Greeneville** U.S.A.
139 E2 **Greenfield** U.S.A.
129 D2 **Green Lake** Can.
127 J2 **Greenland** *terr.* N. America
160 L2 **Greenland Basin** *sea feature*
Arctic Ocean
160 R2 **Greenland Sea** *sea*
Greenland/Svalbard
96 B3 **Greenock** U.K.
97 C1 **Greenore** Ireland
135 D3 **Green River** *UT* U.S.A.
136 B2 **Green River** *WY* U.S.A.
138 B3 **Greensburg** *IN* U.S.A.
139 D2 **Greensburg** *PA* U.S.A.
141 E2 **Green Swamp** U.S.A.
142 A2 **Green Valley** U.S.A.
114 B4 **Greenville** Liberia
140 C2 **Greenville** *AL* U.S.A.
139 F1 **Greenville** *ME* U.S.A.
140 B2 **Greenville** *MS* U.S.A.
141 E1 **Greenville** *NC* U.S.A.
141 D2 **Greenville** *SC* U.S.A.

143 D2 **Greenville** *TX* U.S.A.
53 D2 **Greenwell Point** Austr.
131 D3 **Greenwood** Can.
140 B2 **Greenwood** *MS* U.S.A.
141 D2 **Greenwood** *SC* U.S.A.
50 B2 **Gregory, Lake** *salt flat* Austr.
51 D1 **Gregory Range** *hills* Austr.
102 C1 **Greifswald** Ger.
101 F2 **Greiz** Ger.
86 C2 **Gremikha** Rus. Fed.
93 F4 **Grenå** Denmark
140 C2 **Grenada** U.S.A.
147 D3 **Grenada** *country* West Indies
104 C3 **Grenade** France
93 F4 **Grenen** *spit* Denmark
53 C2 **Grenfell** Austr.
129 D2 **Grenfell** Can.
105 D2 **Grenoble** France
51 D1 **Grenville, Cape** Austr.
134 B1 **Gresham** U.S.A.
140 B3 **Gretna** *LA* U.S.A.
139 D3 **Gretna** *VA* U.S.A.
100 C1 **Greven** Ger.
111 B2 **Grevena** Greece
100 C2 **Grevenbroich** Ger.
101 E1 **Grevesmühlen** Ger.
136 B2 **Greybull** U.S.A.
128 A1 **Grey Hunter Peak** Can.
131 E2 **Grey Islands** Can.
54 B2 **Greymouth** N.Z.
52 B1 **Grey Range** *hills* Austr.
97 C2 **Greystones** Ireland
123 D2 **Greytown** S. Africa
91 E1 **Gribanovskiy** Rus. Fed.
118 B2 **Gribingui** *r.* C.A.R.
101 D3 **Griesheim** Ger.
141 D2 **Griffin** U.S.A.
53 C2 **Griffith** Austr.
88 C3 **Grigiškės** Lith.
118 C2 **Grimari** C.A.R.
101 F2 **Grimma** Ger.
102 C1 **Grimmen** Ger.
98 C3 **Grimsby** U.K.
128 C2 **Grimshaw** Can.
92 □B2 **Grímsstaðir** Iceland
93 E4 **Grimstad** Norway
93 E4 **Grindsted** Denmark
137 E2 **Grinnell** U.S.A.
123 C3 **Griqualand East** *reg.* S. Africa
122 B2 **Griqualand West** *reg.* S. Africa
122 B2 **Griquatown** S. Africa
127 G1 **Grise Fiord** Can.
Grishino Ukr. *see* Krasnoarmiys'k
99 D4 **Gris Nez, Cap** *c.* France
96 C1 **Gritley** U.K.
123 C2 **Groblersdal** S. Africa
122 B2 **Groblershoop** S. Africa
Grodno Belarus *see* Hrodna
103 D1 **Grodzisk Wielkopolski** Pol.
92 □A3 **Gröf** Iceland
104 B2 **Groix, Île de** *i.* France
100 C1 **Gronau (Westfalen)** Ger.
92 F3 **Grong** Norway
100 C1 **Groningen** Neth.
122 B3 **Groot Brakrivier** S. Africa
122 B2 **Grootdrink** S. Africa
51 C1 **Groote Eylandt** *i.* Austr.
120 A2 **Grootfontein** Namibia
122 A2 **Groot Karas Berg** *plat.* Namibia
122 B3 **Groot Swartberge** *mts* S. Africa
122 B2 **Grootvloer** *salt pan* S. Africa
123 C3 **Groot Winterberg** *mt.* S. Africa
101 D2 **Großenlüder** Ger.
101 E2 **Großer Beerberg** *hill* Ger.
102 C2 **Großer Rachel** *mt.* Ger.
103 C2 **Grosser Speikkogel** *mt.* Austria
108 B2 **Grosseto** Italy
101 D3 **Groß-Gerau** Ger.
102 C2 **Großglockner** *mt.* Austria
100 C1 **Groß-Hesepe** Ger.
101 E2 **Großlohra** Ger.
122 A1 **Gross Ums** Namibia
136 A2 **Gros Ventre Range** *mts* U.S.A.
131 E2 **Groswater Bay** Can.
130 B3 **Groundhog** *r.* Can.
135 B3 **Grover Beach** U.S.A.
140 B3 **Groves** U.S.A.
139 E2 **Groveton** U.S.A.
87 D4 **Groznyy** Rus. Fed.
109 C1 **Grubišno Polje** Croatia
Grudovo Bulg. *see* Sredets
103 D1 **Grudziądz** Pol.
122 A2 **Grünau** Namibia
92 □A3 **Grundarfjörður** Iceland
Gruzinskaya S.S.R. *admin. reg.*
Asia *see* Georgia
89 E3 **Gryazi** Rus. Fed.
89 F2 **Gryazovets** Rus. Fed.
103 D1 **Gryfice** Pol.
102 C1 **Gryfino** Pol.
153 E5 **Grytviken** S. Georgia
146 C2 **Guacanayabo, Golfo de** *b.* Cuba
144 B2 **Guadalajara** Mex.
106 C1 **Guadalajara** Spain
48 H4 **Guadalcanal** *i.* Solomon Is
107 C2 **Guadalope** *r.* Spain
106 B2 **Guadalquivir** *r.* Spain
132 B4 **Guadalupe** *i.* Mex.
106 B2 **Guadalupe, Sierra de** *mts* Spain
142 B2 **Guadalupe Peak** U.S.A.
144 B2 **Guadalupe Victoria** Mex.
144 B2 **Guadalupe y Calvo** Mex.
106 C1 **Guadarrama, Sierra de** *mts*
Spain

147 D3 **Guadeloupe** *terr.* West Indies
147 D3 **Guadeloupe Passage**
Caribbean Sea
106 B2 **Guadiana** *r.* Port./Spain
106 C2 **Guadix** Spain
154 B2 **Guaíra** Brazil
147 C3 **Guajira, Península de la** *pen.* Col.
150 B3 **Gualaceo** Ecuador
59 D2 **Guam** *terr.* N. Pacific Ocean
144 B2 **Guamúchil** Mex.
144 B2 **Guanacevi** Mex.
151 E4 **Guanambi** Brazil
150 C2 **Guanare** Venez.
146 B2 **Guane** Cuba
70 A2 **Guang'an** China
71 B3 **Guangchang** China
71 B3 **Guangdong** *prov.* China
Guanghua China *see* Laohekou
71 A3 **Guangxi Zhuangzu Zizhiqu**
aut. reg. China
70 A2 **Guangyuan** China
71 B3 **Guangzhou** China
155 D1 **Guanhães** Brazil
147 D4 **Guanipa** *r.* Venez.
71 A3 **Guanling** China
65 A1 **Guanshui** China
Guansuo China *see* Guanling
147 C2 **Guantánamo** Cuba
155 C2 **Guapé** Brazil
150 C4 **Guaporé** *r.* Bol./Brazil
155 D2 **Guarapari** Brazil
154 B3 **Guarapuava** Brazil
154 C3 **Guaraqueçaba** Brazil
155 C3 **Guaratinguetá** Brazil
154 C3 **Guaratuba** Brazil
106 B1 **Guarda** Port.
Guardafui, Cape Somalia *see*
Gwardafuy, Gees
154 C1 **Guarda Mor** Brazil
106 C1 **Guardo** Spain
155 C2 **Guarujá** Brazil
144 B2 **Guasave** Mex.
146 A3 **Guatemala** *country*
Central America
Guatemala Guat. *see*
Guatemala City
157 G5 **Guatemala Basin** *sea feature*
N. Pacific Ocean
146 A3 **Guatemala City** Guat.
150 C2 **Guaviare** *r.* Col.
155 C2 **Guaxupé** Brazil
150 B3 **Guayaquil** Ecuador
150 A3 **Guayaquil, Golfo de** *g.* Ecuador
152 B1 **Guayaramerin** Bol.
144 A2 **Guaymas** Mex.
117 B3 **Guba** Eth.
86 E1 **Guba Dolgaya** Rus. Fed.
108 B2 **Gubbio** Italy
89 E3 **Gubkin** Rus. Fed.
73 C3 **Gudivada** India
105 D2 **Guebwiller** France
114 A2 **Guélb er Rîchât** *hill* Maur.
115 C1 **Guelma** Alg.
114 A2 **Guelmine** Morocco
130 B3 **Guelph** Can.
145 C2 **Guémez** Mex.
104 B2 **Guérande** France
115 E2 **Guerende** Libya
104 C2 **Guéret** France
95 C4 **Guernsey** *i.* Channel Is
95 C4 **Guernsey** *terr.* Channel Is
144 A2 **Guerrero Negro** Mex.
131 D2 **Guers, Lac** *l.* Can.
158 D4 **Guiana Basin** *sea feature*
N. Atlantic Ocean
150 C2 **Guiana Highlands** *mts*
Guyana/Venez.
Guichi China *see* Chizhou
118 B2 **Guider** Cameroon
108 B2 **Guidonia-Montecelio** Italy
71 A3 **Guigang** China
100 A3 **Guignicourt** France
123 D1 **Guija** Moz.
99 C4 **Guildford** U.K.
71 B3 **Guilin** China
130 C2 **Guillaume-Delisle, Lac** *l.* Can.
106 B1 **Guimarães** Port.
114 A3 **Guinea** *country* Africa
113 D5 **Guinea, Gulf of** Africa
114 A3 **Guinea-Bissau** *country* Africa
104 B2 **Guingamp** France
104 B2 **Guipavas** France
154 B1 **Guiratinga** Brazil
150 C1 **Güiria** Venez.
151 D2 **Guisanbourg** Fr. Guiana
98 C2 **Guisborough** U.K.
100 A3 **Guise** France
64 B2 **Guiuan** Phil.
71 A3 **Guiyang** China
71 A3 **Guizhou** *prov.* China
104 B3 **Gujan-Mestras** France
74 B2 **Gujarat** *state* India
Gujerat *state* India *see* Gujarat
74 B1 **Gujranwala** Pak.
74 B1 **Gujrat** Pak.
91 D2 **Gukovo** Rus. Fed.
70 A2 **Gulang** China
53 C2 **Gulargambone** Austr.
73 B3 **Gulbarga** India
88 C2 **Gulbene** Latvia
79 C2 **Gulf, The** Asia
Gulf of California Mex. *see*
California, Gulf of
Gulf of Chihli China *see* Bo Hai

111 B3 **Gulf of Corinth** *sea chan.* Greece
140 C2 **Gulfport** U.S.A.
53 C2 **Gulgong** Austr.
69 E1 **Gulian** China
77 C2 **Guliston** Uzbek.
Gulja China *see* Yining
129 D2 **Gull Lake** Can.
111 C3 **Güllük** Turkey
Gulü China *see* Xincai
119 D2 **Gulu** Uganda
120 B2 **Gumare** Botswana
76 B3 **Gumdag** Turkm.
115 C3 **Gumel** Nigeria
75 C2 **Gumla** India
100 C2 **Gummersbach** Ger.
87 C4 **Gümüşhane** Turkey
74 B2 **Guna** India
Gunan China *see* Qijiang
53 C3 **Gundagai** Austr.
111 C3 **Güney** Turkey
118 B3 **Gungu** Dem. Rep. Congo
129 E2 **Gunisao** *r.* Can.
53 D2 **Gunnedah** Austr.
136 B3 **Gunnison** *CO* U.S.A.
135 D3 **Gunnison** *UT* U.S.A.
136 B3 **Gunnison** *r.* U.S.A.
73 B3 **Guntakal** India
73 C3 **Guntur** India
51 C1 **Gununa** Austr.
60 A1 **Gunungsitoli** Indon.
60 A1 **Gunungtua** Indon.
102 C2 **Günzburg** Ger.
102 C2 **Gunzenhausen** Ger.
70 B2 **Guojiaba** China
Guoluezhen China *see* Lingbao
74 B2 **Gurgaon** India
151 E3 **Gurgueia** *r.* Brazil
150 C2 **Guri, Embalse de** *resr* Venez.
154 C1 **Gurinhatã** Brazil
121 C2 **Guro** Moz.
151 E4 **Gurupi** Brazil
151 E3 **Gurupi** *r.* Brazil
74 B2 **Guru Sikhar** *mt.* India
121 C2 **Guruve** Zimbabwe
Gur'yev Kazakh. *see* Atyrau
115 C3 **Gusau** Nigeria
88 B3 **Gusev** Rus. Fed.
65 A2 **Gushan** China
74 A1 **Gushgy** Turkm.
70 B2 **Gushi** China
83 I3 **Gusinoozersk** Rus. Fed.
89 F2 **Gus'-Khrustal'nyy** Rus. Fed.
108 A3 **Guspini** *Sardinia* Italy
128 A2 **Gustavus** U.S.A.
101 F1 **Güstrow** Ger.
101 D2 **Gütersloh** Ger.
143 D1 **Guthrie** U.S.A.
152 B1 **Gutiérrez** Bol.
121 C2 **Gutu** Zimbabwe
75 D2 **Guwahati** India
150 D2 **Guyana** *country* S. America
Guyi China *see* Sanjiang
143 C1 **Guymon** U.S.A.
53 D2 **Guyra** Austr.
70 A2 **Guyuan** China
Guzhou China *see* Rongjiang
144 B1 **Guzmán** Mex.
144 B1 **Guzmán, Lago de** *l.* Mex.
77 C3 **G'uzor** Uzbek.
88 B3 **Gvardeysk** Rus. Fed.
74 A2 **Gwadar** Pak.
Gwador Pak. *see* Gwadar
74 B2 **Gwalior** India
121 B3 **Gwanda** Zimbabwe
117 D3 **Gwardafuy, Gees** *c.* Somalia
97 B1 **Gweebarra Bay** Ireland
97 B1 **Gweedore** Ireland
Gwelo Zimbabwe *see* Gweru
121 B2 **Gweru** Zimbabwe
115 D3 **Gwoza** Nigeria
53 D2 **Gwydir** *r.* Austr.
Gya'gya China *see* Saga
Gyandzha Azer. *see* Gäncä
Gyangkar China *see* Dinngyê
Gyangtse China *see* Gyangzê
75 C2 **Gyangzê** China
75 C1 **Gyaring Co** *l.* China
68 C2 **Gyaring Hu** *l.* China
86 G1 **Gydan Peninsula** *pen.* Rus. Fed.
Gydanskiy Poluostrov *pen.*
Rus. Fed. *see* Gydan Peninsula
Gyêgu China *see* Yushu
62 A1 **Gyigang** China
Gyixong China *see* Gonggar
51 E2 **Gympie** Austr.
62 A2 **Gyobingauk** Myanmar
103 D2 **Gyöngyös** Hungary
103 D2 **Győr** Hungary
136 B3 **Gypsum** U.S.A.
129 E2 **Gypsumville** Can.
131 D2 **Gyrfalcon Islands** Can.
111 B3 **Gytheio** Greece
103 E2 **Gyula** Hungary
81 C1 **Gyumri** Armenia
76 B3 **Gyzylarbat** Turkm.
Gzhatsk Rus. Fed. *see* Gagarin

H

88 B2 **Haapsalu** Estonia
100 B1 **Haarlem** Neth.
122 B3 **Haarlem** S. Africa
101 C2 **Haarstrang** *ridge* Ger.

Heniches'k
199

54 A2 **Haast** N.Z.
74 A2 **Hab** *r.* Pak.
79 C3 **Ḩabarūt** Oman
78 B3 **Habbān** Yemen
81 C2 **Ḩabbānīyah, Hawr al** *l.* Iraq
70 B1 **Habirag** China
67 C4 **Hachijō-jima** *i.* Japan
66 D2 **Hachinohe** Japan
67 C3 **Hachiōji** Japan
121 C3 **Hacufera** Moz.
116 A2 **Ḩaḑabat al Jilf al Kabīr** Egypt
79 C2 **Ḩadd, Ra's al** *pt* Oman
96 C3 **Haddington** U.K.
115 D3 **Hadejia** Nigeria
93 E4 **Haderslev** Denmark
78 B2 **Ḩādhah** Saudi Arabia
79 B3 **Ḩaḑramawt** *reg.* Yemen
79 B3 **Ḩaḑramawt, Wādī** *watercourse* Yemen
91 C1 **Hadyach** Ukr.
65 B2 **Haeju** N. Korea
65 B2 **Haeju-man** *b.* N. Korea
65 B3 **Haenam** S. Korea
78 B2 **Ḩafar al Bāţin** Saudi Arabia
74 B1 **Hafizabad** Pak.
75 D2 **Haflong** India
92 □A3 **Hafnarfjörður** Iceland
78 A3 **Hagar Nish Plateau** Eritrea
59 D2 **Hagåtña** Guam
101 F1 **Hagelberg** *hill* Ger.
100 C2 **Hagen** Ger.
101 E1 **Hagenow** Ger.
128 B2 **Hagensborg** Can.
139 D3 **Hagerstown** U.S.A.
93 F3 **Hagfors** Sweden
134 D1 **Haggin, Mount** U.S.A.
67 B4 **Hagi** Japan
62 B1 **Ha Giang** Vietnam
97 B2 **Hag's Head** *hd* Ireland
104 B2 **Hague, Cap de la** *c.* France
69 F3 **Hahajima-rettō** *is* Japan
119 D3 **Hai** Tanz.
Haicheng China *see* **Haifeng**
70 C1 **Haicheng** China
62 B1 **Hai Dương** Vietnam
80 B2 **Haifa** Israel
71 B3 **Haifeng** China
Haikang China *see* **Leizhou**
71 B3 **Haikou** China
78 B2 **Ḩā'il** Saudi Arabia
Hailar China *see* **Hulun Buir**
Hailong China *see* **Meihekou**
92 H2 **Hailuoto** *i.* Fin.
69 D3 **Hainan** *i.* China
71 A4 **Hainan** *prov.* China
128 A2 **Haines** U.S.A.
128 A1 **Haines Junction** Can.
101 E2 **Hainich** *ridge* Ger.
101 E2 **Hainleite** *ridge* Ger.
62 B1 **Hai Phong** Vietnam
Haiphong Vietnam *see* Hai Phong
147 C3 **Haiti** *country* West Indies
116 B3 **Haiya** Sudan
103 E2 **Hajdúböszörmény** Hungary
103 E2 **Hajdúszoboszló** Hungary
67 C3 **Hajiki-zaki** *pt* Japan
78 B3 **Ḩajjah** Yemen
81 D3 **Ḩājjīābād** Iran
103 E1 **Hajnówka** Pol.
62 A1 **Haka** Myanmar
81 C2 **Hakkârı** Turkey
66 D2 **Hakodate** Japan
122 B2 **Hakseen Pan** *salt pan* S. Africa
Ḩalab Syria *see* **Aleppo**
78 B2 **Ḩalabān** Saudi Arabia
81 C2 **Halabja** Iraq
116 B2 **Halaib** Sudan
78 A2 **Halaib Triangle** *terr.* Egypt/Sudan
79 C3 **Ḩalāniyāt, Juzur al** *is* Oman
78 A2 **Ḩālat 'Ammār** Saudi Arabia
68 C1 **Halban** Mongolia
101 E2 **Halberstadt** Ger.
64 B2 **Halcon, Mount** Phil.
93 F4 **Halden** Norway
101 E1 **Haldensleben** Ger.
75 B2 **Haldwani** India
79 C2 **Ḩāleh** Iran
54 A3 **Halfmoon Bay** N.Z.
139 D1 **Haliburton Highlands** *hills* Can.
131 D3 **Halifax** Can.
98 C3 **Halifax** U.K.
139 D3 **Halifax** U.S.A.
65 B3 **Halla-san** *mt.* S. Korea
127 G2 **Hall Beach** Can.
100 B2 **Halle** Belgium
102 C2 **Hallein** Austria
101 E2 **Halle-Neustadt** Ger.
101 E2 **Halle (Saale)** Ger.
48 G3 **Hall Islands** Micronesia
137 D1 **Hallock** U.S.A.
127 H2 **Hall Peninsula** Can.
50 B1 **Halls Creek** Austr.
59 C2 **Halmahera** *i.* Indon.
93 F4 **Halmstad** Sweden
Hälsingborg Sweden *see* Helsingborg
100 B2 **Halsteren** Neth.
98 B2 **Haltwhistle** U.K.
67 B4 **Hamada** Japan
81 C2 **Hamadān** Iran
80 B2 **Ḩamāh** Syria
67 C4 **Hamamatsu** Japan
93 F3 **Hamar** Norway
116 B2 **Ḩamāţah, Jabal** *mt.* Egypt
73 C4 **Hambantota** Sri Lanka
101 D1 **Hamburg** Ger.
123 C3 **Hamburg** S. Africa
140 B2 **Hamburg** U.S.A.
78 A2 **Ḩamḑ, Wādī al** *watercourse* Saudi Arabia
78 B3 **Ḩamḑah** Saudi Arabia
139 E2 **Hamden** U.S.A.
93 H3 **Hämeenlinna** Fin.
101 D1 **Hameln** Ger.
50 A2 **Hamersley Range** *mts* Austr.
65 B1 **Hamgyŏng-sanmaek** *mts* N. Korea
65 B2 **Hamhŭng** N. Korea
68 C2 **Hami** China
116 B2 **Hamid** Sudan
52 B3 **Hamilton** Austr.
130 C3 **Hamilton** Can.
Hamilton *r.* Can. *see* **Churchill**
54 C1 **Hamilton** N.Z.
96 B3 **Hamilton** U.K.
140 C2 **Hamilton** *AL* U.S.A.
134 D1 **Hamilton** *MT* U.S.A.
138 C3 **Hamilton** *OH* U.S.A.
115 E1 **Hamīm, Wādī al** *watercourse* Libya
93 I3 **Hamina** Fin.
100 C2 **Hamm** Ger.
114 B2 **Hammada du Drâa** *plat.* Alg.
115 D1 **Hammamet, Golfe de** *g.* Tunisia
81 C2 **Ḩammār, Hawr al** *imp. l.* Iraq
101 D2 **Hammelburg** Ger.
92 G3 **Hammerdal** Sweden
92 H1 **Hammerfest** Norway
140 B2 **Hammond** U.S.A.
139 E3 **Hammonton** U.S.A.
139 D3 **Hampton** U.S.A.
139 E2 **Hampton Bays** U.S.A.
79 C2 **Hāmūn-e Jaz Mūrīān** *salt marsh* Iran
74 A2 **Hamun-i-Lora** *dry lake* Pak.
74 A2 **Hamun-i-Mashkel** *salt flat* Pak.
78 A2 **Ḩanak** Saudi Arabia
66 D3 **Hanamaki** Japan
101 D2 **Hanau** Ger.
70 B2 **Hancheng** China
138 B1 **Hancock** U.S.A.
70 B2 **Handan** China
119 D3 **Handeni** Tanz.
135 C3 **Hanford** U.S.A.
68 C1 **Hangayn Nuruu** *mts* Mongolia
Hangchow China *see* **Hangzhou**
Hanggin Houqi China *see* **Xamba**
Hangö Fin. *see* **Hanko**
70 B2 **Hangu** China
70 C2 **Hangzhou** China
70 C2 **Hangzhou Wan** *b.* China
79 B2 **Ḩanīdh** Saudi Arabia
Hanjia China *see* **Pengshui**
Hanjiang China *see* **Yangzhou**
93 H4 **Hanko** Fin.
135 D3 **Hanksville** U.S.A.
54 B2 **Hanmer Springs** N.Z.
128 C2 **Hanna** Can.
136 B2 **Hanna** U.S.A.
137 E3 **Hannibal** U.S.A.
101 D1 **Hannover** Ger.
101 D2 **Hannoversch Münden** Ger.
93 F4 **Hanöbukten** *b.* Sweden
62 B1 **Ha Nôi** Vietnam
Hanoi Vietnam *see* **Ha Nôi**
130 B3 **Hanover** Can.
Hanover Ger. *see* **Hannover**
122 B3 **Hanover** S. Africa
139 E2 **Hanover** *NH* U.S.A.
139 D3 **Hanover** *PA* U.S.A.
92 G2 **Hansnes** Norway
93 E4 **Hanstholm** Denmark
88 C3 **Hantsavichy** Belarus
75 C2 **Hanumana** India
74 B2 **Hanumangarh** India
70 A2 **Hanzhong** China
49 M5 **Hao** *atoll* Fr. Polynesia
75 C2 **Haora** India
92 H2 **Haparanda** Sweden
100 B2 **Hapert** Neth.
131 D2 **Happy Valley-Goose Bay** Can.
78 A2 **Ḩaql** Saudi Arabia
79 B2 **Ḩaraḑh** Saudi Arabia
88 C2 **Haradok** Belarus
78 B3 **Ḩarajā** Saudi Arabia
121 C2 **Harare** Zimbabwe
79 C3 **Ḩarāsīs, Jiddat al** *des.* Oman
69 D1 **Har-Ayrag** Mongolia
115 E3 **Haraze-Mangueigne** Chad
114 A4 **Harbel** Liberia
69 E1 **Harbin** China
138 C2 **Harbor Beach** U.S.A.
131 E3 **Harbour Breton** Can.
74 B2 **Harda** India
92 E4 **Hardangerfjorden** *sea chan.* Norway
61 C1 **Harden, Bukit** *mt.* Indon.
100 C1 **Hardenberg** Neth.
100 B1 **Harderwijk** Neth.
122 A3 **Hardeveld** *mts* S. Africa
134 E1 **Hardin** U.S.A.
128 C1 **Hardisty Lake** Can.
93 E3 **Hareid** Norway
100 C1 **Haren (Ems)** Ger.
117 C4 **Hārer** Eth.
117 C4 **Hargeysa** Somalia
110 C1 **Harghita-Mădăraş, Vârful** *mt.* Romania
68 C2 **Har Hu** *l.* China
88 B2 **Hari kurk** *sea chan.* Estonia
74 B1 **Haripur** Pak.
74 A1 **Hari Rūd** *r.* Afgh./Iran
110 C1 **Hârlău** Romania
100 B1 **Harlingen** Neth.
143 D3 **Harlingen** U.S.A.
99 D4 **Harlow** U.K.
134 E1 **Harlowton** U.S.A.
134 C2 **Harney Basin** U.S.A.
134 C2 **Harney Lake** U.S.A.
93 G3 **Härnösand** Sweden
69 E1 **Har Nur** China
68 C1 **Har Nuur** *l.* Mongolia
96 □ **Haroldswick** U.K.
114 B4 **Harper** Liberia
101 D1 **Harpstedt** Ger.
130 C2 **Harricanaw** *r.* Can.
53 D2 **Harrington** Austr.
131 E2 **Harrington Harbour** Can.
96 A2 **Harris** *pen.* U.K.
96 A2 **Harris, Sound of** *sea chan.* U.K.
138 B3 **Harrisburg** *IL* U.S.A.
134 B2 **Harrisburg** *OR* U.S.A.
139 D2 **Harrisburg** *PA* U.S.A.
123 C2 **Harrismith** S. Africa
140 B1 **Harrison** U.S.A.
131 E2 **Harrison, Cape** Can.
126 B2 **Harrison Bay** U.S.A.
139 D3 **Harrisonburg** U.S.A.
128 B3 **Harrison Lake** Can.
137 E3 **Harrisonville** U.S.A.
98 C3 **Harrogate** U.K.
110 C2 **Hârşova** Romania
92 G2 **Harstad** Norway
122 B2 **Hartbees** *watercourse* S. Africa
103 D2 **Hartberg** Austria
139 E2 **Hartford** *CT* U.S.A.
137 D2 **Hartford** *SD* U.S.A.
99 A4 **Hartland Point** U.K.
98 C2 **Hartlepool** U.K.
Hartley Zimbabwe *see* **Chegutu**
128 B2 **Hartley Bay** Can.
123 B2 **Harts** *r.* S. Africa
141 D2 **Hartwell Reservoir** U.S.A.
68 C1 **Har Us Nuur** *l.* Mongolia
136 C1 **Harvey** U.S.A.
99 D4 **Harwich** U.K.
74 B2 **Haryana** *state* India
101 E2 **Harz** *hills* Ger.
101 E2 **Harzgerode** Ger.
78 B2 **Ḩasan, Jabal** *hill* Saudi Arabia
80 B2 **Hasan Dağı** *mts* Turkey
99 C4 **Haslemere** U.K.
73 B3 **Hassan** India
100 B2 **Hasselt** Belgium
101 E2 **Haßfurt** Ger.
115 C2 **Hassi Bel Guebbour** Alg.
115 C1 **Hassi Messaoud** Alg.
93 F4 **Hässleholm** Sweden
100 B2 **Hastière-Lavaux** Belgium
53 C3 **Hastings** *Vic.* Austr.
54 C1 **Hastings** N.Z.
99 D4 **Hastings** U.K.
137 E2 **Hastings** *MN* U.S.A.
137 D2 **Hastings** *NE* U.S.A.
Hatay Turkey *see* **Antakya**
142 B2 **Hatch** U.S.A.
129 D2 **Hatchet Lake** Can.
110 B1 **Haţeg** Romania
52 B2 **Hatfield** Austr.
68 C1 **Hatgal** Mongolia
62 B2 **Ha Tinh** Vietnam
52 B2 **Hattah** Austr.
141 E1 **Hatteras, Cape** U.S.A.
157 H3 **Hatteras Abyssal Plain** *sea feature* S. Atlantic Ocean
140 C2 **Hattiesburg** U.S.A.
100 C2 **Hattingen** Ger.
63 B3 **Hat Yai** Thai.
117 C4 **Haud** *reg.* Eth.
93 E4 **Haugesund** Norway
93 E4 **Haukeligrend** Norway
92 I2 **Haukipudas** Fin.
54 C1 **Hauraki Gulf** N.Z.
54 A3 **Hauroko, Lake** N.Z.
114 B1 **Haut Atlas** *mts* Morocco
131 D3 **Hauterive** Can.
Haute-Volta *country* Africa *see* Burkina
114 B1 **Hauts Plateaux** Alg.
146 B2 **Havana** Cuba
99 C4 **Havant** U.K.
101 E1 **Havel** *r.* Ger.
101 F1 **Havelberg** Ger.
54 B2 **Havelock** N.Z.
Havelock Swaziland *see* **Bulembu**
54 C1 **Havelock North** N.Z.
99 A4 **Haverfordwest** U.K.
100 C2 **Havixbeck** Ger.
103 D2 **Havlíčkův Brod** Czech Rep.
92 H1 **Havøysund** Norway
111 C3 **Havran** Turkey
134 E1 **Havre** U.S.A.
131 D3 **Havre Aubert** Can.
131 D2 **Havre-St-Pierre** Can.
49 L2 **Hawai'i** *i.* U.S.A.
156 E4 **Hawai'ian Islands** *is* N. Pacific Ocean
78 B2 **Ḩawallī** Kuwait
98 B3 **Hawarden** U.K.
54 A2 **Hawea, Lake** N.Z.
54 B1 **Hawera** N.Z.
98 B2 **Hawes** U.K.
96 C3 **Hawick** U.K.
54 C1 **Hawke Bay** N.Z.
52 A2 **Hawker** Austr.
52 B1 **Hawkers Gate** Austr.
122 A3 **Hawston** S. Africa
135 C3 **Hawthorne** U.S.A.
52 B2 **Hay** Austr.
128 C1 **Hay** *r.* Can.
100 C3 **Hayange** France
81 C2 **Haydarābad** Iran
134 C1 **Hayden** U.S.A.
129 E2 **Hayes** *r. Man.* Can.
126 F2 **Hayes** *r. Nunavut* Can.
79 C3 **Haymā'** Oman
77 C2 **Hayotboshi tog'i** *mt.* Uzbek.
111 C2 **Hayrabolu** Turkey
128 C1 **Hay River** Can.
137 D3 **Hays** U.S.A.
78 B3 **Ḩays** Yemen
90 B2 **Haysyn** Ukr.
135 B3 **Hayward** U.S.A.
99 C4 **Haywards Heath** U.K.
74 A1 **Hazarajat** *reg.* Afgh.
138 C3 **Hazard** U.S.A.
75 C2 **Hazaribagh** India
75 C2 **Hazaribagh Range** *mts* India
104 C1 **Hazebrouck** France
128 B2 **Hazelton** Can.
139 D2 **Hazleton** U.S.A.
135 B3 **Healdsburg** U.S.A.
53 C3 **Healesville** Austr.
159 E7 **Heard Island** Indian Ocean
143 D2 **Hearne** U.S.A.
130 B3 **Hearst** Can.
55 A3 **Hearst Island** Antarctica
70 B2 **Hebei** *prov.* China
53 C1 **Hebel** Austr.
140 B1 **Heber Springs** U.S.A.
70 B2 **Hebi** China
131 D2 **Hebron** Can.
128 A2 **Hecate Strait** Can.
71 A3 **Hechi** China
100 B2 **Hechtel** Belgium
54 C2 **Hector, Mount** N.Z.
93 F3 **Hede** Sweden
100 C1 **Heerde** Neth.
100 B1 **Heerenveen** Neth.
100 B1 **Heerhugowaard** Neth.
100 B2 **Heerlen** Neth.
Ḩefa Israel *see* **Haifa**
70 B2 **Hefei** China
70 B3 **Hefeng** China
69 E1 **Hegang** China
119 D1 **Heiban** Sudan
102 B1 **Heide** Ger.
122 A1 **Heide** Namibia
101 D3 **Heidelberg** Ger.
122 B3 **Heidelberg** S. Africa
69 E1 **Heihe** China
102 B2 **Heilbronn** Ger.
69 E1 **Heilong Jiang** *r.* China/Rus. Fed.
93 I3 **Heinola** Fin.
Hejaz *reg.* Saudi Arabia *see* **Hijaz**
92 A3 **Hekla** *vol.* Iceland
92 F3 **Helagsfjället** *mt.* Sweden
70 A2 **Helan Shan** *mts* China
140 B2 **Helena** *AR* U.S.A.
134 D1 **Helena** *MT* U.S.A.
96 B2 **Helensburgh** U.K.
102 B1 **Helgoland** *i.* Ger.
102 B1 **Helgoländer Bucht** *b.* Ger.
Heligoland *i.* Ger. *see* **Helgoland**
Heligoland Bight *b.* Ger. *see* Helgoländer Bucht
Helixi China *see* **Ningguo**
92 □A3 **Hella** Iceland
100 B2 **Hellevoetsluis** Neth.
107 C2 **Hellín** Spain
Hell-Ville Madag. *see* **Andoany**
76 C3 **Helmand** *r.* Afgh.
101 E2 **Helmbrechts** Ger.
122 A2 **Helmeringhausen** Namibia
100 B2 **Helmond** Neth.
96 C1 **Helmsdale** U.K.
96 C1 **Helmsdale** *r.* U.K.
98 C2 **Helmsley** U.K.
101 E1 **Helmstedt** Ger.
65 B1 **Helong** China
143 D3 **Helotes** U.S.A.
93 F4 **Helsingborg** Sweden
Helsingfors Fin. *see* **Helsinki**
93 F4 **Helsingør** Denmark
93 H3 **Helsinki** Fin.
99 A4 **Helston** U.K.
97 C2 **Helvick Head** *hd* Ireland
99 C4 **Hemel Hempstead** U.K.
101 D1 **Hemmoor** Ger.
92 F2 **Hemnesberget** Norway
70 B2 **Henan** *prov.* China
111 D2 **Hendek** Turkey
138 B3 **Henderson** *KY* U.S.A.
141 E1 **Henderson** *NC* U.S.A.
135 D3 **Henderson** *NV* U.S.A.
143 E2 **Henderson** *TX* U.S.A.
49 O6 **Henderson Island** Pitcairn Is
141 D1 **Hendersonville** U.S.A.
99 C4 **Hendon** U.K.
62 A1 **Hengduan Shan** *mts* China
100 C1 **Hengelo** Neth.
Hengnan China *see* **Hengyang**
71 B3 **Hengshan** China
70 B2 **Hengshui** China
71 A3 **Hengxian** China
71 B3 **Hengyang** China
Hengzhou China *see* **Hengxian**
91 C2 **Heniches'k** Ukr.

139 D3 Henlopen, Cape U.S.A.
100 C2 Hennef (Sieg) Ger.
130 B2 Henrietta Maria, Cape Can.
Henrique de Carvalho Angola see Saurimo
139 D3 Henry, Cape U.S.A.
143 D1 Henryetta U.S.A.
127 H2 Henry Kater, Cape Can.
101 D1 Henstedt-Ulzburg Ger.
120 A3 Hentiesbaai Namibia
101 D3 Heppenheim (Bergstraße) Ger.
71 A3 Hepu China
76 C3 Herāt Afgh.
129 D2 Herbert Can.
54 C2 Herbertville N.Z.
101 D2 Herbstein Ger.
109 C2 Herceg-Novi Serb. and Mont.
99 B3 Hereford U.K.
143 C2 Hereford U.S.A.
101 D1 Herford Ger.
100 C2 Herkenbosch Neth.
96 □ Herma Ness hd U.K.
122 A3 Hermanus S. Africa
53 C2 Hermidale Austr.
134 C1 Hermiston U.S.A.
59 D3 Hermit Islands P.N.G.
144 A2 Hermosillo Mex.
154 B3 Hernandarias Para.
100 C2 Herne Ger.
93 E4 Herning Denmark
104 B2 Hérouville-St-Clair France
106 B2 Herrera del Duque Spain
139 D2 Hershey U.S.A.
99 C4 Hertford U.K.
123 C2 Hertzogville S. Africa
51 E2 Hervey Bay Austr.
101 F2 Herzberg Ger.
101 E3 Herzogenaurach Ger.
71 A3 Heshan China
135 C4 Hesperia U.S.A.
128 A1 Hess r. Can.
101 E1 Hessen Ger.
101 D2 Hessisch Lichtenau Ger.
136 C1 Hettinger U.S.A.
101 E2 Hettstedt Ger.
98 B2 Hexham U.K.
98 B2 Heysham U.K.
71 B3 Heyuan China
52 B3 Heywood Austr.
70 B2 Heze China
71 B3 Hezhou China
141 D3 Hialeah U.S.A.
137 D3 Hiawatha U.S.A.
137 E1 Hibbing U.S.A.
141 D1 Hickory U.S.A.
54 C1 Hicks Bay N.Z.
66 D2 Hidaka-sanmyaku mts Japan
143 D3 Hidalgo Mex.
145 C2 Hidalgo Mex.
144 B2 Hidalgo del Parral Mex.
154 C1 Hidrolândia Brazil
67 A4 Higashi-suidō sea chan. Japan
High Atlas mts Morocco see Haut Atlas
134 B2 High Desert U.S.A.
128 C2 High Level Can.
141 E1 High Point U.S.A.
128 C2 High Prairie Can.
128 C2 High River Can.
129 D2 Highrock Lake Can.
High Tatras mts Pol./Slovakia see Tatry
99 C4 High Wycombe U.K.
88 C2 Hiiumaa i. Estonia
78 A2 Hijaz reg. Saudi Arabia
54 C1 Hikurangi mt. N.Z.
101 E2 Hildburghausen Ger.
100 C2 Hilden Ger.
101 E2 Hilders Ger.
101 D1 Hildesheim Ger.
81 C2 Hillah Iraq
100 B1 Hillegom Neth.
100 C2 Hillesheim Ger.
138 C3 Hillsboro OH U.S.A.
143 D2 Hillsboro TX U.S.A.
53 C2 Hillston Austr.
96 □ Hillswick U.K.
49 L2 Hilo U.S.A.
141 D2 Hilton Head Island U.S.A.
100 B1 Hilversum Neth.
74 B1 Himachal Pradesh state India
68 B2 Himalaya mts Asia
74 B2 Himatnagar India
67 B4 Himeji Japan
123 C2 Himeville S. Africa
67 C3 Himi Japan
Ḩimṣ Syria see Homs
147 C3 Hinche Haiti
51 D1 Hinchinbrook Island Austr.
52 B3 Hindmarsh, Lake dry lake Austr.
74 A1 Hindu Kush mts Afgh./Pak.
73 B3 Hindupur India
134 C2 Hines U.S.A.
141 D2 Hinesville U.S.A.
74 B2 Hinganghat India
81 C2 Hınıs Turkey
92 G2 Hinnøya i. Norway
106 B2 Hinojosa del Duque Spain
100 C1 Hinte Ger.
62 A2 Hinthada Myanmar
128 C2 Hinton Can.
75 C2 Hirakud Reservoir India
Hîrlău Romania see Hârlău
66 D2 Hiroo Japan
66 D2 Hirosaki Japan

67 B4 Hiroshima Japan
101 E3 Hirschaid Ger.
101 E2 Hirschberg Ger.
105 C2 Hirson France
Hîrşova Romania see Hârşova
93 E4 Hirtshals Denmark
74 B2 Hisar India
147 C2 Hispaniola i. Caribbean Sea
81 C2 Hit Iraq
67 D3 Hitachi Japan
67 D3 Hitachinaka Japan
92 E3 Hitra i. Norway
49 N4 Hiva Oa i. Fr. Polynesia
93 G4 Hjälmaren l. Sweden
129 D1 Hjalmar Lake Can.
93 F4 Hjørring Denmark
123 D2 Hlabisa S. Africa
92 □B2 Hlíð Iceland
91 C2 Hlobyne Ukr.
123 C2 Hlohlowane S. Africa
123 C2 Hlotse Lesotho
91 C1 Hlukhiv Ukr.
88 C3 Hlusk Belarus
88 C2 Hlybokaye Belarus
114 C4 Ho Ghana
122 A1 Hoachanas Namibia
120 A2 Hoanib watercourse Namibia
120 A2 Hoarusib watercourse Namibia
51 D4 Hobart Austr.
143 D1 Hobart U.S.A.
143 C2 Hobbs U.S.A.
93 E4 Hobro Denmark
117 C4 Hobyo Somalia
Hô Chi Minh Vietnam see Ho Chi Minh City
63 B2 Ho Chi Minh City Vietnam
114 B3 Hôd reg. Maur.
117 D3 Hodda mt. Somalia
78 B3 Hodeidah Yemen
103 E2 Hódmezővásárhely Hungary
Hoek van Holland Neth. see Hook of Holland
65 B2 Hoeyang N. Korea
101 E2 Hof Ger.
101 E2 Hofheim in Unterfranken Ger.
92 □B3 Höfn Iceland
92 □A2 Höfn Iceland
92 □B3 Hofsjökull ice cap Iceland
67 B4 Hōfu Japan
115 C2 Hoggar plat. Alg.
93 G4 Högsby Sweden
93 E3 Høgste Breakulen mt. Norway
101 D2 Hohe Rhön mts Ger.
100 C2 Hohe Venn moorland Belgium
70 B1 Hohhot China
75 C1 Hoh Xil Shan mts China
63 B2 Hôi An Vietnam
119 D2 Hoima Uganda
62 B1 Hôi Xuân Vietnam
75 D2 Hojai India
54 B2 Hokitika N.Z.
66 D2 Hokkaidō i. Japan
91 C2 Hola Prystan' Ukr.
128 B2 Holberg Can.
53 C3 Holbrook Austr.
142 A2 Holbrook U.S.A.
137 D2 Holdrege U.S.A.
146 C2 Holguín Cuba
92 □B2 Hóll Iceland
103 D2 Hollabrunn Austria
138 B2 Holland U.S.A.
Hollandia Indon. see Jayapura
135 B3 Hollister U.S.A.
103 E2 Hollóháza Hungary
93 I3 Hollola Fin.
100 B1 Hollum Neth.
140 C2 Holly Springs U.S.A.
134 C4 Hollywood U.S.A.
141 D3 Hollywood U.S.A.
92 F2 Holm Norway
126 E2 Holman Can.
92 H3 Holmsund Sweden
122 A2 Holoog Namibia
93 E4 Holstebro Denmark
141 D1 Holston r. U.S.A.
98 A3 Holyhead U.K.
98 C2 Holy Island England U.K.
98 A3 Holy Island Wales U.K.
136 C2 Holyoke U.S.A.
Holy See Europe see Vatican City
101 D2 Holzminden Ger.
62 A1 Homalin Myanmar
101 D2 Homberg (Efze) Ger.
114 B3 Hombori Mali
100 C3 Homburg Ger.
127 H2 Home Bay Can.
140 B2 Homer U.S.A.
141 D3 Homestead U.S.A.
92 F3 Hommelvik Norway
141 D3 Homosassa Springs U.S.A.
80 B2 Homs Syria
89 D3 Homyel' Belarus
Honan prov. China see Henan
122 A3 Hondeklipbaai S. Africa
145 D3 Hondo r. Belize/Mex.
142 B2 Hondo NM U.S.A.
143 D3 Hondo TX U.S.A.
146 B3 Honduras country Central America
146 B3 Honduras, Gulf of Belize/Hond.
93 F3 Hønefoss Norway
135 B2 Honey Lake U.S.A.
104 C2 Honfleur France
62 B1 Hồng Gai Vietnam
70 B3 Honghu China

71 A3 Hongjiang China
71 B3 Hong Kong China
71 B3 Hong Kong special admin. reg. China
Hongqizhen China see Wuzhishan
131 D3 Honguedo, Détroit d' sea chan. Can.
65 B1 Hongwŏn N. Korea
70 B2 Hongze Hu l. China
48 H4 Honiara Solomon Is
99 B4 Honiton U.K.
66 D3 Honjō Japan
92 I1 Honningsvåg Norway
49 L1 Honolulu U.S.A.
67 B3 Honshū i. Japan
134 B1 Hood, Mount vol. U.S.A.
50 A3 Hood Point Austr.
134 B1 Hood River U.S.A.
100 B2 Hoogerheide Neth.
100 C1 Hoogeveen Neth.
100 C1 Hoogezand-Sappemeer Neth.
100 C2 Hoog-Keppel Neth.
100 B2 Hook of Holland Neth.
128 A2 Hoonah U.S.A.
123 C2 Hoopstad S. Africa
100 B1 Hoorn Neth.
49 J5 Hoorn, Îles de is Wallis and Futuna Is
128 B3 Hope Can.
140 B2 Hope U.S.A.
83 N2 Hope, Point U.S.A.
131 D2 Hopedale Can.
Hopei prov. China see Hebei
145 D3 Hopelchén Mex.
131 D2 Hope Mountains Can.
Hopes Advance Bay Can. see Aupaluk
52 B3 Hopetoun Austr.
122 B2 Hopetown S. Africa
139 D3 Hopewell U.S.A.
130 C2 Hopewell Islands Can.
50 B2 Hopkins, Lake salt flat Austr.
138 B3 Hopkinsville U.S.A.
134 B1 Hoquiam U.S.A.
81 C1 Horasan Turkey
93 F4 Hörby Sweden
89 D3 Horki Belarus
91 D2 Horlivka Ukr.
79 D2 Hormak Iran
79 C2 Hormuz, Strait of Iran/Oman
103 D2 Horn Austria
92 □A2 Horn c. Iceland
153 B5 Horn, Cape Chile
139 D2 Hornell U.S.A.
130 B3 Hornepayne Can.
Hornos, Cabo de c. Chile see Horn, Cape
53 D2 Hornsby Austr.
98 C3 Hornsea U.K.
90 B2 Horodenka Ukr.
91 C1 Horodnya Ukr.
90 B2 Horodok Ukr.
90 A2 Horodok Ukr.
90 A1 Horokhiv Ukr.
Horqin Youyi Qianqi China see Ulanhot
131 E2 Horse Islands Can.
52 B3 Horsham Austr.
99 C4 Horsham U.K.
93 F4 Horten Norway
126 D2 Horton r. Can.
117 B4 Hosa'ina Eth.
74 A2 Hoshab Pak.
74 B1 Hoshiarpur India
142 B1 Hosta Butte mt. U.S.A.
75 C1 Hotan China
122 B2 Hotazel S. Africa
92 G3 Hoting Sweden
140 B2 Hot Springs AR U.S.A.
Hot Springs SD U.S.A. see Truth or Consequences
136 C2 Hot Springs SD U.S.A.
128 C1 Hottah Lake Can.
100 B2 Houffalize Belgium
138 B1 Houghton U.S.A.
139 F1 Houlton U.S.A.
70 B2 Houma China
140 B3 Houma U.S.A.
131 D3 Houston Can.
143 D3 Houston U.S.A.
50 A2 Houtman Abrolhos is Austr.
122 B3 Houwater S. Africa
68 C1 Hovd Mongolia
99 C4 Hove U.K.
90 A2 Hoverla, Hora mt. Ukr.
68 C1 Hövsgöl Nuur l. Mongolia
68 C2 Hövüün Mongolia
116 A3 Howar, Wadi watercourse Sudan
98 C3 Howden U.K.
53 C3 Howe, Cape Austr.
123 D2 Howick S. Africa
49 J3 Howland Island terr. N. Pacific Ocean
53 C3 Howlong Austr.
Howrah India see Haora
140 B1 Hoxie U.S.A.
101 D2 Höxter Ger.
96 □ Hoy i. U.K.
93 E3 Høyanger Norway
102 C1 Hoyerswerda Ger.
62 A2 Hpapun Myanmar
103 D1 Hradec Králové Czech Rep.
109 C2 Hrasnica Bos.-Herz.
92 □B2 Hraun Iceland
91 C1 Hrebinka Ukr.

88 B3 Hrodna Belarus
62 A1 Hsi-hseng Myanmar
71 C3 Hsinchu Taiwan
71 C3 Hsinying Taiwan
62 A1 Hsipaw Myanmar
70 A2 Huachi China
150 B4 Huacho Peru
70 B1 Huade China
65 B1 Huadian China
70 B2 Huai'an China
70 B2 Huaibei China
70 B2 Huai He r. China
71 A3 Huaihua China
70 B2 Huainan China
70 B2 Huaiyang China
145 C3 Huajuápan de León Mex.
59 C3 Huaki Indon.
71 C3 Hualien Taiwan
150 B3 Huallaga r. Peru
120 A2 Huambo Angola
150 B4 Huancavelica Peru
150 B4 Huancayo Peru
Huangcaoba China see Xingyi
70 B2 Huangchuan China
Huang Hai sea N. Pacific Ocean see Yellow Sea
Huang He r. China see Yellow River
71 A4 Huangliu China
70 B3 Huangshan China
70 B2 Huangshi China
70 A2 Huangtu Gaoyuan plat. China
71 C3 Huangyan China
70 A2 Huangyuan China
65 B1 Huanren China
150 B3 Huánuco Peru
152 B1 Huanuni Bol.
150 B4 Huaral Peru
150 B3 Huaráz Peru
150 B4 Huarmey Peru
152 A2 Huasco Chile
152 A2 Huasco r. Chile
144 B2 Huatabampo Mex.
145 C3 Huatusco Mex.
71 A3 Huayuan China
62 B1 Huayxay Laos
70 B2 Hubei prov. China
73 B3 Hubli India
100 C2 Hückelhoven Ger.
99 C3 Hucknall U.K.
98 C3 Huddersfield U.K.
93 G3 Hudiksvall Sweden
139 E2 Hudson r. U.S.A.
129 D2 Hudson Bay Can.
127 G3 Hudson Bay sea Can.
128 B2 Hudson's Hope Can.
127 H2 Hudson Strait Can.
63 B2 Huê Vietnam
146 A3 Huehuetenango Guat.
144 B2 Huehueto, Cerro mt. Mex.
145 C2 Huejutla Mex.
106 B2 Huelva Spain
107 C2 Huércal-Overa Spain
107 C1 Huesca Spain
106 C2 Huéscar Spain
51 D2 Hughenden Austr.
50 B3 Hughes Austr.
75 C2 Hugli r. mouth India
143 D2 Hugo U.S.A.
Huhehot China see Hohhot
122 B2 Huhudi S. Africa
122 A2 Huib-Hoch Plateau Namibia
71 B3 Huichang China
Huicheng China see Huilai
65 B1 Huich'ŏn N. Korea
71 B3 Huilai China
120 A2 Huila Plateau Angola
71 A3 Huili China
70 B2 Huimin China
69 E2 Huinan China
Huinan China see Nanhui
93 H3 Huittinen Fin.
145 C3 Huixtla Mex.
71 A3 Huize China
68 C1 Hujirt Mongolia
78 B2 Hujr Saudi Arabia
122 B1 Hukuntsi Botswana
78 B2 Ḩulayfah Saudi Arabia
66 B1 Hulin China
130 C3 Hull Can.
70 C2 Huludao China
69 D1 Hulun Buir China
69 D1 Hulun Nur l. China
91 D2 Hulyaypole Ukr.
69 E1 Huma China
150 C3 Humaitá Brazil
122 B3 Humansdorp S. Africa
98 C2 Humber est. U.K.
143 D3 Humble U.S.A.
129 D2 Humboldt Can.
135 C2 Humboldt NV U.S.A.
140 C1 Humboldt TN U.S.A.
135 C2 Humboldt r. U.S.A.
103 E2 Humenné Slovakia
53 C3 Hume Reservoir Austr.
142 A1 Humphreys Peak U.S.A.
115 D2 Hûn Libya
92 □A2 Húnaflói b. Iceland
71 B3 Hunan prov. China
65 C1 Hunchun China
110 B1 Hunedoara Romania
101 D2 Hünfeld Ger.
103 D2 Hungary country Europe
52 B1 Hungerford Austr.
65 B2 Hüngnam N. Korea
65 A1 Hun He r. China

Hunjiang China *see* Baishan
99 D3 Hunstanton U.K.
101 D1 Hunte *r.* Ger.
48 I6 Hunter Island S. Pacific Ocean
51 N4 Hunter Islands Austr.
99 C3 Huntingdon U.K.
138 B2 Huntington *IN* U.S.A.
138 C3 Huntington *WV* U.S.A.
135 C4 Huntington Beach U.S.A.
54 C1 Huntly N.Z.
96 C2 Huntly U.K.
130 C3 Huntsville Can.
140 C2 Huntsville *AL* U.S.A.
143 D2 Huntsville *TX* U.S.A.
Hunyani *r.* Moz./Zimbabwe *see* Manyame
59 D3 Huon Peninsula P.N.G.
Huoxian China *see* Huozhou
70 B2 Huozhou China
Hupeh *prov.* China *see* Hubei
Hurghada Egypt *see* Al Ghurdaqah
137 D2 Huron U.S.A.
138 C2 Huron, Lake Can./U.S.A.
135 D3 Hurricane U.S.A.
100 C2 Hürth Ger.
92 □B2 Húsavík Iceland
110 C1 Huşi Romania
126 B2 Huslia U.S.A.
78 B3 Husn Āl 'Abr Yemen
102 B1 Husum Ger.
68 C1 Hutag Mongolia
60 A1 Hutanopan Indon.
137 D3 Hutchinson U.S.A.
141 D3 Hutchinson Island U.S.A.
70 B2 Hutuo He *r.* China
100 B2 Huy Belgium
70 C2 Huzhou China
92 □C3 Hvalnes Iceland
92 □B3 Hvannadalshnúkur *vol.* Iceland
109 C2 Hvar Croatia
109 C2 Hvar *i.* Croatia
91 C2 Hvardiys'ke Ukr.
120 B2 Hwange Zimbabwe
Hwang Ho *r.* China *see* Yellow River
136 C2 Hyannis U.S.A.
68 C1 Hyargas Nuur *salt l.* Mongolia
50 A3 Hyden Austr.
73 B3 Hyderabad India
74 A2 Hyderabad Pak.
Hydra *i.* Greece *see* Ydra
105 D3 Hyères France
105 D3 Hyères, Îles d' *is* France
65 B1 Hyesan N. Korea
128 B2 Hyland Post Can.
67 B3 Hyōno-sen *mt.* Japan
99 D4 Hythe U.K.
67 B4 Hyūga Japan
93 H3 Hyvinkää Fin.

I

114 B2 Iabès, Erg *des.* Alg.
150 C3 Iaco *r.* Brazil
110 C2 Ialomiţa *r.* Romania
110 C1 Ianca Romania
110 C1 Iaşi Romania
64 A2 Iba Phil.
115 C4 Ibadan Nigeria
150 B2 Ibagué Col.
154 B2 Ibaiti Brazil
150 B2 Ibarra Ecuador
78 B3 Ibb Yemen
100 C1 Ibbenbüren Ger.
115 C4 Ibi Nigeria
107 C2 Ibi Spain
155 C1 Ibiá Brazil
155 D1 Ibiai Brazil
155 D1 Ibiraçu Brazil
107 D2 Ibiza Spain
107 D2 Ibiza *i.* Spain
151 E4 Ibotirama Brazil
79 C2 Ibrā' Oman
79 C2 Ibri Oman
150 B4 Ica Peru
Icaria *i.* Greece *see* Ikaria
İçel Turkey *see* Mersin
92 □B2 Iceland *country* Europe
160 M4 Iceland Basin *sea feature* N. Atlantic Ocean
160 L3 Icelandic Plateau *sea feature* N. Atlantic Ocean
66 D3 Ichinoseki Japan
91 C1 Ichnya Ukr.
65 B2 Ich'ŏn N. Korea
151 F3 Icó Brazil
155 D2 Iconha Brazil
143 E2 Idabel U.S.A.
115 C4 Idah Nigeria
134 D2 Idaho *state* U.S.A.
134 D2 Idaho Falls U.S.A.
100 C3 Idar-Oberstein Ger.
68 C1 Ideriyn Gol *r.* Mongolia
116 B2 Idfū Egypt
115 D2 Idhān Awbārī *des.* Libya
115 D2 Idhān Murzūq *des.* Libya
Idi Amin Dada, Lake Dem. Rep. Congo/Uganda *see* Edward, Lake
118 B3 Idiofa Dem. Rep. Congo
80 B2 Idlib Syria
123 C3 Idutywa S. Africa
88 B2 Iecava Latvia

154 B2 Iepê Brazil
100 A2 Ieper Belgium
111 C3 Ierapetra Greece
119 D3 Ifakara Tanz.
121 □D3 Ifanadiana Madag.
115 C4 Ife Nigeria
114 C3 Ifôghas, Adrar des *hills* Mali
118 C3 Ifumo Dem. Rep. Congo
61 C1 Igan *Sarawak* Malaysia
119 D2 Iganga Uganda
154 C2 Igarapava Brazil
82 G2 Igarka Rus. Fed.
74 B3 Igatpuri India
81 C2 Iğdır Turkey
108 A3 Iglesias *Sardinia* Italy
127 G2 Igloolik Can.
Igluligaarjuk Can. *see* Chesterfield Inlet
130 A3 Ignace Can.
88 C2 Ignalina Lith.
111 C2 İğneada Turkey
110 C2 İğneada Burnu *pt* Turkey
111 B3 Igoumenitsa Greece
86 E3 Igra Rus. Fed.
86 F2 Igrim Rus. Fed.
154 B3 Iguaçu *r.* Brazil
154 B3 Iguaçu Falls Arg./Brazil
145 C3 Iguala Mex.
107 D1 Igualada Spain
154 C2 Iguape Brazil
154 B2 Iguatemi Brazil
154 B2 Iguatemi *r.* Brazil
151 F3 Iguatu Brazil
118 A3 Iguéla Gabon
114 B2 Iguidi, Erg *des.* Alg./Maur.
119 D3 Igunga Tanz.
121 □D2 Iharaña Madag.
69 D2 Ihbulag Mongolia
121 □D3 Ihosy Madag.
92 I2 Iijoki *r.* Fin.
92 I3 Iisalmi Fin.
67 B4 Iizuka Japan
115 C4 Ijebu-Ode Nigeria
100 B1 IJmuiden Neth.
100 B1 IJssel *r.* Neth.
100 B1 IJsselmeer *l.* Neth.
152 C2 Ijuí Brazil
Ikaahuk Can. *see* Sachs Harbour
123 C2 Ikageleng S. Africa
123 C2 Ikageng S. Africa
111 C3 Ikaria *i.* Greece
118 C3 Ikela Dem. Rep. Congo
110 B2 Ikhtiman Bulg.
67 A4 Iki *i.* Japan
118 A2 Ikom Nigeria
121 □D3 Ikongo Madag.
65 B2 Iksan S. Korea
119 D3 Ikungu Tanz.
114 C2 Ilaferh, Oued *watercourse* Alg.
64 B2 Ilagan Phil.
81 C2 Īlām Iran
75 C2 Ilam Nepal
103 D1 Iława Pol.
79 C2 Ilazārān, Kūh-e *mt.* Iran
129 D2 Île-à-la-Crosse Can.
129 D2 Île-à-la-Crosse, Lac *l.* Can.
118 C3 Ilebo Dem. Rep. Congo
119 D2 Ileret Kenya
99 D4 Ilford U.K.
99 A4 Ilfracombe U.K.
155 D1 Ilhabela Brazil
155 D2 Ilha Grande, Baía da *b.* Brazil
154 B2 Ilha Grande, Represa *resr* Brazil
154 B2 Ilha Solteira, Represa *resr* Brazil
106 B1 Ílhavo Port.
151 F4 Ilhéus Brazil
Ili Kazakh. *see* Kapchagay
126 B3 Iliamna Lake U.S.A.
64 B3 Iligan Phil.
Iliysk Kazakh. *see* Kapchagay
98 C3 Ilkley U.K.
152 A3 Illapel Chile
90 C2 Illichivs'k Ukr.
138 A3 Illinois *r.* U.S.A.
138 B3 Illinois *state* U.S.A.
90 B2 Illintsi Ukr.
115 C2 Illizi Alg.
89 D2 Il'men', Ozero *l.* Rus. Fed.
101 E2 Ilmenau Ger.
150 B4 Ilo Peru
64 B2 Iloilo Phil.
92 J3 Ilomantsi Fin.
115 C4 Ilorin Nigeria
87 D4 Ilovlya Rus. Fed.
53 D1 Iluka Austr.
127 I2 Iulissat Greenland
Iman Rus. Fed. *see* Dal'nerechensk
66 B1 Iman *r.* Rus. Fed.
67 A4 Imari Japan
93 I3 Imatra Fin.
imeni Petra Stuchki Latvia *see* Aizkraukle
117 C4 Īmī Eth.
65 B2 Imjin-gang *r.* N. Korea/S. Korea
141 D3 Immokalee U.S.A.
108 B2 Imola Italy
151 E3 Imperatriz Brazil
108 A2 Imperia Italy
136 C2 Imperial U.S.A.
118 B2 Impfondo Congo
72 D2 Imphal India
111 C2 İmroz Turkey
67 C3 Ina Japan
150 C4 Inambari *r.* Peru

115 C2 In Aménas Alg.
115 C2 In Amguel Alg.
54 B2 Inangahua Junction N.Z.
59 C3 Inanwatan Indon.
92 I2 Inari Fin.
92 I2 Inarijärvi *l.* Fin.
67 D3 Inawashiro-ko *l.* Japan
80 B1 İnce Burun *pt* Turkey
65 B2 Inch'ŏn S. Korea
121 C2 Inchope Moz.
123 D2 Incomati *r.* Moz.
116 B3 Inda Silasē Eth.
144 B2 Indé Mex.
135 C3 Independence *CA* U.S.A.
137 E2 Independence *IA* U.S.A.
137 D3 Independence *KS* U.S.A.
137 E3 Independence *MO* U.S.A.
134 C2 Independence Mountains U.S.A.
76 B2 Inderborskiy Kazakh.
72 B2 India *country* Asia
139 D2 Indiana U.S.A.
138 B2 Indiana *state* U.S.A.
138 B3 Indianapolis U.S.A.
129 D2 Indian Head Can.
159 Indian Ocean
137 E2 Indianola *IA* U.S.A.
140 B2 Indianola *MS* U.S.A.
135 C3 Indian Peak U.S.A.
135 C3 Indian Springs U.S.A.
86 D2 Indiga Rus. Fed.
83 K2 Indigirka *r.* Rus. Fed.
109 D1 Indija Serb. and Mont.
135 C4 Indio U.S.A.
58 B3 Indonesia *country* Asia
74 B2 Indore India
60 B2 Indramayu, Tanjung *pt* Indon.
Indrapura, Gunung *vol.* Indon. *see* Kerinci, Gunung
75 C3 Indravati *r.* India
104 C2 Indre *r.* France
74 A2 Indus *r.* China/Pak.
74 B3 Indus, Mouths of the Pak.
159 E2 Indus Cone *sea feature* Indian Ocean
80 B1 İnebolu Turkey
111 C2 İnegöl Turkey
Infantes Spain *see* Villanueva de los Infantes
144 B3 Infiernillo, Presa *resr* Mex.
51 D1 Ingham Austr.
53 D1 Inglewood Austr.
102 C2 Ingolstadt Ger.
75 C2 Ingraj Bazar India
123 D2 Ingwavuma S. Africa
120 B2 Ingwe Zambia
123 D2 Inhaca Moz.
121 C3 Inhambane Moz.
121 C2 Inhaminga Moz.
151 D2 Inini Fr. Guiana
Inis Ireland *see* Ennis
97 A2 Inishbofin *i.* Ireland
97 A2 Inishmore *i.* Ireland
97 C1 Inishowen *pen.* Ireland
54 B2 Inland Kaikoura Range *mts* N.Z.
Inland Sea Japan *see* Seto-naikai
102 C2 Inn *r.* Europe
127 H1 Innaanganeq *c.* Greenland
52 B1 Innamincka Austr.
70 A1 Inner Mongolia *aut. reg.* China
96 B2 Inner Sound *sea chan.* U.K.
51 D1 Innisfail Austr.
102 C2 Innsbruck Austria
97 C2 Inny *r.* Ireland
154 B1 Inocência Brazil
118 B3 Inongo Dem. Rep. Congo
111 D3 İnönü Turkey
Inoucdjouac Can. *see* Inukjuak
103 D1 Inowrocław Pol.
114 C2 In Salah Alg.
62 A2 Insein Myanmar
110 C2 Însurăţei Romania
86 F2 Inta Rus. Fed.
105 D2 Interlaken Switz.
137 E1 International Falls U.S.A.
63 A2 Interview Island India
130 C2 Inukjuak Can.
126 D2 Inuvik Can.
96 B2 Inveraray U.K.
96 C2 Inverbervie U.K.
54 A3 Invercargill N.Z.
53 D1 Inverell Austr.
96 B2 Invergordon U.K.
128 C2 Invermere Can.
131 D3 Inverness Can.
96 B2 Inverness U.K.
96 C2 Inverurie U.K.
159 F4 Investigator Ridge *sea feature* Indian Ocean
52 A3 Investigator Strait Austr.
77 E1 Inya Rus. Fed.
Inyanga Zimbabwe *see* Nyanga
119 D3 Inyonga Tanz.
87 D3 Inza Rus. Fed.
111 B3 Ioannina Greece
137 D3 Iola U.S.A.
96 A2 Iona *i.* U.K.
111 B3 Ionian Islands Greece
109 C3 Ionian Sea Greece/Italy
Ionioi Nisoi *is* Greece *see* Ionian Islands
111 C3 Ios *i.* Greece
137 E2 Iowa *state* U.S.A.
137 E2 Iowa City U.S.A.
154 C1 Ipameri Brazil
155 D1 Ipatinga Brazil
81 C1 Ipatovo Rus. Fed.

123 C2 Ipelegeng S. Africa
150 B2 Ipiales Col.
151 F4 Ipiaú Brazil
154 B3 Ipiranga Brazil
150 B3 Ipixuna Brazil
60 B1 Ipoh Malaysia
154 B1 Iporá Brazil
118 C2 Ippy C.A.R.
111 C2 İpsala Turkey
53 D1 Ipswich Austr.
99 D3 Ipswich U.K.
127 H2 Iqaluit Can.
152 A2 Iquique Chile
150 B3 Iquitos Peru
Irakleio Greece *see* Iraklion
111 C3 Iraklion Greece
81 D2 Iran *country* Asia
61 C1 Iran, Pegunungan *mts* Indon.
79 D2 Īrānshahr Iran
144 B2 Irapuato Mex.
81 C2 Iraq *country* Asia
154 B3 Irati Brazil
88 B2 Irbe Strait Estonia/Latvia
80 B2 Irbid Jordan
86 F3 Irbit Rus. Fed.
151 E4 Irecê Brazil
97 C2 Ireland *country* Europe
118 C3 Irema Dem. Rep. Congo
76 C2 Irgiz Kazakh.
Iri S. Korea *see* Iksan
Irian Jaya *reg.* Indon. *see* Papua
115 E3 Iriba Chad
114 B3 Irígui *reg.* Mali/Maur.
119 D3 Iringa Tanz.
151 D2 Iriri *r.* Brazil
Irish Free State *country* Europe *see* Ireland
95 B3 Irish Sea Ireland/U.K.
68 C1 Irkutsk Rus. Fed.
160 M4 Irminger Basin *sea feature* N. Atlantic Ocean
139 D2 Irondequoit U.S.A.
52 A2 Iron Knob Austr.
138 B1 Iron Mountain U.S.A.
138 C2 Ironton U.S.A.
138 A1 Ironwood U.S.A.
130 B3 Iroquois Falls Can.
64 B2 Irosin Phil.
67 C4 Irō-zaki *pt* Japan
90 C1 Irpin' Ukr.
62 A2 Irrawaddy *r.* Myanmar
63 A3 Irrawaddy, Mouths of the Myanmar
86 F2 Irtysh *r.* Kazakh./Rus. Fed.
107 C1 Irún Spain
96 B3 Irvine U.K.
143 D2 Irving U.S.A.
64 B3 Isabela Phil.
146 B3 Isabelia, Cordillera *mts* Nic.
92 □A2 Ísafjarðardjúp *est.* Iceland
92 □A2 Ísafjörður Iceland
67 B4 Isahaya Japan
102 C2 Isar *r.* Ger.
96 □1 Isbister U.K.
108 B2 Ischia, Isola d' *i.* Italy
67 C4 Ise Japan
118 C2 Isengi Dem. Rep. Congo
105 C2 Isère *r.* France
100 C2 Iserlohn Ger.
101 D1 Isernhagen Ger.
67 C4 Ise-wan *b.* Japan
114 C4 Iseyin Nigeria
Isfahan Iran *see* Eşfahān
66 D2 Ishikari-wan *b.* Japan
77 D1 Ishim *r.* Kazakh./Rus. Fed.
82 F3 Ishim Rus. Fed.
67 D3 Ishinomaki Japan
67 D3 Ishioka Japan
74 B1 Ishkuchi-san *mt.* Japan
138 B1 Ishkoshim Tajik.
138 B1 Ishpeming U.S.A.
111 C3 Işıklar Dağı *mts* Turkey
111 C3 Işıklı Turkey
123 C2 Isipingo S. Africa
119 C2 Isiro Dem. Rep. Congo
80 B2 İskenderun Turkey
82 G3 Iskitim Rus. Fed.
110 B2 Iskŭr *r.* Bulg.
117 D3 Iskushuban Somalia
128 A2 Iskut *r.* Can.
74 B1 Islamabad Pak.
141 D4 Islamorada U.S.A.
52 A2 Island Lagoon *salt flat* Austr.
129 E2 Island Lake Can.
54 B1 Islands, Bay of N.Z.
Islas Canarias *is* N. Atlantic Ocean *see* Canary Islands
96 A3 Islay *i.* U.K.
98 A2 Isle of Man *i.* Irish Sea
Ismail Ukr. *see* Izmayil
77 D3 Ismoili Somoní, Qullai *mt.* Tajik.
116 B2 Isnā Egypt
121 □D3 Isoanala Madag.
121 C2 Isoka Zambia
93 H3 Isokyrö Fin.
109 C3 Isola di Capo Rizzuto Italy
Ispahan Iran *see* Eşfahān
80 B2 Isparta Turkey
110 C2 Isperikh Bulg.
Ispisar Tajik. *see* Khŭjand
80 B2 Israel *country* Asia
50 B3 Israelite Bay Austr.
105 C2 Issoire France
Issyk-Kul' Kyrg. *see* Balykchy

111 C2 **İstanbul** Turkey
İstanbul Boğazı *str.* Turkey *see* Bosporus
103 D2 **Isten dombja** *hill* Hungary
111 B3 **Istiaia** Greece
141 D3 **Istokpoga, Lake** U.S.A.
Istra *pen.* Croatia *see* Istria
105 C3 **Istres** France
108 B1 **Istria** *pen.* Croatia
155 D2 **Itabapoana** Brazil
151 E4 **Itaberaba** Brazil
154 C1 **Itaberaí** Brazil
155 D1 **Itabira** Brazil
155 D2 **Itabirito** Brazil
151 F4 **Itabuna** Brazil
150 D3 **Itacoatiara** Brazil
155 D2 **Itaguaí** Brazil
154 B2 **Itaguajé** Brazil
154 C2 **Itaí** Brazil
154 C3 **Itaiópolis** Brazil
154 B3 **Itaipu, Represa de** *resr* Brazil
151 D3 **Itaituba** Brazil
154 C3 **Itajaí** Brazil
155 D2 **Itajubá** Brazil
108 B2 **Italy** *country* Europe
155 E1 **Itamaraju** Brazil
155 D1 **Itamarandiba** Brazil
155 D1 **Itambacuri** Brazil
155 D1 **Itambé, Pico de** *mt.* Brazil
75 D2 **Itanagar** India
154 C2 **Itanhaém** Brazil
155 D1 **Itanhém** Brazil
155 D1 **Itaobím** Brazil
154 C1 **Itapajipe** Brazil
155 E1 **Itapebi** Brazil
155 D2 **Itapemirim** Brazil
155 D2 **Itaperuna** Brazil
155 D1 **Itapetinga** Brazil
154 C2 **Itapetininga** Brazil
154 C2 **Itapeva** Brazil
151 F4 **Itapicuru** *r.* Brazil
151 E3 **Itapicuru Mirim** Brazil
155 C2 **Itapira** Brazil
154 C2 **Itaporanga** Brazil
154 C1 **Itapuranga** Brazil
154 C2 **Itararé** Brazil
74 B2 **Itarsi** India
154 B1 **Itarumã** Brazil
155 D2 **Itaúna** Brazil
154 B2 **Itaúnas** Brazil
64 B1 **Itbayat** *i.* Phil.
139 D2 **Ithaca** U.S.A.
101 D1 **Ith Hils** *ridge* Ger.
118 C2 **Itimbiri** *r.* Dem. Rep. Congo
155 D1 **Itinga** Brazil
154 B1 **Itiquira** Brazil
154 A1 **Itiquira** *r.* Brazil
67 C4 **Itō** Japan
154 C2 **Itu** Brazil
150 B3 **Ituí** *r.* Brazil
154 C1 **Ituiutaba** Brazil
119 C3 **Itula** Dem. Rep. Congo
154 C1 **Itumbiara** Brazil
154 C1 **Itumbiara, Barragem** *resr* Brazil
154 B1 **Iturama** Brazil
101 D1 **Itzehoe** Ger.
83 N2 **Iul'tin** Rus. Fed.
155 D2 **Iúna** Brazil
154 B2 **Ivaí** *r.* Brazil
92 I2 **Ivalo** Fin.
88 C3 **Ivanava** Belarus
109 C1 **Ivanec** Croatia
Ivangrad Serb. and Mont. *see* Berane
52 B2 **Ivanhoe** Austr.
90 B1 **Ivankiv** Ukr.
90 A2 **Ivano-Frankivs'k** Ukr.
89 F2 **Ivanovo** Rus. Fed.
88 C3 **Ivatsevichy** Belarus
111 C2 **Ivaylovgrad** Bulg.
86 F2 **Ivdel'** Rus. Fed.
110 C1 **Iveşti** Romania
154 B2 **Ivinheima** Brazil
154 B2 **Ivinheima** *r.* Brazil
127 I2 **Ivittuut** Greenland
Iviza *i.* Spain *see* Ibiza
89 E3 **Ivnya** Rus. Fed.
Ivory Coast *country* Africa *see* Côte d'Ivoire
108 A1 **Ivrea** Italy
111 C3 **İvrindi** Turkey
Ivugivik Can. *see* Ivujivik
127 G2 **Ivujivik** Can.
67 G2 **Iwaki** Japan
67 B4 **Iwakuni** Japan
66 D2 **Iwamizawa** Japan
66 D2 **Iwanai** Japan
66 D3 **Iwate-san** *vol.* Japan
88 C3 **Iwye** Belarus
123 D3 **Ixopo** S. Africa
144 B2 **Ixtlán** Mex.
146 B3 **Izabal, Lago de** *l.* Guat.
145 D2 **Izamal** Mex.
81 C1 **Izberbash** Rus. Fed.
86 E3 **Izhevsk** Rus. Fed.
86 E2 **Izhma** Rus. Fed.
Izhma Rus. Fed. *see* Sosnogorsk
89 E3 **Izmalkovo** Rus. Fed.
90 B2 **Izmayil** Ukr.
111 C3 **İzmir** Turkey
111 C2 **İzmit** Turkey
111 C2 **İznik Gölü** *l.* Turkey
67 A4 **Izuhara** Japan
67 B3 **Izumo** Japan

156 C4 **Izu-Ogasawara Trench** *sea feature* N. Pacific Ocean
67 C4 **Izu-shotō** *is* Japan
90 B1 **Izyaslav** Ukr.
91 D2 **Izyum** Ukr.

J

74 A1 **Jabal as Sirāj** Afgh.
106 C2 **Jabalón** *r.* Spain
75 B2 **Jabalpur** India
50 C1 **Jabiru** Austr.
109 C2 **Jablanica** Bos.-Herz.
151 E2 **Jaboatão** Brazil
154 C2 **Jaboticabal** Brazil
107 C1 **Jaca** Spain
145 C2 **Jacala** Mex.
151 D3 **Jacareacanga** Brazil
155 C2 **Jacareí** Brazil
154 B1 **Jaciara** Brazil
155 D1 **Jacinto** Brazil
139 E1 **Jackman** U.S.A.
140 C2 **Jackson** *AL* U.S.A.
138 C2 **Jackson** *MI* U.S.A.
140 B2 **Jackson** *MS* U.S.A.
140 C1 **Jackson** *TN* U.S.A.
136 A2 **Jackson** *WY* U.S.A.
54 A2 **Jackson Head** *hd* N.Z.
140 B2 **Jacksonville** *AR* U.S.A.
141 D2 **Jacksonville** *FL* U.S.A.
138 A3 **Jacksonville** *IL* U.S.A.
141 E2 **Jacksonville** *NC* U.S.A.
143 D2 **Jacksonville** *TX* U.S.A.
147 C3 **Jacmel** Haiti
74 A2 **Jacobabad** Pak.
151 E4 **Jacobina** Brazil
131 D3 **Jacques Cartier, Mont** *mt.* Can.
151 E3 **Jacunda** Brazil
154 C2 **Jacupiranga** Brazil
101 D1 **Jadebusen** *b.* Ger.
Jadotville Dem. Rep. Congo *see* Likasi
109 C2 **Jadovnik** *mt.* Bos.-Herz.
150 B3 **Jaén** Peru
106 C2 **Jaén** Spain
Jaffa Israel *see* Tel Aviv-Yafo
52 A3 **Jaffa, Cape** Austr.
73 B4 **Jaffna** Sri Lanka
75 C2 **Jagdalpur** India
123 C2 **Jagersfontein** S. Africa
79 C2 **Jaghin** Iran
152 C3 **Jaguarão** Uru.
154 C2 **Jaguariaíva** Brazil
81 D3 **Jahrom** Iran
74 B2 **Jaipur** India
74 B2 **Jaisalmer** India
74 B2 **Jaitgarh** *hill* India
75 C2 **Jajarkot** Nepal
109 C2 **Jajce** Bos.-Herz.
Jajnagar *state* India *see* Orissa
60 B2 **Jakarta** Indon.
128 A1 **Jakes Corner** Can.
92 G2 **Jäkkvik** Sweden
Jakobshavn Greenland *see* Ilulissat
92 H3 **Jakobstad** Fin.
77 D3 **Jalālābād** Afgh.
77 D2 **Jalal-Abad** Kyrg.
74 B1 **Jalandhar** India
145 C3 **Jalapa** Mex.
154 B2 **Jales** Brazil
74 B2 **Jalgaon** India
115 D4 **Jalingo** Nigeria
74 B3 **Jalna** India
74 B2 **Jalore** India
144 B2 **Jalostotitlán** Mex.
144 B2 **Jalpa** Mex.
75 C2 **Jalpaiguri** India
145 C2 **Jalpan** Mex.
115 E2 **Jālū** Libya
146 B3 **Jamaica** *country* West Indies
146 C3 **Jamaica Channel** Haiti/Jamaica
75 C2 **Jamalpur** Bangl.
60 B2 **Jambi** Indon.
137 D2 **James** *r.* ND/SD U.S.A.
139 D3 **James** *r.* VA U.S.A.
130 B2 **James Bay** Can.
52 A2 **Jamestown** Austr.
Jamestown Can. *see* Wawa
123 C3 **Jamestown** S. Africa
137 D1 **Jamestown** ND U.S.A.
139 D2 **Jamestown** NY U.S.A.
74 B1 **Jammu** Jammu and Kashmir
74 B1 **Jammu and Kashmir** *terr.* Asia
74 B2 **Jamnagar** India
74 B2 **Jampur** Pak.
93 I3 **Jämsä** Fin.
78 A2 **Jamsah** Egypt
75 C2 **Jamshedpur** India
75 C2 **Jamuna** *r.* Bangl.
75 C2 **Janakpur** Nepal
155 D1 **Janaúba** Brazil
81 D2 **Jandaq** Iran
114 A2 **Jandia** *hill* Canary Islands
135 B2 **Janesville** *CA* U.S.A.
138 B2 **Janesville** *WI* U.S.A.
154 A2 **Jango** Brazil
82 A2 **Jan Mayen** *i.* Arctic Ocean
122 A3 **Jansenville** S. Africa
155 D1 **Januária** Brazil
74 B2 **Jaora** India
67 C3 **Japan** *country* Asia
66 B3 **Japan, Sea of** N. Pacific Ocean

150 C3 **Japurá** *r.* Brazil
154 C1 **Jaraguá** Brazil
154 C3 **Jaraguá, Serra** *mts* Brazil
154 C3 **Jaraguá do Sul** Brazil
154 B2 **Jaraguari** Brazil
152 C2 **Jardim** Brazil
69 D1 **Jargalant** Mongolia
103 D1 **Jarocin** Pol.
103 E1 **Jarosław** Pol.
92 F3 **Järpen** Sweden
70 A2 **Jartai** China
150 C4 **Jarú** Brazil
Jarud China *see* Lubei
88 C2 **Järvenpää** Fin.
49 K4 **Jarvis Island** *terr.* S. Pacific Ocean
93 G3 **Järvsö** Sweden
79 C2 **Jāsk** Iran
103 E2 **Jasło** Pol.
55 A3 **Jason Peninsula** Antarctica
128 C2 **Jasper** Can.
140 C2 **Jasper** *AL* U.S.A.
138 B3 **Jasper** *IN* U.S.A.
143 E2 **Jasper** *TX* U.S.A.
Jassy Romania *see* Iaşi
103 D2 **Jastrzębie-Zdrój** Pol.
103 D2 **Jászberény** Hungary
154 B1 **Jataí** Brazil
74 A2 **Jati** Pak.
154 C2 **Jaú** Brazil
150 C3 **Jaú** *r.* Brazil
145 C2 **Jaumave** Mex.
75 C2 **Jaunpur** India
154 B1 **Jauru** Brazil
61 B2 **Java** *i.* Indon.
107 C1 **Javalambre, Sierra de** *mts* Spain
69 C1 **Javarthushuu** Mongolia
Java Sea Indon. *see* Laut Jawa
156 B6 **Java Trench** *sea feature* Indian Ocean
Jawa *i.* Indon. *see* Java
117 C4 **Jawhar** Somalia
103 D1 **Jawor** Pol.
103 D1 **Jaworzno** Pol.
59 D3 **Jaya, Puncak** *mt.* Indon.
59 D3 **Jayapura** Indon.
79 C2 **Jazirat Maşirah** *i.* Oman
128 B1 **Jean Marie River** Can.
131 D2 **Jeannin, Lac** *l.* Can.
Jebel, Bahr el *r.* Sudan/Uganda *see* White Nile
116 A3 **Jebel Abyad Plateau** Sudan
96 C3 **Jedburgh** U.K.
78 A2 **Jeddah** Saudi Arabia
108 A3 **Jedeida** Tunisia
101 E1 **Jeetze** *r.* Ger.
137 E2 **Jefferson** U.S.A.
135 C3 **Jefferson, Mount** U.S.A.
137 E3 **Jefferson City** U.S.A.
122 B3 **Jeffrey's Bay** S. Africa
88 C2 **Jēkabpils** Latvia
103 D1 **Jelenia Góra** Pol.
88 B2 **Jelgava** Latvia
60 B1 **Jemaja** *i.* Indon.
61 C2 **Jember** Indon.
101 E2 **Jena** Ger.
Jengish Chokusu *mt.* China/Kyrg. *see* Pobeda Peak
80 B2 **Jenin** West Bank
140 B2 **Jennings** U.S.A.
151 E4 **Jequié** Brazil
155 D1 **Jequitaí** Brazil
155 D1 **Jequitinhonha** Brazil
155 E1 **Jequitinhonha** *r.* Brazil
147 C3 **Jérémie** Haiti
144 B2 **Jerez** Mex.
106 B2 **Jerez de la Frontera** Spain
109 D3 **Jergucat** Albania
115 C1 **Jerid, Chott el** *salt l.* Tunisia
134 D2 **Jerome** U.S.A.
95 C4 **Jersey** *i.* Channel Is
95 C4 **Jersey** *terr.* Channel Is
151 E3 **Jerumenha** Brazil
80 B2 **Jerusalem** Israel/West Bank
53 D3 **Jervis Bay Territory** *admin. div.* Austr.
108 B1 **Jesenice** Slovenia
108 B2 **Jesi** Italy
Jesselton Malaysia *see* Kota Kinabalu
101 F2 **Jessen** Ger.
75 C2 **Jessore** Bangl.
141 D2 **Jesup** U.S.A.
137 D3 **Jesus, Mount** *hill* U.S.A.
145 C3 **Jesús Carranza** Mex.
100 C1 **Jever** Ger.
74 B2 **Jhalawar** India
74 B1 **Jhang** Pak.
74 B2 **Jhansi** India
75 C2 **Jharkhand** *state* India
75 C2 **Jharsuguda** India
74 B1 **Jhelum** *r.* India/Pak.
74 B1 **Jhelum** Pak.
74 B2 **Jhunjhunun** India
70 C2 **Jiading** China
69 E1 **Jiamusi** China
71 B3 **Ji'an** *Jiangxi* China
65 B1 **Ji'an** *Jilin* China
Jianchang China *see* Nancheng
62 A2 **Jianchuan** China
71 B3 **Jiande** China
Jiangling China *see* Jingzhou
71 B3 **Jiangmen** China
70 B2 **Jiangsu** *prov.* China
71 B3 **Jiangxi** *prov.* China
70 A2 **Jiangyou** China

70 B3 **Jianli** China
70 B2 **Jianqiao** *Hebei* China
71 B3 **Jianyang** *Fujian* China
70 A2 **Jianyang** *Sichuan* China
69 E2 **Jiaohe** *Jilin* China
Jiaojiang China *see* Taizhou
70 C2 **Jiaozhou** China
70 B2 **Jiaozuo** China
Jiashan China *see* Mingguang
70 C2 **Jiaxing** China
68 C2 **Jiayuguan** China
Jiddah Saudi Arabia *see* Jeddah
92 G2 **Jiehkkevárri** *mt.* Norway
70 B2 **Jiexiu** China
70 A2 **Jigzhi** China
103 D2 **Jihlava** Czech Rep.
115 C1 **Jijel** Alg.
117 C4 **Jijiga** Eth.
117 C4 **Jilib** Somalia
69 E2 **Jilin** China
65 B1 **Jilin** *prov.* China
65 A1 **Jilin Hada Ling** *mts* China
117 B4 **Jima** Eth.
110 B1 **Jimbolia** Romania
144 B2 **Jiménez** Mex.
143 C3 **Jiménez** Mex.
145 C2 **Jiménez** Mex.
70 B2 **Jinan** China
70 A2 **Jinchang** China
70 B2 **Jincheng** China
Jinchuan China *see* Jinchang
53 C3 **Jindabyne** Austr.
103 D2 **Jindřichův Hradec** Czech Rep.
Jin'e China *see* Longchang
70 A2 **Jingbian** China
71 B3 **Jingdezhen** China
62 B1 **Jinghong** China
53 C3 **Jingellic** Austr.
71 B3 **Jinggangshan** China
62 B1 **Jinghong** China
70 B2 **Jingmen** China
70 A2 **Jingning** China
Jingsha China *see* Jingzhou
70 A2 **Jingtai** China
71 A3 **Jingxi** China
Jingxian China *see* Jingzhou
65 B1 **Jingyu** China
70 A2 **Jingyuan** China
70 B2 **Jingzhou** China
70 B2 **Jingzhou** *Hubei* China
71 A3 **Jingzhou** *Hunan* China
70 B1 **Jinhua** China
70 B1 **Jining** *Nei Mongol* China
70 B2 **Jining** *Shandong* China
119 D2 **Jinja** Uganda
117 B4 **Jinka** Eth.
146 B3 **Jinotega** Nic.
146 B3 **Jinotepe** Nic.
71 A3 **Jinping** China
Jinsha Jiang *r.* China *see* Yangtze
Jinshi China *see* Xinning
70 B2 **Jinshi** China
Jinxi China *see* Lianshan
70 B2 **Jinzhong** China
70 C1 **Jinzhou** China
150 C3 **Jiparaná** *r.* Brazil
75 C1 **Jirang** India
116 B2 **Jirjā** Egypt
79 C2 **Jiroft** Iran
79 C2 **Jirwān** Saudi Arabia
71 A3 **Jishou** China
110 B2 **Jiu** *r.* Romania
70 A2 **Jiuding Shan** *mt.* China
70 B3 **Jiujiang** China
Jiulian China *see* Mojiang
79 D2 **Jiwani** Pak.
66 B1 **Jixi** China
78 B3 **Jīzān** Saudi Arabia
77 C2 **Jizzax** Uzbek.
155 D1 **Joaíma** Brazil
João Belo Moz. *see* Xai-Xai
151 F3 **João Pessoa** Brazil
155 C1 **João Pinheiro** Brazil
74 B2 **Jodhpur** India
92 I3 **Joensuu** Fin.
67 C3 **Jōetsu** Japan
121 C3 **Jofane** Moz.
88 C2 **Jõgeva** Estonia
Jogjakarta Indon. *see* Yogyakarta
123 C2 **Johannesburg** S. Africa
134 C2 **John Day** U.S.A.
134 B1 **John Day** *r.* U.S.A.
128 C2 **John d'Or Prairie** Can.
141 E1 **John H. Kerr Reservoir** U.S.A.
96 C1 **John o'Groats** U.K.
141 D1 **Johnson City** U.S.A.
128 A1 **Johnson's Crossing** Can.
50 B3 **Johnston, Lake** *salt flat* Austr.
49 J2 **Johnston Atoll** N. Pacific Ocean
96 B3 **Johnstone** U.K.
Johnstone Lake Can. *see* Old Wives Lake
139 D2 **Johnstown** U.S.A.
60 B1 **Johor Bahru** Malaysia
88 C2 **Jõhvi** Estonia
154 C3 **Joinville** Brazil
105 D2 **Joinville** France
55 B3 **Joinville Island** Antarctica
92 G2 **Jokkmokk** Sweden
92 □B2 **Jökulsá á Fjöllum** *r.* Iceland
138 B2 **Joliet** U.S.A.
130 C3 **Joliette** Can.
64 B3 **Jolo** Phil.

64 B3 **Jolo** *i.* Phil.
61 C2 **Jombang** Indon.
75 C2 **Jomsom** Nepal
88 B2 **Jonava** Lith.
140 B1 **Jonesboro** *AR* U.S.A.
140 B2 **Jonesboro** *LA* U.S.A.
139 F2 **Jonesport** U.S.A.
127 G1 **Jones Sound** *sea chan.* Can.
93 F4 **Jönköping** Sweden
131 C3 **Jonquière** Can.
145 C3 **Jonuta** Mex.
137 E3 **Joplin** U.S.A.
80 B2 **Jordan** *country* Asia
80 B2 **Jordan** *r.* Asia
134 E1 **Jordan** U.S.A.
155 D1 **Jordânia** Brazil
134 C2 **Jordan Valley** U.S.A.
72 D2 **Jorhat** India
101 D1 **Jork** Ger.
93 E4 **Jørpeland** Norway
115 C4 **Jos** Nigeria
145 C3 **José Cardel** Mex.
131 D2 **Joseph, Lac** *l.* Can.
50 B1 **Joseph Bonaparte Gulf** Austr.
115 C4 **Jos Plateau** Nigeria
93 E3 **Jotunheimen** *mts* Norway
122 B3 **Joubertina** S. Africa
123 C2 **Jouberton** S. Africa
104 C2 **Joué-lès-Tours** France
93 I3 **Joutseno** Fin.
134 B1 **Juan de Fuca Strait** Can./U.S.A.
149 B6 **Juan Fernández Islands** S. Pacific Ocean
Juanshui China *see* Tongcheng
145 B2 **Juárez** Mex.
144 A1 **Juárez, Sierra de** *mts* Mex.
151 E3 **Juàzeiro** Brazil
151 F3 **Juàzeiro do Norte** Brazil
117 B4 **Juba** Sudan
117 C5 **Jubba** *r.* Somalia
78 B2 **Jubbah** Saudi Arabia
Jubbulpore India *see* Jabalpur
107 C2 **Júcar** *r.* Spain
145 C3 **Juchitán** Mex.
155 E1 **Jucuruçu** Brazil
102 C2 **Judenburg** Austria
155 E1 **Juerana** Brazil
101 D2 **Jühnde** Ger.
146 B3 **Juigalpa** Nic.
150 D4 **Juína** Brazil
100 C1 **Juist** *i.* Ger.
155 D2 **Juiz de Fora** Brazil
136 C2 **Julesburg** U.S.A.
150 B4 **Juliaca** Peru
Julianatop *mt.* Indon. *see* Mandala, Puncak
151 D2 **Juliana Top** *mt.* Suriname
Jullundur India *see* Jalandhar
107 C2 **Jumilla** Spain
75 C2 **Jumla** Nepal
Jumna *r.* India *see* Yamuna
74 B2 **Junagadh** India
143 D2 **Junction** U.S.A.
137 D3 **Junction City** U.S.A.
154 C2 **Jundiaí** Brazil
128 A2 **Juneau** U.S.A.
53 C2 **Junee** Austr.
105 D2 **Jungfrau** *mt.* Switz.
139 D2 **Juniata** *r.* U.S.A.
153 B3 **Junín** Arg.
92 G3 **Junsele** Sweden
134 C2 **Juntura** U.S.A.
Junxi China *see* Datian
Junxian China *see* Danjiangkou
154 B2 **Jupiá, Represa** *resr* Brazil
141 D3 **Jupiter** U.S.A.
154 C2 **Juquiá** Brazil
117 A4 **Jur** *r.* Sudan
105 D2 **Jura** *mts* France/Switz.
96 B2 **Jura** *i.* U.K.
96 B3 **Jura, Sound of** *sea chan.* U.K.
88 B2 **Jurbarkas** Lith.
88 B2 **Jūrmala** Latvia
150 C3 **Juruá** *r.* Brazil
150 D3 **Juruena** *r.* Brazil
154 C2 **Jurumirim, Represa de** *resr* Brazil
151 D3 **Juruti** Brazil
154 B1 **Jussara** Brazil
150 C3 **Jutaí** *r.* Brazil
101 F2 **Jüterbog** Ger.
154 B2 **Juti** Brazil
145 D3 **Jutiapa** Guat.
93 E4 **Jutland** *pen.* Denmark
146 B2 **Juventud, Isla de la** *i.* Cuba
70 B2 **Juxian** China
81 D3 **Jūyom** Iran
122 B1 **Jwaneng** Botswana
Jylland *pen.* Denmark *see* Jutland
93 I3 **Jyväskylä** Fin.

K

74 B1 **K2** *mt.* China/Jammu and Kashmir
Kaakhka Turkm. *see* Kaka
92 I2 **Kaamanen** Fin.
61 D2 **Kabaena** *i.* Indon.
119 C3 **Kabalo** Dem. Rep. Congo
119 C3 **Kabambare** Dem. Rep. Congo
119 C3 **Kabare** Dem. Rep. Congo
119 C3 **Kabemba** Dem. Rep. Congo
130 B3 **Kabinakagami Lake** Can.

118 C3 **Kabinda** Dem. Rep. Congo
118 B2 **Kabo** C.A.R.
120 B2 **Kabompo** Zambia
119 C3 **Kabongo** Dem. Rep. Congo
77 C3 **Kābul** Afgh.
64 B3 **Kaburuang** *i.* Indon.
121 B2 **Kabwe** Zambia
109 D2 **Kačanik** Serb. and Mont.
74 A2 **Kachchh, Gulf of** India
83 I3 **Kachug** Rus. Fed.
81 C1 **Kaçkar Dağı** *mt.* Turkey
111 C2 **Kadıköy** Turkey
52 A2 **Kadina** Austr.
114 B3 **Kadiolo** Mali
Kadiyevka Ukr. *see* Stakhanov
73 B3 **Kadmat** *i.* India
89 F2 **Kadnikov** Rus. Fed.
121 B2 **Kadoma** Zimbabwe
63 A2 **Kadonkani** Myanmar
117 A3 **Kadugli** Sudan
115 C3 **Kaduna** Nigeria
89 E2 **Kaduy** Rus. Fed.
86 E2 **Kadzherom** Rus. Fed.
114 A3 **Kaédi** Maur.
118 B3 **Kaélé** Cameroon
65 B2 **Kaesŏng** N. Korea
118 C3 **Kafakumba** Dem. Rep. Congo
114 A3 **Kaffrine** Senegal
111 B3 **Kafireas, Akra** *pt* Greece
80 B2 **Kafr ash Shaykh** Egypt
121 B2 **Kafue** Zambia
120 B2 **Kafue** *r.* Zambia
67 C3 **Kaga** Japan
118 B2 **Kaga Bandoro** C.A.R.
91 C2 **Kagal'nitskaya** Rus. Fed.
Kaganovichi Pervyye Ukr. *see* Polis'ke
60 A2 **Kagologolo** Indon.
67 B4 **Kagoshima** Japan
Kagul Moldova *see* Cahul
119 D3 **Kahama** Tanz.
90 C2 **Kaharlyk** Ukr.
61 C2 **Kahayan** *r.* Indon.
118 B3 **Kahemba** Dem. Rep. Congo
101 E2 **Kahla** Ger.
79 C2 **Kahnūj** Iran
92 H2 **Kahperusvaarat** *mts* Fin.
80 B2 **Kahramanmaraş** Turkey
79 C2 **Kahūrak** Iran
59 C3 **Kai, Kepulauan** *is* Indon.
115 C4 **Kaiama** Nigeria
54 B2 **Kaiapoi** N.Z.
59 C3 **Kai Besar** *i.* Indon.
70 B2 **Kaifeng** China
Kaihua China *see* Wenshan
122 B2 **Kaiingveld** *reg.* S. Africa
59 C3 **Kai Kecil** *i.* Indon.
54 B2 **Kaikoura** N.Z.
114 A4 **Kailahun** Sierra Leone
Kailas Range *mts* China *see* Gangdisê Shan
71 A3 **Kaili** China
59 C3 **Kaimana** Indon.
54 C1 **Kaimanawa Mountains** N.Z.
72 C2 **Kaimur Range** *hills* India
88 B2 **Käina** Estonia
67 C4 **Kainan** Japan
115 C3 **Kainji Reservoir** Nigeria
54 B1 **Kaipara Harbour** N.Z.
74 B2 **Kairana** India
115 D1 **Kairouan** Tunisia
100 C3 **Kaiserslautern** Ger.
55 I2 **Kaiser Wilhelm II Land** *reg.* Antarctica
54 B1 **Kaitaia** N.Z.
54 C1 **Kaitawa** N.Z.
Kaitong China *see* Tongyu
59 C3 **Kaiwatu** Indon.
65 A1 **Kaiyuan** *Liaoning* China
71 A3 **Kaiyuan** *Yunnan* China
92 I3 **Kajaani** Fin.
51 D2 **Kajabbi** Austr.
76 B3 **Kaka** Turkm.
122 B2 **Kakamas** S. Africa
119 D2 **Kakamega** Kenya
114 A4 **Kakata** Liberia
91 C2 **Kakhovka** Ukr.
91 C2 **Kakhovs'ke Vodoskhovyshche** *resr* Ukr.
Kakhul Moldova *see* Cahul
73 C3 **Kakinada** India
128 C1 **Kakisa** Can.
67 B4 **Kakogawa** Japan
119 C3 **Kakoswa** Dem. Rep. Congo
126 C2 **Kaktovik** U.S.A.
Kalaallit Nunaat *terr.* N. America *see* Greenland
59 C3 **Kalabahi** Indon.
120 B2 **Kalabo** Zambia
91 E1 **Kalach** Rus. Fed.
119 D2 **Kalacha Dida** Kenya
87 D4 **Kalach-na-Donu** Rus. Fed.
62 A1 **Kaladan** *r.* India/Myanmar
120 B3 **Kalahari Desert** Africa
92 H3 **Kalajoki** Fin.
123 C1 **Kalamare** Botswana
111 B3 **Kalamaria** Greece
111 B3 **Kalamata** Greece
138 B2 **Kalamazoo** U.S.A.
111 B3 **Kalampaka** Greece
88 B2 **Kalana** Estonia
91 C2 **Kalanchak** Ukr.
61 C2 **Kalao** *i.* Indon.
61 C2 **Kalaotoa** *i.* Indon.
63 B2 **Kalasin** Thai.

77 C3 **Kalāt** Afgh.
79 C2 **Kalāt** Iran
74 A2 **Kalat** Pak.
50 A2 **Kalbarri** Austr.
111 C3 **Kale** Turkey
80 B1 **Kalecik** Turkey
118 C3 **Kalema** Dem. Rep. Congo
119 C3 **Kalemie** Dem. Rep. Congo
62 A1 **Kalemyo** Myanmar
86 C2 **Kalevala** Rus. Fed.
Kalgan China *see* Zhangjiakou
50 B3 **Kalgoorlie** Austr.
109 C2 **Kali** Croatia
110 C2 **Kaliakra, Nos** *pt* Bulg.
60 A2 **Kaliet** Indon.
119 C3 **Kalima** Dem. Rep. Congo
61 C2 **Kalimantan** *reg.* Indon.
Kalinin Rus. Fed. *see* Tver'
88 B3 **Kaliningrad** Rus. Fed.
91 D2 **Kalininskaya** Rus. Fed.
88 C3 **Kalinkavichy** Belarus
134 D1 **Kalispell** U.S.A.
103 D1 **Kalisz** Pol.
91 E2 **Kalitva** *r.* Rus. Fed.
92 H2 **Kalix** Sweden
92 H2 **Kalixälven** *r.* Sweden
111 C3 **Kalkan** Turkey
120 A3 **Kalkfeld** Namibia
100 C2 **Kall** Ger.
92 I3 **Kallavesi** *l.* Fin.
92 F3 **Kallsjön** *l.* Sweden
93 G4 **Kalmar** Sweden
93 G4 **Kalmarsund** *sea chan.* Sweden
73 C4 **Kalmunai** Sri Lanka
119 C3 **Kalole** Dem. Rep. Congo
120 B2 **Kalomo** Zambia
128 B2 **Kalone Peak** Can.
74 B1 **Kalpa** India
73 B3 **Kalpeni** *i.* India
75 B2 **Kalpi** India
126 B2 **Kaltag** U.S.A.
101 D1 **Kaltenkirchen** Ger.
115 D3 **Kaltungo** Nigeria
89 E3 **Kaluga** Rus. Fed.
93 F4 **Kalundborg** Denmark
74 B1 **Kalur Kot** Pak.
90 A2 **Kalush** Ukr.
74 B3 **Kalyan** India
89 E2 **Kalyazin** Rus. Fed.
111 C3 **Kalymnos** Greece
111 C3 **Kalymnos** *i.* Greece
119 C3 **Kama** Dem. Rep. Congo
62 A2 **Kama** Myanmar
86 E3 **Kama** *r.* Rus. Fed.
66 D3 **Kamaishi** Japan
80 B2 **Kaman** Turkey
120 A2 **Kamanjab** Namibia
78 B3 **Kamarān** *i.* Yemen
Kamaran Island Yemen *see* Kamarān
74 A2 **Kamarod** Pak.
50 B3 **Kambalda** Austr.
119 C4 **Kambove** Dem. Rep. Congo
160 C4 **Kamchatka Basin** *sea feature* Bering Sea
83 L3 **Kamchatka Peninsula** Rus. Fed.
110 C2 **Kamchiya** *r.* Bulg.
108 D2 **Kamenjak, Rt** *pt* Croatia
76 B1 **Kamenka** Kazakh.
86 D2 **Kamenka** Rus. Fed.
87 D3 **Kamenka** Rus. Fed.
66 C2 **Kamenka** Rus. Fed.
91 D1 **Kamenka** Rus. Fed.
Kamenka-Strumilovskaya Ukr. *see* Kam"yanka-Buz'ka
91 E3 **Kamennomostskiy** Rus. Fed.
91 E2 **Kamenolomni** Rus. Fed.
Kamenongue Angola *see* Camanongue
83 M2 **Kamenskoye** Rus. Fed.
Kamenskoye Ukr. *see* Dniprodzerzhyns'k
91 E2 **Kamensk-Shakhtinskiy** Rus. Fed.
86 F3 **Kamensk-Ural'skiy** Rus. Fed.
89 F2 **Kameshkovo** Rus. Fed.
75 B1 **Kamet** *mt.* China
75 B1 **Kamet** *mt.* China
122 A3 **Kamiesberge** *mts* S. Africa
122 A3 **Kamieskroon** S. Africa
129 D1 **Kamilukuak Lake** Can.
119 C3 **Kamina** Dem. Rep. Congo
129 E1 **Kaminak Lake** Can.
90 A1 **Kamin'-Kashyrs'kyy** Ukr.
119 C3 **Kamituga** Dem. Rep. Congo
128 B2 **Kamloops** Can.
54 B1 **Kamo** N.Z.
116 B3 **Kamob Sanha** Sudan
118 C3 **Kamonia** Dem. Rep. Congo
119 D2 **Kampala** Uganda
60 B1 **Kampar** *r.* Indon.
60 B1 **Kampar** Malaysia
100 B1 **Kampen** Neth.
119 C3 **Kampene** Dem. Rep. Congo
63 A2 **Kamphaeng Phet** Thai.
63 B2 **Kâmpóng Cham** Cambodia
63 B2 **Kâmpóng Chhnāng** Cambodia
Kâmpóng Saôm Cambodia *see* Sihanoukville
63 B2 **Kâmpóng Spœ** Cambodia
63 B2 **Kâmpôt** Cambodia
Kampuchea *country* Asia *see* Cambodia
129 D2 **Kamsack** Can.
86 E3 **Kamskoye Vodokhranilishche** *resr* Rus. Fed.

117 C4 **Kamsuuma** Somalia
90 B2 **Kam"yanets'-Podil's'kyy** Ukr.
90 A1 **Kam"yanka-Buz'ka** Ukr.
88 B3 **Kamyanyets** Belarus
91 D2 **Kamyshevatskaya** Rus. Fed.
87 D3 **Kamyshin** Rus. Fed.
135 D3 **Kanab** U.S.A.
118 C3 **Kananga** Dem. Rep. Congo
87 D3 **Kanash** Rus. Fed.
138 C3 **Kanawha** *r.* U.S.A.
67 C3 **Kanazawa** Japan
62 A1 **Kanbalu** Myanmar
63 A2 **Kanchanaburi** Thai.
73 B3 **Kanchipuram** India
77 C3 **Kandahār** Afgh.
86 C2 **Kandalaksha** Rus. Fed.
74 A2 **Kandangan** Indon.
74 A2 **Kandhkot** Pak.
114 C3 **Kandi** Benin
74 A2 **Kandiaro** Pak.
74 B2 **Kandla** India
53 C2 **Kandos** Austr.
121 □D2 **Kandreho** Madag.
73 C4 **Kandy** Sri Lanka
76 C4 **Kandyagash** Kazakh.
127 H1 **Kane Bassin** *b.* Greenland
91 D2 **Kanevskaya** Rus. Fed.
122 B1 **Kang** Botswana
127 I2 **Kangaatsiaq** Greenland
114 B3 **Kangaba** Mali
80 B2 **Kangal** Turkey
79 C2 **Kangān** Iran
60 B1 **Kangar** Malaysia
52 A3 **Kangaroo Island** Austr.
93 H3 **Kangasala** Fin.
81 C2 **Kangāvar** Iran
75 C2 **Kangchenjunga** *mt.* India/Nepal
70 A2 **Kangding** China
65 B2 **Kangdong** N. Korea
61 C2 **Kangean, Kepulauan** *is* Indon.
119 D2 **Kangeq** *c.* Greenland
127 J2 **Kangeq** *c.* Greenland
127 I2 **Kangerlussuaq** *inlet* Greenland
127 I2 **Kangerlussuaq** *inlet* Greenland
127 I2 **Kangersuatsiaq** Greenland
65 B1 **Kanggye** N. Korea
131 D2 **Kangiqsualujjuaq** Can.
127 H2 **Kangiqsujuaq** Can.
131 C1 **Kangirsuk** Can.
75 C2 **Kangmar** China
65 B2 **Kangnŭng** S. Korea
65 A1 **Kangping** China
72 D2 **Kangto** *mt.* China/India
62 A1 **Kani** Myanmar
118 C3 **Kaniama** Dem. Rep. Congo
61 C1 **Kanibongan** *Sabah* Malaysia
86 D2 **Kanin, Poluostrov** *pen.* Rus. Fed.
86 D2 **Kanin Nos** Rus. Fed.
86 D2 **Kanin Nos, Mys** *c.* Rus. Fed.
91 C2 **Kaniv** Ukr.
52 B3 **Kaniva** Austr.
93 H3 **Kankaanpää** Fin.
138 B2 **Kankakee** U.S.A.
114 B3 **Kankan** Guinea
75 C2 **Kanker** India
Kannur India *see* Cannanore
115 C3 **Kano** Nigeria
122 B3 **Kanonpunt** *pt* S. Africa
67 B4 **Kanoya** Japan
75 C2 **Kanpur** India
136 C3 **Kansas** *r.* U.S.A.
137 D3 **Kansas** *state* U.S.A.
137 E3 **Kansas City** *KS* U.S.A.
137 E3 **Kansas City** *MO* U.S.A.
83 H3 **Kansk** Rus. Fed.
Kansu *prov.* China *see* Gansu
63 B2 **Kantaralak** Thai.
114 C3 **Kantchari** Burkina
91 D2 **Kantemirovka** Rus. Fed.
49 J4 **Kanton** *i.* Kiribati
97 B2 **Kanturk** Ireland
123 D2 **KaNyamazane** S. Africa
123 C1 **Kanye** Botswana
71 C3 **Kaohsiung** Taiwan
120 A2 **Kaokoveld** *plat.* Namibia
114 A3 **Kaolack** Senegal
120 B2 **Kaoma** Zambia
118 C3 **Kapanga** Dem. Rep. Congo
88 C3 **Kapatkyevichy** Belarus
77 D2 **Kapchagay** Kazakh.
77 D2 **Kapchagayskoye Vodokhranilishche** *resr* Kazakh.
100 B2 **Kapellen** Belgium
121 B2 **Kapiri Mposhi** Zambia
127 I2 **Kapisillit** Greenland
130 B2 **Kapiskau** *r.* Can.
61 C1 **Kapit** *Sarawak* Malaysia
63 A3 **Kapoe** Thai.
117 B4 **Kapoeta** Sudan
103 D2 **Kaposvár** Hungary
102 B1 **Kappeln** Ger.
65 B1 **Kapsan** N. Korea
Kapsukas Lith. *see* Marijampolė
61 B2 **Kapuas** *r.* Indon.
52 A2 **Kapunda** Austr.
130 B3 **Kapuskasing** Can.
53 D2 **Kaputar** *mt.* Austr.
103 D2 **Kapuvár** Hungary
88 C3 **Kapyl'** Belarus
77 D3 **Kaqung** China
114 C4 **Kara** Togo
111 C3 **Kara Ada** *i.* Turkey
77 D2 **Kara-Balta** Kyrg.
76 C1 **Karabalyk** Kazakh.

76 C3 **Karabil', Vozvyshennost'** *hills* Turkm.
Kara-Bogaz-Gol Turkm. *see* Karabogazkel'
76 B2 **Kara-Bogaz-Gol, Zaliv** *b.* Turkm.
76 B2 **Karabogazkel'** Turkm.
80 B1 **Karabük** Turkey
76 C2 **Karabutak** Kazakh.
111 C2 **Karacabey** Turkey
111 C2 **Karacaköy** Turkey
81 C1 **Karachayevsk** Rus. Fed.
89 D3 **Karachev** Rus. Fed.
74 A2 **Karachi** Pak.
77 D2 **Karaganda** Kazakh.
77 D2 **Karagayly** Kazakh.
83 L3 **Karaginskiy Zaliv** *b.* Rus. Fed.
81 D2 **Karaj** Iran
Kara-Kala Turkm. *see* Garrygala
64 B3 **Karakelong** *i.* Indon.
Karaklis Armenia *see* Vanadzor
77 D2 **Kara-Köl** Kyrg.
77 D2 **Karakol** Kyrg.
74 B1 **Karakoram Range** *mts* Asia
72 B1 **Karakoram Range** *mts* Asia
117 B3 **Kara K'orē** Eth.
Karakum, Peski *des.* Kazakh. *see* Karakum Desert
76 B2 **Karakum Desert** *des.* Kazakh.
76 C3 **Karakum Desert** Turkm.
Karakumy, Peski *des.* Turkm. *see* Karakum Desert
80 B2 **Karaman** Turkey
77 E2 **Karamay** China
54 B2 **Karamea** N.Z.
54 B2 **Karamea Bight** *b.* N.Z.
80 B2 **Karapınar** Turkey
122 A2 **Karasburg** Namibia
86 F1 **Kara Sea** Rus. Fed.
92 I2 **Karasjok** Norway
Kara Strait Rus. Fed. *see* Karskiye Vorota, Proliv
111 D2 **Karasu** Turkey
Karasubazar Ukr. *see* Bilohirs'k
77 D1 **Karasuk** Rus. Fed.
77 D2 **Karatau** Kazakh.
77 C2 **Karatau, Khrebet** *mts* Kazakh.
86 F2 **Karatayka** Rus. Fed.
67 A4 **Karatsu** Japan
111 B3 **Karavas** Greece
60 B2 **Karawang** Indon.
81 C2 **Karbalā'** Iraq
103 E2 **Karcag** Hungary
Kardeljevo Croatia *see* Ploče
111 B3 **Karditsa** Greece
88 B2 **Kärdla** Estonia
122 B3 **Kareeberge** *mts* S. Africa
75 B2 **Kareli** India
88 C3 **Karelichy** Belarus
92 H2 **Karesuando** Sweden
Karghalik China *see* Yecheng
74 B1 **Kargil** Jammu and Kashmir
Kargilik China *see* Yecheng
86 C2 **Kargopol'** Rus. Fed.
118 B1 **Kari** Nigeria
121 B2 **Kariba** Zimbabwe
121 B2 **Kariba, Lake** *resr* Zambia/Zimbabwe
60 B2 **Karimata, Pulau-pulau** *is* Indon.
60 B2 **Karimata, Selat** *str.* Indon.
73 B3 **Karimnagar** India
61 C2 **Karimunjawa, Pulau-pulau** *is* Indon.
91 C2 **Karkinits'ka Zatoka** *g.* Ukr.
91 D2 **Karlivka** Ukr.
Karl-Marx-Stadt Ger. *see* Chemnitz
109 C1 **Karlovac** Croatia
102 C1 **Karlovy Vary** Czech Rep.
Karlsburg Romania *see* Alba Iulia
93 F4 **Karlshamn** Sweden
93 F4 **Karlskoga** Sweden
93 G4 **Karlskrona** Sweden
102 B2 **Karlsruhe** Ger.
93 F4 **Karlstad** Sweden
101 D3 **Karlstadt** Ger.
89 D3 **Karma** Belarus
93 E4 **Karmøy** *i.* Norway
75 D2 **Karnafuli Reservoir** Bangl.
74 B2 **Karnal** India
110 C2 **Karnobat** Bulg.
74 A2 **Karodi** Pak.
121 B2 **Karoi** Zimbabwe
121 C2 **Karonga** Malawi
116 B3 **Karora** Eritrea
111 C3 **Karpathos** Greece
111 C3 **Karpathos** *i.* Greece
111 B3 **Karpenisi** Greece
Karpilovka Belarus *see* Aktsyabrski
86 B2 **Karpogory** Rus. Fed.
50 A2 **Karratha** Austr.
81 C1 **Kars** Turkey
88 C2 **Kārsava** Latvia
76 B2 **Karshi** Turkm.
Karshi Uzbek. *see* Qarshi
111 C2 **Karşıyaka** Turkey
86 E2 **Karskiye Vorota, Proliv** *str.* Rus. Fed.
Karskoye More *sea* Rus. Fed. *see* Kara Sea
101 E1 **Karstädt** Ger.
111 C2 **Kartal** Turkey
87 F3 **Kartaly** Rus. Fed.
81 C2 **Kārūn, Rūd-e** *r.* Iran

73 B3 **Karwar** India
83 I3 **Karymskoye** Rus. Fed.
111 B3 **Karystos** Greece
111 C3 **Kaş** Turkey
130 B2 **Kasabonika Lake** Can.
118 C3 **Kasaï, Plateau du** Dem. Rep. Congo
118 C4 **Kasaji** Dem. Rep. Congo
121 C2 **Kasama** Zambia
120 B2 **Kasane** Botswana
118 B3 **Kasangulu** Dem. Rep. Congo
73 B3 **Kasaragod** India
129 D1 **Kasba Lake** Can.
120 B2 **Kasempa** Zambia
119 C4 **Kasenga** Dem. Rep. Congo
119 C3 **Kasese** Dem. Rep. Congo
119 D2 **Kasese** Uganda
Kasevo Rus. Fed. *see* Neftekamsk
81 D2 **Kāshān** Iran
77 D3 **Kashi** China
67 D3 **Kashima-nada** *b.* Japan
89 E2 **Kashin** Rus. Fed.
89 E3 **Kashira** Rus. Fed.
89 E3 **Kashirskoye** Rus. Fed.
67 C3 **Kashiwazaki** Japan
76 B3 **Kāshmar** Iran
Kashmir *terr.* Asia *see* Jammu and Kashmir
74 A2 **Kashmor** Pak.
119 C3 **Kashyukulu** Dem. Rep. Congo
89 F3 **Kasimov** Rus. Fed.
138 B3 **Kaskaskia** *r.* U.S.A.
93 H3 **Kaskinen** Fin.
119 C3 **Kasongo** Dem. Rep. Congo
118 B3 **Kasongo-Lunda** Dem. Rep. Congo
111 C3 **Kasos** *i.* Greece
Kaspiyskiy Rus. Fed. *see* Lagan'
116 B3 **Kassala** Sudan
101 D2 **Kassel** Ger.
115 C1 **Kasserine** Tunisia
80 B1 **Kastamonu** Turkey
111 B3 **Kastelli** Greece
Kastellorizon *i.* Greece *see* Megisti
111 B2 **Kastoria** Greece
89 D3 **Kastsyukovichy** Belarus
119 D3 **Kasulu** Tanz.
121 C2 **Kasungu** Malawi
139 F1 **Katahdin, Mount** U.S.A.
118 C3 **Katako-Kombe** Dem. Rep. Congo
119 D2 **Katakwi** Uganda
50 A3 **Katanning** Austr.
63 A3 **Katchall** *i.* India
111 B2 **Katerini** Greece
119 D3 **Katesh** Tanz.
128 A2 **Kate's Needle** *mt.* Can./U.S.A.
121 C2 **Katete** Zambia
62 A1 **Katha** Myanmar
50 C1 **Katherine** Austr.
50 C1 **Katherine** *r.* Austr.
74 B2 **Kathiawar** *pen.* India
123 C2 **Kathlehong** S. Africa
75 C2 **Kathmandu** Nepal
122 B2 **Kathu** S. Africa
74 B1 **Kathua** Jammu and Kashmir
114 B3 **Kati** Mali
75 C2 **Katihar** India
54 C1 **Katikati** N.Z.
123 C3 **Kati-Kati** S. Africa
120 B2 **Katima Mulilo** Namibia
114 B4 **Katiola** Côte d'Ivoire
Katmandu Nepal *see* Kathmandu
111 B3 **Kato Achaïa** Greece
119 C3 **Katompi** Dem. Rep. Congo
53 D2 **Katoomba** Austr.
103 D1 **Katowice** Pol.
80 B3 **Kātrīnā, Jabal** *mt.* Egypt
93 G4 **Katrineholm** Sweden
115 C3 **Katsina** Nigeria
115 C4 **Katsina-Ala** Nigeria
67 D3 **Katsuura** Japan
77 C3 **Kattaqo'rg'on** Uzbek.
93 F4 **Kattegat** *str.* Denmark/Sweden
100 B1 **Katwijk aan Zee** Neth.
101 D3 **Katzenbuckel** *hill* Ger.
49 L1 **Kaua'i** *i.* U.S.A.
93 H3 **Kauhajoki** Fin.
88 B3 **Kaunas** Lith.
115 C3 **Kaura-Namoda** Nigeria
92 H2 **Kautokeino** Norway
109 D2 **Kavadarci** Macedonia
109 C2 **Kavajë** Albania
111 B2 **Kavala** Greece
66 C2 **Kavalerovo** Rus. Fed.
73 C3 **Kavali** India
73 B3 **Kavaratti** *i.* India
110 C2 **Kavarna** Bulg.
59 E3 **Kavieng** P.N.G.
81 D2 **Kavir, Dasht-e** *des.* Iran
67 C3 **Kawagoe** Japan
54 B1 **Kawakawa** N.Z.
67 C3 **Kawanishi** Japan
67 C3 **Kawasaki** Japan
54 C1 **Kawerau** N.Z.
63 A2 **Kawkareik** Myanmar
62 A1 **Kawlin** Myanmar
63 A2 **Kawmapyin** Myanmar
116 B2 **Kawm Umbū** Egypt
63 A2 **Kawthaung** Myanmar
Kaxgar China *see* Kashi
77 D3 **Kaxgar He** *r.* China

114 B3 **Kaya** Burkina
111 C3 **Kayacı Dağı** *hill* Turkey
121 C1 **Kayambi** Zambia
61 C1 **Kayan** *r.* Indon.
136 B2 **Kaycee** U.S.A.
Kaydanovo Belarus *see* Dzyarzhynsk
142 A1 **Kayenta** U.S.A.
114 A3 **Kayes** Mali
77 D2 **Kaynar** Kazakh.
80 B2 **Kayseri** Turkey
134 D2 **Kaysville** U.S.A.
60 B2 **Kayuagung** Indon.
Kazakhskaya S.S.R. *admin. reg.* Asia *see* Kazakhstan
77 D1 **Kazakhskiy Melkosopochnik** *plain* Kazakh.
76 B2 **Kazakhskiy Zaliv** *b.* Kazakh.
76 C2 **Kazakhstan** *country* Asia
Kazakhstan Kazakh. *see* Aksay
87 D3 **Kazan'** Rus. Fed.
Kazandzhik Turkm. *see* Gazandzhyk
110 C2 **Kazanlŭk** Bulg.
Kazan-rettō Japan *see* Volcano Islands
76 A2 **Kazbek** *mt.* Georgia/Rus. Fed.
81 D3 **Kāzerūn** Iran
103 E2 **Kazincbarcika** Hungary
118 C3 **Kazumba** Dem. Rep. Congo
66 D2 **Kazuno** Japan
86 F2 **Kazymskiy Mys** Rus. Fed.
111 B3 **Kea** *i.* Greece
97 C1 **Keady** U.K.
137 D2 **Kearney** U.S.A.
142 A2 **Kearny** U.S.A.
115 C1 **Kebili** Tunisia
116 A3 **Kebkabiya** Sudan
92 G2 **Kebnekaise** *mt.* Sweden
117 C4 **K'ebrī Dehar** Eth.
60 B2 **Kebumen** Indon.
128 B2 **Kechika** *r.* Can.
111 D3 **Keçiborlu** Turkey
103 D2 **Kecskemét** Hungary
88 B2 **Kėdainiai** Lith.
114 A3 **Kédougou** Senegal
103 D1 **Kędzierzyn-Koźle** Pol.
128 B1 **Keele** *r.* Can.
128 A1 **Keele Peak** Can.
Keelung Taiwan *see* Chilung
139 E2 **Keene** U.S.A.
122 A2 **Keetmanshoop** Namibia
129 E3 **Keewatin** Can.
Kefallonia *i.* Greece *see* Cephalonia
59 C3 **Kefamenanu** Indon.
92 □A3 **Keflavik** Iceland
77 D2 **Kegen** Kazakh.
128 C2 **Keg River** Can.
88 C2 **Kehra** Estonia
62 A1 **Kehsi Mansam** Myanmar
98 C3 **Keighley** U.K.
88 B2 **Keila** Estonia
122 B2 **Keimoes** S. Africa
92 I3 **Keitele** *l.* Fin.
52 B3 **Keith** Austr.
96 C2 **Keith** U.K.
128 B1 **Keith Arm** *b.* Can.
134 B2 **Keizer** U.S.A.
103 E2 **Kékes** *mt.* Hungary
117 C4 **K'elafo** Eth.
Kelang Malaysia *see* Klang
92 J2 **Keles-Uayv, Gora** *hill* Rus. Fed.
102 C2 **Kelheim** Ger.
76 C3 **Kelifskiy Uzboy** *marsh* Turkm.
80 B1 **Kelkit** *r.* Turkey
128 B1 **Keller Lake** Can.
134 C1 **Kellogg** U.S.A.
92 I2 **Kelloselkä** Fin.
97 C2 **Kells** Ireland
88 B2 **Kelmė** Lith.
115 D4 **Kelo** Chad
128 C3 **Kelowna** Can.
96 C3 **Kelso** U.K.
134 B1 **Kelso** U.S.A.
60 B1 **Keluang** Malaysia
129 D2 **Kelvington** Can.
86 C2 **Kem'** Rus. Fed.
Ke Macina Mali *see* Massina
128 B2 **Kemano** Can.
118 C2 **Kembé** C.A.R.
111 C3 **Kemer** Turkey
82 G3 **Kemerovo** Rus. Fed.
92 H2 **Kemi** Fin.
92 I2 **Kemijärvi** Fin.
92 I2 **Kemijärvi** *l.* Fin.
92 I2 **Kemijoki** *r.* Fin.
136 A2 **Kemmerer** U.S.A.
92 I3 **Kempele** Fin.
55 G2 **Kemp Land** *reg.* Antarctica
55 A2 **Kemp Peninsula** Antarctica
53 D2 **Kempsey** Austr.
130 C3 **Kempt, Lac** *l.* Can.
102 C2 **Kempten (Allgäu)** Ger.
123 C2 **Kempton Park** S. Africa
61 C2 **Kemujan** *i.* Indon.
126 B2 **Kenai** U.S.A.
129 D2 **Kendall** Can.
98 B2 **Kendal** U.K.
141 D3 **Kendall** U.S.A.
61 D2 **Kendari** Indon.
60 C2 **Kendawangan** Indon.
115 D3 **Kendégué** Chad
114 A4 **Kenema** Sierra Leone
118 B3 **Kenge** Dem. Rep. Congo

62 A1 **Kengtung** Myanmar
122 B2 **Kenhardt** S. Africa
114 B1 **Kénitra** Morocco
97 B3 **Kenmare** Ireland
136 C1 **Kenmare** U.S.A.
97 A3 **Kenmare River** *inlet* Ireland
100 C3 **Kenn** Ger.
143 C2 **Kenna** U.S.A.
139 F2 **Kennebec** *r.* U.S.A.
Kennedy, Cape U.S.A. *see* Canaveral, Cape
140 B3 **Kenner** U.S.A.
99 C4 **Kennet** *r.* U.K.
137 E3 **Kennett** U.S.A.
130 A3 **Kenora** Can.
138 B2 **Kenosha** U.S.A.
142 C2 **Kent** U.S.A.
77 C2 **Kentau** Kazakh.
138 B3 **Kentucky** *r.* U.S.A.
138 C3 **Kentucky** *state* U.S.A.
138 B3 **Kentucky Lake** U.S.A.
140 B2 **Kentwood** U.S.A.
119 D2 **Kenya** *country* Africa
119 D3 **Kenya, Mount** *mt.* Kenya
60 B1 **Kenyir, Tasik** *resr* Malaysia
137 E2 **Keokuk** U.S.A.
75 C2 **Keonjhar** India
111 C3 **Kepsut** Turkey
52 B3 **Kerang** Austr.
91 D2 **Kerch** Ukr.
59 D3 **Kerema** P.N.G.
128 C3 **Keremeos** Can.
116 B3 **Keren** Eritrea
81 C2 **Kerend** Iran
159 E7 **Kerguélen, Îles** *is* Indian Ocean
159 E7 **Kerguelen Plateau** *sea feature* Indian Ocean
119 D3 **Kericho** Kenya
54 B1 **Kerikeri** N.Z.
60 B2 **Kerinci, Gunung** *vol.* Indon.
Kerintji *vol.* Indon. *see* Kerinci, Gunung
100 C2 **Kerkrade** Neth.
111 A3 **Kerkyra** Greece
Kerkyra *i.* Greece *see* Corfu
116 B3 **Kerma** Sudan
49 J7 **Kermadec Islands** S. Pacific Ocean
79 C1 **Kermān** Iran
81 C2 **Kermānshāh** Iran
Kermine Uzbek. *see* Navoiy
143 C2 **Kermit** U.S.A.
135 C3 **Kern** *r.* U.S.A.
114 B4 **Kérouané** Guinea
100 C2 **Kerpen** Ger.
129 D2 **Kerrobert** Can.
143 D2 **Kerrville** U.S.A.
97 B2 **Kerry Head** *hd* Ireland
Keryneia Cyprus *see* Kyrenia
130 B2 **Kesagami Lake** Can.
111 C2 **Keşan** Turkey
66 D3 **Kesennuma** Japan
74 B2 **Keshod** India
100 C2 **Kessel** Neth.
98 B2 **Keswick** U.K.
103 D2 **Keszthely** Hungary
82 G3 **Ket'** *r.* Rus. Fed.
60 C2 **Ketapang** Indon.
128 A2 **Ketchikan** U.S.A.
134 D2 **Ketchum** U.S.A.
114 B4 **Kete Krachi** Ghana
118 B2 **Kétté** Cameroon
99 C3 **Kettering** U.K.
138 C3 **Kettering** U.S.A.
134 C1 **Kettle River Range** *mts* U.S.A.
93 H3 **Keuruu** Fin.
100 C2 **Kevelaer** Ger.
138 B2 **Kewanee** U.S.A.
138 B1 **Keweenaw Bay** U.S.A.
138 B1 **Keweenaw Peninsula** U.S.A.
141 D3 **Key Largo** U.S.A.
99 B4 **Keynsham** U.K.
139 D3 **Keyser** U.S.A.
141 D4 **Key West** U.S.A.
123 C2 **Kgotsong** S. Africa
69 F1 **Khabarovsk** Rus. Fed.
91 D3 **Khadyzhensk** Rus. Fed.
75 D2 **Khagrachari** Bangl.
74 A2 **Khairpur** Pak.
122 B1 **Khakhea** Botswana
76 B3 **Khalilabad** Iran
86 F2 **Khal'mer-Yu** Rus. Fed.
68 C1 **Khamar-Daban, Khrebet** *mts* Rus. Fed.
74 B2 **Khambhat** India
74 B3 **Khambhat, Gulf of** India
74 B2 **Khamgaon** India
79 C2 **Khamir** Iran
78 B3 **Khamir** Yemen
78 B3 **Khamis Mushayṭ** Saudi Arabia
77 C3 **Khānābād** Afgh.
74 B2 **Khandwa** India
83 K2 **Khandyga** Rus. Fed.
74 B1 **Khanewal** Pak.
Khan Hung Vietnam *see* Soc Trăng
83 J3 **Khani** Rus. Fed.
66 B2 **Khanka, Lake** China/Rus. Fed.
115 C2 **Khannfoussa** *hill* Alg.
74 B2 **Khanpur** Pak.
77 D2 **Khantau** Kazakh.
83 H2 **Khantayskoye, Ozero** *l.* Rus. Fed.
86 F2 **Khanty-Mansiysk** Rus. Fed.
63 A3 **Khao Chum Thong** Thai.
63 A2 **Khao Laem Reservoir** Thai.

74 B1 **Khapalu** Jammu and Kashmir
87 D4 **Kharabali** Rus. Fed.
75 C2 **Kharagpur** India
79 C2 **Khārān** *r.* Iran
Kharga Oasis Egypt *see* Khārijah, Wāḩāt al
74 B2 **Khargon** India
116 B2 **Khārijah, Wāḩāt al** Egypt
91 D2 **Kharkiv** Ukr.
Khar'kov Ukr. *see* Kharkiv
111 C2 **Kharmanli** Bulg.
89 F2 **Kharovsk** Rus. Fed.
116 B3 **Khartoum** Sudan
87 D4 **Khasav'yurt** Rus. Fed.
79 D2 **Khāsh** Iran
86 F2 **Khashgort** Rus. Fed.
78 A3 **Khashm el Girba** Sudan
78 A3 **Khashm el Girba Dam** Sudan
81 C1 **Khashuri** Georgia
75 D2 **Khasi Hills** India
111 C2 **Khaskovo** Bulg.
83 H2 **Khatanga** Rus. Fed.
123 C3 **Khayamnandi** S. Africa
78 A2 **Khaybar** Saudi Arabia
122 A3 **Khayelitsha** S. Africa
62 B2 **Khê Bo** Vietnam
107 D2 **Khemis Miliana** Alg.
63 B2 **Khemmarat** Thai.
115 C1 **Khenchela** Alg.
81 D3 **Kherämeh** Iran
91 C2 **Kherson** Ukr.
83 H2 **Kheta** *r.* Rus. Fed.
69 D1 **Khilok** Rus. Fed.
89 E2 **Khimki** Rus. Fed.
89 E3 **Khlevnoye** Rus. Fed.
63 B2 **Khlung** Thai.
90 D1 **Khmel'nyts'kyy** Ukr.
Khmer Republic *country* Asia *see* Cambodia
76 B1 **Khobda** Kazakh.
Khodzheyli Uzbek. *see* Xo'jayli
89 E3 **Khokhol'skiy** Rus. Fed.
74 B2 **Khokhropar** Pak.
74 A1 **Kholm** Afgh.
89 D2 **Kholm** Rus. Fed.
89 D2 **Kholm-Zhirkovskiy** Rus. Fed.
122 A1 **Khomas Highland** *hills* Namibia
89 E3 **Khomutovo** Rus. Fed.
79 C2 **Khonj** Iran
63 B2 **Khon Kaen** Thai.
62 A1 **Khonsa** India
83 K2 **Khonuu** Rus. Fed.
86 E2 **Khoreyver** Rus. Fed.
69 D1 **Khorinsk** Rus. Fed.
120 A3 **Khorixas** Namibia
66 B2 **Khorol** Rus. Fed.
91 C2 **Khorol** Ukr.
81 C2 **Khorramābād** Iran
81 C2 **Khorramshahr** Iran
77 D3 **Khorugh** Tajik.
Khotan China *see* Hotan
90 B2 **Khotyn** Ukr.
114 B1 **Khouribga** Morocco
77 C3 **Khowst** Afgh.
88 C3 **Khoyniki** Belarus
62 A1 **Khreum** Myanmar
76 B1 **Khromtau** Kazakh.
Khrushchev Ukr. *see* Svitlovods'k
90 B2 **Khrystynivka** Ukr.
123 B1 **Khudumelapye** Botswana
77 C2 **Khŭjand** Tajik.
63 B2 **Khu Khan** Thai.
78 A2 **Khulays** Saudi Arabia
75 C2 **Khulna** Bangl.
Khūnīnshahr Iran *see* Khorramshahr
81 D2 **Khunsar** Iran
79 B2 **Khurayş** Saudi Arabia
74 B1 **Khushab** Pak.
90 A2 **Khust** Ukr.
123 C2 **Khutsong** S. Africa
74 A2 **Khuzdar** Pak.
81 D3 **Khvormūj** Iran
81 C2 **Khvoy** Iran
89 D2 **Khvoynaya** Rus. Fed.
77 D3 **Khyber Pass** Afgh./Pak.
53 D2 **Kiama** Austr.
64 B3 **Kiamba** Phil.
119 C3 **Kiambi** Dem. Rep. Congo
Kiangsi *prov.* China *see* Jiangxi
Kiangsu *prov.* China *see* Jiangsu
119 D3 **Kibaha** Tanz.
119 D3 **Kibaya** Tanz.
119 D3 **Kibiti** Tanz.
119 C3 **Kibombo** Dem. Rep. Congo
119 D3 **Kibondo** Tanz.
119 D2 **Kibre Mengist** Eth.
119 D3 **Kibungo** Rwanda
111 B2 **Kičevo** Macedonia
114 C3 **Kidal** Mali
99 B3 **Kidderminster** U.K.
114 A3 **Kidira** Senegal
74 B1 **Kidmang** Jammu and Kashmir
54 C1 **Kidnappers, Cape** N.Z.
102 C1 **Kiel** Ger.
103 E1 **Kielce** Pol.
98 B2 **Kielder Water** *resr* U.K.
119 C4 **Kienge** Dem. Rep. Congo
90 C1 **Kiev** Ukr.
114 A3 **Kiffa** Maur.
119 D3 **Kigoma** Tanz.
88 B2 **Kihnu** *i.* Estonia
92 I2 **Kiiminki** Fin.

67 B4 **Kii-suidō** *sea chan.* Japan
109 D1 **Kikinda** Serb. and Mont.
119 C3 **Kikondja** Dem. Rep. Congo
59 D3 **Kikori** P.N.G.
59 D3 **Kikori** *r.* P.N.G.
118 B3 **Kikwit** Dem. Rep. Congo
65 B1 **Kilchu** N. Korea
97 C2 **Kilcock** Ireland
97 C2 **Kildare** Ireland
118 B3 **Kilembe** Dem. Rep. Congo
143 E2 **Kilgore** U.S.A.
119 D3 **Kilifi** Kenya
119 D3 **Kilimanjaro** *vol.* Tanz.
119 D3 **Kilindoni** Tanz.
80 B2 **Kilis** Turkey
90 B2 **Kiliya** Ukr.
97 B2 **Kilkee** Ireland
97 D1 **Kilkeel** U.K.
97 C2 **Kilkenny** Ireland
111 B2 **Kilkis** Greece
97 B1 **Killala** Ireland
97 B1 **Killala Bay** Ireland
97 B2 **Killaloe** Ireland
128 C2 **Killam** Can.
97 B2 **Killarney** Ireland
143 D2 **Killeen** U.S.A.
96 B2 **Killin** U.K.
131 D1 **Killiniq** Can.
97 B2 **Killorglin** Ireland
97 B1 **Killybegs** Ireland
96 B3 **Kilmarnock** U.K.
53 B3 **Kilmore** Austr.
119 D3 **Kilosa** Tanz.
97 B2 **Kilrush** Ireland
119 C3 **Kilwa** Dem. Rep. Congo
119 D3 **Kilwa Masoko** Tanz.
119 D3 **Kimambi** Tanz.
52 A2 **Kimba** Austr.
136 C2 **Kimball** U.S.A.
128 C3 **Kimberley** Can.
122 B2 **Kimberley** S. Africa
50 B1 **Kimberley Plateau** Austr.
65 B1 **Kimch'aek** N. Korea
65 B2 **Kimch'ŏn** S. Korea
65 B2 **Kimhae** S. Korea
127 H2 **Kimmirut** Can.
89 E3 **Kimovsk** Rus. Fed.
118 C3 **Kimpanga** Dem. Rep. Congo
118 B3 **Kimpese** Dem. Rep. Congo
89 E2 **Kimry** Rus. Fed.
61 C1 **Kinabalu, Gunung** *mt.* Sabah Malaysia
128 C2 **Kinbasket Lake** Can.
96 C1 **Kinbrace** U.K.
130 B3 **Kincardine** Can.
62 A1 **Kinchang** Myanmar
119 C3 **Kinda** Dem. Rep. Congo
98 C3 **Kinder Scout** *hill* U.K.
129 D2 **Kindersley** Can.
114 A3 **Kindia** Guinea
119 C3 **Kindu** Dem. Rep. Congo
89 F2 **Kineshma** Rus. Fed.
118 B3 **Kingandu** Dem. Rep. Congo
51 E2 **Kingaroy** Austr.
135 B3 **King City** U.S.A.
130 C2 **King George Islands** Can.
88 C2 **Kingisepp** Rus. Fed.
51 D3 **King Island** Austr.
Kingisseppa Estonia *see* Kuressaare
50 B1 **King Leopold Ranges** *hills* Austr.
142 A1 **Kingman** U.S.A.
135 B3 **Kings** *r.* U.S.A.
52 A3 **Kingscote** Austr.
97 C2 **Kingscourt** Ireland
99 D3 **King's Lynn** U.K.
50 B1 **King Sound** *b.* Austr.
134 D2 **Kings Peak** U.S.A.
141 D1 **Kingsport** U.S.A.
51 D4 **Kingston** Austr.
130 C3 **Kingston** Can.
146 C3 **Kingston** Jamaica
139 E2 **Kingston** U.S.A.
52 A3 **Kingston South East** Austr.
98 C3 **Kingston upon Hull** U.K.
147 D3 **Kingstown** St Vincent
143 D3 **Kingsville** U.S.A.
99 B4 **Kingswood** U.K.
96 B2 **Kingussie** U.K.
126 F2 **King William Island** Can.
123 C3 **King William's Town** S. Africa
67 D3 **Kinka-san** *i.* Japan
92 I3 **Kinna** Sweden
97 B3 **Kinsale** Ireland
118 B3 **Kinshasa** Dem. Rep. Congo
141 E1 **Kinston** U.S.A.
88 B2 **Kintai** Lith.
114 B4 **Kintampo** Ghana
96 C1 **Kintore** U.K.
96 B3 **Kintyre** *pen.* U.K.
119 D3 **Kiomboi** Tanz.
130 C3 **Kipawa, Lac** *l.* Can.
119 D3 **Kipembawe** Tanz.
119 D3 **Kipengere Range** *mts* Tanz.
129 D2 **Kipling** Can.
Kipling Station Can. *see* Kipling
119 C4 **Kipushi** Dem. Rep. Congo
119 C4 **Kipushia** Dem. Rep. Congo
101 D2 **Kirchhain** Ger.
101 D3 **Kirchheim-Bolanden** Ger.
83 I3 **Kirenga** *r.* Rus. Fed.
83 I3 **Kirensk** Rus. Fed.
89 E3 **Kireyevsk** Rus. Fed.

Kirghizia *country* Asia *see* Kyrgyzstan
77 D2 **Kirghiz Range** *mts* Asia
Kirgizskaya S.S.R. *admin. reg.* Asia *see* Kyrgyzstan
49 J4 **Kiribati** *country* Pacific Ocean
80 B2 **Kırıkkale** Turkey
89 E2 **Kirillov** Rus. Fed.
89 E2 **Kirin** China *see* Jilin
Kirin *prov.* China *see* Jilin
Kirinyaga Kenya *see* Kenya, Mount
89 D2 **Kirishi** Rus. Fed.
48 L3 **Kiritimati** *i.* Kiribati
111 C3 **Kırkağaç** Turkey
98 B3 **Kirkby** U.K.
98 B2 **Kirkby Stephen** U.K.
96 C2 **Kirkcaldy** U.K.
96 B3 **Kirkcudbright** U.K.
92 J2 **Kirkenes** Norway
88 B1 **Kirkkonummi** Fin.
130 B3 **Kirkland Lake** Can.
111 C2 **Kırklareli** Turkey
137 E2 **Kirksville** U.S.A.
81 C2 **Kirkūk** Iraq
96 C1 **Kirkwall** U.K.
Kirov Kazakh. *see* Balpyk Bi
89 D3 **Kirov** Rus. Fed.
86 D3 **Kirov** Rus. Fed.
Kirovabad Azer. *see* Gäncä
Kirovakan Armenia *see* Vanadzor
Kirovo Ukr. *see* Kirovohrad
86 E3 **Kirovo-Chepetsk** Rus. Fed.
Kirovo-Chepetskiy Rus. Fed. *see* Kirovo-Chepetsk
91 C2 **Kirovohrad** Ukr.
86 C2 **Kirovsk** Rus. Fed.
91 D2 **Kirovs'ke** Ukr.
Kirovskiy Kazakh. *see* Balpyk Bi
66 B1 **Kirovskiy** Rus. Fed.
96 C2 **Kirriemuir** U.K.
86 E3 **Kirs** Rus. Fed.
87 D3 **Kirsanov** Rus. Fed.
80 B2 **Kırşehir** Turkey
74 A2 **Kirthar Range** *mts* Pak.
92 H2 **Kiruna** Sweden
67 C3 **Kiryū** Japan
89 E2 **Kirzhach** Rus. Fed.
119 D3 **Kisaki** Tanz.
119 C2 **Kisangani** Dem. Rep. Congo
118 B3 **Kisantu** Dem. Rep. Congo
60 A1 **Kisaran** Indon.
82 G3 **Kiselevsk** Rus. Fed.
75 C2 **Kishanganj** India
115 C4 **Kishi** Nigeria
Kishinev Moldova *see* Chişinău
67 C4 **Kishiwada** Japan
77 D1 **Kishkenekol'** Kazakh.
75 C2 **Kishoreganj** Bangl.
74 B1 **Kishtwar** Jammu and Kashmir
119 D3 **Kisii** Kenya
103 D2 **Kiskunfélegyháza** Hungary
103 D2 **Kiskunhalas** Hungary
87 D4 **Kislovodsk** Rus. Fed.
117 C5 **Kismaayo** Somalia
Kismayu Somalia *see* Kismaayo
119 C3 **Kisoro** Uganda
114 A4 **Kissidougou** Guinea
141 D3 **Kissimmee** U.S.A.
141 D3 **Kissimmee, Lake** U.S.A.
129 D2 **Kississing Lake** Can.
Kistna *r.* India *see* Krishna
119 D3 **Kisumu** Kenya
103 E2 **Kisvárda** Hungary
Kisykkamys Kazakh. *see* Dzhangala
114 B3 **Kita** Mali
67 D3 **Kitaibaraki** Japan
66 D3 **Kitakami** Japan
66 D3 **Kitakami-gawa** *r.* Japan
67 B4 **Kita-Kyūshū** Japan
119 D2 **Kitale** Kenya
66 D2 **Kitami** Japan
130 B3 **Kitchener** Can.
93 J3 **Kitee** Fin.
119 D2 **Kitgum** Uganda
128 B2 **Kitimat** Can.
118 B3 **Kitona** Dem. Rep. Congo
92 H2 **Kittilä** Fin.
141 E1 **Kitty Hawk** U.S.A.
119 D3 **Kitunda** Tanz.
128 B2 **Kitwanga** Can.
121 B2 **Kitwe** Zambia
102 C2 **Kitzbühel** Austria
101 E3 **Kitzingen** Ger.
59 D3 **Kiunga** P.N.G.
92 I3 **Kiuruvesi** Fin.
92 I2 **Kivalo** *ridge* Fin.
90 B1 **Kivertsi** Ukr.
88 C2 **Kiviõli** Estonia
91 D2 **Kivsharivka** Ukr.
119 C3 **Kivu, Lake** Dem. Rep. Congo/Rwanda
111 C2 **Kıyıköy** Turkey
86 E3 **Kizel** Rus. Fed.
111 C3 **Kızıla Dağ** *mt.* Turkey
80 B1 **Kızılırmak** *r.* Turkey
87 D4 **Kizlyar** Rus. Fed.
Kizyl-Arbat Turkm. *see* Gyzylarbat
92 I1 **Kjøllefjord** Norway
92 G2 **Kjøpsvik** Norway
102 C1 **Kladno** Czech Rep.
102 C2 **Klagenfurt** Austria
88 B2 **Klaipėda** Lith.
94 B1 **Klaksvík** Faroe Is

134 B2 **Klamath** *r.* U.S.A.
134 B2 **Klamath Falls** U.S.A.
134 B2 **Klamath Mountains** U.S.A.
60 B1 **Klang** Malaysia
102 C2 **Klatovy** Czech Rep.
122 A3 **Klawer** S. Africa
128 A2 **Klawock** U.S.A.
128 B2 **Kleena Kleene** Can.
122 B2 **Kleinbegin** S. Africa
122 A2 **Klein Karas** Namibia
122 A2 **Kleinsee** S. Africa
123 C2 **Klerksdorp** S. Africa
90 B1 **Klesiv** Ukr.
89 D3 **Kletnya** Rus. Fed.
100 C2 **Kleve** Ger.
88 C3 **Klichaw** Belarus
89 D3 **Klimavichy** Belarus
89 D3 **Klimovo** Rus. Fed.
89 E2 **Klimovsk** Rus. Fed.
89 E2 **Klin** Rus. Fed.
101 F2 **Klingenthal** Ger.
101 F2 **Klínovec** *mt.* Czech Rep.
93 G4 **Klintehamn** Sweden
89 D3 **Klintsy** Rus. Fed.
109 C2 **Ključ** Bos.-Herz.
103 D1 **Kłodzko** Pol.
100 C1 **Kloosterhaar** Neth.
103 D2 **Klosterneuburg** Austria
101 E2 **Klötze (Altmark)** Ger.
128 A1 **Kluane Lake** Can.
Kluang Malaysia *see* Keluang
103 D1 **Kluczbork** Pol.
Klukhori Rus. Fed. *see* Karachayevsk
128 A2 **Klukwan** U.S.A.
74 A2 **Klupro** Pak.
89 F2 **Klyaz'ma** *r.* Rus. Fed.
88 C3 **Klyetsk** Belarus
83 L3 **Klyuchi** Rus. Fed.
98 C2 **Knaresborough** U.K.
93 F3 **Knästen** *hill* Sweden
129 E2 **Knee Lake** Can.
101 E1 **Knesebeck** Ger.
101 E3 **Knetzgau** Ger.
109 C2 **Knin** Croatia
103 C2 **Knittelfeld** Austria
109 D2 **Knjaževac** Serb. and Mont.
Knob Lake Can. *see* Schefferville
97 B3 **Knockaboy** *hill* Ireland
100 A2 **Knokke-Heist** Belgium
141 D1 **Knoxville** U.S.A.
127 H1 **Knud Rasmussen Land** *reg.* Greenland
122 B3 **Knysna** S. Africa
60 B2 **Koba** Indon.
67 C4 **Kōbe** Japan
København Denmark *see* Copenhagen
100 C2 **Koblenz** Ger.
59 C3 **Kobroör** *i.* Indon.
88 B3 **Kobryn** Belarus
Kocaeli Turkey *see* İzmit
111 B2 **Kočani** Macedonia
111 C2 **Kocasu** *r.* Turkey
109 B1 **Kočevje** Slovenia
75 C2 **Koch Bihar** India
89 F3 **Kochetovka** Rus. Fed.
Kochi India *see* Cochin
67 B4 **Kōchi** Japan
87 D4 **Kochubey** Rus. Fed.
75 C2 **Kodarma** India
126 B3 **Kodiak** U.S.A.
126 B3 **Kodiak Island** U.S.A.
123 C1 **Kodibeleng** Botswana
117 B4 **Kodok** Sudan
90 B2 **Kodyma** Ukr.
111 C2 **Kodzhaele** *mt.* Bulg./Greece
122 A2 **Koës** Namibia
122 C2 **Koffiefontein** S. Africa
114 B4 **Koforidua** Ghana
67 C3 **Kōfu** Japan
131 D2 **Kogaluk** *r.* Can.
114 B3 **Kogoni** Mali
74 B1 **Kohat** Pak.
72 D2 **Kohima** India
88 C2 **Kohtla-Järve** Estonia
128 A1 **Koidern** Can.
Kokand Uzbek. *see* Qo'qon
88 B2 **Kökar** Fin.
Kokchetav Kazakh. *see* Kokshetau
122 A2 **Kokerboom** Namibia
88 C3 **Kokhanava** Belarus
89 F2 **Kokhma** Rus. Fed.
92 H3 **Kokkola** Fin.
88 C2 **Koknese** Latvia
138 B2 **Kokomo** U.S.A.
122 B1 **Kokong** Botswana
123 C2 **Kokosi** S. Africa
77 E2 **Kokpekti** Kazakh.
77 C1 **Kokshetau** Kazakh.
131 D2 **Koksoak** *r.* Can.
123 C3 **Kokstad** S. Africa
Koktokay China *see* Fuyun
61 D2 **Kolaka** Indon.
86 C2 **Kola Peninsula** Rus. Fed.
92 H2 **Kolari** Fin.
Kolarovgrad Bulg. *see* Shumen
114 A3 **Kolda** Senegal
93 E4 **Kolding** Denmark
119 C2 **Kole** Dem. Rep. Congo
107 D2 **Koléa** Alg.
86 D2 **Kolguyev, Ostrov** *i.* Rus. Fed.
73 B3 **Kolhapur** India
88 B2 **Kolkasrags** *pt* Latvia

75 C2 **Kolkata** India
Kollam India see Quilon
100 C1 **Kollum** Neth.
Köln Ger. see Cologne
103 D1 **Koło** Pol.
103 D1 **Kołobrzeg** Pol.
114 B3 **Kolokani** Mali
89 E2 **Kolomna** Rus. Fed.
90 B2 **Kolomyya** Ukr.
114 B3 **Kolondiéba** Mali
61 D2 **Kolonedale** Indon.
122 B2 **Kolonkwane** Botswana
82 G3 **Kolpashevo** Rus. Fed.
89 E3 **Kolpny** Rus. Fed.
Kol'skiy Poluostrov pen. Rus. Fed. see Kola Peninsula
78 B3 **Koluli** Eritrea
92 F3 **Kolvereid** Norway
119 C4 **Kolwezi** Dem. Rep. Congo
83 L2 **Kolyma** r. Rus. Fed.
Kolyma Lowland Rus. Fed. see Kolymskaya Nizmennost'
Kolyma Range mts Rus. Fed. see Kolymskiy, Khrebet
83 L2 **Kolymskaya Nizmennost'** lowland Rus. Fed.
83 M2 **Kolymskiy, Khrebet** mts Rus. Fed.
122 A2 **Komaggas** S. Africa
67 C3 **Komaki** Japan
83 M3 **Komandorskiye Ostrova** is Rus. Fed.
103 D2 **Komárno** Slovakia
123 D2 **Komati** r. Swaziland
123 D2 **Komatipoort** S. Africa
67 C3 **Komatsu** Japan
120 A2 **Kombat** Namibia
119 C3 **Kombe** Dem. Rep. Congo
Kominternivs'ke Ukr. see Marhanets'
90 C2 **Kominternivs'ke** Ukr.
109 C2 **Komiža** Croatia
103 D2 **Komló** Hungary
Kommunarsk Ukr. see Alchevs'k
118 B3 **Komono** Congo
111 C2 **Komotini** Greece
Kompong Som Cambodia see Sihanoukville
Komrat Moldova see Comrat
122 B3 **Komsberg** mts S. Africa
83 H1 **Komsomolets, Ostrov** i. Rus. Fed.
89 F2 **Komsomol'sk** Rus. Fed.
91 C2 **Komsomol's'k** Ukr.
83 M2 **Komsomol'skiy** Rus. Fed.
Komsomol'skiy Rus. Fed. see Yugorsk
87 D4 **Komsomol'skiy** Rus. Fed.
83 K3 **Komsomol'sk-na-Amure** Rus. Fed.
89 E2 **Konakovo** Rus. Fed.
75 C3 **Kondagaon** India
86 F2 **Kondinskoye** Rus. Fed.
Kondinskoye Rus. Fed. see Oktyabr'skoye
119 D3 **Kondoa** Tanz.
86 C2 **Kondopoga** Rus. Fed.
89 E3 **Kondrovo** Rus. Fed.
127 J2 **Kong Christian IX Land** reg. Greenland
127 K2 **Kong Christian X Land** reg. Greenland
127 J2 **Kong Frederik VI Kyst** coastal area Greenland
65 B2 **Kongju** S. Korea
119 C3 **Kongolo** Dem. Rep. Congo
93 E4 **Kongsberg** Norway
93 F3 **Kongsvinger** Norway
77 D3 **Kongur Shan** mt. China
100 C2 **Königswinter** Ger.
103 D1 **Konin** Pol.
109 C2 **Konjic** Bos.-Herz.
122 A2 **Konkiep** watercourse Namibia
86 D2 **Konosha** Rus. Fed.
91 C1 **Konotop** Ukr.
103 E1 **Końskie** Pol.
Konstantinograd Ukr. see Krasnohrad
102 B2 **Konstanz** Ger.
115 C3 **Kontagora** Nigeria
63 B2 **Kon Tum** Vietnam
63 B2 **Kontum, Plateau du** Vietnam
80 B2 **Konya** Turkey
77 D2 **Konyrat** Kazakh.
100 C3 **Konz** Ger.
86 E3 **Konzhakovskiy Kamen', Gora** mt. Rus. Fed.
134 C1 **Kooskia** U.S.A.
128 C3 **Kootenay Lake** Can.
53 D2 **Kootingal** Austr.
122 B3 **Kootjieskolk** S. Africa
92 □B2 **Kópasker** Iceland
108 B1 **Koper** Slovenia
93 G4 **Köping** Sweden
123 C1 **Kopong** Botswana
93 G4 **Kopparberg** Sweden
109 C1 **Koprivnica** Croatia
89 F3 **Korablino** Rus. Fed.
73 C3 **Koraput** India
75 C2 **Korba** India
101 D2 **Korbach** Ger.
109 D2 **Korçë** Albania
109 C2 **Korčula** Croatia
109 C2 **Korčula** i. Croatia
65 B1 **Korea, North** country Asia
65 B2 **Korea, South** country Asia
70 C2 **Korea Bay** g. China/N. Korea
65 B3 **Korea Strait** Japan/S. Korea
89 D3 **Korenevo** Rus. Fed.

91 D2 **Korenovsk** Rus. Fed.
Korenovskaya Rus. Fed. see Korenovsk
90 B1 **Korets'** Ukr.
111 C2 **Körfez** Turkey
114 B4 **Korhogo** Côte d'Ivoire
Korinthos Greece see Corinth
103 D2 **Kóris-hegy** hill Hungary
109 D2 **Koritnik** mt. Albania
Koritsa Albania see Korçë
67 D3 **Kōriyama** Japan
87 F3 **Korkino** Rus. Fed.
111 D3 **Korkuteli** Turkey
77 E2 **Korla** China
103 D2 **Körmend** Hungary
49 I5 **Koro** i. Fiji
114 B3 **Koro** Mali
131 D2 **Koroc** r. Can.
91 D1 **Korocha** Rus. Fed.
119 D3 **Korogwe** Tanz.
59 C2 **Koror** Palau
103 E2 **Körös** r. Romania
90 B1 **Korosten'** Ukr.
90 B1 **Korostyshiv** Ukr.
115 D3 **Koro Toro** Chad
93 H3 **Korpo** Fin.
66 D1 **Korsakov** Rus. Fed.
91 C2 **Korsun'-Shevchenkivs'kyy** Ukr.
103 E1 **Korsze** Pol.
116 B3 **Korti** Sudan
100 A2 **Kortrijk** Belgium
83 L3 **Koryakskaya, Sopka** vol. Rus. Fed.
83 M2 **Koryakskiy Khrebet** mts Rus. Fed.
86 D2 **Koryazhma** Rus. Fed.
65 B2 **Koryŏng** S. Korea
91 C1 **Koryukivka** Ukr.
111 C3 **Kos** Greece
111 C3 **Kos** i. Greece
91 D2 **Kosa Biryuchyy Ostriv** i. Ukr.
65 B2 **Kosan** N. Korea
103 D1 **Kościan** Pol.
Kosciusko, Mount Austr. see Kosciuszko, Mount
53 C3 **Kosciuszko, Mount** Austr.
77 E2 **Kosh-Agach** Rus. Fed.
67 A4 **Koshikijima-rettō** is Japan
103 E2 **Košice** Slovakia
92 H2 **Koskullskulle** Sweden
65 B2 **Kosŏng** N. Korea
109 D2 **Kosovo** prov. Serb. and Mont.
109 D2 **Kosovska Mitrovica** Serb. and Mont.
48 H3 **Kosrae** atoll Micronesia
114 B4 **Kossou, Lac de** l. Côte d'Ivoire
76 C1 **Kostanay** Kazakh.
110 B2 **Kostenets** Bulg.
123 C2 **Koster** S. Africa
116 B3 **Kosti** Sudan
92 J3 **Kostomuksha** Rus. Fed.
90 B1 **Kostopil'** Ukr.
89 F2 **Kostroma** Rus. Fed.
89 F2 **Kostroma** r. Rus. Fed.
102 C1 **Kostrzyn** Pol.
91 D2 **Kostyantynivka** Ukr.
103 D1 **Koszalin** Pol.
103 D2 **Kőszeg** Hungary
74 B2 **Kota** India
60 B2 **Kotaagung** Indon.
61 C2 **Kotabaru** Indon.
61 C1 **Kota Belud** Sabah Malaysia
60 B1 **Kota Bharu** Malaysia
60 B2 **Kotabumi** Indon.
61 C1 **Kota Kinabalu** Sabah Malaysia
75 C3 **Kotaparh** India
61 C1 **Kota Samarahan** Sarawak Malaysia
86 D3 **Kotel'nich** Rus. Fed.
87 D4 **Kotel'nikovo** Rus. Fed.
83 K1 **Kotel'nyy, Ostrov** i. Rus. Fed.
91 C1 **Kotel'va** Ukr.
101 E2 **Köthen (Anhalt)** Ger.
119 D2 **Kotido** Uganda
93 I3 **Kotka** Fin.
86 D2 **Kotlas** Rus. Fed.
126 B2 **Kotlik** U.S.A.
115 C3 **Kotorkoshi** Nigeria
109 C2 **Kotor Varoš** Bos.-Herz.
87 D3 **Kotovo** Rus. Fed.
91 E1 **Kotovsk** Rus. Fed.
90 B2 **Kotovs'k** Ukr.
73 C3 **Kottagudem** India
118 C2 **Kotto** r. C.A.R.
83 H2 **Kotuy** r. Rus. Fed.
126 B2 **Kotzebue** U.S.A.
126 B2 **Kotzebue Sound** sea chan. U.S.A.
114 A3 **Koubia** Guinea
100 A2 **Koudekerke** Neth.
114 B3 **Koudougou** Burkina
122 B3 **Kougaberge** mts S. Africa
118 B3 **Koulamoutou** Gabon
114 B3 **Koulikoro** Mali
118 B2 **Koumra** Chad
118 B2 **Koumra** Chad
114 A3 **Koundâra** Guinea
Kounradskiy Kazakh. see Konyrat
151 D2 **Kourou** Fr. Guiana
114 B3 **Kouroussa** Guinea
115 D3 **Kousséri** Cameroon
114 B3 **Koutiala** Mali
93 I3 **Kouvola** Fin.
109 D1 **Kovačica** Serb. and Mont.
92 J2 **Kovdor** Rus. Fed.
90 A1 **Kovel'** Ukr.
Kovno Lith. see Kaunas
89 F2 **Kovrov** Rus. Fed.

51 D1 **Kowanyama** Austr.
54 B2 **Kowhitirangi** N.Z.
111 C3 **Köyceğiz** Turkey
86 D2 **Koyda** Rus. Fed.
126 B2 **Koyukuk** r. U.S.A.
111 B2 **Kozani** Greece
90 C1 **Kozelets'** Ukr.
89 E3 **Kozel'sk** Rus. Fed.
Kozhikode India see Calicut
90 B2 **Kozyatyn** Ukr.
63 A2 **Kra, Isthmus of** Thai.
63 A3 **Krabi** Thai.
63 A2 **Kra Buri** Thai.
63 B2 **Krâchéh** Cambodia
93 E4 **Kragerø** Norway
100 B1 **Kraggenburg** Neth.
109 D2 **Kragujevac** Serb. and Mont.
60 B2 **Krakatau** i. Indon.
103 D1 **Kraków** Pol.
109 D2 **Kraljevo** Serb. and Mont.
91 D2 **Kramators'k** Ukr.
93 G3 **Kramfors** Sweden
111 B3 **Kranidi** Greece
102 C2 **Kranj** Slovenia
123 D2 **Kranskop** S. Africa
86 E1 **Krasino** Rus. Fed.
88 C2 **Kráslava** Latvia
101 F2 **Kraslice** Czech Rep.
89 D3 **Krasnapolle** Belarus
89 D3 **Krasnaya Gora** Rus. Fed.
89 F2 **Krasnaya Gorbatka** Rus. Fed.
Krasnoarmeysk Kazakh. see Tayynsha
87 D3 **Krasnoarmeysk** Rus. Fed.
Krasnoarmeyskaya Rus. Fed. see Poltavskaya
91 D2 **Krasnoarmiys'k** Ukr.
86 D2 **Krasnoborsk** Rus. Fed.
91 D2 **Krasnodar** Rus. Fed.
91 D2 **Krasnodon** Ukr.
88 C2 **Krasnogorodskoye** Rus. Fed.
91 D1 **Krasnogvardeyskoye** Rus. Fed.
91 C2 **Krasnohvardiys'ke** Ukr.
86 E3 **Krasnokamsk** Rus. Fed.
89 D2 **Krasnomayskiy** Rus. Fed.
91 C2 **Krasnoperekops'k** Ukr.
87 D3 **Krasnoslobodsk** Rus. Fed.
86 F3 **Krasnotur'insk** Rus. Fed.
86 E3 **Krasnoufimsk** Rus. Fed.
86 E2 **Krasnovishersk** Rus. Fed.
Krasnovodsk Turkm. see Turkmenbashi
83 H3 **Krasnoyarsk** Rus. Fed.
89 E3 **Krasnoye** Rus. Fed.
83 M2 **Krasnoye, Ozero** l. Rus. Fed.
89 F2 **Krasnoye-na-Volge** Rus. Fed.
103 E1 **Krasnystaw** Pol.
89 D3 **Krasnyy** Rus. Fed.
Krasnyy Kamyshanik Rus. Fed. see Komsomol'skiy
89 E2 **Krasnyy Kholm** Rus. Fed.
91 D2 **Krasnyy Luch** Ukr.
91 E2 **Krasnyy Sulin** Rus. Fed.
90 B2 **Krasyliv** Ukr.
Kraulshavn Greenland see Nuussuaq
100 C2 **Krefeld** Ger.
91 C2 **Kremenchuk** Ukr.
91 C2 **Kremenchuts'ka Vodoskhovyshche** resr Ukr.
90 B1 **Kremenets'** Ukr.
103 D2 **Křemešník** hill Czech Rep.
Kremges Ukr. see Svitlovods'k
91 C2 **Kreminna** Ukr.
136 B2 **Kremmling** U.S.A.
103 D2 **Krems an der Donau** Austria
89 D2 **Kresttsy** Rus. Fed.
88 B2 **Kretinga** Lith.
100 C2 **Kreuzau** Ger.
101 C2 **Kreuztal** Ger.
118 A2 **Kribi** Cameroon
123 C2 **Kriel** S. Africa
111 B3 **Krikellos** Greece
66 D1 **Kril'on, Mys** c. Rus. Fed.
111 B3 **Krios, Akra** pt Greece
73 C3 **Krishna** r. India
73 C3 **Krishna, Mouths of the** India
75 C2 **Krishnanagar** India
93 E4 **Kristiansand** Norway
93 F4 **Kristianstad** Sweden
92 E3 **Kristiansund** Norway
93 F4 **Kristinehamn** Sweden
Kristinopol' Ukr. see Chervonohrad
110 B2 **Kriti** i. Greece see Crete
110 B2 **Kriva Palanka** Macedonia
Krivoy Rog Ukr. see Kryvyy Rih
109 C1 **Križevci** Croatia
108 B1 **Krk** i. Croatia
92 F3 **Krokom** Sweden
91 C1 **Krolevets'** Ukr.
89 E3 **Kromy** Rus. Fed.
101 E2 **Kronach** Ger.
63 B2 **Krŏng Kaôh Kŏng** Cambodia
127 J2 **Kronprins Frederik Bjerge** nunataks Greenland
123 C2 **Kroonstad** S. Africa
91 E2 **Kropotkin** Rus. Fed.
103 E2 **Krosno** Pol.
103 D1 **Krotoszyn** Pol.
60 B2 **Krui** Indon.
122 B3 **Kruisfontein** S. Africa
109 C2 **Krujë** Albania
111 C2 **Krumovgrad** Bulg.

88 C3 **Krupki** Belarus
109 D2 **Kruševac** Serb. and Mont.
101 E2 **Krušné Hory** mts Czech Rep.
128 A2 **Kruzof Island** U.S.A.
89 D3 **Krychaw** Belarus
91 D2 **Krylovskaya** Rus. Fed.
91 D3 **Krymsk** Rus. Fed.
Krymskaya Rus. Fed. see Krymsk
Kryms'kyy Pivostriv pen. Ukr. see Crimea
Krystynopol Ukr. see Chervonohrad
111 C3 **Krytiko Pelagos** sea Greece
91 C2 **Kryvyy Rih** Ukr.
90 B2 **Kryzhopil'** Ukr.
114 B2 **Ksabi** Alg.
107 D2 **Ksar el Boukhari** Alg.
114 B1 **Ksar el Kebir** Morocco
Ksar-es-Souk Morocco see Er Rachidia
89 E3 **Kshenskiy** Rus. Fed.
78 B2 **Kū', Jabal al** hill Saudi Arabia
61 C1 **Kuala Belait** Brunei
Kuala Dungun Malaysia see Dungun
60 B1 **Kuala Kangsar** Malaysia
60 B1 **Kuala Kerai** Malaysia
60 B1 **Kuala Lipis** Malaysia
60 B1 **Kuala Lumpur** Malaysia
61 C2 **Kualapembuang** Indon.
60 B2 **Kuala Terengganu** Malaysia
60 B2 **Kualatungal** Indon.
61 C1 **Kuamut** Sabah Malaysia
65 A1 **Kuandian** China
60 B1 **Kuantan** Malaysia
91 D2 **Kuban'** r. Rus. Fed.
89 E2 **Kubenskoye, Ozero** l. Rus. Fed.
110 C2 **Kubrat** Bulg.
60 B2 **Kubu** Indon.
61 C1 **Kubuang** Indon.
60 C1 **Kuching** Sarawak Malaysia
109 C2 **Kuçovë** Albania
61 C1 **Kudat** Sabah Malaysia
61 C2 **Kudus** Indon.
102 C2 **Kufstein** Austria
127 G2 **Kugaaruk** Can.
91 D2 **Kugey** Rus. Fed.
126 E2 **Kugluktuk** Can.
126 D2 **Kugmallit Bay** Can.
92 I3 **Kuhmo** Fin.
79 C2 **Kührān, Kūh-e** mt. Iran
122 A1 **Kuis** Namibia
Kuitin China see Kuytun
120 A2 **Kuito** Angola
92 I2 **Kuivaniemi** Fin.
65 B2 **Kujang** N. Korea
66 D2 **Kuji** Japan
67 B4 **Kujū-san** vol. Japan
109 D2 **Kukës** Albania
76 B3 **Kukurtli** Turkm.
111 C3 **Kula** Turkey
89 G3 **Kula Kangri** mt. Bhutan
76 B2 **Kulandy** Kazakh.
88 B2 **Kuldīga** Latvia
Kuldja China see Yining
122 B1 **Kule** Botswana
101 E2 **Kulmbach** Ger.
77 C3 **Kŭlob** Tajik.
76 B2 **Kul'sary** Kazakh.
111 D3 **Külübe Tepe** mt. Turkey
77 D1 **Kulunda** Rus. Fed.
77 D1 **Kulundinskoye, Ozero** salt l. Rus. Fed.
127 J2 **Kulusuk** Greenland
67 C3 **Kumagaya** Japan
67 B4 **Kumamoto** Japan
67 C4 **Kumano** Japan
110 B2 **Kumanovo** Macedonia
114 B4 **Kumasi** Ghana
118 A2 **Kumba** Cameroon
78 B2 **Kumdah** Saudi Arabia
87 E3 **Kumertau** Rus. Fed.
65 B2 **Kumi** S. Korea
119 D2 **Kumi** Uganda
111 C3 **Kumkale** Turkey
93 G4 **Kumla** Sweden
115 D3 **Kumo** Nigeria
62 A1 **Kumon Range** mts Myanmar
62 B2 **Kumphawapi** Thai.
Kumul China see Hami
120 A2 **Kunene** r. Angola/Namibia
77 D2 **Kungei Alatau** mts Kazakh./Kyrg.
93 F4 **Kungsbacka** Sweden
118 B2 **Kungu** Dem. Rep. Congo
86 E3 **Kungur** Rus. Fed.
62 A1 **Kunhing** Myanmar
62 A1 **Kunlong** Myanmar
75 B1 **Kunlun Shan** mts China
71 A3 **Kunming** China
65 B2 **Kunsan** S. Korea
50 B1 **Kununurra** Austr.
101 D3 **Künzelsau** Ger.
92 I3 **Kuopio** Fin.
109 C1 **Kupa** r. Croatia/Slovenia
59 C3 **Kupang** Indon.
88 B2 **Kupiškis** Lith.
111 C2 **Küplü** Turkey
128 A2 **Kupreanof Island** U.S.A.
91 D2 **Kup"yans'k** Ukr.
77 E2 **Kuqa** China
81 C2 **Kür** r. Azer.

67 B4 **Kurashiki** Japan
75 C2 **Kurasia** India
67 B3 **Kurayoshi** Japan
89 E3 **Kurchatov** Rus. Fed.
77 E2 **Kurchum** Kazakh.
111 C2 **Kŭrdzhali** Bulg.
67 B4 **Kure** Japan
57 T7 **Kure Atoll** U.S.A.
88 B2 **Kuressaare** Estonia
87 F3 **Kurgan** Rus. Fed.
 Kuria Muria Islands Oman *see*
  Ḩalāniyāt, Juzur al
93 H3 **Kurikka** Fin.
156 C2 **Kuril Basin** *sea feature*
  Sea of Okhotsk
69 F1 **Kuril Islands** *is* Rus. Fed.
69 F1 **Kuril'sk** Rus. Fed.
 Kuril'skiye Ostrova Rus. Fed. *see*
  Kuril Islands
156 C3 **Kuril Trench** *sea feature*
  N. Pacific Ocean
89 E3 **Kurkino** Rus. Fed.
 Kurmashkino Kazakh. *see*
  Kurchum
117 B3 **Kurmuk** Sudan
73 B3 **Kurnool** India
67 D3 **Kuroiso** Japan
101 E2 **Kurort Schmalkalden** Ger.
53 D2 **Kurri Kurri** Austr.
88 B2 **Kuršėnai** Lith.
78 B2 **Kursh, Jabal** *hill* Saudi Arabia
89 E3 **Kursk** Rus. Fed.
109 D2 **Kuršumlija** Serb. and Mont.
122 B2 **Kuruman** S. Africa
122 B2 **Kuruman** *watercourse* S. Africa
67 B4 **Kurume** Japan
83 I3 **Kurumkan** Rus. Fed.
73 C4 **Kurunegala** Sri Lanka
81 D1 **Kuryk** Kazakh.
111 C3 **Kuşadası** Turkey
111 C3 **Kuşadası Körfezi** *b.* Turkey
111 C2 **Kuş Gölü** *l.* Turkey
91 D2 **Kushchevskaya** Rus. Fed.
66 D2 **Kushiro** Japan
 Kushka Turkm. *see* Gushgy
76 C1 **Kushmurun** Kazakh.
75 C2 **Kushtia** Bangl.
126 B2 **Kuskokwim** *r.* U.S.A.
126 B2 **Kuskokwim Mountains** U.S.A.
66 D2 **Kussharo-ko** *l.* Japan
 Kustanay Kazakh. *see* Kostanay
63 B2 **Kut, Ko** *i.* Thai.
111 C3 **Kütahya** Turkey
81 C1 **K'ut'aisi** Georgia
 Kutaraja Indon. *see* Banda Aceh
 Kutch, Gulf of India *see*
  Kachchh, Gulf of
109 C1 **Kutjevo** Croatia
103 D1 **Kutno** Pol.
118 B3 **Kutu** Dem. Rep. Congo
116 A3 **Kutum** Sudan
126 E2 **Kuujjua** *r.* Can.
131 D2 **Kuujjuaq** Can.
130 C2 **Kuujjuarapik** Can.
92 I2 **Kuusamo** Fin.
120 A2 **Kuvango** Angola
89 D2 **Kuvshinovo** Rus. Fed.
78 B2 **Kuwait** *country* Asia
78 B2 **Kuwait** Kuwait
82 G3 **Kuybyshev** Rus. Fed.
 Kuybyshev Rus. Fed. *see* Samara
91 D2 **Kuybysheve** Ukr.
 Kuybyshevka-Vostochnaya
  Rus. Fed. *see* Belogorsk
87 D3 **Kuybyshevskoye**
  Vodokhranilishche *resr* Rus. Fed.
77 E2 **Kuytun** China
111 C3 **Kuyucak** Turkey
87 D3 **Kuznetsk** Rus. Fed.
90 B1 **Kuznetsovs'k** Ukr.
86 C2 **Kuzomen'** Rus. Fed.
92 H1 **Kvalsund** Norway
123 D2 **KwaMashu** S. Africa
61 D1 **Kwandang** Indon.
 Kwangchow China *see* Guangzhou
65 B2 **Kwangju** S. Korea
 Kwangtung *prov.* China *see*
  Guangdong
65 B1 **Kwanmo-bong** *mt.* N. Korea
123 C3 **Kwanobuhle** S. Africa
123 C3 **KwaNojoli** S. Africa
122 B3 **Kwanonzame** S. Africa
123 C3 **Kwatinidubu** S. Africa
123 C3 **KwaZamokhule** S. Africa
122 B3 **Kwazamukucinga** S. Africa
123 C2 **KwaZanele** S. Africa
123 D2 **Kwazulu-Natal** *prov.* S. Africa
 Kweichow *prov.* China *see*
  Guizhou
 Kweiyang China *see* Guiyang
121 B2 **Kwekwe** Zimbabwe
118 B3 **Kwenge** *r.* Dem. Rep. Congo
123 C3 **Kwezi-Naledi** S. Africa
103 D1 **Kwidzyn** Pol.
59 D3 **Kwikila** P.N.G.
118 B3 **Kwilu** *r.* Angola/Dem. Rep. Congo
59 C3 **Kwoka** *mt.* Indon.
118 B2 **Kyabé** Chad
53 C3 **Kyabram** Austr.
62 A2 **Kyaikto** Myanmar
63 A2 **Kya-in Seikkyi** Myanmar
68 D1 **Kyakhta** Rus. Fed.
62 A1 **Kyancutta** Austr.
62 A1 **Kyaukpadaung** Myanmar
62 A2 **Kyaukpyu** Myanmar

88 B3 **Kybartai** Lith.
62 A2 **Kyebogyi** Myanmar
54 B3 **Kyeburn** N.Z.
62 A2 **Kyeintali** Myanmar
74 B1 **Kyelang** India
 Kyiv Ukr. *see* Kiev
 Kyklades *is* Greece *see* Cyclades
129 D2 **Kyle** Can.
96 B2 **Kyle of Lochalsh** U.K.
100 C3 **Kyll** *r.* Ger.
111 B3 **Kyllini** *mt.* Greece
111 B3 **Kymi** Greece
52 B3 **Kyneton** Austr.
119 D2 **Kyoga, Lake** Uganda
53 D1 **Kyogle** Austr.
65 B2 **Kyŏnggi-man** *b.* S. Korea
65 B2 **Kyŏngju** S. Korea
67 C4 **Kyōto** Japan
111 B3 **Kyparissia** Greece
111 B3 **Kyparissiakos Kolpos** *b.* Greece
111 B3 **Kyra Panagia** *i.* Greece
80 B2 **Kyrenia** Cyprus
77 D2 **Kyrgyzstan** *country* Asia
101 F1 **Kyritz** Ger.
93 H3 **Kyrönjoki** *r.* Fin.
86 E2 **Kyrta** Rus. Fed.
86 D2 **Kyssa** Rus. Fed.
83 J2 **Kytalyktakh** Rus. Fed.
111 B3 **Kythira** *i.* Greece
111 B3 **Kythnos** *i.* Greece
128 B2 **Kyuquot** Can.
67 B4 **Kyūshū** *i.* Japan
110 B2 **Kyustendil** Bulg.
62 A2 **Kywebwe** Myanmar
90 C1 **Kyyivs'ke Vodoskhovyshche** *resr*
  Ukr.
92 H3 **Kyyjärvi** Fin.
68 C1 **Kyzyl** Rus. Fed.
76 C2 **Kyzylkum Desert** Kazakh./Uzbek.
77 C2 **Kyzylorda** Kazakh.
 Kzyl-Orda Kazakh. *see* Kyzylorda
 Kzyltu Kazakh. *see*
  Kishkenekol'

L

145 C3 **La Angostura, Presa de** *resr* Mex.
117 C4 **Laascaanood** Somalia
117 C3 **Laasgoray** Somalia
150 C1 **La Asunción** Venez.
114 A2 **Laâyoune** Western Sahara
87 D4 **Laba** *r.* Rus. Fed.
144 B2 **La Babia** Mex.
61 D2 **Labala** Indon.
152 B2 **La Banda** Arg.
61 C1 **Labang** *Sarawak* Malaysia
104 B2 **La Baule-Escoublac** France
102 C1 **Labe** *r.* Czech Rep.
114 A3 **Labé** Guinea
128 A1 **Laberge, Lake** Can.
128 C2 **La Biche, Lac** *l.* Can.
108 B1 **Labin** Croatia
87 D4 **Labinsk** Rus. Fed.
64 B2 **Labo** Phil.
104 B3 **Labouheyre** France
153 B3 **Laboulaye** Arg.
131 D2 **Labrador** *reg.* Can.
131 D2 **Labrador City** Can.
127 I2 **Labrador Sea** Can./Greenland
150 C3 **Lábrea** Brazil
61 C1 **Labuan** Malaysia
61 C2 **Labuhanbajo** Indon.
60 B1 **Labuhanbilik** Indon.
59 C3 **Labuna** Indon.
63 A2 **Labutta** Myanmar
86 F2 **Labytnangi** Rus. Fed.
109 C2 **Laç** Albania
 La Calle Alg. *see* El Kala
105 C2 **La Capelle** France
73 B3 **Laccadive Islands** India
129 C2 **Lac du Bonnet** Can.
146 B3 **La Ceiba** Hond.
52 A3 **Lacepede Bay** Austr.
134 B1 **Lacey** U.S.A.
105 D2 **La Chaux-de-Fonds** Switz.
53 B2 **Lachlan** *r.* Austr.
146 C4 **La Chorrera** Panama
139 E1 **Lachute** Can.
105 D3 **La Ciotat** France
128 C2 **Lac La Biche** Can.
 Lac la Martre Can. *see* Wha Ti
139 E1 **Lac-Mégantic** Can.
128 C2 **Lacombe** Can.
146 B4 **La Concepción** Panama
145 C3 **La Concordia** Mex.
108 A3 **Laconi** *Sardinia* Italy
139 E2 **Laconia** U.S.A.
128 C2 **La Crete** Can.
138 A2 **La Crosse** U.S.A.
144 B2 **La Cruz** Mex.
144 B2 **La Cuesta** Mex.
155 D1 **Ladainha** Brazil
74 B1 **Ladakh Range** *mts* India
122 B3 **Ladismith** S. Africa
79 D2 **Lādīz** Iran
89 D1 **Ladoga, Lake** Rus. Fed.
 Ladozhskoye Ozero *l.* Rus. Fed.
  see Ladoga, Lake
141 D2 **Ladson** U.S.A.
123 C3 **Lady Grey** S. Africa
128 D3 **Ladysmith** Can.
123 C2 **Ladysmith** S. Africa
59 D3 **Lae** P.N.G.

143 C3 **La Encantada, Sierra** *mts* Mex.
152 B2 **La Esmeralda** Bol.
93 F4 **Læsø** *i.* Denmark
 Lafayette Alg. *see* Bougaa
141 C2 **La Fayette** U.S.A.
138 B2 **Lafayette** *IN* U.S.A.
115 C4 **Lafia** Nigeria
104 B2 **La Flèche** France
141 D1 **La Follette** U.S.A.
130 C2 **Laforge** Can.
79 C2 **Lāft** Iran
108 A3 **La Galite** *i.* Tunisia
87 D4 **Lagan'** Rus. Fed.
151 F4 **Lagarto** Brazil
118 B2 **Lagdo, Lac de** *l.* Cameroon
119 E2 **Lagh Bor** *watercourse*
  Kenya/Somalia
115 C1 **Laghouat** Alg.
151 F4 **Lagoa Santa** Brazil
114 A2 **La Gomera** *i.* Canary Is
114 C4 **Lagos** Nigeria
106 B2 **Lagos** Port.
134 C1 **La Grande** U.S.A.
130 C2 **La Grande 2, Réservoir** *resr* Can.
130 C2 **La Grande 3, Réservoir** *resr* Can.
130 C2 **La Grande 4, Réservoir** *resr* Can.
50 B1 **Lagrange** Austr.
141 C2 **La Grange** U.S.A.
150 C2 **La Gran Sabana** *plat.* Venez.
152 D2 **Laguna** Brazil
144 A2 **Laguna, Picacho de la** *mt.* Mex.
150 B3 **Lagunas** Peru
147 C3 **Lagunillas** Venez.
 La Habana Cuba *see* Havana
61 C1 **Lahad Datu** *Sabah* Malaysia
60 B2 **Lahat** Indon.
78 B3 **Lahij** Yemen
81 C2 **Lāhījān** Iran
100 C2 **Lahnstein** Ger.
74 B1 **Lahore** Pak.
74 A2 **Lahri** Pak.
93 I3 **Lahti** Fin.
115 D4 **Laï** Chad
53 D1 **Laidley** Austr.
104 C2 **L'Aigle** France
122 B3 **Laingsburg** S. Africa
93 H2 **Lainioälven** *r.* Sweden
96 B2 **Lairg** U.K.
108 B1 **Laives** Italy
70 B2 **Laiwu** China
70 C2 **Laiyang** China
70 B2 **Laiyuan** China
70 B2 **Laizhou** China
70 B2 **Laizhou Wan** *b.* China
50 C1 **Lajamanu** Austr.
152 C2 **Lajes** Brazil
144 B2 **La Junta** Mex.
136 C3 **La Junta** U.S.A.
117 B4 **Lake Abaya** *l.* Eth.
103 D2 **Lake Balaton** *l.* Hungary
53 C2 **Lake Cargelligo** Austr.
53 D2 **Lake Cathie** Austr.
140 B2 **Lake Charles** U.S.A.
141 D2 **Lake City** *FL* U.S.A.
141 E2 **Lake City** *SC* U.S.A.
128 B3 **Lake Cowichan** Can.
 Lake Harbour Can. *see* Kimmirut
142 A2 **Lake Havasu City** U.S.A.
143 D3 **Lake Jackson** U.S.A.
50 A3 **Lake King** Austr.
141 D3 **Lakeland** U.S.A.
128 C2 **Lake Louise** Can.
134 B1 **Lake Oswego** U.S.A.
54 A2 **Lake Paringa** N.Z.
140 B2 **Lake Providence** U.S.A.
53 C3 **Lakes Entrance** Austr.
117 B3 **Lake Tana** *l.* Eth.
134 B2 **Lakeview** U.S.A.
137 E2 **Lakeville** U.S.A.
136 B3 **Lakewood** *CO* U.S.A.
139 E2 **Lakewood** *NJ* U.S.A.
141 D3 **Lake Worth** U.S.A.
74 A2 **Lakhpat** India
74 B1 **Lakhri** India
111 B3 **Lakonikos Kolpos** *b.* Greece
114 B4 **Lakota** Côte d'Ivoire
92 H1 **Lakselv** Norway
146 A3 **La Libertad** Guat.
106 B1 **Lalín** Spain
106 B2 **La Línea de la Concepción** Spain
74 B2 **Lalitpur** India
 Lalitpur Nepal *see* Patan
129 D2 **La Loche** Can.
100 B2 **La Louvière** Belgium
108 A2 **La Maddalena** *Sardinia* Italy
61 C1 **Lamag** *Sabah* Malaysia
 La Manche str. France/U.K. *see*
  English Channel
136 C3 **Lamar** U.S.A.
79 C2 **Lamard** Iran
108 A3 **La Marmora, Punta** *mt.* *Sardinia*
  Italy
128 C1 **La Martre, Lac** *l.* Can.
104 B2 **Lamballe** France
118 B3 **Lambaréné** Gabon
122 A3 **Lambert's Bay** S. Africa
92 □A2 **Lambeyri** Iceland
106 B1 **Lamego** Port.
131 D3 **Lamèque, Île** *i.* Can.
150 B4 **La Merced** Peru
52 B2 **Lameroo** Austr.
143 C2 **Lamesa** U.S.A.
111 B3 **Lamia** Greece
137 E2 **Lamoni** U.S.A.

62 A2 **Lampang** Thai.
143 D2 **Lampasas** U.S.A.
145 B2 **Lampazos** Mex.
99 A3 **Lampeter** U.K.
62 A2 **Lamphun** Thai.
119 E3 **Lamu** Kenya
105 D3 **La Mure** France
96 C3 **Lanark** U.K.
63 A2 **Lanbi Kyun** *i.* Myanmar
62 A1 **Lancang** China
 Lancang Jiang *r.* China *see*
  Mekong
98 B2 **Lancaster** U.K.
135 C4 **Lancaster** *CA* U.S.A.
138 C3 **Lancaster** *OH* U.S.A.
139 D2 **Lancaster** *PA* U.S.A.
141 D2 **Lancaster** *SC* U.S.A.
127 G2 **Lancaster Sound** *str.* Can.
50 A3 **Lancelin** Austr.
 Lanchow China *see* Lanzhou
102 C2 **Landeck** Austria
136 B2 **Lander** U.S.A.
99 A4 **Land's End** *pt* U.K.
102 C2 **Landshut** Ger.
93 F4 **Landskrona** Sweden
141 C2 **Lanett** U.S.A.
122 B2 **Langberg** *mts* S. Africa
137 D1 **Langdon** U.S.A.
93 F4 **Langeland** *i.* Denmark
101 D1 **Langen** Ger.
100 C1 **Langeoog** Ger.
100 C1 **Langeoog** *i.* Ger.
82 G2 **Langepas** Rus. Fed.
70 B2 **Langfang** China
101 D2 **Langgöns** Ger.
96 C3 **Langholm** U.K.
92 □A3 **Langjökull** *ice cap* Iceland
60 A1 **Langkawi** *i.* Malaysia
105 C3 **Langogne** France
104 B3 **Langon** France
106 B1 **Langreo** Spain
105 D2 **Langres** France
60 A1 **Langsa** Indon.
62 B1 **Lang Son** Vietnam
105 C3 **Languedoc** *reg.* France
101 D1 **Langwedel** Ger.
129 D2 **Lanigan** Can.
153 A3 **Lanín, Volcán** *vol.* Arg./Chile
81 C2 **Länkäran** Azer.
104 B2 **Lannion** France
138 B1 **L'Anse** U.S.A.
139 E1 **L'Anse-St-Jean** Can.
138 C2 **Lansing** U.S.A.
71 B3 **Lanxi** China
117 B4 **Lanya** Sudan
114 A2 **Lanzarote** *i.* Canary Is
70 A2 **Lanzhou** China
64 B2 **Laoag** Phil.
62 B1 **Lao Cai** Vietnam
70 B2 **Laohekou** China
 Laojunmiao China *see* Yumen
65 B1 **Laoling** China
65 B1 **Lao Ling** *mts* China
105 C2 **Laon** France
62 B2 **Laos** *country* Asia
65 B1 **Laotougou** China
66 A2 **Laoye Ling** *mts* China
154 C3 **Lapa** Brazil
114 A2 **La Palma** *i.* Canary Is
146 C4 **La Palma** Panama
150 C2 **La Paragua** Venez.
152 B1 **La Paz** Bol.
145 D3 **La Paz** Hond.
144 A2 **La Paz** Mex.
150 C3 **La Pedrera** Col.
138 C2 **Lapeer** U.S.A.
66 D1 **La Pérouse Strait**
  Japan/Rus. Fed.
145 C2 **La Pesca** Mex.
144 B2 **La Piedad** Mex.
153 C3 **La Plata** Arg.
153 C3 **La Plata, Río de** *sea chan.*
  Arg./Uru.
92 H3 **Lappajärvi** *l.* Fin.
93 I3 **Lappeenranta** Fin.
92 G2 **Lappland** *reg.* Europe
111 C2 **Lâpseki** Turkey
 Laptevo Rus. Fed. *see*
  Yasnogorsk
83 J1 **Laptev Sea** Rus. Fed.
 Laptevykh, More *sea* Rus. Fed.
  see Laptev Sea
93 H3 **Lapua** Fin.
152 B3 **La Quiaca** Arg.
108 B2 **L'Aquila** Italy
135 C4 **La Quinta** U.S.A.
79 C2 **Lār** Iran
114 B1 **Larache** Morocco
136 B2 **Laramie** U.S.A.
136 B2 **Laramie Mountains** U.S.A.
154 B3 **Laranjeiras do Sul** Brazil
61 D2 **Larantuka** Indon.
59 C3 **Larat** *i.* Indon.
107 D2 **Larba** Alg.
 L'Ardenne, Plateau de Belgium
  see Ardennes
106 C1 **Laredo** Spain
143 D3 **Laredo** U.S.A.
141 D3 **Largo** U.S.A.
96 B3 **Largs** U.K.
115 C1 **L'Ariana** Tunisia
152 B2 **La Rioja** Arg.
111 B3 **Larisa** Greece
74 A2 **Larkana** Pak.
80 B2 **Larnaca** Cyprus

Larnaka Cyprus see Larnaca
97 D1 Larne U.K.
100 B2 La Roche-en-Ardenne Belgium
104 B2 La Rochelle France
104 B2 La Roche-sur-Yon France
107 C2 La Roda Spain
147 D3 La Romana Dom. Rep.
129 D2 La Ronge Can.
129 D2 La Ronge, Lac l. Can.
50 C1 Larrimah Austr.
55 A3 Larsen Ice Shelf Antarctica
93 F4 Larvik Norway
136 C3 Las Animas U.S.A.
Las Anod Somalia see Laascaanood
130 C3 La Sarre Can.
142 B2 Las Cruces U.S.A.
152 A2 La Serena Chile
153 C3 Las Flores Arg.
153 B3 Las Heras Arg.
62 A1 Lashio Myanmar
76 C3 Lashkar Gāh Afgh.
109 C3 La Sila reg. Italy
152 B2 Las Lomitas Arg.
106 B2 Las Marismas marsh Spain
144 B2 Las Nieves Mex.
114 A2 Las Palmas de Gran Canaria Canary Is
108 A2 La Spezia Italy
153 C3 Las Piedras Uru.
153 B4 Las Plumas Arg.
155 D1 Lassance Brazil
129 D2 Last Mountain Lake Can.
152 B2 Las Tórtolas, Cerro mt. Chile
118 B3 Lastoursville Gabon
109 C2 Lastovo i. Croatia
144 A2 Las Tres Vírgenes, Volcán vol. Mex.
146 C2 Las Tunas Cuba
144 B2 Las Varas Mex.
144 B2 Las Varas Mex.
142 B1 Las Vegas NM U.S.A.
135 C3 Las Vegas NV U.S.A.
131 E2 La Tabatière Can.
80 B2 Latakia Syria
104 B3 La Teste France
108 B2 Latina Italy
147 D3 La Tortuga, Isla i. Venez.
64 B2 La Trinidad Phil.
89 E2 Latskoye Rus. Fed.
130 C3 La Tuque Can.
88 D2 Latvia country Europe
Latviyskaya S.S.R. admin. reg. Europe see Latvia
59 E3 Lau P.N.G.
102 C1 Lauchhammer Ger.
101 E3 Lauf an der Pegnitz Ger.
105 D2 Laufen Switz.
92 □A3 Laugarás Iceland
127 H1 Lauge Koch Kyst reg. Greenland
142 C1 Laughlin Peak U.S.A.
51 D4 Launceston Austr.
99 A4 Launceston U.K.
62 A1 Launggyaung Myanmar
153 A4 La Unión Chile
51 D1 Laura Austr.
140 C2 Laurel MS U.S.A.
134 E1 Laurel MT U.S.A.
96 C2 Laurencekirk U.K.
109 C2 Lauria Italy
141 E2 Laurinburg U.S.A.
105 D2 Lausanne Switz.
60 B1 Laut i. Indon.
61 C2 Laut i. Indon.
61 C2 Laut Bali Indon.
101 D2 Lautersbach (Hessen) Ger.
60 C2 Laut Jawa Indon.
61 C2 Laut Kecil, Kepulauan is Indon.
59 C3 Laut Maluku Indon.
61 D2 Laut Sawu Indon.
59 C3 Laut Seram Indon.
100 C1 Lauwersmeer l. Neth.
139 E1 Laval Can.
104 B2 Laval France
81 D2 Lāvar Meydān salt marsh Iran
50 B2 Laverton Austr.
155 D2 Lavras Brazil
123 D2 Lavumisa Swaziland
61 C1 Lawas Sarawak Malaysia
78 B3 Lawdar Yemen
62 A1 Lawksawk Myanmar
114 B3 Lawra Ghana
138 B3 Lawrence IN U.S.A.
137 D3 Lawrence KS U.S.A.
139 E2 Lawrence MA U.S.A.
140 C1 Lawrenceburg U.S.A.
141 D2 Lawrenceville U.S.A.
143 D2 Lawton U.S.A.
78 A2 Lawz, Jabal al mt. Saudi Arabia
93 F4 Laxå Sweden
122 B2 Laxey S. Africa
78 B2 Laylá Saudi Arabia
109 D2 Lazarevac Serb. and Mont.
144 A1 Lázaro Cárdenas Mex.
144 B3 Lázaro Cárdenas Mex.
88 B3 Lazdijai Lith.
66 B2 Lazo Rus. Fed.
83 K2 Lazo Rus. Fed.
136 C2 Lead U.S.A.
129 D2 Leader Can.
136 B3 Leadville U.S.A.
Leaf Bay Can. see Tasiujaq
129 D2 Leaf Rapids Can.
143 D3 League City U.S.A.
143 D3 Leakey U.S.A.

99 C3 Leamington Spa, Royal U.K.
97 B2 Leane, Lough l. Ireland
137 E3 Leavenworth U.S.A.
64 B1 Lebak Phil.
80 B2 Lebanon country Asia
137 B3 Lebanon MO U.S.A.
139 E2 Lebanon NH U.S.A.
134 B2 Lebanon OR U.S.A.
139 D2 Lebanon PA U.S.A.
140 C1 Lebanon TN U.S.A.
89 E3 Lebedyan' Rus. Fed.
91 C1 Lebedyn Ukr.
130 C3 Lebel-sur-Quévillon Can.
104 C2 Le Blanc France
103 D1 Lębork Pol.
123 C1 Lebowakgomo S. Africa
106 B2 Lebrija Spain
153 A3 Lebu Chile
104 C3 Le Bugue France
109 C2 Lecce Italy
108 A1 Lecco Italy
102 C2 Lech r. Austria/Ger.
111 B3 Lechaina Greece
71 B3 Lechang China
102 B1 Leck Ger.
140 B2 Lecompte U.S.A.
105 C2 Le Creusot France
104 C3 Lectoure France
106 B1 Ledesma Spain
104 C2 Le Dorat France
128 C2 Leduc Can.
97 B3 Lee r. Ireland
137 E1 Leech Lake U.S.A.
98 C3 Leeds U.K.
99 B3 Leek U.K.
97 B2 Leenane Ireland
100 C1 Leer (Ostfriesland) Ger.
141 D3 Leesburg U.S.A.
140 B2 Leesville U.S.A.
53 C2 Leeton Austr.
122 B3 Leeu-Gamka S. Africa
100 B1 Leeuwarden Neth.
50 A3 Leeuwin, Cape Austr.
147 D3 Leeward Islands Caribbean Sea
111 B3 Lefkada Greece
111 B3 Lefkada i. Greece
Lefkosia Cyprus see Nicosia
64 B2 Legaspi Phil.
103 E1 Legionowo Pol.
108 B1 Legnago Italy
103 D1 Legnica Pol.
74 B1 Leh Jammu and Kashmir
104 C2 Le Havre France
101 E1 Lehre Ger.
122 B1 Lehututu Botswana
74 B1 Leiah Pak.
103 D2 Leibnitz Austria
99 C3 Leicester U.K.
51 C1 Leichhardt r. Austr.
51 D2 Leichhardt Range mts Austr.
100 B1 Leiden Neth.
100 A2 Leie r. Belgium
52 A2 Leigh Creek Austr.
97 C2 Leighlinbridge Ireland
99 C4 Leighton Buzzard U.K.
93 E3 Leikanger Norway
101 D1 Leine r. Ger.
50 B2 Leinster Austr.
97 C2 Leinster reg. Ireland
97 C2 Leinster, Mount hill Ireland
101 F2 Leipzig Ger.
92 F2 Leiranger Norway
106 B2 Leiria Port.
93 E4 Leirvik Norway
97 C2 Leixlip Ireland
71 B3 Leiyang China
71 B3 Leizhou China
71 A3 Leizhou Bandao pen. China
118 B3 Lékana Congo
122 A2 Lekkersing S. Africa
140 B2 Leland U.S.A.
Leli China see Tianlin
100 B1 Lelystad Neth.
153 B5 Le Maire, Estrecho de sea chan. Arg.
Léman, Lac France/Switz. see Geneva, Lake
104 C2 Le Mans France
137 D2 Le Mars U.S.A.
102 B2 Lemberg mt. Ger.
154 C2 Leme Brazil
Lemesos Cyprus see Limassol
101 D1 Lemförde Ger.
127 H2 Lcmieux Islands Can.
136 C1 Lemmon U.S.A.
135 C3 Lemoore U.S.A.
131 D2 Le Moyne, Lac l. Can.
62 A1 Lemro r. Myanmar
109 C2 Le Murge hills Italy
83 J2 Lena r. Rus. Fed.
100 C1 Lengerich Ger.
70 A2 Lenglong Ling mts China
71 B3 Lengshuijiang China
71 B3 Lengshuitan China
Leninabad Tajik. see Khüjand
Leninakan Armenia see Gyumri
91 D2 Lenine Ukr.
Leningrad Rus. Fed. see St Petersburg
91 D2 Leningradskaya Rus. Fed.
Leninobod Tajik. see Khüjand
77 E1 Leninogorsk Kazakh.
77 D3 Lenin Peak Kyrg./Tajik.
Leninsk Kazakh. see Baykonyr
89 E3 Leninskiy Rus. Fed.

53 D1 Lennox Head Austr.
141 D1 Lenoir U.S.A.
100 A2 Lens Belgium
105 C1 Lens France
83 I2 Lensk Rus. Fed.
103 D2 Lenti Hungary
109 C3 Lentini Sicily Italy
114 B3 Léo Burkina
103 D2 Leoben Austria
Leodhais, Eilean i. U.K. see Lewis, Isle of
99 B3 Leominster U.K.
144 B2 León Mex.
146 B3 León Nic.
106 B1 León Spain
122 A1 Leonardville Namibia
108 B3 Leonforte Sicily Italy
53 C3 Leongatha Austr.
50 B2 Leonora Austr.
Léopold II, Lac l. Dem. Rep. Congo see Mai-Ndombe, Lac
155 D2 Leopoldina Brazil
Léopoldville Dem. Rep. Congo see Kinshasa
90 B2 Leova Moldova
Leovo Moldova see Leova
123 C1 Lephalale S. Africa
123 C1 Lephepe Botswana
123 C3 Lephoi S. Africa
71 B3 Leping China
77 D2 Lepsy Kazakh.
105 C2 Le Puy-en-Velay France
123 C1 Lerala Botswana
123 C2 Leratswana S. Africa
150 B3 Lérida Col.
Lérida Spain see Lleida
106 C1 Lerma Spain
111 C3 Leros i. Greece
130 C2 Le Roy, Lac l. Can.
93 F4 Lerum Sweden
96 □ Lerwick U.K.
111 C3 Lesbos i. Greece
147 C3 Les Cayes Haiti
104 C3 Les Escaldes Andorra
139 F1 Les Escoumins Can.
107 D1 Le Seu d'Urgell Spain
70 A3 Leshan China
104 B2 Les Herbiers France
86 D2 Leshukonskoye Rus. Fed.
Leskhimstroy Ukr. see Syeverodonets'k
109 D2 Leskovac Serb. and Mont.
104 B2 Lesneven France
Lesnoy Rus. Fed. see Umba
89 E2 Lesnoye Rus. Fed.
83 H3 Lesosibirsk Rus. Fed.
123 C2 Lesotho country Africa
66 B1 Lesozavodsk Rus. Fed.
104 B2 Les Sables-d'Olonne France
147 D3 Lesser Antilles is Caribbean Sea
81 C1 Lesser Caucasus mts Asia
Lesser Khingan Mountains China see Xiao Hinggan Ling
128 C2 Lesser Slave Lake Can.
105 C3 Les Vans France
Lesvos i. Greece see Lesbos
103 D1 Leszno Pol.
123 D1 Letaba S. Africa
99 C4 Letchworth U.K.
128 C3 Lethbridge Can.
150 D2 Lethem Guyana
59 C3 Leti, Kepulauan is Indon.
150 C3 Leticia Col.
120 B3 Letlhakane Botswana
123 C1 Letlhakeng Botswana
104 C1 Le Touquet-Paris-Plage France
99 D4 Le Tréport France
123 C1 Letsitele S. Africa
63 A2 Letsok-aw Kyun i. Myanmar
123 C2 Letsopa S. Africa
97 C1 Letterkenny Ireland
105 C3 Leucate, Étang de l. France
Leukas Greece see Lefkada
60 A1 Leuser, Gunung mt. Indon.
100 B2 Leuven Belgium
111 B3 Levadeia Greece
92 F3 Levanger Norway
143 C2 Levelland U.S.A.
50 B1 Lévêque, Cape Austr.
96 A2 Leverburgh U.K.
100 C2 Leverkusen Ger.
103 D2 Levice Slovakia
54 C2 Levin N.Z.
131 C3 Lévis Can.
139 E2 Levittown U.S.A.
89 E3 Lev Tolstoy Rus. Fed.
99 D4 Lewes U.K.
96 A1 Lewis, Isle of i. U.K.
139 D2 Lewisburg PA U.S.A.
140 C1 Lewisburg TN U.S.A.
138 C1 Lewisburg WV U.S.A.
134 D1 Lewis Range mts U.S.A.
134 C1 Lewiston ID U.S.A.
139 E2 Lewiston ME U.S.A.
134 E1 Lewistown U.S.A.
138 B3 Lexington KY U.S.A.
136 D2 Lexington NE U.S.A.
143 D1 Lexington OK U.S.A.
139 D3 Lexington VA U.S.A.
64 B2 Leyte i. Phil.
109 C2 Lezhë Albania
89 F2 Lezhnevo Rus. Fed.
89 E3 L'gov Rus. Fed.
75 C2 Lhagoi Kangri mt. China

75 D1 Lharigarbo China
75 D2 Lhasa China
75 C2 Hazê China
60 A1 Lhokseumawe Indon.
Lhünzê China see Xingba
67 B3 Liancourt Rocks i. N. Pacific Ocean
Liangzhou China see Wuwei
70 B2 Liangzi Hu l. China
Lianhe China see Qianjiang
71 B3 Lianhua China
71 B3 Lianjiang China
Lianran China see Anning
70 C1 Lianshan China
Liantang China see Nanchang
Lianxian China see Lianzhou
70 B2 Lianyungang China
71 B3 Lianzhou China
Lianzhou China see Hepu
70 B2 Liaocheng China
70 C1 Liaodong Bandao pen. China
70 C1 Liaodong Wan b. China
65 A1 Liao He r. China
70 C1 Liaoning prov. China
70 C1 Liaoyang China
65 B1 Liaoyuan China
128 B1 Liard r. Can.
134 C1 Libby U.S.A.
118 B2 Libenge Dem. Rep. Congo
136 B2 Liberal U.S.A.
103 D1 Liberec Czech Rep.
114 B4 Liberia country Africa
146 B3 Liberia Costa Rica
150 C2 Libertad Venez.
137 E3 Liberty U.S.A.
100 B3 Libin Belgium
64 B2 Libmanan Phil.
71 A3 Libo China
123 C3 Libode S. Africa
119 E2 Liboi Kenya
104 B3 Libourne France
100 B3 Libramont Belgium
142 A3 Libre, Sierra mts Mex.
118 A2 Libreville Gabon
115 D2 Libya country Africa
115 E2 Libyan Desert Egypt/Libya
116 A1 Libyan Plateau Egypt
108 B3 Licata Sicily Italy
Licheng China see Lipu
99 C3 Lichfield U.K.
121 C2 Lichinga Moz.
101 E2 Lichte Ger.
123 C2 Lichtenburg S. Africa
101 E2 Lichtenfels Ger.
88 C3 Lida Belarus
93 F4 Lidköping Sweden
50 C2 Liebig, Mount U.S.A.
105 D2 Liechtenstein country Europe
100 B2 Liège Belgium
92 J3 Lieksa Fin.
119 C2 Lienart Dem. Rep. Congo
102 C2 Lienz Austria
88 B2 Liepāja Latvia
100 B1 Lier Belgium
102 C2 Liezen Austria
97 C2 Liffey r. Ireland
97 C1 Lifford Ireland
53 C1 Lightning Ridge Austr.
121 C2 Ligonha r. Moz.
105 C3 Ligurian Sea France/Italy
119 C4 Likasi Dem. Rep. Congo
118 C2 Likati Dem. Rep. Congo
128 B2 Likely Can.
Likhachevo Ukr. see Pervomays'kyy
Likhachyovo Ukr. see Pervomays'kyy
89 E2 Likhoslavl' Rus. Fed.
60 B1 Liku Indon.
105 D3 L'Île-Rousse Corsica France
71 B3 Liling China
93 F4 Lilla Edet Sweden
100 B2 Lille Belgium
105 C1 Lille France
Lille Bælt sea chan. Denmark see Little Belt
93 F3 Lillehammer Norway
93 F4 Lillestrøm Norway
128 B2 Lillooet Can.
121 C2 Lilongwe Malawi
64 B3 Liloy Phil.
150 B4 Lima Peru
138 C2 Lima U.S.A.
155 D2 Lima Duarte Brazil
79 C2 Limah Oman
80 B2 Limassol Cyprus
97 C1 Limavady U.K.
153 B3 Limay r. Arg.
101 F2 Limbach-Oberfrohna Ger.
88 B2 Limbaži Latvia
118 A2 Limbe Cameroon
101 D2 Limburg an der Lahn Ger.
122 B2 Lime Acres S. Africa
154 C2 Limeira Brazil
97 B2 Limerick Ireland
93 E4 Limfjorden sea chan. Denmark
92 I3 Liminka Fin.
111 C3 Limnos i. Greece
104 C2 Limoges France
146 B3 Limon U.S.A.
104 C3 Limoux France
123 C1 Limpopo prov. S. Africa
121 C3 Limpopo r. S. Africa/Zimbabwe
64 A2 Linapacan i. Phil.

153 A3 Linares Chile
145 C2 Linares Mex.
106 C2 Linares Spain
108 A3 Linas, Monte *mt. Sardinia* Italy
62 B1 Lincang China
Linchuan China *see* Fuzhou
98 C3 Lincoln U.K.
138 B2 Lincoln *IL* U.S.A.
139 F1 Lincoln *ME* U.S.A.
137 D2 Lincoln *NE* U.S.A.
134 B2 Lincoln City U.S.A.
151 D2 Linden Guyana
140 C1 Linden U.S.A.
119 C3 Lindi *r.* Dem. Rep. Congo
119 D3 Lindi Tanz.
Lindisfarne *i.* U.K. *see* Holy Island
111 C3 Lindos Greece
130 C3 Lindsay Can.
48 K3 Line Islands Kiribati
70 B2 Linfen China
64 B2 Lingayen Phil.
70 B2 Lingbao China
Lingcheng China *see* Lingshan
Lingcheng China *see* Lingshui
123 C3 Lingelethu S. Africa
123 C3 Lingelihle S. Africa
100 C1 Lingen (Ems) Ger.
60 B2 Lingga *i.* Indon.
60 B2 Lingga, Kepulauan *is* Indon.
71 A3 Lingshan China
71 A4 Lingshui China
114 A3 Linguère Senegal
155 D1 Linhares Brazil
70 A1 Linhe China
Linjiang China *see* Shanghang
65 B1 Linjiang China
93 G4 Linköping Sweden
66 B2 Linkou China
71 B3 Linli China
96 B2 Linnhe, Loch *inlet* U.K.
70 B2 Linqing China
154 C2 Lins Brazil
136 C1 Linton U.S.A.
69 D2 Linxi China
70 A2 Linxia China
70 B2 Linyi *Shandong* China
70 B2 Linyi *Shandong* China
70 B2 Linying China
102 C2 Linz Austria
90 A1 Lioboml' Ukr.
105 C3 Lion, Golfe du *g.* France
Lions, Gulf of France *see*
Lion, Golfe du
109 B3 Lipari Italy
108 B3 Lipari, Isole *is* Italy
89 E3 Lipetsk Rus. Fed.
110 B1 Lipova Romania
101 D2 Lippstadt Ger.
53 C2 Liptrap, Cape Austr.
71 B3 Lipu China
119 D2 Lira Uganda
108 B2 Liri *r.* Italy
76 C1 Lisakovsk Kazakh.
118 C2 Lisala Dem. Rep. Congo
Lisboa Port. *see* Lisbon
106 B2 Lisbon Port.
97 C1 Lisburn U.K.
97 B2 Liscannor Bay Ireland
97 B2 Lisdoonvarna Ireland
Lishi China *see* Dingnan
71 B3 Lishui China
104 C2 Lisieux France
99 A4 Liskeard U.K.
89 E3 Liski Rus. Fed.
53 D1 Lismore Austr.
97 C2 Lismore Ireland
97 C1 Lisnaskea U.K.
97 B2 Listowel Ireland
71 A3 Litang *Guangxi* China
68 C2 Litang *Sichuan* China
138 B3 Litchfield *IL* U.S.A.
137 E1 Litchfield *MN* U.S.A.
53 D2 Lithgow Austr.
111 B3 Lithino, Akra *pt* Greece
88 B2 Lithuania *country* Europe
111 B2 Litochoro Greece
102 C1 Litoměřice Czech Rep.
Litovskaya S.S.R. *admin. reg.*
Europe *see* Lithuania
146 C2 Little Abaco *i.* Bahamas
73 D3 Little Andaman *i.* India
141 E3 Little Bahama Bank *sea feature*
Bahamas
93 E4 Little Belt *sea chan.* Denmark
146 B3 Little Cayman *i.* Cayman Is
142 A1 Little Colorado *r.* U.S.A.
138 C1 Little Current Can.
137 E1 Little Falls U.S.A.
143 C2 Littlefield U.S.A.
99 C3 Littlehampton U.K.
122 A2 Little Karas Berg *plat.* Namibia
122 B3 Little Karoo *plat.* S. Africa
96 A2 Little Minch *sea chan.* U.K.
136 C1 Little Missouri *r.* U.S.A.
73 D4 Little Nicobar *i.* India
140 B2 Little Rock U.S.A.
139 E2 Littleton U.S.A.
121 C2 Litunde Moz.
90 B2 Lityn Ukr.
Liuchow China *see* Liuzhou
70 B2 Liujiachang China
Liupanshui China *see* Lupanshui
121 C2 Liupo Moz.
71 A3 Liuzhou China
88 C2 Līvāni Latvia

141 D2 Live Oak U.S.A.
50 B1 Liveringa Austr.
142 C2 Livermore, Mount U.S.A.
53 D2 Liverpool Austr.
131 D3 Liverpool Can.
98 B3 Liverpool U.K.
127 G2 Liverpool, Cape Can.
53 C2 Liverpool Range *mts* Austr.
96 C3 Livingston U.K.
134 D1 Livingston *MT* U.S.A.
143 E2 Livingston *TX* U.S.A.
143 D2 Livingston, Lake U.S.A.
120 B2 Livingstone Zambia
55 A3 Livingston Island Antarctica
109 C2 Livno Bos.-Herz.
89 E3 Livny Rus. Fed.
138 C2 Livonia U.S.A.
108 B2 Livorno Italy
119 D3 Liwale Tanz.
99 A5 Lizard Point U.K.
108 B1 Ljubljana Slovenia
93 G3 Ljugan *r.* Sweden
93 F4 Ljungby Sweden
93 G3 Ljusdal Sweden
93 G3 Ljusnan *r.* Sweden
99 B4 Llandeilo U.K.
99 B4 Llandovery U.K.
99 B3 Llandrindod Wells U.K.
98 B3 Llandudno U.K.
99 A4 Llanelli U.K.
106 C1 Llanes Spain
98 A3 Llangefni U.K.
99 B3 Llangollen U.K.
99 B3 Llangurig U.K.
143 C2 Llano Estacado *plain* U.S.A.
150 C2 Llanos *reg.* Col./Venez.
107 D1 Lleida Spain
99 A3 Lleyn Peninsula U.K.
107 C2 Lliria Spain
106 C1 Llodio Spain
128 B2 Lloyd George, Mount Can.
129 D2 Lloyd Lake Can.
129 C2 Lloydminster Can.
152 B2 Llullaillaco, Volcán *vol.* Chile
154 B2 Loanda Brazil
123 C2 Lobatse Botswana
103 D1 Łobez Pol.
120 A2 Lobito Angola
101 F1 Loburg Ger.
96 B2 Lochaber *mts* U.K.
96 B2 Lochaline U.K.
96 A1 Loch a' Tuath U.K.
Loch Baghasdail U.K. *see*
Lochboisdale
96 A2 Lochboisdale U.K.
104 C2 Loches France
96 B2 Lochgilphead U.K.
96 B1 Lochinver U.K.
96 A2 Lochmaddy U.K.
96 C2 Lochnagar *mt.* U.K.
Loch nam Madadh U.K. *see*
Lochmaddy
96 B3 Lochranza U.K.
52 A2 Lock Austr.
96 C3 Lockerbie U.K.
53 C3 Lockhart Austr.
143 D3 Lockhart U.S.A.
51 D1 Lockhart River Austr.
139 D2 Lock Haven U.S.A.
139 D2 Lockport U.S.A.
63 B2 Lộc Ninh Vietnam
105 C3 Lodève France
86 C2 Lodeynoye Pole Rus. Fed.
74 B2 Lodhran Pak.
108 A1 Lodi Italy
135 B3 Lodi U.S.A.
92 F2 Lødingen Norway
92 G2 Lødingen Norway
93 H3 Loimaa Fin.
104 B2 Loire *r.* France
150 B3 Loja Ecuador
106 C2 Loja Spain
92 I2 Lokan tekojärvi *l.* Fin.
100 B2 Lokeren Belgium
122 B1 Lokgwabe Botswana
91 C1 Lokhvytsya Ukr.
119 D2 Lokichar Kenya
119 D2 Lokichokio Kenya
93 E4 Løkken Denmark
89 D2 Loknya Rus. Fed.
115 C4 Lokoja Nigeria
89 D3 Lokot' Rus. Fed.
88 C2 Loksa Estonia
127 H2 Loks Land *i.* Can.
114 B4 Lola Guinea
93 F5 Lolland *i.* Denmark
119 D3 Lollondo Tanz.
118 C2 Lolo Dem. Rep. Congo

122 B2 Lolwane S. Africa
110 B2 Lom Bulg.
93 E3 Lom Norway
119 C2 Lomami *r.* Dem. Rep. Congo
153 C3 Lomas de Zamora Arg.
50 B1 Lombadina Austr.
61 C2 Lombok *i.* Indon.
61 C2 Lombok, Selat *sea chan.* Indon.
114 C4 Lomé Togo
118 C3 Lomela *r.* Dem. Rep. Congo
100 B2 Lommel Belgium
96 B2 Lomond, Loch *l.* U.K.
88 C2 Lomonosov Rus. Fed.
160 A1 Lomonosov Ridge *sea feature*
Arctic Ocean
61 C2 Lompobattang, Gunung *mt.*
Indon.
135 B4 Lompoc U.S.A.
63 B2 Lom Sak Thai.
103 E1 Łomża Pol.
130 B3 London Can.
99 C4 London U.K.
138 C3 London U.S.A.
97 C1 Londonderry U.K.
50 B1 Londonderry, Cape Austr.
154 B2 Londrina Brazil
135 C3 Lone Pine U.S.A.
83 M2 Longa, Proliv *sea chan.* Rus. Fed.
61 C1 Long Akah *Sarawak* Malaysia
141 E2 Long Bay U.S.A.
135 C4 Long Beach U.S.A.
71 A3 Longchang China
99 C3 Long Eaton U.K.
97 C2 Longford Ireland
96 C1 Longhope U.K.
119 D3 Longido Tanz.
61 C2 Longiram Indon.
147 C2 Long Island Bahamas
130 C2 Long Island Can.
59 D3 Long Island P.N.G.
139 E2 Long Island U.S.A.
130 B3 Longlac Can.
130 B3 Long Lake Can.
71 A3 Longli China
71 A3 Longming China
136 B2 Longmont U.S.A.
Longping China *see* Luodian
138 C2 Long Point Can.
71 B3 Longquan China
131 E3 Long Range Mountains Can.
51 D2 Longreach Austr.
Longshan China *see* Longli
99 D3 Long Stratton U.K.
98 B2 Longtown U.K.
105 D2 Longuyon France
143 E2 Longview *TX* U.S.A.
134 B1 Longview *WA* U.S.A.
61 C1 Longwai Indon.
70 A2 Longxi China
Longxian China *see* Wengyuan
71 B3 Longxi Shan *mt.* China
63 B2 Long Xuyên Vietnam
71 B3 Longyan China
82 C1 Longyearbyen Svalbard
108 B1 Lonigo Italy
100 C1 Löningen Ger.
105 D2 Lons-le-Saunier France
141 E2 Lookout, Cape U.S.A.
119 D3 Loolmalasin *vol. crater* Tanz.
50 B3 Loongana Austr.
97 B2 Loop Head *hd* Ireland
Lopasnya Rus. Fed. *see* Chekhov
63 B2 Lop Buri Thai.
64 B2 Lopez Phil.
118 A3 Lopez, Cap *c.* Gabon
68 C2 Lop Nur *salt l.* China
118 B2 Lopori *r.* Dem. Rep. Congo
92 H1 Lopphavet *b.* Norway
106 B2 Lora del Rio Spain
138 C2 Lorain U.S.A.
74 A1 Loralai Pak.
107 C2 Lorca Spain
51 E3 Lord Howe Island Austr.
142 B2 Lordsburg U.S.A.
155 C2 Lorena Brazil
59 D3 Lorengau P.N.G.
59 D3 Lorentz *r.* Indon.
152 B1 Loreto Bol.
144 A2 Loreto Mex.
104 B2 Lorient France
96 B2 Lorn, Firth of *est.* U.K.
52 B3 Lorne Austr.
105 D2 Lorraine *reg.* France
142 B1 Los Alamos U.S.A.
143 D3 Los Aldamas Mex.
153 A3 Los Ángeles Chile
135 C4 Los Angeles U.S.A.
135 B3 Los Banos U.S.A.
152 B2 Los Blancos Arg.
89 F3 Losevo Rus. Fed.
108 B2 Lošinj *i.* Croatia
144 B2 Los Mochis Mex.
118 B2 Losombo Dem. Rep. Congo
106 B2 Los Pedroches *plat.* Spain
147 D3 Los Roques, Islas *is* Venez.
96 C2 Lossiemouth U.K.
150 C1 Los Teques Venez.
59 E3 Losuia P.N.G.
152 A3 Los Vilos Chile
104 C3 Lot *r.* France
96 C1 Loth U.K.
134 D1 Lothair U.S.A.
Lothringen *reg.* France *see*
Lorraine
119 D2 Lotikipi Plain Kenya

118 C3 Loto Dem. Rep. Congo
89 E2 Lotoshino Rus. Fed.
62 B1 Louangnamtha Laos
62 B2 Louangphabang Laos
118 B3 Loubomo Congo
104 B2 Loudéac France
71 B3 Loudi China
118 B3 Loudima Congo
114 A3 Louga Senegal
99 C3 Loughborough U.K.
97 B2 Loughrea Ireland
105 D2 Louhans France
97 B2 Louisburgh Ireland
51 E1 Louisiade Archipelago *is* P.N.G.
140 B2 Louisiana *state* U.S.A.
123 C1 Louis Trichardt S. Africa
138 B3 Louisville *KY* U.S.A.
140 C2 Louisville *MS* U.S.A.
86 C2 Loukhi Rus. Fed.
118 B3 Loukoléla Congo
106 B2 Loulé Port.
118 A2 Loum Cameroon
130 C2 Loups Marins, Lacs des *lakes*
Can.
104 B3 Lourdes France
151 D2 Lourenço Brazil
Lourenço Marques Moz. *see*
Maputo
106 B1 Lousã Port.
53 C2 Louth Austr.
98 C3 Louth U.K.
Louvain Belgium *see* Leuven
122 A1 Louwater-Suid Namibia
89 D2 Lovat' *r.* Rus. Fed.
110 B2 Lovech Bulg.
136 B2 Loveland U.S.A.
136 B2 Lovell U.S.A.
135 C2 Lovelock U.S.A.
88 C1 Loviisa Fin.
143 C2 Lovington U.S.A.
86 C2 Lovozero Rus. Fed.
119 C3 Lowa Dem. Rep. Congo
139 E2 Lowell U.S.A.
119 D2 Lowelli Sudan
128 C3 Lower Arrow Lake Can.
Lower California *pen.* Mex. *see*
Baja California
54 B2 Lower Hutt N.Z.
97 C1 Lower Lough Erne *l.* U.K.
128 B2 Lower Post Can.
137 E1 Lower Red Lake U.S.A.
Lower Tunguska *r.* Rus. Fed. *see*
Nizhnyaya Tunguska
99 D3 Lowestoft U.K.
103 D1 Łowicz Pol.
139 D2 Lowville U.S.A.
52 B2 Loxton Austr.
Loyang China *see* Luoyang
48 H6 Loyauté, Îles New Caledonia
89 D3 Loyew Belarus
92 F2 Løypskardtinden *mt.* Norway
109 C2 Loznica Serb. and Mont.
91 D2 Lozova Ukr.
120 B2 Luacano Angola
70 B2 Lu'an China
120 A1 Luanda Angola
63 B3 Luang, Thale *lag.* Thai.
121 C2 Luangwa *r.* Zambia
121 B2 Luanshya Zambia
Luao Angola *see* Luau
120 B1 Luarca Spain
120 B2 Luau Angola
103 E1 Lubaczów Pol.
103 D1 Lubań Pol.
64 A1 Lubang Islands Phil.
120 A2 Lubango Angola
119 C3 Lubao Dem. Rep. Congo
103 E1 Lubartów Pol.
101 D1 Lübbecke Ger.
102 C1 Lübben Ger.
143 C2 Lubbock U.S.A.
101 E1 Lübeck Ger.
69 E2 Lubei China
76 B1 Lubenka Kazakh.
119 C3 Lubero Dem. Rep. Congo
103 D1 Lubin Pol.
103 E1 Lublin Pol.
91 C1 Lubny Ukr.
61 C1 Lubok Antu *Sarawak* Malaysia
101 E1 Lübow Ger.
101 E1 Lübtheen Ger.
119 C3 Lubudi Dem. Rep. Congo
60 B2 Lubuklinggau Indon.
119 C4 Lubumbashi Dem. Rep. Congo
120 B2 Lubungu Zambia
119 C3 Lubutu Dem. Rep. Congo
120 A1 Lucala Angola
97 C2 Lucan Ireland
120 B1 Lucapa Angola
108 B2 Lucca Italy
96 B3 Luce Bay U.K.
154 B3 Lucélia Brazil
64 B1 Lucena Phil.
106 C2 Lucena Spain
103 D2 Lučenec Slovakia
109 C2 Lucera Italy
105 D2 Lucerne Switz.
66 B1 Luchegorsk Rus. Fed.
101 E1 Lüchow Ger.
120 A2 Lucira Angola
Łuck Ukr. *see* Luts'k
101 F1 Luckenwalde Ger.
122 B2 Luckhoff S. Africa
75 C2 Lucknow India
120 A1 Lucunga Angola

Lucusse
210

120 B2 Lucusse Angola
Lüda China see Dalian
100 C2 Lüdenscheid Ger.
101 E1 Lüder Ger.
120 A3 Lüderitz Namibia
119 D4 Ludewa Tanz.
74 B1 Ludhiana India
138 B2 Ludington U.S.A.
99 B3 Ludlow U.K.
135 C4 Ludlow U.S.A.
110 C2 Ludogorie reg. Bulg.
93 G3 Ludvika Sweden
102 B2 Ludwigsburg Ger.
101 F1 Ludwigsfelde Ger.
101 D3 Ludwigshafen am Rhein Ger.
101 E1 Ludwigslust Ger.
88 C2 Ludza Latvia
118 C3 Luebo Dem. Rep. Congo
120 A2 Luena Angola
70 A2 Lüeyang China
71 B3 Lufeng China
119 C3 Lufira r. Dem. Rep. Congo
143 E2 Lufkin U.S.A.
88 C2 Luga Rus. Fed.
88 C2 Luga r. Rus. Fed.
105 D2 Lugano Switz.
121 C2 Lugenda r. Moz.
106 B1 Lugo Spain
110 B1 Lugoj Romania
91 D2 Luhans'k Ukr.
119 D3 Luhombero Tanz.
90 B1 Luhyny Ukr.
120 B2 Luiana Angola
Luichow Peninsula China see Leizhou Bandao
118 C3 Luilaka r. Dem. Rep. Congo
Luimneach Ireland see Limerick
105 D2 Luino Italy
92 I2 Luiro r. Fin.
118 C3 Luiza Dem. Rep. Congo
70 B2 Lujiang China
Lukapa Angola see Lucapa
109 C2 Lukavac Bos.-Herz.
118 B3 Lukenie r. Dem. Rep. Congo
142 A2 Lukeville U.S.A.
89 E3 Lukhovitsy Rus. Fed.
Lukou China see Zhuzhou
103 E1 Łuków Pol.
120 B2 Lukulu Zambia
92 H2 Luleå Sweden
92 H2 Luleälven r. Sweden
111 C2 Lüleburgaz Turkey
70 B2 Lüliang Shan mts China
143 D3 Luling U.S.A.
Luluabourg Dem. Rep. Congo see Kananga
61 C2 Lumajang Indon.
75 C1 Lumajangdong Co salt l. China
Lumbala Angola see Lumbala Kaquengue
Lumbala Angola see Lumbala N'guimbo
120 B2 Lumbala Kaquengue Angola
120 B2 Lumbala N'guimbo Angola
140 C2 Lumberton MS U.S.A.
141 E2 Lumberton NC U.S.A.
61 C1 Lumbis Indon.
106 B1 Lumbrales Spain
63 B2 Lumphăt Cambodia
129 D2 Lumsden Can.
54 A3 Lumsden N.Z.
93 F4 Lund Sweden
121 C2 Lundazi Zambia
99 A4 Lundy U.K.
101 E1 Lüneburg Ger.
101 E1 Lüneburger Heide reg. Ger.
100 C2 Lünen Ger.
105 D2 Lunéville France
120 B2 Lunga r. Zambia
114 A4 Lungi Sierra Leone
Lungleh India see Lunglei
75 D2 Lunglei India
97 C2 Lungnaquilla Mountain hill Ireland
120 B2 Lungwebungu r. Zambia
74 B2 Luni r. India
88 C3 Luninyets Belarus
104 C3 L'Union France
114 A4 Lunsar Sierra Leone
77 E2 Luntai China
71 A3 Luodian China
71 B3 Luoding China
70 B2 Luohe China
70 B2 Luoyang China
118 B3 Luozi Dem. Rep. Congo
121 B2 Lupane Zimbabwe
71 A3 Lupanshui China
110 B1 Lupeni Romania
121 C2 Lupilichi Moz.
101 F2 Luppa Ger.
95 B3 Lurgan U.K.
Luring China see Gêrzê
121 D2 Lúrio Moz.
121 D2 Lurio r. Moz.
92 F2 Lurøy Norway
121 B2 Lusaka Zambia
118 C3 Lusambo Dem. Rep. Congo
109 C2 Lushnjë Albania
70 C2 Lüshun China
123 C3 Lusikisiki S. Africa
136 C2 Lusk U.S.A.
Luso Angola see Luena
76 B3 Lut, Dasht-e des. Iran
101 F2 Lutherstadt Wittenberg Ger.
99 C4 Luton U.K.
61 C1 Lutong Sarawak Malaysia
129 C1 Łutselk'e Can.
90 B1 Luts'k Ukr.
55 F3 Lützow-Holm Bay Antarctica
122 B2 Lutzputs S. Africa
122 A3 Lutzville S. Africa
117 C4 Luuq Somalia
137 D2 Luverne U.S.A.
119 C3 Luvua r. Dem. Rep. Congo
120 B2 Luvuei Angola
123 D1 Luvuvhu r. S. Africa
119 D3 Luwegu r. Tanz.
119 D2 Luwero Uganda
61 D2 Luwuk Indon.
100 C3 Luxembourg country Europe
100 C3 Luxembourg Lux.
105 D2 Luxeuil-les-Bains France
62 A1 Luxi China
123 C3 Luxolweni S. Africa
116 B2 Luxor Egypt
100 B2 Luyksgestel Neth.
86 D2 Luza Rus. Fed.
Luzern Switz. see Lucerne
62 B1 Luzhai China
71 A3 Luzhi China
71 A3 Luzhou China
154 C1 Luziânia Brazil
151 E3 Luzilândia Brazil
64 B2 Luzon i. Phil.
64 B1 Luzon Strait Phil.
109 C3 Luzzi Italy
90 A2 L'viv Ukr.
L'vov Ukr. see L'viv
Lwów Ukr. see L'viv
88 C3 Lyakhavichy Belarus
Lyallpur Pak. see Faisalabad
89 D2 Lychkovo Rus. Fed.
92 G3 Lycksele Sweden
55 C2 Lyddan Island Antarctica
123 D2 Lydenburg S. Africa
88 C3 Lyel'chytsy Belarus
88 C3 Lyepyel' Belarus
136 A2 Lyman U.S.A.
99 B4 Lyme Bay U.K.
99 B4 Lyme Regis U.K.
139 D3 Lynchburg U.S.A.
52 A2 Lyndhurst Austr.
129 D2 Lynn Lake Can.
134 B1 Lynnwood U.S.A.
129 D1 Lynx Lake Can.
105 C2 Lyon France
Lyons France see Lyon
89 D2 Lyozna Belarus
103 E1 Łysica hill Pol.
86 E3 Lys'va Rus. Fed.
91 D2 Lysychans'k Ukr.
87 D3 Lysyye Gory Rus. Fed.
98 B3 Lytham St Anne's U.K.
88 C3 Lyuban' Belarus
90 C2 Lyubashivka Ukr.
89 E2 Lyubertsy Rus. Fed.
90 B1 Lyubeshiv Ukr.
89 F2 Lyubim Rus. Fed.
91 D2 Lyubotyn Ukr.
89 D2 Lyubytino Rus. Fed.
89 D3 Lyudinovo Rus. Fed.

M

80 B2 Ma'ān Jordan
70 B2 Ma'anshan China
88 C2 Maardu Estonia
78 B3 Ma'āriḍ, Banī des. Saudi Arabia
80 B2 Ma'arrat an Nu'mān Syria
100 B1 Maarssen Neth.
100 B2 Maas r. Neth.
100 B2 Maaseik Belgium
64 B2 Maasin Phil.
100 B2 Maastricht Neth.
121 C3 Mabalane Moz.
78 B3 Ma'bar Yemen
150 D2 Mabaruma Guyana
98 D3 Mablethorpe U.K.
123 C2 Mabopane S. Africa
121 C3 Mabote Moz.
122 B2 Mabule Botswana
122 B1 Mabutsane Botswana
155 D2 Macaé Brazil
121 C2 Macaloge Moz.
126 F2 MacAlpine Lake Can.
151 D2 Macapá Brazil
150 B3 Macará Ecuador
155 D1 Macarani Brazil
Macassar Indon. see Makassar
Macassar Strait Indon. see Makassar, Selat
121 C2 Macatanja Moz.
151 F3 Macau Brazil
71 B3 Macau special admin. reg. China
121 C3 Maccaretane Moz.
98 B3 Macclesfield U.K.
50 B2 Macdonald, Lake salt flat Austr.
50 C2 Macdonnell Ranges mts Austr.
130 A2 MacDowell Lake Can.
96 C2 Macduff U.K.
106 B1 Macedo de Cavaleiros Port.
52 B3 Macedon mt. Austr.
111 B2 Macedonia country Europe
151 F3 Maceió Brazil
108 B2 Macerata Italy
52 A2 Macfarlane, Lake salt flat Austr.
97 B3 Macgillycuddy's Reeks mts Ireland
74 A2 Mach Pak.
155 C2 Machado Brazil
121 C3 Machaila Moz.
119 D3 Machakos Kenya
150 B3 Machala Ecuador
121 C3 Machanga Moz.
Machaze Moz. see Chitobe
70 B2 Macheng China
138 B2 Machesney Park U.S.A.
139 F2 Machias U.S.A.
73 C3 Machilipatnam India
121 C2 Machinga Malawi
150 B1 Machiques Venez.
150 B4 Machupicchu Peru
99 B3 Machynlleth U.K.
123 D2 Macia Moz.
Macias Nguema i. Equat. Guinea see Bioco
110 C1 Măcin Romania
53 D1 Macintyre r. Austr.
51 D2 Mackay Austr.
50 B2 Mackay, Lake salt flat Austr.
128 C1 MacKay Lake Can.
128 B2 Mackenzie Can.
128 A1 Mackenzie r. Can.
Mackenzie Guyana see Linden
Mackenzie atoll Micronesia see Ulithi
55 H3 Mackenzie Bay Antarctica
126 C2 Mackenzie Bay Can.
126 E1 Mackenzie King Island Can.
128 A1 Mackenzie Mountains Can.
Mackillop, Lake salt flat Austr. see Yamma Yamma, Lake
129 D2 Macklin Can.
53 D2 Macksville Austr.
53 D1 Maclean Austr.
123 C3 Maclear S. Africa
50 A2 MacLeod, Lake imp. l. Austr.
138 A2 Macomb U.S.A.
108 A2 Macomer Sardinia Italy
121 D2 Macomia Moz.
105 C2 Mâcon France
141 D2 Macon GA U.S.A.
137 E3 Macon MO U.S.A.
140 C2 Macon MS U.S.A.
53 C2 Macquarie r. Austr.
48 G9 Macquarie Island S. Pacific Ocean
53 C2 Macquarie Marshes Austr.
53 C2 Macquarie Mountain Austr.
156 D9 Macquarie Ridge sea feature S. Pacific Ocean
55 H2 Mac. Robertson Land reg. Antarctica
97 B3 Macroom Ireland
52 A1 Macumba watercourse Austr.
145 C3 Macuspana Mex.
144 B2 Macuzari, Presa resr Mex.
123 D2 Madadeni S. Africa
121 □D3 Madagascar country Africa
159 D5 Madagascar Ridge sea feature Indian Ocean
115 D2 Madama Niger
111 B2 Madan Bulg.
59 D3 Madang P.N.G.
139 D1 Madawaska r. Can.
62 A1 Madaya Myanmar
150 D3 Madeira r. Brazil
114 A1 Madeira terr. N. Atlantic Ocean
131 D3 Madeleine, Îles de la is Can.
99 B3 Madeley U.K.
144 B2 Madera Mex.
135 B3 Madera U.S.A.
73 B3 Madgaon India
74 B2 Madhya Pradesh state India
123 C2 Madibogo S. Africa
118 B3 Madingou Congo
121 □D2 Madirovalo Madag.
138 B3 Madison IN U.S.A.
137 D2 Madison SD U.S.A.
138 B2 Madison WI U.S.A.
138 C3 Madison WV U.S.A.
134 D1 Madison r. U.S.A.
138 B3 Madisonville U.S.A.
61 C2 Madiun Indon.
119 D2 Mado Gashi Kenya
68 C2 Madoi China
88 C2 Madona Latvia
78 A2 Madrakah Saudi Arabia
79 C3 Madrakah, Ra's c. Oman
Madras India see Chennai
134 B2 Madras U.S.A.
145 C2 Madre, Laguna lag. Mex.
143 D3 Madre, Laguna lag. U.S.A.
150 C4 Madre de Dios r. Peru
145 B3 Madre del Sur, Sierra mts Mex.
144 B2 Madre Occidental, Sierra mts Mex.
145 B2 Madre Oriental, Sierra mts Mex.
106 C1 Madrid Spain
106 C2 Madridejos Spain
61 C2 Madura i. Indon.
61 C2 Madura, Selat sea chan. Indon.
73 B4 Madurai India
121 B2 Madziwadzido Zimbabwe
67 C3 Maebashi Japan
62 A2 Mae Hong Son Thai.
62 A1 Mae Sai Thai.
62 A2 Mae Sariang Thai.
99 B4 Maesteg U.K.
62 A2 Mae Suai Thai.
121 □D2 Maevatanana Madag.
Mafeking S. Africa see Mafikeng
123 C2 Mafeteng Lesotho
53 C3 Maffra Austr.
119 D3 Mafia Island Tanz.
123 C2 Mafikeng S. Africa
119 D3 Mafinga Tanz.
154 C3 Mafra Brazil
83 L3 Magadan Rus. Fed.
Magallanes Chile see Punta Arenas
Magallanes, Estrecho de Chile see Magellan, Strait of
150 B2 Magangue Col.
140 B1 Magazine Mountain hill U.S.A.
114 A4 Magburaka Sierra Leone
69 E1 Magdagachi Rus. Fed.
144 A1 Magdalena Mex.
142 B2 Magdalena U.S.A.
144 A2 Magdalena, Bahía b. Mex.
101 E1 Magdeburg Ger.
153 A5 Magellan, Strait of sea chan. Chile
Maggiore, Lago Italy see Maggiore, Lake
108 A1 Maggiore, Lake l. Italy
116 B2 Maghāghah Egypt
97 C1 Magherafelt U.K.
87 E3 Magnitogorsk Rus. Fed.
140 B2 Magnolia U.S.A.
121 C2 Màgoé Moz.
130 C3 Magog Can.
131 D2 Magpie, Lac l. Can.
114 A3 Magṭa' Laḥjar Maur.
119 D3 Magu Tanz.
151 E3 Maguarinho, Cabo c. Brazil
123 D2 Magude Moz.
90 B2 Măgura, Dealul hill Moldova
62 A1 Magwe Myanmar
81 C2 Mahābād Iran
74 B2 Mahajan India
121 □D2 Mahajanga Madag.
61 C2 Mahakam r. Indon.
123 C1 Mahalapye Botswana
121 □D2 Mahalevona Madag.
75 C2 Mahanadi r. India
121 □D2 Mahanoro Madag.
74 B3 Maharashtra state India
63 B2 Maha Sarakham Thai.
121 □D2 Mahavavy r. Madag.
68 B3 Mahbubnagar India
78 B2 Mahd adh Dhahab Saudi Arabia
107 D2 Mahdia Alg.
150 D2 Mahdia Guyana
113 I6 Mahé i. Seychelles
75 C3 Mahendragiri mt. India
119 D3 Mahenge Tanz.
54 B3 Maheno N.Z.
74 B2 Mahesana India
74 B2 Mahi r. India
54 C1 Mahia Peninsula N.Z.
89 D3 Mahilyow Belarus
107 D2 Mahón Spain
114 B3 Mahou Mali
Mahsana India see Mahesana
74 B2 Mahuva India
111 C2 Mahya Dağı mt. Turkey
106 B1 Maia Port.
Maiaia Moz. see Nacala
147 C3 Maicao Col.
129 D2 Maidstone Can.
99 D4 Maidstone U.K.
115 D3 Maiduguri Nigeria
75 D2 Maijdi Bangl.
75 C2 Mailani India
101 D2 Main r. Ger.
118 B3 Mai-Ndombe, Lac l. Dem. Rep. Congo
101 E3 Main-Donau-Kanal canal Ger.
139 F1 Maine state U.S.A.
131 D3 Maine, Gulf of Can./U.S.A.
62 A1 Maingkwan Myanmar
96 C1 Mainland i. Orkney Is, Scotland U.K.
96 □ Mainland i. Shetland Is, Scotland U.K.
121 □D2 Maintirano Madag.
101 D2 Mainz Ger.
150 C1 Maiquetía Venez.
120 B3 Maitengwe Botswana
53 D2 Maitland N.S.W. Austr.
52 A2 Maitland S.A. Austr.
146 B3 Maíz, Islas del is Nic.
67 C3 Maizuru Japan
109 C2 Maja Jezercë mt. Albania
61 C2 Majene Indon.
119 D2 Majī Eth.
107 D2 Majorca i. Spain
Majunga Madag. see Mahajanga
123 C2 Majwemasweu S. Africa
118 B3 Makabana Congo
61 C2 Makale Indon.
119 C3 Makamba Burundi
77 E2 Makanchi Kazakh.
118 B2 Makanza Dem. Rep. Congo
90 B1 Makariv Ukr.
69 F1 Makarov Rus. Fed.
160 B1 Makarov Basin sea feature Arctic Ocean
109 C2 Makarska Croatia
61 C2 Makassar Indon.
61 C2 Makassar, Selat Indon.
76 B2 Makat Kazakh.
119 D3 Makatapora Tanz.
123 D2 Makatini Flats lowland S. Africa
114 A4 Makeni Sierra Leone
120 B3 Makgadikgadi salt pan Botswana
87 D4 Makhachkala Rus. Fed.
76 B2 Makhambet Kazakh.
119 D3 Makindu Kenya
77 D1 Makinsk Kazakh.
91 D2 Makiyivka Ukr.

131 E2	Makkah Saudi Arabia see Mecca	
103 E2	Makkovik Can.	
118 B2	Makó Hungary	
119 D3	Makokou Gabon	
122 B2	Makongolosi Tanz.	
119 C2	Makopong Botswana	
118 B3	Makoro Dem. Rep. Congo	
111 B3	Makoua Congo	
79 D2	Makrakomi Greece	
74 A2	Makran reg. Iran/Pak.	
89 E2	Makran Coast Range mts Pak.	
81 C2	Maksatikha Rus. Fed.	
62 A1	Mākū Iran	
67 B4	Makum India	
115 C4	Makurazaki Japan	
92 G2	Makurdi Nigeria	
146 B4	Malá Sweden	
73 B3	Mala, Punta pt Panama	
118 A2	Malabar Coast India	
155 D1	Malabo Equat. Guinea	
60 A1	Malacacheta Brazil	
134 D2	Malacca Malaysia see Melaka	
88 C3	Malacca, Strait of Indon./Malaysia	
106 C2	Malad City U.S.A.	
121 □D3	Maladzyechna Belarus	
	Málaga Spain	
	Malagasy Republic country Africa see Madagascar	
121 □D3	Malaimbandy Madag.	
48 H4	Malaita i. Solomon Is	
117 B4	Malakal Sudan	
48 H5	Malakula i. Vanuatu	
61 D2	Malamala Indon.	
61 C2	Malang Indon.	
	Malange Angola see Malanje	
120 A1	Malanje Angola	
93 G4	Mälaren l. Sweden	
153 B3	Malargüe Arg.	
130 C3	Malartic Can.	
88 B3	Malaryta Belarus	
80 B2	Malatya Turkey	
121 C2	Malawi country Africa	
	Malawi, Lake Africa see Nyasa, Lake	
89 D2	Malaya Vishera Rus. Fed.	
64 B3	Malaybalay Phil.	
81 C2	Malāyer Iran	
60 B1	Malaysia country Asia	
81 C2	Malazgirt Turkey	
103 D1	Malbork Pol.	
101 F1	Malchin Ger.	
100 A2	Maldegem Belgium	
48 L4	Malden Island Kiribati	
56 C5	Maldives country Indian Ocean	
99 D4	Maldon U.K.	
56 I9	Male Maldives	
111 B3	Maleas, Akra pt Greece	
103 D2	Malé Karpaty hills Slovakia	
119 C3	Malela Dem. Rep. Congo	
116 A3	Malha Sudan	
134 C2	Malheur Lake U.S.A.	
114 B3	Mali country Africa	
114 A3	Mali Guinea	
59 C3	Maliana East Timor	
58 C3	Malili Indon.	
97 C1	Malin Ireland	
119 E3	Malindi Kenya	
97 C1	Malin Head hd Ireland	
97 B1	Malin More Ireland	
111 C2	Malkara Turkey	
88 C3	Mal'kavichy Belarus	
110 C2	Malko Tŭrnovo Bulg.	
53 C3	Mallacoota Austr.	
53 C3	Mallacoota Inlet b. Austr.	
96 D2	Mallaig U.K.	
116 B2	Mallawi Egypt	
129 E1	Mallery Lake Can.	
	Mallorca i. Spain see Majorca	
97 B2	Mallow Ireland	
92 F3	Malm Norway	
92 H2	Malmberget Sweden	
100 C2	Malmédy Belgium	
122 A3	Malmesbury S. Africa	
93 F4	Malmö Sweden	
71 A3	Malong China	
118 C4	Malonga Dem. Rep. Congo	
86 C2	Maloshuyka Rus. Fed.	
93 E3	Måløy Norway	
89 E2	Maloyaroslavets Rus. Fed.	
89 E2	Maloye Borisovo Rus. Fed.	
86 D2	Malozemel'skaya Tundra lowland Rus. Fed.	
125 J9	Malpelo, Isla de i. N. Pacific Ocean	
84 F5	Malta country Europe	
88 C2	Malta Latvia	
134 E1	Malta U.S.A.	
122 A1	Maltahöhe Namibia	
98 C2	Malton U.K.	
	Maluku is Indon. see Moluccas	
93 F3	Malung Sweden	
123 C2	Maluti Mountains Lesotho	
73 B3	Malvan India	
140 B2	Malvern U.S.A.	
117 B4	Malwal Sudan	
90 B1	Malyn Ukr.	
83 L2	Malyy Anyuy r. Rus. Fed.	
	Malyy Kavkaz mts Asia see Lesser Caucasus	
83 K2	Malyy Lyakhovskiy, Ostrov i. Rus. Fed.	
123 C2	Mamafubedu S. Africa	
151 F3	Mamanguape Brazil	
64 B3	Mambajao Phil.	
119 C2	Mambasa Dem. Rep. Congo	
118 B2	Mambéré r. C.A.R.	
64 B2	Mamburao Phil.	
123 C2	Mamelodi S. Africa	
118 A2	Mamfe Cameroon	
135 C3	Mammoth Lakes U.S.A.	
88 A3	Mamonovo Rus. Fed.	
150 C4	Mamoré r. Bol./Brazil	
114 A3	Mamou Guinea	
114 B4	Mampong Ghana	
61 C2	Mamuju Indon.	
114 B4	Man Côte d'Ivoire	
98 A2	Man, Isle of i. Irish Sea	
150 C3	Manacapuru Brazil	
107 D2	Manacor Spain	
59 C2	Manado Indon.	
146 B3	Managua Nic.	
121 □D3	Manakara Madag.	
78 B3	Manākhah Yemen	
79 C2	Manama Bahrain	
59 D3	Manam Island P.N.G.	
121 □D3	Mananara r. Madag.	
121 □D2	Mananara Avaratra Madag.	
121 □D3	Mananjary Madag.	
114 A3	Manantali, Lac de l. Mali	
54 A3	Manapouri, Lake N.Z.	
77 E2	Manas Hu l. China	
75 C2	Manaslu mt. Nepal	
	Manastir Macedonia see Bitola	
59 C3	Manatuto East Timor	
62 A2	Man-aung Kyun Myanmar	
150 C3	Manaus Brazil	
80 B2	Manavgat Turkey	
116 A3	Manawashei Sudan	
98 B3	Manchester U.K.	
139 E2	Manchester CT U.S.A.	
139 E2	Manchester NH U.S.A.	
140 C1	Manchester TN U.S.A.	
81 D3	Mand, Rūd-e r. Iran	
117 A4	Manda, Jebel mt. Sudan	
121 □D3	Mandabe Madag.	
93 E4	Mandal Norway	
59 D3	Mandala, Puncak mt. Indon.	
62 A1	Mandalay Myanmar	
68 D1	Mandalgovĭ Mongolia	
136 C1	Mandan U.S.A.	
118 B1	Mandara Mountains Cameroon/Nigeria	
108 A3	Mandas Sardinia Italy	
119 E2	Mandera Kenya	
100 C2	Manderscheid Ger.	
74 B1	Mandi India	
114 B3	Mandiana Guinea	
74 B1	Mandi Burewala Pak.	
	Mandidzuzure Zimbabwe see Chimanimani	
75 C2	Mandla India	
121 □D2	Mandritsara Madag.	
74 B2	Mandsaur India	
50 A3	Mandurah Austr.	
73 B3	Mandya India	
108 B1	Manerbio Italy	
90 B1	Manevychi Ukr.	
109 C2	Manfredonia Italy	
109 C2	Manfredonia, Golfo di g. Italy	
114 B3	Manga Burkina	
118 B3	Mangai Dem. Rep. Congo	
49 L6	Mangaia i. Cook Is	
54 C1	Mangakino N.Z.	
110 C2	Mangalia Romania	
73 B3	Mangalore India	
123 C2	Mangaung S. Africa	
60 B2	Manggar Indon.	
	Mangghyshlaq Kazakh. see Mangystau	
61 C1	Mangkalihat, Tanjung pt Indon.	
68 C2	Mangnai China	
121 C2	Mangochi Malawi	
59 C3	Mangole i. Indon.	
54 B1	Mangonui N.Z.	
	Mangshi China see Luxi	
106 B1	Mangualde Port.	
154 B3	Mangueirinha Brazil	
69 E1	Mangui China	
	Mangyshlak Kazakh. see Mangystau	
76 B2	Mangystau Kazakh.	
137 D3	Manhattan U.S.A.	
121 C3	Manhica Moz.	
155 D2	Manhuaçu Brazil	
121 □D2	Mania r. Madag.	
108 B1	Maniago Italy	
121 C2	Maniamba Moz.	
150 C3	Manicoré Brazil	
131 D3	Manicouagan r. Can.	
131 D2	Manicouagan, Réservoir resr Can.	
79 B2	Manīfah Saudi Arabia	
49 K5	Manihiki atoll Cook Is	
64 B2	Manila Phil.	
53 D2	Manilla Austr.	
	Manipur India see Imphal	
111 C3	Manisa Turkey	
107 C2	Manises Spain	
98 A2	Man, Isle of i. Irish Sea	
138 B2	Manistee U.S.A.	
138 B1	Manistique U.S.A.	
129 E2	Manitoba prov. Can.	
129 E2	Manitoba, Lake Can.	
138 B1	Manitou Islands U.S.A.	
130 B3	Manitoulin Island Can.	
136 C3	Manitou Springs U.S.A.	
130 B3	Manitouwadge Can.	
138 B2	Manitowoc U.S.A.	
130 C3	Maniwaki Can.	
150 B2	Manizales Col.	
121 □D3	Manja Madag.	
121 C3	Manjacaze Moz.	
137 E2	Mankato U.S.A.	
114 B4	Mankono Côte d'Ivoire	
129 D3	Mankota Can.	
73 C4	Mankulam Sri Lanka	
74 B2	Manmad India	
52 A2	Mannahill Austr.	
73 B4	Mannar Sri Lanka	
73 B4	Mannar, Gulf of India/Sri Lanka	
101 D3	Mannheim Ger.	
128 C2	Manning Can.	
52 A2	Mannum Austr.	
129 C2	Mannville Can.	
59 C3	Manokwari Indon.	
119 C3	Manono Dem. Rep. Congo	
63 A2	Manoron Myanmar	
105 D3	Manosque France	
131 C2	Manouane, Lac l. Can.	
65 B1	Map'o N. Korea	
107 D1	Manresa Spain	
121 B2	Mansa Zambia	
127 G2	Mansel Island Can.	
92 I2	Mansel'ky'a ridge Fin./Rus. Fed.	
53 C3	Mansfield Austr.	
98 C3	Mansfield U.K.	
140 B1	Mansfield AR U.S.A.	
140 B2	Mansfield LA U.S.A.	
138 C2	Mansfield OH U.S.A.	
139 D2	Mansfield PA U.S.A.	
150 A3	Manta Ecuador	
64 A3	Mantalingajan, Mount Phil.	
155 D1	Mantena Brazil	
141 E1	Manteo U.S.A.	
104 C2	Mantes-la-Jolie France	
155 C2	Mantiqueira, Serra da mts Brazil	
	Mantova Italy see Mantua	
88 C1	Mäntsälä Fin.	
108 B1	Mantua Italy	
86 D3	Manturovo Rus. Fed.	
151 D3	Manuelzinho Brazil	
61 D2	Manui i. Indon.	
54 B1	Manukau N.Z.	
59 D3	Manus Island P.N.G.	
140 B2	Many U.S.A.	
121 C2	Manyame r. Moz./Zimbabwe	
119 D3	Manyara, Lake salt l. Tanz.	
	Manyas Gölü l. Turkey see Kuş Gölü	
87 D4	Manych-Gudilo, Ozero l. Rus. Fed.	
142 B1	Many Farms U.S.A.	
119 D3	Manyoni Tanz.	
106 C2	Manzanares Spain	
146 C2	Manzanillo Cuba	
144 B3	Manzanillo Mex.	
119 C3	Manzanza Dem. Rep. Congo	
69 D1	Manzhouli China	
123 D2	Manzini Swaziland	
115 D3	Mao Chad	
	Maó Spain see Mahón	
59 D3	Maoke, Pegunungan mts Indon.	
123 C2	Maokeng S. Africa	
65 A1	Maokui Shan mt. China	
70 A2	Maomao Shan mt. China	
71 B3	Maoming China	
121 C2	Mapai Moz.	
75 C1	Mapam Yumco l. China	
61 D2	Mapane Indon.	
145 C3	Mapastepec Mex.	
144 B2	Mapimí Mex.	
144 B2	Mapimí, Bolsón de des. Mex.	
64 A3	Mapin i. Phil.	
121 C3	Mapinhane Moz.	
129 D3	Maple Creek Can.	
156 D4	Mapmakers Seamounts sea feature N. Pacific Ocean	
59 D3	Maprik P.N.G.	
123 D1	Mapulanguene Moz.	
121 C3	Maputo Moz.	
123 D2	Maputo r. Moz./S. Africa	
123 C2	Maputsoe Lesotho	
114 A2	Maqteïr reg. Maur.	
75 C2	Maquan He r. China	
120 A1	Maquela do Zombo Angola	
153 B4	Maquinchao Arg.	
137 E2	Maquoketa U.S.A.	
123 C1	Mara S. Africa	
150 C3	Maraã Brazil	
151 E3	Maraba Brazil	
151 D2	Maracá, Ilha de i. Brazil	
150 B1	Maracaibo Venez.	
	Maracaibo, Lago de Venez. see Maracaibo, Lake	
150 B2	Maracaibo, Lake l. Venez.	
154 A2	Maracaju Brazil	
154 A2	Maracaju, Serra de hills Brazil	
150 C1	Maracay Venez.	
115 D2	Marādah Libya	
115 C3	Maradi Niger	
81 C2	Marāgheh Iran	
150 C2	Marahuaca, Cerro mt. Venez.	
151 E3	Marajó, Baía de est. Brazil	
151 D3	Marajó, Ilha de i. Brazil	
79 C2	Marākī Iran	
119 D2	Maralal Kenya	
	Maralbashi China see Bachu	
50 C3	Maralwexi China see Bachu	
142 A2	Marana U.S.A.	
81 C2	Marand Iran	
	Marandellas Zimbabwe see Marondera	
150 B3	Marañón r. Peru	
	Maraş Turkey see Kahramanmaraş	
110 C1	Mărăşeşti Romania	
130 B3	Marathon Can.	
141 D4	Marathon U.S.A.	
106 C2	Marbella Spain	
50 A2	Marble Bar Austr.	
123 C1	Marble Hall S. Africa	
123 D3	Marburg S. Africa	
101 D2	Marburg an der Lahn Ger.	
103 D2	Marcali Hungary	
137 E3	Marceline U.S.A.	
99 D3	March U.K.	
100 B2	Marche-en-Famenne Belgium	
106 B2	Marchena Spain	
152 B3	Mar Chiquita, Laguna l. Arg.	
150 B4	Marcona Peru	
139 E2	Marcy, Mount U.S.A.	
74 B1	Mardan Pak.	
153 C3	Mar del Plata Arg.	
81 C2	Mardin Turkey	
96 B2	Maree, Loch l. U.K.	
51 D1	Mareeba Austr.	
108 B3	Marettimo, Isola i. Sicily Italy	
89 D2	Marevo Rus. Fed.	
142 C2	Marfa U.S.A.	
	Margao India see Madgaon	
50 A3	Margaret River Austr.	
150 E1	Margarita, Isla de i. Venez.	
123 D3	Margate S. Africa	
99 D4	Margate U.K.	
62 A1	Margherita	
	Margherita, Lake Eth. see Lake Abaya	
119 C2	Margherita Peak Dem. Rep. Congo/Uganda	
76 C3	Mărgow, Dasht-e des. Afgh.	
91 C2	Marhanets' Ukr.	
62 A1	Mari Myanmar	
152 B2	Maria Elena Chile	
156 C5	Mariana Trench sea feature N. Pacific Ocean	
	Mariánica, Cordillera mts Spain see Morena, Sierra	
140 B2	Marianna AR U.S.A.	
141 C2	Marianna FL U.S.A.	
102 C2	Mariánské Lázně Czech Rep.	
144 B2	Marías, Islas is Mex.	
78 B3	Ma'rib Yemen	
109 C1	Maribor Slovenia	
	Maricourt Can. see Kangiqsujuaq	
117 B3	Maridi Sudan	
117 A4	Maridi watercourse Sudan	
55 P2	Marie Byrd Land reg. Antarctica	
147 D3	Marie-Galante i. Guadeloupe	
93 G3	Mariehamn Fin.	
122 A1	Mariental Namibia	
93 F4	Mariestad Sweden	
141 D2	Marietta GA U.S.A.	
138 C3	Marietta OH U.S.A.	
105 D3	Marignane France	
83 K3	Marii, Mys pt Rus. Fed.	
88 B3	Marijampolė Lith.	
154 C2	Marília Brazil	
106 B1	Marín Spain	
135 B3	Marina U.S.A.	
109 C3	Marina di Gioiosa Ionica Italy	
88 C3	Mar"ina Horka Belarus	
138 B1	Marinette U.S.A.	
154 B2	Maringá Brazil	
106 B2	Marinha Grande Port.	
138 B2	Marion IN U.S.A.	
138 C3	Marion OH U.S.A.	
141 E2	Marion SC U.S.A.	
138 C3	Marion VA U.S.A.	
141 D2	Marion, Lake U.S.A.	
52 A3	Marion Bay Austr.	
152 B2	Mariscal José Félix Estigarribia Para.	
105 D3	Maritime Alps mts France/Italy	
110 C2	Maritsa r. Bulg.	
91 D2	Mariupol' Ukr.	
117 C4	Marka Somalia	
68 C3	Markam China	
123 C1	Marken S. Africa	
100 B1	Markermeer l. Neth.	
98 C3	Market Rasen U.K.	
98 C3	Market Weighton U.K.	
83 I2	Markha r. Rus. Fed.	
139 D2	Markham Can.	
91 D2	Markivka Ukr.	
118 B2	Markounda C.A.R.	
140 B2	Marksville U.S.A.	
101 D3	Marktheidenfeld Ger.	
101 D3	Marktredwitz Ger.	
100 C2	Marl Ger.	
51 C2	Marla Austr.	
100 A3	Marle France	
143 D2	Marlin U.S.A.	
53 C3	Marlo Austr.	
104 C3	Marmande France	
111 C2	Marmara, Sea of g. Turkey	
	Marmara Denizi g. Turkey see Marmara, Sea of	
111 C3	Marmaris Turkey	
105 C2	Marne r. France	
105 C2	Marne-la-Vallée France	
118 B2	Maro Chad	
121 □D2	Maroantsetra Madag.	
54 B1	Marokopa N.Z.	
101 E1	Maroldsweisach Ger.	
121 □D2	Maromokotro mt. Madag.	
121 C2	Marondera Zimbabwe	
151 D2	Maroni r. Fr. Guiana	
51 E2	Maroochydore Austr.	
61 C2	Maros Indon.	
49 M6	Marotiri is Fr. Polynesia	

118 B1 **Maroua** Cameroon
121 ☐D2 **Marovoay** Madag.
49 N4 **Marquesas Islands** Fr. Polynesia
141 D4 **Marquesas Keys** *is* U.S.A.
155 D2 **Marquês de Valença** Brazil
138 B1 **Marquette** U.S.A.
116 A3 **Marra, Jebel** *mt.* Sudan
123 D2 **Marracuene** Moz.
114 B1 **Marrakech** Morocco
Marrakesh Morocco *see*
Marrakech
116 A3 **Marra Plateau** Sudan
52 A1 **Marree** Austr.
86 F2 **Marresale** Rus. Fed.
121 C2 **Marromeu** Moz.
121 C2 **Marrupa** Moz.
116 B2 **Marsá al 'Alam** Egypt
115 D1 **Marsa al Burayqah** Libya
119 D2 **Marsabit** Kenya
78 A2 **Marsa Delwein** Sudan
108 B3 **Marsala** *Sicily* Italy
116 A1 **Marsá Maṭrūḥ** Egypt
101 D2 **Marsberg** Ger.
108 B2 **Marsciano** Italy
53 C2 **Marsden** Austr.
100 B1 **Marsdiep** *sea chan.* Neth.
105 D3 **Marseille** France
Marseilles France *see* **Marseille**
140 B1 **Marshall** *AR* U.S.A.
137 D2 **Marshall** *MN* U.S.A.
137 E3 **Marshall** *MO* U.S.A.
143 E2 **Marshall** *TX* U.S.A.
48 H2 **Marshall Islands** *country*
N. Pacific Ocean
137 E2 **Marshalltown** U.S.A.
138 A2 **Marshfield** U.S.A.
146 C2 **Marsh Harbour** Bahamas
140 B3 **Marsh Island** U.S.A.
93 G4 **Märsta** Sweden
Martaban, Gulf of Myanmar *see*
Mottama, Gulf of
61 C2 **Martapura** Indon.
60 B2 **Martapura** Indon.
139 E2 **Martha's Vineyard** *i.* U.S.A.
105 D2 **Martigny** Switz.
103 D2 **Martin** Slovakia
136 C2 **Martin** U.S.A.
145 C2 **Martínez** Mex.
141 D2 **Martínez** U.S.A.
155 C1 **Martinho Campos** Brazil
147 D3 **Martinique** *terr.* West Indies
147 D3 **Martinique Passage**
Dominica/Martinique
139 D3 **Martinsburg** U.S.A.
138 D3 **Martinsville** U.S.A.
54 C2 **Marton** N.Z.
107 D1 **Martorell** Spain
106 C2 **Martos** Spain
76 B1 **Martuk** Kazakh.
81 D3 **Marv Dasht** Iran
105 C3 **Marvejols** France
76 C3 **Mary** Turkm.
51 E2 **Maryborough** Austr.
122 B2 **Marydale** S. Africa
139 D3 **Maryland** *state* U.S.A.
98 B2 **Maryport** U.K.
137 D3 **Marysville** U.S.A.
137 E2 **Maryville** *MO* U.S.A.
141 D1 **Maryville** *TN* U.S.A.
119 D3 **Masai Steppe** *plain* Tanz.
119 D3 **Masaka** Uganda
61 C2 **Masalembu Besar** *i.* Indon.
61 D2 **Masamba** Indon.
65 B2 **Masan** S. Korea
119 D4 **Masasi** Tanz.
64 B2 **Masbate** Phil.
64 B2 **Masbate** *i.* Phil.
107 D2 **Mascara** Alg.
155 E1 **Mascote** Brazil
123 C2 **Maseru** Lesotho
Mashaba Zimbabwe *see* **Mashava**
121 C3 **Mashava** Zimbabwe
76 B3 **Mashhad** Iran
123 C3 **Masibambane** S. Africa
79 C3 **Masilah, Wādī al** *watercourse*
Yemen
123 C2 **Masilo** S. Africa
118 B3 **Masi-Manimba** Dem. Rep. Congo
119 D2 **Masindi** Uganda
122 B3 **Masinyusane** S. Africa
Masira, Gulf of Oman *see*
Maṣīrah, Khalīj
79 C3 **Maṣīrah, Khalīj** Oman
81 C2 **Masjed Soleymān** Iran
97 B2 **Mask, Lough** *l.* Ireland
121 ☐E2 **Masoala, Tanjona** *c.* Madag.
137 E2 **Mason City** U.S.A.
Masqaṭ Oman *see* **Muscat**
108 B2 **Massa** Italy
139 E2 **Massachusetts** *state* U.S.A.
139 E2 **Massachusetts Bay** U.S.A.
115 D3 **Massaguet** Chad
115 D3 **Massakory** Chad
121 C3 **Massangena** Moz.
120 A1 **Massango** Angola
116 B3 **Massawa** Eritrea
139 E2 **Massena** U.S.A.
115 D3 **Massenya** Chad
128 A2 **Masset** Can.
105 C2 **Massif Central** *mts* France
115 C3 **Massif de l'Aïr** *mts* Niger
138 C2 **Massillon** U.S.A.
114 B3 **Massina** Mali
121 C3 **Massinga** Moz.
123 D1 **Massingir** Moz.

78 A2 **Mastābah** Saudi Arabia
54 C2 **Masterton** N.Z.
74 B1 **Mastuj** Pak.
74 A2 **Mastung** Pak.
78 A2 **Mastūrah** Saudi Arabia
88 B3 **Masty** Belarus
67 B4 **Masuda** Japan
Masuku Gabon *see* **Franceville**
121 C3 **Masvingo** Zimbabwe
119 D3 **Maswa** Tanz.
118 B3 **Matadi** Dem. Rep. Congo
146 B3 **Matagalpa** Nic.
130 C3 **Matagami** Can.
130 C3 **Matagami, Lac** *l.* Can.
143 D3 **Matagorda Island** U.S.A.
143 D3 **Matagorda Peninsula** U.S.A.
120 A2 **Matala** Angola
114 A3 **Matam** Senegal
54 C1 **Matamata** N.Z.
144 B2 **Matamoros** Mex.
145 C2 **Matamoros** Mex.
119 D3 **Matandu** *r.* Tanz.
131 D3 **Matane** Can.
146 B2 **Matanzas** Cuba
Matapan, Cape *pt* Greece *see*
Tainaro, Akra
73 C4 **Matara** Sri Lanka
61 C2 **Mataram** Indon.
50 C1 **Mataranka** Austr.
107 D1 **Mataró** Spain
123 C3 **Matatiele** S. Africa
54 A3 **Mataura** N.Z.
54 A3 **Mataura** *r.* N.Z.
54 C1 **Matawai** N.Z.
152 B1 **Mategua** Bol.
145 B2 **Matehuala** Mex.
109 C2 **Matera** Italy
108 A3 **Mateur** Tunisia
129 E2 **Matheson Island** Can.
143 D3 **Mathis** U.S.A.
74 B2 **Mathura** India
64 B3 **Mati** Phil.
145 C3 **Matías Romero** Mex.
98 C3 **Matlock** U.K.
150 D4 **Mato Grosso** Brazil
154 B1 **Mato Grosso, Planalto do** *plat.*
Brazil
123 D2 **Matola** Moz.
106 B1 **Matosinhos** Port.
Matou China *see* **Pingguo**
79 C2 **Maṭraḥ** Oman
67 B3 **Matsue** Japan
66 D2 **Matsumae** Japan
67 C3 **Matsumoto** Japan
67 C4 **Matsusaka** Japan
71 C3 **Matsu Tao** *i.* Taiwan
67 B4 **Matsuyama** Japan
130 B2 **Mattagami** *r.* Can.
130 C3 **Mattawa** Can.
105 D2 **Matterhorn** *mt.* Italy/Switz.
134 C2 **Matterhorn** *mt.* U.S.A.
141 D1 **Matthews** U.S.A.
79 C2 **Maṭṭī, Sabkhat** *salt pan*
Saudi Arabia
138 B3 **Mattoon** U.S.A.
150 C2 **Maturín** Venez.
91 D2 **Matveyev Kurgan** Rus. Fed.
123 C2 **Matwabeng** S. Africa
105 C1 **Maubeuge** France
104 C3 **Maubourguet** France
55 E3 **Maud Seamount** *sea feature*
S. Atlantic Ocean
49 L1 **Maui** *i.* U.S.A.
141 D2 **Mauldin** U.S.A.
138 C2 **Maumee** *r.* U.S.A.
61 D2 **Maumere** Indon.
120 B2 **Maun** Botswana
75 C2 **Maunath Bhanjan** India
123 C1 **Maunatlala** Botswana
62 A1 **Maungdaw** Myanmar
75 B2 **Mau Ranipur** India
50 C2 **Maurice, Lake** *salt flat* Austr.
114 A3 **Mauritania** *country* Africa
113 I8 **Mauritius** *country* Indian Ocean
120 B2 **Mavinga** Angola
123 C3 **Mavuya** S. Africa
78 B2 **Māwān, Khashm** *hill* Saudi Arabia
118 B3 **Mawanga** Dem. Rep. Congo
71 B3 **Mawei** China
62 A1 **Mawkmai** Myanmar
62 A1 **Mawlaik** Myanmar
63 A2 **Mawlamyaing** Myanmar
78 B2 **Mawqaq** Saudi Arabia
55 L3 **Mawson Peninsula** Antarctica
78 B3 **Mawza** Yemen
108 A3 **Maxia, Punta** *mt.* Sardinia Italy
121 C3 **Maxixe** Moz.
54 B1 **Maxwell** N.Z.
83 J2 **Maya** *r.* Rus. Fed.
147 C2 **Mayaguana** *i.* Bahamas
147 D3 **Mayagüez** Puerto Rico
81 D2 **Mayamey** Iran
96 B3 **Maybole** U.K.
116 B3 **Maych'ew** Eth.
117 C3 **Maydh** Somalia
100 C2 **Mayen** Ger.
104 B2 **Mayenne** France
104 B2 **Mayenne** *r.* France
128 C2 **Mayerthorpe** Can.
138 B3 **Mayfield** U.S.A.
91 E3 **Maykop** Rus. Fed.
128 A1 **Mayo** Can.
118 B3 **Mayoko** Congo
Mayo Landing Can. *see* **Mayo**
64 B2 **Mayon** *vol.* Phil.

121 D2 **Mayotte** *terr.* Africa
83 J3 **Mayskiy** Rus. Fed.
138 C3 **Maysville** U.S.A.
118 B3 **Mayumba** Gabon
137 D1 **Mayville** U.S.A.
120 B2 **Mazabuka** Zambia
Mazagan Morocco *see* **El Jadida**
151 D3 **Mazagão** Brazil
104 C3 **Mazamet** France
74 B1 **Mazar** China
108 B3 **Mazara del Vallo** *Sicily* Italy
77 C3 **Mazār-e Sharīf** Afgh.
107 C2 **Mazarrón** Spain
107 C2 **Mazarrón, Golfo de** *b.* Spain
144 A2 **Mazatán** Mex.
146 A3 **Mazatenango** Guat.
144 B2 **Mazatlán** Mex.
88 B2 **Mažeikiai** Lith.
88 B2 **Mazirbe** Latvia
121 B3 **Mazunga** Zimbabwe
103 E1 **Mazurskie, Pojezierze** *reg.* Pol.
88 C3 **Mazyr** Belarus
123 D2 **Mbabane** Swaziland
118 B2 **Mbaïki** C.A.R.
118 B2 **Mbakaou, Lac de** *l.* Cameroon
121 C1 **Mbala** Zambia
121 B3 **Mbalabala** Zimbabwe
119 D2 **Mbale** Uganda
118 B2 **Mbalmayo** Cameroon
118 B3 **Mbandaka** Dem. Rep. Congo
118 B2 **Mbandjok** Cameroon
118 A2 **Mbanga** Cameroon
120 A1 **M'banza Congo** Angola
118 B3 **Mbanza-Ngungu** Dem. Rep. Congo
119 D3 **Mbarara** Uganda
118 B2 **Mbé** Cameroon
119 D3 **Mbeya** Tanz.
119 D4 **Mbinga** Tanz.
119 D3 **Mbizi Mountains** Tanz.
119 C2 **Mboki** C.A.R.
118 B2 **Mbomo** Congo
118 B2 **Mbouda** Cameroon
114 A3 **Mbour** Senegal
114 A3 **Mbout** Maur.
118 C3 **Mbuji-Mayi** Dem. Rep. Congo
119 D3 **Mbuyuni** Tanz.
139 F1 **McAdam** Can.
143 D2 **McAlester** U.S.A.
143 D3 **McAllen** U.S.A.
128 B2 **McBride** Can.
134 C2 **McCall** U.S.A.
143 C2 **McCamey** U.S.A.
126 F2 **McClintock Channel** Can.
126 E2 **McClure Strait** Can.
140 B2 **McComb** U.S.A.
136 C2 **McConaughy, Lake** U.S.A.
136 C2 **McCook** U.S.A.
134 C2 **McDermitt** U.S.A.
159 E7 **McDonald Islands** Indian Ocean
134 D1 **McDonald Peak** U.S.A.
135 D3 **McGill** U.S.A.
126 B2 **McGrath** U.S.A.
134 D1 **McGuire, Mount** U.S.A.
121 C2 **Mchinji** Malawi
140 C1 **McKenzie** U.S.A.
51 D2 **McKinlay** Austr.
134 B2 **McKinleyville** U.S.A.
128 C2 **McLennan** Can.
128 B2 **McLeod Lake** Can.
134 B1 **McMinnville** *OR* U.S.A.
140 C1 **McMinnville** *TN* U.S.A.
137 D3 **McPherson** U.S.A.
128 C1 **McTavish Arm** *b.* Can.
123 C3 **Mdantsane** S. Africa
135 D3 **Mead, Lake** *resr* U.S.A.
136 C3 **Meade** U.S.A.
129 D2 **Meadow Lake** Can.
138 C2 **Meadville** U.S.A.
66 D2 **Meaken-dake** *vol.* Japan
106 B1 **Mealhada** Port.
131 E2 **Mealy Mountains** Can.
128 C2 **Meander River** Can.
78 A2 **Mecca** Saudi Arabia
139 D3 **Mechanicsville** U.S.A.
100 B2 **Mechelen** Belgium
100 B2 **Mechelen** Neth.
100 C2 **Mechernich** Ger.
100 C2 **Meckenheim** Ger.
101 E1 **Mecklenburgische Seenplatte**
reg. Ger.
106 B1 **Meda** Port.
60 A1 **Medan** Indon.
153 B4 **Medanosa, Punta** *pt* Arg.
73 C4 **Medawachchiya** Sri Lanka
107 D2 **Médéa** Alg.
150 B2 **Medellín** Col.
115 D1 **Medenine** Tunisia
134 B2 **Medford** U.S.A.
110 C2 **Medgidia** Romania
110 B1 **Mediaş** Romania
136 B2 **Medicine Bow Mountains** U.S.A.
136 B2 **Medicine Bow Peak** U.S.A.
129 C2 **Medicine Hat** Can.
137 D3 **Medicine Lodge** U.S.A.
155 D1 **Medina** Brazil
78 A2 **Medina** Saudi Arabia
106 C1 **Medinaceli** Spain
106 C1 **Medina del Campo** Spain
106 B1 **Medina de Rioseco** Spain
75 C2 **Medinipur** India
84 E5 **Mediterranean Sea**
129 C2 **Medley** Can.
87 E3 **Mednogorsk** Rus. Fed.
62 A1 **Mêdog** China
88 B2 **Medvėgalio kalnis** *hill* Lith.

83 L2 **Medvezh'i, Ostrova** *is* Rus. Fed.
86 C2 **Medvezh'yegorsk** Rus. Fed.
50 A2 **Meekatharra** Austr.
136 B2 **Meeker** U.S.A.
74 B2 **Meerut** India
100 A2 **Meetkerke** Belgium
119 C2 **Mēga** Eth.
60 B2 **Mega** *i.* Indon.
119 D2 **Mega Escarpment** Eth./Kenya
111 B3 **Megalopoli** Greece
75 ☐U2 **Meghalaya** *state* India
75 C2 **Meghasani** *mt.* India
111 C3 **Megisti** *i.* Greece
92 I1 **Mehamn** Norway
50 A2 **Meharry, Mount** Austr.
137 E3 **Mehlville** U.S.A.
79 C2 **Mehrān** *watercourse* Iran
74 B1 **Mehtar Lām** Afgh.
119 D3 **Meia Meia** Tanz.
154 C1 **Meia Ponte** *r.* Brazil
118 B2 **Meiganga** Cameroon
65 B1 **Meihekou** China
Meijiang China *see* **Ningdu**
62 A1 **Meiktila** Myanmar
101 E2 **Meiningen** Ger.
102 C1 **Meißen** Ger.
Meixian China *see* **Meizhou**
71 B3 **Meizhou** China
152 B3 **Mejicana** *mt.* Arg.
152 A2 **Mejillones** Chile
118 B2 **Mékambo** Gabon
65 B1 **Mek'elē** Eth.
114 C2 **Mekerrhane, Sebkha** *salt pan* Alg.
114 B1 **Meknès** Morocco
63 B2 **Mekong** *r.* Asia
63 B3 **Mekong, Mouths of the** Vietnam
60 B1 **Melaka** Malaysia
156 D6 **Melanesia** *is* Pacific Ocean
156 D5 **Melanesian Basin** *sea feature*
Pacific Ocean
53 B3 **Melbourne** Austr.
141 D3 **Melbourne** U.S.A.
108 A2 **Mele, Capo** *c.* Italy
Melekess Rus. Fed. *see*
Dimitrovgrad
89 F2 **Melenki** Rus. Fed.
131 C2 **Mélèzes, Rivière aux** *r.* Can.
115 D3 **Mélfi** Chad
109 C2 **Melfi** Italy
129 D2 **Melfort** Can.
92 F3 **Melhus** Norway
106 B1 **Melide** Spain
114 B1 **Melilla** N. Africa
129 C3 **Melita** Can.
91 D2 **Melitopol'** Ukr.
119 D2 **Melka Guba** Eth.
101 D1 **Melle** Ger.
93 F4 **Mellerud** Sweden
101 E2 **Mellrichstadt** Ger.
101 D1 **Mellum** *i.* Ger.
123 D2 **Melmoth** S. Africa
152 C3 **Melo** Uru.
115 C1 **Melrhir, Chott** *salt l.* Alg.
96 C1 **Melrose** U.K.
Melsetter Zimbabwe *see*
Chimanimani
52 B3 **Melton** Austr.
99 C3 **Melton Mowbray** U.K.
105 C2 **Melun** France
129 D2 **Melville** Can.
51 D1 **Melville, Cape** Austr.
131 E2 **Melville, Lake** Can.
50 C1 **Melville Island** Austr.
126 E1 **Melville Island** Can.
127 G2 **Melville Peninsula** Can.
61 C2 **Memboro** Indon.
102 C2 **Memmingen** Ger.
60 B1 **Mempawah** Indon.
80 B3 **Memphis** *tourist site* Egypt
140 B1 **Memphis** *TN* U.S.A.
143 C2 **Memphis** *TX* U.S.A.
91 C1 **Mena** Ukr.
140 B2 **Mena** U.S.A.
121 ☐D3 **Menabe** *mts* Madag.
114 C3 **Ménaka** Mali
Mènam Khong *r.* Laos/Thai. *see*
Mekong
105 C3 **Mende** France
117 B4 **Mendebo Mountains** Eth.
116 B3 **Mendefera** Eritrea
160 B1 **Mendeleyev Ridge** *sea feature*
Arctic Ocean
145 C2 **Méndez** Mex.
117 B4 **Mendī** Eth.
59 D3 **Mendi** P.N.G.
99 B3 **Mendip Hills** U.K.
138 B2 **Mendota** U.S.A.
153 B3 **Mendoza** Arg.
111 C3 **Menemen** Turkey
100 A2 **Menen** Belgium
70 B2 **Mengcheng** China
60 B2 **Menggala** Indon.
71 A3 **Mengzi** China
131 D2 **Menihek** Can.
52 B2 **Menindee** Austr.
52 B2 **Menindee Lake** Austr.
52 A3 **Meningie** Austr.
104 C2 **Mennecy** France
138 B1 **Menominee** U.S.A.
120 A2 **Menongue** Angola
Menorca *i.* Spain *see* **Minorca**
61 C1 **Mensalong** Indon.
60 A1 **Mentawai, Kepulauan** *is* Indon.
60 B2 **Mentok** Indon.
61 C1 **Menyapa, Gunung** *mt.* Indon.

108 A3 Menzel Bourguiba Tunisia
50 B2 Menzies Austr.
144 B2 Meoqui Mex.
100 C1 Meppel Neth.
100 C1 Meppen Ger.
121 C3 Mepuze Moz.
123 C2 Meqheleng S. Africa
138 B2 Mequon U.S.A.
108 B1 Merano Italy
59 D3 Merauke Indon.
52 B2 Merbein Austr.
Merca Somalia see Marka
107 D2 Mercadal Spain
135 B3 Merced U.S.A.
152 C2 Mercedes Arg.
143 D3 Mercedes U.S.A.
127 H2 Mercy, Cape Can.
143 C1 Meredith, Lake U.S.A.
91 D2 Merefa Ukr.
116 A3 Merga Oasis Sudan
63 A2 Mergui Archipelago is Myanmar
110 C2 Meriç r. Greece/Turkey
111 C2 Meriç Turkey
145 D2 Mérida Mex.
106 B2 Mérida Spain
150 B2 Mérida Venez.
147 C4 Mérida, Cordillera de mts Venez.
134 C2 Meridian ID U.S.A.
140 C2 Meridian MS U.S.A.
143 D2 Meridian TX U.S.A.
104 B3 Mérignac France
93 H3 Merikarvia Fin.
53 C3 Merimbula Austr.
88 B3 Merkinė Lith.
116 B3 Merowe Sudan
50 A3 Merredin Austr.
96 B3 Merrick hill U.K.
138 B1 Merrill U.S.A.
138 B2 Merrillville U.S.A.
136 C2 Merriman U.S.A.
128 C2 Merritt Can.
53 C2 Merrygoen Austr.
116 C3 Mersa Fatma Eritrea
100 C3 Mersch Lux.
101 E2 Merseburg (Saale) Ger.
98 B2 Mersey r. U.K.
80 B2 Mersin Turkey
60 B1 Mersing Malaysia
99 D4 Mers-les-Bains France
74 B2 Merta India
99 B4 Merthyr Tydfil U.K.
119 D2 Merti Plateau Kenya
106 B2 Mértola Port.
76 B2 Mertvyy Kultuk, Sor dry lake Kazakh.
119 D3 Meru vol. Tanz.
122 B3 Merweville S. Africa
80 B1 Merzifon Turkey
100 C3 Merzig Ger.
142 A2 Mesa AZ U.S.A.
142 C2 Mesa NM U.S.A.
137 E1 Mesabi Range hills U.S.A.
109 C2 Mesagne Italy
142 B2 Mescalero U.S.A.
143 C2 Mescalero Ridge U.S.A.
101 D2 Meschede Ger.
89 E3 Meshchovsk Rus. Fed.
Meshed Iran see Mashhad
91 E2 Meshkovskaya Rus. Fed.
142 B2 Mesilla U.S.A.
111 B2 Mesimeri Greece
111 B3 Mesolongi Greece
115 C1 Messaad Alg.
121 D2 Messalo r. Moz.
109 C3 Messina Sicily Italy
109 C3 Messina, Strait of str. Italy
Messina, Stretta di Italy see Messina, Strait of
111 B3 Messini Greece
111 B3 Messiniakos Kolpos b. Greece
111 B2 Mesta r. Bulg.
Mesta r. Greece see Nestos
150 C2 Meta r. Col./Venez.
130 C3 Métabetchouan Can.
127 H2 Meta Incognita Peninsula Can.
140 B3 Metairie U.S.A.
152 B2 Metán Arg.
111 B3 Methoni Greece
109 C2 Metković Croatia
121 C2 Metoro Moz.
60 B2 Metro Indon.
100 C3 Mettlach Ger.
135 C3 Mettler U.S.A.
117 B4 Metu Eth.
105 D2 Metz France
100 B2 Meuse r. Belgium/France
143 D2 Mexia U.S.A.
144 A1 Mexicali Mex.
144 B2 Mexico country Central America
México Mex. see Mexico City
137 E3 Mexico U.S.A.
125 I7 Mexico, Gulf of Mex./U.S.A.
145 C3 Mexico City Mex.
81 D2 Meybod Iran
101 F1 Meyenburg Ger.
76 C3 Meymaneh Afgh.
83 M2 Meynypil'gyno Rus. Fed.
86 D2 Mezen' Rus. Fed.
86 D2 Mezen' r. Rus. Fed.
86 E1 Mezhdusharskiy, Ostrov i. Rus. Fed.
103 E2 Mezőtúr Hungary
144 B2 Mezquital r. Mex.
144 B2 Mezquitic Mex.
88 C2 Mežvidi Latvia

121 C2 Mfuwe Zambia
89 D3 Mglin Rus. Fed.
123 D2 Mhlume Swaziland
74 B2 Mhow India
145 C3 Miahuatlán Mex.
106 B2 Miajadas Spain
141 D3 Miami FL U.S.A.
143 E1 Miami OK U.S.A.
141 D3 Miami Beach U.S.A.
81 C2 Miandowāb Iran
121 □D2 Miandrivazo Madag.
81 C2 Miāneh Iran
71 A3 Mianning China
74 B1 Mianwali Pak.
Mianyang China see Xiantao
70 A2 Mianyang China
121 □D2 Miarinarivo Madag.
87 F3 Miass Rus. Fed.
103 D1 Miastko Pol.
128 C2 Mica Creek Can.
103 E2 Michalovce Slovakia
138 B1 Michigan state U.S.A.
138 B2 Michigan, Lake U.S.A.
138 B2 Michigan City U.S.A.
138 B1 Michipicoten Bay Can.
130 B3 Michipicoten Island Can.
130 B3 Michipicoten River Can.
Michurin Bulg. see Tsarevo
89 F3 Michurinsk Rus. Fed.
156 D5 Micronesia is Pacific Ocean
48 G3 Micronesia, Federated States of country N. Pacific Ocean
158 E6 Mid-Atlantic Ridge sea feature Atlantic Ocean
100 A2 Middelburg Neth.
123 C3 Middelburg E. Cape S. Africa
123 C2 Middelburg Mpumalanga S. Africa
100 B2 Middelharnis Neth.
134 B2 Middle Alkali Lake U.S.A.
73 D3 Middle Andaman i. India
Middle Congo country Africa see Congo
136 D2 Middle Loup r. U.S.A.
138 C3 Middlesboro U.S.A.
98 C2 Middlesbrough U.K.
139 E2 Middletown NY U.S.A.
138 C3 Middletown OH U.S.A.
78 B3 Midī Yemen
130 C3 Midland Can.
138 C2 Midland MI U.S.A.
143 C2 Midland TX U.S.A.
97 B3 Midleton Ireland
Midnapore India see Medinipur
94 B1 Miðvágur Faroe Is
57 I/ Midway Islands terr. N. Pacific Ocean
Midway Oman see Thamarīt
109 D2 Midzhur mt. Bulg./Serb. and Mont.
103 E1 Mielec Pol.
110 C1 Miercurea-Ciuc Romania
106 B1 Mieres Spain
101 E1 Mieste Ger.
75 D1 Migriggyangzham Co l. China
145 C3 Miguel Alemán, Presa resr Mex.
144 B2 Miguel Auza Mex.
144 B2 Miguel Hidalgo, Presa resr Mex.
63 A2 Migyaunglaung Myanmar
67 B4 Mihara Japan
89 E3 Mikhaylov Rus. Fed.
Mikhaylovgrad Bulg. see Montana
66 B2 Mikhaylovka Rus. Fed.
Mikhaylovka Rus. Fed. see Kimovsk
87 D3 Mikhaylovka Rus. Fed.
77 D1 Mikhaylovskiy Rus. Fed.
93 I3 Mikkeli Fin.
86 E2 Mikun' Rus. Fed.
67 C3 Mikuni-sanmyaku mts Japan
67 C4 Mikura-jima i. Japan
73 B4 Miladhunmadulu Atoll Maldives
108 A1 Milan Italy
Milan Italy see Milan
121 C2 Milange Moz.
111 C3 Milas Turkey
137 D1 Milbank U.S.A.
99 D3 Mildenhall U.K.
52 B2 Mildura Austr.
71 A3 Mile China
136 B1 Miles City U.S.A.
139 D3 Milford DE U.S.A.
135 D3 Milford UT U.S.A.
99 A4 Milford Haven U.K.
54 A2 Milford Sound N.Z.
Milḩ, Baḩr al l. Iraq see Razāzah, Buḩayrat ar
107 D2 Miliana Alg.
50 C1 Milikapiti Austr.
51 C1 Milingimbi Austr.
134 E1 Milk r. U.S.A.
116 B3 Milk, Wadi el watercourse Sudan
83 L3 Mil'kovo Rus. Fed.
128 C3 Milk River Can.
105 C3 Millau France
141 D2 Milledgeville U.S.A.
137 E1 Mille Lacs lakes U.S.A.
130 A3 Mille Lacs, Lac des l. Can.
Millennium Island Kiribati see Caroline Island
137 D2 Miller U.S.A.
91 E2 Millerovo Rus. Fed.
52 A2 Millers Creek Austr.
96 B3 Milleur Point U.K.
52 B3 Millicent Austr.
140 C1 Millington U.S.A.
139 F1 Millinocket U.S.A.

55 J3 Mill Island Antarctica
53 D1 Millmerran Austr.
98 B2 Millom U.K.
136 B2 Mills U.S.A.
128 C1 Mills Lake Can.
111 B3 Milos i. Greece
89 E3 Miloslavskoye Rus. Fed.
91 E2 Milove Ukr.
52 B1 Milparinka Austr.
54 A3 Milton N.Z.
99 C3 Milton Keynes U.K.
138 B2 Milwaukee U.S.A.
158 C3 Milwaukee Deep sea feature Caribbean Sea
104 B3 Mimizan France
118 B3 Mimongo Gabon
155 D2 Mimoso do Sul Brazil
79 C2 Mināb Iran
61 D1 Minahasa, Semenanjung pen. Indon.
Minahassa Peninsula Indon. see Minahasa, Semenanjung
79 C2 Mina Jebel Ali U.A.E.
Minaker Can. see Prophet River
60 B1 Minas Indon.
153 C3 Minas Uru.
79 B2 Mīnā' Sa'ūd Kuwait
145 C3 Minas, Cerro de las mt. Hond.
155 D1 Minas Novas Brazil
145 C3 Minatitlán Mex.
62 A1 Minbu Myanmar
64 B3 Mindanao i. Phil.
52 B2 Mindarie Austr.
101 D1 Minden Ger.
140 B2 Minden LA U.S.A.
137 D2 Minden NE U.S.A.
64 B2 Mindoro i. Phil.
64 A2 Mindoro Strait Phil.
118 B3 Mindouli Congo
99 B4 Minehead U.K.
154 B1 Mineiros Brazil
143 D2 Mineral Wells U.S.A.
75 C1 Minfeng China
119 C4 Minga Dem. Rep. Congo
81 C1 Mingäçevir Azer.
131 D2 Mingan Can.
52 B2 Mingary Austr.
70 B2 Mingguang China
62 A1 Mingin Myanmar
107 C2 Minglanilla Spain
119 D4 Mingoyo Tanz.
69 E1 Mingshui China
96 A2 Mingulay i. U.K.
71 B3 Mingxi China
Mingzhou China see Suide
70 A2 Minhe China
41 I/ Minicoy r. India
50 A2 Minilya Austr.
114 B3 Mininian Côte d'Ivoire
131 D2 Minipi Lake Can.
130 A2 Miniss Lake Can.
52 A2 Minlaton Austr.
115 C4 Minna Nigeria
137 E2 Minneapolis U.S.A.
129 E2 Minnedosa Can.
137 E2 Minnesota r. U.S.A.
137 E1 Minnesota state U.S.A.
106 B1 Miño r. Port./Spain
107 D1 Minorca i. Spain
136 C1 Minot U.S.A.
88 C3 Minsk Belarus
103 E1 Mińsk Mazowiecki Pol.
96 D2 Mintlaw U.K.
131 D3 Minto Can.
130 C1 Minto, Lac l. Can.
68 C1 Minusinsk Rus. Fed.
62 A1 Minutang India
70 A2 Minxian China
155 D1 Mirabela Brazil
155 D1 Miralta Brazil
131 D2 Miramichi Can.
111 C3 Mirampelou, Kolpos b. Greece
152 C2 Miranda Brazil
152 C1 Miranda r. Brazil
Miranda Moz. see Macaloge
106 C1 Miranda de Ebro Spain
106 B1 Mirandela Port.
154 B2 Mirandópolis Brazil
154 B2 Mirante, Serra do hills Brazil
79 C3 Mirbāţ Oman
61 C1 Miri Sarawak Malaysia
153 C3 Mirim, Lagoa l. Brazil
79 D2 Mīrjāveh Iran
89 D3 Mirnyy Rus. Fed.
83 I2 Mirnyy Rus. Fed.
101 F1 Mirow Ger.
74 A2 Mirpur Khas Pak.
Mirtoan Sea Greece see Mirtoö Pelagos
111 B3 Mirtoö Pelagos sea Greece
65 B2 Miryang S. Korea
Mirzachirla Turkm. see Murzechirla
Mirzachul Uzbek. see Guliston
75 C2 Mirzapur India
77 E3 Misalay China
66 B1 Mishan China
51 E3 Misima Island P.N.G.
146 B3 Miskitos, Cayos is Nic.
103 E2 Miskolc Hungary
59 C3 Misoöl i. Indon.
115 D1 Mişrātah Libya
130 B1 Missinaibi r. Can.
130 B3 Missinaibi Lake Can.
128 B3 Mission Can.

130 B2 Missisa Lake Can.
140 C3 Mississippi r. Can.
140 C3 Mississippi state U.S.A.
140 C3 Mississippi Delta U.S.A.
140 C2 Mississippi Sound sea chan. U.S.A.
Missolonghi Greece see Mesolongi
134 D1 Missoula U.S.A.
137 E3 Missouri r. U.S.A.
137 E3 Missouri state U.S.A.
130 C3 Mistassibi r. Can.
130 C3 Mistassini, Lac l. Can.
131 D2 Mistastin Lake Can.
103 D2 Mistelbach Austria
131 D2 Mistinibi, Lac l. Can.
130 C2 Mistissini Can.
51 D2 Mitchell Austr.
51 D1 Mitchell r. Austr.
136 C2 Mitchell NE U.S.A.
137 D2 Mitchell SD U.S.A.
97 B2 Mitchelstown Ireland
74 A2 Mithi Pak.
67 D3 Mito Japan
119 D3 Mitole Tanz.
53 D2 Mittagong Austr.
101 E2 Mittelhausen Ger.
101 D1 Mittellandkanal canal Ger.
101 F3 Mitterteich Ger.
Mittimatalik Can. see Pond Inlet
150 B2 Mitú Col.
119 C4 Mitumba, Chaîne des mts Dem. Rep. Congo
119 C3 Mitumba, Monts mts Dem. Rep. Congo
119 C3 Mitwaba Dem. Rep. Congo
118 B3 Mitzic Gabon
78 B2 Miyah, Wādī al watercourse Saudi Arabia
67 C4 Miyake-jima i. Japan
66 D3 Miyako Japan
67 B4 Miyakonojō Japan
76 B2 Miyaly Kazakh.
Miyang China see Mile
67 B4 Miyazaki Japan
67 C3 Miyazu Japan
115 D1 Mizdah Libya
97 B3 Mizen Head hd Ireland
90 A2 Mizhhir"ya Ukr.
Mizo Hills state India see Mizoram
75 D2 Mizoram state India
93 G4 Mjölby Sweden
93 F3 Mjøsa l. Norway
119 D3 Mkomazi Tanz.
103 C1 Mladá Boleslav Czech Rep.
109 D2 Mladenovac Serb. and Mont.
103 E1 Mława Pol.
109 C2 Mljet i. Croatia
123 C3 Mlungisi S. Africa
90 B1 Mlyniv Ukr.
123 C2 Mmabatho S. Africa
123 C2 Mmathethe Botswana
93 E3 Mo Norway
135 E3 Moab U.S.A.
123 D2 Moamba Moz.
54 B2 Moana N.Z.
118 B3 Moanda Gabon
97 C2 Moate Ireland
119 C3 Moba Dem. Rep. Congo
118 C2 Mobayi-Mbongo Dem. Rep. Congo
137 E3 Moberly U.S.A.
140 C2 Mobile U.S.A.
140 C2 Mobile Bay U.S.A.
140 C2 Mobile Point U.S.A.
136 C1 Mobridge U.S.A.
Mobutu, Lake Dem. Rep. Congo/Uganda see Albert, Lake
Mobutu Sese Seko, Lake Dem. Rep. Congo/Uganda see Albert, Lake
121 C2 Moçambicano, Planalto plat. Moz.
121 D2 Moçambique Moz.
Moçâmedes Angola see Namibe
62 B1 Mộc Châu Vietnam
78 B3 Mocha Yemen
123 C1 Mochudi Botswana
121 D2 Mocimboa da Praia Moz.
101 D3 Möckmühl Ger.
150 B2 Mocoa Col.
154 C2 Mococa Brazil
144 B2 Mocorito Mex.
144 B1 Moctezuma Mex.
145 C2 Moctezuma Mex.
144 B2 Moctezuma Mex.
121 C2 Mocuba Moz.
105 D2 Modane France
122 B2 Modder r. S. Africa
108 B2 Modena Italy
135 B3 Modesto U.S.A.
109 B3 Modica Sicily Italy
123 C1 Modimolle S. Africa
53 C3 Moe Austr.
Moero, Lake Dem. Rep. Congo/Zambia see Mweru, Lake
100 C2 Moers Ger.
96 C3 Moffat U.K.
117 C4 Mogadishu Somalia
Mogador Morocco see Essaouira
106 B1 Mogadouro, Serra de mts Port.
123 C1 Mogalakwena r. S. Africa
62 A1 Mogaung Myanmar
Mogilev Belarus see Mahilyow
154 C2 Mogi-Mirim Brazil
83 I3 Mogocha Rus. Fed.

Mogoditshane

214

123 C1 **Mogoditshane** Botswana
62 A1 **Mogok** Myanmar
142 A2 **Mogollon Plateau** U.S.A.
103 D2 **Mohács** Hungary
123 C3 **Mohale's Hoek** Lesotho
107 D2 **Mohammadia** Alg.
142 A2 **Mohave Mountains** U.S.A.
139 E2 **Mohawk** *r.* U.S.A.
62 A1 **Mohnyin** Myanmar
119 D3 **Mohoro** Tanz.
90 B2 **Mohyliv Podil's'kyy** Ukr.
123 C1 **Moijabana** Botswana
110 C1 **Moinești** Romania
Mointy Kazakh. *see* **Moyynty**
92 F2 **Mo i Rana** Norway
88 C2 **Mõisaküla** Estonia
104 C3 **Moissac** France
135 C3 **Mojave** U.S.A.
135 C3 **Mojave Desert** U.S.A.
62 B1 **Mojiang** China
155 C2 **Moji das Cruzes** Brazil
154 C2 **Moji-Guaçu** *r.* Brazil
109 C2 **Mojkovac** Serb. and Mont.
54 B1 **Mokau** N.Z.
123 C2 **Mokhotlong** Lesotho
83 J2 **Mokhsogollokh** Rus. Fed.
118 B1 **Mokolo** Cameroon
123 C1 **Mokopane** S. Africa
65 B3 **Mokp'o** S. Korea
109 C2 **Mola di Bari** Italy
145 C2 **Molango** Mex.
Moldavia *country* Europe *see* **Moldova**
Moldavskaya S.S.R. *admin. reg.* Europe *see* **Moldova**
93 E3 **Molde** Norway
90 B2 **Moldova** *country* Europe
110 B2 **Moldova Nouă** Romania
110 B1 **Moldoveanu, Vârful** *mt.* Romania
110 B1 **Moldovei, Podișul** *plat.* Romania
90 B2 **Moldovei Centrale, Podișul** *plat.* Moldova
123 C1 **Molepolole** Botswana
88 C2 **Molėtai** Lith.
109 C2 **Molfetta** Italy
Molière Alg. *see* **Bordj Bounaama**
107 C1 **Molina de Aragón** Spain
107 C2 **Molina de Segura** Spain
119 D3 **Moliro** Dem. Rep. Congo
150 B4 **Mollendo** Peru
93 F4 **Mölnlycke** Sweden
91 D2 **Molochna** *r.* Ukr.
89 E2 **Molokovo** Rus. Fed.
53 C2 **Molong** Austr.
122 B2 **Molopo** *watercourse* Botswana/S. Africa
Molotov Rus. Fed. *see* **Perm'**
Molotovsk Rus. Fed. *see* **Severodvinsk**
Molotovsk Rus. Fed. *see* **Nolinsk**
118 B2 **Moloundou** Cameroon
59 C3 **Moluccas** *is* Indon.
Molucca Sea Indon. *see* **Laut Maluku**
52 B2 **Momba** Austr.
119 D3 **Mombasa** Kenya
154 B1 **Mombuca, Serra da** *hills* Brazil
111 C2 **Momchilgrad** Bulg.
93 F4 **Møn** *i.* Denmark
105 D3 **Monaco** *country* Europe
96 B2 **Monadhliath Mountains** U.K.
97 C1 **Monaghan** Ireland
143 C2 **Monahans** U.S.A.
147 D3 **Mona Passage** Dom. Rep./Puerto Rico
120 A1 **Mona Quimbundo** Angola
Monastir Macedonia *see* **Bitola**
89 D3 **Monastyrshchina** Rus. Fed.
90 B2 **Monastyryshche** Ukr.
118 B2 **Monatélé** Cameroon
66 D2 **Monbetsu** Japan
108 A1 **Moncalieri** Italy
86 C2 **Monchegorsk** Rus. Fed.
100 C2 **Mönchengladbach** Ger.
144 B2 **Monclova** Mex.
131 D3 **Moncton** Can.
106 B1 **Mondego** *r.* Port.
118 C2 **Mondjamboli** Dem. Rep. Congo
123 D2 **Mondlo** S. Africa
108 A2 **Mondovì** Italy
106 C1 **Mondragón-Arrasate** Spain
111 B3 **Monemvasia** Greece
66 D1 **Moneron, Ostrov** *i.* Rus. Fed.
139 D1 **Monet** Can.
137 E3 **Monett** U.S.A.
108 B1 **Monfalcone** Italy
106 B1 **Monforte** Spain
119 D2 **Mongbwalu** Dem. Rep. Congo
62 B1 **Mông Cai** Vietnam
62 A1 **Mong Hang** Myanmar
Monghyr India *see* **Munger**
75 C2 **Mongla** Bangl.
62 B1 **Mong Lin** Myanmar
62 A1 **Mong Nawng** Myanmar
115 D3 **Mongo** Chad
68 C1 **Mongolia** *country* Asia
74 B1 **Mongora** Pak.
62 A1 **Mong Pawk** Myanmar
62 A1 **Mong Ping** Myanmar
120 B2 **Mongu** Zambia
135 C3 **Monitor Range** *mts* U.S.A.
103 E1 **Mońki** Pol.
99 B4 **Monmouth** U.K.
114 C4 **Mono** *r.* Togo
135 C3 **Mono Lake** U.S.A.
109 C2 **Monopoli** Italy
107 C1 **Monreal del Campo** Spain
140 B2 **Monroe** *LA* U.S.A.
138 C2 **Monroe** *MI* U.S.A.
138 B2 **Monroe** *WI* U.S.A.
140 C2 **Monroeville** U.S.A.
114 A4 **Monrovia** Liberia
100 A2 **Mons** Belgium
155 E1 **Monsarás, Ponta de** *pt* Brazil
100 C2 **Montabaur** Ger.
122 B3 **Montagu** S. Africa
109 C3 **Montalto** *mt.* Italy
110 B2 **Montana** Bulg.
134 E1 **Montana** *state* U.S.A.
105 C2 **Montargis** France
104 C3 **Montauban** France
139 E2 **Montauk Point** U.S.A.
123 C2 **Mont-aux-Sources** *mt.* Lesotho
105 C2 **Montbard** France
105 D2 **Montbéliard** France
105 D2 **Mont Blanc** *mt.* France/Italy
105 C2 **Montbrison** France
100 B3 **Montcornet** France
104 B3 **Mont-de-Marsan** France
104 C2 **Montdidier** France
151 D3 **Monte Alegre** Brazil
154 C1 **Monte Alegre de Minas** Brazil
139 E1 **Montebello** Can.
154 B3 **Montecarlo** Arg.
105 D3 **Monte-Carlo** Monaco
154 C1 **Monte Carmelo** Brazil
152 C3 **Monte Caseros** Arg.
123 C1 **Monte Christo** S. Africa
108 B2 **Montecristo, Isola di** *i.* Italy
146 C3 **Montego Bay** Jamaica
105 C3 **Montélimar** France
109 C2 **Montella** Italy
145 C2 **Montemorelos** Mex.
104 B2 **Montendre** France
Montenegro *aut. rep.* Serb. and Mont. *see* **Crna Gora**
121 C2 **Montepuez** Moz.
108 B2 **Montepulciano** Italy
135 B3 **Monterey** U.S.A.
135 B3 **Monterey Bay** U.S.A.
150 B2 **Montería** Col.
152 B1 **Montero** Bol.
145 B2 **Monterrey** Mex.
109 C2 **Montesano sulla Marcellana** Italy
109 C2 **Monte Sant'Angelo** Italy
151 F4 **Monte Santo** Brazil
108 A2 **Monte Santu, Capo di** *c. Sardinia* Italy
155 D1 **Montes Claros** Brazil
153 C3 **Montevideo** Uru.
137 D2 **Montevideo** U.S.A.
136 B3 **Monte Vista** U.S.A.
140 C2 **Montgomery** U.S.A.
100 B3 **Monthermé** France
105 D2 **Monthey** Switz.
140 B2 **Monticello** *AR* U.S.A.
141 D2 **Monticello** *FL* U.S.A.
135 E3 **Monticello** *UT* U.S.A.
104 C2 **Montignac** France
100 B2 **Montignies-le-Tilleul** Belgium
106 B2 **Montijo** Port.
106 B2 **Montijo** Spain
106 C2 **Montilla** Spain
154 B1 **Montividiu** Brazil
131 D3 **Mont-Joli** Can.
130 C3 **Mont-Laurier** Can.
104 C2 **Montluçon** France
131 C3 **Montmagny** Can.
104 C2 **Montmorillon** France
51 E2 **Monto** Austr.
134 D2 **Montpelier** *ID* U.S.A.
139 E2 **Montpelier** *VT* U.S.A.
105 C3 **Montpellier** France
130 C3 **Montréal** Can.
129 D2 **Montreal Lake** Can.
129 D2 **Montreal Lake** *l.* Can.
99 D4 **Montreuil** France
105 D2 **Montreux** Switz.
96 C2 **Montrose** U.K.
136 B3 **Montrose** U.S.A.
147 D3 **Montserrat** *terr.* West Indies
62 A1 **Monywa** Myanmar
108 A1 **Monza** Italy
107 D1 **Monzón** Spain
123 C1 **Mookane** Botswana
52 A1 **Moolawatana** Austr.
52 B1 **Moomba** Austr.
53 D1 **Moonie** Austr.
53 C1 **Moonie** *r.* Austr.
52 A2 **Moonta** Austr.
50 A3 **Moora** Austr.
50 A2 **Moore, Lake** *salt flat* Austr.
137 D1 **Moorhead** U.S.A.
53 C3 **Mooroopna** Austr.
122 A3 **Moorreesburg** S. Africa
130 B2 **Moose** *r.* Can.
130 B2 **Moose Factory** Can.
139 F1 **Moosehead Lake** U.S.A.
129 D2 **Moose Jaw** Can.
137 E1 **Moose Lake** U.S.A.
129 D2 **Moosomin** Can.
130 B2 **Moosonee** Can.
52 B2 **Mootwingee** Austr.
107 E2 **M'Oukal** Alg.
123 C1 **Mopane** S. Africa
114 B3 **Mopti** Mali
150 B4 **Moquegua** Peru
103 D2 **Mór** Hungary
118 B1 **Mora** Cameroon
93 F3 **Mora** Sweden
137 E1 **Mora** U.S.A.
74 B2 **Moradabad** India
121 □D2 **Morafenobe** Madag.
121 □D2 **Moramanga** Madag.
136 A2 **Moran** U.S.A.
51 D2 **Moranbah** Austr.
103 D2 **Morava** *r.* Europe
96 B2 **Moray Firth** *b.* U.K.
100 C3 **Morbach** Ger.
74 B2 **Morbi** India
93 G4 **Mörbylånga** Sweden
104 B3 **Morcenx** France
69 E1 **Mordaga** China
129 E3 **Morden** Can.
89 F3 **Mordovo** Rus. Fed.
98 B2 **Morecambe** U.K.
98 B2 **Morecambe Bay** U.K.
53 C1 **Moree** Austr.
59 D3 **Morehead** P.N.G.
138 C3 **Morehead** U.S.A.
141 E2 **Morehead City** U.S.A.
145 B3 **Morelia** Mex.
107 C1 **Morella** Spain
74 B2 **Morena** India
106 B2 **Morena, Sierra** *mts* Spain
110 C2 **Moreni** Romania
142 A3 **Moreno** Mex.
128 A2 **Moresby, Mount** Can.
128 A2 **Moresby Island** Can.
53 D1 **Moreton Island** Austr.
52 A2 **Morgan** Austr.
140 B3 **Morgan City** U.S.A.
141 D1 **Morganton** U.S.A.
139 D3 **Morgantown** U.S.A.
105 D2 **Morges** Switz.
68 C2 **Mori** China
66 D2 **Mori** Japan
53 C1 **Moriarty's Range** *hills* Austr.
128 B2 **Morice Lake** Can.
66 D3 **Morioka** Japan
53 D2 **Morisset** Austr.
104 B2 **Morlaix** France
98 C3 **Morley** U.K.
157 G9 **Mornington Abyssal Plain** *sea feature* S. Atlantic Ocean
51 C1 **Mornington Island** Austr.
59 D3 **Morobe** P.N.G.
114 B1 **Morocco** *country* Africa
119 D3 **Morogoro** Tanz.
64 B3 **Moro Gulf** Phil.
122 B2 **Morokweng** S. Africa
121 □D3 **Morombe** Madag.
68 C1 **Mörön** Mongolia
121 □D3 **Morondava** Madag.
106 B2 **Morón de la Frontera** Spain
121 D2 **Moroni** Comoros
59 C2 **Morotai** *i.* Indon.
119 D2 **Moroto** Uganda
98 C2 **Morpeth** U.K.
140 B1 **Morrilton** U.S.A.
154 C1 **Morrinhos** Brazil
54 C1 **Morrinsville** N.Z.
129 E3 **Morris** Can.
137 D1 **Morris** U.S.A.
141 D1 **Morristown** U.S.A.
154 C2 **Morro Agudo** Brazil
155 E1 **Morro d'Anta** Brazil
55 K3 **Morse, Cape** Antarctica
87 D3 **Morshanka** Rus. Fed.
Morshansk Rus. Fed. *see* **Morshanka**
151 C3 **Mortes, Rio das** *r.* Brazil
52 B3 **Mortlake** Austr.
48 G3 **Mortlock Islands** Micronesia
138 B2 **Morton** U.S.A.
53 C2 **Morundah** Austr.
53 D3 **Moruya** Austr.
96 B2 **Morvern** *reg.* U.K.
Morvi India *see* **Morbi**
53 C3 **Morwell** Austr.
101 D3 **Mosbach** Ger.
89 E2 **Moscow** Rus. Fed.
134 C1 **Moscow** U.S.A.
100 C2 **Mosel** *r.* Ger.
122 B2 **Moselebe** *watercourse* Botswana
105 D2 **Moselle** *r.* France
134 C1 **Moses Lake** U.S.A.
92 □A3 **Mosfellsbær** Iceland
54 B3 **Mosgiel** N.Z.
88 C2 **Moshchnyy, Ostrov** *i.* Rus. Fed.
89 D2 **Moshenskoye** Rus. Fed.
119 D3 **Moshi** Tanz.
92 F2 **Mosjøen** Norway
Moskva Rus. Fed. *see* **Moscow**
89 E2 **Moskva** *r.* Rus. Fed.
103 D2 **Mosonmagyaróvár** Hungary
146 B4 **Mosquitos, Golfo de los** *b.* Panama
93 F4 **Moss** Norway
Mossâmedes Angola *see* **Namibe**
122 B3 **Mossel Bay** S. Africa
122 B3 **Mossel Bay** *b.* S. Africa
118 B3 **Mossendjo** Congo
52 B2 **Mossgiel** Austr.
51 D1 **Mossman** Austr.
151 F3 **Mossoró** Brazil
53 D2 **Moss Vale** Austr.
102 C1 **Most** Czech Rep.
114 C1 **Mostaganem** Alg.
109 C2 **Mostar** Bos.-Herz.
152 C3 **Mostardas** Brazil
106 C1 **Móstoles** Spain
81 C2 **Mosul** Iraq
145 D3 **Motagua** *r.* Guat.
93 G4 **Motala** Sweden
123 C2 **Motetema** S. Africa
96 C3 **Motherwell** U.K.
75 C2 **Motihari** India
107 C2 **Motilla del Palancar** Spain
122 B1 **Motokwe** Botswana
106 C2 **Motril** Spain
110 B2 **Motru** Romania
136 C1 **Mott** U.S.A.
63 A2 **Mottama** Myanmar
63 A2 **Mottama, Gulf of** Myanmar
54 B2 **Motueka** N.Z.
145 D2 **Motul** Mex.
49 L5 **Motu One** *atoll* Fr. Polynesia
114 A3 **Moudjéria** Maur.
111 C3 **Moudros** Greece
118 B3 **Mouila** Gabon
52 B3 **Moulamein** Austr.
105 C2 **Moulins** France
141 D2 **Moultrie** U.S.A.
141 E2 **Moultrie, Lake** U.S.A.
138 B3 **Mound City** U.S.A.
115 D4 **Moundou** Chad
138 C3 **Moundsville** U.S.A.
137 E3 **Mountain Grove** U.S.A.
140 B1 **Mountain Home** *AR* U.S.A.
134 C2 **Mountain Home** *ID* U.S.A.
141 D1 **Mount Airy** U.S.A.
123 C3 **Mount Ayliff** S. Africa
52 A3 **Mount Barker** Austr.
53 C3 **Mount Beauty** Austr.
97 B2 **Mount Bellew** Ireland
121 C2 **Mount Darwin** Zimbabwe
139 F2 **Mount Desert Island** U.S.A.
123 C3 **Mount Fletcher** S. Africa
123 C3 **Mount Frere** S. Africa
52 B3 **Mount Gambier** Austr.
59 D3 **Mount Hagen** P.N.G.
53 C2 **Mount Hope** Austr.
51 C2 **Mount Isa** Austr.
52 A3 **Mount Lofty Range** *mts* Austr.
50 A2 **Mount Magnet** Austr.
52 B2 **Mount Manara** Austr.
54 C1 **Mount Maunganui** N.Z.
97 C2 **Mountmellick** Ireland
111 B2 **Mount Olympus** *mt.* Greece
137 E2 **Mount Pleasant** *IA* U.S.A.
138 C2 **Mount Pleasant** *MI* U.S.A.
141 E2 **Mount Pleasant** *SC* U.S.A.
143 E2 **Mount Pleasant** *TX* U.S.A.
135 D3 **Mount Pleasant** *UT* U.S.A.
99 A4 **Mount's Bay** U.K.
134 B2 **Mount Shasta** U.S.A.
54 B2 **Mount Somers** N.Z.
138 B3 **Mount Vernon** *IL* U.S.A.
138 C2 **Mount Vernon** *OH* U.S.A.
134 B1 **Mount Vernon** *WA* U.S.A.
51 D2 **Moura** Austr.
106 B2 **Moura** Port.
115 E3 **Mourdi, Dépression du** *depr.* Chad
97 C1 **Mourne Mountains** *hills* U.K.
100 A2 **Mouscron** Belgium
115 D3 **Moussoro** Chad
61 D1 **Moutong** Indon.
115 C2 **Mouydir, Monts du** *plat.* Alg.
100 B3 **Mouzon** France
97 B1 **Moy** *r.* Ireland
117 B4 **Moyale** Eth.
Moyen Congo *country* Africa *see* **Congo**
123 C3 **Moyeni** Lesotho
76 B2 **Mo'ynoq** Uzbek.
119 D2 **Moyo** Uganda
77 D2 **Moyynkum** Kazakh.
77 D2 **Moyynty** Kazakh.
121 C3 **Mozambique** *country* Africa
113 G8 **Mozambique Channel** Africa
81 C1 **Mozdok** Rus. Fed.
89 E2 **Mozhaysk** Rus. Fed.
119 D3 **Mpanda** Tanz.
121 C2 **Mpika** Zambia
118 B2 **Mpoko** *r.* C.A.R.
121 C1 **Mporokoso** Zambia
123 C2 **Mpumalanga** *prov.* S. Africa
119 D3 **Mpwapwa** Tanz.
62 A1 **Mrauk-U** Myanmar
115 D1 **M'Saken** Tunisia
119 D3 **Msambweni** Kenya
119 D3 **Msata** Tanz.
88 C2 **Mshinskaya** Rus. Fed.
115 C1 **M'Sila** Alg.
89 D2 **Msta** *r.* Rus. Fed.
89 D2 **Mstinskiy Most** Rus. Fed.
89 D3 **Mstsislaw** Belarus
Mtoko Zimbabwe *see* **Mutoko**
89 E3 **Mtsensk** Rus. Fed.
123 D2 **Mtubatuba** S. Africa
119 E4 **Mtwara** Tanz.
151 E3 **Muana** Brazil
118 B3 **Muanda** Dem. Rep. Congo
62 B1 **Muang Hiam** Laos
62 B2 **Muang Hinboun** Laos
63 B2 **Muang Không** Laos
63 B2 **Muang Khôngxédôn** Laos
62 B1 **Muang Ngoy** Laos
62 B2 **Muang Pakbeng** Laos
63 B2 **Muang Phalan** Laos
62 B2 **Muang Phôn-Hông** Laos
62 B1 **Muang Sing** Laos
62 B2 **Muang Vangviang** Laos
60 B1 **Muar** Malaysia
60 B2 **Muarabungo** Indon.
60 B2 **Muaradua** Indon.
61 C2 **Muaralaung** Indon.

60 A2 Muarasiberut Indon.
60 B2 Muaratembesi Indon.
61 C2 Muarateweh Indon.
Muara Tuang Malaysia see
Kota Samarahan
119 D2 Mubende Uganda
115 D3 Mubi Nigeria
120 B2 Muconda Angola
120 A2 Mucope Angola
121 C2 Mucubela Moz.
155 E1 Mucuri Brazil
155 E1 Mucuri r. Brazil
66 A2 Mudanjiang China
66 A1 Mudan Jiang r. China
111 C2 Mudanya Turkey
136 B2 Muddy Gap U.S.A.
101 E1 Müden (Örtze) Ger.
53 C2 Mudgee Austr.
63 A2 Mudon Myanmar
80 B1 Mudurnu Turkey
121 C2 Mueda Moz.
121 B2 Mufulira Zambia
120 B2 Mufumbwe Zambia
111 C3 Muğla Turkey
116 B2 Muhammad Qol Sudan
Muhammarah Iran see
Khorramshahr
101 F2 Mühlberg Ger.
101 E2 Mühlhausen (Thüringen) Ger.
88 B2 Muhu i. Estonia
63 B3 Mui Ca Mau c. Vietnam
97 C2 Muine Bheag Ireland
96 B3 Muirkirk U.K.
121 C2 Muite Moz.
65 B2 Muju S. Korea
Mukačevo Ukr. see Mukacheve
90 A2 Mukacheve Ukr.
61 C1 Mukah Sarawak Malaysia
79 B3 Mukalla Yemen
63 B2 Mukdahan Thai.
Mukden China see Shenyang
Mukhtuya Rus. Fed. see Lensk
50 A3 Mukinbudin Austr.
60 B2 Mukomuko Indon.
121 C2 Mulanje, Mount Malawi
101 F2 Mulde r. Ger.
119 D3 Muleba Tanz.
144 A2 Mulegé Mex.
143 C2 Muleshoe U.S.A.
106 C2 Mulhacén mt. Spain
100 C2 Mülheim an der Ruhr Ger.
105 D2 Mulhouse France
62 B1 Muli China
66 B2 Muling China
66 B1 Muling He r. China
96 B2 Mull i. U.K.
53 C2 Mullaley Austr.
136 C2 Mullen U.S.A.
61 C1 Muller, Pegunungan mts Indon.
50 A2 Mullewa Austr.
97 C2 Mullingar Ireland
96 B3 Mull of Galloway c. U.K.
96 B3 Mull of Kintyre hd U.K.
96 A3 Mull of Oa hd U.K.
53 D1 Mullumbimby Austr.
120 B2 Mulobezi Zambia
74 B1 Multan Pak.
86 F2 Mulym'ya Rus. Fed.
74 B3 Mumbai India
120 B2 Mumbeji Zambia
120 B2 Mumbwa Zambia
61 D2 Muna i. Indon.
145 D2 Muna Mex.
101 E2 Münchberg Ger.
München Ger. see
Munich
München-Gladbach Ger. see
Mönchengladbach
138 B2 Muncie U.S.A.
50 B3 Mundrabilla Austr.
138 B3 Munfordville U.S.A.
119 C2 Mungbere Dem. Rep. Congo
75 C2 Munger India
52 A1 Mungeranie Austr.
53 C1 Mungindi Austr.
102 C2 Munich Ger.
155 D2 Muniz Freire Brazil
101 E1 Münster Ger.
100 C2 Münster Ger.
97 B2 Munster reg. Ireland
100 C2 Münsterland reg. Ger.
62 B1 Mương Nhie Vietnam
92 H2 Muonio Fin.
92 H2 Muonioälven r. Fin./Sweden
Muqdisho Somalia see Mogadishu
155 D2 Muqui Brazil
103 D2 Mur r. Austria
67 C3 Murakami Japan
119 C3 Muramvya Burundi
119 D3 Murang'a Kenya
86 D3 Murashi Rus. Fed.
81 B2 Murat r. Turkey
111 C2 Muratlı Turkey
67 D3 Murayama Japan
50 A2 Murchison watercourse Austr.
107 C2 Murcia Spain
107 C2 Murcia reg. Spain
136 C2 Murdo U.S.A.
131 D3 Murdochville Can.
110 B1 Mureşul r. Romania
104 C3 Muret France
140 C1 Murfreesboro U.S.A.
77 C3 Murghab r. Afgh.
77 D3 Murghob Tajik.

155 D2 Muriaé Brazil
120 B1 Muritz l. Ger.
101 F1 Müritz l. Ger.
92 J2 Murmansk Rus. Fed.
86 C2 Murmanskiy Bereg coastal area
Rus. Fed.
87 D3 Murom Rus. Fed.
66 D2 Muroran Japan
106 B1 Muros Spain
67 B4 Muroto Japan
67 B4 Muroto-zaki pt Japan
141 D1 Murphy U.S.A.
53 C1 Murra Murra Austr.
52 A3 Murray r. Austr.
128 B2 Murray r. Can.
138 B3 Murray r. U.S.A.
59 D3 Murray, Lake P.N.G.
141 D2 Murray, Lake U.S.A.
52 A3 Murray Bridge Austr.
122 B3 Murraysburg S. Africa
52 B3 Murrayville Austr.
52 B2 Murrumbidgee r. Austr.
53 C2 Murrumburrah Austr.
121 C2 Murrupula Moz.
53 D2 Murrurundi Austr.
109 C1 Murska Sobota Slovenia
54 C1 Murupara N.Z.
49 N6 Mururoa atoll Fr.
Polynesia
75 C2 Murwara India
53 D1 Murwillumbah Austr.
76 C3 Murzechirla Turkm.
115 D2 Murzūq Libya
103 D2 Mürzzuschlag Austria
81 C2 Muş Turkey
110 B2 Musala mt. Bulg.
65 B1 Musan N. Korea
78 B3 Musaymir Yemen
79 C2 Muscat Oman
Muscat and Oman country Asia
see Oman
137 E2 Muscatine U.S.A.
50 C2 Musgrave Ranges mts Austr.
118 B3 Mushie Dem. Rep. Congo
60 B2 Musi r. Indon.
123 D1 Musina S. Africa
138 B2 Muskegon U.S.A.
138 B2 Muskegon r. U.S.A.
138 C3 Muskingum r. U.S.A.
143 D1 Muskogee U.S.A.
139 D1 Muskoka, Lake Can.
128 B2 Muskwa r. Can.
74 A1 Muslimbagh Pak.
116 B3 Musmar Sudan
119 D3 Musoma Tanz.
59 D3 Mussau Island P.N.G.
96 C3 Musselburgh U.K.
117 C4 Mustahil Eth.
88 B2 Mustjala Estonia
53 D2 Muswellbrook Austr.
116 A2 Mūţ Egypt
121 C2 Mutare Zimbabwe
121 C2 Mutoko Zimbabwe
66 D2 Mutsu Japan
66 D2 Mutsu-wan b. Japan
121 C2 Mutuali Moz.
155 D1 Mutum Brazil
92 I2 Muurola Fin.
70 A2 Mu Us Shamo des. China
120 A1 Muxaluando Angola
86 C2 Muyezerskiy Rus. Fed.
119 D3 Muyinga Burundi
74 B1 Muzaffargarh Pak.
75 C2 Muzaffarpur India
123 D1 Muzamane Moz.
155 C2 Muzambinho Brazil
144 B2 Múzquiz Mex.
75 C1 Muz Tag mt. China
117 A4 Mvolo Sudan
119 C3 Mwanza Dem. Rep.
Congo
119 D3 Mwanza Tanz.
118 C3 Mweka Dem. Rep. Congo
121 B2 Mwenda Zambia
118 C3 Mwene-Ditu Dem. Rep. Congo
121 C3 Mwenezi Zimbabwe
121 C3 Mwenezi r. Zimbabwe
119 C3 Mweru, Lake
Dem. Rep. Congo/Zambia
121 B1 Mweru Wantipa, Lake Zambia
118 C3 Mwimba Dem. Rep. Congo
120 B2 Mwinilunga Zambia
88 C3 Myadzyel Belarus
62 A2 Myanaung Myanmar
62 A1 Myanmar country Asia
63 A2 Myaungmya Myanmar
63 A2 Myeik Myanmar
Mergui Archipelago is Myanmar
see Mergui Archipelago
62 A1 Myingyan Myanmar
62 A1 Myitkyina Myanmar
90 A2 Mykolayiv Ukr.
91 C2 Mykolayiv Ukr.
111 C3 Mykonos Greece
111 C3 Mykonos i. Greece
86 E2 Myla Rus. Fed.
75 C2 Mymensingh Bangl.
65 B1 Myŏnggan N. Korea
88 C3 Myory Belarus
92 □B3 Mýrdalsjökull ice cap Iceland
92 G2 Myre Norway
91 C1 Myrhorod Ukr.
111 C3 Myrina Greece
90 C2 Myronivka Ukr.
141 E2 Myrtle Beach U.S.A.

53 C3 Myrtleford Austr.
134 B2 Myrtle Point U.S.A.
89 E2 Myshkin Rus. Fed.
Myshkino Rus. Fed. see Myshkin
103 C1 Myślibórz Pol.
73 B3 Mysore India
83 N2 Mys Shmidta Rus. Fed.
63 B2 My Tho Vietnam
111 C3 Mytilini Greece
89 E3 Mytishchi Rus. Fed.
123 C3 Mzamomhle S. Africa
121 C2 Mzimba Malawi
121 C2 Mzuzu Malawi

N

101 F3 Naab r. Ger.
100 B1 Naarden Neth.
97 C2 Naas Ireland
122 A2 Nababeep S. Africa
87 E3 Naberezhnyye Chelny Rus. Fed.
59 D3 Nabire Indon.
80 B2 Nāblus West Bank
123 C1 Naboomspruit S. Africa
121 D2 Nacala Moz.
119 D4 Nachingwea Tanz.
103 D1 Náchod Czech Rep.
73 D3 Nachuge India
143 E2 Nacogdoches U.S.A.
144 B1 Nacozari de García Mex.
Nada China see Danzhou
74 B2 Nadiad India
90 A2 Nadvirna Ukr.
86 C2 Nadvoitsy Rus. Fed.
86 G2 Nadym Rus. Fed.
93 F4 Næstved Denmark
111 B3 Nafpaktos Greece
111 B3 Nafplio Greece
115 D1 Nafūsah, Jabal hills Libya
78 B2 Nafy Saudi Arabia
64 B2 Naga Phil.
130 B2 Nagagami r. Can.
67 C3 Nagano Japan
67 C3 Nagaoka Japan
75 D2 Nagaon India
74 B1 Nagar India
74 B2 Nagar Parkar Pak.
A4 Nagasaki Japan
67 B4 Nagato Japan
74 B2 Nagaur India
73 B4 Nagercoil India
74 A2 Nagha Kalat Pak.
74 B2 Nagina India
67 C3 Nagoya Japan
75 B2 Nagpur India
75 D1 Nagqu China
141 E1 Nags Head U.S.A.
82 E1 Nagurskoye Rus. Fed.
103 D2 Nagyatád Hungary
103 D2 Nagykanizsa Hungary
128 B1 Nahanni Butte Can.
81 C2 Nahāvand Iran
101 E1 Nahrendorf Ger.
153 A4 Nahuel Huapí, Lago l. Arg.
141 D2 Nahunta U.S.A.
131 D2 Nain Can.
81 D2 Nā'īn Iran
121 C2 Naiopué Moz.
96 C2 Nairn U.K.
119 D3 Nairobi Kenya
Naissus Serb. and Mont. see Niš
119 D3 Naivasha Kenya
81 D2 Najafābād Iran
78 B2 Najd reg. Saudi Arabia
106 C1 Nájera Spain
65 C1 Najin N. Korea
78 B3 Najrān Saudi Arabia
119 D2 Nakasongola Uganda
67 C3 Nakatsugawa Japan
78 A3 Nakfa Eritrea
66 B2 Nakhodka Rus. Fed.
63 B2 Nakhon Nayok Thai.
63 B2 Nakhon Pathom Thai.
62 B2 Nakhon Phanom Thai.
63 B2 Nakhon Ratchasima Thai.
63 B2 Nakhon Sawan Thai.
A3 Nakhon Si Thammarat Thai.
Nakhrachi Rus. Fed. see
Kondinskoye
130 B2 Nakina Can.
126 B3 Naknek U.S.A.
121 C1 Nakonde Zambia
93 F5 Nakskov Denmark
119 D3 Nakuru Kenya
128 C2 Nakusp Can.
75 D2 Nalbari India
87 D4 Nal'chik Rus. Fed.
115 D1 Nālūt Libya
123 D2 Namaacha Moz.
123 C2 Namahadi S. Africa
81 D2 Namak, Daryācheh-ye salt flat
Iran
76 B3 Namak, Kavir-e salt flat Iran
79 C1 Namakzar-e Shadad salt flat Iran
77 D2 Namangan Uzbek.
119 D3 Namanyere Tanz.
122 A2 Namaqualand reg. S. Africa
51 E2 Nambour Austr.
53 D2 Nambucca Heads Austr.
63 B3 Năm Căn Vietnam
75 D1 Nam Co salt l. China
62 B1 Nam Đinh Vietnam
121 C2 Namialo Moz.

120 A3 Namib Desert Namibia
120 A2 Namibe Angola
120 A3 Namibia country Africa
72 D2 Namjagbarwa Feng mt. China
59 C3 Namlea Indon.
62 B2 Nam Ngum Reservoir Laos
53 C2 Namoi r. Austr.
134 C2 Nampa U.S.A.
114 B3 Nampala Mali
65 B2 Namp'o N. Korea
121 C2 Nampula Moz.
72 D2 Namrup India
62 A1 Namsang Myanmar
92 F3 Namsos Norway
92 F3 Namsskogan Norway
63 A2 Nam Tok Thai.
83 J2 Namtsy Rus. Fed.
62 A1 Namtu Myanmar
121 C2 Namuno Moz.
100 B2 Namur Belgium
120 B2 Namwala Zambia
65 B2 Namwŏn S. Korea
62 A1 Namya Ra Myanmar
62 B2 Nan Thai.
128 B3 Nanaimo Can.
71 B3 Nan'an China
122 A1 Nananib Plateau Namibia
Nan'ao China see Dayu
67 C3 Nanao Japan
71 B3 Nanchang Jiangxi China
71 B3 Nanchang Jiangxi China
71 B3 Nancheng China
70 A2 Nanchong China
63 A3 Nancowry i. India
105 D2 Nancy France
75 C1 Nanda Devi mt. India
71 A3 Nandan China
74 B3 Nanded India
Nander India see Nanded
53 C2 Nandewar Range mts Austr.
74 B2 Nandurbar India
73 B3 Nandyal India
71 B3 Nanfeng China
62 A1 Nang China
118 B2 Nanga Eboko Cameroon
61 C2 Nangahpinoh Indon.
77 D3 Nanga Parbat mt.
Jammu and Kashmir
61 C2 Nangatayap Indon.
62 A3 Nangin Myanmar
65 B1 Nangnim-sanmaek mts N. Korea
70 B2 Nangong China
119 D3 Nangulangwa Tanz.
70 C2 Nanhui China
70 B2 Nanjing China
Nanking China see Nanjing
67 B4 Nankoku Japan
120 A2 Nankova Angola
70 B2 Nanle China
71 B3 Nan Ling mts China
71 A3 Nanning China
127 I2 Nanortalik Greenland
71 A3 Nanpan Jiang r. China
75 C2 Nanpara India
71 B3 Nanping China
Nanpu China see Pucheng
Nansei-shotō Japan see
Ryukyu Islands
160 I1 Nansen Basin sea feature
Arctic Ocean
126 F1 Nansen Sound sea chan. Can.
104 B2 Nantes France
70 C2 Nantong China
139 F2 Nantucket U.S.A.
139 F2 Nantucket Island U.S.A.
99 B3 Nantwich U.K.
49 I4 Nanumea i. Tuvalu
155 D1 Nanuque Brazil
64 B3 Nanusa, Kepulauan is Indon.
71 B3 Nanxiong China
70 B2 Nanyang China
119 D3 Nanyuki Kenya
70 B2 Nanzhang China
Nanzhao China see Zhao'an
107 D2 Nao, Cabo de la c. Spain
131 C2 Naococane, Lac l. Can.
74 A2 Naokot Pak.
71 B3 Naozhou Dao i. China
135 B3 Napa U.S.A.
126 E2 Napaktulik Lake Can.
139 D2 Napanee Can.
127 I2 Napasoq Greenland
137 F2 Naperville U.S.A.
54 C1 Napier N.Z.
108 B2 Naples Italy
141 D3 Naples U.S.A.
150 B3 Napo r. Ecuador
Napoli Italy see Naples
Napug China see Gê'gyai
114 B3 Nara Mali
88 C3 Narach Belarus
52 B3 Naracoorte Austr.
53 C2 Naradhan Austr.
145 C2 Naranjos Mex.
63 B3 Narathiwat Thai.
74 B3 Narayangaon India
105 C3 Narbonne France
63 A2 Narcondam Island India.
127 H1 Nares Strait Can./Greenland
103 E1 Narew r. Pol.
122 A1 Narib Namibia
87 D4 Narimanov Rus. Fed.
67 D3 Narita Japan
74 B2 Narmada r. India
74 B2 Narnaul India

108 B2 **Narni** Italy
86 F2 **Narodnaya, Gora** *mt.* Rus. Fed.
90 B1 **Narodychi** Ukr.
89 E2 **Naro-Fominsk** Rus. Fed.
53 D3 **Narooma** Austr.
88 C3 **Narowlya** Belarus
93 H3 **Närpes** Fin.
53 C2 **Narrabri** Austr.
53 C2 **Narrandera** Austr.
53 C2 **Narromine** Austr.
67 B4 **Naruto** Japan
88 C2 **Narva** Estonia
88 C2 **Narva Bay** Estonia/Rus. Fed.
92 G2 **Narvik** Norway
88 C2 **Narvskoye Vodokhranilishche** *resr* Estonia/Rus. Fed.
86 E2 **Nar'yan-Mar** Rus. Fed.
77 D2 **Naryn** Kyrg.
74 B2 **Nashik** India
139 E2 **Nashua** U.S.A.
140 C1 **Nashville** U.S.A.
137 E1 **Nashwauk** U.S.A.
109 C1 **Našice** Croatia
117 B4 **Nasir** Sudan
Nasirabad Bangl. *see* Mymensingh
119 C4 **Nasondoye** Dem. Rep. Congo
76 B3 **Naşrābād** Iran
128 B2 **Nass** *r.* Can.
146 C2 **Nassau** Bahamas
116 B2 **Nasser, Lake** *resr* Egypt
93 F4 **Nässjö** Sweden
130 C2 **Nastapoca** *r.* Can.
130 C2 **Nastapoka Islands** Can.
89 D2 **Nasva** Rus. Fed.
120 B3 **Nata** Botswana
151 F3 **Natal** Brazil
60 A1 **Natal** Indon.
Natal *prov.* S. Africa *see* Kwazulu-Natal
159 D6 **Natal Basin** *sea feature* Indian Ocean
143 D3 **Natalia** U.S.A.
131 D2 **Natashquan** Can.
131 D2 **Natashquan** *r.* Can.
140 B2 **Natchez** U.S.A.
140 B2 **Natchitoches** U.S.A.
53 C3 **Nathalia** Austr.
107 D1 **Nati, Punta** *pt* Spain
114 C3 **Natitingou** Benin
151 E4 **Natividade** Brazil
67 D3 **Natori** Japan
119 D3 **Natron, Lake** *salt l.* Tanz.
60 B1 **Natuna, Kepulauan** *is* Indon.
60 B1 **Natuna Besar** *i.* Indon.
122 A1 **Nauchas** Namibia
101 F1 **Nauen** Ger.
64 B2 **Naujan** Phil.
88 B2 **Naujoji Akmenė** Lith.
101 E2 **Naumburg (Saale)** Ger.
48 H34 **Nauru** *country* S. Pacific Ocean
150 B3 **Nauta** Peru
145 C2 **Nautla** Mex.
88 C3 **Navahrudak** Belarus
106 B2 **Navalmoral de la Mata** Spain
106 B2 **Navalvillar de Pela** Spain
97 C2 **Navan** Ireland
Navangar India *see* Jamnagar
88 C2 **Navapolatsk** Belarus
83 M2 **Navarin, Mys** *c.* Rus. Fed.
153 B5 **Navarino, Isla** *i.* Chile
107 C1 **Navarra** *reg.* Spain
Navarre *aut. comm.* Spain *see* Navarra
96 B1 **Naver** *r.* U.K.
89 D3 **Navlya** Rus. Fed.
110 C2 **Năvodari** Romania
77 C2 **Navoiy** Uzbek.
144 B2 **Navojoa** Mex.
144 B2 **Navolato** Mex.
74 A2 **Nawabshah** Pak.
75 C2 **Nawada** India
62 A1 **Nawnghkio** Myanmar
62 A1 **Nawngleng** Myanmar
81 C2 **Naxçıvan** Azer.
111 C3 **Naxos** Greece
111 C3 **Naxos** *i.* Greece
144 B2 **Nayar** Mex.
66 D2 **Nayoro** Japan
80 B2 **Nazareth** Israel
144 B2 **Nazas** Mex.
144 B2 **Nazas** *r.* Mex.
150 B4 **Nazca** Peru
157 H7 **Nazca Ridge** *sea feature* S. Pacific Ocean
111 C3 **Nazilli** Turkey
117 B4 **Nazrēt** Eth.
79 C2 **Nazwá** Oman
121 B2 **Nchelenge** Zambia
122 B1 **Ncojane** Botswana
120 A1 **N'dalatando** Angola
118 C2 **Ndélé** C.A.R.
118 B3 **Ndendé** Gabon
115 D3 **Ndjamena** Chad
118 A3 **Ndogo, Lagune** *lag.* Gabon
121 B2 **Ndola** Zambia
97 C1 **Neagh, Lough** *l.* U.K.
50 C2 **Neale, Lake** *salt flat* Austr.
111 B3 **Neapoli** Greece
111 B2 **Nea Roda** Greece
99 B4 **Neath** U.K.
119 D2 **Nebbi** Uganda
53 C1 **Nebine Creek** *r.* Austr.
150 C2 **Neblina, Pico da** *mt.* Brazil
135 D3 **Nebo, Mount** U.S.A.

89 D2 **Nebolchi** Rus. Fed.
136 C2 **Nebraska** *state* U.S.A.
137 D2 **Nebraska City** U.S.A.
108 B3 **Nebrodi, Monti** *mts Sicily* Italy
143 E3 **Neches** *r.* U.S.A.
156 E4 **Necker Island** U.S.A.
153 C3 **Necochea** Arg.
143 E3 **Nederland** U.S.A.
100 B2 **Neder Rijn** *r.* Neth.
130 C2 **Nedlouc, Lac** *l.* Can.
139 E2 **Needham** U.S.A.
135 D4 **Needles** U.S.A.
74 B2 **Neemuch** India
129 E2 **Neepawa** Can.
87 E3 **Neftekamsk** Rus. Fed.
82 F2 **Nefteyugansk** Rus. Fed.
108 A3 **Nefza** Tunisia
120 A1 **Negage** Angola
117 B4 **Negēlē** Eth.
109 D2 **Negotin** Serb. and Mont.
111 B2 **Negotino** Macedonia
150 A3 **Negra, Punta** *pt* Peru
155 D1 **Negra, Serra** *mts* Brazil
63 A2 **Negrais, Cape** Myanmar
153 B4 **Negro** *r.* Arg.
150 D3 **Negro** *r.* S. America
152 C3 **Negro** *r.* Uru.
106 B2 **Negro, Cabo** *c.* Morocco
64 B3 **Negros** *i.* Phil.
79 D1 **Nehbandān** Iran
69 E1 **Nehe** China
70 A3 **Neijiang** China
129 D2 **Neilburg** Can.
150 B2 **Neiva** Col.
129 E2 **Nejanilini Lake** Can.
Nejd *reg.* Saudi Arabia *see* Najd
117 B4 **Nek'emtē** Eth.
89 D2 **Nekrasovskoye** Rus. Fed.
89 D2 **Nelidovo** Rus. Fed.
73 B3 **Nellore** India
128 C3 **Nelson** Can.
129 E2 **Nelson** *r.* Can.
54 B2 **Nelson** N.Z.
52 B3 **Nelson, Cape** Austr.
53 D2 **Nelson Bay** Austr.
129 E2 **Nelson House** Can.
134 E1 **Nelson Reservoir** U.S.A.
123 D2 **Nelspruit** S. Africa
114 B3 **Néma** Maur.
88 B2 **Neman** Rus. Fed.
105 C2 **Nemours** France
66 D2 **Nemuro** Japan
90 B2 **Nemyriv** Ukr.
97 B2 **Nenagh** Ireland
99 D3 **Nene** *r.* U.K.
69 E1 **Nenjiang** China
137 E3 **Neosho** U.S.A.
75 C2 **Nepal** *country* Asia
75 C2 **Nepalganj** Nepal
139 D1 **Nepean** Can.
135 D3 **Nephi** U.S.A.
97 B1 **Nephin** *hill* Ireland
97 B1 **Nephin Beg Range** *hills* Ireland
131 D3 **Nepisiguit** *r.* Can.
119 C2 **Nepoko** *r.* Dem. Rep. Congo
139 E2 **Neptune** U.S.A.
108 B2 **Nera** *r.* Italy
104 C3 **Nérac** France
53 D1 **Nerang** Austr.
69 D1 **Nerchinsk** Rus. Fed.
89 F2 **Nerekhta** Rus. Fed.
109 C2 **Neretva** *r.* Bos.-Herz./Croatia
120 B2 **Neriquinha** Angola
88 B3 **Neris** *r.* Lith.
89 E2 **Nerl'** *r.* Rus. Fed.
86 F2 **Nerokhi** Rus. Fed.
154 C1 **Nerópolis** Brazil
83 J3 **Neryungri** Rus. Fed.
92 □C2 **Neskaupstaður** Iceland
96 B2 **Ness, Loch** *l.* U.K.
136 D3 **Ness City** U.S.A.
Nesterov Ukr. *see* Zhovkva
111 B3 **Nestos** *r.* Greece
100 B1 **Netherlands** *country* Europe
147 D3 **Netherlands Antilles** *terr.* West Indies
127 H2 **Nettilling Lake** Can.
101 F1 **Neubrandenburg** Ger.
105 D2 **Neuchâtel** Switz.
105 D2 **Neuchâtel, Lac de** *l.* Switz.
100 C2 **Neuerburg** Ger.
100 B3 **Neufchâteau** Belgium
105 D2 **Neufchâteau** France
104 C2 **Neufchâtel-en-Bray** France
101 D2 **Neuhof** Ger.
101 E3 **Neumarkt in der Oberpfalz** Ger.
102 B1 **Neumünster** Ger.
100 C3 **Neunkirchen** Ger.
153 B3 **Neuquén** Arg.
153 B3 **Neuquén** *r.* Arg.
101 F1 **Neuruppin** Ger.
100 C2 **Neuss** Ger.
101 D1 **Neustadt am Rübenberge** Ger.
101 E3 **Neustadt an der Aisch** Ger.
Neustadt an der Hardt Ger. *see* Neustadt an der Weinstraße
101 D3 **Neustadt an der Weinstraße** Ger.
101 E1 **Neustadt-Glewe** Ger.
101 F1 **Neustrelitz** Ger.
99 D5 **Neuville-lès-Dieppe** France
100 C2 **Neuwied** Ger.
137 E3 **Nevada** U.S.A.
135 C3 **Nevada** *state* U.S.A.
106 C2 **Nevada, Sierra** *mts* Spain
135 B2 **Nevada, Sierra** *mts* U.S.A.

88 C2 **Nevaišių kalnis** *hill* Lith.
88 C2 **Nevel'** Rus. Fed.
105 C2 **Nevers** France
53 C2 **Nevertire** Austr.
109 C2 **Nevesinje** Bos.-Herz.
87 D4 **Nevinnomyssk** Rus. Fed.
80 B2 **Nevşehir** Turkey
99 C4 **New Addington** U.K.
128 B2 **New Aiyansh** Can.
119 D4 **Newala** Tanz.
138 B3 **New Amsterdam** Guyana
151 D2 **New Amsterdam** Guyana
139 E2 **Newark** NJ U.S.A.
138 C2 **Newark** OH U.S.A.
99 C3 **Newark-on-Trent** U.K.
139 E2 **New Bedford** U.S.A.
141 B1 **New Bern** U.S.A.
138 B1 **Newberry** MI U.S.A.
141 D2 **Newberry** SC U.S.A.
143 E2 **New Boston** U.S.A.
143 D3 **New Braunfels** U.S.A.
97 C2 **Newbridge** Ireland
59 D3 **New Britain** *i.* P.N.G.
131 D3 **New Brunswick** *prov.* Can.
99 C4 **Newbury** U.K.
48 H6 **New Caledonia** *terr.* S. Pacific Ocean
156 D7 **New Caledonia Trough** *sea feature* Tasman Sea
53 D2 **Newcastle** Austr.
123 C2 **Newcastle** S. Africa
97 D1 **Newcastle** U.K.
138 C2 **New Castle** U.S.A.
136 C2 **Newcastle** U.S.A.
99 B3 **Newcastle-under-Lyme** U.K.
98 C1 **Newcastle upon Tyne** U.K.
51 C1 **Newcastle Waters** Austr.
97 B2 **Newcastle West** Ireland
74 B2 **New Delhi** India
128 C3 **New Denver** Can.
53 D2 **New England Range** *mts* Austr.
157 H3 **New England Seamounts** *sea feature* N. Atlantic Ocean
131 E3 **Newfoundland** *i.* Can.
131 E2 **Newfoundland and Labrador** *prov.* Can.
96 B3 **New Galloway** U.K.
48 G4 **New Georgia Islands** Solomon Is
131 D3 **New Glasgow** Can.
59 D3 **New Guinea** *i.* Indon./P.N.G.
78 A3 **New Halfa** Sudan
139 E2 **New Hampshire** *state* U.S.A.
59 E3 **New Hanover** *i.* P.N.G.
139 E2 **New Haven** U.S.A.
128 B2 **New Hazelton** Can.
New Hebrides *country* S. Pacific Ocean *see* Vanuatu
156 D7 **New Hebrides Trench** *sea feature* S. Pacific Ocean
140 B2 **New Iberia** U.S.A.
59 E3 **New Ireland** *i.* P.N.G.
139 E3 **New Jersey** *state* U.S.A.
130 C3 **New Liskeard** Can.
138 B2 **New London** U.S.A.
50 A2 **Newman** Austr.
54 C2 **Newman** N.Z.
97 B2 **Newmarket** Ireland
99 D3 **Newmarket** U.K.
97 B2 **Newmarket-on-Fergus** Ireland
142 B2 **New Mexico** *state* U.S.A.
141 D2 **Newnan** U.S.A.
140 B3 **New Orleans** U.S.A.
138 C2 **New Philadelphia** U.S.A.
54 B1 **New Plymouth** N.Z.
99 C4 **Newport** England U.K.
99 B4 **Newport** Wales U.K.
140 B1 **Newport** AR U.S.A.
134 B2 **Newport** OR U.S.A.
139 E2 **Newport** RI U.S.A.
141 D1 **Newport** TN U.S.A.
139 E2 **Newport** VT U.S.A.
134 C1 **Newport** WA U.S.A.
139 D3 **Newport News** U.S.A.
141 E3 **New Providence** *i.* Bahamas
99 A4 **Newquay** U.K.
140 B2 **New Roads** U.S.A.
97 C2 **New Ross** Ireland
97 C1 **Newry** U.K.
83 K1 **New Siberia Islands** Rus. Fed.
52 C2 **New South Wales** *state* Austr.
137 E2 **Newton** IA U.S.A.
137 D3 **Newton** KS U.S.A.
99 B4 **Newton Abbot** U.K.
98 C2 **Newton Aycliffe** U.K.
96 B3 **Newton Mearns** U.K.
96 B2 **Newtonmore** U.K.
97 B2 **Newton Stewart** U.K.
99 B3 **Newtown** Ireland
99 B3 **Newtown** U.K.
136 C1 **New Town** U.S.A.
97 D1 **Newtownabbey** U.K.
97 D1 **Newtownards** U.K.
Newtownbarry Ireland *see* Bunclody
97 C1 **Newtownbutler** U.K.
96 C3 **Newtown St Boswells** U.K.
97 C1 **Newtownstewart** U.K.
137 E2 **New Ulm** U.S.A.
139 E2 **New York** U.S.A.
139 D2 **New York** *state* U.S.A.
54 B2 **New Zealand** *country* Oceania
86 D3 **Neya** Rus. Fed.
81 D3 **Neyrīz** Iran
76 B3 **Neyshābūr** Iran
145 C3 **Nezahualcóyotl, Presa** *resr* Mex.

60 B1 **Ngabang** Indon.
118 B3 **Ngabé** Congo
75 C2 **Ngamring** China
119 D2 **Ngangala** Sudan
75 C1 **Nangla Ringco** *salt l.* China
75 C1 **Nganglong Kangri** *mt.* China
75 C1 **Nganglong Kangri** *mts* China
75 C1 **Ngangzê Co** *salt l.* China
62 A2 **Ngao** Thai.
118 B2 **Ngaoundal** Cameroon
118 B2 **Ngaoundéré** Cameroon
54 C1 **Ngaruawahia** N.Z.
62 A2 **Ngathainggyaung** Myanmar
Ngiva Angola *see* Ondjiva
118 B3 **Ngo** Congo
63 B2 **Ngoc Linh** *mt.* Vietnam
115 D4 **Ngol Bembo** Nigeria
115 D3 **Ngourti** Niger
115 D3 **Nguigmi** Niger
59 D2 **Ngulu** *atoll* Micronesia
61 C2 **Ngunut** Indon.
Ngunza Angola *see* Sumbe
Ngunza-Kabolu Angola *see* Sumbe
115 D3 **Nguru** Nigeria
62 B1 **Nguyên Binh** Vietnam
123 C2 **Ngwathe** S. Africa
123 D2 **Ngwelezana** S. Africa
121 C2 **Nhamalabué** Moz.
120 A2 **N'harea** Angola
63 B2 **Nha Trang** Vietnam
52 B3 **Nhill** Austr.
123 D2 **Nhlangano** Swaziland
51 C1 **Nhulunbuy** Austr.
139 D2 **Niagara Falls** Can.
114 C3 **Niamey** Niger
119 C2 **Niangara** Dem. Rep. Congo
114 B3 **Niangay, Lac** *l.* Mali
119 C2 **Nia-Nia** Dem. Rep. Congo
60 A1 **Nias** *i.* Indon.
88 C2 **Nica** Latvia
146 B3 **Nicaragua** *country* Central America
Nicaragua, Lago de Nic. *see* Nicaragua, Lake
146 B3 **Nicaragua, Lake** *l.* Nic.
109 C3 **Nicastro** Italy
105 D3 **Nice** France
73 D4 **Nicobar Islands** India
80 B2 **Nicosia** Cyprus
146 B4 **Nicoya, Golfo de** *b.* Costa Rica
88 B2 **Nida** Lith.
103 E1 **Nidzica** Pol.
102 B1 **Niebüll** Ger.
101 D2 **Niederaula** Ger.
118 B2 **Niefang** Equat. Guinea
101 F1 **Niemegk** Ger.
101 D1 **Nienburg (Weser)** Ger.
103 C1 **Niesky** Ger.
100 B1 **Nieuwegein** Neth.
100 B1 **Nieuwe-Niedorp** Neth.
151 D2 **Nieuw Nickerie** Suriname
122 A3 **Nieuwoudtville** S. Africa
100 A2 **Nieuwpoort** Belgium
80 B2 **Niğde** Turkey
115 C3 **Niger** *country* Africa
115 C4 **Niger** *r.* Africa
115 C4 **Niger, Mouths of the** Nigeria
115 C4 **Nigeria** *country* Africa
130 B3 **Nighthawk Lake** Can.
111 B2 **Nigrita** Greece
67 C3 **Niigata** Japan
67 B4 **Niihama** Japan
67 C4 **Nii-jima** *i.* Japan
67 B4 **Niimi** Japan
67 C3 **Niitsu** Japan
107 C2 **Níjar** Spain
100 B1 **Nijkerk** Neth.
100 B2 **Nijmegen** Neth.
100 C1 **Nijverdal** Neth.
92 J2 **Nikel'** Rus. Fed.
Nikolayev Ukr. *see* Mykolayiv
87 D3 **Nikolayevsk** Rus. Fed.
Nikolayevskiy Rus. Fed. *see* Nikolayevsk
86 D3 **Nikol'sk** Rus. Fed.
Nikol'skiy Kazakh. *see* Satpayev
83 M3 **Nikol'skoye** Rus. Fed.
Nikol'skoye Rus. Fed. *see* Sheksna
91 C2 **Nikopol'** Ukr.
80 B1 **Niksar** Turkey
79 D2 **Nīkshahr** Iran
109 C2 **Nikšić** Serb. and Mont.
Nîl, Bahr el *r.* Africa *see* Nile
135 C4 **Niland** U.S.A.
116 B1 **Nile** *r.* Africa
138 B2 **Niles** U.S.A.
Nimach India *see* Neemuch
105 C3 **Nîmes** France
53 C3 **Nimmitabel** Austr.
117 B4 **Nimule** Sudan
Nimwegen Neth. *see* Nijmegen
53 C1 **Nindigully** Austr.
73 B4 **Nine Degree Channel** India
53 C3 **Ninety Mile Beach** Austr.
54 B1 **Ninety Mile Beach** N.Z.
70 C3 **Ningbo** China
71 B3 **Ningde** China
71 B3 **Ningdu** China
70 B2 **Ningguo** China
71 C3 **Ninghai** China
72 D2 **Ninging** India
Ningjiang China *see* Songyuan
70 A2 **Ningjing Shan** *mts* China
70 A2 **Ningxia Huizu Zizhiqu** *aut. reg.* China

70 B2 **Ningyang** China
62 B1 **Ninh Binh** Vietnam
63 B2 **Ninh Hoa** Vietnam
66 D2 **Ninohe** Japan
137 D2 **Niobrara** r. U.S.A.
62 A1 **Nioko** India
114 B3 **Niono** Mali
114 B3 **Nioro** Mali
104 B2 **Niort** France
129 D2 **Nipawin** Can.
130 B3 **Nipigon** Can.
130 B3 **Nipigon, Lake** Can.
131 C2 **Nipishish Lake** Can.
130 C3 **Nipissing, Lake** Can.
135 C3 **Nipton** U.S.A.
151 E4 **Niquelândia** Brazil
74 B3 **Nirmal** India
109 D2 **Niš** Serb. and Mont.
109 D2 **Nišava** r. Serb. and Mont.
108 B3 **Niscemi** Sicily Italy
67 B4 **Nishino-omote** Japan
90 B2 **Nisporeni** Moldova
155 D2 **Niterói** Brazil
96 C3 **Nith** r. U.K.
103 D2 **Nitra** Slovakia
49 K5 **Niue** terr. S. Pacific Ocean
92 H3 **Nivala** Fin.
100 B2 **Nivelles** Belgium
73 B3 **Nizamabad** India
87 E3 **Nizhnekamsk** Rus. Fed.
87 E3 **Nizhnekamskoye Vodokhranilishche** resr Rus. Fed.
83 H3 **Nizhneudinsk** Rus. Fed.
82 G2 **Nizhnevartovsk** Rus. Fed.
Nizhnevolzhsk Rus. Fed. see Narimanov
83 K2 **Nizhneyansk** Rus. Fed.
Nizhniye Kresty Rus. Fed. see Cherskiy
Nizhniye Ustriki Pol. see Ustrzyki Dolne
89 F3 **Nizhniy Kislyay** Rus. Fed.
87 D3 **Nizhniy Lomov** Rus. Fed.
87 D3 **Nizhniy Novgorod** Rus. Fed.
86 E2 **Nizhniy Odes** Rus. Fed.
86 E3 **Nizhniy Tagil** Rus. Fed.
83 G2 **Nizhnyaya Tunguska** r. Rus. Fed.
86 E3 **Nizhnyaya Tura** Rus. Fed.
91 C1 **Nizhyn** Ukr.
103 E1 **Nizina Mazowiecka** reg. Pol.
121 D2 **Njazidja** i. Comoros
119 D3 **Njinjo** Tanz.
119 D3 **Njombe** Tanz.
118 B2 **Nkambe** Cameroon
119 D4 **Nkhata Bay** Malawi
121 C2 **Nkhotakota** Malawi
118 A3 **Nkomi, Lagune** lag. Gabon
119 D3 **Nkondwe** Tanz.
118 A2 **Nkongsamba** Cameroon
123 C3 **Nkululeko** S. Africa
123 C3 **Nkwenkwezi** S. Africa
67 B4 **Nobeoka** Japan
138 B2 **Noblesville** U.S.A.
52 B1 **Noccundra** Austr.
144 A1 **Nogales** Mex.
142 A2 **Nogales** U.S.A.
104 C2 **Nogent-le-Rotrou** France
83 H2 **Noginsk** Rus. Fed.
89 E2 **Noginsk** Rus. Fed.
83 K3 **Nogliki** Rus. Fed.
74 B2 **Nohar** India
100 C3 **Nohfelden** Ger.
104 B2 **Noires, Montagnes** hills France
104 B2 **Noirmoutier, Île de** i. France
104 B2 **Noirmoutier-en-l'Île** France
67 C4 **Nojima-zaki** c. Japan
74 B2 **Nokha** India
93 H3 **Nokia** Fin.
74 A2 **Nok Kundi** Pak.
118 B2 **Nola** C.A.R.
86 D3 **Nolinsk** Rus. Fed.
126 A2 **Nome** U.S.A.
123 C3 **Nomonde** S. Africa
123 D2 **Nondweni** S. Africa
Nonghui China see Guang'an
62 B2 **Nong Khai** Thai.
75 D2 **Nongstoin** India
52 A2 **Nonning** Austr.
144 B2 **Nonoava** Mex.
65 B2 **Nonsan** S. Korea
63 B2 **Nonthaburi** Thai.
122 B3 **Nonzwakazi** S. Africa
100 B1 **Noordwijk-Binnen** Neth.
77 C3 **Norak** Tajik.
130 C3 **Noranda** Can.
82 C1 **Nordaustlandet** i. Svalbard
128 C2 **Nordegg** Can.
100 C1 **Norden** Ger.
83 H1 **Nordenshel'da, Arkhipelag** is Rus. Fed.
Nordenskjold Archipelago is Rus. Fed. see Nordenshel'da, Arkhipelag
100 C1 **Norderney** Ger.
100 C1 **Norderney** i. Ger.
101 E1 **Norderstedt** Ger.
93 E3 **Nordfjordeid** Norway
Nordfriesische Inseln Ger. see North Frisian Islands
101 E2 **Nordhausen** Ger.
101 D1 **Nordholz** Ger.
100 C1 **Nordhorn** Ger.
Nordkapp Norway see North Cape
92 F3 **Nordli** Norway
102 C2 **Nördlingen** Ger.

92 G3 **Nordmaling** Sweden
94 B1 **Norðoyar** i. Faroe Is
97 C2 **Nore** r. Ireland
88 B3 **Noreikiškės** Lith.
137 D2 **Norfolk** NE U.S.A.
139 D3 **Norfolk** VA U.S.A.
48 H6 **Norfolk Island** terr. S. Pacific Ocean
93 E3 **Norheimsund** Norway
82 G2 **Noril'sk** Rus. Fed.
75 C2 **Norkyung** China
143 D1 **Norman** U.S.A.
Normandes, Îles is English Chan. see Channel Islands
150 D2 **Normandia** Brazil
Normandie reg. France see Normandy
104 B2 **Normandy** reg. France
51 D1 **Normanton** Austr.
128 B1 **Norman Wells** Can.
93 G4 **Norrköping** Sweden
93 G4 **Norrtälje** Sweden
50 B3 **Norseman** Austr.
92 G3 **Norsjö** Sweden
55 M2 **North, Cape** Antarctica
98 C2 **Northallerton** U.K.
50 A3 **Northam** Austr.
50 A2 **Northampton** Austr.
99 C3 **Northampton** U.K.
73 D3 **North Andaman** i. India
159 F4 **North Australian Basin** sea feature Indian Ocean
129 C2 **North Battleford** Can.
130 C2 **North Bay** Can.
130 C2 **North Belcher Islands** Can.
96 C2 **North Berwick** U.K.
North Borneo state Malaysia see Sabah
92 I1 **North Cape** c. Norway
54 B1 **North Cape** N.Z.
130 A2 **North Caribou Lake** Can.
141 E3 **North Carolina** state U.S.A.
130 B3 **North Channel** lake channel Can.
96 A3 **North Channel** U.K.
141 E2 **North Charleston** U.S.A.
128 B3 **North Cowichan** Can.
136 C1 **North Dakota** state U.S.A.
99 C4 **North Downs** hills U.K.
157 E3 **Northeast Pacific Basin** sea feature N. Pacific Ocean
141 E3 **Northeast Providence Channel** Bahamas
101 D2 **Northeim** Ger.
122 A2 **Northern Cape** prov. S. Africa
Northern Dvina r. Rus. Fed. see Severnaya Dvina
129 E2 **Northern Indian Lake** Can.
97 C1 **Northern Ireland** prov. U.K.
59 D1 **Northern Mariana Islands** terr. N. Pacific Ocean
Northern Rhodesia country Africa see Zambia
50 C1 **Northern Territory** admin. div. Austr.
Northern Transvaal prov. S. Africa see Limpopo
96 C2 **North Esk** r. U.K.
137 E2 **Northfield** U.S.A.
99 D4 **North Foreland** c. U.K.
102 B1 **North Frisian Islands** is Ger.
54 B1 **North Island** N.Z.
129 E2 **North Knife Lake** Can.
65 B1 **North Korea** country Asia
72 D2 **North Lakhimpur** India
North Land is Rus. Fed. see Severnaya Zemlya
128 B1 **North Nahanni** r. Can.
136 C3 **North Platte** U.S.A.
136 C2 **North Platte** r. U.S.A.
96 C1 **North Ronaldsay** i. U.K.
129 D2 **North Saskatchewan** r. Can.
94 D2 **North Sea** Europe
63 A2 **North Sentinel Island** India
130 A2 **North Spirit Lake** Can.
53 D1 **North Stradbroke Island** Austr.
131 D3 **North Sydney** Can.
54 B1 **North Taranaki Bight** b. N.Z.
130 C2 **North Twin Island** Can.
98 B2 **North Tyne** r. U.K.
96 A2 **North Uist** i. U.K.
131 D3 **Northumberland Strait** Can.
99 D3 **North Walsham** U.K.
123 C2 **North West** prov. S. Africa
158 D1 **Northwest Atlantic Mid-Ocean Channel** sea chan. N. Atlantic Ocean
50 A2 **North West Cape** Austr.
156 D3 **Northwest Pacific Basin** sea feature N. Pacific Ocean
141 E3 **Northwest Providence Channel** Bahamas
131 E2 **North West River** Can.
128 B1 **Northwest Territories** admin. div. Can.
98 C2 **North York Moors** moorland U.K.
138 C3 **Norton** U.S.A.
121 C3 **Norton** Zimbabwe
Norton de Matos Angola see Balombo
126 B2 **Norton Sound** sea chan. U.S.A.
55 H2 **Norvegia, Cape** Antarctica
138 C2 **Norwalk** U.S.A.
93 F3 **Norway** country Europe
129 E2 **Norway House** Can.
160 L3 **Norwegian Basin** sea feature N. Atlantic Ocean
92 E2 **Norwegian Sea** N. Atlantic Ocean

99 D3 **Norwich** U.K.
139 E2 **Norwich** CT U.S.A.
139 E2 **Norwich** NY U.S.A.
66 D2 **Noshiro** Japan
91 C1 **Nosivka** Ukr.
122 B2 **Nosop** watercourse Africa
86 E2 **Nosovaya** Rus. Fed.
79 C2 **Noşratābād** Iran
121 □D2 **Nosy Bé** i. Madag.
121 □E2 **Nosy Boraha** i. Madag.
103 D1 **Noteć** r. Pol.
93 E4 **Notodden** Norway
67 C3 **Noto-hantō** pen. Japan
131 D3 **Notre Dame, Monts** mts Can.
131 E3 **Notre Dame Bay** Can.
130 C2 **Nottaway** r. Can.
99 C3 **Nottingham** U.K.
114 A2 **Nouâdhibou** Maur.
114 A3 **Nouakchott** Maur.
114 A3 **Nouâmghâr** Maur.
63 B2 **Nouei** Vietnam
48 H6 **Nouméa** New Caledonia
114 B3 **Nouna** Burkina
122 B3 **Noupoort** S. Africa
Nouveau-Comptoir Can. see Wemindji
Nouvelle Anvers Dem. Rep. Congo see Makanza
Nouvelles Hébrides country S. Pacific Ocean see Vanuatu
Nova Chaves Angola see Muconda
154 B2 **Nova Esperança** Brazil
Nova Freixa Moz. see Cuamba
155 D1 **Nova Friburgo** Brazil
109 C1 **Nova Gradiška** Croatia
154 C2 **Nova Granada** Brazil
155 D2 **Nova Iguaçu** Brazil
91 C2 **Nova Kakhovka** Ukr.
155 D1 **Nova Lima** Brazil
Nova Lisboa Angola see Huambo
154 B2 **Nova Londrina** Brazil
91 C2 **Nova Odesa** Ukr.
150 C2 **Nova Paraíso** Brazil
154 C2 **Nova Ponte** Brazil
108 A1 **Novara** Italy
151 E3 **Nova Remanso** Brazil
131 D3 **Nova Scotia** prov. Can.
155 D1 **Nova Venécia** Brazil
83 K1 **Novaya Sibir', Ostrov** i. Rus. Fed.
86 E1 **Novaya Zemlya** is Rus. Fed.
107 C2 **Novelda** Spain
103 D2 **Nové Zámky** Slovakia
Novgorod Rus. Fed. see Velikiy Novgorod
91 C1 **Novhorod-Sivers'kyy** Ukr.
110 B2 **Novi Iskŭr** Bulg.
66 D1 **Novikovo** Rus. Fed.
108 A1 **Novi Ligure** Italy
109 D2 **Novi Pazar** Serb. and Mont.
109 C1 **Novi Sad** Serb. and Mont.
Novoalekseyevka Kazakh. see Khobda
87 D3 **Novoanninskiy** Rus. Fed.
150 C2 **Novo Aripuanã** Brazil
91 C2 **Novoazovs'k** Ukr.
91 E2 **Novocherkassk** Rus. Fed.
89 D2 **Novodugino** Rus. Fed.
86 D2 **Novodvinsk** Rus. Fed.
Novoekonomicheskoye Ukr. see Dymytrov
152 C2 **Novo Hamburgo** Brazil
154 C2 **Novo Horizonte** Brazil
90 B1 **Novohrad-Volyns'kyy** Ukr.
Novokazalinsk Kazakh. see Ayteke Bi
91 E1 **Novokhopersk** Rus. Fed.
68 D1 **Novokuznetsk** Rus. Fed.
109 C1 **Novo Mesto** Slovenia
91 D3 **Novomikhaylovskiy** Rus. Fed.
89 E3 **Novomoskovsk** Rus. Fed.
91 C2 **Novomoskovs'k** Ukr.
91 C2 **Novomyrhorod** Ukr.
Novonikolayevsk Rus. Fed. see Novosibirsk
91 C2 **Novooleksiyivka** Ukr.
91 E2 **Novopokrovskaya** Rus. Fed.
91 D2 **Novopskov** Ukr.
Novo Redondo Angola see Sumbe
91 D3 **Novorossiysk** Rus. Fed.
88 C2 **Novorzhev** Rus. Fed.
87 E3 **Novosergiyevka** Rus. Fed.
91 D2 **Novoshakhtinsk** Rus. Fed.
82 G3 **Novosibirsk** Rus. Fed.
Novosibirskiye Ostrova is Rus. Fed. see New Siberia Islands
89 E3 **Novosil'** Rus. Fed.
89 D2 **Novosokol'niki** Rus. Fed.
91 C2 **Novotroyits'ke** Ukr.
91 C2 **Novoukrayinka** Ukr.
90 A1 **Novovolyns'k** Ukr.
89 E3 **Novovoronezh** Rus. Fed.
Novovoronezhskiy Rus. Fed. see Novovoronezh
89 D2 **Novozybkov** Rus. Fed.
103 D2 **Nový Jičín** Czech Rep.
86 E2 **Novyy Bor** Rus. Fed.
91 C2 **Novyy Buh** Ukr.
Novyy Donbass Ukr. see Dymytrov
Novyye Petushki Rus. Fed. see Petushki
Novyy Margelan Uzbek. see Farg'ona
89 E2 **Novyy Nekouz** Rus. Fed.

91 D1 **Novyy Oskol** Rus. Fed.
86 G2 **Novyy Port** Rus. Fed.
86 G2 **Novyy Urengoy** Rus. Fed.
69 E1 **Novyy Urgal** Rus. Fed.
Novyy Uzen' Kazakh. see Zhanaozen
103 D1 **Nowogard** Pol.
Noworadomsk Pol. see Radomsko
53 D2 **Nowra** Austr.
81 D2 **Now Shahr** Iran
74 B1 **Nowshera** Pak.
103 E2 **Nowy Sącz** Pol.
103 E2 **Nowy Targ** Pol.
82 G2 **Noyabr'sk** Rus. Fed.
105 C2 **Noyon** France
121 B2 **Nsanje** Malawi
121 B2 **Nsombo** Zambia
118 B3 **Ntandembele** Dem. Rep. Congo
123 C2 **Ntha** S. Africa
118 A2 **Ntoum** Gabon
119 D3 **Ntungamo** Uganda
Nuanetsi r. Zimbabwe see Mwenezi
79 C2 **Nu'aym** reg. Oman
116 B2 **Nubian Desert** Sudan
150 B4 **Nudo Coropuna** mt. Peru
143 D3 **Nueces** r. U.S.A.
129 E1 **Nueltin Lake** Can.
150 B2 **Nueva Loja** Ecuador
153 A4 **Nueva Lubecka** Arg.
145 B2 **Nueva Rosita** Mex.
144 B1 **Nuevo Casas Grandes** Mex.
144 B2 **Nuevo Ideal** Mex.
145 C2 **Nuevo Laredo** Mex.
117 C4 **Nugaal** watercourse Somalia
105 C2 **Nuits-St-Georges** France
Nu Jiang r. China/Myanmar see Salween
Nukha Azer. see Şäki
49 J6 **Nuku'alofa** Tonga
49 M4 **Nuku Hiva** i. Fr. Polynesia
48 G4 **Nukumanu Islands** P.N.G.
76 B2 **Nukus** Uzbek.
50 B2 **Nullagine** Austr.
50 C3 **Nullarbor** Austr.
50 B3 **Nullarbor Plain** Austr.
115 D4 **Numan** Nigeria
67 C3 **Numazu** Japan
51 C1 **Numbulwar** Austr.
93 E3 **Numedal** val. Norway
59 C3 **Numfoor** i. Indon.
53 C3 **Numurkah** Austr.
Nunap Isua c. Greenland see Farewell, Cape
127 G2 **Nunavik** reg. Can.
129 E1 **Nunavut** admin. div. Can.
99 C3 **Nuneaton** U.K.
127 G2 **Nunavik** reg. Can.
126 A3 **Nunivak Island** U.S.A.
106 B1 **Nuñomoral** Spain
108 A2 **Nuoro** Sardinia Italy
78 B2 **Nuqrah** Saudi Arabia
77 C1 **Nura** r. Kazakh.
101 E3 **Nuremberg** Ger.
52 A2 **Nuriootpa** Austr.
92 I3 **Nurmes** Fin.
Nürnberg Ger. see Nuremberg
53 C2 **Nurri, Mount** hill Austr.
62 A1 **Nu Shan** mts China
74 A2 **Nushki** Pak.
127 I2 **Nuuk** Greenland
127 I2 **Nuussuaq** Greenland
127 I2 **Nuussuaq** pen. Greenland
80 B3 **Nuwaybi' al Muzayyinah** Egypt
122 A3 **Nuwerus** S. Africa
122 B3 **Nuweveldberge** mts S. Africa
86 Г2 **Nyagan'** Rus. Fed.
75 C2 **Nyainqêntanglha Feng** ml. China
75 D2 **Nyainqêntanglha Shan** mts China
Nyakh Rus. Fed. see Nyagan'
117 A3 **Nyala** Sudan
119 D4 **Nyamtumbo** Tanz.
Nyande Zimbabwe see Masvingo
86 D2 **Nyandoma** Rus. Fed.
118 B3 **Nyanga** Congo
118 B3 **Nyanga** r. Gabon
121 C2 **Nyanga** Zimbabwe
121 C1 **Nyasa, Lake** Africa
Nyasaland country Africa see Malawi
88 C3 **Nyasvizh** Belarus
62 A2 **Nyaunglebin** Myanmar
93 F4 **Nyborg** Denmark
92 I1 **Nyborg** Norway
93 G4 **Nybro** Sweden
Nyenchen Tanglha Range mts China see Nyainqêntanglha Shan
119 D3 **Nyeri** Kenya
75 C1 **Nyima** China
68 C3 **Nyingchi** China
103 E2 **Nyíregyháza** Hungary
93 F5 **Nykøbing** Denmark
93 G4 **Nyköping** Sweden
53 C2 **Nymagee** Austr.
93 G4 **Nynäshamn** Sweden
53 C2 **Nyngan** Austr.
88 B3 **Nyoman** r. Belarus/Lith.
105 D3 **Nyons** France
86 E2 **Nyrob** Rus. Fed.
103 D1 **Nysa** Pol.
134 C2 **Nyssa** U.S.A.
119 C3 **Nyunzu** Dem. Rep. Congo
83 I2 **Nyurba** Rus. Fed.
91 C2 **Nyzhni Sirohozy** Ukr.
91 C2 **Nyzhn'ohirs'kyy** Ukr.

118 B3 **Nzambi** Congo
119 D3 **Nzega** Tanz.
119 B4 **Nzérékoré** Guinea
120 A1 **N'zeto** Angola

O

136 C2 **Oahe, Lake** U.S.A.
49 L1 **O'ahu** *i.* U.S.A.
52 B2 **Oakbank** Austr.
140 B2 **Oakdale** U.S.A.
53 D1 **Oakey** Austr.
138 B3 **Oak Grove** U.S.A.
99 C3 **Oakham** U.K.
134 B1 **Oak Harbor** U.S.A.
138 C3 **Oak Hill** U.S.A.
135 B3 **Oakland** *CA* U.S.A.
139 D3 **Oakland** *MD* U.S.A.
138 B2 **Oak Lawn** U.S.A.
136 C3 **Oakley** U.S.A.
50 B2 **Oakover** *r.* Austr.
134 B2 **Oakridge** U.S.A.
141 D1 **Oak Ridge** U.S.A.
54 B3 **Oamaru** N.Z.
64 B2 **Oas** Phil.
145 C3 **Oaxaca** Mex.
86 F2 **Ob'** *r.* Rus. Fed.
Ob, Gulf of *sea chan.* Rus. Fed.
see **Obskaya Guba**
88 C2 **Obal'** Belarus
118 B2 **Obala** Cameroon
96 B2 **Oban** U.K.
106 B1 **O Barco** Spain
Obbia Somalia *see* **Hobyo**
136 C3 **Oberlin** U.S.A.
53 C2 **Oberon** Austr.
101 F3 **Oberviechtach** Ger.
59 C3 **Obi** *i.* Indon.
151 D3 **Óbidos** Brazil
66 D2 **Obihiro** Japan
69 E1 **Obluch'ye** Rus. Fed.
89 E2 **Obninsk** Rus. Fed.
119 C2 **Obo** C.A.R.
117 C3 **Obock** Djibouti
103 D1 **Oborniki** Pol.
118 B3 **Obouya** Congo
89 E3 **Oboyan'** Rus. Fed.
86 D2 **Obozerskiy** Rus. Fed.
144 B2 **Obregón, Presa** *resr* Mex.
109 D2 **Obrenovac** Serb. and Mont.
134 B2 **O'Brien** U.S.A.
87 E3 **Obshchiy Syrt** *hills* Rus. Fed.
86 G2 **Obskaya Guba** *sea chan.* Rus. Fed.
114 B4 **Obuasi** Ghana
90 C1 **Obukhiv** Ukr.
86 D2 **Ob"yachevo** Rus. Fed.
141 D3 **Ocala** U.S.A.
144 B2 **Ocampo** Mex.
106 C2 **Ocaña** Spain
150 B2 **Occidental, Cordillera** *mts* Col.
150 B4 **Occidental, Cordillera** *mts* Peru
139 D3 **Ocean City** *MD* U.S.A.
139 E3 **Ocean City** *NJ* U.S.A.
128 B2 **Ocean Falls** Can.
135 C4 **Oceanside** U.S.A.
91 C2 **Ochakiv** Ukr.
86 E3 **Ocher** Rus. Fed.
101 E3 **Ochsenfurt** Ger.
110 B1 **Ocna Mureș** Romania
90 B2 **Ocnița** Moldova
141 D2 **Oconee** *r.* U.S.A.
145 C3 **Ocosingo** Mex.
141 E1 **Ocracoke Island** U.S.A.
October Revolution Island
Rus. Fed. *see*
Oktyabr'skoy Revolyutsii, Ostrov
59 C3 **Ocussi** *enclave* East Timor
116 B2 **Oda, Jebel** *mt.* Sudan
66 D2 **Ōdate** Japan
67 C3 **Odawara** Japan
93 E3 **Odda** Norway
106 B2 **Odemira** Port.
111 C3 **Ödemiş** Turkey
93 F4 **Odense** Denmark
101 D3 **Odenwald** *reg.* Ger.
102 C1 **Oder** *r.* Ger.
102 C1 **Oderbucht** *b.* Ger.
90 C2 **Odesa** Ukr.
143 C2 **Odessa** U.S.A.
114 B4 **Odienné** Côte d'Ivoire
89 E3 **Odoyev** Rus. Fed.
103 D1 **Odra** *r.* Pol.
151 E3 **Oeiras** Brazil
101 D2 **Oelde** Ger.
136 C2 **Oelrichs** U.S.A.
101 F2 **Oelsnitz** Ger.
100 B1 **Oenkerk** Neth.
137 E3 **O'Fallon** U.S.A.
109 C2 **Ofanto** *r.* Italy
101 D2 **Offenbach am Main** Ger.
102 B2 **Offenburg** Ger.
66 C3 **Oga** Japan
117 C4 **Ogadēn** *reg.* Eth.
66 C3 **Oga-hantō** *pen.* Japan
67 C3 **Ōgaki** Japan
136 C2 **Ogallala** U.S.A.
Ogasawara-shotō Japan *see*
Bonin Islands
115 C4 **Ogbomosho** Nigeria
136 D2 **Ogden** U.S.A.
139 D2 **Ogdensburg** U.S.A.
126 C2 **Ogilvie** *r.* Can.
126 C2 **Ogilvie Mountains** Can.

141 D2 **Oglethorpe, Mount** U.S.A.
130 B2 **Ogoki** *r.* Can.
130 B2 **Ogoki Reservoir** Can.
88 B2 **Ogre** Latvia
109 C1 **Ogulin** Croatia
81 D2 **Ogurchinskiy, Ostrov** *i.* Turkm.
115 C2 **Ohanet** Alg.
138 B3 **Ohio** *r.* U.S.A.
138 C2 **Ohio** *state* U.S.A.
101 E2 **Ohrdruf** Ger.
101 F2 **Ohře** *r.* Czech Rep.
111 D2 **Ohrid** Macedonia
151 D2 **Oiapoque** Brazil
139 D2 **Oil City** U.S.A.
100 A3 **Oise** *r.* France
67 B4 **Ōita** Japan
144 B2 **Ojinaga** Mex.
152 B2 **Ojos del Salado, Nevado** *mt.*
Arg./Chile
89 F2 **Oka** *r.* Rus. Fed.
120 A3 **Okahandja** Namibia
120 A3 **Okakarara** Namibia
128 C3 **Okanagan Falls** Can.
128 C3 **Okanagan Lake** Can.
134 C1 **Okanogan** U.S.A.
134 C1 **Okanogan** *r.* U.S.A.
74 B1 **Okara** Pak.
120 B2 **Okavango** *r.* Botswana/Namibia
120 B2 **Okavango Delta** *swamp* Botswana
67 C3 **Okaya** Japan
67 B4 **Okayama** Japan
67 C4 **Okazaki** Japan
141 D3 **Okeechobee** U.S.A.
141 D3 **Okeechobee, Lake** U.S.A.
141 D2 **Okefenokee Swamp** U.S.A.
99 A4 **Okehampton** U.K.
115 C4 **Okene** Nigeria
101 E1 **Oker** *r.* Ger.
74 A2 **Okha** India
83 K3 **Okha** Rus. Fed.
75 C2 **Okhaldhunga** Nepal
83 K3 **Okhotka** *r.* Rus. Fed.
83 K3 **Okhotsk** Rus. Fed.
83 K3 **Okhotsk, Sea of** Japan/Rus. Fed.
Okhotskoye More *sea*
Japan/Rus. Fed. *see*
Okhotsk, Sea of
91 C1 **Okhtyrka** Ukr.
69 E3 **Okinawa** *i.* Japan
67 B3 **Oki-shotō** *is* Japan
143 D1 **Oklahoma** *state* U.S.A.
143 D1 **Oklahoma City** U.S.A.
143 D1 **Okmulgee** U.S.A.
Oknitsa Moldova *see* **Ocnița**
78 A2 **Oko, Wadi** *watercourse* Sudan
118 B3 **Okondja** Gabon
128 C2 **Okotoks** Can.
89 D3 **Okovskiy Les** *for.* Rus. Fed.
118 B3 **Okoyo** Congo
92 H1 **Øksfjord** Norway
62 A2 **Oktwin** Myanmar
Oktyabr' Kazakh. *see* **Kandyagash**
Oktyabr'sk Kazakh. *see*
Kandyagash
86 D2 **Oktyabr'skiy** Rus. Fed.
83 L3 **Oktyabr'skiy** Rus. Fed.
87 E3 **Oktyabr'skiy** Rus. Fed.
86 F2 **Oktyabr'skoye** Rus. Fed.
83 H1 **Oktyabr'skoy Revolyutsii, Ostrov**
i. Rus. Fed.
89 D2 **Okulovka** Rus. Fed.
66 C2 **Okushiri-tō** *i.* Japan
92 □B2 **Ólafsfjörður** Iceland
92 □A3 **Ólafsvík** Iceland
88 B2 **Olaine** Latvia
93 G4 **Öland** *i.* Sweden
52 B2 **Olary** Austr.
136 B3 **Olathe** *CO* U.S.A.
137 E3 **Olathe** *KS* U.S.A.
153 B3 **Olavarría** Arg.
103 D1 **Oława** Pol.
108 A2 **Olbia** *Sardinia* Italy
126 C2 **Old Crow** Can.
101 D1 **Oldenburg** Ger.
102 C1 **Oldenburg in Holstein** Ger.
100 C1 **Oldenzaal** Neth.
98 B3 **Oldham** U.K.
97 B3 **Old Head of Kinsale** *hd* Ireland
96 C2 **Oldmeldrum** U.K.
128 C2 **Olds** Can.
129 D2 **Old Wives Lake** Can.
139 D2 **Olean** U.S.A.
103 E1 **Olecko** Pol.
83 J2 **Olekminsk** Rus. Fed.
91 C2 **Oleksandrivka** Ukr.
Oleksandrivs'k Ukr. *see*
Zaporizhzhya
91 C2 **Oleksandriya** Ukr.
86 C2 **Olenegorsk** Rus. Fed.
83 I2 **Olenek** Rus. Fed.
83 I2 **Olenek** *r.* Rus. Fed.
89 D2 **Olenino** Rus. Fed.
Olenivs'ki Kar"yery Ukr. *see*
Dokuchayevs'k
Olenya Rus. Fed. *see* **Olenegorsk**
90 B1 **Olevs'k** Ukr.
106 B2 **Olhão** Port.
123 D1 **Olifants** *r.* Moz./S. Africa
122 A2 **Olifants** *watercourse* Namibia
123 D1 **Olifants** *r.* S. Africa
122 A3 **Olifants** *r.* S. Africa
122 B2 **Olifantshoek** S. Africa
154 C2 **Olímpia** Brazil

151 F3 **Olinda** Brazil
123 C1 **Oliphants Drift** S. Africa
107 C2 **Oliva** Spain
155 D2 **Oliveira** Brazil
Olivença Moz. *see* **Lupilichi**
106 B2 **Olivenza** Spain
140 B2 **Olla** U.S.A.
152 B2 **Ollagüe** Chile
77 C2 **Olmaliq** Uzbek.
106 C1 **Olmedo** Spain
105 D3 **Olmeto** *Corsica* France
150 B3 **Olmos** Peru
138 B3 **Olney** U.S.A.
103 D2 **Olomouc** Czech Rep.
86 C2 **Olonets** Rus. Fed.
64 B2 **Olongapo** Phil.
104 B3 **Oloron-Ste-Marie** France
107 D1 **Olot** Spain
69 D1 **Olovyannaya** Rus. Fed.
100 C2 **Olpe** Ger.
103 E1 **Olsztyn** Pol.
110 B2 **Olt** *r.* Romania
110 C2 **Oltenița** Romania
143 C2 **Olton** U.S.A.
81 C1 **Oltu** Turkey
Ol'viopol' Ukr. *see* **Pervomays'k**
111 B3 **Olympia** *tourist site* Greece
134 B1 **Olympia** U.S.A.
Olympus, Mount Greece *see*
Mount Olympus
134 B1 **Olympus, Mount** U.S.A.
83 M2 **Olyutorskiy** Rus. Fed.
83 M3 **Olyutorskiy, Mys** *c.* Rus. Fed.
66 D2 **Ōma** Japan
97 C1 **Omagh** U.K.
137 D2 **Omaha** U.S.A.
79 C2 **Oman** *country* Asia
79 C2 **Oman, Gulf of** Asia
54 A2 **Omarama** N.Z.
120 A3 **Omaruru** Namibia
120 B2 **Omatako** *watercourse* Namibia
122 B2 **Omaweneno** Botswana
116 B3 **Omdurman** Sudan
53 C3 **Omeo** Austr.
145 C3 **Ometepec** Mex.
78 A3 **Om Hajēr** Eritrea
81 C2 **Omīdīyeh** Iran
128 B2 **Omineca Mountains** Can.
120 A3 **Omitara** Namibia
67 C3 **Ōmiya** Japan
100 C1 **Ommen** Neth.
83 L2 **Omolon** *r.* Rus. Fed.
100 B3 **Omont** France
82 F3 **Omsk** Rus. Fed.
83 L2 **Omsukchan** Rus. Fed.
110 C1 **Omu, Vârful** *mt.* Romania
67 A4 **Ōmura** Japan
138 A2 **Onalaska** U.S.A.
139 D3 **Onancock** U.S.A.
138 C1 **Onaping Lake** Can.
131 C3 **Onatchiway, Lac** *l.* Can.
63 A2 **Onbingwin** Myanmar
120 A2 **Oncócua** Angola
122 B3 **Onderstedorings** S. Africa
120 A2 **Ondjiva** Angola
69 D1 **Öndörhaan** Mongolia
122 B1 **One Botswana**
86 C2 **Onega** Rus. Fed.
86 C2 **Onega** *r.* Rus. Fed.
86 C2 **Onega, Lake** Rus. Fed.
128 B2 **100 Mile House** Can.
139 D2 **Oneida Lake** U.S.A.
137 D2 **O'Neill** U.S.A.
139 D2 **Oneonta** U.S.A.
110 C1 **Onești** Romania
Onezhskoye Ozero *l.* Rus. Fed. *see*
Onega, Lake
122 B2 **Ongers** *watercourse* S. Africa
65 B2 **Ongjin** N. Korea
73 C3 **Ongole** India
121 □D3 **Onilahy** *r.* Madag.
115 C4 **Onitsha** Nigeria
120 A3 **Onjati Mountain** Namibia
67 C3 **Ōno** Japan
122 A2 **Onseepkans** S. Africa
50 A2 **Onslow** Austr.
141 E2 **Onslow Bay** U.S.A.
130 A2 **Ontario** *prov.* Can.
134 C2 **Ontario** U.S.A.
139 D2 **Ontario, Lake** Can./U.S.A.
107 C2 **Ontinyent** Spain
51 C2 **Oodnadatta** Austr.
Oostende Belgium *see* **Ostend**
100 B2 **Oosterhout** Neth.
100 A2 **Oosterschelde** *est.* Neth.
100 B1 **Oost-Vlieland** Neth.
128 B2 **Ootsa Lake** Can.
128 B2 **Ootsa Lake** *l.* Can.
118 C3 **Opala** Dem. Rep. Congo
130 C2 **Opataca, Lac** *l.* Can.
103 D2 **Opava** Czech Rep.
141 C2 **Opelika** U.S.A.
140 B2 **Opelousas** U.S.A.
117 A4 **Opienge** Dem. Rep. Congo
130 C2 **Opinaca, Réservoir** *resr* Can.
131 D2 **Opiscotéo, Lac** *l.* Can.
88 C2 **Opochka** Rus. Fed.
144 A2 **Opodepe** Mex.
103 D1 **Opole** Pol.
106 B1 **Oporto** Port.
54 C1 **Opotiki** N.Z.
93 E3 **Oppdal** Norway
134 C1 **Opportunity** U.S.A.
54 B1 **Opunake** N.Z.
120 A2 **Opuwo** Namibia

110 B1 **Oradea** Romania
109 D2 **Orahovac** Serb. and Mont.
114 B1 **Oran** Alg.
152 B2 **Orán** Arg.
65 B1 **Ŏrang** N. Korea
53 C2 **Orange** Austr.
105 C3 **Orange** France
122 A2 **Orange** *r.* Namibia/S. Africa
143 E2 **Orange** U.S.A.
141 D2 **Orangeburg** U.S.A.
Orange Free State *prov.* S. Africa
see **Free State**
141 D2 **Orange Park** U.S.A.
138 C2 **Orangeville** Can.
145 D3 **Orange Walk** Belize
101 F1 **Oranienburg** Ger.
122 A2 **Oranjemund** Namibia
147 C3 **Oranjestad** Aruba
120 B3 **Orapa** Botswana
110 B1 **Orăștie** Romania
Orașul Stalin Romania *see* **Brașov**
108 B2 **Orbetello** Italy
53 C3 **Orbost** Austr.
141 D3 **Orchid Island** U.S.A.
111 B3 **Orchomenos** Greece
50 B1 **Ord, Mount** *hill* Austr.
106 B1 **Ordes** Spain
70 B2 **Ordos** China
80 B1 **Ordu** Turkey
Ordzhonikidze Rus. Fed. *see*
Vladikavkaz
91 C2 **Ordzhonikidze** Ukr.
93 G4 **Örebro** Sweden
134 B2 **Oregon** *state* U.S.A.
134 B1 **Oregon City** U.S.A.
141 E1 **Oregon Inlet** U.S.A.
87 C3 **Orekhovo-Zuyevo** Rus. Fed.
89 E3 **Orel** Rus. Fed.
83 K3 **Orel', Ozero** *l.* Rus. Fed.
135 D2 **Orem** U.S.A.
111 C3 **Ören** Turkey
87 E3 **Orenburg** Rus. Fed.
54 A3 **Orepuki** N.Z.
111 C2 **Orestiada** Greece
93 F4 **Öresund** *str.* Denmark/Sweden
Oretana, Cordillera *mts* Spain *see*
Toledo, Montes de
99 D3 **Orford Ness** *hd* U.K.
89 F2 **Orgtrud** Rus. Fed.
74 A1 **Orgūn** Afgh.
111 C3 **Orhaneli** Turkey
111 C2 **Orhangazi** Turkey
68 D1 **Orhon Gol** *r.* Mongolia
152 B1 **Oriental, Cordillera** *mts* Bol.
150 B2 **Oriental, Cordillera** *mts* Col.
150 B4 **Oriental, Cordillera** *mts* Peru
107 C2 **Orihuela** Spain
91 C2 **Orikhiv** Ukr.
130 C3 **Orillia** Can.
93 I3 **Orimattila** Fin.
150 C2 **Orinoco** *r.* Col./Venez.
150 C2 **Orinoco Delta** Venez.
75 C2 **Orissa** *state* India
88 B2 **Orissaare** Estonia
108 A3 **Oristano** *Sardinia* Italy
93 I3 **Orivesi** *l.* Fin.
151 D3 **Oriximiná** Brazil
145 C3 **Orizaba** Mex.
145 C3 **Orizaba, Pico de** *vol.* Mex.
154 C1 **Orizona** Brazil
92 E3 **Orkanger** Norway
93 F4 **Örkelljunga** Sweden
93 E3 **Orkla** *r.* Norway
96 C1 **Orkney Islands** U.K.
154 C2 **Orlândia** Brazil
141 D3 **Orlando** U.S.A.
104 C2 **Orléans** France
139 F2 **Orléans** Can.
139 E1 **Orléans, Île d'** *i.* Can.
Orléansville Alg. *see*
Ech Chélif
74 A2 **Ormara** Pak.
64 B2 **Ormoc** Phil.
141 D3 **Ormond Beach** U.S.A.
98 B3 **Ormskirk** U.K.
104 B2 **Orne** *r.* France
92 F2 **Ørnes** Norway
92 G3 **Örnsköldsvik** Sweden
114 B3 **Orodara** Burkina
134 C1 **Orofino** U.S.A.
139 F2 **Orono** U.S.A.
Oroqen Zizhiqi China *see* **Alihe**
64 B3 **Oroquieta** Phil.
108 A2 **Orosei** *Sardinia* Italy
108 A2 **Orosei, Golfo di** *b. Sardinia* Italy
103 E2 **Orosháza** Hungary
135 B3 **Oroville** U.S.A.
52 A2 **Orroroo** Austr.
93 F3 **Orsa** Sweden
89 D3 **Orsha** Belarus
87 E3 **Orsk** Rus. Fed.
110 B2 **Orșova** Romania
93 E3 **Ørsta** Norway
106 B1 **Ortegal, Cabo** *c.* Spain
104 B3 **Orthez** France
106 B1 **Ortigueira** Spain
108 B1 **Ortles** *mt.* Italy
108 B2 **Ortona** Italy
137 D1 **Ortonville** U.S.A.
83 J2 **Orulgan, Khrebet** *mts* Rus. Fed.
Orūmīyeh Iran *see* **Urmia**
Orūmīyeh, Daryācheh-ye *salt l.*
Iran *see* **Urmia, Lake**
152 B1 **Oruro** Bol.
104 B2 **Orvault** France

108 B2 **Orvieto** Italy
93 F3 **Os** Norway
146 B4 **Osa, Península de** *pen.* Costa Rica
137 E3 **Osage** *r.* U.S.A.
137 D3 **Osage City** U.S.A.
67 C4 **Ōsaka** Japan
77 D1 **Osakarovka** Kazakh.
101 E1 **Oschersleben (Bode)** Ger.
108 A2 **Oschiri** *Sardinia* Italy
138 C2 **Oscoda** U.S.A.
89 E3 **Osetr** *r.* Rus. Fed.
139 D1 **Osgoode** Can.
77 D2 **Osh** Kyrg.
120 A2 **Oshakati** Namibia
130 C3 **Oshawa** Can.
120 A2 **Oshikango** Namibia
66 C2 **Ō-shima** *i.* Japan
67 C4 **Ō-shima** *i.* Japan
138 B2 **Oshkosh** U.S.A.
81 C2 **Oshnoviyeh** Iran
115 C4 **Oshogbo** Nigeria
118 B3 **Oshwe** Dem. Rep. Congo
109 C1 **Osijek** Croatia
128 B2 **Osilinka** *r.* Can.
108 B2 **Osimo** Italy
123 D2 **Osipenko** Ukr. *see* Berdyans'k
123 D2 **Osizweni** S. Africa
137 E2 **Oskaloosa** U.S.A.
93 G4 **Oskarshamn** Sweden
89 E3 **Oskol** *r.* Rus. Fed.
93 F4 **Oslo** Norway
93 F4 **Oslofjorden** *sea chan.* Norway
80 B1 **Osmancık** Turkey
111 C2 **Osmaneli** Turkey
80 B2 **Osmaniye** Turkey
88 C2 **Os'mino** Rus. Fed.
101 D1 **Osnabrück** Ger.
153 A4 **Osorno** Chile
106 C1 **Osorno** Spain
128 C3 **Osoyoos** Can.
100 B2 **Oss** Neth.
51 D4 **Ossa, Mount** Austr.
83 L3 **Ossora** Rus. Fed.
89 D2 **Ostashkov** Rus. Fed.
101 D1 **Oste** *r.* Ger.
100 A2 **Ostend** Belgium
101 E1 **Osterburg (Altmark)** Ger.
93 F3 **Österdalälven** *l.* Sweden
101 D1 **Osterholz-Scharmbeck** Ger.
101 E2 **Osterode am Harz** Ger.
92 F3 **Östersund** Sweden
      Ostfriesische Inseln *is* Ger. *see* East Frisian Islands
100 C1 **Ostfriesland** *reg.* Ger.
93 G3 **Östhammar** Sweden
103 D2 **Ostrava** Czech Rep.
103 D1 **Ostróda** Pol.
89 E3 **Ostrogozhsk** Rus. Fed.
90 B1 **Ostroh** Ukr.
103 E1 **Ostrołęka** Pol.
101 F2 **Ostrov** Czech Rep.
88 C2 **Ostrov** Rus. Fed.
      Ostrovets Pol. *see* Ostrowiec Świętokrzyski
89 F2 **Ostrovskoye** Rus. Fed.
103 E1 **Ostrowiec Świętokrzyski** Pol.
103 E1 **Ostrów Mazowiecka** Pol.
      Ostrowo Pol. *see* Ostrów Wielkopolski
103 D1 **Ostrów Wielkopolski** Pol.
109 C2 **Ostuni** Italy
110 B2 **Osŭm** *r.* Bulg.
67 B4 **Ōsumi-kaikyō** *sea chan.* Japan
67 B4 **Ōsumi-shotō** *is* Japan
106 B2 **Osuna** Spain
139 D2 **Oswego** U.S.A.
99 B3 **Oswestry** U.K.
67 C3 **Ōta** Japan
54 B3 **Otago Peninsula** N.Z.
54 C2 **Otaki** N.Z.
77 D2 **Otar** Kazakh.
66 D2 **Otaru** Japan
120 A2 **Otavi** Namibia
67 D3 **Ōtawara** Japan
92 G2 **Oteren** Norway
134 C1 **Othello** U.S.A.
120 A3 **Otjiwarongo** Namibia
109 C2 **Otočac** Croatia
117 B3 **Otoro, Jebel** *mt.* Sudan
      Otpor Rus. Fed. *see* Zabaykal'sk
93 E4 **Otra** *r.* Norway
109 C2 **Otranto, Strait of** Albania/Italy
67 C3 **Ōtsu** Japan
93 E3 **Otta** Norway
130 C3 **Ottawa** Can.
130 C3 **Ottawa** *r.* Can.
138 B2 **Ottawa** *IL* U.S.A.
137 D3 **Ottawa** *KS* U.S.A.
130 B2 **Ottawa Islands** Can.
98 B2 **Otterburn** U.K.
130 B2 **Otter Rapids** Can.
100 B2 **Ottignies** Belgium
100 A2 **Ottumwa** U.S.A.
150 B3 **Otuzco** Peru
140 B2 **Otway, Cape** Austr.
140 B2 **Ouachita** *r.* U.S.A.
140 B2 **Ouachita, Lake** U.S.A.
140 B2 **Ouachita Mountains** U.S.A.
118 C2 **Ouadda** C.A.R.
115 D3 **Ouaddaï** *reg.* Chad
114 B3 **Ouagadougou** Burkina
114 B3 **Ouahigouya** Burkina

114 B3 **Oualâta** Maur.
118 C2 **Ouanda-Djallé** C.A.R.
114 B2 **Ouarâne** *reg.* Maur.
115 C1 **Ouargla** Alg.
114 B1 **Ouarzazate** Morocco
100 A2 **Oudenaarde** Belgium
122 B3 **Oudtshoorn** S. Africa
107 C2 **Oued Tlélat** Alg.
114 B1 **Oued Zem** Morocco
104 A2 **Ouessant, Île d'** *i.* France
118 B2 **Ouesso** Congo
97 B2 **Oughterard** Ireland
118 B2 **Ouham** *r.* C.A.R./Chad
114 B1 **Oujda** Morocco
92 H3 **Oulainen** Fin.
107 D2 **Ouled Farès** Alg.
92 I2 **Oulu** Fin.
92 I3 **Oulujärvi** *l.* Fin.
108 A1 **Oulx** Italy
115 C3 **Oum-Chalouba** Chad
115 D3 **Oum-Hadjer** Chad
115 C3 **Ounianga Kébir** Chad
100 B2 **Oupeye** Belgium
100 C3 **Our** *r.* Lux.
106 B1 **Ourense** Spain
154 C2 **Ourinhos** Brazil
155 D2 **Ouro Preto** Brazil
100 B2 **Ourthe** *r.* Belgium
98 C3 **Ouse** *r.* U.K.
      Outaouais, Rivière des *r.* Can. *see* Ottawa
131 D3 **Outardes** *r.* Can.
131 D2 **Outardes Quatre, Réservoir** *resr* Can.
96 A2 **Outer Hebrides** *is* U.K.
      Outer Mongolia *country* Asia *see* Mongolia
120 A3 **Outjo** Namibia
129 D2 **Outlook** Can.
92 I3 **Outokumpu** Fin.
52 B3 **Ouyen** Austr.
108 A2 **Ovace, Punta d'** *mt.* Corsica France
152 A3 **Ovalle** Chile
106 B1 **Ovar** Port.
92 H2 **Överkalix** Sweden
137 E3 **Overland Park** U.S.A.
135 D3 **Overton** U.S.A.
92 H2 **Övertorneå** Sweden
106 B1 **Oviedo** Spain
141 D3 **Oviedo** U.S.A.
88 B2 **Oviŝrags** *hd* Latvia
93 E3 **Øvre Årdal** Norway
93 E3 **Øvre Rendal** Norway
90 B1 **Ovruch** Ukr.
118 B3 **Owando** Congo
67 C4 **Owase** Japan
143 D1 **Owasso** U.S.A.
137 E2 **Owatonna** U.S.A.
139 D2 **Owego** U.S.A.
138 B3 **Owensboro** U.S.A.
135 C3 **Owens Lake** U.S.A.
130 B3 **Owen Sound** Can.
51 D1 **Owen Stanley Range** *mts* P.N.G.
115 C4 **Owerri** Nigeria
115 C4 **Owo** Nigeria
138 C2 **Owosso** U.S.A.
134 C2 **Owyhee** U.S.A.
134 C2 **Owyhee** *r.* U.S.A.
129 D3 **Oxbow** Can.
54 B2 **Oxford** N.Z.
99 C4 **Oxford** U.K.
140 C2 **Oxford** U.S.A.
129 E2 **Oxford Lake** Can.
145 D2 **Oxkutzcab** Mex.
52 B2 **Oxley** Austr.
      Ox Mountains *hills* Ireland *see* Slieve Gamph
135 C4 **Oxnard** U.S.A.
67 C3 **Oyama** Japan
118 B2 **Oyem** Gabon
129 C2 **Oyen** Can.
105 D2 **Oyonnax** France
77 C2 **Oyoqquduq** Uzbek.
64 B3 **Ozamiz** Phil.
140 C2 **Ozark** *AL* U.S.A.
137 E3 **Ozark** *MO* U.S.A.
137 E3 **Ozark Plateau** U.S.A.
137 E3 **Ozarks, Lake of the** U.S.A.
83 L3 **Ozernovskiy** Rus. Fed.
88 B3 **Ozersk** Rus. Fed.
89 E3 **Ozery** Rus. Fed.
87 D3 **Ozinki** Rus. Fed.

P

127 I2 **Paamiut** Greenland
122 A3 **Paarl** S. Africa
103 D1 **Pabianice** Pol.
75 C2 **Pabna** Bangl.
88 C3 **Pabradė** Lith.
74 A2 **Pab Range** *mts* Pak.
150 B3 **Pacasmayo** Peru
142 B2 **Pacheco** Mex.
109 C3 **Pachino** *Sicily* Italy
145 C2 **Pachuca** Mex.
135 B3 **Pacifica** U.S.A.
157 E9 **Pacific-Antarctic Ridge** *sea feature* S. Pacific Ocean
156 **Pacific Ocean**
61 C2 **Pacitan** Indon.
52 B2 **Packsaddle** Austr.

103 D1 **Paczków** Pol.
60 B2 **Padang** Indon.
60 B1 **Padang Endau** Malaysia
60 B2 **Padangpanjang** Indon.
60 A1 **Padangsidimpuan** Indon.
101 D2 **Paderborn** Ger.
      Padova Italy *see* Padua
143 D3 **Padre Island** U.S.A.
99 A4 **Padstow** U.K.
52 B3 **Padthaway** Austr.
108 B1 **Padua** Italy
138 B3 **Paducah** *KY* U.S.A.
143 C2 **Paducah** *TX* U.S.A.
65 B1 **Paegam** N. Korea
      Paektu-san *mt.* China/N. Korea *see* Baotou Shan
65 A2 **Paengnyŏng-do** *i.* S. Korea
54 C1 **Paeroa** N.Z.
      Pafos Cyprus *see* Paphos
109 C2 **Pag** Croatia
109 B2 **Pag** *i.* Croatia
64 B3 **Pagadian** Phil.
60 B2 **Pagai Selatan** *i.* Indon.
60 B2 **Pagai Utara** *i.* Indon.
59 D1 **Pagan** *i.* N. Mariana Is
61 C2 **Pagatan** Indon.
142 A1 **Page** U.S.A.
88 B2 **Pagėgiai** Lith.
153 E5 **Paget, Mount** S. Georgia
136 B3 **Pagosa Springs** U.S.A.
88 C2 **Paide** Estonia
99 B4 **Paignton** U.K.
93 I3 **Päijänne** *l.* Fin.
75 C1 **Paikü Co** *l.* China
60 B2 **Painan** Indon.
138 C2 **Painesville** U.S.A.
142 A1 **Painted Desert** U.S.A.
      Paint Hills Can. *see* Wemindji
96 B3 **Paisley** U.K.
92 H2 **Pajala** Sweden
150 A3 **Pájaro** Ecuador
150 D2 **Pakaraima Mountains** *mts* Brazil
150 D2 **Pakaraima Mountains** Guyana
74 A2 **Pakistan** *country* Asia
62 A1 **Pakokku** Myanmar
88 B2 **Pakruojis** Lith.
103 D2 **Paks** Hungary
130 A2 **Pakwash Lake** Can.
62 B2 **Pakxan** Laos
63 B2 **Pakxé** Laos
115 D4 **Pala** Chad
60 B2 **Palabuhanratu, Teluk** *b.* Indon.
111 C3 **Palaikastro** Greece
111 B3 **Palaiochora** Greece
      Palakkad India *see* Palghat
122 B1 **Palamakoloi** Botswana
107 D1 **Palamós** Spain
83 L3 **Palana** Rus. Fed.
64 B2 **Palanan** Phil.
61 C2 **Palangkaraya** Indon.
74 B2 **Palanpur** India
123 C1 **Palapye** Botswana
83 L2 **Palatka** Rus. Fed.
141 D3 **Palatka** U.S.A.
59 C2 **Palau** *country* N. Pacific Ocean
63 A2 **Palaw** Myanmar
64 A3 **Palawan** *i.* Phil.
64 A3 **Palawan Passage** *str.* Phil.
88 B2 **Paldiski** Estonia
89 F2 **Palekh** Rus. Fed.
60 B2 **Palembang** Indon.
106 C1 **Palencia** Spain
145 C3 **Palenque** Mex.
108 B3 **Palermo** *Sicily* Italy
143 D2 **Palestine** U.S.A.
62 A1 **Paletwa** Myanmar
73 B3 **Palghat** India
74 B2 **Pali** India
48 G4 **Palikir** Micronesia
109 C2 **Palinuro, Capo** *c.* Italy
111 B3 **Paliouri, Akra** *pt* Greece
100 B3 **Paliseul** Belgium
92 I3 **Paljakka** *hill* Fin.
88 C2 **Palkino** Rus. Fed.
73 B4 **Palk Strait** India/Sri Lanka
      Palla Bianca *mt.* Austria/Italy *see* Weißkugel
54 C2 **Palliser, Cape** N.Z.
157 F7 **Palliser, Îles** *is* Fr. Polynesia
106 B2 **Palma del Río** Spain
107 D2 **Palma de Mallorca** Spain
154 B2 **Palmas** Brazil
151 E4 **Palmas** *Tocantins* Brazil
154 B3 **Palmas, Campos de** *hills* Brazil
114 B4 **Palmas, Cape** Liberia
141 D3 **Palm Bay** U.S.A.
135 C4 **Palmdale** U.S.A.
154 C3 **Palmeira** Brazil
151 E3 **Palmeirais** Brazil
126 C2 **Palmer** U.S.A.
55 A2 **Palmer Land** *reg.* Antarctica
49 K5 **Palmerston** *atoll* Cook Is
54 C2 **Palmerston North** N.Z.
109 C3 **Palmi** Italy
145 C2 **Palmillas** Mex.
150 B2 **Palmira** Col.
154 B2 **Palmital** Brazil
135 C4 **Palm Springs** U.S.A.
      Palmyra Syria *see* Tadmur
49 K3 **Palmyra Atoll** N. Pacific Ocean
135 B3 **Palo Alto** U.S.A.
117 B3 **Paloich** Sudan
145 C3 **Palomares** Mex.
61 D2 **Palopo** Indon.
107 C2 **Palos, Cabo de** *c.* Spain

92 I3 **Paltamo** Fin.
61 C2 **Palu** Indon.
83 M2 **Palyavaam** *r.* Rus. Fed.
150 B3 **Pamar** Col.
121 C3 **Pambarra** Moz.
104 C3 **Pamiers** France
77 D3 **Pamir** *mts* Asia
141 E1 **Pamlico Sound** *sea chan.* U.S.A.
152 B1 **Pampa** Bol.
153 A4 **Pampas** *reg.* Arg.
150 B2 **Pamplona** Col.
107 C1 **Pamplona** Spain
111 D2 **Pamukova** Turkey
60 B2 **Panaitan** *i.* Indon.
73 B3 **Panaji** India
146 B4 **Panama** *country* Central America
      Panamá Panama *see* Panama City
      Panamá, Golfo de Panama *see* Panama, Gulf of
146 C4 **Panama, Gulf of** *g.* Panama
146 C4 **Panama Canal** *canal* Panama
146 C4 **Panama City** Panama
140 C2 **Panama City** U.S.A.
135 C3 **Panamint Range** *mts* U.S.A.
60 B1 **Panarik** Indon.
64 B2 **Panay** *i.* Phil.
109 D2 **Pančevo** Serb. and Mont.
64 B2 **Pandan** Phil.
64 B2 **Pandan** Phil.
75 C2 **Pandaria** India
73 B3 **Pandharpur** India
88 B2 **Panevėžys** Lith.
      Panfilov Kazakh. *see* Zharkent
61 C2 **Pangkalanbuun** Indon.
60 A1 **Pangkalansusu** Indon.
60 B2 **Pangkalpinang** Indon.
60 B2 **Pangkalsiang, Tanjung** *pt* Indon.
127 H2 **Pangnirtung** Can.
86 G2 **Pangody** Rus. Fed.
89 F3 **Panino** Rus. Fed.
74 B2 **Panipat** India
74 A2 **Panjgur** Pak.
      Panjim India *see* Panaji
118 A2 **Pankshin** Nigeria
65 C1 **Pan Ling** *mts* China
75 C2 **Panna** India
50 A2 **Pannawonica** Austr.
154 B2 **Panorama** Brazil
65 B1 **Panshi** China
152 C1 **Pantanal** *reg.* Brazil
145 C2 **Pánuco** Mex.
145 C2 **Pánuco** *r.* Mex.
71 A3 **Panxian** China
62 B1 **Panzhihua** China
109 C3 **Paola** Italy
118 B2 **Paoua** C.A.R.
63 B2 **Paôy Pêt** Cambodia
103 D2 **Pápa** Hungary
54 B2 **Papakura** N.Z.
145 C2 **Papantla** Mex.
96 □ **Papa Stour** *i.* U.K.
54 B1 **Papatoetoe** N.Z.
49 M5 **Papeete** Fr. Polynesia
100 C1 **Papenburg** Ger.
80 B2 **Paphos** Cyprus
137 D2 **Papillion** U.S.A.
59 D3 **Papua** *reg.* Indon.
59 D3 **Papua, Gulf of** P.N.G.
59 D3 **Papua New Guinea** *country* Oceania
89 F3 **Para** *r.* Rus. Fed.
50 A2 **Paraburdoo** Austr.
154 C1 **Paracatu** Brazil
155 C1 **Paracatu** *r.* Brazil
52 A2 **Parachilna** Austr.
109 D2 **Paraćin** Serb. and Mont.
155 D1 **Pará de Minas** Brazil
151 C2 **Paradise** Guyana
135 B3 **Paradise** U.S.A.
140 B1 **Paragould** U.S.A.
151 D3 **Paraguai** *r.* Brazil
147 C3 **Paraguaná, Península de** *pen.* Venez.
152 C2 **Paraguay** *r.* Arg./Para.
152 C2 **Paraguay** *country* S. America
155 D2 **Paraíba do Sul** *r.* Brazil
154 B1 **Paraíso** Brazil
145 C3 **Paraíso** Mex.
114 C4 **Parakou** Benin
52 A2 **Parakylia** Austr.
151 D2 **Paramaribo** Suriname
83 L3 **Paramushir, Ostrov** *i.* Rus. Fed.
152 B3 **Paraná** Arg.
154 A3 **Paraná** *r.* S. America
154 B3 **Paraná, Serra do** *hills* Brazil
154 B2 **Paranaíba** Brazil
154 B1 **Paranaíba** *r.* Brazil
154 B2 **Paranapanema** *r.* Brazil
154 B2 **Paranapiacaba, Serra** *mts* Brazil
154 B2 **Paranavaí** Brazil
90 A2 **Parângul Mare, Vârful** *mt.* Romania
54 B2 **Paraparaumu** N.Z.
155 D2 **Parati** Brazil
52 A2 **Paratoo** Austr.
151 D3 **Parauaquara, Serra** *hill* Brazil
154 B1 **Paraúna** Brazil
105 D2 **Paray-le-Monial** France
74 B2 **Parbati** *r.* India
74 B3 **Parbhani** India
101 E1 **Parchim** Ger.
103 E1 **Parczew** Pol.
155 E1 **Pardo** *r.* Brazil
154 B2 **Pardo** *r.* Brazil

154 C2 Pardo r. Brazil
103 D1 Pardubice Czech Rep.
152 C1 Parecis, Serra dos hills Brazil
130 C3 Parent Can.
130 C3 Parent, Lac l. Can.
61 C2 Parepare Indon.
89 D2 Parfino Rus. Fed.
111 B3 Parga Greece
109 C3 Parghelia Italy
147 D3 Paria, Gulf of Trin. and Tob./Venez.
150 C2 Parima, Serra mts Brazil
151 D3 Parintins Brazil
104 C2 Paric France
140 C1 Paris TN U.S.A.
143 D2 Paris TX U.S.A.
93 H3 Parkano Fin.
142 A2 Parker U.S.A.
138 C3 Parkersburg U.S.A.
53 C2 Parkes Austr.
138 A1 Park Falls U.S.A.
134 B1 Parkland U.S.A.
137 D1 Park Rapids U.S.A.
106 C1 Parla Spain
108 B2 Parma Italy
134 C2 Parma U.S.A.
151 E3 Parnaíba Brazil
151 E3 Parnaíba r. Brazil
111 B3 Parnassos mt. Greece
54 B2 Parnassus N.Z.
111 B3 Parnon mts Greece
88 B2 Pärnu Estonia
65 B2 P'aro-ho l. S. Korea
52 B2 Paroo watercourse Austr.
76 C3 Paropamisus mts Afgh.
111 C3 Paros i. Greece
135 D3 Parowan U.S.A.
153 A3 Parral Chile
53 D2 Parramatta Austr.
144 B2 Parras Mex.
126 C2 Parry, Cape Can.
126 E1 Parry Islands Can.
130 B3 Parry Sound Can.
137 D3 Parsons U.S.A.
108 B3 Partanna Sicily Italy
101 D2 Partenstein Ger.
104 B2 Parthenay France
108 B3 Partinico Sicily Italy
66 B2 Partizansk Rus. Fed.
97 B2 Partry Mountains hills Ireland
151 D3 Paru r. Brazil
131 E3 Pasadena Can.
135 C4 Pasadena CA U.S.A.
143 D3 Pasadena TX U.S.A.
62 A2 Pasawng Myanmar
140 C2 Pascagoula U.S.A.
110 C1 Paşcani Romania
134 C1 Pasco U.S.A.
155 E1 Pascoal, Monte hill Brazil
      Pascua, Isla de i. S. Pacific Ocean
      see Easter Island
      Pas de Calais str. France/U.K. see
      Dover, Strait of
102 C1 Pasewalk Ger.
129 D2 Pasfield Lake Can.
89 D1 Pasha Rus. Fed.
64 B2 Pasig Phil.
60 B1 Pasir Putih Malaysia
103 D1 Pasłęk Pol.
74 A2 Pasni Pak.
153 A4 Paso Río Mayo Arg.
135 B3 Paso Robles U.S.A.
97 B2 Passage West Ireland
155 D2 Passa Tempo Brazil
102 C2 Passau Ger.
152 C2 Passo Fundo Brazil
155 C2 Passos Brazil
88 C2 Pastavy Belarus
150 B3 Pastaza r. Peru
150 B2 Pasto Col.
74 B1 Pasu Jammu and Kashmir
61 C2 Pasuruan Indon.
88 B2 Pasvalys Lith.
103 D2 Pásztó Hungary
153 A5 Patagonia reg. Arg.
75 C2 Patan Nepal
54 B1 Patea N.Z.
139 C2 Paterson U.S.A.
74 B1 Pathankot India
      Pathein Myanmar see Bassein
136 B2 Pathfinder Reservoir U.S.A.
61 C2 Pati Indon.
74 B1 Patiala India
62 A1 Patkai Bum mts India/Myanmar
111 C3 Patmos i. Greece
75 C2 Patna India
81 C2 Patnos Turkey
154 B3 Pato Branco Brazil
152 C3 Patos, Lagoa dos l. Brazil
155 C1 Patos de Minas Brazil
152 B3 Patquía Arg.
      Patra Greece see Patras
111 B3 Patras Greece
75 C2 Patratu India
154 C1 Patrocínio Brazil
63 B3 Pattani Thai.
63 B2 Pattaya Thai.
128 B2 Pattullo, Mount Can.
129 D2 Patuanak Can.
146 B3 Patuca r. Hond.
144 B3 Pátzcuaro Mex.
104 B3 Pau France
104 B3 Pauillac France
150 C3 Pauini Brazil
62 A1 Pauk Myanmar
126 D2 Paulatuk Can.

      Paulis Dem. Rep. Congo see Isiro
151 E3 Paulistana Brazil
151 F3 Paulo Afonso Brazil
123 D2 Paulpietersburg S. Africa
143 D1 Pauls Valley U.S.A.
62 A2 Paungde Myanmar
155 D1 Pavão Brazil
108 A1 Pavia Italy
88 B2 Pāvilosta Latvia
110 C2 Pavlikeni Bulg.
77 D1 Pavlodar Kazakh.
91 D2 Pavlohrad Ukr.
91 E1 Pavlovsk Rus. Fed.
91 D2 Pavlovskaya Rus. Fed.
139 E2 Pawtucket U.S.A.
111 B3 Paxoi i. Greece
60 B2 Payakumbuh Indon.
134 C2 Payette U.S.A.
134 C2 Payette r. U.S.A.
86 F2 Pay-Khoy, Khrebet hills Rus. Fed.
      Payne Can. see Kangirsuk
130 C2 Payne, Lac l. Can.
152 C3 Paysandú Uru.
81 C1 Pazar Turkey
110 B2 Pazardzhik Bulg.
111 C3 Pazarköy Turkey
108 B1 Pazin Croatia
63 A2 Pe Myanmar
128 C2 Peace r. Can.
128 C2 Peace River Can.
53 C2 Peak Hill N.S.W. Austr.
50 A2 Peak Hill W.A. Austr.
135 E3 Peale, Mount U.S.A.
140 C2 Pearl r. U.S.A.
71 B3 Pearl River r. China
143 D3 Pearsall U.S.A.
126 F1 Peary Channel Can.
121 C2 Pebane Moz.
109 D2 Peć Serb. and Mont.
155 D1 Peçanha Brazil
154 C3 Peças, Ilha das i. Brazil
92 J2 Pechenga Rus. Fed.
86 E2 Pechora Rus. Fed.
86 E2 Pechora r. Rus. Fed.
      Pechora Sea Rus. Fed. see
      Pechorskoye More
86 E2 Pechorskoye More sea Rus. Fed.
88 C2 Pechory Rus. Fed.
142 B1 Pecos NM U.S.A.
143 C2 Pecos TX U.S.A.
143 C3 Pecos r. U.S.A.
103 D2 Pécs Hungary
142 B3 Pedernales Mex.
155 D1 Pedra Azul Brazil
154 C2 Pedregulho Brazil
151 E3 Pedreiras Brazil
73 C4 Pedro, Point Sri Lanka
151 E3 Pedro Afonso Brazil
152 B2 Pedro de Valdivia Chile
154 B1 Pedro Gomes Brazil
152 C2 Pedro Juan Caballero Para.
106 B1 Pedroso Port.
96 C3 Peebles U.K.
141 E2 Pee Dee r. U.S.A.
126 D2 Peel r. Can.
98 A2 Peel Isle of Man
128 C2 Peerless Lake Can.
54 B2 Pegasus Bay N.Z.
101 E3 Pegnitz Ger.
62 A2 Pegu Myanmar
62 A2 Pegu Yoma mts Myanmar
153 B3 Pehuajó Arg.
101 E1 Peine Ger.
88 C2 Peipus, Lake Estonia/Rus. Fed.
      Peiraias Greece see Piraeus
154 B2 Peixe r. Brazil
155 C2 Peixoto, Represa resr Brazil
151 D4 Peixoto de Azevedo Brazil
123 C2 Peka Lesotho
60 B2 Pekalongan Indon.
60 B1 Pekan Malaysia
60 B1 Pekanbaru Indon.
      Peking China see Beijing
130 B3 Pelee Island Can.
61 D2 Peleng i. Indon.
103 D2 Pelhřimov Czech Rep.
92 I2 Pelkosenniemi Fin.
122 A2 Pella S. Africa
137 E2 Pella U.S.A.
59 D3 Pelleluhu Islands P.N.G.
92 H2 Pello Fin.
128 A1 Pelly r. Can.
      Pelly Bay Can. see Kugaaruk
128 A1 Pelly Mountains Can.
152 C3 Pelotas Brazil
152 C3 Pelotas, Rio das r. Brazil
139 F1 Pemadumcook Lake U.S.A.
60 B2 Pemangkat Indon.
60 A1 Pematangsiantar Indon.
121 D2 Pemba Moz.
120 B2 Pemba Zambia
119 D3 Pemba Island Tanz.
128 B2 Pemberton Can.
137 D1 Pembina r. Can.
137 D1 Pembina r. U.S.A.
130 C3 Pembroke Can.
99 A4 Pembroke U.K.
141 D3 Pembroke Pines U.S.A.
106 C1 Peñalara mt. Spain
154 B2 Penápolis Brazil
106 B1 Peñaranda de Bracamonte Spain
107 C1 Peñarroya mt. Spain
106 B2 Peñarroya-Pueblonuevo Spain
106 B1 Peñas, Cabo de c. Spain
153 A4 Penas, Golfo de g. Chile

106 B1 Peña Ubiña mt. Spain
111 C2 Pendik Turkey
134 C1 Pendleton U.S.A.
128 B2 Pendleton Bay Can.
134 C1 Pend Oreille Lake U.S.A.
      Penfro U.K. see Pembroke
74 B3 Penganga r. India
118 C3 Penge Dem. Rep. Congo
123 D1 Penge S. Africa
70 C2 Penglai China
71 A3 Pengshui China
106 B2 Peniche Port.
96 C3 Penicuik U.K.
60 B1 Peninsular Malaysia pen.
      Malaysia
108 B2 Penne Italy
52 A3 Penneshaw Austr.
98 B2 Pennines hills U.K.
139 D2 Pennsylvania state U.S.A.
127 H2 Penny Icecap Can.
89 D2 Peno Rus. Fed.
139 F2 Penobscot r. U.S.A.
52 B3 Penola Austr.
50 C3 Penong Austr.
157 E6 Penrhyn Basin sea feature
      S. Pacific Ocean
53 D2 Penrith Austr.
98 B2 Penrith U.K.
140 C2 Pensacola U.S.A.
55 S1 Pensacola Mountains Antarctica
61 C1 Pensiangan Sabah Malaysia
128 C3 Penticton Can.
96 C1 Pentland Firth sea chan. U.K.
99 B3 Penygadair hill U.K.
87 D3 Penza Rus. Fed.
99 A4 Penzance U.K.
83 L2 Penzhinskaya Guba b. Rus. Fed.
142 A2 Peoria AZ U.S.A.
138 B2 Peoria IL U.S.A.
107 C1 Perales del Alfambra Spain
111 B3 Perama Greece
131 D3 Percé Can.
50 B2 Percival Lakes salt flat Austr.
51 E2 Percy Isles Austr.
107 D1 Perdido, Monte mt. Spain
154 C1 Perdizes Brazil
86 F2 Peregrebnoye Rus. Fed.
150 B2 Pereira Col.
154 B2 Pereira Barreto Brazil
      Pereira de Eça Angola see Ondjiva
90 A2 Peremyshlyany Ukr.
89 E2 Pereslavl'-Zalesskiy Rus. Fed.
91 C1 Pereyaslav-Khmel'nyts'kyy Ukr.
153 B3 Pergamino Arg.
92 H3 Perhonjoki r. Fin.
131 C2 Péribonka, Lac l. Can.
152 B2 Perico Arg.
144 B2 Pericos Mex.
104 C2 Périgueux France
150 B2 Perija, Sierra de mts Venez.
111 B3 Peristerio Greece
153 A4 Perito Moreno Arg.
101 E1 Perleberg Ger.
86 E3 Perm' Rus. Fed.
109 D2 Përmet Albania
      Pernambuco Brazil see Recife
52 A2 Pernatty Lagoon salt flat Austr.
110 B2 Pernik Bulg.
      Pernov Estonia see Pärnu
105 C2 Péronne France
145 C3 Perote Mex.
105 C3 Perpignan France
99 A4 Perranporth U.K.
      Perrégaux Alg. see
      Mohammadia
141 D2 Perry FL U.S.A.
141 D2 Perry GA U.S.A.
137 E2 Perry IA U.S.A.
143 D1 Perry OK U.S.A.
138 C2 Perrysburg U.S.A.
143 C1 Perryton U.S.A.
137 F3 Perryville U.S.A.
      Pershnotravnevoye Ukr. see
      Pershotravens'k
99 B3 Pershore U.K.
91 D2 Pershotravens'k Ukr.
      Persia country Asia see Iran
      Persian Gulf Asia see The Gulf
50 A3 Perth Austr.
96 C2 Perth U.K.
159 F5 Perth Basin sea feature
      Indian Ocean
86 C2 Pertominsk Rus. Fed.
105 D3 Pertuis France
108 A2 Pertusato, Capo c. Corsica
      France
150 B3 Peru country S. America
138 B2 Peru U.S.A.
157 H6 Peru Basin sea feature
      S. Pacific Ocean
157 H7 Peru-Chile Trench sea feature
      S. Pacific Ocean
108 B2 Perugia Italy
154 C2 Peruíbe Brazil
100 A2 Péruwelz Belgium
90 C2 Pervomays'k Ukr.
91 C2 Pervomays'ke Ukr.
      Pervomayskiy Rus. Fed. see
      Novodvinsk
89 F3 Pervomayskiy Rus. Fed.
91 D2 Pervomays'kyy Ukr.
108 B2 Pesaro Italy
108 B2 Pescara Italy
108 B2 Pescara r. Italy
74 B1 Peshawar Pak.

109 D2 Peshkopi Albania
109 C1 Pesnica Slovenia
104 B3 Pessac France
89 E2 Pestovo Rus. Fed.
140 C2 Petal U.S.A.
100 B3 Pétange Lux.
147 D3 Petare Venez.
144 B3 Petatlán Mex.
121 C2 Petauke Zambia
130 C3 Petawawa Can.
138 B2 Petenwell Lake U.S.A.
52 A2 Peterborough Austr.
130 C3 Peterborough Can.
99 C3 Peterborough U.K.
96 D2 Peterhead U.K.
55 R3 Peter I Island Antarctica
129 E1 Peter Lake Can.
50 B2 Petermann Ranges mts Austr.
129 D2 Peter Pond Lake Can.
128 A2 Petersburg AK U.S.A.
139 D3 Petersburg VA U.S.A.
101 D1 Petershagen Ger.
      Peter the Great Bay Rus. Fed. see
      Petra Velikogo, Zaliv
      Petitjean Morocco see
      Sidi Kacem
131 D2 Petit Lac Manicouagan l. Can.
131 C2 Petit Mécatina r. Can.
145 D2 Peto Mex.
138 C1 Petoskey U.S.A.
80 B2 Petra tourist site Jordan
66 B2 Petra Velikogo, Zaliv b. Rus. Fed.
111 B2 Petrich Bulg.
      Petroaleksandrovsk Uzbek. see
      To'rtko'l
88 C2 Petrodvorets Rus. Fed.
      Petrokov Pol. see
      Piotrków Trybunalski
151 E3 Petrolina Brazil
77 C1 Petropavlovsk Kazakh.
83 L3 Petropavlovsk-Kamchatskiy
      Rus. Fed.
110 B1 Petroşani Romania
      Petrovskoye Rus. Fed. see
      Svetlograd
89 F3 Petrovskoye Rus. Fed.
89 D2 Petrovskoye Rus. Fed.
86 C2 Petrovsk-Zabaykal'skiy Rus. Fed.
86 C2 Petrozavodsk Rus. Fed.
123 C2 Petrusburg S. Africa
123 C2 Petrus Steyn S. Africa
122 B3 Petrusville S. Africa
      Petsamo Rus. Fed. see Pechenga
87 F3 Petukhovo Rus. Fed.
89 E2 Petushki Rus. Fed.
60 A1 Peureula Indon.
83 M2 Pevek Rus. Fed.
102 B2 Pforzheim Ger.
102 C2 Pfunds Austria
101 D3 Pfungstadt Ger.
123 C2 Phahameng Free State S. Africa
123 C1 Phahameng Limpopo S. Africa
123 D1 Phalaborwa S. Africa
74 B2 Phalodi India
63 A3 Phangnga Thai.
63 B2 Phan Rang Vietnam
63 B2 Phan Thiết Vietnam
63 B3 Phatthalung Thai.
62 A2 Phayao Thai.
129 D2 Phelps Lake Can.
141 C2 Phenix City U.S.A.
63 A2 Phet Buri Thai.
63 B2 Phetchabun Thai.
63 B2 Phichit Thai.
139 D3 Philadelphia U.S.A.
136 C2 Philip U.S.A.
      Philip Atoll Micronesia see Sorol
      Philippeville Alg. see Skikda
100 B2 Philippeville Belgium
51 C2 Philippi, Lake salt flat Austr.
100 A2 Philippine Neth.
156 C4 Philippine Basin sea feature
      N. Pacific Ocean
64 B2 Philippines country Asia
64 B2 Philippine Sea N. Pacific Ocean
126 C2 Philip Smith Mountains U.S.A.
122 B3 Philipstown S. Africa
53 C3 Phillip Island Austr.
137 D3 Phillipsburg U.S.A.
63 B2 Phimun Mangsahan Thai.
123 C2 Phiritona S. Africa
63 B2 Phitsanulok Thai.
63 B2 Phnom Penh Cambodia
      Phnum Pénh Cambodia see
      Phnom Penh
142 A2 Phoenix U.S.A.
49 J4 Phoenix Islands Kiribati
63 B2 Phon Thai.
62 B2 Phong Nha Vietnam
62 B1 Phôngsali Laos
62 B1 Phong Thô Vietnam
62 B2 Phrae Thai.
      Phu Cuong Vietnam see
      Thu Dâu Môt
120 B3 Phuduhudu Botswana
63 A3 Phuket Thai.
63 B2 Phumĭ Kâmpóng Trâlach
      Cambodia
63 B2 Phumĭ Sâmraông Cambodia
63 B2 Phu Nhon Vietnam
63 B2 Phu Quôc, Đao i. Vietnam
123 C2 Phuthaditjhaba S. Africa
      Phu Vinh Vietnam see Tra Vinh
62 A2 Phyu Myanmar
108 A1 Piacenza Italy

108 B2 **Pianosa, Isola** *i.* Italy
110 C1 **Piatra Neamţ** Romania
151 E3 **Piauí** *r.* Brazil
108 B1 **Piave** *r.* Italy
117 B4 **Pibor** *r.* Sudan
117 B4 **Pibor Post** Sudan
104 C2 **Picardie** *reg.* France *see* Picardy
104 C2 **Picardy** *reg.* France
140 C2 **Picayune** U.S.A.
152 B2 **Pichanal** Arg.
144 A2 **Pichilingue** Mex.
98 C2 **Pickering** U.K.
130 A2 **Pickle Lake** Can.
151 E3 **Picos** Brazil
153 B4 **Pico Truncado** Arg.
53 D2 **Picton** Austr.
54 B2 **Picton** N.Z.
73 C4 **Pidurutalagala** *mt.* Sri Lanka
154 C2 **Piedade** Brazil
145 C3 **Piedras Negras** Guat.
145 B2 **Piedras Negras** Mex.
150 C4 **Piedras, Río de las** *r.* Peru
93 I3 **Pieksämäki** Fin.
92 I3 **Pielinen** *l.* Fin.
136 C2 **Pierre** U.S.A.
105 C3 **Pierrelatte** France
123 D2 **Pietermaritzburg** S. Africa
123 D2 **Pietersaari** Fin. *see* Jakobstad
Pietersburg S. Africa *see* Polokwane
123 D2 **Piet Retief** S. Africa
110 B1 **Pietrosa** *mt.* Romania
110 C1 **Pietrosu, Vârful** *mt.* Romania
128 C2 **Pigeon Lake** Can.
137 F1 **Pigeon River** U.S.A.
153 B3 **Pigüé** Arg.
93 I3 **Pihlajavesi** *l.* Fin.
92 I3 **Pihtipudas** Fin.
145 C3 **Pijijiapan** Mex.
89 D2 **Pikalevo** Rus. Fed.
130 A2 **Pikangikum** Can.
136 C3 **Pikes Peak** U.S.A.
122 A3 **Piketberg** S. Africa
138 C3 **Pikeville** U.S.A.
103 D1 **Piła** Pol.
153 C3 **Pilar** Arg.
152 C2 **Pilar** Para.
75 B2 **Pilibhit** India
53 C2 **Pilliga** Austr.
154 C1 **Pilões, Serra dos** *mts* Brazil
150 C4 **Pimenta Bueno** Brazil
88 C3 **Pina** *r.* Belarus
153 C3 **Pinamar** Arg.
60 B1 **Pinang** *i.* Malaysia
80 B2 **Pınarbaşı** Turkey
146 B2 **Pinar del Río** Cuba
64 B2 **Pinatubo, Mount** *vol.* Phil.
103 E1 **Pińczów** Pol.
151 E3 **Pindaré** *r.* Brazil
Pindos Greece *see* Pindus Mountains
111 B2 **Pindus Mountains** *mts* Greece
140 B2 **Pine Bluff** U.S.A.
136 C2 **Pine Bluffs** U.S.A.
50 C1 **Pine Creek** Austr.
136 B2 **Pinedale** U.S.A.
86 D2 **Pinega** Rus. Fed.
129 D2 **Pinehouse Lake** Can.
111 B3 **Pineios** *r.* Greece
141 D3 **Pine Islands** FL U.S.A.
141 D4 **Pine Islands** FL U.S.A.
128 C1 **Pine Point** Can.
136 C2 **Pine Ridge** U.S.A.
108 A2 **Pinerolo** Italy
Pines, Isle of *i.* Cuba *see* Juventud, Isla de la
123 D2 **Pinetown** S. Africa
140 B2 **Pineville** U.S.A.
70 B2 **Pingdingshan** China
70 B2 **Pingdu** China
62 B1 **Pingguo** China
71 B3 **Pingjiang** China
70 A2 **Pingliang** China
70 B1 **Pingquan** China
71 C3 **P'ingtung** Taiwan
Pingxi China *see* Yuping
71 A3 **Pingxiang** *Guangxi* China
71 B3 **Pingxiang** *Jiangxi* China
70 B2 **Pingyin** China
155 C2 **Pinhal** Brazil
151 E3 **Pinheiro** Brazil
52 B3 **Pinnaroo** Austr.
101 D1 **Pinneberg** Ger.
Pinos, Isla de *i.* Cuba *see* Juventud, Isla de la
145 C3 **Pinotepa Nacional** Mex.
48 H6 **Pins, Île des** *i.* New Caledonia
88 C3 **Pinsk** Belarus
152 B2 **Pinto** Arg.
135 D3 **Pioche** U.S.A.
119 C3 **Piodi** Dem. Rep. Congo
108 B2 **Piombino** Italy
86 F2 **Pionerskiy** Rus. Fed.
103 E1 **Pionki** Pol.
103 D1 **Piotrków Trybunalski** Pol.
137 D2 **Pipestone** U.S.A.
131 C3 **Pipmuacan, Réservoir** *resr* Can.
154 B2 **Piquiri** *r.* Brazil
154 C1 **Piracanjuba** Brazil
154 C2 **Piracicaba** Brazil
155 D1 **Piracicaba** *r.* Brazil
154 C2 **Piraçununga** Brazil
111 B3 **Piraeus** Greece
154 C2 **Piraí do Sul** Brazil
154 C2 **Piraju** Brazil

154 C2 **Pirajuí** Brazil
154 B1 **Piranhas** Brazil
151 F3 **Piranhas** *r.* Brazil
155 D1 **Pirapora** Brazil
154 C1 **Pirenópolis** Brazil
154 C1 **Pires do Rio** Brazil
Pirineos *mts* Europe *see* Pyrenees
151 E3 **Piripiri** Brazil
109 D2 **Pirot** Serb. and Mont.
59 C3 **Piru** Indon.
108 B2 **Pisa** Italy
152 A1 **Pisagua** Chile
150 B4 **Pisco** Peru
102 C2 **Písek** Czech Rep.
79 D2 **Pīshīn** Iran
74 A1 **Pishin** Pak.
145 D2 **Pisté** Mex.
109 C2 **Pisticci** Italy
108 B2 **Pistoia** Italy
106 C1 **Pisuerga** *r.* Spain
134 B2 **Pit** *r.* U.S.A.
114 A3 **Pita** Guinea
154 B2 **Pitanga** Brazil
155 D1 **Pitangui** Brazil
49 O6 **Pitcairn Island** S. Pacific Ocean
49 O6 **Pitcairn Islands** *terr.* S. Pacific Ocean
92 H2 **Piteå** Sweden
92 H2 **Piteälven** *r.* Sweden
110 B2 **Piteşti** Romania
75 C2 **Pithoragarh** India
142 A2 **Pitiquito** Mex.
86 C2 **Pitkyaranta** Rus. Fed.
96 C2 **Pitlochry** U.K.
128 B2 **Pitt Island** Can.
137 E3 **Pittsburg** U.S.A.
138 D2 **Pittsburgh** U.S.A.
139 E2 **Pittsfield** U.S.A.
53 D1 **Pittsworth** Austr.
155 C2 **Piumhi** Brazil
150 A3 **Piura** Peru
90 C2 **Pivdennyy Buh** *r.* Ukr.
131 E3 **Placentia** Can.
135 B3 **Placerville** U.S.A.
146 C2 **Placetas** Cuba
143 C2 **Plains** U.S.A.
143 C2 **Plainview** U.S.A.
60 B2 **Plaju** Indon.
61 C2 **Plampang** Indon.
154 C1 **Planaltina** Brazil
137 D2 **Plankinton** U.S.A.
143 D2 **Plano** U.S.A.
154 C2 **Planura** Brazil
140 B2 **Plaquemine** U.S.A.
106 B1 **Plasencia** Spain
109 C3 **Plaški** Croatia
147 C4 **Plato** Col.
137 D2 **Platte** *r.* U.S.A.
138 A2 **Platteville** U.S.A.
139 E2 **Plattsburgh** U.S.A.
101 F1 **Plau** Ger.
101 F2 **Plauen** Ger.
101 F1 **Plauer See** *l.* Ger.
89 E3 **Plavsk** Rus. Fed.
106 B2 **Playa de Castilla** *coastal area* Spain
63 B2 **Plây Cu** Vietnam
129 E2 **Playgreen Lake** Can.
153 B3 **Plaza Huincul** Arg.
143 D3 **Pleasanton** U.S.A.
54 B2 **Pleasant Point** N.Z.
138 B3 **Pleasure Ridge Park** U.S.A.
104 C2 **Pleaux** France
130 B2 **Pledger Lake** Can.
54 C1 **Plenty, Bay of** *g.* N.Z.
136 C1 **Plentywood** U.S.A.
86 D2 **Plesetsk** Rus. Fed.
131 C2 **Plétipi, Lac** *l.* Can.
100 C2 **Plettenberg** Ger.
122 B3 **Plettenberg Bay** S. Africa
110 B2 **Pleven** Bulg.
Plevna Bulg. *see* Pleven
109 C2 **Pljevlja** Serb. and Mont.
108 A2 **Ploaghe** *Sardinia* Italy
109 C2 **Ploče** Croatia
103 D1 **Płock** Pol.
109 C2 **Pločno** *mt.* Bos.-Herz.
104 B2 **Ploemeur** France
110 C2 **Ploieşti** Romania
Ploeşti Romania *see* Ploieşti
89 F2 **Ploskoye** Rus. Fed.
104 B2 **Plouzané** France
110 B2 **Plovdiv** Bulg.
Plozk Pol. *see* Płock
121 B3 **Plumtree** Zimbabwe
88 B2 **Plungė** Lith.
144 B2 **Plutarco Elías Calles, Presa** *resr* Mex.
88 C3 **Plyeshchanitsy** Belarus
147 D3 **Plymouth** Montserrat
99 A4 **Plymouth** U.K.
138 B2 **Plymouth** U.S.A.
99 B3 **Plynlimon** *hill* U.K.
88 C2 **Plyussa** Rus. Fed.
102 C2 **Plzeň** Czech Rep.
114 B3 **Pô** Burkina
108 B1 **Po** *r.* Italy
61 C1 **Po, Tanjung** *pt* Malaysia
77 E2 **Pobedy, Pik** *mt.* China/Kyrg.
Pobeda Peak China/Kyrg. *see* Pobedy, Pik
140 B1 **Pocahontas** U.S.A.
134 D2 **Pocatello** U.S.A.
90 B1 **Pochayiv** Ukr.

89 D3 **Pochep** Rus. Fed.
89 D3 **Pochinok** Rus. Fed.
145 C3 **Pochutla** Mex.
139 D3 **Pocomoke City** U.S.A.
155 C2 **Poços de Caldas** Brazil
89 D2 **Poddor'ye** Rus. Fed.
91 D1 **Podgorenskiy** Rus. Fed.
109 C2 **Podgorica** Serb. and Mont.
82 G3 **Podgornoye** Rus. Fed.
83 H2 **Podkamennaya Tunguska** *r.* Rus. Fed.
89 E2 **Podol'sk** Rus. Fed.
109 D2 **Podujevo** Serb. and Mont.
122 A2 **Pofadder** S. Africa
89 D3 **Pogar** Rus. Fed.
105 E3 **Poggibonsi** Italy
109 D2 **Pogradec** Albania
66 B2 **Pogranichnyy** Rus. Fed.
65 B2 **Po Hai** *g.* China *see* Bo Hai
65 B2 **P'ohang** S. Korea
48 G3 **Pohnpei** *atoll* Micronesia
90 B2 **Pohrebyshche** Ukr.
110 B2 **Poiana Mare** Romania
118 C3 **Poie** Dem. Rep. Congo
118 B3 **Pointe-Noire** Congo
128 C1 **Point Hope** U.S.A.
128 C1 **Point Lake** Can.
138 C3 **Point Pleasant** U.S.A.
104 C2 **Poitiers** France
104 C2 **Poitou, Plaines et Seuil du** *plain* France
74 B2 **Pokaran** India
53 C1 **Pokataroo** Austr.
75 C2 **Pokhara** Nepal
119 C2 **Poko** Dem. Rep. Congo
83 J2 **Pokrovsk** Rus. Fed.
91 D2 **Pokrovskoye** Rus. Fed.
142 A1 **Polacca** U.S.A.
106 B1 **Pola de Lena** Spain
106 B1 **Pola de Siero** Spain
103 D1 **Poland** *country* Europe
55 C1 **Polar Plateau** Antarctica
80 B2 **Polatlı** Turkey
88 C2 **Polatsk** Belarus
77 C3 **Pol-e Khomri** Afgh.
61 C2 **Polewali** Indon.
118 B2 **Poli** Cameroon
102 C1 **Police** Pol.
109 C2 **Policoro** Italy
105 D2 **Poligny** France
64 B2 **Polillo Islands** Phil.
80 B2 **Polis** Cyprus
90 B1 **Polis'ke** Ukr.
109 C3 **Polistena** Italy
103 D1 **Polkowice** Pol.
107 D2 **Pollença** Spain
109 C3 **Pollino, Monte** *mt.* Italy
86 F2 **Polnovat** Rus. Fed.
91 D2 **Polohy** Ukr.
123 C1 **Polokwane** S. Africa
90 B1 **Polonne** Ukr.
134 D1 **Polson** U.S.A.
91 C2 **Poltava** Ukr.
91 D2 **Poltavka** Rus. Fed.
91 D2 **Poltavskaya** Rus. Fed.
88 C2 **Põltsamaa** Estonia
88 C2 **Põlva** Estonia
Polyanovgrad Bulg. *see* Karnobat
92 J2 **Polyarnyy** Rus. Fed.
86 C2 **Polyarnyye Zori** Rus. Fed.
111 B2 **Polygyros** Greece
111 B2 **Polykastro** Greece
156 E6 **Polynesia** *is* Pacific Ocean
106 B2 **Pombal** Port.
108 B2 **Pomezia** Italy
92 I2 **Pomokaira** *reg.* Fin.
110 C2 **Pomorie** Bulg.
102 C1 **Pomorska, Zatoka** *b.* Pol.
155 C1 **Pompéu** Brazil
143 D1 **Ponca City** U.S.A.
147 D3 **Ponce** Puerto Rico
73 B3 **Pondicherry** India
127 G2 **Pond Inlet** Can.
Ponds Bay Can. *see* Pond Inlet
106 B1 **Ponferrada** Spain
117 A4 **Pongo** *watercourse* Sudan
123 D2 **Pongola** *r.* S. Africa
123 D2 **Pongolapoort Dam** *l.* S. Africa
128 C2 **Ponoka** Can.
154 B3 **Ponta Grossa** Brazil
154 C1 **Pontalina** Brazil
105 D2 **Pont-à-Mousson** France
154 A2 **Ponta Porã** Brazil
105 D2 **Pontarlier** France
104 B2 **Pontcharra** France
140 B2 **Pontchartrain, Lake** U.S.A.
154 B1 **Ponte de Pedra** Brazil
106 B2 **Ponte de Sor** Port.
154 B1 **Ponte do Rio Verde** Brazil
98 C2 **Pontefract** U.K.
129 D3 **Ponteix** Can.
155 D2 **Ponte Nova** Brazil
150 D4 **Pontes-e-Lacerda** Brazil
106 B1 **Pontevedra** Spain
Ponthierville Dem. Rep. Congo *see* Ubundu
138 B2 **Pontiac** IL U.S.A.
138 C2 **Pontiac** MI U.S.A.
60 B2 **Pontianak** Indon.
Pontine Islands *is* Italy *see* Ponziane, Isole
104 B2 **Pontivy** France
151 D2 **Pontoetoe** Suriname

104 C2 **Pontoise** France
129 E2 **Ponton** Can.
99 B4 **Pontypool** U.K.
99 B4 **Pontypridd** U.K.
108 B2 **Ponziane, Isole** *is* Italy
99 C4 **Poole** U.K.
Poona India *see* Pune
52 B2 **Pooncarie** Austr.
152 B1 **Poopó, Lago de** *l.* Bol.
150 B2 **Popayán** Col.
83 I2 **Popigay** *r.* Rus. Fed.
52 B2 **Popiltah** Austr.
129 E2 **Poplar** *r.* Can.
137 D3 **Poplar Bluff** U.S.A.
145 C3 **Popocatépetl, Volcán** *vol.* Mex.
118 B3 **Popokabaka** Dem. Rep. Congo
Popovichskaya Rus. Fed. *see* Kalininskaya
110 C2 **Popovo** Bulg.
103 E2 **Poprad** Slovakia
151 E4 **Porangatu** Brazil
74 A2 **Porbandar** India
126 C2 **Porcupine** *r.* Can./U.S.A.
108 B1 **Pordenone** Italy
108 B1 **Poreč** Croatia
154 B2 **Porecatu** Brazil
114 C3 **Porga** Benin
93 H3 **Pori** Fin.
54 B2 **Porirua** N.Z.
88 C2 **Porkhov** Rus. Fed.
104 B2 **Pornic** France
83 K3 **Poronaysk** Rus. Fed.
75 D1 **Porong** China
111 B3 **Poros** Greece
92 I1 **Porsangerfjorden** *sea chan.* Norway
93 E4 **Porsgrunn** Norway
111 D3 **Porsuk** *r.* Turkey
97 C1 **Portadown** U.K.
97 C1 **Portaferry** U.K.
138 B2 **Portage** U.S.A.
129 E3 **Portage la Prairie** Can.
128 B3 **Port Alberni** Can.
106 B2 **Portalegre** Port.
143 C2 **Portales** U.S.A.
128 A2 **Port Alexander** U.S.A.
128 B2 **Port Alice** Can.
140 B2 **Port Allen** U.S.A.
134 B1 **Port Angeles** U.S.A.
97 C2 **Portarlington** Ireland
51 D4 **Port Arthur** Austr.
Port Arthur China *see* Lüshun
143 E3 **Port Arthur** U.S.A.
96 A3 **Port Askaig** U.K.
52 A2 **Port Augusta** Austr.
147 C3 **Port-au-Prince** Haiti
131 E2 **Port aux Choix** Can.
122 B3 **Port Beaufort** S. Africa
73 D3 **Port Blair** India
52 B3 **Port Campbell** Austr.
131 D2 **Port-Cartier** Can.
54 B2 **Port Chalmers** N.Z.
141 D3 **Port Charlotte** U.S.A.
147 C3 **Port-de-Paix** Haiti
128 A2 **Port Edward** Can.
155 D1 **Porteirinha** Brazil
151 D3 **Portel** Brazil
130 B3 **Port Elgin** Can.
123 C3 **Port Elizabeth** S. Africa
96 A3 **Port Ellen** U.K.
98 A2 **Port Erin** Isle of Man
122 A3 **Porterville** S. Africa
135 C3 **Porterville** U.S.A.
Port Étienne Maur. *see* Nouâdhibou
52 B3 **Port Fairy** Austr.
54 C1 **Port Fitzroy** N.Z.
Port Francqui Dem. Rep. Congo *see* Ilebo
118 A3 **Port-Gentil** Gabon
115 C4 **Port Harcourt** Nigeria
128 B2 **Port Hardy** Can.
Port Harrison Can. *see* Inukjuak
131 D3 **Port Hawkesbury** Can.
99 B4 **Porthcawl** U.K.
50 A2 **Port Hedland** Austr.
Port Herald Malawi *see* Nsanje
99 A3 **Porthmadog** U.K.
131 E2 **Port Hope Simpson** Can.
138 C2 **Port Huron** U.S.A.
106 B2 **Portimão** Port.
Port Keats Austr. *see* Wadeye
Port Láirge Ireland *see* Waterford
53 C2 **Portland** *N.S.W.* Austr.
52 B3 **Portland** *Vic.* Austr.
139 E2 **Portland** ME U.S.A.
134 B1 **Portland** OR U.S.A.
143 D3 **Portland** TX U.S.A.
99 B4 **Portland, Isle of** *pen.* U.K.
128 A2 **Portland Canal** *inlet* Can.
97 C2 **Portlaoise** Ireland
143 D3 **Port Lavaca** U.S.A.
52 A2 **Port Lincoln** Austr.
114 A4 **Port Loko** Sierra Leone
113 I8 **Port Louis** Mauritius
Port-Lyautrey Morocco *see* Kénitra
52 B3 **Port MacDonnell** Austr.
53 D2 **Port Macquarie** Austr.
Portmadoc U.K. *see* Porthmadog
128 B2 **Port McNeill** Can.
131 D3 **Port-Menier** Can.
59 D3 **Port Moresby** P.N.G.
96 A3 **Portnahaven** U.K.
96 A1 **Port Ness** U.K.

Port Nis U.K. see Port Ness
122 A2 Port Nolloth S. Africa
Port-Nouveau-Québec Can. see Kangiqsualujjuaq
Porto Port. see Oporto
150 C3 Porto Acre Brazil
154 B2 Porto Alegre Brazil
152 C3 Porto Alegre Brazil
Porto Alexandre Angola see Tombua
Porto Amélia Moz. see Pemba
151 D4 Porto Artur Brazil
154 B2 Porto Camargo Brazil
151 D4 Porto dos Gaúchos Óbidos Brazil
150 D4 Porto Esperidião Brazil
108 B2 Portoferraio Italy
151 E3 Porto Franco Brazil
147 D3 Port of Spain Trin. and Tob.
108 B1 Portogruaro Italy
108 B2 Portomaggiore Italy
154 B2 Porto Mendes Brazil
152 C2 Porto Murtinho Brazil
151 E4 Porto Nacional Brazil
114 C4 Porto-Novo Benin
154 B2 Porto Primavera, Represa resr Brazil
134 B2 Port Orford U.S.A.
151 D3 Porto Santana Brazil
154 B2 Porto São José Brazil
108 A3 Portoscuso Sardinia Italy
155 E1 Porto Seguro Brazil
108 B2 Porto Tolle Italy
108 A2 Porto Torres Sardinia Italy
154 B3 Porto União Brazil
105 D3 Porto-Vecchio Corsica France
150 C3 Porto Velho Brazil
150 A3 Portoviejo Ecuador
96 B3 Portpatrick U.K.
52 B3 Port Phillip Bay Austr.
52 A2 Port Pirie Austr.
96 A2 Portree U.K.
128 B3 Port Renfrew Can.
97 C1 Portrush U.K.
116 B1 Port Said Egypt
123 D3 Port Shepstone S. Africa
99 C4 Portsmouth U.K.
139 E2 Portsmouth NH U.S.A.
138 C3 Portsmouth OH U.S.A.
139 D3 Portsmouth VA U.S.A.
153 B5 Port Stephens Falkland Is
97 C1 Portstewart U.K.
141 C3 Port St Joe U.S.A.
123 C3 Port St Johns S. Africa
141 D3 Port St Lucie City U.S.A.
116 B3 Port Sudan Sudan
140 C3 Port Sulphur U.S.A.
99 B4 Port Talbot U.K.
134 B1 Port Townsend U.S.A.
106 B2 Portugal country Europe
Portugália Angola see Chitato
Portuguese Guinea country Africa see Guinea-Bissau
Portuguese Timor country Asia see East Timor
Portuguese West Africa country Africa see Angola
97 B2 Portumna Ireland
105 C3 Port-Vendres France
48 H5 Port Vila Vanuatu
52 A2 Port Wakefield Austr.
50 B1 Port Warrender Austr.
153 A5 Porvenir Chile
93 I3 Porvoo Fin.
65 B2 Poryŏng S. Korea
152 C2 Posadas Arg.
89 E2 Poshekhon'ye Rus. Fed.
Poshekhon'ye-Volodarsk Rus. Fed. see Poshekhon'ye
92 I2 Posio Fin.
61 D2 Poso Indon.
151 E4 Posse Brazil
101 E2 Pößneck Ger.
143 C2 Post U.S.A.
Poste-de-la-Baleine Can. see Kuujjuarapik
122 B2 Postmasburg S. Africa
108 B1 Postojna Slovenia
114 C2 Post Weygand Alg.
Postysheve Ukr. see Krasnoarmiys'k
109 C2 Posušje Bos.-Herz.
123 C2 Potchefstroom S. Africa
143 E1 Poteau U.S.A.
109 C2 Potenza Italy
108 B2 Potenza r. Italy
151 E3 Poti r. Brazil
81 C1 P'ot'i Georgia
155 E1 Potiraguá Brazil
115 D3 Potiskum Nigeria
139 D3 Potomac, South Branch r. U.S.A.
152 B1 Potosí Bol.
64 B2 Pototan Phil.
142 C3 Potrero del Llano Mex.
101 F1 Potsdam Ger.
139 E2 Potsdam U.S.A.
139 D2 Pottstown U.S.A.
139 D2 Pottsville U.S.A.
131 E3 Pouch Cove Can.
139 E2 Poughkeepsie U.S.A.
98 B3 Poulton-le-Fylde U.K.
155 E1 Pouso Alegre Brazil
63 B2 Poŭthĭsăt Cambodia
103 D2 Považská Bystrica Slovakia
109 C2 Povlen mt. Serb. and Mont.
106 B1 Póvoa de Varzim Port.

136 B2 Powell U.S.A.
135 D3 Powell Lake resr U.S.A.
128 B3 Powell River Can.
154 B1 Poxoréu Brazil
Poyang China see Boyang
71 B3 Poyang Hu l. China
109 D2 Požarevac Serb. and Mont.
145 C2 Poza Rica Mex.
109 C1 Požega Croatia
109 D2 Požega Serb. and Mont.
79 D2 Pozm Tīāb Iran
103 D1 Poznań Pol.
106 C2 Pozoblanco Spain
152 C2 Pozo Colorado Para.
109 B3 Pozzallo Sicily Italy
108 B2 Pozzuoli Italy
60 B2 Prabumulih Indon.
102 C2 Prachatice Czech Rep.
63 A2 Prachuap Khiri Khan Thai.
103 D1 Praděd mt. Czech Rep.
104 C3 Prades France
155 E1 Prado Brazil
102 C1 Prague Czech Rep.
Praha Czech Rep. see Prague
143 C2 Prairie Dog Town Fork r. U.S.A.
138 A2 Prairie du Chien U.S.A.
60 A1 Prapat Indon.
154 C1 Prata Brazil
108 B2 Prato Italy
137 D3 Pratt U.S.A.
140 C2 Prattville U.S.A.
61 C2 Praya Indon.
63 B2 Preăh Vihear Cambodia
89 F2 Prechistoye Rus. Fed.
129 D2 Preeceville Can.
88 C2 Preili Latvia
53 C2 Premer Austr.
105 C2 Prémery France
101 F1 Premnitz Ger.
102 C1 Prenzlau Ger.
66 B2 Preobrazheniye Rus. Fed.
63 A2 Preparis Island Cocos Is
61 D2 Preparis North Channel Cocos Is
63 A2 Preparis South Channel Cocos Is
103 D2 Přerov Czech Rep.
142 A2 Prescott U.S.A.
142 A2 Prescott Valley U.S.A.
109 D2 Preševo Serb. and Mont.
152 B2 Presidencia Roque Sáenz Peña Arg.
151 E3 Presidente Dutra Brazil
154 B2 Presidente Epitácio Brazil
154 B1 Presidente Murtinho Brazil
155 C1 Presidente Olegário Brazil
154 B2 Presidente Prudente Brazil
142 C3 Presidio U.S.A.
103 E2 Prešov Slovakia
111 B2 Prespa, Lake Europe
139 F1 Presque Isle U.S.A.
101 F2 Pressel Ger.
Pressburg Slovakia see Bratislava
98 B3 Preston U.K.
134 D2 Preston U.S.A.
96 B3 Prestwick U.K.
155 C1 Preto r. Brazil
123 C2 Pretoria S. Africa
Pretoria-Witwatersrand-Vereeniging prov. S. Africa see Gauteng
111 B3 Preveza Greece
63 B2 Prey Vêng Cambodia
124 A4 Pribilof Islands U.S.A.
109 C2 Priboj Serb. and Mont.
135 D3 Price U.S.A.
140 C2 Prichard U.S.A.
106 C2 Priego de Córdoba Spain
88 B3 Prienai Lith.
122 B2 Prieska S. Africa
103 D2 Prievidza Slovakia
109 C2 Prijedor Bos.-Herz.
109 C2 Prijepolje Serb. and Mont.
Prikaspiyskaya Nizmennost' lowland Kazakh./Rus. Fed. see Caspian Lowland
111 B2 Prilep Macedonia
101 F3 Přimda Czech Rep.
91 D2 Primorsko-Akhtarsk Rus. Fed.
129 D2 Primrose Lake Can.
129 D2 Prince Albert Can.
122 B3 Prince Albert S. Africa
126 E2 Prince Albert Peninsula Can.
122 B3 Prince Albert Road S. Africa
126 D2 Prince Alfred, Cape Can.
122 A3 Prince Alfred Hamlet S. Africa
127 G2 Prince Charles Island Can.
55 H2 Prince Charles Mountains Antarctica
131 D3 Prince Edward Island prov. Can.
128 B2 Prince George Can.
51 D1 Prince of Wales Island Austr.
126 F2 Prince of Wales Island Can.
128 A2 Prince of Wales Island U.S.A.
126 E2 Prince of Wales Strait Can.
126 E1 Prince Patrick Island Can.
126 F2 Prince Regent Inlet sea chan. Can.
128 A2 Prince Rupert Can.
51 D1 Princess Charlotte Bay Austr.
55 H2 Princess Elizabeth Land reg. Antarctica
128 B2 Princess Royal Island Can.
128 B3 Princeton Can.
138 B3 Princeton IN U.S.A.
137 E2 Princeton MO U.S.A.
134 B2 Prineville U.S.A.

86 C2 Priozersk Rus. Fed.
Pripet r. Belarus see Prypyats'
90 A1 Pripet Marshes Belarus/Ukr.
109 D2 Priština Serb. and Mont.
101 F1 Pritzwalk Ger.
105 C3 Privas France
109 C2 Privlaka Croatia
89 F2 Privolzhsk Rus. Fed.
109 D2 Prizren Serb. and Mont.
151 D2 Professor van Blommestein Meer resr Suriname
145 C2 Progreso Mex.
81 C1 Prokhladnyy Rus. Fed.
109 D2 Prokuplje Serb. and Mont.
Prome Myanmar see Pyè
154 C2 Promissão Brazil
154 C2 Promissão, Represa resr Brazil
126 D3 Prophet r. Can.
128 B2 Prophet River Can.
51 D2 Proserpine Austr.
Proskurov Ukr. see Khmel'nyts'kyy
103 D2 Prostějov Czech Rep.
89 E3 Protvino Rus. Fed.
110 C2 Provadiya Bulg.
105 D3 Provence reg. France
139 E2 Providence U.S.A.
146 B3 Providencia, Isla de i. Caribbean Sea
83 N2 Provideniya Rus. Fed.
105 C2 Provins France
135 D2 Provo U.S.A.
129 C2 Provost Can.
91 C2 Prubiynyy, Mys pt Ukr.
154 B3 Prudentópolis Brazil
126 C2 Prudhoe Bay U.S.A.
100 C2 Prüm Ger.
105 D3 Prunelli-di-Fiumorbo Corsica France
103 D1 Pruszcz Gdański Pol.
103 E1 Pruszków Pol.
110 C1 Prut r. Europe
88 B3 Pruzhany Belarus
91 D2 Pryazovs'ke Ukr.
91 C1 Pryluky Ukr.
91 D2 Prymors'k Ukr.
91 D2 Prymors'kyy Ukr.
143 D1 Pryor U.S.A.
90 B1 Prypyats' r. Belarus/Ukr.
103 E2 Przemyśl Pol.
103 E1 Przeworsk Pol.
Przheval'sk Kyrg. see Karakol
111 C3 Psara i. Greece
81 C1 Psebay Rus. Fed.
91 D3 Pshekha r. Rus. Fed.
88 C2 Pskov Rus. Fed.
88 C2 Pskov, Lake Estonia/Rus. Fed.
111 B2 Ptolemaïda Greece
109 C1 Ptuj Slovenia
150 B3 Pucallpa Peru
71 B3 Pucheng China
65 B2 Puch'ŏn S. Korea
103 D1 Puck Pol.
92 I2 Pudasjärvi Fin.
70 C2 Pudong China
86 C2 Pudozh Rus. Fed.
Puduchcheri India see Pondicherry
145 C3 Puebla Mex.
136 C3 Pueblo U.S.A.
153 B5 Puelén Arg.
153 A3 Puente Alto Chile
106 C2 Puente-Genil Spain
153 A4 Puerto Aisén Chile
152 B1 Puerto Alegre Bol.
145 C3 Puerto Ángel Mex.
146 B4 Puerto Armuelles Panama
150 C2 Puerto Ayacucho Venez.
146 B3 Puerto Barrios Guat.
146 B3 Puerto Cabezas Nic.
150 C2 Puerto Carreño Col.
153 A4 Puerto Cisnes Chile
144 A2 Puerto Cortés Mex.
145 C3 Puerto Escondido Mex.
152 B1 Puerto Frey Bol.
150 C2 Puerto Inírida Col.
152 C1 Puerto Isabel Bol.
150 B3 Puerto Leguizamo Col.
146 B3 Puerto Lempira Hond.
144 A2 Puerto Libertad Mex.
146 B3 Puerto Limón Costa Rica
106 C2 Puertollano Spain
153 B4 Puerto Madryn Arg.
150 C4 Puerto Maldonado Peru
Puerto México Mex. see Coatzacoalcos
147 D4 Puerto Miranda Venez.
153 A4 Puerto Montt Chile
153 A5 Puerto Natales Chile
150 C2 Puerto Nuevo Col.
150 C2 Puerto Páez Venez.
144 A1 Puerto Peñasco Mex.
152 C2 Puerto Pinasco Para.
147 C3 Puerto Plata Dom. Rep.
150 B3 Puerto Portillo Peru
Puerto Presidente Stroessner Para. see Ciudad del Este
64 A3 Puerto Princesa Phil.
154 A3 Puerto Rico Arg.
147 D3 Puerto Rico terr. West Indies
158 D3 Puerto Rico Trench sea feature Caribbean Sea
146 A3 Puerto San José Guat.
153 B5 Puerto Santa Cruz Arg.
152 C2 Puerto Suárez Bol.
144 B2 Puerto Vallarta Mex.
87 D3 Pugachev Rus. Fed.

74 B2 Pugal India
54 B2 Pukaki, Lake N.Z.
49 K5 Pukapuka atoll Cook Is
129 D2 Pukatawagan Can.
65 B1 Pukchin N. Korea
65 B1 Pukch'ŏng N. Korea
109 C2 Pukë Albania
54 B1 Pukekohe N.Z.
65 B1 Puksubaek-san mt. N. Korea
Pula China see Nyingchi
108 B2 Pula Croatia
108 A3 Pula Sardinia Italy
152 B2 Pulacayo Bol.
103 E1 Puławy Pol.
92 I3 Pulkkila Fin.
134 C1 Pullman U.S.A.
64 B2 Pulog, Mount Phil.
64 B3 Pulutan Indon.
150 A3 Puná, Isla i. Ecuador
54 B2 Punakaiki N.Z.
123 D1 Punda Maria S. Africa
73 B3 Pune India
65 B1 P'ungsan N. Korea
121 C2 Púnguè r. Moz.
119 C3 Punia Dem. Rep. Congo
74 B1 Punjab state India
153 B3 Punta Alta Arg.
153 A5 Punta Arenas Chile
108 A2 Punta Balestrieri mt. Sardinia Italy
153 C3 Punta del Este Uru.
146 B3 Punta Gorda Belize
146 B3 Puntarenas Costa Rica
150 B1 Punto Fijo Venez.
92 I3 Puolanka Fin.
82 G2 Pur r. Rus. Fed.
75 C3 Puri India
100 B1 Purmerend Neth.
75 C2 Purnia India
Purnea India see Purnia
75 C2 Puruliya India
150 C3 Purus r. Peru
61 B2 Purwakarta Indon.
61 C2 Purwodadi Indon.
65 B1 Puryŏng N. Korea
74 B3 Pusad India
65 B2 Pusan S. Korea
89 E3 Pushchino Rus. Fed.
Pushkino Azer. see Biläsuvar
89 E2 Pushkino Rus. Fed.
88 C2 Pushkinskiye Gory Rus. Fed.
88 C2 Pustoshka Rus. Fed.
62 A1 Putao Myanmar
71 B3 Putian China
Puting China see De'an
61 C2 Puting, Tanjung pt Indon.
101 F1 Putlitz Ger.
60 B1 Putrajaya Malaysia
122 B1 Putsonderwater S. Africa
102 C1 Puttgarden Ger.
150 C1 Putumayo r. Col.
61 C1 Putusibau Indon.
90 B2 Putyla Ukr.
91 C1 Putyvl' Ukr.
93 I3 Puula l. Fin.
130 C1 Puvirnituq Can.
70 B2 Puyang China
104 C3 Puylaurens France
119 C3 Pweto Dem. Rep. Congo
99 A3 Pwllheli U.K.
92 J2 Pyaozerskiy Rus. Fed.
63 A2 Pyapon Myanmar
83 G2 Pyasina r. Rus. Fed.
87 D4 Pyatigorsk Rus. Fed.
91 C2 P''yatykhatky Ukr.
62 A2 Pyè Myanmar
88 C3 Pyetrykaw Belarus
93 H3 Pyhäjärvi l. Fin.
92 H3 Pyhäjoki r. Fin.
92 I3 Pyhäsalmi Fin.
62 A1 Pyingaing Myanmar
62 A1 Pyinmana Myanmar
62 A1 Pyin-U-Lwin Myanmar
65 B2 Pyŏksŏng N. Korea
65 B2 P'yŏnggang N. Korea
65 B2 P'yŏngsong N. Korea
65 B2 P'yŏngt'aek S. Korea
65 B2 P'yŏngyang N. Korea
135 C2 Pyramid Lake U.S.A.
80 B3 Pyramids of Giza tourist site Egypt
107 D1 Pyrenees mts Europe
111 B3 Pyrgetos Greece
111 B3 Pyrgi Greece
111 B3 Pyrgos Greece
91 C1 Pyryatyn Ukr.
103 C1 Pyrzyce Pol.
88 C2 Pytalovo Rus. Fed.
111 B3 Pyxaria mt. Greece

Q

Qaanaaq Greenland see Thule
Qabqa China see Gonghe
123 C3 Qacha's Nek Lesotho
69 D2 Qagan Nur China
Qahremānshahr Iran see Kermānshāh
68 C2 Qaidam Pendi basin China
79 C2 Qalamat Abū Shafrah Saudi Arabia

78 A2 Qal'at al Azlam Saudi Arabia
78 A2 Qal'at al Mu'azzam Saudi Arabia
78 B2 Qal'at Bīshah Saudi Arabia
76 C3 Qal'eh-ye Now Afgh.
129 E1 Qamanirjuaq Lake Can.
Qamanittuaq Can. see Baker Lake
79 C3 Qamar, Ghubbat al b. Yemen
68 C2 Qamdo China
78 B3 Qam Hadīl Saudi Arabia
127 I2 Qaqortoq Greenland
80 A3 Qārah Egypt
Qarkilik China see Ruoqiang
Qarqan China see Qiemo
77 C3 Qarshi Uzbek.
78 B2 Qaryat al Ulyā Saudi Arabia
127 I2 Qasigiannguit Greenland
116 A2 Qaṣr al Farāfirah Egypt
79 D2 Qaṣr-e Qand Iran
81 C2 Qaṣr-e Shīrīn Iran
127 I2 Qassimiut Greenland
78 B3 Qa'tabah Yemen
79 C2 Qatar country Asia
116 A2 Qattāra Depression Egypt
Qausuittuq Can. see Resolute
76 B3 Qāyen Iran
81 C1 Qazax Azer.
81 C1 Qazımämmäd Azer.
81 C2 Qazvīn Iran
Qena Egypt see Qinā
127 I2 Qeqertarsuaq Greenland
127 I2 Qeqertarsuaq i. Greenland
127 I2 Qeqertarsuatsiaat Greenland
127 I2 Qeqertarsuup Tunua b. Greenland
79 C2 Qeshm Iran
74 A1 Qeyṣār, Kūh-e mt. Afgh.
70 A3 Qianjiang Chongqing China
70 B2 Qianjiang Hubei China
69 E1 Qianjin China
65 A1 Qian Shan mts China
71 A3 Qianxi China
70 C2 Qidong China
77 E3 Qiemo China
71 A3 Qijiang China
68 C2 Qijiaojing China
127 H2 Qikiqtarjuaq Can.
74 A2 Qila Ladgasht Pak.
68 C2 Qilian Shan mts China
127 J2 Qillak i. Greenland
70 B3 Qimen China
127 H1 Qimusseriarsuaq b. Greenland
116 B2 Qinā Egypt
Qincheng China see Nanfeng
70 C2 Qingdao China
68 C2 Qinghai Hu salt l. China
68 C2 Qinghai Nanshan mts China
Qingjiang China see Huai'an
Qingjiang China see Zhangshu
70 B2 Qingshuihe China
70 A2 Qingtongxia China
70 A2 Qingyang China
71 B3 Qingyuan Guangdong China
Qingyuan China see Yizhou
65 A1 Qingyuan Liaoning China
68 C2 Qingzang Gaoyuan plat. China
70 B2 Qingzhou China
70 B2 Qinhuangdao China
Qinjiang China see Shicheng
70 A2 Qin Ling mts China
Qinting China see Lianhua
70 B2 Qinyang China
71 A3 Qinzhou China
71 B4 Qionghai China
71 B4 Qiongshan China
71 A4 Qiongzhong China
69 E1 Qiqihar China
81 D3 Qīr Iran
Qishan China see Qimen
79 C3 Qishn Yemen
66 B1 Qitaihe China
70 B2 Qixian Henan China
70 B2 Qixian Shanxi China
Qogir Feng mt.
China/Jammu and Kashmir see K2
81 D3 Qom Iran
Qomishēh Iran see Shahrezā
Qomolangma Feng mt.
China/Nepal see Everest, Mount
76 B2 Qo'ng'irot Uzbek.
77 C2 Qo'qon Uzbek.
76 B2 Qoraqalpog'iston Uzbek.
80 B2 Qornet es Saouda mt. Lebanon
81 C2 Qorveh Iran
79 C2 Qoṭbābād Iran
101 C1 Quakenbrück Ger.
53 C2 Quambone Austr.
63 B2 Quang Ngai Vietnam
63 B2 Quang Tri Vietnam
Quan Long Vietnam see Ca Mau
Quan Phu Quoc i. Vietnam see
Phu Quốc, Đao
71 B3 Quanzhou Fujian China
71 B3 Quanzhou Guangxi China
108 A3 Quartu Sant'Elena Sardinia Italy
142 A2 Quartzsite U.S.A.
81 C1 Quba Azer.
76 B3 Quchan Iran
53 C3 Queanbeyan Austr.
131 C3 Québec Can.
131 C2 Québec prov. Can.
101 E2 Quedlinburg Ger.
Queen Adelaide Islands Chile see
Reina Adelaida,
Archipiélago de la

128 A2 Queen Charlotte Can.
128 A2 Queen Charlotte Islands Can.
128 B2 Queen Charlotte Sound sea chan.
Can.
128 B2 Queen Charlotte Strait Can.
126 E1 Queen Elizabeth Islands Can.
55 I2 Queen Mary Land reg. Antarctica
126 F2 Queen Maud Gulf Can.
55 E2 Queen Maud Land reg. Antarctica
55 P1 Queen Maud Mountains
Antarctica
52 B3 Queenscliff Austr.
52 B1 Queensland state Austr.
51 D4 Queenstown Austr.
54 A3 Queenstown N.Z.
Queenstown Ireland see Cóbh
123 C3 Queenstown S. Africa
121 C2 Quelimane Moz.
153 A4 Quellón Chile
Quelpart Island S. Korea see
Cheju-do
142 B2 Quemado U.S.A.
Que Que Zimbabwe see Kwekwe
154 B2 Queréncia do Norte Brazil
145 B2 Querétaro Mex.
101 E2 Querfurt Ger.
128 B2 Quesnel Can.
128 B2 Quesnel Lake Can.
74 A1 Quetta Pak.
146 A3 Quetzaltenango Guat.
64 A3 Quezon Phil.
64 B2 Quezon City Phil.
120 A2 Quibala Angola
150 B2 Quibdó Col.
104 B2 Quiberon France
120 A2 Quilengues Angola
104 C3 Quillan France
153 C3 Quilmes Arg.
73 B4 Quilon India
51 D2 Quilpie Austr.
153 A3 Quilpué Chile
120 A1 Quimbele Angola
152 B2 Quimilí Arg.
104 B2 Quimper France
104 B2 Quimperlé France
135 B3 Quincy CA U.S.A.
141 D2 Quincy FL U.S.A.
137 E3 Quincy IL U.S.A.
139 E2 Quincy MA U.S.A.
63 B2 Qui Nhon Vietnam
107 C1 Quinto Spain
121 D2 Quionga Moz.
120 A2 Quirima Angola
53 D2 Quirindi Austr.
154 B1 Quirinópolis Brazil
131 D3 Quispamsis Can.
121 C3 Quissico Moz.
120 A2 Quitapa Angola
150 B3 Quito Ecuador
151 F3 Quixadá Brazil
71 A3 Qujing China
75 D1 Qumar He r. China
123 C3 Qumrha S. Africa
115 E1 Qunayyin, Sabkhat al salt marsh
Libya
129 E1 Quoich r. Can.
52 A2 Quorn Austr.
79 C2 Qurayat Oman
77 C3 Qŭrghonteppa Tajik.
Quxar China see Lhazê
Quyang China see Jingzhou
71 B3 Quzhou China
Qyteti Stalin Albania see Kuçovë
Qyzyltŭ Kazakh. see Kishkenekol'

R

103 D2 Raab r. Austria
92 H3 Raahe Fin.
100 C1 Raalte Neth.
61 C2 Raas i. Indon.
61 C2 Raba Indon.
114 B1 Rabat Morocco
59 E3 Rabaul P.N.G.
50 C2 Rabbit Flat Austr.
78 A2 Rābigh Saudi Arabia
103 D2 Rabka Pol.
Rābniţa Moldova see Rîbniţa
Rabyānah, Ramlat des. Libya see
Rebiana Sand Sea
131 E3 Race, Cape Can.
140 B3 Raceland U.S.A.
139 E2 Race Point U.S.A.
63 B3 Rach Gia Vietnam
103 D1 Racibórz Pol.
138 B2 Racine U.S.A.
78 B3 Radā' Yemen
110 C1 Rădăuţi Romania
138 B3 Radcliff U.S.A.
74 B2 Radhanpur India
130 C2 Radisson Can.
103 E1 Radom Pol.
103 D1 Radomsko Pol.
90 B1 Radomyshl' Ukr.
111 B2 Radoviš Macedonia
88 B2 Radviliškis Lith.
78 A2 Radwá, Jabal mt. Saudi Arabia
90 B1 Radyvyliv Ukr.
75 C2 Rae Bareli India
128 C1 Rae-Edzo Can.
128 C1 Rae Lakes Can.
100 C2 Raeren Belgium
54 C1 Raetihi N.Z.

78 A2 Rāf hill Saudi Arabia
152 B3 Rafaela Arg.
118 C2 Rafaï C.A.R.
78 B2 Rafhā' Saudi Arabia
79 C1 Rafsanjān Iran
119 C2 Raga Sudan
64 B3 Ragang, Mount vol. Phil.
109 B3 Ragusa Sicily Italy
61 D2 Raha Indon.
88 D3 Rahachow Belarus
78 A3 Rahad r. Sudan
74 B2 Rahimyar Khan Pak.
73 B3 Raichur India
75 C2 Raigarh India
128 C2 Rainbow Lake Can.
134 B1 Rainier, Mount vol. U.S.A.
130 A3 Rainy Lake Can.
129 E3 Rainy River Can.
75 C2 Raipur India
93 H3 Raisio Fin.
88 C2 Raja Estonia
73 C3 Rajahmundry India
61 C1 Rajang r. Sarawak Malaysia
74 B2 Rajanpur Pak.
73 B4 Rajapalaiyam India
74 B2 Rajasthan state India
74 B2 Rajasthan Canal canal India
74 B2 Rajgarh India
60 B2 Rajik Indon.
74 B2 Rajkot India
75 C2 Raj Nandgaon India
74 B2 Rajpur India
75 C2 Rajshahi Bangl.
54 B2 Rakaia r. N.Z.
74 B1 Rakaposhi mt.
Jammu and Kashmir
90 A2 Rakhiv Ukr.
91 D1 Rakitnoye Rus. Fed.
88 C2 Rakke Estonia
88 C2 Rakvere Estonia
141 E1 Raleigh U.S.A.
141 E2 Raleigh Bay U.S.A.
48 H3 Ralik Chain is Marshall Is
75 C2 Ramanuj Ganj India
123 C2 Ramatlabama S. Africa
104 C2 Rambouillet France
99 A4 Rame Head hd U.K.
97 C1 Ramelton Ireland
89 E2 Rameshki Rus. Fed.
74 B2 Ramgarh India
81 C2 Rāmhormoz Iran
110 C1 Râmnicu Sărat Romania
110 B1 Râmnicu Vâlcea Romania
89 E3 Ramon' Rus. Fed.
135 C4 Ramona U.S.A.
123 C1 Ramotswa Botswana
75 B2 Rampur India
62 A2 Ramree Island Myanmar
98 A2 Ramsey Isle of Man
130 B3 Ramsey Lake Can.
99 D4 Ramsgate U.K.
81 C2 Rāmshīr Iran
62 A1 Ramsing Indon.
75 C2 Ranaghat India
61 C1 Ranau Sabah Malaysia
153 A3 Rancagua Chile
154 B2 Rancharia Brazil
75 C2 Ranchi India
93 F4 Randers Denmark
63 B3 Rangae Thai.
75 D2 Rangapara North India
54 B2 Rangiora N.Z.
49 M5 Rangiroa atoll Fr. Polynesia
54 C1 Rangitaiki r. N.Z.
60 B2 Rangkasbitung Indon.
63 A2 Rangoon Myanmar
75 C2 Rangpur Bangl.
129 E1 Rankin Inlet Can.
53 C2 Rankin's Springs Austr.
Rankovićevo Serb. and Mont. see
Kraljevo
96 B2 Rannoch Moor moorland U.K.
74 B2 Rann of Kachchh marsh India
63 A3 Ranong Thai.
59 C3 Ransiki Indon.
61 C2 Rantaupanjang Indon.
60 A1 Rantauprapat Indon.
61 C2 Rantepao Indon.
92 I2 Ranua Fin.
93 E4 Ranum Denmark
78 B2 Ranyah, Wādī watercourse
Saudi Arabia
49 J6 Raoul Island Kermadec Is
49 M6 Rapa i. Fr. Polynesia
108 A2 Rapallo Italy
136 C2 Rapid City U.S.A.
88 B2 Rapla Estonia
74 A2 Rapur India
49 L6 Rarotonga i. Cook Is
153 B4 Rasa, Punta pt Arg.
Ras al Khaimah U.A.E. see
Ra's al Khaymah
79 C2 Ra's al Khaymah U.A.E.
116 B3 Ras Dejen mt. Eth.
88 B2 Raseiniai Lith.
116 B2 Ra's Ghārib Egypt
81 C2 Rasht Iran
74 A2 Ras Koh mt. Pak.
110 C1 Râşnov Romania
88 C2 Rasony Belarus
79 C2 Ra's Şirāb Oman
108 B3 Rass Jebel Tunisia
87 D3 Rasskazovo Rus. Fed.
79 C2 Ras Tannūrah Saudi Arabia
101 D1 Rastede Ger.

48 I2 Ratak Chain is Marshall Is
93 F3 Rätan Sweden
123 C2 Ratanda S. Africa
74 B2 Ratangarh India
63 A2 Rat Buri Thai.
62 A1 Rathedaung Myanmar
101 F1 Rathenow Ger.
97 C1 Rathfriland U.K.
97 C1 Rathlin Island U.K.
97 B2 Rathluirc Ireland
100 C2 Ratingen Ger.
74 B2 Ratlam India
73 B3 Ratnagiri India
73 C4 Ratnapura Sri Lanka
90 A1 Ratne Ukr.
142 C1 Raton U.S.A.
96 C2 Rattray Head hd U.K.
93 G3 Rättvik Sweden
101 E1 Ratzeburg Ger.
78 B2 Raudhatain Kuwait
92 □B2 Raufarhöfn Iceland
54 C1 Raukumara Range mts N.Z.
93 H3 Rauma Fin.
88 C2 Rauna Latvia
61 C1 Raung, Gunung vol. Indon.
75 C2 Raurkela India
66 D2 Rausu Japan
90 B2 Rāut r. Moldova
134 D1 Ravalli U.S.A.
81 C2 Ravānsar Iran
108 B2 Ravenna Italy
102 B2 Ravensburg Ger.
50 B3 Ravensthorpe Austr.
74 B1 Ravi r. Pak.
74 B1 Rawalpindi Pak.
103 D1 Rawicz Pol.
50 B3 Rawlinna Austr.
136 B2 Rawlins U.S.A.
153 B4 Rawson Arg.
75 C2 Rayagada India
69 E1 Raychikhinsk Rus. Fed.
78 B3 Raydah Yemen
87 E3 Rayevskiy Rus. Fed.
134 B1 Raymond U.S.A.
53 D2 Raymond Terrace Austr.
143 D3 Raymondville U.S.A.
129 C2 Raymore Can.
145 C2 Rayón Mex.
63 B2 Rayong Thai.
78 A2 Rayyis Saudi Arabia
104 B2 Raz, Pointe du pt France
81 C2 Razāzah, Buhayrat ar l. Iraq
110 C2 Razgrad Bulg.
110 C2 Razim, Lacul lag. Romania
111 B2 Razlog Bulg.
Raz"yezd 3km Rus. Fed. see
Novyy Urgal
104 B2 Ré, Île de i. France
99 C4 Reading U.K.
138 C3 Reading OH U.S.A.
139 D2 Reading PA U.S.A.
123 C2 Reagile S. Africa
115 E2 Rebiana Sand Sea des. Libya
66 D1 Rebun-tō i. Japan
50 B3 Recherche, Archipelago of the is
Austr.
89 D3 Rechytsa Belarus
151 F3 Recife Brazil
123 C3 Recife, Cape S. Africa
100 C2 Recklinghausen Ger.
152 C2 Reconquista Arg.
137 D1 Red r. Can./U.S.A.
140 B2 Red r. U.S.A.
100 B3 Redange Lux.
141 C1 Red Bank U.S.A.
Red Basin China see
Sichuan Pendi
131 E2 Red Bay Can.
135 B2 Red Bluff U.S.A.
98 C2 Redcar U.K.
129 C2 Redcliff Can.
121 B2 Redcliff Zimbabwe
52 B2 Red Cliffs Austr.
128 C2 Red Deer Can.
126 E3 Red Deer r. Can.
129 D2 Red Deer Lake Can.
135 B2 Redding U.S.A.
99 C3 Redditch U.K.
137 D2 Redfield U.S.A.
137 D3 Red Hills U.S.A.
130 A2 Red Lake Can.
130 A2 Red Lake l. Can.
137 E1 Red Lakes U.S.A.
134 E1 Red Lodge U.S.A.
134 B2 Redmond U.S.A.
137 D2 Red Oak U.S.A.
104 B2 Redon France
106 B1 Redondela Spain
106 B2 Redondo Port.
78 A2 Red Sea Africa/Asia
128 B1 Redstone r. Can.
100 B1 Reduzum Neth.
128 C2 Redwater Can.
137 E2 Red Wing U.S.A.
137 D2 Redwood Falls U.S.A.
97 C2 Ree, Lough l. Ireland
134 B2 Reedsport U.S.A.
54 B2 Reefton N.Z.
143 D3 Refugio U.S.A.
101 E2 Regen Ger.
102 C2 Regensburg Ger.
114 C2 Reggane Alg.
109 C3 Reggio di Calabria Italy
108 B2 Reggio nell'Emilia Italy

110 B1 **Reghin** Romania
129 D2 **Regina** Can.
154 C2 **Registro** Brazil
122 A1 **Rehoboth** Namibia
80 B2 **Rehovot** Israel
101 F2 **Reichenbach** Ger.
141 E1 **Reidsville** U.S.A.
99 C4 **Reigate** U.K.
105 C2 **Reims** France
153 A5 **Reina Adelaida, Archipiélago de la** *is* Chile
101 E1 **Reinbek** Ger.
129 D2 **Reindeer** *r.* Can.
129 E2 **Reindeer Island** Can.
129 D2 **Reindeer Lake** Can.
92 F2 **Reine** Norway
106 C1 **Reinosa** Spain
100 C3 **Reinsfeld** Ger.
123 C2 **Reitz** S. Africa
122 B2 **Reivilo** S. Africa
129 D1 **Reliance** Can.
107 D2 **Relizane** Alg.
52 A2 **Remarkable, Mount** *hill* Austr.
79 C2 **Remeshk** Iran
105 D2 **Remiremont** France
100 C2 **Remscheid** Ger.
102 B1 **Rendsburg** Ger.
139 D1 **Renfrew** Can.
60 B2 **Rengat** Indon.
90 B2 **Reni** Ukr.
52 B2 **Renmark** Austr.
48 H5 **Rennell** *i.* Solomon Is
101 D2 **Rennerod** Ger.
104 B2 **Rennes** France
129 D1 **Rennie Lake** Can.
108 B2 **Reno** *r.* Italy
135 C3 **Reno** U.S.A.
70 A3 **Renshou** China
138 B2 **Rensselaer** U.S.A.
75 C2 **Renukut** India
54 B2 **Renwick** N.Z.
61 D2 **Reo** Indon.
136 D3 **Republican** *r.* U.S.A.
127 G2 **Repulse Bay** Can.
150 B3 **Requena** Peru
107 C2 **Requena** Spain
60 B2 **Resag, Gunung** *mt.* Indon.
111 B2 **Resen** Macedonia
154 B2 **Reserva** Brazil
91 C2 **Reshetylivka** Ukr.
152 C2 **Resistencia** Arg.
110 B1 **Reşita** Romania
126 F2 **Resolute** Can.
127 H2 **Resolution Island** Can.
155 D1 **Resplendor** Brazil
145 C3 **Retalhuleu** Guat.
98 C3 **Retford** U.K.
105 C2 **Rethel** France
111 B3 **Rethymno** Greece
113 I8 **Réunion** *terr.* Indian Ocean
107 D1 **Reus** Spain
 Reut *r.* Moldova *see* Răut
102 B2 **Reutlingen** Ger.
86 C2 **Revda** Rus. Fed.
128 C2 **Revelstoke** Can.
144 A3 **Revillagigedo, Islas** *is* Mex.
128 A2 **Revillagigedo Island** U.S.A.
75 C2 **Rewa** India
134 D2 **Rexburg** U.S.A.
135 B3 **Reyes, Point** U.S.A.
160 M4 **Reykjanes Ridge** *sea feature* N. Atlantic Ocean
92 □A3 **Reykjanestá** *pt* Iceland
92 □A3 **Reykjavík** Iceland
145 C2 **Reynosa** Mex.
 Rezā'īyeh Iran *see* Urmia
 Rezā'īyeh, Daryācheh-ye *salt l.* Iran *see* Urmia, Lake
88 C2 **Rēzekne** Latvia
 Rheims France *see* Reims
 Rhein *r.* Ger. *see* Rhine
100 C1 **Rheine** Ger.
101 F1 **Rheinsberg** Ger.
 Rhin *r.* France *see* Rhine
100 C2 **Rhine** *r.* Europe
138 B1 **Rhinelander** U.S.A.
101 F1 **Rhinluch** *marsh* Ger.
101 F1 **Rhinow** Ger.
108 A1 **Rho** Italy
139 E2 **Rhode Island** *state* U.S.A.
111 C3 **Rhodes** Greece
111 C3 **Rhodes** *i.* Greece
 Rhodesia *country* Africa *see* Zimbabwe
111 B2 **Rhodope Mountains** Bulg./Greece
105 C3 **Rhône** *r.* France/Switz.
 Rhum *i.* U.K. *see* Rum
 Rhuthun U.K. *see* Ruthin
98 B1 **Rhyl** U.K.
155 D1 **Riacho dos Machados** Brazil
154 C1 **Rialma** Brazil
154 C1 **Rianápolis** Brazil
60 B1 **Riau, Kepulauan** *is* Indon.
106 B1 **Ribadeo** Spain
106 B1 **Ribadesella** Spain
154 B2 **Ribas do Rio Pardo** Brazil
121 C2 **Ribáuè** Moz.
98 B3 **Ribble** *r.* U.K.
93 E4 **Ribe** Denmark
154 C2 **Ribeira** *r.* Brazil
154 C2 **Ribeirão Preto** Brazil
104 C2 **Ribérac** France
152 B1 **Riberalta** Bol.
90 B2 **Ribnița** Moldova
102 C1 **Ribnitz-Damgarten** Ger.

138 A1 **Rice Lake** U.S.A.
123 D2 **Richards Bay** S. Africa
143 D2 **Richardson** U.S.A.
126 C2 **Richardson Mountains** Can.
135 D3 **Richfield** U.S.A.
134 C1 **Richland** U.S.A.
138 A2 **Richland Center** U.S.A.
53 D2 **Richmond** N.S.W. Austr.
51 D2 **Richmond** Qld Austr.
134 B1 **Richmond** Can.
54 B2 **Richmond** N.Z.
122 B3 **Richmond** S. Africa
98 C2 **Richmond** U.K.
138 C3 **Richmond** IN U.S.A.
138 C3 **Richmond** KY U.S.A.
139 D3 **Richmond** VA U.S.A.
141 D2 **Richmond Hill** U.S.A.
53 D1 **Richmond Range** hills Austr.
130 C3 **Rideau Lakes** Can.
135 C3 **Ridgecrest** U.S.A.
140 B2 **Ridgeland** U.S.A.
102 C1 **Riesa** Ger.
101 D1 **Rieste** Ger.
123 B2 **Riet** *r.* S. Africa
101 D2 **Rietberg** Ger.
122 B2 **Rietfontein** S. Africa
108 B2 **Rieti** Italy
136 B3 **Rifle** U.S.A.
88 B2 **Rīga** Latvia
88 B2 **Riga, Gulf of** Estonia/Latvia
79 C2 **Rīgān** Iran
134 D2 **Rigby** U.S.A.
131 E2 **Rigolet** Can.
93 H3 **Riihimäki** Fin.
55 **Riiser-Larsen Ice Shelf** Antarctica
108 B1 **Rijeka** Croatia
134 C2 **Riley** U.S.A.
105 C2 **Rillieux-la-Pape** France
78 B2 **Rimah, Wādī al** watercourse Saudi Arabia
103 E2 **Rimavská Sobota** Slovakia
128 C2 **Rimbey** Can.
108 B2 **Rimini** Italy
 Rîmnicu Sărat Romania *see* Râmnicu Sărat
 Rîmnicu Vîlcea Romania *see* Râmnicu Vâlcea
131 D3 **Rimouski** Can.
144 B2 **Rincón de Romos** Mex.
93 F3 **Ringebu** Norway
93 E4 **Ringkøbing** Denmark
92 G2 **Ringvassøya** *i.* Norway
99 C4 **Ringwood** U.K.
101 D1 **Rinteln** Ger.
154 B3 **Rio Azul** Brazil
150 B3 **Riobamba** Ecuador
155 D2 **Rio Bonito** Brazil
150 C4 **Rio Branco** Brazil
154 C3 **Rio Branco do Sul** Brazil
154 B2 **Rio Brilhante** Brazil
155 D2 **Rio Casca** Brazil
154 C2 **Rio Claro** Brazil
153 B3 **Rio Colorado** Arg.
153 B3 **Rio Cuarto** Arg.
155 D2 **Rio de Janeiro** Brazil
153 B5 **Rio Gallegos** Arg.
153 B5 **Rio Grande** Arg.
152 C3 **Rio Grande** Brazil
144 B2 **Rio Grande** Mex.
143 D3 **Rio Grande** *r.* Mex./U.S.A.
143 D3 **Rio Grande City** U.S.A.
150 B1 **Riohacha** Col.
150 B3 **Rioja** Peru
145 D2 **Río Lagartos** Mex.
151 F3 **Rio Largo** Brazil
105 C2 **Riom** France
152 B1 **Río Mulatos** Bol.
154 C3 **Rio Negro** Brazil
155 D1 **Rio Pardo de Minas** Brazil
154 C1 **Rio Preto, Serra do** hills Brazil
142 B1 **Rio Rancho** U.S.A.
150 B3 **Rio Tigre** Ecuador
64 A3 **Rio Tuba** Phil.
154 B1 **Rio Verde** Brazil
145 C2 **Rio Verde** Mex.
154 B1 **Rio Verde de Mato Grosso** Brazil
90 C1 **Ripky** Ukr.
99 C3 **Ripley** U.K.
107 D1 **Ripoll** Spain
98 C2 **Ripon** U.K.
66 D1 **Rishiri-tō** *i.* Japan
 Rîşnov Romania *see* Râşnov
93 E4 **Risør** Norway
122 B2 **Ritchie** S. Africa
73 D3 **Ritchie's Archipelago** *is* India
134 C1 **Ritzville** U.S.A.
152 B2 **Rivadavia** Arg.
108 B1 **Riva del Garda** Italy
146 B3 **Rivas** Nic.
152 C3 **Rivera** Uru.
114 B4 **River Cess** Liberia
129 D2 **Riverhurst** Can.
52 C2 **Riverina** reg. Austr.
122 B3 **Riversdale** S. Africa
135 C4 **Riverside** U.S.A.
136 B2 **Riverton** U.S.A.
131 D3 **Riverview** Can.
105 C3 **Rivesaltes** France
131 D3 **Rivière-au-Renard** Can.
131 D3 **Rivière-du-Loup** Can.
139 F1 **Rivière-Ouelle** Can.
90 B1 **Rivne** Ukr.
108 A1 **Rivoli** Italy
120 B2 **Rivungo** Angola

54 B2 **Riwaka** N.Z.
78 B2 **Riyadh** Saudi Arabia
81 C1 **Rize** Turkey
70 B2 **Rizhao** China
105 C2 **Roanne** France
138 D3 **Roanoke** U.S.A.
141 E1 **Roanoke** U.S.A.
141 E1 **Roanoke Rapids** U.S.A.
135 E3 **Roan Plateau** U.S.A.
146 B3 **Roatán** Hond.
52 A3 **Robe** Austr.
52 A3 **Robe, Mount** hill Austr.
101 F1 **Röbel** Ger.
53 D1 **Roberts, Mount** Austr.
92 H3 **Robertsfors** Sweden
122 A3 **Robertson** S. Africa
114 A4 **Robertsport** Liberia
 Robert Williams Angola *see* Caála
130 C3 **Roberval** Can.
50 A2 **Robinson Range** hills Austr.
52 B2 **Robinvale** Austr.
129 D2 **Roblin** Can.
128 C2 **Robson, Mount** Can.
143 D3 **Robstown** U.S.A.
 Roçadas Angola *see* Xangongo
108 B3 **Rocca Busambra** mt. Sicily Italy
153 C3 **Rocha** Uru.
98 B3 **Rochdale** U.K.
154 B1 **Rochedo** Brazil
100 B2 **Rochefort** Belgium
104 B2 **Rochefort** France
52 B3 **Rochester** Austr.
137 E2 **Rochester** MN U.S.A.
139 E2 **Rochester** NH U.S.A.
139 D2 **Rochester** NY U.S.A.
94 A2 **Rockall** *i.* N. Atlantic Ocean
160 L4 **Rockall Bank** sea feature N. Atlantic Ocean
138 B2 **Rockford** U.S.A.
51 E2 **Rockhampton** Austr.
141 D2 **Rock Hill** U.S.A.
50 A3 **Rockingham** Austr.
138 A2 **Rock Island** U.S.A.
136 B1 **Rock Springs** MT U.S.A.
143 C3 **Rocksprings** U.S.A.
136 B2 **Rock Springs** WY U.S.A.
141 D1 **Rockwood** U.S.A.
136 C3 **Rocky Ford** U.S.A.
141 E1 **Rocky Mount** U.S.A.
128 C2 **Rocky Mountain House** Can.
124 F4 **Rocky Mountains** U.S.A.
100 B3 **Rocroi** France
102 C1 **Rødbyhavn** Denmark
131 E2 **Roddickton** Can.
104 C3 **Rodez** France
 Rodi *i.* Greece *see* Rhodes
89 F2 **Rodniki** Rus. Fed.
 Rodos Greece *see* Rhodes
 Rodos *i.* Greece *see* Rhodes
 Rodosto Turkey *see* Tekirdağ
50 A2 **Roebourne** Austr.
50 B1 **Roebuck Bay** Austr.
123 C1 **Roedtan** S. Africa
100 B2 **Roermond** Neth.
100 A2 **Roeselare** Belgium
127 G2 **Roes Welcome Sound** sea chan. Can.
128 C2 **Rogers** Can.
140 B1 **Rogers** U.S.A.
138 C3 **Rogers, Mount** U.S.A.
138 C1 **Rogers City** U.S.A.
157 G8 **Roggeveen Basin** sea feature S. Pacific Ocean
122 B3 **Roggeveldberge** esc. S. Africa
92 G2 **Rognan** Norway
134 B2 **Rogue** *r.* U.S.A.
74 B2 **Rohtak** India
49 M5 **Roi Georges, Îles du** *is* Fr. Polynesia
88 B2 **Roja** Latvia
60 B1 **Rokan** *r.* Indon.
88 C2 **Rokiškis** Lith.
90 B1 **Rokytne** Ukr.
154 B2 **Rolândia** Brazil
137 E3 **Rolla** U.S.A.
143 C2 **Rolling Prairies** reg. U.S.A.
51 D2 **Roma** Austr.
59 C3 **Roma** *i.* Indon.
 Roma Italy *see* Rome
123 C2 **Roma** Lesotho
143 D3 **Roma** U.S.A.
141 E2 **Romain, Cape** U.S.A.
110 C1 **Roman** Romania
158 E5 **Romanche Gap** sea feature S. Atlantic Ocean
110 B1 **Romania** country Europe
91 C3 **Roman-Kosh** mt. Ukr.
69 D1 **Romanovka** Rus. Fed.
105 D2 **Romans-sur-Isère** France
105 D2 **Rombas** France
64 B2 **Romblon** Phil.
108 B2 **Rome** Italy
141 C2 **Rome** GA U.S.A.
139 D2 **Rome** NY U.S.A.
99 D4 **Romford** U.K.
105 C2 **Romilly-sur-Seine** France
91 C1 **Romny** Ukr.
104 C2 **Romorantin-Lanthenay** France
99 C4 **Romsey** U.K.
134 D1 **Ronan** U.S.A.
96 □ **Ronas Hill** U.K.
151 D4 **Roncador, Serra do** hills Brazil
106 B2 **Ronda** Spain
154 B2 **Rondon** Brazil
154 B1 **Rondonópolis** Brazil

74 B1 **Rondu** Jammu and Kashmir
71 A3 **Rong'an** China
 Rongcheng China *see* Rongxian
 Rongcheng China *see* Jianli
71 A3 **Rongjiang** China
62 A1 **Rongklang Range** mts Myanmar
 Rongmei China *see* Hefeng
71 B3 **Rongxian** China
93 F4 **Rønne** Denmark
93 G4 **Ronneby** Sweden
55 **Ronne Ice Shelf** Antarctica
101 D1 **Ronnenberg** Ger.
100 A2 **Ronse** Belgium
 Rooke Island P.N.G. *see* Umboi
74 B2 **Roorkee** India
100 B2 **Roosendaal** Neth.
62 B2 **Roosevelt** U.S.A.
128 B2 **Roosevelt, Mount** Can.
55 N2 **Roosevelt Island** Antarctica
104 B3 **Roquefort** France
150 C2 **Roraima, Mount** Guyana
93 F3 **Røros** Norway
90 C2 **Ros'** *r.* Ukr.
142 B3 **Rosa, Punta** pt Mex.
106 B2 **Rosal de la Frontera** Spain
153 B3 **Rosario** Arg.
144 A1 **Rosario** Mex.
144 B2 **Rosario** Mex.
144 B2 **Rosario** Mex.
147 C3 **Rosario** Venez.
152 B2 **Rosario de la Frontera** Arg.
151 D4 **Rosário Oeste** Brazil
144 A2 **Rosarito** Mex.
144 A1 **Rosarito** Mex.
142 A3 **Rosarito** Mex.
109 C3 **Rosarno** Italy
143 C2 **Roscoe** U.S.A.
104 B2 **Roscoff** France
97 B2 **Roscommon** Ireland
97 C2 **Roscrea** Ireland
147 D3 **Roseau** Dominica
137 D1 **Roseau** U.S.A.
134 B2 **Roseburg** U.S.A.
96 C2 **Rosehearty** U.K.
143 D3 **Rosenberg** U.S.A.
101 D1 **Rosengarten** Ger.
102 C2 **Rosenheim** Ger.
129 D2 **Rosetown** Can.
122 A2 **Rosh Pinah** Namibia
110 C2 **Roşiori de Vede** Romania
93 F4 **Roskilde** Denmark
89 D3 **Roslavl'** Rus. Fed.
134 B1 **Roslyn** U.S.A.
109 C3 **Rossano** Italy
97 B1 **Rossan Point** Ireland
51 E1 **Rossel Island** P.N.G.
55 N1 **Ross Ice Shelf** Antarctica
131 D3 **Rossignol, Lake** Can.
128 C3 **Rossland** Can.
97 C2 **Rosslare** Ireland
97 C2 **Rosslare Harbour** Ireland
101 F2 **Roßlau** Ger.
101 E2 **Roßleben** Ger.
114 A3 **Rosso** Maur.
105 D3 **Rosso, Capo** c. Corsica France
99 B4 **Ross-on-Wye** U.K.
91 D1 **Rossosh'** Rus. Fed.
128 A1 **Ross River** Can.
55 N2 **Ross Sea** Antarctica
92 F2 **Røssvatnet** l. Norway
81 D3 **Rostāq** Iran
129 D2 **Rosthern** Can.
102 C1 **Rostock** Ger.
89 E2 **Rostov** Rus. Fed.
91 D2 **Rostov-na-Donu** Rus. Fed.
 Rostov-na-Donu Rus. Fed. *see* Rostov-na-Donu
104 B2 **Rostrenen** France
92 G2 **Røsvik** Norway
92 H2 **Rosvik** Sweden
142 C2 **Roswell** U.S.A.
59 D2 **Rota** *i.* N. Mariana Is
59 C3 **Rote** *i.* Indon.
101 D1 **Rotenburg (Wümme)** Ger.
101 E3 **Roth** Ger.
98 C2 **Rothbury** U.K.
101 E3 **Rothenburg ob der Tauber** Ger.
98 C3 **Rotherham** U.K.
96 C2 **Rothes** U.K.
96 B3 **Rothesay** U.K.
53 C2 **Roto** Austr.
105 D3 **Rotondo, Monte** mt. Corsica France
54 C1 **Rotorua** N.Z.
54 C1 **Rotorua, Lake** N.Z.
101 E2 **Rottenbach** Ger.
102 C2 **Rottenmann** Austria
100 B2 **Rotterdam** Neth.
102 B2 **Rottweil** Ger.
49 I5 **Rotuma** *i.* Fiji
105 C1 **Roubaix** France
104 C2 **Rouen** France
 Roulers Belgium *see* Roeselare
53 D2 **Round Mountain** Austr.
131 E3 **Round Pond** l. Can.
143 D2 **Round Rock** U.S.A.
134 E1 **Roundup** U.S.A.
96 C1 **Rousay** l. U.K.
130 C3 **Rouyn-Noranda** Can.
 Rouyuanchengzi China *see* Huachi
92 I2 **Rovaniemi** Fin.
91 D2 **Roven'ki** Rus. Fed.
91 D2 **Roven'ky** Ukr.
108 B1 **Rovereto** Italy
63 B2 **Rôviĕng Tbong** Cambodia

108 B1 Rovigo Italy
108 B1 Rovinj Croatia
53 C1 Rowena Austr.
Równe Ukr. see Rivne
64 B3 Roxas Phil.
64 B2 Roxas Phil.
64 A2 Roxas Phil.
64 B3 Roxas Phil.
52 A2 Roxby Downs Austr.
142 C1 Roy NM U.S.A.
134 D2 Roy UT U.S.A.
138 B1 Royale, Isle i. U.S.A.
104 B2 Royan France
99 C3 Royston U.K.
90 C2 Rozdil'na Ukr.
91 C2 Rozdol'ne Ukr.
103 E2 Rožňava Slovakia
100 B3 Rozoy-sur-Serre France
87 D3 Rtishchevo Rus. Fed.
Ruanda country Africa see Rwanda
54 C1 Ruapehu, Mount vol. N.Z.
54 A3 Ruapuke Island N.Z.
89 D2 Ruba Belarus
79 B3 Rub' al Khālī des. Saudi Arabia
119 D3 Rubeho Mountains Tanz.
91 D2 Rubizhne Ukr.
77 E1 Rubtsovsk Rus. Fed.
126 B2 Ruby U.S.A.
135 C2 Ruby Mountains U.S.A.
76 C3 Rudbar Afgh.
66 C2 Rudnaya Pristan' Rus. Fed.
89 D3 Rudnya Rus. Fed.
76 C1 Rudnyy Kazakh.
Rudolf, Lake salt l. Eth./Kenya see
Turkana, Lake
82 E1 Rudol'fa, Ostrov i. Rus. Fed.
Rudolph Island Rus. Fed. see
Rudol'fa, Ostrov
101 E2 Rudolstadt Ger.
116 B3 Rufa'a Sudan
119 D3 Rufiji r. Tanz.
153 B3 Rufino Arg.
121 B2 Rufunsa Zambia
70 C2 Rugao China
99 C3 Rugby U.K.
136 C1 Rugby U.S.A.
102 C1 Rügen i. Ger.
119 C3 Ruhengeri Rwanda
101 E2 Ruhla Ger.
88 B2 Ruhnu i. Estonia
100 C2 Ruhr r. Ger.
71 C3 Rui'an China
142 B2 Ruidoso U.S.A.
144 B2 Ruiz Mex.
119 D3 Rukwa, Lake Tanz.
96 A2 Rum i. U.K.
109 C1 Ruma Serb. and Mont.
78 B2 Rumāh Saudi Arabia
117 A4 Rumbek Sudan
147 C2 Rum Cay i. Bahamas
139 E2 Rumford U.S.A.
103 D1 Rumia Pol.
105 D2 Rumilly France
50 C1 Rum Jungle Austr.
66 D2 Rumoi Japan
121 C2 Rumphi Malawi
54 B2 Runanga N.Z.
98 B3 Runcorn U.K.
120 A2 Rundu Namibia
119 C2 Rungu Dem. Rep. Congo
119 D3 Rungwa Tanz.
68 B2 Ruoqiang China
130 C2 Rupert r. Can.
134 D2 Rupert U.S.A.
130 C2 Rupert Bay Can.
Rusaddir N. Africa see Melilla
121 C2 Rusape Zimbabwe
110 C2 Ruse Bulg.
137 E1 Rush City U.S.A.
121 C2 Rushinga Zimbabwe
77 D3 Rushon Tajik.
136 C2 Rushville U.S.A.
53 C3 Rushworth Austr.
129 D2 Russell Can.
54 B1 Russell N.Z.
137 D3 Russell U.S.A.
140 C2 Russellville AL U.S.A.
140 B1 Russellville AR U.S.A.
138 B3 Russellville KY U.S.A.
101 D2 Rüsselsheim Ger.
82 F2 Russian Federation country
Asia/Europe
81 C1 Rust'avi Georgia
123 C2 Rustenburg S. Africa
140 B2 Ruston U.S.A.
61 D2 Ruteng Indon.
98 B3 Ruthin U.K.
139 E2 Rutland U.S.A.
Rutog China see Dêrub
119 C3 Rutshuru Dem. Rep. Congo
119 E4 Ruvuma r. Moz./Tanz.
79 C2 Ruweis U.A.E.
89 E2 Ruza Rus. Fed.
77 C1 Ruzayevka Kazakh.
87 D3 Ruzayevka Rus. Fed.
119 C3 Rwanda country Africa
89 E3 Ryazan' Rus. Fed.
89 F3 Ryazhsk Rus. Fed.
86 C2 Rybachiy, Poluostrov pen.
Rus. Fed.
Rybach'ye Kyrg. see Balykchy
89 E2 Rybinsk Rus. Fed.
89 E2 Rybinskoye Vodokhranilishche
resr Rus. Fed.
103 D1 Rybnik Pol.

89 E3 Rybnitsa Moldova see Rîbniţa
89 E2 Rybnoye Rus. Fed.
99 D4 Rye U.K.
Rykovo Ukr. see Yenakiyeve
89 D3 Ryl'sk Rus. Fed.
Ryojun China see Lüshun
67 C3 Ryōtsu Japan
69 B3 Ryukyu Islands is Japan
89 D3 Ryzhikovo Rus. Fed.
103 E1 Rzeszów Pol.
91 E1 Rzhaksa Rus. Fed.
89 D2 Rzhev Rus. Fed.

S

79 C2 Sa'ādatābād Iran
101 E2 Saale r. Ger.
101 E2 Saalfeld Ger.
134 B1 Saanich Can.
100 C3 Saar r. Ger.
102 B2 Saarbrücken Ger.
88 B2 Sääre Estonia
88 B2 Saaremaa i. Estonia
92 I2 Saarenkylä Fin.
93 I3 Saarijärvi Fin.
100 C3 Saarlouis Ger.
80 B2 Sab' Ābār Syria
107 D1 Sabadell Spain
67 C3 Sabae Japan
61 C1 Sabah state Malaysia
61 C1 Sabalana i. Indon.
146 B2 Sabana, Archipiélago de is Cuba
150 B1 Sabanalarga Col.
60 A1 Sabang Indon.
155 D1 Sabará Brazil
108 B2 Sabaudia Italy
122 B3 Sabelo S. Africa
119 D2 Sabena Desert Kenya
115 D2 Sabhā Libya
123 D2 Sabie r. Moz./S. Africa
123 D2 Sabie S. Africa
145 B2 Sabinas Mex.
145 B2 Sabinas Hidalgo Mex.
143 E3 Sabine r. U.S.A.
131 D3 Sable, Cape Can.
141 D3 Sable, Cape U.S.A.
131 E3 Sable Island Can.
106 B1 Sabugal Port.
78 B3 Ṣabyā Saudi Arabia
76 B3 Sabzevār Iran
107 D2 Sa Cabaneta Spain
137 D2 Sac City U.S.A.
120 A2 Sachanga Angola
130 A2 Sachigo Lake Can.
65 B3 Sach'on S. Korea
126 D2 Sachs Harbour Can.
154 C1 Sacramento Brazil
135 B3 Sacramento U.S.A.
135 B3 Sacramento r. U.S.A.
142 B2 Sacramento Mountains U.S.A.
135 B2 Sacramento Valley U.S.A.
110 B1 Săcueni Romania
123 C3 Sada S. Africa
107 C1 Sádaba Spain
Sá da Bandeira Angola see
Lubango
78 B3 Ṣa'dah Yemen
63 B3 Sadao Thai.
79 B3 Ṣadārah Yemen
63 B2 Sa Đec Vietnam
74 B2 Sadiqabad Pak.
72 D2 Sadiya India
67 C3 Sadoga-shima i. Japan
107 D2 Sa Dragonera i. Spain
93 F4 Säffle Sweden
142 B2 Safford U.S.A.
99 D3 Saffron Walden U.K.
114 B1 Safi Morocco
155 D1 Safiras, Serra das mts Brazil
86 D2 Safonovo Rus. Fed.
89 D2 Safonovo Rus. Fed.
78 B2 Safrā' as Sark esc. Saudi Arabia
75 C2 Saga China
67 B4 Saga Japan
62 A1 Sagaing Myanmar
67 C3 Sagamihara Japan
74 B2 Sagar India
Sagarmatha mt. China/Nepal see
Everest, Mount
138 C2 Saginaw U.S.A.
138 C2 Saginaw Bay U.S.A.
Saglouc Can. see Salluit
106 B2 Sagres Port.
146 B2 Sagua la Grande Cuba
139 F1 Saguenay r. Can.
107 C2 Sagunto Spain
76 B2 Sagyndyk, Mys pt Kazakh.
106 B1 Sahagún Spain
114 C3 Sahara des. Africa
Saharan Atlas mts Alg. see
Atlas Saharien
74 B2 Saharanpur India
75 C2 Saharsa India
114 B3 Sahel reg. Africa
74 B1 Sahiwal Pak.
144 B2 Sahuayo Mex.
78 B2 Ṣāḥūq reg. Saudi Arabia
114 C1 Saïda Alg.
Saïda Lebanon see Sidon
75 C2 Saidpur Bangl.
67 B3 Saigō Japan
Saigon Vietnam see
Ho Chi Minh City

75 D2 Saiha India
70 B1 Saihan Tal China
67 B4 Saiki Japan
93 I3 Saimaa l. Fin.
144 B2 Sain Alto Mex.
96 C3 St Abb's Head hd U.K.
131 E3 St Alban's Can.
99 C4 St Albans U.K.
138 C3 St Albans U.S.A.
99 B4 St Alban's Head hd U.K.
St Aldhelm's Head hd U.K. see
St Alban's Head
St-André, Cap pt Madag. see
Vilanandro, Tanjona
96 C2 St Andrews U.K.
131 E2 St Anthony Can.
134 D2 St Anthony U.S.A.
52 B3 St Arnaud Austr.
131 E2 St-Augustin Can.
131 E2 St Augustine r. Can.
141 D3 St Augustine U.S.A.
99 A4 St Austell U.K.
104 C2 St-Avertin France
147 D3 St-Barthélemy i. West Indies
98 B2 St Bees Head hd U.K.
105 D3 St-Bonnet-en-Champsaur France
99 A4 St Bride's Bay U.K.
104 B2 St-Brieuc France
130 C3 St Catharines Can.
141 D2 St Catherines Island U.S.A.
99 C4 St Catherine's Point U.K.
137 E3 St Charles U.S.A.
138 C2 St Clair, Lake Can./U.S.A.
105 D2 St-Claude France
99 A4 St Clears U.K.
137 E2 St Cloud U.S.A.
138 A1 St Croix r. U.S.A.
147 D3 St Croix Virgin Is (U.S.A.)
99 A4 St David's U.K.
99 A4 St David's Head hd U.K.
113 I8 St-Denis r.
104 C2 St-Denis France
St-Denis France
St-Denis-du-Sig Alg. see Sig
105 D2 St-Dié France
105 C2 St-Dizier France
130 C3 Ste-Adèle Can.
131 D3 Ste-Anne-des-Monts Can.
139 E1 Ste-Foy Can.
105 C2 St-Égrève France
128 A1 St Elias Mountains Can.
131 D2 Ste-Marguerite r. Can.
139 E1 Ste-Marie Can.
Ste-Marie, Cap c. Madag. see
Vohimena, Tanjona
Sainte-Marie, Île i. Madag. see
Nosy Boraha
Ste-Rose-du-Dégelé Can. see
Dégelis
129 E2 Ste Rose du Lac Can.
104 B2 Saintes France
105 C2 St-Étienne France
104 C2 St-Étienne-du-Rouvray France
130 C3 St-Félicien Can.
97 D1 Saintfield U.K.
105 D3 St-Florent Corsica France
105 C2 St-Flour France
136 C3 St Francis U.S.A.
104 C3 St-Gaudens France
53 C1 St George Austr.
135 D3 St George U.S.A.
141 D3 St George Island U.S.A.
131 C3 St-Georges Can.
147 D3 St George's Grenada
131 E3 St George's Bay Can.
97 C3 St George's Channel Ireland/U.K.
105 D2 St Gotthard Pass pass Switz.
113 C7 St Helena terr.
S. Atlantic Ocean
122 A3 St Helena Bay S. Africa
122 A3 St Helena Bay b. S. Africa
98 B3 St Helens U.K.
134 B1 St Helens, Mount U.S.A.
95 C4 St Helier Channel Is
100 B2 St-Hubert Belgium
139 E1 St-Hyacinthe Can.
138 C1 St Ignace U.S.A.
130 B3 St Ignace Island Can.
99 A4 St Ives U.K.
St Jacques, Cap Vietnam see
Vung Tau
128 A2 St James, Cape Can.
130 C3 St-Jean, Lac l. Can.
104 B3 St-Jean-d'Angély France
104 B3 St-Jean-de-Luz France
104 B2 St-Jean-de-Monts France
130 C3 St-Jean-sur-Richelieu Can.
139 E1 St-Jérôme Can.
134 C1 St Joe r. U.S.A.
131 D3 Saint John Can.
137 D3 St John U.S.A.
139 F1 St John r. U.S.A.
147 D3 St John's Antigua
131 E3 St John's Can.
142 B2 St Johns U.S.A.
141 D3 St Johns r. U.S.A.
139 E2 St Johnsbury U.S.A.
137 E3 St Joseph U.S.A.
130 A2 St Joseph, Lake Can.
St-Joseph-d'Alma Can. see Alma
130 B3 St Joseph Island Can.
139 E1 St-Jovité Can.
104 C2 St-Junien France
94 B2 St Kilda i. U.K.
147 D3 St Kitts and Nevis country
West Indies

151 D2 St-Laurent-du-Maroni Fr. Guiana
131 E3 St Lawrence Can.
131 D3 St Lawrence inlet Can.
131 D3 St Lawrence, Gulf of Can.
126 A2 St Lawrence Island U.S.A.
104 B2 St-Lô France
114 A3 St-Louis Senegal
137 E3 St Louis U.S.A.
137 E1 St Louis r. U.S.A.
147 D3 St Lucia country West Indies
147 D3 St Lucia Channel
Martinique/St Lucia
123 D2 St Lucia Estuary S. Africa
147 D3 St Maarten i. West Indies
96 □ St Magnus Bay U.K.
104 B2 St-Malo France
104 B2 St-Malo, Golfe de g. France
147 C3 St-Marc Haiti
St Mark's S. Africa see Cofimvaba
147 D3 St-Martin i. West Indies
122 A3 St Martin, Cape S. Africa
129 E2 St Martin, Lake Can.
139 E2 St Marys U.S.A.
124 A3 St Matthew Island U.S.A.
59 D3 St Matthias Group is P.N.G.
130 C3 St-Maurice r. Can.
130 C3 St-Michel-des-Saints Can.
104 B2 St-Nazaire France
104 C1 St-Omer France
129 C2 St Paul Can.
137 E2 St Paul U.S.A.
156 A8 St-Paul, Île i. Indian Ocean
137 E2 St Peter U.S.A.
95 C4 St Peter Port Channel Is
141 D3 St Petersburg U.S.A.
131 E3 St-Pierre St Pierre and Miquelon
139 E1 St-Pierre, Lac l. Can.
131 E3 St Pierre and Miquelon terr.
N. America
104 B2 St-Pierre-d'Oléron France
105 C2 St-Pourçain-sur-Sioule France
131 D3 St Quentin Can.
105 C2 St-Quentin France
105 D3 St-Raphaël France
122 B3 St Sebastian Bay S. Africa
104 B2 St-Sébastien-sur-Loire France
131 D3 St-Siméon Can.
129 E2 St Theresa Point Can.
130 B3 St Thomas Can.
105 D3 St-Tropez France
105 D3 St-Tropez, Cap de c. France
St Vincent, Cape see
São Vicente, Cabo de
52 A3 St Vincent, Gulf Austr.
147 D3 St Vincent and the Grenadines
country West Indies
147 D3 St Vincent Passage
St Lucia/St Vincent
129 C2 St Walburg Can.
104 C2 St-Yrieix-la-Perche France
59 D1 Saipan i. N. Mariana Is
152 B1 Sajama, Nevado mt. Bol.
122 B2 Sak watercourse S. Africa
67 C4 Sakai Japan
67 B4 Sakaide Japan
78 B2 Sakākah Saudi Arabia
136 C1 Sakakawea, Lake U.S.A.
Sakarya Turkey see Adapazarı
111 D2 Sakarya r. Turkey
66 C3 Sakata Japan
65 B1 Sakchu N. Korea
66 C1 Sakhalin i. Rus. Fed.
123 C2 Sakhile S. Africa
81 C1 Şäki Azer.
88 B3 Šakiai Lith.
69 E3 Sakishima-shotō is Japan
62 B2 Sakon Nakhon Thai.
74 A2 Sakrand Pak.
122 B3 Sakrivier S. Africa
67 D3 Sakura Japan
91 C2 Saky Ukr.
93 G4 Sala Sweden
130 C3 Salaberry-de-Valleyfield Can.
88 B2 Salacgriva Latvia
109 C2 Sala Consilina Italy
135 C4 Salada, Laguna salt l. Mex.
152 C2 Saladas Arg.
152 B3 Salado r. Arg.
145 C2 Salado r. Mex.
153 B3 Salado o Chadileo r. Arg.
114 B4 Salaga Ghana
122 B1 Salajwe Botswana
79 C2 Salakh, Jabal mt. Oman
115 D3 Salal Chad
78 A2 Salāla Sudan
79 C3 Şalālah Oman
145 B2 Salamanca Mex.
106 B1 Salamanca Spain
139 D2 Salamanca U.S.A.
106 B1 Salas Spain
63 B2 Salavan Laos
59 C3 Salawati i. Indon.
61 D2 Salayar i. Indon.
157 G7 Sala y Gómez, Isla i.
S. Pacific Ocean
Salazar Angola see N'dalatando
104 C2 Salbris France
88 C3 Šalčininkai Lith.
106 C1 Saldaña Spain
122 A3 Saldanha S. Africa
88 B2 Saldus Latvia
53 C3 Sale Austr.
86 F2 Salekhard Rus. Fed.
73 B3 Salem India
138 B3 Salem IL U.S.A.

137 E3 **Salem** *MO* U.S.A.
134 B2 **Salem** *OR* U.S.A.
137 D2 **Salem** *SD* U.S.A.
96 B2 **Salen** U.K.
109 B2 **Salerno** Italy
108 B2 **Salerno, Golfo di** *g.* Italy
98 B3 **Salford** U.K.
151 E2 **Salgado** *r.* Brazil
103 D2 **Salgótarján** Hungary
151 F3 **Salgueiro** Brazil
136 B3 **Salihli** Turkey
88 C3 **Salihorsk** Belarus
121 C2 **Salima** Malawi
121 C2 **Salimo** Moz.
137 D3 **Salina** *KS* U.S.A.
135 D3 **Salina** *UT* U.S.A.
109 B3 **Salina, Isola** *i.* Italy
145 C3 **Salina Cruz** Mex.
155 D1 **Salinas** Brazil
144 B2 **Salinas** Mex.
135 B3 **Salinas** U.S.A.
135 B3 **Salinas** *r.* U.S.A.
107 C2 **Salines, Cap de ses** *c.* Spain
151 E3 **Salinópolis** Brazil
99 C4 **Salisbury** U.K.
139 D3 **Salisbury** *MD* U.S.A.
141 D1 **Salisbury** *NC* U.S.A.
          Salisbury Zimbabwe *see* Harare
99 B4 **Salisbury Plain** U.K.
151 E3 **Salitre** *r.* Brazil
92 I2 **Salla** Fin.
143 E1 **Sallisaw** U.S.A.
127 G2 **Salluit** Can.
75 C2 **Sallyana** Nepal
81 C2 **Salmās** Iran
128 C3 **Salmo** Can.
134 D1 **Salmon** U.S.A.
134 C1 **Salmon** *r.* U.S.A.
128 C2 **Salmon Arm** Can.
134 C2 **Salmon River Mountains** U.S.A.
100 C3 **Salmtal** Ger.
118 B2 **Salo** C.A.R.
93 H3 **Salo** Fin.
105 D3 **Salon-de-Provence** France
          Salonica Greece *see* Thessaloniki
110 B1 **Salonta** Romania
87 D4 **Sal'sk** Rus. Fed.
122 B3 **Salt** *watercourse* S. Africa
107 D1 **Salt** Spain
142 A2 **Salt** *r.* U.S.A.
152 B2 **Salta** Arg.
99 A4 **Saltash** U.K.
96 B3 **Saltcoats** U.K.
145 B2 **Saltillo** Mex.
134 D2 **Salt Lake City** U.S.A.
154 C2 **Salto** Brazil
152 C3 **Salto** Uru.
155 E1 **Salto da Divisa** Brazil
154 B2 **Salto del Guairá** Para.
135 C4 **Salton Sea** *salt l.* U.S.A.
154 B3 **Salto Osório, Represa** *resr* Brazil
154 B3 **Salto Santiago, Represa de** *resr* Brazil
141 D2 **Saluda** U.S.A.
76 B3 **Saluq, Küh-e** *mt.* Iran
108 A2 **Saluzzo** Italy
151 F4 **Salvador** Brazil
79 C2 **Salwah** Saudi Arabia
62 A2 **Salween** *r.* China/Myanmar
81 C2 **Salyan** Azer.
138 C3 **Salyersville** U.S.A.
122 A1 **Salzbrunn** Namibia
102 C2 **Salzburg** Austria
101 E1 **Salzgitter** Ger.
101 D2 **Salzkotten** Ger.
101 E1 **Salzwedel** Ger.
144 B1 **Samalayuca** Mex.
66 D2 **Samani** Japan
64 B2 **Samar** *i.* Phil.
87 E3 **Samara** Rus. Fed.
          Samarahan Malaysia *see* Sri Aman
59 E3 **Samarai** P.N.G.
61 C2 **Samarinda** Indon.
77 C3 **Samarqand** Uzbek.
81 C2 **Sāmarrā'** Iraq
81 C1 **Şamaxı** Azer.
119 C3 **Samba** Dem. Rep. Congo
61 C1 **Sambaliung** *mts* Indon.
75 C2 **Sambalpur** India
60 C2 **Sambar, Tanjung** *pt* Indon.
60 B1 **Sambas** Indon.
121 □E2 **Sambava** Madag.
74 B2 **Sambhar** India
90 A2 **Sambir** Ukr.
61 C2 **Sambo** Indon.
61 C2 **Samboja** Indon.
153 C3 **Samborombón, Bahía** *b.* Arg.
65 B2 **Samch'ŏk** S. Korea
          Samch'ŏnp'o S. Korea *see* Sach'on
81 C2 **Samdi Dag** *mt.* Turkey
119 D3 **Same** Tanz.
121 B2 **Samfya** Zambia
78 B2 **Samirah** Saudi Arabia
65 B1 **Samjiyŏn** N. Korea
          Sam Neua Laos *see* Xam Nua
48 J5 **Samoa** *country* S. Pacific Ocean
156 E6 **Samoa Basin** *sea feature* S. Pacific Ocean
          Samoa i Sisifo *country* S. Pacific Ocean *see* Samoa
109 C1 **Sambor** Croatia
110 B2 **Samokov** Bulg.
111 C3 **Samos** *i.* Greece

          Samothrace *i.* Greece *see* Samothraki
111 C2 **Samothraki** Greece
111 C2 **Samothraki** *i.* Greece
61 C2 **Sampit** Indon.
119 C3 **Sampwe** Dem. Rep. Congo
143 E2 **Sam Rayburn Reservoir** U.S.A.
62 B2 **Sâm Son** Vietnam
80 B1 **Samsun** Turkey
81 C1 **Samtredia** Georgia
63 B3 **Samui, Ko** *i.* Thai.
63 B2 **Samut Songkhram** Thai.
114 B3 **Sana** Mali
78 B3 **Şan'ā'** Yemen
118 A2 **Sanaga** *r.* Cameroon
81 C2 **Sanandaj** Iran
146 B3 **San Andrés, Isla de** *i.* Caribbean Sea
106 B1 **San Andrés del Rabanedo** Spain
142 B3 **San Andres Mountains** U.S.A.
145 C3 **San Andrés Tuxtla** Mex.
143 C2 **San Angelo** U.S.A.
143 D3 **San Antonio** U.S.A.
135 C4 **San Antonio, Mount** U.S.A.
107 D2 **San Antonio Abad** Spain
152 B2 **San Antonio de los Cobres** Arg.
153 B4 **San Antonio Oeste** Arg.
108 B2 **San Benedetto del Tronto** Italy
144 A3 **San Benedicto, Isla** *i.* Mex.
135 C4 **San Bernardino** U.S.A.
135 C4 **San Bernardino Mountains** U.S.A.
142 B3 **San Blas** Mex.
141 C3 **San Blas, Cape** U.S.A.
146 C4 **San Blas, Punta** *pt* Panama
152 B1 **San Borja** Bol.
144 B2 **San Buenaventura** Mex.
64 B2 **San Carlos** Phil.
147 D4 **San Carlos** Venez.
153 A4 **San Carlos de Bariloche** Arg.
147 C4 **San Carlos del Zulia** Venez.
104 C2 **Sancerrois, Collines du** *hills* France
135 C4 **San Clemente** U.S.A.
135 C4 **San Clemente Island** U.S.A.
105 C2 **Sancoins** France
48 H5 **San Cristobal** *i.* Solomon Is
150 B2 **San Cristóbal** Venez.
145 C3 **San Cristóbal de las Casas** Mex.
146 C2 **Sancti Spíritus** Cuba
123 D1 **Sand** *r.* S. Africa
61 C1 **Sandakan** *Sabah* Malaysia
93 E3 **Sandane** Norway
111 B2 **Sandanski** Bulg.
114 A3 **Sandaré** Mali
96 C1 **Sanday** *i.* U.K.
143 C2 **Sanderson** U.S.A.
150 C4 **Sandia** Peru
135 C4 **San Diego** U.S.A.
111 D3 **Sandıklı** Turkey
93 E4 **Sandnes** Norway
92 F2 **Sandnessjøen** Norway
118 C3 **Sandoa** Dem. Rep. Congo
103 E1 **Sandomierz** Pol.
89 C2 **Sandovo** Rus. Fed.
94 B1 **Sandoy** *i.* Faroe Is
134 C1 **Sandpoint** U.S.A.
71 B3 **Sandu** China
94 B1 **Sandur** Faroe Is
138 C2 **Sandusky** U.S.A.
122 A3 **Sandveld** *mts* S. Africa
122 A2 **Sandverhaar** Namibia
93 F4 **Sandvika** Norway
93 G3 **Sandviken** Sweden
131 E2 **Sandwich Bay** Can.
135 D2 **Sandy** U.S.A.
129 D2 **Sandy Bay** Can.
51 E2 **Sandy Cape** Austr.
130 A2 **Sandy Lake** Can.
130 A2 **Sandy Lake** *l.* Can.
141 D2 **Sandy Springs** U.S.A.
144 A1 **San Felipe** Mex.
145 B2 **San Felipe** Mex.
150 B1 **San Felipe** Venez.
144 A1 **San Fernando** Mex.
145 C2 **San Fernando** Mex.
64 B2 **San Fernando** Phil.
64 B2 **San Fernando** Phil.
106 B2 **San Fernando** Spain
147 D3 **San Fernando** Trin. and Tob.
150 C2 **San Fernando de Apure** Venez.
141 D3 **Sanford** *FL* U.S.A.
139 E2 **Sanford** *ME* U.S.A.
141 E1 **Sanford** *NC* U.S.A.
152 B3 **San Francisco** Arg.
135 B3 **San Francisco** U.S.A.
107 D2 **San Francisco Javier** Spain
74 B3 **Sangamner** India
83 J2 **Sangar** Rus. Fed.
108 A3 **San Gavino Monreale** *Sardinia* Italy
101 E2 **Sangerhausen** Ger.
61 C1 **Sanggau** Indon.
118 B3 **Sangha** *r.* Congo
109 C3 **San Giovanni in Fiore** Italy
59 C2 **Sangir** *i.* Indon.
59 C2 **Sangir, Kepulauan** *is* Indon.
65 B2 **Sangju** S. Korea
63 A2 **Sangkhla Buri** Thai.
61 C1 **Sangkulirang** Indon.
73 B3 **Sangli** India
118 B2 **Sangmélima** Cameroon
121 C3 **Sango** Zimbabwe
          San Gottardo, Passo del *pass* Switz. *see* St Gotthard Pass

136 B3 **Sangre de Cristo Range** *mts* U.S.A.
75 C2 **Sangsang** China
144 A2 **San Hipólito, Punta** *pt* Mex.
145 D3 **San Ignacio** Belize
152 B1 **San Ignacio** Bol.
144 A2 **San Ignacio** Mex.
130 C2 **Sanikiluaq** Can.
71 A3 **Sanjiang** China
          Sanjiang China *see* Jinping
67 C3 **Sanjō** Japan
135 B3 **San Joaquin** *r.* U.S.A.
153 B4 **San Jorge, Golfo de** *g.* Arg.
146 B4 **San José** Costa Rica
64 B2 **San Jose** Phil.
64 B2 **San Jose** Phil.
135 B3 **San Jose** U.S.A.
144 A2 **San José, Isla** *i.* Mex.
144 B2 **San José de Bavicora** Mex.
64 B2 **San Jose de Buenavista** Phil.
144 A2 **San José de Comondú** Mex.
144 B2 **San José del Cabo** Mex.
150 B2 **San José del Guaviare** Col.
152 B3 **San Juan** Arg.
146 B3 **San Juan** *r.* Costa Rica/Nic.
147 C3 **San Juan** Dom. Rep.
147 D3 **San Juan** Puerto Rico
135 D3 **San Juan** *r.* U.S.A.
152 C2 **San Juan Bautista** Para.
107 D2 **San Juan Bautista** Spain
145 C3 **San Juan Bautista Tuxtepec** Mex.
147 D4 **San Juan de los Morros** Venez.
145 C2 **San Juan del Río** Mex.
134 B1 **San Juan Islands** U.S.A.
144 B2 **San Juanito** Mex.
136 B3 **San Juan Mountains** U.S.A.
153 B4 **San Julián** Arg.
75 C2 **Sankh** *r.* India
63 B2 **San Khao Phang Hoei** *mts* Thai.
100 C2 **St Augustin** Ger.
105 D2 **St Gallen** Switz.
105 D2 **St Moritz** Switz.
          Sankt-Peterburg Rus. Fed. *see* St Petersburg
89 D2 **St Petersburg** Rus. Fed.
102 C2 **Sankt Veit an der Glan** Austria
100 C3 **St Wendel** Ger.
80 B2 **Şanlıurfa** Turkey
142 B3 **San Lorenzo** Mex.
106 B2 **Sanlúcar de Barrameda** Spain
144 B2 **San Lucas** Mex.
153 B3 **San Luis** Arg.
145 C2 **San Luis de la Paz** Mex.
142 A2 **San Luisito** Mex.
135 B3 **San Luis Obispo** U.S.A.
135 B3 **San Luis Obispo Bay** U.S.A.
145 B2 **San Luis Potosí** Mex.
144 A1 **San Luis Río Colorado** Mex.
143 D3 **San Marcos** U.S.A.
108 B2 **San Marino** *country* Europe
108 B2 **San Marino** San Marino
144 B2 **San Martín de Bolaños** Mex.
153 A4 **San Martín de los Andes** Arg.
135 B3 **San Mateo** U.S.A.
153 B4 **San Matías, Golfo** *g.* Arg.
70 B2 **Sanmenxia** China
146 B3 **San Miguel** El Salvador
152 B2 **San Miguel de Tucumán** Arg.
135 B4 **San Miguel Island** U.S.A.
145 C3 **San Miguel Sola de Vega** Mex.
71 B3 **Sanming** China
153 B3 **San Nicolás de los Arroyos** Arg.
135 C4 **San Nicolas Island** U.S.A.
110 B1 **Sânnicolau Mare** Romania
123 C2 **Sannieshof** S. Africa
114 B4 **Sanniquellie** Liberia
103 E2 **Sanok** Pol.
64 B2 **San Pablo** Phil.
144 B2 **San Pablo Balleza** Mex.
152 B2 **San Pedro** Arg.
152 B1 **San Pedro** Bol.
114 B4 **San-Pédro** Côte d'Ivoire
144 A2 **San Pedro** Mex.
142 A2 **San Pedro** *watercourse* U.S.A.
106 B2 **San Pedro, Sierra de** *mts* Spain
144 B2 **San Pedro de las Colonias** Mex.
152 C2 **San Pedro de Ycuamandyyú** Para.
142 A3 **San Pedro el Saucito** Mex.
146 B3 **San Pedro Sula** Hond.
108 A3 **San Pietro, Isola di** *i.* Sardinia Italy
96 C3 **Sanquhar** U.K.
144 A1 **San Quintín, Cabo** *c.* Mex.
153 B4 **San Rafael** Arg.
108 A2 **San Remo** Italy
143 D2 **San Saba** U.S.A.
147 C2 **San Salvador** *i.* Bahamas
146 B3 **San Salvador** El Salvador
152 B2 **San Salvador de Jujuy** Arg.
108 B2 **Sansepolcro** Italy
109 C2 **San Severo** Italy
109 C2 **Sanski Most** Bos.-Herz.
152 B1 **Santa Ana** Bol.
146 B3 **Santa Ana** El Salvador
144 A1 **Santa Ana** Mex.
135 C4 **Santa Ana** U.S.A.
152 B1 **Santa Ana de Yacuma** Bol.
144 B2 **Santa Bárbara** Mex.
135 C4 **Santa Barbara** U.S.A.
154 B1 **Santa Bárbara, Serra de** *hills* Brazil
152 B2 **Santa Catalina** Chile
135 C4 **Santa Catalina Island** U.S.A.
150 C3 **Santa Clara** Col.
146 C2 **Santa Clara** Cuba

135 B3 **Santa Clara** U.S.A.
135 C4 **Santa Clarita** U.S.A.
107 D1 **Santa Coloma de Gramanet** Spain
          Santa Comba Angola *see* Waku-Kungo
109 C3 **Santa Croce, Capo** *c.* Sicily Italy
153 B5 **Santa Cruz** *r.* Arg.
152 B1 **Santa Cruz** Bol.
64 B2 **Santa Cruz** Phil.
135 B3 **Santa Cruz** U.S.A.
145 C3 **Santa Cruz Barillas** Guat.
155 E1 **Santa Cruz Cabrália** Brazil
107 C2 **Santa Cruz de Moya** Spain
114 A2 **Santa Cruz de Tenerife** Canary Is
152 C2 **Santa Cruz do Sul** Brazil
135 C4 **Santa Cruz Island** U.S.A.
48 H5 **Santa Cruz Islands** Solomon Is
107 D2 **Santa Eulalia del Río** Spain
152 B3 **Santa Fé** Arg.
142 B1 **Santa Fe** U.S.A.
154 B2 **Santa Fé do Sul** Brazil
154 B1 **Santa Helena de Goiás** Brazil
153 B3 **Santa Isabel** Arg.
          Santa Isabel Equat. Guinea *see* Malabo
48 G4 **Santa Isabel** *i.* Solomon Is
154 B1 **Santa Luisa, Serra de** *hills* Brazil
151 E3 **Santa Luzia** Brazil
144 A2 **Santa Margarita, Isla** *i.* Mex.
152 C2 **Santa Maria** Brazil
144 B1 **Santa Maria** *r.* Mex.
135 B4 **Santa Maria** U.S.A.
123 D2 **Santa Maria, Cabo de** *c.* Moz.
106 B2 **Santa Maria, Cabo de** *c.* Port.
155 C1 **Santa Maria, Chapadão de** *hills* Brazil
151 E3 **Santa Maria das Barreiras** Brazil
109 C3 **Santa Maria di Leuca, Capo** *c.* Italy
155 D1 **Santa Maria do Suaçuí** Brazil
150 B1 **Santa Marta** Col.
135 C4 **Santa Monica** U.S.A.
151 E4 **Sântana** Brazil
110 B1 **Sântana** Romania
106 C1 **Santander** Spain
108 A3 **Sant'Antioco** Sardinia Italy
108 A3 **Sant'Antioco, Isola di** *i.* Sardinia Italy
151 D3 **Santarém** Brazil
106 B2 **Santarém** Port.
154 B1 **Santa Rita do Araguaia** Brazil
153 B4 **Santa Rosa** Arg.
152 C2 **Santa Rosa** Brazil
135 B3 **Santa Rosa** *CA* U.S.A.
142 C2 **Santa Rosa** *NM* U.S.A.
146 B3 **Santa Rosa de Copán** Hond.
135 B4 **Santa Rosa Island** *CA* U.S.A.
140 C2 **Santa Rosa Island** *FL* U.S.A.
144 A2 **Santa Rosalía** Mex.
134 C2 **Santa Rosa Range** *mts* U.S.A.
106 B1 **Santa Uxía de Ribeira** Spain
154 B1 **Santa Vitória** Brazil
107 D1 **Sant Carles de la Ràpita** Spain
135 C4 **Santee** U.S.A.
152 C2 **Santiago** Brazil
153 A3 **Santiago** Chile
147 C3 **Santiago** Dom. Rep.
144 B2 **Santiago** Mex.
146 B4 **Santiago** Panama
64 B2 **Santiago** Phil.
106 B1 **Santiago de Compostela** Spain
146 C2 **Santiago de Cuba** Cuba
144 B2 **Santiago Ixcuintla** Mex.
144 B2 **Santiago Papasquiaro** Mex.
106 C1 **Santillana** Spain
107 D1 **Sant Jordi, Golf de** *g.* Spain
155 C2 **Santo Amaro de Campos** Brazil
154 B2 **Santo Anastácio** Brazil
155 C2 **Santo André** Brazil
152 C2 **Santo Ângelo** Brazil
154 B2 **Santo Antônio da Platina** Brazil
151 F4 **Santo Antônio de Jesus** Brazil
150 C3 **Santo Antônio do Içá** Brazil
155 C2 **Santo Antônio do Monte** Brazil
147 D3 **Santo Domingo** Dom. Rep.
144 A2 **Santo Domingo** Mex.
142 B1 **Santo Domingo Pueblo** U.S.A.
          Santorini *i.* Greece *see* Thira
155 C2 **Santos** Brazil
155 C2 **Santos Dumont** Brazil
157 I7 **Santos Plateau** *sea feature* S. Atlantic Ocean
152 C2 **Santo Tomé** Arg.
153 A4 **San Valentin, Cerro** *mt.* Chile
146 B3 **San Vicente** El Salvador
144 A1 **San Vicente** Mex.
64 B2 **San Vicente** Phil.
150 B4 **San Vicente de Cañete** Peru
108 B2 **San Vincenzo** Italy
108 B3 **San Vito, Capo** *c.* Sicily Italy
71 A4 **Sanya** China
155 C2 **São Bernardo do Campo** Brazil
152 C2 **São Borja** Brazil
154 C2 **São Carlos** Brazil
155 D1 **São Felipe, Serra de** *hills* Brazil
151 D3 **São Félix** Brazil
151 D3 **São Félix** Brazil
155 D2 **São Fidélis** Brazil
155 D1 **São Francisco** Brazil
151 F4 **São Francisco** *r.* Brazil
154 C3 **São Francisco, Ilha de** *i.* Brazil
154 C3 **São Francisco do Sul** Brazil
152 C3 **São Gabriel** Brazil
155 D2 **São Gonçalo** Brazil

Serpa Pinto
227

155 C1 **São Gonçalo do Abaeté** Brazil
155 C1 **São Gotardo** Brazil
154 B1 **São Jerônimo, Serra de** *hills* Brazil
155 D2 **São João da Barra** Brazil
155 C2 **São João da Boa Vista** Brazil
106 B1 **São João da Madeira** Port.
155 D1 **São João da Ponte** Brazil
155 D2 **São João del Rei** Brazil
155 D1 **São João do Paraíso** Brazil
155 D1 **São João Evangelista** Brazil
155 D2 **São João Nepomuceno** Brazil
154 C2 **São Joaquim da Barra** Brazil
152 D2 **São José** Brazil
154 C2 **São José do Rio Preto** Brazil
155 C2 **São José dos Campos** Brazil
154 C3 **São José dos Pinhais** Brazil
154 A1 **São Lourenço** Brazil
155 C2 **São Lourenço** Brazil
151 E3 **São Luís** Brazil
154 C2 **São Manuel** Brazil
154 C1 **São Marcos** *r.* Brazil
151 E3 **São Marcos, Baía de** *b.* Brazil
155 E1 **São Mateus** Brazil
154 B3 **São Mateus do Sul** Brazil
105 C2 **Saône** *r.* France
155 C2 **São Paulo** Brazil
155 D2 **São Pedro da Aldeia** Brazil
151 E3 **São Raimundo Nonato** Brazil
155 C1 **São Romão** Brazil
São Salvador Angola *see* **M'banza Congo**
São Salvador do Congo Angola *see* **M'banza Congo**
155 C2 **São Sebastião, Ilha do** *i.* Brazil
154 C2 **São Sebastião do Paraíso** Brazil
154 B1 **São Simão** Brazil
154 B1 **São Simão, Barragem de** *resr* Brazil
59 C2 **Sao-Siu** Indon.
113 D5 **São Tomé** São Tomé and Príncipe
113 D5 **São Tomé** *i.* São Tomé and Príncipe
155 D2 **São Tomé, Cabo de** *c.* Brazil
113 D5 **São Tomé and Príncipe** *country* Africa
155 C2 **São Vicente** Brazil
106 B2 **São Vicente, Cabo de** *c.* Port.
59 C3 **Saparua** Indon.
107 D2 **Sa Pobla** Spain
89 F3 **Sapozhok** Rus. Fed.
66 D2 **Sapporo** Japan
109 C2 **Sapri** Italy
143 D1 **Sapulpa** U.S.A.
81 C2 **Saqqez** Iran
81 C2 **Sarāb** Iran
63 B2 **Sara Buri** Thai.
Saragossa Spain *see* **Zaragoza**
89 F3 **Sarai** Rus. Fed.
109 C2 **Sarajevo** Bos.-Herz.
87 E3 **Saraktash** Rus. Fed.
62 A1 **Saramati** *mt.* India/Myanmar
139 E2 **Saranac Lake** U.S.A.
109 D3 **Sarandë** Albania
64 B3 **Sarangani Islands** Phil.
87 D3 **Saransk** Rus. Fed.
87 E3 **Sarapul** Rus. Fed.
141 D3 **Sarasota** U.S.A.
90 B2 **Sarata** Ukr.
136 B2 **Saratoga** U.S.A.
139 E2 **Saratoga Springs** U.S.A.
61 C1 **Saratok** *Sarawak* Malaysia
87 D3 **Saratov** Rus. Fed.
79 D2 **Saravan** Iran
61 C1 **Sarawak** *state* Malaysia
111 C2 **Saray** Turkey
111 C3 **Sarayköy** Turkey
79 D2 **Sarbāz** Iran
76 B3 **Sarbīsheh** Iran
74 B2 **Sardarshahr** India
Sardegna *i.* Italy *see* **Sardinia**
108 A2 **Sardinia** *i.* Italy
92 G2 **Sarektjåkkå** *mt.* Sweden
77 C3 **Sar-e Pol** Afgh.
158 C3 **Sargasso Sea** *sea* Atlantic Ocean
74 B1 **Sargodha** Pak.
115 D4 **Sarh** Chad
79 D2 **Sarhad** *reg.* Iran
81 D2 **Sārī** Iran
111 C3 **Sarıgöl** Turkey
81 C1 **Sarıkamış** Turkey
61 C1 **Sarikei** *Sarawak* Malaysia
51 D2 **Sarina** Austr.
115 D2 **Sarīr Tibesti** *des.* Libya
65 B2 **Sariwŏn** N. Korea
111 C2 **Sarıyer** Turkey
77 D2 **Sarkand** Kazakh.
111 C2 **Şarköy** Turkey
104 C3 **Sarlat-la-Canéda** France
59 D3 **Sarmi** Indon.
153 B4 **Sarmiento** Arg.
138 C2 **Sarnia** Can.
90 B1 **Sarny** Ukr.
60 B2 **Sarolangun** Indon.
111 B3 **Saronikos Kolpos** *g.* Greece
111 C2 **Saros Körfezi** *b.* Turkey
103 E2 **Sárospatak** Hungary
87 D3 **Sarova** Rus. Fed.
Sarpan *i.* N. Mariana Is *see* **Rota**
105 D2 **Sarrebourg** France
106 B1 **Sarria** Spain
107 C1 **Sarrión** Spain
105 D3 **Sartène** *Corsica* France
Sartu China *see* **Daqing**
111 C3 **Saruhanlı** Turkey
103 D2 **Sárvár** Hungary
81 D3 **Sarvestān** Iran
76 B2 **Sarykamyshskoye Ozero** *salt l.* Turkm./Uzbek.
77 D2 **Saryozek** Kazakh.
77 D2 **Saryshagan** Kazakh.
77 C2 **Sarysu** *watercourse* Kazakh.
77 D3 **Sary-Tash** Kyrg.
75 C2 **Sasaram** India
67 A4 **Sasebo** Japan
129 D2 **Saskatchewan** *prov.* Can.
129 D2 **Saskatchewan** *r.* Can.
129 D2 **Saskatoon** Can.
83 I2 **Saskylakh** Rus. Fed.
123 C2 **Sasolburg** S. Africa
87 D3 **Sasovo** Rus. Fed.
114 B4 **Sassandra** Côte d'Ivoire
108 A2 **Sassari** *Sardinia* Italy
102 C1 **Sassnitz** Ger.
114 A3 **Satadougou** Mali
136 C3 **Satanta** U.S.A.
73 B3 **Satara** India
123 D1 **Satara** S. Africa
87 E3 **Satka** Rus. Fed.
75 C2 **Satna** India
77 C2 **Satpayev** Kazakh.
74 B2 **Satpura Range** *mts* India
63 B2 **Sattahip** Thai.
110 B1 **Satu Mare** Romania
63 B3 **Satun** Thai.
144 B2 **Saucillo** Mex.
93 E4 **Sauda** Norway
92 □B2 **Sauðárkrókur** Iceland
78 B2 **Saudi Arabia** *country* Asia
105 C3 **Saugues** France
137 E1 **Sauk Center** U.S.A.
105 C2 **Saulieu** France
88 B2 **Saulkrasti** Latvia
130 B3 **Sault Sainte Marie** Can.
138 C1 **Sault Sainte Marie** U.S.A.
77 C1 **Saumalkol'** Kazakh.
59 C3 **Saumlakki** Indon.
104 B2 **Saumur** France
120 B1 **Saurimo** Angola
109 D2 **Sava** *r.* Europe
49 J5 **Savai'i** *i.* Samoa
91 E1 **Savala** *r.* Rus. Fed.
114 C4 **Savalou** Benin
141 D2 **Savannah** *GA* U.S.A.
140 C1 **Savannah** *TN* U.S.A.
141 D2 **Savannah** *r.* U.S.A.
63 B2 **Savannakhét** Laos
130 A2 **Savant Lake** Can.
111 C3 **Savaştepe** Turkey
114 C4 **Savè** Benin
105 D2 **Saverne** France
89 F2 **Savino** Rus. Fed.
86 D2 **Savinskiy** Rus. Fed.
Savoie *reg.* France *see* **Savoy**
108 A2 **Savona** Italy
93 I3 **Savonlinna** Fin.
105 D2 **Savoy** *reg.* France
93 F4 **Sävsjö** Sweden
59 C3 **Savu** *i.* Indon.
92 I2 **Savukoski** Fin.
Savu Sea Indon. *see* **Laut Sawu**
74 B2 **Sawai Madhopur** India
62 A1 **Sawan** Myanmar
62 A2 **Sawankhalok** Thai.
136 B3 **Sawatch Range** *mts* U.S.A.
116 B2 **Sawhāj** Egypt
121 B2 **Sawmills** Zimbabwe
79 C3 **Şawqirah, Dawḩat** *b.* Oman
Şawqirah Bay Oman *see* **Şawqirah, Dawḩat**
53 D2 **Sawtell** Austr.
134 C2 **Sawtooth Range** *mts* U.S.A.
68 C1 **Sayano-Shushenskoye Vodokhranilishche** *resr* Rus. Fed.
76 C3 **Sayat** Turkm.
79 C3 **Sayḩūt** Yemen
93 I3 **Säynätsalo** Fin.
69 D2 **Saynshand** Mongolia
139 D2 **Sayre** U.S.A.
144 B3 **Sayula** Mex.
145 C3 **Sayula** Mex.
128 B2 **Sayward** Can.
Sayyod Turkm. *see* **Sayat**
89 E2 **Sazonovo** Rus. Fed.
114 B2 **Sbaa** Alg.
98 B2 **Scafell Pike** *hill* U.K.
109 C3 **Scalea** Italy
96 □ **Scalloway** U.K.
108 B2 **Scandicci** Italy
96 C1 **Scapa Flow** *inlet* U.K.
96 B2 **Scarba** *i.* U.K.
130 C3 **Scarborough** Can.
147 D3 **Scarborough** Trin. and Tob.
98 C2 **Scarborough** U.K.
64 A2 **Scarborough Shoal** *sea feature* Phil.
96 A2 **Scarinish** U.K.
Scarpanto *i.* Greece *see* **Karpathos**
100 B2 **Schaerbeek** Belgium
105 D2 **Schaffhausen** Switz.
100 B1 **Schagen** Neth.
102 C2 **Schärding** Austria
100 A2 **Scharendijke** Neth.
101 D1 **Scharhörn** *sea feature* Ger.
101 D1 **Scheeßel** Ger.
131 D2 **Schefferville** Can.
135 D3 **Schell Creek Range** *mts* U.S.A.
139 E2 **Schenectady** U.S.A.
143 D3 **Schertz** U.S.A.
101 E3 **Scheßlitz** Ger.
100 C1 **Schiermonnikoog** *i.* Neth.
100 B2 **Schilde** Belgium
108 B1 **Schio** Italy
101 F2 **Schkeuditz** Ger.
101 E1 **Schladen** Ger.
102 C2 **Schladming** Austria
101 E2 **Schleiz** Ger.
102 B1 **Schleswig** Ger.
101 D2 **Schloss Holte-Stukenbrock** Ger.
101 D2 **Schlüchtern** Ger.
101 E3 **Schlüsselfeld** Ger.
101 D2 **Schmallenberg** Ger.
Schmidt Island Rus. Fed. *see* **Shmidta, Ostrov**
101 F2 **Schmölln** Ger.
101 D1 **Schneverdingen** Ger.
101 E1 **Schönebeck (Elbe)** Ger.
101 E1 **Schöningen** Ger.
100 B2 **Schoonhoven** Neth.
59 D3 **Schouten Islands** P.N.G.
97 B3 **Schull** Ireland
101 E3 **Schwabach** Ger.
102 B2 **Schwäbische Alb** *mts* Ger.
101 F3 **Schwandorf** Ger.
61 C2 **Schwaner, Pegunungan** *mts* Indon.
101 E1 **Schwarzenbek** Ger.
101 F2 **Schwarzenberg** Ger.
122 A2 **Schwarzrand** *mts* Namibia
Schwarzwald *mts* Ger. *see* **Black Forest**
102 C2 **Schwaz** Austria
102 C1 **Schwedt an der Oder** Ger.
101 E2 **Schweinfurt** Ger.
101 E1 **Schwerin** Ger.
101 E1 **Schweriner See** *l.* Ger.
105 D2 **Schwyz** Switz.
108 B3 **Sciacca** *Sicily* Italy
95 B4 **Scilly, Isles of** U.K.
138 C3 **Scioto** *r.* U.S.A.
136 B1 **Scobey** U.S.A.
53 D2 **Scone** Austr.
110 B2 **Scorniceşti** Romania
55 C3 **Scotia Ridge** *sea feature* S. Atlantic Ocean
149 F8 **Scotia Sea** S. Atlantic Ocean
96 C2 **Scotland** *admin. div.* U.K.
128 B2 **Scott, Cape** Can.
123 D3 **Scottburgh** S. Africa
136 C3 **Scott City** U.S.A.
136 C2 **Scottsbluff** U.S.A.
140 C2 **Scottsboro** U.S.A.
96 B1 **Scourie** U.K.
139 D2 **Scranton** U.S.A.
98 C3 **Scunthorpe** U.K.
105 E2 **Scuol** Switz.
Scutari Albania *see* **Shkodër**
99 D4 **Seaford** U.K.
98 C2 **Seaham** U.K.
129 E2 **Seal** *r.* Can.
122 B3 **Seal, Cape** S. Africa
52 B3 **Sea Lake** Austr.
143 D3 **Sealy** U.S.A.
140 B1 **Searcy** U.S.A.
98 B2 **Seascale** U.K.
134 B1 **Seattle** U.S.A.
139 E2 **Sebago Lake** U.S.A.
144 A2 **Sebastián Vizcaíno, Bahía** *b.* Mex.
Sebastopol Ukr. *see* **Sevastopol'**
Sebenico Croatia *see* **Šibenik**
110 B1 **Sebeş** Romania
60 B2 **Sebesi** *i.* Indon.
88 C2 **Sebezh** Rus. Fed.
80 B1 **Şebinkarahisar** Turkey
141 D3 **Sebring** U.S.A.
61 C2 **Sebuku** *i.* Indon.
128 B3 **Sechelt** Can.
150 A3 **Sechura** Peru
73 B3 **Secunderabad** India
137 E3 **Sedalia** U.S.A.
105 C2 **Sedan** France
54 B2 **Seddon** N.Z.
114 A3 **Sédhiou** Senegal
142 A2 **Sedona** U.S.A.
101 E2 **Seeburg** Ger.
101 E1 **Seehausen (Altmark)** Ger.
122 A2 **Seeheim** Namibia
104 C2 **Sées** France
101 E2 **Seesen** Ger.
101 E1 **Seevetal** Ger.
114 A4 **Sefadu** Sierra Leone
123 C1 **Sefare** Botswana
93 F3 **Segalstad** Norway
60 B1 **Segamat** Malaysia
86 C2 **Segezha** Rus. Fed.
114 B3 **Ségou** Mali
106 C1 **Segovia** Spain
86 C2 **Segozerskoye, Ozero** *resr* Rus. Fed.
115 D2 **Séguédine** Niger
114 B4 **Séguéla** Côte d'Ivoire
143 D3 **Seguin** U.S.A.
107 C2 **Segura** *r.* Spain
106 C2 **Segura, Sierra de** *mts* Spain
120 B3 **Sehithwa** Botswana
93 H3 **Seinäjoki** Fin.
104 C2 **Seine** *r.* France
104 B2 **Seine, Baie de** *b.* France
105 C2 **Seine, Val de** *val.* France
103 E1 **Sejny** Pol.
60 B2 **Sekayu** Indon.
114 B4 **Sekondi** Ghana
134 B1 **Selah** U.S.A.
59 C3 **Selaru** *i.* Indon.
61 C2 **Selatan, Tanjung** *pt* Indon.
126 B2 **Selawik** U.S.A.
98 C3 **Selby** U.K.
136 C1 **Selby** U.S.A.
111 C3 **Selçuk** Turkey
120 B3 **Selebi-Phikwe** Botswana
Selebi-Pikwe Botswana *see* **Selebi-Phikwe**
105 D2 **Sélestat** France
Seletyteniz, Oz. *salt l.* Kazakh. *see* **Siletiteniz, Ozero**
92 □A3 **Selfoss** Iceland
114 A3 **Sélibabi** Maur.
142 A1 **Seligman** U.S.A.
116 A2 **Selīma Oasis** Sudan
111 C3 **Selimiye** Turkey
114 B3 **Sélingué, Lac de** *l.* Mali
89 D2 **Selizharovo** Rus. Fed.
93 E4 **Seljord** Norway
129 E2 **Selkirk** Can.
96 C3 **Selkirk** U.K.
128 C2 **Selkirk Mountains** Can.
142 A2 **Sells** U.S.A.
140 C2 **Selma** *AL* U.S.A.
135 C3 **Selma** *CA* U.S.A.
105 D2 **Selongey** France
99 C4 **Selsey Bill** *hd* U.K.
89 D3 **Sel'tso** Rus. Fed.
Selukwe Zimbabwe *see* **Shurugwi**
150 B3 **Selvas** *reg.* Brazil
134 C1 **Selway** *r.* U.S.A.
129 D1 **Selwyn Lake** Can.
128 A1 **Selwyn Mountains** Can.
51 C2 **Selwyn Range** *hills* Austr.
60 B2 **Semangka, Teluk** *b.* Indon.
61 C2 **Semarang** Indon.
60 B1 **Sematan** *Sarawak* Malaysia
118 B2 **Sembé** Congo
81 C2 **Şemdinli** Turkey
91 C1 **Semenivka** Ukr.
87 D3 **Semenov** Rus. Fed.
61 C2 **Semeru, Gunung** *vol.* Indon.
91 E2 **Semikarakorsk** Rus. Fed.
89 E3 **Semiluki** Rus. Fed.
136 B2 **Seminoe Reservoir** U.S.A.
143 C2 **Seminole** U.S.A.
141 D2 **Seminole, Lake** U.S.A.
77 E1 **Semipalatinsk** Kazakh.
61 C1 **Semitau** Indon.
Sem Kolodezey Ukr. *see* **Lenine**
81 D2 **Semnān** Iran
61 C1 **Semporna** *Sabah* Malaysia
105 C2 **Semur-en-Auxois** France
Semyonovskoye Rus. Fed. *see* **Bereznik**
Semyonovskoye Rus. Fed *see* **Ostrovskoye**
150 C3 **Sena Madureira** Brazil
120 B2 **Senanga** Zambia
67 B4 **Sendai** Japan
67 D3 **Sendai** Japan
141 D2 **Seneca** U.S.A.
114 A3 **Senegal** *country* Africa
114 A3 **Sénégal** *r.* Maur./Senegal
102 C1 **Senftenberg** Ger.
119 D3 **Sengerema** Tanz.
151 E4 **Senhor do Bonfim** Brazil
103 D2 **Senica** Slovakia
108 B2 **Senigallia** Italy
109 B2 **Senj** Croatia
92 G2 **Senja** *i.* Norway
122 B2 **Senlac** S. Africa
105 C2 **Senlis** France
63 B2 **Senmonorom** Cambodia
116 B3 **Sennar** Sudan
130 C3 **Senneterre** Can.
123 C3 **Senqu** *r.* Lesotho
105 C2 **Sens** France
109 D1 **Senta** Serb. and Mont.
128 B2 **Sentinel Peak** Can.
75 B2 **Seoni** India
65 B2 **Seoul** S. Korea
155 D2 **Sepetiba, Baía de** *b.* Brazil
59 D3 **Sepik** *r.* P.N.G.
61 C1 **Sepinang** Indon.
131 D2 **Sept-Îles** Can.
87 D4 **Serafimovich** Rus. Fed.
100 B2 **Seraing** Belgium
59 C3 **Seram** *i.* Indon.
60 B2 **Serang** Indon.
60 B1 **Serasan, Selat** *sea chan.* Indon.
Serbia *aut. rep.* Serb. and Mont. *see* **Srbija**
109 D2 **Serbia and Montenegro** *country* Europe
117 C3 **Serdo** Eth.
89 E3 **Serebryanyye Prudy** Rus. Fed.
60 B1 **Seremban** Malaysia
119 D3 **Serengeti Plain** Tanz.
121 C2 **Serenje** Zambia
90 B2 **Seret** *r.* Ukr.
87 D3 **Sergach** Rus. Fed.
86 F2 **Sergino** Rus. Fed.
89 E2 **Sergiyev Posad** Rus. Fed.
Sergo Ukr. *see* **Stakhanov**
61 C1 **Seria** Brunei
61 C1 **Serian** *Sarawak* Malaysia
111 B3 **Serifos** *i.* Greece
80 B2 **Serik** Turkey
59 C3 **Sermata, Kepulauan** *is* Indon.
Sernyy Zavod Turkm. *see* **Kukurtli**
86 F3 **Serov** Rus. Fed.
120 B3 **Serowe** Botswana
106 B2 **Serpa** Port.
Serpa Pinto Angola *see* **Menongue**

Serpukhov
228

89 E3 Serpukhov Rus. Fed.
155 D2 Serra Brazil
155 C1 Serra das Araras Brazil
108 A3 Serramanna Sardinia Italy
154 B1 Serranópolis Brazil
100 A3 Serre r. France
111 B2 Serres Greece
151 F4 Serrinha Brazil
155 D1 Sêrro Brazil
154 C2 Sertãozinho Brazil
59 D3 Serui Indon.
120 B3 Serule Botswana
61 C2 Seruyan r. Indon.
68 C2 Sêrxü China
120 A2 Sesfontein Namibia
108 B2 Sessa Aurunca Italy
108 A2 Sestri Levante Italy
105 C3 Sète France
155 D1 Sete Lagoas Brazil
92 G2 Setermoen Norway
93 E4 Setesdal val. Norway
115 C1 Sétif Alg.
67 B4 Seto-naikai sea Japan
114 B1 Settat Morocco
98 B2 Settle U.K.
106 B2 Setúbal Port.
106 B2 Setúbal, Baía de b. Port.
130 A2 Seul, Lac l. Can.
81 C1 Sevan Armenia
76 A2 Sevan, Lake Armenia
Sevana Lich l. Armenia see Sevan, Lake
91 C3 Sevastopol' Ukr.
Seven Islands Can. see Sept-Îles
131 D2 Seven Islands Bay Can.
99 D4 Sevenoaks U.K.
105 C3 Sévérac-le-Château France
130 B2 Severn r. Can.
122 B2 Severn S. Africa
99 B4 Severn r. U.K.
86 D2 Severnaya Dvina r. Rus. Fed.
83 H1 Severnaya Zemlya is Rus. Fed.
86 D2 Severnyy Rus. Fed.
86 F2 Severnyy Rus. Fed.
83 I3 Severobaykal'sk Rus. Fed.
86 C2 Severodvinsk Rus. Fed.
83 L3 Severo-Kuril'sk Rus. Fed.
92 J2 Severomorsk Rus. Fed.
86 C2 Severoonezhsk Rus. Fed.
83 H2 Severo-Yeniseyskiy Rus. Fed.
91 D3 Severskaya Rus. Fed.
135 D3 Sevier r. U.S.A.
135 D3 Sevier Lake U.S.A.
Sevilla Spain see Seville
106 B2 Seville Spain
Sevlyush Ukr. see Vynohradiv
89 D3 Sevsk Rus. Fed.
126 C2 Seward U.S.A.
126 B2 Seward Peninsula U.S.A.
128 A2 Sewell Inlet Can.
128 C2 Sexsmith Can.
144 B2 Sextín r. Mex.
86 G1 Seyakha Rus. Fed.
113 I6 Seychelles country Indian Ocean
92 □C2 Seyðisfjörður Iceland
Seyhan Turkey see Adana
80 B2 Seyhan r. Turkey
91 C1 Seym r. Rus. Fed./Ukr.
83 L2 Seymchan Rus. Fed.
53 C3 Seymour Austr.
123 C3 Seymour S. Africa
138 B3 Seymour IN U.S.A.
143 D2 Seymour TX U.S.A.
105 C2 Sézanne France
108 B2 Sezze Italy
111 B3 Sfakia Greece
110 C1 Sfântu Gheorghe Romania
115 D1 Sfax Tunisia
Sfîntu Gheorghe Romania see Sfântu Gheorghe
's-Gravenhage Neth. see The Hague
96 A2 Sgurr Alasdair hill U.K.
70 A2 Shaanxi prov. China
Shabani Zimbabwe see Zvishavane
91 D2 Shabel'sk Rus. Fed.
77 D3 Shache China
55 C1 Shackleton Range mts Antarctica
74 A2 Shadadkot Pak.
86 F3 Shadrinsk Rus. Fed.
99 B4 Shaftesbury U.K.
126 B2 Shageluk U.S.A.
Shāhābād Iran see Eslāmābād-e Gharb
75 C2 Shahdol India
77 C3 Shah Fuladi mt. Afgh.
75 B2 Shahjahanpur India
76 B3 Shāh Kūh mt. Iran
81 D2 Shahr-e Bābak Iran
81 D2 Shahr-e Kord Iran
81 D2 Shahrezā Iran
77 C3 Shahrisabz Uzbek.
Shāhrūd Iran see Emāmrūd
79 B2 Shaj'ah, Jabal hill Saudi Arabia
89 E2 Shakhovskaya Rus. Fed.
Shakhterskoye Ukr. see Pershotravens'k
Shakhty Rus. Fed. see Gusinoozersk
91 E2 Shakhty Rus. Fed.
Shakhtyorskoye Ukr. see Pershotravens'k
86 D3 Shakhun'ya Rus. Fed.
114 C4 Shaki Nigeria
66 D2 Shakotan-hantō pen. Japan
66 D2 Shakotan-misaki c. Japan
76 B2 Shalkar Kazakh.
68 C2 Shaluli Shan mts China
129 E2 Shamattawa Can.
143 C1 Shamrock U.S.A.
70 A2 Shandan China
70 B2 Shandong prov. China
70 C2 Shandong Bandao pen. China
121 B2 Shangani Zimbabwe
121 B2 Shangani r. Zimbabwe
70 B1 Shangdu China
70 C2 Shanghai China
70 C2 Shanghai mun. China
71 B3 Shanghang China
70 A2 Shangluo China
70 B2 Shangnan China
71 B3 Shangrao China
70 B2 Shangshui China
77 E2 Shangyou Shuiku resr China
70 C2 Shangyu China
69 E1 Shangzhi China
Shangzhou China see Shangluo
134 B1 Shaniko U.S.A.
97 B2 Shannon r. Ireland
97 B2 Shannon, Mouth of the Ireland
62 A1 Shan Plateau Myanmar
Shansi prov. China see Shanxi
71 B3 Shantou China
Shantung prov. China see Shandong
70 B2 Shanxi prov. China
71 B3 Shaoguan China
71 B3 Shaowu China
70 C2 Shaoxing China
71 B3 Shaoyang China
96 C1 Shapinsay i. U.K.
116 C2 Shaqrā' Saudi Arabia
90 B2 Sharhorod Ukr.
79 C2 Sharjah U.A.E.
88 C2 Sharkawshchyna Belarus
50 A2 Shark Bay Austr.
78 A2 Sharm ash Shaykh Egypt
138 C2 Sharon U.S.A.
86 D3 Shar'ya Rus. Fed.
121 B3 Shashe r. Botswana/Zimbabwe
117 B4 Shashemenē Eth.
Shashi China see Jingzhou
134 B2 Shasta, Mount vol. U.S.A.
134 B2 Shasta Lake U.S.A.
115 D2 Shāṭi', Wādī ash watercourse Libya
Shatilki Belarus see Svyetlahorsk
89 E2 Shatura Rus. Fed.
129 D3 Shaunavon Can.
138 B2 Shawano U.S.A.
130 C3 Shawinigan Can.
143 D1 Shawnee U.S.A.
83 M2 Shayboveyem r. Rus. Fed.
50 B2 Shay Gap Austr.
89 E3 Shchekino Rus. Fed.
89 E2 Shchelkovo Rus. Fed.
Shcherbakov Rus. Fed. see Rybinsk
Shcherbinovka Ukr. see Dzerzhyns'k
89 E3 Shchigry Rus. Fed.
91 C1 Shchors Ukr.
88 B3 Shchuchyn Belarus
91 D1 Shebekino Rus. Fed.
77 C3 Sheberghān Afgh.
138 B2 Sheboygan U.S.A.
91 D3 Shebsh r. Rus. Fed.
97 C2 Sheelin, Lough l. Ireland
136 B3 Sheep Mountain U.S.A.
99 D4 Sheerness U.K.
98 C3 Sheffield U.K.
143 C2 Sheffield U.S.A.
Sheikh Othman Yemen see Ash Shaykh 'Uthman
Shekhem West Bank see Nāblus
89 E2 Sheksna Rus. Fed.
89 E2 Sheksninskoye Vodokhranilishche resr Rus. Fed.
83 M2 Shelagskiy, Mys pt Rus. Fed.
131 D3 Shelburne Can.
138 B2 Shelby MI U.S.A.
134 D1 Shelby MT U.S.A.
141 D1 Shelby NC U.S.A.
138 B3 Shelbyville IN U.S.A.
140 C1 Shelbyville TN U.S.A.
83 L2 Shelikhova, Zaliv g. Rus. Fed.
126 B3 Shelikof Strait U.S.A.
129 D2 Shellbrook Can.
Shelter Bay Can. see Port-Cartier
134 B1 Shelton U.S.A.
137 D2 Shenandoah U.S.A.
139 D3 Shenandoah r. U.S.A.
139 D3 Shenandoah Mountains U.S.A.
118 A2 Shendam Nigeria
Shengli Feng mt. China/Kyrg. see Pobeda Peak
86 D2 Shenkursk Rus. Fed.
70 B2 Shenmu China
Shensi prov. China see Shaanxi
70 C1 Shenyang China
71 B3 Shenzhen China
90 B1 Shepetivka Ukr.
53 C3 Shepparton Austr.
99 D4 Sheppey, Isle of i. U.K.
131 D3 Sherbrooke N.S. Can.
130 C3 Sherbrooke Que. Can.
97 C2 Shercock Ireland
116 B3 Shereiq Sudan
136 B2 Sheridan U.S.A.
52 A2 Sheringa Austr.
86 F2 Sherkaly Rus. Fed.
143 D2 Sherman U.S.A.
100 B2 's-Hertogenbosch Neth.
96 □ Shetland Islands U.K.
76 B2 Shetpe Kazakh.
Shevchenko Kazakh. see Aktau
91 D2 Shevchenkove Ukr.
137 D1 Sheyenne r. U.S.A.
79 B3 Shibām Yemen
67 C3 Shibata Japan
66 D2 Shibetsu Japan
Shibotsu-jima i. Rus. Fed. see Zelenyy, Ostrov
71 B3 Shicheng China
70 C2 Shidao China
96 B2 Shiel, Loch l. U.K.
Shigatse China see Xigazê
77 E2 Shihezi China
Shihkiachwang China see Shijiazhuang
Shijiao China see Fogang
70 B2 Shijiazhuang China
Shijiusuo China see Rizhao
74 A2 Shikarpur Pak.
67 B4 Shikoku i. Japan
66 D2 Shikotsu-ko l. Japan
86 D2 Shilega Rus. Fed.
75 C2 Shiliguri India
97 C2 Shillelagh Ireland
75 D2 Shillong India
89 F3 Shilovo Rus. Fed.
69 E1 Shimanovsk Rus. Fed.
117 C3 Shimbiris mt. Somalia
67 C3 Shimizu Japan
74 B1 Shimla India
67 C4 Shimoda Japan
73 B3 Shimoga India
66 D2 Shimokita-hantō pen. Japan
67 B4 Shimonoseki Japan
89 D2 Shimsk Rus. Fed.
96 B1 Shin, Loch l. U.K.
62 A1 Shingbwiyang Myanmar
67 C4 Shingū Japan
123 D1 Shingwedzi S. Africa
123 D1 Shingwedzi r. S. Africa
66 D3 Shinjō Japan
119 D3 Shinyanga Tanz.
67 D3 Shiogama Japan
67 C4 Shiono-misaki c. Japan
71 A3 Shiping China
98 C3 Shipley U.K.
142 B1 Shiprock U.S.A.
71 A3 Shiqian China
Shiqizhen China see Zhongshan
70 A2 Shiquan China
78 B2 Shi'r, Jabal hill Saudi Arabia
67 C3 Shirane-san mt. Japan
67 C3 Shirane-san vol. Japan
81 D3 Shīrāz Iran
66 D2 Shiretoko-misaki c. Japan
66 D2 Shiriya-zaki c. Japan
76 B3 Shīrvān Iran
74 B2 Shiv India
74 B2 Shivpuri India
70 B2 Shiyan China
70 A2 Shizuishan China
67 C3 Shizuoka Japan
89 D3 Shklow Belarus
109 C2 Shkodër Albania
83 H1 Shmidta, Ostrov i. Rus. Fed.
67 B4 Shōbara Japan
Sholapur India see Solapur
158 F8 Shona Ridge sea feature S. Atlantic Ocean
77 C3 Sho'rchi Uzbek.
74 B1 Shorkot Pak.
135 C3 Shoshone CA U.S.A.
134 D2 Shoshone ID U.S.A.
135 C3 Shoshone Mountains U.S.A.
123 C1 Shoshong Botswana
91 C1 Shostka Ukr.
70 B2 Shouxian China
78 A3 Showak Sudan
142 A2 Show Low U.S.A.
91 C2 Shpola Ukr.
140 B2 Shreveport U.S.A.
99 B3 Shrewsbury U.K.
77 D2 Shu Kazakh.
Shuangjiang China see Tongdao
62 A1 Shuangjiang China
Shuangxi China see Shunchang
66 B1 Shuangyashan China
87 E4 Shubarkuduk Kazakh.
116 B1 Shubrā al Khaymah Egypt
89 D2 Shugozero Rus. Fed.
Shuidong China see Dianbai
120 B2 Shumba Zimbabwe
110 C2 Shumen Bulg.
87 F3 Shumikha Rus. Fed.
88 C2 Shumilina Belarus
143 C3 Shumla U.S.A.
89 D3 Shumyachi Rus. Fed.
71 B3 Shunchang China
126 B2 Shungnak U.S.A.
78 B3 Shuqrah Yemen
121 C2 Shurugwi Zimbabwe
89 F2 Shushkodom Rus. Fed.
81 C2 Shushtar Iran
128 C2 Shuswap Lake Can.
89 F2 Shuya Rus. Fed.
89 F2 Shuyskoye Rus. Fed.
62 A1 Shwebo Myanmar
62 A1 Shwedwin Myanmar
62 A2 Shwegun Myanmar
62 A2 Shwegyin Myanmar
62 A1 Shweli r. Myanmar
77 C2 Shymkent Kazakh.
74 B1 Shyok r. India
91 C2 Shyroke Ukr.
90 C2 Shyryayeve Ukr.
59 C3 Sia Indon.
74 A2 Siahan Range mts Pak.
74 B1 Sialkot Pak.
Siam country Asia see Thailand
Sian China see Xi'an
64 B3 Siargao i. Phil.
64 B3 Siasi Phil.
88 B2 Šiauliai Lith.
123 D1 Sibasa S. Africa
109 C2 Šibenik Croatia
83 G2 Siberia reg. Rus. Fed.
60 A2 Siberut i. Indon.
74 A2 Sibi Pak.
Sibir' reg. Rus. Fed. see Siberia
118 B3 Sibiti Congo
110 B1 Sibiu Romania
60 A1 Sibolga Indon.
62 A1 Sibsagar India
61 C1 Sibu Sarawak Malaysia
118 B2 Sibut C.A.R.
64 A3 Sibutu i. Phil.
64 B2 Sibuyan i. Phil.
64 B2 Sibuyan Sea Phil.
128 C2 Sicamous Can.
63 A3 Sichon Thai.
70 A2 Sichuan prov. China
70 A3 Sichuan Pendi basin China
105 D3 Sicié, Cap c. France
Sicilia i. Italy see Sicily
108 B3 Sicilian Channel Italy/Tunisia
108 B3 Sicily i. Italy
150 B4 Sicuani Peru
74 B2 Siddhapur India
111 C3 Sideros, Akra pt Greece
122 B3 Sidesaviwa S. Africa
75 C2 Sidhi India
107 D2 Sidi Aïssa Alg.
107 D2 Sidi Ali Alg.
114 B1 Sidi Bel Abbès Alg.
114 A2 Sidi Ifni Morocco
114 B1 Sidi Kacem Morocco
60 A1 Sidikalang Indon.
111 B2 Sidirokastro Greece
96 C2 Sidlaw Hills U.K.
99 B4 Sidmouth U.K.
134 B1 Sidney Can.
136 C1 Sidney MT U.S.A.
136 C2 Sidney NE U.S.A.
138 C2 Sidney OH U.S.A.
141 D2 Sidney Lanier, Lake U.S.A.
61 D1 Sidoan Indon.
80 B2 Sidon Lebanon
154 B2 Sidrolândia Brazil
103 E1 Siedlce Pol.
100 C2 Sieg r. Ger.
101 D2 Siegen Ger.
63 B2 Siěmréab Cambodia
Siem Reap Cambodia see Siěmréab
108 B2 Siena Italy
103 D1 Sieradz Pol.
142 B2 Sierra Blanca U.S.A.
153 B4 Sierra Grande Arg.
114 A4 Sierra Leone country Africa
158 E4 Sierra Leone Basin sea feature N. Atlantic Ocean
158 E4 Sierra Leone Rise sea feature N. Atlantic Ocean
144 B2 Sierra Mojada Mex.
142 A2 Sierra Vista U.S.A.
105 D2 Sierre Switz.
116 C3 Sīfenī Eth.
111 B3 Sifnos i. Greece
107 C2 Sig Alg.
127 I2 Sigguup Nunaa pen. Greenland
110 B1 Sighetu Marmaţiei Romania
110 B1 Sighişoara Romania
60 A1 Sigli Indon.
92 □B2 Siglufjörður Iceland
102 B2 Sigmaringen Ger.
100 B3 Signy-l'Abbaye France
106 C1 Sigüenza Spain
114 B3 Siguiri Guinea
88 B2 Sigulda Latvia
63 B2 Sihanoukville Cambodia
92 I3 Siilinjärvi Fin.
81 C2 Siirt Turkey
60 B2 Sijunjung Indon.
74 B2 Sikar India
74 A1 Sikaram mt. Afgh.
114 B3 Sikasso Mali
111 B2 Sikea Greece
137 F3 Sikeston U.S.A.
66 B2 Sikhote-Alin' mts Rus. Fed.
111 C3 Sikinos i. Greece
103 D2 Siklós Hungary
65 A2 Sikuaishi China
88 B2 Šilalė Lith.
144 B2 Silao Mex.
101 D1 Silberberg hill Ger.
75 D2 Silchar India
77 D1 Siletiteniz, Ozero salt l. Kazakh.
75 C2 Silgarhi Nepal
80 B2 Silifke Turkey
75 C1 Siling Co salt l. China
110 C2 Silistra Bulg.
111 C2 Silivri Turkey
93 F3 Siljan l. Sweden
93 E4 Silkeborg Denmark
88 C2 Sillamäe Estonia

98 B2 **Silloth** U.K.
140 B1 **Siloam Springs** U.S.A.
123 D2 **Silobela** S. Africa
60 B1 **Siluas** Indon.
88 B2 **Šilutė** Lith.
81 C2 **Silvan** Turkey
154 C1 **Silvânia** Brazil
74 B2 **Silvassa** India
137 E1 **Silver Bay** U.S.A.
142 B2 **Silver City** U.S.A.
136 B3 **Silverton** U.S.A.
62 B1 **Simao** China
130 C3 **Simàrd, Lac** l. Can.
111 C3 **Simav** Turkey
111 C3 **Simav Dağları** mts Turkey
118 C2 **Simba** Dem. Rep. Congo
138 C2 **Simcoe** Can.
139 D2 **Simcoe, Lake** Can.
78 A3 **Simēn** Eth.
60 A1 **Simeulue** i. Indon.
91 C3 **Simferopol'** Ukr.
75 C2 **Simikot** Nepal
135 C4 **Simi Valley** U.S.A.
        Simla India see Shimla
110 B1 **Şimleu Silvaniei** Romania
100 C3 **Šimmern (Hunsrück)** Ger.
92 I2 **Simo** Fin.
129 D2 **Simonhouse** Can.
60 B2 **Simpang** Indon.
51 C2 **Simpson Desert** Austr.
93 F4 **Simrishamn** Sweden
60 A1 **Sinabang** Indon.
116 B2 **Sinai** pen. Egypt
105 E3 **Sinalunga** Italy
71 A3 **Sinan** China
65 B2 **Sinanju** N. Korea
62 A1 **Sinbo** Myanmar
62 A1 **Sinbyugyun** Myanmar
150 B2 **Sincelejo** Col.
60 B2 **Sindangbarang** Indon.
111 C3 **Sındırgı** Turkey
86 E2 **Sindor** Rus. Fed.
111 C2 **Sinekçi** Turkey
106 B2 **Sines** Port.
106 B2 **Sines, Cabo de** c. Port.
116 B3 **Singa** Sudan
75 C2 **Singahi** India
60 B1 **Singapore** country Asia
61 C2 **Singaraja** Indon.
63 B2 **Sing Buri** Thai.
119 D3 **Sigida** Tanz.
62 A1 **Singkaling Hkamti** Myanmar
61 C2 **Singkang** Indon.
60 B1 **Singkawang** Indon.
60 B2 **Singkep** i. Indon.
60 A1 **Singkil** Indon.
53 D2 **Singleton** Austr.
        Sin'gosan N. Korea see Kosan
62 A1 **Singu** Myanmar
        Sining China see Xining
108 A2 **Siniscola** Sardinia Italy
109 C2 **Sinj** Croatia
61 D2 **Sinjai** Indon.
116 B3 **Sinkat** Sudan
151 D2 **Sinnamary** Fr. Guiana
        Sînnicolau Mare Romania see
        Sânnicolau Mare
        Sinoia Zimbabwe see Chinhoyi
80 B1 **Sinop** Turkey
65 B1 **Sinp'o** N. Korea
61 C1 **Sintang** Indon.
100 B2 **St Anthonis** Neth.
100 A2 **St-Laureins** Belgium
100 B2 **St-Niklaas** Belgium
143 D3 **Sinton** U.S.A.
100 C2 **St-Vith** Belgium
65 A1 **Sinŭiju** N. Korea
64 B3 **Siocon** Phil.
103 D2 **Siófok** Hungary
105 D2 **Sion** Switz.
137 D2 **Sioux Center** U.S.A.
137 D2 **Sioux City** U.S.A.
137 D2 **Sioux Falls** U.S.A.
130 A2 **Sioux Lookout** Can.
65 A1 **Siping** China
129 E2 **Sipiwesk Lake** Can.
55 P2 **Siple, Mount** Antarctica
55 P2 **Siple Island** Antarctica
        Sipolilo Zimbabwe see Guruve
60 A2 **Sipura** i. Indon.
64 B3 **Siquijor** Phil.
93 E4 **Sira** r. Norway
        Siracusa Italy see Syracuse
51 C1 **Sir Edward Pellew Group**
        is Austr.
110 C1 **Siret** Romania
110 C1 **Siret** r. Romania
79 C2 **Sīrīk** Iran
61 C1 **Sirik, Tanjung** pt Malaysia
62 B2 **Siri Kit Dam** Thai.
128 B1 **Sir James MacBrien, Mount**
        Can.
79 C2 **Sīrjān** Iran
81 C2 **Şırnak** Turkey
74 B2 **Sirohi** India
60 A1 **Sirombu** Indon.
74 B2 **Sirsa** India
115 D1 **Sirte** Libya
115 D1 **Sirte, Gulf of** Libya
88 B2 **Širvintos** Lith.
108 C1 **Sisak** Croatia
63 B2 **Sisaket** Thai.
145 C2 **Sisal** Mex.
122 B2 **Sishen** S. Africa
81 C2 **Sisian** Armenia

127 I2 **Sisimiut** Greenland
129 D2 **Sisipuk Lake** Can.
63 B2 **Sisŏphŏn** Cambodia
105 D3 **Sisteron** France
        Sitang China see Sinan
75 C2 **Sitapur** India
111 C3 **Siteia** Greece
123 D2 **Siteki** Swaziland
128 A2 **Sitka** U.S.A.
100 B2 **Sittard** Neth.
62 A1 **Sittaung** Myanmar
62 A2 **Sittaung** r. Myanmar
62 A1 **Sittwe** Myanmar
61 C2 **Situbondo** Indon.
80 B2 **Sivas** Turkey
111 C3 **Sivaslı** Turkey
80 B2 **Siverek** Turkey
88 D2 **Siverskiy** Rus. Fed.
91 D2 **Sivers'kyy Donets'** r. Ukr.
80 B2 **Sivrihisar** Turkey
116 A2 **Siwah** Egypt
75 B1 **Siwalik Range** mts India/Nepal
116 A2 **Siwah, Wāḩāt** Egypt
        Siwa Oasis Egypt see Sīwah,
        Wāḩāt
105 D3 **Six-Fours-les-Plages** France
70 B2 **Sixian** China
123 C2 **Siyabuswa** S. Africa
        Sjælland i. Denmark see Zealand
109 D2 **Sjenica** Serb. and Mont.
92 G2 **Sjøvegan** Norway
91 C2 **Skadovs'k** Ukr.
93 F4 **Skagen** Denmark
93 E4 **Skagerrak** str. Denmark/Norway
134 B1 **Skagit** r. U.S.A.
128 A2 **Skagway** U.S.A.
92 G2 **Skaland** Norway
93 F4 **Skara** Sweden
74 B1 **Skardu** Jammu and Kashmir
103 E1 **Skarżysko-Kamienna** Pol.
103 D2 **Skawina** Pol.
114 A2 **Skaymat** Western Sahara
128 B2 **Skeena** r. Can.
128 B2 **Skeena Mountains** Can.
98 D3 **Skegness** U.K.
92 H3 **Skellefteå** Sweden
92 H3 **Skellefteälven** r. Sweden
97 C2 **Skerries** Ireland
93 F4 **Ski** Norway
111 B3 **Skiathos** i. Greece
97 B3 **Skibbereen** Ireland
92 □B2 **Skíðadals-jökull** glacier
        Iceland
98 B2 **Skiddaw** hill U.K.
93 E4 **Skien** Norway
103 E1 **Skierniewice** Pol.
115 C1 **Skikda** Alg.
52 B3 **Skipton** Austr.
98 B3 **Skipton** U.K.
93 E4 **Skive** Denmark
92 H1 **Skjervøy** Norway
        Skobelev Uzbek. see Farg'ona
111 B3 **Skopelos** i. Greece
89 E3 **Skopin** Rus. Fed.
111 B2 **Skopje** Macedonia
111 C3 **Skoutaros** Greece
93 F4 **Skövde** Sweden
83 J3 **Skovorodino** Rus. Fed.
139 F2 **Skowhegan** U.S.A.
92 H2 **Skröven** Sweden
88 B2 **Skrunda** Latvia
128 A1 **Skukum, Mount** Can.
123 D1 **Skukuza** S. Africa
88 B2 **Skuodas** Lith.
90 B2 **Skvyra** Ukr.
96 A2 **Skye** i. U.K.
111 B3 **Skyros** Greece
111 B3 **Skyros** i. Greece
93 F4 **Slagelse** Denmark
60 B2 **Slamet, Gunung** vol. Indon.
97 C2 **Slaney** r. Ireland
88 C2 **Slantsy** Rus. Fed.
109 C1 **Slatina** Croatia
110 B2 **Slatina** Romania
143 C2 **Slaton** U.S.A.
129 C1 **Slave** r. Can.
114 C4 **Slave Coast** Africa
128 C2 **Slave Lake** Can.
77 D1 **Slavgorod** Rus. Fed.
88 C2 **Slavkovichi** Rus. Fed.
        Slavonska Požega Croatia see
        Požega
109 C1 **Slavonski Brod** Croatia
90 C1 **Slavuta** Ukr.
90 C1 **Slavutych** Ukr.
66 B2 **Slavyanka** Rus. Fed.
        Slavyanskaya Rus. Fed. see
        Slavyansk-na-Kubani
91 D2 **Slavyansk-na-Kubani** Rus. Fed.
89 D3 **Slawharad** Belarus
103 D1 **Sławno** Pol.
99 C3 **Sleaford** U.K.
97 A2 **Slea Head** hd Ireland
130 C2 **Sleeper Islands** Can.
97 D1 **Slieve Donard** hill U.K.
97 B1 **Slieve Gamph** hills
        Ireland
96 A2 **Sligachan** U.K.
        Sligeach Ireland see Sligo
97 B1 **Sligo** Ireland
97 B1 **Sligo Bay** Ireland
93 G4 **Slite** Sweden
110 C2 **Sliven** Bulg.
        Sloboda Rus. Fed. see Ezhva
110 C2 **Slobozia** Romania

128 C3 **Slocan** Can.
88 C3 **Slonim** Belarus
100 B1 **Sloten** Neth.
99 C3 **Slough** U.K.
103 D2 **Slovakia** country Europe
108 B1 **Slovenia** country Europe
91 D2 **Slov"yans'k** Ukr.
102 C1 **Słubice** Pol.
90 B1 **Sluch** r. Ukr.
100 A2 **Sluis** Neth.
103 D1 **Słupsk** Pol.
88 C3 **Slutsk** Belarus
97 A2 **Slyne Head** hd Ireland
68 C1 **Slyudyanka** Rus. Fed.
131 D2 **Smallwood Reservoir** Can.
88 C3 **Smalyavichy** Belarus
88 C3 **Smarhon'** Belarus
129 D2 **Smeaton** Can.
109 D2 **Smederevo** Serb. and Mont.
109 D2 **Smederevska Palanka**
        Serb. and Mont.
91 C2 **Smila** Ukr.
88 C2 **Smilavichy** Belarus
88 C2 **Smiltene** Latvia
137 D3 **Smith Center** U.S.A.
128 B2 **Smithers** Can.
141 E1 **Smithfield** NC U.S.A.
134 D2 **Smithfield** UT U.S.A.
139 D3 **Smith Mountain Lake** U.S.A.
130 C3 **Smiths Falls** Can.
53 D2 **Smithton** Austr.
53 C2 **Smoky Cape** Austr.
137 D3 **Smoky Hills** U.S.A.
92 E3 **Smøla** i. Norway
89 D3 **Smolensk** Rus. Fed.
89 D3 **Smolensko-Moskovskaya
        Vozvyshennost'** hills Rus. Fed.
111 B2 **Smolyan** Bulg.
66 B2 **Smolyoninovo** Rus. Fed.
130 B3 **Smooth Rock Falls** Can.
        Smyrna Turkey see İzmir
91 D2 **Smyrnove** Ukr.
92 □B3 **Snæfell** mt. Iceland
98 A2 **Snaefell** hill Isle of Man
128 A1 **Snag** Can.
134 C1 **Snake** r. U.S.A.
134 D2 **Snake River Plain** U.S.A.
        Snare Lakes Can. see Wekweti
92 F3 **Snåsvatn** l. Norway
100 B1 **Sneek** Neth.
97 B3 **Sneem** Ireland
122 B3 **Sneeuberge** mts S. Africa
        Snegurovka Ukr. see Tetiyiv
103 D1 **Sněžka** mt. Czech Rep.
108 B1 **Snežnik** mt. Slovenia
103 E1 **Śniardwy, Jezioro** l. Pol.
        Snieckus Lith. see Visaginas
91 C2 **Snihurivka** Ukr.
93 E3 **Snøhetta** mt. Norway
        Snovsk Ukr. see Shchors
129 D1 **Snowbird Lake** Can.
99 A3 **Snowdon** mt. U.K.
        Snowdrift Can. see Łutselk'e
129 C1 **Snowdrift** r. Can.
142 A2 **Snowflake** U.S.A.
129 D2 **Snow Lake** Can.
134 C1 **Snowshoe Peak** U.S.A.
52 A2 **Snowtown** Austr.
53 C3 **Snowy** r. Austr.
53 C3 **Snowy Mountains** Austr.
143 C2 **Snyder** U.S.A.
121 □D2 **Soalala** Madag.
121 □D2 **Soanierana-Ivongo** Madag.
90 B2 **Sob** r. Ukr.
65 B2 **Sobaek-sanmaek** mts S. Korea
117 B4 **Sobat** r. Sudan
100 C3 **Sobernheim** Ger.
89 F2 **Sobinka** Rus. Fed.
151 E4 **Sobradinho, Barragem de** resr
        Brazil
151 E3 **Sobral** Brazil
91 D3 **Sochi** Rus. Fed.
65 B2 **Sŏch'ŏn** S. Korea
49 L5 **Society Islands** Fr. Polynesia
150 B2 **Socorro** Col.
142 B2 **Socorro** NM U.S.A.
142 B2 **Socorro** TX U.S.A.
144 A3 **Socorro, Isla** i. Mex.
56 B4 **Socotra** i. Yemen
63 B3 **Soc Trăng** Vietnam
106 C2 **Socuéllamos** Spain
92 I2 **Sodankylä** Fin.
134 D2 **Soda Springs** U.S.A.
93 G3 **Söderhamn** Sweden
93 G4 **Södertälje** Sweden
116 A3 **Sodiri** Sudan
117 B4 **Sodo** Eth.
93 G3 **Södra Kvarken** str. Fin./Sweden
123 C1 **Soekmekaar** S. Africa
        Soerabaia Indon. see Surabaya
101 D2 **Soest** Ger.
53 C2 **Sofala** Austr.
110 B2 **Sofia** Bulg.
121 □D2 **Sofia** r. Madag.
        Sofiya Bulg. see Sofia
        Sofiyevka Ukr. see Vil'nyans'k
75 D1 **Sog** China
93 E3 **Sognefjorden** inlet Norway
111 D2 **Söğüt** Turkey
        Sohâg Egypt see Sawhāj
        Sohar Oman see Şuḩār
100 B2 **Soignies** Belgium
105 C2 **Soissons** France
90 A1 **Sokal'** Ukr.
65 B2 **Sokch'o** S. Korea

111 C3 **Söke** Turkey
81 C1 **Sokhumi** Georgia
114 C4 **Sokodé** Togo
89 F2 **Sokol** Rus. Fed.
101 F2 **Sokolov** Czech Rep.
115 C3 **Sokoto** Nigeria
115 C3 **Sokoto** r. Nigeria
90 B2 **Sokyryany** Ukr.
73 B3 **Solapur** India
135 B3 **Soledad** U.S.A.
89 F2 **Soligalich** Rus. Fed.
99 C3 **Solihull** U.K.
86 E3 **Solikamsk** Rus. Fed.
87 E3 **Sol'-Iletsk** Rus. Fed.
100 C2 **Solingen** Ger.
122 A1 **Solitaire** Namibia
92 G3 **Sollefteå** Sweden
93 G4 **Sollentuna** Sweden
107 D2 **Sóller** Spain
101 D2 **Solling** hills Ger.
89 E2 **Solnechnogorsk** Rus. Fed.
60 B2 **Solok** Indon.
48 H4 **Solomon Islands** country
        S. Pacific Ocean
48 G3 **Solomon Sea** P.N.G./Solomon Is
61 D2 **Solor, Kepulauan** is Indon.
105 D2 **Solothurn** Switz.
81 D2 **Soltānābād** Iran
101 D1 **Soltau** Ger.
89 D2 **Sol'tsy** Rus. Fed.
96 C3 **Solway Firth** est. U.K.
120 B2 **Solwezi** Zambia
111 C3 **Soma** Turkey
117 C4 **Somalia** country Africa
120 B1 **Sombo** Angola
109 C1 **Sombor** Serb. and Mont.
144 B2 **Sombrerete** Mex.
138 C3 **Somerset** U.S.A.
123 C3 **Somerset East** S. Africa
126 F2 **Somerset Island** Can.
122 A3 **Somerset West** S. Africa
110 B1 **Someş** r. Romania
101 E2 **Sömmerda** Ger.
146 B3 **Somoto** Nic.
75 C2 **Son** r. India
93 E5 **Sønderborg** Denmark
101 E2 **Sondershausen** Ger.
        Søndre Strømfjord inlet Greenland
        see Kangerlussuaq
108 A1 **Sondrio** Italy
63 B2 **Sông Cau** Vietnam
62 B1 **Sông Da, Hồ** resr Vietnam
119 D4 **Songea** Tanz.
65 B1 **Sŏnggan** N. Korea
65 B1 **Songhua Hu** resr China
65 B1 **Songjianghe** China
        Sŏngjin N. Korea see Kimch'aek
63 B3 **Songkhla** Thai.
65 B2 **Sŏngnam** S. Korea
65 B2 **Songnim** N. Korea
120 A1 **Songo** Angola
121 C2 **Songo** Moz.
        Songololo Dem. Rep. Congo see
        Mbanza-Ngungu
69 E1 **Songyuan** China
        Sonid Youqi China see Saihan Tal
74 B2 **Sonipat** India
89 E2 **Sonkovo** Rus. Fed.
62 B1 **Son La** Vietnam
74 A2 **Sonmiani** Pak.
74 A2 **Sonmiani Bay** Pak.
101 E2 **Sonneberg** Ger.
142 A2 **Sonoita** Mex.
144 A2 **Sonora** r. Mex.
135 B3 **Sonora** CA U.S.A.
143 C2 **Sonora** TX U.S.A.
146 B3 **Sonsonate** El Salvador
        Soochow China see Suzhou
117 A4 **Sopo** watercourse Sudan
103 D2 **Sopron** Hungary
74 B1 **Sopur** Jammu and Kashmir
108 B2 **Sora** Italy
130 C3 **Sorel** Can.
51 D4 **Sorell** Austr.
106 C1 **Soria** Spain
90 B2 **Soroca** Moldova
154 C2 **Sorocaba** Brazil
87 E3 **Sorochinsk** Rus. Fed.
        Soroki Moldova see Soroca
59 D2 **Sorol** atoll Micronesia
59 C3 **Sorong** Indon.
119 D2 **Soroti** Uganda
92 H1 **Sørøya** i. Norway
108 B2 **Sorrento** Italy
92 G2 **Sorsele** Sweden
64 B2 **Sorsogon** Phil.
86 C2 **Sortavala** Rus. Fed.
92 G2 **Sortland** Norway
65 B2 **Sŏsan** S. Korea
123 C2 **Soshanguve** S. Africa
89 E3 **Sosna** r. Rus. Fed.
153 B3 **Sosneado** mt. Arg.
86 E2 **Sosnogorsk** Rus. Fed.
86 D2 **Sosnovka** Rus. Fed.
88 C2 **Sosnovyy Bor** Rus. Fed.
103 D1 **Sosnowiec** Pol.
91 C1 **Sosnytsya** Ukr.
86 F3 **Sos'va** Rus. Fed.
91 D2 **Sosyka** r. Rus. Fed.
145 C2 **Soto la Marina** Mex.
118 B2 **Souanké** Congo
111 B3 **Souda** Greece
104 C3 **Souillac** France
        Sŏul S. Korea see Seoul
104 B2 **Soulac-sur-Mer** France

104 B3 **Soulom** France
　 Soûr Lebanon see Tyre
107 D2 **Sour el Ghozlane** Alg.
129 D3 **Souris** Man. Can.
131 D3 **Souris** P.E.I. Can.
129 E3 **Souris** r. Can.
151 F3 **Sousa** Brazil
115 D1 **Sousse** Tunisia
104 B3 **Soustons** France
122 B3 **South Africa, Republic of** country Africa
99 C4 **Southampton** U.K.
129 F1 **Southampton, Cape** Can.
129 F1 **Southampton Island** Can.
73 D3 **South Andaman** i. India
52 A1 **South Australia** state Austr.
140 B2 **Southaven** U.S.A.
142 B2 **South Baldy** mt. U.S.A.
130 B3 **South Baymouth** Can.
138 B2 **South Bend** U.S.A.
141 D2 **South Carolina** state U.S.A.
58 B2 **South China Sea** N. Pacific Ocean
　 South Coast Town Austr. see Gold Coast
136 C2 **South Dakota** state U.S.A.
99 C4 **South Downs** hills U.K.
159 E6 **Southeast Indian Ridge** sea feature Indian Ocean
55 O2 **Southeast Pacific Basin** sea feature S. Pacific Ocean
129 D2 **Southend** Can.
99 D4 **Southend-on-Sea** U.K.
54 B2 **Southern Alps** mts N.Z.
50 A3 **Southern Cross** Austr.
129 E2 **Southern Indian Lake** Can.
159 D7 **Southern Ocean**
141 E1 **Southern Pines** U.S.A.
　 Southern Rhodesia country Africa see Zimbabwe
96 B3 **Southern Uplands** hills U.K.
55 J2 **South Geomagnetic Pole** Antarctica
149 G8 **South Georgia** terr. S. Atlantic Ocean
149 G8 **South Georgia and South Sandwich Islands** terr. S. Atlantic Ocean
138 B2 **South Haven** U.S.A.
129 E1 **South Henik Lake** Can.
119 D2 **South Horr** Kenya
54 B2 **South Island** N.Z.
65 B2 **South Korea** country Asia
135 B3 **South Lake Tahoe** U.S.A.
55 K3 **South Magnetic Pole** Antarctica
149 F9 **South Orkney Islands** S. Atlantic Ocean
136 C2 **South Platte** r. U.S.A.
98 B3 **Southport** U.K.
141 E2 **Southport** U.S.A.
130 C3 **South River** Can.
96 C1 **South Ronaldsay** i. U.K.
123 D3 **South Sand Bluff** pt S. Africa
149 H8 **South Sandwich Islands** S. Atlantic Ocean
55 C4 **South Sandwich Trench** sea feature S. Atlantic Ocean
129 D2 **South Saskatchewan** r. Can.
129 E2 **South Seal** r. Can.
149 E9 **South Shetland Islands** Antarctica
98 C2 **South Shields** U.K.
54 B1 **South Taranaki Bight** b. N.Z.
156 C8 **South Tasman Rise** sea feature Southern Ocean
130 C2 **South Twin Island** Can.
96 A2 **South Uist** i. U.K.
　 South-West Africa country Africa see Namibia
　 Southwest Peru Ridge sea feature S. Pacific Ocean see Nazca Ridge
53 D2 **South West Rocks** Austr.
99 D3 **Southwold** U.K.
109 C3 **Soverato** Italy
88 B2 **Sovetsk** Rus. Fed.
86 F2 **Sovetskiy** Rus. Fed.
91 C2 **Sovyets'kyy** Ukr.
123 C2 **Soweto** S. Africa
66 D1 **Sōya-misaki** c. Japan
65 B2 **Soyang-ho** l. S. Korea
104 C2 **Soyaux** France
90 C1 **Sozh** r. Europe
110 C2 **Sozopol** Bulg.
100 B2 **Spa** Belgium
106 C1 **Spain** country Europe
　 Spalato Croatia see Split
99 C3 **Spalding** U.K.
135 D2 **Spanish Fork** U.S.A.
　 Spanish Guinea country Africa see Equatorial Guinea
97 B2 **Spanish Point** Ireland
　 Spanish Sahara terr. Africa see Western Sahara
146 C3 **Spanish Town** Jamaica
108 B3 **Sparagio, Monte** mt. Sicily Italy
135 C3 **Sparks** U.S.A.
138 A2 **Sparta** U.S.A.
141 D2 **Spartanburg** U.S.A.
111 B3 **Sparti** Greece
109 C3 **Spartivento, Capo** c. Italy
89 D3 **Spas-Demensk** Rus. Fed.
89 F2 **Spas-Klepiki** Rus. Fed.
66 B2 **Spassk-Dal'niy** Rus. Fed.
89 F3 **Spassk-Ryazanskiy** Rus. Fed.
111 B3 **Spatha, Akra** pt Greece
96 B2 **Spean Bridge** U.K.
136 C2 **Spearfish** U.S.A.

143 C1 **Spearman** U.S.A.
　 Spence Bay Can. see Taloyoak
137 D2 **Spencer** IA U.S.A.
134 D2 **Spencer** ID U.S.A.
52 A2 **Spencer Gulf** est. Austr.
98 C2 **Spennymoor** U.K.
54 B2 **Spenser Mountains** N.Z.
101 D3 **Spessart** reg. Ger.
96 C2 **Spey** r. U.K.
101 D3 **Speyer** Ger.
100 C1 **Spiekeroog** i. Ger.
100 B2 **Spijkenisse** Neth.
100 B3 **Spincourt** France
128 C2 **Spirit River** Can.
103 E2 **Spišská Nová Ves** Slovakia
82 C1 **Spitsbergen** i. Svalbard
102 C2 **Spittal an der Drau** Austria
93 E3 **Spjelkavik** Norway
109 C2 **Split** Croatia
129 E2 **Split Lake** Can.
129 E2 **Split Lake** l. Can.
134 C1 **Spokane** U.S.A.
138 A1 **Spooner** U.S.A.
102 C1 **Spree** r. Ger.
122 A2 **Springbok** S. Africa
131 E3 **Springdale** Can.
140 B1 **Springdale** U.S.A.
101 D1 **Springe** Ger.
142 C1 **Springer** U.S.A.
142 B2 **Springerville** U.S.A.
136 C3 **Springfield** CO U.S.A.
138 B3 **Springfield** IL U.S.A.
139 E2 **Springfield** MA U.S.A.
137 E3 **Springfield** MO U.S.A.
138 C3 **Springfield** OH U.S.A.
134 B2 **Springfield** OR U.S.A.
140 C1 **Springfield** TN U.S.A.
123 C3 **Springfontein** S. Africa
131 D3 **Springhill** Can.
141 D3 **Spring Hill** U.S.A.
54 B2 **Springs Junction** N.Z.
51 D2 **Springsure** Austr.
135 D2 **Springville** U.S.A.
98 D3 **Spurn Head** hd U.K.
128 B3 **Squamish** Can.
109 C3 **Squillace, Golfo di** g. Italy
109 C2 **Srbija** aut. rep. Serb. and Mont.
108 C2 **Srebrenica** Bos.-Herz.
110 C2 **Sredets** Bulg.
83 L3 **Sredinnyy Khrebet** mts Rus. Fed.
83 L2 **Srednekolymsk** Rus. Fed.
　 Sredne-Russkaya Vozvyshennost' hills Rus. Fed. see Central Russian Upland
　 Sredne-Sibirskoye Ploskogor'ye Rus. Fed. see Central Siberian Plateau
110 B2 **Srednogorie** Bulg.
69 D1 **Sretensk** Rus. Fed.
61 C1 **Sri Aman** Sarawak Malaysia
73 B4 **Sri Jayewardenepura Kotte** Sri Lanka
73 C3 **Srikakulam** India
73 C4 **Sri Lanka** country Asia
74 B1 **Srinagar** Jammu and Kashmir
73 B3 **Srivardhan** India
101 D1 **Stade** Ger.
101 E1 **Stadensen** Ger.
100 C1 **Stadskanaal** Neth.
101 D2 **Stadtallendorf** Ger.
101 D1 **Stadthagen** Ger.
101 E2 **Staffelstein** Ger.
99 B3 **Stafford** U.K.
99 C4 **Staines** U.K.
91 D2 **Stakhanov** Ukr.
　 Stakhanovo Rus. Fed. see Zhukovskiy
　 Stalin Bulg. see Varna
　 Stalinabad Tajik. see Dushanbe
　 Stalingrad Rus. Fed. see Volgograd
　 Staliniri Georgia see Ts'khinvali
　 Stalino Ukr. see Donets'k
　 Stalinogorsk Rus. Fed. see Novomoskovsk
　 Stalinogród Pol. see Katowice
　 Stalinsk Rus. Fed. see Novokuznetsk
103 E1 **Stalowa Wola** Pol.
138 B1 **Stambaugh** U.S.A.
99 C3 **Stamford** U.K.
139 E2 **Stamford** CT U.S.A.
143 D2 **Stamford** TX U.S.A.
　 Stampalia i. Greece see Astypalaia
122 A1 **Stampriet** Namibia
92 F2 **Stamsund** Norway
123 C2 **Standerton** S. Africa
138 C2 **Standish** U.S.A.
123 D2 **Stanger** S. Africa
　 Stanislav Ukr. see Ivano-Frankivs'k
　 Stanke Dimitrov Bulg. see Dupnitsa
153 C5 **Stanley** Falkland Is
136 C1 **Stanley** U.S.A.
　 Stanleyville Dem. Rep. Congo see Kisangani
　 Stann Creek Belize see Dangriga
111 B3 **Stanos** Greece
83 I3 **Stanovoye Nagor'ye** mts Rus. Fed.
83 J3 **Stanovoy Khrebet** mts Rus. Fed.
53 D1 **Stanthorpe** Austr.
137 E1 **Staples** U.S.A.

103 E1 **Starachowice** Pol.
　 Stara Planina mts Bulg./Serb. and Mont. see Balkan Mountains
89 D2 **Staraya Russa** Rus. Fed.
89 D2 **Staraya Toropa** Rus. Fed.
110 C2 **Stara Zagora** Bulg.
49 L4 **Starbuck Island** Kiribati
103 D1 **Stargard Szczeciński** Pol.
89 D2 **Staritsa** Rus. Fed.
141 D3 **Starke** U.S.A.
140 C2 **Starkville** U.S.A.
102 C2 **Starnberg** Ger.
91 D2 **Starobil's'k** Ukr.
89 D3 **Starodub** Rus. Fed.
103 D1 **Starogard Gdański** Pol.
90 B2 **Starokostyantyniv** Ukr.
91 D2 **Starominskaya** Rus. Fed.
91 D2 **Staroshcherbinovskaya** Rus. Fed.
91 D2 **Starotitarovskaya** Rus. Fed.
89 F3 **Staroyur'yevo** Rus. Fed.
89 E3 **Starozhilovo** Rus. Fed.
99 B4 **Start Point** U.K.
88 C3 **Staryya Darohi** Belarus
86 G2 **Staryy Nadym** Rus. Fed.
89 E3 **Staryy Oskol** Rus. Fed.
101 E2 **Staßfurt** Ger.
103 E1 **Staszów** Pol.
139 D2 **State College** U.S.A.
141 D1 **Statesville** U.S.A.
160 L1 **Station Nord** Greenland
139 D3 **Staunton** U.S.A.
93 E4 **Stavanger** Norway
87 D4 **Stavropol'** Rus. Fed.
　 Stavropol'-na-Volge Rus. Fed. see Tol'yatti
87 D4 **Stavropol'skaya Vozvyshennost'** hills Rus. Fed.
52 B3 **Stawell** Austr.
123 C2 **Steadville** S. Africa
136 B2 **Steamboat Springs** U.S.A.
101 E2 **Stedten** Ger.
128 C2 **Steen River** Can.
134 C2 **Steens Mountain** U.S.A.
100 C1 **Steenwijk** Neth.
126 E2 **Stefansson Island** Can.
　 Stegi Swaziland see Siteki
110 B1 **Ştei** Romania
101 E3 **Steigerwald** mts Ger.
128 B2 **Stein** Neth.
129 E3 **Steinbach** Can.
101 E2 **Steinfurt** Ger.
120 A3 **Steinhausen** Namibia
92 F3 **Steinkjer** Norway
122 A2 **Steinkopf** S. Africa
122 B2 **Stella** S. Africa
123 C3 **Stellenbosch** S. Africa
105 D3 **Stello, Monte** mt. Corsica France
105 D2 **Stenay** France
101 E1 **Stendal** Ger.
　 Steornabhagh U.K. see Stornoway
　 Stepanakert Azer. see Xankändi
52 B2 **Stephens Creek** Austr.
129 E2 **Stephens Lake** Can.
131 E3 **Stephenville** Can.
143 D2 **Stephenville** U.S.A.
　 Stepnoy Rus. Fed. see Elista
122 B3 **Sterling** S. Africa
136 C2 **Sterling** CO U.S.A.
138 B2 **Sterling** IL U.S.A.
136 C1 **Sterling** ND U.S.A.
138 C2 **Sterling Heights** U.S.A.
87 E3 **Sterlitamak** Rus. Fed.
101 E1 **Sternberg** Ger.
128 C2 **Stettler** Can.
138 C2 **Steubenville** U.S.A.
99 C4 **Stevenage** U.K.
129 E2 **Stevenson Lake** Can.
138 B2 **Stevens Point** U.S.A.
126 C2 **Stevens Village** U.S.A.
134 D1 **Stevensville** U.S.A.
128 B2 **Stewart** Can.
128 A1 **Stewart** r. Can.
54 A3 **Stewart Island** N.Z.
127 G2 **Stewart Lake** Can.
123 C3 **Steynsburg** S. Africa
102 C2 **Steyr** Austria
122 B3 **Steytlerville** S. Africa
128 A2 **Stikine** r. Can.
128 A2 **Stikine Plateau** Can.
122 B3 **Stilbaai** S. Africa
137 E1 **Stillwater** MN U.S.A.
143 D1 **Stillwater** OK U.S.A.
135 C3 **Stillwater Range** mts U.S.A.
109 D2 **Štip** Macedonia
96 C2 **Stirling** U.K.
52 A2 **Stirling North** Austr.
92 F3 **Stjørdalshalsen** Norway
103 D2 **Stockerau** Austria
93 G4 **Stockholm** Sweden
98 B3 **Stockport** U.K.
135 B3 **Stockton** U.S.A.
98 C2 **Stockton-on-Tees** U.K.
143 C2 **Stockton Plateau** U.S.A.
63 B2 **Stœng Trêng** Cambodia
96 B1 **Stoer, Point of** U.K.
99 B3 **Stoke-on-Trent** U.K.
98 C2 **Stokesley** U.K.
92 F2 **Stokmarknes** Norway
110 B2 **Stol** mt. Serb. and Mont.
109 C2 **Stolac** Bos.-Herz.
100 C2 **Stolberg (Rheinland)** Ger.

82 E2 **Stolbovoy** Rus. Fed.
88 C3 **Stolin** Belarus
101 F2 **Stollberg** Ger.
101 D1 **Stolzenau** Ger.
96 C2 **Stonehaven** U.K.
99 C4 **Stonehenge** tourist site U.K.
129 E2 **Stonewall** Can.
129 D2 **Stony Rapids** Can.
92 G2 **Storavan** l. Sweden
　 Store Bælt sea chan. Denmark see Great Belt
92 F3 **Støren** Norway
92 I1 **Storfjordbotn** Norway
92 F2 **Storforshei** Norway
126 E2 **Storkerson Peninsula** Can.
137 D2 **Storm Lake** U.S.A.
93 E3 **Stornosa** mt. Norway
96 A1 **Stornoway** U.K.
86 E2 **Storozhevsk** Rus. Fed.
90 B2 **Storozhynets'** Ukr.
92 F3 **Storsjön** l. Sweden
92 H2 **Storslett** Norway
92 G2 **Storuman** Sweden
92 G2 **Storuman** l. Sweden
99 C4 **Stour** r. England U.K.
99 C4 **Stour** r. England U.K.
99 C3 **Stour** r. England U.K.
130 A2 **Stout Lake** Can.
88 C3 **Stowbtsy** Belarus
99 D3 **Stowmarket** U.K.
97 C1 **Strabane** U.K.
102 C2 **Strakonice** Czech Rep.
102 C1 **Stralsund** Ger.
122 A3 **Strand** S. Africa
93 E3 **Stranda** Norway
97 D1 **Strangford Lough** inlet U.K.
96 B3 **Stranraer** U.K.
105 D2 **Strasbourg** France
130 B3 **Stratford** Can.
54 B1 **Stratford** N.Z.
143 C1 **Stratford** U.S.A.
99 C3 **Stratford-upon-Avon** U.K.
128 C2 **Strathmore** Can.
96 C2 **Strathspey** val. U.K.
102 C2 **Straubing** Ger.
134 C2 **Strawberry Mountain** U.S.A.
51 C3 **Streaky Bay** Austr.
138 B2 **Streator** U.S.A.
99 B4 **Street** U.K.
110 B2 **Strehaia** Romania
94 B1 **Streymoy** i. Faroe Is.
82 G2 **Strezhevoy** Rus. Fed.
101 F3 **Stříbro** Czech Rep.
111 B2 **Strimonas** r. Greece
153 B4 **Stroeder** Arg.
101 D1 **Ströhen** Ger.
109 C3 **Stromboli, Isola** i. Italy
96 B2 **Stromeferry** U.K.
96 C1 **Stromness** U.K.
92 G3 **Strömsund** Sweden
96 C1 **Stronsay** i. U.K.
53 D2 **Stroud** Austr.
99 B4 **Stroud** U.K.
100 C1 **Strücklingen (Saterland)** Ger.
111 B2 **Struga** Macedonia
88 C2 **Strugi-Krasnyye** Rus. Fed.
122 B3 **Struis Bay** S. Africa
111 B2 **Struma** r. Bulg.
99 A3 **Strumble Head** hd U.K.
111 B2 **Strumica** Macedonia
122 B2 **Strydenburg** S. Africa
93 E3 **Stryn** Norway
90 A2 **Stryy** Ukr.
90 A2 **Stryy** r. Ukr.
128 B2 **Stuart Lake** Can.
53 C2 **Stuart Town** Austr.
　 Stuchka Latvia see Aizkraukle
　 Stučka Latvia see Aizkraukle
130 A2 **Stull Lake** Can.
89 E3 **Stupino** Rus. Fed.
55 M3 **Sturge Island** Antarctica
138 B2 **Sturgeon Bay** U.S.A.
130 C3 **Sturgeon Falls** Can.
130 A3 **Sturgeon Lake** Can.
138 B2 **Sturgis** MI U.S.A.
136 C2 **Sturgis** SD U.S.A.
52 B1 **Sturt, Mount** hill Austr.
50 B1 **Sturt Creek** watercourse Austr.
50 C1 **Sturt Plain** Austr.
52 B1 **Sturt Stony Desert** Austr.
123 C3 **Stutterheim** S. Africa
102 B2 **Stuttgart** Ger.
140 B2 **Stuttgart** U.S.A.
92 □A2 **Stykkishólmur** Iceland
90 B1 **Styr** r. Belarus/Ukr.
155 D1 **Suaçuí Grande** r. Brazil
116 B3 **Suakin** Sudan
71 C3 **Suao** Taiwan
78 A3 **Suara, Mount** Eritrea
60 B1 **Subi Besar** i. Indon.
109 C1 **Subotica** Serb. and Mont.
110 C1 **Suceava** Romania
　 Suchan Rus. Fed. see Partizansk
97 B2 **Suck** r. Ireland
152 B1 **Sucre** Bol.
154 B2 **Sucuriú** r. Brazil
　 Suczawa Romania see Suceava
89 E2 **Suda** Rus. Fed.
91 C3 **Sudak** Ukr.
116 A3 **Sudan** country Africa
130 B3 **Sudbury** Can.
99 D3 **Sudbury** U.K.
117 A4 **Sudd** swamp Sudan
89 F2 **Sudislavl'** Rus. Fed.

89 F2 **Sudogda** Rus. Fed.
94 B1 **Suðuroy** *i.* Faroe Is
89 E3 **Sudzha** Rus. Fed.
107 C2 **Sueca** Spain
116 B2 **Suez** Egypt
116 B2 **Suez, Gulf of** Egypt
80 B2 **Suez Canal** *canal* Egypt
139 D3 **Suffolk** U.S.A.
140 A3 **Sugar Land** U.S.A.
139 E1 **Sugarloaf Mountain** U.S.A.
53 D2 **Sugarloaf Point** Austr.
70 A2 **Suhait** China
79 C2 **Ṣuḥār** Oman
68 D1 **Sühbaatar** Mongolia
101 E2 **Suhl** Ger.
109 C1 **Suhopolje** Croatia
70 B2 **Suide** China
66 B2 **Suifenhe** China
69 E1 **Suihua** China
70 A2 **Suining** China
70 B2 **Suiping** China
97 C2 **Suir** *r.* Ireland
 Suixian China *see* Suizhou
70 B2 **Suiyang** China
70 B2 **Suizhou** China
74 B2 **Sujangarh** India
74 B1 **Sujanpur** India
74 A2 **Sujawal** Pak.
60 B2 **Sukabumi** Indon.
60 B2 **Sukadana** Indon.
67 D3 **Sukagawa** Japan
60 C2 **Sukaraja** Indon.
 Sukarnapura Indon. *see* Jayapura
 Sukarno, Puntjak *mt.* Indon. *see* Jaya, Puncak
89 E3 **Sukhinichi** Rus. Fed.
89 F2 **Sukhona** *r.* Rus. Fed.
62 A2 **Sukhothai** Thai.
74 A2 **Sukkur** Pak.
89 E2 **Sukromny** Rus. Fed.
59 C3 **Sula, Kepulauan** *is* Indon.
74 A1 **Sulaiman Range** *mts* Pak.
 Sulawesi *i.* Indon. *see* Celebes
101 D1 **Sulingen** Ger.
150 A3 **Sullana** Peru
138 B3 **Sullivan** *IN* U.S.A.
137 E3 **Sullivan** *MO* U.S.A.
140 B2 **Sulphur** U.S.A.
143 D2 **Sulphur Springs** U.S.A.
138 C1 **Sultan** Can.
 Sultanabad Iran *see* Arāk
64 B3 **Sulu Archipelago** *is* Phil.
64 A3 **Sulu Sea** N. Pacific Ocean
101 E3 **Sulzbach-Rosenberg** Ger.
79 C2 **Sumāil** Oman
 Sumatera *i.* Indon. *see* Sumatra
60 A1 **Sumatra** *i.* Indon.
61 D2 **Sumba** *i.* Indon.
61 C2 **Sumba, Selat** *sea chan.* Indon.
61 C2 **Sumbawa** *i.* Indon.
61 C2 **Sumbawabesar** Indon.
119 D3 **Sumbawanga** Tanz.
120 A2 **Sumbe** Angola
96 □ **Sumburgh** U.K.
96 □ **Sumburgh Head** *hd* U.K.
119 C2 **Sumeih** Sudan
61 C2 **Sumenep** Indon.
67 D4 **Sumisu-jima** *i.* Japan
131 D3 **Summerside** Can.
138 C3 **Summersville** U.S.A.
141 D2 **Summerville** U.S.A.
137 D1 **Summit** U.S.A.
128 B2 **Summit Lake** Can.
103 D2 **Šumperk** Czech Rep.
81 C1 **Sumqayıt** Azer.
141 D2 **Sumter** U.S.A.
91 C1 **Sumy** Ukr.
75 D2 **Sunamganj** Bangl.
65 B2 **Sunan** N. Korea
79 C2 **Şunaynah** Oman
52 B3 **Sunbury** Austr.
139 D2 **Sunbury** U.S.A.
65 B2 **Sunch'ŏn** N. Korea
65 B3 **Sunch'ŏn** S. Korea
123 C2 **Sun City** S. Africa
93 H3 **Sund** Fin.
60 B2 **Sunda, Selat** *str.* Indon.
136 C2 **Sundance** U.S.A.
75 C2 **Sundarbans** *reg.* Bangl./India
74 B1 **Sundarnagar** India
 Sunda Strait Indon. *see* Sunda, Selat
 Sunda Trench *sea feature* Indian Ocean *see* Java Trench
98 C2 **Sunderland** U.K.
128 C2 **Sundre** Can.
93 G3 **Sundsvall** Sweden
123 D2 **Sundumbili** S. Africa
60 B2 **Sungailiat** Indon.
60 B2 **Sungaipenuh** Indon.
60 B1 **Sungai Petani** Malaysia
80 B1 **Sungurlu** Turkey
75 C2 **Sun Kosi** *r.* Nepal
93 E3 **Sunndalsøra** Norway
134 C1 **Sunnyside** U.S.A.
135 B3 **Sunnyvale** U.S.A.
141 D3 **Sunrise** U.S.A.
83 I2 **Suntar** Rus. Fed.
74 A2 **Suntsar** Pak.
114 B4 **Sunyani** Ghana
92 I3 **Suomussalmi** Fin.
67 B4 **Suō-nada** *b.* Japan
142 A2 **Suoyarvi** Rus. Fed.
142 A2 **Superior** *AZ* U.S.A.
137 D2 **Superior** *NE* U.S.A.

138 A1 **Superior** *WI* U.S.A.
138 B1 **Superior, Lake** Can./U.S.A.
63 B2 **Suphan Buri** Thai.
81 C2 **Süphan Dağı** *mt.* Turkey
89 D3 **Suponevo** Rus. Fed.
81 C2 **Sūq ash Shuyūkh** Iraq
70 B2 **Suqian** China
78 A2 **Sūq Suwayq** Saudi Arabia
 Suquṭrā *i.* Yemen *see* Socotra
79 C2 **Şūr** Oman
74 A2 **Surab** Pak.
61 C2 **Surabaya** Indon.
61 C2 **Surakarta** Indon.
74 B2 **Surat** India
74 B2 **Suratgarh** India
63 A3 **Surat Thani** Thai.
89 D3 **Surazh** Rus. Fed.
109 D2 **Surdulica** Serb. and Mont.
100 C3 **Sûre** *r.* Lux.
74 B2 **Surendranagar** India
82 F2 **Surgut** Rus. Fed.
64 B3 **Surigao** Phil.
63 B2 **Surin** Thai.
151 D2 **Suriname** *country* S. America
75 C2 **Surkhet** Nepal
 Surt Libya *see* Sirte
 Surt, Khalij *g.* Libya *see* Sirte, Gulf of
60 B2 **Surulangun** Indon.
81 C2 **Süsangerd** Iran
89 F2 **Susanino** Rus. Fed.
135 B2 **Susanville** U.S.A.
80 B1 **Suşehri** Turkey
139 D3 **Susquehanna** *r.* U.S.A.
131 D3 **Sussex** Can.
101 D1 **Süstedt** Ger.
100 C1 **Sustrum** Ger.
83 K2 **Susuman** Rus. Fed.
111 C3 **Susurluk** Turkey
74 B1 **Sutak** Jammu and Kashmir
53 D2 **Sutherland** Austr.
122 B3 **Sutherland** S. Africa
136 C2 **Sutherland** U.S.A.
134 B2 **Sutherlin** U.S.A.
74 B2 **Sutlej** *r.* India/Pak.
138 C3 **Sutton** U.S.A.
99 C3 **Sutton Coldfield** U.K.
98 C3 **Sutton in Ashfield** U.K.
66 D2 **Suttsu** Japan
49 I5 **Suva** Fiji
 Suvalki Pol. *see* Suwałki
89 E3 **Suvorov** Rus. Fed.
90 B2 **Suvorove** Ukr.
103 E1 **Suwałki** Pol.
141 D3 **Suwanee Sound** *b.* U.S.A.
63 B2 **Suwannaphum** Thai.
141 D3 **Suwannee** *r.* U.S.A.
 Suways, Qanât as *canal* Egypt *see* Suez Canal
65 B2 **Suwŏn** S. Korea
79 C2 **Sūzā** Iran
89 F2 **Suzdal'** Rus. Fed.
89 D3 **Suzemka** Rus. Fed.
70 B2 **Suzhou** *Anhui* China
70 C2 **Suzhou** *Jiangsu* China
67 C3 **Suzu** Japan
67 C3 **Suzu-misaki** *pt* Japan
82 B1 **Svalbard** *terr.* Arctic Ocean
90 A2 **Svalyava** Ukr.
92 H2 **Svappavaara** Sweden
91 D2 **Svatove** Ukr.
63 B2 **Svay Riêng** Cambodia
93 F3 **Sveg** Sweden
88 C2 **Švenčionys** Lith.
93 F4 **Svendborg** Denmark
 Sverdlovsk Rus. Fed. *see* Yekaterinburg
111 B3 **Sveti Nikole** Macedonia
66 C1 **Svetlaya** Rus. Fed.
88 B3 **Svetlogorsk** Rus. Fed.
87 D4 **Svetlograd** Rus. Fed.
88 B3 **Svetlyy** Rus. Fed.
93 I3 **Svetogorsk** Rus. Fed.
103 E2 **Svidník** Slovakia
111 C2 **Svilengrad** Bulg.
110 B2 **Svinecea Mare, Vârful** *mt.* Romania
110 C2 **Svishtov** Bulg.
88 B3 **Svislach** Belarus
103 D2 **Svitavy** Czech Rep.
91 C2 **Svitlovods'k** Ukr.
69 E1 **Svobodnyy** Rus. Fed.
110 B2 **Svoge** Bulg.
92 F2 **Svolvær** Norway
88 C3 **Svyetlahorsk** Belarus
141 D2 **Swainsboro** U.S.A.
120 A3 **Swakopmund** Namibia
52 B3 **Swan Hill** Austr.
128 C2 **Swan Hills** Can.
129 D2 **Swan Lake** Can.
97 C1 **Swanlinbar** Ireland
129 D2 **Swan River** Can.
53 D2 **Swansea** Austr.
99 B4 **Swansea** U.K.
122 B3 **Swartkolkvloer** *salt pan* S. Africa
123 C2 **Swartruggens** S. Africa
 Swatow China *see* Shantou
123 D2 **Swaziland** *country* Africa
93 G3 **Sweden** *country* Europe
143 C2 **Sweetwater** U.S.A.
136 B2 **Sweetwater** *r.* U.S.A.
122 B3 **Swellendam** S. Africa
103 D1 **Świdnica** Pol.
103 D1 **Świdwin** Pol.
103 D1 **Świebodzin** Pol.

103 D1 **Świecie** Pol.
129 D2 **Swift Current** Can.
97 C1 **Swilly, Lough** *inlet* Ireland
99 C4 **Swindon** U.K.
102 C1 **Świnoujście** Pol.
105 D2 **Switzerland** *country* Europe
97 C2 **Swords** Ireland
88 C3 **Syanno** Belarus
89 D1 **Syas'troy** Rus. Fed.
89 D2 **Sychevka** Rus. Fed.
53 D2 **Sydney** Austr.
131 D3 **Sydney** Can.
131 D3 **Sydney Mines** Can.
91 D2 **Syeverodonets'k** Ukr.
86 E2 **Syktyvkar** Rus. Fed.
140 C2 **Sylacauga** U.S.A.
75 D2 **Sylhet** Bangl.
102 B1 **Sylt** *i.* Ger.
138 C2 **Sylvania** U.S.A.
51 C1 **Sylvester, Lake** *salt flat* Austr.
111 C3 **Symi** *i.* Greece
91 D2 **Synel'nykove** Ukr.
90 C2 **Synyukha** *r.* Ukr.
109 C3 **Syracuse** *Sicily* Italy
136 C3 **Syracuse** *KS* U.S.A.
139 D2 **Syracuse** *NY* U.S.A.
77 C2 **Syrdar'ya** *r.* Asia
80 B2 **Syria** *country* Asia
80 B2 **Syrian Desert** Asia
111 B3 **Syros** *i.* Greece
91 D2 **Syvash, Zatoka** *lag.* Ukr.
91 C2 **Syvas'ke** Ukr.
87 D3 **Syzran'** Rus. Fed.
102 C1 **Szczecin** Pol.
103 D1 **Szczecinek** Pol.
103 E1 **Szczytno** Pol.
 Szechwan *prov.* China *see* Sichuan
103 E2 **Szeged** Hungary
103 D2 **Székesfehérvár** Hungary
103 D2 **Szekszárd** Hungary
103 E2 **Szentes** Hungary
103 D2 **Szentgotthárd** Hungary
103 E2 **Szerencs** Hungary
103 D2 **Szigetvár** Hungary
103 E2 **Szolnok** Hungary
103 D2 **Szombathely** Hungary
 Sztálinváros Hungary *see* Dunaújváros

T

117 C4 **Taagga Duudka** *reg.* Somalia
64 B2 **Tabaco** Phil.
78 B2 **Tābah** Saudi Arabia
108 A3 **Tabarka** Tunisia
76 B3 **Ṭabas** Iran
79 C1 **Tābāsīn** Iran
81 D3 **Tābask, Kūh-e** *mt.* Iran
150 C3 **Tabatinga** Brazil
154 C2 **Tabatinga** Brazil
114 B2 **Tabelbala** Alg.
128 C3 **Taber** Can.
64 B2 **Tablas** *i.* Phil.
102 C2 **Tábor** Czech Rep.
119 D3 **Tabora** Tanz.
114 B4 **Tabou** Côte d'Ivoire
81 C2 **Tabrīz** Iran
48 L3 **Tabuaeran** *i.* Kiribati
78 A2 **Tabūk** Saudi Arabia
93 G4 **Täby** Sweden
77 E2 **Tacheng** China
102 C2 **Tachov** Czech Rep.
64 B2 **Tacloban** Phil.
150 B4 **Tacna** Peru
134 B1 **Tacoma** U.S.A.
152 C3 **Tacuarembó** Uru.
142 B3 **Tacupeto** Mex.
114 C2 **Tademaït, Plateau du** Alg.
 Tadjikistan *country* Asia *see* Tajikistan
117 C3 **Tadjoura** Djibouti
80 B2 **Tadmur** Syria
129 E2 **Tadoule Lake** Can.
 Tadzhikskaya S.S.R. *admin. reg.* Asia *see* Tajikistan
65 B2 **T'aebaek-sanmaek** *mts* N. Korea/S. Korea
 Taech'ŏn S. Korea *see* Poryŏng
65 B2 **Taegu** S. Korea
65 B2 **Taejŏn** S. Korea
65 B2 **Taejŏng** S. Korea
65 B2 **T'aepaek** S. Korea
69 E1 **Ta'erqi** China
107 C1 **Tafalla** Spain
152 B2 **Tafí Viejo** Arg.
79 D2 **Taftān, Kūh-e** *mt.* Iran
91 D2 **Taganrog** Rus. Fed.
91 D2 **Taganrog, Gulf of** Rus. Fed./Ukr.
62 A1 **Tagaung** Myanmar
64 B2 **Tagaytay City** Phil.
64 B3 **Tagbilaran** Phil.
64 B2 **Tagudin** Phil.
51 E1 **Tagula Island** P.N.G.
64 B3 **Tagum** Phil.
106 B2 **Tagus** *r.* Port./Spain
60 B1 **Tahan, Gunung** *mt.* Malaysia
115 C2 **Tahat, Mont** *mt.* Alg.
69 E1 **Tahe** China
49 M5 **Tahiti** *i.* Fr. Polynesia
143 E1 **Tahlequah** U.S.A.
135 B3 **Tahoe, Lake** U.S.A.
135 B3 **Tahoe City** U.S.A.

126 E2 **Tahoe Lake** Can.
115 C3 **Tahoua** Niger
79 C2 **Tahrūd** Iran
128 B3 **Tahsis** Can.
116 B2 **Ṭaḥṭā** Egypt
64 B3 **Tahuna** Indon.
70 B2 **Tai'an** China
70 A2 **Taibai Shan** *mt.* China
 Taibus Qi China *see* Baochang
71 C3 **T'aichung** Taiwan
70 B2 **Taihang Shan** *mts* China
54 C1 **Taihape** N.Z.
71 B3 **Taihe** China
70 C2 **Tai Hu** *l.* China
52 A3 **Tailem Bend** Austr.
71 C3 **T'ainan** Taiwan
111 B3 **Tainaro, Akra** *pt* Greece
155 D1 **Taiobeiras** Brazil
71 C3 **T'aipei** Taiwan
 Taiping China *see* Chongzuo
60 B1 **Taiping** Malaysia
 Tairbeart U.K. *see* Tarbert
71 B3 **Taishan** China
70 B2 **Tai Shan** *hills* China
119 D3 **Taita Hills** Kenya
153 A4 **Taitao, Península de** *pen.* Chile
71 C3 **T'aitung** Taiwan
92 I2 **Taivalkoski** Fin.
92 H2 **Taivaskero** *hill* Fin.
71 C3 **Taiwan** Asia
 Taiwan Shan *mts* Taiwan *see* Chungyang Shanmo
71 B3 **Taiwan Strait** China/Taiwan
70 B2 **Taiyuan** China
70 B2 **Taizhou** *Jiangsu* China
71 C3 **Taizhou** *Zhejiang* China
78 B3 **Ta'izz** Yemen
145 C3 **Tajumulco, Volcán de** *vol.* Guat.
77 C3 **Tajikistan** *country* Asia
74 B2 **Taj Mahal** *tourist site* India
 Tajo *r.* Spain *see* Tagus
63 A2 **Tak** Thai.
54 B2 **Takaka** N.Z.
115 C2 **Takalous, Oued** *watercourse* Alg.
67 B3 **Takamatsu** Japan
67 C3 **Takaoka** Japan
54 B1 **Takapuna** N.Z.
67 C3 **Takasaki** Japan
122 B1 **Takatokwane** Botswana
122 B1 **Takatshwane** Botswana
67 C3 **Takayama** Japan
67 C3 **Takefu** Japan
60 A1 **Takengon** Indon.
63 B2 **Takêv** Cambodia
 Takhiatash Uzbek. *see* Taxiatosh
63 B2 **Ta Khmau** Cambodia
74 B1 **Takht-i-Sulaiman** *mt.* Pak.
66 D2 **Takikawa** Japan
128 B2 **Takla Lake** Can.
128 B2 **Takla Landing** Can.
 Takla Makan *des.* China *see* Taklimakan Desert
77 E3 **Taklimakan Desert** *des.* China
 Taklimakan Shamo China *see* Taklimakan Desert
128 A2 **Taku** *r.* Can./U.S.A.
63 A3 **Takua Pa** Thai.
115 C4 **Takum** Nigeria
88 C3 **Talachyn** Belarus
74 B1 **Talagang** Pak.
146 B4 **Talamanca, Cordillera de** *mts* Costa Rica
150 A3 **Talara** Peru
59 C2 **Talaud, Kepulauan** *is* Indon.
106 C2 **Talavera de la Reina** Spain
153 A3 **Talca** Chile
153 A3 **Talcahuano** Chile
89 E2 **Taldom** Rus. Fed.
77 D2 **Taldykorgan** Kazakh.
 Taldy-Kurgan Kazakh. *see* Taldykorgan
59 C3 **Taliabu** *i.* Indon.
64 B2 **Talisay** Phil.
61 C2 **Taliwang** Indon.
81 C2 **Tall 'Afar** Iraq
141 C2 **Tallahassee** U.S.A.
53 C3 **Tallangatta** Austr.
88 B2 **Tallinn** Estonia
140 B2 **Tallulah** U.S.A.
104 B2 **Talmont-St-Hilaire** France
90 C2 **Tal'ne** Ukr.
117 B3 **Talodi** Sudan
74 A1 **Tāloqān** Afgh.
91 E1 **Talovaya** Rus. Fed.
126 F2 **Taloyoak** Can.
88 B2 **Talsi** Latvia
152 A2 **Taltal** Chile
129 C1 **Taltson** *r.* Can.
60 A1 **Talu** Indon.
53 C1 **Talwood** Austr.
114 B4 **Tamale** Ghana
115 C2 **Tamanrasset** Alg.
99 A4 **Tamar** *r.* U.K.
 Tamatave Madag. *see* Toamasina
144 B2 **Tamazula** Mex.
145 C2 **Tamazunchale** Mex.
114 A3 **Tambacounda** Senegal
60 B1 **Tambelan, Kepulauan** *is* Indon.
86 G1 **Tambey** Rus. Fed.
61 C2 **Tambisan** *Sabah* Malaysia
61 C2 **Tambora, Gunung** *vol.* Indon.
91 E1 **Tambov** Rus. Fed.
119 C2 **Tambura** Sudan
62 A1 **Tamenglong** India

145 C2 **Tamiahua, Laguna de** *lag.* Mex.
Tammerfors Fin. *see* Tampere
141 D3 **Tampa** U.S.A.
141 D3 **Tampa Bay** U.S.A.
93 H3 **Tampere** Fin.
145 C2 **Tampico** Mex.
69 D1 **Tamsagbulag** Mongolia
102 C2 **Tamsweg** Austria
53 D2 **Tamworth** Austr.
99 C3 **Tamworth** U.K.
119 E3 **Tana** *r.* Kenya
Tana, Lake Eth. *see* Lake Tana
67 C4 **Tanabe** Japan
92 I1 **Tana Bru** Norway
60 A2 **Tanahbala** *i.* Indon.
61 C2 **Tanahgrogot** Indon.
61 D2 **Tanahjampea** *i.* Indon.
60 A2 **Tanahmasa** *i.* Indon.
50 C1 **Tanami Desert** Austr.
63 B2 **Tân An** Vietnam
126 B2 **Tanana** U.S.A.
Tananarive Madag. *see* Antananarivo
108 A1 **Tanaro** *r.* Italy
65 B1 **Tanch'ŏn** N. Korea
64 B3 **Tandag** Phil.
110 C2 **Țăndărei** Romania
153 C3 **Tandil** Arg.
74 A2 **Tando Adam** Pak.
74 A2 **Tando Muhammmad Khan** Pak.
52 B2 **Tandou Lake** *imp. l.* Austr.
67 B4 **Tanega-shima** *i.* Japan
114 B2 **Tanezrouft** *reg.* Alg./Mali
119 D3 **Tanga** Tanz.
75 C2 **Tangail** Bangl.
Tanganyika *country* Africa *see* Tanzania
119 C3 **Tanganyika, Lake** Africa
55 F3 **Tange Promontory** *hd* Antarctica
Tanger *see* Tangier
101 E1 **Tangermünde** Ger.
75 D1 **Tanggulashan** China
75 C1 **Tanggula Shan** *mts* China
114 B1 **Tangier** Morocco
75 C1 **Tangra Yumco** *salt l.* China
70 B2 **Tangshan** China
68 C2 **Taniantaweng Shan** *mts* China
59 C3 **Tanimbar, Kepulauan** *is* Indon.
64 B3 **Tanjay** Phil.
61 C2 **Tanjung** Indon.
60 A1 **Tanjungbalai** Indon.
Tanjungkarang-Telukbetung Indon. *see* Bandar Lampung
60 B2 **Tanjungpandan** Indon.
60 B1 **Tanjungpinang** Indon.
61 C1 **Tanjungredeb** Indon.
61 C1 **Tanjungselor** Indon.
74 B1 **Tank** Pak.
48 H5 **Tanna** *i.* Vanuatu
115 C3 **Tanout** Niger
75 C2 **Tansen** Nepal
116 B1 **Țanța** Egypt
114 A2 **Tan-Tan** Morocco
145 C2 **Tantoyuca** Mex.
119 D3 **Tanzania** *country* Africa
Tao'an China *see* Taonan
Taocheng China *see* Yongchun
Taolanaro Madag. *see* Tôlañaro
69 E1 **Taonan** China
109 C3 **Taormina** *Sicily* Italy
142 B1 **Taos** U.S.A.
114 B2 **Taoudenni** Mali
114 B1 **Taounate** Morocco
114 B1 **Taourirt** Morocco
88 C2 **Tapa** Estonia
145 C3 **Tapachula** Mex.
151 D3 **Tapajós** *r.* Brazil
60 A1 **Tapaktuan** Indon.
145 C3 **Tapanatepec** Mex.
150 C3 **Tapauá** Brazil
152 C2 **Tapera** Brazil
114 B4 **Tapeta** Liberia
74 B2 **Tapi** *r.* India
139 D3 **Tappahannock** U.S.A.
54 B2 **Tapuaenuku** *mt.* N.Z.
150 C3 **Tapurucuara** Brazil
154 B1 **Taquaral, Serra do** *hills* Brazil
154 A1 **Taquari** *r.* Brazil
154 B1 **Taquari, Serra do** *hills* Brazil
154 C2 **Taquaritinga** Brazil
53 D1 **Tara** Austr.
115 D4 **Taraba** *r.* Nigeria
Țarābulus Libya *see* Tripoli
54 C1 **Taradale** N.Z.
61 C1 **Tarakan** Indon.
111 D2 **Taraklı** Turkey
88 A3 **Taran, Mys** *pt* Rus. Fed.
54 B1 **Taranaki, Mount** *vol.* N.Z.
106 C1 **Tarancón** Spain
109 C2 **Taranto** Italy
109 C2 **Taranto, Golfo di** *g.* Italy
150 B3 **Tarapoto** Peru
90 C2 **Tarashcha** Ukr.
91 E2 **Tarasovskiy** Rus. Fed.
150 B3 **Tarauacá** Brazil
150 C3 **Tarauacá** *r.* Brazil
48 I3 **Tarawa** *atoll* Kiribati
54 C1 **Tarawera** N.Z.
77 D2 **Taraz** Kazakh.
107 C1 **Tarazona** Spain
77 E2 **Tarbagatay, Khrebet** *mts* Kazakh.
96 C2 **Tarbat Ness** *pt* U.K.
97 B2 **Tarbert** Ireland
96 A2 **Tarbert** *Scotland* U.K.
96 B3 **Tarbert** *Scotland* U.K.

104 C3 **Tarbes** France
96 B2 **Tarbet** U.K.
141 E1 **Tarboro** U.S.A.
51 C3 **Tarcoola** Austr.
53 D2 **Taree** Austr.
110 C2 **Târgovişte** Romania
110 B1 **Târgu Frumos** Romania
110 B1 **Târgu Jiu** Romania
110 B1 **Târgu Lăpuş** Romania
110 B1 **Târgu Mureş** Romania
110 C1 **Târgu Neamţ** Romania
110 C1 **Târgu Ocna** Romania
79 C2 **Tarif** U.A.E.
152 B2 **Tarija** Bol.
79 B3 **Tarim** Yemen
77 E3 **Tarim Basin** *basin* China
119 D3 **Tarime** Tanz.
77 E2 **Tarim He** *r.* China
Tarim Pendi China *see* Tarim Basin
77 C3 **Tarin Kowt** Afgh.
59 D3 **Taritatu** *r.* Indon.
123 C3 **Tarkastad** S. Africa
82 G2 **Tarko-Sale** Rus. Fed.
114 B4 **Tarkwa** Ghana
64 B2 **Tarlac** Phil.
105 C3 **Tarn** *r.* France
92 G2 **Tärnaby** Sweden
77 C3 **Tarnak** *r.* Afgh.
110 B1 **Tărnăveni** Romania
103 E1 **Tarnobrzeg** Pol.
Tarnopol Ukr. *see* Ternopil'
103 E1 **Tarnów** Pol.
51 D2 **Taroom** Austr.
114 B1 **Taroudannt** Morocco
141 D3 **Tarpon Springs** U.S.A.
108 B2 **Tarquinia** Italy
107 D1 **Tarragona** Spain
107 D1 **Tàrrega** Spain
80 B2 **Tarsus** Turkey
152 B2 **Tartagal** Arg.
104 B3 **Tartas** France
88 C2 **Tartu** Estonia
80 B2 **Țarțūs** Syria
155 D1 **Tarumirim** Brazil
89 E3 **Tarusa** Rus. Fed.
90 B2 **Tarutyne** Ukr.
108 B1 **Tarvisio** Italy
Tashauz Turkm. *see* Dashoguz
75 D2 **Tashigang** Bhutan
81 D3 **Tashk, Daryācheh-ye** *l.* Iran
77 C2 **Tashkent** Uzbek.
130 C2 **Tasialujjuaq, Lac** *l.* Can.
130 C2 **Tasiat, Lac** *l.* Can.
131 D2 **Tasiujaq** Can.
77 E2 **Taskesken** Kazakh.
54 B2 **Tasman Bay** N.Z.
51 D4 **Tasmania** *state* Austr.
54 B2 **Tasman Mountains** N.Z.
54 A1 **Tasman Sea** S. Pacific Ocean
115 C2 **Tassili du Hoggar** *plat.* Alg.
115 C2 **Tassili n'Ajjer** *plat.* Alg.
61 C2 **Tataba** Indon.
103 D2 **Tatabánya** Hungary
90 B2 **Tatarbunary** Ukr.
83 K3 **Tatarskiy Proliv** *str.* Rus. Fed.
Tatar Strait Rus. Fed. *see* Tatarskiy Proliv
67 C4 **Tateyama** Japan
128 C1 **Tathlina Lake** Can.
78 B3 **Tathlith** Saudi Arabia
78 B2 **Tathlīth, Wādī** *watercourse* Saudi Arabia
53 C3 **Tathra** Austr.
62 A1 **Tatkon** Myanmar
128 B2 **Tatla Lake** Can.
103 D2 **Tatra Mountains** *mts* Pol./Slovakia
Tatry *mts* Pol./Slovakia *see* Tatra Mountains
74 A2 **Tatta** Pak.
154 C2 **Tatuí** Brazil
143 C2 **Tatum** U.S.A.
81 C2 **Tatvan** Turkey
151 E3 **Tauá** Brazil
155 C2 **Taubaté** Brazil
101 D3 **Tauberbischofsheim** Ger.
54 C1 **Taumarunui** N.Z.
122 B2 **Taung** S. Africa
62 A1 **Taunggyi** Myanmar
62 A2 **Taung-ngu** Myanmar
62 A2 **Taungup** Myanmar
74 B1 **Taunsa** Pak.
99 B4 **Taunton** U.K.
101 C2 **Taunus** *hills* Ger.
54 C1 **Taupo** N.Z.
54 C1 **Taupo, Lake** N.Z.
88 B2 **Tauragė** Lith.
54 C1 **Tauranga** N.Z.
139 E1 **Taureau, Réservoir** *resr* Can.
80 B2 **Taurus Mountains** *mts* Turkey
111 C3 **Tavas** Turkey
86 F3 **Tavda** Rus. Fed.
106 B2 **Tavira** Port.
99 A4 **Tavistock** U.K.
63 A2 **Tavoy** Myanmar
111 C3 **Tavşanlı** Turkey
99 A4 **Taw** *r.* U.K.
138 C2 **Tawas City** U.S.A.
61 C1 **Tawau** *Sabah* Malaysia
64 A3 **Tawitawi** *i.* Phil.
71 C3 **Tawu** Taiwan
145 C3 **Taxco** Mex.
76 B2 **Taxiatosh** Uzbek.
77 D3 **Taxkorgan** China

96 C2 **Tay** *r.* U.K.
96 C2 **Tay, Firth of** *est.* U.K.
96 B2 **Tay, Loch** *l.* U.K.
128 B2 **Taylor** Can.
138 C2 **Taylor** *MI* U.S.A.
143 D2 **Taylor** *TX* U.S.A.
138 B3 **Taylorville** U.S.A.
78 A2 **Taymā'** Saudi Arabia
83 H2 **Taymura** *r.* Rus. Fed.
83 H2 **Taymyr, Ozero** *l.* Rus. Fed.
Taymyr, Poluostrov Rus. Fed. *see* Taymyr Peninsula
83 G2 **Taymyr Peninsula** *pen.* Rus. Fed.
63 B2 **Tây Ninh** Vietnam
96 C2 **Tayport** U.K.
64 A2 **Taytay** Phil.
76 C3 **Tayyebād** Iran
77 C1 **Tayynsha** Kazakh.
82 G2 **Taz** *r.* Rus. Fed.
114 B1 **Taza** Morocco
129 D2 **Tazin Lake** Can.
86 G2 **Tazovskaya Guba** *sea chan.* Rus. Fed.
81 C1 **T'bilisi** Georgia
91 E2 **Tbilisskaya** Rus. Fed.
118 B3 **Tchibanga** Gabon
115 C3 **Tchin-Tabaradene** Niger
118 B2 **Tchollíré** Cameroon
103 D1 **Tczew** Pol.
144 B2 **Teacapán** Mex.
54 A3 **Te Anau** N.Z.
54 A3 **Te Anau, Lake** N.Z.
145 C3 **Teapa** Mex.
54 C1 **Te Awamutu** N.Z.
115 C1 **Tébessa** Alg.
60 B2 **Tebingtinggi** Indon.
60 A1 **Tebingtinggi** Indon.
144 A1 **Tecate** Mex.
114 B4 **Techiman** Ghana
144 B3 **Tecomán** Mex.
144 B2 **Tecoripa** Mex.
144 B2 **Tecuala** Mex.
110 C1 **Tecuci** Romania
76 C3 **Tedzhen** Turkm.
76 C3 **Tedzhen** *r.* Turkm.
68 C1 **Teeli** Rus. Fed.
98 C2 **Tees** *r.* U.K.
111 C3 **Tefenni** Turkey
60 B2 **Tegal** Indon.
146 B3 **Tegucigalpa** Hond.
115 C3 **Teguidda-n-Tessoumt** Niger
129 E1 **Tehek Lake** Can.
Teheran Iran *see* Tehrān
114 B4 **Téhini** Côte d'Ivoire
81 D2 **Tehrān** Iran
145 C3 **Tehuacán** Mex.
Tehuantepec, Golfo de Mex. *see* Tehuantepec, Gulf of
145 C3 **Tehuantepec, Gulf of** *g.* Mex.
145 C3 **Tehuantepec, Istmo de** *isth.* Mex.
114 A2 **Teide, Pico del** *vol.* Canary Islands
99 A3 **Teifi** *r.* U.K.
Teixeira de Sousa Angola *see* Luau
Tejo *r.* Port. *see* Tagus
145 B3 **Tejupilco** Mex.
54 B2 **Tekapo, Lake** N.Z.
145 D2 **Tekax** Mex.
116 B3 **Tekezë Wenz** *r.* Eritrea/Eth.
111 C2 **Tekirdağ** Turkey
54 C1 **Te Kuiti** N.Z.
75 C1 **Tel** *r.* India
81 C1 **T'elavi** Georgia
80 B2 **Tel Aviv-Yafo** Israel
145 D2 **Telchac Puerto** Mex.
128 A2 **Telegraph Creek** Can.
154 B2 **Telêmaco Borba** Brazil
61 C1 **Telen** *r.* Indon.
50 B2 **Telfer Mining Centre** Austr.
99 B3 **Telford** U.K.
128 B2 **Telkwa** Can.
60 A2 **Telo** Indon.
86 E2 **Tel'pos-Iz, Gora** *mt.* Rus. Fed.
88 B2 **Telšiai** Lith.
60 B2 **Telukbatang** Indon.
60 A1 **Telukdalam** Indon.
60 B1 **Teluk Intan** Malaysia
114 C4 **Tema** Ghana
130 C3 **Temagami Lake** Can.
60 C2 **Temanggung** Indon.
123 C2 **Temba** S. Africa
83 H2 **Tembenchi** *r.* Rus. Fed.
60 B2 **Tembilahan** Indon.
123 C2 **Tembisa** S. Africa
120 A1 **Tembo Aluma** Angola
Tembué Moz. *see* Chifunde
99 B3 **Teme** *r.* U.K.
135 C4 **Temecula** U.S.A.
63 B3 **Temengor, Tasik** *resr* Malaysia
60 B1 **Temerluh** Malaysia
77 D1 **Temirtau** Kazakh.
139 D1 **Témiscamingue, Lac** *l.* Can.
53 C2 **Temora** Austr.
142 A2 **Tempe** U.S.A.
143 D2 **Temple** U.S.A.
97 C2 **Templemore** Ireland
102 C1 **Templin** Ger.
145 C2 **Tempoal** Mex.
120 A2 **Tempué** Angola
91 D2 **Temryuk** Rus. Fed.
91 D2 **Temryukskiy Zaliv** *b.* Rus. Fed.
153 A3 **Temuco** Chile

54 B2 **Temuka** N.Z.
145 C2 **Tenabo** Mex.
143 E2 **Tenaha** U.S.A.
73 C3 **Tenali** India
63 A2 **Tenasserim** Myanmar
99 A4 **Tenby** U.K.
117 C3 **Tendaho** Eth.
105 D3 **Tende** France
105 D3 **Tende, Col de** *pass* France/Italy
73 D4 **Ten Degree Channel** India
114 A3 **Te-n-Dghâmcha, Sebkhet** *salt marsh* Maur.
67 D3 **Tendō** Japan
114 B3 **Ténenkou** Mali
115 C2 **Ténéré** *reg.* Niger
115 D3 **Ténéré, Erg du** *des.* Niger
115 D2 **Ténéré du Tafassâsset** *des.* Niger
114 A2 **Tenerife** *i.* Canary Is
107 D2 **Ténès** Alg.
61 C2 **Tengah, Kepulauan** *is* Indon.
Tengcheng China *see* Tengxian
62 A1 **Tengchong** China
61 C2 **Tenggarong** Indon.
70 A2 **Tengger Shamo** *des.* China
77 C1 **Tengiz, Ozero** *salt l.* Kazakh.
71 B3 **Tengxian** China
119 C4 **Tenke** Dem. Rep. Congo
114 B3 **Tenkodogo** Burkina
51 C1 **Tennant Creek** Austr.
140 C1 **Tennessee** *r.* U.S.A.
140 C1 **Tennessee** *state* U.S.A.
61 C1 **Tenom** *Sabah* Malaysia
145 C3 **Tenosique** Mex.
61 D2 **Tenteno** Indon.
53 D1 **Tenterfield** Austr.
141 D3 **Ten Thousand Islands** U.S.A.
154 B2 **Teodoro Sampaio** Brazil
155 D1 **Teófilo Otôni** Brazil
145 C3 **Teopisca** Mex.
59 C3 **Tepa** Indon.
144 B2 **Tepache** Mex.
54 B1 **Te Paki** N.Z.
144 B3 **Tepalcatepec** Mex.
144 B2 **Tepatitlán** Mex.
144 B2 **Tepehuanes** Mex.
109 D2 **Tepelenë** Albania
144 B2 **Tepic** Mex.
102 C1 **Teplice** Czech Rep.
89 E3 **Teploye** Rus. Fed.
90 B2 **Teplyk** Ukr.
54 C1 **Te Puke** N.Z.
144 B2 **Tequila** Mex.
49 K3 **Teraina** *i.* Kiribati
108 B2 **Teramo** Italy
52 B3 **Terang** Austr.
89 E3 **Terbuny** Rus. Fed.
90 B2 **Terebovlya** Ukr.
87 D4 **Terek** *r.* Rus. Fed.
154 C2 **Terenos** Brazil
151 E3 **Teresina** Brazil
155 D2 **Teresópolis** Brazil
63 A3 **Teressa Island** India
100 A3 **Tergnier** France
80 B1 **Terme** Turkey
108 B3 **Termini Imerese** *Sicily* Italy
145 C3 **Términos, Laguna de** *lag.* Mex.
77 C3 **Termiz** Uzbek.
109 B2 **Termoli** Italy
59 C2 **Ternate** Indon.
100 A2 **Terneuzen** Neth.
66 C1 **Terney** Rus. Fed.
108 B2 **Terni** Italy
90 B2 **Ternopil'** Ukr.
52 A2 **Terowie** Austr.
69 F1 **Terpeniya, Mys** *c.* Rus. Fed.
69 F1 **Terpeniya, Zaliv** *g.* Rus. Fed.
128 B2 **Terrace** Can.
130 B3 **Terrace Bay** Can.
122 B2 **Terra Firma** S. Africa
140 B3 **Terrebonne Bay** U.S.A.
138 B3 **Terre Haute** U.S.A.
131 E3 **Terrenceville** Can.
100 B1 **Terschelling** *i.* Neth.
108 A3 **Tertenia** *Sardinia* Italy
107 C1 **Teruel** Spain
92 H2 **Tervola** Fin.
109 C2 **Tešanj** Bos.-Herz.
116 B3 **Teseney** Eritrea
66 D3 **Teshio** Japan
66 D2 **Teshio-gawa** *r.* Japan
128 A1 **Teslin** Can.
128 A1 **Teslin Lake** Can.
154 B1 **Tesouro** Brazil
115 C3 **Tessaoua** Niger
99 C4 **Test** *r.* U.K.
121 C2 **Tete** Moz.
90 C1 **Teteriv** *r.* Ukr.
101 F1 **Teterow** Ger.
90 B2 **Tetiyiv** Ukr.
114 B1 **Tétouan** Morocco
110 B2 **Tetovo** Macedonia
Tetyukhe Rus. Fed. *see* Dal'negorsk
Teuchezhsk Rus. Fed. *see* Adygeysk
152 B2 **Teuco** *r.* Arg.
144 B2 **Teul de González Ortega** Mex.
101 D1 **Teutoburger Wald** *hills* Ger.
Tevere *r.* Italy *see* Tiber
54 A3 **Teviot** N.Z.
96 C3 **Teviot** *r.* U.K.
96 C3 **Teviothead** U.K.
61 C2 **Tewah** Indon.
51 E2 **Tewantin** Austr.

54 C2 **Te Wharau** N.Z.
99 B4 **Tewkesbury** U.K.
143 E2 **Texarkana** U.S.A.
53 D1 **Texas** Austr.
143 D2 **Texas** *state* U.S.A.
143 D2 **Texas** U.S.A.
143 E3 **Texas City** U.S.A.
145 C3 **Texcoco** Mex.
100 B1 **Texel** *i.* Neth.
143 D2 **Texoma, Lake** U.S.A.
123 C2 **Teyateyaneng** Lesotho
87 F2 **Teykovo** Rus. Fed.
89 F2 **Teza** *r.* Rus. Fed.
75 D4 **Tezpur** India
72 D2 **Tezu** India
129 E1 **Tha-anne** *r.* Can.
123 C2 **Thabana-Ntlenyana** *mt.* Lesotho
123 C2 **Thaba Nchu** S. Africa
123 C2 **Thaba Putsoa** *mt.* Lesotho
123 C2 **Thaba-Tseka** Lesotho
123 C1 **Thabazimbi** S. Africa
123 C2 **Thabong** S. Africa
63 A2 **Thagyettaw** Myanmar
62 B1 **Thai Binh** Vietnam
63 B2 **Thailand** *country* Asia
63 B2 **Thailand, Gulf of** Asia
62 B1 **Thai Nguyên** Vietnam
62 B2 **Thakèk** Laos
74 B1 **Thal** Pak.
63 A3 **Thalang** Thai.
74 B1 **Thal Desert** Pak.
101 E2 **Thale (Harz)** Ger.
62 B2 **Tha Li** Thai.
53 C1 **Thallon** Austr.
123 C1 **Thamaga** Botswana
78 B3 **Thamar, Jabal** *mt.* Yemen
79 C3 **Thamarit** Oman
130 B3 **Thames** *r.* Can.
54 C1 **Thames** N.Z.
99 C4 **Thames** *est.* U.K.
99 C4 **Thames** *r.* U.K.
79 B3 **Thamūd** Yemen
Thana India *see* Thane
63 A2 **Thanbyuzayat** Myanmar
62 A1 **Thandwè** Myanmar
74 B3 **Thane** India
62 B2 **Thanh Hoa** Vietnam
73 B3 **Thanjavur** India
63 A2 **Thanlyin** Myanmar
74 A2 **Thano Bula Khan** Pak.
62 B1 **Than Uyen** Vietnam
74 A2 **Thar Desert** India/Pak.
52 B1 **Thargomindah** Austr.
81 C2 **Tharthār, Buḩayrat ath** *l.* Iraq
111 B2 **Thasos** Greece
111 B2 **Thasos** *i.* Greece
62 B1 **Thât Khê** Vietnam
62 A2 **Thaton** Myanmar
62 A1 **Thaungdut** Myanmar
62 A2 **Thayawadi** Myanmar
63 A2 **Thayetchaung** Myanmar
62 A2 **Thayetmyo** Myanmar
62 A1 **Thazi** Myanmar
146 C2 **The Bahamas** *country* West Indies
98 B2 **The Cheviot** *hill* U.K.
134 B1 **The Dalles** U.S.A.
136 C2 **Thedford** U.S.A.
53 D2 **The Entrance** Austr.
99 C3 **The Fens** *reg.* U.K.
114 A3 **The Gambia** *country* Africa
52 B3 **The Grampians** *mts* Austr.
The Great Oasis Egypt *see*
Wāḩāt al Khārijah
79 C2 **The Gulf** Asia
100 B1 **The Hague** Neth.
129 E1 **Thelon** *r.* Can.
101 E2 **Themar** Ger.
123 C2 **Thembalihle** S. Africa
96 A1 **The Minch** *sea chan.* U.K.
97 A1 **The Mullet** *b.* Ireland
99 C4 **The Needles** *stack* U.K.
150 C3 **Theodore Roosevelt** *r.* Brazil
129 D2 **The Pas** Can.
111 B2 **Thermaïkos Kolpos** *g.* Greece
136 B2 **Thermopolis** U.S.A.
53 C3 **The Rock** Austr.
The Skaw *spit* Denmark *see*
Grenen
99 C4 **The Solent** *str.* U.K.
130 B3 **Thessalon** Can.
111 B2 **Thessaloniki** Greece
99 D3 **Thetford** U.K.
131 C3 **Thetford Mines** Can.
62 A1 **The Triangle** *mts* Myanmar
147 D3 **The Valley** Anguilla
131 D2 **Thévenet, Lac** *l.* Can.
99 D3 **The Wash** *b.* U.K.
99 D4 **The Weald** *reg.* U.K.
143 D2 **The Woodlands** U.S.A.
140 B3 **Thibodaux** U.S.A.
129 E2 **Thicket Portage** Can.
137 D1 **Thief River Falls** U.S.A.
Thiel Neth. *see* Tiel
105 C2 **Thiers** France
114 A3 **Thiès** Senegal
119 D3 **Thika** Kenya
73 B4 **Thiladhunmathi Atoll** Maldives
75 C2 **Thimphu** Bhutan
105 D2 **Thionville** France
111 C3 **Thira** Greece
111 C3 **Thira** *i.* Greece
98 C2 **Thirsk** U.K.
Thiruvananthapuram India *see*
Trivandrum
93 E4 **Thisted** Denmark
129 E1 **Thlewiaza** *r.* Can.

63 B3 **Thô Chu, Đao** *i.* Vietnam
62 A2 **Thoen** Thai.
123 D1 **Thohoyandou** S. Africa
101 E1 **Thomasburg** Ger.
97 C2 **Thomastown** Ireland
140 C2 **Thomasville** *AL* U.S.A.
141 D2 **Thomasville** *GA* U.S.A.
100 C2 **Thommen** Belgium
129 E2 **Thompson** Can.
128 E3 **Thompson** *r.* U.S.A.
134 C1 **Thompson Falls** U.S.A.
128 B2 **Thompson Sound** Can.
51 D2 **Thomson** *watercourse* Austr.
141 D2 **Thomson** U.S.A.
63 B2 **Thon Buri** Thai.
63 A2 **Thongwa** Myanmar
142 B1 **Thoreau** U.S.A.
96 C3 **Thornhill** U.K.
136 C3 **Thornton** U.S.A.
55 F2 **Thorshavnheiane** *reg.* Antarctica
123 C2 **Thota-ea-Moli** Lesotho
104 B2 **Thouars** France
62 A1 **Thoubal** India
134 D1 **Three Forks** U.S.A.
128 C2 **Three Hills** Can.
63 A2 **Three Pagodas Pass**
Myanmar/Thai.
114 B4 **Three Points, Cape** Ghana
138 B2 **Three Rivers** *MI* U.S.A.
143 D3 **Three Rivers** *TX* U.S.A.
Thrissur India *see* Trichur
63 B2 **Thu Dâu Môt** Vietnam
100 B2 **Thuin** Belgium
Thule *see* Qaanaaq
121 B3 **Thuli** Zimbabwe
102 B2 **Thun** Switz.
130 B3 **Thunder Bay** Can.
130 B3 **Thunder Bay** *b.* Can.
63 A3 **Thung Song** Thai.
101 E2 **Thüringer Becken** *reg.* Ger.
101 E2 **Thüringer Wald** *mts* Ger.
Thuringian Forest *mts* Ger. *see*
Thüringer Wald
97 C2 **Thurles** Ireland
59 D3 **Thursday Island** Austr.
96 C1 **Thurso** U.K.
96 C1 **Thurso** *r.* U.K.
55 R2 **Thurston Island** Antarctica
101 D1 **Thüster Berg** *hill* Ger.
121 C2 **Thyolo** Malawi
Thysville Dem. Rep. Congo *see*
Mbanza-Ngungu
79 C2 **Tiāb** Iran
151 E3 **Tianguá** Brazil
70 B2 **Tianjin** China
70 B2 **Tianjin** *mun.* China
71 A3 **Tianlin** China
70 B2 **Tianmen** China
69 E2 **Tianshan** China
70 A2 **Tianshui** China
70 A2 **Tianzhu** China
107 D2 **Tiaret** Alg.
114 B4 **Tiassalé** Côte d'Ivoire
154 B2 **Tibagi** Brazil
154 B2 **Tibagi** *r.* Brazil
118 B2 **Tibati** Cameroon
108 B2 **Tiber** *r.* Italy
Tiberias, Lake Israel *see*
Galilee, Sea of
115 D2 **Tibesti** *mts* Chad
75 C1 **Tibet** *aut. reg.* China
Tibet, Plateau of China *see*
Qingzang Gaoyuan
52 B1 **Tibooburra** Austr.
144 A2 **Tiburón, Isla** *i.* Mex.
114 B3 **Tichît** Maur.
114 A2 **Tichla** Western Sahara
105 D2 **Ticino** *r.* Italy/Switz.
139 E2 **Ticonderoga** U.S.A.
145 D2 **Ticul** Mex.
114 A3 **Tidjikja** Maur.
100 B2 **Tiel** Neth.
70 C1 **Tieling** China
75 B1 **Tielongtan** Aksai Chin
100 A2 **Tielt** Belgium
100 B2 **Tienen** Belgium
68 B2 **Tien Shan** *mts* China/Kyrg.
Tientsin China *see* Tianjin
Tientsin *mun.* China *see* Tianjin
93 G3 **Tierp** Sweden
145 C3 **Tierra Blanca** Mex.
145 C3 **Tierra Colorada** Mex.
153 B5 **Tierra del Fuego, Isla Grande de**
i. Arg./Chile
106 B1 **Tiétar, Valle de** *val.* Spain
154 C2 **Tietê** Brazil
154 B2 **Tietê** *r.* Brazil
138 C2 **Tiffin** U.S.A.
Tiflis Georgia *see* T'bilisi
141 D2 **Tifton** U.S.A.
90 B2 **Tighina** Moldova
75 C2 **Tigiria** India
118 B2 **Tignère** Cameroon
131 D3 **Tignish** Can.
150 B3 **Tigre** *r.* Ecuador/Peru
81 C2 **Tigris** *r.* Asia
114 A3 **Tiguent** Maur.
114 B2 **Tiguesmat** *hills* Maur.
115 D3 **Tigui** Chad
145 C2 **Tihuatlán** Mex.
144 A1 **Tijuana** Mex.
91 E2 **Tikhoretsk** Rus. Fed.
89 D2 **Tikhvin** Rus. Fed.
89 D2 **Tikhvinskaya Gryada** *ridge*
Rus. Fed.

157 F7 **Tiki Basin** *sea feature*
S. Pacific Ocean
54 C1 **Tikokino** N.Z.
81 C2 **Tikrīt** Iraq
83 J2 **Tiksi** Rus. Fed.
100 B2 **Tilburg** Neth.
152 B2 **Tilcara** Arg.
52 B1 **Tilcha** Austr.
114 C3 **Tilemsi, Vallée du** *watercourse*
Mali
114 C3 **Tillabéri** Niger
134 B1 **Tillamook** U.S.A.
63 A3 **Tillanchong Island** India
111 C3 **Tilos** *i.* Greece
52 B2 **Tilpa** Austr.
86 F2 **Til'tim** Rus. Fed.
89 E3 **Tim** Rus. Fed.
86 D2 **Timanskiy Kryazh** *ridge*
Rus. Fed.
54 C2 **Timaru** N.Z.
91 D2 **Timashevsk** Rus. Fed.
Timashevskaya Rus. Fed. *see*
Timashevsk
114 B3 **Timbedgha** Maur.
50 C1 **Timber Creek** Austr.
114 B3 **Timbuktu** Mali
115 C3 **Timia** Niger
114 C2 **Timimoun** Alg.
110 B1 **Timiş** *r.* Romania
110 B1 **Timişoara** Romania
130 B3 **Timmins** Can.
89 E2 **Timokhino** Rus. Fed.
151 E3 **Timon** Brazil
59 C3 **Timor** *i.* Indon.
59 C3 **Timor Sea** Austr./Indon.
Timor Timur *country* Asia *see*
East Timor
93 G3 **Timrå** Sweden
78 B2 **Tin, Jabal** *hill* Saudi Arabia
114 B2 **Tindouf** Alg.
53 D1 **Tingha** Austr.
75 C2 **Tingri** China
93 F4 **Tingsryd** Sweden
92 E3 **Tingvoll** Norway
Tingzhou China *see* Changting
59 D2 **Tinian** *i.* N. Mariana Is
Tinnelvelly India *see* Tirunelveli
152 B2 **Tinogasta** Arg.
111 C3 **Tinos** Greece
111 C3 **Tinos** *i.* Greece
100 A3 **Tinqueux** France
115 C2 **Tinrhert, Plateau du** Alg.
62 A1 **Tinsukia** India
52 B3 **Tintinara** Austr.
136 C1 **Tioga** U.S.A.
107 D2 **Tipasa** Alg.
97 B2 **Tipperary** Ireland
151 E3 **Tiracambu, Serra do** *hills* Brazil
109 C2 **Tirana** Albania
Tiranë Albania *see* Tirana
108 B1 **Tirano** Italy
52 A1 **Tirari Desert** Austr.
90 B2 **Tiraspol** Moldova
122 A2 **Tiraz Mountains** Namibia
111 C3 **Tire** Turkey
96 A2 **Tiree** *i.* U.K.
Tîrgovişte Romania *see* Târgovişte
Tîrgu Frumos Romania *see*
Târgu Frumos
Tîrgu Jiu Romania *see* Târgu Jiu
Tîrgu Lăpuş Romania *see*
Târgu Lăpuş
Tîrgu Mureş Romania *see*
Târgu Mureş
Tîrgu Neamţ Romania *see*
Târgu Neamţ
Tîrgu Ocna Romania *see*
Târgu Ocna
74 B1 **Tirich Mir** *mt.* Pak.
Tîrnăveni Romania *see* Târnăveni
155 C1 **Tiros** Brazil
118 C2 **Tiroungoulou** C.A.R.
73 B3 **Tiruchchirappalli** India
73 B4 **Tirunelveli** India
73 B3 **Tirupati** India
73 B3 **Tiruppattur** India
73 B3 **Tiruppur** India
109 D1 **Tisa** *r.* Europe
Tisa *r.* Hungary *see* Tisza
129 D2 **Tisdale** Can.
107 D2 **Tissemsilt** Alg.
75 C2 **Tista** *r.* India
103 E2 **Tisza** *r.* Hungary
55 L1 **Titan Dome** *ice feature* Antarctica
Titicaca, Lago Bol./Peru *see*
Titicaca, Lake
152 B1 **Titicaca, Lake** *l.* Bol./Peru
75 C2 **Titlagarh** India
Titograd Serb. and Mont. *see*
Podgorica
Titova Mitrovica Serb.
and Mont. *see* Kosovska Mitrovica
Titovo Užice Serb. and
Mont. *see* Užice
Titovo Velenje Slovenia *see*
Velenje
Titov Veles Macedonia *see* Veles
Titov Vrbas Serb. and
Mont. *see* Vrbas
110 C2 **Titu** Romania
141 D3 **Titusville** U.S.A.
99 B4 **Tiverton** U.K.
108 B2 **Tivoli** Italy
79 C2 **Ţīwī** Oman

63 A2 **Ti-ywa** Myanmar
145 D2 **Tizimín** Mex.
107 D2 **Tizi Ouzou** Alg.
114 B2 **Tiznit** Morocco
92 G2 **Tjaktjajaure** *l.* Sweden
Tjirebon Indon. *see* Cirebon
145 C3 **Tlacotalpán** Mex.
144 B2 **Tlahualilo** Mex.
145 C3 **Tlalnepantla** Mex.
145 C3 **Tlapa** Mex.
145 C3 **Tlaxcala** Mex.
145 C3 **Tlaxiaco** Mex.
114 B1 **Tlemcen** Alg.
123 C1 **Tlokweng** Botswana
128 B2 **Toad River** Can.
121 D2 **Toamasina** Madag.
60 A1 **Toba, Danau** *l.* Indon.
Toba, Lake Indon. *see*
Toba, Danau
74 A1 **Toba and Kakar Ranges** *mts* Pak.
147 D3 **Tobago** *i.* Trin. and Tob.
59 C2 **Tobelo** Indon.
130 B3 **Tobermory** Can.
96 A2 **Tobermory** U.K.
129 D2 **Tobin Lake** Can.
60 B2 **Toboali** Indon.
76 C1 **Tobol** *r.* Kazakh./Rus. Fed.
86 F3 **Tobol'sk** Rus. Fed.
Tobruk Libya *see* Tubruq
151 E3 **Tocantinópolis** Brazil
151 E3 **Tocantins** *r.* Brazil
141 D2 **Toccoa** U.S.A.
108 A1 **Toce** *r.* Italy
152 A2 **Tocopilla** Chile
53 C3 **Tocumwal** Austr.
59 C3 **Todeli** Indon.
108 B2 **Todi** Italy
144 A2 **Todos Santos** Mex.
128 B3 **Tofino** Can.
96 □ **Toft** U.K.
61 D2 **Togian** *i.* Indon.
61 D2 **Togian, Kepulauan** *is* Indon.
Togliatti Rus. Fed. *see* Tol'yatti
114 C4 **Togo** *country* Africa
74 B2 **Tohana** India
141 D3 **Tohopekaliga, Lake** U.S.A.
126 C2 **Tok** U.S.A.
116 B3 **Tokar** Sudan
69 E3 **Tokara-rettō** *is* Japan
91 E1 **Tokarevka** Rus. Fed.
80 B1 **Tokat** Turkey
49 J4 **Tokelau** *terr.* S. Pacific Ocean
91 D2 **Tokmak** Ukr.
77 D2 **Tokmok** Kyrg.
54 C1 **Tokoroa** N.Z.
68 B2 **Toksun** China
67 B4 **Tokushima** Japan
67 C3 **Tōkyō** Japan
121 D3 **Tôlañaro** Madag.
Tolbukhin Bulg. *see* Dobrich
154 B2 **Toledo** Brazil
106 C2 **Toledo** Spain
138 C2 **Toledo** U.S.A.
106 C2 **Toledo, Montes de** *mts* Spain
140 B2 **Toledo Bend Reservoir** U.S.A.
121 D3 **Toliara** Madag.
Toling China *see* Zanda
61 D1 **Tolitoli** Indon.
108 B1 **Tolmezzo** Italy
108 B1 **Tolmin** Slovenia
103 D2 **Tolna** Hungary
104 B3 **Tolosa** Spain
145 C3 **Toluca** Mex.
87 D3 **Tol'yatti** Rus. Fed.
138 A2 **Tomah** U.S.A.
138 B1 **Tomahawk** U.S.A.
66 D2 **Tomakomai** Japan
61 D2 **Tomali** Indon.
61 C1 **Tomani** *Sabah* Malaysia
103 E1 **Tomar** Port.
103 E1 **Tomaszów Lubelski** Pol.
103 E1 **Tomaszów Mazowiecki** Pol.
144 B3 **Tomatlán** Mex.
154 C2 **Tomazina** Brazil
140 C2 **Tombigbee** *r.* U.S.A.
120 A1 **Tomboco** Angola
155 D2 **Tombos** Brazil
Tombouctou Mali *see* Timbuktu
142 A2 **Tombstone** U.S.A.
120 A2 **Tombua** Angola
123 C1 **Tom Burke** S. Africa
106 C2 **Tomelloso** Spain
53 C2 **Tomingley** Austr.
61 D2 **Tomini, Teluk** *g.* Indon.
109 C2 **Tomislavgrad** Bos.-Herz.
103 D2 **Tompa** Hungary
50 A2 **Tom Price** Austr.
82 G3 **Tomsk** Rus. Fed.
93 F4 **Tomtabacken** *hill* Sweden
83 K2 **Tomtor** Rus. Fed.
145 C3 **Tonalá** Mex.
150 C3 **Tonantins** Brazil
99 D4 **Tonbridge** U.K.
59 C2 **Tondano** Indon.
49 J5 **Tonga** *country* S. Pacific Ocean
123 D2 **Tongaat** S. Africa
49 J6 **Tongatapu Group** *is* Tonga
71 B3 **Tongcheng** China
70 A2 **Tongchuan** China
71 A3 **Tongdao** China
65 B2 **Tongduch'ŏn** S. Korea
100 B2 **Tongeren** Belgium
65 B2 **Tonghae** S. Korea
71 A3 **Tonghai** China
65 B1 **Tonghua** China

65 B2 Tongjosŏn-man *b.* N. Korea
62 B1 Tongking, Gulf of China/Vietnam
69 E2 Tongliao China
70 B2 Tongling China
52 B2 Tongo Austr.
Tongquan China *see* Malong
71 A3 Tongren China
75 D2 Tongsa Bhutan
70 B2 Tongshan China
Tongshi China *see* Wuzhishan
Tongtian He *r.* China *see* Yangtze
96 B1 Tongue U.K.
Tongxian China *see* Tongzhou
65 B3 T'ongyŏng S. Korea
69 E2 Tongyu China
65 A1 Tongyuanpu China
70 B2 Tongzhou China
71 A3 Tongzi China
119 C2 Tonj Sudan
74 B2 Tonk India
81 D2 Tonkābon Iran
Tônlé Sab *l.* Cambodia *see* Tonle Sap
63 B2 Tonle Sap *l.* Cambodia
135 C3 Tonopah U.S.A.
93 F4 Tønsberg Norway
135 D2 Tooele U.S.A.
52 B3 Tooleybuc Austr.
53 D1 Toowoomba Austr.
137 D3 Topeka U.S.A.
144 B2 Topia Mex.
144 B2 Topolobampo Mex.
86 C2 Topozero, Ozero *l.* Rus. Fed.
134 B1 Toppenish U.S.A.
111 C3 Torbalı Turkey
76 B3 Torbat-e Heydariyeh Iran
76 C3 Torbat-e Jām Iran
131 E3 Torbay Can.
106 C1 Tordesillas Spain
107 C1 Tordesilos Spain
92 H2 Töre Sweden
107 D1 Torelló Spain
100 B1 Torenberg *hill* Neth.
Toretam Kazakh. *see* Baykonyr
101 F2 Torgau Ger.
100 A2 Torhout Belgium
Torino Italy *see* Turin
67 D1 Tori-shima *i.* Japan
117 B4 Torit Sudan
154 B1 Torixoreu Brazil
89 D2 Torkovichi Rus. Fed.
106 B1 Tormes *r.* Spain
92 H2 Torneälven *r.* Sweden
131 D2 Torngat Mountains Can.
92 H2 Tornio Fin.
106 B1 Toro Spain
130 C3 Toronto Can.
89 D2 Toropets Rus. Fed.
119 D2 Tororo Uganda
Toros Dağları Turkey *see* Taurus Mountains
52 B3 Torquay Austr.
99 B4 Torquay U.K.
135 C4 Torrance U.S.A.
106 B2 Torrão Port.
106 B1 Torre *mt.* Port.
107 D1 Torreblanca Spain
106 C1 Torrecerredo *mt.* Spain
106 B1 Torre de Moncorvo Port.
106 C1 Torrelavega Spain
106 C2 Torremolinos Spain
52 A2 Torrens, Lake *salt flat* Austr.
107 C2 Torrent Spain
144 B2 Torreón Mex.
106 B2 Torres Novas Port.
156 C6 Torres Strait Austr.
106 B2 Torres Vedras Port.
107 C2 Torrevieja Spain
96 B2 Torridon U.K.
96 B2 Torridon, Loch *b.* U.K.
106 C2 Torrijos Spain
139 E2 Torrington *CT* U.S.A.
136 C2 Torrington *WY* U.S.A.
107 D1 Torroella de Montgrí Spain
94 B3 Tórshavn Faroe Is
76 C2 To'rtko'l Uzbek.
108 A3 Tortolì *Sardinia* Italy
108 A2 Tortona Italy
107 D1 Tortosa Spain
81 D2 Torūd Iran
103 D1 Toruń Pol.
97 B1 Tory Island Ireland
97 B1 Tory Sound *sea chan.* Ireland
89 D2 Torzhok Rus. Fed.
67 B4 Tosashimizu Japan
122 B2 Tosca S. Africa
108 A2 Toscano, Arcipelago *is* Italy
Toshkent *see* Tashkent
89 D2 Tosno Rus. Fed.
68 C1 Tosontsengel Mongolia
152 B2 Tostado Arg.
101 D1 Tostedt Ger.
80 B1 Tosya Turkey
86 D3 Tot'ma Rus. Fed.
151 D2 Totness Suriname
67 B3 Tottori Japan
114 B4 Touba Côte d'Ivoire
114 B1 Toubkal, Jbel *mt.* Morocco
118 B2 Touboro Cameroon
114 B3 Tougan Burkina
115 C1 Touggourt Alg.
105 D2 Toul France
71 C3 Touliu Taiwan
105 D3 Toulon France
104 C3 Toulouse France

Tourane Vietnam *see* Đa Năng
104 B2 Tourlaville France
100 A2 Tournai Belgium
115 D2 Tourndo, Oued *watercourse* Alg./Niger
105 C2 Tournus France
151 F3 Touros Brazil
104 C2 Tours France
115 D2 Toussidé, Pic *mt.* Chad
122 B3 Touwsrivier S. Africa
150 B2 Tovar Venez.
66 D2 Towada Japan
134 D1 Townsend U.S.A.
51 D1 Townsville Austr.
61 D2 Towori, Teluk *b.* Indon.
77 E2 Toxkan He *r.* China
66 D2 Tōya-ko *l.* Japan
67 C3 Toyama Japan
67 C4 Toyohashi Japan
67 C3 Toyota Japan
115 C1 Tozeur Tunisia
81 C1 Tqvarch'eli Georgia
Trâblous Lebanon *see* Tripoli
80 B1 Trabzon Turkey
106 B2 Trafalgar, Cabo *c.* Spain
128 C3 Trail Can.
88 B3 Trakai Lith.
97 B2 Tralee Ireland
Trá Li Ireland *see* Tralee
97 C2 Tramore Ireland
93 F4 Tranås Sweden
63 A3 Trang Thai.
59 C3 Trangan *i.* Indon.
55 L2 Transantarctic Mountains Antarctica
110 B1 Transylvanian Alps *mts* Romania
108 B3 Trapani *Sicily* Italy
53 C3 Traralgon Austr.
63 B2 Trat Thai.
102 C2 Traunstein Ger.
54 B2 Travers, Mount N.Z.
138 B2 Traverse City U.S.A.
63 B3 Tra Vinh Vietnam
103 D2 Třebíč Czech Rep.
109 C2 Trebinje Bos.-Herz.
103 E2 Trebišov Slovakia
Trebizond Turkey *see* Trabzon
109 C1 Trebnje Slovenia
Trefynwy U.K. *see* Monmouth
153 C3 Treinta y Tres Uru.
153 B4 Trelew Arg.
93 F4 Trelleborg Sweden
130 C3 Tremblant, Mont *hill* Can.
109 C2 Tremiti, Isole *is* Italy
134 D2 Tremonton U.S.A.
107 D1 Tremp Spain
103 D2 Trenčín Slovakia
153 B3 Trenque Lauquén Arg.
Trent Italy *see* Trento
98 C3 Trent *r.* U.K.
108 B1 Trento Italy
139 D2 Trenton Can.
137 E2 Trenton *MO* U.S.A.
139 E2 Trenton *NJ* U.S.A.
131 E3 Trepassey Can.
153 B3 Tres Arroyos Arg.
155 C2 Três Corações Brazil
154 B2 Três Irmãos, Represa *resr* Brazil
154 B2 Três Lagoas Brazil
153 A4 Tres Lagos Arg.
155 C1 Três Marias, Represa *resr* Brazil
155 C2 Três Pontas Brazil
153 B4 Tres Puntas, Cabo *c.* Arg.
155 D2 Três Rios Brazil
101 F1 Treuenbrietzen Ger.
Treves Ger. *see* Trier
108 A1 Treviglio Italy
108 B1 Treviso Italy
99 A4 Trevose Head *hd* U.K.
109 C3 Tricase Italy
Trichinopoly India *see* Tiruchchirappalli
73 B3 Trichur India
53 C2 Trida Austr.
100 C3 Trier Ger.
108 B1 Trieste Italy
108 B1 Triglav *mt.* Slovenia
111 B3 Trikala Greece
59 D3 Trikora, Puncak *mt.* Indon.
97 C2 Trim Ireland
73 C4 Trincomalee Sri Lanka
154 C1 Trindade Brazil
148 H5 Trindade, Ilha da *i.* S. Atlantic Ocean
152 B1 Trinidad Bol.
147 D3 Trinidad *i.* Trin. and Tob.
136 C3 Trinidad U.S.A.
147 D3 Trinidad and Tobago *country* West Indies
143 E3 Trinity *r.* U.S.A.
131 E3 Trinity Bay Can.
111 B3 Tripoli Greece
80 B2 Tripoli Lebanon
115 D1 Tripoli Libya
75 D2 Tripura *state* India
113 B9 Tristan da Cunha *i.* S. Atlantic Ocean
73 B4 Trivandrum India
108 B2 Trivento Italy
103 D2 Trnava Slovakia
59 E3 Trobriand Islands P.N.G.
92 F2 Trofors Norway
109 C2 Trogir Croatia
109 C2 Troia Italy

100 C2 Troisdorf Ger.
106 C2 Trois Fourches, Cap des *c.* Morocco
130 C3 Trois-Rivières Can.
87 F3 Troitsk Rus. Fed.
86 E2 Troitsko-Pechorsk Rus. Fed.
151 D3 Trombetas *r.* Brazil
Tromelin Island Micronesia *see* Fais
123 C3 Trompsburg S. Africa
92 G2 Tromsø Norway
92 F3 Trondheim Norway
96 B3 Troon U.K.
89 E3 Trosna Rus. Fed.
97 C1 Trostan *hill* U.K.
128 C2 Trout Lake Alta Can.
128 B1 Trout Lake *l.* N.W.T. Can.
130 A2 Trout Lake *l.* Ont. Can.
99 B4 Trowbridge U.K.
140 C2 Troy *AL* U.S.A.
139 E2 Troy *NY* U.S.A.
105 C2 Troyes France
135 C3 Troy Peak U.S.A.
109 D2 Trstenik Serb. and Mont.
89 D3 Trubchevsk Rus. Fed.
Truc Giang Vietnam *see* Bên Tre
106 B1 Truchas Spain
Trucial Coast *country* Asia *see* United Arab Emirates
79 C2 Trucial Coast Asia
Trucial States *country* Asia *see* United Arab Emirates
146 B3 Trujillo Hond.
150 B3 Trujillo Peru
106 B2 Trujillo Spain
147 C4 Trujillo Venez.
Trujillo, Monte *mt.* Dom. Rep. *see* Duarte, Pico
140 B1 Trumann U.S.A.
131 D3 Truro Can.
99 A4 Truro U.K.
61 C1 Trus Madi, Gunung *mt.* Malaysia
142 B2 Truth or Consequences U.S.A.
103 D1 Trutnov Czech Rep.
93 F3 Trysil Norway
103 D1 Trzebiatów Pol.
103 D1 Trzebnica Pol.
68 B1 Tsagaannuur Mongolia
Tsaidam Basin China *see* Qaidam Pendi
121 □D2 Tsaratanana, Massif du *mts* Madag.
110 C2 Tsarevo Bulg.
122 A2 Tsaukaib Namibia
Tselinograd Kazakh. *see* Astana
Tsementnyy Rus. Fed. *see* Fokino
122 A2 Tses Namibia
122 B1 Tsetseng Botswana
68 C1 Tsetserleg Mongolia
Tsetserleg Mongolia *see* Halban
122 B2 Tshabong Botswana
122 B1 Tshane Botswana
91 D2 Tschikskoye Vodokhranilishche *resr* Rus. Fed.
118 B3 Tshela Dem. Rep. Congo
118 C3 Tshikapa Dem. Rep. Congo
118 C3 Tshikapa *r.* Dem. Rep. Congo
123 C2 Tshing S. Africa
123 D1 Tshipise S. Africa
118 C3 Tshitanzu Dem. Rep. Congo
120 B3 Tshootsha Botswana
118 C3 Tshuapa *r.* Dem. Rep. Congo
Tshwane S. Africa *see* Pretoria
87 D4 Tsimlyanskoye Vodokhranilishche *resr* Rus. Fed.
Tsinan China *see* Jinan
Tsingtao China *see* Qingdao
Tsining China *see* Jining
121 □D2 Tsiroanomandidy Madag.
Tsitsihar China *see* Qiqihar
76 A2 Ts'khinvali Georgia
123 C3 Tsomo S. Africa
67 C4 Tsu Japan
67 D3 Tsuchiura Japan
66 D2 Tsugarū-kaikyō *str.* Japan
Tsugaru Strait Japan *see* Tsugarū-kaikyō
120 A2 Tsumeb Namibia
122 A1 Tsumis Park Namibia
120 B2 Tsumkwe Namibia
67 C3 Tsuruga Japan
66 C3 Tsuruoka Japan
67 A4 Tsushima *is* Japan
67 B3 Tsuyama Japan
123 C2 Tswelelang S. Africa
88 C3 Tsyelyakhany Belarus
91 C2 Tsyurupyns'k Ukr.
Tthenaagoo Can. *see* Nahanni Butte
59 C3 Tual Indon.
97 B2 Tuam Ireland
54 A3 Tuapeka Mouth N.Z.
91 D3 Tuapse Rus. Fed.
54 A3 Tuatapere N.Z.
142 A1 Tuba City U.S.A.
61 C2 Tuban Indon.
152 D2 Tubarão Brazil
102 B2 Tübingen Ger.
115 E1 Tubruq Libya
49 L6 Tubuai Islands *is* Fr. Polynesia
144 A1 Tubutama Mex.
152 C2 Tucavaca Bol.
128 B1 Tuchitua Can.

142 A2 Tucson U.S.A.
143 C1 Tucumcari U.S.A.
150 C2 Tucupita Venez.
151 E1 Tucuruí Brazil
151 E1 Tucuruí, Represa *resr* Brazil
107 C1 Tudela Spain
106 B1 Tuela *r.* Port.
157 F2 Tufts Abyssal Plain *sea feature* N. Pacific Ocean
123 C3 Tugela *r.* S. Africa
64 B2 Tuguegarao Phil.
106 B1 Tui Spain
59 C3 Tukangbesi, Kepulauan *is* Indon.
126 D2 Tuktoyaktuk Can.
88 B2 Tukums Latvia
119 D3 Tukuyu Tanz.
145 C2 Tula Mex.
89 E3 Tula Rus. Fed.
Tulach Mhór Rep. of Ireland *see* Tullamore
145 C2 Tulancingo Mex.
135 C3 Tulare U.S.A.
142 B2 Tularosa U.S.A.
110 C1 Tulcea Romania
90 B2 Tul'chyn Ukr.
129 E1 Tulemalu Lake Can.
143 C2 Tulia U.S.A.
128 B1 Tulita Can.
140 C1 Tullahoma U.S.A.
53 C2 Tullamore Austr.
97 C2 Tullamore Ireland
104 C2 Tulle France
97 C2 Tullow Ireland
51 D1 Tully Austr.
143 D1 Tulsa U.S.A.
126 B2 Tuluksak U.S.A.
83 H3 Tulun Rus. Fed.
150 B2 Tumaco Col.
123 C2 Tumahole S. Africa
93 G4 Tumba Sweden
118 B3 Tumba, Lac *l.* Dem. Rep. Congo
61 C2 Tumbangtiti Indon.
53 C3 Tumbarumba Austr.
150 A3 Tumbes Peru
128 B2 Tumbler Ridge Can.
52 A2 Tumby Bay Austr.
65 B1 Tumen China
150 C2 Tumereng Guyana
64 A3 Tumindao *i.* Phil.
74 A2 Tump Pak.
151 D2 Tumucumaque, Serra *hills* Brazil
53 C3 Tumut Austr.
99 D4 Tunbridge Wells, Royal U.K.
80 B2 Tunceli Turkey
53 D2 Tuncurry Austr.
118 A1 Tundun-Wada Nigeria
119 D3 Tunduru Tanz.
110 C2 Tundzha *r.* Bulg.
128 B1 Tungsten Can.
115 D1 Tunis Tunisia
108 B3 Tunis, Golfe de *g.* Tunisia
115 C1 Tunisia *country* Africa
150 B2 Tunja Col.
92 F3 Tunnsjøen *l.* Norway
Tunxi China *see* Huangshan
154 B2 Tupã Brazil
154 C1 Tupaciguara Brazil
140 C2 Tupelo U.S.A.
152 B2 Tupiza Bol.
83 H2 Tura Rus. Fed.
86 F3 Tura *r.* Rus. Fed.
78 B2 Turabah Saudi Arabia
83 H3 Turana, Khrebet *mts* Rus. Fed.
54 C1 Turangi N.Z.
76 B2 Turan Lowland Asia
77 D2 Turar Ryskulov Kazakh.
78 A1 Turayf Saudi Arabia
88 B2 Turba Estonia
74 A2 Turbat Pak.
150 B2 Turbo Col.
110 B1 Turda Romania
Turfan China *see* Turpan
76 C2 Turgay Kazakh.
76 C1 Turgayskaya Stolovaya Strana *reg.* Kazakh.
110 C2 Tŭrgovishte Bulg.
111 C3 Turgutlu Turkey
80 B1 Turhal Turkey
107 C2 Turia *r.* Spain
108 A1 Turin Italy
86 F3 Turinsk Rus. Fed.
90 A1 Turiya *r.* Ukr.
90 A1 Turiys'k Ukr.
90 A2 Turka Ukr.
119 D2 Turkana, Lake *salt l.* Eth./Kenya
77 D2 Turkestan Kazakh.
103 E2 Türkeve Hungary
80 B2 Turkey *country* Asia/Europe
50 B1 Turkey Creek Austr.
76 B2 Turkmenabat Turkm.
76 B2 Turkmenbashi Turkm.
76 B2 Turkmenistan *country* Asia
Turkmeniya *country* Asia *see* Turkmenistan
Turkmenskaya S.S.R. *admin. reg.* Asia *see* Turkmenistan
147 C2 Turks and Caicos Islands *terr.* West Indies
147 C2 Turks Islands Turks and Caicos Is
93 H3 Turku Fin.
119 D2 Turkwel *watercourse* Kenya
135 B3 Turlock U.S.A.
155 D1 Turmalina Brazil
54 C2 Turnagain, Cape N.Z.

146 B3 **Turneffe Islands** Belize
100 B2 **Turnhout** Belgium
129 D2 **Turnor Lake** Can.
Tŭrnovo Bulg. *see* Veliko Tŭrnovo
110 B2 **Turnu Măgurele** Romania
68 B2 **Turpan** China
96 C2 **Turriff** U.K.
64 A3 **Turtle Islands** Phil.
77 D2 **Turugart Pass** China/Kyrg.
82 G2 **Turukhansk** Rus. Fed.
140 C2 **Tuscaloosa** U.S.A.
140 C2 **Tuskegee** U.S.A.
81 C2 **Tutak** Turkey
89 E2 **Tutayev** Rus. Fed.
73 B4 **Tuticorin** India
121 C1 **Tutubu** Tanz.
49 J5 **Tutuila** *i.* American Samoa
120 B3 **Tutume** Botswana
93 H3 **Tuusula** Fin.
49 I4 **Tuvalu** *country* S. Pacific Ocean
78 B2 **Tuwayq, Jabal** *hills* Saudi Arabia
78 B2 **Tuwayq, Jabal** *mts* Saudi Arabia
78 A2 **Tuwwal** Saudi Arabia
144 B2 **Tuxpan** Mex.
145 C3 **Tuxpan** Mex.
145 C3 **Tuxtla Gutiérrez** Mex.
62 B1 **Tuyên Quang** Vietnam
63 B2 **Tuy Hoa** Vietnam
80 B2 **Tuz, Lake** *salt l.* Turkey
Tuz Gölü *salt l.* Turkey *see* Tuz, Lake
81 C2 **Tuz Khurmātū** Iraq
109 C2 **Tuzla** Bos.-Herz.
91 E2 **Tuzlov** *r.* Rus. Fed.
89 E2 **Tver'** Rus. Fed.
98 B2 **Tweed** *r.* U.K.
53 D1 **Tweed Heads** Austr.
122 A2 **Twee Rivier** Namibia
135 C4 **Twentynine Palms** U.S.A.
131 E3 **Twillingate** Can.
134 D2 **Twin Falls** U.S.A.
54 B2 **Twizel** *South I.* N.Z.
137 E1 **Two Harbors** U.S.A.
128 C2 **Two Hills** Can.
Tyddewi U.K. *see* St David's
143 D2 **Tyler** U.S.A.
83 J3 **Tynda** Rus. Fed.
Tyndinskiy Rus. Fed. *see* Tynda
96 B2 **Tyndrum** U.K.
98 C2 **Tyne** *r.* England U.K.
95 C2 **Tyne** *r.* Scotland U.K.
93 F3 **Tynset** Norway
80 B2 **Tyre** Lebanon
69 E1 **Tyrma** Rus. Fed.
111 B3 **Tyrnavos** Greece
52 B3 **Tyrrell, Lake** *dry lake* Austr.
108 B2 **Tyrrhenian Sea** France/Italy
76 B2 **Tyub-Karagan, Mys** *pt* Kazakh.
87 E3 **Tyul'gan** Rus. Fed.
86 F3 **Tyumen'** Rus. Fed.
83 J2 **Tyung** *r.* Rus. Fed.
Tyuratam Kazakh. *see* Baykonyr
99 A4 **Tywi** *r.* U.K.
123 D1 **Tzaneen** S. Africa

U

Uaco Congo Angola *see* Waku-Kungo
120 B2 **Uamanda** Angola
150 C3 **Uarini** Brazil
150 C3 **Uaupés** Brazil
155 D2 **Ubá** Brazil
155 D1 **Ubaí** Brazil
151 F4 **Ubaitaba** Brazil
118 B3 **Ubangi** *r.* C.A.R./ Dem. Rep. Congo
Ubangi-Shari *country* Africa *see* Central African Republic
67 B4 **Ube** Japan
106 C2 **Úbeda** Spain
154 C1 **Uberaba** Brazil
154 C1 **Uberlândia** Brazil
123 D2 **Ubombo** S. Africa
63 B2 **Ubon Ratchathani** Thai.
119 C3 **Ubundu** Dem. Rep. Congo
150 B3 **Ucayali** *r.* Peru
100 B2 **Uccle** Belgium
74 B2 **Uch** Pak.
77 E2 **Ucharal** Kazakh.
66 D2 **Uchiura-wan** *b.* Japan
76 C2 **Uchquduq** Uzbek.
83 J3 **Uchur** *r.* Rus. Fed.
99 D4 **Uckfield** U.K.
128 B3 **Ucluelet** Can.
83 I2 **Udachnyy** Rus. Fed.
74 B2 **Udaipur** India
91 C1 **Uday** *r.* Ukr.
93 F4 **Uddevalla** Sweden
92 G2 **Uddjaure** *l.* Sweden
100 B2 **Uden** Neth.
74 B1 **Udhampur** Jammu and Kashmir
108 B1 **Udine** Italy
89 E2 **Udomlya** Rus. Fed.
62 B2 **Udon Thani** Thai.
73 B3 **Udupi** India
83 K3 **Udyl', Ozero** *l.* Rus. Fed.
67 C3 **Ueda** Japan
61 D2 **Uekuli** Indon.
118 C2 **Uele** *r.* Dem. Rep. Congo
83 N2 **Uelen** Rus. Fed.
101 E1 **Uelzen** Ger.
119 C2 **Uere** *r.* Dem. Rep. Congo

87 E3 **Ufa** Rus. Fed.
119 D3 **Ugalla** *r.* Tanz.
119 D2 **Uganda** *country* Africa
69 F1 **Uglegorsk** Rus. Fed.
89 E2 **Uglich** Rus. Fed.
89 D2 **Uglovka** Rus. Fed.
66 B2 **Uglovoye** Rus. Fed.
89 D3 **Ugra** Rus. Fed.
103 D2 **Uherské Hradiště** Czech Rep.
Uibhist a' Deas *i.* U.K. *see* South Uist
Uibhist a' Tuath *i.* U.K. *see* North Uist
101 E2 **Uichteritz** Ger.
96 A2 **Uig** U.K.
120 A1 **Uíge** Angola
65 B2 **Ŭijŏngbu** S. Korea
65 A1 **Ŭiju** N. Korea
135 D2 **Uinta Mountains** U.S.A.
120 A3 **Uis Mine** Namibia
65 B2 **Ŭisŏng** S. Korea
123 C3 **Uitenhage** S. Africa
100 C1 **Uithuizen** Neth.
131 D2 **Uivak, Cape** Can.
Ujiyamada Japan *see* Ise
74 B2 **Ujjain** India
Ujung Pandang Indon. *see* Makassar
89 F3 **Ukholovo** Rus. Fed.
Ukhta Rus. Fed. *see* Kalevala
86 E2 **Ukhta** Rus. Fed.
135 B3 **Ukiah** U.S.A.
127 I2 **Ukkusissat** Greenland
88 B2 **Ukmergė** Lith.
90 C2 **Ukraine** *country* Europe
Ukrainskaya S.S.R. *admin. reg.* Europe *see* Ukraine
Ulaanbaatar Mongolia *see* Ulan Bator
68 C1 **Ulaangom** Mongolia
59 E3 **Ulamona** P.N.G.
70 A2 **Ulan** China
69 D1 **Ulan Bator** Mongolia
Ulanhad China *see* Chifeng
69 E1 **Ulanhot** China
87 D4 **Ulan-Khol** Rus. Fed.
69 D1 **Ulan-Ude** Rus. Fed.
75 D1 **Ulan Ul Hu** *l.* China
65 B2 **Ulchin** S. Korea
Uleåborg Fin. *see* Oulu
88 C2 **Ülenurme** Estonia
74 B3 **Ulhasnagar** India
69 D1 **Uliastai** China
68 C1 **Uliastay** Mongolia
59 D2 **Ulithi** *atoll* Micronesia
53 D3 **Ulladulla** Austr.
96 B2 **Ullapool** U.K.
98 B2 **Ullswater** *l.* U.K.
65 C2 **Ullŭng-do** *i.* S. Korea
102 B2 **Ulm** Ger.
65 B2 **Ulsan** S. Korea
96 □ **Ulsta** U.K.
97 C1 **Ulster** *reg.* Ireland/U.K.
52 B3 **Ultima** Austr.
145 D3 **Ulúa** *r.* Hond.
111 C3 **Ulubey** Turkey
111 D3 **Uluborlu** Turkey
111 C2 **Uludağ** *mt.* Turkey
123 D2 **Ulundi** S. Africa
77 E2 **Ulungur Hu** *l.* China
Uluqsaqtuuq Can. *see* Holman
50 C2 **Uluru** *hill* Austr.
98 B2 **Ulverston** U.K.
90 C2 **Ul'yanovka** Ukr.
87 D3 **Ul'yanovsk** Rus. Fed.
136 C3 **Ulysses** U.S.A.
90 C2 **Uman'** Ukr.
86 C2 **Umba** Rus. Fed.
59 D3 **Umboi** *i.* P.N.G.
59 D3 **Umbukul** P.N.G.
92 H3 **Umeå** Sweden
92 H3 **Umeälven** *r.* Sweden
123 D2 **Umhlanga Rocks** S. Africa
127 J2 **Umiiviip Kangertiva** *inlet* Greenland
126 E2 **Umingmaktok** Can.
123 D2 **Umlazi** S. Africa
78 A2 **Umm al Birak** Saudi Arabia
79 C2 **Umm as Samīm** *salt flat* Oman
116 A3 **Umm Keddada** Sudan
78 A2 **Umm Lajj** Saudi Arabia
78 A2 **Umm Mukhbār, Jabal** *hill* Saudi Arabia
116 B3 **Umm Ruwaba** Sudan
115 E1 **Umm Sa'ad** Libya
134 B2 **Umpqua** *r.* U.S.A.
120 A2 **Umpulo** Angola
Umtali Zimbabwe *see* Mutare
123 C3 **Umtata** S. Africa
123 D3 **Umtentweni** S. Africa
154 B3 **Umuarama** Brazil
123 C3 **Umzimkulu** S. Africa
109 C1 **Una** *r.* Bos.-Herz./Croatia
155 E1 **Una** Brazil
154 C1 **Unaí** Brazil
126 B2 **Unalakleet** U.S.A.
78 B2 **'Unayzah** Saudi Arabia
136 B3 **Uncompahgre Peak** U.S.A.
52 B3 **Underbool** Austr.
136 C1 **Underwood** U.S.A.
89 D3 **Unecha** Rus. Fed.
53 C2 **Ungarie** Austr.
52 A2 **Ungarra** Austr.
127 H2 **Ungava, Péninsule d'** *pen.* Can.
131 D2 **Ungava Bay** Can.

65 C1 **Ungeny** Moldova *see* Ungheni
90 B2 **Ungheni** Moldova
Unguja *i.* Tanz. *see* Zanzibar Island
119 E3 **Ungwana Bay** Kenya
154 B3 **União da Vitória** Brazil
150 C3 **Unini** *r.* Brazil
134 C1 **Union** U.S.A.
140 C1 **Union City** U.S.A.
122 B3 **Uniondale** S. Africa
139 D3 **Uniontown** U.S.A.
79 C2 **United Arab Emirates** *country* Asia
United Arab Republic *country* Africa *see* Egypt
95 C3 **United Kingdom** *country* Europe
United Provinces *state* India *see* Uttar Pradesh
133 B3 **United States of America** *country* N. America
129 D2 **Unity** Can.
100 C2 **Unna** Ger.
96 □ **Unst** *i.* U.K.
101 E2 **Unstrut** *r.* Ger.
89 E3 **Upa** *r.* Rus. Fed.
119 C3 **Upemba, Lac** *l.* Dem. Rep. Congo
122 B2 **Upington** S. Africa
74 B2 **Upleta** India
49 J5 **Upolu** *i.* Samoa
134 B2 **Upper Alkali Lake** U.S.A.
128 C2 **Upper Arrow Lake** Can.
54 C2 **Upper Hutt** N.Z.
134 B2 **Upper Klamath Lake** U.S.A.
128 B1 **Upper Liard** Can.
97 C1 **Upper Lough Erne** *l.* U.K.
137 E1 **Upper Red Lake** U.S.A.
Upper Tunguska *r.* Rus. Fed. *see* Angara
Upper Volta *country* Africa *see* Burkina
93 G4 **Uppsala** Sweden
78 B2 **'Uqlat aş Şuqūr** Saudi Arabia
Urad Qianqi China *see* Xishanzui
76 B2 **Ural** *r.* Kazakh./Rus. Fed.
53 D2 **Uralla** Austr.
87 E3 **Ural Mountains** Rus. Fed.
76 B1 **Ural'sk** Kazakh.
Ural'skiy Khrebet *mts* Rus. Fed. *see* Ural Mountains
119 D3 **Urambo** Tanz.
53 C3 **Urana** Austr.
129 D2 **Uranium City** Can.
86 F2 **Uray** Rus. Fed.
98 C2 **Ure** *r.* U.K.
86 D3 **Uren'** Rus. Fed.
82 G2 **Urengoy** Rus. Fed.
144 A2 **Ures** Mex.
Urfa Turkey *see* Şanlıurfa
76 C2 **Urganch** Uzbek.
100 B1 **Urk** Neth.
111 C3 **Urla** Turkey
110 C2 **Urlaţi** Romania
81 C2 **Urmia** Iran
81 C2 **Urmia, Lake** *salt l.* Iran
109 D2 **Uroševac** Serb. and Mont.
144 B2 **Uruáchic** Mex.
151 E4 **Uruaçu** Brazil
144 B3 **Uruapan** Mex.
150 B4 **Urubamba** *r.* Peru
151 D3 **Urucara** Brazil
151 E3 **Uruçuí** Brazil
151 E3 **Uruçuí, Serra do** *hills* Brazil
151 D3 **Urucurituba** Brazil
152 C2 **Uruguaiana** Brazil
153 C3 **Uruguay** *country* S. America
Urumchi China *see* Ürümqi
68 B2 **Ürümqi** China
Urundi *country* Africa *see* Burundi
53 D2 **Urunga** Austr.
78 B3 **'Urūq al Awārik** *des.* Saudi Arabia
119 D3 **Urvira** Tanz.
110 C2 **Urziceni** Romania
67 B4 **Usa** Japan
86 E2 **Usa** *r.* Rus. Fed.
111 C3 **Uşak** Turkey
120 A3 **Usakos** Namibia
88 C3 **Ushachy** Belarus
82 G1 **Ushakova, Ostrov** *i.* Rus. Fed.
77 D2 **Ushtobe** Kazakh.
Ush-Tyube Kazakh. *see* Ushtobe
153 B5 **Ushuaia** Arg.
86 E2 **Usinsk** Rus. Fed.
99 B4 **Usk** U.K.
99 B4 **Usk** *r.* U.K.
88 C3 **Uskhodni** Belarus
89 E3 **Usman'** Rus. Fed.
86 D2 **Usogorsk** Rus. Fed.
104 C2 **Ussel** France
66 C1 **Ussuri** *r.* China/Rus. Fed.
66 B2 **Ussuriysk** Rus. Fed.
Ust'-Abakanskoye Rus. Fed. *see* Abakan
Ust'-Balyk Rus. Fed. *see* Nefteyugansk
91 E2 **Ust'-Donetskiy** Rus. Fed.
108 B3 **Ustica, Isola di** *i.* Sicily Italy
83 H3 **Ust'-Ilimsk** Rus. Fed.
86 E2 **Ust'-Ilych** Rus. Fed.
102 C1 **Ústí nad Labem** Czech Rep.
Ustinov Rus. Fed. *see* Izhevsk
103 D1 **Ustka** Pol.
83 L3 **Ust'-Kamchatsk** Rus. Fed.
77 E2 **Ust'-Kamenogorsk** Kazakh.
86 F2 **Ust'-Kara** Rus. Fed.
86 E2 **Ust'-Kulom** Rus. Fed.

83 I3 **Ust'-Kut** Rus. Fed.
91 D2 **Ust'-Labinsk** Rus. Fed.
Ust'-Labinskaya Rus. Fed. *see* Ust'-Labinsk
88 C2 **Ust'-Luga** Rus. Fed.
86 E2 **Ust'-Nem** Rus. Fed.
83 K2 **Ust'-Nera** Rus. Fed.
83 I2 **Ust'-Olenek** Rus. Fed.
83 K2 **Ust'-Omchug** Rus. Fed.
83 H3 **Ust'-Ordynskiy** Rus. Fed.
103 E2 **Ustrzyki Dolne** Pol.
86 E2 **Ust'-Tsil'ma** Rus. Fed.
86 D2 **Ust'-Ura** Rus. Fed.
76 B2 **Ustyurt Plateau** Kazakh./Uzbek.
89 E2 **Ustyuzhna** Rus. Fed.
146 B3 **Usulután** El Salvador
Usumbura Burundi *see* Bujumbura
89 D2 **Usvyaty** Rus. Fed.
135 D3 **Utah** *state* U.S.A.
135 D2 **Utah Lake** U.S.A.
88 C2 **Utena** Lith.
119 D3 **Utete** Tanz.
63 B2 **Uthai Thani** Thai.
74 A2 **Uthal** Pak.
139 D2 **Utica** U.S.A.
107 C2 **Utiel** Spain
128 C2 **Utikuma Lake** Can.
100 B1 **Utrecht** Neth.
123 D2 **Utrecht** S. Africa
106 B2 **Utrera** Spain
92 I2 **Utsjoki** Fin.
67 C3 **Utsunomiya** Japan
87 D4 **Utta** Rus. Fed.
62 B2 **Uttaradit** Thai.
75 B1 **Uttaranchal** *state* India
75 B2 **Uttar Pradesh** *state* India
Uummannaq Greenland *see* Dundas
127 I2 **Uummannaq** Greenland
127 I2 **Uummannaq Fjord** *inlet* Greenland
93 H3 **Uusikaupunki** Fin.
120 A2 **Uutapi** Namibia
143 D3 **Uvalde** U.S.A.
81 D1 **Uval Karabaur** *hills* Uzbek.
119 D3 **Uvinza** Tanz.
123 D3 **Uvongo** S. Africa
68 C1 **Uvs Nuur** *salt l.* Mongolia
67 B4 **Uwajima** Japan
78 A2 **'Uwayriḍ, Ḥarrat al** *lava field* Saudi Arabia
116 A2 **Uweinat, Jebel** *mt.* Sudan
83 H3 **Uyar** Rus. Fed.
115 C4 **Uyo** Nigeria
79 B2 **Uyun** Saudi Arabia
152 B2 **Uyuni** Bol.
152 B2 **Uyuni, Salar de** *salt flat* Bol.
76 C2 **Uzbekistan** *country* Asia
Uzbekskaya S.S.R. *admin. reg.* Asia *see* Uzbekistan
Uzbek S.S.R. *admin. reg.* Asia *see* Uzbekistan
104 C2 **Uzerche** France
105 C3 **Uzès** France
90 C1 **Uzh** *r.* Ukr.
90 A2 **Uzhhorod** Ukr.
Užhorod Ukr. *see* Uzhhorod
109 C2 **Užice** Serb. and Mont.
89 E3 **Uzlovaya** Rus. Fed.
111 C3 **Üzümlü** Turkey
111 C2 **Uzunköprü** Turkey

V

123 B2 **Vaal** *r.* S. Africa
92 I3 **Vaala** Fin.
123 C2 **Vaal Dam** S. Africa
123 C1 **Vaalwater** S. Africa
92 H3 **Vaasa** Fin.
103 D2 **Vác** Hungary
152 C3 **Vacaria** Brazil
154 B2 **Vacaria, Serra** *hills* Brazil
135 B3 **Vacaville** U.S.A.
74 B2 **Vadodara** India
92 I1 **Vadsø** Norway
105 D2 **Vaduz** Liechtenstein
94 B1 **Vágar** *i.* Faroe Is
94 B1 **Vágur** Faroe Is
103 D2 **Váh** *r.* Slovakia
49 I4 **Vaiaku** Tuvalu
88 B2 **Vaida** Estonia
136 B3 **Vail** U.S.A.
77 C3 **Vakhsh** Tajik.
Vakhstroy Tajik. *see* Vakhsh
79 C2 **Vakilābād** Iran
108 B1 **Valdagno** Italy
Valdai Hills Rus. Fed. *see* Valdayskaya Vozvyshennost'
89 D2 **Valday** Rus. Fed.
89 D2 **Valdayskaya Vozvyshennost'** *hills* Rus. Fed.
106 B2 **Valdecañas, Embalse de** *resr* Spain
93 G4 **Valdemarsvik** Sweden
105 C2 **Val-de-Meuse** France
106 C2 **Valdepeñas** Spain
153 B4 **Valdés, Península** *pen.* Arg.
126 C2 **Valdez** U.S.A.
153 A3 **Valdivia** Chile
130 C3 **Val-d'Or** Can.
141 D2 **Valdosta** U.S.A.
128 C2 **Valemount** Can.
152 E1 **Valença** Brazil

105 C3 **Valence** France
107 C2 **Valencia** Spain
107 C2 **Valencia** *aut. Comm.* Spain
150 C1 **Valencia** Venez.
107 D2 **Valencia, Golfo de** *g.* Spain
106 B1 **Valencia de Don Juan** Spain
97 A3 **Valencia Island** Ireland
105 C1 **Valenciennes** France
136 C2 **Valentine** U.S.A.
64 B2 **Valenzuela** Phil.
150 B2 **Valera** Venez.
88 C2 **Valga** Estonia
109 C2 **Valjevo** Serb. and Mont.
88 C2 **Valka** Latvia
93 H3 **Valkeakoski** Fin.
100 B2 **Valkenswaard** Neth.
91 D2 **Valky** Ukr.
55 G2 **Valkyrie Dome** *ice feature* Antarctica
145 C3 **Valladolid** Mex.
106 C1 **Valladolid** Spain
107 C2 **Valle de Uxó** Spain
93 E4 **Valle** Norway
145 C2 **Vallecillos** Mex.
150 C2 **Valle de la Pascua** Venez.
150 B1 **Valledupar** Col.
145 C2 **Valle Hermoso** Mex.
135 B3 **Vallejo** U.S.A.
152 A2 **Vallenar** Chile
84 F5 **Valletta** Malta
137 D1 **Valley City** U.S.A.
134 B2 **Valley Falls** U.S.A.
128 C2 **Valleyview** Can.
107 D1 **Valls** Spain
129 D3 **Val Marie** Can.
88 C2 **Valmiera** Latvia
104 B2 **Valognes** France
88 C2 **Valozhyn** Belarus
154 B2 **Valparaíso** Brazil
153 A3 **Valparaíso** Chile
105 C3 **Valréas** France
59 D3 **Vals, Tanjung** *c.* Indon.
74 B2 **Valsad** India
122 B2 **Valspan** S. Africa
91 D1 **Valuyki** Rus. Fed.
106 B2 **Valverde del Camino** Spain
81 C2 **Van** Turkey
81 C2 **Van, Lake** *salt l.* Turkey
81 C1 **Vanadzor** Armenia
83 H2 **Vanavara** Rus. Fed.
140 B1 **Van Buren** *AR* U.S.A.
139 F1 **Van Buren** *ME* U.S.A.
Van Buren U.S.A. *see* Kettering
128 B3 **Vancouver** Can.
134 B1 **Vancouver** U.S.A.
128 B3 **Vancouver Island** Can.
138 B3 **Vandalia** *IL* U.S.A.
138 C3 **Vandalia** *OH* U.S.A.
123 C2 **Vanderbijlpark** S. Africa
128 B2 **Vanderhoof** Can.
122 B3 **Vanderkloof Dam** *resr* S. Africa
50 C1 **Van Diemen Gulf** Austr.
88 C2 **Vändra** Estonia
Väner, Lake Sweden *see* Vänern
93 F4 **Vänern** *l.* Sweden
93 F4 **Vänersborg** Sweden
121 □D3 **Vangaindrano** Madag.
Van Gölü *salt l.* Turkey *see* Van, Lake
142 C2 **Van Horn** U.S.A.
59 D3 **Vanimo** P.N.G.
83 K3 **Vanino** Rus. Fed.
104 B2 **Vannes** France
Vannovka Kazakh. *see* Turar Ryskulov
59 D3 **Van Rees, Pegunungan** *mts* Indon.
122 A3 **Vanrhynsdorp** S. Africa
93 H3 **Vantaa** Fin.
49 I5 **Vanua Levu** *i.* Fiji
48 H5 **Vanuatu** *country* S. Pacific Ocean
138 C2 **Van Wert** U.S.A.
122 B3 **Vanwyksvlei** S. Africa
122 B2 **Van Zylsrus** S. Africa
75 C2 **Varanasi** India
92 I1 **Varangerfjorden** *sea chan.* Norway
92 I1 **Varangerhalvøya** *pen.* Norway
88 C2 **Varapayeva** Belarus
109 C1 **Varaždin** Croatia
93 F4 **Varberg** Sweden
111 B3 **Varda** Greece
111 B2 **Vardar** *r.* Macedonia
93 E4 **Varde** Denmark
92 J1 **Vardø** Norway
101 D1 **Varel** Ger.
88 B3 **Varėna** Lith.
139 E1 **Varennes** Can.
108 A1 **Varese** Italy
155 C2 **Varginha** Brazil
93 I3 **Varkaus** Fin.
110 C2 **Varna** Bulg.
93 F4 **Värnamo** Sweden
155 D1 **Várzea da Palma** Brazil
86 C2 **Varzino** Rus. Fed.
Vasa Fin. *see* Vaasa
88 C3 **Vasilyevichy** Belarus
88 C2 **Vasknarva** Estonia
110 C1 **Vaslui** Romania
93 G4 **Västerås** Sweden
93 G3 **Västerdalälven** *r.* Sweden
88 A2 **Västerhaninge** Sweden
93 G4 **Västervik** Sweden
108 B2 **Vasto** Italy
91 D2 **Vasylivka** Ukr.

90 C1 **Vasyl'kiv** Ukr.
91 D2 **Vasyl'kivka** Ukr.
104 C2 **Vatan** France
111 B3 **Vathia** Greece
108 B2 **Vatican City** Europe
92 □B3 **Vatnajökull** *ice cap* Iceland
110 C1 **Vatra Dornei** Romania
Vätter, Lake Sweden *see* Vättern
93 F4 **Vättern** *l.* Sweden
142 B2 **Vaughn** U.S.A.
105 C3 **Vauvert** France
121 □D2 **Vavatenina** Madag.
49 J5 **Vava'u Group** *is* Tonga
88 B3 **Vawkavysk** Belarus
93 F4 **Växjö** Sweden
Vayenga Rus. Fed. *see* Severomorsk
86 E1 **Vaygach, Ostrov** *i.* Rus. Fed.
154 C1 **Vazante** Brazil
101 D1 **Vechta** Ger.
110 C2 **Vedea** *r.* Romania
100 C1 **Veendam** Neth.
100 B1 **Veenendaal** Neth.
92 F2 **Vega** *i.* Norway
128 C2 **Vegreville** Can.
106 B2 **Vejer de la Frontera** Spain
93 E4 **Vejle** Denmark
110 B2 **Velbůzhdki Prohod** *pass* Macedonia
122 A3 **Velddrif** S. Africa
100 B2 **Veldhoven** Neth.
109 C2 **Velebit** *mts* Croatia
100 C2 **Velen** Ger.
109 C1 **Velenje** Slovenia
109 D2 **Veles** Macedonia
106 C2 **Vélez-Málaga** Spain
155 D1 **Velhas** *r.* Brazil
109 D2 **Velika Plana** Serb. and Mont.
88 C2 **Velikaya** *r.* Rus. Fed.
89 D2 **Velikiye Luki** Rus. Fed.
89 D2 **Velikiy Novgorod** Rus. Fed.
86 D2 **Velikiy Ustyug** Rus. Fed.
110 C2 **Veliko Tŭrnovo** Bulg.
108 B2 **Veli Lošinj** Croatia
89 D2 **Velizh** Rus. Fed.
108 B2 **Velletri** Italy
73 B3 **Vellore** India
86 D2 **Vel'sk** Rus. Fed.
101 F1 **Velten** Ger.
91 D1 **Velykyy Burluk** Ukr.
Velykyy Tokmak Ukr. *see* Tokmak
159 E4 **Vema Trench** *sea feature* Indian Ocean
108 B2 **Venafro** Italy
154 C2 **Venceslau Bráz** Brazil
104 C2 **Vendôme** France
108 B1 **Veneta, Laguna** *lag.* Italy
89 E3 **Venev** Rus. Fed.
Venezia Italy *see* Venice
150 C2 **Venezuela** *country* S. America
150 B1 **Venezuela, Golfo de** *g.* Venez.
108 B1 **Venice** Italy
141 D3 **Venice** U.S.A.
108 B1 **Venice, Gulf of** Europe
100 C2 **Venlo** Neth.
93 E4 **Vennesla** Norway
100 B2 **Venray** Neth.
88 B2 **Venta** *r.* Latvia/Lith.
88 B2 **Venta** Lith.
123 C2 **Ventersburg** S. Africa
123 C3 **Venterstad** S. Africa
108 A2 **Ventimiglia** Italy
99 C4 **Ventnor** U.K.
88 B2 **Ventspils** Latvia
135 C4 **Ventura** U.S.A.
143 C3 **Venustiano Carranza, Presa** *resr* Mex.
107 C2 **Vera** Spain
154 C2 **Vera Cruz** Brazil
145 C3 **Veracruz** Mex.
74 B2 **Veraval** India
108 A1 **Verbania** Italy
108 A1 **Vercelli** Italy
105 D2 **Vercors** *reg.* France
92 F3 **Verdalsøra** Norway
154 B1 **Verde** *r.* Brazil
154 B2 **Verde** *r.* Brazil
144 B2 **Verde** *r.* Mex.
142 A2 **Verde** *r.* U.S.A.
155 D1 **Verde Grande** *r.* Brazil
101 D1 **Verden (Aller)** Ger.
154 B1 **Verdinho, Serra do** *mts* Brazil
105 C3 **Verdon** *r.* France
105 D2 **Verdun** France
123 C2 **Vereeniging** S. Africa
106 B1 **Verín** Spain
91 D1 **Verkhnebakanskiy** Rus. Fed.
89 D3 **Verkhnedneprovskiy** Rus. Fed.
92 J2 **Verkhnetulomskiy** Rus. Fed.
92 J2 **Verkhnetulomskoye Vodokhranilishche** *resr* Rus. Fed.
87 D4 **Verkhniy Baskunchak** Rus. Fed.
91 E1 **Verkhniy Mamon** Rus. Fed.
86 D2 **Verkhnyaya Toyma** Rus. Fed.
89 E3 **Verkhov'ye** Rus. Fed.
90 B2 **Verkhovyna** Ukr.
83 J2 **Verkhoyanskiy Khrebet** *mts* Rus. Fed.
129 C2 **Vermilion** Can.
137 D2 **Vermillion** U.S.A.
130 A3 **Vermillion Bay** Can.
139 E2 **Vermont** *state* U.S.A.
135 E2 **Vernal** U.S.A.
122 B2 **Verneuk Pan** *salt pan* S. Africa

128 C2 **Vernon** Can.
143 D2 **Vernon** U.S.A.
141 D3 **Vero Beach** U.S.A.
111 B2 **Veroia** Greece
108 B1 **Verona** Italy
138 B2 **Verona** U.S.A.
104 C2 **Versailles** France
104 B2 **Vertou** France
123 D2 **Verulam** S. Africa
100 B2 **Verviers** Belgium
105 C2 **Vervins** France
105 D3 **Vescovato** *Corsica* France
87 E3 **Veselaya, Gora** *mt.* Rus. Fed.
91 C2 **Vesele** Ukr.
91 E2 **Veselyy** Rus. Fed.
105 D2 **Vesoul** France
140 C2 **Vestavia Hills** U.S.A.
92 F2 **Vesterålen** *is* Norway
92 F2 **Vestfjorden** *sea chan.* Norway
94 B1 **Vestmanna** Faroe Is
92 □A3 **Vestmannaeyjar** Iceland
92 □A3 **Vestmannaeyjar** *is* Iceland
93 E3 **Vestnes** Norway
Vesuvio *vol.* Italy *see* Vesuvius
108 B2 **Vesuvius** *vol.* Italy
89 E2 **Ves'yegonsk** Rus. Fed.
103 D2 **Veszprém** Hungary
93 G4 **Vetlanda** Sweden
86 D3 **Vetluga** Rus. Fed.
86 D3 **Vetluzhskiy** Rus. Fed.
100 A2 **Veurne** Belgium
119 D2 **Veveno** *r.* Sudan
105 D2 **Vevey** Switz.
91 D1 **Veydelevka** Rus. Fed.
80 B1 **Vezirköprü** Turkey
Vialar Alg. *see* Tissemsilt
152 C3 **Viamao** Brazil
151 E3 **Viana** Brazil
106 B1 **Viana do Castelo** Port.
62 B1 **Viangchan** Laos *see* Vientiane
62 B1 **Viangphoukha** Laos
154 C1 **Vianópolis** Brazil
108 B2 **Viareggio** Italy
93 E4 **Viborg** Denmark
Viborg Rus. Fed. *see* Vyborg
109 C3 **Vibo Valentia** Italy
107 D1 **Vic** Spain
144 A1 **Vicente Guerrero** Mex.
108 B1 **Vicenza** Italy
89 F2 **Vichuga** Rus. Fed.
105 C2 **Vichy** France
140 B2 **Vicksburg** U.S.A.
155 D2 **Viçosa** Brazil
52 A3 **Victor Harbor** Austr.
50 C1 **Victoria** *r.* Austr.
52 B3 **Victoria** *state* Austr.
Victoria Cameroon *see* Limbe
128 B3 **Victoria** Can.
153 A3 **Victoria** Chile
Victoria Malaysia *see* Labuan
113 I6 **Victoria** Seychelles
143 D3 **Victoria** U.S.A.
119 D3 **Victoria, Lake** Africa
52 B2 **Victoria, Lake** Austr.
62 A1 **Victoria, Mount** Myanmar
59 D3 **Victoria, Mount** P.N.G.
154 B3 **Victoria, Sierra de la** *hills* Arg.
120 B2 **Victoria Falls** *waterfall* Zambia/Zimbabwe
120 B2 **Victoria Falls** Zimbabwe
126 E2 **Victoria Island** Can.
55 M2 **Victoria Land** *coastal area* Antarctica
50 C1 **Victoria River Downs** Austr.
139 E1 **Victoriaville** Can.
122 B3 **Victoria West** S. Africa
135 C4 **Victorville** U.S.A.
141 D2 **Vidalia** U.S.A.
110 C2 **Videle** Romania
92 □A2 **Viðidalsá** Iceland
110 B2 **Vidin** Bulg.
74 B2 **Vidisha** India
140 B2 **Vidor** U.S.A.
153 B4 **Viedma** Arg.
153 A4 **Viedma, Lago** *l.* Arg.
102 C2 **Viehberg** *mt.* Austria
107 D1 **Vielha** Spain
100 B2 **Vielsalm** Belgium
101 E2 **Vienenburg** Ger.
103 D2 **Vienna** Austria
138 C3 **Vienna** U.S.A.
105 C2 **Vienne** France
104 C2 **Vienne** *r.* France
62 B2 **Vientiane** Laos
100 C2 **Viersen** Ger.
104 C2 **Vierzon** France
144 B2 **Viesca** Mex.
109 C2 **Vieste** Italy
62 B2 **Vietnam** *country* Asia
62 B1 **Viêt Tri** Vietnam
64 B2 **Vigan** Phil.
108 A1 **Vigevano** Italy
106 B1 **Vigo** Spain
Viipuri Rus. Fed. *see* Vyborg
92 □B3 **Vík** Iceland
111 B2 **Vikhren** *mt.* Bulg.
128 C2 **Viking** Can.
92 F3 **Vikna** *i.* Norway
Vila Alferes Chamusca Moz. *see* Guija
Vila Arriaga Angola *see* Bibala
Vila Bugaço Angola *see* Camanongue

Vila Cabral Moz. *see* Lichinga
Vila da Ponte Angola *see* Kuvango
Vila de Aljustrel Angola *see* Cangamba
Vila de Almoster Angola *see* Chiange
Vila de João Belo Moz. *see* Xai-Xai
Vila de Trego Morais Moz. *see* Chókwé
Vila Fontes Moz. *see* Caia
106 B2 **Vila Franca de Xira** Port.
106 B1 **Vilagarcía de Arousa** Spain
123 D1 **Vila Gomes da Costa** Moz.
106 B1 **Vilalba** Spain
Vila Luísa Moz. *see* Marracuene
Vila Marechal Carmona Angola *see* Uíge
121 □D2 **Vilanandro, Tanjona** *pt* Madag.
88 C2 **Viļāni** Latvia
106 B1 **Vila Nova de Gaia** Port.
107 D1 **Vilanova i la Geltrú** Spain
Vila Paiva de Andrada Moz. *see* Gorongosa
Vila Pery Moz. *see* Chimoio
106 B1 **Vila Real** Port.
106 B1 **Vilar Formoso** Port.
Vila Salazar Angola *see* N'dalatando
Vila Salazar Zimbabwe *see* Sango
Vila Teixeira de Sousa Angola *see* Luau
155 D2 **Vila Velha** Brazil
150 B4 **Vilcabamba, Cordillera** *mts* Peru
82 F1 **Vil'cheka, Zemlya** *i.* Rus. Fed.
92 G3 **Vilhelmina** Sweden
150 C4 **Vilhena** Brazil
88 C2 **Viljandi** Estonia
123 C2 **Viljoenskroon** S. Africa
88 B3 **Vilkaviškis** Lith.
83 H1 **Vil'kitskogo, Proliv** *str.* Rus. Fed.
144 B1 **Villa Ahumada** Mex.
106 B1 **Villablino** Spain
102 C2 **Villach** Austria
Villa Cisneros Western Sahara *see* Ad Dakhla
144 B2 **Villa de Cos** Mex.
152 B3 **Villa Dolores** Arg.
145 C3 **Villa Flores** Mex.
153 C3 **Villa Gesell** Arg.
145 C2 **Villagrán** Mex.
145 C3 **Villahermosa** Mex.
144 A2 **Villa Insurgentes** Mex.
107 C2 **Villajoyosa - La Vila Joíosa** Spain
152 B3 **Villa María** Arg.
153 B3 **Villa Mercedes** Arg.
152 B2 **Villa Montes** Bol.
144 B2 **Villanueva** Mex.
106 B2 **Villanueva de la Serena** Spain
106 C2 **Villanueva de los Infantes** Spain
152 C2 **Villa Ocampo** Arg.
142 B3 **Villa Ocampo** Mex.
108 A3 **Villaputzu** *Sardinia* Italy
152 C2 **Villarrica** Para.
106 C2 **Villarrobledo** Spain
Villasalazar Zimbabwe *see* Sango
152 B2 **Villa Unión** Arg.
144 B2 **Villa Unión** Mex.
144 B2 **Villa Unión** Mex.
150 B2 **Villavicencio** Col.
152 B2 **Villazon** Bol.
104 C3 **Villefranche-de-Rouergue** France
105 C2 **Villefranche-sur-Saône** France
107 C2 **Villena** Spain
100 A2 **Villeneuve-d'Ascq** France
104 C3 **Villeneuve-sur-Lot** France
140 B2 **Ville Platte** U.S.A.
100 A3 **Villers-Cotterêts** France
105 C2 **Villeurbanne** France
123 C2 **Villiers** S. Africa
102 B2 **Villingen** Ger.
137 E2 **Villisca** U.S.A.
88 C3 **Vilnius** Lith.
91 C2 **Vil'nohirs'k** Ukr.
91 D2 **Vil'nyans'k** Ukr.
100 B2 **Vilvoorde** Belgium
88 C3 **Vilyeyka** Belarus
83 J2 **Vilyuy** *r.* Rus. Fed.
93 G4 **Vimmerby** Sweden
153 A3 **Viña del Mar** Chile
107 D1 **Vinaròs** Spain
138 B3 **Vincennes** U.S.A.
55 J3 **Vincennes Bay** Antarctica
139 D3 **Vineland** U.S.A.
62 B2 **Vinh** Vietnam
63 B2 **Vinh Long** Vietnam
143 D1 **Vinita** U.S.A.
90 B2 **Vinnytsya** Ukr.
55 R2 **Vinson Massif** *mt.* Antarctica
93 E3 **Vinstra** Norway
108 B1 **Vipiteno** Italy
64 B2 **Virac** Phil.
74 B2 **Viramgam** India
80 B2 **Viranşehir** Turkey
129 D3 **Virden** Can.
104 B2 **Vire** France
120 A2 **Virei** Angola
155 D1 **Virgem da Lapa** Brazil
142 A1 **Virgin** *r.* U.S.A.
123 C2 **Virginia** S. Africa
137 E1 **Virginia** U.S.A.
139 D3 **Virginia** *state* U.S.A.
139 D3 **Virginia Beach** U.S.A.

135 C3 **Virginia City** U.S.A.
147 D3 **Virgin Islands (U.K.)** *terr.*
West Indies
147 D3 **Virgin Islands (U.S.A.)** *terr.*
West Indies
63 B2 **Virôchey** Cambodia
109 C1 **Virovitica** Croatia
100 B3 **Virton** Belgium
88 B2 **Virtsu** Estonia
73 B4 **Virudhunagar** India
109 C2 **Vis** *i.* Croatia
88 C2 **Visaginas** Lith.
135 C3 **Visalia** U.S.A.
74 B2 **Visavadar** India
64 B2 **Visayan Sea** Phil.
93 G4 **Visby** Sweden
126 E2 **Viscount Melville Sound**
sea chan. Can.
151 E3 **Viseu** Brazil
106 B1 **Viseu** Port.
110 B1 **Vişeu de Sus** Romania
73 C3 **Vishakhapatnam** India
88 C2 **Viški** Latvia
109 C2 **Visoko** Bos.-Herz.
103 D1 **Vistula** *r.* Pol.
Vitebsk Belarus *see* Vitsyebsk
108 B2 **Viterbo** Italy
49 I5 **Viti Levu** *i.* Fiji
83 I3 **Vitim** *r.* Rus. Fed.
155 D2 **Vitória** Brazil
151 E4 **Vitória da Conquista** Brazil
106 C1 **Vitoria-Gasteiz** Spain
104 B2 **Vitré** France
105 C2 **Vitry-le-François** France
89 D2 **Vitsyebsk** Belarus
105 D2 **Vittel** France
108 B3 **Vittoria** *Sicily* Italy
108 B1 **Vittorio Veneto** Italy
106 B1 **Viveiro** Spain
136 C2 **Vivian** U.S.A.
Vizagapatam India *see*
Vishakhapatnam
142 A3 **Vizcaíno, Desierto de** *des.* Mex.
144 A2 **Vizcaíno, Sierra** *mts* Mex.
111 C2 **Vize** Turkey
73 C3 **Vizianagaram** India
100 B2 **Vlaardingen** Neth.
87 D4 **Vladikavkaz** Rus. Fed.
89 F2 **Vladimir** Rus. Fed.
66 B2 **Vladivostok** Rus. Fed.
109 D2 **Vlasotince** Serb. and Mont.
100 B1 **Vlieland** *i.* Neth.
100 A2 **Vlissingen** Neth.
109 C2 **Vlorë** Albania
102 C1 **Vltava** *r.* Czech Rep.
102 C2 **Vöcklabruck** Austria
109 C2 **Vodice** Croatia
Vogelkop Peninsula Indon. *see*
Doberai, Jazirah
101 D2 **Vogelsberg** *hills* Ger.
Vohémar Madag. *see* Iharaña
Vohibinany Madag. *see*
Ampasimanolotra
Vohimarina Madag. *see* Iharaña
121 □D3 **Vohimena, Tanjona** *c.* Madag.
121 □D3 **Vohipeno** Madag.
119 D3 **Voi** Kenya
105 D2 **Voiron** France
131 D2 **Voisey Bay** Can.
109 C1 **Vojvodina** *prov.* Serb. and Mont.
92 J3 **Voknavolok** Rus. Fed.
Volcano Bay Japan *see*
Uchiura-wan
69 F3 **Volcano Islands** *is* Japan
Volchansk Ukr. *see* Vovchans'k
89 E2 **Volga** Rus. Fed.
89 F2 **Volga** *r.* Rus. Fed.
87 D4 **Volgodonsk** Rus. Fed.
87 D4 **Volgograd** Rus. Fed.
87 D4 **Volgogradskoye**
Vodokhranilishche *resr* Rus. Fed.
89 D2 **Volkhov** Rus. Fed.
89 D1 **Volkhov** *r.* Rus. Fed.
101 E2 **Volkstedt** Ger.
91 C2 **Volnovakha** Ukr.
90 B2 **Volochys'k** Ukr.
91 D2 **Volodars'ke** Ukr.
Volodarskoye Kazakh. *see*
Saumalkol'
90 B1 **Volodars'k-Volyns'kyy** Ukr.
90 B1 **Volodymyrets'** Ukr.
90 A1 **Volodymyr-Volyns'kyy** Ukr.
89 E2 **Vologda** Rus. Fed.
89 E2 **Volokolamsk** Rus. Fed.
91 D1 **Volokonovka** Rus. Fed.
111 B3 **Volos** Greece
88 C2 **Volosovo** Rus. Fed.
89 D2 **Volot** Rus. Fed.
89 E3 **Volovo** Rus. Fed.
87 D3 **Vol'sk** Rus. Fed.
114 C4 **Volta** *r.* Ghana
114 C4 **Volta, Lake** *resr* Ghana
155 D2 **Volta Redonda** Brazil
110 C2 **Voluntari** Romania
87 D4 **Volzhskiy** Rus. Fed.
92 □C2 **Vopnafjörður** Iceland
88 C3 **Voranava** Belarus
160 K3 **Voring Plateau** *sea feature*
N. Atlantic Ocean
86 F2 **Vorkuta** Rus. Fed.
88 B2 **Vormsi** *i.* Estonia
83 G2 **Vorogovo** Rus. Fed.
89 E3 **Voronezh** Rus. Fed.
89 E3 **Voronezh** *r.* Rus. Fed.
91 E1 **Vorontsovka** Rus. Fed.

Voroshilov Rus. Fed. *see* Ussuriysk
Voroshilovgrad Ukr. *see* Luhans'k
Voroshilovsk Rus. Fed. *see*
Stavropol'
Voroshilovsk Ukr. *see* Alchevs'k
91 C2 **Vorskla** *r.* Rus. Fed.
88 C2 **Võrtsjärv** *l.* Estonia
88 C2 **Võru** Estonia
122 B3 **Vosburg** S. Africa
105 D2 **Vosges** *mts* France
89 E2 **Voskresensk** Rus. Fed.
93 E3 **Voss** Norway
86 C2 **Vostochnaya Litsa** Rus. Fed.
Vostochno-Sibirskoye More *sea*
Rus. Fed. *see* East Siberian Sea
83 H3 **Vostochnyy Sayan** *mts* Rus. Fed.
66 C1 **Vostok** Rus. Fed.
49 L5 **Vostok Island** Kiribati
86 E3 **Votkinsk** Rus. Fed.
86 E3 **Votkinskoye Vodokhranilishche**
resr Rus. Fed.
154 C2 **Votuporanga** Brazil
105 C2 **Vouziers** France
91 D1 **Vovchans'k** Ukr.
92 J2 **Voynitsa** Rus. Fed.
86 E2 **Voyvozh** Rus. Fed.
91 C2 **Voznesens'k** Ukr.
76 B2 **Vozrozhdenya Island** *i.* Uzbek.
93 E4 **Vrådal** Norway
90 C2 **Vradiyivka** Ukr.
66 B2 **Vrangel'** Rus. Fed.
83 N2 **Vrangelya, Ostrov** *i.* Rus. Fed.
109 D2 **Vranje** Serb. and Mont.
110 C2 **Vratnik** *pass* Bulg.
110 B2 **Vratsa** Bulg.
109 C1 **Vrbas** *r.* Bos.-Herz.
109 C1 **Vrbas** Serb. and Mont.
122 A3 **Vredenburg** S. Africa
122 A3 **Vredendal** S. Africa
100 B3 **Vresse** Belgium
100 C1 **Vriezenveen** Neth.
109 D1 **Vršac** Serb. and Mont.
122 B2 **Vryburg** S. Africa
123 D2 **Vryheid** S. Africa
89 D1 **Vsevolozhsk** Rus. Fed.
109 D2 **Vučitrn** Serb. and Mont.
109 C1 **Vukovar** Croatia
86 E2 **Vuktyl'** Rus. Fed.
123 C2 **Vukuzakhe** S. Africa
90 B2 **Vulcănești** Moldova
109 B3 **Vulcano, Isola** *i.* Italy
Vulkaneshty Moldova *see*
Vulcănești
63 B2 **Vung Tau** Vietnam
92 H2 **Vuollerim** Sweden
92 I2 **Vuotso** Fin.
74 B2 **Vyara** India
Vyarkhowye Belarus *see* Ruba
Vyatka Rus. Fed. *see* Kirov
89 D2 **Vyaz'ma** Rus. Fed.
88 C1 **Vyborg** Rus. Fed.
88 C1 **Vyborgskiy Zaliv** *b.* Rus. Fed.
86 D2 **Vychegda** *r.* Rus. Fed.
88 C2 **Vyerkhnyadzvinsk** Belarus
89 D3 **Vyetka** Belarus
86 C2 **Vygonichi** Rus. Fed.
86 C2 **Vygozero, Ozero** *l.* Rus. Fed.
87 D3 **Vyksa** Rus. Fed.
90 B2 **Vylkove** Ukr.
90 A2 **Vynohradiv** Ukr.
89 D2 **Vypolzovo** Rus. Fed.
91 D2 **Vyritsa** Rus. Fed.
91 D2 **Vyselki** Rus. Fed.
90 C1 **Vyshhorod** Ukr.
89 D2 **Vyshnevolotskaya Gryada** *ridge*
Rus. Fed.
89 D2 **Vyshnyy-Volochek** Rus. Fed.
103 D2 **Vyškov** Czech Rep.
89 E2 **Vysokovsk** Rus. Fed.
86 C2 **Vytegra** Rus. Fed.

W

114 B3 **Wa** Ghana
100 B2 **Waal** *r.* Neth.
100 B2 **Waalwijk** Neth.
119 D2 **Waat** Sudan
128 C2 **Wabasca** *r.* Can.
128 C2 **Wabasca-Desmarais** Can.
138 B3 **Wabash** *r.* U.S.A.
117 C4 **Wabē Gestro** *r.* Eth.
117 C4 **Wabē Shebelē Wenz** *r.* Eth.
129 E2 **Wabowden** Can.
103 D1 **Wąbrzeźno** Pol.
141 D3 **Waccasassa Bay** U.S.A.
101 D2 **Wächtersbach** Ger.
143 D2 **Waco** U.S.A.
74 A2 **Wad** Pak.
115 D2 **Waddān** Libya
Waddeneilanden *is* Neth. *see*
West Frisian Islands
Wadden Islands Neth. *see*
West Frisian Islands
100 B1 **Waddenzee** *sea chan.* Neth.
128 B2 **Waddington, Mount** Can.
100 B1 **Waddinxveen** Neth.
129 D2 **Wadena** Can.
137 D1 **Wadena** U.S.A.
50 B1 **Wadeye** Austr.
Wadhwan India *see* Surendranagar
116 B2 **Wadi Halfa** Sudan
116 B3 **Wad Medani** Sudan
122 B3 **Waenhuiskrans** S. Africa

70 C2 **Wafangdian** China
100 B2 **Wageningen** Neth.
127 G2 **Wager Bay** Can.
53 C3 **Wagga Wagga** Austr.
137 D2 **Wagner** U.S.A.
74 B1 **Wah** Pak.
137 D2 **Wahoo** U.S.A.
137 D1 **Wahpeton** U.S.A.
54 B2 **Waiau** *r.* N.Z.
59 C3 **Waigeo** *i.* Indon.
61 C2 **Waikabubak** Indon.
54 C1 **Waikaremoana, Lake** N.Z.
52 A2 **Waikerie** Austr.
54 B2 **Waimate** N.Z.
75 B3 **Wainganga** *r.* India
61 D2 **Waingapu** Indon.
129 C2 **Wainwright** Can.
126 B2 **Wainwright** U.S.A.
54 C1 **Waiouru** N.Z.
54 B2 **Waipara** N.Z.
54 C1 **Waipawa** N.Z.
54 B2 **Wairau** *r.* N.Z.
54 C1 **Wairoa** N.Z.
54 B2 **Waitaki** *r.* N.Z.
54 B1 **Waitara** N.Z.
54 B1 **Waiuku** N.Z.
67 C3 **Wajima** Japan
119 E2 **Wajir** Kenya
67 C3 **Wakasa-wan** *b.* Japan
54 A3 **Wakatipu, Lake** N.Z.
129 D2 **Wakaw** Can.
67 C4 **Wakayama** Japan
136 D3 **WaKeeney** U.S.A.
54 B2 **Wakefield** N.Z.
98 C3 **Wakefield** U.K.
Wakeham Can. *see*
Kangiqsujuaq
48 H2 **Wake Island** *terr.* N. Pacific Ocean
66 D1 **Wakkanai** Japan
123 D2 **Wakkerstroom** S. Africa
120 A2 **Waku-Kungo** Angola
103 D1 **Wałbrzych** Pol.
53 D2 **Walcha** Austr.
100 C1 **Walchum** Ger.
103 D1 **Wałcz** Pol.
99 B3 **Wales** *admin. div.* U.K.
53 C2 **Walgett** Austr.
119 C3 **Walikale** Dem. Rep. Congo
135 C3 **Walker Lake** U.S.A.
134 C1 **Wallace** *ID* U.S.A.
141 E2 **Wallace** *NC* U.S.A.
52 A2 **Wallaroo** Austr.
98 B3 **Wallasey** U.K.
134 C1 **Walla Walla** U.S.A.
101 D3 **Walldürn** Ger.
122 A3 **Wallekraal** S. Africa
53 C2 **Wallendbeen** Austr.
49 J5 **Wallis, Îles** *is* Wallis and Futuna Is.
49 J5 **Wallis and Futuna Islands** *terr.*
S. Pacific Ocean
96 □ **Walls** U.K.
98 B2 **Walney, Isle of** *i.* U.K.
99 C3 **Walsall** U.K.
136 C3 **Walsenburg** U.S.A.
101 D1 **Walsrode** Ger.
141 D2 **Walterboro** U.S.A.
120 A3 **Walvis Bay** Namibia
158 F6 **Walvis Ridge** *sea feature*
S. Atlantic Ocean
119 C2 **Wamba** Dem. Rep. Congo
52 B1 **Wanaaring** Austr.
54 A2 **Wanaka** N.Z.
54 A2 **Wanaka, Lake** N.Z.
71 B3 **Wan'an** China
130 B3 **Wanapitei Lake** Can.
154 B3 **Wanda** Arg.
66 D1 **Wanda Shan** *mts* China
62 A1 **Wanding** China
Wandingzhen China *see* Wanding
54 C1 **Wanganui** N.Z.
54 B1 **Wanganui** *r.* N.Z.
53 C3 **Wangaratta** Austr.
65 B1 **Wangqing** China
62 A1 **Wan Hsa-la** Myanmar
Wankie Zimbabwe *see* Hwange
71 B4 **Wanning** China
100 B2 **Wanroij** Neth.
99 C4 **Wantage** U.K.
70 A2 **Wanxian** China
70 A2 **Wanyuan** China
117 A4 **Warab** Sudan
73 B3 **Warangal** India
101 D2 **Warburg** Ger.
50 B2 **Warburton** Austr.
52 A1 **Warburton** *watercourse* Austr.
74 B2 **Wardha** India
96 C1 **Ward Hill** U.K.
128 B2 **Ware** Can.
101 F1 **Waren** Ger.
101 C2 **Warendorf** Ger.
53 D1 **Warialda** Austr.
122 A2 **Warmbad** Namibia
135 C3 **Warm Springs** U.S.A.
134 C2 **Warner Lakes** U.S.A.
134 B2 **Warner Mountains** U.S.A.
141 D2 **Warner Robins** U.S.A.
152 B1 **Warnes** Bol.
52 B3 **Warracknabeal** Austr.
53 C3 **Warrandyte** Austr.
53 C2 **Warrego** *r.* Austr.
53 C2 **Warren** Austr.
140 B2 **Warren** *AR* U.S.A.
138 C2 **Warren** *OH* U.S.A.
139 D2 **Warren** *PA* U.S.A.
97 C1 **Warrenpoint** U.K.

137 E3 **Warrensburg** U.S.A.
122 B2 **Warrenton** S. Africa
115 C4 **Warri** Nigeria
98 B3 **Warrington** U.K.
52 B3 **Warrnambool** Austr.
103 E1 **Warsaw** Pol.
138 B2 **Warsaw** U.S.A.
Warszawa Pol. *see* Warsaw
103 C1 **Warta** *r.* Pol.
53 D1 **Warwick** Austr.
99 C3 **Warwick** U.K.
139 E2 **Warwick** U.S.A.
134 D3 **Wasatch Range** *mts* U.S.A.
135 C3 **Wasco** U.S.A.
136 C1 **Washburn** U.S.A.
139 D3 **Washington** *DC* U.S.A.
137 E2 **Washington** *IA* U.S.A.
138 B2 **Washington** *IL* U.S.A.
138 B3 **Washington** *IN* U.S.A.
137 E3 **Washington** *MO* U.S.A.
141 E1 **Washington** *NC* U.S.A.
138 C2 **Washington** *PA* U.S.A.
135 D3 **Washington** *UT* U.S.A.
134 B1 **Washington** U.S.A.
139 E2 **Washington, Mount** U.S.A.
138 C3 **Washington Court House** U.S.A.
74 A2 **Washuk** Pak.
130 C2 **Waskaganish** Can.
129 E2 **Waskaiowaka Lake** Can.
122 A2 **Wasser** Namibia
101 D2 **Wasserkuppe** *hill* Ger.
130 C3 **Waswanipi, Lac** *l.* Can.
61 D2 **Watampone** Indon.
Watenstadt-Salzgitter Ger. *see*
Salzgitter
139 E2 **Waterbury** U.S.A.
129 D2 **Waterbury Lake** Can.
97 C2 **Waterford** Ireland
97 C2 **Waterford Harbour** Ireland
100 B2 **Waterloo** Belgium
137 E2 **Waterloo** U.S.A.
99 C4 **Waterlooville** U.K.
123 C1 **Waterpoort** S. Africa
139 D2 **Watertown** *NY* U.S.A.
137 D2 **Watertown** *SD* U.S.A.
138 B2 **Watertown** *WI* U.S.A.
97 A3 **Waterville** Ireland
139 F2 **Waterville** U.S.A.
99 C4 **Watford** U.K.
136 C1 **Watford City** U.S.A.
129 D2 **Wathaman** *r.* Can.
Watling Island Bahamas *see*
San Salvador
143 D1 **Watonga** U.S.A.
129 D2 **Watrous** Can.
119 C2 **Watsa** Dem. Rep. Congo
138 B2 **Watseka** U.S.A.
118 C3 **Watsi Kengo** Dem. Rep. Congo
128 B1 **Watson Lake** Can.
135 B3 **Watsonville** U.S.A.
59 C3 **Watubela, Kepulauan** *is* Indon.
59 D3 **Wau** P.N.G.
117 A4 **Wau** Sudan
53 D2 **Wauchope** Austr.
138 B2 **Waukegan** U.S.A.
138 B2 **Waukesha** U.S.A.
143 D2 **Waurika** U.S.A.
138 B2 **Wausau** U.S.A.
99 D3 **Waveney** *r.* U.K.
137 E2 **Waverly** U.S.A.
130 B3 **Wawa** Can.
141 D2 **Waycross** U.S.A.
137 D2 **Wayne** U.S.A.
141 D2 **Waynesboro** *GA* U.S.A.
139 D3 **Waynesboro** *VA* U.S.A.
137 E3 **Waynesville** *MO* U.S.A.
141 D1 **Waynesville** *NC* U.S.A.
74 B1 **Wazirabad** Pak.
60 A1 **We, Pulau** *i.* Indon.
98 C2 **Wear** *r.* U.K.
143 D1 **Weatherford** *OK* U.S.A.
143 D2 **Weatherford** *TX* U.S.A.
134 B2 **Weaverville** U.S.A.
143 D3 **Webb** U.S.A.
130 B2 **Webequie** Can.
117 C4 **Webi Shabeelle** *r.* Somalia
137 D1 **Webster** U.S.A.
137 E2 **Webster City** U.S.A.
55 C3 **Weddell Abyssal Plain** *sea feature*
Southern Ocean
55 B3 **Weddell Sea** Antarctica
123 D2 **Weenen** S. Africa
100 B2 **Weert** Neth.
53 C2 **Weethalle** Austr.
53 C2 **Wee Waa** Austr.
100 C2 **Wegberg** Ger.
103 E1 **Węgorzewo** Pol.
103 E1 **Węgrów** Pol.
70 B1 **Weichang** China
101 F3 **Weiden in der Oberpfalz** Ger.
Weidongmen China *see* Qianjin
70 B2 **Weifang** China
70 C2 **Weihai** China
70 B2 **Wei He** *r.* China
53 C1 **Weilmoringle** Austr.
101 E2 **Weimar** Ger.
143 D3 **Weimar** U.S.A.
70 A2 **Weinan** China
71 A3 **Weining** China
51 D1 **Weipa** Austr.
53 C1 **Weir** *r.* Austr.
138 C2 **Weirton** U.S.A.
62 B1 **Weishan** China
101 E2 **Weiße Elster** *r.* Ger.
101 E2 **Weißenfels** Ger.

102 C2 **Weißkugel** *mt.* Austria/Italy
71 A3 **Weixin** China
Weizhou China *see* Wenchuan
103 D1 **Wejherowo** Pol.
128 C1 **Wekweti** Can.
138 C3 **Welch** U.S.A.
117 B3 **Weldiya** Eth.
123 C2 **Welkom** S. Africa
99 C3 **Welland** *r.* U.K.
51 C1 **Wellesley Islands** Austr.
99 C3 **Wellingborough** U.K.
53 C2 **Wellington** Austr.
54 B2 **Wellington** N.Z.
122 A3 **Wellington** S. Africa
136 B2 **Wellington** *CO* U.S.A.
137 D3 **Wellington** *KS* U.S.A.
135 D3 **Wellington** *UT* U.S.A.
153 A4 **Wellington, Isla** *i.* Chile
53 C2 **Wellington, Lake** Austr.
128 B2 **Wells** Can.
99 B4 **Wells** U.K.
134 D2 **Wells** U.S.A.
50 B2 **Wells, Lake** *salt flat* Austr.
54 B1 **Wellsford** N.Z.
99 D3 **Wells-next-the-Sea** U.K.
142 A2 **Wellton** U.S.A.
102 C2 **Wels** Austria
99 B3 **Welshpool** U.K.
Welwitschia Namibia *see*
Khorixas
123 C2 **Wembesi** S. Africa
130 C2 **Wemindji** Can.
134 B1 **Wenatchee** U.S.A.
71 B4 **Wenchang** China
114 B4 **Wenchi** Ghana
Wenchow China *see* Wenzhou
70 A2 **Wenchuan** China
70 C2 **Wendeng** China
101 E1 **Wendisch Evern** Ger.
117 B4 **Wendo** Eth.
135 D2 **Wendover** U.S.A.
71 B3 **Wengyuan** China
Wenhua China *see* Weishan
Wenlan China *see* Mengzi
Wenlin China *see* Renshou
71 C3 **Wenling** China
Wenquan China *see* Yingshan
71 A3 **Wenshan** China
52 B2 **Wentworth** Austr.
71 C3 **Wenzhou** China
123 C2 **Wepener** S. Africa
122 B2 **Werda** Botswana
101 D3 **Werdau** Ger.
100 C2 **Wesel** Ger.
101 E1 **Wesendorf** Ger.
101 D1 **Weser** *r.* Ger.
101 D1 **Weser** *sea chan.* Ger.
51 C1 **Wessel, Cape** Austr.
51 C1 **Wessel Islands** Austr.
123 C2 **Wesselton** S. Africa
55 P2 **West Antarctica** *reg.*
Antarctica
156 B7 **West Australian Basin**
sea feature Indian Ocean
80 B2 **West Bank** *terr.* Asia
138 B2 **West Bend** U.S.A.
75 C2 **West Bengal** *state* India
99 C3 **West Bromwich** U.K.
139 E2 **Westbrook** U.S.A.
137 E2 **West Des Moines** U.S.A.
100 C2 **Westerburg** Ger.
100 C1 **Westerholt** Ger.
139 E2 **Westerly** U.S.A.
50 B2 **Western Australia** *state* Austr.
122 B3 **Western Cape** *prov.* S. Africa
116 A2 **Western Desert** Egypt
Western Dvina *r.* Europe *see*
Zapadnaya Dvina
73 B3 **Western Ghats** *mts* India
114 A2 **Western Sahara** *terr.* Africa
Western Samoa *country*
S. Pacific Ocean *see* Samoa
Western Sayan Mountains *reg.*
Rus. Fed. *see* Zapadnyy Sayan
100 A2 **Westerschelde** *est.* Neth.
100 C1 **Westerstede** Ger.
101 C2 **Westerwald** *hills* Ger.
153 B5 **West Falkland** *i.* Falkland Is
138 B3 **West Frankfort** U.S.A.
100 B1 **West Frisian Islands** Neth.
96 C2 **Westhill** U.K.
55 I3 **West Ice Shelf** Antarctica
147 D2 **West Indies** *is* Caribbean Sea
100 A2 **Westkapelle** Neth.
96 A1 **West Loch Roag** *b.* U.K.
128 C2 **Westlock** Can.
100 B2 **Westmalle** Belgium
Westman Islands Iceland *see*
Vestmannaeyjar
53 C1 **Westmar** Austr.
156 C4 **West Mariana Basin** *sea feature*
N. Pacific Ocean
140 B1 **West Memphis** U.S.A.
138 C3 **Weston** U.S.A.
99 B4 **Weston-super-Mare** U.K.
141 K3 **West Palm Beach** U.S.A.
137 E3 **West Plains** U.S.A.
137 D2 **West Point** U.S.A.

54 B2 **Westport** N.Z.
97 B2 **Westport** Ireland
129 D2 **Westray** Can.
96 C1 **Westray** *i.* U.K.
82 G2 **West Siberian Plain** *plain*
Rus. Fed.
100 B1 **West-Terschelling** Neth.
136 A2 **West Thumb** U.S.A.
97 B1 **West Town** Ireland
135 D2 **West Valley City** U.S.A.
138 C3 **West Virginia** *state* U.S.A.
53 C2 **West Wyalong** Austr.
134 D2 **West Yellowstone** U.S.A.
59 C3 **Wetar** *i.* Indon.
128 C2 **Wetaskiwin** Can.
119 D3 **Wete** Tanz.
101 D2 **Wetzlar** Ger.
59 D3 **Wewak** P.N.G.
97 C2 **Wexford** Ireland
97 C2 **Wexford Harbour** *b.* Ireland
129 D2 **Weyakwin** Can.
129 D3 **Weyburn** Can.
101 D1 **Weyhe** Ger.
99 B4 **Weymouth** U.K.
54 C1 **Whakatane** N.Z.
129 E1 **Whale Cove** Can.
96 □ **Whalsay** *i.* U.K.
54 B1 **Whangamomona** N.Z.
54 B1 **Whangaparaoa** N.Z.
54 B1 **Whangarei** N.Z.
98 C3 **Wharfe** *r.* U.K.
143 D3 **Wharton** U.S.A.
128 C1 **Wha Ti** Can.
136 B2 **Wheatland** U.S.A.
138 B2 **Wheaton** U.S.A.
140 C2 **Wheeler Lake** *resr* U.S.A.
135 D3 **Wheeler Peak** *NM* U.S.A.
135 D3 **Wheeler Peak** *NV* U.S.A.
138 C2 **Wheeling** U.S.A.
98 B2 **Whernside** *hill* U.K.
128 B2 **Whistler** Can.
98 C2 **Whitby** U.K.
128 A1 **White** *r.* Can./U.S.A.
140 B2 **White** *r.* *AR* U.S.A.
138 B3 **White** *r.* *IN* U.S.A.
50 B2 **White, Lake** *salt flat* Austr.
131 E3 **White Bay** Can.
136 C1 **White Butte** *mt.* U.S.A.
52 B2 **White Cliffs** Austr.
128 C2 **Whitecourt** Can.
134 D1 **Whitefish** U.S.A.
98 B2 **Whitehaven** U.K.
97 D1 **Whitehead** U.K.
128 A1 **Whitehorse** Can.
140 B3 **White Lake** U.S.A.
51 D4 **Whitemark** Austr.
135 C3 **White Mountain Peak** U.S.A.
116 B3 **White Nile** *r.* Sudan/Uganda
White Russia *country* Europe *see*
Belarus
86 C2 **White Sea** Rus. Fed.
134 D1 **White Sulphur Springs** U.S.A.
141 E2 **Whiteville** U.S.A.
114 B3 **White Volta** *watercourse*
Burkina/Ghana
136 B3 **Whitewater** U.S.A.
142 B2 **Whitewater Baldy** *mt.* U.S.A.
130 B2 **Whitewater Lake** Can.
129 D2 **Whitewood** Can.
96 B3 **Whithorn** U.K.
54 C1 **Whitianga** N.Z.
135 C3 **Whitney, Mount** U.S.A.
99 D4 **Whitstable** U.K.
51 D2 **Whitsunday Island** Austr.
53 C3 **Whittlesea** Austr.
52 A2 **Whyalla** Austr.
62 A2 **Wiang Pa Pao** Thai.
100 A2 **Wichelen** Belgium
137 D3 **Wichita** U.S.A.
143 D2 **Wichita Falls** U.S.A.
143 D2 **Wichita Mountains** U.S.A.
96 C1 **Wick** U.K.
142 A2 **Wickenburg** U.S.A.
97 C2 **Wicklow** Ireland
97 D2 **Wicklow Head** *hd*
Ireland
97 C2 **Wicklow Mountains** Ireland
98 B3 **Widnes** U.K.
101 D1 **Wiehengebirge** *hills* Ger.
100 C2 **Wiehl** Ger.
103 D1 **Wieluń** Pol.
Wien Austria *see* Vienna
103 D2 **Wiener Neustadt** Austria
100 B1 **Wieringerwerf** Neth.
101 D2 **Wiesbaden** Ger.
100 C1 **Wiesmoor** Ger.
103 D1 **Wieżyca** *hill* Pol.
98 B3 **Wigan** U.K.
99 C3 **Wight, Isle of** *i.* U.K.
96 B3 **Wigtown** U.K.
100 B2 **Wijchen** Neth.
130 B3 **Wikwemikong** Can.
52 B2 **Wilcannia** Austr.
Wilczek Land *i.* Rus. Fed. *see*
Vil'cheka, Zemlya
123 C3 **Wild Coast** S. Africa
101 D1 **Wildeshausen** Ger.
136 C2 **Wild Horse Hill** *mt.* U.S.A.
123 C2 **Wilge** *r.* S. Africa
48 F4 **Wilhelm, Mount** P.N.G.
101 D1 **Wilhelmshaven** Ger.
139 D2 **Wilkes-Barre** U.S.A.
55 K3 **Wilkes Land** *reg.* Antarctica
129 D2 **Wilkie** Can.
134 B1 **Willamette** *r.* U.S.A.

134 B1 **Willapa Bay** U.S.A.
142 B2 **Willcox** U.S.A.
100 B2 **Willebroek** Belgium
147 D3 **Willemstad** Neth. Antilles
52 B2 **William, Mount** Austr.
52 A1 **William Creek** Austr.
142 A1 **Williams** U.S.A.
138 C3 **Williamsburg** *KY* U.S.A.
139 D3 **Williamsburg** *VA* U.S.A.
128 B2 **Williams Lake** Can.
138 C3 **Williamson** U.S.A.
139 D2 **Williamsport** U.S.A.
141 E1 **Williamston** U.S.A.
122 B3 **Williston** S. Africa
136 C1 **Williston** U.S.A.
128 B2 **Williston Lake** Can.
135 B3 **Willits** U.S.A.
137 D1 **Willmar** U.S.A.
122 B3 **Willowmore** S. Africa
135 B3 **Willows** U.S.A.
123 C3 **Willowvale** S. Africa
50 B2 **Wills, Lake** *salt flat* Austr.
52 A3 **Willunga** Austr.
52 A2 **Wilmington** Austr.
139 D2 **Wilmington** *DE* U.S.A.
141 E2 **Wilmington** *NC* U.S.A.
138 C3 **Wilmington** *OH* U.S.A.
141 D2 **Wilmington Island** U.S.A.
Wilno Lith. *see* Vilnius
101 D2 **Wilnsdorf** Ger.
101 D1 **Wilseder Berg** *hill* Ger.
141 E1 **Wilson** U.S.A.
53 C3 **Wilson's Promontory** *pen.* Austr.
100 B3 **Wiltz** Lux.
50 B2 **Wiluna** Austr.
99 D4 **Wimereux** France
123 C2 **Winburg** S. Africa
99 B4 **Wincanton** U.K.
99 C4 **Winchester** U.K.
138 C3 **Winchester** *KY* U.S.A.
139 D3 **Winchester** *VA* U.S.A.
98 B2 **Windermere** *l.* U.K.
122 A1 **Windhoek** Namibia
137 D2 **Windom** U.S.A.
51 D2 **Windorah** Austr.
136 B2 **Wind River Range** *mts* U.S.A.
53 D2 **Windsor** Austr.
130 B3 **Windsor** Can.
147 D3 **Windward Islands** Caribbean Sea
147 C3 **Windward Passage** Cuba/Haiti
137 D3 **Winfield** U.S.A.
100 A2 **Wingene** Belgium
53 D2 **Wingham** Austr.
130 B2 **Winisk** Can.
130 B2 **Winisk** *r.* Can.
130 B2 **Winisk Lake** Can.
63 A2 **Winkana** Myanmar
129 E3 **Winkler** Can.
114 B4 **Winneba** Ghana
138 B2 **Winnebago, Lake** U.S.A.
134 C2 **Winnemucca** U.S.A.
136 C2 **Winner** U.S.A.
140 B2 **Winnfield** U.S.A.
137 E1 **Winnibigoshish, Lake** U.S.A.
129 E3 **Winnipeg** Can.
129 E2 **Winnipeg** *r.* Can.
129 E2 **Winnipeg, Lake** Can.
129 D2 **Winnipegosis, Lake** Can.
139 E2 **Winnipesaukee, Lake** U.S.A.
140 B2 **Winnsboro** U.S.A.
137 E2 **Winona** *MN* U.S.A.
140 C2 **Winona** *MS* U.S.A.
100 C1 **Winschoten** Neth.
101 D1 **Winsen (Aller)** Ger.
101 E1 **Winsen (Luhe)** Ger.
142 A1 **Winslow** U.S.A.
141 D1 **Winston-Salem** U.S.A.
101 D2 **Winterberg** Ger.
141 D3 **Winter Haven** U.S.A.
100 C2 **Winterswijk** Neth.
105 D2 **Winterthur** Switz.
51 D2 **Winton** Austr.
54 A3 **Winton** N.Z.
52 A2 **Wirrabara** Austr.
52 A2 **Wirraminna** Austr.
99 D3 **Wisbech** U.K.
138 A2 **Wisconsin** *r.* U.S.A.
138 B2 **Wisconsin** *state* U.S.A.
138 B2 **Wisconsin Rapids** U.S.A.
Wisła *r.* Pol. *see* Vistula
101 E1 **Wismar** Ger.
123 C2 **Witbank** S. Africa
122 A2 **Witbooisvlei** Namibia
98 D3 **Witham** *r.* U.K.
98 D3 **Withernsea** U.K.
100 B1 **Witmarsum** Neth.
99 C4 **Witney** U.K.
123 D2 **Witrivier** S. Africa
123 C3 **Witteberg** *mts* S. Africa
101 E1 **Wittenberge** Ger.
101 E1 **Wittenburg** Ger.
50 A2 **Wittenoom** Austr.
101 E1 **Wittingen** Ger.
100 C3 **Wittlich** Ger.
100 C1 **Wittmund** Ger.
101 F1 **Wittstock** Ger.
122 A1 **Witvlei** Namibia
101 D2 **Witzenhausen** Ger.
103 D1 **Władysławowo** Pol.
103 D1 **Włocławek** Pol.
103 E1 **Włodawa** Pol.
59 C3 **Wokam** *i.* Indon.
62 A1 **Wokha** India
99 C4 **Woking** U.K.
101 F2 **Wolfen** Ger.

101 E1 **Wolfenbüttel** Ger.
101 D2 **Wolfhagen** Ger.
136 B1 **Wolf Point** U.S.A.
101 E1 **Wolfsburg** Ger.
100 C3 **Wolfstein** Ger.
131 D3 **Wolfville** Can.
102 C1 **Wolgast** Ger.
102 C1 **Wolin** Pol.
129 D2 **Wollaston Lake** Can.
129 D2 **Wollaston Lake** *l.* Can.
126 E2 **Wollaston Peninsula** Can.
53 D2 **Wollongong** Austr.
101 E2 **Wolmirsleben** Ger.
101 E1 **Wolmirstedt** Ger.
100 C1 **Wolvega** Neth.
99 B3 **Wolverhampton** U.K.
65 B2 **Wŏnju** S. Korea
128 B2 **Wonowon** Can.
65 B2 **Wŏnsan** N. Korea
53 C3 **Wonthaggi** Austr.
52 A2 **Woocalla** Austr.
51 C1 **Woodah, Isle** *i.* Austr.
99 D3 **Woodbridge** U.K.
134 B1 **Woodburn** U.S.A.
136 B3 **Woodland Park** U.S.A.
138 A3 **Wood River** U.S.A.
50 C2 **Woodroffe, Mount** Austr.
51 C1 **Woods, Lake** *salt flat* Austr.
129 E3 **Woods, Lake of the** Can./U.S.A.
53 C3 **Woods Point** Austr.
131 D3 **Woodstock** *N.B.* Can.
138 C2 **Woodstock** *Ont.* Can.
54 C2 **Woodville** N.Z.
143 D1 **Woodward** U.S.A.
98 B2 **Wooler** U.K.
53 D2 **Woolgoolga** Austr.
52 A2 **Woomera** Austr.
138 C2 **Wooster** U.S.A.
122 A3 **Worcester** S. Africa
99 B3 **Worcester** U.K.
139 E2 **Worcester** U.S.A.
102 C2 **Wörgl** Austria
98 B2 **Workington** U.K.
98 C3 **Worksop** U.K.
136 B2 **Worland** U.S.A.
101 D3 **Worms** Ger.
99 A4 **Worms Head** *hd* U.K.
122 A1 **Wortel** Namibia
99 C4 **Worthing** U.K.
137 D2 **Worthington** U.S.A.
61 D2 **Wotu** Indon.
61 D2 **Wowoni** *i.* Indon.
Wrangel Island *see* Vrangelya,
Ostrov
128 A2 **Wrangell** U.S.A.
96 B1 **Wrath, Cape** U.K.
136 C2 **Wray** U.S.A.
122 A2 **Wreck Point** S. Africa
Wrecsam U.K. *see* Wrexham
99 B3 **Wrexham** U.K.
136 B2 **Wright** U.S.A.
63 A2 **Wrightmyo** India
142 A2 **Wrightson, Mount** U.S.A.
128 B1 **Wrigley** Can.
103 D1 **Wrocław** Pol.
103 D1 **Września** Pol.
70 B2 **Wu'an** China
Wuchow China *see* Wuzhou
70 A2 **Wudu** China
70 A2 **Wuhai** China
70 B2 **Wuhan** China
70 B2 **Wuhu** China
71 A3 **Wu Jiang** *r.* China
Wujin China *see* Changzhou
115 C4 **Wukari** Nigeria
75 D1 **Wuli** China
62 B1 **Wuliang Shan** *mts* China
59 C3 **Wuliaru** *i.* Indon.
118 B2 **Wum** Cameroon
71 A3 **Wumeng Shan** *mts* China
101 D1 **Wümme** *r.* Ger.
130 B2 **Wunnummin Lake** Can.
101 F2 **Wunsiedel** Ger.
101 D1 **Wunstorf** Ger.
62 A1 **Wuntho** Myanmar
100 C2 **Wuppertal** Ger.
122 A3 **Wuppertal** S. Africa
101 E2 **Wurzbach** Ger.
101 D3 **Würzburg** Ger.
101 F2 **Wurzen** Ger.
101 D2 **Wüstegarten** *hill* Ger.
59 D3 **Wuvulu Island** P.N.G.
70 A2 **Wuwei** China
70 A2 **Wuxi** *Chongqing* China
70 C2 **Wuxi** *Jiangsu* China
Wuxing China *see* Huzhou
71 A3 **Wuxuan** China
Wuyang China *see* Zhenyuan
69 E1 **Wuyiling** China
71 B3 **Wuyishan** China
71 B3 **Wuyi Shan** *mts* China
70 A1 **Wuyuan** China
71 A4 **Wuzhishan** China
70 A2 **Wuzhong** China
71 B3 **Wuzhou** China
51 D2 **Wyandra** Austr.
53 C2 **Wyangala Reservoir** Austr.
52 B3 **Wycheproof** Austr.
99 B4 **Wye** *r.* U.K.
50 B1 **Wyndham** Austr.
52 B3 **Wyndham-Werribee** Austr.
140 B1 **Wynne** U.S.A.
129 D2 **Wynyard** Can.
138 B2 **Wyoming** U.S.A.
136 B2 **Wyoming** *state* U.S.A.

Yushe
239

53 D2 **Wyong** Austr.
103 E1 **Wyszków** Pol.
138 C3 **Wytheville** U.S.A.

X

117 D3 **Xaafuun** Somalia
62 B2 **Xaignabouli** Laos
121 C3 **Xai-Xai** Moz.
70 A1 **Xamba** China
62 B1 **Xam Nua** Laos
120 A1 **Xá-Muteba** Angola
120 A2 **Xangongo** Angola
81 C2 **Xankändi** Azer.
111 B2 **Xanthi** Greece
154 B3 **Xanxerê** Brazil
150 C4 **Xapuri** Brazil
107 C2 **Xátiva** Spain
120 B3 **Xhumo** Botswana
Xiaguan China *see* **Dali**
71 B3 **Xiamen** China
70 A2 **Xi'an** China
70 A3 **Xianfeng** China
62 A1 **Xiangcheng** China
70 B2 **Xiangfan** China
62 A1 **Xianggelila** China
Xianghuang Qi China *see* Xin Bulag
Xiangjiang China *see* **Huichang**
71 B3 **Xiang Jiang** *r.* China
62 B2 **Xiangkhoang** Laos
71 B3 **Xiangtan** China
Xiangyang China *see* **Xiangfan**
71 B3 **Xiangyin** China
70 B3 **Xianning** China
70 B2 **Xiantao** China
70 A2 **Xianyang** China
70 B2 **Xiaogan** China
69 E1 **Xiao Hinggan Ling** *mts* China
70 C2 **Xiaoshan** China
70 B2 **Xiaowutai Shan** *mt.* China
Xiayingpan China *see* **Luzhi**
Xibu China *see* **Dongshan**
71 A3 **Xichang** China
145 C2 **Xicohténcatl** Mex.
70 A2 **Xifeng** *Gansu* China
71 A3 **Xifeng** *Guizhou* China
Xifengzhen China *see* **Xifeng**
75 C2 **Xigazê** China
71 A3 **Xilin** China
69 D2 **Xilinhot** China
68 C2 **Ximiao** China
70 B3 **Xin'anjiang Shuiku** *resr* China
70 B1 **Xin Bulag** China
70 B2 **Xincai** China
Xincun China *see* **Dongchuan**
Xindi China *see* **Honghu**
71 B3 **Xing'an** China
62 A1 **Xingba** China
68 C2 **Xinghai** China
70 B2 **Xinghua** China
71 B3 **Xingning** China
70 A2 **Xingping** China
70 B2 **Xingtai** China
151 D3 **Xingu** *r.* Brazil
151 D3 **Xinguara** Brazil
71 A3 **Xingyi** China
71 B3 **Xinhua** China
70 A2 **Xining** China
75 C1 **Xinjiang** *aut. reg.* China
Xinjing China *see* **Jingxi**
65 A1 **Xinmin** China
71 B3 **Xinning** China
71 A3 **Xinping** China
Xinshiba China *see* **Ganluo**
70 B2 **Xintai** China
Xinxian China *see* **Xinzhou**
70 B2 **Xinxiang** China
70 B2 **Xinyang** China
71 A4 **Xinying** China
71 B3 **Xinyu** China
77 E2 **Xinyuan** China
69 D2 **Xinzhou** *Shanxi* China
70 B2 **Xinzhou** *Shanxi* China
106 B1 **Xinzo de Limia** Spain
Xiongshan China *see* **Zhenghe**
Xiongzhou China *see* **Nanxiong**
70 A2 **Xiqing Shan** *mts* China
151 E4 **Xique Xique** Brazil
70 A1 **Xishanzui** China
71 A3 **Xiushan** China
Xiushan China *see* **Tonghai**
71 B3 **Xiushui** China
71 B3 **Xiuying** China
70 B2 **Xixia** China
76 B2 **Xo'jayli** Uzbek.
63 B2 **Xom Duc Hanh** Vietnam
70 B2 **Xuancheng** China
70 B1 **Xuanhua** China
71 A3 **Xuanwei** China
Xuanzhou China *see* **Xuancheng**
70 B2 **Xuchang** China
Xucheng China *see* **Xuwen**
117 C4 **Xuddur** Somalia
Xuefeng China *see* **Mingxi**
Xujiang China *see* **Guangchang**
71 B3 **Xun Jiang** *r.* China
71 B3 **Xunwu** China
71 B3 **Xuwen** China
71 A3 **Xuyong** China
Xuzhou China *see* **Tongshan**
111 B3 **Xylokastro** Greece
70 A2 **Ya'an** China

Y

117 B4 **Yabēlo** Eth.
69 D1 **Yablonovyy Khrebet** *mts* Rus. Fed.
141 D1 **Yadkin** *r.* U.S.A.
75 C2 **Yadong** China
70 A1 **Yagan** China
55 A4 **Yaghan Basin** *sea feature* S. Atlantic Ocean
89 E2 **Yagnitsa** Rus. Fed.
83 K2 **Yagodnoye** Rus. Fed.
118 B1 **Yagoua** Cameroon
128 C3 **Yahk** Can.
91 C1 **Yahotyn** Ukr.
144 B2 **Yahualica** Mex.
80 B2 **Yahyalı** Turkey
67 C4 **Yaizu** Japan
134 B1 **Yakima** U.S.A.
134 C1 **Yakima** *r.* U.S.A.
74 A2 **Yakmach** Pak.
114 B3 **Yako** Burkina
66 D2 **Yakumo** Japan
67 B4 **Yaku-shima** *i.* Japan
126 C3 **Yakutat** U.S.A.
128 A2 **Yakutat Bay** U.S.A.
83 J2 **Yakutsk** Rus. Fed.
91 D2 **Yakymivka** Ukr.
63 B3 **Yala** Thai.
118 C2 **Yalinga** C.A.R.
53 C3 **Yallourn** Austr.
111 C2 **Yalova** Turkey
90 B2 **Yalpuh, Ozero** *l.* Ukr.
91 C3 **Yalta** Ukr.
65 A1 **Yalu Jiang** *r.* China/N. Korea
86 F3 **Yalutorovsk** Rus. Fed.
67 D3 **Yamagata** Japan
67 B4 **Yamaguchi** Japan
Yamal, Poluostrov Rus. Fed. *see* Yamal Peninsula
86 F1 **Yamal Peninsula** *pen.* Rus. Fed.
Yamankhalinka Kazakh. *see* Makhambet
53 D1 **Yamba** Austr.
150 B2 **Yambi, Mesa de** *hills* Col.
117 A4 **Yambio** Sudan
110 C2 **Yambol** Bulg.
86 G2 **Yamburg** Rus. Fed.
62 A1 **Yamethin** Myanmar
88 C2 **Yamm** Rus. Fed.
51 D2 **Yamma Yamma, Lake** *salt flat* Austr.
114 B4 **Yamoussoukro** Côte d'Ivoire
91 C1 **Yampil'** Ukr.
90 B2 **Yampil'** Ukr.
75 C2 **Yamuna** *r.* India
62 A1 **Yamzho Yumco** *l.* China
83 K2 **Yana** *r.* Rus. Fed.
70 A2 **Yan'an** China
150 B4 **Yanaoca** Peru
78 A2 **Yanbu' al Baḩr** Saudi Arabia
70 C2 **Yancheng** China
50 A3 **Yanchep** Austr.
114 B3 **Yanfolila** Mali
118 C2 **Yangambi** Dem. Rep. Congo
70 B2 **Yangcheng** China
71 B3 **Yangchun** China
65 B2 **Yangdok** N. Korea
71 B3 **Yangjiang** China
Yangôn Myanmar *see* **Rangoon**
70 B2 **Yangquan** China
71 B3 **Yangshuo** China
62 B1 **Yangtouyan** China
70 C23 **Yangtze** *r.* China
70 C2 **Yangtze, Mouth of the** China
Yangtze Kiang *r.* China *see* Yangtze
70 A2 **Yangxian** China
70 B2 **Yangzhou** China
65 B1 **Yanji** China
137 D2 **Yankton** U.S.A.
83 K2 **Yano-Indigirskaya Nizmennost'** *lowland* Rus. Fed.
70 B1 **Yanqing** China
71 A3 **Yanshan** China
83 K2 **Yanskiy Zaliv** *g.* Rus. Fed.
53 C1 **Yantabulla** Austr.
70 C2 **Yantai** China
118 B2 **Yaoundé** Cameroon
59 D2 **Yap** *i.* Micronesia
59 D3 **Yapen** *i.* Indon.
59 D3 **Yapen, Selat** *sea chan.* Indon.
144 A2 **Yaqui** *r.* Mex.
51 D2 **Yaraka** Austr.
86 D3 **Yaransk** Rus. Fed.
48 H4 **Yaren** Nauru
78 B3 **Yarīm** Yemen
Yarkand China *see* **Shache**
Yarkant China *see* **Shache**
77 D3 **Yarkant He** *r.* China
Yarlung Zangbo *r.* China *see* Brahmaputra
131 D3 **Yarmouth** Can.
142 A2 **Yarnell** U.S.A.
86 F2 **Yarongo** Rus. Fed.
89 E2 **Yaroslavl'** Rus. Fed.
66 B2 **Yaroslavskiy** Rus. Fed.
53 C3 **Yarra Junction** Austr.
53 C3 **Yarram** Austr.
89 D2 **Yartsevo** Rus. Fed.
89 E3 **Yasnogorsk** Rus. Fed.
63 B2 **Yasothon** Thai.
53 C2 **Yass** Austr.
81 D2 **Yāsūj** Iran
111 C3 **Yatağan** Turkey
119 D3 **Yata Plateau** Kenya
129 E1 **Yathkyed Lake** Can.
67 B4 **Yatsushiro** Japan
150 C3 **Yavari** *r.* Brazil/Peru
73 B2 **Yavatmal** India
90 A2 **Yavoriv** Ukr.
67 B4 **Yawatahama** Japan
62 A1 **Yawng-hwe** Myanmar
Yaxian China *see* **Sanya**
81 D2 **Yazd** Iran
140 B2 **Yazoo** *r.* U.S.A.
140 B2 **Yazoo City** U.S.A.
111 B3 **Ydra** Greece
111 B3 **Ydra** *i.* Greece
63 A2 **Ye** Myanmar
77 D3 **Yecheng** China
107 C2 **Yecla** Spain
144 B2 **Yécora** Mex.
Yedintsy Moldova *see* **Edineţ**
89 E3 **Yefremov** Rus. Fed.
91 E2 **Yegorlykskaya** Rus. Fed.
89 E2 **Yegor'yevsk** Rus. Fed.
117 B4 **Yei** Sudan
86 F3 **Yekaterinburg** Rus. Fed.
Yekaterinodar Rus. Fed. *see* Krasnodar
Yekaterinoslav Ukr. *see* Dnipropetrovs'k
Yekaterinovskaya Rus. Fed. *see* Krylovskaya
Yelenovskiye Kar'yery Ukr. *see* Dokuchayevs'k
89 E3 **Yelets** Rus. Fed.
89 D2 **Yeligovo** Rus. Fed.
114 A3 **Yélimané** Mali
Yelizavetgrad Ukr. *see* Kirovohrad
96 □ **Yell** *i.* U.K.
128 C1 **Yellowknife** Can.
53 C2 **Yellow Mountain** *hill* Austr.
70 B2 **Yellow River** *r.* China
69 E2 **Yellow Sea** N. Pacific Ocean
136 C1 **Yellowstone** *r.* U.S.A.
136 A2 **Yellowstone Lake** U.S.A.
88 C3 **Yel'sk** Belarus
78 B3 **Yemen** *country* Asia
90 B1 **Yemil'chyne** Ukr.
86 E2 **Yemva** Rus. Fed.
91 D2 **Yenakiyeve** Ukr.
62 A1 **Yenangyaung** Myanmar
62 B1 **Yên Bai** Vietnam
114 B4 **Yendi** Ghana
111 C3 **Yenice** Turkey
111 C3 **Yenifoça** Turkey
68 C1 **Yenisey** *r.* Rus. Fed.
Yeotmal India *see* **Yavatmal**
53 C2 **Yeoval** Austr.
99 B4 **Yeovil** U.K.
51 E2 **Yeppoon** Austr.
Yeraliyev Kazakh. *see* **Kuryk**
83 I2 **Yerbogachen** Rus. Fed.
81 C1 **Yerevan** Armenia
77 D1 **Yereymentau** Kazakh.
Yermentau Kazakh. *see* Yereymentau
143 C3 **Yermo** Mex.
135 C4 **Yermo** U.S.A.
89 D3 **Yershichi** Rus. Fed.
87 D3 **Yershov** Rus. Fed.
150 B4 **Yerupaja** *mt.* Peru
Yerushalayim Israel/West Bank *see* Jerusalem
65 B2 **Yesan** S. Korea
77 C1 **Yesil'** Kazakh.
111 C3 **Yeşilova** Turkey
83 H2 **Yessey** Rus. Fed.
99 A4 **Yes Tor** *hill* U.K.
53 D1 **Yetman** Austr.
62 A1 **Ye-U** Myanmar
104 B2 **Yeu, Île d'** *i.* France
87 D4 **Yevlax** Azer.
91 C2 **Yevpatoriya** Ukr.
Yexian China *see* **Laizhou**
91 D2 **Yeysk** Rus. Fed.
88 C2 **Yezyaryshcha** Belarus
Y Fenni U.K. *see* **Abergavenny**
154 A2 **Ygatimí** Para.
71 A3 **Yibin** China
70 B2 **Yichang** China
69 E1 **Yichun** *Heilong.* China
71 B3 **Yichun** *Jiangxi* China
Yidu China *see* **Qingzhou**
66 A1 **Yilan** China
110 C2 **Yıldız Dağları** *mts* Turkey
80 B2 **Yıldızeli** Turkey
Yilong China *see* **Shiping**
70 A2 **Yinchuan** China
65 B1 **Yingchengzi** China
71 B3 **Yingde** China
70 C1 **Yingkou** China
70 B2 **Yingshan** *Hubei* China
70 A2 **Yingshan** *Sichuan* China
71 B3 **Yingtan** China
Yining China *see* **Xiushui**
77 E2 **Yining** China
62 A1 **Yinmabin** Myanmar
70 A1 **Yin Shan** *mts* China
117 B4 **Yirga Alem** Eth.
119 D2 **Yirga Ch'efē** Eth.
119 D2 **Yirol** Sudan
Yishan China *see* **Yizhou**
70 B2 **Yishui** China
62 A1 **Yi Tu, Nam** *r.* Myanmar
68 C2 **Yiwu** China
70 C1 **Yixian** China
70 B2 **Yixing** China
71 B3 **Yiyang** China
71 B3 **Yizhang** China
71 A3 **Yizhou** China
Yizhou China *see* **Yixian**
92 I2 **Yli-Kitka** *l.* Fin.
92 H2 **Ylitornio** Fin.
92 H3 **Ylivieska** Fin.
93 H3 **Ylöjärvi** Fin.
83 K2 **Ynykchanskiy** Rus. Fed.
Ynys Môn *i.* U.K. *see* **Anglesey**
61 C2 **Yogyakarta** Indon.
118 B2 **Yokadouma** Cameroon
118 B2 **Yoko** Cameroon
67 C3 **Yokohama** Japan
66 D3 **Yokote** Japan
115 D4 **Yola** Nigeria
67 D3 **Yonezawa** Japan
71 B3 **Yong'an** China
Yongbei China *see* **Yongsheng**
71 B3 **Yongchun** China
70 A2 **Yongdeng** China
65 B2 **Yŏngdŏk** S. Korea
65 B2 **Yŏnghŭng** N. Korea
Yongjing China *see* **Xifeng**
65 B2 **Yŏngju** S. Korea
71 C3 **Yongkang** China
Yongle China *see* **Zhen'an**
62 B1 **Yongren** China
62 B1 **Yongsheng** China
71 B3 **Yongzhou** China
139 E2 **Yonkers** U.S.A.
105 C2 **Yonne** *r.* France
150 B2 **Yopal** Col.
50 A3 **York** Austr.
98 C3 **York** U.K.
140 C2 **York** *AL* U.S.A.
137 D2 **York** *NE* U.S.A.
139 D3 **York** *PA* U.S.A.
51 D1 **York, Cape** Austr.
52 A3 **Yorke Peninsula** Austr.
52 A3 **Yorketown** Austr.
98 C3 **Yorkshire Wolds** *hills* U.K.
129 D2 **Yorkton** Can.
87 D3 **Yoshkar-Ola** Rus. Fed.
97 C3 **Youghal** Ireland
53 C2 **Young** Austr.
52 A3 **Younghusband Peninsula** Austr.
138 C2 **Youngstown** U.S.A.
114 B3 **Youvarou** Mali
71 A3 **Youyang** China
77 E2 **Youyi Feng** *mt.* China/Rus. Fed.
80 B2 **Yozgat** Turkey
154 A2 **Ypé-Jhú** Para.
134 B2 **Yreka** U.S.A.
Yr Wyddfa *mt.* U.K. *see* **Snowdon**
59 D3 **Ysabel Channel** P.N.G.
105 C2 **Yssingeaux** France
93 F4 **Ystad** Sweden
Ysyk-Köl Kyrg. *see* **Balykchy**
77 D2 **Ysyk-Köl** *salt l.* Kyrg.
Y Trallwng U.K. *see* **Welshpool**
92 □A3 **Ytri-Rangá** *r.* Iceland
83 J2 **Ytyk-Kyuyel'** Rus. Fed.
71 A3 **Yuanbao Shan** *mt.* China
71 A3 **Yuanjiang** China
62 B1 **Yuan Jiang** *r.* China
71 B3 **Yuanling** China
71 A3 **Yuanmou** China
70 B2 **Yuanping** China
135 B3 **Yuba City** U.S.A.
66 D2 **Yūbari** Japan
145 C3 **Yucatán** *pen.* Mex.
146 B2 **Yucatan Channel** Cuba/Mex.
Yuci China *see* **Jinzhong**
50 C2 **Yuendumu** Austr.
71 C3 **Yueqing** China
71 B3 **Yueyang** China
86 F2 **Yugorsk** Rus. Fed.
Yugoslavia *country* Europe *see* Serbia and Montenegro
71 B3 **Yujiang** China
83 L2 **Yukagirskoye Ploskogor'ye** *plat.* Rus. Fed.
89 E3 **Yukhnov** Rus. Fed.
126 B2 **Yukon** *r.* Can./U.S.A.
143 D1 **Yukon** U.S.A.
128 A1 **Yukon Territory** *admin. div.* Can.
50 C2 **Yulara** Austr.
71 B3 **Yulin** *Guangxi* China
70 A2 **Yulin** *Shaanxi* China
62 B1 **Yulong Xueshan** *mt.* China
142 A2 **Yuma** *AZ* U.S.A.
136 C2 **Yuma** *CO* U.S.A.
135 D4 **Yuma Desert** U.S.A.
68 C2 **Yumen** China
80 B2 **Yunak** Turkey
70 B2 **Yuncheng** China
71 B3 **Yunfu** China
71 A3 **Yungui Gaoyuan** *plat.* China
Yunjinghong China *see* **Jinghong**
Yunling China *see* **Yunxiao**
71 A3 **Yunnan** *prov.* China
52 A2 **Yunta** Austr.
71 B3 **Yunxiao** China
70 B2 **Yunyang** China
71 A3 **Yuping** China
Yuping China *see* **Libo**
82 G3 **Yurga** Rus. Fed.
150 B3 **Yurimaguas** Peru
75 C1 **Yurungkax He** *r.* China
Yuryev Estonia *see* **Tartu**
71 C3 **Yü Shan** *mt.* Taiwan
70 B2 **Yushe** China

68 C2 Yushu China
Yushuwan China see Huaihua
81 C1 Yusufeli Turkey
75 C1 Yutian China
71 A3 Yuxi China
89 F2 Yuza Rus. Fed.
83 K3 Yuzhno-Sakhalinsk Rus. Fed.
91 C2 Yuzhnoukrayinsk Ukr.
70 B2 Yuzhou China
Yuzovka Ukr. see Donets'k
105 D2 Yverdon Switz.
104 C2 Yvetot France

Z

100 B1 Zaandam Neth.
69 D1 Zabaykal'sk Rus. Fed.
119 C2 Zabia Dem. Rep. Congo
78 B3 Zabid Yemen
79 D1 Zābol Iran
79 D2 Zāboli Iran
145 D3 Zacapa Guat.
144 B3 Zacapu Mex.
144 B2 Zacatecas Mex.
145 C3 Zacatepec Mex.
145 C3 Zacatlán Mex.
111 B3 Zacharo Greece
91 D2 Zachepylivka Ukr.
144 B2 Zacoalco Mex.
145 C2 Zacualtipán Mex.
109 C2 Zadar Croatia
63 A3 Zadetkyi Kyun i. Myanmar
89 E3 Zadonsk Rus. Fed.
80 B3 Za'farānah Egypt
106 B2 Zafra Spain
Zagazig Egypt see Az Zaqāziq
114 B1 Zagora Morocco
Zagorsk Rus. Fed. see
Sergiyev Posad
109 C1 Zagreb Croatia
Zagros, Kūhhā-ye Iran see
Zagros Mountains
81 C2 Zagros Mountains mts Iran
79 D2 Zāhedān Iran
80 B2 Zahlé Lebanon
78 B3 Zahrān Saudi Arabia
Zaire country Africa see Congo,
Democratic Republic of the
109 D2 Zaječar Serb. and Mont.
121 C3 Zaka Zimbabwe
89 E3 Zakharovo Rus. Fed.
81 C2 Zākhō Iraq
86 C2 Zakhrebetnoye Rus. Fed.
111 B3 Zakynthos Greece
111 B3 Zakynthos i. Greece
103 D2 Zalaegerszeg Hungary
110 B1 Zalău Romania
78 B2 Zalim Saudi Arabia
116 A3 Zalingei Sudan
90 B2 Zalishchyky Ukr.
78 A2 Zalmā, Jabal az mt. Saudi Arabia
128 C2 Zama City Can.
Zambeze r. Moz. see Zambezi
120 B2 Zambezi r. Africa
120 B2 Zambezi Zambia
120 B2 Zambezi Escarpment
Zambia/Zimbabwe
120 B2 Zambia country Africa
64 B3 Zamboanga Phil.
64 B3 Zamboanga Peninsula Phil.
103 E1 Zambrów Pol.
106 B1 Zamora Spain
144 B3 Zamora de Hidalgo Mex.
103 E1 Zamość Pol.
Zamost'ye Pol. see Zamość
75 B1 Zanda China
100 B3 Zandvliet Belgium
100 B1 Zandvoort Neth.
138 C3 Zanesville U.S.A.
77 D3 Zangguy China
75 C1 Zangsêr Kangri mt. China
81 C2 Zanjān Iran
74 B1 Zanskar Mountains India
Zante i. Greece see Zakynthos
119 D3 Zanzibar Tanz.

119 D3 Zanzibar Island Tanz.
89 E3 Zaokskiy Rus. Fed.
115 C2 Zaouatallaz Alg.
Zaouet el Kahla Alg. see
Bordj Omer Driss
70 B2 Zaoyang China
83 H3 Zaozernyy Rus. Fed.
70 B2 Zaozhuang China
89 D2 Zapadnaya Dvina r. Europe
89 D2 Zapadnaya Dvina Rus. Fed.
Zapadno-Sibirskaya Ravnina
Rus. Fed. see West Siberian Plain
68 B1 Zapadnyy Sayan reg. Rus. Fed.
143 D3 Zapata U.S.A.
92 J2 Zapolyarnyy Rus. Fed.
91 D2 Zaporizhzhya Ukr.
101 E2 Zappendorf Ger.
81 C1 Zaqatala Azer.
Zara Croatia see Zadar
80 B2 Zara Turkey
145 B2 Zaragoza Mex.
107 C1 Zaragoza Spain
79 C1 Zarand Iran
76 C3 Zaranj Afgh.
88 C2 Zarasai Lith.
89 E3 Zaraysk Rus. Fed.
150 C2 Zaraza Venez.
115 C3 Zaria Nigeria
90 B1 Zarichne Ukr.
81 D3 Zarqān Iran
66 B2 Zarubino Rus. Fed.
103 D1 Żary Pol.
115 D1 Zarzis Tunisia
88 C3 Zaslawye Belarus
123 C3 Zastron S. Africa
Zavitaya Rus. Fed. see Zavitinsk
69 E1 Zavitinsk Rus. Fed.
89 F2 Zavolzhsk Rus. Fed.
Zavolzh'ye Rus. Fed. see
Zavolzhsk
103 D1 Zawiercie Pol.
115 E1 Zāwiyat Masūs Libya
77 E2 Zaysan Kazakh.
77 E2 Zaysan, Lake l. Kazakh.
Zaysan, Ozero Kazakh. see
Zaysan, Lake
90 B2 Zbarazh Ukr.
90 B1 Zdolbuniv Ukr.
93 F4 Zealand i. Denmark
100 A2 Zedelgem Belgium
100 A2 Zeebrugge Belgium
123 C2 Zeerust S. Africa
101 F1 Zehdenick Ger.
50 C2 Zeil, Mount Austr.
101 F2 Zeitz Ger.
109 C2 Zelena Gora mt. Bos.-Herz.
87 D3 Zelenodol'sk Rus. Fed.
88 C1 Zelenogorsk Rus. Fed.
89 E2 Zelenograd Rus. Fed.
88 B3 Zelenogradsk Rus. Fed.
88 C3 Zel'va Belarus
119 D2 Zémio C.A.R.
107 D2 Zemmora Alg.
145 C3 Zempoaltépetl, Nudo de mt. Mex.
109 D2 Zemun Serb. and Mont.
65 B1 Zengfeng Shan mt. China
109 C2 Zenica Bos.-Herz.
107 D2 Zenzach Alg.
101 F2 Zerbst Ger.
105 D2 Zermatt Switz.
91 E2 Zernograd Rus. Fed.
Zernovoy Rus. Fed. see
Zernograd
101 E2 Zeulenroda Ger.
101 D1 Zeven Ger.
100 C2 Zevenaar Neth.
100 B2 Zevenbergen Neth.
83 J3 Zeya Rus. Fed.
79 C2 Zeydābād Iran
79 C2 Zeynalābād Iran
83 J3 Zeyskoye Vodokhranilishche resr
Rus. Fed.
103 D1 Zgierz Pol.
88 B3 Zhabinka Belarus
Zhabye Ukr. see Verkhovyna
Zhaksy Sarysu watercourse
Kazakh. see Sarysu

76 A2 Zhalpaktal Kazakh.
77 C1 Zhaltyr Kazakh.
Zhambyl Kazakh. see Taraz
76 B2 Zhanaozen Kazakh.
Zhangaqazaly Kazakh. see
Ayteke Bi
Zhangde China see Anyang
Zhangdian China see Zibo
66 A1 Zhangguangcai Ling
mts China
71 B3 Zhangjiajie China
70 B1 Zhangjiakou China
71 B3 Zhangping China
71 B3 Zhangshu China
65 A1 Zhangwu China
70 A2 Zhangye China
68 C2 Zhangye China
71 B3 Zhangzhou China
76 A2 Zhanibek Kazakh.
71 B3 Zhanjiang China
71 B3 Zhao'an China
69 E1 Zhaodong China
Zhaoge China see Qixian
71 B3 Zhaoqing China
71 A3 Zhaotong China
75 C1 Zhari Namco salt l. China
77 E2 Zharkent Kazakh.
89 D2 Zharkovskiy Rus. Fed.
77 E2 Zharma Kazakh.
90 C2 Zhashkiv Ukr.
Zhaxi China see Weixin
77 D2 Zhayrem Kazakh.
Zhdanov Ukr. see Mariupol'
71 C3 Zhejiang prov. China
82 F1 Zhelaniya, Mys c. Rus. Fed.
Zheleznodorozhnyy Rus. Fed. see
Yemva
Zheleznodorozhnyy Uzbek. see
Qo'ng'irot
89 E3 Zheleznogorsk Rus. Fed.
Zheltyye Vody Ukr. see
Zhovti Vody
70 A2 Zhen'an China
70 A2 Zhenba China
71 A3 Zheng'an China
71 B3 Zhenghe China
70 B2 Zhengzhou China
Zhenjiang China see Dantu
71 A3 Zhenyuan China
91 E1 Zherdevka Rus. Fed.
86 D2 Zheshart Rus. Fed.
77 C2 Zhezkazgan Kazakh.
77 C2 Zhezkazgan Kazakh.
83 J2 Zhigansk Rus. Fed.
70 B2 Zhijiang China
76 C1 Zhitikara Kazakh.
89 D3 Zhizdra Rus. Fed.
88 B3 Zhlobin Belarus
90 B2 Zhmerynka Ukr.
74 A2 Zhob Pak.
88 C3 Zhodzina Belarus
83 L1 Zhokhova, Ostrov i. Rus. Fed.
Zholkva Ukr. see Zhovkva
Zhongba China see Jiangyou
75 C2 Zhongba China
Zhongduo China see Youyang
Zhonghe China see Xiushan
70 A2 Zhongning China
Zhongping China see Huize
71 B3 Zhongshan China
Zhongshan China see
Lupanshui
70 A2 Zhongwei China
Zhongxin China see
Xianggelila
70 B2 Zhoukou China
70 B2 Zhoushan China
90 A1 Zhovka Ukr.
91 C2 Zhovti Vody Ukr.
65 A2 Zhuanghe China
70 B2 Zhucheng China
89 D3 Zhukovka Rus. Fed.
89 E2 Zhukovskiy Rus. Fed.
70 B2 Zhumadian China
Zhuoyang China see Suiping
71 B3 Zhuzhou Hunan China
71 B3 Zhuzhou Hunan China

90 A2 Zhydachiv Ukr.
88 C3 Zhytkavichy Belarus
90 B1 Zhytomyr Ukr.
103 D2 Žiar nad Hronom Slovakia
70 B2 Zibo China
103 D1 Zielona Góra Pol.
100 A2 Zierikzee Neth.
62 A1 Zigaing Myanmar
115 E2 Zighan Libya
71 A3 Zigong China
Zigui China see Guojiaba
114 A3 Ziguinchor Senegal
144 B3 Zihuatanejo Mex.
103 D2 Žilina Slovakia
115 D2 Zillah Libya
83 H3 Zima Rus. Fed.
145 C2 Zimapán Mex.
121 B2 Zimbabwe country Africa
114 A4 Zimmi Sierra Leone
110 C2 Zimnicea Romania
86 C2 Zimniy Bereg coastal area
Rus. Fed.
115 C3 Zinder Niger
78 B3 Zinjibār Yemen
91 C1 Zin'kiv Ukr.
Zinoyevsk Ukr. see Kirovohrad
150 B2 Zipaquirá Col.
103 D2 Zirc Hungary
75 D2 Ziro India
79 C2 Zir Rūd Iran
103 D2 Zistersdorf Austria
145 B3 Zitácuaro Mex.
103 C1 Zittau Ger.
87 E3 Zlatoust Rus. Fed.
103 D2 Zlín Czech Rep.
115 D1 Zlīţan Libya
103 D1 Złotów Pol.
89 D3 Zlynka Rus. Fed.
89 E3 Zmiyevka Rus. Fed.
91 D2 Zmiyiv Ukr.
89 E3 Znamenka Rus. Fed.
91 E1 Znamenka Rus. Fed.
91 C2 Znam"yanka Ukr.
103 D2 Znojmo Czech Rep.
122 B3 Zoar S. Africa
70 A2 Zoigê China
91 D1 Zolochiv Ukr.
90 A2 Zolochiv Ukr.
91 C2 Zolotonosha Ukr.
89 E3 Zolotukhino Rus. Fed.
121 C2 Zomba Malawi
118 B2 Zongo Dem. Rep. Congo
80 B1 Zonguldak Turkey
105 D3 Zonza Corsica France
114 B3 Zorgho Burkina
114 B4 Zorzor Liberia
115 D2 Zouar Chad
114 A2 Zouérat Maur.
109 D1 Zrenjanin Serb. and Mont.
89 D2 Zubtsov Rus. Fed.
105 D2 Zug Switz.
81 C1 Zugdidi Georgia
Zuider Zee l. Neth. see
IJsselmeer
106 B2 Zújar r. Spain
100 C2 Zülpich Ger.
100 A2 Zulte Belgium
121 C2 Zumbo Moz.
145 C3 Zumpango Mex.
142 B1 Zuni Mountains U.S.A.
71 A3 Zunyi China
109 C1 Županja Croatia
105 D2 Zürich Switz.
105 D2 Zürichsee l. Switz.
100 C1 Zutphen Neth.
115 D1 Zuwārah Libya
90 C2 Zvenyhorodka Ukr.
121 C3 Zvishavane Zimbabwe
103 D2 Zvolen Slovakia
109 C2 Zvornik Bos.-Herz.
114 B4 Zwedru Liberia
123 C3 Zwelitsha S. Africa
103 D2 Zwettl Austria
101 F2 Zwickau Ger.
100 C1 Zwolle Neth.
83 L2 Zyryanka Rus. Fed.
77 E2 Zyryanovsk Kazakh.

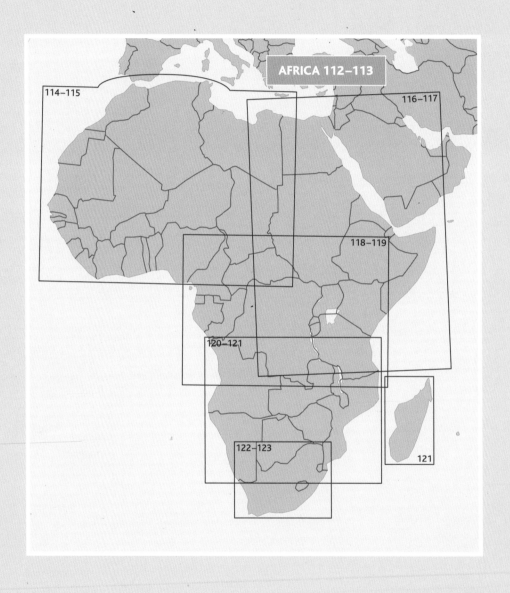

AFRICA 112–113

114–115

116–117

118–119

120–121

121

122–123